The
Bowker
Annual

The Bowker Annual

Library and Book Trade Almanac™

2006 | 51st Edition

Editor Dave Bogart
Consultant Julia C. Blixrud

 Information Today, Inc.

Published by Information Today, Inc.
Copyright © 2006 Information Today, Inc.
All rights reserved

International Standard Book Number 1-57387-250-4
International Standard Serial Number 0068-0540
Library of Congress Catalog Card Number 55-12434

Information Today, Inc.
143 Old Marlton Pike
Medford, NJ 08055-8750
Phone: 800-300-9868 (customer service)
         800-409-4929 (editorial queries)
Fax: 609-654-4309
E-mail (orders): custserv@infotoday.com
Web Site: http://www.infotoday.com

Printed and bound in the United States of America

US $199.95
ISBN 1-57387-250-4

9 781573 872508   19995>

Contents

Part 2
Legislation, Funding, and Grants

Part 3
Library/Information Science
Education, Placement, and Salaries

Part 4
Research and Statistics

Part 5
Reference Information

Part 6
Directory of Organizations

Directory of Library and Related Organizations

Directory of Book Trade and Related Organizations

Preface

Welcome to the 51st edition of the *Bowker Annual,* a compilation of informed analysis and practical information of interest to the library, information, and book trade communities.

This edition records another challenging year as librarians and publishers continued to grapple with problems ranging from post-September 11 privacy issues to book piracy and natural disasters.

Our Special Reports spotlight four areas of interest:

- Robert L. Oakley reviews developments in the realm of copyright law as it adapts to today's increasingly electronic environment.
- Harold Relyea looks closely at efforts to strike a balance between public access to government information and the proper protection of government information for security purposes.
- In an accompanying report, Jamie P. Horsley looks at the trend toward more openness regarding access to government information in the People's Republic of China.
- Kathleen Kern explores virtual reference and how it has come of age as a mainstream library service.

Also in Part 1 are reviews of the year's news and trends in public libraries, school libraries, and publishing, followed by reports on the activities of federal agencies, federal libraries, and national and international library and publishing organizations.

Legislation and regulations affecting libraries and publishing are detailed in Part 2, as are the activities of grant-making agencies and funding programs.

Part 3 is made up of professional information for librarians, from guides to sources of scholarships and employment to a listing of the year's major scholarship and award winners.

Part 4 contains an abundance of statistics and research—tables of library acquisition expenditures, book and periodicals prices, detailed data on publishing, and reports on noteworthy research projects and research tools.

Reference information fills Part 5: lists of bestsellers, recommended books and other media, the roster of the past year's major literary prize winners, and guidance on how to obtain an ISBN, ISSN, and SAN.

Part 6 is our directory of library and publishing organizations at the state, national, and international levels, plus a calendar of major upcoming events.

The *Bowker Annual* represents the work of many people, and our gratitude goes to all those who contributed articles, assembled reports, supplied statistics, and responded to our requests for information. Particular thanks are due Consultant Editor Julia C. Blixrud and Contributing Editor Catherine Barr.

We are confident that you will find this edition a valuable and frequently used resource and, as always, we welcome your comments and suggestions for future editions.

Dave Bogart
Editor

Part 1
Reports from the Field

News of the Year

The Year in Public Libraries: Legal Issues, Natural Disasters, Emerging Social Technologies

Kathy Dempsey

Many of 2005's headlines carried bad news. There seemed to be a constant stream of challenges on everything from copyright to civil liberties to funding, even challenges to the very existence of some libraries. It was a difficult year, but not without hope.

Legal Issues that Affected Libraries

Google's 'Book Search' Causes Stir

Some of the biggest stories of the year were those covering the continuing controversies surrounding Internet search giant Google. The one with the greatest effect on public libraries was Google Print for Libraries, a major digitizing project later renamed Google Book Search (http://books.google.com). In December 2004 Google announced its plan to scan millions of books from libraries around the world. It had made arrangements with several publishers to scan books into its Google Print database. But when the company began scanning scores of books owned by libraries without first getting copyright permission from the authors or publishers, trouble wasn't far behind.

The Association of American University Presses began the challenge, which was joined by the Association of American Publishers (AAP), the Association of Learned and Professional Society Publishers, and others. In late September the Authors Guild launched a class action federal lawsuit against Google, claiming that there was a willful infringement of copyright in Google's plan "to make the full text of the world's books searchable by anyone in the world." AAP filed another suit a month later. At year's end, words were still being carefully exchanged but everyone could read between the lines: This project and this case have the potential to change the information industry; not only in libraries but also for publishers, information aggregators, search companies, and database vendors. Watch for developments in 2006.

Kathy Dempsey is editor-in-chief of *Computers in Libraries* and editor of *Marketing Library Services* newsletter, both published by Information Today, Inc.

Patriot Act Concerns Continue

Librarians and their professional organizations are still embroiled in controversy over the USA Patriot Act.

There was a lot of discussion in the library press and in the general media about the act, in part because some of its provisions were set to expire at the end of 2005. As Congress began to discuss whether to change sections of the act, the American Library Association (ALA) and its Washington Office encouraged members to lobby their congressional representatives. In early August ALA's *Washington Office Newsline* (*ALAWON*) carried a sample letter for library supporters to send, along with talking points for those who wanted to compose their own letters. One of those points summed up ALA's position succinctly:

> The library profession does not oppose the entire [USA Patriot Act]. Libraries are places for the free flow and exchange of ideas essential to an informed citizenry. Therefore, the library profession opposes only those sections (specifically Section 215 and Section 505) of the [act] that currently hinder the free flow of ideas and that infringe on rights guaranteed under the Constitution.

Proponents of the act argued to keep the legislation as strong as it already was—or to make it even stronger—saying that the government wasn't even using the provisions of the act that were of highest concern. They said that librarians and civil libertarians need not be concerned about library patrons' privacy being violated, and that secret demands for information were not being made under Patriot Act powers. However, ALA refuted that claim in June. As part of its efforts to scale back government power to obtain information without warrants, ALA spent $300,000 on a study to examine how frequently federal, state, and local law enforcement officials were demanding patron records from librarians. The survey could not ask for specific details on government Patriot Act inquiries (because admitting that you've been involved in one is a crime in itself under the act); instead, it asked about the frequency of such inquiries, and the responses suggested that it was happening far more than federal officials had acknowledged.

The survey went to 5,500 libraries. Of these, 1,500 were public (33 percent replied) and 4,000 were academic (23 percent replied). The respondents reported a total of 137 formal Patriot Act requests or demands for information. Public libraries reported 63 legally executed requests and academics reported 74 between October 2001, when the act went into effect, and the time of the survey. The full report on the survey, *Impact and Analysis of Law Enforcement Activity in Academic and Public Libraries,* released on August 26, 2005, is at http://www.ala.org/ala/washoff/oitp/LawRptFinal.pdf.

ALA put these results before Congress, and, according to a June 20 article in the *New York Times,* "The library issue . . . was at the center of last week's vote in the House approving a measure to restrict investigators' access to libraries." Earlier, in April 2005, newly appointed U.S. Attorney General Alberto Gonzales had told Congress that the government had never used Section 215 to request library records. Since ALA's survey could not specifically ask how many of the inquiries fell under Section 215, the study did not prove that Gonzales was wrong. In a June 21 editorial, the *New York Times* commented that: "The library association's study does not prove that Mr. Gonzales misstated the record, but it does show that civil libertarians' worries about library privacy are well founded."

In July, on the last day before its summer recess, the Senate passed S. 1389 (the [USA Patriot] Improvement and Reauthorization Act of 2005) on "unanimous consent (meaning no debate, no amendments, no roll call vote)," according to *ALAWON*. That bill added many of the safeguards the library community had been seeking. A week earlier, the House had passed H.R. 3199, and the Senate bill differed in a few important ways.

- H.R. 3199 extended the sunset of Section 215 to the year 2015; S. 1389 extended the sunset only to 2009.
- House legislation allowed the FBI to get library records of anyone "relevant" to a counter-terrorism or counter-espionage investigation; the Senate legislation required the FBI to give facts showing reason to believe that the records sought were "relevant" to such an investigation.
- The House bill allowed a recipient of a Section 215 order to challenge it via a special "petition review panel" of the Foreign Intelligence Surveillance Act (FISA) court; the Senate bill allowed a recipient of a Section 215 order to challenge both the order itself and the secrecy or "gag" order that prevents a recipient of the Section 215 order from telling anyone about the request.

By December the House of Representatives and the Senate still had not reached a compromise on their differing versions. House and Senate negotiators did agree on December 8 that they would extend the Patriot Act before its end-of-month expiration. Congressional bickering ensued. The American Civil Liberties Union—which had previously been active in opposing provisions of the act—again stepped in and asked the lawmakers to reject the legislation because it "intrudes too far into the privacy of innocent Americans," according to an Associated Press account. So the fight continued. On December 16 the Senate rejected the reauthorization attempts, unable to muster the 60 votes necessary to overcome a threatened filibuster. This was a defeat for Gonzales and President Bush and many other Republicans who had lobbied to make most of the act's expiring provisions permanent.

The shift in thinking may have been affected by reports that appeared in the *New York Times* on the same day that the compromise was being voted on in the Senate. The newspaper reported that the Bush administration had authorized wiretapping, without court approval, to eavesdrop on American citizens' overseas telephone calls.

Patriot Act opponents asked for only a short extension of the law—rather than the six-month extension proposed earlier—to allow for further debate, and won that on December 21. The next day, *ALAWON* released a statement from ALA President Michael Gorman, which said, in part: "A bipartisan majority in the Senate guaranteed a continuation of debate last night, reflecting the American public's ever-increasing concern about the [Patriot Act]'s overreaching provisions." On the last day of its 2005 session, the House agreed to a one-month extension, until Feb. 3, 2006. It was a short-term victory; the battle was lost on March 7, when the House voted 280–138 to renew the act with its troublesome library and bookstore provisions intact.

Financial Issues

Federal Funding

The 109th Congress, during its final week, approved some funding for libraries. The Labor-HHS-Education Appropriations bill funded a couple of important programs. The Improving Literacy Through School Libraries program kept its funding level at $19.68 million, although ALA was expecting that a 1 percent across-the-board cut would lower this amount to $19.49 million.

The Library Services and Technology Act (LSTA) was one of few programs to get a funding increase. Its approved funding of $210.6 million ($5 million higher than the previous fiscal year) includes $163.7 million for the state grant program that so many public libraries rely upon.

Salary Survey

The salary story was unclear, at least in terms of the ALA Librarian Salary Survey for 2005. The numbers were reported in the December 2005 issue of *American Libraries,* ALA's monthly magazine, but because of major changes in survey methodology it is difficult to compare them with the figures from the 2004 survey. Regional mean salaries reported ranged from $78,054 for directors down to $36,486 for beginning librarians. In some categories, particularly non-supervising librarians in all sizes of public and academic libraries, the range was very broad; the mean was $47,246.

Mixed Picture in Library Funding

American Libraries reported continued problems in individual library funding across the country; many libraries had to cut hours and/or staff. But the reports were mixed. On the down side was the report that the Buffalo and Erie County (New York) Public Library was planning to close 16 of its 52 branches and to lay off nearly a third of its employees. On the up side, three branches of the Salinas (California) Public Library were able to stay open thanks to voters who approved a half-cent sales tax to increase the city's funding for libraries, recreation, and public safety services.

Awards

While the library world has countless awards, the two mentioned here are among the most widely recognized and widely welcoming—their winners don't have to be in any specific specialty, division, chapter, or school.

Library Journal's 2005 "librarian of the year" was Susan K. Nutter, vice provost (since 1995) and director of libraries (since 1987) at North Carolina State University. Her many accomplishments include making the university libraries central to the school's academic process, investing time and money to build staff, starting a fellows program, and helping to make a new $70 million research library a major funding priority. She has put high values on library education, mentoring, professional development, and aggressive recruitment.

The counterpart to that award is "paraprofessional of the year," which *Library Journal* awarded to Trish Palluck, resource sharing specialist at the Wyoming State Library. The magazine explained how she started as a page 26 years ago and moved up to library assistant. Palluck spent a lot of time typing catalog cards before becoming deeply involved in implementing interlibrary loan software and supporting statewide resource sharing. She also started the Paraprofessional/Support Staff Section of the Wyoming Library Association.

Technology Trends

Blogs and Wikis

Many of the emerging and growing technology trends are about "social software"—the software used to share information and build communities around topics. Blogs and Wikis figured prominently.

Blogs were hotter than ever in 2005, and it seemed everyone had one. Broadcast news programs were updating their news via blogs, political bloggers were being quoted on television shows and in news magazines, library literature was recommending that everyday librarians start blogs at work, and major industry conferences not only had blogging sessions but were being blogged simultaneously as well. The year also saw the growing popularity of such blog alternatives as vlogs (video blogs) and podcasts (broadcasting essays, logs, classes, and so forth over iPod mobile devices).

The term "Wikis" is derived from *Wikipedia*, the collaborative encyclopedia Web site where anyone can post or change an entry online. There was a high-profile incident in December in which John Seigenthaler, Sr., discovered a biography of himself on the site that contained considerable misinformation. Seigenthaler, a First Amendment scholar and a former editorial page editor of *USA Today,* corrected the entry, but as it was four months old some of its inaccurate material had already been "mined" and used on other sites. Obviously, it is impossible to trace all the places that Internet information has reached, so the incident highlighted the questionable validity of some *Wikipedia* entries as well as other online information. The story made national headlines and was, at the very least, a good chance for the news media to spotlight the simplicity of posting erroneous data online.

Emerging Technologies

Several interesting technologies were gaining recognition in 2005 and were expected to become even more popular in 2006.

Social software has gained acceptance with the general public, and librarians are learning to embrace it as well. Much of it is Web-based sharing software such as Flickr (http://www.flickr.com, a photo-sharing site), del.icio.us (http://del.icio.us, a bookmarking, annotating, site-sharing tool), and Gather (http://www.gather.org, a "next-generation blogging platform" designed to share user-generated content). Two Internet sources of more information on this topic are LLRX.com (http://www.llrx.com/features/socialsoftware.htm) and the Social Software Weblog (http://socialsoftware.weblogsinc.com).

Mobile computing is no longer just for business travelers; teenagers and others are carrying all sorts of devices that let them listen to music, download information, search databases from remote locations, keep up with e-mail, make stock trades, and more. While this may seem to be a very consumer-oriented trend, librarians are learning that they need to enable such services if they want to avoid becoming obsolete. The year's library literature carried plenty of articles about catering to wireless users by allowing them to use free wireless Internet access, to surf Web pages that have been reformatted for small-screen viewing, and to use research databases at the point of need (especially in medical organizations). As more and more people depend on wireless devices to access all kinds of data, librarians will no longer be able to consider such services as "extras" offered for a select few. Creating and pushing content to mobile devices will become more necessary in 2006 and beyond.

Open source applications have been around for years, but they are no longer the domain of computer science geeks and code-happy programmers. More and more libraries are using open source software for various jobs. There are operating systems such as Linux and UNIX, as well as software packages that mimic off-the-shelf word processors, database builders, spreadsheets, and more. There are many library-specific applications written by people who weren't satisfied with their vendor-built options. There are even open source integrated library systems that do the work of the traditional OPAC, cataloging module, and so on. Librarians need to be aware that although many of these tools are still free (or available for a donation to the cause), regular for-profit companies have emerged that continue to improve and support the software in exchange for maintenance fees. It is possible, in fact, to contract support for many open source solutions. And as the software gets better and budgets get tighter, this option is likely to become more attractive even to those who aren't necessarily adventurous.

Open access is also gaining momentum. Open access, OpenURL linking, and open platforms are basically go-betweens, translators that allow unrelated machines or applications to "talk" to each other and to share information. Common library actions such as cross-database searching and interlibrary loan benefit greatly from "open" tools that enable a researcher to enter one search, get results lists from multiple sources, and see which items are actually available at his own institution. With so many benefits, few libraries will be able to remain outside the open access movement for much longer. Most will need to implement such tools soon in order to keep from being isolated from peer networks and to deliver the technological capabilities that tomorrow's computer users will expect.

Library 2.0 and *Web 2.0* are related terms that people are beginning to talk about, although there don't seem to be any clear, satisfying definitions of either. The idea involves serving users better by determining what they really want, providing it via technology, and then upgrading the service to keep up with the users while simultaneously repeating these steps for other topics on a constant basis. The terms are going to be addressed in conference sessions in 2006.

Games in Libraries

One technology that emerged years ago is finally making its way onto the information industry's radar screen—electronic games. These products are steadily improving and becoming more sophisticated, and they have devotees of all ages. Why should librarians care? One *Library Journal* article (April 15, 2005) put it this way: "For starters, games are the 'medium of choice' for many . . . with broad participation among the 30-and-under population. . . . Game cultures feature participation in a collective intelligence, blur the distinction between the production and consumption of information, emphasize expertise rather than status, and promote international and cross-cultural media and communities." More simply, gaming is a way to draw young people into public libraries. Wizards of the Coast, creators of the popular Dungeons & Dragons (D&D) game, made a splash at the 2005 ALA Annual Conference with its cozy-living-room booth and game-giveaway program. It would give any interested library a free start-up package containing a complete D&D board game along with advice on how to host games and how to attract young patrons to play. Some libraries have started gaming programs that are so successful that participants have become regular book-borrowers and even library volunteers or advisory board members.

More evidence of this emerging trend came in the form of a gaming symposium for librarians held in Illinois in December for an enthusiastic crowd. Attendees learned about various games and how best to promote them to teenagers. They even got to practice playing some games during their breaks. It seems that games, especially the electronic variety, are poised to burst onto the library scene.

Perceptions of Libraries

What do people think of libraries? OCLC (the Online Computer Library Center) commissioned a major study of Internet users around the world and released a book-length report last fall, *Perceptions of Libraries and Information Resources.* The report—available at http://www.oclc.org/reports/2005perceptions.htm or in print—deserves study, recognition, and discussion.

One of the its main messages is that most people don't perceive libraries the way many in the industry wish they did. They still equate libraries with books; they're often unaware of the higher-level services that are available; they find it more convenient to go through the Internet (rather than through the library) to get information. The bottom line is that libraries need to do a lot more advocating and educating to help the public understand what they are and what they offer. The report makes the point that even if a library has what people want, if people aren't aware of this fact they will continue to perceive the library as irrelevant.

Natural Disasters Devastate Libraries Worldwide

Many will remember 2005 as a year of natural disasters; tsunamis, wildfires, hurricanes, and earthquakes affected hundreds of thousands around the world. Libraries in the stricken areas suffered badly.

Blogs Aid Tsunami Response

When a devastating earthquake and tsunami struck nations around the Indian Ocean in late December 2004, countless individuals and organizations began sending aid as soon as they could, and librarians were among them, collecting materials and money for the affected communities in Indonesia, Malaysia, Thailand, India, Sri Lanka, and Somalia. An interesting phenomenon was the way blogs came into play. Information professionals and others used them to distribute news, to find help, direct donations, identify survivors, and coordinate volunteers. So many blogs sprang up in the wake of the disaster that Yahoo! created registries for them.

Earthquake in Pakistan

The intense earthquake that hit a remote area of Pakistan and Kashmir in October 2005 was not only a disaster in terms of human injury and loss of life; it also destroyed the Khurshid National Library, which held a notable collection on Kashmir's history.

Nuzhat Rahman of the Library of Congress field office in Islamabad, Pakistan, told *American Libraries* what eyewitnesses had told him: The quake had been so ferocious that "the ground and hills were moving up and down like huge waves of water, causing mountains to move and break. At several places, the crevasses opened wide enough to swallow whole buildings, and that is what happened with the library."

Aid from around the world was still making its way into the region at year's end.

Devastation on the Gulf Coast

Another series of disasters hit closer to home. A fierce hurricane season in the Atlantic Ocean produced more named storms than any other year on record. The U.S. Gulf Coast was battered repeatedly, with Hurricanes Rita and Katrina causing the most damage. The city of New Orleans was particularly hard hit and the situation there received international headlines. But damage in parts of Florida, Mississippi, Alabama, and Texas, and elsewhere in Louisiana, was similarly severe.

In New Orleans, many of the city's public libraries were flooded so badly that both the buildings and their contents will have to be replaced. About 90 percent of the system's employees were laid off in the aftermath. ALA followed the progress closely, publishing news on the status of as many libraries as possible (see http://www.ala.org/ala/alonline/hurricanekatrinanews/hurricanenewsarchive/hurricanearchive.htm).

ALA itself was affected by the devastation in New Orleans; its Annual Conference is slated to be held in the city in June 2006. ALA decided that the city and its facilities would be sufficiently restored and that plans would not need to be changed.

Hurricane recovery efforts continued well into 2006. ALA started an "Adopt a Library" program to pair unaffected libraries with devastated ones in order to speed material and other support. Many organizations found other ways to help.

For example, the library network PALINET sent its December holiday greetings electronically, donating its $5,000 in estimated print savings to ALA's Hurricane Katrina Library Relief Fund.

Librarians across the country have rallied to help sustain the stricken communities and residents to rebuild their lives. In Texas, especially, librarians were lauded for helping the hurricane victims temporarily relocated there. Through libraries, the displaced used the Internet to connect to family and friends, to get help with government assistance forms, to keep up with the news, and to make decisions for their futures. The Houston Public Library even created a temporary library in the city's convention center, which was being used to shelter evacuees. The Library of Congress and First Book—a nonprofit organization whose mission is to provide disadvantaged children with new books—said they would provide 5 million books to people displaced by Hurricane Katrina. Other libraries from around the country offered jobs to librarians in need.

This is historically the basic task of librarians and other information professionals—finding answers that will help people, whether they need something as simple as the right children's book or as complicated as a whole new life.

Technology, Blogs, Wikis at Forefront for School Librarians

Walter Minkel

The current generation of children and teenagers in America's K–12 schools are living in the online world in a way no previous generation could because of the spread of the Internet—in particular the high-speed Internet connection—into their homes and their schools.

The Internet has been available to the general public since 1992, and the number of Internet connections in schools has exploded since then. This means that for all but the oldest of K–12 students, the Internet has always been there.

Recent Pew Internet in American Life Project studies show that 87 percent of all young people between the ages of 12 and 17—about 21 million young people—use the Internet ("The Internet at School," August 2005, http://www.pew internet.org/PPF/r/163/report_display.asp). Of those 21 million teenagers, 78 percent—about 16 million—said they used the Internet at school. By comparison, the Pew Internet Project survey in late 2000 found that 73 percent of those aged 12 to 17 used the Internet, and that 47 percent of them used the Internet at school, showing a growth rate of about 45 percent in the number using the Internet at school.

A minority of students in the 2005 survey, about 18 percent, had access to the Internet through school but not at home (usually because of low family income). Approximately half of American teenagers did not have home Internet access in 2000, and this change means that the "digital divide" between higher-income "technology haves" and lower-income "technology have-nots" had shrunk significantly in five years.

Even more significant was the number of teenagers who, instead of the passive consumers of online material they had been five years earlier, had become online content creators. Another Pew study, "Teen Content Creators and Consumers" (November 2005), said this was primarily due to the explosive growth of Weblogs (blogs) and customizable Web sites, such as the MySpace.com site. Of the teenagers surveyed, 57 percent had posted photos, comments, poetry, artwork, videos, and music online for others to see. More than half of this 57 percent ran their own blogs or similar sites that let them share their works and ideas with others. As part of the same study, the Pew researchers also asked teens about downloading copyrighted content, primarily music and video files. Seventy-five percent of teens agreed with this statement: "Music downloading and file-sharing is so easy to do, it's unrealistic to expect people not to do it." Only 23 percent of the teens disagreed, even though half of those surveyed thought that downloading copyrighted music was wrong.

Another interesting statistic from the 2005 study: Thirty-seven percent of teenagers surveyed said that "too many" of their peers were using the Internet to cheat on their schoolwork—for example, through copying and pasting text directly from Web sites into research papers or other assignments.

Walter Minkel is supervising librarian at the Early Childhood Resources and Information Center at the New York Public Library and former technology editor of *School Library Journal*.

Generation M

In March 2005 the Kaiser Family Foundation released "Generation M: Media in the Lives of 8–18-year-olds" (http://www.kff.org/entmedia/upload/Executive-Summary-Generation-M-Media-in-the-Lives-of-8-18-Year-olds.pdf). This study revealed that 28 percent of those polled said they often go online while watching television. Anywhere from a quarter to a third said they use another medium "most of the time" while watching TV (24 percent); reading (28 percent); listening to music (33 percent); or using a computer (33 percent).

These findings appeared to be soil for growing a new generation of school library media specialists, and some school library activists were promoting both more use of new technology and more information literacy instruction to help students use that new technology effectively.

Blogging

The year 2005 was a watershed for blogging everywhere, and many ordinary Americans became aware of the ubiquity of blogs for the first time. Blogs were suddenly everywhere in the media, and their stories were chronicled in the print magazines and on commercial Web sites. New blogs from all sorts of people—school library media specialists included—appeared every day (and disappeared, too; many blogs had insect-like lifespans). But the best new blogs in any field attracted plenty of attention, and almost all of the best school library blogs did their best to advocate for the importance of school libraries, and to carry as many media specialists as possible right out to the cutting edge.

Among the successful media specialist bloggers was Jacquie Henry, librarian at Ruben A. Cirillo High School in Walworth, New York. In her blog, "Wanderings . . . Random thoughts about libraries, information literacy, and information technology" (http://nlcommunities.com/communities/wanderings), she played the devil's advocate when she asked, "Now that everyone 'Googles,' who needs librarians?" But she added that "Whenever someone says this, I wonder if the person has been inside a library lately. Libraries are busier than ever." She was also interested in blogs as a way to reach the multitasking students she served, and to transcend her—and their—physical locations.

Henry was particularly interested in Web 2.0, the term used for an online environment that stresses collaboration using server-based and Web-based, rather than individual-computer-based, software and systems. To demonstrate how things were changing quickly, she compared the more limited library of the year 2000 and the potential of the Web-based library of five years later this way:

> Let's have a little competition at our school library and get ready for the future. I will use a laptop, interactive Library/Web 2.0 tools, a library Web page with access to subscription databases, plus unfiltered access to the Internet. You will use a desktop computer, no subscription databases, a filtered Internet connection, and no interactive technologies—not even e-mail. Are you ready?

She goes on to stress that the up-to-date librarian uses such tools as blogs to collaborate with peers and experts all over the world. It is clear that she wants to do everything she can with these collaborative tools and is working hard to spread the message around.

Doug Johnson, director of media and technology for the Mankato (Minnesota) Public Schools and a frequent writer and speaker on issues concerning school librarianship and educational technology, runs the Blue Skunk Blog at http://doug-johnson.squarespace.com/blue-skunk-blog. A recent Blue Skunk post suggested that school librarians should be in charge of technology at their schools because they had "a whole-school view" of the building and its resources. They also, said Johnson, understood the ethical issues involved in using technology, such as how to avoid plagiarism and respect copyright.

In another post, he asked, jokingly, "So how do you know you're a librarian in 2005? When . . . 1. You have to remind kindergarteners to turn off their cell phones before the story starts. 2. You know what an IP number [Internet Protocol address] is but not an ISBN number. 3. You have a student who does a better job troubleshooting the circulation system than the district technician . . ."

One of the best known of the forward-looking, technology-oriented school librarians is Joyce Valenza, Springfield Township (Pennsylvania) High School librarian. Her blog is "Joyce Valenza's NeverEnding Search," at http://joyce valenza.edublogs.org, and she has jumped into the mix of cutting-edge technology and learning with both feet. "I have to be the scout," she comments, meaning the one in the school who finds the best technical developments and learning strategies, "and if I'm not the scout, I'm not doing what I need to do." Rather than passively watching technology develop and then using whatever products the ed-tech companies choose to sell, she believes strongly that media specialists and teachers can develop their own ways to help young people learn. "What's very exciting," Valenza says, "is we're in the beginning of something we as educators could help frame."

One development she points to that she feels shows great promise is "wiki textbooks." Since the great success of *Wikipedia* (http://en.wikipedia.org), the online encyclopedia written and edited by its users, communities of Web site developers have been using easily available wiki software to speedily create wiki-documents of their own.

The word "wiki," Hawaiian for "quick" or "fast," now signifies collaborative Web sites. One definition: "Wiki is a piece of server software that allows users to freely create and edit Web page content using any Web browser. Wiki supports hyperlinks and has a simple text syntax for creating new pages and crosslinks between internal pages "on the fly" (http://wiki.org/wiki.cgi?WhatIsWiki).

In the context of K–12 education, wiki textbooks are online documents created by groups of teachers and media specialists that can supplement, or even replace, the hard-copy texts used in the typical classroom. A wiki on genetic research or contemporary foreign relations for advanced placement students, for example, can be available to all students with online access everywhere, free of charge. Valenza recommends that librarians and teachers interested in the topic of wiki textbooks could listen to the podcasts (online downloadable recordings) of discussions by the educational mavens at EdTechTalk (http://edtechtalk.com). A sample discussion on wiki textbooks with Danny Wool of the Wikimedia Foundation, the organization that publishes *Wikipedia,* can be found at http://edtechtalk.com/WikiTextbooks4. Although wiki textbooks wouldn't be difficult to create with current software, whether they would run the gauntlet of contemporary educational bureaucracy is another question. In the chat room discussion that followed this podcast, one participant suggested that wiki textbooks might be a first step toward a U.S. national curriculum—something that state governments have traditionally strongly opposed—and might become a hotly debated topic in future educational policy.

Valenza is also a booster of blogs as an educational tool that any teacher can create. She worked, for example, with Sarah Small, a Springfield Township High School teacher, on a curriculum blog unit on author Zora Neale Hurston (http://hurston.learnerblogs.org/about). Along with the blog, the two built a "Webquest" (a Web-based assignment) for students on Hurston's *Their Eyes Were Watching God,* which can be found at http://mciu.org/~spjvweb/hurston2.html.

Diane Chen, a school library information specialist in Nashville, is another thinking-on-the-edge librarian with a blog. "Deep Thinking" (http://deepthinking.blogsome.com) offers collaborative ideas and meditations, and Chen looks for them everywhere in the collaborative Web 2.0 world. In one post, Chen said she had read a inspirational post titled "Incremental vs. Revolutionary Changes" on Kathy Sierra's "Creating Passionate Users" blog (http://headrush.typepad.com/creating_passionate_users), which deals more with computer book publishing than anything else. Sierra said that "The true art of product or service development might come down to this: Knowing when it's appropriate to make incremental improvements and knowing when you need a revolutionary leap." The article inspired Chen to try something new. Her library assistant had been cut to half time, but she still needed to meet her goals, making sure her elementary students learned their library skills. So when doing her library classes, she told her students, "You are responsible for everyone learning this strategy. If one doesn't get it, none of you got it. If you have truly learned it, you can help teach it to your teammate." She gives each team a star or no star—roughly equivalent to an A or an F. Now, she wrote, she sees students from a successful team go over to teach another team that needs help.

One of the most forward-thinking and well-established bloggers, one to whom media specialists pay attention, is David Warlick, a former ed-tech administrator who is now a popular writer and speaker and a favorite at school library media conferences. His blog, "2 Cents Worth: Occasional Thoughts About Education, Teaching, Learning, and the 21st Century" (http://davidwarlick.com/2cents), tracks his adventures as he works with other educators on blogs and wikis and discusses new strategies for teaching. Many educators and their bosses, he writes, are telling the same stories over and over that don't reflect current American school—or workplace—reality.

Addressing teachers and librarians, he says, "We're still teaching like it's all our children will ever need to learn. We need to start helping students learn to teach themselves." The way we do that is to teach students how to manage information wisely.

To the public, he suggests that teachers and librarians start saying, "At some point, sooner than we believe, virtually all practical day-to-day information will be available digitally and through a network, and almost exclusively through digital technology. Anyone without convenient (at hand) access to a networked, digital device and the skills to use that device, may as well not know how to read. We've decided how important it is to learn to read. How about the tech part?"

Warlick assumes that most of his readers know the ins and outs of podcasts, wikis, and blogs, or of sites that many of his readers' students know. But if they don't, he always encourages them to familiarize themselves with these techniques, creating their own blogs and podcasts or to posting pictures on Flickr (http://www.flickr.com)—a Web 2.0 service for posting digital photographs. At a recent conference, Warlick said he was shocked to find that none of the supposedly tech-savvy educators in attendance raised a hand when he asked how many had posted photos on Flickr. (However, there are librarians up there—Flickr had a group of photos of librarians of all types titled "Librarian Trading Cards" at http://flickr.com/groups/librariancards/pool. Those librarians were tech-savvy and obviously having fun, and the page was worth a visit.)

Warlick is fond of saying, when he speaks to school librarians and others, that the current generation of librarians and teachers—the baby boomers and Gen-Xers—are "immigrants" in the country of technology who speak technology "with an accent." But the young people in K–12 schools in 2005—the ones surveyed in the Pew Internet studies—are "natives." Valenza, Johnson, and the others described here are attempting to remake school librarianship, and education itself, in a way that will help students learn more effectively in their native language.

Storms, Censorship, and Political Change

Among other top 2005 news in school librarianship:

Weathering the Storms

Hurricanes Katrina and Rita ripped through Louisiana and surrounding Gulf Coast states in late August and September, together making one of the biggest news stories of the year. While most of the attention focused on the flooding of New Orleans and the displacement of thousands of people from that city, many libraries and schools were damaged by wind and flooding. For example, eight schools in Louisiana's Orleans Parish, nine in Jefferson Parish, and 15 in St. Bernard Parish were destroyed. The American Library Association and the Louisiana Library Association collected thousands of dollars in cash, computers, and books to replace what was lost, but by the end of 2005 many areas were still without libraries and many students and staff were living, working, and going to school far from their previous homes while government committees and commissions wrangled over who was at fault for the mismanagement and delays.

Switch in Education Secretaries

The year began with a new U.S. secretary of education, Margaret Spellings, who had previously been President Bush's domestic policy adviser and had been a big fan of Bush's federal education law, No Child Left Behind (NCLB), from its beginning. Her predecessor, Rod Paige, who had guided NCLB through much controversy, had announced his retirement in November 2004. Even before Spellings was sworn in, she incited the ire of many librarians when she spoke out against an episode of the PBS children's television show "Postcards from Buster," based on characters from author Marc Brown's Arthur series. The episode in question focused on a family with lesbian mothers, and criticism from Spellings and other conservative and religious spokespeople resulted in PBS pulling the episode from its schedule.

One of Rod Paige's last duties as secretary of education was to unveil the Department of Education's National Education Technology Plan (http://www. nationaledtechplan.org), which outlines seven "action steps" to lead to more-effective use of technology in America's schools. These steps included increasing the amount of broadband Internet access, supporting e-learning and virtual schools, and moving toward more digital content, such as online textbooks. Unfortunately, although libraries were mentioned, they were not given a strong, specific role—such as the best resources for information literacy instruction—in the plan.

Digital Copyright Concerns
Lead 2005 Publishing News

Jim Milliot

Business and News Director, *Publishers Weekly*

The issue that drew most attention in 2005 was 2006—and beyond. Publisher concerns about copyright infringement, triggered by the late 2004 announcement by Google that it planned to scan the book collections of five libraries into its search engines, turned to action when both the Association of American Publishers (AAP) and the Authors Guild filed separate lawsuits against the giant search company.

The Authors Guild struck first, filing a class action lawsuit in September charging that Google's Print for Libraries project violated copyright laws by making copies of copyright-protected titles without permission. About a month later, McGraw-Hill, Pearson Education, Penguin, Simon & Schuster, and John Wiley, in a lawsuit coordinated by AAP, filed their own legal action against Google on grounds similar to those of the Authors Guild.

Google defended the library project by claiming that its actions are protected by the fair use doctrine of the copyright law. Google maintained that because it was showing only "snippets" of a book's material on its site, even though it was copying the entire book, the scanning project fell within the bounds of fair use. Google also argued that it was acting within copyright law because publishers and authors have the right to opt out of the scanning program.

The legal battle between publishers and authors and Google was expected to be protracted, with both sides seeing the question of fair use—which has yet to be defined in the digital world—as central to their future businesses.

The way in which book content in digital form will be sold over the Internet began to take shape in 2005. Late in the year, Google approached publishers about some sort of digital book rental program, while Amazon announced that it would begin a page-per-view program some time in 2006. Dubbed Amazon Pages, the program would allow customers to pay a few cents per page to view book material online.

Other giant search and software companies, specifically Yahoo! and Microsoft, also entered the book-scanning business in 2005. Yahoo! and Microsoft both said their copying efforts would respect copyright laws. [For more on book scanning and copyright, see the Special Report "Developments in Copyright, 2005: Exploring the Boundaries" later in Part 1 and "Legislation and Regulations Affecting Publishing in 2005" in Part 2—*Ed.*]

As companies outside traditional publishing circles showed increasing interest in book content, publishers began to draw up their own business models. Random House was the first off the mark, announcing the terms of a sales program for the digital market that has as its core the expectation that it will earn four cents per page for any book viewed online. In December HarperCollins announced that, in an effort to take more control of its books in digital form, it will create a digital warehouse containing the electronic files for all new books; companies such as Amazon and Google will use the files from the Harper warehouse rather than making their own files. While neither Random nor Harper said they had immediate plans to sell content online themselves, both made it clear they could enter the business at some point.

Used Book Sales On Rise

The digital arena was not the only area posing potential problems for the publishing industry. In late September the Book Industry Study Group (BISG) issued a report that documented the growth and size of the market for used books. The study found that sales of used books rose 11 percent in 2004, to $2.22 billion. Sales of used college textbooks were pegged at $1.63 billion, a finding that caused little surprise among educational publishers, which have long grappled with the problem of used book sales. More surprising was the size of the trade market, which the study estimated at $589 million, a significant increase over 2003. The primary factor driving the sale of used trade books is the sale of used books over the Internet. Online sales via the Web jumped by 33 percent in 2004, fueled by higher sales of used books through Amazon and other online stores as well as the growth of online marketplaces such as Abebooks and Alibris. Although the BISG report made no firm predictions about the growth of used book sales, the study suggested that trade book sales will steadily increase as consumers become more comfortable about buying used titles online. The forecast was troubling to publishers and authors, who receive no compensation for the sale of used books.

Looking to capitalize on the growth in online shopping, Simon & Schuster (S&S) and Random House joined Penguin in selling books directly to consumers from their own Web sites. And by the end of the year, most—though not all—publishers were selling books to consumers from their own sites, with many offering substantial discounts on list prices.

In another initiative to lure consumers to buy books, Penguin, S&S, and Harlequin were among the paperback publishers that began selling mass market paperbacks in a larger trim size in 2005. The larger editions feature larger print, which publishers hope will keep aging baby boomers buying mass market titles. The new editions were generally selling at $2 more than regular mass market versions.

Expanding and Acquiring

To keep pace with competition for the entertainment dollar, publishers large and small engaged in a range of initiatives and deals in 2005. The nation's largest trade publisher, Random House, acquired minority stakes in cell phone provider Vocel and in the reading-standards enterprise American Reading Company. Late in the year Random announced the formation of Random House Films, which will produce a limited number of movies annually in cooperation with Focus Features. Random's Doubleday Broadway division invested in talent late in the year when it lured Julie Grau and Cindy Spiegel from their posts as copublishers of Penguin's Riverhead imprint to form a new division at the company.

S&S's largest investment in 2005 was the purchase of Strebor Books, the publisher of African American titles that was owned by bestselling S&S author

Zane. Meanwhile, to expand its presence in the conservative book field, S&S struck a deal with Republican strategist Mary Matalin to form Threshold Books. S&S's Pocket Book division announced plans for an early 2007 launch of G-Unit Books, which will involve rapper 50 Cent. In S&S's children's group, Steve Weitzen was brought in to head a new merchandising group, while Rubin Pfeffer joined as senior vice president and publisher of trade publishing. In another deal that targeted the African American market, Harlequin acquired BET Books from Black Entertainment Television.

The Time Warner Book Group formed a number of new imprints in 2005. The one that generated the most notoriety was Warner Twelve, launched by a former Random House editorial director, Jonathan Karp. Its first titles are to be released in 2007. Other imprints formed by Time Warner included one aimed at baby boomers titled Springboard. Warner Wellness will focus on health-related books, while Solona will be devoted to books of interest to Hispanic and Latino women. Little, Brown children's group started the LB Kids imprint in fall 2005.

Among the acquisitions involving independent publishers in 2005, Interweave Press was acquired by Aspire Media, a new company looking to build a multimedia firm centered around book and magazine hobby publishers. Andrews McMeel made its largest purchase ever, buying Accord Publishing. MBI Publishing also made a significant purchase, acquiring Voyageur Press. One of the largest independent publishers in the country, F&W Publications, changed hands, with the equity firm Abry Partners buying the house from another equity firm. Also in the independent world, the McEvoy Group, parent company of Chronicle Books, bought packager becker&mayer! Ltd. Roman & Littlefield added M. Evans to its publishing lineup. A new player in the publishing market, Big Earth Publishers, made three purchases: Johnson Books, Bleak House, and Intrigue Press. Another publishing newcomer, Steve Floyd, led a group that bought children's publisher August House. Online book marketplace Abebooks bought Bookfinder.

Among the larger houses, John Wiley paid $11 million for computer book publisher Sybex. HarperCollins acquired the trade properties of Smithsonian Institution Press. Perseus Books acquired the distribution company CDS; resulting in the elimination of 12 jobs and the departure of president Gilbert Perlman. In another vertical expansion deal, Amazon bought on-demand printer BookSurge. Thomson Delmar Learning acquired computer book publisher Charles River. Facts on File, acquired by the investment banking firm Veronis Suhler Stevenson in April, bought Chelsea House in August.

In a rebirth of his career, Michael Viner, founder of Dove Audio and New Millennium, founded Phoenix Books and Tapes, with much of the inventory coming from his old firms. Another industry veteran, John Whalen, left Running Press to form Cider Mill Press. After extended negotiations, the Weinstein brothers ended their association with Miramax and Disney to form their own film and book company. Rob Weisbach was named to run the book unit.

There was a fair amount of action in the children's market in 2005. Random House children's group hired veteran S&S children's books editor Anne Schwartz to start her own imprint. Former Dorling Kindersley executives Joanna Bicknell and Danny Gurr launched Make Believe Ideas, which is based in Britain and publishes education-oriented titles. Michael di Capua announced late in the year that he was moving his imprint from Hyperion to Scholastic.

On the education side, School Specialty acquired Delta Education from Wicks Learning Group for $272 million. Earlier in the year, Wicks had acquired EMC/Paradigm Publishing for $44 million.

People

After nearly 30 years with Warner Books, Time Warner Books chief Larry Kirshbaum announced in May that he would be leaving his corporate office and hanging out an agent's shingle by the end of the year. David Young, head of Time Warner's British division, was named to succeed him. At Reader's Digest, Tom Ryder stepped down as CEO and was succeeded by Eric Schrier. Ryder will remain chairman through 2006. Health concerns prompted Peter Jovanovich to step down as head of Pearson's educational publishing group. Another president who stepped down in the year was PublicAffairs' Peter Osnos, who remained editor-at-large. Susan Weinberg, former publisher of the HarperCollins flagship imprint, was named to succeed Osnos as publisher. YS Chi left his spot at Random House Asia to become vice chairman of Elsevier. Ted Nardin, former head of McGraw-Hill's professional group, was named CEO of Springer Publishing.

A changing of the guard at Scholastic's trade publishing division took place when Lisa Holton, publisher of Disney's children group, was named to succeed Barbara Marcus, who retired as president in July. Later in the year, longtime trade division publisher Jean Feiwel left the company, and Holton brought in former Houghton Mifflin children's publisher Andrea Pinkney as publisher; Alan Smagler had been appointed Houghton Mifflin children's group publisher earlier in the year.

The steady makeover of Bookspan continued in 2005. In February editor-in-chief Brigitte Weeks left the company. Later in the year, Seth Radwell, president of Bookspan's editorial and marketing group, resigned to head up Scholastic's Internet efforts. Carole Baron, publisher at Putnam, moved to Bookspan shortly after Radwell's departure as senior vice president and publishing director. Penguin named Warner's Ivan Held to succeed Baron at Putnam. Another Bookspan editor, David Rosen, left at the end of the year to join Harry Abrams as editorial director. Kristy Melville, one-time publisher of indie house Ten Speed Press, was named publisher of Andrew McMeel's book division.

Major shifts in the religion market included the promotion of Michael Hyatt to CEO of Thomas Nelson, succeeding Sam Moore. At rival Zondervan, Doug Lockhart was named president, succeeding Bruce Ryskamp. Cris Doornbos left Zondervan to become president of Cook Communications. Bill Barry, president of DK Publishing, returned to Doubleday as head of Doubleday Religion with a mandate to double the size of the company. Barry was succeeded at DK by Gary June.

Among industry publications, David Ulin took over as editor of the *Los Angeles Times* book review in October after his predecessor, Steve Wasserman, left the job to become an agent. David Kipen, book critic for the *San Francisco Chronicle,* resigned in the fall to become director of literature for the National Endowment for the Arts, succeeding the late Cliff Becker. Former *Publishers Weekly* (*PW*) editor-in-chief Nora Rawlinson joined Time Warner as head of its library marketing unit. Karen Holt, editor with *The Book Standard*, joined *PW* as deputy editor. After 20 years, Anne Larsen resigned as editor of *Kirkus Reviews*. In the fair world, Juergen Boos took control of the Frankfurt Book Fair.

Doug Jones was named head of marketing at Putnam and Riverhead, succeeding Dan Harvey, who had resigned. Suzanne Murphy left her marketing post at S&S children's group to become head of trade marketing at Scholastic. Former S&S marketing head Craig Herman took over the marketing at Running Press.

Newly appointed executive editors in the year included Amy Scheibe, who heads Counterpoint's editorial operations, and Brenda Copeland, who moved from Atria Books to Hyperion. Atria had its share of changes, with Karen Mender stepping down as associate publisher. Also at S&S, longtime editor Michael Korda announced his retirement. After more than a decade at Farrar, Straus & Giroux, John Glusman stepped down as editor-in-chief.

A major change in the distribution business saw Gary Rautenstrauch, former CEO of Baker & Taylor, named president of Blackwell's Book Services.

Downsizing

The bankruptcy that had the largest repercussion in the industry was that of Koen Book Distributors, which closed its doors in the fall, costing publishers millions of dollars. Following Koen's closure, Levy Home Entertainment formed Koen-Levy Distribution, a new distribution company, with Koen founder Bob Koen. Meanwhile, Baker & Taylor bought Koen's inventory in the bankruptcy auction and returned many of those titles to publishers.

On the editorial side, HarperCollins closed its Fourth Estate imprint early in 2005 and phased out its ThorsonsElement U.S. imprint. Penguin downsized its Chamberlain Bros. unit, with imprint founder Carlo DeVito leaving the company. Early in 2005 Penguin cut about 40 positions throughout the company following disappointing sales growth. The DK unit cut another 44 positions, mainly in Britain. Soft library sales resulted in the elimination of 30 positions in Scholastic's library division.

One of the nation's longest-running street fairs, New York Is Book Country, suspended its run with its future direction uncertain.

Among the major developments in independent bookselling, Atlanta's Chapter 11 Books closed 6 of its 13 stores as part of a Chapter 11 bankruptcy filing. In California, Kepler's avoided going out of business when the local community rallied to support the 50-year-old institution. New England's Buck-a-Book closed the last of its stores, which once numbered 30, during 2005.

Although comics and graphic novels have been a growth area, there were a few casualties in 2005. DreamWave Productions shut down early in the year, and ComicsOne transferred the rights of its most popular titles to a new company. Manga publisher Central Park Media cut six people early in the year as competition stiffened in the market.

Feminist press Spinsters Ink closed in January, but was reborn two months later as an imprint of Bella Books. Another once-hot small press, UglyTown, went on hiatus until spring 2006 as a result of cash flow problems following the closure of Words distribution company.

In the manufacturing segment, Phoenix Color closed its Book Technology Park division, which had employed about 200 people.

Bestsellers

In a year when a new Harry Potter is released, it would be big news if it weren't that year's top seller. *Harry Potter and the Half-Blood Prince,* released in July, sold more than 6.5 million copies in its first weekend and nearly 10 million for all of 2005, making it the biggest seller for the year. James Frey's *A Million Little Pieces* sold more than 2 million copies in trade paperback after Oprah Winfrey made it the first nonfiction selection for her club, but early in 2006 the veracity of some of Frey's story was called into question, fueling an industry-wide debate over an author's—and publisher's—responsibility to stick to the facts in a memoir.

Joining *Half-Blood Prince* among the top sellers of the year were some old favorites, including *The Da Vinci Code,* which sold 12 million copies through 2005. *The Purpose-Driven Life* and *Your Best Life Now* continued to sell well in nonfiction, while a self-published book, *Natural Cures,* which benefited from a series of infomercials, had a total of 4 million copies in print. Dan Brown and John Grisham topped the mass market paperback charts, while *The Kite Runner* by Khaled Hosseini joined *A Million Little Pieces* as a trade paperback standout.

The number of books hitting the *PW* bestsellers list rose noticeably in 2005, up to 442 from 421 in 2004. That increase meant that bestsellers tended to stay on the list for a shorter time.

The Time Warner Book Group, which had a good 2004 bestseller performance in hardcover, did even better in 2005, putting 24 books on the hardcover bestseller lists; this gave it a 16.6 percent share of hardcover bestsellers, up 6.6 percent over 2004. The number of Random House hardcover bestsellers fell slightly in the year, from 75 to 72, and its market share fell 5.9 percent to 22.5 percent. The number of HarperCollins bestsellers increased in 2005, and its market share had a solid increase, moving up 5.1 percent to 17.9 percent. Rounding out the top five publishers, Penguin had 50 hardcover bestsellers and a 13.7 percent market share, a 0.4 percent increase. S&S's hardcover market share fell 3.6 percent, dropping to an 11.2 percent share.

Paperback bestseller rankings held to the status quo in 2005. Random House had 63 paperbacks reach the *PW* bestsellers lists, down only 0.3 percent from 2004. Penguin placed 46 paperbacks on the list, giving it a 17.4 percent market share compared with 17.6 percent in 2004. S&S had the strongest paperback bestseller performance in 2005, increasing its market share 2.6 percent to 15.3 percent.

For the second holiday season in a row, retailers depended on a range of titles to lift sales rather than on hot new books. Books-A-Million reported an 8.9 percent sales increase in the holiday season, beating expectations. Borders also did better than expected, posting a 1.4 percent sales increase as weak music sales offset good book results. Barnes & Noble holiday sales came in as projected, up about 5 percent. Independent booksellers reported gains in the low single digits.

Federal Agency and Federal Library Reports

Library of Congress

10 First St. S.E., Washington, DC 20540
202-707-5000, World Wide Web http://www.loc.gov

James H. Billington
Librarian of Congress

The Library of Congress was established in 1800 to serve the research needs of the U.S. Congress. For more than two centuries, the library has grown both in the size of its collection (now totaling more than 132 million items) and in its mission. As the largest library in the world and the oldest federal cultural institution in the nation, the Library of Congress serves not only Congress but also government agencies, libraries around the world, and scholars and citizens in the United States and abroad. At the forefront of technology, the library now serves patrons on-site in its three buildings on Capitol Hill in Washington, D.C., and worldwide through its highly acclaimed Web site. More than 1.4 million people visited the library in 2005, and more than 3.7 billion "hits" were recorded on the library's Web site.

Highlights of the Year

- The Federal Library and Information Center Committee (FLICC) marked its 40th anniversary in March 2005.
- In May the library, in partnership with the National Science Foundation, awarded research grants totaling $3 million to ten universities and their partner institutions to undertake cutting-edge research in the field of digital preservation and access.
- In June Librarian of Congress James H. Billington proposed an initiative to develop a public and private partnership to build a World Digital Library; in November Google, Inc. became the first private partner with a donation of $3 million.
- Blues musician B. B. King and composer Gunther Schuller were awarded the Living Legend Medal in honor of their achievements.

Report compiled by Audrey Fischer, Public Affairs Specialist, Library of Congress.

- On September 24 the library sponsored the fifth National Book Festival on the National Mall in Washington, D.C., once again hosted by First Lady Laura Bush.
- The library launched its Creativity Across America initiative in December, with the first stop in an 11-city Song of America tour featuring renowned baritone Thomas Hampson performing works from the library's music collections.

Legislative Support to Congress

Serving Congress is the library's highest priority, particularly in the area of legislative support. During the year, the library provided Congress with the most current research and analysis relevant to the war on terrorism, homeland security, and many other issues of national and international concern.

In 2005 Congress called on the library's Congressional Research Service (CRS) for objective and authoritative research and analysis on significant and far-reaching public policy issues such as the continuing U.S. presence in Iraq and Afghanistan, the Supreme Court nominations, and the federal response to Hurricanes Katrina and Rita. CRS delivered 906,000 research responses to members of Congress and committees during the year.

The Legislative Information System (LIS), developed solely for use by Congress and congressional staff members, continued to provide access to information on past and current legislation through all facets of the lawmaking process. LIS received an array of display enhancements to its nine databases to coincide with the start of the 109th Congress.

The Library of Congress Law Library, the world's largest, provided Congress with comprehensive international, comparative, and foreign law research based on the most current information available. During the year, law library staff produced 1,132 written reports for Congress. The law library also kept Congress informed on matters pertaining to international law through the online publication of the *World Law Bulletin*. The Global Legal Information Network (GLIN) also provided Congress with access to the laws of 43 member nations.

The Copyright Office provided policy advice and technical assistance to Congress on important copyright laws and related issues such as piracy of intellectual property, preservation of orphan works, and the Copyright Royalty Distribution Reform Act of 2004 (Public Law 108-419). Under this legislation, effective on May 31, 2005, the Copyright Arbitration Royalty Panels (CARPs) were replaced by the Copyright Royalty Board. Appointed by the Librarian of Congress in consultation with the Register of Copyrights, the Copyright Royalty Board is composed of three copyright royalty judges. It sets rates and terms for various statutory licenses and determines the distribution of royalty fees collected by the Copyright Office.

The Congressional Relations Office (CRO) assisted members of Congress and their staff in making use of the library's collections, services, and facilities. CRO and other library offices worked with member and committee offices on current issues of legislative concern such as the library's appropriations, the construction of a Capitol Visitor Center, the National Digital Information Infrastructure and Preservation Program, the Veterans History Project, and reauthorization of the National Film Preservation Program.

Security

With generous support from Congress, the library developed further its security in a climate of heightened alert while continuing to carry out its mission of sustaining, preserving, and making accessible its universal collections. In coordination with other agencies on Capitol Hill, the library continued upgrading its perimeter security, entrance and exit screening procedures, emergency preparedness capabilities, and internal controls safeguarding the library's collections. The Employee Emergency Action Guide was updated and a new Computer Emergency Notification System was procured. The library also moved forward on plans to implement a state-of-the-art public address system.

The library continued to implement systems and policies to ensure the availability, reliability, and integrity of its computer systems, applications, and data. Building on the new Information Technology Security Policy, which was issued in 2004, the Information Technology Services Office (ITS) issued a dozen directives outlining the procedures that service units need to follow to fulfill their role in protecting library resources. ITS developed an IT security plan and refined the continuity-of-operations plan. ITS also created the Security Operations Center (SOC) within the newly formed IT Security Group. SOC, which serves the entire library, is responsible for incident handling and response. Working with the library's Office of Management and Training, ITS created an online security awareness course that all library staff, contractors, and other personnel are required to complete.

Budget

The library received a total of $584,870,304 in appropriations for fiscal year (FY) 2005. Under the Legislative Branch Appropriations Act of 2005 (Public Law 108-447), which was signed into law on December 8, 2004, the library was to receive $589,587,000, including authority to spend $39,827,000 in receipts. This legislation included a 0.8 percent across-the-board rescission of federal agency budgets, which resulted in FY 2005 appropriations for the library of $584,870,304, including authority to spend $39,508,384 in receipts.

Development

During FY 2005 the library's fund-raising activities brought in a total of $12 million, made up of 750 gifts from 639 donors. The donor categories included 476 individuals giving $2 million; 48 foundations giving $7.2 million; 62 corporations giving $1.8 million; and 53 trusts, estates, associations, councils, and societies giving $1 million.

Those gifts, including $500,000 received through the library's Planned Giving Program, were made to 64 different library funds and consisted of $3.7 million in cash gifts, $7.9 million in new pledges, and approximately $400,000 in in-kind gifts. The library forged new partnerships with 232 first-time donors, including 181 individuals; 22 trusts, estates, associations, councils, and societies; 17 corporations; and 12 foundations. These new donors gave $1 million, representing 8 percent of the gifts received. Six new gift and trust funds were established.

Private gifts supported a variety of new and continuing programs throughout the library, including exhibitions, acquisitions, symposia and other scholarly programs, and the fifth National Book Festival (supported by $1.5 million in private funds).

The James Madison Council, the library's first private-sector advisory group, continued to provide substantial support for a number of library initiatives. Gifts from Madison Council members in FY 2005 totaled $8.8 million, bringing total support since 1990 to $167.8 million. The major part of the council's contributions in 2005 provided support for two of the library's new initiatives: Thomas Hampson's Song of America tour and seed money for the library's Creativity Across America project.

The Leaders Circle, a dynamic group of library supporters, was officially launched on May 4, 2005, at a reception hosted by Mr. and Mrs. William N. Cafritz. The Leaders Circle is dedicated to making the Library of Congress and its collections, programs, and resources universally known and accessible and to increasing involvement with the library through the talent, creativity, influence, and resources of a new generation of philanthropic leadership.

Collections

During 2005 the size of the library's collections grew to more than 132 million items, an increase of more than 2 million over the previous year. The total figure includes more than 30 million cataloged books and other print materials, 59 million manuscripts, 14 million microforms, 5.2 million maps, 5.4 million items in the music collection, 14 million visual materials, 2.8 million audio materials, and more than 1 million items in miscellaneous formats.

Integrated Library System

The Library of Congress Integrated Library System (ILS) performs routine library functions such as circulation, acquisitions, and serials check-in. ILS also provides access to the library's Online Public Access Catalog (OPAC). In November the library converted its database of more than 34 million records to Unicode, thereby allowing bibliographic records to display in non-roman scripts. The library has been cataloging in non-roman scripts for more than 20 years, but the software was unable to display non-roman characters until this upgrade.

Arrearage Reduction/Cataloging

During the year the Bibliographic Access Divisions and Serial Record Division cataloged a record total of 312,818 bibliographic volumes.

Production of full- and core-level original cataloging totaled 185,531 bibliographic records. Cataloging staff also created 55,925 copy cataloging records and 28,993 minimal-level cataloging records.

With the library serving as the secretariat for the international Program for Cooperative Cataloging, member institutions created 171,988 new name authorities and 5,916 new or updated subject and classification authorities. In addition, the library contributed 88,828 new name authorities, 9,056 new series authorities, and 6,678 new subject headings.

Secondary Storage

The library continued to fill new storage units at Fort Meade, Maryland. During the year, Module 1 at Fort Meade was filled to capacity with nearly 1.6 million monographs and bound periodicals. Module 2 was completed in May 2005 with a capacity of 3.3 million monographs and bound serials.

Planning continued for the National Audio-Visual Conservation Center (NAVCC) in Culpeper, Virginia, scheduled to open in November 2006. The 45-acre NAVCC campus is being built with private-sector support from the Packard Humanities Institute and will consist of four building components totaling 420,000 square feet of space for the library's recorded sound, videotape, safety film, and nitrate film collections. The site will also consolidate the activities of the library's Motion Picture, Broadcasting, and Recorded Sound Division in one location.

Important Acquisitions

The library receives millions of items each year from copyright deposits, federal agencies, and purchases, exchanges, and gifts. Significant acquisitions made possible by the Madison Council during the year included retrospective acquisitions, among them a rare photograph of Texas historical figure Sam Houston; the *Middlesex Gazette* (Middletown, Connecticut) edition of December 27, 1799; a set of eight circa 1904 "White House Views" from the Detroit Publishing Company; and a Philip Trager "Taos Church" photograph.

In addition, the library acquired the following significant items and collections in 2005:

- Papers of Supreme Court Justices John Paul Stevens, Sandra Day O'Connor, and Ruth Bader Ginsburg
- Papers of the late Katharine Graham, former publisher of the *Washington Post*
- More than 20,000 items including drawings, models, and business papers from renowned architect I. M. Pei
- Significant additions to the Iranian collections, including 20 books given by the National Library of Iran to the Librarian of Congress marking his visit to Iran in November
- Nearly 20,000 individual submissions to the Veterans History Project, comprising some 80,000 items documenting the experiences of the nation's war veterans

- The first group of digitally recorded interviews, capturing personal histories of Americans from all walks of life, as part of the StoryCorps Project

Digital Projects and Planning

National Digital Information Infrastructure and Preservation Program

The National Digital Information Infrastructure and Preservation Program (NDI-IPP) was established in FY 2001 and funded with an appropriation of $99.8 million from Congress. Its goal is to encourage shared responsibility for the collection, selection, and organization of historically significant cultural materials regardless of evolving formats; the long-term storage, preservation, and authentication of those collections; and rights-protected access for the public to the digital heritage of the American people.

In 2004 eight institutions and their partners were awarded $14 million to identify, collect, and preserve historically important digital materials. These partners—36 institutions—met twice in 2005 to discuss issues of mutual concern.

In May 2005 the library, in partnership with the National Science Foundation, awarded research grants totaling $3 million to ten university teams to undertake cutting-edge research in the field of digital preservation and access.

In October the library announced a $3 million grant award to Ithaka, a nonprofit organization, for the development of Portico, an electronic archiving service. The project will begin by archiving electronic journals. The award advances two fundamental goals of the library's massive digital preservation program: to develop a technical infrastructure to support long-term preservation of digital content and to foster the development of new business models for digital preservation services.

World Digital Library

In June the Librarian of Congress introduced the concept of a world digital library during a speech delivered at Georgetown University to the newly established U.S. National Commission for UNESCO. He proposed that public research institutions and libraries work with private organizations to digitize significant primary materials of different cultures from institutions across the globe. In November Google, Inc. agree to donate $3 million as the first partner in this public-private initiative.

Internet Resources

The library continued to expand its electronic services to Congress and the nation through its award-winning Web site. During the year, more than 3.7 billion transactions were recorded on the library's computer systems. The following are selected resources available on the Web site.

American Memory. At year's end, more than 10 million American historical items were available on the American Memory Web site. In 2005 seven new multimedia historical collections were added to the site, bringing the total to 133. Five existing collections were expanded with new content. American Memory registered 825 million hits in FY 2005, an increase of more than 33 percent over the previous year.

America's Library. Work continued to expand the content and features available on America's Library, an interactive Web site for children and families that draws upon the library's vast online resources. The site has won numerous awards and is one of the most popular online offerings of the library. America's Library logged more than 239 million transactions during the year, compared with 218 million in 2004.

Exhibitions. Nine new library exhibitions were added to the library's Web site in 2005, bringing the total to 63. This feature allows users who are unable to visit the library in person to view many of its past and current exhibitions online.

Global Gateway. Four new collections were added to the Global Gateway Web site, a portal to the library's unparalleled international collections and those of other major repositories worldwide through collaborative digitization projects. These included the library's collection of 38 cuneiform tablets, which were digitized and added to the site.

Global Legal Information Network. During the year, the Library of Congress Law Library implemented an enhanced version of the Global Legal Information Network (GLIN), a network of government agencies and international institutions that contribute official texts of laws and related legal materials to a database that is accessible over the Internet. Through the contributions of 27 countries and international institutions and the addition of laws for 16 other countries by the staff of the law library, GLIN provides timely access to the laws of 43 of the world's governing bodies. The upgraded system provides new features, including multilingual input and search capabilities in English, French, Spanish, and Portuguese. Since the launch of the new system in February, approximately 2.4 million transactions were recorded on the GLIN site.

Online Catalog. The library continued to provide global access to its online public access catalog (OPAC). The site recorded more than 4 million transactions during the year.

Prints and Photographs Online Catalog. A milestone was reached in 2005 with the addition of the one-millionth image from the library's Prints and Photographs Division to the online catalog.

THOMAS. The public legislative information system known as THOMAS continued to be a popular resource, with 210 million transactions recorded in 2005 compared with 150 million in 2004. The system was upgraded and enhanced in November to provide a more visually appealing home page, to improve navigation, and to be accessible to persons with disabilities in compliance with Section 508 of the Americans With Disabilities Act.

Wise Guide. The library's Web magazine, *Wise Guide,* is a portal to the millions of resources from the library available online. Each month, readers are offered seven articles with links to the most interesting materials on the library's various Web sites.

Reference Service

In addition to serving Congress, the library provides reference service to the public in its 21 reading rooms and via its Web site. During the year, the library's staff handled more than 667,000 reference requests that were received in person, over the telephone, and through written and electronic correspondence. Nearly 1.3 million items were circulated for use within the library.

Digital Reference

The library is a leader in providing Web-based reference and information services. Initiated in 1999 as the Collaborative Digital Reference Service, its successor, QuestionPoint, has grown to a membership of more than 800 libraries around the world, providing reference service to patrons at any time of the day or night through their local libraries' Web sites. This service, which is available to libraries by subscription, is free for library patrons. During the year the library's digital reference team answered more than 26,000 Web-based inquiries.

The library also continued to operate the "Ask a Librarian" service, by which a question can be submitted directly by a patron and answered (within five business days) through an interactive form on the library's Web site. The service, which is supported by the QuestionPoint software, includes a live chat feature that allows researchers to consult a reference librarian in real time via e-mail. During the year, the digital reference team conducted 1,274 live chat sessions.

Preservation

In 2005 the library's Preservation Directorate completed more than 12 million assessments, treatments, rehousings, and reformattings for books, codices, manuscripts, maps, cartoons, political posters, palm leaves, architectural drawings, photographs, newspapers, discs, films, magnetic tapes, and artifacts. A total of 7,143,845 items were repaired, mass deacidified, or microfilmed—a 70 percent increase over the previous year.

The library took action to preserve its collections by

- Deacidifying 296,119 books and 1,012,599 sheets of paper as part of its 30-year (one generation) mass deacidification plan to stabilize 8.5 million general collection books and 30 million pages of manuscripts (since the project's inception in 1995, the library has deacidified 1.4 million bound volumes and nearly 3 million sheets of manuscript materials)
- Using a single-sheet treatment cylinder on site at the library to deacidify paper-based nonbook materials that were too valuable to be transported to the mass deacidification vendor plant near Pittsburgh
- Surveying 3.7 million special collection items for treatment, digitization, exhibition, and relocation to off-site storage
- Rehousing 786,676 documents, photographs, discs, film, and magnetic tape reels and cassettes
- Converting 4,664,992 documents, newspaper pages, and motion picture reels to microfilm and digital format

- Treating 4,188 items for mounting on the Library's Web site
- Treating 577 items for display in library exhibitions
- Preservation microfilming of 2.7 million exposures (4.6 million pages)
- Working in partnership with other organizations to develop the NDIIPP to sort, acquire, describe, and preserve electronic materials

The library continued to play a leadership role in the preservation of materials in a variety of formats such as photographs, newspapers, films, and sound recordings. It also played an outreach role in the preservation of the nation's heritage through several oral history projects. Highlights of these included

Photographs. In August the Andrew W. Mellon Foundation awarded a $40,000 grant to the library's preservation directorate to undertake a comprehensive assessment of its photograph collections, create and evaluate a database structure to use as an assessment tool, and make recommendations to address the needs identified in the survey. The survey of the library's approximately 13.9 million photographs will allow photo conservators to plan and conduct photo preservation activities effectively and efficiently with limited staff and resources, and will provide a model that can be used to survey other photograph collections in large research institutions.

Newspapers. Over the past 22 years, access to American newspapers has been greatly enhanced through the efforts of the United States Newspaper Program (USNP) to catalog and preserve on microfilm approximately 67.5 million historical newspaper pages. In 2005 the library continued to provide technical support to USNP grant recipients under an interagency agreement with the National Endowment for the Humanities (NEH), which announced USNP awards of $1.4 million to fund continuing projects in California, Illinois, and Virginia. To date, NEH has provided more than $52 million in support of USNP projects in each of the 50 states, the District of Columbia, Puerto Rico, and the U.S. Virgin Islands.

Building on the soon-to-be-completed USNP, the library and NEH established the National Digital Newspaper Program in October 2005 with the awarding of more than $1.9 million in grants to six institutions to develop an Internet-based, searchable database of U.S. newspapers now in the public domain. Two-year projects in California, Florida, Kentucky, New York, Utah, and Virginia each will digitize 100,000 or more pages of each state's most historically significant newspapers published between 1900 and 1910. The digitized newspapers will be made available through the library's Web site.

Films. The library continued its commitment to preserving the nation's film heritage. On April 27, 2005, President Bush signed into law the Family Entertainment and Copyright Act of 2005 (Public Law 109-9), which included a provision reauthorizing the library's National Film Preservation Board program. The act authorized the National Film Registry, the National Film Preservation Board, and the National Film Preservation Foundation until October 11, 2009, and increased the foundation's annual federal matching fund level from $250,000 to $530,000. The 25 films listed below were named to the National Film Registry in 2005, bringing the total to 425. The library works to ensure that the films listed on the registry are preserved either through the library's motion picture preservation program at Dayton, Ohio, or through collaborative ventures with other archives, motion picture studios, and independent film makers.

Baby Face (1933)
The Buffalo Creek Flood: An Act of Man (1975)
The Cameraman (1928)
Commandment Keeper Church, Beaufort South Carolina, May 1940 (1940)
Cool Hand Luke (1967)
The Fall of the House of Usher (1960)
Fast Times at Ridgemont High (1982)
The French Connection (1971)
Giant (1956)
H2O (1929)
Hands Up (1926)
Hoop Dreams (1994)
Imitation of Life (1934)
Jeffries-Johnson World's Championship Boxing Contest (1910)
Making of an American (1920)
Miracle on 34th Street (1947)
Mom and Dad (1944)
The Music Man (1962)
Power of the Press (1928)
A Raisin in the Sun (1961)
The Rocky Horror Picture Show (1975)
San Francisco Earthquake and Fire, April 18, 1906 (1906)
The Sting (1973)
A Time for Burning (1966)
Toy Story (1995)

Sound Recordings. In October the library announced the results of its commissioned study on the nation's audio heritage. The study, Survey of Reissues of U.S. Recordings, found that most of America's historical sound recordings have become virtually inaccessible, available neither commercially nor in the public domain. Laws still protect the rights to fully 84 percent of recordings made in the United States between 1890 and 1964 of interest to scholars and collectors. Of those protected, rights-holders have reissued only 14 percent on compact disc. This means that the vast majority of historically important sound recordings are available for hearing only through private collectors or at research libraries that collect the nation's audio heritage and have the equipment to play obsolete recordings.

Despite this report, during the year the library's Motion Picture, Broadcasting and Recorded Sound Division (MBRS) discovered a seminal jazz tape featuring the Thelonious Monk Quartet with saxophonist John Coltrane, recorded at Carnegie Hall in November 1957. No recording of this landmark concert had been thought to exist until it was discovered as part of the library's Voice of America Collection, preserved in the MBRS recording lab. Blue Note records released a CD of the recording in September, to public and critical acclaim.

In April 2005 the Librarian of Congress announced the 2004 additions to the National Recording Registry. Under the terms of the National Recording Preservation Act of 2000, the librarian is responsible for selecting 50 recordings annually that are "culturally, historically, or aesthetically significant." The recordings are

"Gypsy Love Song," Eugene Cowles (1898)

"Some of These Days," Sophie Tucker (1911)

"The Castles in Europe One-Step" ("Castle House Rag"), Europe's Society Orchestra (1914)

"Swanee," Al Jolson (1920)

Armistice Day broadcast by Woodrow Wilson (1923)

"See See Rider Blues," Gertrude "Ma" Rainey (1923)

"Charleston," Golden Gate Orchestra (1925)

"Fascinating Rhythm" from "Lady, Be Good!" Fred and Adele Astaire; George Gershwin, piano (1926)

NBC radio broadcast coverage of pioneer aviator Charles A. Lindbergh's arrival and reception in Washington, D.C. (1927)

"Stardust," Hoagy Carmichael (1927)

"Blue Yodel (T for Texas)," Jimmie Rodgers (1927)

"Ain't Misbehavin'," Thomas "Fats" Waller (1929)

"Gregorio Cortez," Trovadores Regionales (1929)

Sergei Rachmaninoff "Piano Concerto No. 2 in C minor," Sergei Rachmaninoff, piano; Leopold Stokowski, conductor; Philadelphia Orchestra (1929)

"The Suncook Town Tragedy," Mabel Wilson Tatro of Springfield, Vt. (July 1930)

Rosina Cohen oral narrative from the Lorenzo D. Turner Collection (1932)

"Stormy Weather," Ethel Waters (1933)

"Body and Soul," Coleman Hawkins (1939)

Sergei Prokofiev "Peter and the Wolf," Serge Koussevitzky, conductor; Richard Hale, narrator; Boston Symphony Orchestra (1939)

"In the Mood," Glenn Miller and His Orchestra (1939)

Edward R. Murrow news broadcast from London (1940)

"We Hold These Truths" radio broadcast (1941)

Peter Ilich Tchaikovsky "Piano Concerto No. 1, op. 23, B minor," Vladimir Horowitz, piano; Arturo Toscanini; conductor; NBC Symphony Orchestra (1943)

"Down by the Riverside," Sister Rosetta Tharpe (1944)

"U.S. Highball (A Musical Account of a Transcontinental Hobo Trip)," Harry Partch; Gate 5 Ensemble (1946)

"Four Saints in Three Acts," Virgil Thomson, composer, with members of original 1934 cast (1947)

"Manteca," Dizzy Gillespie Big Band with Chano Pozo (1947)

Jack Benny radio program of March 28, 1948

"Foggy Mountain Breakdown," Lester Flatt and Earl Scruggs (1949)

"Lovesick Blues," Hank Williams (1949)

"Guys and Dolls," original cast recording (1950)

"Old Soldiers Never Die (Farewell Address to Congress)," Gen. Douglas A. MacArthur (1951)

"Songs by Tom Lehrer" (1953)

"I'm Your Hoochie Coochie Man," Muddy Waters (1954)

"Earth Angel (Will You Be Mine)," The Penguins (1954)

Tuskegee Institute Choir Sings Spirituals, directed by William L. Dawson (1955)

"Messiah," Eugene Ormandy, conductor; Richard Condie, choir director, Mormon Tabernacle Choir; Philadephia Orchestra (1958)

"Giant Steps," John Coltrane (1959)

"Drums of Passion," Michael Babatunde Olatunji (1960)

"Peace Be Still," James Cleveland (1962)

"The Girl from Ipanema," Stan Getz, Joao Gilberto, Antonio Carlos Jobim, Astrud Gilberto (1963)

"Live at the Apollo," James Brown (1965)

"Pet Sounds," The Beach Boys (1966)

King James version of the Bible, Alexander Scourby (1966)

Remarks from Apollo 11 astronaut Neil Armstrong's broadcast from the moon (1969)

"The Allman Brothers Band at Fillmore East" (1971)

"Star Wars" (soundtrack), John Williams (1977)

"Fear of a Black Planet," Public Enemy (1989)

Recordings of Asian elephants by Katharine Payne (1989)

"Nevermind," Nirvana (1991)

Oral History. The American Folklife Center (AFC) continued its mandate to "preserve and present American folklife" through a number of outreach and oral history programs such as the Veterans History Project (VHP) and StoryCorps. The purpose of VHP, established by Congress in 2000, is to record and preserve first-person accounts of armed services personnel who served during wartime, including members of Congress. During the year VHP staff continued to gather veterans' stories and make them accessible on the project's Web site at http://www.loc.gov/vets. During the year the project acquired an additional 20,000 submissions comprising 80,000 items, bringing the total to 40,000 submissions comprising more than 160,000 items. On Veterans Day 2005, VHP published *Forever a Soldier: Unforgettable Stories of Wartime Service,* its second in a series of books based on these submissions.

During the year the American Folklife Center (AFC) acquired its first installment of oral histories through the StoryCorps project. This national oral history project to instruct and inspire Americans to record one another's oral stories was conceived by David Isay of Sound Portraits Productions. Isay was inspired by library's collection of oral history recordings made by the Works Progress Administration (WPA) during the late 1930s and early 1940s. The StoryCorps interviews, a contemporary corollary to the WPA recordings, are the AFC's first "born digital" collection.

Copyright

The Copyright Office received 600,535 new claims to copyright during the year, covering more than 1 million works. It registered 531,720 claims. The office received more than 20,000 full electronic claims for textual works and music. The office recorded 11,874 documents covering more than 350,000 titles. The copyright public record, available for searching online, grew with the cataloging of 643,735 registrations and the indexing of thousands of parties and titles of works contained in documents recorded. The office also continued major initiatives to re-engineer its core business processes and use information technology to increase the efficiency of operations and the timeliness of public services.

The Americana collections of the Library of Congress have been created largely through the copyright system. The Copyright Office annually transfers to the library about 1 million deposit copies in all formats. In 2005 the Copyright Office forwarded 1,098,420 copies of works with a net worth of $39,649,813 to the library, including 562,588 items that were received from publishers under the mandatory deposit provisions of the copyright law.

National Library Service for the Blind and Physically Handicapped

Established by an act of Congress in 1931, the National Library Service for the Blind and Physically Handicapped (NLS) has grown to a program that supplies 23 million recorded discs and braille materials to more than 500,000 readers through a network of nearly 134 cooperating libraries around the country.

During the year work continued toward replacing outmoded analog audiotapes and cassette players with state-of-the-art digital talking books (DTBs). The project calls for the incremental phasing in of DTB playback machines and media in 2008 and the gradual elimination of obsolete analog cassettes and equipment. During the year NLS arranged for Battelle, a major technology innovation firm, to lead a consortium of expert subcontractors to design and develop its next-generation audiobook system. The complete playback system will include a solid-state digital talking-book machine and a flash-memory cartridge, about the size of a credit card and labeled in both print and braille, that stores the audiobook. It will be lightweight, portable, and durable enough for ten years of daily use, largely maintenance-free.

NLS contracted with ManTech Advanced Systems International for a study of distribution systems for the new DTBs. ManTech evaluated three distribution models and selected as the most appropriate a hybrid model that would combine mass circulation and on-demand duplication.

Now in its sixth year, the Internet-based Web-Braille service continued to provide access to braille books, magazines, and music scores online. In addition to providing access to braille material to users with a special braille keyboard and screen, the system allows a library that has lost a braille volume to order a new bound copy and put the title back in circulation. The Web-Braille site is password-protected, and all files are in an electronic form of contracted braille, requiring the use of special equipment to gain access.

Web-Braille began with approximately 2,600 titles and only a few hundred registered users. At year's end, the system offered more than 7,000 titles from the national collection, 600 music scores, 29 NLS-produced magazines, and 6 sports schedules. Books and magazines from eight regional libraries were also available. The number of users exceeded 4,000.

John W. Kluge Center

The John W. Kluge Center was established in fall 2000 with a gift of $60 million from John W. Kluge, Metromedia president and founding chairman of the James Madison Council. Located within the library's Office of Scholarly Programs, the center's goal is to bring the world's best thinkers to the Library of Congress where they can use the institution's unparalleled resources and interact with public policymakers.

In the wake of Hurricane Katrina's devastation of many educational institutions along the Gulf Coast, the Kluge Center provided interim research space to William C. Brumfield, professor of Slavic Studies at Tulane University in New Orleans. Brumfield, an internationally recognized expert on Russian architecture and acclaimed photographer, has contributed extensively to the library's Web-based Meeting of Frontiers project and the Prokudin-Gorskii Collection.

The Kluge Center Scholars' Council met September 12–13. The scholars' council is a body of international scholars appointed by the Librarian of Congress to advise on matters related to the Kluge Center and the Kluge Prize. During the formal session, the librarian explored some of the key plans for the library's future, such as the Creativity Across America initiative. He sought the council's ideas and participation and led a discussion in which members suggested the issues that might be of most significance in their field during the next 20 years.

Publications

The Publishing Office produced more than 20 books, calendars, and other products describing the library's collections in 2005, many in cooperation with trade publishers.

The library's American Folklife Center collections are the subject of a new illustrated guide. Made possible by the support of the James Madison Council, the illustrated guides to the library's collections feature materials in various formats. They include guides to the library's collections of manuscripts; prints and photographs; rare books; cartographic materials; music, theater, and dance;

motion pictures, broadcasting, and recorded sound; and Asian, African, Middle Eastern, Hispanic and Portuguese, and European materials.

In collaboration with National Geographic Books, the library published the second in a series of books based on the Veterans History Project collection and the American Folklife Center.

Released on Veterans Day 2005, *Forever a Soldier: Unforgettable Stories of Wartime Service* features personal accounts of veterans and civilians from World War I to the Gulf War of 1990–1991 gathered by the library's Veterans History Project. It joins *Voices of War: Stories of Service from the Home Front and the Front Lines,* which was published in 2004.

Theaters, the third volume of the Norton/Library of Congress Visual Source-books Architectural, Design, and Engineering series, features the architecture of American theaters. Earlier volumes in the series include *Barns* and *Canals.* The architecture of the nation's capital is featured in *Capital Drawings: Architectural Designs for Washington, D.C., from the Library of Congress,* published in 2005 by the library in cooperation with Johns Hopkins University Press.

Exhibitions

Major exhibitions featured rare books, maps, manuscripts, and other objects from the early exploration of the Americas ("The Cultures and History of the Americas: The Jay I. Kislak Collection at the Library of Congress"), color photographs from the Depression era ("Bound for Glory: America in Color, 1939–43"), rare illustrated books from the Medieval and early Renaissance period ("A Heavenly Craft: The Woodcut in Early Printed Books"), and personal stories from the Civil Rights era ("Voices of Civil Rights").

In keeping with conservation and preservation standards, several rotational changes were made in the continuing "American Treasures of the Library of Congress" exhibition. Special displays mounted in the exhibition in 2005 included "'I Do Solemnly Swear . . .' Inaugural Materials from the Collections of the Library of Congress"; "Revising Himself: Walt Whitman and Leaves of Grass," to mark the 150th anniversary of the publication of that collection of poetry; and "Benjamin Franklin: In His Own Words," to mark the 300th anniversary of Franklin's birth.

Special Events

A variety of special events, such as literary events, concerts, and symposia, were held at the library throughout the year, many of them cybercast on the library's Web site.

National Book Festival. The library organized and sponsored the 2005 National Book Festival, which was held on September 24, 2005, on the National Mall. Hosted once again by First Lady Laura Bush, the event drew the largest crowd yet, an estimated 100,000-plus. The event, which was free and open to the public, featured 79 award-winning authors, illustrators, and poets. In addition to author readings and book discussions, the festival included book sales and signings and appearances by children's storybook characters.

Other Literary Events. The library marked several literary milestones during the year. The 150th anniversary of the publication of Walt Whitman's *Leaves of Grass* was celebrated with an exhibition, symposium, poetry reading, concert, and a dramatic reading of Whitman's lecture on the "Death of Lincoln" delivered by poet, playwright, and biographer Daniel Mark Epstein. The 200th anniversary of Hans Christian Andersen's birth was celebrated in April with a lecture and small display.

During the year the library's Poetry and Literature Center sponsored a number of programs featuring new and renowned poets reading from their works. In March the library hosted "An Evening with John Prine and Ted Kooser" to discuss the work of the songwriter and the poet laureate. In April the Librarian of Congress announced the reappointment of Kooser as the library's 2005–2006 Poet Laureate Consultant in Poetry. The same month, Kooser received the 2005 Pulitzer Prize for Poetry for his book *Delights and Shadows.* During his first term (2004–2005) Kooser, with the support of the Poetry Foundation, inaugurated the program "American Life in Poetry," which offers a free weekly column to local newspapers across the country. It features the work of contemporary American poets with a sentence or two of introduction by Kooser. During its first year, the column was featured in 134 newspapers nationwide, and the Web site (http://www.americanlifeinpoetry.org) had a "circulation" of 9.6 million.

The library sponsored numerous book talks, many offered as part of the Books and Beyond lecture series sponsored by the library's Center for the Book. [For more information about the center, see "Center for the Book" later in Part 1—*Ed.*] Civil rights leaders Robert L. Carter and John Hope Franklin each discussed their recent memoirs.

Concerts. The library's 2005–2006 season marked the 80th anniversary of the Concerts from the Library of Congress series, which was established in 1925 by philanthropist and music patron Elizabeth Sprague Coolidge. Since its inception, the series has offered more than 2,000 concerts in the library's Coolidge Auditorium. During its 32-concert season, the series featured an evening dedicated to the 250th anniversary of Wolfgang Amadeus Mozart's birth.

In March the National Library Service for the Blind and Physically Handicapped sponsored the American concert debut of blind Italian pianist Enrico Lisi in the Coolidge Auditorium. The event, cosponsored by the National Federation of the Blind, the Friends of Libraries for Blind and Physically Handicapped Individuals in North America, and the North America/Caribbean Region of the World Blind Union, featured a program of selections by Schubert, Liszt, Granados, Saint-Saëns, and Chopin.

Sponsored by the American Folklife Center, the outdoor concert series titled "Homegrown: The Music of America" (April–December) continued with diverse performances by Irish fiddlers, cowboy singers from Montana, Navajo dancers, and an African American gospel quartet, among others.

Symposia and Lectures. A number of symposia held at the library were developed in conjunction with library exhibitions. These included "The Woodcut in Early Printed Books," "The World of Joseph Smith," and "Whitman and Place." Other symposia marked significant events such as the 60th anniversary of the end of World War II. During the year the library sponsored a number of lectures, several delivered in conjunction with various heritage month celebrations. These included Congressman Melvin Watt (D-N.C.) (African American Heritage Month); feminist Betty Friedan (Women's History Month); Senator Daniel Akaka (Asian Pacific American Heritage Month); Jacqueline Johnson, executive director of the National Congress of American Indians (Native American Heritage Month); and Ruben Barrales, deputy assistant to the president and director of the Office of Intergovernmental Affairs (Hispanic Heritage Month).

The Office of Scholarly Programs and the Kluge Center sponsored more than 40 events, such as symposia, book talks, and conferences, as well as talks by fellows and scholars on their particular areas of research. Highlights include a lecture series titled "Managing Knowledge and Creativity in a Digital Context" organized by Derrick de Kerckhove, the library's Papamarkou Chair in Education and Technology; a conference on neuroethics organized by Columbia University Medical School with the support of the Dana Foundation; and several seminars that introduced educators to the library's collections and will result in greater use of this material in college classrooms throughout the nation.

The fourth annual Kissinger Lecture was delivered on February 22, 2005, by former Brazilian president and former Kluge Scholar Fernando Henrique Cardoso. His lecture, "The Need for Global Democratic Governance: A Perspective from Latin America," was filmed and added to the library's growing number of online Webcasts.

Václav Havel, playwright and former president of the Czech Republic (1989–1992), delivered a human rights lecture on May 24. Titled "The Emperor Has No Clothes," the lecture focused on the contradiction between what nations proclaim about human rights and how they actually treat their citizens, with particular attention to Cuba, China, Belarus, and Burma.

The first Jay I. Kislak Lecture was delivered on September 20 by Jared Diamond, Pulitzer Prize-winning author, evolutionary biologist, physiologist, and biogeographer. The inaugural lecture, "Collapse: How Societies Choose to Fail or Succeed," discussed why some civilizations collapsed in the past and what might be learned from their experiences.

Outreach. The library continued to share its treasures both nationally and internationally on its Web site, through its Learning Page for teachers, traveling exhibitions program, and other programs such as the Song of America tour, which launched the library's Creativity Across America initiative.

Additional Sources of Information

Library of Congress telephone numbers for public information:

Main switchboard (with menu)	202-707-5000
Reading room hours and locations	202-707-6400
General reference	202-707-3399
	TTY 202-707-4210

Visitor information	202-707-8000
	TTY 202-707-6200
Exhibition hours	202-707-4604
Reference assistance	202-707-6500
Copyright information	202-707-3000
Copyright hotline (to order forms)	202-707-9100
Sales shop (credit card orders)	888-682-3557

Center for the Book

John Y. Cole
Director, Center for the Book

Library of Congress, Washington, DC 20540
World Wide Web http://www.loc.gov/cfbook

With its network of affiliated centers in 50 states and the District of Columbia and more than 80 organizations serving as national reading promotion partners, the Center for the Book is one of the Library of Congress's most dynamic and visible educational outreach programs. Since its creation in 1977, it has used the resources and prestige of the Library of Congress to stimulate public interest in books, reading, literacy, and libraries, and to encourage the study of books, reading, and the printed word. The Center for the Book is a successful public-private partnership. The Library of Congress supports its four full-time positions, but all of its activities must be funded through contributions from individuals, corporations, and foundations, or by transfers of funds from other government agencies.

Highlights of 2005

- A major contribution to the success of the 2005 National Book Festival, held on the National Mall on September 24
- Sponsorship of more than 20 author talks and book signings at the Library of Congress
- Family literacy program grants to 12 public libraries and their community partners through the Center for the Book/Viburnum Foundation "Reading Powers the Mind" project
- Publication and promotion of the *Encyclopedia of the Library of Congress: For Congress, the Nation and the World*

Themes and Campaigns

The Center for the Book creates and publicizes national reading promotion themes that stimulate interest and support for reading and literacy projects that benefit all age groups. Used by affiliated state centers, national organizational partners, and schools and libraries across the nation, the themes remind Americans of the fundamental importance of books, reading, and libraries in today's world. The center's current national reading promotion theme, "Telling America's Stories," is widely used; ideas are available in a Center for the Book brochure and on the center's Web site. Previous themes still promoted by the center and often used by its affiliates and partners include "Books Change Lives," "Books Make a Difference," "Building a Nation of Readers," "Read More About It!" and "Explore New Worlds—READ!"

State Centers for the Book

The state partnership affiliation program began in 1984 when the Florida Center for the Book, hosted by the Broward County Library, was approved as the first state center. Today there are affiliated centers in all 50 states and the District of Columbia. Most of them are hosted by state libraries, large public library systems, state humanities councils, or universities. Each works with the national center to promote books, reading, and libraries, as well as the state's own literary and intellectual heritage. Each also develops and funds its own operation and projects, making use of Library of Congress themes and assistance as appropriate. State centers must apply every three years to renew their affiliate status. In 2005 renewal applications were approved from Alaska, Arizona, Arkansas, California, Delaware, the District of Columbia, Florida, Indiana, Maryland, Massachusetts, Minnesota, Missouri, Nebraska, New Hampshire, New Mexico, North Dakota, Ohio, Pennsylvania, Rhode Island, South Carolina, Tennessee, Texas, and Virginia. The Maryland Humanities Council became the host institution for the Maryland Center for the Book, and the North Dakota Humanities Commission became the home of the North Dakota Center for the Book.

On May 3 and 4, 2005, state center representatives participated in idea-sharing sessions at the Library of Congress. Principal discussion topics were fund raising, the center's "Letters About Literature" program and "Reading Powers the Mind" project, "one book" community reading and discussion projects, state book awards programs, state book festivals, and the National Book Festival. Ruth F. Boorstin, wife of former Librarian of Congress Daniel J. Boorstin, who established the Center for the Book in 1977, presented Boorstin Awards for innovative reading promotion projects to five state centers. The awards, each including a $1,000 stipend, went to Massachusetts, Michigan, Montana, Pennsylvania, and Texas.

In December three state centers (Arkansas, Florida, and South Dakota) received grants from the National Endowment for the Arts for new "one book" community reading and discussion projects.

Reading Promotion Partners

The Center for the Book is part of several reading, education, and literacy promotion networks, including the National Coalition for Literacy and the Department of Education's Federal Interagency Committee on Education. In addition, more than 80 civic, educational, and governmental organizations are "reading promotion partners" of the center, helping to promote books, reading, literacy, and libraries in ways that are compatible with their own organizational goals.

New center partners in 2005 included BrailleInk, In2Books, Phi Beta Phi fraternity, Reader to Reader, and the Read to Me International Foundation. On March 8, 2005, representatives of most of the partner organizations met at the Library of Congress to exchange information and promotion ideas.

Events and Projects

For the fifth straight year, the center played a key role in the National Book Festival, which is organized and sponsored by the Library of Congress and was hosted again in 2005 by First Lady Laura Bush. The center develops, coordinates, and oversees arrangements for the presentations by the festival's featured guests, and manages the festival's Pavilion of the States. Held on the National Mall on September 24, the 2005 festival attracted a crowd of more than 100,000. Seventy-nine authors, illustrators, and poets made presentations and signed books. The Pavilion of the States featured reading and literacy promotion programs from all 50 states, the District of Columbia, American Samoa, Guam, Puerto Rico, and the U.S. Virgin Islands.

"Letters About Literature," a national reading and writing promotion program for children and young adults, broke new records in 2005. Sponsored nationally by Target Stores and directed by center consultant Cathy Gourley, the program in 2005 saw more than 45,000 students write letters to their favorite authors, explaining why that writer's book helped shape their life. State centers throughout the country honored state winners; six national winners were selected from among the state winners, and Target brought them, their parents, and their teachers to Washington for the festival. The winners read their letters in the Teens and Children Pavilion in a program moderated by Librarian of Congress James H. Billington. Target placed full-page color advertisements congratulating state and national "Letters About Literature" winners in their hometown newspapers.

During 2005 the center hosted more than 20 book talks and signings at the Library of Congress. Each featured the author of a newly published book that was based on the library's collections or focused on a library project or program. Each was cosponsored with either a Library of Congress division or a reading promotion partner. Authors included journalists Robert MacNeil and Nick Kotz; historians Susan Ware, A. Roger Ekrich, Dane Kennedy, and John Hope Franklin; literary scholar Richard Layman; editor and translator Lori Marie Carlson; former ambassador Gordon S. Brown; poet Jorie Graham; and biographer Edmund Morris. All of the talks can be seen as Webcasts on the center's Web site.

Twelve public library literacy programs received $3,000 grants in 2005 as part of "Reading Powers the Mind," the center's family literacy project supported by the Viburnum Foundation and directed by center consultant Virginia H. Mathews. The libraries were: Ozark-Dale (Alabama) Public Library; Tucson-Pima (Arizona) Public Library; Crawford County (Arkansas) Library System; Ohoopee (Georgia) Regional Library; East Baton Rouge (Louisiana) Parish Library; Columbus-Lowndes (Mississippi) Public Library; Belen (New Mexico) Public Library; Pioneer Library System, Norman, Oklahoma; Colleton County (South Carolina) Memorial Library; Gibson County (Tennessee) Memorial Library; Longview (Texas) Public Library; and Hamlin-Lincoln County (West Virginia) Public Library.

All 12 libraries and their community partners took part in the Reading Powers the Mind family literacy workshop hosted by the Center for the Book at the Library of Congress August 3–5. In addition to sharing information about their projects, participants heard from more than a dozen distinguished speakers from government agencies and national nonprofit organizations dedicated to family literacy issues. The keynote speaker was Kathleen Strottman, an early childhood policy adviser to U.S. Sen. Mary Landrieu (D-La.).

Outreach and Publications

Center for the Book Director John Y. Cole made presentations during visits to 12 states in 2005. He made two presentations at the annual meeting of the Russian Library Association in St. Petersburg, held May 23–28, 2005, and participated in the 72nd General Conference of the International Federation of Library Associations and Institutions (IFLA) in Oslo August 9–20. A member of the IFLA Standing Committee on Reading, he also edits the IFLA *Section on Reading Newsletter,* which is produced and distributed twice a year by the Center for the Book.

In February 2005 the Library of Congress announced the publication of the *Encyclopedia of the Library of Congress: For Congress, the Nation and the World,* an authoritative and well-illustrated 569-page reference work of newly written and researched essays, articles, and statistical appendices. Edited by Cole and historian Jane Aikin, the volume describes the historical development of the library's collections, functions, and services from 1800 to 2004. To promote the volume, published jointly by the Library of Congress and Bernan Press, the center undertook a program of presentations and appearances by the editors that lasted throughout 2005.

Federal Library and Information Center Committee

101 Independence Ave. S.E., Room 217, Washington, DC 20540-4935
202-707-4800, fax 202-707-4818, e-mail flicc@loc.gov

Roberta I. Shaffer
Executive Director

Highlights of the Year

During fiscal year (FY) 2005, the Federal Library and Information Center Committee (FLICC) continued its mission "to foster excellence in federal library and information services through interagency cooperation and to provide guidance and direction for FEDLINK."

FLICC's annual information policy forum, "Evolving Information Policy: Open Access and New Constraints," focused on the new opportunities of electronic publishing and the Web to expand access to literature resulting from federally funded research and to archive those materials to ensure their availability. The morning session featured a talk by Elias A. Zerhouni, director of the National Institutes of Health (NIH) on NIH's new policy to make available all final results of research supported in whole or in part by NIH funding. The afternoon discussion centered on the threat of terrorism, other information security issues, and Executive Order 13233, which implements the Presidential Records Act and authorizes indefinite restriction of public access to archived presidential documents that previously had been largely available to the public after 12 years.

The FLICC working groups completed an ambitious agenda in FY 2005. Notably, the Human Resources Working Group renewed its efforts to redefine the Office of Personnel Management's (OPM) 1410 Qualification Standards and the Classification Standards in order to remove the occupation of librarian from OPM's "services" directory and have it established as a "professional" occupation. The Education Working Group presented a variety of seminars and workshops, including a leadership and management education series for current and potential federal library managers; other workshops, seminars, and institutes were on cataloging, copyright law, digital licensing, and other information science policy issues. The Content Management Working Group sponsored a content management update on the future of the federal library and workshops on information architecture, taxonomy, and e-government.

The FLICC Awards Working Group announced the following awards:

- Federal Library/Information Center of the Year—large library/information center category (staff of 11 or more), Dudley Knox Library at the Naval Postgraduate School, Monterey, California; small library/information center category (staff of 10 or fewer), Edwards Air Force Base Library, Air Force Materiel Command, Edwards Air Force Base, California.
- Federal Librarian of the Year—Barbara D. Wrinkle, chief of the Air Force Libraries Branch at the Air Force Library and Information System.
- Federal Library Technician of the Year—Mary Alice B. Mendez of the Defense Language Institute, English Language Center Library at Lackland Air Force Base, Texas.

FLICC added five new programs to its online video library on topics ranging from information architecture, metadata, and controlled vocabularies to e-government and taxonomies, ontologies, and the semantic Web.

FLICC also continued its collaboration with the Library of Congress General Counsel on a series of meetings between federal agency legal counsels and agency librarians. Now in their seventh year, the forums grew out of the recognition that federal attorneys and librarians face many of the same questions concerning copyright law, privacy law, the Freedom of Information Act, and other laws, with regard both to using information within the agency and to publishing the agency's information. These meetings have enhanced the relationship between agency attorneys and librarians and have helped them develop contacts with their counterparts at other agencies. This year's quarterly series featured discussions on the role of the Government Accountability Office (GAO) in the federal appropriations process, e-records management, policies for federal agency Web sites, and legal issues relating to the public access policy.

FLICC's cooperative network, FEDLINK, continued to enhance its fiscal operations while providing its members $65.3 million in transfer-pay services, $8.4 million in direct-pay services, and an estimated $30.7 million in Direct Express services, saving federal agencies more than $11 million in vendor volume discounts and approximately $7.8 million more in cost avoidance.

To meet the requirements of the Fiscal Operations Improvement Act of 2000 (P.L. 106-481), which created new statutory authority for FEDLINK's fee-based activities, FEDLINK governing bodies and staff members developed a five-year business plan in FY 2002 that entered its fourth year in FY 2005. Program work in FY 2005 continued to take advantage of the increased opportunities of FEDLINK's authority as a revolving fund. Staff members made significant progress on goals relating to improving processes and expanding marketing initiatives.

In FY 2005 FEDLINK continued to give federal agencies cost-effective access to an array of automated information-retrieval services for online research, cataloging, and interlibrary loan (ILL). FEDLINK members also procured print serials, electronic journals, books and other publications, CD-ROMs, and document delivery via Library of Congress/FEDLINK contracts with more than 120 major vendors. The program obtained further discounts for customers through consortia and enterprise-wide licenses for journals, aggregated information retrieval services, and electronic books. FEDLINK awarded new contracts for monograph acquisitions with 26 companies and renewed six. FEDLINK implemented competition for agencies' serials services under new contracts with seven serial subscription agents. A number of national conferences highlighted FEDLINK programs, including the Military Librarians Workshop, Defense Technical Information Center Users Group meetings, and FOSE, the largest and longest-running government technology showcase.

FY 2005 also saw innovative educational initiatives including workshops and seminars on cataloging, information architecture, taxonomy, e-government, serials holdings, copyright law, digital licensing, and other information science policy issues. Staff members sponsored 37 seminars and workshops for 1,426 participants, 33 on-site training classes for 216 participants, and 10 off-site programs for 89 participants. These included workshops on the Online Computer

Library Center (OCLC) and acquisitions provided to Army and Air Force library staff members in Germany.

FEDLINK continued to customize and configure software and support services for electronic invoicing and to increase online access to financial information for member agencies and vendors. FEDLINK's continuing financial management efforts ensured that FEDLINK successfully passed the Library of Congress financial audit of FY 2004 transactions.

FLICC also had a change of leadership in FY 2005. Susan M. Tarr retired after 10 years as executive director, and was succeeded in August by Roberta I. Shaffer.

FLICC Quarterly Membership Meetings

Beyond regular FLICC Working Group updates and reports from FLICC/FEDLINK staff members, each FLICC Quarterly Meeting included a special focus on a new or developing trend in federal libraries or a guest speaker. The February 2005 meeting featured the University of Maryland Masters of Information Management study team's progress report on performance metrics; the June meeting included an update on "Libraries and Google: Improving Access to Information" by Catherine Gordon, business development director of Google, Inc.; and the September 2005 meeting's focus was a presentation on "Digitization for Preservation: A Federal Government Perspective" by Judy Russell, managing director, information dissemination (Superintendent of Documents), U.S. Government Printing Office.

FLICC Executive Board

The FLICC Executive Board (FEB) focused its efforts on a number of initiatives related to FLICC's 40th anniversary and the FLICC Forum. Early in the year, the board selected the FLICC Awards winners and updated the FLICC Bylaws. FEB then contacted the Secretary of the Navy in support of re-establishing the position of Librarian of the Navy, worked with the Department of Housing and Urban Development on its library closure, and began discussions with representatives from the Environmental Protection Agency libraries on a letter of support and to explore cooperative endeavors.

FLICC Working Group Highlights

Awards Working Group

To honor the many ways in which federal libraries, librarians, and library technicians fulfill the information demands of government, business, research, scholarly communities, and the American public, the Awards Working Group administers a series of national awards for federal librarianship.

The award for 2004 Federal Library/Information Center of the Year (for a large library/information center with a staff of 11 or more employees) went to the Dudley Knox Library at the Naval Postgraduate School, Monterey, California. FLICC recognized the library as a national leader in the delivery of government and defense information. Knox Library provides an information-rich environment for both the Naval Postgraduate School's student body and the greater Department of Defense worldwide.

The award for small library/information center (staff of 10 or fewer) went to Edwards Air Force Base Library, Air Force Materiel Command, Edwards Air Force Base, California. FLICC recognized the library for the innovative services and superior customer services it offered in FY 2004. The library has demonstrated its ability to combine creativity and innovation to meet the needs of its military and civilian customers and the overall mission of its agency.

The award for 2004 Federal Librarian of the Year was won by Barbara D. Wrinkle, chief of the Air Force Libraries Branch at the Air Force Library and Information System. She was recognized for her professional knowledge and expertise and for undertaking initiatives that have greatly improved the Air Force library systems and provided improved information services to military personnel and their families around the world.

Federal Library Technician of the Year for 2004 was Mary Alice B. Mendez of the Defense Language Institute, English Language Center Library at Lackland Air Force Base, Texas, who was recognized for her dedication to service excellence in support of the mission of the library. As the sole staff member of the library, she carried out the normal duties of a technician but also the duties typically performed by a professional librarian, including collection development, acquisitions, cataloging, reference, and ILL.

The Librarian of Congress presented the awards at the annual FLICC Forum on Federal Information Policies in March 2005.

Budget and Finance Working Group

The Budget and Finance Working Group developed the FY 2006 FEDLINK budget and fee structure in the spring quarter. The group produced an online budget questionnaire for FEDLINK members and used the results to verify assumptions for the budget for FY 2006. The final budget for FY 2006 kept membership fees for transfer-pay customers at FY 2005 levels: 7.75 percent on accounts up to $300,000 and 7 percent on amounts exceeding $300,000. Direct-pay fees also remained at FY 2005 levels, as did Direct Express fees of 0.75 percent for all participating commercial online information services vendors. Library of Congress officials approved the budget in August 2005.

Competitive Sourcing Working Group

The Competitive Sourcing Working Group sponsored a brown bag session in January 2005, "Competitive Sourcing: A Catalyst for Change," which featured a discussion of the competitive sourcing process and possible outcomes. Experienced librarians from a number of federal agencies provided an overview of the process, introduced vocabulary, clarified acronyms, and shared resources.

Group members also began preparations for a survey on competitive sourcing to collect basic information concerning the history of outsourcing in federal libraries, and revised Chapter 5 of the *FLICC Handbook of Federal Librarianship,* which covers competitive sourcing.

Content Management Working Group

The Content Management Working Group sponsored brown bag discussions on e-government, federated search technologies, information architecture, and metadata and controlled vocabularies. Members also coordinated the 2005 Content Management Update, "The Future of the Federal Library," which attracted more than 100 attendees. The group upgraded its Web site, offering links to a list of content management resources by topic, and centered its discussions on such issues as Open Archives Initiative (OAI) Rights Expression Language and the NISO Open Digital Language.

Education Working Group

The Education Working Group, in collaboration with other FLICC working groups, sponsored a total of 37 seminars, workshops, and lunchtime discussions for 1,426 members of the federal library and information center community concerning cataloging, copyright issues, statistics, information access, communication skills, and leadership development.

The working group responded to the educational agenda developed by the FLICC membership in 2001 by continuing its seminar series from the American Management Association with a multiple-day session on communication and a "mini-MBA" series for federal library directors.

Human Resources Working Group

The Human Resources Working Group continued its focus on the critical areas of core competencies, recruitment and retention of federal librarians, professional development, and advancement for federal librarians. The group continued negotiating with the Office of Personnel Management (OPM) on removing "librarian" as a category in the Department of Labor's Directory of Occupations under the Contracts Services Act and redefining the OPM 1410 Qualification and Classification Standards.

Nominating Working Group

The Nominating Working Group oversaw the 2005 election process for FLICC rotating members, FLICC Executive Board members, and the FEDLINK Advisory Council. Librarians representing a variety of federal agencies agreed to place their names in nomination for these positions.

Working Group on Federal Libraries/GPO Partnership

Early in 2005, nine librarians on the ad hoc Federal Libraries/GPO Partnership Working Group met with the Superintendent of Documents to discuss issues relating to the future of the depository program within the federal library context. In the succeeding months, the group received proposals from GPO via its closed listserv and commented on GPO plans from a federal library perspective.

Preservation and Binding Working Group

The Preservation and Binding Working Group completed its efforts on a statement of work for developing a standard federal conservation/preservation service contract that opened for bids in the spring. After members of the working group reviewed bidders' proposals for conservation and preservation services, Library of Congress Contracts and Grants Management (LC/C&G) awarded basic ordering agreements to 13 preservation services vendors. The working group also held an informational session on the GPO binding contract.

Publications and Education Office

In FY 2005 FLICC supported an ambitious publication schedule, producing six issues of *FEDLINK Technical Notes* and two issues of the *FLICC Quarterly Newsletter*.

FLICC revised mission-critical materials and developed targeted resources to support the FEDLINK program, including the electronic-only FY 2006 *FEDLINK Registration Pamphlet* and four FEDLINK Information Alerts. FLICC also produced the minutes of the four FY 2005 FLICC Quarterly Meetings and six FLICC Executive Board meetings, and all FLICC Education Program promotional and support materials, including the FLICC forum announcement, forum attendee and speaker badges, press advisories, speeches and speaker remarks, and forum collateral materials. FLICC produced 47 FLICC meeting announcements to promote FLICC education programs, FEDLINK membership and OCLC users' meetings, brown bag discussion series and education institutes, along with other supporting materials.

FLICC and FEDLINK staff members continued to manage, support, and update the FLICC/FEDLINK Web site of more than 1,000 pages of content, video, and resource links. Special Web projects during the year included updating the html code on all new and revised Web pages to meet both the library's and the World Wide Web Consortium's html code validation and access requirements and revisions to the federal library resources site. Staff members worked closely with the FLICC working groups, updating the Awards, Preservation and Binding, and Human Resources Working Groups pages and completing a new Content Management Working Group page. FLICC staff members continued to convert all publications, newsletters, announcements, alerts, member materials, meeting minutes, and working group resources into html and pdf formats, uploading current materials within days of their being printed. Staff members maintained the many Web links throughout the FLICC/FEDLINK Web site and enhanced and expanded the site via an inter-unit Web team of content, design, editorial, and technical personnel.

FLICC increased its distance-learning offerings by providing on-demand Web videos of both the fall and spring FEDLINK Membership meetings, and the annual FLICC Information Policy Forum, the FLICC Awards Ceremony, the Joint Spring Workshop, and a number of content-management events. Staff members now also routinely incorporate electronic versions of PowerPoint and other presentation materials to enhance access to the resources available at educational programs.

FLICC staff members recorded five outstanding educational programs to provide videos on ILL through the National Library of Education. Staff members also recorded presentations at the FLICC Quarterly Membership Meetings and distributed copies in DVD format for viewing by members who were unable to attend.

In collaboration with FEDLINK Network Operations staff members, FLICC Publications staff continued to offer dynamic resources including OCLC Usage Analysis Reports, pricing data, and many other new documents, including the FY 2005 budget questionnaire and ballot and a variety of training resources. Staff also worked with Library of Congress Contracts and Gifts staff to make electronic versions of FEDLINK's Requests for Proposals available online for prospective vendors.

In FY 2005 Publications staff continued to support the Member Services Unit and its Online Registration/Online Interagency Agreement (IAG) system. The Online Registration site also included an updated screen regarding serials subscriptions services competitions with enhanced interactive forms and detailed instructions.

In conjunction with the FLICC Working Groups, FLICC offered a total of 37 seminars, workshops, and lunchtime discussions to 1,426 members of the federal library and information center community. Multiple-day institutes looked at cataloging, organizational communication, and international and online copyright management; one-day sessions offered hands-on and theoretical knowledge on e-government, basic serials and MARC cataloging, taxonomy, statistics, content management, Library of Congress subject headings, and virtual reference. FLICC was also the host to four General Counsel forums on appropriations, electronic records management, e-government, NIH information access, and fair use, and three Federal Webmaster forums on emerging technology issues relating to e-government initiatives. FLICC also collaborated with the consortium CAPCON on educational events by co-promoting programs and opening events to each other's members when additional space was available.

FLICC demonstrated its ongoing commitment to library technicians' continuing education by hosting a teleconference series, "Soaring to . . . Excellence," produced by the College of DuPage. Federal and academic librarians also joined FLICC professionals to discuss various areas of librarianship, including taxonomies, acquisitions, cataloging, copyright laws, reference, and automation.

FLICC also provided organizational, promotional, and logistical support for FEDLINK meetings and events including the FEDLINK Fall and Spring Membership Meetings, two FEDLINK OCLC Users Group meetings, and 47 vendor presentations with 374 customers attending.

FEDLINK

In FY 2005 FEDLINK (the Federal Library and Information Network) continued to give federal agencies cost-effective access to an array of automated information retrieval services for online research, cataloging, and ILL. FEDLINK members also procured print serials, electronic journals, books and other publications, CD-ROMs, and document delivery via Library of Congress/FEDLINK contracts with more than 120 major vendors. The program obtained further discounts for customers through consortia and enterprise-wide licenses for journals, aggregated information retrieval services, and electronic books. FEDLINK awarded new contracts for monograph acquisitions to 26 companies and renewed six.

FEDLINK also initiated competition for federal agencies' serials services under new contracts with seven serial subscription agents. To market these products and services to current and potential FEDLINK customers, staff members participated and exhibited in a number of national conferences including the Military Librarians Workshop, Defense Technical Information Center (DTIC) Users Group, and FOSE, the premier exposition of technology for the government.

The FEDLINK Advisory Council (FAC) met eight times during the fiscal year. In addition to its general oversight activities, FAC advised FEDLINK managers on priorities for the fourth year of the five-year business plan, provided valuable insight into trends in the information industry, and supported adoption of the proposed FY 2006 budget. It also provided feedback on the administration of consortial purchases and gave insight to FEDLINK staff members on customer requirements.

The annual Fall FEDLINK Membership meeting featured Carrie Russell, copyright specialist with the American Library Association's (ALA) Office for Information Technology Policy, who presented "Copyright in the Digital Age." FEDLINK staff members also presented information about new services at this meeting.

The Spring 2005 FEDLINK Membership meeting featured Carol Bursik, chair of the FLICC Budget and Finance Working Group, who presented the proposed FY 2006 budget; a presentation by Miriam Nisbet, ALA legislative counsel, on "ALA's Perspective on the Principles for Fair Electronic Commerce Transactions"; and a discussion of issues affecting federal agencies' licensing of electronic content presented by a panel of federal librarians from the Environmental Protection Agency, the Armed Forces Medical Library, and the Naval Research Laboratory Library.

FEDLINK/OCLC Network Activity

Both FEDLINK OCLC Users Group meetings, held in October and May, provided in-depth presentations on OCLC's expanded Web services including improved interfaces for cataloging, ILL, reference databases, and full text in FirstSearch, NetLibrary, and QuestionPoint, the Library of Congress-OCLC cooperative digital reference system.

FEDLINK staff members supplemented these biannual OCLC meetings with six "OCLC News" articles in *FEDLINK Technical Notes,* postings on electronic lists, extensive telephone consultations, and e-mail. They provided demonstrations and lectures at agency meetings, such as Navy and Air Force library meetings, the Military Librarians Workshop, and the DTIC Users Group meeting. Staff members also monitored OCLC usage, posted usage data monthly to FEDLINK's online account management system, ALIX-FS, and reduced deficits in OCLC accounts.

Eleanor Frierson, deputy director of the National Agricultural Library, represented FEDLINK on the OCLC Membership Council, adding a federal perspective to the larger issues in librarianship and information science and contributing to future plans that meet the cooperative needs of libraries and similar institutions. Frierson was re-elected for a second three-year term in spring 2005. Suzanne Ryder, associate librarian, Naval Research Laboratory Library, was elected alternate delegate.

Training Program

The 2005 FEDLINK training program included 33 on-site training classes for 216 students and 10 off-site programs for 89 participants. These included workshops on OCLC and acquisitions provided to Army and Air Force library staff members in Germany.

FEDLINK promoted its training agreements with other OCLC networks so that FEDLINK customers could fund training accounts for workshops held by the consortia Amigos, BCR, CAPCON, Michigan Library Consortium, Missouri Library Network Corporation, NYLINK, OCLC Western, PALINET, and SOLINET. FEDLINK also brokered the Computers in Libraries conference at a discounted rate for more than 250 attendees, saving the government approximately $49,000.

Procurement Program

During FY 2005 staff worked closely with LC/C&G to issue a request for proposal for monograph acquisitions, resulting in basic ordering agreements with 11 additional book jobbers for FY 2006, bringing the total to 32. Staff also worked with LC/C&G to compete individual libraries' serials subscription services for 123 libraries.

FEDLINK staff members continued to support consortial arrangements for services such as INSPEC, LexisNexis, and West.

FEDLINK Fiscal Operations

FLICC's cooperative network, FEDLINK, continued to enhance its fiscal operations while providing its members with $65.3 million in transfer-pay services, $8.4 million in direct-pay services, and an estimated $30.7 million in the new Direct Express services, saving federal agencies more than $11 million in vendor volume discounts and approximately $7.8 million more in cost avoidance.

To meet the requirements of the Fiscal Operations Improvement Act of 2000 (P.L. 106-481), which created new statutory authority for FEDLINK's fee-based activities, FEDLINK governing bodies and staff members developed a five-year business plan in FY 2002 that entered its fourth year in FY 2005. Program work in FY 2005 continued to take advantage of the increased opportunities of FEDLINK's authority as a revolving fund. Staff members made significant progress on goals relating to improving processes and expanding marketing initiatives to attract high-volume customers through a pilot initiative that lowered fees for their vendor accounts in excess of $1 million.

FEDLINK Vendor Services

Total FEDLINK vendor service dollars for FY 2005 comprised $65.3 million for transfer-pay customers, $8.4 million for direct-pay customers and $30.7 million of estimated vendor billings to Direct Express customers. Database retrieval services, available only through the transfer-pay and Direct Express options, represented $28.9 million and $30.7 million, respectively. Within this service category, online services composed the largest procurement for transfer-pay and Direct Express customers, representing $27.1 million and $28.9 million, respectively. Publication acquisition services, available only through the transfer-pay and standard direct-pay options, represented $29 million and $8.4 million, respectively. Within this service category, serials subscription services composed the largest procurement for transfer-pay and direct-pay customers, representing $20 million and $8.2 million, respectively. Library support and other miscellaneous services, available only through the transfer-pay option, represented $7.4 million. Within this service category, bibliographic utilities made up the largest procurement area, representing $5 million.

Accounts Receivable and Member Services

FEDLINK processed FY 2005 registrations from federal libraries, information centers, and other federal offices for a total of 518 signed interagency agreements (IAGs). In addition, FEDLINK processed 2,002 IAG amendments (1,001 for FY 2005 and 1,001 for prior years) for agencies that added, adjusted, or ended service funding. These IAGs and IAG amendments represented 7,238 individual service requests to begin, move, convert, or cancel service from FEDLINK vendors. FEDLINK executed service requests by generating 7,054 delivery orders that LC/C&G issued to vendors. For FY 2005 alone, FEDLINK processed $65.3 million in service dollars for 2,238 transfer-pay accounts and $8.4 million in service dollars for 28 direct-pay accounts.

Included in the above member service transactions were 731 member requests to move prior-year (no-year and multiple-year) funds across FY boundaries. These no-year and multiple-year service request transactions represented an additional contracting volume of $4.1 million.

Transfer-Pay Accounts Payable Services

For transfer-pay users, FEDLINK processed 55,962 invoices for payment during FY 2005 for both current-year and prior-year orders. Staff members efficiently processed vendor invoices and earned $19,989 in discounts in excess of interest payment penalties levied for the late payment of invoices to FEDLINK vendors. FEDLINK rejected 7,995 invoices due to the following reasons: insufficient customer funds, 33 percent; duplicate vendor invoices, 30 percent; no authority (such as IAG and/or Delivery Order), 29 percent; and unidentified customer and other, 8 percent. FEDLINK continued to maintain open accounts for three prior years to pay publications service invoices ("bill laters" and "back orders") for members using books and serials services.

Staff members issued 86,919 statements to members (22,323 for the current year and 64,596 for prior years). FEDLINK generated current fiscal year statements for electronic information retrieval service accounts on the 30th or last working day of each month and publications and acquisitions account statements on the 15th of each month. In support of closing obligations for expired FY 2000 appropriations, FEDLINK issued final FY 2000 statements and quarterly statements for prior fiscal years while supporting the reconciliation of FY 2001

FEDLINK vendor service accounts. FEDLINK issued the final call for FY 2001 and 2002 invoices to vendors September 2005.

Direct Express Services

The FEDLINK Direct Express Program now includes 59 vendors offering database-retrieval services. Direct Express began as a pilot program with just five vendors in FY 2003. FEDLINK established the program to provide customers similar procurement and payment options to those available through the General Services Administration, where vendors pay a quarterly service fee based on customer billings for usage. Customers and vendors need only cite the FEDLINK contract terms and conditions and then benefit by simplifying the process of establishing a FEDLINK IAG for the direct purchase of online services.

Direct Express generated 114 percent of the fee revenue initially anticipated in the budget and the forecast for FY 2005. FEDLINK attributes the successful performance to the implementation of revised procedures that strengthened program communication and control while improving the timeliness of vendor reporting and payment to FEDLINK.

Budget and Revenue

FEDLINK FY 2005 fee revenue from signed IAGs increased 6.7 percent, or $311,859 above FY 2004 levels, and was 1.2 percent, or $56,777, more than anticipated by the FY 2005 budget. FY 2005 expenditure obligations, however, are expected to exceed FEDLINK fee revenue by $150,648.

Reserves and Risks

FEDLINK estimates its reserve carryover for FY 2005 will be $1,569,000, exceeding the program's reserve requirement by $111,000. Required reserves are intended for the following risk mitigation items: annual leave, $160,000, and shut-down costs, $797,000.

Financial Management, Reporting, and Control

FEDLINK successfully passed the Library of Congress financial audit of FY 2004 transactions and completed vulnerability assessments of program financial risks for Library Services. As a follow-up requirement, staff members completed detailed control reviews of program financial operations for Library Services, Office of Management and Training, and Office of the Inspector General review. Support for these audits includes financial systems briefings, documented review and analysis of financial system, testing and verification of account balances in the central and subsidiary financial system, financial statement preparation support, security briefings, and reviews and research and documented responses to follow-up audit questions and findings.

FEDLINK continued to provide central accounting for customer agency account balances to meet Treasury Department reporting requirements. FEDLINK also completed all aspects of its revolving fund status reporting, including preparation, review, and forecasting of revenue and expenses for the accounting period.

National Agricultural Library

U.S. Department of Agriculture
NAL Bldg., 10301 Baltimore Ave., Beltsville, MD 20705-2351
E-mail agref@nal.usda.gov
World Wide Web http://www.nal.usda.gov

Len Carey
Public Affairs Officer

The U.S. Department of Agriculture's National Agricultural Library (NAL) is the largest and most accessible agricultural research library in the world. NAL was created with the U.S. Department of Agriculture (USDA) in 1862 and established as a national library by Congress (7 USCS § 3125a) as the primary agricultural information resource of the United States.

Congress assigned to the library the responsibilities to

- Acquire, preserve, and manage information resources relating to agriculture and to allied sciences
- Organize agricultural information products and services
- Provide agricultural information products and services within the United States and internationally
- Plan, coordinate, and evaluate information and library needs relating to agricultural research and education
- Cooperate with and coordinate efforts toward development of a comprehensive agricultural library and information network
- Coordinate the development of specialized subject information services among the agricultural and library information communities

NAL is the only library in the United States with the mandate to carry out these national and international responsibilities for the agricultural community. The library's vision is "advancing access to global information for agriculture."

NAL is located in Beltsville, Maryland, near Washington, D.C., on the grounds of USDA's Henry A. Wallace Beltsville Agricultural Research Center. The library's 15-story Abraham Lincoln Building is named in honor of the president who created the Department of Agriculture and signed many of the major U.S. laws affecting agriculture.

Today, NAL employs about 160 librarians, information specialists, computer specialists, administrators, and clerical personnel, supplemented by about 80 contract staff, cooperators from NAL partnering organizations, and a few volunteers.

The library's expert staff, leadership in delivering information services, collaborations with other U.S. and international agricultural research and information organizations, extensive collection of agricultural information, AGRICOLA bibliographic database of citations to the agricultural literature, and advanced information technology infrastructure contribute to NAL's status as one of the world's foremost agricultural libraries.

The Collection

The origin of the NAL collection dates to the congressionally approved 1839 purchase of books for the Agricultural Division of the Patent Office, predating the 1862 establishment of USDA itself. Today NAL provides access to billions of pages of agricultural information—an immense collection of scientific literature, books and journals, audiovisuals, reports, theses, artifacts, and images—and to a widening array of digital media, databases, and other information resources.

The library's collection contains more than 3.5 million items dating from the 16th century to the present, including the most complete repository of USDA publications and the most extensive set of materials anywhere on the history of agriculture in the United States. The collection covers all aspects of agriculture and related sciences, making it a comprehensive resource for agricultural scientists, policy makers, regulators, and scholars.

Networks of Cooperation

NAL collections and information resources are further expanded via networks of cooperation, including arrangements with agricultural libraries at U.S. land-grant universities, other U.S. national libraries, and agricultural libraries in other countries.

NAL staff serves as secretariat for the Agriculture Network Information Center (AgNIC) Alliance, a collaborative partnership that hosts a discipline-specific, distributed network of agricultural information Web sites (http://www.agnic.org). AgNIC provides high-quality agricultural information selected by an alliance of partners involving NAL, land-grant universities, and other institutions. In 2005 AgNIC celebrated its tenth anniversary and welcomed six new members. AgNIC's 56 member institutions offer 52 subject-specific sites. During the year AgNIC released a new Web portal supporting distributed input by a geographically dispersed membership, a fully updated database, and a redesigned calendar interface.

As the U.S. node of an international agricultural information system, the library also serves as a gateway to U.S. agricultural libraries and resources for international agricultural libraries and information centers.

Building NAL Collections

NAL annually acquires more than 18,000 serial titles, including licenses for more than 2,700 electronic serials in the agricultural sciences. The library has primary responsibility for collecting and retaining all publications of USDA and its agencies, and is the only U.S. national library legally mandated to collect comprehensively in plant and animal sciences, agricultural economics, statistics, chemistry and engineering, agronomy, forestry, forest products, food, and nutrition. In addition to these core subjects, the NAL collection contains extensive materials in such related subjects as biology, physics, natural history, wildlife ecology, pollution, genetics, natural resources, meteorology, and fisheries.

Since the mid-1800s NAL has carried out a strong global program for the acquisition of publications through international exchange. The types of publications received on exchange are often difficult to acquire through established subscription vendors and constitute a valuable body of "gray literature" that is not widely available in other U.S. libraries. Currently, NAL initiates and coordinates these exchanges with more than 5,000 partners from 106 countries worldwide.

NAL's collection development policy outlines the scope of subjects collected and the degree of coverage for each subject. The policy is continually revised to include emerging subject areas and incorporate guidelines for collecting new formats, especially digital formats. NAL's collection policies reflect and differentiate the collecting responsibilities of the National Library of Medicine and the Library of Congress. The current policy is found at http://www.nal.usda.gov/acq/cdpolicy.htm.

In general, NAL's acquisition program and its collection development policy are based upon the library's responsibility to provide service to the staff of USDA, to U.S. land-grant universities, and to the general public in all subjects pertaining to agriculture.

Since the mid-1990s NAL has increasingly collected and distributed more agricultural information resources in electronic formats, making a transition toward a future "National Digital Library for Agriculture." Accordingly, NAL has continually revised its collection development strategies to emphasize electronic formats and World Wide Web resources, and to integrate networked resources to be added to the online catalog.

Special Collections

The NAL special collections program emphasizes access to and preservation of rare and unique materials documenting the history of agriculture and its sciences. These collections include rare books, manuscripts, nursery and seed trade catalogs, posters, and photographs, plus other rare or unique materials documenting agricultural subjects. The materials cover more than four centuries.

Detailed information about NAL special collections is available at http://www.nal.usda.gov/speccoll. NAL special collections of note include:

- The U.S. Department of Agriculture History Collection (http://www.nal.usda.gov/speccoll/collect/history.html), assembled over 80 years by USDA historians, which includes letters, memoranda, reports, and papers of USDA officials, plus photographs, oral histories, and clippings covering the activities of the department from its founding through the early 1990s.

- The U.S. Department of Agriculture Pomological Watercolor Collection (http://www.nal.usda.gov/speccoll/collect/pomology.html), including more than 7,000 expertly detailed, botanically accurate watercolor illustrations of fruits and nuts representing newly introduced varieties, healthy and diseased fruits, and depictions of various stages of development. Created between 1880 and 1915, the watercolor illustrations served as official documentation of the work of the office of the pomologist and were used for creation of chromolithographs in publications distributed widely by the department. Although created for scientific accuracy, the works in this collection constitute artistic treasures in their own right.

- The Henry G. Gilbert Nursery and Seed Trade Catalog Collection (http://www.nal.usda.gov/speccoll/collect/nursery.html), a rich collection of historic catalogs of the nursery and seed trade. Started in 1904 by Percy L. Ricker, economic botanist for the department, the collection is used by researchers to document the introduction of plants to the United States, to study economic trends, and to illustrate early developments in American landscape design. The earliest catalogs document the trade to the mid-1700s. NAL continues to collect nursery and seed catalogs.
- The Rare Book Collection (http://www.nal.usda.gov/speccoll/collect/rare book.html), which highlights agriculture's printed historical record and covers a wide variety of agricultural subjects. The collection, international in scope, documents early agricultural practices in Britain and Europe as well as the Americas.
- NAL offers access to more than 300 manuscript collections (http://www.nal.usda.gov/speccoll/collectionsguide/mssindextemp.shtml) documenting the story of American agriculture and its influence on the world.

In recent years, NAL has enhanced access to its special collections by digitizing Web-accessible reformatted images. The library provides in-house research and reference services for its special collections and offers fee-based duplication services. Detailed indexes to the content of many manuscript collections are produced and made available in print as well as on the Web. AGRICOLA, NAL's catalog and index to its collections, includes bibliographic entries for special collection items, manuscripts, and rare books.

During 2005 NAL collaborated with the Hunt Institute for Botanical Documentation on a significant exhibition, "Inspiration and Translation: Botanical and Horticultural Lithographs of Joseph Prestele and Sons." The exhibition opened at the Hunt Institute in Pittsburgh in September 2005 and at NAL in March 2006.

The exhibition, featuring mostly botanical and horticultural illustration, draws from the collections of both institutions as well as the Smithsonian Institution and includes items on loan from the descendants of the Prestele family. The exhibition includes watercolors, drawings, lithographs, and account books documenting the family's work for botanists and horticulturalists of the late 1800s. The Prestele family served as a major resource for USDA and the Smithsonian Institution, as well as for the nursery and seed trade. A significant group of Prestele manuscript materials from NAL's collection received conservation treatment for this exhibition.

Preservation

NAL is pursuing a long-term strategy to ensure that the growing body of agricultural information is systematically identified, prioritized, preserved, and archived. NAL has digitized a growing collection of USDA publications, including *Home and Garden Bulletin, Agriculture Information Bulletin,* and *Yearbook of the United States Department of Agriculture.* Online access to these and other full-text publications will be available in 2006 when NAL initiates a pilot digital repository site.

NAL is committed to the preservation of its print collections and strives to improve its environmental quality to extend the longevity of all materials in the collection.

AGRICOLA

AGRICOLA (AGRICultural OnLine Access) is the catalog and index to NAL collections, as well as a primary public source for worldwide access to agricultural information. AGRICOLA is searchable on the Web (http://www.nal.usda.gov/landing_pages/webvoy.htm); it can also be accessed on a fee basis through several commercial vendors, both online and on CD-ROM. In addition, users can subscribe to the AGRICOLA file on a fee basis from the National Technical Information Service, part of the U.S. Department of Commerce.

The AGRICOLA database covers materials in all formats, including printed works dating back several centuries. The records describe publications and resources encompassing all aspects of agriculture and allied disciplines. Thousands of AGRICOLA records contain Web links to networked resources.

The AGRICOLA database is organized into two components, updated with newly cataloged and indexed materials, searchable separately or together:

- NAL Public Access Catalog, containing citations to books, audiovisual materials, serial titles, and other materials in the NAL collection; AGRICOLA also contains some bibliographic records for items cataloged by other libraries but not held in NAL's collection
- NAL Article Citation Database, which includes citations to serial articles, book chapters, reports, and reprints

AGRICOLA's scope has eroded since 1985 as NAL's appropriated funding has been insufficient to acquire content needed to maintain a comprehensive index of agricultural literature. Qualitative evaluation of AGRICOLA has documented gaps in continuous coverage due to index backlogs. Currently, about 65,000 AGRICOLA index records are added annually, contrasting with the estimated publication output of almost 200,000 English-language articles appearing each year on agricultural topics.

As a result, NAL in 2005 began to redefine the scope of the AGRICOLA index to reflect realistic capacity and capabilities. Rather than pursue a goal of comprehensiveness, the AGRICOLA index in the future will likely focus on publications of USDA and USDA agencies, and on articles authored by USDA scientists, as well as on electronic and printed content material in the agricultural sciences that is not indexed by commercial indexing services. The re-scoped AGRICOLA index will continue to serve as the search tool to access NAL's collections.

Electronic Repository of Agricultural Literature

In 2005 NAL began development of an Electronic Repository of Agricultural Literature (ERAL) as a key component of the NAL collections. Initially, this institutional repository will preserve digital copies of articles authored by Agricultural Research Service (ARS) and other USDA researchers, but also will contain presentations and other unpublished works authored by USDA scientists as well as digital copies of USDA publications. By preserving the scientific work of USDA scientists, this repository will enable NAL to provide access to this information via the Web.

NAL has instituted planning for ERAL through a pilot project involving the storage and display of serial articles authored by scientists in two ARS laboratories. NAL plans the initial development of ERAL for 2006.

Information Management and Information Technology

Over the last quarter century NAL has been a leader in applying information technology to support its core function of managing and providing access to a diverse array of agricultural information. Technological developments spearheaded by NAL date back to the 1940s and 1950s, when Director Ralph Shaw invented "electronic machines" such as the photocharger, rapid selector, and photoclerk. There have been numerous technological improvements at NAL since.

NAL implemented the Voyager integrated library management system (produced by Endeavor Information Systems) over the last two years to organize, manage, and provide access to the library's collection. The system supports ordering, receiving, and invoice processing for purchases; creating and maintaining indexing and cataloging records for AGRICOLA; and circulation.

In 2005 NAL examined ways to increase the speed and productivity of its indexing program, exploring machine-aided indexing; broadened use of publisher-supplied data; and streamlined the indexing process. These measures reduced a backlog of articles waiting indexing.

NAL is known for its expertise in development and use of a thesaurus or controlled vocabulary, a critical component of effective electronic information systems. The NAL Agricultural Thesaurus (NALT) is an online vocabulary for agricultural and biological terms (http://agclass.nal.usda.gov/agt/agt.shtml). Updated yearly, NALT broadly defines the subject scope of agriculture, organized according to 17 subject categories. Biological nomenclature comprises most terms in the thesaurus, although it includes terminology in the supporting biological, physical, and social sciences. Suggestions for new terms or definitions can be sent to thes@nal.usda.gov.

Originally prepared to meet the needs of ARS scientists, NALT has been adopted to aid retrieval in agricultural information systems within USDA and elsewhere. NALT is the indexing vocabulary for NAL's bibliographic database of 3.75 million article citations to agricultural resources included in the AGRICOLA database.

NAL released the fifth edition of NALT in early January 2006, adding 400 new definitions for a total of 66,417 terms. Terminology associated with herbal dietary supplements was expanded with the fifth edition, including botanical nomenclature, common names, and bioactive compounds. The taxonomic classification of insects and other arthropods was reviewed and updated according to the recommendation of the Entomological Society of America.

Library Services

NAL serves the agricultural information needs of customers through traditional library reference, document delivery, and information center services. The main reading rooms in NAL's Beltsville facility house a walk-up service desk, an extensive reference collection, a current periodicals collection, an electronic services center, and a selection of full-text scientific journals. NAL also operates a walk-in reference and electronic services center at USDA headquarters in downtown Washington, D.C. Services at both NAL facilities are available 8:30 A.M. to 4:30 P.M. Monday through Friday, except federal holidays.

The library makes most of its information resources available to customers worldwide via the NAL Web site. In 2005 the library delivered nearly 80 million direct customer services throughout the world via the Web site and other Internet-based services, a 12 percent increase over the previous year.

During 2005 NAL reference and information center staffs completed participation in a one-year test of a virtual-reference project for the U.S. Department of Homeland Security (DHS). The 24 federal libraries and information centers that participated in this project provided electronic information services, including live chat, to the estimated 80 percent of DHS staff who lacked direct access to library services.

Also during 2005, an NAL-wide team created an online resource guide focused on Asian soybean rust (http://www.nal.usda.gov/services/pubs/soyrust.shtml). The guide comprises an extensive bibliography of relevant research, links to important resources online, and automated searches of AGRICOLA, USDA, and ARS Web sites and the Internet.

Information Centers

Operating within the overall NAL program structure, NAL's several national information centers offer portals to reliable sources of science-based information in key areas of American agriculture. By collaborating with other organizations throughout government, the centers provide timely, accurate, comprehensive, and in-depth coverage in their specialized subject areas. Staffs of these information centers make specialized information available through the NAL Web site and help library users find answers to specific questions and begin more extensive research programs.

Each information center has its own Web site and is a partner in the Agriculture Network Information Center (AgNIC). Presently, NAL has seven information centers:

- The Alternative Farming Systems Information Center (AFSIC), which specializes in farming methods that maintain the health and productivity of the entire farming enterprise, including the natural resource base
- The Animal Welfare Information Center (AWIC), which provides scientific information and referrals to help ensure the proper care and treatment of animals used in biomedical research, in teaching, in exhibition, and by animal dealers
- The Food and Nutrition Information Center (FNIC), which helps consumers, educators, health professionals, the media, researchers, and others locate scientific information relating to food and human nutrition; FNIC maintains a staff of information specialists with training in food science and human nutrition
- The Food Safety Information Center, which provides links to intergovernmental information resources about food safety, in addition to links to nongovernmental food safety research resources, and information on the risk of food-borne illness and on safe food handling and preparation
- The Rural Information Center, which provides to organizations and individuals information and referral services regarding community economic development, small business development, healthcare access and financing, housing, environment, quality of life, community leadership, and education to organizations and individuals
- The Technology Transfer Information Center, which works to "get results of research into the hands of those individuals and organizations that can put it into practical use"; the center helps individuals and organizations locate information and promote new products and processes
- The Water Quality Information Center (WQIC), which collects, organizes, and communicates scientific findings, educational methodologies, and public policy issues relating to water resources and agriculture

Web-Based Products and Services

NAL continues to emphasize the expansion of its presence on the World Wide Web to provide broader access to information for its global clientele on an every-hour-of-every-day basis. In 2005 NAL's Web site received an average of 4.3 million hits each month.

In late 2005 NAL launched a redesigned core Web site to implement USDA Web standards and meet U.S. Office of Management and Budget guidelines to focus on customer needs. NAL anticipates that Web site usage will increase in response to the site's user-friendly design, enhanced searching capabilities, and the redesign of subsidiary sites.

Designed with customer preferences in mind, the new NAL site brings a fresh look and faster access to an array of agriculture-related information. The site offers several pages with information focused on the needs of specific audiences, including children and teenagers, librarians, and USDA employees. Visitors to the home page of the newly designed core site can browse information on popular agricultural topics supported by the new navigational taxonomy. Each follow-on Web page leads quickly to more information. Visitors can use other areas of the redesigned site to access NAL's most popular library services, see where NAL representatives are exhibiting or appearing, or get information about some of the most current concerns in agriculture.

In 2006 NAL is adding enhanced searching capabilities and introducing redesigned Web sites on food safety, water quality, invasive species, human nutrition, alternative farming systems, animal welfare, and technology transfer.

Nutrition.gov

In late 2004 the secretary of agriculture launched an NAL-developed nutrition Web site (http://www.nutrition.gov) for the general public. Nutrition.gov includes databases, recipes, interactive tools, and specialized information for infants and children, adult men and women, and seniors. The site links to information on the USDA food pyramid, dietary guidelines, dietary supplements, fitness, and food safety. It provides a comprehensive source of information on nutrition and dietary guidance from several federal agencies.

Nutrition.gov received more than 2 million hits in 2005. In order of popularity, the top three subjects were "Smart Nutrition 101," weight management, and food composition.

A team of dietitians and nutrition information specialists at NAL's Food and Nutrition Information Center maintain Nutrition.gov and provide reference services to answer questions on food and nutrition issues. This NAL site is an important tool for developing food- and exercise-based strategies for weight management and for coordinating the work of federal agencies in a national obesity-prevention effort.

DigiTop

NAL's DigiTop, the digital desktop library for USDA, provides online access to thousands of journals in full text, several citation databases, and hundreds of newspapers from around the world, plus significant additional digital reference resources. DigiTop is available to all USDA employees and contractors worldwide—more than 110,000 people—24 hours a day. A proxy server enables employees not on the USDA backbone network to have the same level of access from their locations through their own Internet providers.

Comparing the number of full-text journal articles accessed through DigiTop with the cost of providing the same number of articles through traditional document-supply channels yields a favorable return on investment. With more than 675,000 article downloads from DigiTop to USDA users in 2005—an increase of more than 10 percent from the previous year—this return on investment is yielding significant cost efficiencies.

Document Delivery Services

NAL's document delivery operation responds to requests from around the world for agricultural information materials. For USDA employees, NAL acquires needed information materials not otherwise available from the NAL collections.

In April 2005 NAL began using the Relais Enterprise document-request system, integrated with NAL's Voyager integrated library system, to support its document delivery. This means NAL customers can both request and receive materials electronically and check on the status of their requests via the Internet. NAL no longer accepts document requests submitted via e-mail, Agricultural Research Information Express Loan (ARIEL), fax, or mail; all documents must be requested via the Web, using AGRICOLA or blank request forms. NAL also accepts requests via OCLC (NAL's symbol is AGL) and DOCLINE (NAL's libid is MDUNAL).

To deliver documents, NAL uses an array of methods as requested by its customers. Library staff, contractors, and cooperators work together to fill document delivery and interlibrary loan requests and deliver them to customers via the Internet through ARIEL, fax, mail, courier, and other means.

NAL cooperates via reciprocal agreements with other libraries and information centers and consortia. It is part of the Agricultural Libraries Network (AGLINET), a voluntary network of agricultural libraries around the world with strong regional/country coverage and other comprehensive or very specialized subject resource collections, and also is part of the United Nations information system.

National Library of Medicine

8600 Rockville Pike, Bethesda, MD 20894
301-496-6308, 888-346-3656, fax 301-496-4450
E-mail publicinfo@nlm.nih.gov
World Wide Web http://www.nlm.nih.gov

Robert Mehnert
Director, Office of Communications and Public Liaison

The National Library of Medicine (NLM), a part of the U.S. Department of Health and Human Services' National Institutes of Health in Bethesda, Maryland, is the world's largest library of the health sciences.

Although we live in an increasingly "virtual" world, NLM takes great pride in collecting and preserving the many forms of the literature of the biosciences. The library, as a public institution, welcomes patrons of all kinds—students, scientists, health practitioners, and the general public—and has many services and resources they can use in their search for health-related information. NLM has more than 8 million books, journals, manuscripts, audiovisuals, and other forms of medical information on its shelves, making it the world's largest health science library. Patrons also have access to a remarkable collection of books, manuscripts, and art relating to the history of the health sciences. Used not only by scholars, these materials are frequently integrated into exhibitions and displays for visitors. Traveling versions of NLM exhibitions attract crowds across the country.

In 1994 NLM introduced its Web site—one of the first in the federal government. Today, via the Web site,

- Researchers and health professionals have instantaneous access to more than 15 million scientific articles on virtually any medical subject via the PubMed/Medline database
- The general public consults MedlinePlus, which has consumer-friendly information from the National Institutes of Health (NIH) and other trusted sources
- Those with more-specialized needs have access to the library's databases about clinical trials, the environment, the history of the health sciences, and genomic information and molecular sequence data
- Special populations—American Indians, Asian Americans, those who live in the Arctic, the elderly, and those whose primary language is Spanish—have access to information tailored to their needs and requirements

NLM's key partner in making information available is the National Network of Libraries of Medicine. The network consists of 5,500 member institutions, including eight regional medical libraries that receive NLM support, 125 resource libraries connected to medical schools, and more than 5,000 libraries located primarily in hospitals and clinics. This network is of inestimable value in helping NLM to reach out to the community. Network institutions hold workshops and provide backup services for public libraries and other community organizations, demonstrate NLM databases to the public, and exhibit at meetings and conventions on behalf of NLM, thus providing the personal element that can be so important in connecting users to high-quality information.

Information Services for the Public

MedlinePlus

NLM's MedlinePlus Web site (http://www.medlineplus.gov) provides access to an extensive range of authoritative consumer health information. Much of this material comes from the NIH Institutes and, although the information is based on the medical research the institutes sponsor and carry out, the text and graphics have been carefully written and formatted to be easily understood.

In the seven years since its introduction, MedlinePlus has grown tremendously both in terms of its coverage of health information and its usage by the public. In November 2005 there were 68 million page-views by 8.7 million unique visitors.

The heart of MedlinePlus is the more than 700 "health topics," containing, for example, overview information; material on prevention, management, therapies, pertinent clinical trials, the latest research, and alternative medicine; and the latest health-related news from the print media. There are also links to the scientific literature through PubMed/Medline. In addition to the health topics, there are medical dictionaries, a medical encyclopedia, extensive information about prescription and over-the-counter drugs, directories of hospitals and providers, and interactive, easily understood "tutorials" with images and sound.

The newest addition to MedlinePlus is a series of surgical videos that show common surgical procedures being performed. MedlinePlus en Español was introduced in 2002 and has grown to virtual parity with the English version. Another aspect of MedlinePlus is Go Local, a service to link users from the MedlinePlus health topics to related health and social services in their communities. Ten states are represented in Go Local, and more are coming online all the time. MedlinePlus and MedlinePlus en Español are the federal Web sites most highly ranked by the independent American Customer Satisfaction Index.

ClinicalTrials.gov

Launched in February 2000, ClinicalTrials.gov (http://www.ClinicalTrials.gov) was created to provide easy public access to information about human research studies. ClinicalTrials.gov has proven popular, with some 20,000 visitors a day and about 7 million page-views a month. Without question, it has also helped investigators to recruit patients. The site contains information on more than 23,500 federally and privately supported trials. It includes summaries of the purpose of each study, the recruiting status, criteria for patient participation, location(s) of the trial, and specific contact information. New features were introduced in 2005 to help users find studies in different ways, such as geographical area (browse by map) and patient recruitment status (browse by status).

NIHSeniorHealth.gov

Another Web site for consumers, NIHSeniorHealth.gov (http://www.NIHSenior Health.gov), is maintained by NLM in collaboration with the National Institute on Aging. At present there are 22 topics of interest to seniors, among them Alzheimer's disease, balance problems, macular degeneration, shingles, and stroke. The topics are prepared in cooperation with nine NIH institutes, and more are in preparation. There are also videos of inspiring "exercise stories" from seniors 90 and older. NIHSeniorHealth.gov contains information in a format that is especially usable by seniors. For example, the site features large-print and easy-to-read segments of information repeated in a variety of formats, such as open-captioned videos and short quizzes, to increase the likelihood it will be remembered. NIHSeniorHealth.gov also has a "talking" function that allows users the option of reading the text or listening to it as it is read to them.

Genetics Home Reference

Findings from the Human Genome Project have greatly increased the public's interest in genetics, but the technical data resulting from the project can be overwhelming for those without formal training. Genetics Home Reference is a Web-based information system intended to help with this problem. It provides brief, consumer-friendly summaries of genetic conditions and related genes and chromosomes. At its launch in February 2003 by NLM's Lister Hill National Center for Biomedical Communications, Genetics Home Reference covered a handful of diseases that had a prominent genetic component. As of October 2005 it covered about 450 topics grouped in categories—for example, brain and nervous system, lungs and breathing, digestive system, and cancers.

Understandability is a primary consideration for information in Genetics Home Reference, and all topics receive close review by experts before they are put in the database. An online handbook to help consumers understand genetics has been created and made available in the process.

Profiles in Science

The Profiles in Science Web site makes the archival collections of a growing number of pioneering biomedical scientists available to the public. The site (http://profiles.nlm.nih.gov) was launched in September 1998 and promotes the use of the Internet for research and teaching in the history of biomedical science. The collections contain published and unpublished items, including books, journal volumes, pamphlets, diaries, letters, manuscripts, photographs, audiotapes, video clips, and other materials. During the past year, the papers of former U.S. Surgeon General C. Everett Koop were added to Profiles in Science, as were those of Wilbur A. Sawyer, a key figure in preventive medicine and international public health.

Tox Town

The colorful Tox Town is among a number of Web-based information services developed by NLM's Division of Specialized Information Services. Tox Town looks at an ordinary town and points out many harmful substances and environmental hazards that might exist there. Users can click on a town location—the school, for example—and see a colorful dollhouse-style cutaway view of the building. Toxic chemicals that might be found in the school are listed, along with links to selected Internet resources about school environments. There are similar cutaways for offices, factories, parks, and other locations. NLM has introduced several other versions of Tox Town that concentrate on the special problems found in a big city, the U.S.-Mexico border area, and a farm. There is also a new special section with information on toxic chemicals and disaster health concerns in the wake of hurricanes Katrina and Rita.

A related database, TOXMAP, is an interactive Web site that shows, on maps, the amount and location of certain toxic chemicals released into the environment in the United States. Unlike Tox Town, which is hypothetical, TOXMAP actually focuses on the geographic distribution of chemical releases, their relative amounts, and their trends over time. This release data comes from industrial facilities around the United States, as reported annually to the Environmental Protection Agency. TOXMAP is being used by public health professionals, public health students and faculty, librarians, community health nurses, and citizens who are concerned about the location of toxic chemicals in their neighborhood.

Household Products Database

Another consumer information resource created by the Division of Specialized Information Services is the Household Products Database. This is a guide that provides easy-to-understand data on the potential health effects of more than 2,000 ingredients contained in more than 6,000 common household products. The database provides information on many of these substances and their potential health effects in consumer-friendly language. For convenience in searching, the products are categorized—automobile, personal care, pet care, and so forth. The database has proven to be a popular subject with the media, and there have been a number of newspaper and magazine articles about it.

Information Services for the Scientific Community

PubMed/Medline

PubMed/Medline is NLM's free Web-based service for the worldwide scientific community, a database of more than 15 million references and abstracts for medical journal articles from the 1950s to the present. New citations are added weekly, and the database expands at the rate of more than 600,000 records a year. PubMed also links to the sites of participating publishers so that users can retrieve full-text articles from about 5,000 journals. Where links to electronic full text are not available, the user can use PubMed to place an online order for an article directly from a library in the National Network of Libraries of Medicine. PubMed allows users to customize their access, for example with an option to automatically update and e-mail search results from user-saved searches. A spell-check feature was added to PubMed that provides the user with choices of alternative spellings for search terms.

The ability of medical scientists and health professionals to have instant access to scientific articles (some free, some at a small charge) is unparalleled and not matched by any other scientific discipline. The National Institutes of Health Web site is the second-most-heavily trafficked site in the federal government, and the NLM databases account for the major share of that use. Usage of PubMed/Medline by the scientific and lay communities has grown considerably since its introduction in 1997, to more than 2.8 million searches a day.

PubMed Central

PubMed Central (PMC) (http://www.pubmedcentral.nih.gov) is a Web-based repository of biomedical journal literature providing free and unrestricted access to the full text of articles. This repository is based on a natural integration with the existing PubMed biomedical literature database of references and abstracts. Currently, PMC contains more than 500,000 full-text articles from 214 biomedical journals. Recent additions have come from newly published material as well as from digitizing back issues that previously were available only in printed form. In addition to creating a digital copy of every page in the backfiles, the digitization process is also creating a pdf file for every discrete item (article, editorial, letter, advertisement, and so forth) in the archive, and using optical character recognition (OCR) technology to generate searchable text. Creating such digital archives as PubMed Central to ensure that the world's biomedical literature is properly recorded and available for future generations is an important NLM responsibility.

GenBank

GenBank is the NIH genetic sequence database, an annotated collection of all publicly available DNA sequences. NLM's National Center for Biotechnology Information (NCBI) is responsible for all phases of GenBank production, support, and distribution. Integrated retrieval tools allow seamless searching of the sequence data housed in GenBank and provide links to related sequences, bibliographic citations, and other resources. Such features allow the database to serve as a critical research tool in the analysis and discovery of gene function as well as discoveries that can potentially lead to identification and cures for a number of diseases. GenBank reached a total of 100 billion gigabases in 2005, a milestone for the database and its international collaborators. Access GenBank at http://www.ncbi.nl.mnih.gov/genbank/index.html.

One recent example of the use of NCBI sequence databases was in the identification in November 2005 of the first polio case in the United States since 1999. The state health laboratory in Minnesota had isolated an unknown virus from a hospitalized child from an Amish community. When laboratory staff determined the virus's DNA code, they went to the Web, searched against the 55 million DNA sequences at NCBI, found a match to the polio virus used in the Sabin oral vaccine, and "Bingo!" said the laboratory's director, "It was a 98 percent match. We knew we had nailed it."

NCBI is working with others at NIH on the Influenza Genome Sequencing Project, which aims to deposit a large number of influenza sequences into GenBank. By the end of 2005, the project had generated more than 3,000 influenza sequences, including those for more than 150 complete influenza genomes. Initial work reveals the process of influenza viral evolution to be complex, and further progress depends on the collection of more extensive datasets and the further integration of new sequence data with other biological information. As the data accumulates and the analyses progress, the discoveries made will lead to better prediction of large-scale outbreaks, more-effective vaccine design, and the saving of many human lives.

PubChem

PubChem is a new database developed by NCBI that serves as a repository for what are called "small molecules," which are crucial in drug development. Small molecules are responsible for the most basic chemical processes that are essential for life, such as those that produce energy for a cell and those that carry messages to cells and their components. Most therapeutic drugs are small molecules. PubChem links the small molecules to their biological functions and to the macromolecules with which they interact. At present, PubChem, which is a key component of the NIH Roadmap initiative, includes more than 7.5 million records for small molecules, with more than 5 million molecular structures. Access PubChem at http://pubchem.ncbi.nlm.nih.gov.

Areas of Special Interest

Information Management and Disaster Planning

NLM has been involved in disaster response and management since the late 1960s, when its Specialized Information Services Division was established as the U.S. government focal point for information on toxic substances and environmental health. NLM's services in this area have been used in such emergencies as the gas leak disaster in Bhopal, India, in the 1980s and the earthquakes in Central America in the 1990s. In the aftermath of the terrorist attacks of September 11, 2001, NLM increased its focus on use of information services and technology to enhance disaster response and management (defined to encompass all types of natural and manmade disasters). Some of these activities include

- Development of the software package OSIRIS (Open Source Independent Review and Interpretation System) to identify victims' remains via DNA (the software is now being tested within five collaborating forensic DNA laboratories, and it is being used to assist in the analysis and validation of forensic data from the Gulf Coast states in the aftermath of Hurricane Katrina)
- Four grant programs to support information management during natural disasters or terrorist attacks, including one named Informatics for Disaster Management Grants
- WISER (Wireless Information System for Emergency Responders), which provides information via handheld mobile devices to help identify unknown harmful substances to those responding to chemical emergencies; WISER was used in Louisiana after Hurricane Katrina

NLM also has taken steps to protect its databases and information services from outside attack or interference, including establishing an extensive off-site backup facility.

Standards for Electronic Health Records

As part of its Unified Medical Language System (UMLS) project, NLM produces and distributes vocabulary databases and software tools to be applied in automated interpretation and integration of medical knowledge and health data. UMLS serves as a common distribution vehicle for standard code sets and vocabularies needed for administrative transactions and electronic health records, as well as a resource for advanced natural language processing, automated indexing, and enhanced information retrieval. Chief among UMLS resources is the Metathesaurus, which links and provides 4.7 million concept names for 1.2 million concepts from 114 vocabularies in a single database format. NLM works closely with the Office of the National Coordinator for Health Information Technology and relevant federal agencies and organizations to align health data standards into an effective interlocking set and to promote more-rapid adoption of standards-based electronic health records in an effort to facilitate patient care, public health surveillance, and clinical research.

Grants

NLM's Extramural Programs are authorized by the Medical Library Assistance Act. The act allows the library to award grants for research, training and fellowships, medical library assistance, improving access to information, and publications. For more than 20 years, NLM has supported the training of medical informaticians at universities across the nation. In the early years, the program focused on training of informaticians for clinical care; today the training programs have added opportunities for training in bioinformatics, the field of biomedical computing for the large datasets characteristic of modern research. At present NLM provides 18 grants for biomedical informatics training at 27 universities, supporting 300 trainees. NLM also participates in NIH Roadmap activities, almost all of which have major emphasis on biomedical computing. For example, training is an important requirement of the National Centers for Biomedical Computing, an initiative for which NLM is a key leader. Training as embedded in Roadmap activities is expected to become a significant complement to NLM's traditional support of informatics training.

Planning

Twenty years ago the library published a long-range plan that has proved to be of great benefit to the institution. Out of it grew such initiatives as the Visible Human Project, the National Center for Biotechnology Information, and the recommendation that NLM engage in an outreach campaign to reach minority and other underserved health professionals. The library is now engaged in a similar planning exercise for the next quarter century. Leaders from across the spectrum of health and medicine are meeting at the library to consider four major themes: NLM resources and infrastructure for the 21st century, NLM outreach to the underserved in the 21st century, NLM support for clinical and public health systems for the 21st century, and NLM support for genomics in the 21st century. The plan will be reviewed by the NLM Board of Regents and published in 2006.

Administration

The director of NLM, Donald A. B. Lindberg, M.D., is guided in matters of policy by a board of regents consisting of 10 appointed and 11 ex officio members.

Table 1 / Selected NLM Statistics*

Library Operation	Volume
Collection (book and nonbook)	8,566,000
Items cataloged	21,700
Serial titles received	21,000
Articles indexed for MEDLINE	606,000
Circulation requests processed	593,000
For interlibrary loan	341,000
For on-site users	252,000
Computerized searches (Medline/PubMed)	884,200,000
Budget authority	$331,431,000
Staff	640

*For the year ending September 30, 2005

United States Government Printing Office

732 North Capitol St. N.W., Washington, DC 20401
202-512-1957, e-mail vmeter@gpo.gov
World Wide Web http://www.gpo.gov

Veronica Meter
Director, Office of Public Relations

The U.S. Government Printing Office (GPO) is the federal government's primary centralized resource for gathering, cataloging, producing, providing, and preserving published information in all its forms. Since its inception, GPO has offered Congress, the courts, and government agencies a set of centralized services to enable them to easily and cost-effectively produce printed documents according to a uniform set of federal government specifications. In addition, GPO has offered these publications for sale to the public and made them widely available at no cost through the Federal Depository Library Program (FDLP). It is poised to perform its function in an increasingly digital future.

GPO is part of the legislative branch of the federal government and operates under the authority of the public printing and documents chapters of Title 44 of the U.S. Code. In addition to Congress, approximately 130 federal departments and agencies rely on GPO's services. Congressional documents, U.S. Supreme Court decisions, federal regulations and reports, IRS tax forms, and U.S. passports are all produced by or through GPO.

GPO's headquarters, which includes a bookstore, is in Washington, D.C. Nationwide, GPO maintains 16 field locations and a major distribution facility in Pueblo, Colorado.

GPO's information dissemination activities include FDLP, which disseminates information products from all three branches of the federal government to more than 1,250 libraries nationwide; GPO Access, which provides online access to titles on GPO servers as well as links to titles on other federal Web sites; and a publications sales program that sells government publications to the public. Together, these activities disseminate one of the world's largest volumes of published information. This report focuses on GPO's role as the disseminator of government information in print and electronic formats.

Future Digital System

GPO's Future Digital System (FDsys) will manage, preserve, provide version control and access to, and disseminate authentic government information. As outlined in GPO's *A Strategic Vision for the 21st Century* (http://www.gpo.gov/congressional/pdfs/04strategicplan.pdf), FDsys will allow federal content creators to easily create and submit content that can then be preserved, authenticated, managed, and delivered upon request. This digital content system will form the core of GPO's future operations.

Whether first published in print or born digital, this content will be entered into the system and then authenticated and cataloged according to GPO metadata and document-creation standards. In addition to text and associated graphics, it will include video, sound, and other forms of content that emerge. Materials will be available for Web searching and Internet viewing, downloading and printing, and as document masters for conventional and on-demand printing or other dissemination methods. GPO will introduce FDsys in phases, with full system operation expected by December 2007.

A contractor will serve as the "master integrator" for building FDsys, working collaboratively with GPO to develop the FDsys functions and to integrate the various components, technology, and applications into a world-class information management system.

For more on FDsys, see http://www.gpo.gov/projects/fdsys.htm.

Authentication/PKI

GPO is engaged in a major authentication initiative designed to assure users that the information made available by GPO is official and authentic and that trust relationships exist between all participants in electronic transactions. This authentication initiative, which employs public key infrastructure (PKI) technology, will allow users to determine that files are unchanged since GPO authenticated them.

GPO is procuring the necessary tools and capabilities to automate the application of digital signatures on Adobe Acrobat portable document format (pdf) files. This will enable application of digital signatures in a more timely, efficient, and cost-effective manner than can be achieved manually. GPO also intends to procure a validation mechanism that will enable users to easily view authentication information for digitally signed pdf documents.

GPO has also begun applying a "seal of authenticity" to various print publications, giving users assurance that publications are coming from an official source and reinforcing the integrity of the publications.

Disaster Recovery

GPO has made strides in the planning and development of a disaster recovery (DR) site to ensure that electronic data is protected and remains accessible in event of a system failure or catastrophe.

It has completed the first phase of the DR project, which includes a global off-site backup of GPO Access data, static content delivery of the gpo.gov and bookstore.gpo.gov domains, and a proof of concept for five GPO Access applications (*Federal Register, Code of Federal Regulations, Congressional Record,* Congressional Bills, and Congressional Hearings) that emulate the current search system while providing faster performance and improved search results. A second phase of the DR project will result in the migration of the remaining wide area information system (WAIS), at which time GPO will have a complete backup system that will offer assured availability to all of GPO's Web services and also maintain an archival copy of GPO's data for redundant off-site storage.

Federal Depository Library Program

Integrated Library System

The enhanced online *Catalog of U.S. Government Publications* (*CGP*) for the National Bibliography of U.S. Government Publications is now operational. The national bibliography is a comprehensive index of public documents from all three branches of the federal government. In the online information environment, the new *CGP* is essential to GPO's core mission to ensure that the public has access to government information. The enhanced *CGP* is a component of a modernization plan to replace older legacy systems with GPO's recently acquired integrated library system.

The enhanced *CGP* provides more records and data than previous applications. It contains more than 500,000 records dating from July 1976 to the present and will become more far-reaching in the future. It replaces previous versions, as well as New Electronic Titles (NET) and Locate Libraries. The "other catalogs to search" feature provides access to the Congressional Serial Set, periodicals, and Internet publications.

In addition to more extensive information, the enhanced *CGP* is a robust search-and-retrieval tool that offers fielded searches and indexing to help with depository administrative functions. Direct links to online publications and to related records are provided within the bibliographic record. GPO processing information and holdings also are available.

Registry of Digitization Projects

GPO has launched the Registry of U.S. Government Publication Digitization Projects, a locator tool for publicly accessible collections of digitized U.S. government publications. Volunteer contributors can input records about their institution's projects that include digitized copies of publications originating from the federal government.

GPO's Digitization Specification 3.2 is currently under development. Version 3.2 is a result of multiple internal reviews and two focused external reviews by federal agencies and universities involved in preservation-quality digitization. This specification will be used to support GPO's plan to convert legacy documents into preservation masters that will subsequently be used to create derivative "access" files that support user requirements.

The specification will continue to evolve as technological advancements and digitization requirements occur in the digital imaging industry.

More information about the legacy digitization project, including a link to Specification 3.0, is available at http://www.gpoaccess.gov/legacy.

LOCKSS

The GPO LOCKSS (Lots of Copies Keep Stuff Safe) pilot project was launched in June 2005. As of early 2006, GPO had made the current volumes of several government e-journals available to the 19 libraries participating in the pilot. The *Treasury Bulletin, Social Security Bulletin, Journal of Research of the National Institute of Standards and Technology, Humanities, Survey of Current Business, Monthly Labor Review,* and *Monthly Energy Review* were the first made available under the program. LOCKSS is open source software that provides institutions with a way to collect, store, and preserve access to their own local copies of e-journal content. LOCKSS was developed by Stanford University and is currently maintained by the Stanford University LOCKSS Program Management Office with support from the LOCKSS Alliance. The purpose of the GPO LOCKSS pilot project is to investigate whether LOCKSS, or similar software, can be used to manage, disseminate, and preserve access to federal government e-journals that are within the scope of FDLP, as well as those distributed via the International Exchange Service, which allows for the official exchange of public documents between the United States and foreign governments.

Measures of success for LOCKSS include harvesting ten e-journals from federal government Web sites, providing access to those e-journals via LOCKSS, and collecting information from pilot partners about their experiences with LOCKSS.

Additional information and news about the GPO LOCKSS Pilot Project is available at http://www.access.gpo.gov/su_docs/fdlp/lockss/index.html.

CD-ROM Data-Migration Strategy

GPO is working to devise a data-migration strategy to ensure that information on the CD-ROMs that have been distributed to depository libraries remains accessible. After an initial review, GPO selected three agencies to use as case studies: the Department of Education, the Department of Justice, and the United States Geological Survey. These agencies were selected because the number of discs produced appeared to be a manageable sample, yet varied enough to cover a good cross-section of considerations for migration. GPO wanted a sample that would include serials and monographic discs, a variety of file formats and system requirements, and databases and discs containing static documents.

A list of depository CD-ROMs from these agencies was prepared and reviewed to see which ones were available via the Internet. GPO will soon release a list of the discs reviewed, indicating which are available online and which are considered migration candidates. Discs considered to be migration candidates will be tested, and the results will be used to devise a migration strategy for other depository discs.

Web Discovery and Harvesting

GPO is continuing its efforts to discover and retrieve publications from federal agency Web sites that fall within the scope of FDLP and the National Bibliography Program. It is currently exploring a solution for the discovery, harvesting, and assessment of documents and publications from Web sites utilizing Web crawler and data-mining technologies.

As a first step in learning about available methodologies and technologies, GPO is working with the Environmental Protection Agency (EPA) on a pilot project for Web discovery and harvesting of all EPA Web sites. In addition to locating electronic content for FDLP, the information gained through this pilot will be utilized in developing a set of long-term requirements and specifications for Web discovery and harvesting in conjunction with the implementation of GPO's FDsys.

During the pilot project, three separate crawls of the EPA Web site will be conducted in a six-month period. The results from each will be compared to develop criteria for targeting in-scope materials on other agency Web sites for inclusion in GPO's information dissemination programs.

Recent Developments in FDLP Partnerships

GPO currently has 15 partnerships with depository libraries and federal agencies. A complete list is available at http://www.access.gpo.gov/su_docs/fdlp/partners/index.html. Any depository interested in exploring the possibility of a partnership is encouraged to contact GPO.

GPO formed two new partnerships in 2005.

- GPO and the Federal Reserve Bank of St. Louis implemented a partnership in April to provide depository access to federal government information in the Federal Reserve Archival System for Economic Research (FRASER) service.
- GPO and the Robert Muldrow Cooper Library of Clemson University formed a partnership in June to facilitate the migration of tangible publications distribution to electronic dissemination for federal depository libraries while assessing the operational and service implications of a regional federal depository library with a primarily electronic collection.

Sales of GPO Cataloging Records

GPO has begun selling the GPO Cataloging Records previously available as a monthly subscription service from the Library of Congress. The cataloging records are available in MARC format via ftp. The cost for the monthly service is $1,920 a year. For more information, contact the GPO Contact Center at askGPO @gpo.gov.

Distribution and Other Statistics

While more than 92 percent of the new titles made available through FDLP are available in electronic form, whether or not they are also available in tangible form, GPO continues to distribute a large volume of tangible publications to federal depository libraries. In fiscal year (FY) 2005 GPO distributed a total of 5,285,169 tangible copies (including maps, CD-ROMs, microfiche, and print) of 10,303 titles to FDLP libraries. Of that total, 7,940 titles were produced in tangible form only, while the balance (including maps) were produced in both tangible and electronic formats but distributed in a tangible format. GPO distributed a total of 35,966 tangible and electronic titles.

Titles available through GPO Access are up substantially. In FY 2005, GPO added 18,834 titles, an increase in titles of 6,902 (58 percent) over FY 2004. In addition, 6,432 publications were acquired for the electronic archive in FY 2005 via harvest from agency Web sites. The project is being pursued as an alternative to manual harvesting, and it is anticipated that there will be a substantial increase in the number of harvested titles in FY 2006.

GPO produced 15,194 bibliographic records (including 2,094 ONIX records) in FY 2005.

GPO Access

GPO Access (http://www.gpoaccess.gov) provides access to electronic information products from all three branches of the federal government. Since its inception in 1994, GPO Access retrievals have exceeded 2.45 billion. June 2005 set an all-time record with more than 39 million retrievals. The total number of retrievals in FY 2005 was 431 million. Through November, more than 52.67 million documents had been retrieved in FY 2006.

GPO Access provides a number of free tools to assist users in searching or browsing for government information. In order to provide more visibility, the finding aids have been further integrated into the pages of a redesign of GPO Access. These tools act as a portal to information available on government Web sites. They can be used to conduct government-wide searches, locate government publications online and in print, and find agency Web sites based on broad subject areas. A complete list of finding aids can be found at http://www.gpoaccess. gov/branches.html#federal.

Ben's Guide to U.S. Government (http://bensguide.gpo.gov), designed for students from kindergarten to 12th grade, continues to flourish in the tercentenary year of Benjamin Franklin's birth. Ben's Guide strives to introduce and explain the workings of all three branches of the federal government. Through the use of primary source materials, grade-appropriate explanations, and a stimulating site design, Ben's Guide not only increases public access to and knowledge of the federal government, but makes learning fun.

The site is divided into four grade levels (K–2, 3–5, 6–8, and 9–12) and also provides an area for parents and educators. Ben's Guide includes historical documents and information on the legislative and regulatory processes, elections, and citizenship. The site also features learning activities and a list of federal Web sites designed for students, parents, and educators.

New and on the Horizon

GPO Access "What's New" RSS feed—A new RSS (Rich Site Summary/Really Simple Syndication) feed for "What's New" on GPO Access is available at http:// www.gpoaccess.gov.

RSS is a small XML file that notifies users when a Web site has been updated. Users subscribe to an RSS feed and receive a notification message that alerts them to additions to the "What's New" feature.

Supreme Court Nomination Hearings—The Senate Committee on the Judiciary's Supreme Court nomination hearing transcripts (1971–forward), in their entirety, are now available on GPO Access at http://www.gpoaccess.gov/ congress/senate/judiciary/scourt.html.

Bound Congressional Record—A full-text, searchable, and browseable 1999 bound *Congressional Record* is now available as a GPO Access application at http://www.gpoaccess.gov/crecordbound/index.html. At the end of each session of Congress, all of the daily editions of the *Congressional Record* are collected, repaginated, and reindexed into a permanent bound edition. Volume 145 (1999, first session of the 106th Congress) is now available; additional volumes will be added in the near future.)

U.S. Code—The United States Code, 2000 Edition, Supplement 2, is now available on GPO Access at http://www.gpoaccess.gov/uscode/search.html. The United States Code is the codification by subject matter of the general and permanent laws of the United States, based on what is printed in the *United States Statutes at Large*. It is divided by broad subjects into 50 titles and published by the Office of the Law Revision Counsel of the House of Representatives.

Statutes at Large—GPO plans to release a *United States Statutes at Large* (Volume 117, 108th Congress) application in 2006, with future volumes to follow, after final review and approval by the Office of the Federal Register.

Selling Government Publications

GPO's sales program currently offers approximately 6,000 government publications on a wide array of subjects. These are sold principally via electronic, e-mail, telephone, fax, and mail order. The program operates on a cost-recovery basis. Publications for sale include books, forms, posters, pamphlets, maps, CD-ROMs, computer diskettes, and magnetic tapes. Subscription services for both dated periodicals and basic-and-supplement services (involving an initial volume and supplemental issues) are also offered.

Express service, which includes priority handling and Federal Express delivery, is available for orders placed by telephone for domestic delivery. Orders placed before noon Eastern time for in-stock publications and single-copy subscriptions will be delivered within two working days. Some quantity restrictions apply. Call the telephone order desk toll-free at 866-512-1800 (or 202-512-1800 within the Washington, D.C., area) for more information.

Consumer-oriented publications are also either sold or distributed at no charge through the Federal Citizen Information Center in Pueblo, Colorado, which GPO operates on behalf of the General Services Administration.

The GPO sales program has begun using print-on-demand technology to increase the long-term availability of publications and begin testing the capabilities of a number of vendors. The sales program is also engaged in bringing its bibliographic practices more in line with those of the commercial publishing sector by utilizing ONIX (online information exchange), the standard electronic format for sharing product data with wholesale and retail booksellers, other publishers, and anyone else involved in the sale of books. ONIX enables GPO to have government publications listed, promoted, and sold by commercial book dealers worldwide.

GPO has launched an improved U.S. Government Online Bookstore that adds additional services for sales customers. The Online Bookstore now uses Pay.gov, a secure governmentwide financial management transaction portal available around the clock for more timely and efficient processing of GPO credit card and deposit account orders. The improved Online Bookstore also gives customers the option of expedited shipping via USPS Priority and Express Mail, new and improved order confirmation e-mails, and expanded ordering options for international customers; it also allows customers to save their online shopping carts.

Customers can also register to receive e-mail updates when new publications become available for sale from the Superintendent of Documents through the

New Titles by Topic e-mail alert service. Anyone can sign up for one or more of these lists free of charge. This service can be accessed at http://bookstore.gpo.gov/alertservice.html.

The sales program also lists selected titles on Amazon.com, Barnesandnoble.com, and other online commercial book selling sites.

Outsourcing Under Study

GPO is exploring opportunities to outsource all or parts of its sales program, and is seeking potential vendors' recommendations for an entirely new publications sales and distribution operation. GPO's aim is to improve service to its customers and continue to fulfill its mission to keep America informed through the sale of public documents.

National Technical Information Service

Technology Administration
U.S. Department of Commerce, Springfield, VA 22161
800-553-NTIS (6847) or 703-605-6000
World Wide Web http://www.ntis.gov

Linda Davis
Marketing Communications

The National Technical Information Service (NTIS) serves as the nation's largest central source and primary disseminator of scientific, technical, engineering, and business information produced or sponsored by U.S. and international government sources. NTIS is a federal agency within the Technology Administration of the U.S. Department of Commerce.

Since 1945 the NTIS mission has been to operate a central U.S. government access point for scientific and technical information useful to American industry and government. NTIS maintains a permanent archive of this declassified information for researchers, businesses, and the public to access quickly and easily. Release of the information is intended to promote American economic growth and development and to increase U.S. competitiveness in the world market.

The NTIS collection of approximately 3 million titles contains products available in various formats. Such information includes reports describing research conducted or sponsored by federal agencies and their contractors; statistical and business information; U.S. military publications; multimedia training programs; computer software and electronic databases developed by federal agencies; and technical reports prepared by research organizations worldwide. Approximately 60,000 new titles are added and indexed annually. NTIS maintains a permanent repository of its information products.

More than 200 U.S. government agencies contribute to the NTIS collection, including the National Aeronautics and Space Administration, Environmental Protection Agency, the departments of Agriculture, Commerce, Defense, Energy, Health and Human Services, Interior, Labor, Treasury, Veterans Affairs, Housing and Urban Development, Education, Transportation, and numerous other agencies. International contributors include Canada, Japan, Britain, and several European countries.

NTIS E-Government Virtual Library

NTIS offers Web-based access to the latest government scientific and technical research information products. Visitors to http://www.ntis.gov can search more than 600,000 NTIS database records dating back to 1990 free of charge. NTIS also provides access links to documents online at other government agency Web sites when available, downloading capability for many technical reports, and purchase of the publications on CD.

NTIS Database

The NTIS Database (listings of information products acquired by NTIS since 1964) offers unparalleled bibliographic coverage of U.S. government and worldwide government-sponsored research. Its contents represent hundreds of billions of research dollars and cover a range of important topics including agriculture, biotechnology, business, communication, energy, engineering, the environment, health and safety, medicine, research and development, science, space, technology, transportation, and more.

Most records include abstracts. Database summaries describe technical reports, datafiles, multimedia/training programs, and software. These titles are often unique to NTIS and generally are difficult to locate from any other source. The complete NTIS Database provides instant access to more than 2 million records.

Free 30-day trials of the NTIS Database are available through the GOV. Research_Center (http://grc.ntis.gov). The NTIS Database can be leased directly from NTIS, and it can also be accessed through the following commercial services: Cambridge Scientific Abstracts, 800-843-7751, http://www.csa.com; DATA-STAR (DIALOG), 800-334-2564, http://www.dialog.com; EBSCO Publishing, 800-653-2726, http://www.epnet.com; Engineering Information (Ei), 800-221-1044, http://www.ei.org; Knowledge EXPRESS, 800-529-5337, http://www.knowledgeexpress.com; NERAC, Inc., 860-872-7000, http://www.nerac.com; Ovid Technologies, Inc., 800-950-2035, http://www.ovid.com; SilverPlatter Information, Inc., 800-343-0064, http://www.silverplatter.com; and STN International/CAS, 800-848-6533, http://www.cas.org. For an updated list of organizations offering NTIS Database products, see http://www.ntis.gov/products/types/databases/commercial.asp.

To lease the NTIS Database directly from NTIS, contact the NTIS Subscriptions Department at 800-363-2068 or 703-605-6060. For more information, see http://www.ntis.gov/products/types/databases/ntisdb.asp

Other Databases Available from NTIS

NTIS offers several valuable research-oriented database products. To find out more about accessing the databases, visit http://www.ntis.gov/products/types/databases/data.asp.

FEDRIP

The Federal Research in Progress Database (FEDRIP) provides access to information about ongoing federally funded projects in the fields of the physical sciences, engineering, and life sciences. The ongoing research announced in FEDRIP is an important component of the technology transfer process in the United States; FEDRIP's uniqueness lies in its structure as a nonbibliographic information source of research in progress. Project descriptions generally include project title, keywords, start date, estimated completion date, principal investigator, performing and sponsoring organizations, summary, and progress report. Record content varies depending on the source agency.

There are many reasons to search FEDRIP. Among these are to avoid research duplication, locate sources of support, identify leads in the literature, stimulate ideas for planning, identify gaps in areas of investigation, and locate individuals with expertise. To access an updated list of organizations offering FEDRIP Database products, see http://www.ntis.gov/products/types/databases/fedrip.asp.

AGRICOLA

As one of the most comprehensive sources of U.S. agricultural and life sciences information, the Agricultural Online Access Database (AGRICOLA) contains bibliographic records for documents acquired by the National Agricultural Library (NAL) of the U.S. Department of Agriculture. The complete database dates from 1970 and contains more than 4 million citations to journal articles, monographs, theses, patents, software, audiovisual materials, and technical reports relating to agriculture. AGRICOLA serves as the document locator and bibliographic control system for the NAL collection. The extensive file provides comprehensive coverage of newly acquired worldwide publications in agriculture and related fields. AGRICOLA covers the field of agriculture in the broadest sense. Subjects include Agricultural Economics, Agricultural Education, Agricultural Products, Animal Science, Aquaculture, Biotechnology, Botany, Cytology, Energy, Engineering, Feed Science, Fertilizers, Fibers and Textiles, Food and Nutrition, Forestry, Horticulture, Human Ecology, Human Nutrition, Hydrology, Hydroponics, Microbiology, Natural Resources, Pesticides, Physiology, Plant and Animal, Plant Sciences, Public Health, Rural Sociology, Soil Sciences, Veterinary Medicine, Water Quality, and more. To access an updated list of organizations offering AGRICOLA Database products, see http://www.ntis.gov/products/types/databases/agricola.asp.

AGRIS

The International Information System for the Agricultural Science and Technology (AGRIS) Database is a cooperative system for collecting and disseminating information on the world's agricultural literature in which more than 100 national and multinational centers take part. References to citation for U.S. publications given coverage in the AGRICOLA Database are not included in AGRIS. A large number of citations in AGRIS are not found in any other database. References to nonconventional literature (documents not commercially available) contain a note where a copy can be obtained. AGRIS can be used to find citations to agricultural information from around the world. Much of this information includes government documents, technical reports, and nonconventional literature that have their source in both developed and developing countries and that can be found nowhere else. To access an updated list of organizations offering AGRIS Database products, see http://www.ntis.gov/products/types/databases/agris.asp.

Energy Science and Technology

The Energy Science and Technology Database (EDB) is a multidisciplinary file containing worldwide references to basic and applied scientific and technical research literature. The information is collected for use by government managers, researchers at the national laboratories, and other research efforts sponsored by the U.S. Department of Energy, and the results of this research are transferred to the public. Abstracts are included for records from 1976 to the present. EDB also contains the Nuclear Science Abstracts, a comprehensive abstract and index collection to the international nuclear science and technology literature for the period 1948–1976. Included are scientific and technical reports of the U.S. Atomic Energy Commission, U.S. Energy Research and Development Administration and its contractors, other agencies, universities, and industrial and research organizations. Approximately 25 percent of the records in the file contain abstracts. Nuclear Science Abstracts contains more than 900,000 bibliographic records. The entire EDB contains more than 3 million bibliographic records. To access an updated list of organizations offering EDB products, see http://www.ntis.gov/products/types/databases/engsci.asp.

Immediately Dangerous to Life or Health Concentrations Database

The NIOSH (National Institute for Occupational Safety and Health) documentation for the Immediately Dangerous to Life or Health Concentrations (IDLHs) Database contains air concentration values used by NIOSH as respirator-selection criteria. This compilation is the rationale and source of information used by NIOSH during the original determination of 387 IDLHs and their subsequent review and revision in 1994. Toxicologists, persons concerned with use of respirators, industrial hygienists, persons concerned with indoor air quality, and emergency response personnel will find this product beneficial. This database will enable users to compare NIOSH limits with other limits and will be an important resource for those concerned with acute chemical exposures. To access an updated list of organizations offering IDLHs Database products, see http://www.ntis.gov/products/types/databases/idlhs.asp.

NIOSH Manual of Analytical Methods Database

The NIOSH Manual of Analytical Methods (NMAM) Database is a compilation of methods for sampling and analysis of contaminants in workplace air and in the bodily fluids of workers who are occupationally exposed to that air. These methods have been developed specifically to have adequate sensitivity to detect the lowest concentrations and sufficient flexibility of range to detect concentrations exceeding safe levels of exposure, as regulated by the Occupational Safety and Health Administration and recommended by NIOSH. The Threshold Values and Biological Exposure Indices of the American Conference of Governmental Industrial Hygienists are also cited. To access an updated list of organizations offering NIOSH Manual of Analytical Methods Database products, see http://www.ntis.gov/products/types/databases/nmam.asp.

NIOSH Pocket Guide to Chemical Hazards Database

The NIOSH Pocket Guide to Chemical Hazards (NPG) Database is intended as a source of general industrial hygiene information that is quick and convenient for workers, employers, and occupational health professionals. NPG presents in abbreviated tabular form key information and data on chemicals or substance groupings (e.g., cyanides, fluorides, manganese compounds) that are found in the work environment. The industrial hygiene information found in NPG should help users recognize and control occupational chemical hazards. The information in NPG includes chemical structures or formulas, identification codes, synonyms, exposure limits, chemical and physical properties, incompatibilities and reactivities, measurement methods, recommended respirator selections, signs and symptoms of exposure, and procedures for emergency treatment. Industrial hygienists, industrial hygiene technicians, safety professionals, occupational health physicians and nurses, and hazardous materials managers will find the database a versatile and indispensable tool. For an updated list of organizations offering Pocket Guide to Chemical Hazards Database products, see http://www.ntis.gov/products/types/databases/npgfacts.asp.

NIOSHTIC

NIOSHTIC is a bibliographic database of literature in the field of occupational safety and health developed by NIOSH. Although the file has been static since 1998, it contains retrospective information, some dating back to the 19th century. Because NIOSH examines all aspects of adverse effects experienced by workers, much of the information contained in NIOSHTIC has been selected from sources that do not have a primary occupational safety and health orientation. NIOSHTIC subject coverage includes the behavioral sciences; biochemistry, physiology, and metabolism; biological hazards; chemistry; control technology; education and training; epidemiological studies of disease/disorders; ergonomics; hazardous waste; health physics; occupational medicine; pathology and histology; safety; toxicology; and more. To access an updated list of organizations offering NIOSHTIC products, visit http://www.ntis.gov/products/types/databases/nioshtic.asp.

Registry of Toxic Effects of Chemical Substances Databases

The Registry of Toxic Effects of Chemical Substances Databases (RTECS) is a compendium of data extracted from the open scientific literature. The data are recorded in the format developed by the RTECS staff and arranged in alphabetical order by prime chemical name. No attempt has been made to evaluate the studies cited in RTECS; the user has the responsibility of making such assessments. To access an updated list of organizations offering RTECS Database products, visit http://www.ntis.gov/products/types/databases/rtecs.asp.

Specialized Online Subscriptions

Those wishing to expand their access to subject-specific resources through use of the Internet are likely to benefit from the NTIS online options highlighted below. Online subscriptions offer quick, convenient online access to the most current information available.

Government Research Center

The GOV.Research_Center (GRC) is a collection of well-known government-sponsored research databases available on the World Wide Web via an online subscription service. Customers can subscribe to a single GRC Database product or to several databases. The following databases made available at the GOV. Research_Center by NTIS and the National Information Services Corporation (NISC) are searchable at the site utilizing NISC's Biblioline search engine. These database subscription products include the NTIS Database, FEDRIP, NIOSHTIC, EDB, Nuclear Science Abstracts Database, AgroBase, AGRICOLA, and RTECS. NTIS and NISC are constantly improving the content and features of GRC. Online ordering allows ordering of documents directly from the NTIS Database by using a credit card or NTIS deposit account; cross-database searching allows use of a single search query across all databases within a subscription plan. Limited day-pass access to the NTIS Database is available for a nominal fee.

For more information, visit the GOV.Research_Center at http://grc.ntis.gov.

World News Connection

World News Connection (WNC) is an NTIS online news service accessible only via the World Wide Web. WNC makes available English-language translations of time-sensitive news and information from thousands of non-U.S. media. Particularly effective in its coverage of local media, WNC provides the power to identify what is happening in a specific country or region. The information is obtained from speeches, television and radio broadcasts, newspaper articles, periodicals, and books. The subject matter focuses on socioeconomic, political, scientific, technical, and environmental issues, and events.

The information in WNC is provided to NTIS by the Foreign Broadcast Information Service (FBIS), a U.S. government agency. For more than 60 years, analysts from FBIS's domestic and overseas bureaus have monitored timely and pertinent open-source material, including gray literature. Uniquely, WNC allows subscribers to take advantage of the intelligence-gathering experience of FBIS.

WNC is updated every government-business day. Generally, new information is available within 24 to 72 hours of the time of original publication or broadcast.

Subscribers can conduct unlimited interactive searches and have the ability to set up automated searches known as profiles. When a profile is created, a search is run against WNC's latest news feed to identify articles relevant to a subscriber's topic of interest. The results are automatically sent to the subscriber's e-mail address.

Access to WNC is available through Dialog Corporation. To use the service, complete the WNC form at http://www.dialog.com/contacts/forms/wnc.shtml.

U.S. Export Administration Regulations

U.S. Export Administration Regulations (EAR) provides the latest rules controlling the export of U.S. dual-use commodities, technology, and software. Step by step, EAR explains when an export license is necessary and when it is not, how to obtain an export license, policy changes as they are issued, new restrictions on exports to certain countries and of certain types of items, and where to obtain further help.

This information is now available through NTIS in looseleaf form, on CD-ROM, and online. An e-mail update notification service is also available.

For more information, see http://bxa.fedworld.gov.

Davis-Bacon Wage Determination Database

The Davis-Bacon Wage Determination Database subscription product contains wage determinations issued by the U.S. Department of Labor under the mandate of the Davis-Bacon Act and related legislation. The department determines prevailing wage rates for construction-related occupations in most counties in the United States. All federal government construction contracts and most contracts for federally assisted construction over $2,000 must abide by the wage structure as provided for in the Davis-Bacon wage determinations. This product offers such value-added features as electronic delivery of modified wage decisions directly to the user's desktop, the ability to access wage decisions issued earlier in the year, and extensive help desk support.

A variety of access plans are available. For more information, see http://davisbacon.fedworld.gov.

Service Contract Act Wage Determination Database

The Service Contract Act Wage Determination (SCA) Database contains unsigned copies of the latest wage determinations developed by the U.S. Department of Labor. These wage determinations, issued by the Wage and Hour Division in response to specific notices filed, set the minimum wage on federally funded service contracts. SCA is updated each Tuesday with all wage determinations that were added or revised by the preceding Thursday.

For federal agencies participating under a memorandum of understanding with the department's Wage and Hour Division, and meeting all of its requirements, SCA can be used in the procurement process. For all other users, the wage determinations are for information only. They are not considered official wage determinations for specific solicitations or contracts and are not to be used to set prevailing wage rates on federal service contracts, but these data form a convenient and accurate basis upon which rates can be compared by occupation and geography.

A variety of access plans are available. For more information, see http://servicecontract.fedworld.gov.

Special Subscription Services

NTIS Alerts

More than 1,000 new titles are added to the NTIS collection every week. NTIS Alerts were developed in response to requests from customers to search and tap into this newly obtained information. NTIS prepares a list of search criteria that is run against all new studies and R&D reports in 16 subject areas. An NTIS Alert provides a twice-monthly information briefing service covering a wide range of technology topics.

An NTIS Alert provides numerous benefits: efficient, economical, and timely access to the latest U.S. government technical studies; concise, easy-to-read summaries; information not readily available from any other source; contributions from more than 100 countries; and subheadings within each issue designed to identify essential information quickly.

For more information, call the NTIS Subscriptions Department at 703-605-6060 or see http://www.ntis.gov/new/alerts_printed.asp.

Automatic Delivery Products

Selected Research In Microfiche (SRIM) is an inexpensive, tailored information service that delivers full-text microfiche copies of technical reports based on a customer's needs. Customers choose from Standard SRIM Service (selecting one or more of the 320 existing subject areas) or use Custom SRIM Service, which creates a new subject area to meet their particular needs. Custom SRIM Service requires a one-time fee to cover the cost of strategy development and computer programming to set up a profile. Except for this fee, the cost of Custom SRIM is the same as the Standard SRIM. Through this ongoing subscription service, customers receive microfiche copies of new reports pertaining to their field(s) of interest, as NTIS obtains the reports.

The SRIM service is now available in CD-ROM format—Science and Technology on CD. Documents are digitized and stored in pdf format that can easily be viewed using free Adobe Acrobat Reader software. With Science and Technology on CD, NTIS can provide more publications—those that cannot be rendered on microfiche, such as colorized illustrations or oversized formats.

For more information, see http://www.ntis.gov/products/auto-products.asp. To place an order, call 800-363-2068 or 703-605-6060.

Also at NTIS

NTIS Homeland Security Information Center

NTIS is a valuable resource for scientific and technical information relating to homeland security. It provides a Web-based finding aid in the following homeland security categories: health and medicine, food and agriculture, biological and chemical warfare, preparedness and response, and safety training. For more information, see http://www.ntis.gov/hs.

NTIS FedWorld

Since 1992 NTIS FedWorld Information Technologies has served as the online locator service for a comprehensive inventory of information disseminated by the federal government. FedWorld assists federal agencies and the public in electronically locating federal government information, both information housed within the NTIS repository and information FedWorld makes accessible through an electronic gateway to other government agencies. FedWorld is currently meeting the information needs of tens of thousands of customers daily. Examples of electronic information available on FedWorld include EPA auto emissions information, federal job searches, and Supreme Court decisions. Visit FedWorld at http://www.fedworld.gov.

NTIS Customer Service

NTIS's automated systems keep it at the forefront when it comes to customer service. Shopping online at NTIS is safe and secure; its secure socket layer (SSL) software is among the best available today.

Electronic document storage is fully integrated with NTIS's order-taking process, allowing it to provide rapid reproduction for the most recent additions to the NTIS document collection. Most orders for shipment are filled and delivered anywhere in the United States in five to seven business days. Rush service is available for an additional fee.

Key NTIS Contacts for Ordering

Order by Phone

Sales Desk	800-553-6847
8:00 A.M.–6:00 P.M. Eastern time, Monday–Friday	or 703-605-6000
Subscriptions	800-363-2068
8:30 A.M.–5:00 P.M. Eastern time, Monday–Friday	or 703-605-6060
TDD (hearing impaired only)	703-487-4639
8:30 A.M.–5:00 P.M. Eastern time, Monday–Friday	

Order by Fax

24 hours a day, seven days a week	703-605-6900
To verify receipt of fax, call	703-605-6090
7:00 A.M.–5:00 P.M. Eastern time Monday–Friday	

Order by Mail

National Technical Information Service
5285 Port Royal Road
Springfield, VA 22161

RUSH Service (available for an additional fee)	800-553-6847
	or 703-605-6000

Note: If requesting RUSH Service, please do not mail your order

Order Via World Wide Web

Direct and secure online ordering	http://www.ntis.gov

Order Via E-Mail

24 hours a day	orders@ntis.gov.

For Internet security, customers placing an order by e-mail can register their credit card in advance. To do so, call 703-605-6070 between 7:00 A.M. and 5:00 P.M. Eastern time, Monday through Friday.

National Archives and Records Administration

8601 Adelphi Rd., College Park, MD 20740
866-272-6272, 301-837-2000, fax 301-837-0483
E-mail form http://www.archives.gov/contact/inquire-form.html
World Wide Web http://www.archives.gov

Susan M. Ashtianie
Director, Policy and Planning Staff

The National Archives and Records Administration (NARA), an independent federal agency, ensures for the citizen, the public servant, the president, Congress, and the courts ready access to essential evidence that documents the rights of American citizens, the actions of federal officials, and the national experience.

NARA is singular among the world's archives as a unified federal institution that accessions and preserves materials from all three branches of government. NARA assists federal agencies in documenting their activities, administering records management programs, scheduling records, and retiring noncurrent records to federal records centers. The agency also manages the presidential libraries; assists the National Historical Publications and Records Commission in its grant program for state and local records and edited publications of the papers of prominent Americans; publishes the laws, regulations, presidential documents, and other official notices of the federal government; and oversees classification and declassification policy in the federal government through the Information Security Oversight Office. NARA constituents include the federal government, educators at all levels, a history-minded public, the media, the archival community, and a broad spectrum of professional associations and researchers in such fields as history, political science, law, library and information services, and genealogy.

The size and breadth of NARA's holdings are staggering. Together, NARA's facilities hold 28 million cubic feet (equivalent to more than 83 billion pieces of paper) of original textual and nontextual materials from the executive, legislative, and judicial branches of the federal government. Its multimedia collections include more than 114,000 motion picture films; nearly 7 million maps, charts, and architectural drawings; nearly 250,000 sound and video recordings; more than 25 million aerial photographs; more than 19 million still pictures and posters; and more than 8 billion electronic records.

Strategic Directions

NARA's strategic priorities are laid out in *Ready Access to Essential Evidence: The Strategic Plan of the National Archives and Records Administration, 1997–2008*, revised in 2003. Success for the agency as envisioned in the plan will mean reaching five strategic goals:

- Essential evidence will be created, identified, appropriately scheduled, and managed for as long as needed.

- Electronic records will be controlled, preserved, and made accessible for as long as needed.
- Essential evidence will be easy to access, regardless of where it is or where users are, for as long as needed.
- All records will be preserved in an appropriate environment for use as long as needed.
- NARA will strategically manage and align staff, technology, and processes to achieve its mission.

The plan lays out strategies for reaching these goals, sets milestone targets for accomplishments through 2008, and identifies measurements for gauging progress. The targets and measurements are further delineated in NARA's Annual Performance Plans.

The Strategic Plan and NARA's Annual Performance Plans and Reports are available on the NARA web site at http://www.archives.gov/about/plans-reports or by calling the Policy and Planning staff at 301-837-1850.

Records and Access

Internet

NARA's Web site, http://www.archives.gov, provides the most widely available means of electronic access to information about NARA via portals designed to support the particular needs of genealogists, veterans and their families, educators and students, researchers, the general public, records managers, journalists, information security specialists, members of Congress, and federal employees.

The site includes directions on how to contact NARA and do research at its facilities; descriptions of its holdings in an online catalog; direct access to certain archival electronic records (see http://www.archives.gov/aad); digital copies of selected archival documents; electronic versions of Federal Register publications; online exhibits; and classroom resources for students and teachers. There are also online tools, such as the Web-based, interactive inquiry program at http://www. archives.gov/veterans/evetrecs that allows veterans and the next-of-kin of deceased veterans to complete and print, for mail-in submission, requests for their service records. There is an Internet contact form, at http://www.archives. gov/contact/inquire-form.html, for customer questions, reference requests, comments, compliments, and complaints. Copies of military pension records from the American Revolution through World War I and other family history records in NARA's holdings can also be ordered at http://www.archives.gov/research/order/orderonline.html.

NARA also plays a key role in a nationwide civics initiative called Our Documents (at http://www.ourdocuments.gov), which features 100 milestone documents of American history drawn primarily from NARA's holdings and provides guidance for their use in the classroom.

In cooperation with several federal agencies, NARA also has established a Web portal, http://www.regulations.gov, on which anyone can find, view, and comment on rules and regulations promulgated by all federal agencies.

Archival Research Catalog

As a result of NARA's Archival Research Catalog (ARC), anyone with a computer connected to the Internet can search descriptions of NARA's nationwide holdings and view digital copies of some of its most popular documents. A significant piece of the electronic access strategy outlined in NARA's Strategic Plan, this single online catalog includes holdings in the regional archives and presidential libraries. Because of the vast extent of NARA holdings, it will take several years to populate ARC, but it already contains more than 600,000 descriptions of archival holdings and more than 124,000 digital copies of high-interest documents, representing about 42 percent of NARA's collection. The documents available online include many of the holdings highlighted in the Public Vaults, NARA's permanent interactive exhibition. The catalog is available at http://www.archives.gov/research/arc.

Electronic Records Archives

An unprecedented number of electronic records are being created by the government's departments and agencies. The most important of them will be preserved and made accessible indefinitely as the result of a new partnership between NARA and Lockheed Martin to create the Electronic Records Archives (ERA). ERA is driving the development of new technologies that will enable organizations to keep and use electronic records permanently while taking advantage of improvements in information technology. Its development will have far-reaching benefits that spread across the federal government and beyond. [For an in-depth report on ERA, see the following article, "NARA'S Electronic Records Archives—Preserving Information in the Face of Ever-Changing Technology—*Ed.*]

National Archives Experience

In September 2003 NARA reopened the Rotunda for the Charters of Freedom at the National Archives Building in Washington, D.C. It had been closed for renovation since July 2001. Returned to display were the Declaration of Independence, the Constitution, and the Bill of Rights, known collectively as the Charters of Freedom, which had received conservation treatment and were placed in new state-of-the-art encasements. For the first time, all four pages of the Constitution are on permanent display, and all the documents are now displayed so that they are easier to view by young visitors and those using wheelchairs. The reopening of the rotunda launched the National Archives Experience, a set of interconnected resources—made possible by a public-private partnership between NARA and the Foundation for the National Archives—that provide a variety of ways of exploring the power and importance of America's records.

The National Archives Experience continued to expand in 2004 with the opening of the William G. McGowan Theater, the unveiling of the Public Vaults, and the inauguration of the Lawrence F. O'Brien Gallery. The 290-seat McGowan Theater is a state-of-the-art showplace for NARA's extensive audiovisual holdings and serves as a forum for lectures and discussion. It also is home to the new Guggenheim Center for the Documentary Film. The Public Vaults is a 9,000-square-foot permanent exhibition that conveys the feeling of going beyond the walls of the rotunda and into the stacks and vaults of the working archives. Dozens of individual exhibits, many of them interactive, reveal the breadth and variety of NARA's holdings. Complementing the Public Vaults, the O'Brien Gallery hosts a changing array of topical exhibits based on National Archives records. Additions will include a learning center, scheduled to open in 2006, that will use the documentary resources of the National Archives to engage and inspire children to connect to the nation's past.

A set of Web pages now makes the entire National Archives Experience available on the Internet. An illustrated history of the Charters of Freedom can be found, as well as information on events and exhibits. For more information, see "The National Archives Experience" at http://www.archives.gov/national-archives-experience.

Warner Research Center

Another highlight of the renovation of the National Archives Building is the Robert M. Warner Research Center, which opened in October 2003. It consolidated on one floor many of the research services previously scattered throughout the building and offered a number of new services for researchers.

Archives Library Information Center

The Archives Library Information Center (ALIC) provides access to information on American history and government, archival administration, information management, and government documents. ALIC is physically located in two traditional libraries in the National Archives Building in Washington and the National Archives at College Park, Maryland. Customers also can visit ALIC on the Internet at http://www.archives.gov/research/alic, where they will find "Reference at Your Desk" (organized access to a variety of Internet reference tools), staff-compiled bibliographies and publications, an online library catalog, and more. ALIC can be reached by telephone at 202-357-5018 in Washington and 301-837-3415 in College Park.

Government Documents

U.S. government publications are generally available to researchers at many of the 1,250 congressionally designated federal depository libraries throughout the United States. A record set of these publications also is part of NARA's archival holdings. Publications of the U.S. Government (Record Group 287) is a collection of selected publications of U.S. government agencies, arranged by the classification system (SuDoc System) devised by the Office of the Superintendent of Documents, Government Printing Office (GPO). The core of the collection is a library established in 1895 by GPO's Public Documents Division. By 1972, when NARA acquired the library, it included official publications dating from the early years of the federal government and selected publications produced for and by federal government agencies. Since 1972 the 25,000-cubic-foot collection has been augmented periodically with accessions of U.S. government publications selected by the Office of the Superintendent of Documents as a byproduct of its cataloging activity. As with the federal depository library collections, the holdings in NARA's Record Group 287 compose only a portion of all U.S. government publications.

NARA Publications

NARA publishes guides and indexes to various portions of its archival holdings; catalogs of microfilmed records; informational leaflets and brochures; general interest books about NARA and its holdings that will appeal to anyone with an interest in U.S. history; more-specialized publications that will be useful to scholars, archivists, records managers, historians, researchers, and educators; facsimiles of certain documents; and *Prologue,* a scholarly journal published quarterly. Some NARA publications are available through the National Archives Fax-on-Demand System described below. Some are also available on NARA's Web site, at http://www.archives.gov/publications/online.html. Many are available from NARA's Customer Service Center in College Park by telephoning 800-234-8861 or 866-272-6272 (301-837-2000 in the Washington, D.C., area) or faxing 301-837-0483. The NARA Web site's publications home page, http://www.archives.gov/publications, provides more-detailed information about available publications and ordering.

Fax-on-Demand

NARA customers can request faxed copies of select informational materials at any time by calling NARA's interactive fax retrieval system at 301-837-0990. By following the voice-activated instructions, customers will receive copies of the materials stored digitally on the hard drive of an agency computer. Among the materials available by fax are general information leaflets, other fact sheets about various NARA holdings, programs, and facilities; instructions, forms, and vendor lists for ordering copies of records; and finding aids for some textual, audiovisual, and micrographic records. Instructions and a listing of currently available documents are found at http://www.archives.gov/publications/ordering/fax.html. There are no charges for using this service except for the cost of long-distance telephone calls.

Federal Register

The *Federal Register* is the daily newspaper of the federal government and includes proposed and final regulations, agency notices, and presidential legal documents. It is published by the Office of the Federal Register and printed and distributed by GPO. The two agencies collaborate in the same way to produce the annual revisions of the *Code of Federal Regulations* (*CFR*). Free access to the full text of the electronic version of the *Federal Register* and *CFR* is available through the GPO Access service, on the Internet at http://www.gpoaccess.gov.

In addition to these publications, the full texts of other Federal Register publications are available through GPO Access, including the *Weekly Compilation of Presidential Documents, Public Papers of the President,* slip laws, *U.S. Statutes at Large,* and *United States Government Manual.* All of these publications also are maintained at all federal depository libraries. The *Electronic Code of Federal Regulations* (*eCFR*) is an unofficial, currently updated online publication also available through the GPO Access service. Public Law Electronic Notification Service is a free subscription e-mail service available for notification of recently enacted public laws. The Federal Register Table of Contents Service is a free e-mail service available for delivery of the daily table of contents from the *Federal Register* with direct links to documents.

The Office of the Federal Register also publishes information about its ministerial responsibilities associated with the operation of the Electoral College and ratification of constitutional amendments and provides access to related records. Publication information concerning laws, regulations, and presidential documents and services is available from the Office of the Federal Register by calling 202-741-6000. Information about and additional finding aids for Federal Register publications, the Electoral College, and constitutional amendments also are available via the Internet at http://www.archives.gov/federal-register. Publications also can be ordered from GPO by writing to New Orders, Superintendent of Documents, P.O. Box 371954, Pittsburgh, PA 15250-7954.

Customer Service

Customers

NARA's Customer Service Standards, available free of charge in its research rooms nationwide and on its Web site at http://www.archives.gov/about/customer-service/standards.html, lists the many types of customers NARA serves and describes NARA's standards for customer service. Few records repositories serve as many customers as NARA. In fiscal year 2005, there were more than 167,000 research visits to NARA facilities nationwide, including archives, presidential libraries, and federal records centers. At the same time, more than a million customers requested information in writing. NARA also served the executive agencies of the federal government, the courts, and Congress by providing records storage, reference service, training, advice, and guidance on many issues relating to records management. Federal records centers replied to nearly 10 million requests for information and records, including more than 750,000 requests for information from other agencies for military and civilian government service records provided by the National Personnel Records Center in St. Louis. NARA also provided informative public programs at its various facilities for more than 245,000 people. More than a million visited the National Archives Experience in Washington, and exhibits in the presidential library museums were visited by nearly 1.7 million people. NARA's customer service accomplishments are detailed in its annual performance and accountability reports.

Customer Opinion

Among the specific strategies published in NARA's Strategic Plan is an explicit commitment to expanding the opportunities of its customers to inform NARA about information and services that they need. In support of that strategy, NARA continues to survey, hold focus groups, and meet with customers to evaluate and constantly improve services. For example, the agency continuously surveys visitors to the Web site and users of military service records. NARA also maintains an Internet form (http://www.archives.gov/contact/inquire-form.html) to facilitate continuous feedback from customers about what is most important to them and what NARA might do better to meet their needs.

Grants

The National Historical Publications and Records Commission (NHPRC) is the grant-making affiliate of NARA. The Archivist of the United States chairs the commission and makes grants on its recommendation. NHPRC's 14 other members represent the president of the United States (two appointees), the Supreme Court, the Senate and House of Representatives, the Departments of State and Defense, the Librarian of Congress, the American Association for State and Local History, the American Historical Association, the Association for Documentary Editing, the National Association of Government Archives and Records Administrators, the Organization of American Historians, and the Society of American Archivists.

NHPRC carries out a statutory mission to ensure understanding of the nation's past by promoting nationwide the identification, preservation, and dissemination of essential historical documentation. It supports the creation and publication of documentary editions, including eight from the nation's founding era, and basic and applied research in the management and preservation of authentic electronic records, and it works in partnership with a national network of state historical records advisory boards to develop a national archival infrastructure. NHPRC grants help state and local governments and archives, universities, historical societies, professional organizations, and other nonprofit organizations to establish or strengthen archival programs, improve training and techniques, preserve and process records collections, and provide access to them through finding aids and documentary editions of the papers of significant historical figures and movements in U.S. history.

NHPRC contributes to NARA's role as "first preserver" in times of emergency. Through its connection with state and local government archives, NHPRC is able to provide immediate financial assistance through grants for preserving historical records affected by natural disasters, such as flooding. For more information about the commission, see http://www.archives.gov/nhprc.

Administration

NARA employs approximately 3,100 people, of whom about 2,700 are full-time permanent staff. For fiscal year 2006, NARA received a budget of $338,141,000, including $7,500,000 to support NHPRC.

NARA'S Electronic Records Archives— Preserving Information in the Face of Ever-Changing Technology

James Worsham

Editor of Publications, Public Affairs and Communications Staff
National Archives and Records Administration

Move the clock ahead three decades to 2036.

- An Army veteran, now in retirement, wants to apply for the government benefits to which he's entitled. When he contacts the Army, he is told that the medical records from that period in his life are electronic, and—since his file has been inactive for years—there is no way a computer in 2036 can access them. Frustrated, the veteran tries to reconstruct his file using paper documents, but this task will take time, and may not even be possible.

- A woman who spent 2000 to 2010 working as a librarian at a state university needs her personnel records—all electronic—to be able to collect her pension. But the university is unable to access the records because the software in use during the ten years of her employment is no longer available.

- Researchers at the Pentagon, working on new security measures, want to look at archived plans for weaponry from the early years of the 21st century. But they are having trouble opening them as they no longer have the software that was used to create them.

- Historians working on a history of the early 21st century are frustrated in their attempt to consult records of the U.S. presidents from that period because these electronic documents can no longer be accessed.

These hypothetical scenarios raise the specter of a tomorrow that has no yesterday after a wave of technological advances has swept away digital links to the past. But all of this could indeed happen if we do not ensure preservation of the electronic records being created today by government at all levels, day in and day out.

To meet the challenge of preserving authentic and accessible electronic records, the National Archives and Records Administration (NARA) is building an Electronic Records Archives, or ERA. Once ERA begins operating, in 2007, it will be able to accept, preserve, and make accessible—far into the future—any type of electronic document. And it will do this regardless of what hardware and software were used to create the document. ERA will also maintain the authenticity of these records by guarding against tampering, thus ensuring full and accurate representation of the transactions, activities, and facts contained in them.

'Major First Step'

"With the government producing electronic records at such a rapid pace, ERA is absolutely necessary," Archivist of the United States Allen Weinstein told the Association of Research Libraries in October 2005. "The stakes for the country are too high, and failure is simply not an option." Weinstein cautioned that ERA is not the answer to all the problems of preserving electronic records; "It is not a panacea, but a major first step in addressing the management of electronic records," he said.

NARA is charged with preserving and making accessible indefinitely the records of the federal government—no matter what form they are in—that document the rights of all citizens, the actions of government officials, and the national experience. Accordingly, it has taken the lead in finding a way to preserve these federal electronic records, which come in many forms—from text documents and e-mails to Web pages, videotapes, and audio files. And these records can be complex; e-mails often have attachments, Web pages can be interactive, even electronic text documents often have other documents embedded in them or links to supporting documents. Without some means to preserve them, important federal records could be lost or at least become very difficult to access.

The pace at which these records are created is astounding. For example, the eight-year administration of President Bill Clinton created 40 million e-mail messages alone; the George W. Bush administration is expected to leave more than twice that many.

It is not only the records of the federal government that are at risk without the technology that ERA will bring. The records of state and local governments, hospitals and health providers, insurance companies, small businesses and large corporations, courts and law enforcement agencies, public schools and colleges and universities, and banks and financial institutions are equally imperiled. But the technology being developed as part of ERA will be able to be used to permanently preserve these records as well.

Effort Began in 1998

The ERA program dates to 1998, when NARA began seeking to clarify requirements for preserving authentic electronic records and to identify and evaluate emerging technologies that could be used to meet the challenges posed. The agency invested seed money to engage government and private research partners to determine if long-term preservation of electronic records was possible. This research created new techniques that led to the first proof-of-concept in 1999 and demonstrated that electronic records preservation was a possibility. NARA then turned its attention to building a new system that was still subject to computer science research. Early steps included the creation of an ERA Program Management Office and the development of ERA system requirements, with critical input from federal, state, and local governments, professional organizations, scientific communities, and private-sector stakeholders. These research collaborations provide an environment for testing and evaluating new technologies as they emerge.

These institutions or organizations have included San Diego Supercomputer Center, a broad community of scientists, engineers, students, commercial partners, and museums and other facilities working to develop solutions for managing their data needs; the University of Maryland Institute for Advanced Computer Studies, which conducts interdisciplinary research into a wide variety of computing procedures; the National Center for Supercomputing Applications at the University of Illinois, which develops and deploys new computing and software technologies; the Army Research Laboratory, a basic- and applied-research laboratory that provides innovative science, technology, and analysis to enable full-spectrum operations; Georgia Institute of Technology, one of the nation's top research universities; Massachusetts Institute of Technology, a world-renowned research center for the sciences; and Stanford Linear Accelerator Center, a leading research laboratory that has produced many breakthroughs in science and technology.

The ERA program has also partnered with a number of federal agencies, including the National Aeronautics and Space Administration, the National Nuclear Security Agency, the National Institute of Standards and Technology, the National Science Foundation, the Department of Defense, and the National Security Agency.

Other organizations that have worked with NARA on ERA include

- The InterPARES (International Research on Permanent Authentic Records in Electronic Systems) Project, which is developing the theoretical and methodological knowledge for long-term preservation of authentic records in digital form
- The Digital Library Federation, a consortium of libraries and related agencies that are pioneering the use of electronic-information technologies to extend collections and services
- The Federal Geographic Data Committee, which is developing the National Spatial Data Infrastructure (NDSI)—policies, standards, and procedures to cooperatively produce and share geographic data—in cooperation with organizations from state, local, and tribal governments, the academic community, and the private sector
- The Global Grid Forum, the community of users, developers, and vendors leading the global standardization effort for grid computing
- The Institute of Electrical and Electronics Engineers (IEEE), which promotes the engineering process of creating, developing, integrating, sharing, and applying knowledge about electro- and information technologies and sciences
- The National Computational Science Alliance, a leader in the development and deployment of new computing and software technologies for the scientific and engineering community

For ERA, one of the most important tools is the Research Prototype Persistent Archives, also referred to as NARA's ERA "data grid." This is a product of a seven-year research effort that includes contributions from the National Science Foundation, the San Diego Supercomputer Center, and the University of Maryland.

The data grid is a test bed that allows staff to directly access computers and files at the sites of research partners. It gives these partners opportunities to test geographically dispersed records collections, storing collections in a hardware- and software-independent environment, and managing electronic records that are many times larger than those currently held by NARA.

Another tool is the Producer Archive Workflow Network, or PAWN. This prototype application provides tools for the automated transfer of records from the records creators to the National Archives. It allows NARA to look at such issues as ensuring that the records an agency desires to transfer to the National Archives are authorized for such transfer; that the person transferring the records is authorized to do so; and that the records are accompanied by sufficient information to understand what they are, what they are used for, and what types of preservation actions they will require.

Lockheed Martin Lead Contractor

During the past few years, while research continued, NARA held a competition among major U.S. information technology firms for the contract to build ERA. The competition ended in September 2005 when NARA announced that the $308 million contract would go to the Transportation and Security Solutions unit of Lockheed Martin Corporation, based in Bethesda, Maryland.

Said Weinstein in making the announcement, "We have been impressed with [Lockheed's] ability to design a system which addresses in considerable depth NARA's business needs, on the one hand, and on the other hand, a system that entails a modern, service-oriented architecture."

He noted that the ERA contract announcement came "in a climate of urgency" when "an unprecedented number" of electronic records are being created by the federal government, the most important of which will be preserved and made accessible at NARA indefinitely. "This simply must happen," Weinstein said.

The $308 million contract award covers all costs of development, acquisition of hardware and software products, integration, deployment, and operational support through 2012.

As the prime contractor for the ERA project, Lockheed Martin said it would lead a team of companies with archiving and data management expertise. The team includes BearingPoint, Inc., of McLean, Virginia; Fenestra Technologies Corp. of Germantown, Maryland; FileTek, Inc., and History Associates, Inc., of Rockville, Maryland; EDS Corp. of Plano, Texas; Image Fortress Corp. of Westford, Massachusetts; Métier Ltd. of Washington, D.C.; Science Applications International Corp. (SAIC) of San Diego; and Tessella, Inc., of Newton, Massachusetts.

At the same time it awarded the contract to Lockheed Martin, NARA formed the Advisory Committee on the Electronic Records Archives, made up of experts in computer science, information technology, archival science, records management, information science, law, history, genealogy, and education. The committee is headed by Robert Kahn, president and CEO of the Corporation for National Research Initiatives.

Kenneth Thibodeau, director of the ERA Program at NARA: "As we move forward to making the Electronic Records Archives a reality, it is more important than ever that we reach out to obtain advice from a broad spectrum of relevant expertise and interests." As ERA emerges from the drawing board, these experts will advise the National Archives on how well it meets the needs of its customers.

Well before the contract award to Lockheed, NARA was getting ready for a world of electronic records. NARA has been preserving electronic records since the 1970s, but over the past decade the agency's holdings of such records have grown 100 times faster than its holdings of traditional paper records.

Already NARA has started making electronic records available over the Internet at its Web site, http://www.archives.gov. One way has been through Access to Archival Databases (AAD), the first publicly accessible application developed under the ERA Program. With AAD, researchers can access a selection of more than 85 million electronic records created by more than 30 federal agencies on a wide range of topics, from immigration records to prisoner-of-war lists.

Researchers can learn about the widely varied content of the National Archives by searching the Archival Research Catalog (ARC), also accessible at the NARA Web site at http://www.archives.gov/research/arc/index.html. ARC currently contains descriptions of more than 40 percent of all of NARA's holdings nationwide and adds descriptions continuously. ARC's functions will be absorbed into ERA, providing a "one-stop shopping" portal to NARA information and services.

National Security Implications

ERA will also help make the records accessible for other reasons than use by future researchers. The nation's national security—today and well into the future—depends on the deployment of ERA. Federal agencies, state and local governments, and the United States' allies must be able to share information critical to the safety of their citizens, their governments, their infrastructures, and their social and economic fabric. Much of the information being used today to secure the nation's borders and protect its people will be needed long after the computers and software that created the information are obsolete.

The day-to-day operation of what is now referred to as "e-government" depends on reliable management of the rapidly increasing amount of electronic records. A large group of those records—the White House records of the eight years of the administration of George W. Bush, the most digital presidency yet—are to be turned over to NARA on January 20, 2009. In addition to the e-mails, the White House creates countless text documents, digital photographs and other images, videotape, Web snapshots, and other electronic records.

Much of the information that will come to NARA with the Bush White House records—as is the case with all presidents leaving office—consists of sensitive documents dealing with national security. ERA will be able to handle these records and provide the proper access controls as well as the needed preservation services.

ERA will need to free each record from dependence on the program or programs that were used to create it and allow it to be accessed with whatever programs are in use in the future.

"The most fundamental characteristic of ERA is that it must be able to evolve over time, a radically new concept in system design," Thibodeau said. He explained that this would allow new types of electronic records, not yet invented, to be brought into ERA and preserved, and will permit ERA to take advantage of improved technologies over the years.

ERA will be built to guarantee that the electronic records researchers get from the National Archives next year, in five years, or at any time in the future, are not corrupted or distorted by changes in technology. "They will be authentic—as reliable as they were the day they were created," Thibodeau said.

To ensure that electronic records of the federal government are in good order when they reach the National Archives, the agency has been working with departments and agencies on records management issues. NARA is not only helping them to manage their electronic records, long before these records are turned over to the archives, but is also ensuring that these agencies can use and keep active electronic records for many years while taking advantage of advances in information technology. Improved records management in government today, NARA officials note, will make easier the future transfer to NARA of ever-increasing volumes of historically valuable electronic records.

For years, NARA was trying to catch up with the rapidly advancing technology, but now, Weinstein said, the agency has come to a "major milestone" in trying to meet the challenge posed by electronic records. "There has been a race against technology as we watch software become obsolete almost as soon as it is installed in our computers," he said, "but the technology for preserving electronic records is finally catching up with the technology for creating them." At the National Archives, development of ERA is now on what he calls an "urgent schedule."

With Lockheed Martin in place as the company that will build ERA, attention is now turning to how it will actually work. The project is expected to create much new technology, just as the space program brought great technological advances. The new technology resulting from ERA can be scaled and adapted for archives and libraries in businesses and corporations, colleges and universities, state and local governments, banks and financial institutions, and hospitals and medical facilities.

For more information about the Electronic Records Archives Program, contact the ERA Communications Office at 301-837-0740, or send an e-mail to ERA.Program@nara.gov. Additional information is also found at http://www.archives.gov/era.

National Center for Education Statistics Library Statistics Program

U.S. Department of Education, Institute of Education Sciences
1990 K St. N.W., Washington, DC 20006

Adrienne Chute
Elementary/Secondary and Libraries Studies Division

In an effort to collect and disseminate more-complete statistical information about libraries, the National Center for Education Statistics (NCES) initiated a formal library statistics program in 1989 that now includes surveys on academic libraries, public libraries, school library media centers, and state library agencies. The Library Statistics Program (LSP) is administered and funded by NCES, under the leadership of Jeffrey Williams, program director. The U.S. National Commission on Libraries and Information Science (NCLIS) and the U.S. Bureau of the Census work cooperatively with NCES in implementing the program.

The four library surveys conducted by NCES are designed to provide comprehensive nationwide data on the status of libraries. Federal, state, and local officials, professional associations, and local practitioners use these surveys for planning, evaluating, making policy, and drawing samples for special surveys. These data are also available to researchers and educators.

The LSP Web site (http://nces.ed.gov/surveys/libraries) provides links to data-search tools, the latest available data for each survey, other publications, data files, survey definitions, details of new information that is coming up, and a Researchers and Respondents Corner for each survey. This article describes the four library surveys.

Public Libraries

Descriptive statistics for more than 9,000 public libraries are collected and disseminated annually through a voluntary census, the Public Libraries Survey. The survey is conducted by NCES through the Federal-State Cooperative System (FSCS) for Public Library Data. In 2006 FSCS will complete its 18th data collection.

The Public Libraries Survey collects identifying information about public libraries and each of their service outlets, including street address, city, county, zip code, and telephone number. Additional identifying information includes Web address and mailing address. The survey collects data on staffing; type of legal basis; type of geographic boundary; type of administrative structure; type of interlibrary relationship; type and number of public service outlets; operating revenue and expenditures; capital revenue and expenditures; size of collection (including number of electronic books and databases); current serial subscriptions (including electronic); and such service measures as number of reference

*The authorization for the National Center for Education Statistics (NCES) to collect library statistics is included in the Education Sciences Reform Act of 2002 (PL 107-279), under Title I, Part C.

Note: Jeffrey Williams, Elaine Kroe, and Barbara Holton of NCES contributed to this article.

transactions, interlibrary loans, circulation, public service hours, library visits, circulation of children's materials, number of children's programs, children's program attendance, total number of library programs, total attendance at library programs, number of Internet terminals used by the general public, and number of users of electronic resources per year.

This survey also collects several data items about outlets, including the location of an outlet relative to a metropolitan area, number of books-by-mail-only outlets, number of bookmobiles by bookmobile outlet, and square footage of the outlet.

The 50 states and the District of Columbia participate in data collection. Beginning in 1993 the following outlying areas joined the FSCS for Public Library Data: Guam, Commonwealth of the Northern Mariana Islands, Puerto Rico, and the U.S. Virgin Islands. For the collection of fiscal year (FY) 2004 data, the respondents that provided publishable data were the more than 9,000 public libraries identified by state library agencies in the 50 states, the District of Columbia, and the U.S. Virgin Islands. The first release of Public Libraries Survey data occurs with the release of the updated Compare Public Libraries Tool on the LSP Web site. The data used in this Web tool are final, but do not include imputations for missing data (imputation is a statistical means for providing an estimate for each missing data item). The next release is the public use data file, followed by the release of an E.D. Tab (an NCES publication that presents data highlights followed by a succinct presentation of descriptive statistics, including tables) on the NCES Web site. [For a sampling of content from recent E.D. Tabs, see "Highlights of NCES Surveys" in Part 4—Ed.]

Final imputed data files that contain FY 2003 data on more than 9,000 responding libraries and identifying information about their outlets were made available in June 2005 on the LSP Web site. The FY 2003 data were aggregated to state and national levels in the E.D. Tab *Public Libraries in the United States: Fiscal Year 2003* and released in September 2005 on the LSP Web site. NCES expects to release FY 2004 data and an E.D. Tab in summer 2006.

The Compare Public Libraries Tool and the Find Public Libraries Tool have been updated with FY 2003 data. FY 2004 data were expected to be available on these tools in early 2006.

The FSCS for Public Library Data is an example of the synergy that results from combining federal/state cooperation with state-of-the-art technology. The Public Libraries Survey was the first national NCES data collection in which the respondents supplied the data electronically. All Public Libraries Survey data have been collected electronically.

Beginning with the FY 2005 data-collection cycle, descriptive data on public libraries are collected via a Web-based application called WebPLUS. FSCS collects identifying information on all known public libraries and their service outlets. The resulting universe file has been a resource for use in drawing samples for special surveys on such topics as literacy, access for the disabled, and library construction. At the state level and in the outlying areas, data coordinators, appointed by each state or outlying area's chief officer of the state library agency, administer FSCS. FSCS is a working network. State data coordinators collect the requested data from public libraries and submit these data to NCES, and NCES aggregates the data to provide state and national totals. An annual training conference is provided for the state data coordinators, and a steering committee that represents them is active in the development of the Public Libraries Survey and its Web-based data collection. Technical assistance to states is provided by state data coordinators, by NCES staff, by the Bureau of the Census, and by NCLIS. NCES also works cooperatively with NCLIS, the Bureau of the Census, the Institute for Museum and Library Services (IMLS) Office of Library Programs, the Chief Officers of State Library Agencies (COSLA), the American Library Association (ALA), and the U.S. Department of Education's National Library of Education.

Recent Public Library Data Projects

LSP has released its redesigned Compare Public Libraries Tool (updated with FY 2003 data) on its Web site. With this tool, a user can select a library of interest and search for a peer group of libraries by selecting key characteristics to define it (such as all other libraries in the same state with similar total operating expenditures), then view customized reports of the comparison between his or her library and its peers. To use this tool, visit http://nces.ed.gov/surveys/libraries/compare.

Questions about public libraries have also been included in other NCES surveys. For example, in fall 2002 questions about the purposes for which households use public libraries were included as part of a supplement to the Current Population Survey. NCES plans to release a report on these data in 2006.

Additional information on public libraries data is available from Adrienne Chute, Elementary/Secondary and Libraries Studies Division, National Center for Education Statistics, Room 9091, 1990 K St. N.W., Washington, DC 20006 (telephone 202-502-7328, e-mail adrienne.chute@ed.gov).

Academic Libraries

The Academic Libraries Survey (ALS) provides descriptive statistics for approximately 3,700 academic libraries in the 50 states, the District of Columbia, and the outlying areas of the United States. NCES surveyed academic libraries on a three-year cycle between 1966 and 1988. From 1988 to 1998 ALS was a component of the Integrated Postsecondary Education Data System (IPEDS) and was on a two-year cycle. As of FY 2000, ALS is no longer a component of IPEDS, but remains on a two-year cycle. IPEDS and ALS data can still be linked using the unit identification codes of the postsecondary education institutions. In aggregate, these data provide an overview of the status of academic libraries nationally and by state. ALS collects data on libraries in the entire universe of degree-granting postsecondary institutions, using a Web-based data collection system.

ALS has established a working group composed of representatives of the academic library community. Its mission is to improve data quality and the timeliness of data collection, processing, and release. NCES also works cooperatively with ALA, NCLIS, the Association of Research Libraries, the Association of College and Research Libraries, and academic libraries in the collection of ALS.

ALS collects data on total library operating expenditures, full-time-equivalent (FTE) library staff, service outlets, collection size, number of documents digitized by library staff, circulation, interlibrary loans, public service hours, library visits, reference transactions, consortia services, number of presentations, attendance at presentations, and online services. Academic libraries are also asked whether they offer library reference services by e-mail, electronic document delivery to a patron's account-address, and technology for patrons with disabilities. The final data file and documentation for the 2002 ALS were released on the NCES Web site in December 2005.

NCES has developed a Web-based peer analysis tool for ALS that has a number of features similar to the Compare Public Libraries Tool and was updated with FY 2002 unimputed data in 2004.

Additional information on academic library statistics is available from Jeffrey Williams, Elementary/Secondary and Libraries Studies Division, National Center for Education Statistics, Room 9026, 1990 K St. N.W., Washington, DC 20006 (telephone 202-502-7476, e-mail jeffrey.williams@ed.gov).

School Library Media Centers

National surveys of school library media centers in elementary and secondary schools in the United States were conducted in 1958, 1962, 1974, 1978, 1986, 1994, 2000, and 2004. The next survey will take place during the 2007–2008 school year.

NCES, with the assistance of the U.S. Bureau of the Census, conducts the School Library Media Centers Survey as part of the Schools and Staffing Survey (SASS), the nation's largest sample survey of K–12 public and private schools. Data from the school library media center questionnaire provide a national picture of school library staffing, collections, expenditures, technology, and services. *The Status of Public and Private School Library Media Centers in the United States: 1999–2000* (NCES 2004-313), a report based on the 1999–2000 SASS, can be downloaded from the NCES Web site and can be ordered from EDPubs. The report *Schools and Staffing Survey, 1999–2000: Overview of the Data for Public, Private, Public Charter, and Bureau of Indian Affairs Elementary and Secondary Schools* (NCES 2002-313) is also available from the NCES Web site. The restricted-use data file for this survey was released by NCES in January 2003. The 2003–2004 SASS included a Public School Library Media Center Survey, and the data are currently being processed.

NCES also published a historical report about school libraries, *Fifty Years of Supporting Children's Learning: A History of Public School Libraries and Federal Legislation from 1953–2000*. Drawn from more than 50 sources, this report presents descriptive data about public school libraries since 1953. Along with key characteristics of school libraries, the report also presents national and regional standards as well as federal legislation affecting school library media centers. Data from sample surveys are presented at the national, regional, and school levels, and by state.

NCES has included some library-oriented questions on the parent and the teacher instruments of its new Early Childhood Longitudinal Study (ECLS). For more information, visit http://nces.ed.gov/ecls. Library items also appear in National Household Education Survey (NHES) instruments; for more information on that survey, visit http://nces.ed.gov/nhes.

NCES included a questionnaire about high school library media centers in the Education Longitudinal Study of 2002 (ELS: 2002). This survey collected data from tenth graders about their schools, their school library media centers, their communities, and their home life. The report *School Library Media Centers: Selected Results from the Education Longitudinal Study of 2002* (ELS: 2002) (NCES 2005-302) is available on the NCES Web site and can be ordered through EDPubs. For more information about this survey, visit http://nces.ed.gov/surveys/els2002.

Additional information on school library media center statistics is available from Barbara Holton, Elementary/Secondary and Libraries Studies Division, National Center for Education Statistics, Room 9030, 1990 K St. N.W., Washington, DC 20006 (telephone 202-219-7095, e-mail barbara.holton@ed.gov).

State Library Agencies

The State Library Agencies (StLA) Survey collects and disseminates information about the state library agencies in the 50 states and the District of Columbia. A state library agency (StLA) is the official unit of state government charged with statewide library development and the administration of federal funds under the Library Services and Technology Act (LSTA). StLAs' administrative and developmental responsibilities affect the operation of thousands of public, academic, school, and special libraries. StLAs provide important reference and information services to state government and sometimes also provide service to the general public. StLAs often administer state library and special operations such as state archives and libraries for the blind and physically handicapped and the state Center for the Book. The StLA survey began in 1994 as a cooperative effort between NCES, COSLA, and NCLIS. The FY 2004 StLA survey collected data on the following areas: direct library services, adult literacy and family literacy, library development services, resources assigned to allied operations such as archive and records management, organizational and governance structure within which the agency operates, electronic networking, staffing, collections, and expenditures. These data are edited electronically, and prior to FY 1999 missing data were not imputed. Beginning with FY 1999 data, however, national totals included imputations for missing data. Another change is that beginning with FY 1999 data the StLA became a Web-based data collection system. The most recent data available are for FY 2004. The survey database was released in July 2005 and the E.D. Tab *State Library Agencies, Fiscal Year 2004* was released in October 2005. The E.D. Tab was redesigned to include selected findings and eight tables of summary data for 50 states and the District of Columbia; FY 2005 data are being processed.

More information on the State Library Agencies Survey is available from Elaine Kroe, Elementary/Secondary and Libraries Studies Division, Room 9027, National Center for Education Statistics, 1990 K St. N.W., Washington, DC 20006 (telephone 202-502-7379, e-mail patricia.kroe@ed.gov).

How to Obtain Printed and Electronic Products

As a result of its library surveys, NCES regularly publishes E.D. Tabs that contain tables presenting state and national totals, a survey description, and data highlights. NCES also publishes separate, more in-depth studies analyzing these data.

Internet Access

Many NCES publications (including out-of-print publications) and edited raw data files from the library surveys are available for viewing or downloading at no charge through the Electronic Catalog on NCES's Web site at http://nces.ed.gov/pubsearch.

Ordering Printed Products

Many NCES publications are also available in printed format. To order one free copy of recent NCES reports, contact the Education Publications Center (ED Pubs) at

E-mail: customerservice@edpubs.org
Toll-free telephone: 877-4-ED-Pubs (877-433-7827)
TTY/TDD toll-free number 877-576-7734
Fax: 301-470-1244
Mail: ED Pubs, P.O. Box 1398, Jessup, MD 20794-1398

Many publications are available through the Educational Resources Information Center (ERIC) system. For more information on services and products, visit the EDRS Web site at http://www.eric.ed.gov.

Out-of-print publications and data files may be available through the NCES Electronic Catalog on NCES's Web site at http://nces.ed.gov/pubsearch or through one of the 1,400 federal depository libraries throughout the United States (see http://www.gpoaccess.gov/libraries.html). Use the NCES publication number included in the citations for publications and data files to quickly locate items in the NCES Electronic Catalog. Use the GPO number to locate items in a federal depository library.

National Commission on Libraries and Information Science

1800 M St. N.W., Suite 350, Washington, DC 20036-5841
202-606-9200, fax 202-606-9203, e-mail info@nclis.gov
World Wide Web http://www.nclis.gov

Trudi Bellardo Hahn
Executive Director

The law that created the National Commission on Libraries and Information Science (NCLIS), Public Law 91-345 (20 U.S.C. 1501 *et seq.*, signed July 20, 1970), states that "library and information services adequate to meet the needs of the people of the United States are essential to achieve national goals." It is the commission's responsibility to develop and recommend plans that will enable the American people to have adequate library and information services.

For 35 years NCLIS has worked to fulfill its mandated mission of identifying the people's needs for library and information services, translating those needs into recommendations for national policy and advising the president, Congress, state and local governments, and others on implementation of national policy. During that period, NCLIS has engaged in many important initiatives to achieve its statutory mandate and has published a number of reports of its findings, studies, and recommendations.

The commission has also partnered for 20 years with the National Center for Educational Statistics (NCES) to develop and implement the Library Statistics Program (LSP). NCLIS has served as liaison to the library community, organized meetings and training workshops, supported training and technical assistance, monitored trends, and advised NCES on policy matters. The LSP has resulted in the development of standards for library statistics, as well as the accurate and timely collection of relevant statistics to assist in policy development and implementation at the federal, state, and local levels.

Personnel and Funding

NCLIS includes the Librarian of Congress, the director of the Institute of Museum and Library Services (IMLS), and 14 commissioners appointed by the president and confirmed by the Senate for terms not to exceed five years. The law requires that five of the appointees be librarians or information specialists. At least one commissioner must be "knowledgeable with respect to the technological aspects of library and information science and sciences," and one must be "knowledgeable with respect to the library and information science needs of the elderly."

In January 2004 President Bush appointed and the Senate confirmed 12 new commissioners, bringing the commission to full strength. In July 2005 the IMLS director, Robert Martin, stepped down and Mary Chute succeeded him as IMLS acting director and took his place as an ex-officio NCLIS member. In August 2005 the president nominated one commissioner, Sandra Ashworth, whose term had expired, to a second term, and nominated two new commissioners, Jan Cellucci of Massachusetts and Diane Rivers of Alabama, to succeed Joan Challinor and Jack Hightower, whose terms had also expired. The three August nominations were confirmed by the Senate in October and the three new commissioners were sworn in by Chief of Staff Andrew H. Card, Jr. at the White House in December. Thus the commission has been maintained at full strength. Beth Fitzsimmons continues as its chairman.

Commission staff includes the executive director, director of operations, director of statistics and surveys, a management analyst (operations), and a special assistant for technology. Robert Molyneux left the position of director of statistics and surveys in March 2005 and Neal Kaske succeeded him in August. In order to provide additional specialized services, consultants and temporary support staff were engaged. Also, since September, a graduate student intern from the College of Information Studies at the University of Maryland has been working part-time to assist the executive director in supporting the commission's initiatives.

The current financial situation is extremely tight, with insufficient funds to operate fully an independent federal agency. The size of the NCLIS appropriation has not been increased since fiscal year 2001. Even with intense efforts to reduce expenditures, including moving the agency to smaller quarters, rising costs have seriously eroded the appropriation. It has become a challenge to adhere to rules, regulations, reporting procedures, compliance documentation, records management and archiving requirements, and the e-government mandates required of all federal agencies.

2005 Activities

Despite the severe budget constraints, the commission accomplished several important goals during 2005. Using the resources available—which included, in addition to the appropriation, contributions to the gift account, a UNESCO grant made possible by the U.S. Department of State, and offsetting collections from the NCES interagency agreement, as well as the commissioners' volunteer efforts and partnerships with other agencies and organizations—the commission pursued initiatives in the following areas:

Library Services for the Aging

This initiative, a specific statutory responsibility for NCLIS, seeks to identify opportunities to improve library services for the elderly. At the same time, the initiative supports economic development by identifying how libraries might use the skills and experience of older workers as employees.

In February 2005 Commissioner Ashworth wrote an NCLIS position paper for the White House Conference on Aging (WHCoA), which was held in December 2005. Her paper was published on the Web sites of both NCLIS and the American Library Association (ALA). Ashworth and the NCLIS executive director participated in a pre-White House Conference event held at the ALA Annual Conference in June, and Ashworth was a delegate from Idaho to the WHCoA.

International Library and Information Science Issues

During 2005, in an initiative led by Commissioner Challinor, NCLIS continued to examine the role of libraries in sub-Saharan Africa in the battle against HIV/AIDS. With the support of a grant from UNESCO, NCLIS sent a consultant in fall 2004 to Cameroon to study the feasibility of establishing "living libraries" in vans—something like bookmobiles, but staffed by storytellers and actors as well as librarians—to travel the country and visit villages on market days. Another consultant, an expert in information dissemination in developing countries, was tasked with writing a background paper, setting the broader context for the Cameroonian study and making recommendations for implementing similar programs in developing countries struggling with the HIV/AIDS epidemic. The study concluded that libraries in Africa will play a stronger role when they establish partnerships with other organizations already involved in dissemination and education activities. It also recommended that libraries in Africa should expand the scope of the information sources they collect and distribute to include information sources outside the role of traditional libraries.

NCLIS published the final report of this work—*The Role of Libraries in HIV/AIDS Information Dissemination in Sub-Saharan Africa*—in November 2005. It is available as a pdf document on the NCLIS Web site, at http://www.nclis.gov/LibrariesandHIVinfo.pdf, and paper copies are available through the NCLIS office.

Also in the international arena, the executive director and Commissioner Challinor in August attended the World Library and Information Conference held by the International Federation of Library Associations and Institutions (IFLA) in Oslo. In November Challinor represented the commission as a member of the U.S. delegation to the World Summit on the Information Society in Tunis. Her report is on the NCLIS Web site at http://www.nclis.gov/libinter/WSISTUNIS REPORT.pdf

The Role of Libraries in Health Information Literacy

Since 2004 NCLIS has worked toward the goal of encouraging libraries across the country to support Americans' health information needs. The commission believes that the successful implementation of this initiative will result in a healthier population, including a healthier work force. It has been established that if people made even small improvements in their lifestyles, there would be less illness, fewer lost workdays, and the nation's economy would be strengthened simply because the huge percentage of the economy now spent on health care would be significantly reduced.

An NCLIS task force led by Commissioner Mary ("Mitzi") Perdue created Consumer Health Information Recognition Awards for Libraries to recognize libraries that excel in meeting the consumer health needs of American citizens. With the cooperation of the members of COSLA (Chief Officers of State Library Agencies), NCLIS presented awards to 37 libraries in 2004.

In May 2005 the commission hosted a reception at the National Agricultural Library for about 250 people. As with the health recognition awards, the reception was underwritten by donations to the gift account. The purpose of the gala was to celebrate model programs in health information provided by libraries around the nation. Exhibits from 12 agencies or organizations added to the value of the event.

The overall goal of the effort in 2004—and continuing into 2005, 2006, and beyond—is to identify best practices and model programs and to share them with the larger library-management community. In June 2005 a document with detailed descriptions of the 2004 award winners was distributed to the president and Congress and to the library and information science community. This best practices report was also published on the NCLIS Web site for library managers who want to develop or enhance their own libraries' health information programs (see http://www.nclis.gov/info/ModelProgramsReport04-19-05.pdf).

A second round of awards is planned for 2006 that will again recognize outstanding library programs in each state, but will also select nine semifinalists ($1,000 each) and one grand-prize-winning library that will receive $20,000. An all-day forum and awards reception were scheduled for May 2006 at the National Library of Medicine. Forum speakers were to represent the ten top programs and describe the ways in which they were succeeding in bringing health information to their communities, especially to at-risk or underserved populations.

As a consequence of the national scope of this activity, the commission will be able to collect a set of best practices in health communication provided by libraries throughout the nation (e.g., in both rural and urban areas, areas with large elderly populations, communities with many non-English speakers), and to establish a body of knowledge that can be shared with library managers who want to develop or enhance their own libraries' health communication programs. It was anticipated that after the forum in May 2006 NCLIS would publish this body of knowledge and disseminate it widely through presentations at professional meetings, community groups, citizens advocacy groups, and through the NCLIS Web site.

Libraries and Educational Achievement

NCLIS's libraries and educational achievement initiative seeks to identify how school libraries affect classroom learning and to disseminate this information to community organizations, school administrators, local politicians with funding authority, the media, the larger educational community, and all others who have an interest in the topic.

In spring 2005 Commissioner Fitzsimmons sent a letter to First Lady Laura Bush, proposing a mechanism to extend the first lady's efforts to increase public awareness about school libraries' role in educational achievement. Fitzsimmons proposed a school librarian award that would highlight the contributions of school librarians everywhere.

The next step was to approach a major publisher of children's books and supplier of library materials to underwrite the award. Again, the response was positive, and negotiations are under way to set a budget and a plan for implementing the award.

Another aspect of this initiative was executed with a letter from the NCLIS chairman to Secretary of Education Margaret Spellings. In the letter, Fitzsimmons recommended changes to the next version of the No Child Left Behind (NCLB) Act. Secretary Spellings directed her staff to meet with the NCLIS chairman and executive director in mid-summer to discuss and refine the changes. As a result, the commission will continue to work with U.S. Department of Education staff, especially those involved in the Improving Literacy Through School Libraries section of the NCLB Act.

To support both of these initiatives, Commissioner Allison Druin created a flyer titled "Why Care About School Libraries?" The flyer was developed in recognition of the problem that school libraries are not fully appreciated for the value they bring to the educational process. In a succinct format, the flyer conveys the messages that school libraries

- Are critical for student achievement
- Have an important role in teaching
- Are leading the way for technology use in schools
- Inspire literacy

The flyer will be used to convey the findings of existing research to individuals in leadership positions with respect to school libraries. It is available on the NCLIS Web site at http://www.nclis.gov/info/schoollibraryactivities.html.

Libraries and Emergency Preparedness

Another NCLIS initiative involves the role of libraries in emergency preparedness, particularly their role as information distribution centers to help communities prepare for a terrorist attack, respond quickly during an attack, and recover after an attack. In spring 2005 NCLIS partnered with the Government Printing Office and lent staff support to the Special Libraries Association (SLA) for the preparation of a proposal titled "Planning for Critical Emergencies: Training Librarians to Train Citizens for National Preparedness." SLA submitted the proposal for a Department of Homeland Security training grant, but unfortunately the proposal was not funded. However, NCLIS will continue to pursue this initiative to encourage libraries to play significant roles in their local communities' preparation for and response to natural disasters and terrorist attacks.

Assessment and Appraisal

Commissioner José Aponte called for an initiative that seeks to identify new measures to assess the value of libraries to the communities they serve. NCLIS staff organized a group of researchers and leaders in library assessment to study the issue and is planning to publish a summary description of the various innovative assessment measures currently in use or being developed.

Also in the area of statistics and surveys, a study funded in part by the Library Statistics Program was completed and published by SOLINET and the HBCU Library Alliance. The report, "The State of Libraries at Historically Black Colleges and Universities," provides a statistical assessment of the libraries at HCBUs using data collected by the NCES Academic Libraries Survey.

NCLIS as a Federal Agency

As an agency of the federal government, NCLIS must match the President's Management Agenda Initiatives, including investment in such government-wide initiatives as the strategic management of human capital, competitive sourcing, improved financial performance, expanded electronic government, and budget and performance integration. Because of budget limitations, it was a challenge for NCLIS to accomplish most of them, and staff turnover exacerbated the problem. In two areas, however, major effort was made and goals were met in 2005.

Management review. A team of commissioners and the executive director, with support and documentation from the NCLIS director of operations, conducted a thorough review of human resources and budget in spring 2005. The team examined job descriptions, functional areas of responsibility, flow charts of key agency functions, analyses of tasks and approximate time spent by staff, federal management laws, funding availability, federal agency accounting, NCLIS financial accounting and spreadsheets that track details of income and expenses during a fiscal year, the General Agreement for Management Support Services between the Department of Education and NCLIS, and other materials. The team concluded that it is unlikely that there are untapped resources from the appropriation that might support additional commission initiatives. This means, unfortunately, that the commission cannot generate additional resources from refining or reorganizing the administration and management of the agency.

Web site redesign. With contributions of design suggestions and technical expertise from graduate students at the University of Maryland and staff of ProQuest Company, preliminary redesign of the NCLIS Web site was begun in spring 2005 and the new site was unveiled on November 1.

Plans for 2006

In addition to pursuing the initiatives outlined, the commission will examine the roles of libraries in providing access to digitized information. With the University of Michigan, NCLIS cosponsored a national symposium March 2006 in Ann Arbor titled "Scholarship and Libraries in Transition: A Dialogue About the Social and Economic Impacts of Mass Digitization Projects." Its goal was to investigate the impact of mass digitization on libraries, universities, government, information policy, publishing, and education.

The symposium provided a forum to stimulate thinking about the changing information environment and to identify the challenges and opportunities shaping future directions for libraries and scholarly communication at both the national and local level. Six panels, each featuring nationally recognized individuals in their area of expertise, discussed the impact of mass digitization on the economy, learning and teaching, libraries, public policy, publishing, and research.

Funding for this initiative was provided mainly by the University of Michigan and outside sponsors. NCLIS was to prepare and publish a report on the key issues discussed and conclusions reached.

Conclusion

This overview of its work makes clear the broad scope of the NCLIS mission. No other government agency, professional association, trade association, research and development organization, academic institution, or philanthropic organization has the statutory responsibility that is the commission's reason for being—to provide policy advice to the president and Congress with respect to libraries and information science. Of course, other organizations are involved in these matters, and these organizations are invited and encouraged to partner and collaborate with the commission in developing the knowledge that informs NCLIS's recommendations to the president and Congress. All such organizations are solicited to join with NCLIS in sharing this knowledge in the larger society, since such knowledge development and knowledge sharing is for the common good.

Defense Technical Information Center

8725 John J. Kingman Rd., No. 0944, Fort Belvoir, VA 22060
703-767-8217, fax 703-767-8032
World Wide Web http://www.dtic.mil

Sandy Schwalb
Public Affairs Officer

The Defense Technical Information Center (DTIC) has served the information needs of the defense community for more than 60 years. DTIC is the central facility for the collection, storage, retrieval, and dissemination of scientific and technical information for the Department of Defense (DOD). DTIC is a field activity, one of several organizations whose work reaches across all segments of DOD. The center

- Provides controlled access to DOD information
- Is a vital link in the transfer of information among the defense-related government and civilian research and development communities
- Is a primary provider of Web services for organizations within DOD

DTIC is located in the Andrew T. McNamara Headquarters Complex Building at Fort Belvoir, Virginia, and has four regional offices, whose addresses appear at the end of this article.

Leadership Changes

In November 2005 R. Paul Ryan was appointed DTIC's administrator, after serving as acting administrator since November 2004. Ryan has been with DTIC for more than 20 years, holding a number of positions including deputy administrator responsible for daily operations, budget, and personnel. Active in the scientific and technical community at the local, national, and international levels, Ryan is a former president and member of the board of trustees of the National Federation of Abstracting and Information Services (NFAIS). He was chair and deputy chair of the NATO Advisory Group for Aerospace Research and Development (AGARD) Technical Information Panel.

Acting Deputy Administrator K. Pete Suthard was named deputy administrator. Suthard also serves as the center's chief information officer and, as such, oversees information resource management at DTIC.

Carlynn Thompson, director of DTIC's Directorate of Component Information Support, is the center's first chief technology officer (CTO). As CTO, she has a broad overview of DTIC's technology posture and is responsible for managing information support systems, services, and products and for determining the organization's future needs.

Innovation Award

DTIC received the 2005 Innovations in Technology Award from the Special Libraries Association (SLA) for "innovative use and application of technology in a special library setting." Ryan accepted the award during the SLA Annual Conference held in Toronto June 5–8.

SLA's District of Columbia Chapter nominated DTIC for the award because of ". . . sustained contribution to the application of technology to more efficiently serve the needs of their clients, the U.S. Defense community. This contribution is especially worthy of recognition in this critical time for our armed forces as they face the challenges of combat in Iraq." The nomination continued: "Through the application of technology and a commitment to knowledge management, DTIC has insured that the billions of dollars of taxpayers' money invested in research for the Department of Defense are invested wisely and that use of the results can be maximized."

In endorsing the award, SLA's Military Librarians Division commented: "Although DTIC's primary mission has always been to support the research and engineering information needs of the Department of Defense, its contractor and academic partners, and other federal agencies as they relate to defense issues, the organization has made numerous contributions to the special library community."

Research and Engineering Portal

The Research and Engineering (R&E) Portal was launched by DTIC and the Director, Defense Research and Engineering (DDR&E) in April 2005. A working research tool, the portal provides one-stop access to current and historical research and engineering information, including DTIC technical data resources. The portal supports the entire DOD research and development, test, and evaluation community, from the Pentagon to various laboratory activities. It offers a greatly expanded search capability, with customized views of results.

The first of four phases of the portal was accomplished in January 2005 when a gateway to a number of DOD-related databases was built. In April 2005, when the portal was officially rolled out, phase two was completed by adding search tools and a news engine, which is a personalized business page offering relevant news on technologies of interest each day.

Phase three, completed at the end of November 2005, saw the addition of DTIC's own databases, among them technical reports and research summaries. A retrieval engine, Defense Technology Search, was developed and provides the ability to search across several databases simultaneously. In phase four, which will take place in 2006, the goal is to provide the capability for a single sign-on—one user name and password—for all of the resources in the portal.

Access to the portal is controlled by the DTIC registration process and is currently limited to DOD employees and DOD contractors. For more registration information, see https://register.dtic.mil/DTIC. The portal is at https://rdte.osd.mil.

New DTIC Home Page

In order to enhance access to defense information, DTIC created a new home page (http://www.dtic.mil) that links directly to a search engine. The primary goal of the redesign is to focus on DTIC's key mission, which is to deliver defense information. The page provides a new look and feel, similar to the Google interface, and is more in line with what people are accustomed to seeing on other search engines. There are links to other Internet resources, such as Google, first.gov, and science.gov, and the home page offers the ability to search different, large government databases simultaneously. The site features three new search options:

- DTIC Science and Technology—publicly available information from the DTIC Technical Reports collection with an advanced search capability
- DOD-Wide Science and Technology—science- and technology-related sites throughout DOD with the ability to narrow the search to specific organizations
- All DOD Web sites—publicly available defense information throughout the department or by agencies, commands, military services, or other DOD organizations

Several links to the general DTIC Web site (http://www.dtic.mil/dtic/index. html) are available on the search page.

Open Archives Initiative

DTIC launched the Open Archives Initiative (OAI) in 2005 to provide broader access to information in DTIC's collection. OAI is an international effort focused on furthering the interoperability of digital libraries. Its objective is to make it easier to find content stored, but not always readily accessible, on the Internet. Currently, much authoritative information resides on the "deep Web," composed of content-rich databases maintained by universities, libraries, associations, businesses, and government agencies, including DTIC. In most cases, this information cannot be found using commercial search engines such as Google, Yahoo!, and AltaVista.

Security of Information

While there is much publicly accessible material in the DTIC collection (almost one half of DOD's technical reports are publicly available the day they are published), some information is restricted by security classifications. DOD's scientific and technical information is always categorized (or "marked," which is the term used in the defense community) by the office that originates the document. This marking determines how, and to whom, the information can be disseminated.

Some information is marked to protect national security. DTIC's databases contain classified information marked "confidential" and "secret." DTIC's databases also contain information that, although not classified, is still sensitive for various reasons. These documents are marked to show why the information is sensitive and to whom the document can be made available. Such documents are considered "unclassified, limited." Information in DTIC's databases that is neither classified nor limited can be released to the public and is referred to as "unclassified, unlimited."

The information in DTIC's collection is 41 percent "unclassified, unlimited," 51 percent "unclassified, limited," and 8 percent "classified."

Resources

DTIC's holdings include technical reports on completed research; research summaries of planned, ongoing, and completed work; independent research and development summaries; defense technology transfer agreements; DOD planning documents; DOD directives and instructions; conference proceedings; security classification guides; command histories; and special collections that date back to World War II. DOD-funded researchers are required to search DTIC's collections to ensure that they do not "reinvent the wheel" and undertake unnecessary or redundant research.

The scope of DTIC's collection includes areas normally associated with defense research. DOD's interests are widespread, however, and include such areas as agriculture; atmospheric sciences; behavioral and social sciences; human factors engineering; information warfare (safeguarding the survivability, authenticity, and continuity of DOD information systems); mathematic and computer sciences; nuclear science and technology; propulsion, engines, and fuels; radiation studies; and virtual reality.

Registering for Services

DTIC offers its information services to a diverse population of the defense community. Due to the nature of the information DTIC handles, users must qualify for services. To be eligible, a user must be

- An employee of a DOD organization, DOD contractor, or potential DOD contractor
- An employee of a federal government agency or federal government contractor
- Affiliated with a university or college funded by DOD or a federal government agency for research throughout the United States
- A Small Business Innovation Research/Small Business Technology Transfer (SBIR/STTR) Program participant
- A faculty or staff member or student of a Historically Black College and University (HBCU), Hispanic Serving Institution (HSI), Tribal College and University (TCU), or other Minority Institution (MI)

Everyone can search DTIC's publicly accessible collections and display or download such information. Descriptions of the various DTIC databases are below; unless otherwise noted, the databases are available to the public. Registered users can order documents directly from DTIC. Those who are not eligible to register with DTIC can order "unclassified, unlimited" documents by contacting the National Technical Information Service (NTIS) at 800-553-NTIS (6847) or by visiting http://www.ntis.gov.

DTIC's Primary Collections

The Technical Reports database contains more than 2 million reports in print, nonprint (CDs, DVDs, software, data files, databases, and video recordings), and electronic formats conveying the results of defense-sponsored research, development, test, and evaluation efforts. It includes journal articles, DOD-sponsored patent applications, studies, analyses, open source literature from foreign countries, conference proceedings, and theses. Between 25,000 and 30,000 new documents are added annually.

The Research Summaries database contains descriptions of DOD research that provide information on technical content, responsible individuals and organizations, principal investigators, and funding sources at the work-unit level. Available only to certain registered users, this collection is controlled by individual access restrictions. The collection consists of approximately 303,000 active and inactive summaries from 1965 to the present.

The Independent Research and Development database contains more than 171,000 descriptions (dating back to the mid-1970s) of research and development projects initiated and conducted by defense contractors independent of DOD control and without direct DOD funding. More than $3 billion worth of independent research and development projects are submitted to DTIC each year. The database includes basic and applied research, technology development efforts, and systems and concept formulation studies. Defense contractors and potential contractors are encouraged to submit project descriptions to the database. Accessible only by U.S. government organizations, the information is used to identify contractors with expertise in areas of interest to DOD and to avoid DOD duplication of industry research and development efforts.

STINET Services

DTIC's Scientific and Technical Information Network (STINET) is one of DOD's largest repositories of scientific and technical information currently available. There are three versions of the database: Public STINET, Private STINET, and Classified STINET.

Public STINET, available to the general public free of charge, provides access to citations of "unclassified, unlimited" reports that describe the progress or results of research efforts and other scientific and technical information held by DTIC. Many of these documents are available in full text and can be downloaded.

Private STINET is a password-protected, value-added service for individuals who have registered with DTIC. Other information available through Private STINET includes

- Free online limited distribution documents as well as all "unclassified, unlimited" documents in DTIC's Technical Reports database
- The Research Summaries database
- Free access to two international database services—Canada Institute for Scientific and Technical Information's CISTI Source and the British Library Document Supply Centre's "Inside Web"
- Information from the Interagency Gray Literature Working Group
- ProQuest Research Library Complete, an index to journal articles

STINET MultiSearch is available in both Public and Private STINET. A portal to the "deep Web" for government scientific and technical information, it searches content below the "surface" Web for information not accessible through commercial and government search engines.

Classified STINET is located on the Secret Internet Protocol Router Network (SIPRNET). This database contains the complete DTIC collection, including "unclassified, limited" reports and classified citations. In order to use this service, a user must be able to access the SIPRNET and must register with DTIC. Some of the information to be found in Classified STINET includes the DOD Index of Specifications and Standards (DODISS) database, the Militarily Critical Technologies List, and the DOD Index of Security Classification Guides.

New Searching Capability

DTIC launched its Scheduled Search Service in 2005. This new product is free and available to registered users of DTIC's Private STINET. Scheduled searches provide users with the latest information in their subject area of interest. Users determine if they want to save and schedule searches that are particularly useful. DTIC's Technical Reports, Research Summaries, and Independent Research and Development databases can be searched (although access to the Independent Research and Development database is restricted).

Users formulate their own search strategies, save the search, and determine its frequency. These searches can be scheduled to run automatically on a biweekly, monthly, or quarterly schedule. Users receive e-mail alert messages each time a search is executed. Bibliographies are offered in ASCII, HTML, pdf, and XML. The new system also offers the ability to order microfiche.

Training Opportunities

Free training is available to registered users at DTIC's Fort Belvoir, Virginia, headquarters and four regional offices, the addresses of which appear below. Training can be arranged off-site if the instructor's travel costs are borne by the host organization/user. Customized courses can also be provided.

A three-day, hands-on class, "Searching DTIC Databases using Private STINET," covers methods of searching and retrieving scientific, research, and engineering information. The course also provides tools on searching the various databases found within Private STINET.

DTIC offers a three-day course designed to acquaint scientific and technical information (STINFO) managers and other interested personnel with the requirements of the DOD Scientific and Technical Information Program. Marking documents and contract reporting requirements are covered. A one-day STINFO manager overview covers the highlights of the standard three-day class.

A class that examines the rationale and mechanics of marking technical documents is available by arrangement with the instructor.

Additional training information is available at http://www.dtic.mil/dtic/training.

Other DTIC Activities and Programs

Web Hosting Expertise

DTIC, an early pioneer in Internet use for information dissemination, has designed and hosted more than 100 Web sites sponsored by components of the Office of the Secretary of Defense, military service headquarters organizations, and several defense agencies.

In 2005 DTIC partnered with a number of organizations, both within and outside the U.S. government, to create the Iraqi Virtual Science Library (http://www.ivsl.org). The plan for the virtual library is to ensure that Iraqi scientists and engineers have access to information to help rebuild Iraq's infrastructure. A great many scientific information sources were lost before and during the Iraq war. This virtual science library site is being produced under the auspices of the Defense Threat Reduction Agency, the Department of State, the National Academy of Sciences, DDR&E, and DTIC. A number of journal publishers have been asked to provide access to scientific literature.

Information Analysis Centers

DTIC manages and funds contractor-operated joint service-oriented Information Analysis Centers (IACs), which are research organizations. Chartered by DOD, IACs identify, analyze, and use scientific and technical information in specific technology areas. They also develop information and analysis products for the defense science and engineering communities and are staffed by experienced technical area scientists, engineers, and information specialists. The DTIC-managed IACs are AMMTIAC (Advanced Materials, Manufacturing and Testing IAC), CBIAC (Chemical and Biological Defense IAC), CPIAC (Chemical Propulsion IAC), DACS (Data and Analysis Center for Software), IATAC (Information Assurance Technology Analysis Center), SENSIAC (Sensors IAC), RIAC (Reliability IAC), SURVIAC (Survivability IAC), and WSTIAC (Weapons Systems IAC). See http://iac.dtic.mil for more information.

Many of the products and services produced by the IACs are free and include announcements of reports relevant to the particular IAC's field of interest, authoritative bibliographic search reports, the latest scientific and engineering information on specific technical subjects, consultation with or referral to world-recognized technical experts, and status of current technologies.

The Total Electronic Migration System (TEMS), a gateway to the IAC collection, is available online at http://iac.dtic.mil/resources_tems.html. TEMS provides DTIC registered users the ability to perform full-text searches and retrieve mission-critical information.

QuestionPoint

DTIC is a participating member of QuestionPoint, a virtual reference service developed jointly by the Library of Congress and the Online Computer Library Center (OCLC) and supported by cooperating institutions worldwide. This collaborative digital reference service is available at all hours seven days a week and allows libraries and information centers to expand reference services with shared resources and subject specialists around the world. DTIC is part of two QuestionPoint cooperatives: Global Reference Network, a worldwide group of libraries and institutions committed to digital reference, and Defense Digital Library Research Service (DDLRS), an around-the-clock electronic reference assistance for DOD libraries. Questions submitted by patrons via this Web-based digital reference service may be referred to the Global Network or to the cooperatives of DOD or Department of Homeland Security libraries.

2005 Users Conference

"Defense Research and Engineering: Turning Data into Knowledge" was the theme of the 31st annual DTIC Conference in Alexandria, Virginia, April 4–6, 2005. Nearly 300 customers, exhibitors, and DTIC personnel took part. Government and commercial exhibitors demonstrated their latest information services and technologies, and more than 25 conference topics were offered, including "Information and Security after 9/11," "DOD Biometrics," "Creating a Homeland Security Digital Library," "Security Through Knowledge Management," and "Tech Transfer and Commercialization." DTIC customers include scientists, engineers, and professionals in technology research and development, information science, and acquisition from DOD, federal, and contractor communities.

"Defense Research and Engineering: Information for the Warfighter" is the theme of the 2006 conference, scheduled for April 3–5, again in Alexandria.

Customer Surveys

DTIC has surveyed its registered customers since fiscal year 1999 in order to gauge the level of satisfaction among general users and to identify possible areas for improving products and services. Web-based and e-mail surveys are the primary collection methods used. Two surveys are conducted yearly: the Customer Satisfaction (CS) Survey, a complete sampling of all DTIC registered users, and the Top 200 Users Survey, which involves roughly 200 major users of DTIC's products and services.

Based upon the survey findings, the majority of the 2005 survey respondents were satisfied with DTIC services as a whole. DTIC continues to exceed the federal government's American Customer Satisfaction Index (ACSI) baseline/benchmark score. The ACSI survey, conducted in December 2004, showed a customer satisfaction rating of 72 percent. DTIC's rating in the 2005 survey was 76 percent.

Outreach

DTIC customers can host, at their location, a briefing or demonstration of DTIC's products and services tailored to the customer's schedule and information needs. For more information, e-mail bcporder@dtic.mil.

Tours and briefings are available at DTIC's headquarters. Visitors do not need a security clearance to attend, although special arrangements are needed for foreign nationals and employees of foreign governments. For more information, see http://www.dtic.mil/dtic/events/tours_brief.html.

Handle Service

Ensuring the permanent availability of information in the DTIC collection is a high priority. DTIC's Handle Service preserves access to electronic resources on the Web, guaranteeing their availability over time and changing formats. A handle is a permanent identifier, or permanent name, for a digital object regardless of where and how it is stored. It provides long-term access to a digital resource and allows for the reliable management of information on the Internet over long periods of time. Handles have been added to the public information on DTIC's Public and Private STINET services. These handles link directly to full-text pdf documents. Handles will be extended to limited documents, which DTIC registered users can access through Private STINET. Benefits offered by handles include the facts that they do not change, unlike Uniform Resource Locators (URLs); that information will remain available over long periods of time; and that they help in the creation of accurate, "live" links within bibliographies and other research papers.

Publications

DTIC Digest, a Web-based quarterly newsletter, provides information about programs, initiatives, activities, issues, and developments in the technical information arena. This publication is on DTIC's Web site at http://www.dtic.mil/dtic/prodsrvc/review/index.html.

DTIC Review provides the full text of selected technical reports and a bibliography of other references of interest. Each volume provides a sampling of documents from the DTIC collection on a specific topic of current interest. The fall 2005 (Vol. 7 No. 2) issue of the review, for instance, was on "Strategies Against Terrorism."

Cooperation and Collaboration

DTIC works with the information community through many partnerships and affiliations. These include

- Science.gov, a collaboration of scientific and technical organizations in the federal government that is a free gateway to more than 1,700 government information resources about science including technical reports, journal citations, databases, federal Web sites, and fact sheets
- CENDI, an interagency working group of senior scientific and technical information managers from a number of U.S. government departments and agencies, including the departments of Commerce, Energy, Defense, and Interior, the National Aeronautics and Space Administration, and the Government Printing Office
- NFAIS, the National Federation of Abstracting and Information Services
- FLICC, the Federal Library and Information Center Committee
- ASIDIC, Association of Information and Dissemination Centers
- SLA, the Special Libraries Association
- NISO, the National Information Standards Organization

DTIC Regional Offices

Midwestern Regional Office
Wright-Patterson Air Force Base, Ohio
Tel. 937-255-7905, fax 937-986-7002
E-mail dayton@dtic.mil

Northeastern Regional Office
Hanscom Air Force Base
Bedford, Massachusetts
Tel. 781-377-2413, fax 781-377-5627
E-mail boston@dtic.mil

Southwestern Regional Office
Kirtland Air Force Base, New Mexico
Tel. 505-846-6797, fax 505-846-6799
E-mail albuq@dtic.mil

Western Regional Office
El Segundo, California
Tel. 310-363-6642, fax 310-363-6705
E-mail losangel@dtic.mil

Note: DTIC and STINET are registered service marks of the Defense Technical Information Center.

National Library of Education

National Center for Education Evaluation and Regional Assistance
Institute of Education Sciences, U.S. Department of Education
400 Maryland Ave. S.W., Washington, DC 20202
800-424-1616, 202-205-4945, fax 202-401-0547
World Wide Web www.ed.gov/about/offices/list/ies/ncee/nle.html

Christina Dunn
Director, National Library of Education
202-219-1012, e-mail christina.dunn@ed.gov

The year 2005 marked the 11th year of operation for the National Library of Education (NLE). The program is charged with four related responsibilities under the authorizing legislation (Title I of Public Law 107-279, Education Sciences Reform Act of 2002):

- Collecting and archiving information, including products and publications developed through, or supported by, the Institute of Education Sciences; and other relevant and useful education-related research, statistics, and evaluation materials and other information, projects, and publications that are consistent with scientifically valid research or the priorities and mission of the institute, and developed by the department, other federal agencies, or entities
- Providing a central location within the federal government for information about education
- Providing comprehensive reference services on matters relating to education to employees of the Department of Education and its contractors and grantees, other federal employees, and members of the public
- Promoting greater cooperation and resource sharing among providers and repositories of education information in the United States

NLE is part of the National Center for Education Evaluation and Regional Assistance in the Institute of Education Sciences. The center is headed by a commissioner who, among other responsibilities, is charged with managing NLE. In turn, NLE—headed by a director qualified in library science and five federal staff, including the ERIC director—operates the Education Resources Information Center (ERIC) and the U.S. Department of Education (ED) Reference Center. This article covers the ED Reference Center; the ERIC program is covered separately in the following article.

ED Reference Center

The ED Reference Center, with a staff of 11 (four federal staff and seven contract librarians), is housed in ED's headquarters building. Two satellites serving the Office of Vocational and Adult Education and the Institute of Education Sciences are housed in other facilities. The reference center's primary purpose is to serve the information needs of agency staff and contractors. Technical and public services staff are combined in one unit, allowing the organization to be as nimble as possible in responding to user needs.

Use

While its primary customers include department staff and contractors, the reference center also serves the general public, agency grantees, other federal agencies, and other libraries. About 73 percent of all reference center customer requests come from the general public (down 2.3 percent from the previous year), with a little less than 10 percent of these being referrals generated by the ERIC Help Desk or Library of Congress Virtual Reference Desk. The remaining 27 percent of requests come from ED staff, contractors, and grantees (23 percent or a 2 percent increase over the previous year); other libraries (2.5 percent); and other government agencies (1.5 percent). About 64 percent of the general public contacting the reference center in 2005 were K–12 educators, students in institutions of higher education, or researchers; 34 percent were parents—leaving 2 percent unknown. The majority of customers continue to access the reference center by telephone (56 percent) or e-mail (38 percent); only about 6 percent actually visit the reference center or its satellites. The decrease in actual visits is probably due to an increase in the quality and number of the reference center's desktop services.

Collections

The reference center's collection concentrates on education issues, with an emphasis on research and policy. It includes monographs in the field of education published since 1965, as well as related topics such as law, public policy, economics, urban affairs, sociology, history, philosophy, psychology, and library and information science. Periodicals holdings number more than 850 English-language print and electronic journals, including most of the journals indexed by ERIC and other major education and psychology databases. More than one half of all current subscriptions provide journals in electronic format, which is the preferred medium because of limited storage capacity.

The reference center specializes in collecting documents associated with its parent agency, having a complete collection of ERIC microfiche; research reports supporting the work of the What Works Clearinghouse, a project of the Institute of Education Sciences (http://www.whatworks.ed.gov); and current publications of the agency. In addition, it holds historical collections of Department of Education publications and documents spanning more than 100 years, including a special collection of federal education legislation. Other historical collections include documents and archives of the former National Institute of Education and the former U.S. Office of Education, including reports, studies, manuals, statistical publications, speeches, and policy papers. Together, these collections represent a resource covering the history of the U.S. Department of Education and its predecessor agencies. The reference center also serves as a federal depository library under the Government Printing Office program.

Services

While the reference center provides general and legislative reference and statistical information services in response to inquiries from those outside the agency, it provides more in-depth research and document delivery to ED staff and contractors. In 2005 there was an increase in service to this group, but a slight decrease in service to all others. The reference center responded to more than 11,600 inquiries, with most questions coming from the general public and pertaining to U.S. Department of Education programs and statistics, as well as to such current education-related issues as education reform initiatives, student assessment, school and teacher quality, and early literacy. In addition, the reference center serves other libraries by lending books and other materials from its collection. During the past year it made available almost 2,000 items, mostly research reports, to institutions of higher education, federal and state agencies, and other libraries. This is an increase over the number of items loaned in any previous year and is probably due to a stronger collection of current education research reports, including those from other English-speaking countries. ED staff and contractors conducted about 15,000 searches of the library's databases, and the reference center delivered nearly 5,000 documents and journal articles to these customers. Of this number, about 12 percent were borrowed from other libraries.

During 2005 the reference center continued to focus on initiatives started in 2004—improving information services to ED staff and contractors and redesigning its portal available on the department's intranet. New initiatives included implementing an OpenURL link resolver and a federated search service, and adding a significant number of new journal titles and research reports to its collection. Reference center staff continue to work with the ERIC staff to identify agency and other resources for inclusion in the ERIC database.

The ED Reference Center can be reached by e-mail at library@ed.gov or by telephone at 800-424-1616 (toll free), 202-205-5015 or 202-205-5019 (reference desk), or TTY at 202-205-7561. It is open from 9:00 A.M. to 5:00 P.M. weekdays, except federal holidays.

Education Resources Information Center

National Library of Education
National Center for Education Evaluation and Regional Assistance
Institute of Education Sciences, U.S. Department of Education
400 Maryland Ave. S.W., Washington DC 20202
World Wide Web http://www.eric.ed.gov

Luna Levinson

Director, ERIC Program
202-208-2321, e-mail luna.levinson@ed.gov

The Education Resources Information Center (ERIC) provides public access to education research and information through an electronic database of more than 1 million bibliographic records from 1966 to the present as well as links to publishers' Web sites and full-text documents when feasible.

With a 40-year history of serving students, teachers, librarians, administrators, and the general public, ERIC is one of the oldest programs of the U.S. Department of Education. As the world's largest education resource, the ERIC database is distinguished by two hallmarks: free dissemination of bibliographic records and the collection of gray literature such as research conference papers and government contractor reports. This vast collection of education-related material was built by a decentralized network of 16 ERIC clearinghouses with specific collection scopes for database building, publications, and user services.

Changes in ERIC

Modernization of ERIC began in 2003, following the enactment of the Education Sciences Reform Act of 2002 (Sec. 172(a)3 of Public Law 107-279). In the past, legislation had required the continuation of the clearinghouse structure, procedures, and products, but the new legislation envisioned ERIC topics as part of the totality of enhanced dissemination to be conducted by the Institute of Education Sciences (IES). The Department of Education issued a new statement of work for ERIC in 2003 and awarded a single contract for its operation in March 2004.

In September 2004 ERIC launched a new Web site at http://www.eric.ed. gov, providing accessibility to all the database bibliographic records, and a month later added 107,000 full-text non-journal documents (issued 1993–2004) that previously had been sold through the ERIC Document Reproduction Service (EDRS). One of the most significant developments in increasing public access to ERIC resources is the elimination of fee subscriptions for libraries, organizations, and individuals. Improved download performance of the image files is another added convenience.

In 2005 more than 21,000 new records (comprising the majority of 2004–2005 backlog materials) were added to ERIC. The collection continues to be composed of journal and non-journal materials, and accession numbers continue the ED and EJ prefix model established by ERIC some years ago. Roughly 600 journals are currently indexed in ERIC, resulting from more than 450 agreements with publishers and organizations. In addition to the government-sponsored ERIC Web site, the ERIC database is also distributed by commercial database vendors including Cambridge Scientific Abstracts, Thomson Dialog, EBSCO, OCLC, Ovid, ProQuest, and SilverPlatter. ERIC provides monthly content updates to the vendors as well as quarterly updates to the Thesaurus of ERIC Descriptors. Additional access to ERIC records is provided by searching Google and Google Scholar. Usage statistics suggest that ERIC continues to serve a large audience: for the period August to December 2005, there were more than 32 million searches of the ERIC database.

ERIC Mission

The ERIC mission is to provide a comprehensive, easy-to-use, searchable Internet-based bibliographic and full-text database of education research and information for educators, researchers, and the general public. It is

- Comprehensive, consisting of journal articles and non-journal materials, including materials not published by commercial publishers, that are directly related to education
- Easy-to-use and searchable, allowing database users to find the information they need quickly and efficiently
- Electronic, making ERIC operations accessible to the maximum extent feasible and linking to publishers and commercial sources of journal articles
- Bibliographic and full-text, with bibliographic records conveying information in a simple and straightforward manner, and whenever possible including full-text journal articles and non-journal materials free of charge

Following this mission, the overarching goal of ERIC is to increase the availability and quality of research and information for ERIC users.

ERIC Functions

Activities that fulfill the ERIC mission are broadly categorized as collection development, content authorizations and agreements, acquisitions and processing, database and Web site operations, and communications. These five functions continue to evolve and improve as suggestions and guidance are received from a variety of sources, including public comments, online surveys of customer satisfaction, and the ERIC Steering Committee and Content Experts, who are recognized authorities tasked with advising the ERIC contractor on activities designed to ensure database quality.

Database collection development is the core function of ERIC. IES legislation requires the continued inclusion of ERIC topics: early childhood education through higher education, vocational education, and special education, including teaching and teacher education; education administration, assessment and evaluation, counseling, information and technology; the academic areas of reading, mathematics, science and environmental education, languages, and social studies; and materials on closing the achievement gap, educational practices that improve academic achievement, and education research. Curators—subject specialists in education—follow the ERIC selection policy to identify articles for selective database acquisitions and communicate with ERIC Content Experts about comprehensive or cover-to-cover indexing of journals.

Automated systems for acquisition and processing help to reduce the total time required to produce a database record, and most records are processed within 30 days. The ERIC bibliographic file is updated weekly on the ERIC Web site.

Recent Enhancements

All ERIC functions utilize electronic technologies to increase database efficiency. For example, individual authors (copyright holders) register through the ERIC Web site feature My ERIC; follow the steps to enter bibliographic information, abstract, and document files; and submit the electronic document-release form authorizing ERIC to disseminate the materials. Once publishers have signed an ERIC agreement, files can be submitted by e-mail or disk or by upload to ERIC's ftp site.

Recent enhancements to the ERIC Web site increase functionality and support non-duplicative resources. Searchers can mark records for placement in a temporary workspace called My Clipboard. This new feature permits users to print, e-mail, or export records, or save them in a My ERIC account. Another enhancement, in development and testing, is a link to My Library. This feature, based on Open URL technology, enables users to link to electronic resources available in their library. Ten universities are participating in the testing.

ERIC continues to refine the technical architecture to improve system functionality and user satisfaction. Eight rounds of usability tests have been conducted since 2004 with participant groups including librarians, researchers, and students at major association conferences such as the American Library Association and the American Education Research Association. In each database enhancement, the development process contributes to increasing accessibility, efficiency, and quality.

National Association and Organization Reports

American Library Association

50 E. Huron St., Chicago, IL 60611
312-944-6780, 800-545-2433
World Wide Web http://www.ala.org

Michael Gorman
President

Founded in 1876 in Philadelphia and subsequently chartered in the Commonwealth of Massachusetts, the American Library Association (ALA) is the oldest, largest, and most influential library association in the world. The association's membership of more than 66,000 includes not only librarians but also library trustees, publishers, and other interested people from every U.S. state and many nations. The association serves public, state, school, and academic libraries, as well as special libraries for people working in government, commerce and industry, the arts, and the armed services, or in hospitals, prisons, and other institutions.

ALA's mission is "to provide leadership for the development, promotion, and improvement of library and information services and the profession of librarianship in order to enhance learning and ensure access to information for all."

ALA is governed by an elected Council—its policy-making body—and an Executive Board, which acts for the council and administers policies and programs. These are proposed by standing committees, designated as committees of the association or of the council. ALA operations are directed by an executive director and implemented by staff through a structure of programmatic offices and support units.

ALA is home to 11 membership divisions, each focused on a type of library or library function. They are the American Association of School Librarians (AASL), the Association for Library Collections and Technical Services (ALCTS), the Association for Library Service to Children (ALSC), the Association for Library Trustees and Advocates (ALTA), the Association of College and Research Libraries (ACRL), the Association of Specialized and Cooperative Library Agencies (ASCLA), the Library Administration and Management Association (LAMA), the Library and Information Technology Association (LITA), the Public Library Association (PLA), the Reference and User Services Association (RUSA), and the Young Adult Library Services Association (YALSA). ALA also hosts 17 roundtables for members who share interests that do not fall within the scope of any of the divisions. A network of affiliates, chapters, and other organizations enables ALA to reach a broad audience.

Key action areas for ALA include diversity, education and continuous learning, equity of access, intellectual freedom, and 21st-century literacy.

ALA offices are units of the association that address broad interests and issues of concern to ALA members; they track issues and provide information, services, and products for members and the general public. Current ALA offices are the Chapter Relations Office, the Development Office, the Governance Office, the International Relations Office, the Office for Accreditation, the Office for Diversity, the Office for Government Relations, the Office for Human Resource Development and Recruitment, the Office for Information Technology Policy, the Office for Intellectual Freedom, the Office for Literacy and Outreach Services, the Office for Research and Statistics, the Public Information Office, the Public Programs Office, and the Washington (D.C.) Office.

ALA headquarters is in Chicago; the Office for Government Relations and the Office for Information Technology Policy are located in the Washington Office. ALA also has an editorial office in Middletown, Connecticut, for *Choice,* a review journal for academic libraries.

ALA is a 501(c)(3) charitable and educational organization.

Focus on Library Education

During his presidential year, 2005–2006 ALA President Michael Gorman focused on library education, recruitment, accreditation, and certification.

The route to revitalization of library education, Gorman said, is to provide "a relevant education to those who aspire to work in libraries and, thus, satisfy their desires as well as those of potential employers." ALA, he said, "must use existing tools and policies to redefine the field of library studies and regain control of professional education."

Gorman envisioned ALA moving from a descriptive accreditation process, in which library-education programs define what they are trying to achieve and ALA assesses them in terms of that self-definition, to a prescriptive process, in which ALA defines a core library curriculum and then assesses education programs on the basis of how well they teach and conduct research in the core elements of library studies.

This will help the profession face the challenges that lie before it, including how to produce "teachers who are committed to libraries and librarianship," ensure that the profession becomes more diverse and "looks like America," and raise the salaries of all library workers, he said.

Gorman, dean of library services at California State University–Fresno Madden Library, is the third British-born ALA president, following Andrew Keogh (1929–1930) and Eric Moon (1977–1978). He is a prolific contributor to the literature of library science.

Highlights of the Year

ALA and the USA Patriot Act

ALA remained actively involved in 2005 in the fight to amend sections of the USA Patriot Act that infringe on library patron privacy and civil liberties. The

Committee on Legislation and Washington Office staff worked with House and Senate lawmakers in an attempt to guarantee that reauthorization legislation would contain language strengthening reader privacy. The central issue was whether, or for how long, to extend Section 215, which eases restrictions on FBI access to library and business records.

The Campaign for Reader Privacy—which includes ALA, the American Booksellers Association, the Association of American Publishers, and PEN American Center—took an active part in the debate as the dispute grew over provisions of the act that were to expire at the end of the year. ALA 2004–2005 President Carol Brey-Casiano took the issue to the National Press Club on National Legislative Day, and President-Elect Gorman made ALA's position known in letters to the House and Senate judiciary committees and in media interviews.

A compromise on the reauthorization of the act was reached early in 2006 but did little to ameliorate the provisions of Section 215. "We're glad to see that there is still a four-year sunset provision for Section 215, which will allow oversight again in four years, but disappointed that the negotiators just did not go far enough," Gorman said.

Meanwhile, the preliminary results of an ALA survey measuring law enforcement visits to public and academic libraries were released. The study received a great deal of attention from the library community and the press, with coverage of the study appearing in many major news outlets, including an editorial in the *New York Times*. Despite law enforcement's insistence that it has "no interest" in library records, survey respondents reported 137 legally executed searches of public and academic libraries since October 2001. Most libraries do not volunteer information without an official request, the survey revealed, and libraries have made few official changes in policies since passage of the USA Patriot Act in 2001. Interviewees reported that they have made qualitative changes as a result of the act; some libraries keep fewer records and usage statistics.

Librarians Respond to Katrina

After Hurricane Katrina struck the Gulf Coast on Aug. 29, libraries and librarians nationwide played a key role in helping tens of thousands of people who were displaced by the storm.

Katrina took nearly 1,500 lives, made refugees of more than a million people, destroyed as many as 15 library branches in five Louisiana parishes, and severely damaged many others. Librarians throughout the region braved floodwaters to rescue collections, and the National Guard and other emergency responders often used libraries as rescue areas. Thousands of people who fled the hurricane before it hit or were evacuated afterward wound up far from home, and many of them headed for the local library to fill out disaster-assistance applications, look for missing family and friends, or send e-mails letting people know they were all right.

ALA responded by establishing the Hurricane Katrina Relief Fund, which funneled hundreds of thousands of dollars in donations to ALA chapters in the Gulf Coast region through the Louisiana, Mississippi, and Alabama library associations. Some 4,350 libraries signed up for ALA's Adopt-a-Library Program and were matched with public, school, and academic libraries in the Gulf Coast region.

And after six weeks of intense deliberation, ALA decided Oct. 12 to stick with its plans to hold its 2006 Annual Conference, scheduled for June 22–28, in New Orleans. "The best thing that the association and its members can do is to go to New Orleans and lead the reconstruction by example," said ALA President Gorman. "Our conference will provide the jobs and tax revenues needed to help residents reestablish their lives and for the city to fully restore services, including library services," he continued. "We speak often of how libraries build communities, and now we have a chance to show the country and the world that librarians build communities, too."

Internet Access at Public Libraries

Virtually all public libraries in the United States offer public access to the Internet, but many struggle to meet demand for access, according to a study titled "Public Libraries and the Internet 2004: Survey Results and Findings," funded by the ALA Office for Information Technology and Policy and the Bill and Melinda Gates Foundation. Eight-five percent of public libraries reported having insufficient hardware, and only 42 percent were able to offer truly robust high-speed connections, according to the study, which was released at the 2005 Annual Conference. Half of the nation's public libraries reported that their technology budgets stayed the same from 2003 to 2004, while 13 percent reported a decline.

The study was carried out by Florida State University's Information Use Management and Policy Institute and continued a series of surveys begun in 1996.

Legislative Day Focuses on Funding

More than 500 librarians, including 2004–2005 ALA President Brey-Casiano, library trustees, board members, and library friends, traveled to Washington, D.C., in May 2005 to attend National Library Legislative Day events and to speak with their elected representatives about the needs of libraries. The event—cosponsored by the District of Columbia Library Association, the Special Libraries Association, and ALA—drew participants from 45 states. Its theme was "Fund America's Libraries."

Web Site on School/Public Library Partnerships

AASL, ALSC, and YALSA formed a joint task force on school/public library partnerships and created a Web site that includes information on existing school/public library partnerships, a bibliography on school/public library cooperation, and a list of exemplary Web sites. Its address is http://www.ala.org/ala/alsc/alscresources/forlibrarians/SchPLCoopActivities.htm.

School Library Media Brochure

AASL developed a brochure, "Your School Library Media Program and No Child Left Behind," to promote the school library media specialist's role in meeting the requirements of the federal No Child Left Behind (NCLB) Act. The brochure shows how the media specialist is both an ally and asset to school administrators as they face the task of meeting NCLB goals by 2013.

Teen Read Week Participation Soars

Teen Read Week was held Oct. 16–22, 2005, with the theme of "Get Real! @ your library." More than 4,600 librarians and educators participated, an increase of more than 300 percent from 2004, and more than 2,400 online votes were cast for the Teens' Top Ten list of most popular young adult books. The theme for Teen Read Week 2006, scheduled for Oct. 15–21, is "Get Active @ your library."

Certification for Public Library Administrators

The ALA-Allied Professional Association Council approved guidelines that will govern all certifications offered for public library administrators, and the Certified Public Library Administrator program is under way. Librarians with management experience will take courses to fulfill competencies developed by PLA, LAMA, and ASCLA. The guidelines were approved at the 2005 Annual Conference, the program was launched in late 2005, and participants were accepted starting in January 2006. The program's goal is to improve the quality of library service through the provision of practical knowledge and skills essential to successful library management. This certification, the first of its kind to be offered in the United States, is a national program specifically for public librarians who have had at least three years of supervisory experience. The program's standards will allow candidates to demonstrate mastery of the skills needed for library and human resources management.

Record Number of Spectrum Scholarships

A record 67 people received $6,500 Spectrum Scholarships in June 2005 in the eighth year of the program, bringing the total number of recipients to 346 since 1998. Originally created as a three-year initiative, the Spectrum program awarded 50 scholarships from 1998 to 2001 and drew on its endowment to continue support at a lower level in 2002 through 2004. Now, thanks to a grant from the Institute of Museum and Library Services, the program has bounced back and is funded through June 2007. The Spectrum program seeks to improve library services at the local level through the development of a representative work force that reflects the racial and ethnic diversity of the communities served.

PLA approved pilot project funding for five new public librarian Spectrum scholarships to be awarded in conjunction with a mentoring program. PLA also will initiate a pilot national institutional scholarship program that will provide five public libraries with funding to "grow their own" librarians. The Medical Library Association and National Library of Medicine also support a Spectrum scholar.

Focus on Children with Special Needs

An ALSC committee on library service to special-population children and their caregivers has compiled bibliographies of home schooling resources for librarians, resources for librarians serving teen parents, new-immigrant resources, and library programs for children with disabilities. Links are in the "resources" section of the ALSC Web site (http://www.ala.org/ala/alsc/alscresources/resources.htm).

Banned Books Week

"Read Banned Books: It's Your Freedom We're Talking About" was the theme of the 24th annual Banned Books Week, Sept. 24–Oct. 1, 2005. Once again, readings, exhibits, and programs nationwide highlighted this annual celebration of the freedom to read, which gives librarians, teachers, booksellers, and others an opportunity to raise awareness in their communities about the importance of free speech and free expression. Banned Books Week is sponsored by ALA, American Booksellers Association, American Booksellers Foundation for Free Expression, American Society of Journalists and Authors, Association of American Publishers, and National Association of College Stores, and is endorsed by the Center for the Book of the Library of Congress.

We the People Bookshelf

The We the People Bookshelf project is awarding a third round of grants to another 1,000 libraries in 2006; the theme is "Becoming American." The 2005 bookshelf provided sets of 15 classic children's books on the theme of "Freedom" to 1,000 public and K–12 school libraries in 49 states. A program of the National Endowment for the Humanities (NEH) and the ALA Public Programs Office, the initiative aims to encourage young people to read and understand great literature while exploring themes in American history.

Advocacy Honor Roll

ALTA named more than 80 people to the National Advocacy Honor Roll at a banquet held at the 2005 ALA Annual Conference. The honor roll celebrates individuals and groups who have actively supported and strengthened library services at the local, state, or national levels; these individuals' accomplishments provide models for others who wish to expand advocacy efforts. ALTA also partnered with the Public Information Office, Chapter Relations Office, Washington Office, and Friends of Libraries U.S.A. to hold advocacy institutes that provided peer-to-peer modeling to support grassroots advocates as they create and sustain change in their communities.

Bookmobile Celebration

Bookmobiles marked a century-plus of service in public libraries nationwide and had a birthday party at the Diversity Fair at the 2005 Annual Conference. The anniversary celebrated Washington County, Maryland, librarian Mary Titcomb, who used a horse-drawn buggy in 1895 to deliver books to neighboring rural communities.

Campaign for America's Libraries

The ALA board approved a five-year extension of the Campaign for America's Libraries after more than 75 percent of those who participated in an online member survey said they found the three top-level campaign goals "important" or "very important." Nearly half the respondents said they were using campaign materials and participating in nationally sponsored programs, and one third said they were participating in a campaign initiative sponsored by a state library or state association. The trademarked "@ your library" brand is the centerpiece of the Campaign for America's Libraries, ALA's multiyear public awareness and advocacy campaign about the value of libraries, librarians, and library workers.

ALSC's @ your library campaign, focusing on children in grades K–4 and their parents or caregivers, is to be launched in 2006. Focus groups conducted in spring 2005 with children in urban, suburban, and rural settings elicited their opinions of the public library, and the ideas gleaned were incorporated into the campaign's promotion of library services. The Office for Literacy and Outreach Services and the Public Information Office were awarded a $10,000 ALA-World Book Goal Award to support the development of key messaging and a new @ your library toolkit.

PLA launched its Smartest Card campaign at the Brooklyn Public Library with the library's executive director, Ginnie Cooper, PLA President Clara Bohrer, and Theo from PBS's acclaimed children's television series "Between the Lions." The goal of PLA's new campaign, "The Smartest Card. Get It. Use It. @ your library," is to make the library card the most valued card in every wallet. The kickoff event concluded Library Card Sign-up Month and included a program for local bilingual elementary school students. A new public service series starring actor and comedian George Lopez, the campaign spokesperson, was also announced; the print version was placed in national magazines, while television and radio ads were made available to libraries.

Campaign for the World's Libraries

The Campaign for the World's Libraries, cosponsored by ALA and the International Federation of Library Associations and Institutions (IFLA), now includes library associations in nearly 30 countries: Argentina, Armenia, Australia, Azerbaijan, Belarus, Brazil, Bulgaria, Canada, El Salvador, Georgia, Greece, Iceland, Ireland, Italy, Japan, Kazakhstan, Korea, Mexico, Moldova, Nepal, Norway, Nigeria, Portugal, Serbia, Singapore, Turkey, Uruguay, Uzbekistan, and Venezuela. The campaign was showcased during IFLA's World Library and Information Conference in Oslo.

Programs and Partners

Countering Stereotypes About the Elderly

In partnership with George Washington University's Center on Aging, Health, and the Humanities, ALSC surveyed librarians and developed a reading list of children's books that counter negative stereotypes about aging and the elderly. More than 200 librarians, specialists, and consumers of various ages evaluated the completed list of 91 titles, published between 1976 and 2002, that are appropriate for children in pre-kindergarten through grade six.

Campaign Partnerships

In June 2005 ALA announced a new partnership with Investor Protection Trust (IPT), a nonprofit organization dedicated to investor education, and in the fall 20 public libraries started hosting free investor-education seminars as part of "Investor Education @ your library" with materials provided by ALA, IPT, and *Kiplinger's Personal Finance* magazine.

The fourth year of the "Join the Major Leagues @ your library" program, developed with Major League Baseball, was launched on Jackie Robinson Day, April 15, 2005, at the Echo Park Branch of the Los Angeles Public Library. The program featured an online baseball trivia game designed to promote libraries and librarians and to encourage people of all ages to build information literacy skills. ALSC, REFORMA (the National Association to Promote Library and Information Services to Latinos and the Spanish-Speaking), and the Hispanic Heritage Baseball Museum joined PLA and the National Baseball Hall of Fame and Museum as supporters of the program, whose top winner received a free trip to the World Series.

The "Register to Vote @ your library" program, sponsored by ALA and Working Assets, resulted in more than 20,000 new voters registering online through the Your Vote Matters Web site and another 9,000 people updating their registration information. Funded by a grant from Working Assets, this activity produced more than $30,000 for ALA's library advocacy efforts. As part of the program, ALA and Working Assets also offered a $1,000 grant to the library in the zip code with the largest number of registrants; the winner was the San Marcos (Texas) High School library.

The "Be Well Informed @ your library" program, sponsored by ALA and Walgreens, was well under way in 2005. Ten library systems hosted free seminars with local librarians and Walgreens pharmacists on the Medicare prescription drug discount card. The goal was to position each library system as a trusted community resource for up-to-date and credible health information. Each system received a $25,000 grant to host four additional seminars ("Managing the Cost of Your Medicine," "Beyond the Label: Understanding Your Medications," "Over the Counter and into the Mouth," and "Modern Epidemics") and to develop their health collections. RUSA administered the grants.

The fourth year of the "Put It in Writing @ your library" partnership with *Woman's Day* magazine was launched during National Library Week in April with 15 community college and public libraries hosting free writers workshops for the public. That brought to 45 the number of libraries that have hosted workshops, with more than 3,500 attendees. In addition, two winners were chosen for the "Librarian for a Day" editorial outreach initiative and were featured in a four-page article in the March 8 issue of the magazine. ALA has received editorial coverage worth more than $3 million from this partnership.

ABC-TV released seven new public service announcements featuring daytime and prime time stars. The ABC spots feature Zach Levi ("Less than Perfect"), Rebecca Budig ("All My Children"), Evangeline Lily ("Lost"), Kimberly Williams-Paisley ("According to Jim"), Noah Gray-Cabey ("My Wife and Kids"), Masiela Lusha ("George Lopez"), George Lopez ("George Lopez"), and Taylor Atelian and Billi Bruno ("According to Jim"). The end of each announcement was tagged with "The Campaign for America's Libraries" and the ALA Web address.

Public Programs Office Projects

ALA's Public Programs Office (PPO) and National Video Resources named 50 public and academic libraries nationwide as pilot sites for the viewing-and-discussion series based on the documentary film *The World War I Years: America Becomes a World Power.* Twenty-five of the libraries received a $1,300 grant for project expenses, and the project librarian and a local scholar participated in a two-day training workshop in Chicago. This six-week program features scholar-led lectures, documentary film screenings, and readings and discussions.

PPO and Nextbook, an organization that uses its Web site and local programs to promote books illuminating 3,000 years of Jewish civilization, awarded two rounds of new grants for the reading-and-discussion series "Let's Talk About It: Jewish Literature—Identity and Imagination," which explores themes in contemporary and classic Jewish literature. One hundred public and academic libraries now are participating.

Touring Exhibits

PPO received additional grant funding from NEH and the Abraham Lincoln Bicentennial Commission to support two more copies of the exhibit "Forever Free: Abraham Lincoln's Journey to Emancipation," which will travel to 60 libraries from September 2006 through May 2010. PPO also toured three other exhibitions across the country in 2005—"Changing the Face of Medicine: Celebrating America's Women Physicians"; "Elizabeth I: Ruler and Legend"; and "Frankenstein: Penetrating the Secrets of Nature"—and 40 libraries have been chosen to host an exhibit. Two copies of the exhibit "Alexander Hamilton: The Man Who Made Modern America" will be on tour through June 2009; this exhibit is organized by the New York Historical Society, the Gilder Lehrman Institute of American History, and PPO, and is funded by a grant from NEH.

Conferences and Workshops

2005 Annual Conference

U.S. Sen. Barack Obama (D-Ill.) received a standing ovation for his keynote address to the opening general session of the 2005 ALA Annual Conference, which drew a record 27,962 participants to Chicago June 23–29.

Alluding to the federal government "looking over our shoulders in the library," Obama called librarians "full-time defenders of the most fundamental American liberties" and said, "for that, you deserve America's deepest gratitude."

Chicago Mayor Richard M. Daley told the same audience that he wanted to "thank all the librarians for their great public service. . . . You're the ones that have provided this great system that we have, the public library system in America, and we must keep it strong."

ALA 2004–2005 President Brey-Casiano's President's Program, "Coming Full Circle: Library as Place," featured a keynote address by futurist and economist Lowell Catlett and a panel discussion about the role libraries play as community and cultural centers, an idea Brey-Casiano said was central to the design of libraries a century ago. One of the panelists, Karen McPheeters, director of the Farmington (New Mexico) Public Library, said, "People will give libraries support if they feel you're giving them what they need."

A conference within a conference entitled "Empowering Library Support Staff for the 21st Century" drew almost 500 library support staff professionals, including many first-time conference attendees, and plans were begun to carry the new tradition forward to the 2006 and 2007 conferences.

Brey-Casiano held a screening of the film *Unconstitutional*, which examines the effects of the USA Patriot Act on civil liberties, and the audience cheered during a scene in which Santa Cruz (California) Public Library Director Anne Turner collects the library's Internet sign-in sheets and feeds them into a shredder. U.S. Attorney Patrick J. Fitzgerald, who spoke at the conference, said both sides of the Patriot Act battle should "let go of the rhetoric" to encourage different points of view and the sharing of accurate information.

ALA Council approved the association's "ALAhead to 2010" strategic plan, affirming the plan's six goals: advocacy/value of the profession, education, public policy and standards, building the profession, membership, and organizational excellence.

Council also adopted a resolution expressing the association's opposition to all legislative and government attempts to proscribe library materials related to sex, gender identity, or sexual orientation. Another resolution, which called for the withdrawal of U.S. military forces from Iraq, succeeded a year after a similar attempt had failed at the 2004 Annual Conference in Orlando. The 2005 statement, titled "Resolution on the Connection Between the Iraq War and Libraries," overcame objections voiced the previous year that the conflict was not an appropriate matter of concern for ALA.

Minority job seekers discovered helpful career information at the eighth annual Diversity Fair, sponsored by the ALA Office for Literacy and Outreach Services and Demco, Inc.

2006 Midwinter Meeting

More than 11,000 librarians and other library staff, publishers, and guests gathered in San Antonio January 20–25 for ALA's 2006 Midwinter Meeting. The conference concluded with a national call-in effort with library leaders simultaneously phoning members of Congress January 25 at 10 A.M. as part of a nationwide grassroots effort to modify the USA Patriot Act.

ALA Council addressed the "65 percent solution" being considered in many states that would mandate that 65 percent of school funding be spent on "direct classroom instruction," as defined by categories established more than 30 years ago by the National Center for Education Statistics. Council called for a coordinated national effort to classify school librarians as instructional staff rather than support staff and to recognize the impact of state-certified school librarians on student achievement. More than 60 research studies have found a clear link between well-staffed school libraries and increased student achievement.

ALA President Gorman hosted two programs focused on education for librarians. A forum brought together a full house of library practitioners, educators, and students to explore the big issues in library education, including "What is the nature of the profession of librarianship, and what does the 21st-century librarian need to know?"

Nearly 500 people attended the seventh annual Arthur Curley Memorial Lecture, which featured ragtime composer and pianist Reginald R. Robinson, winner of a 2004 MacArthur "genius grant."

ACRL Conference Breaks Records

Several attendance records were broken as nearly 4,000 people from all 50 states and 15 countries attended the ACRL 12th National Conference, "Currents and Convergence: Navigating the Rivers of Change," held in Minneapolis April 7–10, 2005. The number of first-time attendees (1,059) and conference scholarship recipients (94) were new highs. All paid attendees had access to the first-ever ACRL Virtual National Conference, which included live Webcasts of several programs, discussion boards, blogs, listservs, chat rooms, and speaker materials.

Seattle Conference

A conference titled "The Seattle Public Library: Shattering Stereotypes"—jointly sponsored by PLA, the Seattle Public Library, and the Public Libraries International Network—attracted more than 250 participants from the international library community April 27–29, 2005. Attendees explored Seattle's new library facility and discussed best practices from libraries around the world.

Publishing

Booklist

ALA's *Booklist* magazine celebrated its 100th year of publication in 2005 and included many features in honor of the anniversary. In one ongoing feature, "A Century of Books," children's authors and illustrators reminisced about the books that affected their lives and works. In another, "From the *Booklist* Archives," the editors looked back to past reviews, sometimes offering apologies for mistakes ("We're sorry, Mr. White, about how we treated Charlotte"), at other times patting predecessors on the back for work well done. The celebration culminated with the June 2005 anniversary issue and a special feature called "The *Booklist* Century: 100 Books, 100 Years," in which the editors named the most influential books published in each year of *Booklist*'s life.

Meanwhile, the magazine's staff was busy developing a new product, Booklist Online (BOL), a Web site and subscription database that will assist collection development and readers' advisory librarians as well as offer reading and research opportunities to library patrons and general readers.

ALA Editions

ALA Editions published 25 new titles and recorded strong backlist sales, led by *Information Power: Building Partnerships for Learning.* Two books, *Fundamentals of Library Supervision* by Joan Giesecke and *Fundamentals of Children's Services* by Michael Sullivan, introduced the ALA Fundamentals series. ALA Editions also published PLA's *Technology for Results: Developing Service-Based Plans.* Written by Diane Mayo, this book replaces *Wired for the Future* and is another addition to the PLA planning series begun in 1998 with the release of *Planning for Results: A Public Library Transformation Process.* More than 21,500 copies of the "results" books have been sold since 1998.

Another offering was the 2005 *ALA Survey of Librarian Salaries,* a project of the ALA-Allied Professional Association and the ALA Office for Research and Statistics. The 2005 survey was Web-based and had a larger and more inclusive sample size than in previous years to satisfy its new goal of collecting state-level salary data and more information about public libraries serving smaller (10,000–25,000) populations.

American Libraries

American Libraries, ALA's flagship news magazine, published several cover features dealing with newsworthy and controversial professional issues, including the status of library support staff, the Google print digitization project, the opening of the Clinton Presidential Library, and the library funding crisis. Advocacy was also a chief theme during the year, culminating with an August cover story by U.S. Sen. Barack Obama, in which he stated that ". . . our prosperity as a nation is directly correlated to our literacy."

ALA Graphics

ALA Graphics offered several new products in 2005 to help library and school staff extend their reach quickly, easily, and affordably. With the cooperation of OCLC (the Online Computer Library Center), ALA Graphics introduced a Dewey nightshirt to complement the growing line of Dewey products, as well as a product line featuring AASL's popular theme "Every Student Succeeds @ your library."

ALA Graphics has introduced digital art downloads on the ALA Online Store. The collection provides reasonably priced library-friendly art. The best-selling Celebrity READ series has grown to include comic Margaret Cho, baseball player Johnny Damon, Bollywood actress Aishwarya Rai, actor Colin Farrell, actress Keira Knightley, and singer-actor-producer Ice Cube. The author poster series expanded to include Ray Bradbury, Tavis Smiley, and David Sedaris. Children's and young adult characters such as Batman, Maisy, Olive, and Thomas the Tank Engine also have become themed posters for ALA, as has "The Chronicles of Narnia."

Resources for College Libraries

ACRL and R. R. Bowker have signed an agreement to copublish *Resources for College Libraries* (*RCL*), a new core collection of recommended titles for academic libraries that will be the successor to *Books for College Libraries,* third edition. The new *RCL* will be an online product whose coverage will include electronic resources as well as books. *RCL* will be regularly updated and revised, ensuring that it remains current. The target publication date is September 2006.

Leadership

Michael Gorman, who has been dean of library services at California State University–Fresno, Madden Library, since 1988, was inaugurated as ALA's 2005–2006 president at the 2005 Annual Conference in Chicago.

From 1977 to 1988 Gorman worked at the library of the University of Illinois, Urbana-Champaign, serving part of that time as acting university librarian. From 1966 to 1977 Gorman was, successively, head of cataloguing at the British National Bibliography, a member of the British Library Planning Secretariat, and head of the Office of Bibliographic Standards in the British Library. He has taught at library schools in Britain and in the United States, most recently at the University of California, Los Angeles.

Gorman has published hundreds of articles in professional and scholarly journals. He has contributed chapters to a number of books and is the author or editor of other books and monographs. He has given presentations at international, national, and state conferences and has been the recipient of numerous awards.

Leslie Burger, director of the Princeton (New Jersey) Public Library, was elected ALA president-elect in the 2005 election, and is to be inaugurated ALA president at the 2006 Annual Conference in New Orleans. Her presidential activities will focus on the theme "Libraries Transform Communities."

Teri R. Switzer, associate dean, research, operations, and document delivery services, at the University of Colorado at Denver and Health Sciences Center, Auraria Library, continued her term (2004–2007) as ALA treasurer.

ALA Council elected four new members to its executive board at the 2005 Midwinter Meeting to serve three-year terms that will end in June 2008: Francis J. Buckley, Jr., interim director of the District of Columbia Public Library and former U.S. Superintendent of Documents; Terri G. Kirk, school library media specialist at Reidland High School in Paducah, Kentucky; June A. Pinnell-Stephens, collection services manager at the Fairbanks (Alaska) North Star Borough Public Library, and Patricia H. Smith, executive director of the Texas Library Association.

Grants and Contributions

ALA received an $80,000 grant from the Ford Foundation to continue, at the regional level throughout 2007, the advocacy institutes launched by 2004–2005 ALA President Brey-Casiano at the 2005 Midwinter Meeting.

A grant from the W. K. Kellogg Foundation will allow AASL to work with other national organizations, including REFORMA, on the promotion of the El Día de los Niños/El Día de Los Libros (Day of the Child/Day of the Book) celebration each April. The grant will fund education programs, Web site design and maintenance, a tenth anniversary celebration in 2006, and national mailings. The goals of the program are to honor children and their languages and culture, to encourage reading and literacy, and to promote library collections and programs that reflect the nation's plurality.

ALA's PPO and Public and Cultural Programs Advisory Committee raised more than $117,000 in 2005 for the Cultural Communities Fund, an endowment fund to support library cultural programming. The fund has received a $350,000 challenge grant from NEH and more than $250,000 in contributions from individuals and other organizations, including Barnes & Noble, Nextbook, PLA, the Wallace Foundation, the H. W. Wilson Foundation, and more than 250 ALA members and friends. The goal is to raise $5 million for the fund by 2010.

The International Relations Office completed a two-and-a-half-year program under a $125,000 grant from the Carnegie Corporation of New York to "Improve Access to Information in Academic Libraries in the South Caucasus." ALA leveraged the grant to provide more than $500,000 in books, databases, and other resources to Baku State University in Azerbaijan, Yerevan State University in Armenia, and Tbilisi State University in Georgia.

YALSA and PPO received a $50,000 grant from Oprah's Angel Network to fund book-discussion groups in alternative high schools and juvenile-detention centers. The grant was announced on "The Oprah Show" in October. The name of the program is Great Stories C.L.U.B (Connecting Libraries, Underserved teens, and Books).

Major Awards and Honors

Book Awards

The 2005 Newbery Medal, awarded annually by ALSC to the author of the most distinguished contribution to American literature for children, went to *Kira-Kira* (Atheneum), a novel by Cynthia Kadohata about growing up in a Japanese American family. The 2005 Caldecott Medal, awarded annually to the artist of the most distinguished American picture book for children, went to *Kitten's First Full Moon* (HarperCollins), illustrated and written by Kevin Henkes.

Toni Morrison, author of *Remember: The Journey to School Integration* (Houghton Mifflin), and Kadir Nelson, illustrator of *Ellington Was Not a Street* by Ntozake Shange (Simon & Schuster), were the winners of the 2005 Coretta Scott King Awards honoring African American authors and illustrators of outstanding books for children and young adults. The awards are presented annually by ALA's Ethnic Multicultural Information Exchange Round Table to authors and illustrators of African descent whose distinguished books promote an understanding and appreciation of African American culture. They commemorate the life and work of Dr. Martin Luther King, Jr., and honor his widow, Coretta Scott King, for her courage and determination for having continued the work for peace and world brotherhood.

Barbara Hathaway, author of *Missy Violet and Me* (Houghton Mifflin), was the Coretta Scott King/John Steptoe New Talent Author Award winner. Frank Morrison, illustrator of *Jazzy Miz Mozetta* (Farrar, Straus and Giroux), won the Steptoe New Talent Illustrator Award.

How I Live Now (Wendy Lamb Books) by Meg Rosoff won the 2005 Michael L. Printz Award, which honors a book that exemplifies literary excellence in young adult literature. Russell Freedman was the 2005 winner of the Robert F. Sibert Informational Book Award for *The Voice that Challenged a Nation: Marian Anderson and the Struggle for Equal Rights* (Clarion). This award, established by ALSC in 2001, is given annually to the author of the most distinguished informational book published during the preceding year.

Honorary Members

ALA conferred honorary membership, the association's highest honor, on two distinguished members at the 2005 Annual Conference. The honorees were Lotsee F. Patterson and Nettie B. Taylor.

Patterson, cofounder of the American Indian Library Association (AILA), an ALA affiliate, was nominated "in recognition of her lifelong commitment to establishing quality library services and programs for Native Americans, her accomplishments as an advocate for native and indigenous libraries on the regional, national, and international levels, and her contributions as an author, library educator, and mentor." Taylor, who began her library career in 1936 and in 1948 moved to the Maryland State Department of Education where she served for 40 years, was honored "in recognition of her extraordinary career as a librarian and library advocate spanning nearly seven decades" and "her commitment to resource-sharing and library cooperation, her tireless efforts to increase federal funding for libraries, and her influence as a mentor to generations of librarians."

James Madison Award

Richard M. Schmidt, who died in October 2004, was the recipient of the 2005 James Madison Award, presented by ALA to honor those who have championed, protected, and promoted public access to government information and the public's right to know. Schmidt devoted a long and illustrious career to the pursuit of open government and a free press, both of which he considered integral to a flourishing democracy. Throughout his career, which included positions in the legislative and executive branches of government, he strove to push the government toward greater openness and to change attitudes about access. The Madison Award, named for the nation's fifth president, was established in 1986.

Association of American Publishers

71 Fifth Ave., New York, NY 10010
212-255-0200, fax 212-255-7007

50 F St. N.W., Washington, DC 20001
202-347-3375, fax 202-347-3690

World Wide Web http://www.publishers.org

Judith Platt
Director, Communications/Public Affairs

The Association of American Publishers (AAP) is the national trade association of the U.S. book publishing industry. The association was created in 1970 through the merger of the American Book Publishers Council, a trade publishing group, and the American Educational Publishers Institute, an organization of textbook publishers. AAP's more than 300 corporate members include most of the major commercial book publishers in the United States as well as smaller and medium-sized houses, not-for-profit publishers, university presses, and scholarly societies.

AAP members publish hardcover and paperback books in every field including general fiction and nonfiction; poetry; children's books; textbooks; Bibles and other religious works; reference works; scientific, medical, technical, professional, and scholarly books and journals; computer software; and a range of electronic products and services.

AAP also works closely with some 2,000 smaller regional publishers through formal affiliations with the Publishers Association of the West, the Publishers Association of the South, the Florida Publishers Association, the Small Publishers Association of North America, and the Evangelical Christian Publishers Association.

AAP policy is set by a board of directors elected by the membership for four-year terms, under a chair who serves for two years. There is an executive committee composed of the chair, vice chair, secretary, and treasurer and a minimum of two at-large members. Management of the association, within the guidelines set by the board, is the responsibility of AAP's president and CEO, Pat Schroeder.

AAP maintains two offices, in New York and Washington, D.C.

Highlights of 2005

Among the highlights of the year in publishing:

- In a legal action coordinated and funded by AAP, five major publishers sued Google over plans to digitally copy and distribute copyrighted works without permission.
- AAP's 2005 Honors went to *USA Today* for the newspaper's outstanding work in promoting American books and authors.
- Poet Lawrence Ferlinghetti, cofounder of the San Francisco bookstore and publisher City Lights, received the 29th Curtis Benjamin Award for Creative Publishing.

- The Miriam Bass Independent Publishing Award went to Akashic Books Publisher Johnny Temple.
- Anthony Lucki, president and CEO of Houghton Mifflin, was elected to a two-year term as AAP chairman, succeeding HarperCollins CEO Jane Friedman.
- Book sales totaled $23.72 billion in 2004, an increase of 1.3 percent over 2003, according to figures released by AAP in February 2005.
- AAP's School Division gave a special Mary McNulty Award for lifetime service to educational publishing to Peter Jovanovich.
- The 2005 R. R. Hawkins Award for the outstanding professional, scholarly, or reference work was presented to Belknap Press of the Harvard University Press for *Huck's Raft: A History of American Childhood* by Steven Mintz.
- Get Caught Reading began its seventh year with ten new celebrities and a photo shoot on Capitol Hill.
- Turkish publisher Abdullah Keskin was the third recipient of the Jeri Laber International Freedom to Publish Award.
- Working as part of the Campaign for Reader Privacy, AAP scored some important victories in the campaign to modify provisions of the USA Patriot Act.
- The International Freedom to Publish Committee issued strong protests over the persecution of writers in Turkey and in Cuba.
- Members of the former American Medical Publishers Association were welcomed into AAP and its Professional and Scholarly Publishing Division.
- AAP joined with higher education, library, and university presses in issuing *Campus Copyright Rights and Responsibilities: A Basic Guide to Policy Considerations.*

Government Affairs

AAP's Washington office is the industry's front line on matters of federal legislation and government policy. Washington keeps AAP members informed about developments on Capitol Hill and in the executive branch to enable the membership to develop consensus positions on national policy issues. AAP's government affairs professionals serve as the industry's voice in advocating the views and concerns of American publishers on questions of national policy.

A separate report details legislation and regulatory actions affecting book publishers in 2005. [See "Legislation and Regulations Affecting Publishing in 2005" in Part 2—*Ed.*]

Communications/Public Affairs

The Communications and Public Affairs program is AAP's voice, informing the trade press and other media, the AAP membership, and the general public about AAP's work to promote the cause of American publishing and serving as the industry's spokesman on a host of issues. Through the program's regular publica-

tions, press releases and advisories, op-ed pieces, and other means, AAP express-
es the industry's views and provides up-to-the-minute information on subjects of
concern to its members. The Communications/Public Affairs program has primary responsibility for the AAP Web site.

AAP's public affairs activities include outreach and cooperative programs
with such organizations as the Center for the Book in the Library of Congress, the
Arts Advocacy Alliance (supporting the National Endowment for the Arts and
other federal arts programs), PEN American Center and its International Freedom
to Write program, and many literacy and reading-promotion efforts including an
early-childhood literacy initiative, Reach Out and Read. The public affairs program also coordinates AAP's participation in the National Book Festival.

BookExpo America

AAP is a cosponsor of BookExpo America (BEA), the premiere English-language book event. BookExpo 2005 was held in New York June 3–5. Among the
highlights were welcoming remarks by author and comedian Billy Crystal and a
solo turn by comedian Bill Maher to benefit the Book Industry Foundation,
which supports the work of the American Booksellers Foundation for Free Expression (ABFFE) and the Get Caught Reading program.

At BookExpo 2005, AAP joined with ABFFE and the Freedom to Read
Foundation in sponsoring a program featuring U.S. Rep. Jerry Nadler (D-N.Y.)
discussing the USA Patriot Act.

Get Caught Reading

AAP continued its work in 2005 to promote a love of reading with the Get
Caught Reading/¡Ajá, leyendo! campaign. New participating celebrities included
Alicia Keys, Queen Latifah, the Miami Heat, Batman, Marlo Thomas, Gloria
Estefan, Maya and Miguel, George Foreman, Sue Bird, Swin Cash, Tim Duncan,
and Grant Hill.

On May 11, 2005, AAP sponsored another popular "Get Caught Reading
Day on Capitol Hill" with members of the House and Senate having their pictures taken reading a favorite book.

AAP initiated efforts to air a Get Caught Reading public service announcement with Whoopi Goldberg on pro bono airtime offered via ABC Television. To
be aired on ABC network television and its local affiliates, the announcement is
designed to heighten awareness of the importance of books and reading.

AAP met with representatives of Starbucks, which planned to use the Get
Caught Reading theme for a New York City reading initiative in May 2006. Also
involved in the program are the New York City Board of Education's Fund for
Public Schools, the New York Public Library, and Jumpstart, an organization
that pairs college students with young children for reading sessions in an effort to
boost their literacy skills before kindergarten.

Booksellers, educators, and librarians use the Get Caught Reading Web site
(http://www.getcaughtreading.org) as a resource to initiate and equip Get Caught
Reading campaigns in their communities. AAP also continued its Get Caught

Reading partnership with the National Basketball Association, and Get Caught Reading had a presence at the New York Comic-Con Show and continued its involvement with the Harlem Book Fair.

Copyright

The AAP Copyright Committee coordinates efforts to protect and strengthen intellectual property rights and enhance public awareness of the importance of copyright as an incentive to creativity. The committee monitors intellectual property legislation in the United States and abroad and serves as an advisory body to the AAP Board of Directors in formulating policy on legislation and compliance activities, including litigation. The committee coordinates AAP's efforts to promote understanding and compliance with U.S. copyright law on college and university campuses. Bob Bolick (McGraw-Hill) chaired the committee in 2005.

The Family Entertainment and Copyright Act, which was enacted in April 2005 primarily to address the problem of digital piracy of movies, recordings, and computer programs, contained a provision helpful to publishers. Although the statutory language that makes it a felony to engage in "willful pre-commercial online distribution" of an audiovisual work does not cover literary works, the legislation contained a provision calling for regulations to establish a pre-registration procedure to protect works prior to commercial release. AAP submitted comments to the Copyright Office in summer 2005 urging that such protection be extended to literary works, and the regulations issued late in 2005 apply that protection to literary works because such works also have a "history of copyright infringement prior to commercial distribution."

The Digital Media Consumers' Rights Act (H.R. 1201), which AAP opposed in the previous Congress, was reintroduced in 2005. Carefully drafted to fall within the primary jurisdiction of the House Energy and Commerce Committee rather than the Judiciary Committee, the bill again threatens to gut the anticircumvention provisions of the Digital Millennium Copyright Act (DMCA). The legislation's sponsors often justify the bill's provisions by pointing to digital rights management restrictions faced by consumers in their use of purchased e-books. A hearing on fair use was held by the House Energy and Commerce Consumer Protection Subcommittee in an apparent attempt to promote the legislation. AAP continues to oppose the bill.

The opening of the third round of the triennial rulemaking process mandated by DMCA began on December 1, 2005—the deadline for submitting proposals for temporary exemptions from the important provision of DMCA that prohibits the circumvention of technologies used to control access to copyrighted materials. AAP again joined allied organizations representing the copyright-based industries in reviewing and responding to these proposals during the reply round, which ended February 2, 2006.

AAP participated in a number of friend-of-the-court briefs concerning copyright issues in 2005.

In January 2005 AAP joined with a host of groups representing media and professional sports organizations, whose members rely on effective copyright protection for their livelihood, in asking the U.S. Supreme Court to review and overturn the Ninth Circuit ruling in *Metro-Goldwyn-Mayer* v. *Grokster*. That decision would have allowed providers of peer-to-peer file-sharing services to avoid secondary liability for facilitating acts of copyright infringement simply by taking no action to eliminate or minimize the amount of online copyright infringement by users of their service. The Supreme Court ultimately decided the case in a manner that did not fully resolve conflicting rulings of the Ninth and Seventh Circuits, but strongly supported the idea that those who induce others to engage in copyright infringement can themselves be held liable for such infringement.

AAP participated in an amicus brief in *United States* v. *Martignon,* supporting reversal of a Second Circuit ruling holding the anti-bootlegging statute for live music performances unconstitutional because (1) such performances are not "fixed" and thus not "writings," and (2) the protection against bootlegging is not for "a limited time." The brief focused on the first holding, where the court ruled that Congress cannot enact "copyright-like" legislation under any other constitutional grant of legislative authority (such as the Commerce Clause) if the Copyright Clause itself does not authorize the statutory protection at issue.

In July AAP signed onto an amicus brief in the U.S. Supreme Court's review of the Illinois Tool Works case, urging the court to reject the view endorsed by the U.S. Court of Appeals for the Federal Circuit that mere ownership of a copyright gives rise to a presumption of market power for purposes of a tying analysis under antitrust law. The case under review specifically holds that such a presumption exists with respect to patents, but states *in dicta* (an opinion expressed by the bench) that such a presumption also exists with respect to copyrights.

AAP joined an amicus brief in *Kahle* v. *Ashcroft* opposing a request that the Ninth Circuit remand the case to give the lower court an opportunity to determine whether changes that Congress has made (such as elimination of notice, registration and renewal requirements, and imposition of term extension) from an "opt-in" to an "opt-out" copyright system constitute the kind of change in the "traditional contours of copyright" that the Supreme Court, in the *Eldred* decision, implied might justify heightened First Amendment scrutiny of challenges to copyright laws enacted by Congress, such as the Copyright Term Extension Act.

After nearly six years of negotiated drafting, *Campus Copyright Rights and Responsibilities: A Basic Guide to Policy Considerations,* a cooperative effort of AAP, the Association of American Universities, the Association of American University Presses (AAUP), and the Association of Research Libraries, was published in December 2005. Some 1,800 copies of the publication, which was endorsed by the American Council on Education and the Authors Guild, were distributed to universities along with a letter explaining its importance to the university community. The document is posted on the AAP Web site, as well as on the Web sites of the cosponsoring and endorsing organizations and can be downloaded as a pdf file.

In response to a notice of inquiry published by the U.S. Copyright Office seeking public comments on ways to handle the problem of "orphan works" (works whose copyright owners cannot be located by third parties seeking permission to use them), AAP joined with AAUP and the Software and Information Industry Association (SIIA) in filing comments on March 24, 2005. Reflecting the interests of the three groups as both users and owners of copyrighted works, the comments recommended "fine tuning" current U.S. copyright law to limit the liability of the user of an orphan work if, after a "reasonably diligent" search fails to reveal the identity or location of the owner, the owner comes forward after the use has begun. Under such circumstances, the owner would be entitled to a "reasonable licensing fee or royalty" (as determined by market practices), but not to statutory damages, the user's profits, or injunctive relief. The Copyright Office was expected to submit its report and recommendations to Congress by February 2006.

The committee continued to monitor the Google Print for Libraries project (now called Google Book Search). AAP disagreed with Google's view that its activities in scanning copyright-protected books into its search engine database were protected either by fair use under Section 107 of the Copyright Act or the library privileges under Section 108 of the act. After fruitless attempts to negotiate a mutually acceptable approach to the handling of such works, on October 19 five major AAP members filed suit in federal court claiming that Google's plan to digitally copy and distribute copyrighted works without permission of the copyright owners violates U.S. copyright law. The legal action was taken after lengthy discussions broke down between AAP and Google's top management regarding the copyright infringement implications of the Google project. The suit, which was filed in U.S. District Court for the Southern District of New York, seeks a declaration by the court that Google commits infringement when it scans entire books covered by copyright, and a court order preventing Google from doing so without permission of the copyright owner. The lawsuit was filed on behalf of the McGraw-Hill Companies, Pearson Education, Penguin Group (USA), Simon & Schuster, and John Wiley & Sons. The legal action is being coordinated and funded by AAP and has the strong backing of the publishing industry; it was filed following an overwhelming vote of support by the AAP Board.

With the revitalization of the AAP Copyright Committee's Online Piracy Working Group in 2004 under the chairmanship of Keith Titan (Random House), the group continued studying the extent and nature of online book piracy activities in 2005.

The committee has been closely monitoring issues arising from the use of copyrighted works in digital formats on college campuses, including library e-reserves. The committee has been working with the Copyright Clearance Center, which, following substantial research on university and library views regarding "blanket licenses," has implemented an "Electronic Course Content Service" to facilitate the authorized use of such materials.

The Rights and Permissions Advisory Committee (RPAC), which operates under the aegis of the AAP Copyright Committee, sponsors education programs for rights and permissions professionals. Bonnie Beacher (McGraw-Hill) chaired the group in 2005. The committee brought a popular half-day seminar on the "No Child Left Behind" and "TEACH" acts, originally held in New York, to Boston. In May RPAC hosted its annual conference in New York. gathering rights and permissions professionals from around the country. In addition to educational seminars and conferences, RPAC continues to maintain the AAP Imprints List, providing contact details and information on various imprints for those seeking permission. The list can be found at http://www.publishers.org/member/imprints. cfm. RPAC members have also begun to update the *New and Updated Copyright Primer* for its third printing.

The Copyright Education Committee has worked on abbreviating AAP's FAQs on e-reserves and creating other revisions for a new edition of *Q & A on Copyright for the Campus Community*. The committee has also been in contact with the Copyright Clearance Center to discuss joint copyright education and compliance activities on university campuses.

Diversity/Recruit and Retain

AAP's Diversity/Recruit and Retain Committee (DRRC) continued its mission to attract talented, diverse voices to the book publishing industry with its "Book Yourself a Career" campaign. The committee was chaired in 2005 by Bridget Marmion (Houghton Mifflin).

AAP initiated advertising via Google AdWords, resulting in a dramatic increase in traffic to the bookjobs.com (http://www.bookjobs.com) Web site, which serves as a comprehensive database of jobs and internships in the industry as well as a "one-stop-shopping" resource for information about book publishing. The jobs database includes job and internship listings from nearly 300 book publishers of all types—large and small, consumer, professional, and educational. The Web site offers a wealth of information, including types of publishers, material about various companies, types of jobs in publishing, matches between college majors and particular job departments, publishing programs, and events in the industry.

DRRC continued its college outreach initiative in 2005 to publicize the Web site on college campuses, with a focus on schools with high academic standards and a diverse student population.

In 2006 AAP will initiate a retiree mentoring program entitled PRIME (Publishing Resource Information Mentoring Exchange) to provide ongoing mentoring support by publishing retirees to those who may be making a transition from one segment of the publishing industry to another.

Education

AAP's education program is designed to provide educational opportunities for publishing industry personnel. The most popular of these is the intensive "Introduction to Publishing" course, which was held in New York in November 2005. Among other educational programs were "Finance for Editors" and AAP's tax seminar, which features speakers with expertise in finance and taxation. [See also "Higher Education" and "School Division" later in this report—*Ed.*]

Enabling Technologies

The association's Enabling Technologies program works to foster the development and implementation of technologies facilitating print and digital publishing. AAP's director of digital policy, Ed McCoyd, oversees a variety of initiatives serving the interests of all segments of the industry.

The work of the Higher Education Critical Issues Task Force is detailed later in this report. Other initiatives include the following:

ISBN-13

The International Organization for Standardization (ISO) is expanding the International Standard Book Number (ISBN) from a 10- to a 13-digit code. To give publishers adequate time to prepare for the change, AAP successfully negotiated within ISO to delay the implementation date of the 13-digit ISBN (often referred to as "ISBN-13") to January 1, 2007 (the change was originally proposed to occur as early as 2005). On the first day of 2007, ISBN registration agencies will begin issuing a 13-digit ISBN to publishers, rather than the 10-digit ISBN that is currently issued.

In August 2005 AAP sent a letter to more than 7,000 school districts across the country to alert them to the change, the reasons behind it, its implications, and publishers' efforts to facilitate the transition. Information was also posted on AAP's Web site at http://www.publishers.org/isbn-13, and AAP worked with school district depositories on implementation issues, coordinated with ISBN-13 outreach and communications efforts by the Book Industry Study Group (BISG), and gave ISBN-13 presentations to school district representatives at the annual meeting of the National Association of State Textbook Administrators (NASTA). [For more information on the 13-digit ISBN, see "How to Obtain an ISBN" in Part 5—*Ed.*]

PLUS Initiative

AAP formed a task force in 2005 to review and provide input on the glossary being created by the PLUS (Picture Licensing Universal System) Coalition, a group working on standards to facilitate picture licensing worldwide. The glossary will be of terms that publishers and other parties can choose to use in photograph and other image licenses.

One of the goals of the effort to is create codes identifying defined terms in the glossary to be incorporated into picture licenses and, through their association with the glossary, to help avoid contract disputes that can arise from confusion over the meanings of terms in an agreement. PLUS will also create a template for putting licensing provisions in a certain order to foster machine-readability. The AAP task force consists of photo researchers, rights and permissions professionals, and other representatives of publisher members of AAP.

Freedom to Read

The mandate of the AAP Freedom to Read Committee is to protect the free marketplace of ideas for American publishers. The committee serves as the publishing industry's early warning system on such issues as libel, privacy, school and library censorship, journalists' privilege and the right to protect confidential sources, Internet censorship, government regulation of protected speech, third-party liability for protected speech, and efforts to punish speech that "causes harm." The committee coordinates AAP participation in First Amendment cases, sponsors educational programs, plays an active role in the Media Coalition (a trade association of business-oriented groups concerned with censorship issues), and works with groups within and beyond the book community to advance common interests in the area of intellectual freedom. Lisa Drew (Lisa Drew Books/ Scribner) chaired the committee in 2005.

The USA Patriot Act and the Campaign for Reader Privacy

Section 215 of the USA Patriot Act, especially as it applies to library and bookstore records, continued to be a source of concern for publishers and for the larger book community. Over and above the issue of library and bookstore records, publishers have serious business concerns about Section 215. In addition, the issue of national security letters (NSLs) came to the forefront during 2005 as it became evident that these administrative subpoenas, which do not require a warrant, were being widely used by the FBI in efforts to examine library and bookstore records.

Working with allies in the "book community," publishers did a remarkable job in raising awareness of the implications of Section 215 for ordinary citizens. Members of Congress heard from constituents by phone, e-mail, and through the Campaign for Reader Privacy, jointly sponsored by AAP, the American Library Association (ALA), the American Booksellers Association, and PEN American Center. The campaign generated support for legislation in the House (H.R. 1157) to exempt libraries and bookstores from Section 215 searches and for legislation in the Senate (S. 737), a narrowly crafted bipartisan bill that would restore important civil liberties safeguards to the most controversial provisions of the USA Patriot Act.

A high point in the fight came on June 15, 2005, when the House, by a vote of 238–187, and in defiance of both the Republican leadership and the White House, approved Rep. Bernie Sanders's (I-Vt.) amendment to the Justice Department appropriations bill cutting off funds for FBI searches of bookstores and libraries under Section 215. (The amendment was not expected to survive the appropriations conference process, and in November it was stripped from the final appropriations bill.)

Jubilation over passage of the Sanders amendment was short-lived; it ended when the House passed H.R. 3199, extending Section 215 for ten years and making changes that are largely semantic, leaving the door open for potential government abuse of reader privacy. On July 29 the Senate passed by unanimous consent its own version of the USA Patriot Act reauthorization—S. 1389—which had been approved a week earlier by the Senate Judiciary Committee. While reader privacy and civil liberties advocates did not get everything they had hoped for, the Senate bill contained important safeguards for protecting library, bookstore, and publisher records under Section 215. The House/Senate conference, which had been expected shortly after Labor Day, was delayed until November when, after a week of intensive negotiations, there was word that an agreement had been reached. However, the draft conference report ignited a firestorm of protest and a bipartisan group of six senators vowed to fight it. On December 14, the House overwhelmingly approved the conference report, making permanent 14 of the 16 provisions due to expire at the end of 2005 and extending the others for four years. But serious concerns over the lack of civil liberties safeguards in the conference-approved legislation stalled the bill in the Senate. On December 16, a move to shut off debate and bring the act to a final vote failed when four Republican senators joined Democratic colleagues, denying the 60 votes needed to invoke cloture. On December 21, with key provisions of the act due to expire in ten days, a letter signed by 52 senators (including 8 Republicans) was sent to the senate majority leader urging a three-month temporary extension. Late in the evening on December 21, the Senate approved a compromise to extend the expiring provisions for six months, with a commitment to revisit the civil liberties concerns early in the new year. The Bush administration said it would go along with the six-month extension, but when the extension went to the House for approval, Judiciary Committee Chairman James Sensenbrenner (R-Wis.) refused to accept it, asserting that it would allow the Senate "to duck the issue until the last week in June." Instead, on December 22 the House approved Sensenbrenner's recommended five-week extension, carrying the issue over into 2006. [The battle continued until March 7, when the House voted 280–138 to renew the act. The president signed the legislation into law March 9, with its troublesome provisions regarding bookstore and library records intact.—*Ed.*]

Journalists' Privilege

Publishers have watched with growing unease the erosion of fundamental protections for investigative journalists and authors. A number of high-profile cases have underscored an increasing willingness on the part of federal authorities to subpoena journalists and to raise the threat of civil and criminal contempt for refusal to identify confidential sources. Although journalists have fairly strong protection against compelled disclosure in state courts (31 states and the District of Columbia have "shield laws" on the books, and another 18 recognize some degree of common law privilege), this protection has never been codified for federal proceedings. Over the past several years, more than two dozen subpoenas have been issued to obtain reporters' source notes and other materials.

These incidents have underscored the need for federal legislation that would provide journalists with a degree of protection against compelled testimony in federal court. AAP Freedom to Read counsel worked on a task force to develop draft legislation, the "Free Flow of Information Act." Introduced in both the House and the Senate with bipartisan sponsorship, the act would provide some measure of protection for reporters in shielding confidential sources in federal court proceedings and would specifically cover book publishers and authors. AAP will lobby hard for passage of the act in 2006.

In the Courts

- AAP joined with four other Media Coalition members in filing an amicus brief in the California Supreme Court supporting Warner Brothers' motion for summary judgment in *Lyle* v. *Warner Brothers,* a sexual-harassment suit in which a former writer's assistant on the television show "Friends" asserts that the sexual content of conversation in the writers' room, although not directed at her, created a "hostile work environment."
- AAP joined a coalition of media groups in asking the U.S. Supreme Court to review the contempt orders imposed on *New York Times* reporter Judith

Miller and *Time* magazine reporter Matt Cooper for refusing to testify in the grand jury investigation of the leaking of the name of Valerie Plame as covert intelligence officer for the Central Intelligence Agency.

- On May 9 a federal judge in South Carolina issued a permanent injunction barring enforcement of a state statute criminalizing the digital communication of work considered to be harmful to minors, including "depictions of nudity and sexual content." The South Carolina victory was the latest in a series of successful legal challenges to state Internet harmful-to-minors laws spearheaded by the Media Coalition. AAP was one of the plaintiffs in the South Carolina suit, *Southeast Booksellers Association* v. *McMaster,* brought in November 2002.

- Joining with 13 co-plaintiffs, AAP went into federal court in Salt Lake City in June 2005 to challenge Utah's newly enacted Internet harmful-to-minors statute. The statute requires the state attorney general to compile a "blacklist" of Internet sites that contain material considered harmful to minors. Internet service providers would then be required to block access to the sites and Web site operators would be required to rate their sites and control minors' access to material that might be considered harmful to minors. The complaint charges that the statute "imposes severe content-based restriction on the availability, display, and dissemination of constitutionally protected speech on the Internet."

- AAP joined an amicus brief in *Forensic Advisors* v. *Matrixx Initiatives,* a case making its way through the Maryland courts, supporting the right of a journalist and publisher to keep confidential subscriber lists and source material, and the right to read and speak anonymously on the Internet. The amicus brief argues that Maryland's journalists' shield law protects against compelled disclosure of sources and information used in news gathering, and that the First Amendment protects the right to read anonymously.

- AAP joined amicus briefs supporting two separate challenges to Section 205 of the USA Patriot Act dealing with the issuance of National Security Letters (NSLs), administrative subpoenas issued without judicial oversight that give the FBI virtually unlimited power to obtain electronic communications transactions. The first case involves the government's appeal of a ruling by a federal judge in New York that held that NSLs violate the Fourth Amendment's ban on unreasonable searches, and that the gag order prohibiting those receiving an NSL from revealing that fact violates the First Amendment. The second challenge was brought by the American Civil Liberties Union on behalf of an ALA member in Connecticut who received an NSL and sought to have the gag order lifted so that the recipient could participate in the debate over reauthorization of the USA Patriot Act. On September 9, finding that the government could not support its allegation that the gag order was necessary (and underscoring the importance of judicial oversight even when national security is involved), a federal judge in Connecticut lifted the gag order, but stayed the ruling pending the government's appeal. Both cases then went to the Second Circuit Court of Appeals, which heard oral arguments on November 2. There had been no further ruling at the time this report was prepared.

- AAP joined in filing an amicus brief in support of U.S. author Rachel Ehrenfeld's request that a federal court in New York declare unenforceable a British court's default libel judgment against her. The judgment—involving substantial damages, an injunction against publication in Britain of Ehrenfeld's book *Funding Evil,* and a "declaration of falsity" against the book—arose from a libel action brought in Britain by Saudi businessman Khalid Bin Mahfouz although Ehrenfeld's book hadn't been published there. The amicus brief cites "the growing and dangerous threat of 'libel tourism'—the cynical and aggressive use of claimant-friendly libel laws in foreign jurisdictions with no legitimate connection to the challenged publication."

- AAP welcomed a September ruling by the Ontario Court of Appeal in *Bangoura* v. *Washington Post,* a case with far-reaching implications for freedom of speech on the Internet. The ruling overturned the decision of a lower Canadian court that would have allowed a libel suit against the *Washington Post* to proceed in Canada based on the fact that an article accessible through the *Post*'s online archive allegedly defamed a Canadian resident. The Ontario Supreme Court recognized that the refusal of U.S. courts to enforce foreign libel judgments that do not meet the standards established in *New York Times* v. *Sullivan* is "rooted in the guarantees of freedom of speech and of the press under the First Amendment of the U.S. Constitution."

Education Programs

At the BookExpo America trade show in New York, AAP cosponsored a program featuring U.S. Rep. Jerry Nadler (D-N.Y.), who spoke about the need to amend the USA Patriot Act and restore federal judicial oversight to the process of obtaining records, including library and bookstore records, under the act's Section 215.

At the 2005 ALA Annual Conference in Chicago, AAP cosponsored "Intellectual Freedom: A Casualty of War?" exploring the history of intellectual freedom in wartime, the extent to which the current "war on terror" has had an impact on free speech and dissent, and strategies for the book and information communities to help maintain individual liberties during "perilous times." Featured speaker was University of Chicago law professor Geoffrey R. Stone, author of *Perilous Times: Free Speech in Wartime from the Sedition Act of 1798 to the War on Terrorism,* joined by First Amendment legal expert Floyd Abrams.

Higher Education

AAP's Higher Education Committee serves the needs and interests of AAP members who publish for the postsecondary education market. The Higher Education Executive Committee was chaired by John Isley (Pearson Education) in 2005.

AAP continued to fight widespread misunderstanding and misinformation about the price of college textbooks. In February 2005 the Public Interest Research Group (PIRG) issued its second report on college textbooks, *Ripoff 101, 2nd Edition: How the Publishing Industry's Practices Needlessly Drive Up Textbook*

Costs. The report claimed that publishing practices were unnecessarily driving up the price of college textbooks, that college and university faculty were opposed to new editions and supplemental learning materials, and that students were being "ripped off" by being forced to purchase these materials at inflated prices. The report also attacked the practice of selling textbooks at market prices overseas.

Following release of the report, AAP President Pat Schroeder exchanged several letters with PIRG, questioning their charges, and again offering to work with PIRG to develop impartial research and to provide PIRG with sources of independent data. Schroeder and a representative of Zogby International, a nationally recognized polling company, subsequently met with PIRG at the AAP Washington office.

In an effort to communicate with college and university faculty, administrators, and students, AAP and member publishers participated in a series of forums on textbook pricing hosted in the spring by the Georgia University System Board of Regents at which a student, bookstore manager, faculty member, and publishing representative gave short presentations and participated in a discussion with the audience. Many issues were raised at the forums, but most apparent was the range and diversity of opinions surrounding the issue of textbook pricing.

On April 11, Schroeder spoke on behalf of the higher education textbook industry before the New York City Council's Higher Education Committee, identifying potential ways of helping students pay for textbooks.

Prompted by the first PIRG report, several members of Congress in 2004 signed a joint letter in 2004 to the General Accountability Office (GAO) requesting a study of textbook pricing. In August 2005, GAO released its report, attracting nationwide media interest. While AAP endorsed the key conclusions of the report—that the college textbook employs new technologies to enhance the educational experience for instructors and students and that publishers are assuming roles that traditionally belonged to postsecondary institutions—AAP expressed continuing concern that pricing analyses included in the study did not provide a balanced picture of the industry.

As 2005 progressed, PIRG's attacks moved from public relations initiatives to a push for legislation. As a result, an onslaught of textbook-pricing legislation was introduced in 22 states. Working with higher education publishers, AAP began tracking and then working to revise or defeat legislation it felt was ill-conceived.

In October higher education publishers and AAP participated in meetings in Hartford, Connecticut, and Richmond, Virginia—both mandated by the state legislatures—to discuss the cost of college textbooks with professors, bookstores, students, college and school administrators, and state government representatives. Publishing industry representatives discussed their role in the textbook market, outlining the industry's commitment to providing a wide range of textbook choices, providing faculty and students with textbook information, and sponsoring on-campus educational programs.

The central focus of the forums, hearings, GAO report, legislation, and media interviews was on methods of addressing the cost of textbooks. Recommendations included a ban on sales tax for textbooks, a requirement that texts be used for a certain amount of time, an initiative to increase the number of textbooks available through campus libraries, the creation of book vouchers for low-income students, and tax credits for learning materials.

At the federal level, textbook pricing and rental program bills were introduced in connection with the reauthorization of the Higher Education Act, a process that is continuing in 2006. AAP will continue to monitor these bills.

The "accessibility" issue also gained momentum in 2005, with legislators in several states introducing textbook-accessibility legislation that would create a patchwork of state rules and regulations, hindering rather than improving student access to materials. Many of the bills mandated that publishers provide instructional materials to postsecondary institutions in specified digital formats that would require expensive conversions. AAP and the Higher Education Critical Issues Task Force (CITF) worked with representatives of colleges, organizations for the disabled, and legislators to determine the best ways to meet college students' accessibility needs while protecting publishers' rights.

Higher Education Critical Issues Task Force

The Higher Education Critical Issues Task Force (CITF) consists of representatives of publishers of textbooks and other instructional materials for the postsecondary educational market in the United States. It works exclusively on issues involving the provision of accessible instructional materials to students with disabilities in postsecondary education.

Under various federal and state laws, colleges and universities must give disabled students equal and effective access to instructional materials. While services such as human readers are sometimes provided by educational institutions, another approach is to make the materials available in specialized formats (such as braille, audio, or digital text). Consequently, a number of states have passed additional legislation, known as "e-text" laws, requiring that when instructional materials are adopted for use in a course in which a disabled student is enrolled, the publisher will deliver the material to the college in an electronic format that can be either used directly or converted into another specialized format for use by the student with a print disability. Many publishers voluntarily provide e-text to campuses in states without such legislation as well.

Fulfilling electronic file requests often presents publishers with difficult challenges: in some instances, the publisher may not have electronic text of an older title produced through methods that did not require creation of a digital file; or the publisher may not possess the necessary copyright licenses to distribute the book electronically (if the author, illustrator, or photograph licensor, for example, withheld electronic distribution rights in licensing publication rights to the publisher). Converting a production file into the specific format requested can also be very costly. In addition, publishers have concerns about whether the electronic files will be secure against unauthorized reproduction and use by students for whom they were not intended.

CITF's efforts in 2005 included

- Announcing the Alternate Formats Initiative, an AAP effort in conjunction with disabled student services (DSS) professionals, organizations for the disabled, students, and others to develop national solutions to improve print-disabled students' timely access to postsecondary course materials (Rick Bowes, an accessibility expert, was to spearhead the 12-month effort, beginning in February 2006)

- Hosting a stakeholders meeting sponsored by the Association on Higher Education and Disability (AHEAD) E-Text Solutions Group to discuss key issues involved with the provision of accessible instructional materials
- Working with the New York State Education Department to provide upstate and downstate training sessions for campus DSS professionals on the requirements created by New York's postsecondary e-text legislation (known as "Chapter 219") and the implementation guidelines developed by CITF, DSS officials, the education department, advocacy organizations, and others
- Sending a delegation to the spring meeting of the Washington Association on Postsecondary Education and Disability (WAPED) to present AAP's proposed implementation guidelines for Washington State's postsecondary e-text legislation and to discuss colleges' and publishers' issues with DSS representatives from around the state
- Responding to legislative proposals in Georgia, Minnesota, and Oregon
- Giving talks and participating in roundtable discussions at the AHEAD annual conference in Milwaukee

International Sales Committee

The International Sales Committee represents a broad cross-section of the AAP membership with interests in overseas markets, focusing on issues relating to the export of mass market paperbacks. Composed of export sales directors from AAP member houses and chaired in 2005 by David Wolfson (HarperCollins), the group's major concerns are piracy, export online, and distribution and currency issues associated with export sales to the U.S. military, overseas schools, hotels, bookstores, and airports. The group works to facilitate publisher/bookseller/distributor dialogue at major book fairs. In addition to the committee's biannual meetings, members continued a series of meetings started in 2002 with former Frankfurt Book Fair Director Volker Neumann and Frankfurt Book Fair Marketing Director Thomas Minkus. These meetings have kept communication with Frankfurt open and permitted AAP members to have input into future Frankfurt Book Fair changes.

International Copyright Protection

AAP's International Copyright Protection program works to combat the problem of international copyright piracy, to increase fair access to foreign markets, and to strengthen foreign copyright law regimes. The program inaugurated a number of new initiatives in 2005 while continuing activities begun previously. Deborah Wiley (John Wiley & Sons) chaired the International Copyright Protection Committee in 2005.

In carrying out its overseas antipiracy campaign, AAP and the regional representatives of member publishers worked closely together and in cooperation with local government authorities. As a consequence, book pirates in six Asian locations felt the long reach of AAP's antipiracy campaign in a series of raids, educational activities, and policy initiatives coordinated by AAP throughout the year. The association and its members are pursuing legal actions growing out of the raids.

In the People's Republic of China, AAP worked in partnership with Britain's Publishers Association (PA) to conduct research on photocopying practices affecting sales of university textbooks. The survey revealed extensive copying at university-run textbook centers. AAP and PA brought the survey's results to the attention of government authorities and there are ongoing efforts to bring the unauthorized practices under control. In July AAP and PA conducted a market survey of street stalls and book markets in Beijing to reveal the extent of piracy of trade bestsellers. These findings were incorporated into a program held in Beijing in September, cosponsored by AAP, PA, and the Publishers Association of China, to highlight opportunities and challenges for publishers in that country. AAP and PA followed up the seminar with additional research on textbook piracy in October. Throughout the year, AAP also explored the growing phenomenon of trading Internet files containing book content. AAP was also engaged in a number of policy initiatives involving China, participated in the U.S. Ambassador's Intellectual Property Rights Roundtable in Beijing in January 2005, and cosponsored a number of seminars focusing on law reform, especially Internet regulation.

In South Korea, AAP worked with government authorities and the Korea Reprographic and Transmission Rights Center in raids on several illegal operations doing business in close proximity to 20 universities, primarily in the vicinity of Seoul; these resulted in the seizure of hundreds of illegal copies of copyrighted works. Supported by U.S. government policy, AAP succeeded in securing a letter from Korea's minister of education directing all universities in the country to formulate and implement plans to crack down on illegal copying on campuses. Continuing into the fall semester, AAP remained involved in both educational and enforcement initiatives, continuing to press for adherence to the minister of education's letter. In September AAP's investigators and law enforcement personnel raided the Woosung Munhwasa copy shop in Seoul, whose owner admitted that over the previous three years his shop had illegally produced copies of more than 10,000 copyrighted books. The 909 books confiscated in the raid included titles from major publishers including John Wiley & Sons, Thomson Learning, Pearson Education, McGraw-Hill, Blackwell, and Oxford University Press. A criminal complaint was filed. A few days later another raid, conducted against Jip-Hyun-Jeon copy shop, yielded several confiscated illegal copies of major publishers' works, including those of a number of university presses.

In Taiwan, AAP and member company representatives working through the local AAP group, the Taiwan Book Publishers Association (TBPA), and local police, under the supervision of the Ministry of Justice, raided pirate operations in Taipei City, Taoyuan, Taichung, and Tainan. As a follow-up, TBPA worked with a newly formed government group, the Intellectual Property Right Protecting Corps, in raids on several copy shops in March and April resulting in the seizure of hundreds of books belonging to a wide range of AAP members. Again, Taiwan geared up for the fall university term by undertaking a number of actions in September. In the five locations raided, officers seized 29 titles and 179 infringing copies of titles belonging to publishers Thomson Learning, Pearson Education, McGraw-Hill, John Wiley & Sons, Elsevier, and others. Interestingly, the shop pirated roughly equal numbers of English-language and Chinese-language books, showing that the problem is not limited to English-language titles.

Ongoing cooperation between local AAP publishers and the Hong Kong Customs and Excise Department resulted in a series of raids throughout the spring. In May authorities seized more than 150 copies at shops located throughout Hong Kong, in Causeway Bay, Shaukeiwan, and Tsuen Wan. Authorities also confiscated two machines and made three arrests. The Hong Kong government's efforts to combat piracy continued into the fall, not only working with rights-holders on enforcement actions but adapting those actions to the increasingly underground nature of Hong Kong's photocopy facilities. Government authorities also initiated a reward scheme in October in the hope of increasing the number of underground targets. In August law enforcement authorities confiscated four copiers and five binding machines and made seven arrests at four copy shops, seizing illegal copies valued at more than HK$82,000.00. In mid-September, officers seized 179 copies of books and four copiers and arrested three people at an underground copying facility housed in a residential unit. The same day, authorities searched two more shops where they found HK$120,000 worth of illegal commodities, including copying machines, and arrested the two shop owners. The October raid further underscored the seriousness of underground photocopying. In its post-raid press briefing, the Customs and Excise Department revealed that 1,510 infringing photocopies of textbooks and three machines, totaling about HK$200,000 in value, had been confiscated at two residential premises. In line with the enhanced enforcement and monitoring required to combat underground photocopying, the department investigated an additional 12 photocopy centers the following day, confiscating 962 illegal copies of books and three copiers in several cities. In addition to these highly successful enforcement actions, AAP has been engaged with the Hong Kong Commerce, Industry, and Technology Bureau as it looks toward revisions in its criminal piracy and fair use statutes.

In Malaysia, in the first of a series of raids, AAP lawyers working with local authorities seized 53 master copies (used for making hundreds of photocopies) and several copy machines from an illegal operation in Kuala Lumpur on June 23. In collaboration with local authorities, AAP conducted four more raids in July and one in August. The association had initiated a reward scheme in Malaysia earlier in the year and it is producing results. Acting on a tip, authorities raided a facility on July 21, seizing 201 books and illegal copies and two photocopy machines from two small premises. Less than a week later, officers hit three more locations in the vicinity of the National University of Malaysia. Officers found a combined total of about 100 infringing copies and originals. Finally, an enforcement action in Kajang resulted in confiscation of 320 copies of books and two large photocopying machines.

AAP also has been engaged in ongoing education efforts to keep university administrations and students—as well as copy shops—informed about the illegal nature of commercial-scale photocopying.

In the Philippines, the government's attention to the piracy problem was initially generated by the conviction of a copy shop operator through an AAP-sponsored legal action in 2004 that continued into 2005. Despite the sentencing, the pirate operation continued at full speed during the appeals process. As a result, in

August police again raided the operation, known as Multilinks Book Shop, seizing 21 boxes of original books, mostly medical textbooks, three copy machines and a computer. AAP is pushing for resolution of the cases.

In Singapore, AAP cosponsored a seminar on legal reform in January 2005 and has participated in a number of educational initiatives for copy shop owners, as well as ongoing programs by the Intellectual Property Office of Singapore. The association continues to coordinate enforcement issues with the Singapore Police.

In Thailand, pushing for legal reform, AAP worked with U.S. government officials to craft appropriate language to be put forward during the U.S.-Thailand Free Trade Agreement (FTA) negotiations. AAP members are faced with the ongoing problem of an overly broad fair use provision in Thailand, which it is hoped can be corrected as FTA negotiations continue. AAP and its members also began work on an education program aimed at Thai students.

In addition, AAP and its member companies were active in education, policymaking, and related initiatives in countries including India, Pakistan, Vietnam, and Indonesia. AAP worked throughout the year on legal reform and enforcement issues at the political level worldwide, with a notable increase in efforts in Central and South America, Canada, South Asia, and the Middle East.

The Office of the United States Trade Representative (USTR) releases its annual Special 301 Report each year, detailing the adequacy and effectiveness of intellectual property protection in selected countries worldwide. AAP, as a member of the International Intellectual Property Alliance (IIPA), submitted specific recommendations to USTR on February 11, 2005, as part of the annual review. AAP members estimated annual losses of more than $603 million as a result of copyright piracy. The Special 301 process is one of several tools available to the U.S. government to help industries fight to improve legislative and enforcement efforts in key markets in an attempt to stem losses from copyright piracy. AAP works hard to ensure that, in this process and all U.S. government engagements throughout the year, its members' voices are heard.

International Freedom to Publish

AAP's International Freedom to Publish Committee (IFTPC) defends and promotes freedom of written communication worldwide. The committee monitors human rights issues and provides moral support and practical assistance to publishers and authors outside the United States who are denied basic freedoms. The committee carries on its work in close cooperation with other human rights groups, including Human Rights Watch and PEN American Center, and maintains its own Web site at http://www.iftpc.org. Hal Fessenden (Viking Penguin) became chair of the committee in 2004.

In spring 2003 the committee established the Jeri Laber International Freedom to Publish Award, to be given annually to a book publisher outside the United States who has demonstrated courage in the face of political persecution. The award, which carries a $10,000 cash prize, is named in honor of human rights activist Jeri Laber, one of IFTPC's founding members, who continues to direct its work as a consultant to AAP. In 2005 the committee's third annual award went to Turkish publisher Abdullah Keskin of Avesta Publishing House, the first publisher in Turkey to publish in the Kurdish language, and at a time when it was prohibited to do so. More than ten of Avesta's books have been banned, and Keskin has been frequently tried and fined. The award was presented in April 2005 at the PEN gala in New York.

In December 2004, in an effort to encourage and increase the diversity of literary works being published in the United States, the committee offered U.S. publishers a unique opportunity to bring the work of three gifted Iranian authors to an American audience. In consultation with a distinguished group of scholars and writers in the United States and Iran, the committee commissioned partial translations and a precis of several Iranian literary works and secured funding that enabled it to provide $10,000 each to U.S. publishers contracting for English-language rights for each work. The money was used to assist in additional translation costs and for promotion and publicity. The project was completed at the end of 2005. *Strange Times, My Dear: The PEN Anthology of Contemporary Iranian Literature* was published by Arcade Publishing in 2005; Shahmoush Parsipour's *Tooba and the Meaning of Night* will be published in March 2006 by the Feminist Press; and Mahmoud Dowlatabadi's *The Empty House of Solouch* is being published by Melville House.

IFTPC members undertake (at their own expense) missions to meet with writers, publishers, human rights activists, and others in areas where freedom of expression is seriously threatened. Committee chairman Fessenden and member Wendy Wolfe (Viking Penguin) undertook such a mission to Turkey in late 2004. Accompanied by historian Joshua Brown and journalist Dawn Drzal, they spent five days in Istanbul meeting with a wide variety of book publishers, journalists, NGOs, and human rights activists. They found the mood to be generally optimistic but wary. The crisis of a few years ago has abated, in large measure as a result of Turkey's determination to conform to guidelines to gain entrance into the European Union. However, publishers—especially those who deal with Kurdish issues, the Armenian genocide, the military, and arbitrarily defined "insults to the state"—are still being detained, fined, and harassed. In a return visit to Istanbul in November 2005, Fessenden and committee member Bill Strachan attended a freedom-of-expression conference to support writers and publishers in peril, including Orhan Pamuk, Fatih Tas, and Ragip Zarakolu, all of whom faced trials in spring 2006. IFTPC will coordinate with an international community of activists to champion the rights of these writers to free expression.

In February 2005 IFTPC members Fessenden and Peternelle Van Arsdale went to Egypt where they met with Egyptian publishers and discussed the political and religious pressures under which they are forced to operate.

Postal

AAP's Postal Committee coordinates activity in the area of postal rates and regulations, monitors developments at the U.S. Postal Service and the independent Postal Rate Commission, and intervenes on the industry's behalf in formal proceedings before the commission. The committee also directs AAP lobbying activities on postal issues. Paul DeGuisti (McGraw Hill) chaired the committee in 2005.

Professional/Scholarly Publishing

The Professional/Scholarly Publishing (PSP) Division of AAP is composed of AAP members who publish books, journals, and looseleaf and electronic products in technology, science, medicine, business, law, the humanities, the behavioral sciences, and scholarly reference. Professional societies and university presses play an important role in the division. Marc Brodsky (American Institute of Physics) chaired the division in 2005.

The 2005 PSP Annual Conference in Washington, D.C., in February had as its theme "Managing the Publishing Mix: All Media, All Markets" and featured as speakers U.S. Rep. Howard L. Berman (D-Calif.) and Elias A. Zerhouni, director, National Institutes of Health. The division's Electronic Information Committee sponsored a preconference seminar on "How to Survive and Thrive in a Search Engine Culture." The division sponsors an awards program, open only to AAP/PSP members, to acknowledge outstanding achievements in professional, scholarly, and reference publishing. At the 29th annual PSP Awards, the R. R. Hawkins Award for the outstanding professional/scholarly work of the year went to the Harvard University Press for *Huck's Raft: A History of American Childhood,* by Steven Mintz. In addition, book awards were presented in more than 30 subject categories, in design and production, and in journal and electronic publishing.

Among the division's educational activities in 2005, the PSP Journals Committee sponsored a roundtable discussion, "What's the point of XML?" and the ninth biennial Journals Boot Camp was held in Chicago.

The PSP Public Issues Task Force has developed and maintains the *PSP Issues Glossary,* an online reference and research tool for PSP members. This glossary is available through a new link on the home page of the PSP Web site (http://www.pspcentral.org).

The PSP Executive Council directs an ongoing campaign to improve relationships between the PSP communities and user and scholar communities. The campaign explains the role PSP members play and the value they add to the dissemination of scholarly information. In 2005 the executive council established the American Medical Publishers Committee, whose goals are to educate, advocate, engage in outreach and philanthropy, and frame issues of relevance to medical publishers, including promoting a positive image of scientific and medical publishing. The committee is chaired by Maureen DeRosa (American Academy of Pediatrics) and Thane Kerner (Silverchair).

In a lengthy process, PSP, in partnership with author and other publishing organizations, confronted the Office of Foreign Assets Controls (OFAC) within the U.S. Treasury Department about its practice of demanding that publishers seek licenses to process manuscripts from certain embargoed countries. PSP holds that this practice is unconstitutional and illegal. A year of negotiation with OFAC and other government entities yielded little progress until PSP and its partner litigants filed a lawsuit against OFAC seeking to end the practice. Soon thereafter, before ever formally responding to the court about PSP's legal action, OFAC issued regulations freeing publishers to carry on with publishers' review, editing, marketing, and other normal business activities involving the manuscripts in question. PSP is still negotiating details of the new OFAC regulations with the government before withdrawing its lawsuit.

PSP has been actively representing publisher interests in dealing with attempts to use the results of publisher investments on government Web sites that are seeking to republish, modify, and freely deliver articles that are based in part on government-funded research.

In other countries, PSP has cooperated with international publishing associations to find the right balance between fair use of intellectual property and rights holders' needs to be able to realize a fair return for their works. The division has worked with Britain's Publishers Association and the International Scientific, Technical, and Medical Association to produce the first international annual Journals Statistics Survey.

Resources for the Book Publishing Industry

AAP publishes a variety of resources for the book publishing industry, including the Survey on Compensation and Personnel Practices in the Book Publishing Industry, which is widely regarded as the most comprehensive and reliable source of data in this area. AAP's Compensation Committee, composed of senior compensation and human resources professionals, met throughout the year to create job descriptions and manage the survey process.

AAP also publishes industry statistics for all segments of book publishing, on a monthly and annual basis. Committees in the areas of consumer, trade, higher education, and professional publishing met throughout 2005 to revise the program and develop a seamless system for the distribution of electronic monthly reports.

AAP is also working in concert with the Book Industry Study Group (BISG) on how methods in which statistics are compiled and communicated throughout the industry could be more streamlined.

School Division

The AAP School Division is concerned with publishing for the elementary and secondary school (K–12) market. The division works to enhance the role of instructional materials in the education process, to maintain categorical funding for instructional materials and increase the funds available for the purchase of these materials, to simplify and rationalize the process of state adoptions for instructional materials, and to generally improve the climate in which educational publishers do business. The division serves as a bridge between the publishing industry and the educational community, promoting the cause of education at the national and state level, and working closely with an effective lobbying network in key adoption states. Julie McGee (Harcourt Education) chaired the division in 2005.

The year 2005 was a challenging and difficult one for AAP's K–12 publishers, in large measure because of events in Texas, the nation's second-largest textbook market. The sudden and unanticipated resignation of AAP's longtime Texas lobbyist at the beginning of the year could not have come at a worse time—just two weeks before the start of the legislative session, which was to consider measures that could have substantial adverse impact on school publishers. An extensive search resulted in the selection of new, highly qualified lobbying team composed of Louann Martinez (former associate executive director of governmental relations for the Texas Association of School Administrators), David Thompson (former counsel of the Texas Education Agency and one of the state's leading education attorneys), and the law firm Johnson and Johnson. By the time the new team was in place, the legislature was already in session and dealing with such problematic issues as the elimination of categorical funding, elimination of the adoption cycle, and implementation of a program to provide students with laptops at the expense of needed instructional materials.

Another challenge facing AAP members in Texas in 2005 was instructional materials funding. The previous legislative session had deferred appropriating the $327 million needed to purchase materials adopted under Proclamation 2001. In addition, Proclamation 2002, under which schools were due to buy new instructional materials for classes starting in the fall of 2005, needed funding of $387 million. While the funding for Proclamation 2001 was agreed to early in the session, funding for Proclamation 2002 was in doubt for much of 2005, notwithstanding the fact that publishers had, in good faith, printed these textbooks in anticipation of school purchases in the spring of 2005. Further complicating the situation was the fact that Texas's educational funding system had been found unconstitutional and there were major differences between the two bodies of the Texas legislature over how to deal with this issue. AAP priorities such as instructional materials funding and reform of the adoption process were caught up in the broader school finance battle.

Working with the lobbying team, AAP succeeded in having the issue of instructional materials funding raised to a high priority, and in August $295.5 million in funding was approved to pay for Proclamation 2002. Publishers noted with concern, however, that a rider was attached to the budget that directs the State Board of Education to defer issuing future proclamations until the legislature implements state textbook procurement reforms.

Fortunately, developments in California, Florida, and the other significant instructional materials states were less problematic in 2005.

In Florida, AAP lobbying efforts were able to produce a $13.6 million (6 percent) increase in funding for instructional materials. The used-book pilot program AAP helped establish several years ago continued to demonstrate that schools achieved minimal (less than 1 percent) savings by purchasing used textbooks while at the same time losing many of the benefits, such as professional development, that come with buying new programs.

It was a good year for AAP in the nation's largest state for instructional materials, California. Even though K–12 education suffered a cut of $1.8 billion, funding for instructional materials remained stable. In fact, in great measure because of AAP's lobbying efforts, funding for instructional materials in California has actually increased 35 percent over the past four years.

AAP efforts were also effective in two other states: Georgia, where legislation that would have mandated an electronic version of every adopted textbook was defeated; and New York, where funding for instructional materials was increased and efforts to allow schools to use their instructional materials dollars to buy computer hardware were derailed.

In December 2004 major changes to the Individuals with Disabilities Education Act (IDEA) were signed into law. IDEA establishes a new National Instructional Materials Accessibility Standard (NIMAS) that K–12 publishers must use to create an electronic file of their core instructional materials to assist in making these materials more accessible to students with print disabilities. IDEA also established a national repository for these files to facilitate getting the files out to schools that need them.

AAP played an important role in helping craft these instructional accessibility provisions and continues to work on two national advisory panels established to oversee implementation of both the NIMAS file format and the National Instructional Materials Access Center (NIMAC). Steve Driesler, AAP School Division's executive director and Rick Ferrie (Pearson Education), who chairs the division's Serving Students with Disabilities Committee, are the industry's official representatives on both advisory panels.

In 2007 ISBN numbers will be increased from the current 10 to 13 digits. This change has potential implementation problems for publishers, their customers, and the supply chain. To ease this transition, the School Division launched a major effort to educate customers about this coming change and to work to make this transition as smooth as possible. The division did a nationwide informational mailing to school district administrators, purchasing directors, information technology directors, and other school system officials, and has held a number of meetings with textbook depositories and the National Association of State Textbook Administrators (NASTA) on this matter.

In fall 2005 AAP held another of its education summits in Washington, D.C., bringing together publishers, educators, public officials, and academic experts to discuss the important and timely topic of how to improve middle and high school education.

While AAP strongly supported enactment of the Reading First program as part of the No Child Left Behind (NCLB) Act, it raised concerns with then-Secretary of Education Rod Paige about the unfairness of a perceived "approved list" of reading programs eligible for Reading First funding. During the more than five years since the establishment of Reading First, AAP has continued to express concern over potential conflicts of interest with program reviews, the arbitrary way in which programs were reviewed, and—now that few new programs are being reviewed at all by the Technical Advisory Centers established to help implement NCLB—the concern that new products that have been developed are being ignored.

Over the past year, the Reading First Program came under increased scrutiny in Congress and in the press, and the Department of Education's inspector general launched an investigation into publishers' allegations of unfair treatment. Also, the chairman (Sen. Michael B. Enzi, R-Wyo.) and ranking Democrat (Sen. Edward M. Kennedy, D-Mass.) on the Senate Committee on Health, Education, Labor, and Pensions have asked the U.S. Comptroller General for an investigation into Reading First. Although the outcome is yet to be determined, it is evident that AAP's concerns over the implementation of Reading First were well founded.

Trade Publishing

AAP's Trade Publishing Group comprises publishers of fiction, general nonfiction, poetry, children's literature, religious, and reference publications, in hardcover, paperback, and electronic formats. Robert Miller (Hyperion) chaired the committee in 2005.

The group's major areas of attention in 2005 included the ongoing development of a nonfiction book club with ABC Television's "The View" for which AAP will serve as a clearinghouse for titles publishers would like the program to consider. The book club plans to feature entertaining, upbeat, informative books, on topics that coincide with the various interest of the five hosts and the viewing audience, including beauty, health, fashion, celebrity, relationships, literary nonfiction, and others.

In 2005 AAP began work with the National Endowment for the Arts (NEA), providing NEA with proposed communications illustrating the support publishers can provide to organizations working with the endowment on local "city reads" programs via NEA's umbrella "Big Read" campaign. "The Big Read" is intended to foster and facilitate "city reads" programs—in which everyone in a city is encouraged to read a certain book—across the nation.

AAP works to increase awareness of Latino books through its Publishing Latino Voices for America (PLVA) Task Force, which produced the ¡Ajá, leyendo! campaign; the committee also produced a Publishing Latino Voices brochure featuring selected Spanish-language titles, and English titles written by Latinos, which was distributed to booksellers and librarians during Hispanic Heritage Month. A series of sessions for the Spanish and Latin American market were also presented in concert with PLVA at BookExpo America 2005. AAP also met with the Spanish Embassy to discuss partnering on the America Reads Spanish campaign.

AAP also expanded its Adopt-A-School program with the New York City Department of Education. The program has grown to involve an additional 25 schools since its launch in 2004, and gives publishers the opportunity to support city schools by providing specific resources that schools request through AAP, including books, guidance in developing literary publications and yearbooks, author visits and events, field trips to publishing houses, and participation in career fairs at schools.

The AAP Trade Group also works on the AAP Honors program, nominating and electing a candidate from outside the publishing industry who has helped promote American books and authors to be honored at the AAP Annual Meeting. Selection of the 2005 honoree, the book team at *USA Today,* reflected the impact of the media's influence throughout the nation on books and reading. The book team was recognized for its ongoing efforts to heighten editorial focus and its outstanding coverage of books, authors, and reading.

Trade Libraries Committee

AAP's Trade Libraries Committee is made up of representatives of major book publishing houses in partnership with organizations including ALA, Friends of Libraries USA (FOLUSA), and *Library Journal.* In June 2005 AAP announced the launch of a new Web site, Authors @ your library (http://www.AuthorsAt YourLibrary.org), which links publishers and librarians to simplify the process of scheduling library events. Authors @ your library is a free online "matchmaking" service for librarians who want to schedule successful author events, and for publishers who are seeking enthusiastic audiences for their authors.

Other library activities included research on state funding and support initiatives and exploring ways in which publishers might advocate for library funding in select states through lobbying efforts. At the federal level, expressing the publishing industry's support for America's libraries, AAP sent letters to the chairman and ranking member of the House Appropriations Subcommittee on Labor, Health, Human Services, and Education urging full funding for the Library Services and Technology Act (LSTA) and the Improving Literacy Through School Libraries Program, in line with President Bush's budget request.

AAP continues to work with librarian associations including the Public Library Association and ALA on initiatives supporting the library community.

Small and Independent Publishers

AAP's Smaller and Independent Publishing Committee held a seminar in conjunction with AAP's Annual Meeting in March 2005. The all-day program, "Creating a Successful Publishing Strategy: Capitalizing on Your Publishing Niche," included sessions on "Consumer Outlets: Selling Directly to the Consumer," "Maximizing Your Opportunities Through Special Sales," "Trade Outlets: Bookstores, Libraries and Other Traditional Channels," "Spotting Crossover Marketing Potential: Moving a Title from Niche to Mainstream," and "Creating Alternative Formats: Repurposing Titles for a Second Life. Opportunities on the Internet."

AAP awarded its second Miriam Bass Award for Creativity in Independent Publishing. Established in memory of the contributions Miriam Bass made to the industry in her career working with independent publishers, the award carries a $5,000 prize funded by Rowman & Littlefield and National Book Network. The 2005 award went to Johnny Temple of Akashic Books.

Young to Publishing Group

The Young to Publishing Group (YPG) continued its expansion in 2005, growing to 1,000 members, an increase of almost 300 from 2004. The group's brown bag lunch series in New York featured speakers from across the industry, and chapters in Boston and San Diego grew as well. The YPG group hosted several social events in 2005, and continued to publish the popular *YPG Newsletter*.

Annual Meeting Highlights

Just days before AAP's 2005 General Annual Meeting in New York, organizers were scurrying to find larger meeting rooms to accommodate a last-minute registration rush that brought attendance close to 300. By holding a joint meeting in New York, with *Publishers Weekly* as a cosponsor, AAP was apparently able to tap into a reserve of interested publishers who missed out on previous meetings because of travel time but were happy to taxi across town for this year's event. The intensely focused, business-oriented program seemed to generate a good deal of interest.

Speakers included Pulitzer Prize-winning author James Stewart and corporate strategy guru Peter Skarzynski, who led a panel of innovators in a discussion that included the power of "buzz" marketing (David Balter), changes in wholesale distribution driven by changing customer expectations and a renewed interest in the backlist (Jim Chandler), seeking sustainable long-term growth in K–12 publishing and the need not to remain a zero-sum game (Pat Tierney), the need to provide children's content in a range of formats (Deborah Dugan), the need for retailers and publishers to communicate on a level beyond their normal economic relationships (Greg Josefowicz), and the opportunities for creating online content-based businesses for offline brands and content owners (Ben Wolin).

Other speakers included New York City Schools Chancellor Joel Klein, *Publishers Weekly* editor-in-chief Sara Nelson, Latino bookseller and entrepreneur Rueben Martinez, Audible Inc. CEO Donald Katz, graphic novel author/artists Art Spiegelman and Neil Gaiman, and manga maven John Parker.

Ferlinghetti, Jovanovich Receive Awards

The Curtis Benjamin Award for Creative Publishing was presented to Lawrence Ferlinghetti, cofounder of the San Francisco bookstore and publisher City Lights. The octogenarian poet, publisher, and bookseller was unable to make the trip from San Francisco, but sent a note expressing his surprise and gratitude at getting "this prestigious publishers award," saying that he takes the award "as recognition for the accomplishments of the independent presses and the bookstores that support them . . ." The inscription on the plaque reads "For Lawrence Ferlinghetti: courageous publisher and independent spirit, who has challenged complacency and celebrated the right to dissent for half a century.

Peter Jovanovich received a special Mary McNulty Award, the School Division's highest honor, for lifetime service to educational publishing. Jovanovich, who served as AAP chairman from 1998 to 2000, stepped down in 2005 as CEO of Pearson Education.

Lucki, Sarnoff, Sargent Head AAP Board

Anthony Lucki (Houghton Mifflin), Richard Sarnoff (Random House), and John Sargent (Holtzbrinck) were elected AAP officers for fiscal year (FY) 2005–2006, which began April 1, 2005. Lucki will serve a two-year term as chairman of the AAP Board of Directors, succeeding Jane Friedman, with Sarnoff as vice chair and Sargent as treasurer.

Lucki is president and CEO of Houghton Mifflin Company, to which he returned in 2003 after serving as president and CEO of Harcourt, Inc. Lucki, who holds a master's degree in teaching from the University of Louisville, began his publishing career in 1975 as an assistant editor at Allyn & Bacon. He joined Houghton Mifflin in 1977, moving up through the corporate ranks and then moving on, first to Macmillan and then to Harcourt.

Membership Approves Budget

The membership approved an operating budget of $7,294,580 for FY 2005–2006, with $4,269,280 allocated to core programs (including the two committees serving the Trade and International constituencies), $700,000 to the Higher Education Committee, and $2,325,300 to the two divisions ($1,509,800 for the School Division and $815,500 for PSP).

American Booksellers Association

200 White Plains Rd., Tarrytown, NY 10591
914-591-2665, World Wide Web http://www.BookWeb.org

Jill Perlstein
Director of Marketing

Founded in 1900, the American Booksellers Association (ABA) is a not-for-profit trade organization devoted to meeting the needs of its core members—independently owned bookstores with storefront locations—by providing advocacy, opportunities for peer interaction, education, support services, and new business models. ABA actively supports free speech, literacy, and programs that encourage reading. The association also hosts the annual ABA Convention in conjunction with the BookExpo America conference and trade show each spring.

2005 Highlights

An increase in the number of provisional members (individuals planning to open new bookstores) and steady levels of membership retention gave ABA a strong foundation during 2005 for its board and staff to continue the work of helping independent booksellers meet the challenges of a changing retail environment.

In June ABA moved its headquarters to a smaller location in an office complex in Tarrytown, New York.

In September, following the devastating hurricanes that hit the Gulf Coast, ABA established a Bookseller Relief Fund. By the end of the year, the fund had helped more than 40 booksellers cover the cost of such basic needs as food, housing, and transportation. In addition to offering financial relief, ABA provided the means—via its Web site, http://www.BookWeb.org—for booksellers to offer other types of support (such as temporary housing and jobs) to their peers.

Strategic Plan

Although ABA provides programs and services to others in the bookselling industry, its primary focus is on its core members, which provide influential and vital links between authors, readers, publishers, and the community.

Key components of ABA's strategic plan, "Independent Bookselling: Competing in a Changing World," for the years 2003–2007, and how its goals are being met, follow.

Goal 1—Provide independent professional booksellers with access to the education, information, and business services they need to succeed in a changing world.

To fulfill this goal, the association once again conducted the annual ABA Convention in conjunction with BookExpo America (BEA). ABA organized a full day of educational programming at BEA, offering a variety of peer-to-peer and interactive opportunities. New York's Javits Convention Center hosted more than 35,000 book industry professionals. "Hotel ABA"—an exclusive bookseller-only hotel where members get to benefit from group-rate rooms, publisher-sponsored receptions, welcome bags, shuttle buses, and more—was a sold-out success.

In keeping with ABA's focus on education, the association surveyed its members and created an education task force. Both the results of the survey and input from the task force were used as the foundation for creating educational offerings at BEA and throughout the year.

Year three of the relaunched ABACUS project (the financial benchmark study by and for independent booksellers) was completed and continued to provide participants with information essential to improving a bookstore's bottom line. ABA offered several financial-education programs, among them "Increasing Sales," "Increasing Margin," "Cost of Goods 101," "Renegotiating a Lease," and "The 2 Percent Solution—An Introduction to Profitability." In conjunction with bookstore training and consulting group Paz & Associates, the association also sponsored education programs for both prospective booksellers and new booksellers at BEA and at other times during the year. ABA also offered education programs at ten regional trade shows.

Fourteen bookseller forums were organized and facilitated, at least one in every region of the country, with 288 booksellers attending from 192 stores in 39 states. The forums provided members an opportunity to meet with representatives of the ABA board and senior staff to discuss issues of concern and to share ideas, as well as to get an update on the association's activities and to influence future plans.

BookWeb.org—an important source of association news, services, and resources—provides networking opportunities via the online forums "Idea Exchange" and "Ask ABA." An education forum was added in 2005. Booksellers are encouraged to post materials, share experiences, and ask questions. BookWeb.org also provides links to related industry organizations and companies, in addition to educational materials and professional development resources. It is home to the new Booksellers Resource Directory (BRD), a listing of vendors of nonbook products and services. BRD is open to ABA bookstore, provisional, and publisher members. It replaces the former Bookstore Source Guide with an updated database of vendors of sidelines, office supplies, display fixtures, computer hardware and software, design services, and more, in a user-friendly format.

Bookselling This Week (*BTW*) offers weekly news dispatches by e-mail to more than 10,000 subscribers. *BTW* features breaking industry news, in-depth articles, the latest developments in ABA's Book Sense marketing program, and other association news. Industry professionals have access to *BTW* via http://news.BookWeb.org and can create their own easy-to-print editions of the newsletter. "BTW Flashes" alert readers to important developments in a variety of subjects.

The ABA *Book Buyer's Handbook,* available online to members at BookWeb.org, is a source of publishers' discount schedules, return policies, trade terms, and more, including links to publishers' Web sites and e-mail addresses for ordering and general information. Fully searchable and regularly updated, it also lists the latest information on publishers' special offers. In the past year, more than 1,800 publisher records were updated.

Goal II—Serve as the voice of professional independent booksellers and advocate on their behalf on such issues as free expression, trade practices, literacy, and community activism.

ABA continued to play a leading role in the fight to restore the safeguards for the privacy of bookstore and library records that were threatened by the USA Patriot Act. With its partners in the Campaign for Reader Privacy, it achieved several important victories during the year. In June, the House of Representatives approved Rep. Bernie Sanders' (I-Vt.) Freedom to Read Amendment by a vote of 238–187, cutting off funds for bookstore and library searches under Section 215 of the USA Patriot Act. However, the House subsequently approved a bill reauthorizing Section 215 and other expiring sections of the act without including important protections for reader privacy. In July reader privacy advocates won a second important victory when the Senate passed a USA Patriot Act reauthorization bill that restricted bookstore and library searches to the records of people suspected of terrorism. In September the sponsors of the Campaign for Reader Privacy delivered to Capitol Hill petitions bearing more than 200,000 signatures that had been collected in hundreds of bookstores and libraries around the country. However, an effort to reach a compromise between the House and Senate failed in December. [The campaign continued until March 7, when the House voted 280–138 to renew the act. The president signed the legislation into law March 9, with its controversial provisions regarding bookstore and library records intact.—*Ed.*]

ABA also maintained trade practice vigilance through ongoing meetings with publishers, wholesalers, and others. ABA worked with other industry leaders in the continued fight for sales tax equity. It also compiled and disseminated information on the positive economic impact of locally owned businesses, and it continued to build alliances with like-minded independent retailers.

ABA carried on its work with the Book Industry Study Group (BISG) to disseminate information about the 13-digit ISBN, which will begin to affect the industry in 2007. ABA supported this industry initiative by facilitating conversations between booksellers and point-of-sale vendors and by distributing important information. As a BISG board member, ABA represents the concerns of independent booksellers facing industry standardization and global influences.

ABA also worked closely with the Institute for Local Self-Reliance, Home Town Advantage, American Independent Business Alliance (AMIBA), Business Alliance for Local Living Economies (BALLE), and Civic Economics to disseminate information about the importance of locally based independent businesses and how booksellers can form local business alliances. Advertisements promoting the value of shopping locally, based on findings about the importance of locally owned independent businesses, were created and published in a number of Book Sense Picks lists. Materials created by a variety of "local first" groups and regional booksellers associations were disseminated to ABA membership. In addition, ABA organized a series of meetings with independent business associations to examine the issues confronting "Main Street America."

In addition, ABA supported the following industry-wide observances: the Association of American Publishers (AAP) Get Caught Reading campaign and Latino Book Month, the Audio Publishers Association's audio book promotion, the National Book Festival, the American Library Association's Teen Read Week, the Children's Book Council's National Children's Book Week, the Academy of American Poets' National Poetry Month, the Small Press Center's Small Press Month, Banned Books Week, the National Book Awards, the Quill Awards, and the James Patterson PageTurner Awards.

Goal III—Promote the value of independent booksellers as a group through Book Sense and other cooperative activities.

Book Sense ("Independent Bookstores for Independent Minds") is ABA's national branding and marketing program for independent bookstores. The program continued to grow in popularity during 2005 and now has more than 1,200 participating locations in the United States, Bermuda, Puerto Rico, and the Virgin Islands.

In early 2005 the program was relaunched in an effort to broaden its appeal to all types of independent bookstores. The paper gift certificate program was discontinued and the letter of agreement revised. Booksellers currently benefit from two mailings a month. One, the Book Sense Red Box, contains timely marketing materials; the second, the Book Sense White Box, contains publishers' galley proofs, advance reading copies, and promotional materials from Book Sense publisher partners.

The main components of the Book Sense program are

- Book Sense Picks, 25 lists featuring notable titles recommended by independent booksellers. The program includes a monthly "Picks" list of recommendations; three children's lists; the annual Reading Group Guide, Paperback, and Highlights lists; and a number of "top ten" lists.
- The Book Sense Bestseller List, compiled from nearly 500 reporting stores each week. Regional and extended lists are created each week, specialty category lists biweekly.
- Book Sense Book of the Year Awards for adult fiction, nonfiction, children's illustrated, and children's literature.
- The Book Sense Gift Card Program. Consumers can purchase and redeem gift cards in more than 370 locations in 47 states and on some bookstores' Web sites. Book Sense gift cards never expire and carry no inactivity fees or other hidden fees. This year booksellers were offered new card designs featuring Harry Potter, a quote from *To Kill a Mockingbird,* and special-occasion cards.
- BookSense.com, an e-commerce Web site that allows participating stores to offer a secure shopping environment and to market their bookstores. BookSense.com hosts more than 240 independent bookstores' Web sites and offers consumers a choice when shopping online. Cooperative programs, inventory uploads, and easy-to-use tools allow booksellers to create Web sites that reflect their store's personality. BookSense.com has more than 2,000 affiliates.

The Book Sense program benefits its Publisher Partners by offering effective marketing tools, including Advance Access, an e-mail update of available advance reading copies and other materials.

Building on the success of the 2004 publication *Book Sense Best Books: 125 Favorite Books Recommended by Independent Booksellers* (Newmarket Press), Book Sense and Newmarket published *Book Sense Best Children's Books: 240 Favorites for All Ages Recommended by Independent Booksellers,* which featured a foreword by bestselling author Cornelia Funke and an introduction by Book Sense Marketing Director Mark Nichols.

Goal IV—Foster development of new and enhanced business models, systems, and services.

ABA continued to offer business management services to its members. These include services from LIBRIS, which offers casualty and property insurance for booksellers and liability insurance for publishers; Partnership, which provides small and large package shipping services via FedEx Ground, FedEx Express, and Yellow Freight; CDW Computer Centers, providing members with access to computer hardware at reduced prices; Bank of America, which offers members competitive rates for credit card processing; and Constant Contact, which gives members an easy-to-use Web-based e-mail marketing service to create, mail, and manage e-mail newsletter campaigns.

American Booksellers Foundation for Free Expression

The American Booksellers Foundation for Free Expression (ABFFE), the bookseller's voice in the fight against censorship, continued in 2005 to lead the effort to defend the privacy of bookstore customers. Since 2001 ABFFE has worked to educate booksellers about the adverse impact on bookstores of the USA Patriot Act, which eliminated crucial safeguards on the privacy of bookstore records. During 2005 ABFFE's newsletter, *ABFFE Update,* provided regular reports on the fight being waged in Congress to add reader privacy protections to the act.

ABFFE filed a friend-of-the-court brief in an American Civil Liberties Union (ACLU) action defending a Connecticut librarian's challenge to a "national security letter" seeking information about a patron's use of a library computer to search the Internet. ABFFE is participating in two other ACLU cases that involve reader privacy: a challenge in Michigan to the constitutionality of Section 215 of the USA Patriot Act, and an effort to invalidate a national security letter issued to an Internet service provider. Decisions in all three cases were pending at the time this report was prepared.

ABFFE launched a new effort to use bookstores as a forum for educating the public about First Amendment issues. In conjunction with a media group, the MLRC (Media Law Resource Center) Institute, ABFFE offered to provide bookstores with a reporter to talk about how the growing attack on using confidential sources threatens free speech. Booksellers responded enthusiastically; more than 50 have agreed to host programs on "reporters' privilege." They were planned for early 2006.

ABFFE continued to speak out in defense of First Amendment rights. It joined the National Coalition Against Censorship (NCAC) in criticizing a University of Colorado investigation of one of its professors, Ward Churchill. The governor and members of the legislature demanded that Churchill be fired for statements that they viewed as condoning the September 11, 2001, terrorist attacks. No disciplinary action was taken against Churchill. ABFFE and NCAC also joined in condemning the removal of three books on sexuality from school libraries in Fayetteville, Arkansas. The school board restored the books after its lawyer said it was on shaky legal ground based on a 2003 decision that overturned a ban on Harry Potter books in another Arkansas school district. ABFFE had filed an amicus brief in that case as well.

ABFFE joined two Utah bookstores, the King's English and Sam Weller's Zion Bookstore, in challenging a Utah law that bans the display on Web sites of material that is "harmful to minors." ABFFE has participated in lawsuits overturning numerous Internet censorship laws that restrict the ability of booksellers to sell constitutionally protected material on the Internet. In May 2005 a judge struck down a South Carolina law that ABFFE had challenged. ABFFE has also attacked laws that unconstitutionally restrict the display of "harmful" material in "bricks-and-mortar" (non-Internet) bookstores. In February 2005 Arkansas conceded defeat in a case ABFFE had filed in 2003.

ABFFE is a sponsor of Banned Books Week, a national celebration of the freedom to read. In 2005 ABFFE created an online resource manual to make it easier for booksellers to participate. It is available through the ABFFE Web site, http://www.abffe.com.

Association of Research Libraries

21 Dupont Circle N.W., Washington, DC 20036
202-296-2296, e-mail arlhq@arl.org
World Wide Web http://www.arl.org

Duane E. Webster
Executive Director

The Association of Research Libraries (ARL) represents 123 principal research libraries serving major research institutions in the United States and Canada. ARL influences the changing environment of scholarly communication and the public policies that affect research libraries and the communities they serve. ARL pursues this mission by advancing the goals of its member research libraries, providing leadership in public and information policy to the scholarly and higher education communities, fostering the exchange of ideas and expertise, and shaping a future environment that leverages its interests with those of allied organizations.

In November 2004 the ARL Board of Directors approved a new strategic plan for 2005–2009 that describes a three-pronged framework to replace the earlier structure of eight program objectives. ARL will fulfill its mission and build its programs in the coming years along three strategic directions—scholarly communication; public policies affecting research libraries; and the library's role in the transformation of research, teaching, and learning.

The ARL board established an implementation team to identify a process that the association could use to realize the strategic plan. Among its recommendations was a reorganization of membership participation in the association through three Strategic Direction Steering Committees, four board committees (Finance, Membership, Nomination, and Statistics and Assessment), a small number of self-funded initiatives (such as the Initiative to Recruit a Diverse Workforce), and subgroups and task forces as deemed necessary to address the strategic directions. Four enabling capabilities (Research, Statistics, and Measurement; Communications and Alliances; Governance and Membership Meetings; and General Administration) were identified to support the three strategic directions. Issue 238/239 of *ARL: A Bimonthly Report on Research Library Issues and Actions from ARL, CNI, and SPARC* covers the strategic plan and implementation in detail. This issue is available at http://www.arl.org/newsltr/238_239/index.html.

The Strategic Direction Steering Committees were charged with reviewing current program activities and determining whether efforts could be realigned with the new strategic directions, transferred to other organizations, or discontinued. The association's primary focus in 2005 was on implementing the strategic plan while fulfilling commitments to prior ongoing, multiyear projects.

Strategic Direction I

Scholarly Communication

ARL will be a leader in the development of effective, extensible, sustainable, and economically viable models of scholarly communication that provide barrier-free access to quality information in support of teaching, learning, research, and service to the community.

This strategic direction advocates "new and enhanced models of scholarly communication that promote wide availability and enduring access." In early 2002 an ARL task force recommended that the association promote "open access to quality information in support of learning and scholarship." ARL has supported a number of open access efforts since then, among them the National Institutes of Health (NIH) Public Access Policy. The NIH policy requested that, beginning May 2, 2005, all NIH-funded investigators submit to PubMed Central an electronic version of their final manuscripts upon acceptance for publication. In a memo to members, ARL and SPARC included potential actions for libraries to take to provide faculty members and other researchers with information, direction, and support for increased access to scientific information; key points for libraries to consider when developing materials for discussing this new policy; links to resources for more information; and a draft memo for use when contacting researchers about the new policy. Also included in the memo was an author's addendum created by SPARC that encourages authors to retain their rights to make their published articles available in an open, noncommercial, digital archive on the Web, and/or to make copies of the article to use in their classrooms. The SPARC author's addendum is available online at http://www.arl.org/sparc/author/addendum.html. The ARL/SPARC memo on campus response to the NIH Public Access Policy is available at http://www.arl.org/info/publicaccess/nihpolicy/campusresponse.html.

ARL published *Open Access Bibliography: Liberating Scholarly Literature with E-Prints and Open Access Journals* in early 2005. Compiled by Charles W. Bailey, Jr., University of Houston, it presents more than 1,300 selected English-language books, conference papers (including some digital video presentations), debates, editorials, e-prints, journal and magazine articles, news articles, technical reports, and other printed and electronic sources that are useful in understanding the open access movement. Most sources were published between 1999 and August 31, 2004; however, a limited number of key sources published prior to 1999 are also included. Where possible, links are provided to sources that are freely available on the Internet (approximately 78 percent of the bibliography's references have such links). The publication also includes a concise overview of key concepts that are central to the open access movement. The bibliography is available for purchase in soft cover and is freely available online at http://info.lib.uh.edu/cwb/oab.pdf.

In concert with other members of the Open Access Working Group, ARL offered a statement of support in response to the Research Councils UK (RCUK) policy that mandated open access for funded works. ARL's statement notes, "We believe that open access research dissemination is an indispensable part of the overall remedy to the serious problems now facing the system of scholarly communication. Moreover, open access is a necessary ingredient in any plan to fully realize the social benefits of scientific advances. While these advantages are important no matter the source of the funding, it is particularly critical when the research is publicly funded and the resulting output is a public good." The RCUK document is available at http://www.rcuk.ac.uk/access/index.asp.

To build a better understanding of the evolving publishing environment, ARL gathers data and forms alliances to raise awareness of library concerns about the dysfunctions in the scholarly publishing industry. In February the Information Access Alliance (of which ARL is a member) and the American Antitrust Institute hosted an invitational symposium on "Antitrust Issues in Scholarly and Legal Publishing." The meeting presented perspectives from the library community, economists, and antitrust experts in the legal community to an audience of federal and state regulators, economics and antitrust scholars, and librarians. Participants explored issues surrounding consolidation in the scholarly and legal publishing industry and related issues arising from the development of bundling as a pricing strategy. Notes from a follow-up discussion on the "Anticompetitive Implications of Bundling and the Conditions Set by Large STM Publishers" during the May ARL Membership Meeting are available at http://www.arl.org/arl/proceedings/146/antitrustsum.html.

In a follow-up to two surveys conducted in 2002 and 2003 on the issues libraries are facing in ensuring the effective use of electronic resources and in dealing with e-journal licensing, in 2005 ARL surveyed member libraries on their experiences with large bundled collections of journals. The information collected will support the research library community in understanding the market practices for large bundles of journal titles. Survey results will be disseminated in 2006.

To further the goal of promoting "enduring access," the Scholarly Communication Steering Committee sponsored a panel of speakers during the May ARL Membership Meeting who described three different models for preserving licensed journal content: Portico, LOCKSS, and e-Depot. Slides from each of the speakers are posted on the ARL Web site at http://www.arl.org/arl/proceedings/ 147. In addition, ARL endorsed the statement "Urgent Action Needed to Preserve Scholarly Electronic Journals." It reflects ARL's recognition that now is a crucial time for the library community to act in support of initiatives that will ensure enduring access to scholarly e-journals. The statement arose out of a recent meeting of library leaders hosted by the Andrew W. Mellon Foundation and articulates four actions needed to support the development of qualified preservation archives for scholarly e-journals. The statement is available at http://www.arl. org/osc/EjournalPreservation_Final.pdf.

ARL, the Coalition for Networked Information (CNI), the Council on Library and Information Resources (CLIR), and the Digital Library Federation (DLF) sponsored a forum on "Managing Digital Assets: Strategic Issues for Research Libraries" following the October ARL Membership Meeting in Washington, D.C. The forum explored the strategic implications of repositioning research libraries to manage digital assets for their institutions. The keynote address provided a broad overview of several issues and developments surrounding digital-asset management. Three program sessions engaged the audience in discussions of institutional policies, emerging federal policies, and the state of tools available to take on the role of digital-asset management. The forum focused on strategic issues of concern to senior decision makers and policy makers in research institutions, including provosts and vice presidents of research and academic affairs, directors of research libraries and senior library managers, and CIOs and other senior information technology managers.

This strategic direction also focuses on "the development of library professionals who have the expertise and knowledge to contribute to enhanced and transformed systems of scholarly communication." To this end, ARL and the Association of College and Research Libraries (ACRL) agreed to jointly develop an ongoing Institute on Scholarly Communication. The institute will offer an immersive learning experience to library administrators, librarians who work directly with campus faculty, and other constituencies involved in campus program development in the arena of scholarly communication. The institute aims to prepare a pool of experts engaged in developing innovative campus outreach programs for scholarly communication. The first institute is being planned for the summer of 2006.

Strategic Direction II

Public Policies Affecting Research Libraries

ARL will influence information and other public policies, both nationally and internationally, that govern the way information is managed and made available.

Part of the scope of this strategic direction is "influencing laws, public policies, regulations, and judicial decisions that are key to research libraries and their users, such as those governing the use and preservation of copyrighted materials and other intellectual property. . . " In 2005 ARL engaged in a variety of efforts to promote access to copyrighted works.

In March the Library Copyright Alliance (LCA), made up of the five major U.S. library associations, submitted comments on a Notice of Inquiry (NOI) from the U.S. Copyright Office that sought comments on issues concerning "orphan works"—those works whose owners are difficult or impossible to locate. The NOI stated that "the public interest may be harmed when works cannot be made available to the public due to the uncertainty over their copyright ownership and status, even when there is no longer any living person or legal entity claiming ownership of the copyright or the owner no longer has any objection to such use." The NOI also acknowledged that "the uncertainty surrounding ownership of such works might needlessly discourage subsequent creators and users from incorporating such works in new creative efforts or making such works available to the public." The LCA comments are available at http://www.arl.org/info/frn/copy/orphanedworks/LCAcomment0305.pdf. In May LCA joined with 12 other organizations and filed reply comments that are available at http://www.arl.org/info/frn/copy/orphanedworks/orphanreply.pdf.

Also in May, ARL, the Medical Library Association, and the American Association of Law Libraries cosponsored a teleconference on "Orphan Works: Issues and Solutions" during which the presenters addressed a wide range of issues concerning orphan works. Additional resources on orphan works are available at http://www.arl.org/info/frn/copy/orphanedworks/resources.html.

The Digital Millennium Copyright Act calls for a rulemaking every three years on the anticircumvention provisions of the act. The Librarian of Congress, in consultation with the Register of Copyrights and the Assistant Secretary of Commerce for Communications and Information, conducts an "on the record" rulemaking proceeding to determine whether users, including libraries and educational institutions, are, or are likely to be, "adversely affected" in their ability to make noninfringing uses of a particular class of copyrighted works. LCA filed comments along with the Music Library Association on exceptions that the Library of Congress should grant pursuant to 17 U.S.C. section 1201 (a)(1)(C) of the act.

The LCA/Music Library Association comments observed that the Copyright Office seems to have moved away from the rigid applications of the "substantial adverse impact" standard that were articulated in the previous rulemaking. In addition, the Copyright Office qualified the standard for actual harm, changing it from always requiring a showing of "actual instances of verifiable problems" to "generally" requiring such a showing. The comments are available at http://www. arl.org/info/frn/copy/1201comments05.html.

In February the United States Court of Appeals for the District of Columbia Circuit heard arguments in a lawsuit that challenged the Federal Communications Commission's (FCC) authority to mandate a "broadcast flag" copy protection for digital television. Public Knowledge, five library associations including ARL, and consumer groups brought the suit because of concerns that the FCC ruling provides content owners with expanded control over how consumers and users may use electronic content.

In May the court ruled that FCC had overstepped its authority when it issued the regulation in 2003 that would have required consumer electronic devices such as TVs to include a "broadcast flag"—a device that would prevent digital TV shows from being copied and then shared. In an earlier filing before FCC, the library associations noted that the broadcast flag could undermine provisions of the TEACH Act, a law designed to facilitate distance education in the networked environment. The court also found that ARL had standing to file this challenge. Additional information about this issue is available at http://www.arl.org/info/frn/copy/DRMBFR.html.

In an ongoing effort to raise awareness of issues associated with copyright and intellectual property management, ARL joined with others in the public and private sectors during 2005 in filing friend-of-the-court briefs. On March 29 the U.S. Supreme Court heard arguments in the case *Metro-Goldwyn-Mayer* v. *Grokster*. In this case, 28 entertainment companies sued the makers of file-sharing services Grokster, Kazaa, and Morpheus. The Ninth U.S. Circuit Court of Appeals in San Francisco ruled that file-sharing services were not liable for their users' illegal activity. The ruling cited the precedent set in the U.S. Supreme Court decision *Sony Corp.* v. *Universal City Studios* (known as the Sony Betamax decision, 1984) and noted that file-sharing systems have significant noninfringing uses not unlike those of videocassette recorders that allow consumers to make copies of copyrighted works for the purposes of time-shifting.

With four other library associations, the Internet Archive, the American Civil Liberties Union, and Project Gutenberg, ARL filed an amicus brief before the U.S. Supreme Court that presented examples of peer-to-peer applications in the education and library arenas as well as a focus on free speech issues. These organizations also filed an amicus brief when the case was before the Court of Appeals. These briefs are available at http://www.arl.org/info/ctcases/Grokster SupremeCourt.pdf and http://www.arl.org/info/frn/copy/groksterbrief.pdf.

In June the U.S. Supreme Court declared, in a unanimous ruling, that distributors of peer-to-peer (P2P) file-sharing systems may be held liable if they actively induce copyright infringement by users of those P2P systems. Importantly, the court strongly reaffirmed its earlier ruling in *Sony Corp.* v. *Universal City Studios,* which held that technologies could not be outlawed if they were capable of substantial noninfringing uses. By focusing on conduct that induces infringement, rather than on the distribution of technology, the decision ensures the continued availability of new and evolving digital technologies to libraries and their patrons. Additional background information on this case is available at http://www.arl.org/info/frn/copy/ctcases.html.

ARL and other library associations submitted an amici curiae brief in support of the National Geographic Society (NGS) in the case of *Faulkner* v. *National Geographic Society* because a ruling in favor of the freelancers would have required publishers of collective works, and others who legitimately digitize them, to obtain additional copyright permission, a requirement that would hamper the efforts of libraries and others to digitize scholarly collections. In March the U.S. Court of Appeals for the Second Circuit ruled that NGS did not infringe the copyrights of freelance photographers and authors when it digitized their works to create a CD-ROM collection from the entire print version of the NGS magazine in a searchable format. The brief is available at http://www.arl.org/info/frn/amibriefs/faulkner.pdf.

On the legislative front, ARL worked to support H.R. 1201, the Digital Media Consumers' Rights Act of 2005 (DMCRA). DMCRA reaffirms fair use in a networked environment; resolves key concerns regarding hardware and software that permit significant noninfringing uses; allows researchers to engage in the scientific research of technological protection measures; and requires content distributors to notify purchasers that the content is protected by a digital lock that might restrict its use. In November, at a hearing on "Fair Use: Its Effects on Consumers and Industry" convened by the Subcommittee on Commerce, Trade, and Consumer Protection of the U.S. House of Representatives Committee on Energy and Commerce, ARL presented testimony on behalf of LCA about the importance of fair use in libraries and education. The testimony is available at http://www.arl.org/info/frn/copy/109legislation/psa_testimony.pdf.

In two different lawsuits, the Authors Guild and five publishers challenged Google's plan to scan complete library collections. Many legal analyses support Google's claim that the scanning is reasonable as fair use, but the case could ultimately be decided in the Supreme Court. Issue 242 of *ARL: A Bimonthly Report of Research Library Issues and Actions from ARL, CNI, and SPARC* includes an analysis of Google's claim to fair use that concludes that Google has a strong case to make. The article is available at http://www.arl.org/newsltr/242/ARLBR242.pdf.

To assist member libraries with their copyright education activities, ARL engaged a visiting scholar for its Campus Copyright and Intellectual Property projects. Working closely with the Public Policies Steering Committee and key ARL and SPARC staff, the visiting scholar will lead the planning and development of a multiphase ARL Copyright Education Initiative to offer information, resources, and tools that are reflective of library principles and goals and are specifically targeted at major campus constituent groups.

To promote access to government information, ARL, with others in the public interest community, worked in support of the continuation of the PubChem database. In 2005 the American Chemical Society (ACS) asked that NIH terminate, or significantly alter, PubChem, a publicly available database that includes information from disparate public sources about the biological activities of chemical compounds. PubChem is considered the "informatics backbone" of the NIH Molecular Libraries Initiative, an effort launched by NIH in 2004 that focuses on helping scientists use small-molecule chemical compounds in their research. The Molecular Libraries Initiative is a part of NIH's Roadmap Initiative, which seeks to accelerate the development of new research and medical treatments. ACS is concerned that PubChem, as a free publicly available database, will cause economic harm to the society's fee-based Chemical Abstracts Service (CAS). ARL provided members with background on PubChem, an explanation of how it compares to CAS, and talking points that could be used locally to call attention to this effort and to support NIH and PubChem.

When the National Geospatial-Intelligence Agency (NGA) proposed removing a significant amount of geospatial information from public distribution, ARL wrote to NGA expressing deep concerns about the proposal and emphasized the strong and valuable public interest in ensuring that these geospatial resources remain publicly available. Many of the reasons cited by NGA—such as avoiding competition with commercial interests, upholding terms of bilateral data-sharing agreements, and security issues in a post-9/11 environment—when examined closely either lacked merit or were not applicable. Following extensive public comment, NGA decided to remove selected aeronautical information from public distribution, asserting that a growing number of international information providers were claiming intellectual property rights to some of the data. The ARL letter is available at http://www.arl.org/info/frn/gov/arlgeo.html.

In September and October ARL presented two symposia on "The Future of Government Documents in ARL and Regional FDLP Libraries." The symposia convened institutional teams composed of government information librarians and their immediate supervisors (directors or associate university librarians) to discuss issues and describe a preferred future for libraries' role in providing access to government information. During the event, the participants discussed the current conditions shaping the work of government documents librarians, explored new service models, defined the role(s) of government documents librarians for a new era, and generated next steps—for teams and for the group—on how to lead and influence the transition from print-based collections to electronic access.

Strategic Direction III

The Library's Role in Research, Teaching, and Learning

ARL will promote and facilitate new and expanding roles for ARL libraries to engage in the transformations affecting research and undergraduate and graduate education.

In March 2005 ARL presented the Webcast "Teaching, Learning and Research: Libraries and Their Role in the Academic Institution." This Webcast convened library leaders to discuss the role libraries play in academia and highlighted the way one library—at the University of Tennessee—is moving to more fully engage with faculty and students in this process. The Webcast closed with a question-and-answer session between audience and presenters. This exchange, as well as questions that the presenters did not have time to answer online, is available at http://www.arl.org/training/webcast/tlr.

Part of the scope of this strategic direction is "promoting and facilitating the development of library professionals engaged in and leading partnerships that advance research, teaching, and learning." ARL pursues several activities to recruit and educate such professionals for research libraries.

Funded by the Institute of Museum and Library Services (IMLS) and 59 ARL member libraries, the Initiative to Recruit a Diverse Workforce (IRDW) offers a stipend of up to $10,000 over two years, a mentoring relationship with an experienced librarian, and a leadership training curriculum for MLS students from underrepresented groups who are interested in careers in academic and research libraries. This multiyear initiative reflects the commitment of ARL members to create a diverse academic and research library community that will better meet the new challenges of global competition and changing demographics. A list of the 2005–2007 participants is available at http://www.arl.org/arl/pr/initrecruitselects05.html. In April Purdue University hosted IRDW participants for visits to the Purdue University Libraries. This all-expenses-paid component of the initiative was created to increase awareness about issues facing research libraries. In November Harvard College Library hosted seven IRDW participants in an effort to help recruit librarians from underrepresented ethnic minorities into the Harvard University Administrative Fellowship program and to broaden their understanding of the wide range of library careers available at Harvard.

ARL and five member libraries (University of California, Los Angeles; Columbia University; University of Illinois at Urbana-Champaign; University of Texas at Austin; and University of Washington) piloted the ARL Research Library Leadership Fellows (RLLF) Program in 2005. This new executive leadership program identifies the unique demands facing directors of large research libraries and prepares participants to develop the skills and professional networks to move into those positions. Twenty-one emergent leaders were selected in late 2004 to participate in RLLF. A list of the fellows is available at http://www.arl.org/olms/rllf/fellows04.html.

The first of three Strategic Issues Institutes was held in February at the University of Illinois at Urbana-Champaign. The institute created a forum for these future leaders of large ARL libraries to tackle the professional issues of today and develop a vision for the future. The experience exposed fellows to representatives of multiple levels of the library and campus communities. As a follow-up to the institute, fellows created customized learning plans, participated in weeklong site visits to one of the five sponsoring libraries, and began working with a mentor pool.

The second Strategic Issues Institute, with the theme "Complexity, Community, and Collaboration," was hosted by the University of Washington in July. Program fellows spent time discussing major issues in academic libraries and higher education with several key members of the university's administration, including the president and provost, faculty members, and leaders at University of Washington at Tacoma as well as the Seattle Public Library. Values—both institutional and personal—and the importance of understanding and shaping organizational culture were emphasized in every interaction.

The ARL Academy was created to recruit, educate, train, and place in positions within ARL libraries Ph.D. holders or those with specialized educational accomplishments who are interested in transitioning to careers in research libraries. ARL is partnering with three library schools in this IMLS-funded program: Catholic University of America, University of North Carolina at Chapel Hill, and Simmons College. The program was created based on interest expressed among ARL directors for recruitment efforts, and models, that bring the practitioner and educator communities together. As part of this program, all of the fellows—45 over the next three years—will receive either a graduate degree or a certificate in library and information science. Fifteen fellows have been selected and are taking courses at one of the three partner library schools. A complete list of fellows, including biographical statements and expected graduation dates, is available at http://www.arl.org/olms/arlacademy. In September fellows participated in a Leadership Institute in Washington, D.C., to discuss the major issues facing academic and research libraries and to explore opportunities for maximizing their academic backgrounds as they transition to librarianship. One of the final learning experiences will be a fellowship in an ARL library.

ARL hosted a Leadership Symposium for 75 MLIS students at the American Library Association (ALA) Midwinter Meeting in Boston. The symposium focused on transitioning into and building career networks in academic and research libraries. It included presentations by library directors and other leaders on such topics as "Transitioning into a Research Library," "Introduction to the Public Research Library," "Should I consider the Ph.D.?," and "Current Trends in Federal Relations: Information a New Librarian Should Know."

Another part of this strategic direction is "identifying implications for libraries resulting from the changing global (i.e., international, interdisciplinary, intercultural) nature of scholarly and learning communities." In March the first Association of American Universities/ARL Global Resources Network (GRN) Forum, "The Global Record: Ensuring Its Future for Scholarship," was hosted by the Yale University Library and Yale's Center for International and Area Studies. The forum explored emerging scholarly uses of international resources, how these uses may be changing, the consequences in terms of collection gaps and resources needed, and the ways in which GRN might respond. In panel discussions, scholars shared their emerging and innovative uses of traditional and electronic resources and librarians commented on how they are responding to those demands by building stronger collections or providing access to remote resources. Small group discussions permitted the 70-plus participants to think about these issues from their own perspectives. The conference papers are available at http://www.library.yale.edu/mssa/globalrecord/new_web. An essay highlighting the themes of the conference was published in issue 240 of *ARL: A Bimonthly Report on Research Library Issues and Actions from ARL, CNI, and SPARC*. The essay is available at http://www.arl.org/newsltr/240/global.html.

At its July meeting the ARL board approved the transfer of GRN from ARL to the Center for Research Libraries (CRL) effective January 1, 2006. In September the CRL board confirmed the transfer. CRL, under the guidance of the director of international resources, will assume leadership, governance, coordination, and services of GRN. In accordance with the transition plan recommended by the GRN Steering Committee, funding for 2006 activities will be shared by ARL and CRL.

The ARL Special Collections Task Force continued to explore ways of providing greater access to unprocessed manuscript and rare book collections and began exploring a suggestion that the task force initiate conversations with representatives of Historically Black Colleges and Universities (HBCUs) that have large unprocessed collections of valuable materials. A summary of the May meeting of the task force is available at http://www.arl.org/collect/spcoll/tforce/min0505.html. A status report of the progress the task force has made toward its charge over the past several years, along with anticipated next steps, is available at http://www.arl.org/collect/spcoll/tforce/status0705.html.

Research, Statistics, and Measurement

This enabling capability encompasses the Statistics and Measurement Program to identify quantitative and qualitative metrics and assessment tools needed to support all three strategic objectives. The Statistics and Measurement Program seeks to describe and measure the performance of research libraries and their contributions to teaching, research, scholarship, and community service. The program also includes the New Measures Initiative, a series of projects and services to develop new approaches for describing and evaluating library service effectiveness, diversity, and leadership.

Discussions in 2004 on revising the annual *ARL Statistics* survey unearthed differing opinions regarding the way collections can and should be described in an environment in which multiple formats abound, collaborations flourish, and electronic content offers new ways of doing business. Representatives of three former and current ARL standing committees (Statistics and Measurement, Collections and Access, and Membership) formed the Task Force on Measuring Collections to define the issues and propose solutions for measuring research library collections. In 2005 task force members conducted interviews with member directors to develop a consensus on how collections can or should be described and measured to demonstrate library contributions to teaching, learning, research, and public engagement. A major theme of the interviews was the need for ARL to present the research library story more fully, including its relevance to teaching, learning, and research. Interview subjects suggested that ARL should highlight the unique collection content and strong service component of research libraries. Interviewees also felt that statistics are important and will continue to be important for their historical contributions, accountability, and comparison with peer institutions; however, an increasing number of directors noted that the ranking (Membership Criteria Index) published in the *Chronicle of Higher Education* is misleading and unhelpful. Many directors would like to describe the benefits research libraries provide to their communities and the relation of research collections to the success of their users. The need for a framework that recognizes and describes success from a user perspective surfaced repeatedly.

Through a variety of New Measures Initiatives, ARL continues to develop new assessment methods for understanding changes in user behavior. The

LibQUAL+ survey, now in its sixth year, measures user perceptions of, and satisfaction with, library services. More than 250 libraries participated in the survey in 2005 and more than 151,000 responses were gathered and analyzed.

As part of the National Science Digital Library (NSDL)/National Science Foundation (NSF) effort to modify LibQUAL+ for the digital library environment, a pilot project was undertaken across a variety of NSDL digital libraries to collect user feedback using survey questions developed from focus groups with users of these digital libraries. A paper, "Developing the DigiQUAL Protocol for Digital Library Evaluation," describing some of the developments of this research-and-development effort, was presented at the Joint Conference on Digital Libraries in June 2005. The paper is available at http://www.libqual.org/documents/admin/digiqual-jcdl05-v5.pdf. A paper on "User Perspectives into Designs for Both Physical and Digital Libraries: New Insights on Commonalities/Similarities and Differences from the NSDL Digital Libraries and LibQUAL+ Data Bases" was presented at the Seventh Congress of the International Society for Knowledge Organization–Spain in July. The paper is available at http://www.libqual.org/documents/admin/ISKO.pdf.

In the fall ARL libraries were invited to participate in a new program, "Making Library Assessment Work: Practical Approaches for Developing and Sustaining Effective Assessment." The goal of the program is to establish a process to help libraries develop sustainable assessment efforts to demonstrate their contributions to teaching, learning, and research. Initial interest exceeded expectations, so a Phase II was scheduled for those libraries not accommodated in Phase I. During Phase I, site visits to seven ARL libraries were conducted. Based on the experience gained during the year, including feedback from participating libraries, a number of enhancements were added to the program. These include extending the site visit from one day to one and a half days; establishing formal follow-up activities to assist in implementing the recommendations included in the project report and consulting on a specific assessment project; a meeting with a representative of the library during a professional meeting; and providing additional written resources that support practical approaches to sustainable assessment.

Project SAILS (Standardized Assessment of Information Literacy Skills) completed its third phase. About 70 institutions participated in the project, which is a partnership between Kent State University and ARL. Data analysis workshops were provided at ALA conferences for those interested in learning more about Item Response Theory and what additional analyses could be conducted beyond those provided in the project's standard reports. A set of studies was conducted to determine the validity of the test items and skill sets. Kent State received a no-cost extension of its IMLS grant to provide more time for further validation, redesign, and rebuilding of the online testing system, development of a registration and customization system, and automation of all data analyses and report generation. System work was expected to be completed in May 2006 in time for test administration to take place in fall 2006.

The Statistics and Measurement Program also produces a series of annual publications that describe salary compensation and collection, staffing, expenditure, and service trends for research libraries. The series includes the *ARL Annual Salary Survey, ARL Statistics, ARL Academic Law Library Statistics, ARL*

Academic Health Sciences Library Statistics, and *ARL Preservation Statistics.* ARL Interactive Statistics, hosted at the Geostat Center of the University of Virginia, continues to be one of the most popular ways of accessing the annual data collected by ARL. The ranked lists allow users to pick from more than 30 variables for data reports. This site is at http://fisher.lib.virginia.edu/arl/index. html.

The SPEC survey program gathers information on current research library operating practices and policies and publishes the SPEC Kit series as guides for libraries as they face ever-changing management issues. Six SPEC Kits were published in 2005: *SPEC Kit 286 Collaboration for Distance Learning Information Literacy Instruction, SPEC Kit 287 Instructional Improvement Programs, SPEC Kit 288 Scanning Services for Library Users, SPEC Kit 289 Managing Large Projects, SPEC Kit 290 Access Services,* and *SPEC Kit 291 Spatial Data Collections and Services.*

Communications and Alliances

Communications and Alliances is an enabling capability engaged in many activities that support ARL's strategic directions. These include acquainting ARL members with current, important developments of interest to research libraries; influencing policy and decision makers within the higher education, research, and scholarly communities; educating academic communities about issues relating to scholarly communication and research libraries; and providing the library community with information about activities in which research libraries are engaged. Using print and electronic media as well as direct outreach, the communications capability disseminates information about ARL to the higher education and scholarly communities, as well as to ARL member institutions, and publishes a full range of timely, accurate, and informative resources to assist library and higher education communities in their efforts to improve the delivery of scholarly communication. ARL makes many of its titles available electronically via the World Wide Web; some are available in excerpted form for preview before purchase and others are available in their entirety. News about ARL activities and publications is available through the arl-announce list, distributed widely to the library and higher education communities. To subscribe, visit http://www.arl.org/arl/pr/subscription.html.

Governance and Membership Meetings

Representatives of 107 ARL libraries met in Philadelphia at ARL's 146th Membership Meeting in May 2005. The meeting, hosted by Temple University and the University of Pennsylvania, focused on "Strategic Directions for Research Libraries: Innovation and Impact in Times of Change." Speakers and discussion forums advanced one or more of the three strategic directions in the new ARL strategic plan.

A total of 114 member institutions were represented at ARL's 147th Membership Meeting held in Washington, D.C., in October. William G. Bowen, president of the Andrew W. Mellon Foundation, gave the keynote address. He reflected on the lessons learned from JSTOR and other Mellon-funded initiatives for the future of scholarly communication and the role of the library in the digital landscape. Following his remarks, ARL President Ann Wolpert (MIT) presented Bowen with an award in honor of his support of research libraries during his tenure at the foundation. Bowen's paper was published in issue 243 of *ARL: A Bimonthly Report of Research Library Issues and Actions from ARL, CNI, and SPARC* and is also available at http://www.arl.org/arl/proceedings/147. On October 27 Brian E. C. Schottlaender (University of California, San Diego) began his term as ARL president. The board elected Sherrie Schmidt (Arizona State) as vice president/president-elect, and the membership elected three new board members: Brinley Franklin (Connecticut), Charles Lowry (Maryland), and Jennifer Younger (Notre Dame).

SPARC

21 Dupont Circle N.W., Suite 800, Washington, DC 20036
202-296-2296, e-mail sparc@arl.org
World Wide Web http://www.arl.org/sparc

Heather Joseph
SPARC Director

SPARC (the Scholarly Publishing and Academic Resources Coalition), launched in 1998 as an initiative of the Association of Research Libraries (ARL), is an alliance of more than 200 academic and research libraries working to correct imbalances in the scholarly publishing system.

These imbalances have driven the cost of scholarly journals (especially in science, technology, and medicine) to insupportably high levels and have diminished the community's ability to access, share, and use information. At the core of SPARC's mission is the belief that these imbalances inhibit the advancement of scholarship and are at odds with fundamental needs of scholars and the academic enterprise.

Mission

SPARC is a catalyst for action. Its pragmatic agenda stimulates the emergence of new scholarly communication models that expand dissemination of scholarly research and reduce financial pressures on libraries. Action by SPARC in collaboration with other stakeholders builds on the unprecedented opportunities created by the networked digital environment to advance the conduct of scholarship.

Strategy

SPARC strategy seeks to reduce barriers to access, sharing, and use of scholarship; in particular, scientific research. SPARC's highest priority has been on advancing the understanding and implementation of open access to research results. It is important to recognize that primary-journal literature represents just one element of scholarly research and that SPARC's strategy is designed to advance a more open system of scholarship as a whole.

Two key conditions are necessary for fundamental change to occur in scholarly communication: scholars and scientists must actively recognize the benefits of change, and mechanisms to support the cost of scholarly communication must be implemented. SPARC's strategy seeks to address both of these requirements, linking broad advocacy of change with real-world demonstrations of how new models of scholarly communication might actually work.

As a practical matter, SPARC's program activity recognizes that change will play out differently in various disciplines and that, in some areas, the interests of academe may be best served in the near term by affordable subscription-supported publishing solutions. The organization's programs therefore aim at building a broader understanding of opportunities for change in all fields.

SPARC's role in stimulating change focuses on

- Educating stakeholders about the problems facing scholarly communication and the opportunities for change
- Advocating policy changes that advance the potential of technology to advance scholarly communication and that explicitly recognize that dissemination is an essential, inseparable component of the research process
- Incubating real-world demonstrations of business and publishing models that advance changes benefiting scholarship and academe

2006 Priorities

SPARC actions will, foremost, advance the viability and acceptance of a more open system of scholarship, with a primary focus on open access models. Over the past two years, the pace and scope of public policy developments—particularly interest in public access to federally funded research—has accelerated dramatically. It is important that SPARC deploy a focused and disciplined advocacy strategy while remaining sufficiently agile to capitalize on emerging market opportunities that align with its objectives. Reviewed here are the key program activities planned for 2006.

Public policy strategy—following the highly visible success of SPARC's public policy initiative to advance public access to research funded by the National Institutes of Health (NIH), its advocacy program will build on the NIH precedent and further raise the public policy profile of open access by the following means:

- SPARC will attend, and, where appropriate, participate in national advisory committee meetings where public access policies are discussed, including the PubMed Central National Advisory Committee, the Public Access Working Group of the National Library of Medicine, the PubChem Working Group, and other relevant groups.
- SPARC will lead and manage the policy advocacy work of the Open Access Working Group (OAWG), an informal alliance of leading organizations that support open access.[1] Similarly, SPARC will continue to serve as the organizational focal point for the Alliance for Taxpayer Access (ATA), a letterhead alliance that brings together the OAWG communities and patient-advocacy organizations. In 2006 SPARC will re-examine the operating model for ATA and consider alternative scenarios for long-term configuration and support of this entity.
- SPARC expects that in 2006 OAWG/ATA activity will focus on ensuring that the NIH policy implementation results in a satisfactory outcome, and on supporting adoption of positive government-wide policies on public access to published results of publicly funded research.

1. Organizations represented in OAWG are the American Association of Law Libraries, the Association of Academic Health Sciences Libraries, the Association of College and Research Libraries, the American Library Association, the Association of Research Libraries, Creative Commons, the Medical Library Association, the Open Society Institute, Public Knowledge, the Public Library of Science, and SPARC.

- OAWG/ATA work is supported by a public-policy consulting firm retained and supervised by SPARC, and will be closely managed to ensure that the consultant's activities track SPARC's focused objectives.
- SPARC is positioned as an expert source on the issue of public access and will continue to actively and frequently communicate with the press. It will also work to feature more individual scholars as well as patient advocates through its work with OAWG/ATA.
- An active series of presentations on SPARC's advocacy activities will continue with presentations at meetings of both library and publishing organizations in the United States and abroad. SPARC will promote the relevance and importance of the rapidly growing international open access movement and will share information on advocacy strategy and program planning with related library and scholarly groups worldwide, both on its own and in concert with SPARC Europe.
- To raise the profile of libraries as key stakeholders in policy decisions that affect the communication of research results, SPARC will apply for observer status to the World Intellectual Property Organization (WIPO). Decision on observer status is made by WIPO in the fourth quarter of each year.
- SPARC will demonstrate open access's progress by continuing its direct sponsorship of the monthly *SPARC Open Access Newsletter,* written by Peter Suber, and an associated e-mail list, as well as the bimonthly *SPARC e-news.* The support of SPARC and the Open Society Institute also will continue to make possible Suber's "Open Access News" blog, which has become a widely consulted news source for those tracking open access and scholarly communications generally.

Economics of open access—SPARC will partner with SPARC Europe to develop a high-level cost/benefit economic analysis of open access, with an emphasis on the potential benefits of open access to national economies. A scoping meeting for this project, to be attended by economists who will potentially participate in this analysis, was scheduled for March 2006. The meeting was to be supported with funds from the Soros Foundation's Open Society Institute, and securing funding for the larger project will be actively pursued.

Antitrust issues in journal publishing—SPARC will continue to actively participate in the Information Access Alliance (IAA), a group of library organizations working to highlight the budgetary impact of the rapid escalation of the price of information, particularly of scientific, technical, and medical (STM) journals. SPARC will support and promote activities of IAA designed to seek new solutions to the problems associated with publisher bundling practices, and will help to support the work of economists and antitrust scholars interested in looking at an area where unrestrained concentration is rapidly developing.

Model form author's addendum—In concert with partners (Science Commons and, potentially, the SURF Foundation), SPARC will launch a promotional brochure and publicity activities to support a model contract addendum that journal-article authors can append to publishers' copyright agreements to assert key rights, including deposit in institutional repositories. In partnership with Science Commons, SPARC will create a machine-readable form of this addendum, designed to enhance its searchability and usefulness.

The SPARC addendum employs the approach of reserving a "bundle" of rights for an author in one instrument. To supplement this, SPARC expects to consult with Science Commons as it creates and deploys a series of addenda designed to allow authors to reserve individual ("unbundled") rights to ensure legal interoperability of these addenda. SPARC will collect and actively communicate data on the use of these addenda, as well as responses to the addenda by authors and publishers.

International activity—Because change in scholarly communications is needed on a global scale, SPARC will seek to amplify its impact by working in collaboration with global allies such as SPARC Europe, the Canadian Association of Research Libraries, and various national and regional university library associations.

- In partnership with the Japan Association of National and University Libraries, SPARC expects to announce the launch of SPARC Japan by the third quarter of 2006. A full range of promotional activities will be deployed in support of this launch. SPARC will have representation on the governing board of SPARC Japan, and its expectation is that a close cooperative relationship and full slate of collaborative activities will develop among SPARC, SPARC Europe, and SPARC Japan.

- As open access activities grow in scope and importance in developing countries, SPARC will collaborate with appropriate partners, including eIFL.net, an independent foundation that strives to lead, negotiate, support, and advocate for the wide availability of electronic resources to library users in developing countries.

Institutional repositories—SPARC will continue to maintain and expand the content-rich SPARC resource on institutional repositories (www.arl.org/sparc/repos/index.html).

- In 2006 SPARC will cosponsor with SPARC Europe a second workshop on institutional repositories. A follow-up to the successful meeting held in Washington, D.C., in 2004, the workshop will be held in the autumn in Glasgow, Scotland. SPARC will contribute resources toward the planning and implementation of this meeting, tentatively titled "Open Scholarship and Institutional Repositories."

- As the discussion about institutional repositories evolves from issues surrounding their establishment and launch to issues central to identifying and adding content, SPARC will work to advance the understanding of the role that data play in scholarly communications. In 2006 SPARC will commission a white paper on "open data" to explore the implications of practices and policies involving access to data.

Publisher partnership programs—SPARC will support, demonstrate, and promote useful examples of open access or other innovative publishing initiatives via the SPARC Alternative, Leading Edge, and Scientific Communities publishing partnership programs:

- To ensure close collaboration continues and to foster regular, candid dialogue between the library and not-for-profit publishing communities, SPARC will convene a quarterly series of roundtable discussion meetings in Washington, D.C.
- SPARC will identify, support, and promote a robust, community-based venture designed to illustrate an end-to-end open system of data-driven scholarship.
- With the International Coalition of Library Consortia (ICOLC), SPARC will support efforts by the *Stanford Encyclopedia of Philosophy* to build an endowment sufficient to sustain perpetual open access publication.
- Via promotional and other activity (including service on advisory boards), SPARC will continue to aid both BioOne (http//:www.bioone.org) and Cornell University's Project Euclid (http://projecteuclid.org) in evolving sound, sustainable business practices needed to become leading platforms for digital dissemination of independent journals.

Campus education—SPARC encourages and aids libraries' grassroots advocacy efforts, cosponsoring the Create Change program and Web site (http://www.createchange.org) and collaborating with the Association of College and Research Libraries and other organizations to engage beyond the SPARC membership. In 2006 this campaign (Web site and printed material) will be completely updated to reflect a more faculty-focused approach.

Other SPARC activities will support institutionally based scholarly communication programs directed at faculty and administrators in higher education. These will include

- Development and presentation of Webcasts and in-person roundtables on such topics as copyright issues for journal-article authors and the future of society publishing
- Continued support of one quarter of the time of Julia Blixrud—SPARC's assistant executive director, external relations—to serve as a consultant to and speaker at local scholarly communication programs.

Discussion paper on publishing cooperatives—A key cultural barrier to changes in the current journal-publishing model is resistance from many societies and their active members. Their centrality to scientific and scholarly publishing makes understanding the future of society publishing a component of meaningful change to the journal-publishing system. SPARC will develop a paper evaluating alternative models available to society publishers, specifically the potential application of the economic model of cooperatives to the publishing arena. This paper will explore the benefits those models offer publishing societies, their members, and other academic community stakeholders, and will form the basis for stimulating a broader community discussion of the future of societies that SPARC will play out in its campus, media, and other communication initiatives. It will also serve as the basis for the creation of beta projects that can test the viability of such cooperatives.

Business consulting services—SPARC will continue to make available SPARC-subsidized expert advisory services to deserving journals and alternative publishing ventures. In 2005 nearly 20 publishing organizations used this service.

Publishing tools—SPARC will explore the addition of tools to its growing arsenal of practical aids to innovative journal-publishing practice, including an in-depth guide to developing sponsorships in support of journal publications and a series of self-help resources on sound business planning practices for small independent publishing initiatives.

SPARC Organizational Model

SPARC is supported by a membership of more than 200 libraries, mainly in North America and reaching beyond the ranks of ARL member libraries. In addition, several major library organizations around the world are SPARC affiliate members. The allied SPARC Europe organization includes more than 100 additional members and is entirely self-supporting.

SPARC operates under the administrative umbrella and not-for-profit status of ARL. SPARC funds are administered on SPARC's behalf by ARL and are accounted for separately from ARL funds. SPARC pays ARL a negotiated annual fee for administrative services and office space provided by ARL. SPARC receives no ARL financial support.

The SPARC executive director, who reports to the ARL executive director, manages the affairs of the coalition with guidance from a 12-member SPARC Steering Committee that is broadly representative of all SPARC member institutions. Ray English, Oberlin College, chairs the committee for 2006. Its other members are Larry Alford, Temple University; Nancy Baker, University of Iowa; Sherrie Bergman, Bowdoin College; Deb Carver, University of Oregon; Gwendolyn Ebbett, University of Windsor; Diane Graves, Trinity University; John Ober, California Digital Library; Joyce Ogburn, University of Washington; Carolynne Presser, University of Manitoba; Sarah Pritchard, University of California, Santa Barbara; and Bas Savenije, Utrecht University Library.

Financial Strategy

Income—SPARC operations are supported mainly by membership dues, which have not increased since SPARC was founded in 1998. Modest additional income is secured from interest on cash-on-hand. SPARC expects that its overall membership base and income will remain stable in 2006.

Expenses—It is expected that 2006 SPARC annual revenue and expenses will be approximately in balance (i.e., no material deficit or surplus).

Council on Library and Information Resources

1755 Massachusetts Ave. N.W., Suite 500, Washington, DC 20036-2124
202-939-4754, fax 202-939-4765, World Wide Web http://www.clir.org

Kathlin Smith
Director of Communications

The Council on Library and Information Resources (CLIR) is an independent, nonprofit organization dedicated to improving the management of information for research, teaching, and learning. CLIR's mission is to expand access to information, however recorded and preserved, as a public good.

CLIR pursues three primary goals in support of its mission:

- To foster new approaches to the management of digital and nondigital information resources so that they will be available in the future
- To expand leadership capacity in the information professions
- To analyze changes in the information landscape and help practitioners prepare for them

CLIR's program staff develops projects, programs, and publications to advance these goals.

CLIR is supported by fees from sponsoring institutions, grants from public and private foundations, contracts with federal agencies, and donations from individuals. CLIR's board establishes policy, sets goals, and approves strategies for their achievement.

CLIR's activities for 2005 are represented in six program areas: resources for scholarship, preservation awareness, digital libraries, economics of information, leadership, and international developments.

Resources for Scholarship

Scholarly Communication Institute

The third annual Scholarly Communication Institute was held July 17–19, 2005, in cooperation with and on the grounds of the University of Virginia. Three research universities (Emory University, Indiana University, and the University of Virginia) and a liberal arts college (Wheaton College) sent teams to participate. Each team comprised a senior scholar, a senior administrative officer, the college or university librarian, a technologist, and a student.

The institute focused on the sustainability of scholarly digital projects. CLIR asked participants to consider what challenges scholars and institutions face in transforming "mature" digital scholarly projects into sustainable research and teaching programs. Are there common as well as specific strategies for institutions to address the challenges? Participants discussed a range of obstacles: reliable funding, institutional commitment to sustainability, the rewards system, and institutional capacity to create supportive cultures and technologies. Each of the institutional teams drew up a plan for continuing the discussion on sustainability on its home campus and for involving stakeholders not present at the Institute.

Mellon Dissertation Fellowships

The Mellon Dissertation Fellowship program supports original-source doctoral research in libraries and archives, without regard to the location or the format of those sources. Fourteen fellows were selected in 2005 from more than 350 candidates. As in previous years, fellows started their year with a one-day workshop at the Library of Congress on research in archives and special collections. In October 2005, fellows from the 2004–2005 academic year convened at the Library of Congress for a post-fellowship seminar.

Preservation Awareness

Legal and Technical Issues Surrounding Audio Recordings

In response to the mandate set forth in the National Recording Preservation Act of 2000, the Library of Congress asked CLIR to develop and implement the first phase of a national preservation-planning strategy for audio resources. To this end, CLIR is undertaking a range of work that identifies obstacles to the preservation of and access to sound recordings made before 1972. In 2005 CLIR began work on a study to explore the range of factors—from cataloging to physical deterioration to copyright—that threaten future access to the world's recorded-sound heritage. The study will draw heavily on information gathered from interviews with a range of stakeholders, such as curators, scholars, performers, and rights holders.

In 2005 CLIR also published two reports on copyright issues relating to audio preservation and access. The first, by June Besek of Columbia Law School, focuses on commercial sound recordings made before 1972; it was published in December 2005. The second, by Tim Brooks, executive vice president of research for Lifetime Cable Networks, focuses on reissue practices under current U.S. copyright law, looking at all pre-1965 recordings. Brooks's report was published in August 2005. Both reports were commissioned for and sponsored by the National Recording Preservation Board, Library of Congress.

National Digital Information Infrastructure and Preservation Program

CLIR continued in 2005 to provide a range of support to help the Library of Congress coordinate the work of the National Digital Information Infrastructure and Preservation Program (NDIIPP). The NDIIPP legislation, enacted in December 2000, called for a phased approach to building an infrastructure of cooperating institutions to help ensure the long-term preservation of digital content. CLIR has assisted the library's Office of Strategic Initiatives and the NDIIPP Preservation Partnerships by monitoring and providing guidance to two of the program's eight partnerships.

Digital Libraries

CLIR's work at the intersection of libraries, scholarship, and technology is enhanced by the activities of the Digital Library Federation (DLF). DLF is a consortium of 34 members and 5 allied organizations that are pioneering the use of electronic information technologies to extend library collections and services. The full range of DLF's work is described on the DLF Web site at http://www. diglib.org. In May 2005 DLF incorporated to become an independent organization. DLF will remain housed at CLIR, and, to further support coordination with CLIR, DLF appointed a trustee to serve on CLIR's board; CLIR's president also serves as a DLF trustee and ex officio member of the trustee executive committee.

DLF Aquifer

In January 2005 Katherine Kott of Stanford University was appointed full-time director of DLF Aquifer. The primary goal of DLF Aquifer, established in 2004, is to enable distributed content to be used effectively by libraries and scholars for teaching, learning, and research. Starting with a significant, well-bounded collection of digital content in the area of American culture and life, DLF Aquifer is creating a test bed of tools for selecting, collecting, and providing access to high-quality digital content.

Metadata Object Description Schema

DLF Aquifer developed draft guidelines in 2005 for implementing MODS (metadata object description schema) for cultural heritage- and humanities-based scholarly resources. MODS is a descriptive metadata format designed to support the location, identification, and use of resources. Although based on MARC, MODS is encoded in XML and is therefore more readily usable in a Web environment. It is also simpler than MARC and richer than other metadata formats commonly used for describing digital resources, such as Dublin Core. This richness enables more robust end-user service development for improved access, sorting, and browsing across collections.

Open Archives Initiative Best Practices

With support from a national leadership grant from the Institute of Museum and Library Services and in partnership with Emory University, the University of Illinois at Urbana-Champaign, and the University of Michigan, DLF has been working on a project to research, design, and develop prototype "second generation" Open Access Initiative (OAI) finding systems, capitalizing on the lessons learned from the first wave of OAI harvesting and using, as its raw material, collections drawn from across the DLF membership. The aim is to foster better teaching and scholarship through easier, more relevant discovery of digital resources, and to enhance libraries' ability to build more responsive local services on top of a distributed metadata platform. Experts in the field of harvestable metadata have produced a draft of best practices guidelines on how to build harvestable records en masse that work easily in an interoperable manner. The guidelines were scheduled to be published early in 2006.

DLF Services Framework

Formed in November 2004, the DLF Services Framework Working Group has launched an initiative that aims to understand and communicate the business processes of libraries in the new world of digital information and to relate them to emerging services. It is intended to provide the community with a roadmap and a common reference vocabulary around which to organize collective attention to library services in a changing networked environment. In November 2005 DLF announced the appointment of Geneva Henry, executive director of Rice University's Digital Library Initiative, as a DLF Distinguished Fellow. Henry will work with a team of DLF colleagues throughout 2006 to develop the DLF Services Framework.

Preservation-Quality Digital Images

In 2005 DLF commissioned a team from the U.S. National Archives and Records Administration (NARA), the Library of Congress, Kodak, the Swiss Institute of Technology, Harvard University, and elsewhere to build on earlier work by NARA to produce a statement of the best that is collectively known about preservation-quality digital images and the information about them that should be recorded for the long term. It is expected that the group will report its findings in 2006.

Electronic Resources Management Initiative

The Electronic Resources Management Initiative (ERMI) has created and disseminated a common, sharable, XML database record for expressing the content of license agreements, related administrative information, and internal processes associated with collections of licensed electronic resources. Use of the record saves libraries the time-consuming effort of retyping publishers' diverse license terms into their management systems. Publishers are now willing to deliver their licenses to libraries in a common XML record format, and vendors are providing software that makes it simple to load these records into library management systems. In late 2005 DLF pressed forward with the next round of implementation and real-world formalization and testing to move libraries to a more efficient license-expression workflow with planning for the Electronic Resource Management Initiative, Phase 2.

Managing Digital Assets Workshop

CLIR partnered with the Association for Research Libraries, the Coalition for Networked Information, and DLF to hold a one-day workshop, "Managing Digital Assets: Strategic Issues for Research Libraries," on October 28, 2005, in Washington, D.C. The forum focused on issues of concern to senior decision-makers in research institutions, including provosts and vice presidents of research and academic affairs, directors and senior managers of research libraries, chief information officers, and other information technology managers. Forum presenters and participants explored the strategic implications of repositioning research libraries to manage digital assets for their institutions.

Economics of Information

Work-Redesign Project

During 2005 six library consortia completed projects to explore ways to improve work processes and expand services. The six consortia were the Appalachian

College Association; Claremont University Consortium; Five Colleges, Inc.; Five Colleges of Ohio; Tri-College Library Consortium; and the Robert W. Woodruff Library of the Atlanta University Center. CLIR will publish a report on the projects in 2006.

Leadership

CLIR continued several programs in 2005 designed to address evolving leadership needs in the information profession.

Postdoctoral Fellowship Program

The CLIR Postdoctoral Fellowship Program in Scholarly Information Resources in the Humanities, offered in conjunction with a consortium of academic research institutions, seeks to create a new kind of scholarly information professional—one who believes that there are opportunities to develop meaningful linkages among disciplinary scholarship, libraries, archives, and evolving digital tools. The fellowships are open to individuals who have recently completed Ph.D. degrees in a humanities discipline. CLIR awarded four fellowships, each of one to two years in length, for 2005–2006.

Frye Leadership Institute

The Frye Leadership Institute was created to develop leaders who can guide and transform academic information services for higher education. Since its inception in 2000, the institute has trained nearly 300 librarians, faculty members, and technology experts. The 2005 institute was held June 5–17 at the Emory Conference Center in Atlanta. The class of 45 participants came from public and private institutions of all sizes and included one representative each from Canada, Britain, and Australia. CLIR President Nancy Davenport, EDUCAUSE President Brian Hawkins, and CLIR Program Director Susan Perry served as deans of the Institute.

Academic Librarians Advisory Committee

The Academic Librarians Advisory Committee advises CLIR on issues of interest to liberal arts colleges and small research libraries. In February 2005 the committee sponsored a three-day workshop for library and information technology administrators at small and midsize academic libraries seeking in-depth information about the planning, purchase, implementation, and management of digital assets. The workshop, "Managing Digital Assets," focused on trends in digital content management and on how small and midsize academic libraries can incorporate new approaches into their operations.

Chief Information Officers of Liberal Arts Colleges

CLIR's Chief Information Officers (CIO) Group is composed of 34 directors of organizations that have merged their library and technology units on liberal arts college campuses. The group met at Kenyon College in March 2005 for a symposium to which directors of such merged units and staff who report directly to them were invited. Participants explored the issue of whether a merged organization can provide better service to students and faculty than a traditional organization can. To evaluate the services that merged information organizations are providing, the CIO Group endorsed a project to survey users on several campuses. Survey results will allow a college to benchmark its services against those of other schools.

A. R. Zipf Fellowship in Information Management

Richard Swart was the recipient of the 2005 A. R. Zipf Fellowship in Information Management. A Ph.D. student in business information systems and education at Utah State University, Swart is the ninth recipient of the fellowship, which was established in 1997 to recognize a graduate student who shows exceptional promise for leadership and technical achievement in information management. Swart's research areas include semantic integration, management, and security of widely distributed and Web services-enabled data stores, and handling threats from those seeking to disrupt or intercept information flow.

International Developments

Bill and Melinda Gates Foundation Award

Shidhulai Swanirvar Sangstha of Bangladesh received the 2005 Bill and Melinda Gates Foundation Access to Learning Award. The nongovernmental organization was recognized for its use of indigenous boats converted into mobile libraries, schools, and educational units that use generators or solar energy and mobile phones for Internet access. The boats travel to rural communities in a northern Bangladesh watershed, even during monsoon season, to educate women, men, and children on issues ranging from agricultural practices to microenterprise and health concerns.

The award, which totals $1 million, is given annually to public libraries or similar kinds of organizations outside the United States for innovative programs that provide free public access to information technology. The award is intended to inspire others to expand access to information, particularly for the poor, disabled, and minorities. CLIR has managed the award program for the past three years.

Rovelstad Scholarship in International Librarianship

The Rovelstad Scholarship is awarded annually to encourage students who have an interest in international library work and help enable them to participate in activities of the International Federation of Library Associations and Institutions (IFLA) early in their careers. Alison Raab, a graduate student in the School of Information and Library Science at the University of North Carolina–Chapel Hill, was named the third recipient of the Rovelstad Scholarship in International Librarianship. The award, funded by Mathilde and the late Howard Rovelstad and administered by CLIR, provides travel funds for a student of library and information science to attend IFLA's World Library and Information Congress.

CLIR Publications

CLIR published the following in 2005:

Besek, June M. *Copyright Issues Relevant to Digital Preservation and Dissemination of Pre-1972 Commercial Sound Recordings by Libraries and Archives.* Copublished with Library of Congress (December 2005).

Brogan, Martha L., with assistance from Daphnée Rentfrow. *A Kaleidoscope of Digital American Literature.* Copublished with Digital Library Federation (September 2005).

Brooks, Tim. *Survey of Reissues of U.S. Recordings. Copublished with Library of Congress* (August 2005).

Council on Library and Information Resources. *Annual Report 2004–2005* (October 2005).

Council on Library and Information Resources. *Library as Place: Rethinking Roles, Rethinking Space* (February 2005).

Covey, Denise Troll. *Acquiring Copyright Permission to Digitize and Provide Open Access to Books.* Copublished with Digital Library Federation (October 2005).

Jackson, Jack. *Århus Public Libraries: Embracing Diversity, Empowering Citizens in Denmark* (July 2005).

Liu, Geoffrey Z. *Evergreen: Bringing Information Resources to Rural China* (July 2005).

Newsletters

CLIR Issues, nos. 43–48

Association for Library and Information Science Education

1009 Commerce Park Drive, Suite 150, Oak Ridge, TN 37831-4219
Tel. 865-425-0155, fax 865-481-0390, e-mail contact@alise.org
World Wide Web http://www.alise.org

Ken Haycock
President, 2005–2006

The Association for Library and Information Science Education (ALISE) is an independent, nonprofit professional association whose mission is to promote excellence in research, teaching, and service for library and information science (LIS) education through leadership, collaboration, advocacy, and dissemination of research.

ALISE was founded as the Association of American Library Schools. The original association grew out of a series of informal meetings of library school faculty at American Library Association (ALA) conferences that was known as the Round Table of Library School Instructors. The Round Table voted in 1915 to form a permanent organization and to be identified as the Association of American Library Schools. The association has provided a forum for library educators to share ideas, to discuss issues, and to seek solutions to common problems. In 1983 the association changed its name to its present form to reflect more accurately its mission, goals, and membership.

ALISE is now both an institutional and individual membership association. Its institutional members are units within universities—whether departments, programs, or schools—that provide courses and programs designed to educate professionals for libraries and other information agencies. Its personal members are both instructors in the member programs and those who have an interest in education for the library and information professions. While the majority of its institutional members are programs accredited by ALA's Committee on Accreditation, membership is not limited to those programs, and an effort is currently under way to increase its other institutional memberships. In addition, while ALISE is chiefly North American, with a preponderance of its membership drawn from the United States and Canada, it does have international institutional affiliates and personal members. Dues from institutional and personal members are the single largest source of operating funds for the association.

The business of the association is carried out by a board of directors elected by the membership. The board—which establishes policy, sets goals and strategic directions, and provides oversight for association management—consists of a president, vice president/president-elect, past president, secretary/treasurer, and three board members elected on a rotating basis. Each year's slate includes nominees for one board position and for president-elect. Every third year the slate also includes candidates for secretary/treasurer. Thus all board members generally serve three-year terms. The current officers are John Budd (University of Missouri–Columbia), president; Connie Van Fleet (University of Oklahoma), president-elect; Ken Haycock (San Jose State University), past president; Lisa Given (University of Alberta), secretary/treasurer. Board members are Julie Hersberger

(University of North Carolina–Greensboro), director for special interest groups; Heidi Julien (University of Alberta), director for external relations; and Gloria Leckie (University of Western Ontario), director for membership services.

ALISE publishes a journal, the *Journal of Education for Library and Information Science,* under the joint editorship of Cheryl Knott Malone and Anita Sandaram Coleman of the University of Arizona. Annual publications include a membership directory, directory of LIS programs and faculty in the United States and Canada, and the *Library and Information Science Education Statistical Report,* a statistical compendium published in cooperation with ALA's Committee on Accreditation, which gathers data for accreditation purposes. These publications are available for purchase through ALISE.

Annual Conference

The major activity of the association, in addition to its publications, is its Annual Conference, currently held immediately prior to the ALA Midwinter Meeting. The conference serves not only as a venue for sharing scholarship related especially—although not exclusively—to teaching and learning in information and library science, but also as the major opportunity to meet and interview prospective faculty members. A juried doctoral poster session, which in 2005 featured approximately 90 exhibitors, allows established faculty to see the work of doctoral students. In addition, the association distributes applicant résumés and provides space for interviewing candidates.

Conference attendance continues to grow. In 2003 conference registrants totaled 360, in 2004 total registration stood at 353, and in 2005 registration reached 435.

At the 2006 Annual Conference, ALISE focused on research, evidence, and best practice in teaching and learning. More proposals and papers were submitted for the conference than in recent memory. Only one in four was accepted following the refereeing process.

Each year two students are honored with Doctoral Students to ALISE awards on the basis of a short essay and the recommendation of their program head. This award provides complimentary conference registration and a $500 stipend to defray the selected students' conference expenses.

ALISE's special interest groups (SIGs) also meet at the conference, sometimes in informal discussion groups, but more often in order to present panels or papers on topics of interest. SIGs provide a means for individuals to become involved in a relatively small group of people with similar research or teaching interests. The SIGs have been clustered for organizational purposes by area of interest: the Roles and Responsibilities Cluster—Assistant/Associate Deans and Directors, Doctoral Students, New Faculty, and Part-time and Adjunct Faculty; the Teaching and Learning Cluster—Continuing Education, Curriculum, Distance Education, and Teaching Methods; and the Topics and Courses Cluster—Archival/Records Management Education, Gender Issues, Historical Perspectives, Information Ethics, Information Policy, International Library Education, Multicultural, Ethnic and Humanistic Concerns, Preservation Education, Research, Technical Services Education, and Youth Services.

In addition, the Council of Deans, Directors, and Program Chairs, which consists of the chief executive officer of each individual ALISE Institutional member school, plans an annual program to provide a platform for the administrators in library and information science education to address the profession and a structure whereby the executive officers can meet to seek solutions to common problems and to make reports and recommendations to the association.

Strategic Plan

Perhaps most significantly, a strategic planning process was begun in 2004 with member consultation early in 2005 and an approved strategic plan for monitoring and tracking of the organization's directions. The association developed or revised, and approved, vision, mission, and enduring purpose statements, together with five strategic directions with objectives.

Vision

By 2008 ALISE will be the visionary organization in library and information science education. The association will be known for its unique purpose, build its strength, and communicate that strength through vision, voice, and visibility.

Mission

ALISE promotes excellence in research, teaching, and service for library and information science educators through leadership, collaboration, advocacy, and dissemination of research.

Enduring Purpose

ALISE promotes research that informs the scholarship of teaching and learning for library and information science, enabling members to integrate research into teaching and learning.

Strategic Directions

Achieve the association's unique purpose—attaining vision, voice, and visibility through a focus on the scholarship of teaching and learning and the enhancement of research.

The association developed a taxonomy/classification scheme for library and information studies, made conference presentations on the connections between research and teaching and learning, and established a task force on best practices in teaching and learning in LIS education. The task force will provide needed support for quality instruction, especially for newer colleagues and adjunct faculty.

Promote the association's unique purpose through marketing and communication of the ALISE vision.

A student group in an LIS graduate course in marketing worked with the ALISE board to develop a marketing and communications plan. The association also developed a specific marketing plan for adjunct and part-time faculty. These draft plans were presented to the appropriate committees and groups at the annual meeting for consultation and response before implementation begins.

The first-ever LIS Education Pavilion, held at the ALA Annual Conference in 2005, was highly successful based on participation and attendance. The association is developing specific performance measures for 2006 and looks forward to featuring more than 30 graduate programs.

Ensure membership growth to develop the association's unique purpose through strategic development of new special interest groups and targeted growth.

ALISE reinstated a guide to LIS faculty for better connections among members. In addition, the association developed a special interest group for school library media educators, an identified target group for membership development.

In 2003 ALISE membership was 348; in 2004 ALISE membership had grown to 458; in 2005 membership reached 565.

Enhance revenue streams to extend the association's unique purpose through planned development and advancement and new initiatives.

The association established a development and advancement committee with industry representation, introduced a silent auction at its annual conference for contributions to endowed research awards, developed policy and strategy for paid advertisements in publications, and developed a strategy for enhancing conference sponsorships. All of these should contribute to the organization's financial health. Results are beginning to show: at a base level, in 2003 (October–October) ALISE had a fund balance of $1,306; in 2004, $17,364; and in 2005, $50,025.

Restructure to achieve the association's unique purpose, through a realignment of board responsibilities, restructuring and accountability of committees, and translation of the strategic plan into specific, measurable, active, relevant, and timed objectives.

ALISE contracts for association management services with Information International Associates (IIa), headquartered in Oak Ridge, Tennessee. In 2005 the association developed criteria and processes for regular evaluation of the management firm and conducted its first annual assessment. The association identified core services and costs, with incentives for revenue development. It also revised its service agreement with IIa.

The association restructured its operations to ensure ongoing responsibilities for board members and direct connection for committees with the same board member for three years; each of three directors was assigned responsibilities for external relations, member services, and special interest groups. Several existing committees were clustered around awards, research, and publications to develop consistency and coordination; each committee had a specific charge and minimum expectations for the year. A written process was developed for external liaisons and for selecting representatives for liaising with other organizations.

As a primarily North American association, ALISE reviewed and codified relations with the Canadian Association for Information Studies, its Canadian counterpart, to articulate roles and responsibilities for government relations, alumni reunions, and national and international association relationships, resulting in Canadian members paying fees at par in Canadian funds due to reduced services and overhead expenses.

ALISE also developed a conference planning handbook, reviewed and revised its policies and procedures manual, and introduced its first governance committee to review board and association performance.

Two significant changes were incorporated in ALISE culture through the plan. First was to ensure "vision, voice, and visibility" for ALISE, specifically through a focus on the scholarship of teaching and learning. The second was to set aside the ongoing debate over use of the "L" (library) or "I" (information) words and their attendant issues to focus on teaching and learning, a common framework for all ALISE members.

The year 2005 was a transitional year for ALISE, to ensure a strong foundation for the association while beginning the move forward. Previous presidents grappled with enduring structural issues that have now been addressed; future presidents will grapple with new opportunities and competing demands for new programs and services.

Friends of Libraries U.S.A.

1420 Walnut St., Suite 450, Philadelphia, PA 19102
800-936-5872, e-mail friends@folusa.org, World Wide Web http://www.folusa.org

Sally Gardner Reed
Executive Director

Friends of Libraries U.S.A. (FOLUSA) is a national nonprofit organization providing networking opportunities, education, and consultation to local friends-of-the-library groups (friends groups) across the country. Friends groups raise money, awareness, and political support for their libraries, and more than 2,000 friends groups, libraries, and individuals are members of FOLUSA, representing hundreds of thousands of library supporters.

Established in 1979 as a committee of the Library Administration and Management Association of the American Library Association (ALA), FOLUSA is a national leader in library advocacy and support. Its mission is to motivate and support local friends groups in their efforts to preserve and strengthen libraries and to create awareness and appreciation for library services by

- Assisting in developing friends groups in order to generate local, state, and national support
- Providing guidance, education, and consulting services to friends and libraries
- Promoting the development of strong library advocacy programs
- Providing expert information for friends and librarians via toolkits, workshops, and the publication of book and Web-based resources
- Promoting early childhood literacy in partnership with friends groups
- Promoting the appreciation of the nation's literary heritage

Governance

FOLUSA is governed by a 25- to 30-member board of directors. Board members come from all avenues of the library world: friends group members, librarians, leaders of library corporations, publishers, and library supporters.

In June 2005 FOLUSA inaugurated as its president Douglas Roesemann, president of the ReferenceUSA Division of infoUSA, Inc. Vice president/president-elect is Mary K. Dodge, assistant to the dean and liaison to the friends, Auraria Library, Denver; secretary is Margaret Schuster, volunteer services and friends coordinator, Hennepin County (Minnesota) Public Library; and treasurer is Amy Dougherty, executive director, Friends of the Free Library of Philadelphia.

Advocacy and Public Awareness

FOLUSA engages in efforts to raise the political profile of libraries and to help friends and other lay supporters of libraries use the power of their voices to ensure that libraries are supported. FOLUSA is an affiliate of ALA and works closely with its Washington Office and Public Information Office to create programs that engage friends groups and library supporters in library-promotion activities.

In 2003 FOLUSA organized a "virtual march on Washington" to coincide with ALA's National Library Legislation Day, and the virtual march has become an annual event. It helps friends of libraries in contacting their legislative leaders via telephone, Internet, or fax to reinforce the messages that librarians are delivering in person on Capitol Hill that day.

Also on National Library Legislation Day, FOLUSA presents its public service award to a member of Congress who has done the most to support libraries during the previous year. In 2005 the award went to U.S. Rep. Ralph Regula (R-Ohio).

In 2005 FOLUSA partnered with ALA to present the first Advocacy Institute preconference at ALA's Midwinter Meeting in Boston. The institute was held again at the 2005 Annual Conference in Chicago. It focuses on training friends, librarians, and trustees to work together to develop successful local-level advocacy campaigns in the community or on campus.

FOLUSA traveled to more than 15 state and regional library gatherings during the year to work with friends and librarians in creating effective public awareness and advocacy efforts.

Networking Opportunities

Friends groups typically work in isolation from one another. To help them receive advice and counsel from each other and to provide a forum for best practices, FOLUSA hosts a listserv at http://www.folusa.org/html/listserv.html. Approximately 500 friends members and librarians subscribe to and participate on the listserv.

NewsUpdate, FOLUSA's bimonthly newsletter, is another vehicle for the sharing of ideas and best practices. *NewsUpdate,* which has more than 2,500 subscriptions, includes articles and information of interest to friends groups as well as good ideas from groups across the country. Many of these good ideas are archived on FOLUSA's Web site.

Publications and Resources

In addition to *NewsUpdate,* FOLUSA publishes occasional resources and online toolkits to help friends groups increase their effectiveness in serving their libraries.

Toolkits are available free of charge to FOLUSA members via the Friends Zone page of the organization's Web site. They currently include *Starting a New Friends Group or Revitalizing the Group You Have*; *School Media Center Friends Groups: A Prescription for Success*; *Friends and Libraries: Working Effectively Together*; and *Incorporating and Tax Exempting Procedures for Friends.*

Additional resources available to members of FOLUSA include scripts for radio public-service announcements promoting libraries; an organizational chart showing the roles of the players in the library world (librarians, trustees, and friends); "Notable Quotables" (quotes about libraries, books, and reading for use in friends groups' newsletters, Web sites, and other promotions); more than 20 fact sheets on organizational effectiveness and other issues of concern to friends; information about special discount offers for members; and information about FOLUSA award opportunities.

Other publications available to friends and librarians include *101+ Great Ideas for Libraries and Friends, Making Our Voices Heard: Citizens Speak Out for Libraries*, and *Getting Grants in Your Community*.

Programs

FOLUSA presents a variety of literary programs during ALA's Midwinter Meeting and Annual Conference. Working with publisher-sponsors, FOLUSA highlights bestselling authors at its semiannual Author Tea. At annual conferences, additional programs feature first-time published writers in a variety of genres.

At the 2005 Midwinter Meeting, authors taking part in the Author Tea were Aaron Lansky, Frank Delaney, Judith Martin, and Nancy Thayer; at the Annual Conference, they were Ilene Beckerman, Arthur Frommer, Tess Gerritsen, Laura Lippman, and Lisa See.

FOLUSA hosted three additional programs: "First Author, First Book," which included authors Blue Balliett, Kalisha Buckhanon, Robert Kurson, Edward Schwarzchild, Jack Kerley, and John Grogan; "Fighting the Good Fight—Authors on the First Amendment," featuring Floyd Abrams, Linda Greenhouse, and Victor Navasky; and "Street Lit," which featured Darren Coleman, Mister Mann Frisby, Y. Blak Moore, and K'Wan.

Literary Landmarks

In support of its goal to promote appreciation for America's literary heritage, FOLUSA's Literary Landmarks program marks, with foundry-crafted plaques, locations connected to important writers. Begun in 1987, the program has designated 90 landmarks honoring such authors as Willa Cather, Jack London, Theodore Roethke, Zora Neale Hurston, Carl Sandburg, and W. E. B. Dubois.

In 2005 FOLUSA sponsored Literary Landmarks at the William Johnson House in Natchez, Mississippi; at the William Carlos Williams Home in Rutherford, New Jersey; at Tennessee Williams House in New Orleans; at Pearl S. Buck's birthplace in Hillsboro, West Virginia; at Dorothy Parker's birthplace in West End, New Jersey; and honoring Robert McCloskey (at Boston Garden), Upton Sinclair (at Union Stockyard Gate), Randolph Caldecott (at Evergreen Cemetery in St. Augustine, Florida); Richard Bland (at Bland Cemetery in Prince George County, Virginia); and Dashiell Hammett (at an apartment house in which he lived on Post Street in San Francisco).

Books for Babies

Books for Babies is FOLUSA's national literacy program that acquaints parents of newborns with the important role they play in the development of their children. Parents are given a Books for Babies kit containing a book, baby's first library card, and brochures with reading tips for parents and caregivers. Kits are available in English and Spanish.

Library friends groups and women's clubs are among the organizations that purchase Books for Babies packets, often supplementing them with information about local resources, such as library locations and contact information, as well as details about lap-sit and preschool storyhours.

Books for Babies is designed to encourage parents to engage in developmentally appropriate literacy activities with their babies. Parents are a critical part of the developmental equation, and reading aloud to babies is an ideal form of stimulation because it engages visual, auditory, interactive, and attention processes in a pleasurable context. Research shows that babies who are read to and engaged in verbal interaction show superior language and math skills.

The program is believed to have benefited approximately 100,000 babies since its launch in 1992.

International Activities

FOLUSA is extending its reach and expertise to librarians across the world. In 2005 Executive Director Sally Reed traveled to Uzbekistan, Kyrgyzstan, and Turkey to talk about how library friends groups enhance America's libraries and to share ideas with librarians in these countries about how they can connect with their communities and foster citizen support.

These programs, sponsored by the U.S. State Department, are geared toward helping citizens of emerging democracies understand their role in participating in government at the local level and also toward raising community awareness about important resources such as libraries. Although citizen involvement in increasing library support (through fund raising and advocacy) may be a new concept, it is one of great interest to librarians in these countries.

Awards

Several awards are presented to friends groups by FOLUSA each year.

Barbara Kingsolver Award

The Barbara Kingsolver Award is given to a small friends group that has done the most to improve its library. The award includes a $10,000 prize for the purchase of children's books and an expense-paid trip for two of the winning friends group's designees to the ALA Annual Conference. The award, named in honor of author Barbara Kingsolver, is underwritten by HarperCollins Publishers. The 2005 Kingsolver Award went to the Friends of the Effingham (New Hampshire) Public Library who conducted a campaign that resulted in their library going from 4 opening hours a week to 22, creation of an automated catalog, and the hiring of a librarian and children's program director to augment the previously all-volunteer staff.

Baker & Taylor Awards

Baker & Taylor sponsors two awards given annually to friends groups that have distinguished themselves in their support of their libraries and a third award for a friends group that has made the best use of ALA's "@ your library" campaign slogan in its promotional materials. Each of these awards presents $2,000 to the winning friends group, as well as a plaque commemorating its accomplishments. The 2005 winners were: in the small library category, Friends of the Marathon (Texas) Library; in the large library category, Friends of the Solana Beach Branch of the San Diego County Library. The "@ your library" award went to Friends of the Monroe Township (New Jersey) Library.

Best Friends Award

In 2005 FOLUSA launched the Best Friends Award, which will recognize friends groups for print and electronic materials that promote the group and its special programs and projects. The awards do not evaluate the type or scope of the group's programs, only the printed and electronic materials. The winners will be recognized in *NewsUpdate* and on the FOLUSA Web site. Winners also will receive a certificate of recognition from FOLUSA and will be given a press release to help them promote their recognition locally. Winning entries will be posted in the Friends Zone, a members-only section of the FOLUSA Web site, for groups around the country to view. The first awards will be made in 2006.

Authors at Sea

Under an arrangement with the Authors at Sea organization, FOLUSA offers a friends group a free week-long cruise for two to raffle as a fund-raiser. The winning group will be chosen at random from entries submitted to the FOLUSA Web site. The cruise includes deluxe shipboard accommodation and the opportunity to meet and discuss books with bestselling authors. The individual who submits the winning entry to the Web site receives a $100 Target gift certificate and a collection of books for his or her personal library.

FOLUSA's Funding

As a nonprofit organization, FOLUSA receives its funding through three basic revenue streams: corporate sponsorship, membership dues, and the sale of products and services that further its mission. A list of corporate sponsors, as well as membership and sponsorship opportunities, is available at http://www.folusa.org.

International Reports

International Federation of Library Associations and Institutions

P.O. Box 95312, 2509 CH The Hague, Netherlands
Tel. 31-70-314-0884, fax 31-70-383-4827, e-mail ifla@ifla.org
World Wide Web http://www.ifla.org

Beacher Wiggins

Director for Acquisitions and Bibliographic Access, Library of Congress
Library of Congress Representative to the Standing Committee of the
IFLA Section on Bibliography

The International Federation of Library Associations and Institutions (IFLA) is the preeminent international organization representing librarians, other information professionals, and library users. During 2005 IFLA protected the world's cultural and documentary heritage from the ravages of war and natural disaster; broadened participation in its activities by countries with developing economies; expanded the theory and practice of bibliographic control; and promoted equitable access to information without regard to barriers of poverty, handicap, or geographical isolation. Throughout the year, IFLA promoted an understanding of libraries as cultural heritage resources that are the patrimony of every nation.

World Library and Information Conference

More than 3,000 librarians, publishers, and exhibitors from 133 countries took part in the 71st IFLA General Conference and third World Library and Information Conference in Oslo in mid-August. The conference theme, "Libraries—A Voyage of Discovery," was reinforced by the conference logo of a Viking ship. Keynote speaker Francis Sejersted, former chair of the Norwegian Nobel Committee and historian at the University of Oslo, spoke on freedom of expression and libraries, and on the inclusion of a clause on freedom of expression in the Norwegian constitution. The ceremonial high point of the conference was a reception to celebrate the reopening of Norway's restored National Library (Nasjonalbiblioteket) building by King Harald V on Monday, August 15.

The increasingly holistic concept of libraries as part of world cultural heritage was evident in the IFLA National Libraries Section program, "Networking Cultural Heritage: National Libraries, Archives, and Museums Working Together," which included presentations about Library and Archives Canada and the Norwegian Archive, Library, and Museum Authority—two national agencies formed in the past three years by the mergers of more narrowly focused organizations. The library world's increasing experience with digital content was evident in such programs as "Electronic Resources: Different Approaches for End-Users," sponsored by IFLA's Acquisition and Collection Development Section, and "Perspectives on the Supply of Electronic Documents," presented by the Document Delivery and Resource Sharing Section.

Satellite meetings and preconferences offered more-intensive learning opportunities. The Parliamentary Library of Norway sponsored a preconference for the IFLA Library and Research Services for Parliaments Section that stressed the role of parliamentary libraries in educating citizens about their national information structures and in assisting parliamentary libraries in developing countries. The IFLA Africa Section sponsored a workshop on curricula for African schools of library and information science, with attention to online learning tools. The IFLA Newspaper Section reported on work to obtain equipment and locate the master negatives of newspapers in a cooperative project to acquire microfilmed newspapers from Africa for 13 libraries. Other Newspaper Section discussions focused on the importance to libraries of obtaining rights to digitize when acquiring microfilm. Other satellite meetings focused on resisting censorship, continuing professional development for librarians, and statistics and performance measurements in libraries.

Satellite meetings, some of them held in Denmark, England, and Sweden, were a cost-effective way for travelers to combine the general conference with a concentrated learning experience.

The Arctic Circle Conservation Colloquium was a satellite meeting held in Mo i Rana, Norway. This colloquium highlighted state-of-the-art storage and conservation practices at the National Library of Norway's low-oxygen, low-temperature facility at Mo i Rana, where robots are used to retrieve collection materials, clean them, and select materials for deacidification. Low-oxygen storage, which can protect library materials against aging and fire, was also featured at a program on "Housing for Eternity—Sustainable Solutions and Mistakes to Avoid."

The Reading and School Libraries and Resource Centres sections cosponsored an invitational meeting on "Literacy for Life." After several years of work, the Reading Section has issued Guidelines for Library-Based Literacy Programs, a set of practical tips on identifying target audiences and partner institutions, planning and choosing materials, training library staff for literacy promotion initiatives, and measuring program effectiveness. The Reading Section also sponsored a bilingual reading promotion program with the British Council and the Pushkin Library and promoted the United Nations Decade for Literacy, which ends in 2010.

Conference of Directors of National Libraries

The Conference of Directors of National Libraries (CDNL) is an independent association that meets in conjunction with the IFLA Conference to promote cooperation on matters of common interest to national libraries around the world. At the Oslo CDNL meeting, a major focus was on how national libraries are making the content of their collections available on the World Wide Web. The

National Library of Norway is a pioneer in using commercial search engines to access its digital collections, which number nearly 1 million items. Most European national libraries have joined forces in a massive cooperative digitization program, and all were considering how to deal with the impact of Google and other search engines on their operations. European criticisms of "American cultural imperialism" during the CDNL meeting were countered by observations that American libraries collect materials in hundreds of different languages and have worked collaboratively for many years, through the Digital Library Federation and other bodies, to make digital collections generally available.

World Summit on the Information Society

The second World Summit on the Information Society (WSIS) was held in Tunis, Tunisia, November 16–18, 2005. The summit is sponsored by the International Telecommunications Union, a United Nations organization separate from UNESCO, and IFLA was concerned that, without substantial input from the library community, the summit would address only a technical and corporate agenda. To ensure a strong advocacy role for libraries at WSIS, IFLA presidents Kay Raseroka (2003–2005) and Alex Byrne (2005–2007), with past presidents Robert Wedgeworth and Christine Deschamps and new president-elect Claudia Lux, met with 120 librarians at a pre-summit conference in Alexandria, Egypt, to discuss "Libraries—The Information Society in Action." They developed a database of Library Success Stories and drafted IFLA's "Alexandria Manifesto on Libraries, the Information Society in Action." At the actual summit in Tunis, Byrne spoke as a panelist on "The Role of WIPO and NGOs to Balance Intellectual Property Rights" and also addressed the final plenary session. IFLA's advocacy ensured that the concluding WSIS document, the "Tunis Agenda for the Information Society," recognized the role of libraries in providing equitable access to information and knowledge for all and called on governments to support libraries in this role.

Response to War and Natural Disaster

The international library community's concern for the preservation of cultural heritage intensified in 2005 in response to armed conflict in Iraq and natural disasters around the world. In 1996 IFLA joined with three other organizations—the International Council on Archives, the International Council on Monuments and Sites, and the International Council of Museums—to found the International Committee of the Blue Shield (ICBS) to protect cultural property in the event of natural and man-made disasters. In 2005 ICBS worked with UNESCO and Interpol to mitigate damage to cultural and documentary heritage in Iraq and following the massive earthquake that struck Bam, Iran, in December 2003. ICBS paid particular attention to combating illicit trade in Iraqi antiquities in 2005.

When Hurricane Katrina struck the U.S. Gulf Coast on August 29, 2005, ICBS issued a statement expressing "sorrow and solidarity with the American people and in particular with the population of Louisiana, Mississippi, and Alabama for the loss of lives and for the terrible disruption of their livelihood caused by hurricane Katrina and the ensuing floods." ICBS called on the U.S. federal, state, and local governments to draw up and implement plans to ensure the survival and restoration of historic buildings and sites, museum collections, books in libraries, and documents in archives, and urged the international community to support these efforts. In directly practical steps, IFLA began to establish regional centers for preservation and conservation. The North American regional center at the Library of Congress is developing a network of colleague institutions to provide a safety net for library collections during emergencies.

ICBS continued to work toward full international adoption of the 1954 Hague Convention—the Convention for the Protection of Cultural Property in the Event of Armed Conflict—and the two additional protocols of 1954 and 1999. The 1954 Hague Convention requires that cultural property looted during wartime be returned to its rightful owners. The additional protocols define "cultural war crimes" and give ICBS a formal advisory role in the protection of cultural property during armed conflicts. At the end of 2005, 37 countries had become parties to the 1999 protocol, which went beyond specifying legal restrictions in wartime to prescribing practical preparations to be undertaken in peacetime, such as inventorying important cultural property and planning for evacuating such property to safety should armed conflict occur.

Almost immediately after the earthquake and tsunami that devastated parts of South and Southeast Asia on December 26, 2004, IFLA began fund-raising and other efforts to restore some of the hundreds of libraries that were destroyed by the disaster, particularly in Sri Lanka. Rescue work for Sri Lankan and other South Asian libraries will continue for years to come.

Bibliographic Control

IFLA has worked steadily over the decades to improve bibliographic control through practical workshops, support of the International Standard Bibliographic Description, and research that seeks to establish basic principles of bibliographic control and to identify areas where cataloging practice in different cultures can be harmonized to make library catalogs less expensive to produce and easier for patrons to use.

The IFLA Governing Board joined with six national libraries—the British Library, Die Deutsche Bibliothek, the Library of Congress, the National Library of Australia, the Biblioteca Nacional de Portugal, and the Koninklijke Bibliotheek (Netherlands)—and the Conference of Directors of National Libraries (CDNL) to form the IFLA-CDNL Alliance for Bibliographic Standards (ICABS) in 2003. In addition to general issues of bibliographic control, ICABS works to advance the understanding of issues relating to long-term archiving of electronic resources. The first ICABS program took place at the Buenos Aires IFLA conference in 2004. At the Oslo conference in 2005, ICABS presented a session on "Maintaining Access to Digital Collections." The program highlighted the central role of metadata and of format registries in ensuring long-term accessibility of digital content as online formats continue to evolve rapidly.

The FRANAR (Functional Requirements and Numbering of Authority Records) Working Group, supported by the ICABS initiative, released its report

Functional Requirements for Authority Records for worldwide review in the summer. The FRANAR model aims to show how library authority records currently function and how authority control might be improved in the future. The FRANAR group moved away from the notion of a "standard authority data number" and envisioned a future in which there is no longer a single authorized form for each entity in a catalog.

The third International Meeting of Experts on an International Cataloging Code (IME ICC) was held in Cairo December 12–14, 2005. The IME ICC meetings are a series of five regional invitational conferences planned by the IFLA Cataloguing Section to explore similarities and differences in current national and regional cataloging rules, in an attempt to clarify where variations for languages and cultural differences may be needed and where rules might be the same. The first meeting was held in Frankfurt in 2003 for experts from Europe and North America; the second took place in Buenos Aires in conjunction with the 2004 World Library and Information Conference and IFLA General Conference. The goal is to increase the ability to share cataloging information worldwide by promoting standards for the content of bibliographic and authority records used in library catalogs.

Grants and Awards

IFLA continues to collaborate with corporate partners and national libraries to maintain programs and opportunities that would otherwise not be possible, especially for librarians and libraries in developing countries. The IFLA/OCLC Early Career Development Fellowships bring library and information science professionals from countries with developing economies who are in the early stages of their careers to the United States for four weeks of intensive experience in librarianship. In 2005 the Fellows were from China, Colombia, Georgia, and Malawi. Announced in Oslo in 2005, the Fellows for 2006 will be from Brazil, Indonesia, Kenya, Moldova, and Trinidad and Tobago. The American Theological Library Association is now a third sponsor of the program, and one of the Fellows must be a theological librarian.

The Frederick Thorpe Award was established in 2003, administered by the IFLA Libraries for the Blind Section and the Ulverscroft Foundation of Leicester, England, which Thorpe founded to support the visually impaired. In 2004 this £15,000 grant took the form of three £5,000 travel stipends awarded to Wendy Patricia Ling of the South African Library for the Blind; Ademike Olorundore, librarian at the Anglo-Nigerian Welfare Association for the Blind; and Sarah Home, operations and development manager at Britain's National Library for the Blind. They carried out their travel between November 2004 and October 2005. No award was made in 2005, but the Ulverscroft Foundation agreed to renew the program as the Ulverscroft/IFLA Best Practice Awards (Frederick Thorpe Awards) in 2006.

The Bill and Melinda Gates Foundation Access to Learning Award was presented during the Oslo conference to Shidhulai Swanirvar Sangstha, a nongovernmental organization in Bangladesh, recognized for its pioneering approach to bridging the digital divide and its commitment to providing free public access to computers and the Internet. This annual award, managed by the Council on Library and Information Resources, presents up to $1 million to libraries, library agencies, or comparable organizations outside the United States that have been innovative in providing free public access to information. Shidhulai Swanirvar Sangstha planned to use the award money to double its fleet of boat libraries, which bring Internet technology and other library services to remote communities in northern Bangladesh.

In 2002, 2003, and 2004, IFLA and 3M Library Systems cosponsored the International Marketing Awards to recognize best practices in library marketing and public relations. In 2005 IFLA and SirsiDynix announced plans to renew the award program for 2006. The marketing award includes a stipend and travel to the annual IFLA Conference, which in 2006 will be held in Seoul.

Membership

IFLA has approximately 1,700 members in 150 countries. Initially established at a conference in Edinburgh in 1927, it has been registered in the Netherlands since 1971 and has headquarters facilities at the Koninklijke Bibliotheek (Royal Library) in The Hague. Although IFLA did not hold a General Conference outside Europe and North America until 1980, there has since been steadily increasing participation from Asia, Africa, South America, and Australia. The federation now maintains regional offices for Africa (in Dakar); Asia and Oceania (in Singapore); and Latin America and the Caribbean (in Rio de Janeiro). The organization has five working languages—English, French, German, Russian, and Spanish—and offers six membership categories: international library associations, national library associations, other associations (generally regional or special library associations), institutions, personal affiliates, and student affiliates. Association and institution members have voting rights in the IFLA General Council and may nominate candidates for IFLA offices; personal affiliates have no voting rights, but may run for any office. In addition, more than two dozen corporations in the information industry have formed a working relationship with IFLA as corporate partners, providing financial and in-kind support. UNESCO has given IFLA formal associate relations status, the highest level of relationship accorded to nongovernmental organizations by UNESCO.

Personnel, Structure, and Governance

The secretary general of IFLA is Peter Johan Lor. Sjoerd M. J. Koopman is coordinator of professional activities, an IFLA headquarters position, and also served as acting secretary general until Lor assumed this role on a permanent basis on February 15, 2005.

The current president of IFLA is Alex Byrne, university librarian of the University of Technology, Sydney, who began his two-year term at the close of the Oslo conference. The president-elect is Claudia Lux, director general, Zentral- und Landesbibliothek Berlin. The treasurer is Gunnar Sahlin, National Librarian of Sweden.

Under revised statutes that took effect in 2001, IFLA's former executive board and professional board were combined in a new governing board. The 21-member board (plus the secretary general, ex officio) is responsible for IFLA's general policies, management and finance, and external communications. The current members, in addition to Byrne, Lux, Sahlin, and Lor, are Barbara J. Ford (United States), Sang-wan Han (Republic of Korea), Bob McKee (United Kingdom), Vinyet Panyella (Spain), Adolfo Rodriguez Gallardo (Mexico), Shawky Salem (Egypt), Réjean Savard (Canada), Tiiu Valm (Estonia), and Zhang Xiaolin (China), plus the chair and members of the professional committee, named below. In addition, Keith Michael Fiels, executive director of the American Library Association, and Gary Strong, university librarian, University of California, Los Angeles, were co-opted to the governing board, with their terms extended to cover 2005 and 2006.

The governing board delegates responsibility for overseeing the direction of IFLA between board meetings, within the policies established by the board, to the IFLA Executive Committee, which includes the president, president-elect, treasurer, chair of the professional committee, two members of the governing board (elected every two years by members of the board from among its elected members), and IFLA's secretary general, ex officio. The current elected governing board members of the executive committee are Nancy Gwinn (United States) and McKee.

The IFLA Professional Committee monitors the planning and programming of professional activities carried out by IFLA's two types of bodies: professional groups (eight divisions, 48 sections, and discussion groups) and core activities, formerly called core programs. The professional committee is composed of one elected officer from each division plus a chair elected by the incoming members; the president-elect and the coordinator of professional activities; and two elected members of the governing board, currently Panyella and Zhang. Jacinta Were, systems librarian, University of Nairobi Library, Kenya, chairs the professional committee.

The eight divisions of IFLA and their representatives on the professional committee are: I: General Research Libraries (Donna Scheeder, United States); II: Special Libraries (Nancy Bolt, United States); III: Libraries Serving the General Public (Torny Kjekstad, Norway); IV: Bibliographic Control (Barbara Tillett, United States); V: Collections and Services (Edward Swanson, United States); VI: Management and Technology (Nancy E. Gwinn, United States); VII: Education and Research (Gwynneth Evans, Canada); and VIII: Regional Activities (Maria Isabel Cabral da Franca, Brazil). Each division has interest sections such as Statistics and Evaluation, Library Theory and Research, and Management and Marketing; other sections focus on particular types of libraries or parts of the world.

The six core activities are Advancement of Librarianship (ALP), Preservation and Conservation (PAC), IFLA-CDNL Alliance for Bibliographic Standards (ICABS), IFLA UNIMARC Programme (UP), Committee on Free Access to Information and Freedom of Expression (FAIFE), and Committee on Copyright and Other Legal Matters (CLM).

IFLA's Three Pillars: Society, Members, and Profession

In December 2004 the IFLA Governing Board endorsed a new operational model for IFLA based on three pillars: society, membership, and professional matters. A review of IFLA's core activities, conducted in 2003 and 2004, showed that all of the federation's core functions related to three strategic factors: the societal contexts in which libraries and information services operate, the membership of the federation, and the library profession.

Although the three pillars and the infrastructure of IFLA are interdependent, they can be roughly analyzed as follows: The society pillar focuses on the role and impact of libraries and information services in society. Activities supported by the society pillar include FAIFE, CLM, Blue Shield, and IFLA's presence at the World Summit on the Information Society. The profession pillar focuses on the activities covered by IFLA's sections and divisions and its core activities ALP, ICABS, PAC, and UP. The members pillar includes IFLA's member services, conferences, and publications. The federation's operational infrastructure—consisting of IFLA headquarters, the IFLANET Web site, and the IFLA governance structure—supports and receives strategic direction from these three pillars.

Within the framework of the three pillars, the president and governing board positioned IFLA for significant change. In 2005, working parties focused on the society pillar, improved the IFLANET Web site, and began to articulate a new approach to budget management. The federation's major periodical publication, *IFLA Journal,* was published by Sage Publications beginning in January 2005; it had been published by K. G. Saur since 1978. Beyond these immediate changes, the three pillars will provide a focus for IFLA's future budgets and management decisions.

Canada's Libraries in 2005:
Legal Issues, Funding, Openings Lead Year's News

Karen G. Adams

Director of Library Services and Information Resources
University of Alberta Libraries

After a year and five months in office, Canada's minority federal Liberal government fell on November 28, 2005. The cause was a no-confidence motion triggered by concerns over a patronage scandal in Quebec that was the subject of a public inquiry. On January 23, 2006, voters elected a Conservative minority government with Stephen Harper becoming the nation's 22nd prime minister. The new government was Canada's smallest minority government (in terms of the percentage of seats held by the governing party) since confederation more than a century ago.

Canada's gross domestic product (GDP) rose 3 percent from November 2004 to November 2005. The greatest increases over the period were in wholesale trade and the category "arts, entertainment, and recreation." Information and cultural industries also experienced above-average growth. In October 2005 Statistics Canada released its data on cultural spending in the 2003–2004 fiscal year by all three levels of government—federal, provincial/territorial, and municipal. The data identified total expenditures of C$7.3 billion, an increase of 4.1 percent over 2002–2003. The federal government spent C$11 per capita, with cultural industries (broadcasting, the film and video industries, book and periodical publishing, and the sound recording industry) and heritage (museums, archives, nature parks, and historic sites) being the major recipients. The provincial/territorial governments spent C$69 per capita, and the municipal governments C$63 per capita. Public libraries continued to dominate provincial/territorial and municipal budgets for culture, receiving some C$856 million in total from the provinces and territories, an increase of 6 percent overall, along with C$1.5 billion from municipalities, an increase of 5.9 percent.[1,2]

In fiscal year 2005–2006, the majority of provinces and territories continued the trend of increasing expenditures on libraries. Provincial grants to public libraries in Saskatchewan increased by 2 percent in 2005–2006, and an additional C$300,000 was allocated from Saskatchewan Learning to foster collaborative projects between school divisions and public library systems relating to joint planning for library collections, programs, or services. British Columbia's public libraries saw a modest increase in per capita operating grants and continued to benefit from the infusion of C$12 million over three years as announced in November 2004 to support the strategic plan, Libraries Without Walls. As part of that plan, C$1.8 million was allocated to British Columbia's public libraries. Half of the new funding for libraries was intended to support literacy programs, such as training staff to deliver early literacy, helping libraries purchase special collections in other languages, and supporting libraries' partnerships at the local level with other literacy services. The remaining C$900,000 was earmarked for technology to help libraries participate in electronic opportunities. In Alberta, provincial operating funding remained constant, with a special allocation of C$1.7 million to cover the annual cost of connecting public libraries to the Alberta SuperNet. In Manitoba, public library grants increased 1.6 percent to enable the province to match increased municipal contributions under the provincial formula.

In Ontario, provincial operating grants to libraries remained constant despite a reduction of C$1.2 million in library funds within the Ontario Ministry of Culture. The two Ontario Library Services (OLS-North and SOLS) offices operated by the ministry assumed C$700,000 of the reductions. The Ontario Ministry of Education announced $61 million in dedicated funding for elementary and secondary school libraries, covering materials including textbooks and learning resource materials. The program's goal was to provide equal treatment for small schools that have been traditionally disadvantaged by per capita formulas for distribution of funding.[3]

British Columbia also announced funding for school libraries and learning resources as part of its C$150 million investment in schools. Funding was contingent on school boards having a plan to ensure student access to school libraries, learning resources, music and arts programs, and improved services for special needs students.[4]

Postsecondary libraries in Alberta were allocated C$30 million from the endowed Access to the Future Fund announced as part of Bill 1. The allocation, intended to be annual, will support the development of the Lois Hole Campus Alberta Digital Library, a digital library that will allow postsecondary students and faculty across the province to access the digitized resources and knowledge currently held in the individual libraries of postsecondary institutions. This initiative was centered on the work already under way at the University of Calgary, with administration through the Alberta Library.[5]

Studies

Library and Archives Canada (LAC) released the results of its consultations early in 2005 and found general support within the community for proposed new directions: a new kind of knowledge institution; a truly national institution, providing Canadians with access to the whole of their documentary heritage through working with others; and a prime learning destination. Libraries sought the continuation of certain programs, such as AMICUS, at no cost; the library book rate; interlibrary loan; coordination of ISBN, ISSN, and ISMN programs; and core library statistics. Libraries sought more LAC leadership in meeting the challenges of digital information and in balancing the traditional library with new opportunities resulting from the digital environment.[6]

Results of the first national study of human resource issues in Canadian libraries (informally known as the 8Rs project) were published in 2005. *The Future of Human Resources in Canadian Libraries* documents retirement plans among librarians and paraprofessionals and notes the need for librarians able to perform managerial functions and to assume leadership roles. As a result, the report recommends inclusion of the concept of the "librarian as manager" into the socialization process of library education. The next phase of the project will consist of a gap analysis of library education and workplace competencies for librarians and library technicians.[7]

In May Statistics Canada released data from its *Information and Communications Technology in Schools* survey showing that 93.3 percent of schools had libraries and that the median expenditure on new materials was C$2,000. The mean expenditure on electronic resources was C$513. Few schools had a full-time teacher-librarian (0.25 teacher-librarians per school was the average); slightly more library technicians were reported (an average of 0.26 per school). Schools with teacher-librarians were more likely to use technology applications in teaching, and those with full-time teacher-librarians were roughly three times more likely than those with part-time teacher-librarians to have links to the library on the school's Web site.[8]

A report commissioned by the Canadian Association of Research Libraries (CARL) found that the use of electronic learning in Canadian universities has increased by 30 percent over the past five years. The report, *Libraries and E-Learning—Final Report of the CARL E-Learning Working Group,* noted that in 2002–2003 more than 330,000 students at CARL universities took advantage of instruction in using electronic library resources.[9]

The Canadian Library Association (CLA) released its report on the establishment of a national network for equitable library service, enhanced alternative format collections, and standards for service and collections. The report, *Opening the Book: A Strategy for a National Network for Equitable Library Service for Canadians with Print Disabilities,* was sent to the federal government for its response.[10]

In a report released in March 2005, *Reading and Buying Books for Pleasure: 2005 National Survey Final Report,* Canadian Heritage found that reading for pleasure remains a solidly established habit of Canadians with little or no change since the previous survey, in 1991. A total of 54 percent of Canadians surveyed read books for pleasure regularly (almost every day), and 33 percent read occasionally; 87 percent read at least one book a year. The three social variables that correlated with reading for pleasure were gender (women read more than men); education (those who have completed university read more regularly than those who have not completed postsecondary education); and language (francophones with French as their mother tongue have lower reading rates than anglophones). The study found that the growth of home Internet use has not been at the expense of reading for pleasure, but there was a negative impact reported in regard to television viewing and reading newspapers and magazines.[11]

An analysis of data gathered during the 2001 federal census found that 48 percent of Canadian households spent C$1.1 billion on books, compared with the 63 percent of households that spent C$1.2 billion on newspapers, and the 61 percent of households that spent C$1.2 billion on movie admissions. The highest proportion of book-buying households (53 percent) were in the prairie provinces; the lowest (41 percent) in Quebec. In contrast, Canadians spent C$451 million on live sports events.[12]

In another study, *Online News and Information Seeking: What the Future Holds,* Ipsos Reid found that the amount of time Internet-using Canadians are spending actively using the Internet is on the rise, averaging 12.7 hours a week (up 46 percent from 8.7 hours in 2002). This increase appears to have come at the expense of radio; the typical Internet-using adult now spends 11 hours a week listening to the radio, down from 16 hours a week in 2002. Television retained the number-one position among media sources with Internet-using Canadians averaging 14.3 hours of viewing per week. The gap between Internet and television usage appeared to be closing (a difference of 1.6 hours per week compared with 4.5 hours in 2002), with the Internet threatening to overtake television should the trend continue.[13]

International and National Information Policy Issues

GATS

CLA continued to monitor the General Agreement on Trade in Services (GATS) situation with respect to library services and prepared the *GATS and Libraries Pathfinder*. Canada has made no commitment that library services fall under GATS rules; on the other hand, it has not granted libraries any specific protection. The United States has committed its libraries to GATS rules, but has reassured the community that "public" library services will be safe. The Ontario government also has an FAQ on GATS and libraries, and notes its view that the risk of a challenge to libraries in Canada under GATS is relatively low.[14, 15]

Library Book Rate

Once again, Canada Post announced its plan to end the library book rate, with one year's notice, in April 2006; once again, the library community fought back, and the decision was reversed. On July 22 National Revenue Minister John McCallum announced that the program would continue in spite of the expiration of the agreement between Canada Post and the Department of Canadian Heritage. The library book rate was also an action item at the first meeting of the provincial ministers responsible for public library services (see below). The value of the subsidy to libraries is estimated at C$13 million.[16]

Copyright

The copyright reform process that stalled in 2004 began again in 2005 with the tabling by Industry Minister David Emerson and Canadian Heritage Minister Liza Frulla of the government's response to the Standing Committee on Canadian Heritage, including proposals for reform. Bill C-60, An Act to Amend the Copyright Act, was introduced June 20 with amendments relating to World Intellectual Property Organization (WIPO) issues, Internet service provider (ISP) liability, educational and research access issues, and photography issues. The government also signaled its intention to begin a public consultation process on educational use of publicly available Internet material.

Access Copyright, the licensing collective for print materials, has been an advocate for licensing of material on the Internet, while the Council of Ministers of Education and other education groups were advocates for continuing the current practice of open, no-cost access to material publicly available on the Internet. The government also announced that it would to continue to work on private copying (the regime that allows private copying of music onto discs and tapes with royalties through a levy on the blank media) and on reproductions made by broadcasters. The major reform with respect to libraries included document delivery directly to patron desktops, a service explicitly prohibited under current legislation. In general, the response of those interested in copyright reform to the bill was lukewarm, perhaps the most positive response that can be expected on a matter as divisive as copyright. It was expected that the bill would receive a second reading during the fall session of Parliament and be referred to a legislative committee that would hold hearings and receive briefs from the public, but the copyright reform process was halted once again when, on November 29, the government fell and the January election was called.[17]

As noted above, the private copying regime was to have been part of the copyright reform agenda. The Canadian Private Copying Collective (CPCC) has collected a levy on audio cassettes (C29 cents), CD-R and CD-RW (C21 cents), and CD-R Audio and CD-RW Audio MiniDiscs (C77 cents) and redistributed the royalties to rights-holders in music. From January 2003 to January 2005, C$33.2 million in royalties was distributed to music authors, music publishers, recording artists, musicians, and record companies. In December 2003, CPCC added a levy on nonremovable memory, including both flash memory and hard drives embedded in digital audio recorders at rates from C$2 to C$25 based on the capacity in gigabytes. In late December 2004 the Federal Court of Appeal concluded that the levy on memory was invalid because the tariff-setting body, the Copyright Board of Canada, did not have the jurisdiction to impose the levy. The court subsequently decided that CPCC could keep the C$4.1 million in levies collected pending its application for leave to appeal to the Supreme Court of Canada. In July 2005 the Supreme Court denied CPCC's application, with the result that the C$4.1 million in levies must be reimbursed to the companies that submitted them.[18]

Digital Divide Funding

Although the Community Access Program (CAP) has been Industry Canada's showcase program for eliminating the digital divide, libraries anticipated that 2005–2006 marked the last year of funding for public libraries. The 2005–2006 funds were to be distributed on a competitive basis, with the priorities being support for the delivery of public access; support in reaching Canadians who face the digital divide; support for other online service delivery by the federal government; and support for improved access for people with disabilities. CAP was one of a series of programs operating under the now-defunct rubric "Connecting Canadians;" funding support for broadband and satellite connectivity in remote and northern communities and for connecting Canadian francophone communities continues. CLA responded to the last year of CAP with an advocacy campaign and a resolution at its June annual meeting. In October 2005 the federal government announced two individual initiatives relating to the digital divide. The Digital Inclusion Program includes the private sector and charitable organizations as partners, with the intention of improving access to information technology by providing hardware, software, and technical support in shelters for the homeless. The Computers for Schools Program announced a successful pilot in Manitoba's Headingley Correctional Centre, where aboriginal inmates were trained to refurbish computers for the program.[19, 20, 21, 22, 23]

Censorship

The lengthy legal fight over the ability of Canada Customs to block importation of books and magazines at the border on the grounds of obscenity continued. Little Sisters Book and Art Emporium in Vancouver won the right to appeal to the Supreme Court of Canada and to argue that the federal government should be funding its legal battles with Canada Customs. Normally such funding is reserved for cases in which constitutional matters are at stake and individual litigants cannot afford to fund the case on their own. Estimated legal costs are C$500,000 to C$1 million.[24]

In June a collection of photographs on display at the Côte Saint-Luc library was shut down by the municipal council, following a public complaint that the exhibit was pro-Palestinian. The photographs were the work of Montreal-based Zahra Kazemi, who died while in the custody of police in Tehran in July 2003.[25]

Depository Services Program

After some months of investigation, the LAC Depository Services Program (DSP) Steering Committee announced in August to the DSP Library Advisory Committee that a transfer of DSP to LAC would not be cost effective, noting special issues involving warehousing, customer service functions, and the e-bookstore. DSP will form part of a new organization, Service Canada.[26]

Events

Ministers Meet

The first meeting of the ministers responsible for public library services took place in Calgary in June 2005 during the CLA annual conference. In addition to discussing the role of public libraries in early-childhood learning, supporting cultural communities, providing electronic access to government information, and creating the digital Canadian memory, the ministers agreed to express their concerns about the threatened cancellation of the library book rate to the federal government and to meet again in June 2006 in Ottawa.[27]

Grande Bibliothèque Opens

The Grande Bibliothèque du Québec opened to the public on May 10, 2005, after four years under construction. The building provides access to more than 4 million documents published in a variety of formats, primarily in French but also in English and other languages, and constructed as two collections. The first, the national collection, contains everything published in Quebec, and about Quebec; this collection is for in-library use only. The second is the universal lending and reference collection, entirely for lending purposes, consisting of the collections of the Bibliothèque Centrale de Montréal (including those of the Phonothèque), the sound recordings and braille books of the Institut Nazareth et Louis-Braille and the Magnétothèque, and nearly a half million new acquisitions purchased specifically for the facility. The Grande Bibliothèque has received accolades for its interior design and its furnishings. The total cost was C$97.6 million for construction, design, furniture, and equipment.[28, 29]

Barber Learning Centre Progresses

In early October the first phase of the C$68 million Irving K. Barber Learning Centre opened at the University of British Columbia. It features Canada's first and North America's largest library robot as part of its automated storage and retrieval system for books and other library materials. This new construction replaced the original north wing of the main library, built in 1948; a second phase to replace the center and south wings was begun.[30]

Milestone in Winnipeg

Winnipeg Public Library opened its Millennium Library on November 8 after years of fund raising by the Winnipeg Library Foundation and renovation and construction activities since 2003. The new construction added 40,000 square feet to the existing 140,000 square feet to create a state-of the-art facility. The year also saw the celebration of the 90th anniversaries of the two remaining Carnegie libraries in Winnipeg, the Cornish Library and the St. John's Library, both of which opened in June 1915.[31, 32]

Ottawa Opening Delayed

The Library of Parliament in Ottawa did not reopen as planned in August; the renovation was six months behind schedule, and well over budget (C$136 million rather than C$83 million). The delays were caused by the fact that original construction took place from 1859 to 1876, and the original plans provided little detail about what was under and inside the building. The renovation will add three new basements, including mobile shelving units for rare books.[33]

Vanishing Bookmobiles

Another of the handful of remaining bookmobiles in Canada stopped running at the end of June, this one the last in the service of Saskatoon Public Library where it was once one of three used to take library service to smaller neighborhoods.[36]

Privacy Decision

Based on a case in Parkland Regional Library, the Alberta Information and Privacy Commissioner ruled in June that keystroke-logging software installed without an employee's knowledge violated the employee's privacy rights.[37]

Name Change

The School of Information Management (SIM) was approved by Dalhousie University as the new name of the university's School of Library and Information Studies, effective May 9, 2005. The new name is intended to reflect and promote the breadth of the education and research conducted by members of the school, and to emphasize that the school recruits and educates for a wide array of information management positions.[34]

Leadership Conference

Canada's library leadership event, the Northern Exposure to Leadership Institute, was held September 29–October 4 at Emerald Lake, British Columbia. The institute was the eighth of its kind, and 24 librarians who received their library degrees within the past seven years attended.[38]

Canadian Library Week

Canadian Library Week took place October 17–24 with the theme "Lifelong Libraries: Discover Us/Les Bibliothèques C'est Pour la Vie: Découvrez-Les." Sarmite Bulte, parliamentary secretary to the minister of Canadian heritage, launched the week on October 20, reading a statement in the House of Commons to encourage all members of Parliament and all Canadians to discover their local libraries. In communities across the country, celebrations brought people to the library. In Clarington, Ontario, the library held a reception. In Newfoundland and Labrador, librarians organized a poetry contest and offered schools games and puzzles to underscore the role libraries play. In Saskatchewan, Canadian Library Week served as part of an invitation to rediscover the province through local public libraries. Also celebrated during Canadian Library Week was National School Library Day, held on October 24.[39]

Ontario Marks First Nations Library Week

Ontario First Nations celebrated First Nations Public Library Week in February 2005; the week pays tribute to First Nations (aboriginal) oral tradition by respecting and building on community storytelling traditions. The Ontario Ministry of Culture supported the development of library services in the province's First Nations communities with annual funding of C$798,800 through its First Nations Library Development Program.[35]

Innovations and Initiatives

AlouetteCanada

The Canadian Association of Research Libraries (CARL) launched the Open Canada Digitization Initiative, known familiarly as AlouetteCanada, on November 17. The initiative was the result of a meeting that included CARL members and representatives from the public library, museum, and archive communities. AlouetteCanada is a component of the Open Content Alliance and plans to work in concert with the Canadian digital information strategy being developed by LAC. The launch was preceded by a meeting in October sponsored by LAC that brought together content producers, libraries and archives, federal departments and agencies, university-based digital initiatives, educators, and the municipal sector to explore the possibility of collaboratively developing a national digital information strategy.[40, 41]

Information Literacy Portal

CARL also launched its Information Literacy Portal in 2005, to encourage the sharing of resources and the promotion of best practices in information literacy. The site provides an inventory of Canadian practice as well as links to relevant sites.[42]

'New Direction' in Regina

After a period of controversial deliberations about the fate of its branches and services, Regina Public Library issued its plan for the future, "A New Direction," in March 2005. The plan details the options under consideration for each branch, as well as the Dunlop Art Gallery and the Prairie History Room, both of which had been threatened with closure during budget discussions.[43]

Initiatives at LAC

LAC announced two projects intended to improve service. The first, which began on November 1 as a pilot, will test allowing clients to use their own photographic equipment and LAC microform printers and scanners to copy documents held by LAC for purposes of research and private study. The second initiative saw LAC offering access to free wireless Internet service in the reference rooms and consultation rooms at its main Ottawa site.[44, 45]

Partnership in Ottawa

Ottawa Public Library received an unsolicited proposal from DCR/Phoenix Group of Companies to build a new $150 million central library for the City of Ottawa and the Ottawa Public Library Board under a public-private partnership agreement. The city has needed a new central library for many years to replace the current 90,000-square-foot facility; the proposal would construct a new library of some 271,000 square feet. In essence, the developer would finance the construction, lease it back to the city for 35 years, and then assume ownership.[46]

New Journal

Canada's second journal in library and information science was launched in fall 2005 by the University of Alberta Libraries. *Evidence Based Library and Information Practice* is a new open access, peer-reviewed journal scheduled to begin publication in 2006. The purpose of the journal is to provide a forum for librarians to discover research that can contribute to decision making supported by best practices.[47]

Librarians Without Borders

Librarians Without Borders (LWB) was founded by the MLIS program at the University of Western Ontario with the following mission: "LWB is an organization that strives to improve access to information resources regardless of language, by forming partnerships with community organizations in developing countries." The group's first project was in Angola, helping to develop a medical library.[48]

Distance-Education Group Grows

The Partnership, a collaboration of library associations that delivers distance-education programming to libraries, grew to include the British Columbia Library Association, the Library Association of Alberta, the Saskatchewan Library Association, the Ontario Library Association, the Atlantic Provinces Library Association, and the Nova Scotia Library Association. Associations share the profits earned by the programs and services of the Partnership, based on the participation of their members.[49]

ASIN Portal

The 17 postsecondary library members of the Atlantic Scholarly Information Network (ASIN) are continuing to develop the ASIN portal, established to make it easy for readers to access both licensed and free electronic information resources held by the Council of Atlantic University Libraries.[50]

Cards for Preschoolers

As part of its strategy to increase the number of New Brunswickers with a public library card, New Brunswick Public Library Service (NBPLS) issued library cards to all preschool children attending a registered day care in the province. Parents were required to take the child and card to the nearest library or bookmobile to activate the card. NBPLS also launched its provincewide online reference service, Quaestio, on August 22. The goal of the service is to support lifelong learning for everyone in the province, regardless of location.[51, 52]

Reading Partnerships in PEI

The Prince Edward Island Provincial Library Service launched a number of community-based partnerships in 2005. A partnership with selected publishers supported a three-month pilot to provide children's e-books as part of the TD Summer Reading Program. In October the PEI Reads Project gave parents of children in grades one to three a 24-page guide to help them help their children learn to read; the children each received a new public library card. Also in October, a partnership with the PEI Active Living Alliance enabled PEI residents to borrow pedometers from the 26 library branches across the province. The loan included a workbook on healthy lifestyles and a logbook to record activity.[53, 54, 55]

Adopt-A-Library

Nova Scotia also launched a partnership, the Adopt-a-Library Literacy Program, which saw public and school libraries partnering with local policing agencies to promote literacy. In a community within Eastern Counties Regional Library, a Royal Canadian Mounted Police cruiser arrived at an education center with lights flashing and siren wailing. The RCMP was taking part in Operation Read 'n' Ride, a part of the Adopt-A-Library Reading Club at the Sherbrooke Branch Library. The constable provided a ride to school for two children as the grand prize for the library's fall reading club.[56, 57]

Well Overdue

A book of sermons borrowed from the Niagara-on-the-Lake Public Library during the War of 1812 was returned, 193 years overdue. The book was found in the collection of an Anglican church as the church library was being packed for a move to a new location. Had the library not set a cap on fines of $20, the fines on this overdue book would have been $10,036. The library waived the fines and let the church keep the book.[58]

Early Bible

A gift to St. John's College at the University of Manitoba in 1897 has been verified to be one of 50 copies of the first edition of the King James Bible printed in 1611. A card within the book indicates that King James I himself used the specific copy.[59]

Notes

1. http://www.statcan.ca/Daily/English/051031/d051031b.htm.

2. http://www.statcan.ca/Daily/English/060131/d060131.pdf.

3. http://ogov.newswire.ca/ontario/GPOE/2005/05/26/c3700.html?lmatch=&lang=_e.html.

4. http://www2.news.gov.bc.ca/archive/2001-2005/2005BCED0006-000070.htm.

5. http://www.gov.ab.ca/acn/200503/17659735E1CB9-13B4-4DEF-8540A14FE2DCCB0D.html.

6. http://www.collectionscanada.ca/consultation/012012-300-e.html.

7. http://www.ls.ualberta.ca/8rs.

8. http://www.statcan.ca/Daily/English/050504/d050504a.htm.

9. http://www.carl-abrc.ca/projects/e_learning/pdf/communique-e.pdf.

10. http://www.cla.ca/issues/nnels_final.htm.

11. http://www.pch.gc.ca/pc-ch/pubs/lalpd-rbbp/pdf/study.pdf.

12. http://www.hillstrategies.com/resources_details.php?resUID=1000080&lang=0.

13. http://www.ipsos-na.com/news/pressrelease.cfm?id=2749.

14. http://www.cla.ca/resources/GATS_Pathfinder.pdf.

15. http://www.culture.gov.on.ca/english/culdiv/library/gats-faq.htm.

16. http://www.cbc.ca/story/arts/national/2005/07/22/Arts/bookrate050722.html.

17. http://www.pch.gc.ca/newsroom/index_e.cfm?fuseaction=displayDocument&DocIDCd=4N0345.

18. http://cpcc.ca/english/news.htm.

19. http://www.thealbertalibrary.ab.ca/taltales/tt06/TAL_tales_Jan06.pdf.

20. http://www.cla.ca/issues/advocacy_cap_lbr.htm.

21. http://cap.ic.gc.ca/pub/funding/index.html.

22. http://www.connect.gc.ca/index.htm.

23. http://cfs-ope.ic.gc.ca/cfs-ope/default.asp?lang=en&id=7.

24. http://www.arvayfinlay.com/news/news-nov-18-2005.htm

25. http://cbc.ca/story/arts/national/2005–2006/07/Arts/Kazemiexhibit050607.html?ref=rss.

26. http://dsp-psd.pwgsc.gc.ca/nw-nv/minute-e.html.

27. Personal correspondence from Punch Jackson, director, Libraries, Community and Voluntary Sector Services Branch, Alberta government, February 2, 2006.

28. http://www.bnquebec.ca/portal/dt/a_propos_bnq/communiques/courants/com_2005_05_10.htm

29. "Definitely One for the Books," *Globe and Mail,* May 14, 2005, p. R6.

30. http://www.publicaffairs.ubc.ca/media/releases/2005/mr-05-118.html.

31. "Turning a Page in the History of Our City," *@The Library: Your Guide to the Winnipeg Public Library,* November/December 2005, pp. 2–3.

32. "Stories in the Stacks," *Winnipeg Free Press,* May 28, 2005, p. F3

33. http://www.cbc.ca/story/canada/national/2005/08/15/Library_of_Parliament_reno_overbudget.

34. http://www.library.ns.ca/publications/disseminator/index_2005/dissv.12n.3.htm

35. http://ogov.newswire.ca/ontario/GPOE/2005/02/14/c3938.html?lmatch=&lang=_e.html.

36. http://cbc.ca/story/arts/national/2005–2006/08/Arts/book050608.html?ref=rss.

37. http://www.cbc.ca/edmonton/story/ed-privacy-computer20050707.html.

38. http://www.ls.ualberta.ca/neli.

39. http://www.cla.ca/clw/index.htm.

40. http://www.carl-abrc.ca/new/pdf/OCDI_communique-e.pdf.

41. http://www.collectionscanada.ca/cdis/index-e.html.

42. http://www.carl-abrc.ca/projects/information_literacy/information_literacy-e.html.

43. http://reginalibrary.ca/anewdirection.html.

44. http://www.collectionscanada.ca/services/005-211-e.html.

45. http://www.collectionscanada.ca/whats-new/013-246-e.html.

46. "Ottawa Offered Unsolicited Library," *Library Journal,* November 15, 2005, p.20

47. http://ejournals.library.ualberta.ca/index.php/EBLIP.

48. http://www.librarianactivist.org/2005–2006/23/librarians-without-borders.

49. http://www.accessola.com/site/showPage.cgi?page=headlinesarchive/headlines0502.html.

50. http://www.upei.ca/~library/html/whatsnew.html

51. http://www.gnb.ca/cnb/news/edu/2005e0560ed.htm.

52. http://www.gnb.ca/cnb/news/edu/2005e1060ed.htm.

53. http://www.gov.pe.ca/news/getrelease.php3?number=4191.

54. http://www.gov.pe.ca/news/getrelease.php3?number=4337.

55. http://www.gov.pe.ca/news/getrelease.php3?number=4346.

56. http://www.library.ns.ca/publications/disseminator/index_2005/dissv.12n.1.htm.

57. http://www.library.ns.ca/publications/disseminator/index_2005/dissv.12n.2.htm.

58. "Library Book of Sermons 193 Years Overdue," *Edmonton Journal,* June 24, 2005, p. A5.

59. http://www.ala.org/al_onlineTemplate.cfm?Section=alonline&template=/Content Management/ContentDisplay.cfm&ContentID=111954.

Canadian Library Association

328 Frank St., Ottawa, ON K2P 0X8
613-232-9625, fax 613-563-9895
E-mail info@cla.ca
World Wide Web http://www.cla.ca

Don Butcher
Executive Director

The Canadian Library Association (CLA) is Canada's national professional and sector association for the library and information community. Its mission: "CLA is my advocate and public voice, educator and network. We build the Canadian library and information community and advance its information professionals."

Membership is composed both of individuals (librarians and other information professionals, library board trustees) and of institutions (mainly libraries, but also encompassing suppliers to the library and information community). It is predominantly English-language, with selected activities also in French.

CLA's activities are driven by its values:

- We believe that libraries and the principles of intellectual freedom and free universal access to information are key components of an open and democratic society.
- Diversity is a major strength of our association.
- An informed and knowledgeable membership is central in achieving library and information policy goals.
- Effective advocacy is based upon understanding the social, cultural, political, and historical contexts in which libraries and information services function.

Founded in 1946, CLA is a federally incorporated not-for-profit organization. It is governed by an 11-person executive council, which is advised by 14 standing committees and as-needed task forces.

Much of CLA's work is done through its five divisions:

- Canadian Association of College and University Libraries (CACUL), including the Community and Technical College Libraries (CTCL) section
- Canadian Association of Public Libraries (CAPL), including the Canadian Association of Children's Librarians (CACL) section
- Canadian Library Trustees Association
- Canadian Association for School Libraries
- Canadian Association of Special Libraries and Information Services (CASLIS), which has geographic chapters in Calgary, Edmonton, Ottawa, Toronto, Manitoba, and Atlantic Canada.

The presidents of the five divisions are among the 11 members of the CLA's national executive council.

In 2005 each of Canada's six English-language library and information science (LIS) university-level schools had a CLA student chapter, and the first student chapter in a library technician program was founded. The city of Montreal also has a CLA chapter.

To facilitate sharing of information on specific areas of interest, CLA has 21 interest groups on topics as diverse as access to government information, action for literacy, library and information needs of native peoples, new librarians and information professionals, and rural and remote libraries. Two new interest groups were founded during 2005, dealing with information commons and evidence-based librarianship.

Governance

In June 2005 CLA inaugurated as its president Barbara Clubb, city librarian of the Ottawa Public Library, who has a wide range of experience in a number of Canadian provinces. Her theme for the year is to highlight the important role that libraries play in developing their communities—the geographic community of a public library, or the institutional community of a university, school, or corporation. Clubb succeeded Stephen Abram of SirsiDynix in the presidency.

Also serving as officers for 2005–2006 are Linda Cook, vice president; A. A. ("Sandy") Cameron, treasurer; and Don Butcher, executive director.

Major Activities of 2005

The year 2005 was an implementation year for CLA. The current strategic plan had been completed in 2004, and in 2005 the organization concentrated on implementing activities toward the plan's identified objectives.

Advocacy

As the major national umbrella association for the Canadian library and information community, CLA is expected to lead in advocating the value of libraries and information professionals on a national level.

In the latter half of 2005, CLA released—with the assistance of its French-language counterpart, l'Assocation pour l'Avancement des Sciences et des Techniques de la Documentation (ASTED)—a bilingual kit to assist librarians in their advocacy efforts. The kit focused on two current access-to-information issues: the library book rate and the community access program.

The library book rate is a discounted rate provided to libraries by Canada's postal service for interlibrary loan. It was scheduled to end March 31, 2006. Because of extensive media coverage sparked by a librarian and led by CLA, the government of Canada made a commitment to continue the rate past that date, although long-range plans had not been announced at the time this report was prepared.

The federal government's Community Access Program, which helps public libraries provide Internet access, also was scheduled to sunset at the end of March 2006, and CLA has lobbied extensively for it to continue.

Advocacy continued on potential revisions to the copyright act. A report proposing amendments harmful to information users was overridden by proposed legislation that was more balanced between creators, rights holders, and users. CLA continues to push for the rights of information users, both on its own and as part of a coalition of user organizations, through the Copyright Forum.

As the year ended, Canada was once again holding a federal election and CLA was working with its members and others to keep issues including literacy and access to information in the public eye. As part of its election advocacy, CLA joined a coalition, led by booksellers, against the national sales tax levied on books.

CLA's advocacy for a nationwide network of equitable public library service for the print-disabled took a major step forward with the release of a report outlining a model by which this service could be delivered. The federal government's 2005 budget allocated $1 million a year for three years, starting in 2006, to Library and Archives Canada to pilot the network, and tangible progress has been made. CLA also received a government grant to pilot a clearinghouse for electronic text to facilitate the production of alternate (nonprint) format materials.

Continuing Professional Development

CLA's Annual Conference continues to be the association's major vehicle for continuing professional development. The 2005 conference was held in Calgary, and delegate and exhibitor attendance was excellent, allowing financial results to meet expectations. An addition to the programming in 2005 was program "tracks": two day-long, limited registration, mini-institutes exploring two topics (technology, and leadership and management) in depth. Keynote speeches were delivered by Dave Snowden of the Cynefin Centre on social complexity, "sense-making," and narrative; David Bollier, an independent policy strategist and author, on librarians as stewards of the information commons; and Sharon Wood, the first North American woman to climb Mount Everest, on teamwork and perseverance.

CLA furthered its commitment to expanding continuing professional development for its members late in 2004 by hiring, as a two-year pilot program, a staff person specifically for that purpose. A series of distance education offerings attracted not only Canadians but others from around the world.

Support for Library Community

Following the release of the groundbreaking study of human resources in Canadian libraries by the 8Rs Research Team headed by the University of Alberta, CLA undertook to make the study results meaningful for libraries and librarians through a CLA president's council. The council's work teams are developing toolkits and communications pieces that will directly benefit practitioners in dealing with issues of recruitment, retention, and rejuvenation of the library work force.

CLA continued to supply books and other resources to the Canadian library and information community as the exclusive distributor of American Library Association Editions in Canada and by publishing or distributing Canadian publications. Added to the CLA booklist in 2005 was *Opening the Doors to Children,* the results of an extensive research project on children's use of public libraries. All proceeds from the sale of these books goes to CLA's book awards program for children's and young adult authors and illustrators.

International Activities

CLA continued its leadership of Canadian participation in the International Federation of Library Associations and Institutions (IFLA). Its activities included chairing IFLA's Canadian caucus and supporting ASTED as it prepares to host IFLA's World Library and Information Congress in Quebec City in 2008.

In response to the devastation to libraries caused by the December 26, 2004, tsunami in the Indian Ocean, CLA created a tsunami relief fund and has been accepting financial contributions. CLA is working with IFLA to ensure that the funding reaches libraries in need.

CLA also created a hurricane relief fund to assist libraries on the U.S. Gulf Coast devastated by hurricanes Katrina and Rita. These funds are forming the basis of a more permanent disaster relief and development program.

Member Communications

As information professionals, Canadian librarians depend on timely and attractive publications from their professional association.

CLA's bimonthly publication *Feliciter* continued to explore core themes in the library community: library education; convergence of library, archives, and records management; special libraries; international librarianship; and community librarianship. Each edition had a volunteer guest editor and generous contributors.

The CLA electronic membership newsletter, *CLA Digest,* continues to communicate with members by presenting synopses of articles that are presented more fully on CLA's Web site, http://www.cla.ca.

CLA Presidents Stephen Abram and Barbara Clubb each undertook extensive travel on behalf of CLA in 2005. Independently, they visited public, academic, school, and special libraries in virtually every province. They continued the practice started by one of their predecessors of visiting the library schools across Canada to advise students on the role of professional associations, including CLA, in their careers. They also represented CLA at international conferences and events in the United States and Europe.

Awards and Honors

Because the strength and power of any community comes down to its people, CLA recognized several individuals from the Canadian library and information community with awards and honors in 2005.

CLA's highest honor, the Outstanding Services to Librarianship award, went to Pat Cavill of Calgary. Over her 32-year career, Cavill has demonstrated leadership both as a senior administrator for public and provincial libraries and as a consultant to libraries. She is well known as an outstanding advocate both for libraries and librarians in school and public libraries. Hundreds of librarians, technicians, library staff, and trustees have taken advantage of her work through the Library Advocacy Now! training programs.

The CLA/Information Today award for Innovative Technology was presented to the Red Deer (Alberta) Public Library for its project in building a world-class information technology infrastructure.

The CLA Student Article contest was won by Anne Dorsey, who wrote on accessibility in public library service in "Open Wide the Library Doors."

The CLA Award for the Advancement of Intellectual Freedom was presented to David Wyman, a graphic designer from Toronto who has donated the designs for six posters for the annual Freedom to Read Week. His work has been fundamental to the program's continued success.

The Book of the Year for Children Award was presented to Anne Laurel Carter for *Last Chance Bay* (Penguin), the Amelia Frances Howard Gibbon Illustrators Award went to Wallace Edwards for *Monkey Business* (Kids Can), and the Young Adult Canadian Book Award went to Miriam Toews for *A Complicated Kindness* (Knopf Canada).

Conclusion

A modest increase in active membership numbers to about 2,600 and balanced financial results suggest that CLA is on a solid course as it provides leadership to the Canadian library and information community. As libraries are at the heart of their respective communities, CLA is endeavoring to be at the heart of the Canadian library and information community.

Library and Archives Canada

Ian E. Wilson
Librarian and Archivist of Canada

395 Wellington St., Ottawa, ON K1A 0N4
866-578-7777, fax 613-995-6274
World Wide Web http://www.collectionscanada.ca

Library and Archives Canada (LAC) continues its forward momentum, establishing itself as an innovative knowledge institution for the 21st century, accessible to all and combining the roles of a national library, a national archives, and a national portrait museum.

LAC was created in May 2004, replacing the former National Archives (dating back to 1872) and National Library of Canada (established in 1953). The Library and Archives of Canada Act introduced the concept of Canada's documentary heritage, including publications and records in all media. LAC will make this heritage accessible using a broad spectrum of channels—on site, through traveling exhibits, and with a major investment in online services. One initiative to highlight one aspect of the LAC collection is the new Portrait Gallery of Canada, which will feature portraits of people from all walks of life who have contributed to and continue to contribute to the development of Canada.

Mandate

LAC has accomplished the behind-the-scenes groundwork to determine what the institution will be—defining its framework, its long-term vision, its systems and ways of working, and its very organization—and has moved on to the next stage, the implementation of its mandate:

- To preserve the documentary heritage of Canada for the benefit of present and future generations
- To serve as a source of enduring knowledge accessible to all, contributing to the cultural, social, and economic advancement of Canada as a free and democratic society
- To facilitate cooperation among the communities involved in the acquisition, preservation, and diffusion of knowledge
- To serve as the continuing memory of the government of Canada and its institutions

Digital Information

LAC is responsible for a collection of extraordinary range, depth, and magnitude. The comprehensive collection contains, among other items, Canadian books, periodicals, newspapers, and government publications; manuscript collections of individuals and organizations of national significance; kilometers of government records; millions of visual artifacts, including photographs, prints, drawings, portraits, plans, and maps; and thousands of hours of films, videos, and sound recordings, as well as a unique music collection.

Yet the history that is made today, and which must be preserved for future generations, has become a kind of shape-shifter, increasingly hard to capture and preserve. We live in a volatile age—one in which libraries and archives around the world are re-evaluating their role and exploring the infinite possibilities of digital information, along with its myriad challenges. It would be impossible for LAC to transform itself as a prime learning destination—an institution with national presence and a greater capacity to serve Canadians of all ages, cultures, and regions, a leader in terms of information management within the government of Canada—without taking on the digital realm we live in.

Digital information is becoming the raw material that engages our curiosity and fuels our experience, and a great deal of that experience takes place online. How does LAC respond? How does it preserve a reality that is becoming more fleeting by the minute?

The scope is daunting. As a library and as an archives, LAC wants to support the development of Canadian digital content and to explore the relationship between the public and the private sector in a digitized environment. There are many questions. What about authenticity, information security, and the need for trusted digital repositories? What about access and rights management? What do the ultimate end users of digital information want and need?

LAC posed some of these questions at a mini-summit in October 2005 in preparation for a national symposium to be held in fall 2006. Like many other countries—among them Britain, the United States, the Netherlands, and Australia—Canada is coping with the explosive growth of information on the Internet and the need to manage it appropriately. But despite the resources being poured into the creation of digital information, its stewardship in Canada is fragmented. At the same time, Google and other private-sector companies are aggressively offering new ways to access information.

LAC recognized the fundamental need for a collective national strategy on digital information, one that would be developed in close collaboration with industry, government, such heritage institutions as the Canadian Historical Association and the Canadian Association of Research Libraries, universities and research organizations, and the pan-Canadian network of libraries and archives. It also realized that for a strategy to work it would need to respond to a wide variety of needs; those of creators, publishers, end users, governments, students, industry, government, academics, and, of course, libraries and archives themselves.

More than 50 Canadian organizations, including representatives of industry and the federal government, participated in the mini-summit and discussed the creation of a strategy. While opinions varied on how to get there, consensus emerged on the need to ensure that Canada's digital information assets are created, protected, preserved, and made accessible into the future. The participants agreed that more focused and collaborative activity was required to make more digital content available for Canadians and to preserve it over time. As one participant put it, we need to think of digital information as the country's "intellectual and information capital" and invest in its growth, longevity, and accessibility.

What we decide now will influence how we are seen and understood by future generations, and this is no small challenge. As Canada's leading knowledge institution and one of the few integrated libraries and archives in the world, LAC is ready to take that challenge on. It is holding thematic workshops across the country focusing on optimizing digital production, creating a digital preservation infrastructure, and fostering access and use within a rights framework, as a lead-in to a national symposium in the fall.

Information Management

Canada has described itself as the most connected country in the world, but if it is to maintain this status and preserve its cultural heritage in its new form, it cannot afford to sit still. In 2005 LAC also hosted the Canadian Metadata Forum in an effort to explore and highlight some of the latest research into metadata and bring together key decision-makers and leaders in the field of information resource management. More than 200 people attended the forum, including experts from the Canadian metadata community, both government and non-government, as well as libraries, archives, museums, educational and research institutions, academia, and multimedia producers. Participants discussed the challenges of metadata implementation, including how to influence metadata policy. LAC is now developing a single framework for using metadata, which will enable it to reduce description backlogs and make Canada's documentary heritage more accessible on the Internet.

While access remains a cornerstone of LAC's mandate, it is also responsible for ensuring that information and knowledge are effectively managed within the government of Canada. The Librarian and Archivist of Canada serves as information management (IM) champion within the government community. Information management is a hallmark of good, effective, accountable, and citizen-centered government. LAC initiated a study in 2005 of the current state of IM in government, and as a result LAC will be working closely with other departments to create an IM strategy so that the management of information across government is fully integrated and part of a common vision that truly reflects the values and ethics of Canadians.

Four 'Catalytic' Initiatives

Powerful computers, mega databases, sophisticated indexes, and the ability to search thousands of years of history with a couple of clicks of a mouse have truly changed expectations, especially for libraries and archives. It is impossible in this day and age to separate the content needs of users from the technology that will make that content accessible to them. This is one of the reasons LAC continued to develop four integrated "catalytic" initiatives in 2005: digital collection, metadata strategy, service-delivery transformation, and the integration of its core business systems, such as AMICAN, which supports the intellectual and physical management of and access to LAC holdings online.

Working together, these four initiatives will achieve a number of user-friendly results:

- All of LAC's holdings will be presented in a single database, providing seamless access to the collection in all media.
- A single uniform search engine interface will provide first-stop access to all of LAC's documentary heritage and resources.
- A comprehensive LAC-wide reference program featuring full consultation and genealogy services, interlibrary and inter-institutional loans, and the Canadian Book Exchange Centre will improve LAC's service to Canadians of all ages, cultures, and regions.

As part of improved service delivery, LAC also launched a number of pilot projects, including a self-service digital copying service that allows clients to use their own photographic equipment and LAC microform printers and scanners to copy certain documents in the collection for research or private study. LAC is considering offering this service permanently, as well as allowing clients to order copies of textual, photographic, cartographic, and architectural records, and even works of art, online.

In December 2005 LAC also provided access to free wireless Internet service in its reference and consultation rooms in Ottawa, allowing clients to use their own laptops to gain direct access to the vast resources of the Internet and LAC's Web site. In addition, LAC is reorganizing its public research areas to provide a truly client-centered service through a comprehensive approach to the dissemination of Canada's documentary heritage.

Collection Development Framework

The year 2005 was one of preparation, creating a kind of launchpad for the new institution. The process of transformation was taking place throughout the institution and in all aspects of its work, including how it builds the LAC collection as part of the nation's documentary heritage.

The Collection Development Framework, produced in 2005, created a new policy direction for the institution and provided a unique basis for LAC collection-development activities. As a result, all collection activities will now be grounded in the idea of "one LAC collection"—an integrated collection that reflects the goals and vision of a truly national institution. LAC's collection activities will also reflect the diversity of the nation's aboriginal cultures, as well as its multicultural diversity. In addition, the framework recognizes the need for LAC to be as adept in collecting documentary heritage materials in digital form as it has long been with analog media—and this will require change at all levels, including policies, procedures, technology, and staff skills.

Summer Reading Program

Because the work of libraries and archives has become so technologically sophisticated, it is easy to forget one of their most basic and compelling features—books. The year 2005 was a banner year for thousands of children who participated in the TD Summer Reading Club, a joint initiative between LAC and the Toronto

Dominion Bank Financial Group. Now in its third year with LAC, the program promotes the love of reading among school-age children by encouraging them to continue reading during the summer. Operating in public libraries in seven provinces and all three territories, the estimated number of children's materials circulating within participating library systems reached nearly 6.1 million in 2005, and at least 2 million books were read as a direct result of the program.

1911 Census

While books tell one kind of story, records can tell another, and the combination of stories, records, and technology can inform an entire generation. Some 7.2 million men, women, and children were enumerated in Canada on June 1, 1911, and the release of these census records in 2005 provided a fascinating glimpse of a critical time in the nation's history. In the decade between 1901 and 1911, more than 1.8 million immigrants arrived in Canada from every corner of the globe, laying the foundations of today's multicultural society. For the vast majority of these new arrivals, the information in the 1911 census is the only documentation available. These records, now online—totaling 135 reels of microfilm—provide individuals' names, occupations, and year of birth, but more importantly they tell their stories. Activity on the site is about 15 downloads a second and on the rise, as people explore the threads of their history online.

New Acquisitions

The integration of LAC was also the reason behind the donation of an unusual fonds—that of Canadian photojournalist Jock Carroll. From 1950 to 1968 Carroll worked in the Toronto bureau of Montreal-based *Weekend Magazine,* a national weekly newspaper supplement. Perhaps best known for the photos he took of Marilyn Monroe when she was a young starlet, Carroll covered a wide range of topics from the Korean War to celebrities to everyday life. The fonds is unusual because of the large quantity of textual records it contains that are connected with the photographs, offering unique insights into the working life of a photojournalist. Since Carroll himself did not wish to split up the collection, the legacy of this fonds, representing approximately 12 meters of textual documents, 21,000 photographs, first-edition books, and audiovisual components, would not have been possible without the combined institution.

Another major achievement of 2005 was the acquisition of the Peter Winkworth Collection of Canadiana, a spectacular and invaluable collection of Canadian documentary art. The collection includes portraits of aboriginal peoples, colonial administrators, explorers, and politicians; flora and fauna depicted by such artists as Audubon; scenes of settlements, towns and cities, battles, shipwrecks, fires and floods; and maps, atlases, and architectural drawings. Much of the collection is unique.

Portrait Gallery of Canada

As part of LAC, the Portrait Gallery of Canada will have access to all of the institution's collections, such as the photographs of Yousef Karsh, and will borrow portraits in public and private collections from across Canada and internationally. The concept designs for the gallery were unveiled in March 2005, paving the way for construction to begin in December in a building in Ottawa that was originally opened in 1932 as the United States Embassy.

The gallery will be part of a network of federal and cultural agencies along Confederation Boulevard. The Gallery is set to open in 2007. In November it launched its loans program in Saint John's at The Rooms, Newfoundland and Labrador's newest public cultural space, with portraits of Sir John Berry (1635–1690) and his wife. Berry was one of the founding fathers of Newfoundland and Labrador, and the two portraits are the earliest identified oil portraits in LAC's collection.

Exhibitions and Events

LAC also celebrated Saskatchewan's centennial year in 2005, showcasing the rich and varied work of the province's traditional and nontraditional visual, literary, and performing artists. The exhibition included everything from cookbooks to political records. LAC helped such Canadian filmmakers as Ali Kazimi and launched numerous Web sites, featuring everything from eccentric Canadiana to records of reported encounters with UFOs.

Conclusion

LAC has already attracted international attention for the direction it is taking, and is now poised at a critical phase in its transformation. Joining the responsibilities, collections, services, and staff of the National Archives and the National Library was a bold move, offering unprecedented opportunities for helping Canadians and for the world to learn about Canada. It has fostered seamless research by its clients, for example through the acclaimed Canadian Genealogy Centre and the Canadian Postal Archives Web sites. It has streamlined and strengthened its provision of service by integrating access and sharpening its focus. It has refused to be a passive repository of information, making efforts to connect with Canadians not only through its own networks, but also through Canada's 3,600 public library service points across the country, its 800 archives, and its strong network of academic libraries.

LAC is becoming a knowledge institution that is more than the sum of its parts. The momentum gained through directions for change will sustain its efforts to be measured not by the number of items it holds, but by the way it contributes to the continued cultural, social, and economic success of Canadian society.

Special Reports

Developments in Copyright, 2005: Exploring the Boundaries

Robert L. Oakley

Director, Law Library, and Professor of Law, Georgetown University Law Center

Looking back at 2005, it may be that we have finally seen a turning point in the development of new copyright principles for the digital age. After years of skirmishing, some serious moves may now be under way to define or redefine the boundaries of acceptable uses of copyrighted material in the electronic environment. How these discussions will unfold and what results they will yield, remain to be seen, but at least the discussions are taking place.

Copyright Office Initiatives

Early in 2005 the United States Copyright Office signaled a significant new interest in resolving some of the problems faced by libraries under the Copyright Act. In relatively quick succession, the office announced two major initiatives, one concerning the use of works whose owners cannot be identified or found, and the other concerning the adequacy of the statutory exemption for certain library uses as set out in Section 108 of the act.

Orphan Works

For many years, librarians and others have expressed concern about the difficulty of identifying and locating copyright owners in order to get permission to copy an item beyond what is clearly permitted under the Copyright Act. In libraries, this problem comes up most often in the context of preservation, but it arises in numerous other contexts as well, including classroom use, preparation of student papers and theses, copying of sheet music for private study or use, and the digitization of both video images and historical sound recordings. Authors and publishers, who may want to incorporate some or all of an earlier work into a subsequent work, also experience difficulty in finding copyright owners to get their permission for use.

As a result of the concerns expressed by librarians, authors, filmmakers, and publishers, among others, the Copyright Office published a notice of inquiry in the *Federal Register* in January 2005 concerning "orphan works."[1] Orphan works were defined as "copyrighted works whose owners are difficult or even impossible to locate." In its notice, the Copyright Office observed that the

> uncertainty created by copyright in orphan works has the potential to harm an important public policy behind copyright: to promote the dissemination of works by creating incentives for their creation and dissemination to the public. First, the economic incentive to create may be undermined by the imposition of additional costs on subsequent creators . . . Subsequent creators may be dissuaded from creating new works incorporating existing works for which the owner cannot be found because they cannot afford the risk . . . Second, the public interest may be harmed when works cannot be made available to the public due to uncertainty over its copyright ownership and status, even when there is no longer any living person or legal entity claiming ownership . . .

Recognizing all this, the notice of inquiry sought input on the question of how to remedy the problem. The library community filed a statement providing numerous concrete examples of how the problem affects them and their users and endorsing an approach that would (a) allow for use of an orphan work provided that reasonable efforts had been made to identify the owner and (b) limit any monetary remedy for uses begun after such a search had been made.

The inquiry from the Copyright Office brought an outpouring of 716 submissions. Remarkably, more than 90 percent of the submissions supported some type of action to solve the problem. Even more striking was the degree of consensus among the submissions. Participants noted how unusual it was for librarians and publishers to be in substantial agreement on a copyright issue. In fact, in this case, the vast majority of commenters agreed that orphan works presented a problem that needed to be solved, and that it affected both published and unpublished works, without regard to the age of the work. There was also a consensus that whatever remedy is developed should apply to all types of uses; it should not be restricted to nonprofit uses, nor should it be limited to analog uses.

In essence, it was generally agreed that if a party had made a reasonable effort and failed to identify and locate a copyright owner, they should be allowed to go ahead with the proposed use, even a commercial use, provided that there would be some remedy available should the copyright owner show up later and want to exert their rights in the work.

The issue of the remedy—rather than what would be allowed under an orphan works exception—is where the publishers and librarians parted company. Publishers thought that the copyright owner should be entitled to payment of a "reasonable royalty" to be negotiated between the parties. The librarians thought that an uncapped royalty was too open-ended and favored a cap on any such royalty payments at a relatively low level, perhaps $100. Visual artists also noted that their works might present special difficulties, because photographers and graphic artists often produce hundreds or even thousands of images, and those images rarely carry any identifying information, making them appear to be orphaned from the very beginning.

As this article was being written, the report from the Register of Copyrights was released. The document, more than 200 pages long, is available at http://www.copyright.gov/orphan/orphan-report-full.pdf. By means of a limitation on the remedies for an infringement claim, the report recommends

- That users be permitted to use orphan works provided they have made a "good faith, reasonably diligent" search
- That the user of an orphan work provide attribution to the copyright holder whenever possible
- That no monetary remedy be available against a noncommercial user, provided that they take down (or cease using) the work in question if a copyright owner surfaces and asserts a claim of right
- That compensation be limited to "reasonable compensation" under the circumstances for commercial uses or if a noncommercial user does not wish to take down or cease using the work
- That no injunctive relief be permitted where a new work has been created that uses the orphan in a work "with a significant amount of the infringer's expression" added, provided that reasonable compensation is paid and attribution is given
- That injunctive relief be available in other cases, but before issuing the injunction, the court should consider harm to the user from its reliance on the orphan works provision of the Copyright Act.

Based upon an initial review, these recommendations seem to strike a reasonable compromise among the various interests, although they may not address the concerns of the visual artists. Very importantly, also left undefined is what constitutes a "good faith, reasonably diligent" search. The report adopts a general "reasonableness" standard because such a search is likely to vary with a variety of factors: whether the work is a photograph or a book, whether the name of the owner is indicated somewhere on the work, the age of the work, and so forth. Moreover, the nature of the search might depend on the proposed use. One might be expected to go further if one is turning a work into a major motion picture than if one is simply copying it for preservation purposes in a library. In any case, the report suggests that interest groups might develop their own statements of best practices:

> Ideally these would be collaborative between user and owner groups, but they could also be separate endeavors. In either case, the individual groups could publish the results of their efforts for users to consult when conducting searches. For example, a library association could publish its best practices or guidelines for users trying to find the owner of a photograph, and a photography association could publish its own separate set of guidelines. None of these guidelines would be definitive and dispositive . . . [2]

If this proposed legislation passes—and with publishers and librarians in substantial agreement, passage seems likely—interest groups like libraries would be well advised to develop their own statements of best practices, consistent with the spirit of the Register of Copyright's report. This legislation would be a breakthrough, freeing up for preservation and other purposes millions of essentially abandoned works in library collections around the country.

In saying that, however, it must be recognized that allowing the use of a work because a copyright owner cannot be found is not at all the same thing as putting the work into the public domain, and it is extremely important to recognize the difference.

Review of Section 108 of the Copyright Act, which permits, under certain circumstances, reproductions by libraries and archives

Because fair use is an uncertain standard, when the Copyright Act of 1976 was passed it included in Section 108 a series of "safe harbor" provisions for certain library activities, including preservation of unpublished works, replacement of damaged or deteriorating published works, interlibrary lending, and copying for a user. The section also contains a number of conditions under which each of these library privileges applies, exempts libraries from the liability for the actions of their users, and indicates that the library section does not negate fair use as a separate privilege.

When the act was passed it was widely considered to be medium-neutral; that is, the principles of the law were stated generally and were not supposed to change with the format of a work. With hindsight, however, it now appears that Section 108, at least, was written with a print (or at least analog) paradigm in mind. Thus the preservation and replacement sections were originally written to permit only a single copy, thinking obviously, in terms of a photocopy. Later those sections were amended to permit up to three copies, reflecting a newer standard for preservation microfilm. At the same time, however, the law was also updated to permit the use of digital technology for preservation and replacement copying, but that further change actually made the three-copy limit inappropriate. In the digital environment three copies is not sufficient, because many copies may be made in the course of processing, and additional copies may be made every time a work is accessed. These additional copies are often temporary and ephemeral and certainly do not affect the market for the work, but they do exceed the literal terms of the statute. Moreover, under the terms of the amended act, any digital copies made under these sections were restricted to use on the library premises (again, inappropriately reflecting the analog model), while in many cases today they are likely to be available on the library or campus network.

Similarly, the limits in Section 108 of the act and the associated guidelines for interlibrary lending and borrowing reflect paper delivery models, not digital, which may again require additional transitory copies. The guidelines developed at the time, and widely followed in libraries to this day, certainly reflect the time when libraries had individual subscriptions to individual titles, not the currently evolving model of subscriptions to large aggregated bundles of journals available through a major database supplier. Activity that might have been considered a "substitute for a purchase" in the individual subscription model can in no way be seen as a substitute for a purchase of a major database.

These and many other similar questions gave rise to a need to review Section 108 to determine whether it still meets the needs of libraries, and, if not, what changes should be made. In spring 2005 the Register of Copyrights appointed a study committee—under the sponsorship of the National Digital Information Infrastructure and Preservation Program and consisting of representatives of the content community as well as libraries, archives, and museums—to review the issues and make recommendations for legislative change. The committee's Web site is http://www.loc.gov/section108/index.html.

The group first met in April 2005 to plan its work and to list a range of possible issues for future discussion. By the end of the year, it had spent considerable time discussing issues relating to

- Who would be eligible for the Section 108 exceptions
- What amendments might be needed to the preservation and replacement exceptions in subsections (b) and (c), including possible amendments to the three-copy limit, the 108(c) triggers (should the privilege be limited to when a work is "damaged, deteriorating, lost, or stolen," or is it then already too late), the on-site access restrictions, and the separate treatment of unpublished works
- Proposals for a new exception to permit the creation of restricted-access preservation copies, which would become available only upon some trigger event such as the loss of the original from the publisher
- The possibility of a new exception for the preservation of Web sites and other online content

While the committee continues its discussions, it was planning to hold a series of roundtables on these issues in spring 2006 to obtain input from the wider copyright community. Other topics that remained to be discussed by the committee include, among others, making copies upon patron request, interlibrary loans, e-reserves, and licensing.

The group hopes to finish its work by the end of 2006. It will issue a report containing background, analysis, and—hopefully—legislative recommendations.

E-Reserves

The area of electronic reserves continues to be one where there is substantial disagreement. In the analog environment, library reserves consisted of a limited number of copies of mostly supplemental readings that students had to use on site. Although such reserves were not generally seen as a problem, publishers drew the line at so-called coursepacks, where photocopies were used for the basic class readings, thus making it unnecessary for the students to buy the original works. More than once, publishers have taken the creators of coursepacks to court. In 1991 a federal court ruled that a publisher's copyright was infringed when a Kinko's copy shop reprinted portions of a book in an academic coursepack.[3] The court said that reprinting copyrighted materials in academic coursepacks was not a fair use and that permission was required. This case was followed by a later case in Michigan, though in both cases the commercial nature of the copy shop was an important factor.

Copyright owners see no difference between traditional coursepacks and electronic coursepacks, such as might be provided through an electronic courseware system such as Blackboard. Moreover, to the extent that library electronic reserve systems begin to resemble electronic coursepacks—by virtue of the number of documents included, the length of the documents, and whether or not they are "supplemental" or constitute the bulk of the readings in the course—publishers are equally concerned about the library role. To the extent that an e-reserve system "looks like" a coursepack and contains a similar range of material, it can be expected that publishers will take note.

In late 2004 and early 2005 the Association of American Publishers contacted the University of California, objecting to the e-reserves on the university's San Diego campus, saying that they are "offering too much, that electronic reserves had become more like coursepacks." The university counsel investigated and found that the library's practice "conforms with the principles of fair use."[4] The issue seemed to quiet down in the second part of the year, but it would be a mistake for librarians to think that this issue is settled.

Peer-to-Peer File Sharing

Peer-to-peer file sharing has many important and clearly legal uses, including online distribution of public domain works, distribution of materials prepared by students or a faculty member for class, and many others. Unfortunately, peer-to-peer file sharing has also been used in ways that many have found questionable, most notably for the distribution of copyrighted music without restriction over the Internet. Several cases in 2005 began to define more carefully what constitutes an unlawful use of the technology and made it clear that the technology, itself, is not legally to blame.

Before the rulings highlighted below were announced, there was significant concern that the courts would begin to hold technology manufacturers liable for the way in which their product was used, thus putting future technological developments in doubt. Fortunately, the courts have steered clear of that approach—and focused instead on the culpable behavior of the creation and marketing of some systems. This approach ensures that technology developments will continue. However, in making these rulings, the courts have undoubtedly created new uncertainties, some of which, it might be argued, might at least put a chill on the development and marketing of new information technologies.

Metro-Goldwyn-Mayer v. Grokster[5]

In 1984 the Supreme Court decided the landmark case of *Sony* v. *Universal Studios*,[6] holding that the manufacturer of a VCR would not be held secondarily liable for alleged copyright violations in the use of its product, so long as the product was capable of substantial non-infringing uses. This standard—"substantial non-infringing uses"—has been important for the continued development of information technology in the years since the case was decided. Without it, would the personal computer have evolved in the same way? Would the Internet be what it is today? Would iPods be the ubiquitous presence that they are? Undoubtedly not. And yet, as much as the electronics industry has relied upon the standard, it is also one that the content community—especially the entertainment industry—has tried to roll back, limit, or at least blunt, using whatever means it could, including with legislation (for example, the Digital Millennium Copyright Act), technological protection measures (such as a proposed digital protection "flag" to be built into every digital television broadcast), and even with license agreements. With peer-to-peer file-sharing technology, the entertainment industry hoped that at last it had found a technology that was so egregious that it could achieve a ban on technologies that permitted uncontrolled copying of copyrighted works. In the case of *MGM* v. *Grokster,* the industry argued strongly that since almost all of the use of the peer-to-peer technology was infringing, the court could not find that there was no substantial non-infringing use, and that, therefore, the technology had no other purpose than copyright infringement, and that its creators should be held secondarily liable for the millions of infringements that had allegedly occurred.

In an important case decided in June 2005, the court disagreed with this view and found another way to approach the issue.[7] Although Grokster lost the case, and the entertainment industry claimed a big win, in fact it was actually a big win for technology development in general and file sharing in particular.

In *Grokster,* the defendant distributed peer-to-peer file-sharing software that enabled users to download music and other copyrighted works from the Internet without permission. The lower courts in the case relied on *Sony* and found that the software was capable of substantial non-infringing uses. As a result, they refused to shut down the system or hold the defendants liable for the actions of their users.

In the oral argument before the Supreme Court, the justices were clearly looking for another approach. They did not seem to want to overrule *Sony,* because they appeared to be worried about harming technological development. Yet they also did not like what Grokster had done to establish a business model that was dependent on infringing other people's rights. At oral argument, the justices spent much of the time questioning the advocates about how to deal with that dilemma. Their chief concern seemed to be that the defendants didn't just create a technology, they actually actively encouraged copyright infringement.

Writing for a unanimous court, Justice David Souter wrote

> We hold that one who distributes a device with the object of promoting its use to infringe copyright, as shown by clear expression or other affirmative steps taken to foster infringement, is liable for the resulting acts of infringement by third parties.[8]

He further noted that

> One infringes contributorily by intentionally inducing or encouraging direct infringement.[9]

Thus the court created a new category of infringement for "intentional inducement or encouragement of infringement." This suggests that it was the behavior and the business model of Grokster, not the technology, that was the problem. The court cited three aspects of the evidence of intent that it said were particularly notable:

- First, by the way the service was marketed and from internal e-mail documentation, it was clear that the company was trying to reach a known source of demand for copyright infringement; that is, the users of the former Napster service, which went out of business after it was found guilty of copyright infringement.

- Second, the company made no effort to develop filtering techniques to diminish the level of infringing activity.
- Third, because the company made its money from advertising, its revenue was increased with a high volume of use of the system. And since the vast majority of use of the system was for infringement, increasing the volume of use also meant increasing the amount of infringement.

With this explanation of why the court found infringement in this case, if a library or its parent institution wants to make use of peer-to-peer technology, it should

- Make sure that marketing material and other written documentation (including internal correspondence during development) does not say anything that might appear to encourage infringement
- Ensure that its user sign-up agreement specifically encourages users not to engage in infringing activity
- To whatever extent possible and feasible, make efforts to filter or prevent the sharing of copyrighted material

As a technical matter, the plaintiffs won this case and ultimately shut down Grokster. On the other hand, the victory is a narrow one, legally. Rather than a broad ruling banning peer-to-peer technology, as requested by the plaintiffs, the court instead focused on the narrower issue of "intentional inducement." Since "intent" can be difficult to prove, future plaintiffs in similar cases will need to show not only that the plaintiff enabled the infringement, and that the technology does not have substantial non-infringing purposes, but they will also have to show that the state of mind of the defendant was to encourage infringement. Although electronics companies are worried that this decision will have a chilling effect on further technological developments, it appears that they will continue to develop—so long as there is no obvious intent to encourage infringement.

BMG Music v. Gonzalez[10]

Following the decision in *Grokster,* Judge Frank Easterbrook, in the Seventh Circuit, rejected a claim of fair use against an individual user of Kazaa, another peer-to-peer file-sharing system. In that case, the defendant had downloaded more than 1,300 songs, which she retained on her computer, claiming that she had downloaded them for purposes of sampling prior to purchase. This activity she analogized to time-shifting, which had been specifically approved in the Sony case. Unfortunately, her time-shifting analogy was weakened because she had not removed the downloaded songs from her hard drive after the sampling was done, and Judge Easterbrook flat-out rejected the claim:

> A copy downloaded, played, and retained on one's hard drive for future use is a direct substitute for a purchased copy—and without the benefit of the license fee paid to the broadcaster . . . The files that Gonzalez obtained, by contrast, were posted in violation of copyright law; there was no license governing a single transmission—and, to repeat, Gonzalez kept the copies. Time-shifting by an authorized recipient this is not.[11]

Easterbrook went on to note that if Gonzalez had wanted to sample the material, there were other authorized ways to do so:

> Licensed Internet sellers, such as the iTunes Music Store, offer samples—but again they pay authors a fee for the right to do so . . . Other intermediaries offer licensed access to large collections of music [and] new technologies, such as SNOCAP, enable authorized trials over peer-to-peer systems . . .

> Authorized previews share the feature of evanescence: if a listener decides not to buy (or stops paying the rental fee), no copy remains behind. With all these means available to consumers who want to choose where to spend their money, downloading full copies of copyrighted material without compensation to authors cannot be deemed "fair use."[12]

Universal Music v. Sharman License Holdings[13]

In Australia, a federal court used reasoning similar to that in the Grokster case to conclude that the Kazaa file-sharing system was infringing under Australian law and that to continue in operation, the company needed to take certain steps to protect the interests of the copyright owners.

Under Australian law, it is a violation to "authorize" infringement, and Judge Murray Wilcox found that Sharman, the company that controls Kazaa, had authorized infringements by users of the file-sharing software. He found that both the posted warnings and the license agreement were insufficient and ineffective at preventing—or even curtailing—infringements by users of the system. He also noted that the company could have used technological protection measures to reduce infringements. Instead, he found, the company had actually encouraged users to increase their file sharing and to ignore copyright.

Like the U.S. Supreme Court, Judge Wilcox understood that the technology could be used for lawful purposes when it does not interfere with an owner's copyright interests. With that in mind, he went on to say that Kazaa could continue in operation if it either

- Adopted a filtering system to filter out specific songs or other works that a copyright owner had notified them were protected and not available for distribution (this would allow the system to be used by those who wanted such a distribution mechanism, for instance by up-and-coming artists who wanted to find a way to gain a wider distribution of their works), or
- Modified the search component of the system so that the search results displayed would be limited to licensed works

Digitization

Two decisions in 2001 created doubt over the future of efforts to digitize and make available back runs of journals and other serials.[14] In *Greenberg* v. *National Geographic Society*,[15] the 11th Circuit held that a CD-ROM version of the magazine was a new work, not a "revision" of the original, and that, therefore, use of the plaintiff's photographs without compensation was an infringement. To distinguish this case from microfilm, which had been around for a long time and which was clearly permitted under the Copyright Act, the court relied on the fact that software was required to use the CD and that with the software, some new features were added—such as search capability—and an opening, continually changing, montage. These additions, said the court, made this a new work, requiring new compensation to the original contributors.

New York Times v. *Tasini*[16] was decided by the Supreme Court after the National Geographic case. It, too, found for the plaintiff, but the rationale was quite different. In *Tasini,* a freelance author sued over the inclusion of his works in large-scale online databases such as LexisNexis and Westlaw. Instead of relying on the existence of a software program, the court looked at both how the material was stored and how it was displayed to the user. They noted that the material was disaggregated from other surrounding material in the original and stored separately as individual items. This meant that while individual items could be retrieved, they would not be presented in the same way as they were shown in the original. Moreover, the presentation looked nothing like the original; graphics were usually missing, ads were left out, the text was just text rather than an image. You could not "turn the pages" to see what was on the preceding and following pages. In short, the court felt these databases were totally unlike microfilm and were, therefore, again a new work requiring compensation.

In both of these cases, plaintiffs won. This left some doubt about the future of large-scale digitization programs. Would organizations like J-Stor, Hein Online, and others have to go back and get permission from every author? That would make such an effort almost impossible. In 2005 another case against National Geographic resolved the issue in the Second Circuit by applying the reasoning of *Tasini* to the CD-ROM/image case and coming up with a different result.

National Geographic v. Faulkner[17]

In *National Geographic* v. *Faulkner,* a number of freelance authors and photographers accused National Geographic of copyright infringement when it created and sold sets of CD-ROMs containing the entire backfile of the magazine, back to 1888. The three-judge panel observed that in *Tasini* the articles were both stored separately and presented out of their original context. In this new case, the court suggested that the presentation was more like microfilm. The entire work is there, displayed exactly as it was in the magazine. You can turn the pages, see the ads, and see all the photographs and other graphics, just as you could in the original. This, said the second circuit, made the work more like microfilm and less like the large databases in *Tasini.* Accordingly, the court concluded that just as a microfilm version of a complete work was allowed, so too was the electronic equivalent in the form of an image-based product.

In December 2005 the Supreme Court refused to hear the appeal of the Faulkner case, thus letting this precedent stand as the last word on the topic.[18] As of now, despite the earlier questions, it appears that it is allowable for a publisher to digitize the retrospective files of serial publications, so long as the digital version is image-based, complete, and the works are shown in their original context.

Google Book Search

In December 2004 Google announced that it was planning to digitize the collections of four major academic libraries—those of Stanford, Harvard, Oxford, and the University of Michigan—and the New York Public Library under a new program called Google Print for Libraries (now called Google Book Search). New York Public and Oxford stated that they would make available for scanning only those materials that were already in the public domain. But Michigan indicated that its entire collection would be digitized—including works still under copyright—and Harvard and Stanford had not indicated what they would do in this regard.

Prior to the announcement of Google Print for Libraries, the company had been negotiating with publishers to index their works in another program called Google Print for Publishers (now called the Partners Program). This program would allow search and retrieval of, at most, a few pages of a book, together with a link that would enable a user to purchase the work. Since this program is being done by means of a contract agreement with the publisher, it is noncontroversial. It is the Google Print for Libraries Program that has provoked both much discussion and two lawsuits.

The Google library project is, itself, divided into two parts. For those materials that are clearly in the public domain, Google will make available the entire work, if desired. For materials that are not in the public domain, however, Google will only make available "snippets" of the work. The term "snippet" is not defined, but Google says that it is much less than a page, perhaps only a sentence or two on either side of the search terms. In addition to displaying the "snippet," Google will also provide information about where the complete work can be found, either through purchase or in a library. Google argues that displaying the "snippets" is clearly a fair use of the work and that far from harming a publisher's market, the availability of this material through a major online search engine is likely to enhance the market and stimulate sales.

Publishers, on the other hand, say that it is not up to Google to decide how best to market their works; it is up to the copyright owners to decide. Moreover, even if the "snippet" is a fair use, the original copying of the complete work into the database is not. Publishers say that it is fine to put these materials into the database, so long as the publisher agrees, but not otherwise.

In response to this, in August Google offered publishers an opportunity to "opt out" by telling them which titles they did not want included, and they promised that upon receiving such notification, those titles would be removed. Publishers say that this approach is backward; that the copyright law does not permit large-scale copying subject to the copyright owner's coming forward to have an item removed. Rather, the copyright law says if you want to copy a work in this way, you have to get permission from the owner first. Publishers therefore favor an opt-in approach instead.

In response to the Google Book Search project, two lawsuits have been filed, both in the Southern District of New York. On September 20 the Authors Guild filed a lawsuit and sought class-action status, so as to represent other authors similarly situated. On October 9 five book publishers filed a similar complaint in the same court, alleging that the Google Print for Libraries program infringes copyright. None of the partner libraries have been named as defendants in the cases.

Because of the unique facts of this case, there is very little applicable case law. The most relevant case, which found in favor of fair use, is from the Ninth Circuit, *Kelly* v. *Arriba Soft*.[19] In this case, the defendant copied photographic images from the plaintiff's Web site and displayed them as thumbnails to provide an online index. The court did not reach the question of whether a full-sized display of the work would have been infringing, but limited its holding to the thumbnails, which are analogous to the "snippets" being provided by Google. In *Kelly* v. *Arriba Soft* the court found that the thumbnails did not interfere with the market, and that it was necessary to copy the entire work in the first place to provide the beneficial result of the online index. On balance, the court found that the indexing and display of thumbnails was a fair use.

On the other hand, the District Court for the Southern District of New York (where the Google cases were filed) decided the case of *UMG* v. *MP3.com*[20] and rejected the claim of fair use. In that case, MP3.com provided a music storage service, allowing consumers the ability to copy and store online the content of purchased CDs. However, the court found that MP3.com also purchased tens of thousands of popular CDs and copied them directly onto its servers, so as to be able to replay the recording without authorization. It should be noted that in this case there was no claim that only snippets or thumbnails were available. In language not unrelated to the Google claims, the court wrote:

> Any allegedly positive impact of defendant's activities on plaintiffs' prior market in no way frees defendant to usurp a further market that directly derives from reproduction of the plaintiffs' copyrighted works.

Google has tried to meet the publishers part way by allowing them to participate in the Partners program, by allowing them to opt out, if they so desire, and by allowing them to share in some of the context-based advertising revenue that will result. Nonetheless, the publishers (and authors) seem to want either a "better deal" or simply to reassert their control in the matter. This case will be an important one to watch for the future of print-based information, the future of libraries, and the future of information delivery via the Web.

International Treaty Development

In 2005 an international effort began that has the potential to reform copyright worldwide. This effort faces an uphill battle and may never succeed, but even having the effort under discussion is reshaping and refocusing the agenda.

The World Intellectual Property Organization (WIPO) is a United Nations body that has as its essential purpose

> (i) to promote the protection of intellectual property throughout the world . . . [21]

Moreover, the current statement of vision and strategic direction provides that

> 3. The main objectives of the Medium-term Plan, as expressed in the past remain constant: maintenance and further development of the respect for intellectual property throughout the

world. This means that any erosion of the existing protection should be prevented, and that both the acquisition of the protection and, once acquired, its enforcement, should be simpler, cheaper and more secure.[22]

With a sense that these long-standing objectives did not provide an appropriate balance or meet the needs of less-developed countries of the world, in fall 2004 the General Assembly of WIPO adopted a resolution asking WIPO to take further steps to consider making a "development agenda" a part of the agenda for WIPO.[23]

With that decision as a mandate, but with the need to be much more specific, a meeting of experts was called in Geneva in January 2005 to begin to determine what the agenda should be when WIPO took up the issues later in the year. In preparation for the Geneva meeting, the library community developed a one-page statement of "Library-Related Principles"[24] for possible inclusion in later discussions or a treaty yet to be formulated. These principles were endorsed by all the major library associations in the United States and many non-U.S. library associations as well, including the International Federation of Library Associations and Institutions (IFLA). The statement of principles has so far been translated into seven languages. The full text of the principles is set out as an appendix to this article. The major categories are:

- Support for a robust and growing public domain
- Support for specific exemptions for libraries and education, as well as for private research and study
- Support for technological progress and innovation
- Support for the priority of these principles over conflicting provisions in trade agreements or in contracts

Following the meeting of experts in Geneva, a treaty was drafted for presentation to WIPO during the summer. The proposed treaty is known as a Treaty on Access to Knowledge[25] (shorthand, A2K), and its basic purpose is:

to protect and enhance access to knowledge, and to facilitate the transfer of technology to developing countries.

It contains sections on

- Enhancing the knowledge commons
- Exemptions and limitations to the rights of copyright owners
- First sale
- Technological protection measures
- Orphan works

WIPO scheduled three inter-sessional meetings during summer 2005 specifically to consider the possibility of a development agenda and what it might include. In addition, the issue was considered during a meeting of the WIPO Standing Committee on Copyright and Related Rights in November. According to reports from those in attendance at these meetings, progress stalled, largely because of opposition from the developed countries, led by the United States, the United Kingdom, and Japan. As of this writing, international attention on copyright issues had shifted its focus elsewhere. However, additional meetings were scheduled for February and June of 2006. Even though progress may appear to be glacial, it is important to recognize that the Treaty on Access to Knowledge is an important initiative, both in concept and in its implications for intellectual property law reform. It should be watched for future developments that may take many years to materialize.

Appendix

Library-Related Principles for the International Development Agenda of the World Intellectual Property Organization

Goal 1: A robust and growing public domain to provide new opportunities for creativity, research, and scholarship.

- 1.1. All works created by governmental authorities should be in the public domain.
- 1.2. Published works resulting from government-funded research should be publicly available at no charge within a reasonable time frame.
- 1.3. Facts and other public domain materials, and works lacking in creativity, should not be subject to copyright or copyright-like protections.
- 1.4. Consistent with the Berne Convention, the term of copyright should be the life of the author plus 50 years. The term of copyright should not be extended retroactively.

Goal 2: Effective library programs and services as a means of advancing knowledge.

- 2.1. A library may make copies of published and unpublished works in its collection for purposes of preservation or to migrate content to a new format.
- 2.2. A work that has been lawfully acquired by a library may be lent to others without further transaction fees to be paid by the library.
- 2.3. A work that has been lawfully acquired by a library or other educational institution may be made available over a network in support of classroom teaching or distance education in a manner that does not unreasonably prejudice the rights holder.
- 2.4. Subject to appropriate limitations, a library or educational institution may make copies of a work in support of classroom teaching.
- 2.5. A library may convert material from one format to another to make it accessible to persons with disabilities.
- 2.6. In support of preservation, education or research, libraries and educational institutions may make copies of works still in copyright but not currently the subject of commercial exploitation.

Goal 3: High levels of creativity and technological progress resulting from individual research and study.

- 3.1. Copyright laws should not inhibit the development of technology where the technology in question has substantial non-infringing uses.
- 3.2. Copying of individual items for or by individual users should be permitted for personal research and study.
- 3.3. It should be permissible to circumvent a technological protection measure for the purpose of making a non-infringing use of a work.

Goal 4: Harmonization of copyright.

- 4.1 The goals and policies set out in this document should not be over-ridden by other bi-lateral or multi-lateral agreements.
- 4.2 The goals and policies set out in this document are important statements of national and international principle and should not be varied by contract.

January 26, 2005

The foregoing principles were developed in December 2004 and were initially endorsed by the following library associations: American Association of Law Libraries, American Library Association, Association of Research Libraries, International Federation of Library Associations and Institutions, Medical Library Association, and the Special Libraries Association. They have since been adopted by many other library associations, worldwide. These principles were prepared for use in discussions at the World Intellectual Property Organization concerning the impact of intellectual property protection on economic development and the significance of copyright exceptions for libraries, educational institutions, and the disabled. These principles are not intended to serve as statutory language and thus do not reflect limitations and qualifications that would appear in such language.

Notes

1. 70 *Fed.Reg.* 3739 (January 26, 2005).
2. *Report on Orphan Works: a Report of the Register of Copyrights, United States Copyright Office,* Library of Congress, http://www.loc.gov/section108/index.html, p. 110 (January 2006).
3. *Basic Books Inc.* v. *Kinko's Graphics Corp.,* 758 F.Supp. 1522 (S.D. N.Y. 1991).
4. "Legal Battle Brews Over Availability of Texts on Online Reserve at U. of California Library," *Chronicle of Higher Education,* April 22, 2005.
5. 545 U.S. ___ , 125 S.Ct. 2764 (2005).
6. 464 U.S. 417 (1984).
7. See note 6, above.
8. Id. at 2770.
9. Id. at 2776.

10. ___ F.3d ___ (2005), available at http://www.ca7.uscourts.gov/tmp/QF0RFYTE.pdf (last visited February 14, 2006).

11. Id. at ___.

12. Id. at ___.

13. 2005 FCA 1242 (2005), available at http://www.fedcourt.gov.au.

14. See discussion of *New York Times* v. *Tasini* and *National Geographic Society* v. *Greenberg* in Oakley, "Copyright 2001, Exploring the Implications of Technology," 2002 *Bowker Annual*, 287–289 (2002).

15. 244 F.3d 1267 (11th Cir. 2001).

16. *New York Times* v. *Tasini* 533 U.S. 483 (2001).

17. *Faulkner* v. *National Geographic Society, Inc.* (2d Cir. 2005).

18. ___U.S. ___, 126 S.Ct. 833 (December 2005). It should be noted that this ruling also leaves standing the apparently conflicting opinion in *Greenberg*. However, unless or until another opinion is handed down, it it likely that the Second Circuit opinion in *Faulkner* will be regarded as controlling because it is later in time and interprets the Supreme Court's opinion in *Tasini*.

19. *Kelly* v. *Arriba Soft*, 336 F.3d 811 (9th Cir. 2003).

20. *UMG Recordings* v. *MP3.Com, Inc.,* 92 F.Supp.2d 349, (S.D.N.Y., 2000).

21. Convention Establishing the World Intellectual Property Association, Article 3, clause (i) (Signed at Stockholm, July 14, 1967.) available at http://www.wipo.int/treaties/en/convention/trtdocs_wo029.html (last visited February 14, 2006).

22. "Medium Term Plan for WIPO Program Activities—Vision and Strategic Direction of WIPO, 2006–2009," available at: http://www.wipo.int/about-wipo/en/dgo/pub487.htm (last visited February 13, 2006).

23. General Assembly Decision on a Development Agenda for WIPO, October 24, 2004, available at http://www.cptech.org/ip/wipo/wipo10042004.html (last visited February 13, 2006).

24. "Library-Related Principles for the International Development Agenda of the World Intellectual Property Organization," available at http://www.arl.org/info/frn/copy/intl/wipoprinciples.html (last visited February 13, 2006).

25. For text of the draft treaty, dated May 9, 2005, see http://www.cptech.org/a2k/consolidatedtext-may9.pdf (last visited February 13, 2006).

Access to Federal Government Information: A Status Report

Harold C. Relyea

Specialist in American National Government
Congressional Research Service, Library of Congress

During the latter half of the past century, various efforts were made to improve public access to federal government information. With the end of global warfare in 1945, American journalism organizations increasingly sought unfettered access to government officials, proceedings, and records. The federal bureaucracy, however, conditioned by the official secrets experience of World War II and the subsequent cold war, and threatened by demobilization work force reductions and discomfiting loyalty investigations, was not eager to have its activities and operations disclosed to the public, the press, or other government entities. Prevailing law tolerated this situation. A housekeeping law, dating to 1789, regarding the custody, use, and preservation of the records, papers, and property of executive entities, was often invoked to preclude access to documentary materials.[1] Moreover, Section 3 of the Administrative Procedure Act of 1946, while indicating that matters of official record could be made available to "persons properly and directly concerned," allowed agencies to restrict such access "for good cause found" or "in the public interest."[2] After a decade of executive branch resistance to pleas from various quarters for access to unpublished agency records, a House Special Subcommittee on Government Information was established and, on November 7, 1955, launched an inquiry into the availability of information from federal departments and agencies. These hearings continued until April 1959; they were paralleled, and succeeded, by subcommittee staff investigations and reports, which continued until the enactment of the Freedom of Information Act (FOIA) in 1966.[3] The statute was designed to enable any person—individual or corporate, regardless of citizenship—to request, without explanation or justification, presumptive access to existing, identifiable, unpublished, executive branch agency records on any topic. It specified nine categories of information that might be permissibly exempted from the rule of disclosure. Disputes over the accessibility of requested records could be ultimately settled in court.

Thereafter, the House subcommittee and its successors worked with counterpart Senate panels to strengthen FOIA through amendments in 1974, 1976, 1986, and 1996. FOIA was soon joined by other open-government laws providing presumptive access to advisory and policy deliberation meetings and to one's personally identifiable records, chief among these being the Federal Advisory Committee Act of 1972,[4] the Privacy Act of 1974,[5] and the Government in the Sunshine Act of 1976.[6] Building on the reform effort of President Dwight D. Eisenhower, Presidents Richard M. Nixon, Jimmy Carter, and Bill Clinton issued executive orders, respectively, in March 1972, June 1978, and April 1995, successively narrowing the bases and discretion for the security classification of executive branch records and information.

Note: The views expressed in this report are solely those of the author and are not attributable to the Library of Congress or the Congressional Research Service.

This legacy of information access and open-government law and policy was much affected by the events of September 11, 2001. There can be little doubt that the terrorist attacks on the World Trade Center and the Pentagon prompted rethinking, as well as continuing concern, about various aspects of the internal security—or homeland security—of the United States, not the least of which included the public availability of information of potential value to terrorists for either the commission of their acts or forewarning them of ways of their being detected. Oftentimes, it has not been clear to what extent, if any, an attempt was made to weigh citizen needs for information vis-à-vis denying its availability to terrorists, or if thoughtful consideration was given to alternative limits short of total restriction. "At the very least," a Heritage Foundation report observed not long ago, "such wholesale withdrawal of information seems arbitrary and undermines important values of government openness, the development of electronic government (e-gov) to speed the delivery and lower the costs of government services, and public trust."[7] Some aspects of the withdrawal of information from public availability in the aftermath of the September 11 terrorist attacks were examined in a special report appearing in the 2003 edition of the *Bowker Annual*.[8] The report provided here assesses the status of public access to government information at the close of 2005.

Secrecy currently permeates the executive branch of the federal government, more so in some places than in others. Were it not for the effects of a few open-government laws—especially FOIA—the situation would be closely comparable to the cold war era of the 1950s. Information-access retrenchment in response to the September 11 terrorist attacks, however, is not the only factor contributing to this situation. While President George W. Bush has indicated that he believes in open government, he has also cloaked some of his policies, decision making, and actions in secrecy as a matter of military necessity because, as he often stresses, the United States is engaged in a war.[9] Take the example of the president secretly ordering the National Security Agency (NSA) to conduct warrantless electronic surveillance of United States persons outside of the framework of the Foreign Intelligence Surveillance Act (FISA) that was established to authorize such monitoring.[10] Although it was later discovered that NSA had initially acted on its own authority in the weeks after the September 11 terrorist attacks to pursue such surveillance operations,[11] and was capturing purely domestic communications in some cases,[12] President Bush, in remarks at a December 19, 2005, press conference reacting to the revelation of this activity as reported in the *New York Times*,[13] justified it in terms of "defending the country against an enemy that declared war against the United States." Continuing, he said:

> As President and commander-in-chief, I have the constitutional responsibility and the constitutional authority to protect our country. Article II of the Constitution gives me that responsibility and that authority necessary to fulfill it. And after September the 11th, the United States Congress also granted me additional authority to use military force against al Qaeda.[14]

His reliance upon Article II authority and the congressional joint resolution of September 18, 2001, authorizing the use of all necessary and appropriate force against those responsible for the terrorist attacks of the previous week, while ignoring FISA arrangements, has been called into question in various quarters.

Regarding the secrecy surrounding his order to NSA and its expanded surveillance effort, the president said: "My personal opinion is it was a shameful act for someone to disclose this very important program in a time of war. The fact that we're discussing this program," he maintained, "is helping the enemy." Concerning the leak, the president commented: "We're at war, and we must protect America's secrets. And so the Justice Department, I presume, will proceed forward with a full investigation." Secrecy also figured prominently in his consideration of modifying FISA to accommodate the kind of expanded surveillance he had ordered NSA to perform. He appeared to reject the constitutionally prescribed legislative process in this regard with the comment that "an open debate about law would say to the enemy, here is what we are going to do. And this is an enemy which adjusts." Reiterating this view in a response to another question, he added: "This is a war." [15]

Contributing, as well, is the president's view of the "unitary executive." In one regard, this means that the president has managerial control over all executive branch information. In another, President Bush and Vice President Richard B. Cheney, from the outset of their tenure, have justified taking certain actions in secret and otherwise declining to respond to congressional demands for information as part of a broader effort to reassert powers of the presidency that they believe had been dangerously eroded in the years after the Vietnam conflict and the Watergate fiasco. In remarks at a March 13, 2002, White House press conference when the General Accounting Office (GAO; later renamed the Government Accountability Office) was initially seeking records concerning the deliberations of the vice president's energy task force, President Bush, indicating he was "not going to let Congress erode the power of the executive branch," said: "I have a duty to protect the executive branch from legislative encroachment. I mean, for example, when the GAO demands documents from us, we're not going to give them to them." He then reiterated that he had "an obligation to make sure that the presidency remains robust and the legislative branch doesn't end up running the executive branch." [16]

Secrecy impedes access to information, but, as history has surely revealed, in the American experience, it is not absolute; it is both temporal and varietal. Concerning the first of these conditions, while some secrecy may prevail for a long time, very little secrecy lasts forever. This realization may not be comforting for various reasons, not the least of which is the recognition that information has timely value. A spoiled fruit or a stale cookie is not very satisfying to the palate. There is, as well, another important dimension to this realization. In a democracy, representatives of the citizenry, whether elected or appointed, may momentarily cloak their decision making and their policies in secrecy for the good of the nation—to protect it from enemies and to assure its survival. Those representatives must remember that the secrecy they impose is only momentary and that the shrouded decisions and policies they make, once made known to the citizenry, must be acceptable to them. The citizenry, in turn, accept such secrecy only in limited instances and on a momentary basis in order to have the confidence that their representatives are making decisions and policies acceptable to them. A government failing to honor these arrangements, we have been warned, may well be one "not worth the cost of preservation." [17]

Concerning the second of the two conditions, secrecy may be realized for reasons other than national security. Personal privacy, for some, may be considered a form of secrecy. Trade secrecy practices, as formally recognized in American law, serve to protect formulas, patterns, devices, or compilations of information used in business that provide an opportunity to obtain a market advantage over competitors. In the absence of such protection, entrepreneurs would be disadvantaged in both domestic and international markets.

These considerations, among others, enter into the information-access review set out in this report. FOIA, of course, recognizes that some types of information—such as that which is properly classified, a trade secret, or personally identifiable—may require protection from public disclosure. Likewise, security classification policy and procedure, prescribed in a presidential executive order, recognizes that some officially secret records may require protection beyond the threshold established for many others. These considerations are offered as an introduction to the review that follows.

Freedom of Information

The Bush administration's FOIA policy, which was in formulation before the September 11 terrorist attacks, was issued a few weeks thereafter in an October 12, 2001, memorandum from Attorney General John Ashcroft to the heads of all federal departments and agencies.[18] The memorandum appeared to ignore the statute's presumptive right of records access and seemed to regard the application of its exemptions to the rule of disclosure to be mandatory rather than permissive. The memorandum assured readers that the Department of Justice and "this Administration," in addition to being "committed to full compliance with the Freedom of Information Act [FOIA]," were "equally committed to protecting other fundamental values that are held by our society," including "safeguarding our national security, enhancing the effectiveness of our law enforcement agencies, protecting sensitive business information and, not least, preserving personal privacy." The attorney general encouraged each agency "to carefully consider the protection of all such values and interests when making disclosure determinations under the FOIA." Furthermore, the agencies were advised, when "making these decisions, you should consult with the Department of Justice's Office of Information and Privacy when significant FOIA issues arise, as well as with our Civil Division on FOIA litigation matters." Readers were assured that "the Department of Justice will defend your decisions unless they lack a sound legal basis or present an unwarranted risk of adverse impact on the ability of other agencies to protect other important records."

The new policy was not well received by users of the act, such as journalists and public-interest organizations, or by at least one congressional overseer. The House Committee on Government Reform, in its March 2002 version of *A Citizen's Guide on Using the Freedom of Information Act,* pointedly noted that "the statute requires Federal agencies to provide the fullest possible disclosure of information to the public." Continuing, it said:

> The history of the act reflects that it is a disclosure law. It presumes that requested records will be disclosed, and the agency must make its case for withholding in terms of the act's exemp-

tions to the rule of disclosure. The application of the act's exemptions is generally permissive—to be done if information in the requested records requires protection—not mandatory. Thus, when determining whether a document or set of documents should be withheld under one of the FOIA exemptions, an agency should withhold those documents only in those cases where the agency reasonably foresees that disclosure would be harmful to an interest protected by the exemption. Similarly, when a requestor asks for a set of documents, the agency should release all documents, not a subset or selection of those documents. *Contrary to the instructions issued by the Department of Justice on October 12, 2001, the standard should not be to allow the withholding of information whenever there is merely a "sound legal basis" for doing so.*[19]

That same month, a memorandum from White House Chief of Staff Andrew H. Card, Jr., to the heads of executive departments and agencies, reminding them that they had "an obligation to safeguard Government records regarding weapons of mass destruction," was accompanied by guidance from the Information Security Oversight Office and the Justice Department's Office of Information and Privacy, in the words of the Card memo, "for reviewing Government information in your department or agency regarding weapons of mass destruction, as well as other information that could be misused to harm the security of our Nation and the safety of our people." The agencies were directed "to safeguard sensitive but unclassified information related to America's homeland security." Failing to define such information, it disingenuously stated that "the Freedom of Information Act recognizes the concept by authorizing agencies to withhold from public disclosure several categories of 'sensitive but unclassified' information." It also advised the agencies to follow the attorney general's October 12, 2001, memorandum "by giving full and careful consideration to all applicable FOIA exemptions," and made certain in a question-and-answer exchange that they understood that the Bush administration wanted them to remove from their Web sites information "regarding weapons of mass destruction, as well as other information that could be misused to harm the security of our Nation and the safety of our people."[20]

Subsequently, GAO assessed the impact of the Ashcroft "careful consideration" policy for making discretionary FOIA disclosures and the "sound legal basis" standard for defending agencies that withhold information based on FOIA exemptions. As part of its evaluation, GAO surveyed 205 FOIA officers at 25 agencies, which together handle more than 97 percent of FOIA requests government-wide, and received responses from 183 officers from 23 of the sample agencies. The following findings were offered in a September 2003 report.

When asked about views regarding the effects of the new policy, FOIA officers most frequently reported that they did not notice changes in their agencies' responses to FOIA requests when compared with previous years. Of the FOIA officers surveyed, 48 percent [88 of 183] reported that they did not notice a change with regard to the likelihood of their agency making discretionary disclosures. About one third of the FOIA officers [57 of 183] reported a decreased likelihood; and of these officers, 75 percent [43 of 57] cited the new policy as a top factor influencing the change. When FOIA officers were asked about changes in the use of particular FOIA exemptions, 62 percent [114 of 183] reported no change with regard to the use of these exemptions. One fourth of the officers [45 of 183] reported a change in this regard. Among these respondents, the two factors cited most frequently as influencing this change were the policy stated in the Ashcroft memorandum and concerns over protecting critical infrastructure information and other sensitive information related to homeland security.[21]

Almost two years later, a GAO representative, testifying at an oversight hearing by a House subcommittee, described FOIA trends in the following terms:

First, citizens have been requesting and receiving an ever-increasing amount of information from the Federal Government through FOIA. Based on data reported by the agencies, the number of requests received increased by 71 percent from 2002 to 2004.

In recent years, the Veterans Administration [VA] and the Social Security Administration have accounted for many of the total requests. In 2004 these two agencies accounted for about 82 percent of total requests.

As more requests come in, agencies also report that they have been processing more of them, 68 percent more in 2002 to 2004. However, at the same time the number of pending requests carried over from year to year, also known as the backlog, has also been increasing, rising 14 percent since 2002.

In 2004 about 92 percent of FOIA requests Government-wide were reported to have been granted in full. A relatively small number were partially granted and about 1 percent were denied.

Without VA and Social Security 61 percent of requests were granted in full; 15 percent partially granted and 2 percent denied. However, the number of fully granted requests varied widely among the agencies in fiscal year 2004. For example, three agencies, [Department of] State, CIA and the National Science Foundation make full grants of requested records in less than 20 percent of the cases they processed. We also saw this variation in previous years as well.

In regard to timeliness, reported time required to process requests varied considerably by agency. For example, 11 agency components reported processing simple requests in median times of less than 10 days. However, other agency components are taking much more time to process simple requests and in some cases reported median processing time in excess of 100 days.[22]

On the latter point concerning timeliness in FOIA request processing, journalists have traditionally been quite critical of FOIA administration. Of interest in this regard is a September 2005 assessment of environmental reporters' experiences with the act. Based on interviews with 55 journalists belonging to the Society of Environmental Journalists, the results "revealed growing shortcomings in the way the government is treating FOIA requests," including

- Significant delays in receiving responsive records, some exceeding a year
- Frequent failure to respond promptly and fully at the Department of Energy, Department of Defense, Food and Drug Administration, and Mine Safety and Health Administration
- Difficulties, sometimes severe, in monitoring the status of a FOIA request or to determine who is processing it
- Unnecessary requirements to file FOIA requests at the Department of Energy, Federal Energy Regulatory Commission, Environmental Protection Agency, and Mine Safety and Health Administration to obtain routine documents and reports
- Questioning of journalists' receipt of records without charge, resulting in more delay
- Disappointing quality and quantities of records provided in FOIA responses

- Reluctance to use FOIA due to unfamiliarity with its requirements, "horror stories" told by other reporters regarding their experience with it, and ability to substitute other means to obtain desired information effectively[23]

Legislative Proposals

To address some of these problems, as well as others, remedial legislation has been introduced in both houses of Congress. On February 16, 2005, Sen. John Cornyn (R-Texas) introduced legislation on behalf of himself and Sen. Patrick Leahy (D-Vt.) to "significantly expand the accessibility, accountability, and openness of the Federal Government." Acknowledged to be "a bipartisan effort to improve and update our public information laws—particularly the Freedom of Information Act," S. 394, denominated the Openness Promotes Effectiveness in Our National Government Act of 2005 or OPEN Government Act of 2005, was referred to the Committee on the Judiciary. Senator Leahy is the ranking minority member on the committee, and Senator Cornyn chairs its Subcommittee on Terrorism, Technology, and Homeland Security, which held the initial hearing on the measure.[24] Senator Cornyn noted that the bill "is supported by a broad coalition across the ideological spectrum," and placed in the *Congressional Record* "endorsement letters from dozens of watchdog groups."[25]

In his related remarks, Senator Leahy characterized S. 394 as "a collection of common sense modifications designed to update FOIA and improve the timely processing of FOIA requests by Federal agencies."[26] That same day, a companion bill, H.R. 867, was introduced in the House by Rep. Lamar Smith (R-Texas) and was referred to the Committee on Government Reform.

The following matters are among those addressed in the provisions of the bills, as introduced.

- Clarifying that independent journalists are not barred from obtaining fee waivers solely because they lack an institutional affiliation with a recognized news media organization.
- Clarifying that a complainant has substantially prevailed in an FOIA lawsuit, and is eligible to recover attorney fees, if the complainant has obtained a substantial part of his or her requested relief through a judicial or administrative order or if the pursuit of a claim was the catalyst for the voluntary or unilateral change in position by the opposing party.[27]
- Requiring that the attorney general, whenever a court finds that agency personnel have acted arbitrarily or capriciously with respect to withholding records sought under FOIA, notify both the Office of Special Counsel and Congress of such court finding, and requiring the Office of Special Counsel to report annually to Congress on any actions taken by its personnel to investigate such cases.[28]
- Clarifying that the 20-day time limit on responding to an FOIA request commences on the date on which the request is initially received by the agency, and providing that, if an agency fails to comply with the time limit requirement, it may not assert any exemption under Section 552(b)

to the request unless disclosure would endanger national security or disclose personal information protected by the Privacy Act or proprietary information, or is otherwise prohibited by law.[29]

- Requiring agencies to establish tracking systems, with each FOIA request receiving a tracking number, and to notify requesters of their tracking numbers within 10 days of receiving a request, and to establish a telephone or Internet system to allow requesters to obtain information on the status of their individual requests, including an estimated date on which action on the request will be completed by the agency.

- Providing that statutory provisions protecting records relative to the third exemption of the FOIA which are enacted subsequent to the enactment of the bill must do so explicitly and cite directly to the third exemption, thereby conveying congressional intent to create an information protection within the scope of the exemption.[30] This provision was later offered in separate legislation (see below).

- Expanding agency reporting requirements on FOIA administration to include data on the 10 oldest active requests pending at each agency, including the amount of time that has elapsed since each such request was originally filed; calculated average response times and the range of response times for FOIA requests; and the number of fee status requests that are granted and denied, and the average number of days for adjudicating fee status determinations.

- Clarifying that agency records kept by private contractors licensed by the federal government to undertake recordkeeping functions remain subject to FOIA.

- Establishing an Office of Government Information Services within the Administrative Conference of the United States to review agency policies and procedures, audit agency performance, recommend policy changes, and mediate disputes between FOIA requesters and agencies with a view to alleviating the need for litigation, but not limiting the ability of requesters to litigate FOIA claims.[31]

- Requiring reports to Congress by the Comptroller General of the United States on the implementation and use of the Critical Infrastructure Information Act of 2002, including the number of private-sector persons and state and local government agencies that voluntarily furnished critical infrastructure information (CII) records to the Department of Homeland Security, the number of requests for access to CII records granted or denied, and the results of an examination of whether the nondisclosure of CII has led to the increased protection of critical infrastructure.[32]

- Requiring the Office of Personnel Management to examine how FOIA can be better administered at the agency level, including an assessment of whether FOIA performance should be considered as a factor in personnel performance reviews, whether a job classification series specific to FOIA and the Privacy Act should be considered, and whether FOIA awareness training should be provided to federal employees.

Referred to the Committee on the Judiciary, S. 394 was the subject of hearings before the Subcommittee on Terrorism, Technology, and Homeland Security on March 15, 2005. Witnesses included representatives of the Texas Open Records Division, Heritage Foundation Center for Media and Public Policy, American Civil Liberties Union, and National Security Archive.

Of related interest is S. 589, the Faster FOIA Act of 2005, introduced by Senator Cornyn with Senator Leahy on March 10, 2005.[33] This legislation would establish a temporary commission to examine, and make recommendations concerning, FOIA request-processing delays. Of the 16 members of the panel, 3 each would be appointed by the chairman and ranking minority member of the Senate Committee on the Judiciary and House Committee on Government Reform, with the 4 remaining members being appointed by the attorney general, director of the Office of Management and Budget, Archivist of the United States, and comptroller general of the United States. At least four members of the commission must be from groups with experience submitting FOIA requests on behalf of nonprofit groups or media organizations. Referred to the Committee on the Judiciary, the bill was reported from committee without amendment or a written report on March 17, 2005, and was placed on the Senate legislative calendar. A companion bill, H.R. 1620, was introduced in the House by Rep. Brad Sherman (D-Calif.), with Rep. Lamar Smith, on April 13, 2005, and was referred to the Committee on Government Reform.

Senator Leahy also introduced another related bill, S. 622, the Restoration of Freedom of Information Act of 2005, on March 15, 2005, for himself and Senators Carl Levin (D-Mich.), Russell Feingold (D-Wis.), and Joseph Lieberman (D-Ct.). The proposal would amend the Homeland Security Act to prohibit a record pertaining to the vulnerability of, and threats to, critical infrastructure that is furnished voluntarily to the Department of Homeland Security (DHS) from being made available to the public pursuant to FOIA if (1) the provider would not customarily make the record available to the public, and (2) the record is designated and certified by the provider as confidential and not customarily made available to the public. The measure also prohibits other federal agencies in receipt of such a record furnished to DHS from making the record publicly available, and allows a provider of such a record to withdraw the confidential designation at any time. When introducing the legislation, Senator Leahy indicated that the bill would "protect Americans' right to know while simultaneously providing security to those in the private sector who voluntarily submit critical infrastructure records to the Department of Homeland Security." He called the current protective arrangement "an extraordinarily broad exemption to FOIA in exchange for the cooperation of private companies in sharing information with the government regarding vulnerabilities in the nation's critical infrastructure."[34] The legislation was referred to the Committee on the Judiciary.

On May 12, 2005, Rep. Henry Waxman (D-Calif.) introduced, on behalf of himself and 19 initial cosponsors, H.R. 2331, the Restore Open Government Act of 2005. The measure contains sections promoting the public disclosure of government information, revoking Bush administration memoranda regarded to encourage the withholding of information, fostering better managed use of information-control markings outside the security classification regime, restoring public access to presidential records, prohibiting the use of secret advisory committees within the executive branch, promoting the timely declassification of information, and improving the operation of FOIA. The bill was referred to the Committee on Government Reform and the Committee on Homeland Security.

On June 7, Senator Cornyn, with Senator Leahy, introduced S. 1181, which included a provision from S. 394 stating that statutory provisions protecting records relative to the third exemption of FOIA that are enacted subsequent to passage of the bill must do so explicitly and cite directly to the third exemption, thereby conveying congressional intent to create an information protection within the scope of the exemption.[35] The bill cleared the Committee on the Judiciary on a voice vote on June 9, 2005. The Senate passed the bill by unanimous consent on June 24, and the measure was then sent to the House, where it was referred to the Committee on Government Reform.[36]

The Bush administration does not appear to have taken a position on pending legislation to amend FOIA. Responding to questions at the American Society of Newspaper Editors convention on April 14, 2005, the president stated that, in processing FOIA requests, "the presumption ought to be that citizens ought to know as much as possible about the government decision making," and said, "I think that FOIA requests ought to be dealt with as expeditiously as possible." He also referred to Senator Cornyn, calling him "a good friend," and, though his remark was somewhat unclear, may have indicated he looked forward "to analyzing and working with legislation" offered by the senator to improve FOIA administration.[37]

Presidential Initiative

On December 14, 2005, President Bush signed an executive order, E.O. 13392, on improving agency disclosure of information.[38] The order required each agency to designate, from existing personnel, a chief FOIA officer by mid-January 2006. While many agencies already have an official who is responsible, in whole or in part, for FOIA administration, they are not at the assistant secretary or equivalent level prescribed for the new chief FOIA officers. Officials at the assistant secretary or equivalent level, however, are likely to be presidential appointees and may serve a brief tenure. Also, those designated as the chief FOIA officer will have other duties that will compete for their attention.

Following their designation, the chief FOIA officers are directed to conduct a review of their agency's FOIA operations and draft a plan for improvement with concrete milestones for fiscal year (FY) 2006 and FY 2007. By mid-June 2006, each chief FOIA officer is to submit to the Department of Justice, with a copy to the Office of Management and Budget (OMB), and to post on the agency's Web site a summary of the agency review and FOIA improvement plan. Follow-up reports in February 2007 and February 2008 are to include information on the agency's performance in meeting the milestones of its FOIA improvement plan. While these arrangements have a potential for realizing meaningful upgrading of FOIA administration, there is also the possibility that agency improvement plans will set a few modest, easily achievable milestones for what is asserted to be an already well-functioning administration of FOIA.

Finally, the order directs each agency to establish one or more FOIA Requester Service Centers to enable those seeking information pursuant to the statute to learn about the status of their request and the agency's FOIA response, and to place contact information for the service center on the agency's Web site. The chief FOIA officer for each agency is also to designate one or more public liaisons to serve as supervisory officials to whom a FOIA requester can pose concerns about the service received from the service center. Agency Web sites will have contact information for these public liaisons.

Some of the innovations mandated by the president's order may abate some of the current shortcomings of FOIA administration identified in the Society of Environmental Journalists survey—failure to have the receipt of a request acknowledged, lengthy delays in obtaining responsive records, and difficulties with monitoring the status of a FOIA request or determining who is processing it. Pending legislation, of course, also addresses some of these problems. Indeed, there are some who regard the executive order as an attempt to weaken the need for such legislation while keeping policymaking for FOIA administration in the hands of the president, and, perhaps, even strengthening the unitary executive in its managerial control over information provided to the public pursuant to FOIA.

Security Classification

A couple of weeks after Senator Cornyn saw one of his FOIA reform proposals receive the approval of his colleagues, the *New York Times* observed editorially that the "Bush Administration is classifying the documents to be kept from public scrutiny at the rate of 125 a minute. The move toward greater secrecy," it continued, "has nearly doubled the number of documents annually hidden from public view—to well more than 15 million last year, nearly twice the number classified in 2001."[39] As the number of classification actions has been increasing, the editorial also noted, the volume of declassified material has been decreasing, as the data in Table 1 indicate.[40]

Table 1 / Information Moving In and Out of Classified Status

Fiscal Year	New Classification Actions	Declassified Pages
2001	8,650,735	100,104,990
2002	11,271,618	44,365,711
2003	14,228,020	43,093,233
2004	15,645,237	28,413,690

These activities, of course, have related costs. Security classification expenses—which include personnel security, physical security, education and training, and management and planning—far exceed expenditures for declassification, which, as the data in Table 2 reflect, are declining.[41]

Table 2 / Cost Estimates for Information Security Activities

Fiscal Year	Classification	Declassification
2001	$4.5 billion	$232 million
2002	$5.5 billion	$113 million
2003	$6.4 billion	$54 million
2004	$7.1 billion	$48.3 million

As noted earlier, Presidents Nixon and Carter issued executive orders during their tenures that built on the security classification reforms inaugurated by President Eisenhower. The results of their efforts were a successive narrowing of the bases and discretion for security-classifying executive branch records and information. Then, on April 2, 1982, this trend was reversed with E.O. 12356, issued by President Ronald Reagan.[42] This order expanded the categories of classifiable information, mandated that information falling within these categories be classified, authorized the reclassification of previously declassified documents, admonished classifiers to err on the side of classification, and eliminated automatic declassification arrangements.

President Clinton returned security classification policy and procedure to the reform trend of the Eisenhower, Nixon, and Carter administrations with E.O. 12958 of April 17, 1995.[43] Adding impetus to the development and issuance of the new order were changing world conditions: the democratization of many eastern European countries, the demise of the Soviet Union, and the end of the cold war. Accountability and cost considerations were also significant influences. In 1985 the temporary Department of Defense Security Review Commission, chaired by retired General Richard G. Stilwell, declared that there were "no verifiable figures as to the amount of classified material produced in DOD and in defense industry each year." Nonetheless, it was concluded that "too much information appears to be classified and much at higher levels than is warranted."[44] In October 1993 the cost of the security classification program became clearer when GAO reported that it was "able to identify government-wide costs directly applicable to national security information totaling over $350 million for 1992." After breaking this figure down—it included only $6 million for declassification work—the report added that "the U.S. government also spends additional billions of dollars annually to safeguard information, personnel, and property."[45] E.O. 12958 set limits for the duration of classification, prohibited the reclassification of properly declassified records, authorized government employees to challenge the classification status of documents, reestablished the balancing test of the Carter order weighing the need to protect information vis-à-vis the public interest in its disclosure, and created two review panels—one on classification and declassification actions and one to advise on policy and procedures.

On March 25, 2003, President Bush signed E.O. 13292 amending E.O. 12958.[46] The product of a review and reassessment initiated in the summer of 2001, the directive, among other changes, eliminated the Clinton order's standard that information should not be classified if there is "significant doubt" about the need to do so; treated information obtained in confidence from foreign governments as classified; and authorized the vice president, "in the performance of executive duties," to classify information originally. It also added "infrastructures" and "protection services" to the categories of classifiable information; eased the reclassification of declassified records; postponed the automatic declassification of protected records 25 or more years old from beginning on April 17, 2003, to beginning on December 31, 2006; eliminated the requirement that agencies prepare plans for declassifying records; and permitted the director of central intelligence to block declassification actions of the Interagency Security Classification Appeals Panel (ISCAP), unless overruled by the president.

Created by the Clinton order, ISCAP is composed of senior-level representatives of the secretary of state, secretary of defense, attorney general, director of central intelligence, archivist of the United States, and assistant to the president for national security affairs. The president selects the panel's chair from among its members. The director of the Information Security Oversight Office (ISOO), which is the government-wide overseer of the security classification program, serves as the ISCAP executive secretary. The panel makes final determinations on classification challenges appealed to it; approves, denies, or amends exemptions from automatic declassification sought by agencies; makes final determinations on mandatory declassification review requests appealed to it; and generally advises and assists the president in the discharge of his discretionary authority to protect the national security of the United States. The recent review activities of ISCAP are detailed in Table 3.[47]

Table 3 / ISCAP Decisions

Year	Documents Reviewed	Declassified in Full	Declassified in Part	Affirmed Classification
2001	34 (100%)	8 (23%)	21 (62%)	5 (15%)
2002	49 (100%)	9 (18%)	17 (35%)	23 (47%)
2003	106 (100%)	3 (3%)	80 (75%)	23 (22%)
2004	159 (100%)	11 (7%)	30 (19%)	118 (74%)

As suggested by these data, the trend generally appears to be that, as more documents are reviewed, fewer are being declassified in whole or in part.

In addition to the growing quantity of security classified records and associated rising costs of the past few years, controversy has developed from time to time over what some regard to be zealous use of security classification to make segments of investigative reports officially secret. The ISOO director, William Leonard, took issue with the classification of portions of Major General Antonio M. Taguba's report on his investigation of prisoner interrogation conditions at Abu Ghraib Prison, and called the action a "bureaucratic impulse" to "almost reflexively reach out to the classification system."[48]

Problems with security-classifiable information in investigative reports also arose when the House Permanent Select Committee on Intelligence and the Senate Select Committee on Intelligence prepared to publish the findings from their joint inquiry into intelligence community activities prior to, and after, the September 11 terrorist attacks.[49] "It took more than six months of wrangling," according to a *Washington Post* editorial, "for the congressional joint committee investigating the Sept. 11 attacks to extract approval to publish its report—and

even then it had to black out an entire section involving Saudi Arabia."[50] A similar experience occurred with the July 9, 2004, release of the Senate Intelligence
Committee's report on the intelligence community's prewar intelligence assessments on Iraq.[51] According to one account, an estimated 20 percent of the draft
report was deleted at the request of the Central Intelligence Agency (CIA) prior
to its publication.[52] "It could have been worse, though," editorialized the *Washington Post*: "If Intelligence officials had their way, nearly half of the 511-page
report would have been redacted, rather than the 15 percent or so that was ex-
cised in the final version."[53]

These developments prompted calls for the creation of an independent panel
for the impartial and expeditious resolution of disputes over whether or not to
declassify portions of the sensitive content of official reports prior to their publication. In a July 2004 editorial on the matter, the *Washington Post* said:

> No one wants to insist on the release of information that could aid terrorists or other enemies
> of the United States. Clearly, some information reviewed by lawmakers or other investigators
> must remain secret. But the way the system is structured, no one can have confidence that the
> judgments to keep information classified are being made on the basis of national security
> alone—and there is ample evidence to the contrary. The reports already produced have offered
> a powerful, even chastening demonstration of the importance of outside oversight and review;
> it's hard to see what the arguments for classifying parts of those documents would have been.
> Among other effects, this undermines the credibility of the classifiers when it comes to pro-
> tecting real secrets.[54]

Shortly thereafter, Sen. Ron Wyden (D-Ore.) sought to remedy the situation
with legislation creating a three-member board that would, prior to publication,
review official reports containing information in dispute regarding its need to be
classified and render a final decision regarding the matter.[55] Several weeks later,
he proposed amending omnibus intelligence reform legislation, then under consideration in the Senate, with the language of his bill.[56] The floor manager for the
intelligence reform bill noted that "the administration has expressed grave reser-
vations about the amendment as it is now drafted," and suggested that some reconciliation of it with other points in the bill might be in order. She proposed
some staff-level adjustment of the amendment.[57]

Two days later, Senator Wyden offered a revised version of his original
amendment. It sought to empower an existing presidential information security
advisory board to review, at the request of the leaders of congressional armed
services, foreign policy, and intelligence committees, existing or proposed classification actions and to make recommendations to the president regarding the continued need for such classification. Not later than 60 days after receiving the
board's recommendations, the president, if he did not accept and implement
them, would be required to transmit to Congress a written justification for his
decision. The Wyden amendment, as modified, was agreed to by the Senate,[58]
and remained in the intelligence reform bill given Senate approval on a 96-2 vote
on October 6, and was subsequently sent to conference.[59] The conferees further
modified the amendment, rewriting it to indicate that the board is authorized to
"review and make recommendations to the President in a timely manner with
respect to any congressional request, made by the committee of jurisdiction, to
declassify certain records or to reconsider a declination to declassify specific

records," and that, if requested by the president, the board "shall review in a timely manner certain records or declinations to declassify specific records, the declassification of which has been the subject of specific congressional request." While the board is obligated to advise a requesting congressional committee as to whether or not it intends to conduct a declassification review, it is not required to inform the committee of the results of such a review, which is left to the president's discretion.[60] These modifications appeared to strengthen the president's control over the board's conduct of declassification reviews requested by congressional committees and the findings resulting from such reviews as are conducted. On December 7, the House, on a 336–75 vote, agreed to the conference committee report; the Senate gave its approval the following day on an 89–2 vote, clearing the intelligence reform legislation for the president's signature on December 17, 2004.[61] At that time, however, the panel, formally known as the Public Interest Declassification Board, was inactive. Originally mandated in 2000 in the closing weeks of the Clinton administration, the board had no members until September 2004, when President Bush named five nominees; the other four members are designated by congressional leaders, but only two had been selected by the end of 2005. Furthermore, the board did not receive an appropriation until the end of 2005 when $1 million was allocated for its operations in the Department of Defense appropriations act for FY 2006.[62]

Information-Control Markings

Adding a considerable measure of confusion to the current information access situation are an array of information-control markings—some 50 or more varieties—the vast majority of which have no statutory authorization and many of which have a weak management regime. They have been regarded by some as a form of "overclassification," or the over-protection of information, and by others as "pseudo-classification."[63] The security classification program has evolved over 65 years. One may not agree with all of its rules and requirements, but, as an expression of policy and procedure, its attention to detail is commendable. The operative presidential directive, as amended, defines its principal terms. Those who are authorized to exercise original classification authority are identified. Exclusive categories of classifiable information are specified, as are the terms of the duration of classification, as well as classification prohibitions and limitations. Classified information is required to be marked appropriately along with the identity of the original classifier, the agency or office of origin, and a date or event for declassification. Authorized holders of classified information who believe that its protected status is improper are "encouraged and expected" to challenge that status through prescribed arrangements. Mandatory declassification reviews are also authorized to determine if protected records merit continued classification at their present level, a lower level, or at all. Unsuccessful classification challenges and mandatory declassification reviews are subject to review by the Interagency Security Classification Appeals Panel. General restrictions on access to classified information are prescribed, as are distribution controls for classified information. An entity, ISOO, is mandated to provide central management and oversight of the security classification program. If the director of ISOO finds that a violation, of the order or its implementing directives, has occurred, it must be reported to the head of the agency or to the appropriate senior agency official so that corrective steps, if appropriate, can be taken.

In the closing days of January 2005, *GCN Update,* the online news service of *Government Computer News,* reported that "dozens of classified Homeland Security Department documents" had been accidentally made available on a public Internet site for several days because of an apparent security glitch at the Department of Energy. Describing the contents of the compromised materials and reactions to the breach, the account stated the "documents were marked 'for official use only,' the lowest secret-level classification." The documents, of course, were not security classified, because the marking cited is not authorized by E.O. 12958. Interestingly, however, in view of the fact that this misinterpretation appeared in a story to which three reporters contributed, perhaps it reflects, to some extent, the current state of confusion about the origin and status of the various new information-control markings.[64]

The situation, however, is not unprecedented. In March 1972, a subcommittee of the House Committee on Government Operations, now the House Committee on Government Reform, launched the first oversight hearings on the administration and operation of FOIA, which had become operative in July 1967. In the early months of 1972, the Nixon administration was developing new security classification policy and procedure, which would be prescribed in E.O. 11652, issued in early March. The subcommittee's strong interest in this directive is reflected in its unsuccessful attempt to receive testimony from one of the directive's principal architects, David Young, special assistant to the National Security Council. The subcommittee sought his testimony as it examined the way in which the new order "will affect the economic and efficient operation of our security classification system, the rationale behind its various provisions, and alternatives to the present approach."[65] Although Young, through White House counsel John Dean, declined the invitation to testify, the subcommittee was more successful in obtaining department and agency responses to its August 1971 questionnaire, which, among other questions, asked: "What legend is used by your agency to identify records which are *not* classifiable under Executive Order 10501 [the operative order at the time] but which are not to be made available outside the government?"[66] Of 58 information-control markings identified in response to this question, the most common were "For Official Use Only" (11 agencies); "Limited Official Use" (9 agencies) "Official Use Only" (8 agencies); "Restricted Data" (5 agencies); "Administratively Restricted" (4 agencies); "Formerly Restricted Data" (4 agencies); and "Nodis," or no dissemination (4 agencies). Seven other markings were used by two agencies in each case.[67] A review of the agency responses to the question prompted the following observation.

> Often no authority is cited for the establishment or origin of these labels; even when some reference is provided it is a handbook, manual, administrative order, or a circular but not statutory authority. Exceptions to this are the Atomic Energy Commission, the Defense Department and the Arms Control and Disarmament Agency. These agencies cite the Atomic Energy Act, N.A.T.O. related laws, and international agreements as a basis for certain additional labels. The Arms Control and Disarmament Agency acknowledged it honored and adopted State and Defense Department labels.[68]

At a May 1, 1972, hearing on the relationship of FOIA to the security classification system, Rep. William S. Moorhead (D-Pa.), chairman of the House Foreign Operations and Government Information Subcommittee, wondered aloud
how the act's nine exemptions to the rule of disclosure could be expanded to the
multiple information-control markings that the departments and agencies had
indicated they were using.[69] The following day, when the hearing continued, William D. Blair, Jr., deputy assistant secretary for public affairs at the Department
of State, explained that some information-control markings were used to route
otherwise classified information to a limited group of recipients, "those people
who have responsibility for the subject matter concerned." He then addressed the
relationship question raised by Moorhead, saying:

> But if a question came in under the Freedom of Information Act or from the Congress or other
> representative of the public for that given document, the fact that it is marked, let's say,
> NODIS, is not relevant. What is relevant to the making available of that document to the pub-
> lic is whether or not it was properly classified under the Executive order and whether or not
> the Freedom of Information Act, for example, once we have reviewed the document, still per-
> tains, whether we feel that the need for the classification still pertains and whether, in fact, we
> are authorized under the act to withhold it.[70]

A moment thereafter, he explained another marking, which was not applied
to route classified information but apparently had the same effect as a security
classification protective marking.

> "Limited official use" is not a fixed distribution channel, such as some of these other terms
> you have mentioned. It simply is an administrative red flag put on that document which means
> that the document should be given the same degree of protection, physical protection as a clas-
> sified document even though it is not, under the Executive order, classifiable.[71]

However, when asked if, in applying this particular marking, "you mean to
exclude all individuals outside the Department, subject to the Freedom of Information Act, where they can go to court to obtain it," Blair's response indicated
that the use of the marking was somewhat more complicated than functioning as
a parallel security label, when he said:

> Not necessarily sir. That may be the case. For instance, one set of files on which we use
> "Limited official use" quite commonly is personnel files. Well, we would be very likely to
> deny those personnel files if they were requested by a member of the public, on quite different
> grounds from classification—on grounds of invasion of privacy. But on the other hand we
> may use a term like "Limited official use" on an internal advisory document which we may be
> authorized under the Freedom of Information Act to withhold if it were requested; but we
> might decide not to claim that authority.[72]

Although an attempt was made to obtain further explanation of how information-control markings were used, the questioner, a subcommittee staff member, concluded "that all you have convinced me of is to reinforce my belief that a
distribution marking is merely a more restrictive or stricter type of classification
marking."[73]

Later in the hearing, in an exchange with the subcommittee's staff director, Department of Defense General Counsel J. Fred Buzhardt, made another attempt to clarify the use of control markings.

> In the first place, you have a determination as to whether the material is to be classified. Once the decision is made that the information should be classified, then the limitation of access has to do with the protection of that which is classified. We also have the responsibility to control the dissemination. That is what these access limitations are for, to control dissemination, to confine access to the people who have a need to know to work with the information. It is a protection device. We must use protective devices of some sort.[74]

Asked if the control markings, such as "eyes only," were applied to material that was not classified, Buzhardt said:

> I presume you wouldn't find "eyes only" in an authorized way upon any document that was not classified by one of the classifiers. Once it is classified you can use limitations on distribution to protect it. That is a protective device.[75]

To this response, Blair added:

> The purpose of classification is to determine what information is or is not available to the public outside of the government. These labels that you are referring to have nothing to do with that. They have absolutely no value for determining what information or what document may be given to a member of the public. They are simply a mailing device, if you like, a means by which a superior determines which of his subordinates he wishes to deal with this particular matter and be aware of this particular information.[76]

These explanations of information-control markings being used as devices to limit the distribution of classified information within the Department of Defense and the State Department, however, did not appear to extend to all such markings. Blair, for instance, had testified that the "Limited official use" marking was applied, in his words, "quite commonly" to personnel files, which, for the most part, were not security classifiable materials at that time. Several entities indicating they used information-control markings had no original classification authority. These included, among others, the American Revolution Bicentennial Commission (ARBC), the Department of Housing and Urban Development, and the Federal Trade Commission (FTC).[77] Does this situation mean that the control markings of these entities were applied only to limit the distribution of classified information received from other agencies? That is possible, but seems unlikely. The ARBC control marking, "Administratively confidential," appears to have been designed for information of a different character from national security classified materials, while the FTC label, "For staff use only," does not appear to have provided much limitation on the distribution of classified information.

Before this phase of the oversight hearings on FOIA concluded, the subcommittee received testimony from Assistant Attorney General Ralph E. Erickson of the Office of Legal Counsel, Department of Justice, on May 11, 1972. During the course of his appearance before the subcommittee to discuss E.O. 11652, the use of control markings to limit the distribution of classified information was raised with the following question from the subcommittee's staff director.

Can you assure us today that these kinds of distribution access stamps will not be used on unclassified material in any Executive agency or department? If you can guarantee that, then I will go along and say [Section] 4(a) is a big improvement. But I do not think that is going to be the case from other testimony we have had. I think people are going to substitute LIMDIS, NODIS, and all these other stamps for the stamps authorized under the Executive order and we are going to proliferate more and more and more.[78]

Erickson offered a two part response.

First, it is our hope within the Department of Justice and I think in other agencies, too, that the use of this sort of a restricted distribution will be severely limited or removed. But, more importantly, it [Section 4(a)] specifically limits the use of such designations to the point where they must conform with the provision of this order and would have no effect in terms of classification. It will not prevent the information from otherwise being made available. It may in part restrict the distribution within the department but certainly if a request were made under the Freedom of Information Act it has no applicability.[79]

He assured his questioner that control markings used to limit the distribution of classified information "will not have any effect on disclosure" under FOIA, and would not, in themselves, be a bar to disclosure.

Later, in May 1973, when reviewing this phase of the subcommittee's oversight hearings, a report by the parent Committee on Government Operations commented:

One of the difficult problems related to the effective operation of the security classification system has been the widespread use of dozens of special access, distribution, or control labels, stamps, or markings on both classified and unclassified documents. Such control markings were not specifically authorized in Executive Order 10501, but have been utilized for many years by many executive agencies having classification authority and dozens of other agencies who do not possess such authority. The use of such stamps has, in effect, been legitimized in section 9 of the new Executive Order 11652.[80]

On this matter, the report concluded that "while there is a clear rationale for the use of such access or control markings, the basic problem is the effect of the proliferation of their use on the effective operation of the classification system. This problem," it continued, "fully explored with executive branch witnesses during the hearings, is one that this committee believes should be carefully monitored by the [newly created] Interagency Classification Review Committee and by department heads to assure that it does not interfere with the overall effectiveness and integrity of the classification system."[81]

That such interference with the security classification program by these types of information-control markings—in terms of both their confusion and presumed coequal authority with classification markings—has occurred in the post-9-11 environment may be discerned in the recent *GCN Update* story cited earlier. In some instances, the phraseology of the markings is new, and, in at least one case, the asserted authority for the label is, unlike most of those of the past, statutory. Among the problems they generate, however, the one identified more than three decades ago by the House Committee on Government Operations endures.

Broadly considering the contemporary situation regarding information-control markings, a recent information security report by the JASON Program Office of the MITRE Corporation proffered the following assessment.

> The status of sensitive information outside of the present classification system is murkier than ever. . . . "Sensitive but unclassified" data is increasingly defined by the eye of the beholder. Lacking in definition, it is correspondingly lacking in policies and procedures for protecting (or not protecting) it, and regarding how and by whom it is generated and used.[82]

A contemporaneous Heritage Foundation report appeared to agree with this appraisal, saying:

> The process for classifying secret information in the federal government is disciplined and explicit. The same cannot be said for unclassified but security-related information for which there is no usable definition, no common understanding about how to control it, no agreement on what significance it has for U.S. national security, and no means for adjudicating concerns regarding appropriate levels of protection.[83]

Concerning the current "Sensitive But Unclassified" (SBU) marking, a recent report by the Federal Research Division of the Library of Congress commented that guidelines for its use are needed, and noted that "a uniform legal definition or set of procedures applicable to all Federal government agencies does not now exist." Indeed, the report indicates that SBU has been utilized in different contexts with little precision as to its scope or meaning, and, to add a bit of chaos to an already confusing situation, is "often referred to as Sensitive Homeland Security Information."[84]

The array of new information-control markings raises many concerns. Key terms often lack definition. Vagueness exists regarding who is authorized to apply markings, for what reasons, and for how long. Uncertainty prevails concerning who is authorized to remove markings and for what reasons. These markings seem to be confused, in some instances, with security classification markings. They also may constitute a prejudgment regarding the availability of a record, so marked, pursuant to FOIA. Efforts to better understand the use of these markings and the problems they generate are under way. So, too, are attempts to prompt their better management.

Other efforts to improve public access to federal government information—such as the proposed amendments to FOIA and the innovations initiated by President Bush in his information disclosure improvements order—are to be welcomed. Perhaps ISOO or OMB should be enlisted in the effort to instill better management of information-control markings and to oversee agency compliance with those arrangements. Whether or not this responsibility is assigned to ISOO, that entity is probably deserving of more resources to conduct audits and inspections to determine if agencies are implementing the requirements of the classification-declassification program. This might include a permanent on-site presence within the major classifying organizations, such as the Departments of Defense, Homeland Security, Justice, and State. Achieving a balance between public access to government information and the proper protection of government information for security and other legitimate purposes is something of a Sisyphean condition;

there are times when one side of the equation or the other holds sway, but the dynamic is such that actual balance remains elusive.

Notes

1. The section was modified in 1958 (72 Stat. 547) to indicate that it "does not authorize withholding information from the public or limiting the availability of records to the public"; currently found at 5 U.S.C. 301.

2. 60 Stat. 237, at 238; the section was replaced by the provisions of the Freedom of Information Act in 1966.

3. 80 Stat. 250; codified in 1967, 81 Stat. 54; currently found at 5 U.S.C. 552.

4. 5 U.S.C. App.

5. 5 U.S.C. 552a.

6. 5 U.S.C. 552b.

7. James Jay Carafano and David Heyman, "DHS 2.0: Rethinking the Department of Homeland Security," *Heritage Special Report SR-02* (Washington: Dec. 13, 2004), p. 20.

8. See Harold C. Relyea and L. Elaine Halchin, "Homeland Security and Information Management," *Bowker Annual Library and Book Trade Almanac*, 48th edition (Information Today, Inc., 2003), pp. 231–250.

9. Responding to a question at the American Society of Newspaper Editors convention, President Bush said: "I believe in open government. I've always believed in open government." U.S. White House Office, "President Addresses American Society of Newspaper Editors Convention," J. W. Marriott Hotel, Washington, D.C., Apr. 14, 2005, available at http://www.whitehouse.gov/news/releases/2005/04/print/20050414-4.html.

10. See 50 U.S.C. 1801 et seq.

11. Eric Lichtblau and Scott Shane, "Agency First Acted on Its Own to Broaden Spying, Files Show, *New York Times*, Jan. 4, 2006, pp. A1, A13.

12. James Risen and Eric Lichtblau, "Spying Program Snared U.S. Calls," *New York Times*, Dec. 21, 2005, pp. A1, A23.

13. James Risen and Eric Lichtblau, "Bush Lets U.S. Spy on Callers Without Courts," *New York Times*, Dec. 16, 2005, pp. A1, A22.

14. U.S. White House Office, "Press Conference of the President," Washington, D.C., Dec. 19, 2005, available at http://www.whitehouse.gov/news/releases/2005/12/print/20051219-2.html.

15. Ibid.

16. U.S. White House Office, "President Bush Holds Press Conference: Press Conference by the President," Washington, D.C, March 13, 2002, available at http://www.whitehouse.gov/news/releases/2002/03/print/20020313-8html.

17. *Ex parte Milligan*, 71 U.S. 121 (1866). See http://www.constitution.org/ussc/071-002a.htm.

18. U.S. Department of Justice, Office of the Attorney General, "The Freedom of Information Act," Memorandum for the Heads of all Federal Departments and Agencies, Oct. 12, 2001, Washington, D.C.; available at http://www.usdoj.gov/04foia/011012.htm.

19. U.S. Congress, House Committee on Government Reform, *A Citizen's Guide on Using the Freedom of Information Act and the Privacy Act of 1974 to Request Government Records*, 107th Congress, 2nd session, H. Rept. 107-371 (Washington: GPO, 2002), p. 3 (*emphasis added*).

20. White House Office, Chief of Staff, "Action to Safeguard Information Regarding Weapons of Mass Destruction and Other Sensitive Documents Related to Homeland Security," Memorandum for the Heads of Executive Departments and Agencies, Mar. 19, 2002, Washington, D.C., accompanied by Information Security Oversight Office and Department of Justice, Office of Information and Privacy, "Safeguarding Information Regarding Weapons of Mass Destruction and Other Sensitive Records Related to Homeland Security," Memorandum for Departments and Agencies, undated, Washington, D.C.; available at http://www.usdoj.gov/oip/foiapost/2002foiapost10.htm. The version available at this Web site does not include the Q&A clarifications accompanying the original documents.

21. U.S. General Accounting Office, *Freedom of Information Act: Agency Views on Changes Resulting from New Administration Policy,* GAO Report GAO-03-981 (Washington: Sept. 2003), pp. 2–3, 14.

22. U.S. Congress, House Committee on Government Reform, *Information Policy in the 21st Century: A Review of the Freedom of Information Act,* hearing, 109th Cong., 1st sess., May 11, 2005 (Washington: GPO, 2005), p. 78; also produced as U.S. Government Accountability Office, *Information Management: Implementation of the Freedom of Information Act,* GAO Report GAO-05-648T (Washington: May 11, 2005).

23. Society of Environmental Journalists, First Amendment Task Force, *A Flawed Tool: Environmental Reporters' Experiences with the Freedom of Information Act* (Jenkintown, PA: Sept. 12, 2005), pp. 3–4, available at http://www.sej.org/foia/SEJ_FOIA_Report2005.pdf.

24. U.S. Congress, Senate Committee on the Judiciary, *Openness in Government and Freedom of Information: Examining the Open Government Act of 2005,* hearing, 109th Cong., 1st sess., Mar. 15, 2005 (Washington: GPO, 2005).

25. See *Congressional Record,* daily edition, vol. 151, Feb. 16, 2005, pp. S1520–S1524.

26. Ibid., p. S1526.

27. This provision responds to the ruling in *Buckhannon Board and Care Home, Inc.* v. *West Virginia Dep't of Health and Human Services,* 532 U.S. 598 (2001), in which the Supreme Court eliminated the "catalyst theory" of attorney fee recovery under certain federal civil rights laws, and which prompted concern that the holding could be extended to FOIA cases.

28. FOIA requires that, when a court finds that agency personnel have acted arbitrarily or capriciously with respect to withholding records sought under FOIA, the Office of Special Counsel shall determine whether disciplinary action against such personnel is warranted; 5 U.S.C. § 552(a)(4)(F).

29. The Privacy Act may be found at 5 U.S.C. 552a.

30. The third exemption to the rule of disclosure exempts matters that are "specifically exempted from disclosure by statute [other than the Privacy Act], provided that such statute (A) requires that the matters be withheld from the public in such a manner as to leave no discretion on the issue, or (B) establishes particular criteria for withholding or refers to particular types of matters to be withheld"; 5 U.S.C. § 552(b)(3).

31. The authorization for the Administrative Conference lapsed in 1995, but it was recently reauthorized, although it has not been appropriated any funds; see 118 Stat. 2255.

32. The Critical Infrastructure Information Act is Subtitle B of Title II of the Homeland Security Act of 2002; see 116 Stat. 2150.

33. *Congressional Record,* daily edition, vol. 151, Mar. 10, 2005, pp. S2485–S2486.

34. Ibid., Mar. 15, 2005, pp. S2736–S2738.

35. Ibid., June 7, 2005, pp. S6159–S6161.

36. Ibid., June 24, 2005, pp. S7383–S7385.

37. U.S. White House Office, "President Addresses American Society of Newspaper Editors Convention," J. W. Marriott Hotel, Washington, D.C., April 14, 2005, available at http://www.whitehouse.gov/news/releases/2005/04/print/20050414-4.html.

38. See *Federal Register,* vol. 70, Dec. 19, 2005, pp. 75373–75377.

39. Editorial, "The Dangerous Comfort of Secrecy," *New York Times,* July 12, 2005, p. A22.

40. Data from U.S. National Archives and Records Administration, Information Security Oversight Office, *Report to the President 2001* (Washington: Sept. 2002), p. 16; U.S. National Archives and Records Administration, Information Security Oversight Office, *Report to the President 2002* (Washington: June 2003), p. 26; U.S. National Archives and Records Administration, Information Security Oversight Office, *Report to the President 2003* (Washington: Mar. 2004), pp. 20, 25; U.S. National Archives and Records Administration, Information Security Oversight Office, *Report to the President 2004* (Washington: Mar. 2005), pp. 15, 17.

41. Data from U.S. National Archives and Records Administration, Information Security Oversight Office, *Report to the President 2001,* (Washington: Sept. 2002), pp. 7–8; U.S. National Archives and Records Administration, Information Security Oversight Office, *Report to the President 2002,* (Washington: June 2003), pp. 14–15; U.S. National Archives and Records Administration, Information Security Oversight Office, *2003 Report on Cost Estimates for Security Classification Activities* (Washington: July 2004), pp. 2–3; U.S. National Archives and Records Administration, Information Security Oversight Office, *Report on Cost estimates for Security Classification Activities for 2004* (Washington: May 2005), p. 3.

42. 3 C.F.R. 1982 Comp., pp. 166–178.

43. 3 C.F.R., 1995 Comp., pp. 333–356.

44. U.S. Department of Defense, Department of Defense Security Review Commission, *Keeping The Nation's Secrets* (Washington: GPO, 1985), pp. 48–49.

45. U.S. General Accounting Office, *Classified Information: Costs of Protection Are Integrated With Other Security Costs,* GAO Report GAO/NSIAD-94-55 (Washington: Oct. 1993), p. 1.

46. 3 C.F.R., 2003 Comp., pp. 196–218.

47. Data from U.S. National Archives and Records Administration, Information Security Oversight Office, *Report to the President 2001* (Washington: Sept. 2002), p. 5; U.S. National Archives and Records Administration, Information Security Oversight Office, *Report to the President 2002* (Washington: June 2003), p. 9; U.S. National Archives and Records Administration, Information Security Oversight Office, *Report to the President 2003* (Washington: Mar. 2004), p. 9; U.S. National Archives and Records Administration, Information Security Oversight Office, *Report to the President 2004* (Washington: Mar. 2005), p. 7.

48. Shaun Waterman (UPI), "Pentagon Classifying 'Impulse' Criticized," *Washington Times,* July 8, 2004, p. A6.

49. U.S. Congress, Senate Select Committee on Intelligence and House Permanent Select Committee on Intelligence, *Joint Inquiry into Intelligence Community Activities Before and After the Terrorist Attacks of September 11, 2001,,* 107th Cong., 2nd sess., S.Rept. 107-351, H.Rept. 107-792 (Washington: GPO, 2002).

50. Editorial, "Credible Classifications," *Washington Post,* July 13, 2004, p. A14.

51. U.S. Congress, Senate Select Committee on Intelligence, *Report on the U.S. Intelligence Community's Prewar Intelligence Assessments on Iraq,* 108th Cong., 2nd sess. (Washington: GPO, 2004).

52. Neil A. Lewis, "The Committee: C.I.A. Deleted Large Sections, Officials Say," *New York Times,* July 10, 2004, p. A9.

53. Editorial, "Credible Classifications," *Washington Post,* p. A14.

54. Ibid.

55. *Congressional Record,* daily edition, vol. 150, July 15, 2004, pp. S8234–S8237.

56. Ibid., Sept. 27, 2004, pp. S9726–S9728.

57. Ibid., pp. S9714–S9719.

58. Ibid., Sept. 29, 2004, pp. S9911–S9914.

59. Ibid., Oct. 6, 2004, p. S10543.

60. U.S. Congress, House, Committee of Conference, *Intelligence Reform and Terrorism Prevention Act of 2004,* a report to accompany S. 2845, 108th Cong., 2nd sess., H. Rept. 108-796 (Washington: GPO, 2004), p. 64.

61. 118 Stat. 3638.

62. 119 Stat. 2680.

63. U.S. Congress, House Committee on Government Reform, *Emerging Threats: Overclassification and Pseudo-classification,* hearing, 109th Cong., 1st sess., Mar. 2, 2005 (Washington: GPO, 2005).

64. Patience Wait, "DHS Classified Briefings Leaked Through Energy System," *GCN Update,* Jan. 27, 2005, available at http://www.gcn.com/vol1_no1/daily-updates/34907-1.html; credited as contributing to this story were *GCN* staff writers Susan M. Menke and Mary Mosquera.

65. Letter to David Young, Apr. 24, 1972, appearing in U.S. Congress, House Committee on Government Operations, *U.S. Government Information Policies and Practices—Security Classification Problems Involving Subsection (b)(1) of the Freedom of Information Act (Part 7),* hearings, 92nd Cong., 2nd sess. (Washington: GPO, 1972), pp. 2452–2453.

66. Ibid., p. 2930 (emphasis in original).

67. Ibid., pp. 2933–2934.

68. Ibid., p. 2932.

69. Ibid., p. 2284.

70. Ibid., pp. 2477–2478.

71. Ibid., p. 2478.

72. Ibid.

73. Ibid., p. 2479.

74. Ibid., p. 2497.

75. Ibid.

76. Ibid., pp. 2497–2498.

77. Ibid., p. 2935.

78. Ibid., pp. 2705–2706.

79. Ibid., p. 2706.

80. U.S. Congress, House Committee on Government Operations, *Executive Classification of Information—Security Classification Problems Involving Exemption (b)(1) of the Freedom of Information Act (5 U.S.C. 552),* a report, 93rd Cong., 2nd sess., H. Rept. 93-221 (Washington: GPO, 1973), p. 75.

81. Ibid., p. 78.

82. MITRE Corporation, JASON Program Office, *Horizontal Integration: Broader Access Models for Realizing Information Dominance* (McLean, VA: Dec. 2004), p. 5.

83. James Jay Carafano and David Heyman, "DHS 2.0: Rethinking the Department of Homeland Security," *Heritage Special Report SR-02,* p. 20.

84. U.S. Library of Congress, Federal Research Division, *Laws and Regulations Governing the Protection of Sensitive But Unclassified Information,* by Alice R. Buchalter, John Gibbs, and Marieke Lewis (Washington: Sept. 2004), p. i.

Access to Government Information in the People's Republic of China

Jamie P. Horsley

Most observers would not expect that the People's Republic of China—one of the few remaining Communist regimes and frequently chastised in the international media for its suppression of freedom of expression and freedom of the press—would be quietly introducing new mechanisms of more open and participatory government, including unprecedented access to government information.

China's much-criticized delay in announcing the outbreak of the Sudden Acute Respiratory Syndrome (SARS) epidemic in 2003 prompted State Council Premier Wen Jiabao and other leaders to call for improved information disclosure, which created widespread anticipation that China would move quickly to establish more open procedures.[1] While no dramatic change was effected immediately, the State Council—China's cabinet—has decided to begin serious work in 2006 on drafting national regulations on access to government information.

Legislative momentum follows several years of experimentation with increasingly standardized open information mechanisms at both the central ministry and local government levels. The southern commercial hub of Guangzhou (formerly known as Canton) shattered centuries of secretive tradition in late 2002 with municipal rules establishing a presumption of disclosure for government information. Effective January 1, 2003, the Guangzhou Municipal Provisions on Open Government Information (the Guangzhou OGI Provisions), for the first time in Chinese history, give Chinese citizens the right to obtain information from the government upon request and impose a corresponding obligation on government to disclose information it possesses that is not exempted from disclosure under the provisions. Indeed, the Guangzhou OGI Provisions refer to requesters as "persons with the right of access" and government agencies as "persons with the obligation to disclose."

The Guangzhou OGI Provisions are among the first pieces of Chinese legislation to refer to the "right to know." However, that concept has been under development in China for at least two decades, during which China has been gradually encouraging heightened transparency of government operations under the broader policy rubric of "open government affairs." Under the former planned economy established after the Communist party came to power in 1949, the Chinese government monopolized the production, sharing, and use of all kinds of information. As China began to "open up" its economy to foreign investment and market-based reforms 30 years later, in 1979, China's leaders embraced the concept of creating an "information society" in support of economic development. By the late 1990s, programs to make "government affairs" more open and to build "E-government" networks—under which government agencies at all levels would release an ever-increasing amount of information about their functions and activities, and provide services over the Web—had become wide-

Jamie P. Horsley is deputy director of the China Law Center and senior research scholar and lecturer-in-law at the Yale Law School. She lived and worked in China for 15 years as a lawyer, diplomat, and corporate executive and has written and lectured extensively on legal and other developments in China.

spread.[2] China's bilateral trade and economic agreements and, in particular, its accession commitments to the World Trade Organization (WTO) to make trade-related rules and requirements transparent further buttressed the open government trend.[3]

Despite an explosion of information being made available under the "open government affairs" policy, and the establishment of more than 10,000 government Web sites,[4] China still lacks an information-access law and has no developed concept of public records. China's Constitution does not grant a right to information, and existing legislation—including laws on protecting state secrets and archived materials—emphasizes secrecy, not sharing of official information. As long as information disclosure remains a policy and not a legal mandate, government officials will continue to enjoy the discretion to decide what information to make available and what information they want to keep confidential.

However, the Chinese leadership appears ready to begin to "legalize" its open information policy by creating rights and obligations that are to be enforceable against the government. This new kind of information-rights-and-obligations regime is generally, although not always, referred to as "open government information" or OGI. In his work report to the annual meeting of the National People's Congress (NPC) in March 2004, Premier Wen called for the establishment of an OGI system and increased transparency of government work to keep the people informed so that they can better supervise the government.[5] A year later, in March 2005, the party's Central Committee joined the State Council to issue a joint policy "opinion" on promoting open government affairs that specifically advocates speeding up work on national OGI regulations,[6] which could pave the way for an even more authoritative information-access law. Indeed, the drafting of a national law on open government information has been placed on the NPC legislative agenda for the current session running through 2008.

Reform Imperatives

A combination of economic and political motives seems to be driving the authoritarian Communist party leadership toward greater transparency. While China's international and bilateral commitments require greater transparency and provide an additional impetus toward greater openness, the main drivers for information reform seem to be largely domestic.

The economic imperative to permit the free flow of information in order to realize sustainable development and create a more attractive foreign investment environment has been a key consideration spurring the movement toward greater information openness among national leaders. The revered former leader Deng Xiaoping as early as 1984 identified the importance of developing information resources to support economic development efforts and more-efficient government. He recognized all too well that a monopoly on information leads to waste of and inefficient allocation of resources, as well as opportunities for corruption.

The open government affairs policy itself traces its origins to the self-governance program promoted at the most local levels in the country's villages since the early 1980s. Financial oversight of how elected village officials, as well as the village party branch, spent their hard-earned money was the core of villagers' demand for greater transparency and accountability, referred to as "openness in village affairs."[7] The openness in village affairs program gradually spread outward to other sectors and up the administrative hierarchy, evolving by the year 2000 into the nationwide "openness in government affairs" policy.[8]

Open information is clearly also seen as a tool in China's campaign against rampant corruption, which is estimated to cost China some 3 percent to 5 percent of GDP[9] and is a source of much social unrest.[10] The premise underlying adoption in the United States of the Freedom of Information Act and other open government legislation is the belief and experience that transparency is an effective restraint on government abuse of power and corruption, that "sunlight is the best disinfectant."[11] Chinese leaders and academics clearly appreciate that curbing corruption is an important by-product of more-transparent government operations and information, and that greater transparency permits citizens to fulfill their constitutional duty to supervise government actions.[12]

China's leaders further recognize that open information can also help build trust in government and promote social stability. The confusion arising from and criticism of China's initial secretive handling of the SARS outbreak in 2003 highlighted the need for a more-open government system in order to build credibility among the Chinese populace and mobilize effective responses in times of crisis. The SARS experience drove home the truism that keeping information from the public only feeds speculation and panic, whereas providing credible and timely information helped to calm a situation. Growing social demand for information from the consumer rights, environmental protection, property owner, and other sectors, as well as a growing rights consciousness including the nascent "right to know," are fueling the movement toward greater information flow.

Moreover, China's experimentation with new mechanisms of public participation such as public hearings and notice and comment procedures reflect government recognition that providing timely information about plans, products, and government actions—including proposed laws and regulations—to help enlist the public's input and assistance can help create a partnership between government and the people to tackle thorny new problems and challenges as they arise. The current leadership speaks of administration and governance "in accordance with the law" to promote more efficient, "scientific," and competent decision making by the government and the party, programs that emphasize the establishment of open information systems as well as more participatory decision making.[13]

Technological Impetus

"Informatization," the technological side of open information, is now a strategic priority in China's tenth five-year economic plan (2002–2007) and is recognized as key to achieving modernization. Chinese scientists were quick to appreciate the value of emerging digital technologies in the early 1980s and established China's first intranet for academic use. It was not long before government leaders began to focus on the benefits of information technology that permitted greater sharing of and access to widely held government information. Although the initial emphasis was on internal sharing among governmental entities to improve administrative capacity and further state-led economic development, as the market economy began to flourish and non-state actors proliferated, these new technical platforms increasingly began to be used to disseminate information about government functions and regulations to the general public under the "open government affairs" policy.

China's e-government initiative was officially launched in 2000,[14] the same year the open government affairs policy was pronounced at the annual party congress, although the policy directive underlying this program was not made public. By the end of 2005, 96 percent of central government departments and 81 percent of local governments had reportedly established Web sites, although those at the lower levels were still fairly rudimentary, or even dysfunctional.[15] In the more-developed cities such as Beijing and Shanghai, however, these Web sites post an ever-greater amount of information about government organizations, activities, regulations, and policies; offer Web-based administrative services such as applying for licenses, paying taxes, and filing information requests; and provide interactive services such as opinion polls and chat rooms. Chongqing even pioneered the practice of holding online public hearings,[16] and in July 2005 a live online broadcast in East China's Zhejiang Province attracted more than 100,000 "netizens" for the first time to watch a session of the provincial people's congress standing committee, the local legislature, which traditionally has met behind closed doors.[17]

On October 1, 2005, the national government launched a centralized information Web site, http://www.gov.cn. This Web site not only provides information on current affairs and national and local laws and policies, as well as certain online services, it also includes a page called "government affairs interaction" that gives Chinese citizens centralized access to draft rules and regulations on which public comment is being sought both by central government agencies and local governments. The development of notice-and-comment-style rulemaking is a very recent innovation in China. Traditionally, citizens had difficulty learning about even government rules that had been adopted and were in effect, let alone access to those being drafted. As China has opened up, in part due to pressure from international trading partners, various institutions such as the NPC, Supreme People's Court, and State Council have started publishing periodic gazettes containing the text of adopted laws and regulations, selected judicial opinions and interpretations, and the like. These official gazettes are now frequently available online. The latest development is the publication of draft rules and decisions for public input, a trend that is promoted by the central government and the party and supported by local OGI provisions that call for an "advance disclosure system" of draft decisions of interest to the people and for considering their opinions on the drafts.

By the end of 2005, the number of registered Internet users in China hit 111 million, or 8.5 percent of the 1.3 billion Chinese,[18] making China the second-largest Internet user in the world. While the Chinese government still actively seeks to censor what it deems to be politically sensitive or inappropriate content, the Internet in China affords millions of Chinese access to a great deal of information and has helped facilitate the increasingly broad dissemination of government information.

Local Experimentation Breaks New Ground

China often permits and even promotes local experimentation with new ideas and systems before introducing them on a national basis. The Guangzhou OGI Provisions were an example of such centrally authorized innovation. Initiated by reform-minded local officials and scholars who had spent time overseas, Guangzhou's pioneering OGI Provisions aim to "protect the right to know of individuals and organizations, standardize the disclosure of government information, increase the transparency of administrative activities, and supervise government agencies in the exercise of their powers in accordance with the law."[19] They abandon the ingrained convention of government secrecy to establish a presumption of disclosure, stating that government information shall in principle be made public and non-disclosure shall be the exception.[20]

The Guangzhou OGI Provisions introduce basic concepts and mechanisms that establish a framework for the local OGI provisions that followed and may well influence national-level legislation to come. As a threshold matter, they define "government information" as information made, obtained, or possessed by all levels of government and its functional departments and related organizations in the course of managing or providing public services. The disclosure mandate of the provisions thus does not apply to Chinese courts or to the people's congresses, which comprise China's legislature at various levels.

The provisions stipulate that information is to be provided essentially free of charge, subject only to cost-based fees, and made available through two mechanisms: dissemination by government on its own initiative and disclosure upon specific request. Basic categories of information that government agencies are to publish on their own initiative are enumerated. These include a wide range of material, much of which had not been previously made available to the public even under the open government affairs policy, such as development plans, budget information, and government expenses-related and government personnel-related information, as well as rules and regulations, the functions and structure of government agencies, and administrative procedures.

In yet another first, the Guangzhou OGI Provisions give individuals and organizations the unprecedented right to request that government agencies provide them with information that has not already been disseminated, and impose on government the obligation to comply with such requests, subject to specified exemptions. The Guangzhou OGI Provisions further introduce the right of individuals (and organizations) to inspect government records containing information about themselves and to request corrections thereto.[21] Under the planned economy, government files on individuals—including personnel dossiers, or "dang'an," and company records—had not been accessible to the persons concerned. The granting of a right to individuals in particular to review and correct personal information maintained in government-controlled files is increasingly important as China becomes a market-based economy and individuals change jobs, move to other locations, and apply for credit.

Following international practice, Guangzhou carves out certain exceptions to the rule of disclosure. The Guangzhou OGI Provisions list five categories of information that need not be disclosed: an individual's private information, commercial secrets, state secrets, information that is in the course of being deliberated, and government information that is prohibited from disclosure under other laws and regulations.[22] These exemptions may sound unexceptional to information-access practitioners, but in China's context their application in a manner that will not undercut the presumption of disclosure will require clear and authoritative guidance, as discussed below.

The Guangzhou OGI Provisions break additional new ground by calling for an "advance disclosure system" regarding proposed decisions about "matters affecting major interests of individuals or organizations, or that have a major social influence."[23] In a country where government decision making has traditionally been done behind closed doors and announced—if at all—only after the fact, this innovative use of an information-disclosure rule to compel publication of proposed decisions and seek public opinion on them was extraordinary.

The Guangzhou OGI Provisions further suggest various mechanisms for supervising their implementation, including periodic evaluation of government agency performance and setting up hotlines and mailboxes for complaints. They also provide remedies for aggrieved requesters consisting of administrative reconsideration by the agency that denied the request, taking the agency to court, or otherwise seeking compensation.

The Guangzhou OGI Provisions, in sum, were nothing short of revolutionary and took many observers by complete surprise. They are sophisticated in terms of incorporating certain principles of information access being developed in countries around the world, and extremely bold in terms of inaugurating a range of new rights and concepts not contained in previous Chinese legislation. They remain arguably the most liberal of the local OGI regimes adopted to date, even specifically extending access rights to foreigners, subject to a reciprocity clause.

Other localities quickly followed Guangzhou's lead. Shanghai—China's financial center and possibly most internationalized city, which enjoys provincial-level status along with the municipalities of Beijing, Tianjin, and Chongqing—became the first to establish a provincial-level OGI system. The Shanghai OGI Provisions, which went into effect May 1, 2004,[24] follow the basic regulatory framework of the Guangzhou OGI Provisions. While limiting their application to Chinese citizens and entities and not articulating directly the presumption of disclosure, they introduce refinements of the concept of "government information" and certain other matters. They also introduce a balancing test, which weighs the public interest in disclosure against the possible harm when determining whether to withhold information under the specified exemptions, which Shanghai expanded to include one for information relating to enforcement actions.[25]

The Shanghai OGI Provisions further provide greater organizational detail intended to ensure that they are effectively implemented. For example, they establish an Open Government Information Joint Conference led by the city's General Office; call on the municipal Informatization Commission to organize, guide, and promote the new regime; and require that each government agency identify a special office to handle OGI work on a daily basis, including information dissemination and responding to requests.[26] Government agencies are, moreover, to draw up guides on how to access agency information, compile a catalog of the information they possess, and provide reading rooms for the public.[27] Shanghai also added a "non-profiteering" provision prohibiting officials from refusing to disclose information upon request and then essentially selling the same information to others.[28] This provision was intended to curb a trend for government agencies to commercialize and profit from the provision of information that would be considered "public record" in many other countries, such as company registration records. As an additional spur to serious implementation, the Shanghai OGI Provisions follow U.S. federal government practice in requiring that the Informatization Commission compile an annual report on OGI work by the various agencies.[29]

As of January 2006 at least 30 provincial and large municipal-level governments had adopted OGI provisions.[30] Most OGI rules follow the general outlines of the Guangzhou and Shanghai OGI Provisions, with some variations. A few provisions do not specify the right to request information, only stating that citizens and entities may request information and that government agencies should assist them with their requests, and do not detail civil remedies available if government agencies do not comply with disclosure requests.[31] A few places have passed "online OGI" rules that cover only information dissemination and for some reason do not specifically provide a request mechanism at all.[32]

These local governments are being joined by central government departments, including Customs, Construction, Environmental Protection, Labor and Social Security, and the State Grain Administration, that are issuing departmental rules promoting information access in terms and with procedures that borrow from the local government OGI provisions. While these rules frequently refer to both the "right to know" and the "right to participate," they stop short of stipulating civil remedies in the event of agency noncompliance. Central government agencies are also beginning to require information disclosure as a means of regulating private-sector behavior, such as in the areas of direct selling, electric power, and the issuance of public securities.

Implementation Challenges

As might be expected in a country where a presumption of secrecy rather than of disclosure still permeates the approach to information, implementation of new OGI regimes has varied. Despite great fanfare accompanying the adoption of the Guangzhou OGI Provisions in October 2002, no one seems to have thought to utilize these novel provisions to request information from the government concerning the mysterious disease that began to spread throughout Guangdong province in late 2002, and which was later identified as SARS and only announced to the public in a press conference held in mid-February 2003. Three years later, while an ever-increasing amount of information is being publicly disseminated on the government's initiative over the government Web site and other channels, Guangzhou residents reportedly are filing very few information requests.

Voluntary government disclosure may be simpler to promote than encouraging and responding to specific information requests. The capital city of Beijing, for example, has published online OGI provisions calling for dissemination of a wide range of government information.[33] Beijing residents can now obtain free copies of regulations issued by the municipal government at more than 800 locations across the city. The government has installed computers with touchscreens in streets, squares, residential districts, and government service centers to allow inquiries and searches to be made into legal and government information.[34] However, Beijing has yet to adopt rules authorizing information requests.

Affirmative use of the OGI system in Shanghai to date seems to be much more advanced than elsewhere. The first annual report on OGI work required by the Shanghai OGI Provisions covered the period from May 1, 2004, when those provisions went into effect, to the end of the year.[35] The report states that an impressive 8,722 out of 8,799 requests for information received had been dealt with during that eight-month period, leaving only 77 pending. Statistics revealed a 79 percent full disclosure rate for requested information, 5.5 percent partial disclosure, and 15 percent non-disclosure, of which 29 percent was due to nonexistent information, 35 percent due to the information not being held by the agency from which it was requested, 9 percent due to "unclear requests," 6.5 percent due to various exemptions under the OGI Provisions, and 21 percent due to "other reasons." The most requests were directed at the personnel, public security (police), industry and commerce, and labor and social security agencies.

Like many other information-access provisions, the Shanghai OGI Provisions stipulate that dissatisfied requesters can file complaints, seek administrative reconsideration by the agency that denied the request, or file lawsuits in court. In the initial eight-month period covered by Shanghai's first annual OGI report, a total of 38 administrative reconsiderations were filed (24 at the municipal level and 14 at the district/county level), six administrative lawsuits disagreeing with administrative reconsideration or agency decisions were brought, and 10 complaints were lodged with the Shanghai Informatization Committee or the Supervision Committee, which is given oversight responsibilities under the OGI Provisions. Clearly, Shanghai residents are getting the message about the new information-access regime and their rights under it. Some Chinese observers attribute this respectable degree of initial utilization to the high-level political support for the new regime from Shanghai's mayor, as well as media reports and ongoing education campaigns directed at both the public and government agency officials.[36]

Nonetheless, the Shanghai experience highlights some of the challenges to implementing a new access regime in China. The first lawsuit brought under the Shanghai OGI Provisions, the Dong Ming case, represented both a victory and a loss for the Shanghai information initiative.[37] While the Shanghai court ultimately upheld the decision of a district real estate bureau to withhold requested records dating from the period 1947–1968, it also established some important principles simply by agreeing to hear the unprecedented case (Chinese courts frequently decline to accept cases that are deemed politically sensitive or that involve newly asserted legal principles without firm foundation in national law) and by ruling that the Shanghai OGI Provisions do apply to information created and collected prior to their effective date. The court also chastised the defendant agency for failing to follow certain procedural requirements imposed by the Shanghai OGI Provisions, such as responding in time and explaining the reason for its refusal to disclose. However, the case was ultimately decided on the basis that the requested information was "archived materials" and therefore disclosure was subject to the provisions of the more restrictive Archives Law, under which the defendant did not have to disclose the requested records.[38]

The case further raised political sensitivities. Some Shanghai officials apparently feared the requester's motive was to obtain evidence to reclaim real estate confiscated during the excesses of the Great Proletarian Cultural Revolution (1966–1976), during which many citizens lost property. Using information-access laws to reveal and redress past abuses is a phenomenon encountered in both transitional and established countries around the world. Some reform-minded Chinese are concerned that their more-conservative colleagues might take advantage of fears of stirring up public anger and having to deal with a large number of complex historical cases as an excuse to oppose the introduction of more-open information laws in China. Some question whether they can delay addressing the leftover problems of history—which could include those dating back to the original Communist revolution, various political and economic campaigns since then, and the 1989 Tiananmen Square incident—while new practices and more-open attitudes are permitted to take hold going forward. Political sensitivities must surely be among the issues that have delayed adoption of national-level OGI legislation.

Anticipating National Legislation

About the time that Guangzhou began to consider development of its OGI Provisions, the State Council entrusted a group of scholars at the Chinese Academy of Social Sciences (CASS) to prepare a draft of nationwide OGI regulations,[39] possibly in response to proposals for national legislation on open government information that had been raised by deputies at recent National People's Congress sessions. The group had been researching information-access laws in various countries, including the United States, Britain, Japan, and South Korea. By July 2002 CASS had reportedly submitted a 42-article draft (the Scholars' Draft) to the State Council for consideration and revision.[40]

One of the threshold questions that China's policymakers need to address is whether to proceed with a formal law on information access or start, as is common practice, with administrative regulations issued by the State Council in order to gain further experience before adopting a law that would be more difficult to pass and amend. The drawbacks of the regulatory approach include the fact that the State Council cannot bind bodies like the National People's Congress and the people's courts and procuracies. Judicial remedies provided in State Council regulations may lack enforceability, since Chinese courts may be reluctant to enforce novel rights and obligations created by administrative regulation rather than by a law promulgated by the NPC. On the other hand, formulating administrative regulations is quicker than pressing for adoption of a full-blown law by the NPC or its Standing Committee.

What might national OGI regulations or a law look like, and what are the challenges that local experimentation has demonstrated will need to be addressed? The 2005 joint Communist party and State Council policy opinions called for government information to be made available either through dissemination on the government's own initiative or upon request. The opinions further stipulated that "All types of matters concerning administrative management and public services, except those involving state or commercial secrets and individual privacy that are protected by law, shall be disclosed strictly according to facts and in strict compliance with the provisions of laws, regulations and relevant policies."[41] This prescription comes close to establishing a general presumption of disclosure, and the opinions outline a general framework for information access—disclosure through dissemination or upon request of all government information except that relating to state or commercial secrets and individual privacy—that conforms to most open government provisions and that will presumably form the foundation of the national OGI regulations.

The Scholars' Draft was never officially made public. However, the head of the CASS drafting group did publish an annotated proposed draft of national OGI regulations as part of a three-book series on open government in 2003 that is likely very close, if not identical to, the Scholars' Draft.[42] A comparison of the Guangzhou OGI Provisions and the Scholars' Draft reveals some similarities in concept and language, suggesting a certain degree of cross-fertilization between the two drafts, which were formulated in roughly the same time frame. Both stipulate the presumption of disclosure, both apply to "natural persons" rather than being limited to "citizens," and both give individuals the right to access and correct information about themselves (a right Guangzhou also extends to organizations). However, the Scholars' Draft does not provide for an "advance disclosure system," because the main drafter felt that the issue of making draft rules and other proposals public for comment should be covered in a separate regulation.

The Scholars' Draft sets as its legislative purpose the protection of the public's "right to know" and of public participation in the management of state and social affairs, promotion of the flow of government information, and supervision of government agencies in the exercise of their powers in accordance with the law. These purposes sound very similar to those of the Guangzhou and other OGI provisions. Substantially in accord with local legislation passed to date, the Scholars' Draft lists seven exemptions from disclosure[43] that—with the exception of the exemption for "state secrets," which under current law is overly broad—conform generally to international practice. These exemptions are for state secrets (the disclosure of which is clearly prohibited by other laws), internal agency personnel rules, commercial secrets, personal information, information relating to internal deliberations, and information relating to criminal law enforcement.

These seemingly common exemptions from disclosure present some very real challenges in China, however. The definition of "commercial secret" is fairly well understood,[44] although its application in the context of information-access regimes will need to be further developed, as anticipated in the Scholars' Draft, to protect information that companies may be asked to submit to government but for which they seek confidentiality.

The concepts of individual privacy and the protection of personal information, not yet addressed comprehensively in Chinese law, remain to be articulated.[45] Although privacy rights have been asserted in some cases, there is no law clearly establishing and defining the parameters of such rights. Recently promulgated local rules on consumer protection and credit reporting in Shanghai and other places have introduced principles that seek to prevent disclosure of personal information that could embarrass or intrude on one's daily life; lead to discrimination in employment, credit, or other areas; and put at risk the physical safety of the person involved—all interests that privacy laws might typically address. The Scholars' Draft would, in the absence of a stand-alone law, avoid use of the term "privacy" but provide similar general principles with respect to protected "personal information."[46]

Possibly the most problematic exemption under China's emerging information-access regime is that for "state secrets," China's counterpart to a national defense and foreign policy exemption. The cornerstone of China's modern approach to government secrecy is the Law on Safeguarding State Secrets, adopted in 1988.[47] This law defines "state secrets" broadly as being "matters that affect the security and interests of the state," which matters are illustrated with general categories of information such as secrets concerning "important policy decisions on state affairs," "economic and social development," science and technology, and criminal investigations, as well as the more conventional areas of national defense and diplomatic affairs. While the law was intended at least in part to promote increased access to archived materials by identifying particular categories of records that needed to be restricted to a limited range of people for a specific period of time,[48] in practice the law has been interpreted quite broadly to maintain the general presumption of secrecy for a wide range of information.

Information about disasters and about diseases not yet listed by the Ministry of Public Health as a contagion that should be announced to the public has also been treated as a state secret under implementing regulations. Revealing "state secrets" has been used to justify the indictment and imprisonment of Chinese journalists reporting on corruption scandals and citizen protests and of activist lawyers attempting to represent disadvantaged petitioners,[49] with intended chilling effect on such reporting and activities. Recent regulations on Internet content sweepingly ban the online publication of material divulging "state secrets" or that endangers national security or is detrimental to the honor and interests of the state.[50]

Chinese officials as well as legal scholars recognize that the scope of the state secrets law needs to be further narrowed and clarified, both through revision of the law and through practical implementation. For example, in August 2005 the State Secrets Bureau, now under the leadership of a prominent legal scholar, announced at its first-ever press conference that it was removing the total number of deaths from information about disasters that has been classified as secret for many years.[51] In addition to citing practical reasons for making this information publicly available, the surrounding public announcements noted that relaxing application of the state secrets law was in line with the current trend toward greater information openness and would ensure the "people's right to know."[52] The Party Discipline Committee is reportedly drafting guidelines on open information that will establish a framework for reconciling the state secrets law with open government information regulations.[53] As one noted law professor remarked, if the state secrets law is not revised, there is no way that open government information regulations can be carried out, since efforts to disclose information will run into a "stone wall" everywhere.[54]

Apart from officially designated secrets, Chinese government officials are also accustomed to treating virtually everything they work on or read as confidential "work secrets." In fact, the drafters of the Scholars' Draft discovered that the most common grounds for refusing disclosure was an enormous loophole called "work secrets," which had no clear definition in national law at all.[55] While the local government OGI provisions adopted to date do not sanction or even mention "work secrets" as a basis for non-disclosure of information, unfortunately the recently adopted Civil Servants Law of 2005 does require all government personnel to protect "work secrets" as well as state secrets[56]—but without providing guidance on what constitutes a "work secret." Moreover, some central department information-disclosure rules, such as those adopted in December 2005 by Chinese Customs, do list "work secrets" as one of the categories of information exempted from disclosure.

Another major source of potential conflict, under provisions that exempt from disclosure information covered by other laws and regulations, is China's archival system. China has an extensive records system that traces its origins back centuries, with the oldest recorded paper document dated 714 A.D.[57] The modern system is governed by the 1988 Archives Law, which covers the handling of government documents and reference materials that have been placed in official archives at all levels. The law's basic presumption is that archived government information is under state copyright and may not be disclosed to the public for at least 30 years without special approval. To be sure, the Archives Law also contains language providing that the archives should be open to society (including non-Chinese). However, until recently, the archives bureaus at all levels have normally construed this requirement narrowly, granting access primarily to public officials, courts, state-owned work units (for their historical records), and individuals seeking information relating to birth, marriage, and other such certificates.[58]

Nonetheless, in line with the new policy environment of greater openness, central and local authorities have started to announce a more-open access policy to their unclassified documents. Following practices established under local OGI legislation, the Archives Law was amended in 2004 to require, *inter alia,* that archives bureaus compile catalogs of information that has been made open to the public so as to facilitate its access. Also in line with the new policy, formerly confidential "red-titled" guidance documents that used to be accessible only to government officials have been made public at 80 percent of the government archives bureaus at the country level and above,[59] and documents covering China's foreign affairs and the destructive Great Proletarian Cultural Revolution (1966–1976), a period when China was virtually closed off to the rest of the world, are beginning to be released for the first time.[60] Shanghai built a new wing of the municipal archives that opened for public use the same day that Shanghai's OGI Provisions took effect on May 1, 2004, and includes a public reading room.

In spite of some progress in making archived records more accessible, it appears that such records continue to be viewed as different from "government information" that is subject to emerging OGI regimes. In the first lawsuit filed under Shanghai's OGI Provisions, one of the defenses successfully raised by the defendant real estate bureau to disclosure of records relating to a property allegedly owned by plaintiff's father from 1947 to 1968 was that those files had been transferred to the archives and were thus subject to the strictures of the archives regime and not the more recent OGI Provisions.[61] China's forthcoming national information system will need to address the seeming conflict between the traditionally restrictive archives regime and the access-oriented OGI regime by applying to archived records the same presumption of disclosure subject to specified exemptions that applies to non-archived government information.

Institutional Issues

The Scholars' Draft goes beyond local provisions promulgated to date in introducing some institutional reforms such as "chief information officers" (CIOs) in each government agency, specifically to handle information management and the establishment of information commissions at the county level and above. The commissions would be composed of appointed "expert" commissioners and CIOs from same-level government departments, with powers to handle complaints and provide advisory opinions in the event of disputes as an alternative to administrative reconsideration. While local OGI regimes do not use these precise formulations, the foundational concepts are not so far afield from ideas reflected in local OGI provisions adopted to date, such as designating special offices within each agency to handle OGI matters, which helps ensure that someone or some office is going to take responsibility for implementing the new regime, and establishing a "joint conference" or other designated high-level office to supervise implementation of OGI provisions and provide guidance on how to resolve conflicts.

The ultimate challenge for establishing a credible open information system will be the availability of a relatively independent decision-making body that can decide conflicts between requesters and recalcitrant government agencies. China's court system, ultimately subordinate to the NPC Standing Committee and the Communist party, does not enjoy the power to interpret law, only to apply it. When issues are unclear, novel, or politically sensitive, the courts typically seek or defer to political intervention. Nonetheless, a system can be crafted to deal with questions arising in the ordinary course that do not involve alleged state secrets and other politically sensitive issues. Alternatives might include simply training judges to handle these new issues of information access, establishing a specialized tribunal within the courts, or introducing an administrative or combined public-government advisory body.

Chinese scholars and officials have been studying different models, including the U.S. federal system of having one agency (in the U.S. case, the Department of Justice) serve as a coordinating body to provide advice to other agencies and requesters and oversee the system, but without the authority to hear disputes, which are handled by the courts; the establishment of a high-level advisory body without enforcement powers such as the New York State Committee on Open Government, with a permanent executive director who develops sufficient expertise and respect that the director's advisory opinions are frequently complied with or cited as authoritative if the case ends up in court; the independent Connecticut State Freedom of Information Commission, which enjoys adjudicatory and enforcement powers, including the authority to impose fines, subject to limited judicial review of the record for legal error; and various other information commissioner and ombudsman models such as those adopted in Canada at the federal and provincial levels. The different models all involve questions of cost, expertise, procedure, and perceived independence from government or party control. China's challenge is to develop a system that will resolve, or be perceived to resolve, conflicts over information access in a fair and impartial manner.

Related Developments

The evolution of open government information in China has been accompanied by corresponding progress in transparency of legislative and court proceedings. Many local legislatures now permit citizens to sign up to view congressional meetings as "auditors" and solicit public comment on draft legislation through hearings or written notice and comment procedures. The NPC itself is just beginning to experiment with more regular mechanisms of citizen participation. Chinese courts are beginning to open court proceedings and publish selected judicial opinions and interpretations, which are not deemed to be "public record" in China, more regularly. Even the Communist party, which recently announced a policy of "open party affairs,"[62] is making a nod at the trend toward greater transparency to enlist broad popular support for its programs and policies.

Chinese government and party officials are not accustomed to the public give-and-take of Western democratic politics. Until recently, press conferences were rare and completely scripted, held primarily by the Foreign Ministry and other departments closely connected with international affairs, and most leaders refrained from making themselves personally available to the media and the public. The launching by China's State Council Information Office of an expanded government spokesperson system modeled on foreign practices in 2003 was therefore heralded within China as an important advance in open government affairs. Indeed, a number of local OGI provisions, including those adopted in Shanghai, stipulate the periodic holding of press conferences.

By early 2006, 70 central government departments—replicated at lower levels of government in 27 out of 31 provincial-level governments—had established official spokespersons whose function is to meet regularly with the press and announce new policies, report on official activities, and respond to questions. Even the people's courts at all levels are setting up spokesperson systems to strengthen the links between courts, the public, and the media through greater transparency.[63] While such spokespersons have been criticized by some Western observers as just another attempt by the Chinese government to control the flow of information, this new system could help inculcate a new culture of greater openness simply by meeting regularly with media and being required to respond to questions.

Additional concepts recently reflected in national legislation and practice also promote principles of openness. For example, the 2003 Administrative Licensing Law[64] stipulates that the licensing and approval process shall be open, unless state secrets, commercial secrets, or individual privacy are involved, and gives the public the right to inspect agency records relating to the supervision of licensed activities. The National Auditing Office (NAO) decided in 2003 to make all its annual reports public and for the first time released the entire text and posted it on the NAO Web site. In the past these reports had been submitted only to the State Council and the NPC.[65] In 2004 NAO created a national "audit storm" with its public report that 41 ministries under the State Council had misappropriated the equivalent of US$171.56 million, including the embarrassing news that the State General Administration of Sports had embezzled US$15.83 million from the country's 2008 Olympics special construction fund.[66]

Conclusion

The local government and departmental OGI provisions enacted in China to date provide at best a piecemeal approach to making government information more accessible, without an overarching legal framework that would ensure that Chinese government agencies at all levels will respect, and the people's courts will enforce, the presumption of disclosure they are trying to instill. That is what a national information-access statute could provide. The adoption of OGI regulations by the State Council would be an important first step, signaling party and government leadership support and paving the way for a formal law.

China is the first non-democratic country to begin to establish an open government information regime. Economic and social imperatives, as well as growing rights consciousness in China, are driving this trend, but the development of information-access regimes in an authoritarian, one-party state is fraught with contradictions and challenges. Moreover, while the OGI provisions already in force are helping to nurture a fragile culture of openness, they must overcome a 2,000-year-old culture of secrecy that long predates the current Communist party regime. It will be interesting to follow how China crafts its first national government information-access legislation to address common issues faced by governments around the world while taking into account its own unique circumstances.

Notes

1. Sun Yafei, "Feidian: Jiasu xinxi gongkai bufa" ("SARS: Increasing the Pace of Information Openness,") *Nanfang Zhoumo,* April 31, 2003, http://www.nanfangdaily.com.cn/zm/20030501/xw/ttzs/200304300462.asp. See also "SARS: A Valuable Lesson for Chinese Gov't to Learn," in *People's Daily Online* (English version), June 8, 2003, at http://english.people.com.cn/200306/08/eng20030608_117858.shtml.

2. See, e.g., Zhou Hanhua, "Zhongguo de zhengfu xinxihua ji qi mianlin de shijian wenti," February 27, 2004, at http://www.iolaw.org.cn/paper10.asp.

3. China's transparency-related commitments made in connection with its accession to WTO include: only enforcing those laws, regulations, and other measures that have been published and are widely available, and making those materials available to WTO members before enforcement absent emergency conditions; designating an official journal for the publication of laws, regulations, and other measures relating to trade in goods, services, trade-related intellectual property, and control of foreign exchange; providing an opportunity to comment before the measures are implemented (with certain exceptions), and making the journal available to individuals and enterprises; and establishing one or more enquiry points where any individual, enterprise, or WTO member can obtain all information a time for reply of 30 to 45 days. WTO rules do not generally require, as does China's accession protocol, that its members provide a public comment period before a trade measure can be implemented and establish enquiry points. These were specifically negotiated with China in order to compel changes in China's underlying legal system to facilitate greater transparency. See summary in United States General Accounting Office, *World Trade Organization: Analysis of China's Commitments to Other Members* (October 2002) at 9, 47–49 at: http://www.gao.gov/new.items/d034.pdf.

4. "Chinese Government Turns 'Face-to-Face' Online with General Public," Xinhua News Agency, January 1, 2006, at http://english.peopledaily.com.cn/200601/01/text20060101_232118.html.

5. "Section III, Government Self-Improvement; the Chinese text of the Premier's Report on the Work of the Government," delivered March 5, 2004, at http://www.peopledaily.com.cn/GB/shizheng/1024/2394441.html. The official English translation is at http://www.chinadaily.com.cn/english/doc/2004-03/16/content_315302.htm.

6. Zhonggong zhongyang bangongting, Guowuyuan bangongting guanyu jinyibu tuixing zhengwu gongkai de yijian (Opinions of the General Office of the Central Committee of the Chinese Communist Party and of the State Council on Further Promoting Open Government Affairs), March 24, 2005, at http://news.xinhuanet.com/newscenter/2005-04/26/content_2877607.htm.

7. Jamie P. Horsley, "The Democratization of Chinese Governance Through Public Participation and Open Government Information," *Political Civilization and Modernization in China, Vol. 3: The Political Context of China's Transformation* (Renmin University, Beijing, 2004) at 569, and Jamie P. Horsley, "A Legal Perspective on the Development of Electoral Democracy in China: The Case of Village Elections," and sources cited therein, in C. Stephen Hsu, Ed., *Understanding China's Legal System* (New York University Press, 2003), at 309 and 327.

8. The 15th Party Congress in October 2000 encouraged openness in "government affairs" and "factory affairs," as well as "village affairs," thus officially expanding the scope of the "openness" program beyond the village. *Communique of the Fifth Plenum of the Fifteenth Central Committee of the CCP,* October 11, 2000, in Chinese at http://www.people.com.cn/GB/channel1/10/20001012/268296.html; in English at http://english.peopledaily.com.cn/200010/11/eng20001011_52364.html.

9. "China's Corruption Crackdown," FriedlNet.com, March 16, 2003, at http://www.friedlnet.com/news/03031602.html.

10. Edward Cody, "China Takes Aim at Corruption," *Washington Post,* January 8, 2006, p. A21, at http://www.washingtonpost.com/wp-dyn/content/article/2006/01/07/AR2006010701055.html, and "China's Probe of Mining Disasters Finds Corruption, Chaos," *Washington Post,* December 24, 2005, A10, at http://www.washingtonpost.com/wp-dyn/content/article/2005/12/23/AR2005122301472.html.

11. Peter Strauss, *Administrative Justice in the United States* (Carolina Academic Press, 2nd ed. 2002) at 276.

12. See, e.g., Opinions on Further Promoting Open Government Affairs, supra note 6.

13. See, e.g., "Quanmian tuijin yifa xingzheng shishi gangyao" (State Council Outline on Implementing the Comprehensive Promotion of Administration in Accordance with the Law), adopted and effective March 22, 2004, available at http://news.xinhuanet.com/zhengfu/2004-04/21/content_1431232.htm, at paragraph 10. An English-language article generally describing this outline, "Guideline to Build Law-Based Government Publicized," published by china.org.cn on April 22, 2004, is available at http://www.china.org.cn/english/government/93677.htm. See also comments on the need for open information channels between government and the people made by Beijing Mayor Wang Qishan, *China Daily,* December 16, 2005, at http://news.xinhuanet.com/english/2005-12/16/content_3929490.htm.

14. "E-government Spurs Efficiency Drive," *China Daily,* March 22, 2005, at http://service.china.org.cn/link/wcm/Show_Text?info_id=123487&p_qry=archives, and "More Gov't Departments Open Portal Websites," *China View,* January 12, 2006, at http://news.xinhuanet.com/english/2006-01/12/content_4045253.htm.

15. "E-government Spurs Efficiency Drive," *China Daily,* March 22, 2005, at: http://service.china.org.cn/link/wcm/Show_Text?info_id=123487&p_qry=archives; and "More Gov't Departments Open Portal Websites," *China View,* January 12, 2006, at: http://news.xinhuanet.com/english/2006-01/12/content_4045253.htm.

16. "Chongqing juxing quanguo shouce wangshang lifa tingzhenghui" (Chongqing Holds Country's First Online Legislative Hearing), November 14, 2005, at http://www.jcrb.com/zyw/n7/ca433054.htm.

17. "Internet Becoming Part of Chinese People's Life," Xinhua News Agency, October 8, 2005, at http://service.china.org.cn/link/wcm/Show_Text?info_id=144353&p_qry=transparency.

18. "Chinese Internet Users Hit 111 Million in 2005," Reuters, January 17, 2006, at http://today.reuters.com/news/newsArticle.aspx?type=internetNews&storyID=2006-01-18T030843Z_01_SHA66703_RTRUKOC_0_US-CHINA-INTERNET.xml.

19. Provisions of Guangzhou Municipality on Open Government Information, http://www.Freedominfo.org/news/guangzhou/provisions.pdf , Article 1 (hereafter "Guangzhou OGI Provisions"), appended to Jamie P. Horsley, "Guangzhou's Pioneering Foray into Open Government: A Tale of Two Cities," at http://www.freedom.org/news/guangzhou/index.htm.

20. Guangzhou OGI Provisions, supra note 19, Article 6.

21. Guangzhou OGI Provisions, supra note 19, Article 13, paragraph 2.

22. Guangzhou OGI Provisions, supra note 19, Article 14.

23. Guangzhou OGI Provisions, supra note 19, Article 1. A December 2000 policy notice jointly issued by the party and the State Council on open government affairs had included the recommendation that matters should be published in advance before final decisions are made. Circular Zhongfaban [2000] No. 25, December 6, 2000, issued by the General Offices of the CCP Central Committee and the State Council on "Implementing in an All-Around Manner the System of Opening Government Affairs to the Public by Organs of State Power in Towns and Townships Throughout the Nation," Beijing Xinhua Domestic Service in Chinese, translated in FBIS Article ID: CPP2001010500097, December 25, 2000; Chinese text of "Zhonggong zhongyang bangongting, Guowuyuan bangongting guanyu zai quanguo xiangzhen zhengfu jiguan quanmian tuixing zhengwu gongkai zhidu de tongzhi" at http://www.cass.net.cn/chinese/s04_nfs/rdi2/regulation/regulation1.htm.

24. See Jamie P. Horsley, "Shanghai Advances the Cause of Open Government Information in China," April 20, 2004, at http://www.freedominfo.org/news/shanghai/index.htm.

25. Shanghai Municipal Provisions on Open Government Information (hereafter "Shanghai OGI Provisions"), Article 10, effective May 1, 2004, at http://www.freedominfo.org/news/shanghai/shanghai_provisions.pdf.

26. Shanghai OGI Provisions, supra note 25, Article 5.

27. Shanghai OGI Provisions, supra note 25, Articles 22 and 26.

28. Shanghai OGI Provisions, supra note 25, Article 16.

29. Shanghai OGI Provisions, supra note 25, Article 30.

30. The author wishes to thank Yale Law School graduate and O'Melveny & Myers lawyer Kaichen Xu, and Peking University law student and research assistant Wen Zhou, for their help in tracking developments in local OGI legislation.

31. See, e.g., the recent OGI provisions of Shaanxi and Liaoning Provinces, "Liaoning sheng zhengfu xinxi gongkai guiding" (Open Government Information Provisions of Liaoning Province), adopted December 6, 2005, effective February 1, 2006, at http://www.gov.cn/gzdt/2006-02/05/content_177992.htm, and "Shaanxi sheng zhengfu xinxi gongkai guiding" (Open Government Information Provisions of Shaanxi Province), issued December 10, 2005, effective January 10, 2006, at http://www.gov.cn/ziliao/flfg/2005-12/16/content_129149.htm.

32. The first of these were the Shenzhen Municipal Measures for Online Open Government Information ("Shenzhenshi zhengfu xinxi wangshang gongkai banfa"), issued February 25, 2004, and effective April 1, 2004. Other localities with similar rules include the special

municipalities, with provincial status, of Tianjin (effective August 1, 2004) and Beijing (effective October 1, 2005).

33. "Beijingshi Zhengfu Xinsi Wangshang Gongkai Shixing Banfa" (Beijing Municipal Measures on Online Open Government Information for Trial Implementation), issued June 21, 2005, and effective October 1, 2005, at http://www.beijing.gov.cn/fg/zxfggzjwj/t20050707_253728.htm.

34. "Public Center Set Up for Gov't Papers," *China Daily,* November 24, 2004, at http://service.china.org.cn/link/wcm/Show_Text?info_id=113125&p_qry=archives.

35. In Chinese, "2004 nian zhengfu xinxi gongkai niandu baogao" (Annual Report for the Year 2004 on Open Government Information), at http://www.shanghai.gov.cn/shanghai/node2314/node2319/node14868/userobject21ai102389.html. As for staffing, the report indicates that citywide there were 222 employees engaged full time and 1,804 engaged part-time in OGI work, with an average of 2 full-time and 5.2 part-time staff in each municipal-level agency and 6.8 full-time and 81.8 part-time staff in each district- or county-level government.

36. Reporting on OGI implementation elsewhere is spotty. Apparently the city of Wuhan, whose OGI provisions went into effect July 1, 2004, ordered reconsideration of a request for information from the labor bureau by a laid-off worker that had been denied in August 2004. However, no follow-up report could be located.

37. The author is indebted to the analysis of China Law Center Fellow John Balzano, on which she has drawn for the discussion of the Dong Ming case, the intermediate court decision in which is on file with the author.

38. On appeal, the defendant reportedly asserted that it could not even locate the requested records, thus rendering the lawsuit moot.

39. "Woguo zhuoshou zhiding Zhengfu xinxi gongkai taioli" (Our Country Grasps the Formulation of Open Government Information Regulations), *China Youth Daily,* online at http://news.gznet.gov.cn/hot/xxhgk/20030203/200211200073.asp (November 20, 2002).

40. Ibid. One report indicates that the drafting group of about 20 included officials from the Legislative Affairs Commission of the National People's Congress, the State Council Office of Legislative Affairs, the Public Security Bureau, the State Secrets Bureau, and others. Chedi diaocha: "Zhengfu xinxi gongkai tiaoli" de taiqian muhou, http://tech.sina.com.cn/it/e/2002-11-05/1011148038.shtml. During the same period, a group of scholars undertook to draft a proposed Administrative Procedure Law that would also establish information disclosure principles applicable to citizens, "legal persons," and other organizations, and provide for affirmative dissemination of information as well as by request. October 2003. Draft on file with the author.

41. Opinions of the General Office of the Central Committee of the Chinese Communist Party and of the State Council on Further Promoting Open Government Affairs, March 24, 2005, supra note 6.

42. Zhou Hanhua, ed., "Zhengfu Xinxi Gongka Tiaoli Zhuanjia Jianygao" (proposed scholars' draft of open government information regulations) (the "Scholars' Draft") (China Law Publishers, 2003).

43. Scholars' Draft, Article 19, Zhou, supra note 41.

44. Article 10(3) of the Law of the People's Republic of China Against Unfair Competition defines "commercial secrets" broadly to mean "technical information or operating information that is not known by the public, can bring about economic benefits to the rightsholder, has practical utility and about which the rightsholder has adopted secrecy measures." Zhonghua renmin gongheguo fan buzhengdang jingzheng fa, adopted September 2, 1992 and effective December 1, 1993, available at http://www.isinolaw.com/jsp/law/LAW_Articles.jsp?LangID=2&CatID=503&langswitch=1; English translation at http://www.

isinolaw.com/jsp/law/LAW_Articles.jsp?CatID=385&LangID=0&StatutesID=131669& ChapterID=-1.

45. Instead, the Chinese Constitution, Article 38, protects "personal dignity" and Article 40 protects the freedom and privacy of correspondence. Article 101 of the General Principles of Civil Law protects the right of reputation, without defining the concept. Recently, regulations on the use of computers and the Internet prohibit damaging "privacy," again without defining the term. See Yingxi Fu-Tomlinson, "Personal Data Protection in China," *China Business Review* (July-August 2002) at 36. See also the 2004 report by Privacy International on the People's Republic of China, available online at http://www.privacyinternational.org/article.shtml?cmd[347]=x-347-83511.

46. That draft's proposed comparable exemption in Article 14(a) covers: "Personal information that could identify an individual if disclosed, except for (1) personal information that laws and regulations stipulate the public may search and read; (2) personal information that must be disclosed in order to protect life health or property; (3) personal information relevant to the performance of the duties of government agency personnel; and (4) personal information records that the party agrees to disclose, where 'personal information' is defined to mean information such as an individual's name, address, date of birth, personal identification number, medical record, personnel record and photograph that singly or together with other information might specially identify that individual." See Zhou, supra note 42.

47. Adopted September 5, 1988, effective May 1, 1989, English translation at http://www. intellnet.org/documents/000/060/65.pdf; text of Chinese original, "Zhonghua renmin gongheguo baoshou guojia mimifa," available at http://www.sss.net.cn/sassnews.asp?NewsID=766.

48. See Timothy A. Gelatt, "The New Chinese State Secrets Law," 22 *Cornell International Law Journal* 256 (1989).

49. Shanghai lawyer Zheng Enchong, who represented residents evicted under China's version of eminent domain proceedings in more than 500 cases, most notably in a suit against Shanghai tycoon Zhou Zhengyi, was sentenced to three years in prison for "illegally providing state secrets to foreign entities" on October 28, 2003. Amnesty International, "Defenders of the Right to Housing—Zheng Enchong," at http://asiapacific.amnesty.org/apro/aproweb. nsf/pages/ZhengEnchong. The charge against Zheng involved two faxes Zheng was alleged to have sent to the New York-based Human Rights in China (HRIC). One was a publicly available press report by Xinhua, China's official news agency, on a demonstration by laid-off workers in Shanghai that was only subsequently classified as a "state secret" by Shanghai authorities to be used as evidence in court against Zheng. The second document was allegedly an internal report that the court acknowledged HRIC never received.

50. "New Measures to Regulate Online News Service," Xinhua News Agency, September 26, 2005, at http://service.china.org.cn/link/wcm/Show_Text?info_id=143517&p_qry=state%20 and%20secrets.

51. "Woguo dali tuijin zhengwu gongkai, baomi zhidu chongzhi dixian" (Our Country Makes Great Efforts to Promote Open Government Affairs, Secrets System Redefines the Bottom Line), September 20, 2005, at http://www.qzwb.com/gb/content/2005-09/20/content_ 1805804.htm (hereafter "Bottom Line").

52. See, e.g., "Death Toll in Natural Disasters No Longer Kept as Secret," Xinhua News Agency, September 12, 2005, http://service.china.org.cn/link/wcm/Show_Text?info_ id=141604&p_qry=state%20and%20secrets.

53. "Bottom Line," supra note 51. See also, Mao Fei, "Goujian zhengwu xinxi gongkai zhidu geng ying kaimen lifa" (There is Even Greater Need for Open Legislation About Constructing an Open Government Affairs Information System), at http://gb.chinabroadcast.cn/3821/ 2005/09/20/116@708845.htm.

54. Tsinghua University School of Law Assistant Professor Cheng Jie, quoted in "Bottom Line," supra note 51.

55. Interestingly, Guangzhou Municipality does have administrative provisions on the handling of "work secrets," which are defined to include draft regulations and policy documents, minutes of meetings, leaders' speeches, plans, budgets, and policy discussions, that do provide a procedure for determining what is a "work secret" but effectively create an atmosphere where everyone has a responsibility not to disclose work secrets. "Guangzhoushi baoshou gongzuo mimi guiding" (Provisions of Guangzhou Municipality on Safeguarding Work Secrets), adopted July 16, 2001, by the Guangzhou Municipal Government. Chinese text at http://www.gzlo.gov.cn/LawNew/LawNew_Read.asp?id=24.

56. Article 12(6), Zhonghua renmin gongheguo gonwuyuan fa (Civil Servant Law of the People's Republic of China), adopted April 27, 2005. Chinese version at http://politics.people.com.cn/GB/1026/3354665.html. Chinese statistics put the number of civil servants at 6.37 million, with 30 million working for government-funded institutions throughout the country, as of the end of 2003. "New Law Approved to Improve China's Civil Servant System," China Daily, April 27, 2005, at http://www.chinadaily.com.cn/english/doc/2005-04/27/content_438023.htm. This provision seems to track similar provisions in the PRC Judges Law, which in Article 8 requires judges to safeguard work secrets (Chinese text at http://www.cecc.gov/pages/newLaws/judgesLaw.php) and in the PRC Procurators Law, which in Article 8 requires procurators to preserve procuracy work secrets (Chinese text at http://www.chinainnovations.org/read.asp?type01=3&type02=1&type03=1&articleid=964).

57. "Imperial Archives Open to Public," Shanghai Daily, January 18, 2005, at http://service.china.org.cn/link/wcm/Show_Text?info_id=118141&p_qry=archives.

58. William M. Moss, "Research Note: Dang'an: Contemporary Chinese Archives," China Quarterly 1996: 112–129.

59. "Gov't Archives Open to Public," Xinhua News Agency, December 15, 2005, at http://service.china.org.cn/link/wcm/Show_Text?info_id=152066&p_qry=archives.

60. "China Declassifies First Diplomatic Files," Xinhua News Agency, January 19, 2004, at http://news.xinhuanet.com/english/2004-01/19/content_1283797.htm; "Public Gain Access to 'Cultural Revolution' Files," Shenzhen Daily, June 23, 2005, at http://service.china.org.cn/link/wcm/Show_Text?info_id=132952&p_qry=archives, and "Shannxi Opens Archives About Cultural Revolution," Xinhua News Agency, October 2, 2005, at: http://service.china.org.cn/link/wcm/Show_Text?info_id=144102&p_qry=archives.

61. See discussion of the Dong Ming case accompanying notes 37-38, supra.

62. "Chinese Communist party Publishes Key Policy Document on Governance Capability," in People's Daily (English) online, September 26, 2004, at http://english.peopledaily.com.cn/200409/26/print20040926_158378.html; and links to other sections of the policy document "Zhonggong zhongyang guanyu jiaqiang dangde zhizheng nengli jianshe de jueding" at http://www.people.com.cn/GB/shizheng/1026/2809350.html.

63. "Spokesperson System Promotes Judicial Justice," China Daily, January 12, 2006, at http://service.china.org.cn/link/wcm/Show_Text?info_id=154912&p_qry=transparency.

64. "Zhonghua renmin gongheguo xuke fa," adopted September 27, 2003, and effective July 1, 2004, Chinese text at http://www.law-lib.com/law/law_view.asp?id=79264.

65. "Auditing Reports to Open to Public," China Daily, July 5, 2003.

66. "Premier Welcomes Audit Report on Government Departments," People's Daily, July 5, 2004.

Virtual Reference Becoming Mainstream Library Service

M. Kathleen Kern

In the four years since Ilene Rockman wrote "Internet Speed, Library Know-How Intersect in Digital Reference" for the *Bowker Annual,*[1] virtual reference (VR) has gained widespread acceptance as a service concept. Many libraries have added VR services; training opportunities within library schools and as professional development are on the rise; instant messaging (IM) and other developments are expanding opportunities for online communication; and VR is an active area of research. While VR is a changing service, it is also becoming a mainstream library service.

Definitions

VR is also referred to as digital reference, and occasionally as electronic reference. Virtual reference is the preferred term, as it distinguishes the service of providing reference using online communications, whereas digital reference also encompasses use of online resources to answer reference questions. The *Guidelines for Implementing and Maintaining Virtual Reference Services*[2] developed by the Reference and User Services Association (RUSA) of the American Library Association (ALA) provides this definition:

> 1.1 Virtual reference is reference service initiated electronically, often in real-time, where patrons employ computers or other Internet technology to communicate with reference staff, without being physically present. Communication channels used frequently in virtual reference include chat, videoconferencing, Voice over IP [voice-over-Internet protocol], co-browsing, e-mail, and instant messaging.
>
> 1.2 While online sources are often utilized in provision of virtual reference, use of electronic sources in seeking answers is not of itself virtual reference.
>
> 1.3 Virtual reference queries are sometimes followed-up with telephone, fax, in-person and regular mail interactions, even though these modes of communication are not considered virtual.

In addition to VR and digital reference, many libraries and authors use the terms "ask-a" service or "ask-a-librarian" when referring to the concepts embodied in the above definition. When searching for articles about and Web sites of VR services, it is important to keep in mind the variety of terminology used. Some authors give the technology primacy and write of "chat reference services" or "e-mail reference." While these terms are more specific and appropriate when writing about specific technologies, they are too narrow to encompass the entire concept of VR and will quickly become dated as technology changes. In this article, "chat reference" will be used to refer to VR conducted through Web-based chat software; VR will encompass chat, IM, and e-mail.

M. Kathleen Kern is digital services coordinator and assistant reference librarian in Central Reference Services at the University of Illinois at Urbana-Champaign Library and co-manager of the library's chat reference service and instant messaging reference initiative. Her research interests include evaluation of reference service, sustainability and integration of virtual reference with more "traditional" reference services, and education of new librarians.

Whatever the choice of terminology used, the NISO Question/Answer Transaction Protocol (draft status)[3] states the matter succinctly: ". . . the essential characteristic of the service is the ability of the patron to submit questions and to receive answers via electronic means."

Features of Chat Software

Chat reference software has as its core function text-based online communication. The chat software marketed to and used by most library services has a suite of advanced features that contains some or all of the following features.

Co-browsing allows the patron and the librarian to share a Web browser and to interact with the content of Web page together. Co-browsing often allows for viewing what is being typed, which is very useful for instructing a patron in searching a database or the online catalog. *Page-pushing* and *escorting* are less fully interactive forms of screen sharing in that only the librarian controls the screen. The former allows the librarian to send static Web pages one at a time to the patron's browser, while the latter follows every link that the librarian follows and sends the pages to the patron's browser. All of these forms of screen sharing can be used to instruct the patron in the use of resources through demonstrating a search or, preferably, showing the patron the steps to take and offering hints on searching, and then observing the patron's search. Co-browsing has its appeal to librarians, but—given the popularity of IM—may not have the same attraction for patrons.

Canned messages can add speed to the chat interaction and provide uniformity of response (where desired) by providing pre-scripted messages that are inserted into the conversation with one mouse click. An individual library can write its own canned messages, and some systems allow individual librarians to set up their own. Care should be taken that these messages do not sound too cold or robotic.

File sharing enables the librarian to send documents, presentations, video, and so forth to the patron during the chat session. Document delivery can be done through this means, although most reference services (virtual or otherwise) leave document delivery to the interlibrary lending office. The use of file sharing to send tutorials and instruction is more common.

Chat transfer works much like transferring a telephone call. The patron can be passed to another librarian with different expertise, or, in the case of consortia, at a different institution. Chat transfers are "live" and the transferring and receiving librarians must both be logged into the chat software.

Other communication modes such as e-mail, text-messaging (formally known as short message service or SMS), video chat, and so on are supported with varying frequency. E-mail is quite often part of a VR software package, and chat-to e-mail is supported by some systems where a chat can be turned into an e-mail for follow-up at a later point by the same librarian or a different librarian.

Administrative features help libraries with evaluating their VR service. Transcripts are often kept and statistical reports are *de rigueur* with variance among vendors as to the data collected and the extent to which reports can be customized. Survey-pushing (through a pop-up window or by sending a link) at the close of a chat session is also a common feature.

For a comparison of chat software from some of the major commercial vendors, see the Virtual Reference Software Comparison Spreadsheet[4] and the Virtual Reference Software Comparative Review,[5] both by Jody Condit Fagan.

Chat software vendors are continually working to keep up with changing technologies and with patron and librarian preferences. New Web browsers and operating system changes demand new development to ensure operability with many types of computer configurations and patron preferences for Web browsers and settings. Deciding which emerging technologies to pursue is another consideration for vendors (and libraries): Will there be a demand for video chat? Can money be made by integrating IM into commercial chat software? Will patrons actually text-message the library? What is likely to be an enduring technology versus a flash in the pan?

E-Mail Reference

E-mail reference is an important aspect of VR services. It is sometimes overlooked in the literature because it is not as new as chat and IM reference and lacks the exciting aspect of being a synchronous interaction. Many more libraries offer service via e-mail than via the synchronous methods. Some libraries that have ceased operating live VR services have experienced an increase in their e-mail reference traffic.[6] E-mail allows the patron to contact the library at any time, which has led some libraries to claim around-the-clock service, a term that should be reserved for around-the-clock synchronous service. E-mail queries are generally answered during normal hours of reference operation.

One advantage to e-mail is that the librarian has more time to respond to the question and formulate an answer. From the patron's point of view, e-mail can be a nice "drop-and-go" option when they are not in need of an immediate response. The disadvantages to only offering e-mail are that lack of synchronicity results in a flat (or thin) interaction with no reference interview or feedback from the patron, difficulty in providing instruction on use of resources, and perhaps a longer turnaround time for response than the patron desires. Planning for a robust e-mail service includes short and well-advertised response times and marketing of the service. Cross-promotion with other services (in-person, telephone, chat) will allow patrons to choose an available synchronous mode of communication if that better fits their needs or preferences.

Expanding Area of Service

It is impossible to know the pervasiveness of VR services. Coffmann and Arrett[7] estimated there to be more than 3,000 VR services in the United States in 2004, but these figures were based on several now-obsolete registries.[8] Attempts at documenting all of the virtual reference services in existence have been abandoned as the number of services has burgeoned beyond what one individual can track. As of this writing, none of these directories had information more recent than 2003. An up-to-date directory of services would not only provide a census, but allow librarians starting a new service or exploring new software to contact other similar libraries. RUSA's Virtual Reference Committee is working to form a directory of virtual reference services that will allow libraries to input data about what they offer. Hopefully this sharing of responsibility for collection and upkeep of the data between the RUSA committee and the VR community will result in an accurate registry of services.

Even without a census of services, it is evident from conference programs, discussion list activity, and journal articles that VR services are widespread throughout all types of libraries worldwide. New Zealand has a country-wide service (http://anyquestions.co.nz), and New Zealand and Australian libraries are popular English-language partners for U.S. libraries wishing to collaborate across time zones. Because VR demands that both the library and the patron have appropriate Internet infrastructure, its popularity, of course, is mainly within more-developed nations.

Critics and Closures

Not all libraries have had uniformly positive experiences with live (chat or IM) VR, and some libraries have ended their VR services. Low volume of questions is a commonly cited reason, and flat or declining library budgets are also a factor.[9] Coffman and Arrett consider that consortia and around-the-clock arrangements may be a solution to the volume problem, but there have been cooperative VR services that have closed their virtual doors. Conversely, there are single-library services and consortia services with less than around-the-clock operation that do have more than adequate volume to argue for continued existence even in the face of tight budgets. Research into what contributes to the enduring success of some virtual reference services may help existing and nascent services to establish themselves in a sustainable manner.

Reference Consortia

Virtual reference has opened up a new area of collaboration for libraries. The technology supports sharing of reference questions in a way that previous technologies, such as the telephone, did not. There are many types of consortia, organized around the benefits that the participating libraries seek.

- *Multi-type* library consortia expand the variety of expertise available to patrons by bringing together librarians from a variety of libraries (public, academic, medical, state, and so forth). This makes possible assistance on a broader range of subjects.

- *Single-type* groups consist of libraries with similar constituency and focus. The primary objective is to share staffing to achieve a cost-effective service. Patrons and their questions may be more homogenous in this type of arrangement than in a multi-type consortium and electronic resource subscriptions may be similar.

- *Subject-based* consortia consist of libraries with a shared subject focus. A group of experts in a single subject area is available to patrons and provides a depth of knowledge. It also creates a community of practice for the librarians.

- *Geographically centered* consortia organize around proximity. The area can be small (a county or city) or large (a state or country). Administration and funding may be shared or come from a state or national library that leads the organization of the consortium. This focus for collaboration may draw on existing resource-sharing agreements, shared base of funding, and similar culture. It can also facilitate training and meetings if libraries are not too dispersed. Geographical groups may also have multi-type, single-type, or subject-based arrangements.
- *Global* partnerships are arranged for the benefits of distance. The distance may be a few states or around the world. Access to the resources of a particular library may also play a role in these partnerships. Like geographically centered consortia, these may also have a subject focus or be composed of similar or dissimilar types of libraries.

Virtual reference consortia are appealing for many reasons:

- Multiple libraries staffing the service may result in a greater number of hours of availability without significant increase in money allocated to staffing.
- Collaboration across time zones can expand hours of operation for the libraries involved.
- Access is gained to subject experts or librarians in other places for specialized questions.
- Software costs are shared.
- Training is shared.
- A generally higher volume of questions results in more cost-effective service.
- There is a central or designated administration to conduct assessments, scheduling, contract negotiations, and so forth.

There are also potential drawbacks to virtual reference consortia:

- Many questions are best answered locally.
- A wider variety of reference questions puts an increased training burden on staff.
- Difficulty may be encountered when online database subscriptions differ.
- Concerns may arise over quality of response.
- Administration must be assigned and budgeted.
- There may be questions of staffing and cost-sharing equity.

Some libraries feel that they would not be able to offer VR without participation in a consortium, but others do quite well as a single library.[10] The volume of questions received by consortia may increase the cost-effectiveness of VR services. Deciding to join a consortium depends on weighing the benefits and drawbacks and finding a consortium that matches the mission of the library.

Software Market Trends

Much like the publishing market, the VR software market has experienced many mergers and acquisitions. Commercial chat software systems marketed primarily to customer service and catalog order lines and information technology help desks have backed away from promoting themselves to the library market, leaving only three major commercial players in library chat software: QuestionPoint (OCLC), Docutek (SirsiDynix), and Tutor.com. Shareware and open source chat software products, such as RAKIM, are another option.[11] As with all shareware and freeware, the institution using the software is responsible for the hosting and maintenance of the program.

Emergence of IM Reference

Instant messaging (IM) is not a new technology. It has existed since the mid-1990s and has its roots as far back as the 1970s as a text-based talk option on mainframe systems. Despite this long history, IM did not come to libraries' notice until the 2004 publication of a Pew Internet and American Life Project report that revealed the extent to which IM was pervasive, particularly among the 18-to-27 age group.[12] Among all adults, 42 percent of people online reported using IM, and for the Generation Y group (18–27), 62 percent were regular IM users. For 25 percent of online Americans, IM was more frequently used than e-mail. These figures, coupled with the low cost and ease of use of IM software, are motivating libraries to add IM to their reference repertoire.

Sometimes IM takes the place of chat software; for other libraries it is an additional means of communication. This decision depends on the nature of the user population served and its communication preferences, as well as the needs of the library for a more full-featured chat product. IM is considerably more streamlined and lacks advanced features of chat software such as co-browsing, canned messages, statistics reporting, and ability to transfer patrons to another librarian. Since IM requires that a patron already have an account with an IM provider (such as AOL, Google, MSN, or Yahoo!), it can be a barrier to connecting to the library online, particularly for those older than Generation Y. The University of Illinois at Urbana-Champaign has found that undergraduate students are predominant users of IM reference, with 90 percent of the IM questions coming from that group, whereas graduate students and faculty compose almost 50 percent of the users for the chat reference service.[13]

Starting a New VR Service

There are many considerations when starting a VR service. As with any new project, planning is crucial to success. At this point in the development of VR, there are published case studies, online presentations, and books, as well as seasoned experts willing to talk informally or consult for a fee.

ALA's *Guidelines for Implementing and Maintaining Virtual Reference Services*[14] gives an outline of decision points that libraries face when implementing

VR and some guidance about how to approach these questions. Some of the broad categories of elements needed for a VR service, as presented in the guidelines, are

- Administrative support
- Budgeting for equipment, staff, and other resources
- Execution of a marketing plan
- Defining parameters of service (hours of operation, types of questions to be answered, response time for e-mail, and so forth)
- Writing policies for staff and for the public
- Training of staff on software and communications
- Evaluation and assessment of the service
- Protecting patron privacy

The guidelines do leave most of the outcomes of the decision-making process open to the individual library, as each library has its own organizational climate and patron needs. Such decisions such as where, when, and with whom to staff are local decisions, and there is great variance in (successful) practice. Other issues, such as patron privacy and equity of service, have more clearly defined best practices.

Privacy and Legal Issues

Libraries are concerned with the privacy of patron records. Since transcripts are collected by VR software, securing the confidentiality of the patron interaction is important. When choosing a chat software product, libraries should check what information is retained as part of the transcript and that identifying details are stripped from it. Demographic data about patrons should be stored separately and not linked to individual interactions. A retention policy for e-mail (which is likely to include the patron's e-mail address and other information) and for chat transcripts is advisable.

IM software is commercial software not tailored to library use, and transcripts are often kept by the provider of the IM service. This means the library will have no control over the purging of these transcripts or their availability—for instance, to law-enforcement officials. That being noted, users of IM are likely to be discussing more sensitive and personal topics with their friends and family through IM than they are with the library. People using IM have signed end-user agreements with the IM service providers and should already be aware that transcripts are being kept.

Other legal issues in VR involve document delivery of copyrighted material, ownership of questions in knowledge bases, and upholding licensing agreements to subscription databases when co-browsing. The Digital Reference Legal Issues Group and ALA's Office of Information Technology Policy are exploring the extent to which these legal and privacy issues affect libraries and library practice in these areas in hope of providing guidance to VR software vendors and libraries.

Education and Professional Development

As VR services have gained popularity, the demand for training has increased. While it is almost certain that this demand will taper, at present the opportunities for professional development are plentiful. In addition to presentations at various state and national conferences and full-day preconferences, there are some programs dedicated to educating librarians for VR.

Virtual Reference Desk

The Virtual Reference Desk Conference has been a mainstay in the VR community since 1999. With the end of a grant from the Institute of Museum and Library Services in 2005, the future of this conference is uncertain, but there are groups working to continue the conference in some form in 2007.

State Libraries and Consortia

One advantage of consortium membership is the availability of in-person and teleconference group training. Online training is also popular, and state libraries in particular have produced freely available quality online training. This free sharing of information benefits the greater VR community, not just the members of the consortium.[15]

Digital Reference Education Initiative

The Digital Reference Education Initiative (DREI) is an online space for libraries to share policies, training competencies, marketing plans, and so forth to enhance practice. It is also a clearinghouse for workshops, courses, and training. Of particular interest are the sections on Training Programs and Materials and the DREI Rubrics for Digital Reference Service Providers.[16]

Courses in LIS schools

A few library schools (the Information School at the University of Washington is one) have offered courses focused on VR. More commonly, virtual reference is incorporated into the syllabus of an existing reference course as another mode of communication for reference service. This approach is appropriate, but virtual reference should similarly be integrated into other library school courses so that aspects of management, impact on collection development, and technology issues can also be taught.

Future Directions

Communications technologies and preferences are rapidly changing. The challenge for libraries is to keep apprised of the trends and to determine which technologies will reach a critical point of popularity and longevity that make it worth investing in reference services via these methods. Voice-over-IP has been a much-anticipated technology that has yet to be widely used in the daily lives of patrons and has thus not really arrived as a library service. SMS is the technology on the horizon as of this writing as text messaging is a common choice of communication among the millennial and Generation Y age groups. Altarama offers technology to manage SMS communications from within a library's normal e-mail.[17] There are numerous blogs and online sources for keeping up with developments in VR. "Library Success: A Best Practice Wiki" shows early promise of keeping current with new technologies, which libraries are using them, and major vendors.[18]

More than changes in technology, the most important issues for the future of virtual reference are sustainability and integration. Service closings have brought into question VR at the same time that other libraries uniformly report positive patron response to chat and IM. The popularity of IM particularly points toward the need to determine sustainable ways to mainstream VR, in whatever technology incarnation. At issue is reaching patrons where they are, in a way that is integrated with the library's reference service and flexible to changes in technology.

Notes

1. Rockman, Ilene F. "Internet Speed, Library Know-How Intersect in Digital Reference," *Bowker Annual* 2002, 234–248.

2. American Library Association, Reference and User Services Association. *Guidelines for Implementing and Maintaining Virtual Reference Services.* (http://www.ala.org/ala/rusa/ rusaprotools/referenceguide/virtrefguidelines.htm).

3. NISO Committee AZ "Networked Reference Services" (Draft Standard Z39.90-200x) (http://www.loc.gov/standards/netref/qatp-trial.pdf). Arnold, Julie, and Neal Kaske, "Evaluating the Quality of a Chat Service." *portal: Libraries and the Academy* 5, no. 2 (April 2005): 177–193.

4. Fagan, Jody Condit. "Virtual Reference Software Comparison Spreadsheet." http://peregrin. jmu.edu/~faganjc/presentations/VRD2004/ChatRefProductsFinal.xls.

5. Fagan, Jody Condit. *Charleston Advisor* 6, no. 4 (April 2005).

6. Horowitz, Lisa R, Patricia A. Flanagan, and Deborah L. Helman. "The Viability of Live Online Reference: An Assessment." *portal: Libraries and the Academy* 5, no. 2, April 2005, 239–258.

7. Coffman, Steve, and Linda Arrett. "To Chat or Not to Chat—Taking Another Look at Virtual Reference, Part 1." *Searcher,* 12(7), July/August 2004 (http://www.infotoday.com/searcher/ jul04/arret_coffman.shtml), and Coffman, Steve, and Linda Arrett. "To Chat or Not to Chat—Taking Another Look at Virtual Reference, Part 2." *Searcher,* 12(8), 49–56, September 2004 (http://www.infotoday.com/searcher/sep04/arret_coffman.shtml).

8. See Stephen Francouer's "Index of Chat Reference Services" (http://www.teachinglibrarian. org/chatindex.htm), Bernie Sloan's "Collaborative Live Reference Services" in *Teacher Librarian* (http://people.lis.uiuc.edu/~b-sloan/collab.htm), and Gerry McKiernan's "A Registry of Real-Time Digital Reference Services" in *LiveRef* (http://www.public.iastate.edu/ ~cyberstacks/LiveRef.htm).

9. Radford, Marie, and M. Kathleen Kern. "Cyberspace Casualties: An Inquiry into Cases of Discontinued Virtual Reference Services." Presented at the 7th Annual Virtual Reference Desk Conference Recognizing the Success of Reference. November 14–15, 2005, Burlingame, California (http://www.vrd.org/conferences/VRD2005/proceedings).

10. For example, Purdue University and the University of North Carolina have both reported busy VR services and have hours of operation similar to those of the in-person reference desk.

11. http://rakim.sourceforge.net.

12. Pew Internet and American Life Project. "How Americans Use Instant Messaging." September 1, 2004 (http://www.pewinternet.org/pdfs/PIP_Instantmessage_Report.pdf).

13. Ward, David, and M. Kathleen Kern. "Combining IM and Vendor-based Chat Systems: A Case Study" (Currently under review).

14. American Library Association, 2004.

15. See in particular the materials from the Washington State Library's Statewide Virtual Reference Project.

16. Digital Reference Education Initiative (http://drei.syr.edu).

17. Houghton, Sarah. LibrarianInBlack.net (http://librarianinblack.typepad.com/librarianinblack/2005/11/text_a_libraria.html).

18. "Library Success: A Best Practices Wiki." (http://www.libsuccess.org). See particularly the sections on Online Reference, listed under Reference Services and Information Literacy.

Part 2
Legislation, Funding, and Grants

Legislation

Legislation and Regulations Affecting Libraries in 2005

Emily Sheketoff

Executive Director, Washington Office, American Library Association

Library Funding

On February 7, 2005, President Bush released his $2.5 trillion fiscal year (FY) 2006 budget proposing to cut non-defense, non-homeland security spending by nearly 1 percent.

Despite an extremely tight fiscal environment, the president requested $262,240,000 for the Institute of Museum and Library Services (IMLS), an increase of $21,565,000. For the Library Services and Technology Act, the budget included $221,325,000, an increase of $15,374,000 from FY 2005. Within that total was almost $171 million for Grants to State Library Agencies, $26 million for the Librarians for the 21st Century program, $14 million for National Leadership Grants for libraries, and $3.67 million for Improving Library Service to Native Americans.

Overall, the president's FY 2006 budget cut education funding by $530 million, or 0.9 percent, for a total of $56 billion. For school libraries, the budget proposed $19,683,264 for the Improving Literacy Through School Libraries program, the same level as FY 2005 and slightly below FY 2004. It proposed increased funding for Title I, Striving Readers Initiative, and special education.

The budget request cut or eliminated more than 150 programs, 48 of them education programs. Some of those programs proposed for elimination include Even Start ($225 million) and the Enhancing Education Through Technology program ($496 million). The president also proposed cutting funding for Adult Education by $369.7 million, or 63 percent, from $585.4 million in FY 2005 to $215.7 million.

This was the first time since FY 2002 that the Labor/HHS/Education appropriations bill was passed as stand-alone legislation and not included in an "omnibus package." An earlier version of the Labor/HHS/Ed Conference Report failed in November amid a surprising defeat in the House led by members upset about funding cuts in such areas as rural health care and the virtual elimination of roughly $1 billion in congressional earmarks. For the past several years, the level of funding for these earmarks has been increasing, including within IMLS, where last year nearly $40 million was targeted for specific museum and library projects.

Although the final version of the conference budget report did not include earmarks, the necessary votes for passage were found by adding funds for rural health and several other health-related programs. In terms of funding for libraries, the final FY 2006 conference agreement provides $247 million for IMLS.

The president signed the FY 2006 Labor/HHS/Education appropriations bill on December 30, 2005.

Table 1 / Funding for Federal Library and Related Programs, FY 2006
(amounts in thousands)

	Final FY 2005	FY 2006 Budget Request	Final FY 2006
GPO SuDocs	$31,953	$33,837	$33,303
Library of Congress	545,362	590,800	561,751
Institute of Museum and Library Services	280,564	262,240	247,144
Library Services	205,951	221,325	210,597
Museum Programs	34,724	38,951	35,705
National Agricultural Library	22,305	22,455	25,000
National Commission on Libraries and Information Science	993	993	983
National Library of Medicine (includes MLAA)	323,346	318,091	323,028
Library-Related Programs			
Department of Education			
Adult Education and Literacy	569,672	200,000	563,975
Title I, Grants to Local Education Agencies (ESEA)	12,739,571	13,342,309	12,713,125
Even Start (ESEA)	225,095	0	99,000
Educational Technology (ESEA)	496,000	0	272,250
Innovative Education Program Strategies (ESEA)	198,400	100,000	99,000
21st Century Community Learning Centers (ESEA)	991,077	991,077	981,166
Star Schools (ESEA)	20,832	0	14,850
Community Technology Centers (ESEA)	4,960	0	0
Special Education (IDEA) State Grants	10,589,746	11,097,746	10,582,960
Institute of Education Sciences (formerly OERI)	349,198	371,698	345,705
Educational Research	164,194	164,194	162,552
Educational Statistics	91,664	90,931	90,021
Educational Assessment	94,073	116,573	93,132
Institutional Development (HEA)	421,476	418,464	419,629
College Work Study (HEA)	990,257	990,257	980,354
International Education (HEA)	106,819	106,819	105,751
Postsecondary Education Improvement Fund (HEA)	162,604	22,211	21,989
Inexpensive Book Distribution (RIF)	25,296	25,296	25,043
Improving Literacy Through School Libraries (ESEA)	19,683	19,683	19,486
Reading First State Grants (ESEA)	1,041,600	1,041,600	1,029,234
Early Reading First (ESEA)	104,160	104,160	103,118
Other Government Agencies			
Head Start (HHS)	6,843,391	6,888,136	6,876,000
National Archives and Records Administration	264,809	280,975	280,215
National Endowment for the Arts	121,263	121,264	125,001
National Endowment for the Humanities	138,054	138,054	126,328

Workforce Investment Act

While the Workforce Investment Act (WIA) of 1998—which consolidates, coordinates, and improves employment, training, literacy, and vocational rehabilitation programs—was authorized through FY 2003, attempts to complete the reauthorization in the 108th and the First Session of the 109th Congress failed despite significant progress in both the House and Senate.

In the House, H.R. 27, the Job Training Improvement Act, passed on March 2, 2005. The act includes language adding "the employment, training, and literacy services carried out by public libraries" as "additional partners" in various federal employment training and adult education programs.

On September 7, the Senate marked up S. 1021 but was unable to bring the legislation to the floor before the First Session ended. Congress was expected to reconsider the reauthorization of WIA as one of its first agenda items in the Second Session.

Head Start

Head Start has provided comprehensive early childhood development services to millions of low-income children since 1965. The federal program was last reauthorized in 1998 (P.L. 105-285) for fiscal years 1999–2003. Attempts to reauthorize Head Start in the First Session of the 108th Congress were unsuccessful. While both bills (H.R. 2210 and S. 1940) reauthorizing the program in the last Congress included language urging consultation, collaboration, and outreach to libraries, the bills did not list libraries as entities eligible for reimbursement for their efforts with local Head Start centers.

In October 2005 the House passed H.R. 2123, the School Readiness Act of 2005, by a vote of 231–184. The bill encourages Head Start programs to conduct outreach, coordinate, and collaborate with libraries. Further, it includes language that will permit libraries to enter into memoranda of understanding with local Head Start programs, allowing libraries to potentially be reimbursed for any expenditure they make in support of Head Start programs. Report language added to the House bill clarifies the important role libraries play in Head Start programs nationwide and allows libraries to enter into financial agreements for the quality services they offer Head Start programs.

The Senate Health, Education, Labor, and Pensions (HELP) Committee approved S. 1107, the Head Start Improvements for School Readiness Act. Thanks to the support and influence of Sen. Jack Reed (D-R.I.), S. 1107 includes numerous references to libraries and language encouraging increased collaboration and coordination with them. Moreover, it includes language that makes the head of the state library administrative agency a member of the program's state advisory council.

Reauthorization of Head Start was likely to be among the many reauthorizations that the Second Session of the 109th Congress would consider.

Perkins Vocational and Technical Education Act

Authorization of the Carl D. Perkins Vocational and Technical Education Act expired in 2003. While both the House and the Senate introduced bills in the last

Congress reauthorizing the act, no bills made it beyond the House Education and the Workforce Committee or the Senate Health, Education, Labor, and Pensions Committee.

The Senate passed S. 250, the Carl D. Perkins Career and Technical Education Improvement Act of 2005, by a vote of 99–0 on February 1, 2005. The act includes language permitting the use of funds "for leasing, purchasing, upgrading, or adapting instructional equipment, including support for library resources, such as business journals, publications, and other related resources designed to strengthen and support academic and technical skill achievement."

The House introduced a similar bill, H.R. 366, which passed on May 4, 2005, by a vote of 416–9. H.R. 366 expands the permitted use of funds to include "publications." The intent of this change, as explained in the report language, is to clarify the ability of recipients, particularly school libraries, to use a portion of their funding to purchase vocation-related books, materials, and related resources.

The Perkins Act was likely to be considered for reauthorization in the second session.

Telecommunications

Universal Service

In March 2005 the Federal Communications Commission (FCC) announced that it had contracted with the National Academy of Public Administration (NAPA), a nonprofit consulting group, to study the E-rate program to determine if it could be better managed. The study was recommended by FCC's inspector general and was expected to take five to six months to complete.

The American Library Association (ALA) submitted comments and reply comments to FCC responding to a notice of proposed rulemaking. ALA outlined a major simplification for the E-rate program that would make the application and disbursement process less burdensome for library and other applicants. The program provides telecommunications discounts for libraries and K–12 public and private schools.

E-rate and ADA

Thanks to language passed by the House and Senate Appropriations Subcommittee on Commerce, Justice, and Science, the E-rate is exempted from the Anti-Deficiency Act (ADA) until December 31, 2006. ADA is an Office of Management and Budget (OMB) requirement that would prohibit the Universal Service Administrative Corporation (USAC), which administers the E-rate, from sending out commitment letters without all funding for the E-rate program being in the bank at the time the letters are sent to applicants. This is rarely possible because universal service contributions are collected from telecommunications carriers quarterly.

This is the second one-year exemption from ADA rules that E-rate has received. ALA is seeking a permanent solution to this issue in the 109th Congress.

Copyright Legislation and Litigation

S. 167, Family and Entertainment Copyright Act of 2005

In April 2005 the House passed S. 167, a copyright bill that had been approved by the Senate in February. The president signed the bill as Public Law 109-9 on April 27. Libraries supported passage of this bill, which, among other things, amended (in Title IV of the bill, the Preservation of Orphan Works Act) Section 108 of the Copyright Act to allow libraries to engage in preservation, scholarship, and research of musical works, motion pictures, and other audiovisual works during the last 20 years of their copyright term.

H.R. 1201, Digital Media Consumers Rights Act of 2005

Congressmen Rick Boucher (D-Va.), John Doolittle (R-Calif.), and Joe Barton (R-Texas) are cosponsoring a fair use bill, H.R. 1201, the Digital Media Consumers Rights Act of 2005. Introduced in March 2005, this remained the only significant fair use bill at the time this report was prepared. The bill would, among other things

- Amend Section 1201 of the Digital Millennium Copyright Act (DMCA) to allow bypassing a technological "lock" that controls access to and use of a copyrighted work, provided that the circumvention does not result in infringement of the work
- Codify the U.S. Supreme Court's 1984 ruling that a copying technology (in that case, the videocassette recorder) is permissible under the Copyright Act so long as it can be used for non-infringing as well as infringing purposes.

Fair Use Hearing

On November 16, 2005, the House Energy and Commerce Committee held a hearing titled "Fair Use: Its Effects on Consumers and Industry." The lively hearing—convened by the committee's Subcommittee on Commerce, Trade, and Consumer Protection—lasted more than two hours and heard the views of eight witnesses, including testimony on behalf of the Library Copyright Alliance (LCA)—ALA, the Association of Research Libraries (ARL), the American Association of Law Libraries (AALL), the Medical Library Association (MLA), and the Special Libraries Association (SLA)—on fair use, copyright law, and technology. The subcommittee chairman said he intended to hold a hearing in 2006 on H.R. 1201, the Digital Media Consumers Rights Act of 2005, which was pending in the House.

H.R. 2408, Public Domain Enhancement Act

Rep. Zoe Lofgren (D-Calif.) and Rep. Doolittle introduced H.R. 2408, the Public Domain Enhancement Act, in May 2005 to amend the Copyright Act to allow abandoned copyrighted works to enter the public domain after 50 years. The bill would provide a simple mechanism to ensure that abandoned copyrighted works pass into the public domain. Lofgren had introduced a similar bill in the 108th Congress, and it was endorsed by ALA and other library associations. An alternative legislative approach to dealing with abandoned copyrighted works lies with the current inquiry into "orphan works" being conducted by the U.S. Copyright Office.

DMCA Section 1201 Rulemaking

ALA, working as part of LCA, filed comments on December 1 with the Copyright Office. Joined by the Music Library Association, LCA requested exemptions to DMCA's Section 1201 prohibition on circumvention of technological measures that control access to copyrighted works.

The Copyright Office issued its third notice of inquiry in October 2005 to begin the third round of triennial proceedings under Section 1201(a)(1) of DMCA (see http://www.copyright.gov/fedreg/2005/70fr57526.html). DMCA provides that there can be exemptions from the prohibition on circumvention for users of "classes of works" who would be "adversely affected by virtue of such prohibition in their ability to make non-infringing uses" of those works. The rulemaking process to determine the exemptions is to take place every three years. The Library of Congress issued rules in October 2000 and October 2003, and the next rule is to be issued in October 2006.

In their comments, LCA and the Music Library Association requested two new exemptions plus a renewal of the four exemptions granted in 2003 (see http://www.copyright.gov/1201/docs/fedreg-notice-final.pdf).

Copyright Office Inquiry on Orphan Works

The library community has participated in various ways in the ongoing project of the Copyright Office to address "orphan works"—copyrighted works whose owners prove difficult or even impossible to find. On May 9, 2005, ALA, through LCA, filed reply comments with the Copyright Office in further support of a proposal to change copyright law to allow use of orphaned works after a due-diligence search for an owner. In July libraries participated in a public roundtable discussion sponsored by the Copyright Office to air views from many stakeholders. In November library representatives met with officials in the Copyright Office to discuss some of the issues and to make further recommendations from libraries. Libraries also continue to work closely with American University's Washington College of Law on the proposal that it has made (through the Glusko-Samuelson Intellectual Property Clinic) for solving the orphan works problem. The Copyright Office was expected to make a recommendation to Congress early in 2006.

Library of Congress Section 108 Study Group

The Library of Congress in 2005 convened a Section 108 Study Group to prepare findings and make recommendations to the Librarian of Congress by mid-2006 for possible alterations to the law that reflect current technologies. The group, named after the section of the U.S. Copyright Act that provides limited exceptions for libraries and archives, held its inaugural meeting at the Library of Congress in April 2005, a second meeting in New York City in June, its third meeting in Washington in September, and its fourth meeting in New York in November. Meetings are scheduled through October 2006.

S. 2104, American Center for Cures Act

S. 2104, introduced in December 2005 to establish the American Center for Cures within the National Institutes for Health (NIH), includes a provision that would help to make taxpayer-funded biomedical research available to all potential users. Introduced by Senators Joe Lieberman (D-Ct.) and Thad Cochran (R-Miss.), the bipartisan American Center for Cures Act of 2005 would expedite development of new therapies and cures for life-threatening diseases and would require free public access to articles stemming from federally funded research. At the time this report was prepared, the bill was in the hands of the Senate Committee on Health, Education, Labor, and Pensions.

Copyright Court Cases

Psihoyos v. *National Geographic Enterprises*

LCA filed a friends-of-the-court brief in November 2005 with the Supreme Court in the copyright case *Psihoyos* v. *National Geographic Enterprises.* The brief urged the court to grant a petition for certiorari (appeal) and to affirm a decision by the U.S. Court of Appeals for the Second Circuit in favor of the National Geographic Society (NGS). The case concerns whether publishers of collective works can republish those works in a digital format without seeking permission of authors or other contributors. The Second Circuit ruled that copyright law allows NGS to republish the entire print version of the *National Geographic* magazine from 1888 to 1996 in a searchable format (such as CD-ROM or DVD).

On December 12, however, the Supreme Court denied the petition for certiorari. NGS wanted the high court to hear the case, even though it had won in the Second Circuit, hoping that the court would rule in its favor and, by doing so, resolve a confusing situation in which two federal courts of appeals (the other being the Eleventh Circuit) have issued conflicting opinions about this provision of copyright law.

ALA v. *FCC* ("broadcast flag" case)

ALA v. *FCC* is a case in the U.S. Court of Appeals for the District of Columbia Circuit in which libraries and other public interest and consumer groups successfully challenged FCC. In 2004 FCC issued "broadcast flag" copyright protection rules that were to go into effect in July 2005. The order required that all digital electronic devices, such as television sets and personal computers, include code (a "broadcast flag") that accompanies digital television (DTV) signals to prevent redistribution of the digital content over the Internet. The FCC ruling marked another step toward giving content providers extensive control over what users can do with electronic content.

In May 2005 the Court of Appeals issued a unanimous decision striking down FCC's rule, holding that FCC had exceeded its legal authority when it attempted to regulate consumers' use of TV receiver devices after the completion of a broadcast transmission.

However, almost immediately after the court's decision was issued, efforts began to have legislation introduced to authorize FCC to issue a broadcast flag. These efforts are tied into various legislative initiatives arising out of the transition from analog to digital television, which Congress appears ready to mandate to occur by early 2009.

Privacy, Surveillance, and Libraries

USA Patriot Act

ALA continues to be concerned about particular portions of the USA Patriot Act and the effects the act may have on libraries and library users.

One strong focus has been on Section 215 of the act, which allows federal authorities to get an order from the secret Foreign Intelligence Surveillance Act (FISA) Court for "any tangible thing" sought "in relation to a foreign intelligence investigation," which ALA considers a very loose and vague standard.

On July 29, the final day before its summer recess, the Senate passed S. 1389 (the USA Patriot Improvement and Reauthorization Act of 2005) on unanimous consent. The bill added to the act many of the safeguards for library and reader privacy that had been sought by the library community since the passage of the law soon after the terrorist attacks of September 11, 2001, including tougher requirements for searching library records under Section 215. On November 9 House conferees were named, and official conference meetings began on November 10. On November 13 a draft conference report was "unofficially circulated" to organizations working to reform the act. After much work on the part of ALA and others, the draft was withdrawn. Then, on December 8, a new conference report was filed in the House and agreed to on December 14 by a vote of 251–174. The Senate voted on December 16 to allow an extended debate on the conference report in the upper house. On December 21, it extended the expiring provisions of the act for six months, but on December 22 House Judiciary Committee Chair James Sensenbrenner (R-Wis.) refused to accept the six-month extension. The House sent back a bill with a five-week extension, until February 3, 2006. Then a filibuster by Sen. Russ Feingold (D-Wis.) resulted in postponement of further action until mid-March. [The battle ended on March 7, when the House voted 280–138 to renew the act with its troublesome library and bookstore provisions intact; the president signed the legislation two days later—Ed.]

For more on ALA's activity in relation to reauthorization of the USA Patriot Act, see http://www.ala.org/ala/washoff/WOissues/civilliberties/theusapatriotact/usapatriotact.htm.

National Security Letters

On September 9, 2005, U.S. District Court Judge Janet Hall ruled that the FBI must lift a gag order that was preventing an "organization with library records" from participating in the USA Patriot Act debate. The opinion came in a Connecticut case brought by the American Civil Liberties Union (ACLU) challenging a provision of the USA Patriot Act that authorizes the FBI to demand records without judicial review, through a national security letter (NSL).

The decision marked the second time a federal court had dealt a blow to the NSL provision of the USA Patriot Act. The first ruling found that the entire NSL provision was unconstitutional (*John Doe and American Civil Liberties Union* v. *John Ashcroft, Robert Mueller, and Marion E. Bowman,* detailed below.)

In the Connecticut decision, which was stayed pending appeal, Judge Hall wrote that "The statute has the practical effect of silencing those who have the most intimate knowledge of the statute's effect and a strong interest in advocating against the federal government's broad investigative powers . . . The government may intend the non-disclosure provision to serve some purpose other than the suppression of speech. Nevertheless, it has the practical impact of silencing individuals with a constitutionally protected interest in speech and whose voices are particularly important to an ongoing, national debate about the intrusion of governmental authority into individual lives."

Under appeal, the Connecticut case was merged with the *Doe* v. *Ashcroft* case in the United States Court of Appeals for the Second Circuit in New York. In *Doe* v. *Ashcroft,* Judge Victor Marrero of U.S. District Court in New York ruled September 29 that Section 505 of the USA Patriot Act "essentially coerces the reasonable recipient into immediate compliance," which he held was in violation of the Fourth Amendment rule against unreasonable searches. The judge also ruled that the accompanying gag order violated the First Amendment. Marrero invalidated part of the Electronic Communications Privacy Act of 1986, as expanded by the USA Patriot Act, that allowed the FBI to demand a list of e-mail addresses with which a certain subscriber had corresponded and a list of Web pages visited, as well as to read stored e-mails. The judge stayed the order for 90 days to allow time for the government to appeal, and the Justice Department indicated that it would do so.

Civil Liberties and Privacy Oversight Board

As of early 2006, the Civil Liberties and Privacy Oversight Board, a recommendation of the National Commission on Terrorist Attacks Upon the United States (9-11 Commission), continued to lack adequate resources to do its job. Nominations to the board were delayed, some nominees lacked extensive civil liberties credentials, and initial funding for the board was severely inadequate. As of the time this report was prepared, nominations to the board had yet to be confirmed by the Senate and the board therefore had not yet convened.

The board—if funded and staffed—will be responsible for reviewing some of the most sensitive programs in the federal government, such as the National Security Agency's wiretapping of U.S. citizens' international phone calls, the Homeland Security Department's opening of inbound international mail, and the department's screening of airline passengers. It would also look into the limits of secrecy and use of torture in government prisons.

Chief Privacy Officers

Language requiring every federal agency to have a "chief privacy officer" (CPO) was slipped into the Transportation-Treasury Appropriations Act of 2005, one of the nine appropriations bills in the omnibus bill that Congress passed late in November. In a memorandum (M-05-08) to agency heads in February 2005,

OMB had said, "Consistent with the Paperwork Reduction Act, the agency's Chief Information Officer (CIO) may perform this role." It was not immediately apparent how many agencies had complied with even this version of the requirement by designating their CIO to be their CPO.

Surveillance Issues

A November 5, 2005, article in the *Washington Post* revealed that the FBI had issued tens of thousands of national security letters under Section 505 of the USA Patriot Act. The article also indicated that the information gathered through these searches was being retained in government data banks and shared among federal government agencies and beyond. According to the article, in late 2003 the Bush administration reversed a long-standing policy requiring government agents to destroy their files on innocent American citizens, companies, and residents when investigations closed. Late in 2005 President Bush signed Executive Order 13388 expanding access to those files for "state, local, and tribal" governments and for "appropriate private-sector entities," which were not defined.

The *New York Times* reported in December 2005 that the National Security Agency (NSA) was actively conducting warrantless electronic surveillance of American citizens within the United States. Such eavesdropping without a warrant from the Foreign Surveillance Court violates the Foreign Intelligence Surveillance Act (FISA), which Congress intended to be the exclusive framework for electronic surveillance in the United States. The full extent and details of the NSA program were not yet known.

Access to Government Information

E-Government

The deadlines for OMB to implement the requirements of the E-Government Act of 2002 arrived in December 2005. ALA's concern is primarily focused on Section 207(d), "Categorizing of Information." An Interagency Committee on Government Information (ICGI) was required to submit (by December 2004) recommendations on

- Adoption of standards, which are open to the maximum extent feasible, to enable the organization and categorization of government information in a way that is searchable electronically, including by searchable identifiers, and in ways that are interoperable across agencies
- Definition of categories of government information that should be classified under the standards
- Determination priorities and developing schedules for the initial implementation of the standards by agencies

ICGI submitted its report last year, recommending that OMB adopt the ISO Z39.50 international standard for interoperable search and take action to assure that future search technology procured by federal agencies is compliant with this standard.

In September OMB and the General Services Administration (GSA) put out a request for information to "identify and promote the most cost-effective means to search for, identify, locate, retrieve, and share information, and assess the net performance difference (including cost-benefits) of assigning metadata and/or a controlled vocabulary to various types of information versus not doing so." It asks: "Does current search technology perform to a sufficiently high level to make an added investment in metadata tagging unnecessary in terms of cost and benefit?" GSA's response analysis can be read at http://tinyurl.com/9ljc6.

On December 16, OMB issued a memorandum (M-06-02) on "Improving Public Access to and Dissemination of Government Information and Using the Federal Enterprise Architecture Data Reference Model." It identifies "three new requirements" in the area of "organizing and categorizing government information and making it searchable across agencies to improve public access and dissemination." Agencies must now (1) organize and categorize their information intended for public access, make it searchable across agencies, and describe how they use "formal information models" to assist their dissemination activities; (2) review the performance and results of their information dissemination programs and describe the review in their Information Resources Management (IRM) Strategic Plans; and (3) publish their IRM Strategic Plans on their public Web sites.

In regard to (1) above, the memorandum outlines procedures to "cost-effectively" fulfill this requirement:

> (1) When disseminating information to the public-at-large, publish your information directly to the Internet. This procedure exposes information to freely available and other search functions and adequately organizes and categorizes your information.
>
> (2) When interchanging data among specific identifiable groups or disseminating significant information dissemination products, advance preparation, such as using formal information models, may be necessary to ensure effective interchange or dissemination.

The memorandum states that this policy "does not prescribe any new or specific thresholds requiring advance preparation of information or what form such preparation must take. Agencies should continue to meet existing requirements, ensure appropriate consultation with users, and consider the significance of the information dissemination product or data interchange to the agency mission and the level of public interest. As significance increases, so too may the need for advance preparation." It notes that "Specific identifiable groups, also known as user groups and 'communities of interest,' can include any combination of Federal agencies, State, local, and tribal governments, industry, scientific community, academia, and *specific* interested members of the general public" (emphasis added).

An agency's IRM Strategic Plan is "the agency's IT vision or roadmap that will align its information resources with its business strategies and investment decisions. As an example, the IRM Strategic Plan might include the mission of the agency, key business processes, IT challenges, and guiding principles." It is unclear how this meets the requirements of the statute to determine "priorities and developing schedules for the initial implementation of the standards by agencies."

Right to Know

ALA's Washington Office has been actively engaged in promoting the public's "right to know" information created and collected by or for the federal government. This concept is an expansion and strengthening of the long-standing principle that government should make this information available. The public's right to information, however, has come under steady pressure and challenge since September 11, 2001.

NGA Deletions

Extensive databases of aeronautical information that have long been publicly available will be withdrawn from public access in 2006. "The National Geospatial-Intelligence Agency (NGA) will go forward with its previously announced proposal to remove its Flight Information Publications (FLIP) and Digital Aeronautical Flight Information File (DAFIF) from public access," according to an NGA news release issued on November 29. The NGA did not approve another proposal to withdraw certain paper maps from public access: "NGA has decided not to withdraw paper map products to a scale of 1:250,000 to 1:5,000,000. These products will continue to be available to the public," the news release stated.

According to NGA, copyright concerns raised by foreign data sources were the driving factor for the decision to withhold the information from the public. *Secrecy News* quotes a subject matter expert (who requested anonymity because he works with NGA) who calls the move "a very bad precedent" when "the introduction of any copyright-protected material renders a massive public domain database off limits to the public. Many, many other databases are at stake." The expert noted that NGA could have "offered a redacted version of the databases for public sale. DAFIF—a really big database—could easily have been stripped of its Australian-supplied [copyrighted] data and kept public and available." The data withdrawal was to begin in January 2006 and be complete by October 2007.

Toxic Release Inventory Under Threat

The U.S. Environmental Protection Agency (EPA) Toxic Release Inventory (TRI), created in the wake of the 1984 Bhopal disaster in India, is a landmark achievement of the community "right to know" movement that pressed for improved public reporting of toxic chemical hazards. It has functioned successfully for nearly two decades, leading to significant reductions in releases of toxic chemicals. EPA is proposing to drastically reduce the data collected and reported in TRI, beginning with a move to eliminate the current annual reporting requirement in favor of reporting every other year.

'Sensitive But Unclassified' Guidelines

In a December 16, 2005, memorandum, "Guidelines and Requirements in Support of the Information Sharing Environment," the White House told executive branch agencies to develop standard procedures for handling of "sensitive but unclassified" information.

Agencies were told that "To promote and enhance the effective and efficient acquisition, access, retention, production, use, management, and sharing of

Sensitive But Unclassified (SBU) information, including homeland security information, law enforcement information, and terrorism information, procedures and standards for designating, marking, and handling SBU information must be standardized across the Federal Government." Agencies are required to assess their procedures for handling SBU information and report on them to the director of national intelligence within 90 days. Within a year, the director, with other agency heads, is to present recommendations on standardized SBU procedures for the president's approval.

There is, at this point, no generally accepted definition of "sensitive."

Intelligence Budget Secrecy

A federal judge on April 4, 2005, ordered the Central Intelligence Agency (CIA) to disclose its 1963 budget, marking the first time that a court has compelled the CIA to surrender intelligence budget information. The order was issued in response to a motion from the Federation of American Scientists, and over the opposition of the CIA, in the Freedom of Information Act proceeding *Aftergood* v. *CIA* (D.C. District Case No. 01-2524).

Judicial Branch

In late November 2004 ALA—together with other library, archives, journalists', and public-interest organizations—filed a friends-of-the-court brief with the District of Columbia Circuit Court of Appeals supporting public access to information about the makeup of the National Energy Policy Development Group (NEPDG), convened by Vice President Dick Cheney in 2001. The case was brought by the Sierra Club and Judicial Watch and heard by the United States Supreme Court in April 2005. The Supreme Court, recognizing the importance of the issue and the conflicting principles of separation of powers and public accountability, sent the case back to the D.C. Circuit Court of Appeals for adjudication. In May 2005 the D.C. Circuit ruled unanimously in favor of the government. Its opinion included (1) a holding that a government committee whose official members are only government employees will not become subject to the Federal Advisory Committee Act (FACA) merely because an outsider participates in the meetings of the committee, or even does so persuasively (as long as the outsider has no vote on the committee, FACA does not apply); and (2) a holding that the factual record in this case did not establish the participation of any outsiders in the NEPDG meetings, and thus there would be no basis for invoking FACA anyway. Because the plaintiffs never were able to conduct any discovery in the matter, they were never able to get behind the bland assurances in the government's declaration.

Legislation and Regulations Affecting Publishing in 2005

Allan Adler
Vice President, Legal and Governmental Affairs

Emilia Varga-West
Executive Assistant for Government Relations and International Enforcement

Association of American Publishers
50 F St. N.W., Suite 400, Washington, DC 20001
202-347-3375, fax 202-347-3690
E-mail adler@publishers.org or ewest@publishers.org

The First Session of the 109th Congress was marked by an exacerbation of the previous Congress's bitterly partisan election-year politics, which continued to be dominated by inter-party disputes over the Bush administration's Iraqi war policies, high-profile judicial nominations, and a succession of stalemates between the House and Senate over the congressional appropriations process. While most copyright initiatives were put on the legislative back burner pending the Supreme Court's resolution of the Grokster case (*Metro-Goldwyn-Mayer* v. *Grokster*) on secondary liability for peer-to-peer online infringements, a variety of legislative activities of interest to publishers continued to percolate in both houses.

This report focuses on legislative actions that affect book and journal publishing interests, primarily concerning intellectual property protection, freedom of expression, new technologies and "e-commerce," and educational issues. It also reports on significant developments regarding tax and postal matters.

A summary, text, and status report for each piece of referenced legislation, whether enacted or not, can be found online at http://thomas.loc.gov, the legislation-tracking site maintained by the Congressional Research Service of the Library of Congress.

Copyright Issues

Family Entertainment and Copyright Act of 2005

(S. 167; Public Law No.109-9; April 27, 2005)

Introduced by Sen. Orrin Hatch (R-Utah) and cosponsored by four other senators in January 2005, the Family Entertainment and Copyright Act (FECA) primarily addresses copyright protection issues for the motion picture industry, but contains a provision that will also be helpful to book publishers.

Among other things, FECA establishes a new provision amending the U.S. Code to penalize the unauthorized act of using or attempting to use a video camera to transmit or record any audiovisual work in any theater or other exhibition facility. It also makes it a felony to engage in "willful pre-commercial online distribution" of an audiovisual work. Although the statutory provision on prerelease distribution does not specifically cover literary works, a related provision that calls for regulations to establish a pre-registration procedure to protect works prior to commercial release made it possible for literary works to qualify for such pre-registration protection if the Register of Copyrights determined in a subsequent rulemaking that such works had a "history of copyright infringement prior to commercial distribution" similar to that which has plagued motion pictures. The Association of American Publishers (AAP) filed comments in the rulemaking, demonstrating the existence of such a "history" for highly anticipated books prior to their publication, and the Register included literary works as eligible for the pre-registration procedure when rules were issued to govern that process.

Non-Enacted Legislation

Two copyright-related bills of interest to AAP were introduced during the First Session and remained pending before Congress in early 2006.

- The proposed Digital Media Consumers' Rights Act of 2005 (H.R. 1201) would, among other things, amend the Digital Millennium Copyright Act (DMCA) to permit the circumvention of technological access and use controls for non-infringing purposes and to legalize tools that would facilitate such circumvention. Because its sponsors were unable to gain traction in the House Judiciary Committee with earlier versions of this bill, the pending version of this legislation (like a version that died in the 108th Congress) was referred to the House Energy and Commerce Committee based on its inclusion of provisions that would authorize the Federal Trade Commission to regulate unfair and deceptive practices in the sales of digital music disc products through labeling requirements.
- The proposed Public Domain Enhancement Act (H.R. 2408) would establish a copyright "renewal" process that would strip works of their copyright protection and place them in the public domain if the copyright owners fail to renew their rights in compliance with a specified procedure requiring timely payment of a "maintenance fee" within a specific timeframe and every 10 years thereafter until the end of the copyright term. The bill's ostensible purpose is to identify so-called orphan works whose copyright owners cannot be identified or located, or have abandoned any interest in economic exploitation of the works, in order to permit those works to be used in otherwise infringing circumstances without risk of infringement liability for the user. However, the bill's approach to the orphan works issue has been rejected by the Copyright Office in a recent study that concludes with legislative recommendations to codify a different approach to orphan works that has garnered much more support among users and producers of copyrighted works, including book publishers.

Both of these bills would be harmful to the copyright interests of book publishers. AAP will remain alert for any attempts to advance these measures through the legislative process and will continue to oppose their enactment.

Freedom of Expression Issues
Non-Enacted Legislation

Proposals to Amend the USA Patriot Act

Lingering discomfort among members of Congress regarding some of the more controversial provisions of the USA Patriot Act enacted after the terrorist attacks of September 11, 2001, produced a high-visibility public debate over whether Congress should reauthorize certain provisions of the act that were due to expire before the end of 2005. Few issues in this context had a higher profile than the struggle over Section 215 of the act, which provided few safeguards for privacy and freedom of expression in authorizing federal officials to access library, bookstore, and other third-party "business records" as part of an investigation into alleged terrorist activities.

During early spring 2005, the proposed Freedom to Read Protection Act (H.R. 1157) and the proposed Library, Bookseller, and Personal Records Privacy Act (S. 317), reintroduced by Rep. Bernie Sanders (I-Vt.) and Sen. Russell Feingold (D-Wis.), respectively, were among numerous bills that were offered by legislators seeking to strengthen civil liberties protections that were weakened by various provisions of the USA Patriot Act and other antiterrorism legislation. The proposals had in common the restoration of the requirement that federal law enforcement agencies seeking such records must show probable cause to believe that the individual who is the subject of the records is involved in espionage or terrorism-related activities.

Similarly, the proposed Security and Freedom Enhancement (SAFE) Act (S. 737), which was introduced by Sen. Larry Craig (R-Idaho) as a narrowly crafted bipartisan effort to address the most serious concerns with respect to Section 215, would restore a standard of individualized suspicion and establish procedural safeguards to prevent abuse of that statutory authority. Specifically, the act states that (1) the government would need to show there was reason to believe the individual whose records were sought was an agent of a foreign power; (2) the recipient of a Foreign Intelligence Surveillance Act (FISA) order would have the right to quash it; (3) the government would need to demonstrate the need for a gag order; (4) a time limit, which could be extended by the court, would be placed on the gag order; and (5) the individual whose records are sought would have to be notified if the government seeks to use those records in a subsequent proceeding and would have a right to challenge the use of such records. The spring legislation continued with H.R. 1526 (Security and Freedom Ensured Act) and H.R. 2715 (Stop Self-Authorized Secret Searches Act), which to a lesser extent set forth similar provisions to those of SAFE Act.

In June 2005 the House, by a 238–187 vote, approved an amendment offered by Rep. Sanders to the Justice Department's appropriations legislation to cut off funding for FBI searches of bookstores and libraries under Section 215. It was an unexpected victory because the Bush administration had defeated a similar amendment proposed in 2004. AAP's joint Campaign for Reader Privacy with the American Booksellers Association, the American Library Association, and PEN American Center played a significant role in securing the positive vote.

However, the victory proved short-lived, as President Bush threatened to veto the appropriations legislation unless the Sanders amendment was removed, and the House subsequently passed the proposed USA Patriot Improvement and Reauthorization Act of 2005 (H.R. 3199), which would make relatively cosmetic changes to Section 215 that would not satisfy the campaign members. This time, Rep. Sanders was blocked from offering his legislation as an amendment to the bill. At about the same time, an equally insufficient measure to reauthorize Section 215 and other expiring provisions of the USA Patriot Act came out of the Senate Intelligence Committee (S. 1266), which was reported to Senate without any amendment.

The battle took another turn in July when the Senate unanimously passed its own version of the proposed USA Patriot Improvement and Reauthorization Act of 2005 (S. 1389), which included some of the crucial safeguards for protecting library, bookstore, and publisher records that AAP had been advocating for more than two years. The differences between the two proposals were significant. Under the Senate version, the recipient of a Section 215 order would have had the right to consult an attorney and to challenge the order in the FISA court. The FBI would also have had to present facts to the FISA court demonstrating a reason to believe that the records pertain to individuals suspected of espionage or terrorism and those who are in contact with them, thus reducing the possibility of a government "fishing expedition." Regarding library and bookstore records, the agent would have needed prior written approval from the director or deputy director of the FBI before seeking such an order. Under the Senate bill, Section 215 was to "sunset" in four instead of ten years as proposed by the House bill, which would have significantly weakened the opportunity for meaningful congressional oversight.

AAP expressed grave disappointment in the legislation that emerged from the House and Senate conference committee in November because of its failure to provide adequate civil liberties protections for Section 215. The conferees had rejected several key changes sought by AAP and proposed in S. 1389, including the establishment of standard of individualized suspicion as the basis for obtaining bookstore and library records. The final bill failed to provide any meaningful way for a recipient to challenge the secret court order and rejected the four-year "sunset" approved by the Senate, proposing instead to extend the provision for another seven years.

Congress, however, did not pass the conference report in the House and Senate before the First Session of the 109th Congress adjourned. Instead, it enacted S. 2167 (PL. 109-160), extending the expiring provisions of the USA Patriot Act until February 3, 2006, in order to permit Congress to take the issues up again in the Second Session.

[The battle continued until March 7, when the House voted 280–138 to renew the act, just days before 16 major provisions of the old law were to expire. The president signed the legislation March 9. The measure renews the expiring provisions of the original USA Patriot Act, including one that lets federal officials seize "tangible items," such as patron records from libraries and business records from bookstores, in connection with international terrorism investigations.—Ed.]

Bills to Provide Confidential Source Protection for Journalists

In the wake of several highly publicized and publicly criticized "leak" investigations by the Bush administration, the question of whether federal law provides a "confidential source" privilege for journalists has been raised in Congress as well as in the federal courts. In the absence of federal statutory protection, the issue has generally been addressed through state statutes and claims based on the First Amendment. However, in response to recent judicial rulings that have rejected the existence of an unqualified constitutional "reporter's privilege" under the First Amendment, several members of Congress have introduced bills to establish federal statutory protection for confidential news sources.

The proposed Free Flow of Information Act of 2005 (H.R. 581) would permit federal entities to compel a "covered person" (identified as media outlets or their employees) to testify or to provide requested documents only if the testimony could not be obtained from other sources and if it is vital to an investigation, prosecution, or defense in a federal criminal case. At the same time, the bill also specifies that no media person could be required to reveal the identity of a confidential source unless the person received an opportunity to resist such disclosure in federal court. A bill identical to this House measure was pending in the Senate (S. 340).

The proposed Free Speech Protection Act of 2005 (S. 369), introduced by the Senate sponsor of the original House bill, would go one step further by providing that journalists cannot be compelled to disclose any information or documents (including notes, video or sound tapes, out-takes, and photographs) that were acquired during the process of newsgathering but were not disclosed to the public.

Subsequently, the House and Senate sponsors of the original source-protection legislation introduced new versions (H.R. 3323 and S. 419) of those bills containing provisions similar to the additional protection in S. 369, but also specifically limiting press protections by permitting compelled disclosure in cases where "imminent and actual harm to national security" is otherwise expected to result and would outweigh the public interest in protecting the free flow of information.

None of these measures had advanced through committees in the House or Senate by early 2006. Recognizing that authors and publishers of books frequently have reasons to invoke the protection of confidential sources against government efforts to secure compelled disclosure, AAP will continue to monitor the pending legislation and support its enactment.

Bills to Improve Public Access to Federal Agency Records Under FOIA

The freedom to obtain access to information, especially from the executive branch of the federal government, is often an important precondition to the exercise of freedom of expression with respect to federal government activities and policies. Continuing dissatisfaction with the Bush administration's marked penchant for government secrecy, particularly with respect to its stewardship over agency compliance with the federal Freedom of Information Act (FOIA), has led several members of Congress to introduce legislation to strengthen the public's ability to obtain access to federal agency records under FOIA.

The proposed OPEN Government Act, which was simultaneously introduced in the House and Senate (H.R. 867 and S. 394), would amend FOIA to facilitate the granting of fee-waiver requests from freelance journalists and other news media representatives who lack institutional affiliations. The legislation would require federal agencies to take the requester's publication history (including through books, articles, and television and radio broadcasts) into consideration when determining eligibility for a waiver of search and copy fees. Agencies would be required to assign a tracking number to each waiver request, indicate its status in response to an online or telephone inquiry, and make a determination on granting the request within 20 days of its receipt.

When neither of these bills advanced, one of the primary Senate sponsors, Sen. John Cornyn (R-Texas), introduced two other measures that made progress in the Senate. The proposed Faster FOIA Act of 2005 (S. 589)—which would establish a Commission on Freedom of Information Act Processing Delays to study and report to Congress on reducing such delays and ensuring efficient and equitable FOIA administration through the federal government—was reported by the Senate Judiciary Committee and at the time of this report awaited action by the full Senate. Cornyn's second, untitled bill (S. 1181), took a provision from the earlier House and Senate bills and managed not only to get it reported out of committee but passed by the full Senate in June. The provision would require that any future legislation to establish a new exemption from disclosure under FOIA must be explicitly identified as such within the text of bill. The Senate-passed bill, along with a companion measure introduced in the House (H.R. 1620), was pending further action in the House.

Education Issues

Higher Education Extension Act of 2005
(H.R. 3784; Public Law No. 109-81; September 30, 2005)

Second Higher Education Extension Act of 2005
(H.R. 4525; Public Law No. 109-150; December 30, 2005)

Departments of Labor, Health and Human Services, and Education, and Related Agencies Appropriations Act of 2006
(H.R. 3010; Public Law No. 109-149; December 30, 2005)

As the end of the First Session rapidly approached, the prospects for enacting legislation to reauthorize the Higher Education Act of 1965 continued to elude legislators, much as they had in the previous Congress. As a result, Congress was forced to forgo proposals to substantively revise various programs authorized under the act, and to twice enact legislation to extend the current authorization for those programs pending full reauthorization legislation. The first extension provided continued authorization for higher education programs until the end of the year, and the second extension—made necessary by congressional failure to meet that deadline—gave the programs continued authorization through March 31, 2006.

At the same time, Congress enacted legislation (H.R. 3010) to appropriate funds for programs under the aegis of the U.S. Department of Education through the fiscal year ending September 30, 2006.

Non-Enacted Legislation

As noted above, legislation intended to reauthorize the Higher Education Act of 1965 was not enacted in 2005, so Congress extended the current authorization for existing programs under that act. Two bills pending in the House (H.R. 609, the College Access and Opportunity Act of 2005) and Senate (S. 1614, the Higher Education Amendments of 2005) were expected to be the primary vehicles for reauthorization legislation when Congress resumed consideration of the issue in the Second Session. At the time of this report, neither of the bills contained provisions regarding the price of college textbooks.

An investigation of textbook pricing by the Government Accountability Office (GAO), which was initiated at the request of House committee leaders during summer 2004, concluded in June 2005 with somewhat flattering results for the publishing industry's efforts to use new technologies to enhance the learning experience. Still, some of the report's less favorable findings regarding cost increases for textbooks in recent years ensured that negative national media coverage continued.

In Congress, the impact of the GAO report was fairly muted, with no reprise of the House subcommittee hearing held in 2004 and only a single piece of responsive legislation introduced in the House and Senate. The proposed Affordable Books for College Act, which was introduced simultaneously in the House by Rep. Tim Ryan (D-Ohio) (H.R. 3259) and in the Senate by Sen. Charles Schumer (D-N.Y.) (S. 1384), would establish a demonstration program in college bookstores allowing students to rent course materials. This legislation attracted no cosponsors in either body and appeared unlikely to be picked up as an amendment to pending reauthorization legislation.

One additional bill noted by AAP in last year's legislation report raises the specter of censorship in school library programs. The proposed Parental Empowerment Act of 2005 (H.R. 2295), which was introduced by Rep. Walter Jones (R-N.C.) and five Republican cosponsors, was apparently inspired by a popular children's book in which a traditional tale now portrays a prince choosing a male, rather than female, consort. The bill calls for the establishment by all local and state educational agencies of "parent review and empowerment councils" to ensure appropriate oversight and input concerning the acquisition of library and classroom-based instructional materials, excluding textbooks, for elementary schools. The bill would make the establishment and maintenance of such councils a condition for states to receive federal educational funding.

AAP's interest in reauthorization of the Higher Education Act, as well as its interest in appropriations for the Department of Education, is usually limited to the provisions in both pieces of legislation that affect federal student loan and grant programs that provide funding for college students to purchase their books and other instructional materials. In 2005, however, the media coverage of student complaints regarding the price of college textbooks—building on the results of the GAO investigation—raised the possibility that members of Congress might utilize the reauthorization or appropriations legislation as vehicles to propose measures addressing those complaints, which might be inimical to the interests of book publishers.

Tax Issues

Katrina Emergency Tax Relief Act of 2005

(H.R. 3768; Public Law No. 109-73; September 9, 2005)

On several occasions over the last few years, Senate legislation has contained proposals to modify the existing Internal Revenue Code provisions establishing a charitable deduction for contributions of book inventory to organizations for educational purposes. When the Senate passed the Charity Aid, Recovery, and Empowerment (CARE) Act (S. 476) by an overwhelming 95–5 vote in April 2003, it looked as though AAP would score another rare victory on tax issues. That legislation, which was a bipartisan compromise version of President Bush's Faith-based and Community Initiative, included the Contributions of Book Inventory Amendment, sponsored by Senator Hatch. Unfortunately, the House did not take up the Senate-passed version of S. 476 but instead passed its own version of the CARE Act (H.R. 7), which did not include any provision regarding charitable deductions for book inventories.

Originally introduced as a stand-alone bill (S. 680), the Senate amendment would have enhanced the charitable tax deduction incentives under existing law for book publishers to contribute excess book inventory to educational organizations, public libraries, and literacy programs. During the previous Congress, Senator Hatch had made sure that a similar provision was included in the Senate-passed version of the administration's major tax legislation, the Relief Act of 2001, but it was dropped with many other provisions from the final version that the president signed into law. AAP staff had worked with Senator Hatch's staff to improve that version of the inventory contributions provisions, and several of the issues raised by AAP resulted in changes in the amendment as introduced and passed in the Senate.

Under current law, a charitable tax deduction for donation of a taxpayer's inventory is limited to the taxpayer's basis (cost) in the inventory. However, a taxpayer may be eligible for an enhanced deduction, which is equal to the lesser of (1) the basis plus one-half of an item's appreciated value, or (2) two times the basis, if the items donated are to be used "solely for the care of the ill, the needy, or infants." Unfortunately, book publishers are often prohibited from receiving an enhanced deduction for charitable contributions of their book inventories because of the requirement that the donation be used solely for the care of the ill, the needy, or infants rather than that it be made to charitable organizations that can use the books.

Under the revised Senate-passed amendment, a special rule would have been carved out for book publishers to receive an enhanced deduction for charitable contributions of their book inventories to schools, libraries, and literacy programs for educational purposes. For qualified book contributions, the ceiling on the enhanced deduction for book publishers would have been the amount by which the fair market value of the contributed materials exceeds twice the taxpayer's basis in the materials. A "qualified book contribution" would have referred to a charitable contribution of books to (1) an educational organization that normally maintains a regular faculty and curriculum and normally has a regularly enrolled body of pupils or students in attendance at the place where its educational activities are regularly carried on (schools); (2) a public library; or, (3) a 501(c)(3) entity that is organized primarily to make books available to the general public at no cost or to operate a literacy program. "Fair market value" would have been determined by reference to a "bona fide published market price" as determined (1) using the same printing and edition; (2) in the usual market in which the book is customarily sold by the taxpayer; and (3) by the validity of the taxpayer's showing that the taxpayer customarily sold such books in arm's length transactions within seven years preceding the contribution. In practical terms, this meant that the "bona fide published market price" for contributed books could not be based on the price from the publisher's own price list or catalog, but instead must be an independently verifiable reference to actual sales of those books. Under the amendment, the donee organization would have to (1) use the books consistent with their exempt purpose; (2) not transfer the books in exchange for money, other property, or services; and (3) certify in writing both that the donated books are suitable, in terms of currency, content, and quantity, for use in the organization's educational programs, and that the books will be used in such educational programs.

Unfortunately, the lack of necessary offsets to pay for the costs of new charitable tax deductions in the CARE Act apparently doomed the effort by the bill's lead sponsors, Sen. Rick Santorum (R-Pa.) and Sen. Joseph Lieberman (D-Conn.), to attach the bill's provisions to that congressional session's only major tax bill, which Congress eventually enacted as the American Jobs Creation Act.

The same provision, with minor modifications, is now contained in a new CARE Act title of the proposed "Marriage, Opportunity, Relief and Empowerment (MORE) Act" (S. 6), which was introduced by Senator Santorum but saw no movement.

In the aftermath of Hurricane Katrina, bipartisan pressure to provide tax relief to the victims of the storm's devastation led Congress to examine a number of tax relief proposals that were pending but not moving through the legislative process. One of these was the charitable deduction for book inventories. However, in keeping with the narrow focus of disaster relief, Congress did not enact the revised deduction as it has appeared in several successive legislative proposals, but provided only a limited tax deduction for the charitable contribution of book inventories to public schools educating children from kindergarten through grade 12. Intended to help Gulf Coast schools replace lost school library collections, the provisions provided only a limited window for this tax relief, applying only to donations made between August 28 and December 31, 2005.

Although the book inventory charitable donation deduction provisions remained pending as part of the proposed MORE Act legislation, the tight budgetary situation made its enactment highly unlikely.

Postal Issues

Non-Enacted Legislation

Comprehensive Postal Reform Legislation

The proposed Postal Accountability and Enhancement Act (H.R. 22) and its Senate counterpart (S. 662) made it back to Capitol Hill in 2005 after failing to reach the floor in either body during the previous Congress. House passage of H.R. 22 in July and Senate committee approval of S. 662 shortly thereafter gave the legislation's sponsors and supporters hope of securing its enactment during the current Congress. However, substantial obstacles still blocked enactment in early 2006.

Among other things, the legislation features reforms that would (1) shift rate regulation from its current litigation model to one tied to the Consumer Price Index for market-dominant products while permitting flexible market pricing for competitive products; (2) define "postal services" and limit the United States Postal Service (USPS) offering of non-postal products; and (3) give the renamed Postal Regulatory Commission subpoena power and broaden its regulatory and oversight functions. Some of these provisions, particularly those establishing new rules for the postage rate-setting process, continue to be the subject of negotiations.

But the most problematic provisions in the bill, which have raised veto threats from the Bush administration, are clearly those that would eliminate the escrow account and military pension policy implemented with passage of the Postal Civil Service Retirement System (CSRS) Funding Reform Act of 2003. That legislation arose out of a financial analysis that the Office of Personnel Management (OPM) conducted at the request of GAO, revealing that USPS had almost fully funded its retirement obligation for postal employees and that additional payments at the current rate would over-fund USPS liability by approximately $71 billion. The new law was the congressional response to this analysis, and was intended to prevent the overpayment by correcting the statutory formula for the USPS contributions to CSRS, while stipulating that the funds saved were to be used by USPS to (1) pay down its debt to the Treasury Department; (2) maintain current postage rates without any increases until 2006 at the earliest; and (3) fund postal retiree health benefits.

Now, however, the provisions of the legislation that would transfer pension cost obligations connected with military service credit for postal employees from USPS to the Treasury Department, in addition to abolishing the 2006 escrow requirement in order to delay the need for a rate case, have been targeted by the Bush administration as budget-busters. In addition, the administration has also questioned whether the legislation has gone far enough in providing transparency to prevent cross-subsidization of competitive products with monopoly product revenue, as well as in providing flexibility to reduce high labor costs.

Even if, as appears likely, the Senate passes S. 662 during the Second Session, the chances for enactment of this legislation during the current Congress will hinge on resolving the administration's budgetary concerns. At the time of this report, it was not clear how that could be accomplished consistent with the desire of both USPS and Congress to use the escrowed funds to put off the need for another postal rate hike so soon after the increase at the beginning of 2006.

Funding Programs and
Grant-Making Agencies

National Endowment for the Humanities

1100 Pennsylvania Ave. N.W., Washington, DC 20506
202-606-8400, 1-800-634-1121
TDD (hearing impaired) 202-606-8282 or 866-372-2930 (toll free)
E-mail Info@NEH.gov, World Wide Web http://www.neh.gov

Thomas C. Phelps

The National Endowment for the Humanities (NEH) is an independent federal agency created in 1965. It is the largest funder of humanities programs in the United States.

Because democracy demands wisdom, NEH serves and strengthens the republic by promoting excellence in the humanities and conveying the lessons of history to all Americans. It accomplishes this mission by providing grants for high-quality humanities projects in four funding areas: preservation and access, education, research, and public programs.

NEH grants typically go to cultural institutions, such as museums, archives, libraries, colleges, universities, public television and radio stations, and to individual scholars. The grants

- Strengthen teaching and learning in the humanities in schools and colleges
- Facilitate research and original scholarship
- Provide opportunities for lifelong learning
- Preserve and provide access to cultural and educational resources
- Strengthen the institutional base of the humanities

Over the past 40 years, NEH has reached millions of Americans with projects and programs that preserve and study the nation's cultural heritage while providing a foundation for the future.

The endowment's mission is to enrich American cultural life by promoting the study of the humanities. According to the National Foundation on the Arts and Humanities Act, "The term 'humanities' includes, but is not limited to, the study of the following: language, both modern and classical; linguistics; literature; history; jurisprudence; philosophy; archaeology; comparative religion; ethics; the history, criticism, and theory of the arts; those aspects of social sciences which have humanistic content and employ humanistic methods; and the study and application of the humanities to the human environment with particular attention to reflecting our diverse heritage, traditions, and history and to the relevance of the humanities to the current conditions of national life."

The act, adopted by Congress in 1965, provided for the establishment of the National Foundation on the Arts and the Humanities in order to promote progress and scholarship in the humanities and the arts in the United States. The act included the following findings:

- The arts and the humanities belong to all the people of the United States.
- The encouragement and support of national progress and scholarship in the humanities and the arts, while primarily a matter for private and local initiative, are also appropriate matters of concern to the federal government.
- An advanced civilization must not limit its efforts to science and technology alone, but must give full value and support to the other great branches of scholarly and cultural activity in order to achieve a better understanding of the past, a better analysis of the present, and a better view of the future.
- Democracy demands wisdom and vision in its citizens. It must therefore foster and support a form of education, and access to the arts and the humanities, designed to make people of all backgrounds and wherever located masters of their technology and not its unthinking servants.
- It is necessary and appropriate for the federal government to complement, assist, and add to programs for the advancement of the humanities and the arts by local, state, regional, and private agencies and their organizations. In doing so, the government must be sensitive to the nature of public sponsorship. Public funding of the arts and humanities is subject to the conditions that traditionally govern the use of public money. Such funding should contribute to public support and confidence in the use of taxpayer funds. Public funds provided by the federal government must ultimately serve public purposes the Congress defines.
- The arts and the humanities reflect the high place accorded by the American people to the nation's rich cultural heritage and to the fostering of mutual respect for the diverse beliefs and values of all persons and groups.

What NEH Grants Accomplish

Since its founding in 1965, NEH has awarded more than 60,000 grants. Following are some facts about NEH grants and their impact.

Interpretive Exhibitions

Interpretive exhibitions provide opportunities for lifelong learning in the humanities for millions of Americans. Since 1967 NEH has made more than 2,400 grants for interpretive exhibitions, catalogs, and public programs, which are among the most highly visible activities supported by the agency. A total of 151 NEH-funded exhibitions will appear across the United States in 2006.

Renewing Teaching

Over the years, more than 60,000 high school and college teachers have deepened their knowledge of the humanities through intensive summer study supported by NEH; tens of thousands of students benefit from these better-educated teachers every year.

Reading and Discussion Programs

Since 1982 the endowment has supported reading and discussion programs in the nation's libraries, bringing people together to discuss works of literature and history. Scholars in the humanities provide thematic direction for the programs. Using selected texts and themes, such as "Work," "Family," "Diversity," and "Not for Children Only," these programs have attracted more than 1 million Americans to read and talk about what they've read.

Preserving the Nation's Heritage

NEH has launched an innovative program, the National Digital Newspaper Program, which is supporting projects to convert microfilm of historically important U.S. newspapers into fully searchable digital files and to mount these files on the Internet. Developed in partnership with the Library of Congress, this complex, long-term project ultimately will make more than 30 million pages of newspapers accessible online.

Stimulating Private Support

More than $1.3 billion in humanities support has been generated by the NEH Challenge Grants program, which requires most grant recipients to raise $3 or $4 in nonfederal funds for every dollar they receive.

Presidential Papers

Ten presidential papers projects are underwritten by NEH, from George Washington to Dwight D. Eisenhower. The Washington and Eisenhower papers have each leveraged more than $1.8 million in nonfederal contributions. In addition to these ongoing projects, NEH has proposed a major initiative to transcribe, digitize, and mount on the Internet the papers of the nation's first four presidents: George Washington, John Adams, Thomas Jefferson, and James Madison.

New Scholarship

NEH grants enable scholars to do in-depth study: Jack Rakove explored the making of the Constitution in his *Original Meanings* and James McPherson chronicled the Civil War in his *Battle Cry of Freedom.* Both won the Pulitzer Prize, as have 13 other recipients of NEH grants.

History on Screen

Nearly 40 million Americans saw the Ken Burns documentary *The Civil War,* and 750,000 people bought the book. Through 340 other NEH-supported films such as *Liberty!, Jazz,* and *The Invisible Man* and film biographies of Theodore and Franklin Roosevelt, Andrew Carnegie, and Gen. Douglas MacArthur, Americans learn about the events and people that shaped the nation.

Library of America

Millions of books have been sold as part of the Library of America series, a collection of the riches of the nation's literature. Begun with NEH seed money, the more than 170 published volumes include the writings of Henry Adams, Edith Wharton, William James, Eudora Welty, W. E. B. DuBois, and many others.

Science and the Humanities

The scientific past is being preserved with NEH-supported editions of the letters of Charles Darwin, the works of Albert Einstein, and the 14-volume papers of Thomas A. Edison.

Learning Under the Tent

Across the country, state humanities councils bring a 21st-century version of Chautauqua to the public, embracing populations of entire towns, cities, or even regions. Scholars portray significant figures such as Meriwether Lewis, Sojourner Truth, Willa Cather, Teddy Roosevelt, and Sacagawea, first speaking as the historic character and later giving audiences opportunities to ask questions. The give-and-take between the scholar/performer and the audiences provides an entertaining, energetic, and thought-provoking exchange about experiences and attitudes in the present and the past.

Technology and the Classroom

NEH's EDSITEment Web site assembles the best humanities resources on the Web, drawing up to 170,000 visitors every month. Online lesson plans help teachers use more than 100 Web sites to enhance their teaching. Schools across the country are developing curricula to bring digital resources to the classroom.

Special Initiatives

We the People

"We the People" is an initiative launched by NEH to encourage the teaching, studying, and understanding of American history and culture. Under this initiative, the endowment invites scholars, teachers, filmmakers, curators, librarians, and others to submit grant applications that explore significant events and themes in the nation's history and culture and that advance knowledge of the principles that define the United States.

Proposals responding to the initiative can take the form of

- New scholarship
- Projects to preserve and provide access to documents and artifacts
- Educational projects for every level, from kindergarten through college
- Public programs in libraries, museums, and historical societies, including exhibitions, film, radio, and Internet-based programs

NEH will accept "We the People" proposals to all programs and all deadlines. Proposals are expected to meet the guidelines of the program that best fits the character of the project. A list of programs and deadlines is available on NEH's Web site, http://www.neh.gov.

Proposals will be evaluated through NEH's established review process and will not receive special consideration. The chairman of NEH reserves the right to determine which grants will be designated as "We the People" projects.

One of the main components of the program is the "We the People" Bookshelf, an annually selected short list of classic books for young readers to be awarded to schools and libraries for use in local programs. The first bookshelf, on the theme of courage (sample titles: *Little House on the Prairie* and *The Adventures of Huckleberry Finn*), and the second bookshelf, on the theme of freedom (sample titles: *The Tale of Peter Rabbit* and *Fahrenheit 451*), both reached 1,000 libraries. The third bookshelf, on "Becoming American" (sample titles: *Rip Van Winkle* and *Giants in the Earth: A Saga of the Prairie*), is expected to reach 2,000 libraries.

Plans include expanding "We the People" through a grant program to support projects that help schools and universities improve their teaching of American history, government, and civics. The summer seminars and institutes program will be expanded to offer teachers more opportunities to study significant texts.

EDSITEment

EDSITEment, a joint project to share the best humanities Web sites with teachers and students, was launched in 1997. Users of EDSITEment now have access to more than 100 high-quality humanities sites, representing more than 50,000 files searchable through the EDSITEment search engine, http://www.edsitement. neh.gov.

Federal-State Partnership

The Office of Federal-State Partnership links NEH with the nationwide network of 56 humanities councils, which are located in each state, the District of Columbia, Puerto Rico, the U.S. Virgin Islands, the Northern Mariana Islands, American Samoa, and Guam. Each humanities council funds humanities programs in its own jurisdiction. A contact list for all the state councils can be found below.

Directory of State Humanities Councils

Alabama

Alabama Humanities Foundation
1100 Ireland Way, Suite 101
Birmingham, AL 35205-7001
205-558-3980, fax 205-558-3981
http://www.ahf.net
Board Chair Elaine Hughes
Executive Robert Stewart

Alaska

Alaska Humanities Forum
421 W. First Ave., Suite 300
Anchorage, AK 99501
907-272-5341, fax 907-272-3979
http://www.akhf.org
Board Chair Talis J. Colberg
Executive Ira Perman

Arizona

Arizona Humanities Council
Ellis-Shackelford House
1242 N. Central Ave.,
Phoenix, AZ 85004-1887
602-257-0335, fax 602-257-0392
http://www.azhumanities.org
Board Chair Diane Hamilton
Executive Juliana Yoder

Arkansas

Arkansas Humanities Council
10800 Financial Centre Pkwy., Suite 465
Little Rock, AR 72211
501-221-0091, fax 501-221-9860
http://www.arkhums.org
Board Chair Barbara W. Heffington
Executive Robert E. Bailey

California

California Council for the Humanities
312 Sutter St., Suite 601
San Francisco, CA 94108
415-391-1474, fax 415-391-1312
http://www.calhum.org
Board Chair Charlene L. Simmons
Executive James Quay

Colorado

Colorado Endowment for the Humanities
1490 Lafayette St., Suite 101
Denver, CO 80218
303-894-7951, fax 303-864-9361
http://www.ceh.org
Board Chair Marguerite Salazar
Executive Margaret A. Coval

Connecticut

Connecticut Humanities Council
955 S. Main St., Suite E
Middletown, CT 06457
860-685-2260, fax 860-704-0429
http://www.ctculture.org
Board Chair Carol Clapp
Executive Bruce Fraser

Delaware

Delaware Humanities Forum
100 W. Tenth St., Suite 1009
Wilmington, DE 19801
302-657-0650, fax 302-657-0655
http://www.dhf.org
Board Chair Megan Mantzavinos
Executive Marilyn Whittington

District of Columbia

Humanities Council of Washington, D.C.
925 U St. N.W.
Washington, DC 20001
202-387-8393, fax 202-387-8149
http://wdchumanities.org
Board Chair Donald Murray
Executive Joy Austin

Florida

Florida Humanities Council
599 Second St. S.
St. Petersburg, FL 33701-5005
772-553-3800, fax 772-553-3829
http://www.flahum.org
Board Chair Kathleen Deagan
Executive Janine Farver

Georgia

Georgia Humanities Council
50 Hurt Plaza S.E., Suite 595
Atlanta, GA 30303-2915
404-523-6220, fax 404-523-5702
http://www.georgiahumanities.org
Board Chair Steve Wrigley
Executive Jamil Zainaldin

Hawaii

Hawaii Council for the Humanities
First Hawaiian Bank Bldg.
3599 Waialae Ave., Room 23
Honolulu, HI 96816
808-732-5402, fax 808-732-5402
http://www.hihumanities.org
Board Chair Gail Ainsworth
Executive Robert Buss

Idaho

Idaho Humanities Council
217 W. State St.
Boise, ID 83702
208-345-5346, fax 208-345-5347
http://www.idahohumanities.org
Board Chair Marc Johnson
Executive Rick Ardinger

Illinois

Illinois Humanities Council
203 N. Wabash Ave., Suite 2020
Chicago, IL 60601-2417
312-422-5580, fax 312-422-5588
http://www.prairie.org
Board Chair Arthur Sussman
Executive Kristina Valaitis

Indiana

Indiana Humanities Council
1500 N. Delaware St.
Indianapolis, IN 46202
317-638-1500, fax 317-634-9503
http://www.ihc4u.org
Board Chair Larry S. Wechter
Executive Scott T. Massey

Iowa

Humanities Iowa
100 Oakdale Campus, Northlawn
University of Iowa
Iowa City, IA 52242-5000
319-335-4153, fax 319-335-4154
http://www.humanitiesiowa.org
Board Chair John C. Fitzpatrick
Executive Christopher Rossi

Kansas

Kansas Humanities Council
112 S.W. Sixth Ave., Suite 210
Topeka, KS 66603
785-357-0359, fax 785-357-1723
http://www.kansashumanities.org
Board Chair Judy Billings
Executive Marion Cott

Kentucky

Kentucky Humanities Council
206 E. Maxwell St.
Lexington, KY 40508
859-257-5932, fax 859-257-5933
http://www.kyhumanities.org
Board Chair James Parker
Executive Virginia Smith

Louisiana

Louisiana Endowment for the Humanities
938 Lafayette St., Suite 300
New Orleans, LA 70113-1027
504-523-4352, fax 504-529-2358
http://www.leh.org
Board Chair R. Lewis McHenry
Executive Michael Sartisky

Maine

Maine Humanities Council
674 Brighton Ave.
Portland, ME 04102-1012
207-773-5051, fax 207-773-2416
http://www.mainehumanities.org
Board Chair Richard Barnes
Executive Dorothy Schwartz

Maryland

Maryland Humanities Council
108 W. Centre St.,
Baltimore, MD 21201-4565
410-685-0095, fax 410-685-0795
http://www.mdhc.org
Board Chair Stanley C. Gabor
Executive Margaret Burke

Massachusetts

Massachusetts Foundation for the Humanities
66 Bridge St.
Northampton, MA 01060
413-584-8440, fax 413-584-8454
http://www.mfh.org
Board Chair John Dacey
Executive David Tebaldi

Michigan

Michigan Humanities Council
119 Pere Marquette Drive, Suite 3B
Lansing, MI 48912-1270
517-372-7770, fax 517-372-0027
http://michiganhumanities.org
Board Chair James McConnell
Executive Jan Fedewa

Minnesota

Minnesota Humanities Commission
987 E. Ivy Ave.
St. Paul, MN 55106-2046
651-774-0105, fax 651-774-0205
http://www.minnesotahumanities.org
Board Chair Humphrey Doermann
Executive Stanley Romanstein

Mississippi

Mississippi Humanities Council
3825 Ridgewood Rd., Room 311
Jackson, MS 39211
601-432-6752, fax 601-432-6750
http://www.mshumanities.org
Board Chair Willis Lott
Executive Barbara Carpenter

Missouri

Missouri Humanities Council
543 Hanley Industrial Court, Suite 201

St. Louis, MO 63144-1905
314-781-9660, fax 314-781-9681
http://www.mohumanities.org
Board Chair W. Nicholas Knight
Executive Michael Bouman

Montana

Montana Committee for the Humanities
311 Brantly Hall
University of Montana
Missoula, MT 59812-8214
406-243-6022, fax 406-243-4836
http://www.humanities-mt.org
Board Chair Jean Steele
Executive Mark Sherouse

Nebraska

Nebraska Humanities Council
Lincoln Center Bldg., Suite 500
215 Centennial Mall South
Lincoln, NE 68508
402-474-2131, fax 402-474-4852
http://www.nebraskahumanties.org
Board Chair Peter Longo
Executive Jane Renner Hood

Nevada

Nevada Humanities Committee
1034 N. Sierra St.
Reno, NV 89507
775-784-6587, fax 775-784-6527
http://www.nevadahumanities.org
Board Chair Belinda Quilici
Executive Judith K. Winzeler

New Hampshire

New Hampshire Humanities Council
19 Pillsbury St.
P.O. Box 2228
Concord, NH 03302-2228
603-224-4071, fax 603-224-4072
http://www.nhhc.org
Board Chair John P. Resch
Executive Deborah Watrous

New Jersey

New Jersey Council for the Humanities
28 W. State St.
Trenton, NJ 08608

609-695-4838, fax 609-695-4929
http://www.njch.org
Board Chair Zachary M. Narrett
Executive Jane Rutkoff

New Mexico

New Mexico Humanities Council
1 University of New Mexico
Albuquerque, NM 87131-0001
505-277-3705, fax 505-277-6056
http://www.nmeh.org
Board Chair Albert Westwood
Executive Craig L. Newbill

New York

New York Council for the Humanities
150 Broadway, Suite 1700
New York, NY 10038
212-233-1131, fax 212-233-4607
http://www.nyhumanities.org
Board Chair Donn Rogosin
Executive David Cronin

North Carolina

North Carolina Humanities Council
122 N. Elm St., Suite 601
Greensboro, NC 27401
336-334-5325, fax 336-334-5052
http://www.nchumanities.org
Board Chair Lucinda H. MacKethan
Executive Douglas Quin

North Dakota

North Dakota Humanities Council
2900 Broadway East, Suite 3
P.O. Box 2191
Bismarck, ND 58502
701-255-3360, fax 701-223-8724
http://www.nd-humanities.org
Board Chair Janet E. Rowse
Executive Janet Daley

Ohio

Ohio Humanities Council
471 E. Broad St., Suite 1620
Columbus, OH 43215-3857
614-461-7802, fax 614-461-4651
http://www.ohiohumanities.org

Board Chair Allan Winkler
Executive Gale E. Peterson

Oklahoma

Oklahoma Humanities Council
Festival Plaza
428 W. California, Suite 270
Oklahoma City, OK 73102
405-235-0280, fax 405-235-0289
http://www.okhumanitiescouncil.org
Board Chair Ann Frankland
Executive Anita May

Oregon

Oregon Council for the Humanities
812 S.W. Washington St., Suite 225
Portland, OR 97205
503-241-0543, fax 503-241-0024
http://www.oregonhum.org
Board Chair Gene d'Autremont
Executive Christopher Zinn

Pennsylvania

Pennsylvania Humanities Council
325 Chestnut St., Suite 715
Philadelphia, PA 19106-2607
215-925-1005, fax 215-925-3054
http://www.pahumanities.org
Board Chair Michael A. Tomor
Executive Joseph Kelly

Rhode Island

Rhode Island Council for the Humanities
385 Westminster St., Suite 2
Providence, RI 02903
401-273-2250, fax 401-454-4872
http://www.rihumanities.org
Board Chair Eugene B. Mihaly
Executive Sara Archambault

South Carolina

Humanities Council of South Carolina
2711 Middleburg Drive, Suite 308
P.O. Box 5287
Columbia, SC 29254
803-771-2477, fax 803-771-2487
http://www.schumanities.org
Board Chair Byron E. Gipson
Executive Randy L. Akers

South Dakota

South Dakota Humanities Council
Box 7050, University Station
Brookings, SD 57007
605-688-6113, fax 605-688-4531
http://web.sdstate.edu/humanities
Board Chair John A. Lyons
Executive Donald Simmons

Tennessee

Humanities Tennessee
306 Gay St., Suite 306
Nashville, TN 37201
615-770-0006, fax 615-770-0007
http://www.humanitiestennessee.org
Board Chair Jane Walters
Executive Robert Cheatham

Texas

Humanities Texas
Banister Place A
3809 S. Second St.
Austin, TX 78704
512-440-1991, fax 512-440-0115
http://www.humanitiestexas.org
Board Chair Jo Anne Christian
Executive Michael Gillette

Utah

Utah Humanities Council
202 W. 300 North
Salt Lake City, UT 84103-1108
801-359-9670, fax 801-531-7869
http://www.utahhumanities.org
Board Chair Phillip Bimstein
Executive Cynthia Buckingham

Vermont

Vermont Humanities Council
200 Park St.
RR 1, Box 7285
Morrisville, VT 05661
802-888-3183, fax 802-888-1236
http://www.vermonthumanities.org
Board Chair William E. Dakin, Jr.
Executive Peter A. Gilbert

Virginia

Virginia Foundation for the Humanities and
  Public Policy
145 Ednam Drive
Charlottesville, VA 22903-4629
434-924-3296, fax 434-296-4714
http://www.virginia.edu/vfh
Board Chair Elizabeth L. Young
Executive Robert C. Vaughan

Washington

Humanities Washington
615 Second Ave., Suite 300
Seattle, WA 98104
206-682-1770, fax 206-682-4158
http://www.humanities.org
Board Chair Maureen Herward
Acting Executive Amanda Swain

West Virginia

West Virginia Humanities Council
1310 Kanawha Blvd. East
Charleston, WV 25301
304-346-8500, fax 304-346-8504
http://www.wvhumanities.org
Board Chair Jill Wilson
Executive Kenneth Sullivan

Wisconsin

Wisconsin Humanities Council
222 S. Bedford St., Suite F
Madison, WI 53703-3688
608-262-0706, fax 608-263-7970
http://www.wisconsinhumanities.org
Board Chair David Brostrom
Executive Constantine Bakopoulos

Wyoming

Wyoming Council for the Humanities
1315 E. Lewis St.
Laramie, WY 82072-3459
307-721-9244, fax 307-742-4914
http://uwadmnweb.uwyo.edu/humanities
Board Chair Laurie Latta
Executive Marcia Britton

American Samoa

Amerika Samoa Humanities Council
P.O. Box 5800
Pago Pago, AS 96799
684-633-4870, fax 684-633-4873
http://www.ashumanities.org
Board Chair Fonoti Savali Vaeao
Executive Niualama Taifane

Guam

Guam Humanities Council
Bank of Guam Headquarters Bldg., Suite 711
111 Chalan Santo Papa
Hagatna, Guam 96910
671-646-4460, fax 671-472-4465
http://www.guamhumanitiescouncil.org
Board Chair Nick Goetzfridt
Executive Kimberlee Kihleng

Northern Mariana Islands

Northern Mariana Islands Council for the
  Humanities
P.O. Box 506437
Saipan, MP 96950

670-235-4785, fax 670-235-4786
http://cnmi.humanities.org.mp
Board Chair Herman T. Guerrero
Executive Paz C. Younis

Puerto Rico

Fundación Puertorriqueña de las
  Humanidades
109 San Jose St., 3rd floor
Box 9023920
San Juan, PR 00902-3920
787-721-2087, fax 787-721-2684
http://www.fprh.org
Board Chair Miguel Rodriguez
Executive Juan M. González Lamela

Virgin Islands

Virgin Islands Humanities Council
1826 Kongens Gade 5-6, Suite 2
St. Thomas, VI 00802
340-776-4044, fax 340-774-3972
http://www.vihumanities.org
Board Chair Roberta Q. Knowles
Executive Mabel J. Maduro

NEH Overview

Division of Preservation and Access

Grants are made for projects that will create, preserve, and increase the availability of resources important for research, education, and public programming in the humanities.

Projects may encompass books, journals, newspapers, manuscript and archival materials, maps, still and moving images, sound recordings, and objects of material culture held by libraries, archives, museums, historical organizations, and other repositories.

Preservation and Access Projects

Support may be sought to preserve the intellectual content and aid bibliographic control of collections; to compile bibliographies, descriptive catalogs, and guides to cultural holdings; to create dictionaries, encyclopedias, databases, and other types of research tools and reference works; and to stabilize material culture collections through the appropriate housing and storing of objects, improved environmental control, and the installation of security, lighting, and fire-prevention systems. Applications may also be submitted for national and regional education and training projects, regional preservation field service programs, and research and demonstration projects that are intended to enhance institutional practice and the use of technology for preservation and access.

Proposals may combine preservation and access activities within a single project. Historically Black Colleges and Universities with significant institutional collections of primary materials are encouraged to apply.

Eligible applicants: Individuals, nonprofit institutions and cultural organizations, state agencies, and institutional consortia.

Application deadlines: May 15, July 3, July 17, and October 2, 2006

Contact: 202-606-8570, e-mail preservation@neh.gov

Division of Public Programs

This division fosters public understanding and appreciation of the humanities by supporting projects that bring significant insights into these disciplines to general audiences of all ages through interpretive exhibitions, radio and television programs, lectures, symposia, multimedia projects, printed materials, and reading and discussion groups.

Grants support consultation with scholars and humanities programming experts to shape an interpretive project; the planning and production of television and radio programs in the humanities intended for general audiences; the planning and implementation of exhibitions, the interpretation of historic sites, and the production of related publications, multimedia components, and educational programs; and the planning and implementation of projects through the use of books, new technologies, and other resources in the collections of libraries and archives in formats such as reading and discussion programs, lectures, symposia, and interpretive exhibitions of books, manuscripts, and other library resources.

Eligible applicants: Nonprofit institutions and organizations including public television and radio stations and state humanities councils.

Application deadlines: Planning, scripting, implementation, production, March 20, September 12, and November 3, 2006; Consultation grants, March 20 and September 12, 2006

Contact: 202-606-8269, e-mail publicpgms@neh.gov

Division of Research Programs

Through fellowships to individual scholars and grants to support complex, frequently collaborative, research, the Division of Research Programs contributes to the creation of knowledge in the humanities.

Fellowships and Stipends

Grants provide support for scholars to undertake full-time independent research and writing in the humanities. Grants are available for a maximum of one year and a minimum of two months of summer study.

Eligible applicants:	Individuals
Application deadlines:	Fellowships, May 1, 2006; Summer Stipends, October 2, 2006
Contact:	202-606-8200, e-mail (fellowships) fellowships@neh.gov; (summer stipends) stipends@neh.gov

Research

Grants provide up to three years of support for collaborative research in the preparation for publication of editions, translations, and other important works in the humanities, and in the conduct of large or complex interpretive studies including archaeology projects and humanities studies of science and technology. Grants also support research opportunities offered through independent research centers and international research organizations.

Eligible applicants:	Individuals, institutions of higher education, nonprofit professional associations, scholarly societies, and other nonprofit organizations
Application deadlines:	Collaborative Research, November 1, 2006; Fellowship Programs at Independent Research Institutions, September 1, 2006
Contact:	202-606-8200, e-mail research@neh.gov

Division of Education

Through grants to educational institutions, fellowships to scholars and teachers, and through the support of significant research, this division is designed to strengthen sustained, thoughtful study of the humanities at all levels of education.

Grants support curriculum and materials development efforts, faculty study programs within and among educational institutions, and conferences and networks of institutions. The endowment is interested in projects that help teachers use electronic technologies to enhance students' understanding of humanities subjects.

Eligible applicants:	Public and private elementary and secondary schools, school systems, colleges and universities, nonprofit academic associations, and cultural institutions, such as libraries and museums
Application deadlines:	Grants for Teaching and Learning Resources and Curriculum Development, October 2, 2006; Humanities Initiatives for Faculty at Historically Black, Hispanic-Serving, and Tribal Colleges and Universities, June 15, 2006; Landmarks of American History and Culture: Workshops for School Teachers, March 15, 2006; Landmarks of American History and Culture: Workshops for Community College Faculty, March 15, 2006; Faculty Humanities Workshops, September 15, 2006
Contact:	202-606-8500, e-mail education@neh.gov

Seminars and Institutes

Grants support summer seminars and national institutes in the humanities for college and school teachers. These faculty development activities are conducted at colleges and universities across the country. Those wishing to participate in seminars submit their seminar applications to the seminar director.

Eligibility:	Individuals and institutions of higher learning
Application deadlines:	Participants, March 1, 2007, for summer seminars and institutes in 2007; Directors, March 1, 2007, for summer seminars and institutes in 2008
Contact:	202-606-8463, e-mail sem-inst@neh.gov

Office of Challenge Grants

Nonprofit institutions interested in developing new sources of long-term support for educational, scholarly, preservation, and public programs in the humanities may be assisted in these efforts by an NEH Challenge Grant. Grantees are required to raise $3 or $4 in new or increased donations for every federal dollar offered. Both federal and nonfederal funds may be used to establish or increase institutional endowments and thus guarantee long-term support for a variety of humanities needs. Funds may also be used for limited direct capital expenditures where such needs are compelling and clearly related to improvements in the humanities.

Eligible applicants:	Nonprofit postsecondary, educational, research, or cultural institutions and organizations working within the humanities.
Application deadlines:	May 1 and November 1, 2006
Contact:	202-606-8309, e-mail challenge@neh.gov

Institute of Museum and Library Services
Library Programs

1800 M St. N.W., Ninth Floor, Washington, DC 20036-5802
202-653-4657, fax 202-653-4625
World Wide Web http://www.imls.gov

Anne-Imelda Radice

Director

Mission

The Institute of Museum and Library Services (IMLS) is an independent federal agency. Recognizing that lifelong learning is critical to both societal and individual success, IMLS sees as its mission "creating and sustaining a nation of learners." Through its grant making, convenings, research, and publications, IMLS empowers museums and libraries nationwide to provide leadership and services to enhance learning in families and communities, sustain cultural heritage, build 21st-century skills, and provide opportunities for civic participation.

Overview

Libraries and museums help create vibrant, energized learning communities. Our achievement as individuals and our success as a democratic society depend on learning continually, adapting to change readily, and evaluating information critically.

As stewards of cultural heritage, information, and ideas, museums and libraries traditionally have played a vital role in helping people experience, explore, discover, and make sense of the world. That role is now more essential than ever. Through building technological infrastructure and strengthening community relationships, libraries and museums can offer the public unprecedented access and expertise in transforming "information overload" into knowledge.

IMLS provides leadership and funding for the nation's museums and libraries, resources these institutions need to fulfill their mission of becoming centers of learning for life—crucial to achieving personal fulfillment, a productive work force, and an engaged citizenry.

Specifically, the Museum and Library Services Act authorizes IMLS to

Library Services and Technology Act (LSTA)

- Promote improvements in library services in all types of libraries to better serve the people of the United States
- Facilitate access to resources in all types of libraries for the purpose of cultivating an educated and informed citizenry
- Encourage resource sharing among all types of libraries for the purpose of achieving economical and efficient delivery of library services to the public

Museum Services Act

- Encourage and support museums in carrying out their public service role of connecting the whole society to cultural, artistic, historic, natural, and scientific understandings that constitute our heritage
- Encourage and support museums in carrying out their educational role as core providers of learning and in conjunction with schools, families, and communities
- Encourage leadership, innovation, and applications of the most current technologies and practices to enhance museum services
- Assist, encourage, and support museums in carrying out their stewardship responsibilities to achieve the highest standards in conservation and care of the cultural, historic, natural, and scientific heritage of the United States to benefit future generations
- Assist, encourage, and support museums in achieving the highest standards of management and service to the public, and ease the financial burden borne by museums as a result of their increasing use by the public
- Support resource sharing and partnerships among museums, libraries, schools, and other community organizations

In 2005 Congress appropriated $198,933,000 for the programs and administrative support authorized by LSTA. The Office of Library Services within IMLS, under the policy direction of the IMLS director and deputy director, administers LSTA programs. The office comprises the Division of State Programs, which administers the Grants to States program, and the Division of Discretionary Programs, which administers the National Leadership Grants program, the Librarians for the 21st Century program, the Native American Library Services program, the Native Hawaiian Library Services program, and the Partnership for a Nation of Learners Community Collaboration Grants program (a leadership initiative of IMLS and the Corporation for Public Broadcasting). IMLS also presents annual awards to libraries through the National Awards for Museum and Library Service program. Additionally, IMLS is one of the sponsoring organizations supporting the Coming Up Taller awards (in conjunction with the President's Committee on the Arts and the Humanities, the National Endowment for the Arts, and the National Endowment for the Humanities) and Save America's Treasures (in partnership with the National Park Service, the National Trust for Historic Preservation, Heritage Preservation, the National Endowment for the Arts, and the National Park Foundation).

Impact of Museum and Library Services

The Museum and Library Services Act also authorizes IMLS to analyze the impact of library and museum services, in consultation with state library administrative agencies; state, regional, and national library and museum organizations; and other relevant agencies and organizations. The analyses are intended to identify national needs for and trends in museum and library services made available under the act; report on impact and effectiveness of programs conducted with funds made available by IMLS in addressing such needs; and identify and disseminate information on best practices.

State-Administered Programs

In fiscal year (FY) 2005, approximately 80 percent of the annual federal appropriation under LSTA was distributed through the Grants to States program to the state library administrative agencies (SLAAs) according to a population-based formula. The formula consists of a minimum amount set by law plus a supplemental amount based on population. Population data was based on the information available from the Bureau of Census Web site on October 1, 2004. The 2003 reauthorization requires that base allotments of $340,000 to the states and $40,000 to the Pacific Territories be increased to $680,000 for the states and $60,000 for the Pacific Territories if IMLS is fully funded. The new base allotments will be phased in gradually as the total appropriation increases. For 2005 the adjusted base allotment to the states was $537,481; that for the Pacific Territories remained the same.

For FY 2005 the Grants to States program total appropriation was $160,704,000 (see Table 1). State agencies may use the appropriation for statewide initiatives and services. They may also distribute the funds through competitive subgrants or cooperative agreements to public, academic, research, school, or special libraries. For-profit and federal libraries are not eligible applicants. LSTA State Grant funds have been used to meet the special needs of children, parents, teenagers, the unemployed, senior citizens, and the business community, as well as adult learners. Many libraries have partnered with community organizations to provide a variety of services and programs, including access to electronic databases, computer instruction, homework centers, summer reading programs, digitization of special collections, access to e-books and adaptive technology, bookmobile service, and development of outreach programs to the underserved. LSTA limits the amount of funds available for administration at the state level to 4 percent and requires a 34 percent match from nonfederal state or local funds.

Grants to the Pacific Territories and the Freely Associated States (FAS) are funded under a Special Rule, 20 USCA 9131(b)(3), which authorizes a small competitive grants program in the Pacific and the U.S. Virgin Islands. There are seven eligible entities: Guam, American Samoa, and the Commonwealth of Northern Mariana Islands, which together are the Pacific Territories (Insular Areas); the Federated States of Micronesia, the Republic of the Marshall Islands, and the Republic of Palau, which together are the FAS; and the Virgin Islands. The funds for this grant program are taken from the allotments for the FAS, but not from the allotments to the territories. The territories (Guam, American Samoa, the Northern Mariana Islands, and the U.S. Virgin Islands) receive their allotments through the regular program and, in addition, may apply for funds under this program. In FY 2005, $203,404 was available for the seven entities. This amount included a set-aside of 5 percent because Pacific Resources for Education and Learning (PREL), based in Hawaii, facilitated the competition. PREL received the set-aside amount to administer parts of the program. Therefore, the total awarded in FY 2005 was $193,234.

Priorities for funding programs and services that support the goals of LSTA are set by the individual SLAAs based on needs they identify in the statutorily required five-year plans that they submit to IMLS. In response to the Youth Initiative of First Lady Laura Bush, the Grants to States program developed the outcomes-based evaluation Task Force on Summer Reading Programs. This task force will develop evaluation tools that can be used by states that fund summer reading programs. Other task forces are planned to assist IMLS in evaluating LSTA-funded projects.

On a rotating basis, program staff conduct site visits to provide technical support and to monitor the states' success in administering the program. This year, program officers visited Colorado, Connecticut, the District of Columbia, Illinois, Iowa, Montana, and West Virginia.

Discretionary Programs

In 1998 IMLS began administering the discretionary programs of LSTA. In FY 2005, a total of $38,589,000 was allocated for the National Leadership Grants program, the Librarians for the 21st Century program, the Native American Library Services program, and the Native Hawaiian Library Services program. In addition, $7,807,000 was awarded in congressionally directed grants.

The FY 2005 congressional appropriation for discretionary programs included the following:

- National Leadership Grants (including Partnership for a Nation of Learners grants), $12,301,000
- Librarians for the 21st Century, $22,816,000
- Native American Library Services, $2,976,000
- Native Hawaiian Library Services, $496,000

National Leadership Grants Program

The National Leadership Grants program provides funding for innovative model programs to enhance the quality of library services nationwide. National Leadership Grants are competitive and intended to produce results useful for the broader library community.

In 2005 IMLS awarded 28 National Leadership Grants totaling $10,850,995. A total of 147 applications were received, requesting $58,061,717. The projects funded were selected as innovative model projects in the field of library and information science in three categories: Advancing Learning Communities, Building Digital Resources, and Research and Demonstration (see Table 2). These categories replaced the 2004 categories of Continuing Education, Library-Museum Collaboration, Preservation or Digitization, and Research and Demonstration.

Advancing Learning Communities—This category creates new opportunities for libraries and museums to engage with other educational and community organizations to support the educational, economic, and social needs of learners of all ages. Priorities were

- To meet clearly defined community needs through innovative collaborations between museums and libraries, and with other organizations as appropriate
- To promote learning in formal or informal settings through designs based on current research in cognition and learning
- To promote learning through innovative uses of technology to deliver library and/or museum resources
- To effectively engage communities in learning through the services of museums and libraries (communities may include families, teachers, students, caregivers, museum and/or library staff, and others, especially in groups that cross generational and other social boundaries)
- To enhance learning by exploring the relationship between digital and physical learning experiences
- To create learning through innovative approaches to delivering library and museum content and services via the Internet2 network

Building Digital Resources—This category supports the creation, use, preservation, and presentation of significant digital resources as well as the development of tools to manage digital assets. IMLS supported projects that

- Improved or broadened community access to library and museum resources through innovative approaches and improved practice for digital resources
- Demonstrated approaches that effectively preserve or archive digital media
- Helped individuals and organizations manage, present, and use digital assets effectively through authoring, annotation, personalization, or other tools
- Demonstrated and evaluated the effectiveness of large-scale collaborative approaches to managing and preserving digital resources, especially projects of a statewide, multistate, thematic, or national scope
- Tested, or developed and tested, business or service models for sustaining digital assets

Research and Demonstration—This category supports basic and applied research and demonstration projects to test potential solutions to problems in a real-world environment. Priorities were

- To provide knowledge that enhances people's ability to use library and museum resources
- To enhance library or museum services, including preservation, through the effective and efficient use of new and appropriate technologies
- To collaboratively develop new standards for library or museum services

- To evaluate the impact of libraries and library services, and museums and museum services, on users or communities
- To improve knowledge about users' information needs, expectations, and behaviors
- To investigate or develop systems of knowledge organization, such as taxonomies and ontologies, to enhance information discovery
- To investigate issues such as knowledge integration, digital preservation, interoperability, or the integration of digital and physical experiences (see the discussion in "Report of the Workshop on Opportunities for Research on the Creation, Management, Preservation and Use of Digital Content" at http://www.imls.gov/pdf/digitalopp.pdf)
- To investigate how learning takes place in libraries and museums

Partnership for a Nation of Learners

Partnership for a Nation of Learners (PNL) Community Collaboration Grants, a joint funding program of IMLS and the Corporation for Public Broadcasting (CPB), strengthen the ability of libraries, museums, and public broadcasting licensees to work together to help audiences enhance their engagement in community, work, family, and society.

IMLS and CPB created the PNL Community Collaboration Grants program in September 2004. The partnership includes a pilot competitive grant program, a professional development curriculum, and a Web site (http://www.partnership forlearners.org) that will serve as the project's "knowledge commons." In 2005 seven PNL grants were awarded totaling $1,447,022 (see Table 2). The funded projects were models of collaboration in response to local community needs. A total of 132 eligible applications requesting $26,467,615 were received.

The PNL program particularly encourages projects that

- Build or strengthen long-term relationships among the partners and with other community organizations, with an emphasis on how the project meets the documented needs of the community
- Enhance lifelong learning across the potential audience spectrum through innovative programs or services
- Develop or adapt innovative applications of technology for education
- Reach new or underserved audiences and communities

Librarians for the 21st Century

The Librarians for the 21st Century program provides competitive funding to support projects to recruit and educate the next generation of librarians and library leaders, to build institutional capacity in graduate schools of library and information science and develop faculty who will help in this endeavor, to conduct needed research on the demographics and needs of the profession, and to support programs of continuing education and training in library and information science for librarians and library staff.

In FY 2005 IMLS awarded 38 grants totaling $21,477,221 for the Librarians for the 21st Century grant program (see Table 3). (Including an additional $19,980 awarded in two small, out-of-cycle grants, the total awarded increases to $21,497,201 for FY 2005.) Eighty-six applications requesting $47,976,688 were received.

The 2005 priorities for the Librarians for the 21st Century grant funding were as follows:

- Priority 1, Master's Programs—to educate the next generation of librarians; in particular, to increase the number of students enrolled in nationally accredited graduate library programs preparing for careers of service in libraries
- Priority 2, Doctoral Programs—(1) to develop faculty to educate the next generation of library professionals; in particular, to increase the number of students enrolled in doctoral programs that will prepare faculty to teach master's students who will work in school, public, and academic libraries, and (2) to develop the next generation of library leaders; in particular, to increase the number of students enrolled in doctoral programs that will prepare them to assume positions as library managers and administrators
- Priority 3, Preprofessional Programs—to recruit future librarians; in particular, to attract promising junior high, high school, or college students to consider careers in librarianship through statewide or regional pilot projects employing recruitment strategies that are cost-effective and measurable
- Priority 4, Research—to provide the library community with information needed to support successful recruitment and education of the next generation of librarians; in particular, through funded research, to establish baseline data on professional demographics and job availability, and to evaluate current programs in library education for their capacity to meet the identified needs
- Priority 5, Programs to Build Institutional Capacity—to develop or enhance curricula within graduate schools of library and information science; in particular, to develop or enhance courses or programs of study for library, museum, and archives professionals in the creation, management, preservation, presentation, and use of digital assets; to develop or enhance courses or programs of study relating to the development of critical thinking skills, such as organization leadership and research methods; and to broaden the library and information science curriculum by incorporating perspectives from other disciplines and fields of scholarship, such as public policy, ethics, American studies, urban planning, mass communication, and instructional design
- Priority 6, Continuing Education—to develop or enhance programs of continuing education and training in library and information science for librarians and library staff

Native American Library Services Program

The Native American Library Services program provides opportunities for improved library services to an important part of the nation's community of library users. The program offers three types of support to serve the range of needs of Indian tribes and Alaska Native villages. In 2005 IMLS distributed $2,970,000 in grants under the program, which offers three types of support:

- Basic library services grants, in the amount of $5,000, which support core library operations on a noncompetitive basis for all eligible Indian tribes and Alaska Native villages that apply for such support. IMLS awarded basic grants to 62 tribes in 15 states in 2005. The amount of the basic grant was increased from $4,000 in FY 2004 to $5,000 in 2005.
- Basic library services grants with a supplemental education/assessment option of $1,000, totaling $6,000, which were implemented for the first time in 2005. IMLS awarded basic grants with the education/assessment option to 176 tribes in 25 states. The purpose of the education/assessment option is to provide funding for library staff to attend continuing education courses and/or training workshops on site or off site; for library staff to attend or give presentations at conferences relating to library services; and/or to hire a consultant for an on-site professional library assessment. This option replaces the professional assistance grant category.
- Enhancement grants, which support new levels of library service for activities specifically identified under LSTA. In 2005 these competitive awards ranged from $35,273 to $149,986. Of the 41 applications received, IMLS awarded 13 enhancement grants for a total of $1,604,000 (see Table 4).

Native Hawaiian Library Services Program

The Native Hawaiian Library Services program provides opportunities for improved library services through grants to nonprofit organizations that primarily serve and represent Native Hawaiians (as the term "Native Hawaiian" is defined in section 7207 of the Native Hawaiian Education Act, 20 U.S.C. 7517). In 2005 one Native Hawaiian Library Services grant was awarded to Alu Like, Inc., of Honolulu in the amount of $496,000.

National Awards for Museum and Library Service

The National Award for Museum Service was established in 1994, and the National Award for Library Service was first awarded in 2000. These awards honor outstanding American libraries and museums that have made a significant and exceptional contribution to their communities. They recognize libraries and museums that demonstrate extraordinary and innovative approaches to public service, and that reach beyond the expected levels of community outreach and core programs generally associated with such services. The principal criterion for selection is evidence of the library or museum's systematic and ongoing commitment to public service through exemplary and innovative programs and community partnerships. The winning institutions each receive $10,000.

The winners of the 2005 National Awards for Museum and Library Service were COSI Toledo, Toledo, Ohio; Johnson County Library, Overland Park, Kansas; Levine Museum of the New South, Charlotte, North Carolina; Mathews Memorial Library, Mathews, Virginia; Pratt Museum, Homer, Alaska; and Saint Paul Public Library, Saint Paul, Minnesota.

Evaluation of IMLS Programs

IMLS has taken a leadership role in evaluating its programs through incorporating outcomes-based measurement as a tool to document effectiveness of funded projects. Within the state-administered programs, IMLS continued to provide training in outcomes-based evaluation (OBE). LSTA requires that each state library administrative agency independently evaluate its LSTA activities before the end of the state LSTA five-year plan. In addition, IMLS trains new competitive grants recipients in OBE and presents information about evaluation at state, regional, and national professional meetings.

To ensure that it is meeting current public and professional needs in library services, IMLS routinely seeks advice from diverse representatives of the library community, carries out studies of library practice, and evaluates its programs with the assistance of external consultants.

IMLS Conferences and Activities

More than 300 archivists, museum curators, systems scientists, educators, historians, librarians, and technology leaders assembled for the 2005 Web-Wise conference in Washington, D.C., February 16–18, 2005. Experts from across the country shared the latest research and advances in digital collections from the nation's museums and libraries. The focus of the conference was teaching and learning with digital resources. To further extend the benefit of this conference, selected papers were printed in the June 2005 issue of *First Monday* (vol. 10, no. 6) at http://www.firstmonday.org/issues/issue10_6. Streaming video of the conference is available at http://www.uic.edu/depts/lib/webwise/videos.html.

IMLS co-organized a Canada-U.S. Dialogue on Digital Heritage in cooperation with the Department of Canadian Heritage and the Canadian Heritage Information Network on August 30, 2005, and cooperated in organization of a Broadband Discussion Day with the Canadian Heritage Information Network and Library and Archives Canada on August 31 in Gatineau, Quebec.

IMLS participated in the fifth annual National Book Festival, presented in Washington, D.C., by the Library of Congress and hosted by First Lady Laura Bush. The festival took place on the National Mall on September 24. IMLS supported the Pavilion of the States, which featured representatives from library agencies from the 50 states, the District of Columbia, and the U.S. territories.

November 15–17, 2005, IMLS presented "Five-Year Evaluation: Documenting the Impact," its annual conference in Washington, D.C., for state library administrative agencies. The conference focused on preparing for the five-year evaluation report due to IMLS in 2007.

IMLS Web Site and Publications

The IMLS Web site (http://www.imls.gov) provides information on the various grant programs, the National Awards for Museum and Library Service, funded projects, application forms, and staff contacts. The Web site also highlights model projects developed by libraries and museums throughout the country and provides information about IMLS-sponsored conferences, publications, and studies. Through an electronic newsletter, *Primary Source,* IMLS provides timely information on grant deadlines and opportunities. Details on subscribing to the IMLS newsletter are provided on the Web site.

The following recent publications are available on the Web site: the 2006 *Grant Opportunities Guide*; *Charting the Landscape, Mapping New Paths: Museums, Libraries, and K–12 Education*; and guidelines for each of the grant programs.

Table 1 / Library Services and Technology Act, State Allotments, FY 2005
Total Distributed to States: $160,704,000[1]

State	Federal Funds from IMLS (66%)[2]	State Matching Funds (34%)	Total Federal and State Funds
Alabama	$2,556,671	$1,317,073	$3,873,744
Alaska	828,563	426,835	1,255,398
Arizona	3,041,222	1,566,690	4,607,912
Arkansas	1,760,329	906,836	2,667,165
California	16,457,012	8,477,855	24,934,867
Colorado	2,579,074	1,328,614	3,907,688
Connecticut	2,100,240	1,081,942	3,182,182
Delaware	904,235	465,818	1,370,053
Florida	8,172,813	4,210,237	12,383,050
Georgia	4,433,740	2,284,048	6,717,788
Hawaii	1,101,687	567,536	1,669,223
Idaho	1,150,464	592,663	1,743,127
Illinois	6,214,291	3,201,301	9,415,592
Indiana	3,317,057	1,708,787	5,025,844
Iowa	1,858,287	957,299	2,815,586
Kansas	1,759,339	906,326	2,665,665
Kentucky	2,384,878	1,228,574	3,613,452
Louisiana	2,554,689	1,316,052	3,870,741
Maine	1,123,275	578,657	1,701,932
Maryland	3,008,965	1,550,073	4,559,038
Massachusetts	3,423,733	1,763,741	5,187,474
Michigan	5,059,705	2,606,515	7,666,220
Minnesota	2,807,289	1,446,179	4,253,468
Mississippi	1,830,121	942,790	2,772,911
Missouri	3,096,707	1,595,273	4,691,980
Montana	949,157	488,960	1,438,117
Nebraska	1,317,786	678,859	1,996,645
Nevada	1,542,939	794,847	2,337,786
New Hampshire	1,115,181	574,487	1,689,668
New Jersey	4,412,959	2,273,343	6,686,302
New Mexico	1,378,496	710,134	2,088,630

New York	9,146,819	4,711,998	13,858,817
North Carolina	4,309,258	2,219,921	6,529,179
North Dakota	821,842	423,373	1,245,215
Ohio	5,667,969	2,919,863	8,587,832
Oklahoma	2,112,874	1,088,450	3,201,324
Oregon	2,134,437	1,099,558	3,233,995
Pennsylvania	6,085,045	3,134,720	9,219,765
Rhode Island	1,020,285	525,601	1,545,886
South Carolina	2,398,034	1,235,351	3,633,385
South Dakota	880,376	453,527	1,333,903
Tennessee	3,158,288	1,626,997	4,785,285
Texas	10,460,595	5,388,791	15,849,386
Utah	1,592,429	820,342	2,412,771
Vermont	815,233	419,969	1,235,202
Virginia	3,851,240	1,983,972	5,835,212
Washington	3,288,255	1,693,950	4,982,205
West Virginia	1,349,667	695,283	2,044,950
Wisconsin	2,992,540	1,541,612	4,534,152
Wyoming	762,355	392,728	1,155,083
District of Columbia	790,234	407,090	1,197,324
Puerto Rico	2,277,522	1,173,269	3,450,791
American Samoa	65,977	33,988	99,965
Northern Marianas	75,106	38,691	113,797
Guam	114,513	58,992	173,505
Virgin Islands	88,799	45,745	134,544
Pacific Territories[3]	203,404	104,784	308,188
Total	$160,704,000	$82,786,909	$243,490,909

1 The amount available to states is based on the balance remaining after enacted allocations have been subtracted from the total appropriation as follows:

LIBRARY ALLOCATION, FY2005	$205,951,000 P.L. 108-447
Librarians for the 21st Century	$22,816,000
National Leadership Grants	$12,301,000
Native American/Native Hawaiian	$3,472,000
Administration	$6,658,000
Total Distributed to States	$160,704,000

2 Calculation is based on minimum set in the law (P.L. 108-81) and reflects appropriations enacted by P.L. 108-447. Population data are from the Bureau of Census (BOC) estimates. Data used in the state allotment table are the most current published population estimates available the first day of the fiscal year. Therefore, the population data used in the 2005 table are what was available on the BOC Web site http://eire.census.gov/popest/data/states/tables/ on October 1, 2004.

3 Aggregate allotments (including administrative costs) for Palau, Marshall Islands, and Micronesia are awarded on a competitive basis to eligible applicants and are administered by Pacific Resources for Education and Learning (PREL).

Table 2 / National Leadership Grants, FY 2005

Advancing Learning Communities

Minnesota Historical Society $244,500

The Minnesota Historical Society will provide new geography teachers with the tools they need to meet the state's graduation standards for geography through workshops instructing them on finding and using the many geographic resources available online. The project will enhance the value of the state's digital resources by integrating the application of technologies with the needs of students and teachers in grades 4–12. Project products will include a Web-based geospatial information system (GIS) tool. An online curriculum package and repository of the geographic narratives students and teachers will create will also be provided.

Table 2 / National Leadership Grants, FY 2005 *(cont.)*

Oklahoma Department of Libraries $209,000

In collaboration with seven other statewide cultural organizations and a variety of individual librarians, historians, and scholars, the Oklahoma Department of Libraries will sponsor a 27-month project, "Oklahoma Image: 100 Years of Statehood," as part of the state's centennial celebration. The project will produce a series of workshops for librarians, education directors, teachers, and others; public library programs on Oklahoma history; and standards-based study guides for K–12 teachers relating to the use of Oklahoma Image, an online digital image resource of primary sources.

Stephen F. Austin State University, Nacogdoches, Texas $570,288

The Texas Tides Digital Learning Consortium will help eastern Texas build successful learning communities for public schools, colleges, universities, and memory institutions and their patrons. It will increase access for educators, students, and other researchers to primary resources relating to eastern Texas, with emphasis on history, science, and multicultural resources. The initial platform, developed during Phase 1 of the project using state grant funds, features a bilingual Web site with lesson plans for Texas history teachers and students in grades 4–7, with more than 10,000 digitized primary resources, and a fully searchable database of encoded archival description finding aids.

Building Digital Resources

Atlanta Historical Society $116,795

The Atlanta History Center of the Atlanta Historical Society will digitize 7,500 photographs selected from the collections of three historically important *Atlanta Journal* and *Atlanta Constitution* photojournalists—Kenneth G. Rogers, Bill Wilson, and Marion Johnson. The work of these photographers provides a visual documentation of Georgia politics, popular culture, and the developing urban landscape of Atlanta. In addition, the project's technical approach provides an exemplary model for the preservation of and access to photographic media of historical value.

George Mason University $249,420

The university's Center for History and New Media will develop free, open source Web browser tools to enhance the use of digital library and museum collections. These tools will turn a regular browser into SmartFox: The Scholar's Browser for Digital Collections, which will allow users to capture and organize digital scholarly materials. SmartFox will relieve libraries and museums of the need to build personal collection tools for their users and will leverage the substantial investment they have already made in digitizing collection materials.

Indiana University $768,747

Over the past four years, Indiana University has developed an experimental digital music library system known as Variations2, which provides a complete environment in which students and faculty can discover, listen to, view, annotate, and interact with music. The Indiana University Digital Library Program project will now create Variations3, a turnkey digital music library and learning system that can be easily deployed at a wide range of college and university libraries with minimal technical support and at minimal cost to the institutions.

Missouri Botanical Garden $494,216

The Missouri Botanical Garden will create a public-resource computing application that digitizes and automatically indexes vast amounts of scientific literature, ultimately providing users with an integrated Web portal for the discovery of information about plants. SciLINC (Scientific Literature Indexing on Networked Computers) will use Internet-connected personal computers to analyze data when the personal computer is not active, taking advantage of unused computer processing power. SciLINC, freely available to the general public, will analyze text from digitized botanical literature to return a full-text index and a keyword index for each page. These keywords will be annotated with links to other Web pages about a particular plant, allowing users of the portal to search for terms, discover where they reside in a body of digitized literature, view the appropriate pages, and click through to discover other online resources associated with that keyword.

Table 2 / National Leadership Grants, FY 2005 *(cont.)*

Texas State Library and Archives Commission $240,249

Together with 11 partner institutions in the Texas Heritage Digitization Initiative, the Texas State Library and Archives Commission will identify, describe, digitize, preserve, and make broadly accessible special collections materials of history and culture held by libraries, archives, museums, and historical societies throughout the state.

University of Chicago $249,857

The Goodspeed Manuscript Collection Project will produce a digital collection of 65 Greek, Syrian, Ethiopian, Armenian, Arabic, and Latin manuscripts dating from the 7th to the 19th centuries. The digital collection project will allow comparative and cross-cultural textual and iconographic research, free to the public, through open source interfaces for searching, browsing, page-turning, and zooming in and out of high-resolution images.

University of North Carolina at Chapel Hill $505,232

The university library—in collaboration with the Southern Oral History Program, the Center for the Study of the American South, the university's School of Education, and ibiblio (a conservancy of freely available information, including software, music, literature, art, history, science, politics, and cultural studies)—will digitize and make available on the Web 500 oral history interviews that offer personal insights into civil rights, women's rights, politics, and environmental issues. The project will also develop standards-based curriculum materials for teachers and students, as well as reusable learning objects for a range of class levels.

University of Tennessee $928,080

The University of Tennessee and nine partner institutions throughout the state will build a free, full-text searchable electronic database of 10,000 historically significant items from Tennessee libraries, museums, and other repositories. The project will create three regional centers to administer a statewide network of shared resources, provide training opportunities, and develop common technical standards. It will also begin to integrate digitized primary sources into the state's K–12 teaching curricula through user-based assessments. The project will connect libraries, museums, and archives throughout Tennessee directly to teachers, students, researchers, and others.

University System of Georgia $761,427

The University of Georgia and two partners, Georgia Public Broadcasting and the Georgia Humanities Council, will create the Civil Rights Digital Library Initiative to promote an enhanced understanding of the civil rights movement through a digital video archive of historical news film.

WGBH Educational Foundation, Boston $166,500

The WGBH Media Library will integrate three digitized archived television series—the "New Television Workshop," "Say Brother," and the "Ten O'clock News"—into a seamless virtual library that can be searched across the three archives. This Web-accessible collection will be a model for managing rich media resources so that engaging materials can be discovered, used, and reused for a variety of purposes.

Research and Demonstration

American Library Association $239,416

The American Library Association (ALA) Office for Research and Statistics and the Association of Specialized and Cooperative Library Agencies (ASCLA) will survey library networks, consortia, and cooperatives to develop a clear and current understanding of how library networks and cooperatives operate and the many ways these collaborative organizations help advance learning communities. All resources developed in the project will be freely available on the ALA Web site. ASCLA will provide ongoing support and updating of the data after the end of the grant period.

Table 2 / National Leadership Grants, FY 2005 *(cont.)*

Florida State University School of Information Studies $249,979

Florida State University's Information Institute—in partnership with the Omaha Public Library, Baltimore County Public Library, Mid-York Library System, and ALA's Office for Research—will investigate how "best practice" evaluation strategies can demonstrate the value of public libraries to the communities they serve. The project will develop a framework to improve public library evaluation and produce a Web-based Evaluation Decision Management System for public library managers and advocates.

James Madison University $158,593

James Madison University's Libraries and Educational Technologies Department will produce a series of computer games to help students develop health literacy and information literacy skills. The project will be conducted in collaboration with the university's Center for Instructional Technology and will research and evaluate whether traditional information literacy skills can be acquired through game-like experiences and determine if this approach is more effective with university students than current text-based approaches.

Kent State University $327,016

Kent State University will investigate the health-information-seeking behaviors of older adults in northeastern and Appalachian Ohio and make recommendations to help libraries and healthcare providers create more-effective health information programs and services. The researchers will evaluate all aspects of health information for seniors, including information access, decision-making processes, and the practices of community professionals who serve this population.

Rutgers School of Communication, Information, and Library Studies $684,996

The Rutgers School of Communication, Information, and Library Studies and the Online Computer Library Center (OCLC) will research and evaluate the sustainability and relevance of virtual reference (VR) services—human-mediated, Internet-based library information services. The increasing use of VR by the public has increased the demand on libraries to provide reference services online, and this project aims to improve libraries' ability to respond to the demand.

Syracuse University $563,621

Syracuse will extend its successful S.O.S. (Situation, Outcome, Strategies) for Information Literacy program to grades 9–12 and will also create a higher education version. IMLS funded the first S.O.S. project in 2002 for grades K–8, which involved creation of a freely accessible Web-based multimedia resource of standards-based lesson plans, support materials, and examples of "best practice" in teaching information literacy.

University of California, Riverside $999,719

The university library will conduct research aimed at producing better machine-based, automatically generated metadata to improve the search and retrieval of online content. The project will refine and augment services and accompanying software tools supported with previous IMLS funding to expand its automated and semi-automated textual data mining, data extraction, and metadata generation capabilities.

University of Illinois at Urbana-Champaign Library Research Center $495,053

The research center, in partnership with the Pew Internet and American Life Project, will investigate how effectively public libraries and community technology centers provide government information to people with limited access to the Internet. Findings and recommendations for improving services to the public are expected in October 2007.

University of Maine, Orono $249,689

The university's Fogler Library, in partnership with the Department of Spatial Information Science and Engineering, will research the requirements for an open source Commons of Geographic Data (CGD) System. The CGD System will ultimately provide a means to capture

Table 2 / National Leadership Grants, FY 2005 *(cont.)*

and make available the rich but currently largely invisible geographic information resources generated by local, nonfederal sources.

University of Michigan $510,205

The university's School of Information will investigate the development of institutional repositories in colleges and universities to identify models and best practices in administration, technical infrastructure, and access to collections.

University of Nebraska–Lincoln $169,651

The university libraries will use the Walt Whitman Archive project to create a model metadata encoding and transmission standard (METS) profile for digital thematic research collections. By standardizing the way metadata are encoded, creators of digital thematic research collections can make their work more sustainable and universally usable.

University of Tennessee Office of Research $199,995

The University of Tennessee, in partnership with the University of Wisconsin–Milwaukee, will analyze the needs and query behaviors of users who search for information on the Web. The aim of the project is to create new models for information discovery that incorporate algorithms for conceptual matching, allowing users to search for concepts as an alternative to entering search terms.

University of Texas at Austin, Office of Sponsored Projects $157,172

The Open Choice project will create, test, and evaluate an open source Internet content filter for use in libraries.

University of Wisconsin–Milwaukee $189,540

The University of Wisconsin–Milwaukee and Queens College of the City University of New York will investigate the use of automated help systems provided by digital libraries. The project will compare automated help systems with human help interactions to develop effective automated interaction strategies. The project also will develop design principles for automated help systems for the novice user of digital libraries.

University of Wisconsin–Milwaukee $152,039

Researchers at the university's School of Information Studies will create a novel interactive virtual reference (iVR) model and prototype system. The project team will develop a virtual reference assistant that will observe patrons' information-seeking behaviors and adapt to them. The project will make the iVR software freely accessible to the library community.

Partnership for a Nation of Learners Community Collaboration Grants

Avampato Discovery Museum $249,626

"Beginning a Healthy Life," a collaboration between the Avampato Discovery Museum, West Virginia Public Broadcasting System, and the Kanawha County Library System, tackles critical health issues facing the citizens of West Virginia. The goal of the project is to educate young children and their caregivers about the essentials of healthy living and to instill healthy habits at an early age.

Fairbanks Museum and Planetarium $222,623

"Eye on the Night Sky: A Project for Science Literacy" is a partnership between the Fairbanks Museum and Planetarium of St. Johnsbury, Vermont, and Vermont Public Radio (VPR) of Colchester. The project is an extension of the partners' popular "Eye on the Sky" weather program, which reaches more than 150,000 listeners a week in Vermont and parts of New York, New Hampshire, Massachusetts, and Quebec. The grant will fund the production of short daily broadcasts, a new Web site, resources for teachers, and community workshops conducted in public libraries throughout the state.

Table 2 / National Leadership Grants, FY 2005 *(cont.)*

Haines Borough Public Library $212,367

"Perspectives: Issues and Explorations" is a two-year program developed by the Haines Borough (Alaska) Public Library and Lynn Canal Broadcasting (KHNS radio). This multifaceted project focuses on the innovative application of technology to educate rural Alaskans about the impacts of drug and alcohol abuse. Activities will include training for community participants in storytelling through digital audio production, creation of audio diaries illustrating the impacts of substance abuse, dissemination of audio diaries through broadcasts and a Web site, and development of related resources such as curriculum materials for dissemination via the Web site.

Las Vegas Clark County Library District $221,197

The Open Doors project addresses the literacy needs of adults, including young adults 18–24 seeking the GED, parents and caregivers of preschoolers, and native Spanish-speakers. The project will demonstrate how the resources of public libraries and public television can be combined to provide new, cost-effective methods for supporting critical literacy learning among adults and children.

Nebraska State Historical Society $249,837

Through a program modeled on the popular public television show "Antiques Roadshow," the society, Nebraska Library Commission, and statewide public television network Nebraska Educational Telecommunications (NET) will show families and museum and library staff how to preserve their treasures. Professional conservators will offer information and advice at three community-based conservation clinics.

Portland Harbor Museum $41,372

The Portland Harbor Museum in South Portland, Maine, and community radio station WMPG-FM will collaborate to document one of World War II's little-known stories, that of the New England Shipbuilding Corporation, which produced 236 liberty ships for the U.S. Emergency Shipbuilding Program. The collaboration will produce a radio program that will air in five 10-minute segments in early December 2006 and a traveling kiosk exhibit for use by libraries and other community organizations.

WGBH Educational Foundation $250,000

WGBH Boston, Boston Children's Museum, Boston Public Library, Children's Hospital Boston, and the Boston Public Health Commission will launch a major asthma management campaign aimed at black and Latino children in neighborhoods with the highest incidence of asthma. The two-year campaign will build on the appeal of WGBH's popular "Arthur" series, which featured an award-winning episode dealing with asthma.

Table 3 / Librarians for the 21st Century Grants, FY 2005

Priority 1, Master's Level Programs

Denver Public Library $670,315

Denver Public Library will partner with the Emporia State University School of Library and Information Management and the University of Denver College of Education, Library and Information Science division, to conduct an educational program aimed at increasing America's pool of minority and bilingual librarians.

Mansfield University of Pennsylvania School of Library and Information Technologies $981,814

The school will partner with the Colorado Department of Education, the Harrisburg Area School District, and the Pennsylvania Department of Education School of Library Media Division to increase the number of school library media specialists across the nation while building advocacy among school administrators. Forty-five school library media specialists will be recruited, trained, and provided with job opportunities, and 30 principals will be furnished with the background, guidelines, and tools to work effectively with school library media specialists.

Table 3 / Librarians for the 21st Century Grants, FY 2005 (cont.)

Montana State Library $460,044

Montana State Library will educate and employ ten new professional librarians in Montana through the development and implementation of a statewide campaign to promote librarianship as a career. The recruitment and promotion phase of the project will target Native American students and communities to increase the number of Native Americans in the profession. Students will receive scholarships to attend the Information School at the University of Washington in Seattle. Following graduation, four libraries in communities currently not served by professional librarians will receive stipends to hire new graduates.

Old Dominion University $594,709

Old Dominion University in Norfolk, Virginia, will partner with Virginia Educational Region IV and Virginia Educational Region VII to address the critical shortage of licensed school library media specialists in the state by delivering a nationally recognized online professional graduate program to 40 students in the rural and mountainous southern region of the state and the urban northern Virginia region.

Oneida Herkimer Madison Board of Cooperative Educational Services $184,065

The Oneida Herkimer Madison Board of Cooperative Educational Services, New Hartford, New York, will collaborate with other boards of cooperative educational services, participating school districts, and the SUNY University at Buffalo Department of Library and Information Studies to address needs in central and upstate New York for certified library media specialists. The project will recruit nine students who will complete the New York State Education Department-approved library media certification program.

Pratt Institute School of Information and Library Science $591,206

The Pratt Institute School of Information and Library Science will collaborate with the Brooklyn (New York) Historical Society to enhance the training of Pratt students seeking MLIS degrees by arranging supervised internships at the society. Thirty students from diverse communities will complete an archive certificate program covering theory and practice from traditional methods to digital technology and then intern at the society's archives.

San Antonio Public Library $312,400

The library, in collaboration with the City of San Antonio, will recruit 20 candidates from current library staff to a master's degree program. The project will address current diversity and service needs within the San Antonio Public Library system. At least 12 candidates will be bilingual. The program will provide students with a mentor, workshops, individual executive coaching in leadership, and job rotation.

Syracuse University School of Information Studies $999,033

The school will partner with the New York City Board of Education to address the need to educate school library media professionals for service in high-need urban schools by creating a focused, graduate-level school media program in the city. Forty master's-level students will be recruited and will receive partial or total funding for participation.

Texas Woman's University School of Library and Information Studies $905,030

The school will collaborate with the Dallas Independent School District and the Universities Center at Dallas to improve the accessibility and quality of library services for a diverse student population in the Dallas Independent School District. The project will extend the education of newly certified librarians through completion of their professional degrees.

University of Arizona School of Information Resources and Library Science $990,174

The school will recruit 48 Native American and Hispanic students to a master's program in library and information science as part of its Knowledge River initiative. The initiative also will involve 12 second-year scholars for the Knowledge River program and 24 Native American and Hispanic high school students in a Teen Community Health Information Institute to explore health sciences librarianship and provide community health services.

Table 3 / Librarians for the 21st Century Grants, FY 2005 *(cont.)*

*University of North Carolina at Chapel Hill School of Information and
Library Science* $392,295

The school will partner with the Duke University Medical Center Library to recruit two cohorts of medical students into a new dual-degree master's program at UNC Chapel Hill and Duke University. Four physicians will be educated in information and library science to develop medical "informationists."

University of Oklahoma School of Library and Information Science $569,552

The school will partner with Oklahoma City Schools and Tulsa Public Schools to fund 30 master's degree candidates with strong teaching credentials, including teacher certification and experience working with minority students. The partners will provide release time and continued employment of the future school library media specialists.

*University of Rhode Island Graduate School of Library and Information
Science* $504,775

The school will collaborate with the university libraries to build on the university's successful 2000–2002 National Leadership Grant project, Project Prism, which recruited and trained seven master's students in library science. This program will recruit and educate 12 students, focusing on four underrepresented ethnic minority groups, and prepare them to work with diverse populations.

University of South Florida School of Library and Information Science $758,736

The school, in partnership with the University of Central Florida Libraries, Florida Atlantic University Library, and the University of Florida Tampa Campus Library, will recruit 24 future academic librarians from three geographical areas in Florida.

University of Tennessee School of Information Sciences $632,249

The school will collaborate with the U.S. Department of Energy's Oak Ridge National Laboratory and its Office of Scientific and Technical Information, Information International Associates, the University of Tennessee John C. Hodges Library, and the University of Tennessee Pendergrass Agriculture and Veterinary Medicine Library to educate ten science and technology librarians and create a model for the education of subject specialist librarians by combining practice in leading science institutions and libraries with graduate instruction.

University of the Virgin Islands $965,910

The University of the Virgin Islands will collaborate with the University of Pittsburgh School of Information Sciences to fund 25 Virgin Islands residents studying for a master's in library and information science degree through the University of Pittsburgh School of Information Science's "FastTrack" online program.

University of Wisconsin–Milwaukee School of Information Studies $991,246

The school, in collaboration with the Marquette University Libraries, the Milwaukee Public Library, and the University of Wisconsin–Milwaukee Libraries, will produce skilled organization-of-information professionals from diverse backgrounds. Twenty students will be admitted to the school's ALA-accredited master's program in library and information science.

Urban Libraries Council $999,541

In collaboration with 23 partner libraries across the United States, the council will recruit and educate new professional public librarians, providing them with a diverse professional work force that understands neighborhood-based public library staffing and service strategies and the challenges of delivering them in community contexts.

Priority 2, Doctoral Programs

Simmons College Graduate School of Library and Information Science $780,465

The school will establish a Ph.D. program that specializes in managerial leadership in the

Table 3 / Librarians for the 21st Century Grants, FY 2005 *(cont.)*

information professions and focuses on the knowledge, skills, competencies, and personal traits applicable to leadership in libraries, nonprofit organizations, and other information-intensive enterprises. The program will train 15 individuals to lead libraries and information organizations into the future, disseminate a body of scholarly and practice-based research to the profession, and continually update and examine leadership issues in information-related organizations.

University of Maryland at College Park College of Information Studies $370,300

The college, in collaboration with the university's Human Computer Interaction Lab, will recruit and educate four doctoral students to teach and conduct research in the area of children's information resources and services and digital libraries. Emphasis will be placed on recruiting from underrepresented groups or individuals who have interest in meeting the needs of diverse communities.

University of Texas at Austin School of Information $251,910

The school will educate three doctoral students to teach preservation in library and information science programs. Candidates will be recruited for three areas: administration of preservation, preservation and information policy, and preservation of digital information.

Priority 3, Preprofessional Programs

Free Library of Philadelphia Foundation $997,099

The foundation will develop recruitment programs that target high school and college students who work or volunteer at the Free Library. A three-tiered approach to recruitment will reach a total of 370 candidates for careers in librarianship (300 high school students, 45 library interns, and 25 paraprofessional library staff members) through a combination of tuition assistance, educational leave time, internships, mentoring, and training, while providing for more traditionally underrepresented populations in the professional library field.

William H. Welch Medical Library, Johns Hopkins University $639,746

The library will collaborate with the medical libraries of Georgetown University, Howard University, the University of Colorado, the University of Tennessee–Memphis, the Houston Academy of Medicine, Washington University, and Yale University to bring together medical librarians, "informaticians," and diversity counselors to increase the number of underrepresented minorities entering the health information professions.

Simmons College Libraries $661,449

The libraries, in partnership with the University of Massachusetts–Boston, will recruit future librarians by providing internships to 144 Massachusetts high school students, focusing on minorities and those who are the first in their families to attend college.

Priority 4, Research

State University of New York at Albany School of Information Science and Policy $153,767

The school will improve education and training of visual resources professionals by providing the library community with the information necessary to support the development of successful training and education programs for the next generation of visual resources professionals.

University of North Carolina at Chapel Hill School of Library and Information Science $804,344

The school will partner with the university's Institute on Aging to conduct a research project designed to study the career patterns of graduates of library and information science programs by building an in-depth understanding of educational, workplace, career, and retention issues faced by LIS graduates.

Table 3 / Librarians for the 21st Century Grants, FY 2005 (cont.)

Priority 5, Programs to Build Institutional Capacity

Drexel University College of Information Science and Technology $291,492

The college plans to address two needs relating to library and information science education in the management of digital information. The project will enhance the curricula offered by the College of Information Science and Technology and Drexel's College of Media Arts and Design by enriching existing courses and developing new courses in research methods and digital librarianship.

Florida State University College of Information $159,526

The college will develop graduate education opportunities focused on leadership for school library media specialists and integrating the tenets of the National Board for Professional Teaching Standards.

Priority 6, Continuing Education

American Library Association, Association of College and Research Libraries $93,106

The Rare Book and Manuscript Section of the Association of College and Research Libraries (ACRL) will support a major national conference focused on examining issues of mutual interest to special collections library and museum communities and creating greater collaboration between them. Titled "Intersecting Missions, Converging Futures: Libraries and Museums in the Twenty-First Century," the conference will bring together practicing and aspiring professionals from both fields to investigate common concerns and to explore ways in which they can work more closely.

Indiana University $883,171

The university, in a cooperative agreement with IMLS, will develop an online, instructor-mediated course in outcomes-based evaluation for library and museum professionals and students in library and museum education programs. Funding during the three-year project will support course development, testing, and a two-year initial deployment at no cost to course participants.

New York Public Library $178,332

New York Public Library will develop a leadership academy to educate 60 staff members on core concepts of leadership and management, provide staff the opportunity and knowledge to develop a solution to a leadership or management problem, and begin to prepare staff to become the future leaders of the library and the greater library community. Training will focus on leadership, communication, and management and supervision.

Northeast Document Conservation Center $266,425

The center will work in partnership with the Online Computer Library Center (OCLC) to develop, test, and disseminate a training program on digital preservation for staff in libraries, archives, museums, and other cultural heritage organizations. A project advisory committee of digital experts, library school educators, and representatives of state libraries will develop the content for a pilot conference, "Persistence of Memory."

Online Computer Library Center $399,537

OCLC and the J. Paul Getty Trust, in collaboration with IMLS, will co-host the annual IMLS Web-Wise Conference on Libraries and Museums in the Digital World for 2006 and 2007. The conference will be held in Los Angeles in 2006 and in Washington, D.C. in 2007.

Pacific Resources for Education and Learning $652,610

The organization will address the continuing education needs of library staff in the U.S.-affiliated Pacific territories of American Samoa, the Commonwealth of the Northern Mariana Islands, the Federated States of Micronesia, Guam, the Republic of the Marshall Islands, and the Republic of Palau by providing summer institutes for selected segments of the region's preprofessional staff.

Table 3 / Librarians for the 21st Century Grants, FY 2005 (cont.)

University of California–Los Angeles Graduate School of Education and Information Studies $109,147

The school will build the infrastructure to develop the California Rare Book School to meet the needs of the western United States special library community. The goal is to have a permanent program in special collections and to increase the number of educated and trained special-collections librarians.

University of North Texas School of Library and Information Sciences $159,578

The school, in collaboration with the Ysleta Independent School District and the El Paso Independent School District, will create, test, and revise Web-based courseware to be used by school librarians throughout the nation in online continuing education for K–12 librarians and staff.

University of Virginia Rare Book School $122,250

The school will offer 50 full-tuition scholarships to a diversified range of students for each of the next three years. The program will allow the school to increase its current level of scholarship support from less than 4 percent to about 15 percent of those attending, increasing the number and diversity of its student body.

Urban Libraries Council $999,873

The council will recruit 40 emerging leaders in 40 public libraries to attend an 11-month program that includes three instructional workshops, individual leadership assessments, and executive coaches. Participants will be recruited with a focus on diversifying the next generation of public library leaders.

Table 4 / Native American Library Services Enhancement Grants, FY 2005

Assiniboine and Sioux Tribes of the Fort Peck Indian Reservation, Poplar, Montana $134,015

The microfilm, children's programming, and library security projects under this grant will assemble and microfilm the complete run of the newspaper of record for the Fort Peck tribes, the *Wotanin Wowapi*, from 1969 to the present, in partnership with Montana State University-Bozeman. Other priorities include expanding the children's summer reading program and adding a security system to decrease the loss of materials from the library.

Chilkat Indian Village, Klukwan, Alaska $146,692

Chilkat Indian Village and Klukwan School are collaborating in the Klukwan Library Revitalization Project to develop a fully functioning library that serves both students and community members, providing access to an up-to-date collection, the Internet, and specialized Tlingit language and history materials.

Chilkoot Indian Association, Haines, Alaska $149,986

The project, a cooperative effort between the Chilkoot Indian Association Tribal Government and the Haines Borough Public Library, aims at improved efficiency, quality, and quantity of children's and youth services; the expansion of the mentor-based Dragonfly Project to provide community training in word processing, graphic design, filmmaking, security issues, and electronic file management; and providing job training opportunities in library work for tribal members.

Grand Traverse Band of Ottawa and Chippewa Indians, Traverse City, Michigan $148,948

The project, Enhancing the Grand Traverse Band Heritage Library, will provide a full-time librarian who will develop resources and programs to draw tribal members into the library. Students will be trained to teach community members in an intergenerational computer literacy skills program.

Table 4 / Native American Library Services Enhancement Grants, FY 2005 *(cont.)*

Lac Courte Oreilles Band of Lake Superior Chippewa Indians, Hayward,
Wisconsin $149,183

In anticipation of the opening of the new Lac Courte Oreilles Ojibwa College Community Library, this project will ensure that enhanced library services are achieved through increased collection development, installation of a new computer network, and new furnishings.

Makah Indian Tribe, Neah Bay, Washington $40,000

A series of storytelling programs and training will create new services for community members and the general public. Live storytelling sessions and recordings of past expert storytellers will be offered at the Makah Cultural and Research Center. Workshops will instruct interested individuals in the techniques of Makah storytelling.

Native Village of Afognak, Kodiak, Alaska $107,934

The village's Alutiiq Heritage Library Project will enhance its specialized Alutiiq collection, implement an automated catalog, and link to five local libraries and museums for increased access to this unique collection.

Pauma Band of Luiseno Mission Indians, Pauma Valley, California $142,097

The Pauma/AA'Alvikat Library Archive and Enhancement Project will implement an automated library catalog, establish an archive of important tribal material, and increase the number of programs at the library. An archive room will be established to house a special collection of documents pertaining to land use, water rights, archeology, culture, and history.

Red Cliff Band of Lake Superior Chippewa Indians, Bayfield, Wisconsin $35,273

Mazinaaigan Waakaaigan, the Red Cliff Public Library, will establish a stronger and more involved staff and board through staff development and board training, review and update its long-term strategic plan in a series of planning sessions with the goal of meeting state library standards, and continue to strengthen ongoing collaborations with other tribal departments.

Rosebud Sioux Tribe of the Rosebud Indian Reservation, Mission,
South Dakota $149,600

The Unkiciksuyapi and Beyond: Cultural and General Information Literacy for the Sicangu Oyate project will select local and regional historical videotapes from the past 30 years, transfer them to DVD, and make them available to the public in a new media-viewing room in the Sinte Gleske University Library. Families will be encouraged to document and "remember themselves" and their recent ancestors for future generations through the university library's family photo history project and an oral history project.

Saginaw Chippewa Indian Tribe of Michigan $119,810

The tribe will create an extension of its tribal library services at the Tribal College Learning Resource Center Library under the management of the tribal library and the direction of a project team comprising tribal and college staff. The satellite site will include a computer lab with Internet access, audiovisual equipment, and library materials ranging from reference to cultural and leisure reading materials.

Sealaska Corporation, Juneau, Alaska $140,606

The Sealaska Heritage Institute will process, digitize, and make accessible online and on CD several recently acquired collections of materials relating to the 20th-century history of southeast Alaska Native issues and organizations, including the Alaska Native Brotherhood/Sisterhood, which was seminal in Native land claims cases, Alaska Native Claims Settlement Act legislation, and the formation of Native corporations.

Three Affiliated Tribes, New Town, North Dakota $139,856

The Fort Berthold Library at Fort Berthold Community College will enhance its collection on the Mandan, Hidatsa, and Arikara nations as well as improve its general collection, and will acquaint children and teenagers with tribal-specific information available at the library.

Part 3
Library/Information Science Education, Placement, and Salaries

Employment Sources on the Internet

Catherine Barr

Contributing Editor

The library and information science community has always actively shared information about job openings, with individual libraries, professional associations, library schools, and other organizations spreading the word through telephone "joblines" and fax services as well as through advertising in trade journals and use of employment agencies. This activity has naturally progressed to the Internet, and now the World Wide Web and a variety of online listservs and discussion groups have become some of the most useful—and current—resources for library and information professionals seeking jobs within and outside the library profession. Blogs focusing on employment opportunities are a relatively new phenomenon and usually focus on alerting readers to new features on the established sites.

There are now hundreds of job-related sites of interest to library and information professionals. This article makes no attempt to be all-inclusive, but aims instead to point readers to some of the most useful sites.

Many of the sites recommended simply list job openings; some also offer advice on searching for jobs, writing résumés, preparing for interviews, and negotiating salaries.

Before spending a lot of time on any Web site, users should check that the site has been updated recently and that out-of-date job listings no longer appear. If a jobseeker has a particular geographic location or specialized field in mind, he or she may find that the Directory of Organizations in Part 6 of this volume will provide a relevant Web address faster than a search of the Web.

Background Information

One particularly useful print resource, *The Information Professional's Guide to Career Development Online* (Information Today, Inc., 2001), has a companion Web site at http://www.lisjobs.com/careerdev. Both the print and the updated online versions present information on job hunting, networking, and online and continuing education. An article by the same authors—Rachel Singer Gordon and Sarah L. Nesbeitt—titled "Market Yourself Online!" appeared in the October/ November 2001 issue of *Marketing Library Services*. The article presents practical advice on promoting yourself and your abilities on the Web; it is available at http://www.infotoday.com/mls/oct01/gordon&nesbeitt.htm.

The Bureau of Labor Statistics of the Department of Labor provides a thorough overview of the work of a librarian, necessary qualifications, and the job and salary outlook at http://stats.bls.gov/oco/content/ocos068.stm. More-detailed employment and wage estimates can be found at http://stats.bls.gov/oes/current/oes254021.htm

for librarians, at http://stats.bls.gov/oes/current/oes254011.htm for archivists, and at http://stats.bls.gov/oes/current/oes254031.htm for library technicians.

An excellent 2002 *American Libraries* feature article by Linda K. Wallace on the breadth of opportunities available to librarians and information professionals—"Places an MLS Can Take You"—is archived at http://www.ala.org/ala/hrdr/careersinlibraries/al_mls.pdf. The American Library Association (ALA) provides information on specific library careers—law librarian, medical librarian, and so forth—on its Careers in Libraries page (http://www.ala.org/ala/hrdr/careersinlibraries/careerslibraries.htm). And How to Apply for a Library Job (http://www.liswiki.com/wiki/HOWTO:Apply_for_a_library_job) offers thoughtful and practical interview tips.

General Sites/Portals

American Library Association: Human Resource Development and Recruitment http://www.ala.org/ala/hrdr/humanresource.htm
Maintained by ALA.
A useful source of information on library careers, education and professional development, scholarships, and salaries. There is a special section for library support staff. The Guide to Employment Sources in the Library and Information Professions (http://www.ala.org/ala/hrdr/libraryempresources/employmentguide05.htm) provides lots of local, national, and international links and gives easy access to library job ads in *American Libraries* (including its Hot Jobs Online, which is updated daily) and in *C&RLNews*. There are also links to ALA's conference placement service and to information about discrimination and unfair employment practices.

Library Job Postings on the Internet http://www.libraryjobpostings.org
Compiled by Sarah (Nesbeitt) Johnson of Booth Library, Eastern Illinois University, coauthor of *The Information Professional's Guide to Career Development Online* (Information Today, 2001); there is a link to the book's companion Web site.
Provides links to library employment sites in the United States and abroad, with easy access by location and by category of job.

LIScareer.com http://www.liscareer.com
Maintained by Priscilla Shontz, editor of *The Librarian's Career Guidebook* (Scarecrow, 2004).
Subtitled "The Library and Information Science Professional's Career Development Center," this helpful and up-to-date site provides no job listings but offers bibliographies of and, when available, links to resources of interest in the areas of career planning, education, job hunting, experience, work/life balance, networking, mentoring, interpersonal skills, leadership, and publishing.

Lisjobs.com—Jobs for Librarians and Information Professionals http://www.lisjobs.com
Maintained by Rachel Singer Gordon, author of *The Accidental Library Manager* (Information Today, 2005) and coauthor of *The Information Professional's Guide to Career Development Online* (Information Today, 2001).

A searchable database of job listings and guide to online job resources in the United States and abroad. Job seekers can post résumés for a small fee. Also features an advice page and an interesting professional development newsletter, *Info Career Trends.*

The Riley Guide: Employment Opportunities http://www.rileyguide.com
and Job Resources on the Internet
Compiled by Margaret F. Dikel, a private consultant and coauthor with Frances Roehm of *The Guide to Internet Job Searching* (McGraw-Hill, 2002).
A general site rich in advice for the job seeker, from résumé writing and how to target a new employer to tips on networking and interviewing. Links to job sites are organized by discipline; Information Design, Delivery, and Management is found under The Humanities, Social Sciences, and Personal Services.

University of Missouri–Columbia: http://www.coe.missouri.edu/
Library Job Listings ~career/library.html
Maintained by Career and Program Support, College of Education, University of Missouri–Columbia.
A no-frills site with links to sites that list library jobs. Includes a number of state joblines.

Professional Associations

General

Employment Resources: http://slisweb.sjsu.edu/resources/employment.htm
Organizations and Associations
Maintained by San José State University's School of Library and Information Science.
Gives links to organizations that will be of interest to students at the university, including a number of California sites. A related page, Professional Associations in the Information Sciences (http://slisweb.sjsu.edu/resources/orgs.htm), is a comprehensive listing of associations in the United States and abroad.

Public Libraries

Public library openings can be found at all the general sites/portals listed above. The Public Library Association offers information on public librarianship—from educational requirements and salaries to testimonials from public librarians and the opportunity to participate in Job Shadow Day. The URL is http://www.pla. org/ala/pla/projects/publiclibrecruit/publiclibrarian.htm.

School Libraries

School library openings can be found at many of the sites listed above. Sites with interesting material for aspiring school librarians include those listed below. School library jobseekers should read "Interviewing Teacher-Librarian Candidates" by Alice Yucht (*Teacher Librarian*, February 2004.)

AASL: Recruitment to　　　　http://www.ala.org/ala/aasl/aasleducation/
School Librarianship　　　　recruitmentlib/aaslrecruitment.htm
The American Association of School Librarians hosts this site, which offers state-by-state information on licensure, scholarships, library education, job hunting, mentoring, and recruitment efforts.

General education sites usually include school library openings. Among sites with nationwide coverage is

Education America　　　　http://www.educationamerica.net
Library openings can be searched by geographic location.

Special and Academic

AALL Job Placement Hotline　　　　http://www.aallnet.org/hotline/hotline.asp
Maintained by the American Association of Law Librarians.

ACRL: Career Opportunities　　　http://www.ala.org/ala/acrl/acrlpubs/crlnews/
from Across the Country　　　　crlcareeropps/careeropportunities.htm
Online access to job postings placed in *C&RL News* (published by the Association of College and Research Libraries), and to many jobs that can only be found online.

ALISE: Job Placement　　　　http://www.alise.org/jobplacement/index.html
The Association for Library and Information Science Education posts jobs for deans, directors, program chairs, faculty, visiting and summer faculty, and support positions in the field of library and information science.

ASIS&T Jobline Online http://www.jobtarget.com/home/index.cfm?site_id=180
Maintained by the American Society for Information Science and Technology.

Association of Research Libraries:　　　　http://db.arl.org/careers/index.html
Career Resources
In addition to listings of openings at ARL member institutions and at other organizations, there is a database of research library residency and internship programs. There are links to ARL's annual salary survey and to the article "Careers in Research Libraries and Information Science: The Dynamic Role of the Research Librarian."

Chronicle of Higher Education　　　　http://chronicle.com/jobs
Access job openings from more than 1,470 institutions. Listings can be browsed, with geographical options, under the category "Library/information sciences" or searched by simple keyword such as "library."

EDUCAUSE Job Posting Service　　　　http://www.educause.edu/jobpost
EDUCAUSE member organizations post positions "in the broad field of information technology in higher education."

HigherEdJobs.com　　　　http://www.higheredjobs.com
Published by Internet Employment Linkage, Inc. Job openings from nearly 1,300 institutions can be searched by location, job category, or keyword.

MLANet: Careers   http://www.mlanet.org/career/index.html
The Medical Library Association offers much more than job listings here, with brochures on medical librarianship, career tips, a mentor program, and a virtual student group.

SLA: Career Center   http://www.sla.org/content/jobs/index.cfm
In addition to searchable job listings that are available to all users, the Special Libraries Association provides around-the-clock job advice and mentoring to association members. A Career Articles & Resources page offers tips and tools.

Government

Library of Congress   http://www.loc.gov/hr/employment
Current jobs, internships, fellowships, and volunteering.

National Archives and Records   http://www.archives.gov/careers/
Administration
Employment, internships, and volunteering.

Library Support Staff

LibrarySupportStaffJobs http://bowietrek.typepad.com/librarysupportstaffjobs/
Lists job openings for library support staff, library assistants, library technicians, and library clerks.

Miscellaneous

REFORMA Employment   http://www.reforma.org/refoempl.htm
REFORMA (The National Association to Promote Library and Information Services to Latinos and the Spanish-Speaking) collects job postings from listservs and direct mailings. The page is updated weekly. Knowledge of Spanish is required for some jobs listed here.

Library Periodicals

American Libraries: http://www.ala.org/ala/education/empopps/
Hot Jobs Online   careerleadsb/hotjobsonline/hotjobsonline.htm
New ads are posted daily, plus openings scheduled to appear in forthcoming issues of *American Libraries*. "Working Knowledge" is a monthly column about life on the job.

Feliciter   http://www.cla.ca/careers/careeropp.htm
The Canadian Library Association lists openings here; some may have already appeared in the association's publication *Feliciter*.

Library Journal   http://jobs.libraryjournal.com/
Easy access to online job listings. A related JobZone (http://www.libraryjournal.com/community/891/Careers/42799.html) includes the annual salary survey and information for new librarians.

SLJ Career Center   http://www.schoollibraryjournal.com/
                          index.asp?layout=careerCenter
"All about salary, staffing, certification, and more" plus access to the jobs listed on the *Library Journal* site.

Employment Agencies/Commercial Services

A number of employment agencies and commercial services in the United States and abroad specialize in library-related jobs. Among those that keep up-to-date listings on their Web sites are:

ASLIB   http://www.aslib.co.uk/recruitment/index.htm
Lists jobs available in Britain.

Library Associates   http://www.libraryassociates.com/index.php4?page=jobs

TPFL: The Information People: http://www.tfpl.com/permanent_
Recruitment and Executive Search   recruitment/candidates/pjobs.cfm
Specializes in jobs in the fields of knowledge management, library and information management, records management, and Web and content management. Jobs around the world are listed, with an emphasis on Europe.

Listservs

Many listservs allow members to post job openings on a casual basis.

LIBJOBS   http://www.ifla.org/II/lists/libjobs.htm
Managed by the International Federation of Library Associations and Institutions (IFLA). Subscribers to this list receive posted job opportunities by e-mail.

NASIGWeb Job Listings   http://www.nasig.org/jobs/list.htm
This site collects serials-related job openings posted on the following listservs: ACQNET, AUTOCAT, COLLIB-L, INNOPAC, LIBJOBS, LITA-L, PACS-L, SERIALST, SLAJOB, STS-L, and ERIL-L.

PUBLIB   http://sunsite.berkeley.edu/PubLib
Public library job openings often appear on this list.

Blogs

Beyond the Job   http://librarycareers.blogspot.com/
Maintained by Sarah Johnson and Rachel Singer Gordon, this blog focuses on job-hunting advice and professional development.

LIScareers News   http://liscareer.blogspot.com/
Posts alerts to new features on LIScareer.com.

Placements and Salaries 2004: Closing the Gap

Stephanie Maatta

Assistant Professor, University of South Florida
School of Library and Information Science, Tampa

As the U.S. economy strengthened in 2004, so did the outlook for library salaries and job prospects. Graduates of the 2004 class of American Library Association (ALA)-accredited library and information science programs reported salaries that showed modest growth. Though long job searches remained the norm, they resulted for most in a variety of jobs that were increasingly stable as the cobbled part-time positions of the previous class have given way to more full-time spots. The news is best for women and minorities, who are closing the long-standing salary gap with their male counterparts.

Salaries increased fastest in the Southeast and Midwest and saw the greatest gains at academic libraries and vendors. Positions in reference/information services and in school media centers continue to dominate the placement trends for new LIS graduates, but positions in children's and youth services and in "other" types of assignments are on the rise.

Salaries across the board are improving and salary differentials are stabilizing. Some numbers: In 2004 graduates reported an average starting salary of $39,079, an increase of 2.91 percent over the 2003 average of $37,975. This almost matched the combined growth of salaries in 2002 and 2003 ($1,157 for the two years compared to $1,104 in 2004). This remained below the national inflation rate of 3.5 percent and doesn't touch the average annual salary growth of the late 1990s (4.35 percent), but it is a significant improvement over 2003's 1.48 percent increase.

Job Trends

An impressive 1,951 graduates responded to the 2004 *Library Journal* Placements and Salaries Survey, a solid response of 40 percent of the total graduates, the most in 10 years. Of these graduates 1,779 reported employment status of some type (92.8 percent), both within the profession and outside of it. Approximately 78.5 percent of those employed (1,397) are in full-time positions. On another positive note, 14.1 percent of the 2004 graduates had part-time jobs (a slight increase from 2003's 13.35 percent), but less than 1 percent of the graduates held two or more part-time jobs in order to earn a full-time salary (down from 2 percent the previous year).

Of the 1,779 graduates who reported job placement, 36 percent returned to their current employer after graduation (95 percent in libraries), and of these 85.6 percent reaped the benefits of increased salary and responsibility after attaining a master's degree. Unfortunately, a smaller number of graduates found jobs prior to graduation; 23 percent in 2004, down from 30 percent in 2003.

Getting a full-time job in the Southeast and Southwest looked easier. While the inclusion of graduates in the Washington, D.C., area in the total responses

Adapted from *Library Journal*, October 15, 2005.

helped improve numbers in the Southeast, reported full-time placements increased 37 percent from 2003 (201 in 2003 up to 275 in 2004). More significant growth showed up in the Southwest, with reported full-time placements almost doubling between 2003 (73) and 2004 (141). Mirroring patterns of the general U.S. population, an increasing number of graduates moved into the Southeast and Southwest, especially from the Northeast and Midwest.

Minority Placement

The pool of LIS graduates is slowly growing more diverse, with 16 percent of the 2004 LIS graduates claiming minority status, up from approximately 11.5 percent in 2000 and 15 percent in 2003. Approximately 89 percent of graduates claiming minority status reported full-time positions in libraries and other types of agencies, a significant improvement over the 75 percent of the previous year.

Starting salaries for new minority graduates recovered in 2004. Minority graduates reported an average starting salary of $39,795, a healthy 8 percent ($3,129) rise from 2003. And minority graduates earned 2 percent more when compared to the average starting salary of all graduates ($39,079). Surprisingly, minority graduates fared very well in the Southeast, which historically has had the lowest salary ranges overall, with 23 percent reporting placement and an average starting salary of $39,567 (7.64 percent higher than overall reported salaries in the Southeast). The minority graduates in the Southeast reported jobs split evenly among academic and public libraries and school media centers, with approximately 20 percent in each type of library. While 17 percent of the minority graduates found full-time jobs in the Southwest, this is the one region where salaries fell off sharply from the average. Minority salaries in the Southwest were 11 percent below the overall average, $33,161 compared to $36,759.

Improved salaries and placements for minority graduates may be a reflection of the profession's increased awareness of the need for greater diversity in the library work force. One method of attracting strong recruits is to improve salaries and opportunities, and this appears to be happening.

Between the Sexes

In 2004 women comprised 81 percent of the LIS graduates reporting placement, with starting salaries approximately 4.04 percent lower than men. However, the gender gap has narrowed. Women reported average starting salaries of $38,704, while men reported average starting salaries of $40,332. The difference ($1,628) is an improvement over 2003, when the salary gap was $3,071 or 7.59 percent. Additionally, women have experienced salary growth of 3.51 percent compared to 2003, while starting salaries for men have remained relatively flat, decreasing less than 0.5 percent from $40,462 in 2003.

Women were earning higher starting salaries in public libraries ($35,505) and with library vendors ($44,875) compared with starting salaries of men ($34,825 and $38,625, respectively). Additionally, salaries for men fell below

(text continues on page 398)

Table 1 / Status of 2004 Graduates in Library Professions*

	Number of Schools Reporting	Number of Graduates Responding	Permanent Professional	Temporary Professional	Non-professional	Total	Graduates in Nonlibrary Positions	Unemployed or Status Unreported
Northwest	13	570	420	35	41	495	39	36
Southeast	11	351	262	20	23	305	22	24
Midwest	10	621	408	50	47	505	59	57
Southwest	5	174	135	11	5	151	14	9
West	5	178	94	28	22	144	28	6
Canada	2	21	7	8	—	15	1	5
Total	46	1,915**	1,326	152	138	1,616	163	137

* Table based on survey response from schools and individual graduates. Figures will not necessarily be fully consistent with some of the other data reported that came from individual graduates. Tables do not always add up, individually or collectively, since both schools and individuals omitted data in some cases.
** Note that there were 36 individuals who responded but we were unable to identify an affiliation with a region or program for a total of 1,951.

Table 2 / Placements and Full-Time Salaries of 2004 Graduates/Summary by Region*

Region	Number of Placements	Salaries			Low Salary		High Salary		Average Salary			Median Salary		
		Women	Men	Total	Women	Men	Women	Men	Women	Men	All	Women	Men	All
Northeast	410	306	60	366	$18,000	$12,000	$100,000	$90,000	$39,966	$38,204	$39,756	$38,000	$36,800	$38,000
Southeast	275	205	50	255	16,000	14,880	78,000	59,000	36,567	36,455	36,543	35,000	35,000	35,000
Midwest	431	293	86	379	14,000	27,000	82,500	93,000	38,535	43,249	39,617	47,000	40,000	37,400
Southwest	141	108	23	131	20,800	27,000	85,000	60,000	35,135	39,691	36,759	36,000	37,500	36,000
West	116	84	14	98	22,000	38,000	93,000	74,000	43,616	47,779	44,216	42,000	43,750	42,000
Canada/Intl.**	15	11	4	15	18,357	35,048	43,391	38,500	35,009	36,863	35,503	35,048	36,952	35,883
Combined***	1,373	1,007	237	1,244	14,000	12,000	100,000	93,000	38,704	40,332	39,079	37,000	38,000	37,500

* This table represents only salaries reported as full-time. Some data were reported as aggregate without break-down by gender. Comparison with other tables will show different numbers of placements.
** All international salaries converted to U.S. dollars based on conversion rates for August 16, 2005.
***U.S. results.

Table 3 / 2004 Total Graduates/Placements by School*

Schools	Graduates			Employed			Unemployed			Students		
	Women	Men	Total	Women	Men	Total	Women	Men	Total	Women	Men	Total
Alabama	69	15	84	15	2	17	1	—	1	1	—	1
Alberta	33	7	40	—	—	—	—	—	—	—	—	—
California (UCLA)	41	12	53	—	—	—	—	—	—	—	—	—
Cal State Long Beach	15	3	18	1	—	1	—	—	—	—	—	—
Catholic	57	18	75	23	7	30	5	1	6	—	—	—
Clarion	60	17	77	19	2	21	2	—	2	—	—	—
Denver	13	6	19	—	—	—	—	—	—	—	—	—
Dominican	123	30	153	76	11	87	1	—	1	1	—	1
Drexel	151	49	200	6	3	9	—	—	—	—	—	—
Emporia**	39	11	50	36	9	45	3	—	3	—	1	1
Florida State**	19	5	24	18	5	23	1	—	1	2	—	2
Hawaii	49	5	54	9	—	9	—	—	—	—	—	—
Illinois	159	49	208	71	22	93	2	—	2	3	1	4
Indiana	166	63	229	40	14	54	2	1	3	2	1	3
Iowa	20	6	26	17	5	22	2	1	3	—	—	—
Kentucky	76	26	102	21	8	29	—	—	—	—	—	—
Long Island	131	30	161	53	6	59	1	1	2	—	1	1
Louisiana State	68	13	81	36	5	41	1	—	1	1	—	1
Maryland	83	28	111	24	10	34	1	1	2	—	—	—
McGill	54	17	71	15	4	19	—	1	1	—	—	—
Michigan**	63	29	114	53	27	80	—	—	—	10	2	12
Missouri–Columbia	77	19	96	13	3	16	—	—	—	—	—	—
N.C. Chapel Hill	80	38	118	28	4	32	—	—	—	2	—	2

N.C. Greensboro	70	14	84	22	5	27	—	—	—	1	—	1
North Texas	236	59	295	71	18	89	5	1	6	1	—	—
Oklahoma	70	12	82	25	4	29	—	1	—	—	—	—
Pittsburgh	129	35	164	41	8	49	10	1	11	—	—	—
Pratt**	15	6	21	15	6	21	—	1	4	—	—	—
Queens College**	24	9	33	22	8	30	2	1	2	—	—	—
Rhode Island	61	13	74	34	7	41	1	1	4	—	—	—
Rutgers	109	19	128	30	6	36	3	1	4	—	—	1
San Jose	208	59	267	94	23	117	12	3	15	1	—	1
Simmons	247	47	294	145	28	173	2	—	2	—	1	—
South Carolina	154	19	173	44	6	50	—	1	—	—	1	—
South Florida	124	23	147	17	5	22	1	—	2	—	—	—
Southern Connecticut	77	6	83	29	2	31	—	—	—	—	—	—
Southern Mississippi	41	12	53	14	6	20	—	—	—	—	—	—
St. John's	32	6	38	19	3	22	—	—	—	—	—	—
Syracuse	105	9	114	37	1	38	1	—	1	—	—	—
Texas (Austin)	82	24	106	35	10	45	1	—	1	—	—	—
Texas Women's	150	9	159	—	—	—	—	—	—	—	—	—
University of Albany**	4	1	5	4	1	5	—	—	—	—	—	—
Washington**	27	5	32	27	5	32	—	1	7	1	—	—
Wayne State	130	40	170	68	16	84	6	1	7	1	—	1
Wisconsin (Madison)	59	19	78	52	19	71	1	—	1	2	—	2
Wisconsin (Milwaukee)	93	17	110	18	14	32	—	—	—	—	—	—
Total	3,893	959	4,874	1,437	348	1,785	67	16	84	28	7	35

* This table represents placements of any kind. Comparison with other tables will show different numbers of placements.
** For schools that did not fill out the institutional survey, data were taken from graduate surveys, thus there is not full representation of their graduating classes. Unknown status: 2,213 women, 579 men.

Table 4 / Placements by Type of Organization*

Schools	Public		Elementary and Secondary		College and University		Special		Government		Library and Co-op Network		Vendor		Other		Total		
	Women	Men	Women	Men	Women	Men	Women	Men	Women	Men	Women	Men	Women	Men	Women	Men	Women	Men	Total
Alabama	5	—	4	1	4	—	—	—	1	1	—	—	1	—	—	1	15	3	18
Cal State–Long Beach	—	—	1	—	—	—	—	—	—	—	—	—	—	—	—	—	1	—	1
Catholic	5	—	4	—	4	3	6	1	2	—	—	—	—	—	2	3	23	7	30
Clarion	6	1	6	—	5	—	—	1	1	—	—	—	—	—	1	—	19	2	21
Dominican	27	2	16	1	12	3	7	2	—	—	3	—	—	—	—	1	65	9	74
Drexel	1	—	—	1	2	2	1	—	1	—	—	—	—	—	—	—	5	3	8
Emporia State	13	2	4	—	14	6	—	—	2	—	—	—	—	—	—	—	33	8	41
Florida State	4	3	5	—	5	1	1	—	—	—	—	—	—	—	—	—	15	4	19
Hawaii	2	—	3	—	2	—	—	—	—	—	—	—	—	—	—	—	7	—	7
Illinois	20	4	11	2	22	6	3	1	2	1	—	1	1	—	11	1	70	16	86
Indiana	14	5	5	2	8	3	4	1	1	—	—	—	—	—	3	3	35	14	49
Iowa	8	1	2	—	4	2	1	1	—	—	2	—	—	—	—	1	17	5	22
Kentucky	6	5	5	—	5	2	2	1	—	—	1	—	—	—	—	—	19	8	27
Long Island**	18	1	19	1	6	4	4	1	1	—	—	2	—	—	—	—	48	9	57
Louisiana State	6	3	10	—	12	1	2	—	3	1	—	—	4	—	2	—	35	5	40
Maryland	3	3	1	—	2	4	7	2	7	1	—	—	1	—	—	—	24	10	34
McGill	4	2	—	—	4	—	1	—	2	1	—	—	1	—	—	1	12	4	16
Michigan	7	1	5	—	13	3	6	1	1	1	—	—	—	—	21	20	54	26	80
Missouri–Columbia	2	1	5	1	2	1	—	—	1	—	—	1	—	—	—	—	10	4	14
N.C. Chapel Hill	4	—	1	—	14	2	2	—	1	—	—	3	—	—	—	2	22	7	29

Institution																				
N.C. Greensboro	2	2	17	—	2	—	—	1	—	2	—	—	2	—	—	—	—	23	5	28
North Texas	17	4	22	3	18	7	6	—	1	1	—	3	—	—	—	—	2	64	19	83
Oklahoma	10	2	6	1	6	—	1	2	—	1	—	—	1	—	—	—	—	23	4	27
Pittsburgh	11	1	14	1	10	4	4	2	1	—	4	—	—	—	—	1	—	41	8	49
Pratt	5	2	1	—	2	2	4	1	—	1	—	—	—	—	—	—	—	16	5	21
Queens College	7	4	7	1	6	—	2	1	—	—	—	—	—	—	—	—	1	22	8	30
Rhode Island	13	2	12	2	6	—	—	1	—	—	—	2	1	—	—	3	1	34	6	40
Rutgers	12	2	7	—	4	1	1	1	2	1	—	—	—	1	—	7	1	26	7	33
San Jose	37	8	7	1	20	6	11	2	5	2	—	—	—	—	—	6	5	88	21	109
Simmons	38	—	26	1	35	17	18	2	4	2	—	1	1	—	1	1	—	127	26	153
South Carolina	6	4	19	1	7	1	5	—	1	—	—	—	—	—	—	—	—	39	7	46
South Florida	6	3	7	2	1	—	—	—	—	—	—	1	—	—	2	—	—	16	5	21
So. Connecticut	13	—	5	—	7	1	1	—	1	—	—	2	—	—	—	—	—	27	3	30
So. Mississippi	3	3	5	—	4	2	—	—	1	—	—	—	—	—	—	—	—	13	5	18
St. John's	11	—	3	—	3	3	6	—	—	—	—	—	—	—	—	—	—	23	3	26
Syracuse	9	—	20	1	6	—	1	1	—	1	—	—	—	—	1	1	3	37	9	38
Texas (Austin)	9	3	5	—	12	2	—	1	3	—	—	—	1	—	—	3	3	33	9	42
Univ. of Albany	—	—	—	—	3	—	—	—	—	—	—	—	—	—	1	1	—	4	1	5
Washington	8	—	—	—	8	3	1	—	1	—	1	—	1	—	—	5	—	25	3	28
Wayne State	27	4	10	—	17	6	3	1	2	—	—	1	—	1	—	2	2	61	15	76
Wisc. (Madison)	15	3	4	—	8	8	6	—	7	1	1	2	—	—	—	3	3	44	13	57
Wisc. (Milwaukee)	6	1	1	—	6	2	1	—	—	—	—	—	—	—	—	2	—	16	3	19
Total	420	82	305	23	331	108	119	27	54	11	13	19	12	2	19	77	49	1,323	329	1,651

* This table represents only placements reported by type.
** Some individuals omitted placement or gender information, rendering some information unusable. Comparison with other tables will show different numbers of placements.

Table 5 / Average Salary Index Starting Library Positions, 1990–2004

Year	Library Schools*	Average Beginning Salary	Dollar Increase in Average Salary	Salary Index	BLS-CPI**
1990	38	$25,306	$725	143.03	130.7
1991	46	25,583	277	144.59	136.2
1992	41	26,666	1,083	150.71	140.5
1993	50	27,116	450	153.26	144.4
1994	43	28,086	970	158.74	148.4
1995	41	28,997	911	163.89	152.5
1996	44	29,480	483	166.62	159.1
1997	43	30,270	790	171.05	161.6
1998	47	31,915	1,645	180.38	164.3
1999	37	33,976	2,061	192.03	168.7
2000	37	34,871	895	197.26	175.1
2001	40	36,818	1,947	208.09	177.1
2002	30	37,456	638	211.70	179.9
2003	43	37,975	519	214.63	184.0
2004	46	39,079	1,104	220.87	188.9

* Includes U.S. schools only

**U.S. Department of Labor, Bureau of Labor Statistics, Consumer Price index, All Urban Consumers (CPI-U), U.S. city average, all items, 1982-1984=100. The average beginning professional salary for that period was $17,693.

(continued from page 392)

2003 levels in public libraries, school media centers, special libraries, and library vendors. Much like those for minority recruitment, strong advocacy programs at annual and national conferences and through professional organizations build awareness of the salary differentials, and the career-planning workshops offered by many of the LIS programs may be helping graduates negotiate higher salaries.

Women reported the majority of the positions in public libraries (83.7 percent), school media centers (93 percent), and special libraries (89.4 percent). However, men reported 64 percent more full-time postings in public libraries than 2003, indicating a significant increase in the number of men entering public-service-related positions. In 2004, 21.8 percent more women reported full-time placements in academic libraries than the previous year, but their numbers continued to be disproportionately low compared to men and their salaries were lagging (6.41 percent lower).

The Lure of the "Other"

Jobs in the "other" category fill a broad array of areas from private industry and corporate entities to nonprofit agencies and scientific research. Employment opportunities for LIS graduates encompass jobs in nontraditional settings, such as banks and financial institutions, as well as those directly related to traditional library services in government agencies and academic departments. Placements in these types of agencies and positions increased significantly, from 2.61 percent of the total placements in 2003 to 9.08 percent of the placements in 2004.

Table 6 / Salaries of Reporting Professionals by Area of Job Assignment*

Assignment	Number	Percent of Total	Low Salary	High Salary	Average Salary	Median Salary
Acquisitions	20	1.42	$21,000	$45,000	$34,759	$36,000
Administration	82	5.81	20,800	80,000	38,549	36,000
Archives	60	4.25	16,000	60,000	35,286	35,000
Automation/Systems	12	0.85	26,500	90,000	48,736	50,000
Cataloging and Classification	72	5.10	14,880	58,000	36,144	36,050
Children's Services	67	4.75	18,357	50,000	35,739	36,000
Circulation	42	2.97	22,000	48,000	34,461	35,000
Collection Development	17	1.20	30,000	52,000	37,206	35,750
Database Management	12	0.85	25,000	45,000	37,218	37,000
Electronic or Digital Services	34	2.41	28,000	60,000	39,362	38,500
Government Documents	13	0.92	32,000	46,000	39,350	40,000
Indexing/Abstracting	4	0.28	40,000	54,080	44,860	40,500
Info. Technology	37	2.62	25,000	93,000	47,394	45,000
Instruction	34	2.41	25,000	72,000	40,782	39,000
Interlibrary Loans/ Document Delivery	10	0.71	27,600	43,000	34,500	34,000
Other	128	9.07	12,000	100,000	43,242	40,000
Reference/Info. Services	324	22.95	14,000	65,000	37,228	36,500
Research	3	0.21	37,500	40,000	38,750	38,750
School Library Media Specialist	275	19.48	19,000	82,000	41,114	39,080
Solo Librarian	56	3.97	18,000	62,000	37,353	37,000
Tech Services/Serials	5	0.35	18,000	50,600	35,640	35,000
Telecomm.	3	0.21	37,000	42,000	39,333	39,000
Usability/Usability Testing	12	0.85	37,500	85,000	58,778	62,000
Virtual Reference/ Information Services	4	0.28	26,500	44,000	34,375	33,500
Web Services	3	0.21	32,000	57,500	44,750	44,750
Youth Services	83	5.88	24,000	50,000	36,894	35,680
Total	1,412	100.00	12,000	100,000	39,018	37,500

* This table represents only full-time placements reported by job assignment. Some individuals omitted placement information, rendering some information unusable. Comparison with other tables will show different numbers of placements.

The survey suggests that graduates continued to receive significantly higher compensation in these positions, with an annual average of $47,626 in 2004 (17.94 percent higher than the overall average). Women, in particular, were benefiting from these nontraditional settings, with annual salaries approximately 16.14 percent higher than the overall averages ($46,605 compared to $39,079). Salary gaps between men and women in "other" types of agencies decreased significantly between 2002 (28 percent difference) and 2004 (6.1 percent difference).

(text continues on page 404)

Table 7 / Comparison of Salaries by Type of Organization*

	Total Placements	Salaries		Low Salary		High Salary		Average Salary			Median Salary		
		Women	Men	Women	Men	Women	Men	Women	Men	All	Women	Men	All
Public Libraries													
Northeast	107	87	12	$21,450	$27,000	$56,500	$50,000	$36,545	$37,664	$36,694	$36,000	$36,800	$36,000
Southeast	75	49	23	18,000	14,880	55,000	48,000	33,116	31,872	32,719	32,943	32,949	32,946
Midwest	107	76	19	14,000	27,000	53,000	41,092	34,496	35,230	34,643	35,600	35,900	35,900
Southwest	47	38	8	20,800	28,000	45,000	52,000	32,798	37,081	33,543	34,000	34,698	34,000
Canada/International	6	5	1	18,357	35,048	43,391	35,048	34,302	35,048	34,426	38,000	35,408	36,524
All Public	391	293	65	14,000	14,880	56,500	52,000	35,505	34,825	35,393	35,100	34,198	35,000
School Libraries													
Northeast	121	100	8	17,000	29,000	77,000	82,000	42,592	46,431	42,876	40,000	38,724	40,000
Southeast	73	64	5	26,000	34,000	61,000	59,000	36,912	41,000	37,209	35,000	39,000	35,000
Midwest	58	50	3	20,000	32,000	74,000	49,000	40,928	40,333	40,894	40,000	40,000	40,000
Southwest	36	31	3	25,000	35,500	51,238	42,500	38,285	39,333	38,378	39,000	40,000	39,000
West	14	9	2	28,500	49,000	70,000	74,000	47,500	61,500	50,045	48,000	61,500	49,000
Canada/International	4	2	1	26,000	36,000	42,000	36,000	34,000	36,000	34,667	34,000	36,000	36,000
All School	305	256	22	17,000	29,000	77,000	82,000	40,431	44,293	40,737	39,000	39,500	39,000
College/University Libraries													
Northeast	104	68	23	20,000	21,000	80,000	90,000	38,743	38,113	38,671	38,000	38,000	38,000
Southeast	66	40	21	16,700	18,000	44,000	60,000	35,175	40,333	36,951	36,250	40,000	37,500
Midwest	98	67	19	22,000	25,896	72,000	55,000	37,371	39,281	37,778	36,000	38,000	37,000
Southwest	53	40	8	23,000	30,000	49,000	47,500	34,849	37,500	35,291	34,372	35,250	35,000
West	46	29	9	24,960	38,000	56,256	55,000	39,632	47,167	41,417	39,000	49,000	40,500
Canada/International	5	5	—	32,545	—	70,000	—	41,203	—	41,203	34,210	—	34,210
All Academic	374	249	80	16,700	18,000	80,000	90,000	37,323	39,878	37,981	37,000	39,000	38,000
Special Libraries													
Northeast	41	32	6	25,000	30,000	65,000	55,000	42,197	37,500	42,055	41,000	34,000	40,500
Southeast	23	20	3	30,000	35,000	60,000	40,000	40,450	36,800	39,974	40,500	35,400	40,000
Midwest	22	14	6	27,000	28,500	43,700	93,000	33,836	44,170	36,936	34,500	36,500	35,000
Southwest	7	6	1	33,000	27,000	42,000	27,000	39,083	27,000	37,357	40,000	27,000	40,000
West	12	7	2	22,000	40,000	59,600	60,000	38,563	50,000	40,850	36,850	50,000	39,000

Canada/International	8	6	1	30,000	12,000	40,000	12,000	36,152	12,000	32,127	36,878	12,000	36,381
All Special	116	85	19	22,000	12,000	65,000	93,000	39,459	40,221	39,606	39,050	36,000	38,000
Government Libraries													
Northeast	8	6	2	34,000	32,000	53,000	45,000	42,526	38,500	41,520	41,078	38,500	41,078
Southeast	30	24	6	27,600	28,000	58,000	57,000	40,081	43,404	40,592	41,900	44,463	41,900
Midwest	7	6	—	27,040	—	46,000	—	36,622	—	36,622	36,545	—	36,545
Southwest	5	4	—	38,000	—	62,000	—	44,750	—	44,750	39,500	—	39,500
West	8	6	2	21,000	42,000	60,000	42,000	40,500	42,000	40,875	41,500	42,000	42,000
Canada/International	4	1	1	41,724	37,904	41,724	37,904	41,724	37,904	39,814	41,724	37,904	39,814
All Government	63	47	11	21,000	28,000	62,000	57,000	40,437	41,277	40,608	41,600	41,250	41,600
Library Cooperatives/Networks													
Midwest	4	1	3	44,000	30,000	44,000	37,000	44,000	32,333	35,250	44,000	30,000	33,500
West	1	1	—	44,845	—	44,845	—	44,845	—	44,845	44,845	—	44,845
All Co-op./Nets.	5	2	3	44,000	30,000	44,845	37,000	44,423	32,333	37,169	44,423	30,000	37,000
Vendors													
Northeast	3	2	1	40,000	37,000	49,000	37,000	44,500	37,000	42,000	44,500	37,000	40,000
Southeast	1	1	—	50,000	—	50,000	—	50,000	—	50,000	50,000	—	50,000
Midwest	2	1	1	45,000	32,500	45,000	32,500	45,000	32,500	38,750	45,000	32,500	38,750
West	5	3	2	44,000	35,000	52,000	50,000	46,667	42,500	45,000	44,000	42,500	44,000
Canada/International	1	1	—	35,000	—	35,000	—	35,000	—	35,000	35,000	—	35,000
All Vendors	12	8	4	35,000	32,500	52,000	50,000	44,875	38,625	42,792	44,500	36,000	44,000
Other Organizations													
Northeast	25	11	10	25,000	32,000	100,000	67,000	48,725	44,380	46,656	47,474	39,000	45,000
Southeast	24	15	6	16,000	32,000	54,080	62,500	39,053	48,357	42,018	36,500	47,000	40,063
Midwest	38	22	8	23,816	38,000	82,500	90,000	45,048	63,250	49,902	38,750	66,500	42,750
Southwest	12	7	4	25,000	34,000	85,000	60,000	45,000	42,250	44,000	34,000	37,500	35,000
West	22	17	2	29,900	45,000	93,000	60,000	55,876	52,500	55,521	50,000	52,500	50,000
Canada/International	10	2	3	33,000	40,000	37,970	50,000	35,485	44,167	40,694	35,485	42,500	40,000
All Other	131	74	33	16,000	32,000	100,000	90,000	46,605	49,847	47,626	42,250	47,000	43,000

* This table represents only full-time salaries and placements reported by type. Some individuals omitted placement information rendering some information unusable. Comparison with other tables will show different numbers of total placements due to completeness of the data reported by individuals and schools.

Table 8 / Placements and Full-Time Salaries of Reporting 2004 Graduates*

Schools	Placements	Salaries		Low Salary		High Salary		Average Salary			Median Salary		
		Women	Men	Women	Men	Women	Men	Women	Men	All	Women	Men	All
Alabama	16	13	2	$22,000	$34,000	$50,000	$40,500	$36,365	$37,250	$36,483	$39,000	$37,250	$39,000
Catholic	23	15	5	30,000	30,000	61,000	50,000	39,834	39,200	39,676	37,900	36,000	37,450
Clarion	19	14	1	18,000	27,000	52,000	27,000	32,318	27,000	31,963	32,500	27,000	32,000
Dominican	62	51	7	20,000	28,500	53,000	46,000	36,841	37,814	36,958	36,000	38,000	36,200
Drexel	9	5	3	30,000	39,000	42,000	48,000	37,600	42,346	39,380	40,000	40,039	40,020
Emporia	41	25	3	21,000	35,500	52,000	40,000	34,555	37,833	34,907	34,000	38,000	35,180
Florida State	17	10	4	25,000	28,350	48,600	37,000	37,760	33,034	36,410	38,500	33,392	36,750
Hawaii	9	6	—	35,000		58,000		42,333		42,333	37,500		37,500
Illinois	80	56	16	26,000	30,000	55,000	59,000	38,922	41,833	39,569	38,000	39,000	38,000
Indiana	52	33	13	26,000	27,000	67,000	49,000	38,091	37,815	38,011	36,939	37,000	37,000
Iowa	21	8	4	30,000	28,392	54,500	40,000	39,903	34,227	38,011	38,250	34,259	38,250
Kentucky	26	17	7	20,800	14,880	56,256	51,000	38,271	34,240	37,095	35,500	33,500	35,200
Long Island	51	36	6	27,000	27,000	100,000	60,000	47,148	35,589	45,761	44,666	30,366	43,000
Louisiana State	38	31	5	16,000	27,000	45,000	36,800	34,477	29,960	33,849	34,000	28,000	32,969
Maryland	33	22	9	30,764	33,600	78,000	49,000	42,283	39,956	41,607	39,800	40,000	40,000
McGill	19	12	4	18,357	35,048	43,391	38,500	35,009	36,863	35,503	35,048	36,952	35,883
Michigan	78	43	21	25,000	32,500	82,500	90,000	45,244	56,476	48,930	41,000	55,000	43,000
Missouri–Columbia	12	8	3	31,200	32,000	46,000	45,000	35,650	37,667	36,200	33,500	36,000	34,000
N.C. Chapel Hill	27	23	4	25,000	44,000	49,000	59,000	35,986	49,333	37,526	38,500	45,000	39,000

N.C. Greensboro	22	18	2	26,000	22,000	43,000	57,000	33,940	39,500	34,525	33,000	39,500	33,000
North Texas	73	55	11	20,800	28,000	51,238	46,000	36,279	38,013	36,765	36,500	37,245	36,500
Oklahoma	26	22	3	21,000	35,500	45,000	52,000	31,787	41,667	32,972	32,000	37,500	33,000
Pittsburgh	42	28	8	27,000	12,000	55,000	50,000	36,188	31,250	35,026	35,250	35,500	35,250
Pratt	20	13	4	23,000	38,000	59,600	42,500	36,020	40,625	37,104	35,000	41,000	38,000
Queens College	27	18	8	25,000	30,000	69,000	70,000	44,159	40,850	43,141	41,887	34,900	39,900
Rhode Island	30	22	4	25,000	30,000	51,000	37,448	35,281	34,112	35,101	35,000	34,500	35,000
Rutgers	31	26	4	30,240	36,000	75,000	55,000	42,939	45,250	43,247	38,678	45,000	39,175
San Jose	83	56	11	22,000	40,000	93,000	74,000	44,735	49,627	45,538	43,400	50,000	43,800
Simmons	109	84	15	21,500	21,000	80,000	90,000	40,581	37,321	40,110	38,000	35,500	37,000
South Carolina	45	35	6	16,700	25,000	49,000	48,000	34,454	34,000	34,387	34,500	32,000	34,497
South Florida	19	12	5	27,500	32,949	39,000	39,000	34,513	35,610	34,836	33,100	34,000	34,000
So. Connecticut	22	19	1	21,000	37,000	62,000	37,000	37,701	37,000	37,666	37,000	37,000	37,000
So. Mississippi	15	11	3	28,000	28,500	53,000	35,000	34,532	30,667	33,704	32,000	28,500	32,000
St. John's	16	12	3	25,000	32,800	46,800	45,000	37,733	39,267	38,040	38,250	40,000	38,500
Syracuse	35	30	1	22,000	82,000	77,000	82,000	40,020	82,000	41,375	38,000	82,000	38,000
Texas (Austin)	42	32	9	28,000	27,000	85,000	60,000	38,435	41,084	39,016	37,250	40,000	38,000
Univ. of Albany	4	3	1	20,000	32,000	47,474	32,000	34,491	32,000	33,869	36,000	32,000	34,000
Washington	28	22	3	26,000	38,000	52,000	45,000	40,316	41,000	40,398	38,500	40,000	39,000
Wayne State	55	33	7	14,000	35,000	74,000	93,000	38,597	45,800	39,857	37,000	38,603	37,601
Wisc. (Madison)	53	27	14	26,000	25,100	51,000	44,000	36,968	34,745	36,209	36,000	34,625	36,000
Wisc. (Milwaukee)	19	14	2	22,000	34,000	50,000	44,000	34,896	39,000	35,409	34,400	39,000	34,400

* This table represents only placements and salaries reported as full-time. Some individuals or schools omitted some information, rendering information unusable. Comparisons with other tables will show different numbers of placement and salary.

(continued from page 399)

Career Changers

There has long been a sense that many of the graduates of LIS programs were pursuing the degree to change careers. To get a picture of how large this group is, for the first time the 2004 placements and salary survey asked graduates to discuss their backgrounds. A total of 1,611 graduates responded to questions about career aspirations. Some 53 percent of them were seeking a second or third career. First careers in education topped the list at 33 percent. Graduates had taught a wide range of subjects in K–12 schools, including art, biology, music, physical education, and the social sciences. Approximately 3 percent of the graduates were from backgrounds loosely affiliated with library and information services, involved in bookselling, editing, and publishing. The LIS profession draws from many interesting disciplines, including the clergy (especially youth ministry), social work and the allied health fields, air traffic control, agriculture, and environmental policy. These backgrounds bring diversity to the profession and create connections to many other types of agencies.

Innovative Primary Jobs

The 2004 graduates reported jobs in a wide array of primary assignments. Traditional positions continued to be popular, including those in reference/information services and school media centers. However, these two types of assignments decreased again, dropping from 26.50 percent and 21.47 percent, respectively, in 2003 to 22.92 percent and 19.52 percent in 2004. Children's and youth services experienced healthy growth in 2004, with 42.6 percent more graduates reporting these positions. Combined, children's and youth services comprised 10.65 percent of the overall placements of LIS graduates. Salaries for children's and youth services also gained modestly, with an increase of 3.3 percent from 2003.

In their responses, many graduates indicated that they held dual or multiple primary assignments. Several reference librarians reported combined responsibilities in both "subject specializations" and "rights and reproductions" or "reference" and "instruction/instructional design." Children's and youth services librarians also reported dual roles as community outreach coordinators. And many graduates agreed with the one who wrote: "I do it all—everything from adult and reference services to coordinating special events at the library." Trends in specialization are changing for new graduates as they are expected to take on responsibility in multiple areas of the library operation.

"Other" job assignments indicate dynamic and diverse responsibilities. While the overall total is small, several graduates indicated placement with nonprofit agencies other than libraries. They provide assistance with community information technology, archival services, and computer training. Several LIS graduates responded that they are involved in funding and research foundations, including those that focus on public humanities programs. Graduates described challenging positions in information consulting, geospatial information and mapping (GIS), and software development. How did they find these positions? Overwhelmingly, they noted "past experience," "networking and communicating with professionals outside of the field," and "customer service and people skills."

Graduates on the Move

There was a discernable shift in where LIS graduates were finding jobs. Approximately 18 percent had moved from their home regions to other areas of the United States, Canada, and international locales. In 2002 and 2003 the majority of graduates reported placements in the Northeast and in the Midwest. In 2004 placements in the Southeast and Southwest had increased considerably. In 2003 placements in the Northeast comprised 34 percent of the jobs reported; 28 percent of the graduates reported placements in areas of the Northeast in academic year 2004. Placements in the Midwest for 2003 and 2004 followed a similar pattern, with 35 percent of the reported placements in 2003 falling to 31 percent in 2004.

In the Southwest, jobs in public libraries, academic libraries, and school media centers saw the most impressive growth. Public library jobs in the Southwest were up 57 percent from the previous year, but salaries did not follow suit, increasing by only 1.7 percent (up from $32,916 to $33,543 in 2004). More impressive, academic library positions saw an increase of 62 percent in reported positions and 7.28 percent higher salaries ($32,720 to $35,291). Jobs as school media specialists grew by 41 percent in 2004, and salaries for these positions also had modest growth (5 percent) from $36,196 in 2003 to $38,378 in 2004. This follows a similar pattern that was reported nationwide, with public library positions increasing by 22 percent, academic librarians increasing by 15.8 percent, and school media specialists increasing by 15.4 percent.

Public library positions in the Southeast reflected a similar pattern of growth. Graduates reported approximately 22 percent more jobs in public libraries than the prior year. Salaries, while certainly not keeping pace with growth in positions, also measured approximately 3.78 percent higher than 2003, a slightly faster growth than salaries overall (2.91 percent). School media specialists in the Southeast reported 40 percent more placements in 2004 and average annual salaries of $37,209, which was 6.14 percent higher than 2003 ($34,291). Academic positions, on the other hand, saw a significant drop in reported placements (approximately 31.8 percent decrease) even though average salaries increased approximately 6 percent from $34,729 to $36,951.

Finding the Right Job

For graduates who did not return to an employer or who did not find employment prior to graduation, the job search was arduous. As in 2003, graduates reported an average of almost 4.5 months to find the right job. The length of time to gain employment ranged from less than a week to more than 15 months. However, several of the LIS programs pointed out that the graduates who experienced the longest job searches tended to be the ones who were actively seeking jobs outside their home regions.

LIS schools reported that they did not encounter any serious difficulties in placing their 2004 graduates. Of the 46 schools that participated in the survey, 35 percent indicated that the number of jobs available for graduates seemed to increase over the previous year's availability, ranging from 5 percent more to 40 percent more than 2003. The areas where there appeared to be fewer jobs were academic libraries and library cooperatives/networks.

Graduates had mixed emotions about the job search. For some the search took "long, grueling months to find the right job in the right area," while others reported "two or three job offers within a week or two of graduation." Others told about the decision to accept one of multiple job offers. Said one, "My heart was with the public library position, but I couldn't make it on the salary they could offer. I had to take an academic job in order to make ends meet. School loans and life made the decision."

Graduates discussed the resources they consulted to find jobs. The large majority used multiple resources for job announcements, including career placement services offered by the graduate institutions, professional and student listserv announcements, and state/regional library association resources. Professional listserv announcements were by far the most popular choice, while career placement services at state and national professional conferences were the least highly used resources. This corresponded to what the graduate programs were reporting, with approximately 24 percent reporting career counseling services compared to at least 75 percent providing announcements on student listservs. Some other resources included specific Web sites of libraries and corporations, using headhunters, and participating in an internship or fieldwork activity prior to graduation. Academic librarians frequently consulted *The Chronicle of Higher Education* while the school media specialist went directly to the boards of education job lines and Web sites for the school districts.

Networking with professionals continued to be an effective method for locating jobs. Graduates also frequently mentioned that "my people skills" or "my customer service training" helped them to get the job. Experience counted for a lot, with numerous graduates saying that their years of experience were their greatest asset. Graduates advised "perseverance," "flexibility," "a willingness to move," and "old fashioned job hunting."

Further education continued to be an option for a small number of graduates. Perhaps due to a lengthy job search or accepting a nonprofessional position, approximately 2.9 percent of LIS graduates continued their education, with only 39 percent of them seeking advanced graduate studies in library and information science. They suggest that a second master's degree in another discipline is making a difference in who gets the jobs, stating the belief that "the combination of my MLIS and second master's degree will get me the position I want."

The Final Outcome

For 2004 LIS graduates, the job search was lengthy but productive. They experienced modest salary increases compared to their peers from previous years, and they found interesting jobs in dynamic environments as the master's degree in library and information science is being sought by employers outside of the traditional library environment. The patterns are shifting for job availability, with increasing options in the Southeast and Southwest, though job placement continues to be strong in the Northeast and Midwest. This is a positive outlook for the profession and for graduates.

Accredited Master's Programs in Library and Information Studies

This list of graduate programs accredited by the American Library Association is issued by the ALA Office for Accreditation. Regular updates and additional detail appear on the Office for Accreditation's Web site at http://www.ala.org/ala/accreditation/lisdirb/lisdirectory.htm. More than 200 institutions offering both accredited and nonaccredited programs in librarianship are included in the 58th edition of *American Library Directory* (Information Today, Inc., 2005–2006).

Northeast: Conn., D.C., Md., Mass., N.J., N.Y., Pa., R.I.

Catholic University of America, School of Lib. and Info. Science, 620 Michigan Ave. N.E., Washington, DC 20064. Martha Hale, dean. Tel. 202-319-5085, fax 202-219-5574, e-mail cua-slis@cua.edu, World Wide Web http://slis.cua.edu. Admissions contact: Sydney Pierce. Tel. 202-319-5085, e-mail pierce@cua.edu.

Clarion University of Pennsylvania, Dept. of Lib. Science, 210 Carlson Lib. Bldg., 840 Wood St., Clarion, PA 16214. Bernard F. Vavrek, chair. Tel. 866-272-5612, fax 814-393-2150, World Wide Web http://www.clarion.edu/libsci. Admissions contact: Barbara Reed. Tel. 866-272-5612, e-mail reed@clarion.edu.

Drexel University, College of Info. Science and Technology, 3141 Chestnut St., Philadelphia, PA 19104-2875. David E. Fenske, dean. Tel. 215-895-2474, fax 215-895-2494, e-mail info@cis.drexel.edu, World Wide Web http://www.cis.drexel.edu. Admissions contact: Matthew Lechtenburg.

Long Island University, Palmer School of Lib. and Info. Science, C. W. Post Campus, 720 Northern Blvd., Brookville, NY 11548-1300. Mary Westermann-Cicio, acting dean. Tel. 516-299-2866, fax 516-299-4168, e-mail palmer@cwpost.liu.edu, World Wide Web http://www.liu.edu/palmer. Admissions contact: Rosemary Chu. Tel. 516-299-2487, e-mail rchu@liu.edu.

Pratt Institute, School of Info. and Lib. Science, 144 W. 14 St., New York, NY 10011. Tula Giannini, dean. Tel. 212-647-7682, fax 202-367-2492, e-mail infosils@pratt.edu, World Wide Web http://www.pratt.edu/sils. Admissions contact: Virginia Papandrea.

Queens College, City Univ. of New York, Grad. School for Lib. and Info. Studies, Rm. 254, Rosenthal Lib., 65-30 Kissena Blvd., Flushing, NY 11367-1597. Virgil L. P. Blake, dir. Tel. 718-997-3790, fax 718-997-3797, e-mail gslis@qcunix1.qc.edu, World Wide Web http://www.qc.edu/gslis. Admissions contact: Roberta Brody. E-mail roberta_brody@qc.edu.

Rutgers University, Dept. of Lib. and Info. Science, School of Communication, Info., and Lib. Studies, 4 Huntington St., New Brunswick, NJ 08901-1071. Michael Lesk, Chair. Tel. 732-932-7500 ext. 8955, fax 732-932-2644, e-mail scilsmls@scils.rutgers.edu, World Wide Web http://www.scils.rutgers.edu. Admissions contact: Dan O'Connor.

Saint John's University, College of Liberal Arts and Sciences, Div. of Lib. and Info. Science, 8000 Utopia Pkwy., Jamaica, NY 11439. Jeffery E. Olson, dir. Tel. 718-990-6200, fax 718-990-2071, e-mail dlis@stjohns.edu, World Wide Web http://www.stjohns.edu/libraryscience. Admissions contact: Brad Goldberg. Tel. 618-990-6209.

Simmons College, Grad. School of Lib. and Info. Science, 300 The Fenway, Boston, MA 02115. Michelle Cloonan, dean. Tel. 617-521-2800, fax 617-521-3192, e-mail gslis@simmons.edu, World Wide Web http://www.simmons.edu/gslis.

Southern Connecticut State University, School of Communication, Info., and Lib. Science, 501 Crescent St., New Haven, CT 06515. Edward Harris, dean. Tel. 203-392-5781, fax 203-392-5780, e-mail mckayll @southernct.edu, World Wide Web http:// www.southernct.edu/departments/ils. Admissions contact: Arlene Bielefield. Tel. 203-392-5708, e-mail bielefielda1@ southernct.edu.

Syracuse University, School of Info. Studies, 4-206 Center for Science and Technology, Syracuse, NY 13244-4100. Raymond von Dran, dean. Tel. 315-443-2911, fax 315-443-5673, e-mail ist@syr.edu, World Wide Web http://www.ist.syr.edu. Admissions contact: Gisela von Dran. Tel. 315-443-2911, e-mail mls@syr.edu.

University at Albany, State Univ. of New York, School of Info. Science and Policy, Draper 113, 135 Western Ave., Albany, NY 12222. Peter Bloniarz, dean. Tel. 518-442-5110, fax 518-442-5367, e-mail info sci@albany.edu, World Wide Web http:// www.albany.edu/sisp. Admissions contact: Frances Reynolds. E-mail reynolds@ albany.edu.

University at Buffalo, State Univ. of New York, Dept. of Lib. and Info. Studies, School of Informatics, 534 Baldy Hall, Buffalo, NY 14260. Judith Robinson, chair. Tel. 716-645-2412, fax 716-645-3775, e-mail ub-lis@buffalo.edu, World Wide Web http://www.informatics.buffalo. edu/lis. Admissions contact: Donna M. King. Tel. 716-645-2412 ext. 1173, e-mail kingd@acsu.buffalo.edu.

University of Maryland, College of Info. Studies, 4105 Hornbake Lib. Bldg., College Park, MD 20742. Jennifer Preece, dean. Tel. 301-405-2033, fax 301-314-9145, World Wide Web http://www.clis. umd.edu. Admissions e-mail lbscgrad@ deans.umd.edu, tel. 301-405-2038.

University of Pittsburgh, School of Info. Sciences, 135 N. Bellefield Ave., Pittsburgh, PA 15260. Ronald Larsen, dean. Tel. 412-624-5230, fax 412-624-5231, e-mail lising @mail.sis.pitt.edu, World Wide Web http://www.sis.pitt.edu. Admissions con-

tact: Terry Kizina. Tel. 412-624-3988, e-mail tkizina@mail.sis.pitt.edu.

University of Rhode Island, Grad. School of Lib. and Info. Studies, Rodman Hall, 94 W. Alumni Ave., Kingston, RI 02881. W. Michael Havener, dir. Tel. 401-874-2947, fax 401-874-4964, e-mail gslis@etal.uri. edu, World Wide Web http://www.uri.edu/ artsci/lsc.

Southeast: Ala., Fla., Ga., Ky., La., Miss., N.C., S.C., Tenn., P.R.

Florida State University, College of Info., Shores Bldg., Tallahassee, FL 32306-2100. Larry Dennis, dean. Tel. 850-644-5772, fax 850-644-9763, e-mail grad@lis. fsu.edu, World Wide Web http://www.ci. fsu.edu. Admissions contact: Delores Bryant. Tel. 850-645-3280.

Louisiana State University, School of Lib. and Info. Science, 267 Coates Hall, Baton Rouge, LA 70803. Beth Paskoff, dean. Tel. 225-578-3158, fax 225-578-4581, e-mail slis@lsu.edu, World Wide Web http://slis.lsu.edu. Admissions contact: LaToya Coleman Joseph. E-mail lcjoseph @lsu.edu.

North Carolina Central University, School of Lib. and Info. Sciences, 1800 Fayetteville St., Durham, NC 27707. Irene Owens, dean. Tel. 919-530-6485, fax 919-530-6402, e-mail lsis@nccu.edu, World Wide Web http://www.nccuslis.org. Admissions contact: Tysha Jacobs. Tel. 919-530-7320.

University of Alabama, School of Lib. and Info. Studies, Box 870252, Tuscaloosa, AL 35487-0252. Elizabeth Aversa, dir. Tel. 205-348-4610, fax 205-348-3746, e-mail info@slis.ua.edu, World Wide Web http://www.slis.ua.edu. Admissions contact: Linda Hord.

University of Kentucky, College of Communications and Info. Studies, School of Lib. and Info. Science, 502 King Lib., Lexington, KY 40506-0039. Timothy W. Sineath, dir. Tel. 859-257-8876, fax 859-257-4205, World Wide Web http://www.uky.edu/ CIS/SLIS. Admissions contact: Jane Salsman. Tel. 859-257-3317, e-mail salsman@ uky.edu.

University of North Carolina at Chapel Hill, School of Info. and Lib. Science, CB 3360, 100 Manning Hall, Chapel Hill, NC 27599-3360. José-Marie Griffiths, dean. Tel. 919-962-8366, fax 919-962-8071, e-mail info@ils.unc.edu, World Wide Web http://www.ils.unc.edu. Admissions contact: Betty Dye.

University of North Carolina at Greensboro, Dept. of Lib. and Info. Studies, School of Educ., 349 Curry Bldg., Greensboro, NC 27402-6170. Lee Shiflett, chair. Tel. 336-334-3477, fax 336-334-5060, e-mail lis@uncg.edu, World Wide Web http://lis.uncg.edu.

University of Puerto Rico, Graduate School of Info. Sciences and Technologies, Box 21906, San Juan, PR 00931-1906. Nitza Hernández, dir. Tel. 787-763-6199, fax 787-764-2311, e-mail egcti@rrpac.upr.clu.edu, World Wide Web http://egcti.upr.edu. Admissions contact: Migdalia Dávila. Tel. 787-764-0000 ext. 3530, e-mail mdavila2@rrpac.upr.clu.edu.

University of South Carolina, School of Lib. and Info. Science, Davis College, Columbia, SC 29208. Daniel Barron, dir. Tel. 803-777-3858, fax 803-777-7938, e-mail ddbarron@gwm.sc.edu, World Wide Web http://www.libsci.sc.edu. Admissions contact: Ruth Roberts. Tel. 800-304-3153, e-mail rroberts@sc.edu.

University of South Florida, School of Lib. and Info. Science, College of Arts and Sciences, 4202 E. Fowler Ave., CIS 1040, Tampa, FL 33620. Vicki Gregory, dir. Tel. 813-974-3520, fax 813-974-6840, e-mail lis@cas.usf.edu, World Wide Web http://www.cas.usf.edu/lis. Admissions contact: Mel Pace. Tel. 813-974-7650, e-mail tpace@cas.usf.edu.

University of Southern Mississippi, School of Lib. and Info. Science, 118 College Drive, No. 5146, Hattiesburg, MS 39406-0001. M. J. Norton, dir. Tel. 601-266-4228, fax 601-266-5774, e-mail slis@usm.edu, World Wide Web http://www.usm.edu/slis. Admissions tel. 601-266-5137, e-mail graduatestudies@usm.edu,.

University of Tennessee, School of Info. Sciences, 451 Communications Bldg., 1345 Circle Park Drive, Knoxville, TN 37996-0341. Edwin Cortez, dir. Tel. 865-974-2148, fax 865-974-4967, e-mail sis@utk.edu, World Wide Web http://www.sis.utk.edu. Admissions contact: Tanya Arnold.

Midwest: Ill., Ind., Iowa, Kan., Mich., Mo., Ohio, Wis.

Emporia State University, School of Lib. and Info. Management, Campus Box 4025, Emporia, KS 66801. Ann L. O'Neill, dean. Tel. 620-341-5203, fax 620-341-5233, e-mail sliminfo@emporia.edu, World Wide Web http://slim.emporia.edu. Admissions contact: Daniel Roland. Tel. 620-341-5064, e-mail slimapply@emporia.edu.

Indiana University, School of Lib. and Info. Science, LI 011, 1320 E. 10 St., Bloomington, IN 47405-3907. Blaise Cronin, dean. Tel. 812-855-2018, fax 812-855-6166, e-mail slis@indiana.edu, World Wide Web http://www.slis.indiana.edu. Admissions contact: Rhonda Spencer.

Kent State University, School of Lib. and Info. Science, Box 5190, Kent, OH 44242-0001. Richard E. Rubin, dir. Tel. 330-672-2782, fax 330-672-7965, World Wide Web http://www.slis.kent.edu, e-mail inform@slis.kent.edu. Admissions contact: Cheryl Tennant.

Dominican University, Grad. School of Lib. and Info. Science, 7900 W. Division St., River Forest, IL 60305. Susan Roman, dean. Tel. 708-524-6845, fax 708-524-6657, e-mail gslis@dom.edu, World Wide Web http://www.gslis.dom.edu. Admissions contact: Kathleen M. Swantek. Tel. 708-524-6848, e-mail kswantek@dom.edu.

University of Illinois at Urbana-Champaign, Grad. School of Lib. and Info. Science, 501 E. Daniel St., Champaign, IL 61820-6211. John Unsworth, dean. Tel. 217-333-3280, fax 217-244-3302, World Wide Web http://www.lis.uiuc.edu. Admissions contact: Valerie Younger. Tel. 217-333-0734., e-mail apply@alexia.lis.uiuc.edu.

University of Iowa, School of Lib. and Info. Science, 3087 Main Lib., Iowa City, IA 52242-1420. David Eichmann, dir. Tel. 319-335-5707, fax 319-335-5374, e-mail slis@uiowa.edu, World Wide Web http://

www.uiowa.edu/~libsci. Admissions contact: Caroline Austin. E-mail caroline-austin@uiowa.edu.

University of Michigan, School of Info., 304 West Hall Bldg, 1085 S. University Ave., Ann Arbor, MI 48109-1092. John L. King, dean. Tel. 734-763-2285, fax 734-764-2475, e-mail si.admissions@umich.edu, World Wide Web http://www.si.umich.edu. Admissions contact: Laura Elgas. E-mail lauramb@umich.edu.

University of Missouri, College of Educ., School of Info. Science and Learning Technologies, 303 Townsend Hall, Columbia, MO 65211. John Wedman, dir. Tel. 573-882-4546, fax 573-884-0122, e-mail sislt@missouri.edu, World Wide Web http://sislt.missouri.edu.

University of Wisconsin–Madison, School of Lib. and Info. Studies, Rm. 4217, H. C. White Hall, 600 N. Park St., Madison, WI 53706. Louise S. Robbins, dean. Tel. 608-263-2908, fax 608-263-4849, e-mail uw-slis@slis.wisc.edu, World Wide Web http://www.slis.wisc.edu. Admissions contact: Barbara J. Arnold. Tel. 608-263-2909, e-mail bjarnold@wisc.edu.

University of Wisconsin–Milwaukee, School of Info. Studies, P.O. Box 413, Milwaukee, WI 53211. Johannes Britz, dean. Tel. 414-229-4707, fax 414-229-6699, e-mail info@sois.uwm.edu, World Wide Web http://www.sois.uwm.edu.

Wayne State University, Lib. and Info. Science Program, 106 Kresge Lib., Detroit, MI 48202. Joseph J. Mika, dir. Tel. 313-577-1825, fax 313-577-7563, e-mail asklis @wayne.edu, World Wide Web http://www.lisp.wayne.edu. Admissions contact: Matthew Fredericks. Tel. 313-577-2446, e-mail aj8416@wayne.edu.

Southwest: Ariz., Okla., Texas.

Texas Woman's University, School of Lib. and Info. Studies, P.O. Box 425438, Denton, TX 76204-5438. Ling Hwey Jeng, dir. Tel. 940-898-2602, fax 940-898-2611, e-mail slis@twu.edu, World Wide Web http://www.twu.edu/cope/slis. Admissions contact: Patricia Graham. E-mail pgraham @mail.wu.edu.

University of Arizona, School of Info. Resources and Lib. Science, 1515 E. 1 St., Tucson, AZ 85719. Jana Bradley, dir. Tel. 520-621-3565, fax 520-621-3279, e-mail sirls@u.arizona.edu, World Wide Web http://www.sir.arizona.edu. Admissions contact: Polly Mitchell. E-mail pmitch@ email.arizona.edu.

University of North Texas, School of Lib. and Info. Sciences, Box 311068, Denton, TX 76203-1068. Herman Totten, dean. Tel. 940-565-2731, fax 940-565-3101, e-mail slis@unt.edu, World Wide Web http://www.unt.edu/slis. Admissions contact: Toby Faber. Tel. 940-565-2445, e-mail tfaber@lis. admin.unt.edu.

University of Oklahoma, School of Lib. and Info. Studies, College of Arts and Sciences, Rm. 120, 401 W. Brooks, Norman, OK 73019-6032. Kathy Latrobe, interim dir. Tel. 405-325-3921, fax 405-325-7648, e-mail slisinfo@ou.edu, World Wide Web http://www.ou.edu/cas/slis. Admissions contact: Maggie Ryan.

University of Texas at Austin, School of Info., 1 University Sta., D7000, Austin, TX 78712-0391. Andrew Dillon, dean. Tel. 512-471-3821, fax 512-471-3971, e-mail info@ischool.utexas.edu, World Wide Web http://www.ischool.utexas.edu. Admissions contact: Philip Doty. Tel. 512-471-3624, e-mail pdoty@ischool.utexas. edu.

West: Calif., Colo., Hawaii, Wash.

San Jose State University, School of Lib. and Info. Science, 1 Washington Sq., San Jose, CA 95192-0029. Ken Haycock, dir. Tel. 408-924-2490, fax 408-924-2476, e-mail office@slis.sjsu.edu, World Wide Web http://slisweb.sjsu.edu. Admissions contact: Scharlee Phillips. Tel. 408-924-2417, e-mail sphillip@slis.sjsu.edu.

University of California, Los Angeles, Graduate School of Educ. and Info. Studies, Dept. of Info. Studies, Box 951520, Los Angeles, CA 90095-1520. Anne Gilliland, chair. Tel. 310-825-8799, fax 310-206-3076, e-mail info@gseis.ucla.edu, World

Wide Web http://is.gseis.ucla.edu. Admissions contact: Susan Abler. Tel. 310-825-5269, e-mail abler@gseis.ucla.edu.

University of Denver, College of Educ., Lib. and Info. Science Program, Wesley Hall, 2153 E. Wesley, Ste. 103, Denver, CO 80208. Deborah S. Grealy, dir. Tel. 303-871-2747, fax 303-871-3422, World Wide Web http://www.du.edu/lis. Admissions contact: Sandra Snyder-Mondragon. Tel. 303-871-2747, e-mail smondrag@du.edu.

University of Hawaii, Lib. and Info. Science Program, College of Natural Sciences, 2550 McCarthy Mall, Honolulu, HI 96822. Rebecca Knuth, chair. Tel. 808-956-7321, fax 808-956-3548, e-mail slis@hawaii. edu, World Wide Web http://www.hawaii. edu/slis. Admissions contact: Gail Morimoto.

University of Washington, The Info. School, 370 Mary Gates Hall, Box 352840, Seattle, WA 98195-2840. Harry Bruce, dean. Tel. 206-685-9937, fax 206-616-3152, e-mail info@ischool.washington.edu, World Wide Web http://www.ischool. washington.edu. Admissions contact: Lindsay Boswell. Tel. 206-543-1794, e-mail mlis@ischool.washington.edu.

Canada

Dalhousie University, School of Info. Management, Kenneth C. Rowe Management Bldg., Halifax, NS B3H 3J5. Fiona Black, dir. Tel. 902-494-3656, fax 902-494-2451, e-mail sim@dal.ca, World Wide Web http://www.sim.management.dal.ca. Admissions contact: JoAnn Watson. Tel. 902-494-3656, e-mail mlis.coordinator@dal.ca.

McGill University, Grad. School of Lib. and Info. Studies, 3459 McTavish St., Montreal, PQ H3A 1Y1. France Bouthillier, dir. Tel. 514-398-4204, fax 514-398-7193, e-mail gslis@mcgill.ca, World Wide Web

http://www.gslis.mcgill.ca. Admissions contact: Kathryn Hubbard.

Université de Montréal, École de Bibliothéconomie et des Sciences de l'Information, C.P. 6128, Succursale Centre-Ville, Montreal, QC H3C 3J7. Jean-Michel Salaun, dir. Tel. 514-343-6400, fax 514-343-5753, e-mail ebsiinfo@ebsi.umontreal.ca, World Wide Web http://www.ebsi.umontreal.ca. Admissions contact: Diane Mayer. E-mail diane.mayer@umontreal.ca.

University of Alberta, School of Lib. and Info. Studies, 3-20 Rutherford S., Edmonton, AB T6G 2J4. Anna Altmann, dir. Tel. 780-492-4578, fax 780-492-2430, e-mail slis@ualberta.ca, World Wide Web http:// www.slis.ualberta.ca. Admissions contact: Joanne Hilger. Tel. 780-492-4140, e-mail joanne.hilger@ualberta.ca.

University of British Columbia, School of Lib., Archival, and Info. Studies, Ste. 301, 6190 Agronomy Rd., Vancouver, BC V6T 1Z3. Edie Rasmussen, dir. Tel. 604-822-2404, fax 604-822-6006, e-mail slais@ interchange.ubc.ca, World Wide Web http://www.slais.ubc.ca. Admissions contact: Richard Hopkins. E-mail slaisad@ interchange.ubc.ca.

University of Toronto, Faculty of Info. Studies, Rm. 211, 140 George St., Toronto, ON M5S 3G6. Brian Cantwell Smith, dean. Tel. 416-978-3202, fax 416-978-5762, e-mail inquire@fis.utoronto.ca, World Wide Web http://www.fis.utoronto.ca. Admissions contact: Adriana Rossini. Tel. 416-978-8589, e-mail Adriana.rossini@utoronto.ca.

University of Western Ontario, Grad. Programs in Lib. and Info. Science, Faculty of Info. and Media Studies, Rm. 240, North Campus Bldg., 1151 Richmond St., London, ON N6A 5B7. Catherine Ross, dean. Tel. 519-661-4017, fax 519-661-3506, e-mail mlisinfo@uwo.ca, World Wide Web http://fims.uwo.ca. Admissions contact: Shelley Long.

Library Scholarship Sources

For a more complete list of scholarships, fellowships, and assistantships offered for library study, see *Financial Assistance for Library and Information Studies,* published annually by the American Library Association. The document is also available on the ALA Web site at http://www.ala.org/ala/hrdr/educprofdev/financial assistance.htm.

American Association of Law Libraries. (1) A varying number of scholarships of a minimum of $1,000 for graduates of an accredited law school who are degree candidates in an ALA-accredited library school; (2) a varying number of scholarships of varying amounts for library school graduates working on a law degree, non-law graduates enrolled in an ALA-accredited library school, and law librarians taking a course related to law librarianship; (3) the George A. Strait Minority Stipend of $3,500 for varying numbers of minority librarians working toward an advanced degree to further a law library career, and (4) a varying number of $500 scholarships for law librarians taking courses related to law librarianship. For information, write to: Scholarship Committee, AALL, 53 W. Jackson Blvd., Suite 940, Chicago, IL 60604.

American Library Association. (1) The Marshall Cavendish Scholarship of $3,000 for a varying number of students who have been admitted to an ALA-accredited library school; (2) the David H. Clift Scholarship of $3,000 for a varying number of students who have been admitted to an ALA-accredited library school; (3) the Tom and Roberta Drewes Scholarship of $3,000 for a varying number of library support staff; (4) the Mary V. Gaver Scholarship of $3,000 for a varying number of individuals specializing in youth services; (5) the Miriam L. Hornback Scholarship of $3,000 for a varying number of ALA or library support staff; (6) the Christopher J. Hoy/ERT Scholarship of $5,000 for a varying number of students who have been admitted to an ALA-accredited library school; (7) the Tony B. Leisner Scholarship of $3,000 for a varying number of library support staff; (8)

Spectrum Initiative Scholarships of $6,500 for a varying number of minority students admitted to an ALA-accredited library school. For information on all ALA scholarships, write to: ALA Scholarship Clearinghouse, 50 E. Huron St., Chicago, IL 60611. Application can also be made online; see http://www.ala.org/hrdr/scholarship.html.

ALA/American Association of School Librarians. The AASL School Librarians Workshop Scholarship of $3,000 for a candidate admitted to a full-time ALA-accredited MLS or school library media program. For information, write to: ALA Scholarship Clearinghouse, 50 E. Huron St., Chicago, IL 60611, or see http://www.ala.org/hrdr/scholarship.html.

ALA/Association for Library Service to Children. (1) The Bound to Stay Bound Books Scholarship of $6,000 each for two students who are U.S. or Canadian citizens, who have been admitted to an ALA-accredited program, and who will work with children in a library for one year after graduation; (2) the Frederic G. Melcher Scholarship of $6,000 each for two U.S. or Canadian citizens admitted to an ALA-accredited library school who will work with children in school or public libraries for one year after graduation. For information, write to: ALA Scholarship Clearinghouse, 50 E. Huron St., Chicago, IL 60611, or see http://www.ala.org/hrdr/scholarship.html.

ALA/Association of College and Research Libraries and the Institute for Scientific Information. (1) The ACRL Doctoral Dissertation Fellowship of $1,500 for a student who has completed all coursework and submitted a dissertation proposal that has been accepted, in the area of academic librarianship; (2) the Samuel Lazerow Fellowship of $1,000 for a research, travel, or writing project in acquisitions or technical services in an academic or research library; (3) the ACRL and Martinus Nijhoff International West European Specialist Study Grant, which pays travel expenses, room, and board for a ten-day trip to Europe for an ALA member (selection is based on proposal outlining purpose of trip). For information, write to: Megan Bielefeld, ACRL/ALA, 50 E. Huron St., Chicago, IL 60611.

ALA/Association of Specialized and Cooperative Library Agencies. Century Scholarship of up to $2,500 for a varying number of disabled U.S. or Canadian citizens admitted to an ALA-accredited library school. For information, write to: ALA Scholarship Clearinghouse, 50 E. Huron St., Chicago, IL 60611, or see http://www.ala.org/hrdr/scholarship.html.

ALA/International Relations Committee. The Bogle Pratt International Library Travel Fund grant of $1,000 for a varying number of ALA members to attend a first international conference. For information, write to: Michael Dowling, ALA/IRC, 50 E. Huron St., Chicago, IL 60611.

ALA/Library and Information Technology Association. (1) The LITA/Christian Larew Memorial Scholarship of $3,000 for a student who has been admitted to an ALA-accredited program in library automation and information science; (2) the LITA/Sirsi Scholarship in Library and Information Technology of $2,500 for a student who has been admitted to an ALA-accredited program in library automation and information technology; (3) the LITA/OCLC Minority Scholarship in Library and Information Technology of $3,000 for a minority student admitted to an ALA-accredited program; (4) the LITA/LSSI Minority Scholarship of $2,500 for a minority student admitted to an ALA-accredited program. For information, write to: ALA Scholarship Clearinghouse, 50 E. Huron St., Chicago, IL 60611, or see http://www.ala.org/hrdr/scholarship.html.

ALA/Public Library Association. The Demco New Leaders Travel Grant Study Award of up to $1,500 for a varying number of PLA members with MLS degrees and five years or less experience. For information, write to: PLA Awards Program, PLA/ALA, 50 E. Huron St., Chicago, IL 60611.

American-Scandinavian Foundation. Fellowships and grants for 25 to 30 students, in amounts from $3,000 to $18,000, for advanced study in Denmark, Finland, Iceland, Norway, or Sweden. For information, write to: Exchange Division, American-Scandinavian Foundation, 58 Park Ave., New York, NY 10026.

Association for Library and Information Science Education (ALISE). A varying number of research grants of up to $2,500 each for members of ALISE. For information, write to: Association for Library and Information Science Education, Box 7640, Arlington, VA 22207.

Association of Jewish Libraries. (1) The AJL Scholarship Fund offers up to two scholarships of $500 each for MLS students who plan to work as Judaica librarians; (2) the Rosalie Katchen Memorial Award of varying amounts for varying numbers of MLS students to enable them to advance in Hebraica or Judaica cataloging. For information, write to: Deborah Stern, Dir., Kaplan Library, Reconstructionist Rabbinical College, 1299 Church Rd., Wyncote, PA 19095, e-mail dstern@rrc.edu.

Association of Seventh-Day Adventist Librarians. The D. Glenn Hilts Scholarship of $1,000 for a member of the Seventh-Day Adventist Church in a graduate library program. For information, write to: Ms. Wisel, Association of Seventh-Day Adventist Librarians, Columbia Union College, 7600 Flower Ave., Takoma Park, MD 20912.

Beta Phi Mu. (1) The Sarah Rebecca Reed Scholarship of $2,000 for a person accepted in an ALA-accredited library program; (2) the Frank B. Sessa Scholarship of $1,250 for a Beta Phi Mu member for continuing education; (3) the Harold Lancour Scholarship of $1,500 for study in a foreign country related to the applicant's work or schooling; (4) the Blanche E. Woolls Scholarship for School Library Media Service of $1,500 for a person accepted in an ALA-accredited library program; (5) the Doctoral Dissertation Scholarship of $2,000 for a person who has completed course work toward a doctorate; (6) the Eugene Garfield Doctoral Dissertation Scholarship of $3,000 for a person who has approval of a dissertation topic. For information, write to: Wayne Wiegand, Executive Director, Beta Phi Mu, Florida State University, SIS, Tallahassee, FL 32306-2100.

Canadian Association of Law Libraries. The Diana M. Priestly Scholarship of $2,500 for a student with previous law library experience or for entry to an approved Canadian law school or accredited Canadian library school. For information, write to: Ann Rae, Chair, CALL/ACBD Scholarship and Awards Committee, Bora Laskin Law Library, University of Toronto, 78 Queens Park, Toronto, ON M5S 2C5.

Canadian Federation of University Women. (1) The Alice E. Wilson Award of $5,000 for three students enrolled in graduate studies in any field, with special consideration given to candidates returning to study after at least three years; (2) the Margaret McWilliams Pre-Doctoral Fellowship of $11,000 for a full-time student who has completed one full year of study at the doctoral level; (3) the CFUW Memorial Fellowship of $6,500 for a student enrolled in a master's program in science, mathematics, or engineering; (4) the Beverly Jackson Fellowship of $2,000 for a student over age 35 enrolled in graduate work at an Ontario University; (5) the 1989 Polytechnique Commemorative Award of $2,800 for a student enrolled in graduate studies related particularly to women; (6) the Bourse Georgette LeMoyne award of $6,000 for graduate study at a Canadian university where one of the languages of administration and instruction is French; (7) the Dr. Marion Elder Grant Fellowship of $10,000 for a full-time student at the master's or doctoral level; (8) the Margaret Dale Philp Biennial Award of $3,000 for graduate studies in the humanities or social sciences. For information, write to: Fellowships Program Manager, Canadian Federation of University Women, 251 Bank St., Suite 600, Ottawa, ON K2P 1X3, Canada.

Canadian Library Association. (1) The World Book Graduate Scholarship in Library and Information Science of $2,500; (2) the CLA Dafoe Scholarship of $3,000; and (3) the H. W. Wilson Scholarship of $2,000. Each scholarship is given to a Canadian citizen or landed immigrant to attend an accredited Canadian library school; (4) the Library Research and Development Grant of $1,000 for a member of the Canadian Library Association, in support of theoretical and applied research in library and information science. For information, write to: CLA Membership Services Department, Scholarships and Awards Committee, 328 Frank St., Ottawa, ON K2P 0X8, Canada.

Catholic Library Association. (1) The World Book, Inc., Grant of $1,500 divided among no more than three CLA members for continuing education in children's or school librarianship; (2) the Rev. Andrew L. Bouwhuis Memorial Scholarship of $1,500 for a student accepted into a graduate program in library science. For information, write to: Jean R. Bostley, SSJ, Scholarship Chair, Catholic Library Association, 100 North St., Suite 224, Pittsfield, MA 01201-5109.

Chinese American Librarians Association. (1) the Sheila Suen Lai Scholarship and (2) the C. C. Seetoo/CALA Conference Travel Scholarship each offer $500 to a Chinese descendant who has been accepted in an ALA-accredited program. For information, write to: MengXiong Liu, Clark Library, San Jose State University, 1 Washington Sq., San Jose, CA 95192-0028.

Church and Synagogue Library Association. The Muriel Fuller Memorial Scholarship of $200 (including texts) for a correspondence course offered by the University of Utah Continuing Education Division. Open to CSLA members only. For information, write to: CSLA, P.O. Box 19357, Portland, OR 97280-0357.

Council on Library and Information Resources. (1) The Rovelstad Scholarship in International Librarianship, to enable a student enrolled in an accredited LIS program to attend the IFLA Annual Conference; (2) the A. R. Zipf Fellowship in

Information Management of $10,000, awarded annually to a U.S. citizen enrolled in graduate school who shows exceptional promise for leadership and technical achievement. For more information, write to: Council on Library and Information Resources, 1755 Massachusetts Ave. N.W., Suite 500, Washington, DC 20036.

Massachusetts Black Librarians' Network. Two scholarships of at least $500 and $1,000 for minority students entering an ALA-accredited master's program in library science, with no more than 12 semester hours toward a degree. For information, write to: Pearl Mosley, Chair, Massachusetts Black Librarians' Network, 17 Beech Glen St., Roxbury, MA 02119.

Medical Library Association. (1) The Cunningham Memorial International Fellowship of $6,000 plus up to $2,000 travel expenses; (2) a scholarship of $5,000 for a person entering an ALA-accredited library program, with no more than one-half of the program yet to be completed; (3) a scholarship of $5,000 for a minority student for graduate study; (4) a varying number of Research, Development and Demonstration Project Grants of $100 to $1,000 for U.S. or Canadian citizens who are MLA members; (5) the MLA Doctoral Fellowship of $2,000 for doctoral work in medical librarianship or information science; (6) the Rittenhouse Award of $500 for a student enrolled in an ALA-accredited library program or a recent graduate working as a trainee in a library internship program; (7) Continuing Education Grants of $100 to $500 for U.S. or Canadian citizens who are MLA members. For information, write to: Professional Development Department, Medical Library Association, 65 E. Wacker Pl., Suite 1900, Chicago, IL 60601-7298.

Mountain Plains Library Association. (1) A varying number of grants of up to $600 each and (2) a varying number of grants of up to $150 each for MPLA members with at least two years of membership for continuing education. For information, write to: Joseph R. Edelen, Jr., MPLA Executive Secretary, I. D. Weeks Library, University of South Dakota, Vermillion, SD 57069.

Society of American Archivists. The Colonial Dames Awards, two grants of $1,200 each for specific types of repositories and collections. For information, write to: Debra Noland, Society of American Archivists, 521 S. Wells St., 5th fl., Chicago, IL 60607.

Southern Regional Education Board. A varying number of grants of varying amounts to cover in-state tuition for graduate or postgraduate study in an ALA-accredited library school for residents of various southern U.S. states (qualifying states vary year by year). For information, write to: Academic Common Market, c/o Southern Regional Education Board, 592 Tenth St. N.W., Atlanta, GA 30318-5790.

Special Libraries Association. (1) Three $6,000 scholarships for students interested in special-library work; (2) the Plenum Scholarship of $1,000 and (3) the ISI Scholarship of $1,000, each also for students interested in special-library work; (4) the Affirmative Action Scholarship of $6,000 for a minority student interested in special-library work; and (5) the Pharmaceutical Division Stipend Award of $1,200 for a student with an undergraduate degree in chemistry, life sciences, or pharmacy entering or enrolled in an ALA-accredited program. For information on the first four scholarships, write to: Scholarship Committee, Special Libraries Association, 1700 18th St. N.W., Washington, DC 20009-2508; for information on the Pharmaceutical Stipend, write to: Susan E. Katz, Awards Chair, Knoll Pharmaceuticals Science Information Center, 30 N. Jefferson St., Whippany, NJ 07981.

Library Scholarship and Award Recipients, 2005

Scholarships and awards are listed by organization.

American Association of Law Libraries (AALL)

AALL and West Group George A. Strait Minority Scholarships. *Winners:* Michelle Crosby, Wendy Duplechain, Jennifer Frazier.

AALL Scholarships. *Winners:* (Library Degree for Law School Graduates) Timothy Baland; (Library Degree for Non-Law School Graduates) Diana Daleo; (Law Librarians in Continuing Education Courses) Karen Beck.

James F. Connolly/LexisNexis Academic and Library Solutions Scholarship. *Winner:* Jennifer Behrens.

Marian Gould Gallagher Distinguished Service Award. To recognize extended and sustained service to law librarianship. *Winners:* Charles R. Dyer, Roy M. Mersky, Michael S. Miller.

Institute for Court Management Scholarship. *Winner:* Not awarded in 2005.

LexisNexis Grants. *Winners:* Maureen Anderson, Nicole A. Casner, Beth Chamberlain, Miriam D. Childs, Stephanie D. Crawford, Christine Demetros, Donna M. Fisher, Jill A. Fukunaga, N. Jane Goodman, Julienne E. Grant, Deborah K. Hackerson, Margaret F. Hall, Tammy A. Hinderman, Trina T. Holloway, Shan Jiang, Julie M. Jones, Susan Julian, Marguerite Martin, Susan Nevelow Mart, Denise R. Potter, Kevin Reiss, Sarah Shik, Kelly J. Shorrel, Linda M. Sobey, Sergio Stone, Kathleen E. Thomson, Camilla Tubbs, Colleen C. Williams, Gary R. Yessin.

LexisNexis/John R. Johnson Memorial Scholarships. *Winners:* Casey Duncan, Cyril Emery, Emily Janoski, Theresa Leming, Shawn Nevers, Jason Raymond.

Meira Pimsleur Scholarship. *Sponsor:* Arthur W. Diamond Law Library, Columbia Law School. *Winner:* Not awarded in 2005.

Minority Leadership Development Award. *Winner:* Ronald E. Wheeler, Jr.

American Library Association (ALA)

ALA/Information Today Library of the Future Award ($1,500). For a library, consortium, group of librarians, or support organization for innovative planning for, applications of, or development of patron training programs about information technology in a library setting. *Donor:* Information Today, Inc. *Winner:* Oberlin (Ohio) Public Library for its establishment and operation of The Bridge, Oberlin's Community Technology Center.

Leo Albert Spectrum Scholarship. To a designated Spectrum Scholarship recipient. *Donor:* Leo Albert. *Winner:* Toshiba Lynette Burns-Johnson.

Hugh C. Atkinson Memorial Award ($2,000). For outstanding achievement (including risk taking) by academic librarians that has contributed significantly to improvements in library automation, management, and/or development or research. *Offered by:* ACRL, ALCTS, LAMA, and LITA divisions. *Winner:* Paul M. Gherman.

Carroll Preston Baber Research Grant (up to $3,000). For innovative research that could lead to an improvement in library services to any specified group(s) of people. *Donor:* Eric R. Baber. *Winner:* Kristin R. Eschenfelder, University of Wisconsin at Madison, for "Investigating the Impact of Digital Rights Management Systems on the Users of Digital Works: A Pilot Study."

Beta Phi Mu Award ($500). For distinguished service in library education. *Donor:* Beta Phi Mu International Library Science Honorary Society. *Winner:* Lynn Akin.

Bogle/Pratt International Library Travel Fund Award ($1,000). To ALA member(s) to attend their first international conference. *Donors:* Bogle Memorial Fund and Pratt Institute School of Information and Library Science. *Winner:* Irina Tarsis.

W. Y. Boyd Literary Novel Award. *Winner:* See "Literary Prizes, 2005" by Gary Ink.

David H. Clift Scholarship ($3,000). To worthy U.S. or Canadian citizens enrolled in an ALA-accredited program toward an MLS degree. *Winner:* Megan Eberhardt.

Eileen Cooke State and Local James Madison Award. To recognize individuals or groups who have championed public access to government information. *Winner*: Minnesota Coalition on Government Information.

Melvil Dewey Medal. To an individual or group for recent creative professional achievement in library management, training, cataloging and classification, and the tools and techniques of librarianship. *Donor:* OCLC/Forest Press. *Winner:* Joan S. Mitchell.

Tom and Roberta Drewes Scholarship ($3,000). To a library support staff member pursuing a master's degree. *Winner:* Sherry L. Buchanan.

EBSCO/ALA Conference Sponsorship Award (up to $1,000). To enable ten librarians to attend the ALA Annual Conference. *Donor:* EBSCO Subscription Services. *Winners:* Cynthia Bischoff, Michelle Boule, Donna Erisman, Marianne Fitzgerald, Marquita L. Harnett, Anne Hoffman, Robin Imperial, Rowena Li, Nichole Schulert, Joni Stine.

Equality Award ($500). To an individual or group for an outstanding contribution that promotes equality of women and men in the library profession. *Donor:* Scarecrow Press. *Winner:* Alma Dawson.

Freedom to Read Foundation Roll of Honor Award. *Winner:* David Cohen.

Elizabeth Futas Catalyst for Change Award ($1,000). To recognize and honor a librarian who invests time and talent to make positive change in the profession of librarianship. *Donor:* Elizabeth Futas Memorial Fund. *Winner:* Atifa Rawan.

Loleta D. Fyan Public Library Research Grant (up to $10,000). For projects in public library development. *Donor:* Fyan Estate. *Winner:* Cadillac-Wexford County (Michigan) Public Library for "MP3 @ the Library."

Mary V. Gaver Scholarship ($3,000). To a student pursuing an MLS and specializing in youth services. *Winner:* Angelia Maria Mahone.

Louise Giles Spectrum Scholarship. To a designated Spectrum Scholarship recipient. *Donor:* Louise Giles. *Winner:* Karen Annmarie Gordon.

William R. Gordon Spectrum Scholarship. To a designated Spectrum Scholarship recipient. *Donor:* William R. Gordon and friends. *Winner:* Not awarded in 2005.

Grolier Foundation Award ($1,000). For stimulation and guidance of reading by children and young people. *Donor:* Scholastic Library Publishing. *Winner:* Caroline Ward.

Ken Haycock Award ($1,000). For significant contribution to public recognition and appreciation of librarianship through professional performance, teaching, or writing. *Winner:* Sarah Ann Long.

Highsmith Library Literature Award ($500). To an author or coauthors who make an outstanding contribution to library literature issued during the three years preceding the presentation. *Donor:* Highsmith. *Winner:* Not awarded in 2005.

Honorary ALA Membership. *Honorees:* Lotsee Patterson, Nettie B. Taylor.

Miriam L. Hornback Scholarship ($3,000). To an ALA or library support staff person pursuing a master's degree in library science. *Winner:* Sarah Rebekah Krygier.

Paul Howard Award for Courage ($1,000). To a librarian, library board, library group, or an individual who has exhibited unusual courage for the benefit of library programs or services. *Donor:* Paul Howard Memorial Fund. *Winner:* Yongyi Song.

John Ames Humphry/OCLC/Forest Press Award ($1,000). To an individual for significant contributions to international librarianship. *Donor:* OCLC/Forest Press. *Winner:* Marianna Tax Choldin.

Tony B. Leisner Scholarship ($3,000). To a library support staff member pursuing a master's degree program. *Winner:* Sharon Denise Vaughn-Williams.

Joseph W. Lippincott Award ($1,000). To a librarian for distinguished service to the profession. *Donor:* Joseph W. Lippincott, III. *Winner:* Donald J. Sager.

James Madison Award. To recognize efforts to promote government openness. *Winner:* Richard M. Schmidt, general counsel to American Society of Newspaper Editors.

Marshall Cavendish Excellence in Library Programming Award ($2,000). Recognizes either a school library or public library that demonstrates excellence in library programming by providing programs that have community impact and respond to community need. *Winner:* San Diego Public Library for "Stories of Faith: Religion and Diversity in San Diego."

Marshall Cavendish Scholarship ($3,000). To a worthy U.S. or Canadian citizen to begin an MLS degree in an ALA-accredited program. *Winner:* Jennifer Wann.

Schneider Family Book Awards (three awards of $5,000). To authors or illustrators of books that embody artistic expressions of the disability experience for child and adolescent audiences. *Donor:* Katherine Schneider. *Winners:* See "Literary Prizes, 2005" by Gary Ink.

Spectrum Initiative Scholarships ($6,500). Presented to minority students admitted to an ALA-accredited library school. *Winners:* Aryanez Albuquerque, Gabriel Angulo, Ricardo Antoni, Veronica Inez Arellano, Sherlonya Laquisha Augustine, Ofilia Paola Barrera, Eileen Kuan-Veng Bosch, Allison D. Broussard, Tanya Brown, Toshiba Lynette Burns-Johnson, Michael Lamont Butler-Harley, Claire Kaui Card, Maria Magdalena Cortez-Tafolla, Juliette Elaine Douglas, LaToya Charise Eddington, Monique Marie Escamilla, Cheryl Denise Franklin, Kimberly Diane Gales, Lesly Galiana, Nancy Suzanne Gistover, Karen Annmarie Gordon, Michelle Renee Hammond, Regina Lachelle Harris, Corinne Ruth Hatcher, Maria Lucia Hernandez, Gregory Allan-Kingman Hom, Sylvia Estella Johnson, Alice Pin-Lan Ko, Janice Lynn Kowemy, Nghi Lam, Kafi Ayana Laramore-Josey, Richard Kien Le, Tamara Lynne Lee, Yunn-Hwa Lii, Deborah Lois Lilton, Brenda Marisol Linares, Sandra D. Littletree, Shu-Hua Liu, Douglas Cleveland Lyles, Candice Anne Mack,

Josy A. Martinez, Michelle Pantoja McKinney, Eileen Joyce Mendez, Leah Marie Mickens, Gouse S. A. Mohammed, Vani Natarajan, Phuongkhanh Nguyen, Han Ngoc Nguyen, Megan Zoe Perez, Patrice D. Prevost, Margaret Siatafu Reid-Leach, Tezeno Lynette Roberson, Elisabeth Ruth Rodriguez, Melody Ingrid Royster, Brandy S. Sanchez, Beatrice Colastin Skokan, Allen Sweatt, Neely Tang, Lana Marrie Thelen, Chastity Thomas, Joel Thornton, Grisel Torralbas, Anne Tran, Carly Veary, Baasil Wilder, Nicole Williams, Robert Yazzie.

Sullivan Award for Public Library Administrators Supporting Services to Children. To a library supervisor/administrator who has shown exceptional understanding and support of public library services to children. *Donor:* Peggy Sullivan. *Winner:* Wayne Onkst.

Howard M. and Gladys B. Teeple Spectrum Scholarship. To a designated Spectrum Scholarship recipient. *Donor:* The Religion and Ethics Institute. *Winner:* Corinne Ruth Hatcher.

Thomson Gale Financial Development Award ($2,500). To a library organization for a financial development project to secure new funding resources for a public or academic library. *Donor:* Gale Group. *Winner:* Joseph Mark Lauinger Memorial Library, Georgetown University.

Betty J. Turock Spectrum Scholarship. To a designated Spectrum Scholarship recipient. *Donor:* JTBC Foundation. *Winner:* Neely Tang.

H. W. Wilson Library Staff Development Grant ($3,500). To a library organization for a program to further its staff development goals and objectives. *Donor:* H. W. Wilson Company. *Winner:* Broward County (Florida) Library.

World Book–ALA Goal Grant (up to $10,000). To ALA units for the advancement of public, academic, or school library service and librarianship through support of programs that implement the goals and priorities of ALA. *Donor:* World Book. *Winners:* Office for Literacy and Outreach Services, Association for Library Trustees and Advocates, Chapter Relations Office, Public Information Office, Office for Research and Statistics, and Washington Office, for their advocacy for rural, native, and tribal school and public libraries.

ALA/Allied Professional Association

Dynix Award for Outstanding Achievement in Promoting Salaries and Status for Library Workers ($2,500). *Donor:* Dynix. *Winners:* Maurice Freedman, Dorothy Morgan.

Working @ Your Library: For Love or Money Advocacy Video Contest ($250). To the writer and editor of a guide to accompany the video. *Winners:* (writer) Sue Knoche, (editor) Martha Whaley.

American Association of School Librarians (AASL)

AASL/ABC-CLIO Leadership Grant (up to $1,750). For planning and implementing leadership programs at state, regional, or local levels to be given to school library associations that are affiliates of AASL. *Donor:* ABC-CLIO. *Winner:* Wisconsin Educational Media Association.

AASL/Baker & Taylor Distinguished Service Award ($3,000). For outstanding contributions to librarianship and school library development. *Donor:* Baker & Taylor Books. *Winner:* Rebecca Bingham.

AASL Collaborative School Library Media Award ($2,500). For expanding the role of the library in elementary and/or secondary school education. *Donor:* Sagebrush Corporation. *Winner:* Valerie Edwards.

AASL Crystal Apple Award. To an individual or group for a significant impact on school libraries and students. *Winner:* Follett Library Resources.

AASL Distinguished School Administrators Award ($2,000). For expanding the role of the library in elementary and/or secondary school education. *Donor:* ProQuest. *Winner:* Michael Hart, principal, Holy Rosary School, Tacoma, Washington.

AASL Distinguished Service Award ($3,000). For outstanding national contributions to school librarianship and school library development. *Winner:* Rebecca T. Bingham.

AASL/Frances Henne Award ($1,250). To a school library media specialist with five or fewer years in the profession to attend an AASL regional conference or ALA Annual Conference for the first time. *Donor:* Greenwood Publishing Group. *Winner:* John McDonald.

AASL/Highsmith Research Grant (up to $5,000). To conduct innovative research aimed at measuring and evaluating the impact of school library media programs on learning and education. *Donor:* Highsmith, Inc. *Winner:* Joyce Valenza for "School Virtual Libraries: The Influence of Best Practices on High School Students' Information Seeking."

AASL School Librarian's Workshop Scholarship ($3,000). To a full-time student preparing to become a school library media specialist at the preschool, elementary, or secondary level. *Donor:* Jay W. Toor, president, Library Learning Resources. *Winner:* Elizabeth Fisher.

Information Technology Pathfinder Award ($1,000 to the specialist and $500 to the library). To library media specialists for innovative approaches to microcomputer applications in the school library media center. *Donor:* Follett Software Company. *Winners:* (elementary) not awarded in 2005; (secondary) not awarded in 2005.

Intellectual Freedom Award ($2,000, and $1,000 to media center of recipient's choice). To a school library media specialist who has upheld the principles of intellectual freedom. *Donor:* ProQuest. *Winner:* Ann Ewbank, Cholla Middle School, Phoenix, Arizona, and Cholla Middle School Library Media Center.

National School Library Media Program of the Year Award ($10,000 each in three categories). To school districts and a single school for excellence and innovation in outstanding library media programs. *Donor:* Follett Library Resources. *Winners:* (Single School—tie) Downers Grove (Illinois) South High School and Henry M. Brader Elementary School, Newark, Delaware; (Large School District) William Floyd School District, Mastic Beach, New York.

Association for Library Collections and Technical Services (ALCTS)

Hugh C. Atkinson Memorial Award. *See under* American Library Association.

Paul Banks and Carolyn Harris Preservation Award ($1,500). To recognize the contribution of a professional preservation specialist who has been active in the field of preservation and/or conservation for library and/or archival materials. *Donor:* Preservation Technologies. *Winner:* Paul Conway.

Best of *LRTS* Award ($250). To the author(s) of the best paper published each year in the division's official journal. *Winner:* Kristin Antelman for "Identifying the Serial Work as a Bibliographic Entity."

Blackwell's Scholarship Award ($2,000 scholarship to the U.S. or Canadian library school of the recipient's choice). To honor the author(s) of the year's outstanding monograph, article, or original paper in the field of acquisitions, collection development, and related areas of resource development in libraries. *Donor:* Blackwell's. *Winner:* Peggy Johnson for "Fundamentals of Collection Development and Management."

Bowker/Ulrich's Serials Librarianship Award ($1,500). For leadership in serials-related activities. *Donor:* R. R. Bowker. *Winner:* Dan Tonkery.

First Step Award (Wiley Professional Development Grant) ($1,500). For librarians new to the serials field to attend ALA's Annual Conference. *Donor:* John Wiley & Sons. *Winner:* Jennifer Arnold.

Leadership in Library Acquisitions Award ($1,500). For significant contributions by an outstanding leader in the field of library acquisitions. *Donor:* Harrassowitz. *Winner:* Scott Wicks.

Margaret Mann Citation (and $2,000 to the U.S. or Canadian library school of the winning author's choice). To a cataloger or classifier for achievement in the areas of cataloging or classification. *Donor:* Online Computer Library Center. *Winner:* Dorothy McGarry.

Esther J. Piercy Award ($1,500). To a librarian with no more than ten years' experience for contributions and leadership in the field of library collections and technical services. *Donor:* YBP Library Services. *Winner:* Terry Paul Reese.

Association for Library Service to Children (ALSC)

ALSC/BWI Summer Reading Program Grant ($3,000). To an ALSC member for implementation of an outstanding public library summer reading program for children. *Donor:* BWI. *Winner:* Jersey City (New Jersey) Free Public Library.

ALSC/Sagebrush Education Resources Literature Program Award ($1,000 toward ALA Annual Conference attendance). To an ALSC member for the development of an outstanding literature program for children. *Donor:* Sagebrush Corporation. *Winner:* Lisa Sizemore.

May Hill Arbuthnot Honor Lectureship. To an author, critic, librarian, historian, or teacher of children's literature who prepares a paper considered to be a significant contribution to the field of children's literature. *Winner:* Russell Freedman.

Mildred L. Batchelder Award. *Winner:* See "Literary Prizes, 2005" by Gary Ink.

Louise Seaman Bechtel Fellowship ($4,000). For librarians with 12 or more years of professional-level work in children's library collections, to read and study at the Baldwin Library, University of Florida (must be an ALSC member with an MLS from an ALA-accredited program). *Donor:* Bechtel Fund. *Winner:* Sharon Deeds.

Pura Belpré Award. *Winner:* See "Literary Prizes, 2005" by Gary Ink.

Bound to Stay Bound Books Scholarships (scholarships of $6,500 each). For men and women who intend to pursue an MLS or advanced degree and who plan to work in the area of library service to children. *Donor:* Bound to Stay Bound Books. *Winners:* Melissa Brumstead, Donna Colson, Latonya Pegues, Danielle Winn.

Caldecott Medal. *Winner:* See "Literary Prizes, 2005" by Gary Ink.

Andrew Carnegie Medal. To the U.S. producer of the most distinguished video for children in the previous year. *Donor:* Carnegie Corporation of New York. *Winners:* Paul

Gagne and Melissa Reilly (Weston Woods Studios) for *The Dot.*

Carnegie-Whitney Awards (up to $5,000). For the publication of bibliographic aids for research. *Donor:* James Lyman Whitney and Andrew Carnegie Funds. *Winners:* Donald Altschiller, Tiffeni J. Fontno, Carla Levesque, Alice A. Tait, Frances Yates.

Distinguished Service to ALSC Award ($1,000). To recognize significant contributions to, and an impact on, library services to children and/or ALSC. *Winner:* Marilyn Miller.

Frederic G. Melcher Scholarship ($6,000). To two students entering the field of library service to children for graduate work in an ALA-accredited program. *Winners:* Jonathan Hunt, Wendy Torrence.

John Newbery Medal. *Winner:* See "Literary Prizes, 2005" by Gary Ink.

Penguin Young Readers Group Awards ($600). To children's librarians in school or public libraries with ten or fewer years of experience to attend the ALA Annual Conference for the first time. Must be a member of ALSC. *Donor:* Penguin Young Readers Group. *Winners:* Kristine M. Casper, Alison O'Reilly, Sarah Pardi, Amy Schardein.

Robert F. Sibert Medal. To the author of the most distinguished informational book for children published during the preceding year. *Donor:* Bound to Stay Bound Books. *Winner:* See "Literary Prizes, 2005" by Gary Ink.

Laura Ingalls Wilder Medal. To an author or illustrator whose works have made a lasting contribution to children's literature. *Winner:* See "Literary Prizes, 2005" by Gary Ink.

Association for Library Trustees and Advocates (ALTA)

ALTA/Gale Outstanding Trustee Conference Grant Award ($750). *Donor:* Gale Research. *Winners:* Maureen Hayes, Ruby Neely.

ALTA Literacy Award (citation). To a library trustee or an individual who, in a volunteer capacity, has made a significant contribution to addressing the illiteracy problem in the United States. *Winner:* Not awarded in 2005.

ALTA Major Benefactors Honor Award (citation). To individuals, families, or corporate bodies that have made major benefactions to public libraries. *Winners:* the Simon Family, Hemlock Federal Bank, James T. Smith.

Trustee Citations. To recognize public library trustees for individual service to library development on the local, state, regional, or national level. *Winners:* Jim Connor, Robert B. Lyons.

Association of College and Research Libraries (ACRL)

ACRL Academic/Research Librarian of the Year Award ($3,000). For outstanding contribution to academic and research librarianship and library development. *Donor:* YBP Library Services. *Winner:* Ravindra Nath Sharma.

ACRL Distinguished Education and Behavioral Sciences Librarian Award ($1,000). To an academic librarian who has made an outstanding contribution as an education and/or behavioral sciences librarian through accomplishments and service to the profession. *Donor:* John Wiley & Sons. *Winner:* Kate Corby.

ACRL Doctoral Dissertation Fellowship ($1,500). To a doctoral student in the field of academic librarianship whose research has potential significance in the field. *Donor:* Thomson Scientific. *Winner:* Susan Ward Aber.

ACRL Special Presidential Recognition Award (plaque). To recognize an individual's special career contributions to ACRL and the library profession. *Winner:* Richard K. Gardner, founding editor, *Choice.*

ACRL Women's Studies Section Awards for Achievement (two awards of $1,000). To recognize achievements in women's studies librarianship. *Donors:* Greenwood Publishing Group and Routledge. *Winners:* Ellen J. Broidy, Cindy Ingold, Linda Krikos.

Hugh C. Atkinson Memorial Award. *See under* American Library Association.

Best Practices in Marketing @ Your Library Awards ($2,000 and $1,000). To recognize academic and research libraries that demonstrate outstanding best-practices marketing programs. *Donor:* ACRL Friends Committee. *Winners:* (first place) American University; (second place) Illinois State University.

Community College Learning Resources Leadership/Library Achievement Awards ($500). To recognize outstanding achievement in library programs or leadership. *Sponsor:* EBSCO Information Services. *Winners:* (leadership) Susan M. Maltese; (programs) Kate Connell, Suzanne Lo.

Coutts Nijhoff International West European Specialist Study Grant (up to 4,500 euros). Supports research pertaining to West European studies, librarianship, or the book trade. *Sponsor*: Coutts Nijhoff International. *Winner:* Charlene Kellsey.

Miriam Dudley Instruction Librarian Award ($1,000). For contribution to the advancement of bibliographic instruction in a college or research institution. *Donor:* Elsevier Science. *Winner:* Ilene F. Rockman.

Excellence in Academic Libraries Awards ($3,000 plus travel expenses).To recognize an outstanding community college, college, and university library. *Donor:* Blackwell's Book Services. *Winners:* (community college) Pierce College, Lakewood and Puyallup, Washington; (college) Mount Holyoke College, South Hadley, Massachusetts; (university) University of Virginia, Charlottesville.

Haworth Press Distance Learning Librarian Conference Sponsorship Award ($1,200). To an ACRL member working in distance-learning librarianship in higher education. *Winner:* Martha Kreszock.

Instruction Section Innovation Award ($3,000). To librarians or project teams in recognition of a project that demonstrates creative, innovative, or unique approaches to information literacy instruction or programming. *Donor:* LexisNexis. *Winner:* The Library Prize for Undergraduate Research, University of California–Berkeley.

Marta Lange/*Congressional Quarterly* Award ($1,000). To recognize an academic or law librarian for contributions to bibliography and information service in law or political

science. *Donor:* CQ Press. *Winner:* Merle J. Slyhoff.

Samuel Lazerow Fellowship for Research in Acquisitions or Technical Services ($1,000). To foster advances in acquisitions or technical services by providing librarians a fellowship for travel or writing in those fields. *Sponsor:* Thomson Scientific. *Winner:* Kristin R. Eschenfelder for "Investigating the Impact of Digital Rights Management Systems on Libraries: A Pilot Study."

Katharine Kyes Leab and Daniel J. Leab Exhibition Catalog Awards (citations). For the best catalogs published by American or Canadian institutions in conjunction with exhibitions of books and/or manuscripts. *Winners:* (division I–expensive) *Holding In, Holding On: Artist's Books by Martha A. Hall,* Martha Hall and Martin Antonetti, Mortimer Rare Book Room, Smith College; (division II–moderately expensive) *Objects of American Art Education: Highlights from the Diana Korzenik Collection,* Diana Korzenik, Huntington Library, San Marino, California; (division III–inexpensive) *Commentary: An Exhibition of Artwork by Sylvia Ptak,* Sylvia Ptak and Kyo Maclear, Thomas Fisher Rare Book Library, University of Toronto; (division IV–brochures) *Uncle Tom's Cabin in Print: The Collection of Mary C. Schlosser,* Mary Schlosser, Ronald Patkus, and Joyce Bickerstaff, Vassar College; (division V, electronic exhibitions) *Elizabeth I: Ruler and Legend,* Center for Renaissance Studies, Newberry Library, Chicago.

Oberly Award for Bibliography in the Agricultural or Natural Sciences. Biennially, for the best English-language bibliography in the field of agriculture or a related science in the preceding two-year period. *Donor:* Eunice Rockwood Oberly Memorial Fund. *Winner:* Not awarded in 2005.

Publication of the Year Award (citation). Recognizes an outstanding publication or publications relating to instruction in a library environment published in the preceding two years. *Winner: Motivating Students in Information Literacy Classes* by Trudi E. Jacobson and Lijuan Xu (Neal-Schuman, 2004).

Association of Specialized and Cooperative Library Agencies (ASCLA)

ASCLA Century Scholarship (up to $2,500). For a library school student or students with disabilities admitted to an ALA-accredited library school. *Winner:* Ivan Murillo.

ASCLA Exceptional Service Award. To recognize exceptional service to patients; the homebound; inmates; and medical, nursing, and other professional staff in hospitals. *Winner:* Queens Borough (New York) Public Library.

ASCLA Leadership Achievement Award. To recognize leadership and achievement in the areas of consulting, multitype library cooperation, and state library development. *Winner:* Library Development Bureau of the New Jersey State Library.

ASCLA Professional Achievement Award. To recognize professional achievement within the areas of consulting, networking, statewide service, and programs. *Winner:* Not awarded in 2005.

ASCLA Service Award (citation). For outstanding service and leadership to the division. *Winner:* Marilyn Irwin.

Francis Joseph Campbell Award. For a contribution of recognized importance to library service for the blind and physically handicapped. *Winners:* Judith M. Dixon and Wells B. Kormann, National Library Service for the Blind and Physically Handicapped, Library of Congress.

KLAS/National Organization on Disability Award for Library Service to People with Disabilities ($1,000). To a library organization to recognize an innovative project to benefit people with disabilities. *Donor:* Keystone Systems. *Winner:* Johnson County Library, Shawnee Mission, Kansas.

Ethnic and Multicultural Information and Exchange Round Table

David Cohen Multicultural Award ($300). To recognize articles of significant research and publication that increase understanding and promote multiculturalism in North American libraries. *Donor:* Routledge. *Winner:* Not awarded in 2005.

Gale Multicultural Award ($1,000). For outstanding achievement and leadership in serving the multicultural/multiethnic community. *Donor:* Gale Research. *Winner:* Not awarded in 2005.

Exhibits Round Table

Christopher J. Hoy/ERT Scholarship ($5,000). To an individual or individuals who will work toward an MLS degree in an ALA-accredited program. *Donor:* Family of Christopher Hoy. *Winner:* Robin White.

Kohlstedt Exhibit Award (citation). To companies or organizations for the best single, multiple, and island booth displays at the ALA Annual Conference. *Winners:* Not awarded in 2005.

Federal and Armed Forces Librarians Round Table (FAFLRT)

FAFLRT Achievement Award. For achievement in the promotion of library and information service and the information profession in the federal government community. *Winner:* Not awarded in 2005.

Adelaide del Frate Conference Sponsor Award ($1,000). To encourage library school students to become familiar with federal librarianship and ultimately seek work in federal libraries; for attendance at ALA Annual Conference and activities of the Federal and Armed Forces Librarians Round Table. *Winner:* Not awarded in 2005.

Distinguished Service Award (citation). To honor a FAFLRT member for outstanding and sustained contributions to the association and to federal librarianship. *Winner:* Jewel A. Player.

Gay, Lesbian, Bisexual, and Transgendered Round Table (GLBT)

Stonewall Book Awards. *Winners:* See "Literary Prizes, 2005" by Gary Ink.

Government Documents Round Table (GODORT)

James Bennett Childs Award. To a librarian or other individual for distinguished lifetime contributions to documents librarianship. *Winner:* Ernest G. Baldwin, III.

Bernadine Abbott Hoduski Founders Award (plaque). To recognize documents librarians who may not be known at the national level but who have made significant contributions to the field of state, international, local, or federal documents. *Winner:* Sue Selmer.

LexisNexis Documents to the People Award ($3,000). To an individual, library, organization, or noncommercial group that most effectively encourages or enhances the use of government documents in library services. *Winner:* Daniel P. Mahony.

Newsbank/Readex Catharine J. Reynolds Award ($2,000). Grants to documents librarians for travel and/or study in the field of documents librarianship or area of study benefiting performance as documents librarians. *Donor:* Newsbank and Readex Corporation. *Winner:* Not awarded in 2005.

W. David Rozkuszka Scholarship ($3,000). To provide financial assistance to an individual who is currently working with government documents in a library while completing a master's program in library science. *Winner:* Julia Tanis Sayles.

Intellectual Freedom Round Table (IFRT)

John Phillip Immroth Memorial Award for Intellectual Freedom ($500). For notable contribution to intellectual freedom fueled by personal courage. *Winner:* Hayes (Kansas) Public Library Board of Trustees.

Eli M. Oboler Memorial Award ($500). Biennially, to an author of a published work in English or in English translation dealing with issues, events, questions, or controversies in the area of intellectual freedom. *Winner:* Not awarded in 2005.

ProQuest/SIRS State and Regional Achievement Award ($1,000). To an innovative and effective intellectual freedom project covering a state or region during the calendar year. *Donor:* ProQuest Social Issues Resource Series (SIRS). *Winner:* Not awarded in 2005.

Library Administration and Management Association (LAMA)

Hugh C. Atkinson Memorial Award. *See under* American Library Association.

Diana V. Braddom Fundraising and Financial Development Section Scholarship ($1,000). To enable attendance at the ALA Annual Conference. *Donor:* Diana V. Braddom. *Winner:* Alissa Williams.

John Cotton Dana Library Public Relations Awards ($3,500). To libraries or library organizations of all types for public relations programs or special projects ended during the preceding year. *Donor:* H. W. Wilson Company. *Winners:* Riverside County (California) Library System, Seattle Public Library, San Diego State University Library and Information Access, Louisiana Center for the Book, Maricopa County (Arizona) Library District, Calgary (Alberta) Public Library, and North Suburban Library System, Wheeling, Illinois.

LAMA/AIA Library Buildings Award (citation). Biennial awards to recognize excellence in the architectural design and planning of libraries. *Sponsors:* American Institute of Architects and LAMA. *Winners:* R. M. Kliment and Frances Halsband Architects, Mack Scogin Merrill Elam Architects, Wandel and Schnell Architects, Loysen + Kreuthmeier Architects, Hellmuth Obata Kassabaum, Einhorn Yaffee Prescott Architecture and Engineering, Bohlin Cywinski Jackson, VCBO Architecture, Moshe Safdie and Associates, Office for Metropolitan Architecture and LMN Architects.

LAMA Cultural Diversity Grant ($1,000). To support creation and dissemination of resources that will assist library administrators and managers in developing a vision and commitment to diversity. *Winner:* Pikes Peak Library District Cultural Diversity Committee, Colorado Springs.

LAMA Group Achievement Award. To honor LAMA committees or task forces, recognizing outstanding teamwork supporting the goals of LAMA. *Winner:* 2004 National Institute Planning Committee.

LAMA Leadership Award. *Winner:* Don Leslie.

LAMA President's Award. *Winner:* Not awarded in 2005.

LAMA/YBP Student Writing and Development Award ($1,000 grant to attend the ALA Annual Conference). *Donor:* YBP Library Services. *Winner:* Not awarded in 2005.

Library and Information Technology Association (LITA)

Hugh C. Atkinson Memorial Award. *See under* American Library Association.

LITA/Brett Butler Entrepreneurship Award ($5,000). To recognize a librarian or library for demonstrating exemplary entrepreneurship by providing innovative products or services through the application of information technology. *Donor:* Thomson Gale. *Winner:* Dan Chudnov, Yale Center for Medical Informatics.

LITA/Endeavor Student Writing Award ($1,000). For the best unpublished manuscript on a topic in the area of libraries and information technology written by a student or students enrolled in an ALA-accredited library and information studies graduate program. *Donor:* Endeavor Information Systems. *Winner:* Kristin Yiotis for "The Open Access Initiative: New Paradigms for Scholarly Communications."

LITA/Christian Larew Memorial Scholarship ($3,000). To encourage the entry of qualified persons into the library and information technology field. *Sponsor:* Informata.com. *Winner:* Margaret Lawrence.

LITA/Library Hi Tech Award ($1,000). To an individual or institution for a work that shows outstanding communication for continuing education in library and information technology. *Donor:* Emerald Press. *Winner:* William Gosling.

LITA/LSSI Minority Scholarship in Library and Information Science ($2,500). To encourage a qualified member of a principal minority group to work toward an MLS degree in an ALA-accredited program with emphasis on library automation. *Donor:* Library Systems and Services, Inc. *Winner:* Han Nguyen.

LITA/OCLC Frederick G. Kilgour Award for Research in Library and Information Technology ($2,000 and expense-paid atten-

dance at ALA Annual Conference). To bring attention to research relevant to the development of information technologies. *Donor:* OCLC. *Winner:* William E. Moen.

LITA/OCLC Minority Scholarship in Library and Information Technology ($3,000). To encourage a qualified member of a principal minority group to work toward an MLS degree in an ALA-accredited program with emphasis on library automation. *Donor:* OCLC. *Winner:* Andreas E. Ciriello.

LITA Scholarship in Library and Information Technology ($2,500). To encourage the entry of qualified persons into the library automation field who demonstrate a strong commitment to the use of automated systems in libraries. *Winner:* Toshiba Lynette Burns-Johnson.

Library History Round Table (LHRT)

Phyllis Dain Library History Dissertation Award ($500). To the author of a dissertation treating the history of books, libraries, librarianship, or information science. *Winner:* Bonnie Mak.

Donald G. Davis Article Award (certificate). For the best article written in English in the field of U.S. and Canadian library history. *Winner:* Not awarded in 2005.

Eliza Atkins Gleason Book Award. Presented every third year to the author of the best book in English in the field of library history. *Winner:* Not awarded in 2005.

Justin Winsor Prize Essay ($500). To an author of an outstanding essay embodying original historical research on a significant subject of library history. *Winner:* Donald C. Boyd for "The Book Women of Kentucky: The WPA Pack Horse Library Project, 1935–1943."

Library Research Round Table (LRRT)

Ingenta Research Award (up to $6,000). To sponsor research projects about acquisition, use, and preservation of digital information; the award includes $1,000 to support travel to a conference to present the results of that research. *Sponsor:* Ingenta. *Winner:* Patricia K. Galloway for "Institutionalizing a University Department-Level Institutional Repository."

Jesse H. Shera Award for Distinguished Published Research ($500). For a research article on library and information studies published in English during the calendar year. *Winners:* Karen E. Fisher, Joan C. Durrance, and Marian Bouch Hinton for "Information Grounds and the Use of Need-Based Services by Immigrants in Queens, NY: A Context-Based, Outcome Evaluation Approach."

Jesse H. Shera Award for Support of Dissertation Research ($500). To recognize and support dissertation research employing exemplary research design and methods. *Winner:* Doughee Sinn, School of Information Science, University of Pittsburgh, for "Records and the Understanding of Violent Events: Archival Documentation, Historical Perception, and the No Gun Ri Massacre in the Korean War."

Map and Geography Round Table (MAGERT)

MAGERT Honors Award. To recognize lifetime achievement and contributions to map and geography librarianship. *Winner:* Not awarded in 2005.

New Members Round Table (NMRT)

Shirley Olofson Memorial Award ($1,000). To an individual to help defray costs of attending the ALA Annual Conference. *Winner:* Mary Mannix.

Student Chapter of the Year Award. To an ALA student chapter for outstanding contributions to ALA. *Winner:* School of Library and Information Science, Indiana University at Bloomington.

3M Professional Development Grant. To new NMRT members to encourage professional development and participation in national ALA and NMRT activities. *Donor:* 3M. *Winners:* Annis Lee Adams, Philip Anthony Homan, Michal Strutin.

Office for Diversity

Achievement in Diversity Research Honor. To an ALA member who has made significant contributions to diversity research in the profession. *Winner:* Mark Winston.

Diversity Research Grants ($2,500): To the authors of research proposals that address critical gaps in the knowledge of diversity issues within library and information science. *Winners:* Wooseob Jeong, Isabel Espinal, Karen J. Underhill.

Office for Information Technology Policy

L. Ray Patterson Award in Support of Users' Rights. To recognize an individual who supports the constitutional purpose of U.S. copyright law, fair use, and the public domain. *Winner:* Kenneth D. Crews.

Office for Intellectual Freedom

Freedom to Read Foundation Roll of Honor (citation): To recognize individuals who have contributed substantially to the foundation. *Winner:* David Cohen.

Office for Literacy and Outreach Services

Jean E. Coleman Library Outreach Lecture. *Winner:* Sanford Berman.

Diversity Fair Awards ($50 to $500). To outreach librarians for their institutions' diversity-in-action initiatives. *Winners:* (first place) Annisha Jeffries, (second place) Kim Edson, (third place) Jayati Chaudhuri.

Estela and Raúl Mora Award ($1,000 and plaque). For the most exemplary program celebrating Día de Los Niños/Día de Los Libros. *Winner:* REFORMA de Utah, Salt Lake City.

Public Information Office

Scholastic Library/Grolier National Library Week Grant ($5,000). To libraries or library associations of all types for a public awareness campaign in connection with National Library Week in the year the grant is awarded. *Sponsor:* Scholastic Library Publishing. *Winner:* Haverford Township (Pennsylvania) Free Library.

Public Library Association (PLA)

Advancement of Literacy Award (plaque). To a publisher, bookseller, hardware and/or software dealer, foundation, or similar group that has made a significant contribution to the advancement of adult literacy. *Donor: Library Journal. Winner:* Verizon Foundation.

Baker & Taylor Entertainment Audio Music/ Video Product Grant ($2,500 worth of audio music or video products). To help a public library to build or expand a collection of either or both formats. *Donor:* Baker & Taylor. *Winner:* Haines Borough (Alaska) Public Library.

Demco New Leaders Travel Grants (up to $1,500). To PLA members who have not attended a major PLA continuing-education event in the past five years. *Winners:* Wendy Lee, Jennifer Dawson.

EBSCO Excellence in Small and/or Rural Public Service Award ($1,000). Honors a library serving a population of 10,000 or less that demonstrates excellence of service to its community as exemplified by an overall service program or a special program of significant accomplishment. *Donor:* EBSCO Subscription Services. *Winner:* Curtis Township Public Library, Glennie, Michigan.

Highsmith Library Innovation Award ($2,000). To recognize a public library's innovative achievement in planning and implementing a creative community service program. *Donor:* Highsmith. *Winner:* Richmond (British Columbia) Public Library.

Allie Beth Martin Award ($3,000). To honor a public librarian who has demonstrated extraordinary range and depth of knowledge about books or other library materials and has distinguished ability to share that knowledge. *Donor:* Baker & Taylor. *Winner:* Pamela E. Groves.

Public Libraries Magazine Feature Writing Awards ($500 and $300). To public library employees for feature-length articles published during the preceding year. *Winners:* (first prize) Betsy Diamant-Cohen, (second prize) Mark Smith.

Charlie Robinson Award ($1,000). Honors a public library director who, over a period of seven years, has been a risk taker, an innovator, and/or a change agent in a public library. *Donor:* Baker & Taylor. *Winner:* Raymond Santiago.

Women's National Book Association/Ann Heidbreder Eastman Grant ($750). To a librarian to take a course or participate in an institute devoted to aspects of publishing as a profession or to provide reimbursement for such study completed within the past year. *Winner:* Frances Yates.

Reference and User Services Association (RUSA)

ABC-CLIO Online History Award ($3,000). To recognize professional achievement in historical reference and librarianship. *Donor:* ABC-CLIO. *Winner:* Oregon Historical Society.

Virginia Boucher-OCLC Distinguished ILL Librarian Award ($2,000). To a librarian for outstanding professional achievement, leadership, and contributions to interlibrary loan and document delivery. *Winner:* Harry M. Kriz.

Dartmouth Medal. For creating current reference works of outstanding quality and significance. *Donor:* Dartmouth College. *Winner:* Oxford University Press for *The Oxford Dictionary of National Biography* (2004).

Dun & Bradstreet Award for Outstanding Service to Minority Business Communities ($2,000). *Donor:* Dun & Bradstreet. *Winner:* Not awarded in 2005.

Dun & Bradstreet Public Librarian Support Award ($1,000). To support the attendance at the ALA Annual Conference of a public librarian who has performed outstanding business reference service. *Donor:* Dun & Bradstreet. *Winner:* Terry Zarsky.

Genealogical Publishing Company/History Section Award ($1,500). To encourage and commend professional achievement in historical reference and research librarianship. *Donor:* Genealogical Publishing Company. *Winner:* Michael Barren Clegg.

MARS Recognition Certificate. For excellence in service to the Machine-Assisted Reference Section. *Winner:* Elliot Kanter.

Margaret E. Monroe Library Adult Services Award (citation). To a librarian for impact on library service to adults. *Winner:* Gary Warren Niebuhr.

Isadore Gilbert Mudge–R. R. Bowker Award ($5,000). For distinguished contributions to reference librarianship. *Donor:* R. R. Bowker. *Winner:* David Tyckoson.

Reference Service Press Award ($2,500). To the author or authors of the most outstanding article published in *RUSQ* during the preceding two volume years. *Donor:* Reference Service Press. *Winner:* Paul Neuhaus.

John Sessions Memorial Award (plaque). To a library or library system in recognition of work with the labor community. *Donor:* AFL/CIO. *Winner:* Bridgeport (Connecticut) Public Library for its historical collection.

Louis Shores–Greenwood Publishing Group Award ($3,000). To an individual, team, or organization to recognize excellence in reviewing of books and other materials for libraries. *Donor:* Greenwood Publishing Group. *Winner:* Ronald Sukenick, founding editor, *American Book Review* (awarded posthumously).

Thomson Financial Student Travel Award (BRASS) ($1,000). For a student enrolled in an ALA-accredited master's degree program to attend the ALA Annual Conference. *Donor:* Thomson Financial. *Winner:* Jared Howland.

Thomson Gale Award for Excellence in Business Librarianship ($3,000). To an individual for distinguished activities in the field of business librarianship. *Donor:* Thomson Gale. *Winner:* Charles J. Popovich.

Thomson Gale Award for Excellence in Reference and Adult Services ($3,000). To a library or library system for developing an imaginative and unique library resource to meet patrons' reference needs. *Donor:* Thomson Gale. *Winner:* Smithsonian American Art Museum.

Social Responsibilities Round Table (SRRT)

Coretta Scott King Awards. *Winners:* See "Literary Prizes, 2005" by Gary Ink.

Jackie Eubanks Memorial Award ($500). To honor outstanding achievement in promoting the acquisition and use of alternative media in libraries. *Donor:* SRRT Alternatives in Publication Task Force. *Winner:* Not awarded in 2005.

Young Adult Library Services Association (YALSA)

Alex Awards. To the authors of ten books published for adults that have high potential appeal to teenagers. *Sponsor:* Margaret Alexander Edwards Trust. *Winners:* Steve Almond for *Candyfreak: A Journey Through the Chocolate Underbelly of America* (Algonquin), Lynn Cox for *Swimming to Antarctica: Tales of a Long-Distance Swimmer* (Knopf), Brenda Halpin for *Donorboy* (Random), Robert Kurson for *Shadow Divers* (Random), Ken Meyers for *Work of Wolves* (Harcourt), Ann Patchett for *Truth and Beauty: A Friendship* (HarperCollins), Jodi Picoult for *My Sister's Keeper* (Atria), Kit Reed for *Thinner Than Thou* (Tom Doherty Associates), Jim Shepard for *Project X* (Knopf), Robert Sullivan for *Rats: Observations on the History and Habitat of the City's Most Unwanted Inhabitants* (Bloomsbury).

Baker & Taylor/YALSA Conference Grants ($1,000). To young adult librarians in public or school libraries to attend an ALA Annual Conference for the first time. *Donor:* Baker & Taylor. *Winners:* Sophie Brookover, Tori Jensen.

BWI/YALSA Collection Development Grant ($1,000). To YALSA members who represent a public library and work directly with young adults, for collection development materials for young adults. *Donor:* Book Wholesalers, Inc. *Winners:* Kimberly Archer, Christa Gunderson.

Margaret A. Edwards Award ($2,000). To an author whose book or books have provided young adults with a window through which they can view their world and which will help them to grow and to understand themselves and their role in society. *Donor:* School Library Journal. *Winner:* Francesca Lia Block for the Weetzie Bat series (HarperCollins).

Great Book Giveaway (books, videos, CDs, and audio cassettes valued at a total of $25,000). *Winner:* Hardee Senior High School Library, Wauchula, Florida.

Frances Henne/VOYA Research Grant ($500 minimum). To provide seed money to an individual, institution, or group for a project to encourage research on library service to young adults. *Donor:* Scarecrow Press. *Winner:* Not awarded in 2005.

Michael L. Printz Award. *Winner:* See "Literary Prizes, 2005" by Gary Ink.

YALSA/Sagebrush Award ($1,000). For an exemplary young adult reading or literature program. *Donor:* Sagebrush Corporation. *Winner:* Amelia Shelley.

American Society for Information Science and Technology (ASIS&T)

ASIS&T Award of Merit. For an outstanding contribution to the field of information science. *Winner:* Marcia Bates.

ASIS&T Best Information Science Book. *Winner:* Richard Rogers for *Information Politics on the Web* (MIT Press).

ASIS&T Proquest Doctoral Dissertation Award ($1,000 plus expense-paid attendance at ASIS&T Annual Meeting). *Winner:* Weiping Yue.

ASIS&T Research in Information Science Award. For a systematic program of research in a single area at a level beyond the single study, recognizing contributions in the field of information science. *Winner:* Carol Kuhlthau.

ASIS&T Special Award. To recognize long-term contributions to the advancement of information science and technology and enhancement of public access to information and discovery of mechanisms for improved transfer and utilization of knowledge. *Winner:* Not awarded in 2005.

ASIS&T/UMI Doctoral Dissertation Award. *Winner:* Not awarded in 2005.

James M. Cretsos Leadership Award. *Winner:* K. T. L. Vaughan.

Watson Davis Award. *Winner:* Michael Buckland.

Pratt Severn Best Student Research Paper. *Winner:* Mary Gabehart.

John Wiley & Sons Best *JASIST* Paper Award. *Winner:* Soo Young Rieh for "On the Web at Home: Information Seeking and Web Searching in the Home Environment."

Thomson ISI Citation Analysis Research Grant. *Winner:* Dimitris A. Dervos.

Thomson ISI Doctoral Dissertation Proposal Scholarship. *Winner:* Svetlana Symonenko.

Thomson ISI Outstanding Information Science Teacher Award ($500). *Winner:* Peiling Wang, University of Tennessee.

Art Libraries Society of North America (ARLIS/NA)

ARLIS/NA Conference Attendance Award. *Winner:* Katherine Cowan.

ARLIS/NA Internship Award. To provide financial support for students preparing for a career in art librarianship or visual resource librarianship. *Winner:* Lauren Edison.

John Benjamins Award. To recognize research and publication in the study and analysis of periodicals in the fields of the fine arts, literature, and cross-disciplinary studies. *Winner:* Not awarded in 2005.

Andrew Cahan Photography Award. To encourage conference participation of art information professionals in the field of photography. *Winner:* Jane Devine Mejia.

Distinguished Service Award. To honor an individual whose exemplary service in art librarianship, visual resources curatorship, or a related field has made an outstanding national or international contribution to art information and/or art librarianship. *Winner:* Nancy S. Schuller.

Melva J. Dwyer Award. To the creators of exceptional reference or research tools relating to Canadian art and architecture. *Winners:* Jonathan Franklin and the National Gallery of Canada Library for *Index to Nineteenth Century Canadian Catalogues of Art/L'Index des Catalogues d'Art Parus au Canada au XIXe Siècle* (National Gallery of Canada, Otttawa, 2004).

Getty Travel Awards. *Winners:* Marlyn Bonilla Arroyo, Mirta Colon, Gabriela Betsabe Miramonte, Dora Pane, N. P. Salazar Vasquez.

Howard and Beverly Joy Karno Award. To provide financial assistance to a professional art librarian in Latin America through interaction with ARLIS/NA members and conference participation. *Winner:* Taina B. Caragol.

David Mirvish Books/Books on Art Travel Award (C$500). To encourage art librarianship in Canada. *Winner:* Kathy Zimon.

Gerd Muehsam Award. To one or more graduate students in library science programs to recognize excellence in a graduate paper or project. *Winner:* Johanna Woll.

Salander O'Reilly Student Travel Award. To promote participation in ARLIS/NA by supporting travel for a student considering a career in art librarianship. *Winner:* Not awarded in 2005.

Puvill Libros Award. To encourage professional development of European art librarians through interaction with ARLIS/NA colleagues and conference participation. *Winner:* Claudio DiBenedetto.

Research Libraries Group Asia/Oceania Award. To encourage professional development of art information professionals who reside in Asia/Oceania through interaction with ARLIS/NA colleagues and conference participation. *Winner:* Janet Blake.

Research Libraries Group Award. To promote participation in ARLIS/NA by supporting conference travel for an individual who has not attended an ARLIS/NA Annual Conference. *Winner:* Not awarded in 2005.

Student Diversity Award. *Winner:* Juan Wang.

Student Travel Award. *Winner:* Katherine O'Dell.

H. W. Wilson Foundation Research Grant. To support research activities by ARLIS/NA members in the fields of librarianship, visual resources curatorship, and the arts. *Winner:* Alfred Willis for "American Bungalow Books, 1903–1952."

George Wittenborn Memorial Book Award. For outstanding publications in the visual arts and architecture. *Winners:* Richard Shiff, Carol Mancusi-Ungario, and Heidemarie Colsman for *Barnett Newman: A Catalogue Raisonné* (Yale University Press, 2004); Helen C. Evans for *Byzantium: Faith and Power (1261–1557)* (Yale University Press, 2004).

Worldwide Books Award for Electronic Resources. *Winner:* Ed Teague for *The Architecture of the University of Oregon: A History, Bibliography, and Research Guide.*

Worldwide Books Award for Publications. *Winner:* Max Marmor for "From Purgatory to the Primavera: Some Observations on Botticelli and Dante," in *Artibus et Historiae,* no. 48 (XXIV).

Association for Library and Information Science Education (ALISE)

ALISE Award for Teaching Excellence in the Field of Library and Information Science Education. *Winner:* Ann Curry.

ALISE Pratt-Severn Faculty Innovation Award ($1,000). *Winner:* Not awarded in 2005.

ALISE Professional Contribution to Library and Information Science Education Award. *Winners:* Marcia J. Bates, Joan C. Durrance.

ALISE Research Grant Awards (one or more grants totaling $5,000): *Winners:* Youngok Choi and Edie Rasmussen for "Digital Librarians: Who Are They, What Skills Do They Need, and How Can They Be Educated?"

ALISE Service Award. *Winner:* Louise S. Robbins.

ALISE/Bohdan S. Wynar Research Paper Competition. For a research paper concerning any aspect of librarianship or information studies by a member of ALISE. *Winners:* Lokman Meho and Kristina Spurgin for "Ranking the Research Productivity of LIS Faculty and Schools: An Evaluation of Data Sources and Research Methods."

Dialog/ALISE Methodology Paper Competition ($500). *Winner:* Not awarded in 2005.

Doctoral Students to ALISE Award ($400 toward attendance at the ALISE Annual Conference). *Winners:* Karen Cook, Abe Crystal.

Eugene Garfield/ALISE Doctoral Dissertation Awards ($500). *Winners:* Paulette M. Rothbauer for "Finding and Creating Possibility: Reading in the Lives of Lesbian, Bisexual, and Queer Young Women," University of Western Ontario, 2004; Betsy

Van der Veer Martens for "Theories at Work: Functional Characteristics of Theories That Facilitate Their Diffusion Over Time," Syracuse University, 2004.

OCLC/ALISE Library and Information Science Research Grants (up to $15,000). *Winners:* Shawne Miksa, Jun Wang, Peiling Wang.

Beta Phi Mu

Beta Phi Mu Award. *See under* American Library Association.

Elfreda Chatman/Beta Phi Mu Minority Doctoral Student Scholarship ($1,000). *Winner:* Min Song.

Doctoral Dissertation Scholarship. *Winner:* Marcia A. Mardis.

Eugene Garfield Doctoral Dissertation Fellowships ($3,000). *Winner:* Brian Arbogast de Hubert-Miller.

Harold Lancour Scholarship for Foreign Study ($1,000). For graduate study in a foreign country related to the applicant's work or schooling. *Winner:* Tatiana Nikolova-Houston.

Mary Jo Lynch Distinguished Research Award. *Winner:* Mary Lee Kennedy. *Lecture topic:* "Bridging the Gap: Information Behavior and Information Professionals."

Sarah Rebecca Reed Scholarship ($2,000). For study at an ALA-accredited library school. *Winner:* Rachael Holovach.

Frank B. Sessa Scholarship for Continuing Professional Education ($750). For continuing education for a Beta Phi Mu member. *Winner:* Allaina M. Howard.

Blanche E. Woolls Scholarship ($1,000). For a beginning student in school library media services. *Winner:* Maria L. Muhlbauer.

Bibliographical Society of America (BSA)

BSA Fellowships (up to $2,000 a month for two months). For scholars involved in bibliographical inquiry and research in the history of the book trades and in publishing history. *Winners:* Cécile Alduy, Janine Barchas, Michael Everton, Jacqueline Goldsby, Joseph Gwara, John Hench, Edward Jones, Catherine Marsters, Ruth Panofsky, Giuseppina Panzuto, Allen Reddick, Margit Smith, Elizabeth Willingham.

William L. Mitchell Prize for Research on Early British Serials ($1,000). For the best single work published between January 1, 2002, and September 1, 2005. *Winner:* William E. Rivers for his edition of Nicholas Amhurst's *Terrae-Filius or, The Secret History of the University of Oxford (1721–26)* (University of Delaware Press, 2004).

Justin G. Schiller Prize for Bibliographical Work on Pre-20th-Century Children's Books ($2,000). To encourage scholarship in the bibliography of historical children's books. *Winner:* To be awarded in January 2007 and every three years thereafter.

Canadian Library Association (CLA)

Olga B. Bishop Award ($200). To a library school student for the best paper on government information or publications. *Winner:* Not awarded in 2005.

CLA Award for the Advancement of Intellectual Freedom in Canada. *Winner:* David Wyman.

CLA Elizabeth Dafoe Scholarship ($3,000). *Winner:* Manon Lamontagne.

CLA/Ken Haycock Award for Promoting Librarianship ($1,000). To honor an individual for contributing significantly to the public recognition and appreciation of librarianship. *Winner:* To be awarded for the first time in 2006.

CLA/Information Today Award for Innovative Technology. *Donor:* Information Today, Inc. *Winner:* Red Deer (Alberta) Public Library.

CLA Outstanding Service to Librarianship Award. *Donor:* R. R. Bowker. *Winner:* Patricia Cavill.

CLA Research and Development Grant ($1,000). *Winner:* Leona Jacobs.

CLA Student Article Award. *Winner:* Anne Dorsey for "Open Wide the Library Doors."

CLA/3M Award for Achievement in Technical Services ($1,000). *Winner:* Project TRAP-CREPUQ.

W. Kaye Lamb Award for Service to Seniors. *Winner:* Not awarded in 2005.

H. W. Wilson Scholarship ($2,000). *Winner:* Pamela Joanne Wheatley.

World Book Graduate Scholarship in Library Science ($2,500). *Winner:* Not awarded in 2005.

Canadian Association for School Libraries (CASL)

CASL Margaret B. Scott Award of Merit. For the development of school libraries in Canada. *Winner:* Karin E. Paul.

CASL National Book Service Teacher-Librarian of the Year Award. *Winner:* Hazel Clark.

CASL Angela Thacker Memorial Award. For outstanding contribution to teacher-librarianship. *Winner:* River East Transcona School Division.

Chancellor Group Conference Grant. *Winner:* Karen Lindsay.

Canadian Association of College and University Libraries (CACUL)

CACUL/Miles Blackwell Award for Outstanding Academic Librarian. *Sponsor:* Blackwell's. *Winner:* Ethel Auster.

CACUL Innovation Achievement Award ($1,500). *Sponsor:* Sirsi. *Winner:* Ontario Council of University Libraries (OCUL).

CTCL Award for Outstanding College Librarian. *Winner:* Susan Brayford.

CTCL Innovation Achievement Award. *Sponsor:* Micromedia ProQuest. *Winner:* Mohawk College of Applied Arts and Technology.

Canadian Association of Public Libraries (CAPL)

CAPL/Brodart Outstanding Public Library Service Award. *Winner:* Stan Squires.

Canadian Association of Special Libraries and Information Services (CASLIS)

CASLIS Award for Special Librarianship in Canada. *Winner:* Claudette Cloutier.

Canadian Library Trustees Association (CLTA)

CLTA/Stan Heath Achievement in Literacy Award. For an innovative literacy program by a public library board. *Donor:* ABC Canada. *Winner:* Toronto Public Library.

CLTA Merit Award for Distinguished Service as a Public Library Trustee. *Winner:* John Snow.

Chinese-American Librarians Association (CALA)

CALA Distinguished Service Award. To a librarian who has been a mentor, role model, and leader in the fields of library and information science. *Winner:* Susana Juh-mei Liu.

CALA President's Recognition Award. *Winner:* Esther Lee.

CALA Scholarship of Library and Information Science. *Winner:* Donghua Tao.

Sheila Suen Lai Scholarship ($500). *Winner:* Zhi Xian Yi.

C. C. Seetoo/CALA Conference Travel Scholarship ($500). For a student to attend the ALA Annual Conference and CALA program. *Winner:* Hairong Zhu.

Sally T. Tseng Professional Development Grant. *Winners:* Jian Anna Xiong and Liang Ruan (joint application), Yongyi Song.

Huang Tso-ping and Wu Yao-yu Scholarship Memorial Research Grants (total $1,000). *Winner:* Yang Jin.

Church and Synagogue Library Association (CSLA)

CSLA Award for Outstanding Congregational Librarian. For distinguished service to the congregation and/or community through devotion to the congregational library. *Winner:* Anne Greenwood, St. Paul's Episcopal Church, Washington, D.C.

CSLA Award for Outstanding Congregational Library. For responding in creative and innovative ways to the library's mission of reaching and serving the congregation and/or the wider community. *Winner:*

Duluth (Georgia) First United Methodist Church, Cheryl Cutchin, librarian.

CSLA Award for Outstanding Contribution to Congregational Libraries. For providing inspiration, guidance, leadership, or resources to enrich the field of church or synagogue librarianship. *Winner:* Mary Ellen Draper, Briarlake Baptist Church, Decatur, Georgia.

Muriel Fuller Scholarship Award. *Winner:* Not awarded in 2005.

Helen Keating Ott Award for Outstanding Contribution to Children's Literature. *Winner:* Sandra McLeod Humphrey, Oak Knoll Lutheran Church, Minnetonka, Minnesota.

Pat Tabler Memorial Scholarship Award. *Winner:* Eleanor Moore, New Hope Presbyterian Church, Fishers, Indiana.

Coalition for Networked Information

Paul Evan Peters Award. To recognize notable and lasting international achievements relating to high-performance networks and the creation and use of information resources and services that advance scholarship and intellectual productivity. *Winner:* Not awarded in 2005.

Paul Evan Peters Fellowship ($2,500 a year for two years). To a student pursuing a graduate degree in librarianship or the information sciences. *Winner:* Not awarded in 2005.

Council on Library and Information Resources (CLIR)

CLIR Fellowships in Scholarly Information Resources. *Winners:* Marlene Allen, Ali Anooshahr, Kelly Miller, Michelle Morton.

Bill and Melinda Gates Foundation Access to Learning Award ($1 million). To public libraries or similar organizations outside the United States for innovative programs that provide the public free access to information technology. *Winner:* Shidhulai Swanirvar Sangstha of Bangladesh.

Rovelstad Scholarship in International Librarianship. To enable a student enrolled in an accredited LIS program to attend the IFLA World Library and Information Congress. *Winner:* Alison Raab.

A. R. Zipf Fellowship in Information Management ($5,000). To a student enrolled in graduate school who shows exceptional promise for leadership and technical achievement. *Winner:* Richard Swart.

Friends of Libraries USA (FOLUSA)

FOLUSA/Baker & Taylor @ your library Award ($2,000). To a friends group that has made the best use of ALA's "@ your library" campaign slogan in its promotional materials. *Winner:* Friends of the Monroe Township (New Jersey) Library.

FOLUSA/Baker & Taylor Awards ($2,000). To friends groups that have distinguished themselves in support of their libraries. *Winners:* (small library) Friends of the Marathon (Texas) Library; (large library) Friends of the Solana Beach Branch of the San Diego County Library.

Barbara Kingsolver Award ($10,000 for the purchase of children's books). To a small friends-of-the-library group that has done the most to improve its library. *Donor:* HarperCollins Publishers. *Winner:* Friends of the Effingham (New Hampshire) Public Library.

International Federation of Library Associations and Institutions (IFLA)

Hans-Peter Geh Grant. To enable a librarian from the former Soviet Union to attend a conference in Germany or elsewhere. *Winner:* Not awarded in 2005.

Dr. Shawky Salem Conference Grant (up to $1,900). To enable an expert in library and information science who is a national of an Arab country to attend the IFLA Conference for the first time. *Winner:* Ayman Bustanji, Dubai Public Libraries.

Frederick Thorpe Individual Awards (up to £5,000 total). To librarians working in libraries for the blind. *Donor:* Ulverscroft Foundation. *Winners:* Not awarded in 2005.

Frederick Thorpe Organizational Award (up to £15,000). To a library organization for development of service delivery to the visually impaired. *Donor:* Ulverscroft Foundation. *Winner:* Not awarded in 2005.

Medical Library Association (MLA)

Estelle Brodman Award for the Academic Medical Librarian of the Year. To honor significant achievement, potential for leadership, and continuing excellence at mid-career in the area of academic health sciences librarianship. *Winner:* Michele Tennant.

Lois Ann Colaianni Award for Excellence and Achievement in Hospital Librarianship. To a member of MLA who has made significant contributions to the profession in the area of overall distinction or leadership in hospital librarianship. *Winner:* Mary Fran Prottsman.

Cunningham Memorial International Fellowship ($6,000). A six-month grant and travel expenses in the United States and Canada for a foreign librarian. *Winner:* Hanne Caspersen, State and University Library, Aarhus, Denmark.

Louise Darling Medal. For distinguished achievement in collection development in the health sciences. *Winner:* Deborah Blecic.

Janet Doe Lectureship. *Winner:* Julie J. McGowan.

EBSCO/MLA Annual Meeting Grant (up to $1,000). *Winners:* Kelly Klinke, Molly J. Montgomery, Carolyn M. Papa, Paula Whannell.

Ida and George Eliot Prize. For an essay published in any journal in the preceding calendar year that has been judged most effective in furthering medical librarianship. *Donor:* Login Brothers Books. *Winners:* Pamela Sherwill-Navarro and Addajane Wallace for "Research on the Value

of Medical Library Services: Does It Make an Impact in the Health Care Literature?"

Murray Gottlieb Prize. For the best unpublished essay submitted by a medical librarian on the history of some aspect of health sciences or a detailed description of a library exhibit. *Donors:* Ralph and Jo Grimes. *Winner:* Ursula Ellis for "The Japanese Adoption of Western Medicine: From Sakoku to the Meiji Era."

Hospital Libraries Section/MLA Professional Development Grants. *Winners:* Marcy Brown, Sharon Kambeitz.

David A. Kronick Traveling Fellowship ($2,000). *Sponsor:* Bowden-Massey Foundation. *Winner:* Kristine M. Alpi.

Joseph Leiter NLM/MLA Lectureship. *Winner:* former U.S. Surgeon General Joycelyn Elders.

Donald A. B. Lindberg Research Fellowship. *Winner:* Yin Aphinyanaphongs.

Lucretia W. McClure Excellence in Education Award. To an outstanding eduator in the field of health sciences librarianship and informatics. *Winner:* Jo Dorsch.

Majors/MLA Chapter Project of the Year Award. *Sponsor:* Majors Scientific Books. *Winner:* Pacific Northwest Chapter of MLA for its e-journal group project on consortial buying.

Medical Informatics Section/MLA Career Development Grant ($1,500). For up to two individuals to support a career development activity that will contribute to advancement in the field of medical informatics. *Winners:* Ruiling Guo, Christine F. Marton.

MLA Continuing Education Grant ($100–$500). *Winner:* Andrea Ketchum.

MLA Fellowships. *Winners:* Julie J. McGowan, Kent A. Smith, Julia F. Sollenberger, Linda A. Watson, Gail A. Yokote.

MLA President's Award. *Winners:* Patricia L. Thibodeau, Linda A. Watson, Carla J. Funk.

MLA Research, Development, and Demonstration Project Grant ($100 to $1,000). *Winner:* Peggy Mullaly-Quijas.

MLA Scholarship (up to $5,000). For graduate study at an ALA-accredited library school. *Winner:* Teresa Hammett.

MLA Scholarship for Minority Students (up to $5,000). For graduate study at an ALA-accredited library school. *Winner:* Shamsha Damani.

Marcia C. Noyes Award. For an outstanding contribution to medical librarianship. The award is the highest professional distinction of MLA. *Winner:* Judith Messerle.

Rittenhouse Award. For the best unpublished paper on medical librarianship submitted by a student enrolled in, or having been enrolled in, a course in an ALA-accredited library school or a trainee in an internship program in medical librarianship. *Donor:* Rittenhouse Medical Bookstore. *Winner:* Ann Bett-Madhavan for "The Information Needs of Medical Journalists: A Role for Information Specialists."

Thomson ISI/Frank Bradway Rogers Information Advancement Award ($500). For an outstanding contribution to knowledge of health science information delivery. *Winner:* Arizona Health Information Network (AZHIN).

REFORMA (National Association to Promote Library and Information Services to Latinos and the Spanish-Speaking)

REFORMA scholarships ($1,500). To students who qualify for graduate study in library science and who are citizens or permanent residents of the United States. *Winners:* Iris Cotto, Sol Gomez, Yesenia Lopez, Amanda Sherriff.

K. G. Saur (Munich, Germany)

K. G. Saur Award for Best *LIBRI* Student Paper ($500). To author(s) to recognize the most outstanding article published in *LIBRI* during the preceding year. *Donor:* K. G. Saur Publishing. *Winner:* Jack Kormos for "On the Methods by Which We Acquire Information, and the Effectiveness of Libraries in Supporting These Behaviors" (vol. 55, no. 2–3, September 2005).

Society of American Archivists (SAA)

C. F. W. Coker Award for Description. *Winner:* Online Archives of California.

Colonial Dames of America and Donna Cutts Scholarships (up to $1,200). To enable new archivists to attend the Modern Archives Institute of the National Archives and Records Administration. *Winners:* Linda Hocking, Debra Kimok, Charlotte A. Walters.

Council Exemplary Service Award. To recognize exemplary contribution to the profession. *Winner:* Robert S. Martin.

Council Outstanding Service Award. To recognize outstanding service. *Winners:* Philip B. Eppard, Scott Schwartz.

Fellows' Posner Award. For an outstanding essay dealing with a facet of archival administration, history, theory, or methodology, published in *American Archivist*. *Winner:* Elena Danielson for "Privacy Rights and the Rights of Political Victims: Implications of the German Experience."

Philip M. Hamer–Elizabeth Hamer Kegan Award. For individuals and/or institutions that have increased public awareness of a specific body of documents. *Winner:* Survivors of the Shoah Visual History Foundation in recognition of its Web site and online resource featuring information about the Holocaust.

Oliver Wendell Holmes Award. To enable overseas archivists already in the United States or Canada for training to attend the SAA annual meeting. *Winner:* Not awarded in 2005.

J. Franklin Jameson Award. For individuals and/or organizations that promote greater public awareness of archival activities and programs. *Winner:* George F. Farr, Jr.

Sister M. Claude Lane, O.P., Memorial Award. For a significant contribution to the field of religious archives. *Winner:* William Sumners.

Waldo Gifford Leland Prize. For writing of superior excellence and usefulness in the field of archival history, theory, or practice. *Winner:* Richard J. Cox for *No Innocent Deposits: Forming Archives by Rethinking Appraisal* (Scarecrow, 2004).

Theodore Calvin Pease Award. For the best student paper. *Winner:* Ian Craig Breaden for "Sound Practices: Online Audio Exhibits and the Cultural Heritage Archive."

Harold T. Pinkett Minority Student Award. To encourage minority students to consider careers in the archival profession and promote minority participation in SAA. *Winners:* Jenniger Osorio, Paul Sevilla.

Preservation Publication Award. To recognize an outstanding work published in North America that advances the theory or the practice of preservation in archival institutions. *Winner:* National Film Preservation Foundation for *The Film Preservation Guide: The Basics for Archives, Libraries and Museums.*

SAA Fellows. Highest individual distinction awarded to a limited number of members for their outstanding contribution to the archival profession. *Honored*: Nancy Bartlett, Thomas Battle, Connell B. Gallagher, Joan D. Krizack, Richard Pearce-Moses, Megan Sniffin-Marinoff, Helen R. Tibbo, John J. Treanor.

Special Libraries Association (SLA)

Mary Adeline Connor Professional Development Scholarship ($6,000). *Winner:* Jeannie Bail.

John Cotton Dana Award. For exceptional support and encouragement of special librarianship. *Winner:* Sylvia A. E. Piggott.

Diversity Leadership Development Award. *Winners:* Tamika Barnes McCullough, Phebe Poydras, Matildah Misengo Sakala.

Factiva Leadership Award ($2,000). To an SLA member who exemplifies leadership as a special librarian through excellence in personal and professional competencies. *Winner:* Susan Fifer Canby.

Steven I. Goldspiel Memorial Research Grant. *Winners:* Not awarded in 2005.

Hall of Fame Award. To a member or members of the association at or near the end of an active professional career for an extended and sustained period of distinguished service to the association. *Winners:* Carol Ginsburg, Phyllis Waggoner.

Honorary SLA Membership. *Honored:* Susan Tarr.

Innovations in Technology Award. To recognize an SLA member's innovative use of technology in a library setting. *Winner:* Defense Technical Information Center.

SLA Affirmative Action Scholarship. *Winner:* Kelly Lynn Anders.

SLA Fellows. *Honored:* L. Susan Hayes, Tom Rink, Dav Robertson, Hope Tillman, Richard Wallace.

SLA Member Achievement Award. *Winner:* John Latham.

SLA President's Award. *Winner:* Barbie Keiser.

SLA Professional Award. *Winners:* Karen Melville, Judy Russell.

SLA Student Scholarships. For graduate study in librarianship leading to a master's degree in library or information science. *Winners:* Eugene Barsky, Megan Comey, Terry Lynn Kline.

Rose L. Vormelker Award. *Winner:* Tony Stankus.

H. W. Wilson Company Award ($500). For the most outstanding article in the past year's *Information Outlook. Donor:* H. W. Wilson Company. *Winners:* John J. Digilio and Gayle Lynn-Nelson, Laura Gasaway.

Part 4
Research and Statistics

Library Research and Statistics

Research and Statistics on Libraries and Librarianship in 2005

Denise M. Davis

Director, Office for Research and Statistics, American Library Association

The year 2005 will be remembered as a year of disaster and recovery. Louisiana, Mississippi, Alabama, Florida, and other states lost public, school, and academic libraries to storms and floods. The cost of repairing and rebuilding these libraries—and their communities—is unknown, but what is known is the generosity demonstrated to people in need. Thank you.

The event of the year may have been the first national meeting of deans of schools of information science. "The First Conference of the i-School Community—Bridging Disciplines to Confront Grand Challenges" was held at Penn State September 28–30, coordinated by Penn, Syracuse, the University of California–Irvine, the University of Michigan, and the University of Washington. Feedback from attendees indicated a fruitful conference of discussions on ways to improve curriculum. The conference Web site has links to all the papers presented and other useful materials (http://iconference.ist.psu.edu/content/view/12/40).

Research Relevant to all Libraries

Digital Library Archaeology

One of the more interesting articles completed in 2005 was by Scott Nicholson of Syracuse: "Digital Library Archeology: A Conceptual Framework for Understanding Library Use Through Artifact-Based Evaluation." The article appeared in *The Library Quarterly* and is available as a preprint at http://dlist.sir.arizona.edu/885. At the center of Nicholson's work is the premise that moving library science research "toward a hypothesis-based exploration" is an effective method of evaluating digital libraries and their users (collections and services used and user behavior). Librarians and researchers, as digital library archeologists, embrace the concepts of digitized images as artifacts and users as depositors of "data-based artifacts" as evidence of communities in the virtual space. "These shards of virtual pottery such as searches and browsing behavior, and the burial mounds of dead discussion groups hold valuable information if the pieces can be collected, cleaned, organized, and examined," Nicholson writes. The application of three frameworks—traditional archaeology, new archaeology, and postprocessual archaeology—in connection with evidence-based librarianship is both provocative and overwhelming (in an "I leave a virtual trail, therefore I exist" kind of way). It will be interesting to see if the evaluation methods presented are applied to the myriad digital library projects under way.

Cataloger Retention

Joan M. Lysen and Jeanne M. K. Boydston's work on cataloger retention in academic libraries, "Supply and Demand for Catalogers: Present and Future," was published in *Library Resources & Technical Services* (*LRTS* 49(4): 250–265, October 2005). The article presents a useful summary of downward staffing trends in technical services since the 1990s and provides a generous bibliography for additional investigation. Not surprisingly, retirements, budget cuts, and use of paraprofessionals in technical services have impacted the role and responsibilities of catalogers. Much of what is presented here regarding academic libraries may well apply to other types of library settings. Of special note from this research is that libraries will continue to recruit beginning-level librarians into cataloging, but expectations are that their responsibilities will be managerial and administrative in nature. The authors published the survey instrument as an appendix to the article.

ALA Salary Survey

The American Library Association (ALA) continues its annual salary survey, but with some significant changes. The 2005 survey represents a break in the methodology used for the 1982–2004 surveys: the sample of public and academic libraries was stratified by region as well as by state; public libraries serving populations of fewer than 10,000 were invited to participate in the now-Web-based survey; the total sample of public and academic libraries increased 340 percent to 4,343 from 1,275 in 2004; and the 2005 survey reports actual salaries rather than adjusting for an academic year of fewer than 12 months. Salary data for states with response rates of 50 percent or higher by type of library and position are included. A comparative study has been done of librarian salaries from 1982 to 2004 and is available at http://www.ala.org/ala/ors/reports/librariansalaries1982-2003-091605.pdf. Additional information about the 2005 survey is available at http://www.ala.org/ala/ors/reports/reports.htm.

'Return on Investment'

It was a particularly busy year for "return on investment" and "library value" studies. Most notable were the Seattle Public Library and South Carolina studies.

"The Seattle Public Library Central Library: Economic Benefits Assessment," subtitled "The Transformative Power of a Library to Redefine Learning, Community, and Economic Development" (http://www.berkandassociates.com/spl.html), was prepared for the Seattle Public Library Foundation and the City of Seattle Office of Economic Development. This study positions the new library as a tourism stop as well as a city library, and links city, county, and state revenue gains within this model. The estimated spending by out-of-towners in the first year of the library's operation was approximately $16 million.

"The Economic Impact of Public Libraries on South Carolina" was prepared for the University of South Carolina by Daniel D. Barron, Robert V. Williams, Stephen Bajjaly, Jennifer Arns, and Steven Wilson of the School of Library and Information Science, University of South Carolina (http://www.libsci.sc.edu/SCEIS/exsummary.pdf). Among many findings, the study determined that for every $1 spent by state and local governments on South Carolina public libraries, the return on investment was $2.86.

Future of Librarians

"The Future of Librarians in the Workforce" (School of Information and Library Science, University of North Carolina at Chapel Hill) is an enormous undertaking, launching five national surveys to understand librarian salaries, career satisfaction, skills requirements, and career retention. More information about this important study is available at http://libraryworkforce.org/tiki-index.php.

Social Informatics

Research being done in the area of social informatics, especially circumvention of digital content, is growing. Although an issue for the academic library community for some time, it is filtering (no pun intended) more into the mainstream library community. A number of researchers are working in this area, but of particular note is the work being done by Kristin Eschenfelder (University of Wisconsin–Madison). Eschenfelder released a number of articles in 2005, listed in her vitae at http://slisweb.lis.wisc.edu/~kreschen/vitae.html, among them "The Ethics of DeCSS Posting: Toward Assessing the Morality of the Internet Posting of DVD Copyright Circumvention Software" (coauthored with R. G. Howard and A. C. Desai, *Information Research,* forthcoming). *Information Research* is an online, peer-reviewed journal available at http://informationr.net/ir. In addition, the June/July 2005 issue of *Bulletin of the American Society for Information Science and Technology* was a special issue on social informatics. Work from Eschenfelder, Steve Sawyer (Penn State), Alex Halavais (University of Buffalo), Elisabeth Davenport (Napier University, Edinburgh), and Lee S. Strickland (University of Maryland, College Park) appear. W. David Penniman (University of Buffalo) was the guest editor of this special issue.

Academic Libraries

Academic library research in 2005 spanned topics from virtual reference to open source electronic reserves.

Library as Place

The Council on Library and Information Resources produced a report early in the year, *Library as Place: Rethinking Roles, Rethinking Space* (http://www.clir.org/pubs/abstract/pub129abst.html). The report is a compilation of articles addressing the changing needs for and roles of academic and research libraries, and how to plan for the future. Although walk-in library use may be on the decline, these articles reflect the creativity with which academic libraries are addressing increased virtual use and the processes being used to understand future needs.

Assessment

Continuing with assessment, Wanda Dole, Jitka Hurych, and Anne Liebst in "Assessment: A core Competency for Library Leaders" (*Library Administration & Management* 19(3): 125–132) replicated the important work done by Susan Beck (Rutgers University). The findings closely matched those of Beck—that assessment was a valued competency of those in library leadership positions. Dole, Hurych, and Liebst found similar perceptions held by library deans and campus administrators at three Carnegie MA I universities in Kansas and Missouri. Generally, the use of assessment tools by administrators for decision making correlated to their leadership philosophy and organizational culture, among other characteristics. The study provides useful insight into assessment tools used at these institutions, and the extent to which library administrators use available data for decision making. The replicability of this research model is encouraging, and the extent to which it can be applied to governance structures outside of academe will be interesting to discover.

Public Libraries

Normative Data Project

One of the sleepers of 2005 was the SirsiDynix Normative Data Project (NDP) (http://www.librarynormativedata.info). Although designed for its customers, this utility is quite extraordinary. The NDP utility merges the library's own usage data with federal (public library data and census characteristics from the decennial census files) and geospatial tools to map data sets, partnering with Florida State University with its Public Library Geographic Database (PLGDB) Mapping project (http://www.geolib.org/PLGDB.cfm). The result is a live tracking tool of library usage and expenditure, and a comparative tool among libraries in the SirsiDynix data set. Access is provided to all MLIS programs in North America to encourage research. If you haven't tried this site, you are encouraged to do so. [For more on NDP, see the following article, "Two Business Intelligence Tools for Libraries: An Introduction and Preliminary Results"—*Ed.*]

Young Adult Services

Young adult services are finally getting the recognition they deserve. Of particular interest is work done by Mary K. Chelton (Queens College, City College of New York) in her regular column, "Perspectives on YA Practice," in *Young Adult Library Service* (*YALS*), an ALA/Young Adult Library Services Association periodical. Chelton presents ongoing research in the area of YA services in a very readable and applicable way. In the Summer 2005 issue of *YALS,* Chelton evaluates models of YA services and grounds that evaluation both in previous research and current application. This column is a good source of information for those interested in YA service and supporting research.

YA Services History

Also published in 2005 was "Two Hundred Years of Young Adult Library Services History: The Chronology" by Anthony Bernier, Mary K. Chelton, Christine A. Jenkins, and Jennifer Burek Pierce (*Voice of Youth Advocates* 28:2, 106–111). This article provides a useful summary of services to youth in America's libraries, and the full chronology is available online at http://www.voya.com.

Multicultural Awareness

Donna L. Gilton (University of Rhode Island) continues her research in multicultural awareness in library collections and services. To be published in 2006 is *I, Too, Sing America: Multicultural and Ethnic Children's Literature in the U.S.* (Scarecrow Press). Marya Doerfel and Lily Arasaratnam (Rutgers) also published in this area, with "Intercultural Communication Competence: Identifying Key Components from Multicultural Perspectives" (*International Journal of Intercultural Relations*, March 2005, 29(2): 137–163).

YA Information Seeking

Finally, the work of a research project directed by Denise Agosta and Sandra Hughes (Drexel University) is appearing in the literature. Among that work is "People, Places, and Questions: Preliminary Findings From an Investigation of the Everyday Life Information-Seeking Behaviors of Urban Young Adults," *Library and Information Science Research* (2005) 27(2): 141–163. More about this research project is available on Agosta's Web site, http://www.pages.drexel.edu/~dea22.

School Libraries

Collaboration

Collaboration between school media center staff and teachers has long been a focus of research for the American Association of School Librarians (AASL). The 2005 edition of *School Library Media Research,* an online refereed journal of AASL, published a study done by Patricia Montiel-Overall (University of Arizona School of Information Resources and Library Science) titled "Toward a Theory of Collaboration for Teachers and Librarians." Drawing upon research in psychology, education, technology, and corporate management theory, Montiel-Overall presents four models of cooperation: coordination, cooperation/partnership, integrated instruction, and integrated curriculum. The study presents factors that impact the success of collaborative projects and, thereby, the positive impact of collaboration on student achievement. The paper includes an extensive bibliography and is available online at http://www.ala.org/ala/aasl/aaslpubsand journals/slmrb/slmrcontents/volume82005/theory.htm.

Notable Books

Two 2005 books that warrant recognition are *Administering the School Library Media Center* (fourth edition) by Betty J. Morris and *Information Literacy and*

Information Skills Instruction: Applying Research to Practice in the School Library Media Center (second edition) by Nancy Pickering Thomas, both published by Libraries Unlimited. Both titles have been well reviewed and have become key titles for school library media center management.

50 Years of Education Data

The National Center for Education Statistics (NCES) Library Statistics Program released a 50-year compilation of its school library media center data. "Fifty Years of Supporting Children's Learning: A History of Public School and Federal Legislation from 1953 to 2000" (http://nces.ed.gov/pubs2005/2005311.pdf) presents national-level and state-level data for six key measures: number of schools, enrollment, number of media centers, staffing, books per pupil, and expenditures. Not all states participate in each reporting period, and this is reflected in the variation of data by state. The report also includes relevant descriptive information drawn from other NCES studies of school library services during the 50-year period, including standards or guidelines and staff development. Barbara Holton of NCES and Joan Michie of Westat should especially be commended for pulling these data together in such a valuable resource and making them available online.

NCES's 'Build a Table'

We await the release of the NCES 2003–2004 School Library Media Center study, but can use the Common Core of Data "Build a Table" utility to review the most recently released fiscal and nonfiscal data about schools and staffing. The online tool, available at http://nces.ed.gov/ccd/bat, supports table building on a range of characteristics reported by approximately 94,000 primary and secondary schools and 17,000 school districts. The data sets available are 1986–1987 through 2003–2004 (preliminary data). Selected Census Bureau data also are included.

Other Research Benefiting the Profession

There will be research in a number of areas in 2006 that will be of note. Among the more interesting projects are these:

- Rutgers University School of Communication, Information, and Library Studies and OCLC begin a research project to evaluate the need for, and sustainability of, digital virtual reference services.
- Kent State University will study the health-information-seeking behaviors of older adults in rural Ohio in an effort to develop more-effective health information programs in libraries and for healthcare providers.
- Health and information literacy games are being developed for students at James Madison University's Libraries.

Each of these studies is supported by the Institute of Museum and Library Services (IMLS) as part of its National Leadership Grant program.

Blogging

Among the research being done in the area of blogging is that by Susan Herring of Indiana University (http://www.slis.indiana.edu/faculty/spotlight/index. php?facid=009). Of particular note is a coauthored work, "Conversations in the Blogosphere: An Analysis From the Bottom Up" (S. C. Herring, I. Kouper, J. C. Paolillo, L. A. Scheidt, M. Tyworth, P. Welsch, E. Wright, and N. Yu, published in *Proceedings of the 38th Hawaii International Conference on System Sciences (HICCS-38 2005)* (IEEE Press). Also writing in this area is Alex Halavais. Have a look at the online journal *Into the Blogosphere* (University of Minnesota) at http://blog.lib.umn.edu/blogosphere for a useful compilation of research done on blogging. Studies also have been conducted as part of the Pew Internet and American Life Project (http://www.pewinternet.org).

Information Retrieval

Many may be familiar with algorithmic models applied to enhance the Web-based search experience, including results stacking, frequency, guided navigation, visual indexing, and the like. Research of particular interest is from the School of Information Science, University of Pittsburgh: "Testing User Interaction with a Prototype Visualization-Based Information Retrieval System" by Sherry Koshman (*JASIST* 56(8): 824–833, 2005). This study investigated the intuitiveness of visual presentations of information retrieval (IR) systems, specifically of a prototype IR product, Visual Information Browsing Environment (VIBE). Koshman studied whether user expertise affected usability of VIBE. Expertise levels were defined as VIBE experts, online searchers, and novices, and there were 31 participants—12 expert online searchers (librarians), 4 VIBE experts (LIS staff/faculty), and 15 novice users (all of them pursuing MLIS degrees). The study found that repeated use of VIBE increased familiarity, and yielded higher levels of task completion but not necessarily accurate completion. In addition, there was little variation in rate of success between online searchers and novices in the first session using VIBE. Precise visual tasks were more successfully completed than complex ones. It will be interesting to see how systems like VIBE are applied in the future to information retrieval processes.

Awards and Grants that Honor and Support Excellent Research

The professional library associations offer many awards and grants to recognize and encourage research. The 2005 awards and grants here are listed under the name of the sponsoring association, and in the case of ALA by the awarding division, in alphabetical order. More-detailed information about the prizes and prizewinners can be found at the association Web sites.

A new award to honor the contributions of Mary Jo Lynch, former director of the ALA Office for Research and Statistics, was established by Beta Phi Mu's Distinguished Lecture Program and named the Mary Jo Lynch Distinguished Research Award. The first awardee was Mary Lee Kennedy, director of the Knowledge Network Group at Microsoft, whose lecture, "Bridging the Gap: Information Behavior and Information Professionals," was delivered on October

28, 2005. The lecture focused on how technology continues to change the ways in which people create, share, and use information. More information about this award is available at http://www.beta-phi-mu.org/lectures.htm.

American Library Association (ALA)

http://www.ala.org

Carroll Preston Baber Research Grant
Winner: Kristin R. Eschenfelder, University of Wisconsin at Madison, for "Investigating the Impact of Digital Rights Management Systems on the Users of Digital Works: A Pilot Study."

Jesse H. Shera Award for Excellence in Published Research
Winners: Karen E. Fisher, Joan C. Durrance, and Marian Bouch Hinton for "Information Grounds and the Use of Need-Based Services by Immigrants in Queens, N.Y.: A Context-Based, Outcome Evaluation Approach."

Jesse H. Shera Award for Support of Dissertation Research
Winner: Doughee Sinn, School of Information Science, University of Pittsburgh, for "Records and the Understanding of Violent Events: Archival Documentation, Historical Perception, and the No Gun Ri Massacre in the Korean War."

Ingenta Research Award
Winner: Patricia K. Galloway for "Institutionalizing a University Department-Level Institutional Repository."

American Association of School Librarians (AASL)

http://www.ala.org/aasl

AASL/Highsmith Research Grant
Winner: Joyce Valenza for "School Virtual Libraries: The Influence of Best Practices on High School Students' Information Seeking."

Association of College and Research Libraries (ACRL)

http://www.ala.org/acrl

Coutts Nijhoff International West European Specialist Study Grant
Winner: Charlene Kellsey for "The Bibliothèques Municipales of France as Sources for Medieval History of Monastic Institutions: The Case of Arles."

Doctoral Dissertation Fellowship
Winner: Susan Ward Aber for "Information Needs and Behaviors of Geoscience Educators: A Grounded Theory Study."

Instruction Section Publication of the Year Award
Winners: Trudi E. Jacobson and Lijuan Xu for *Motivating Students in Information Literacy Classes* (Neal-Schuman, 2004).

Samuel Lazerow Fellowship for Research in Collections and Technical Services in Academic and Research Libraries
Winner: Kristin R. Eschenfelder for "Investigating the Impact of Digital Rights Management Systems on Libraries: A Pilot Study."

Library and Information Technology Association/OCLC

http://www.ala.org/lita

Frederick G. Kilgour Award for Research in Library and Information Technology
Winner: William E. Moen, University of North Texas.

American Society for Information Science and Technology (ASIS&T)

http://asis.org

ASIS&T Best Information Science Book
Winner: Richard Rogers for *Information Politics on the Web* (MIT Press).

ASIS&T Proquest Doctoral Dissertation Award
Winner: Weiping Yue.

ASIS&T Research in Information Science Award
Winner: Carol Kuhlthau.

Thomson ISI Citation Analysis Research Grant
Winners: Dimitris A. Dervos, Thomas Kalkanis, and Nikolas Samras.

John Wiley & Sons Best *JASIST* Paper Award
Winner: Soo Young Rieh for "On the Web at Home: Information Seeking and Web Searching in the Home Environment."

Association for Library and Information Science Education (ALISE)

http://www.alise.org

Eugene Garfield/ALISE Doctoral Dissertation Award
Winners: Paulette M. Rothbauer for "Finding and Creating Possibility: Reading in the Lives of Lesbian, Bisexual, and Queer Young Women," University of Western Ontario, 2004; Betsy Van der Veer Martens for "Theories at Work: Functional Characteristics of Theories that Facilitate Their Diffusion Over Time," Syracuse University, 2004.

Research Grant Award
Winners: Youngok Choi (SUNY Oswego) and Edie Rasmussen (University of British Columbia) for "Digital Librarians: Who Are They, What Skills Do They Need, and How Can They Be Educated?"

Medical Library Association (MLA)

http://www.mlanet.org

Donald A. B. Lindberg Research Fellowship
Winner: Yin Aphinyanaphongs, Department of Biomedical Informatics, Vanderbilt University.

President's Award
Winners: Patricia L. Thibodeau, AHIP Medical Center Library, Duke University; Linda A. Watson, AHIP Claude Moore Health Sciences Library, University of

Virginia Health System–Charlottesville; and Carla J. Funk, Medical Library Association.

Ida and George Eliot Prize

Winners: Pamela Sherwill-Navarro, AHIP Health Science Center Libraries, University of Florida–Gainesville, and Addajane Wallace, AHIP Medical Library, Halifax Medical Center, Daytona Beach, for "Research on the Value of Medical Library Services: Does It Make an Impact in the Health Care Literature?"

Janet Doe Lectureship

Winner: Julie J. McGowan, AHIP Ruth Lilly Medical Library, Indiana University–Indianapolis.

Two Business Intelligence Tools for Libraries: An Introduction and Preliminary Results

Robert E. Molyneux

Chief Statistician, SirsiDynix

There have been remarkable developments in the business world that make it relatively easy to analyze data well. Terms such as "data mining" and "business intelligence" are used to describe a confluence of developments that have resulted in databases that are easy to use, intuitive, and fast—yet they permit powerful analysis for decision support, planning, and day-to-day management.

This article describes two applications being developed at SirsiDynix that use On-Line Analytical Processing (OLAP). OLAP organizes data into "cubes" of multidimensional data. A result of this technique is that complex analysis can be done at astonishing speeds with mouse clicks and without having to know how to program.

The OLAP applications discussed here are SirsiDynix Director's Station and the Normative Data Project for Libraries (NDP). The purpose of this article is to describe them and to present a few early results from analysis of NDP data. Both applications use OLAP, but each has a different focus. The two are related because they use similar techniques to organize and integrate library data and to ease the data manipulation to see underlying conditions or causes and to generate reports.

Director's Station was developed first. It is a statistical server designed to organize and warehouse data from integrated library systems (ILSs). Public, special, and academic libraries, as well as consortia, are using Director's Station. Although it was originally developed for the SirsiDynix Unicorn Library Management System, libraries running the Horizon library system soon will also be able to use it. NDP integrates data on all U.S. public libraries. In effect, Director's Station looks in while NDP looks out, but the two applications provide the best of modern business intelligence capabilities to library managers.

Each of these applications builds on the fact that modern ILSs keep track of much more than just circulations. They are, as their name suggests, integrated into all aspects of a library's operations. These applications tap the information generated, massage it, and make it available for manipulation.

Director's Station

Typically, Director's Station runs on a server near the library or consortium's ILS server. It will query the ILS in the evening and build the OLAP cubes in time for use by morning. It reports on the myriad activities of the library or consortium recorded by the ILS, such as circulations, disposition of funds, cataloging, and so on. It also allows queries and analysis of those data.

Robert Molyneux has worked on compiling, documenting, and analyzing library data for more than 20 years and has taught a variety of library school classes dealing with the integration of computers and networking technology in libraries.

Given that Director's Station is a tool used at different libraries, SirsiDynix cannot pool the results of the detailed analysis available, but does have anecdotal evidence of its use.

Normative Data Project

The Normative Data Project Web page is http://www.libraryndp.info. This site is used to provide general information on this project, as well as to document discoveries about the data and to share results from investigations into public libraries in the United States.

Contributing Libraries

Currently, NDP is being developed solely around U.S. public libraries. It integrates several kinds of data. One kind comes directly from a set of contributing libraries' ILSs. These data include information on titles held, such as call numbers and type of item (book, DVD, and so on) at these libraries. Another kind of information derived from the ILSs is circulation data. That is, what particular books, DVDs, and the like circulate, what call numbers are most heavily circulated, and what kind of borrower (adult, juvenile, and so on) checks them out, and in what language. It should be noted that there is no personally identifiable information in NDP—just class of borrower.

Those familiar with library-use studies are aware that the question of how library users interact with libraries has been and remains key. Herman H. Fussler and Julian L. Simon's *Patterns in the Use of Books in Large Research Libraries* (University of Chicago Press, 1969) is one of the landmark studies. The data collection problems were daunting and many of their conclusions and those of others who worked on this problem are based on small samples. NDP now has data on nearly a quarter of a billion (and growing) circulation transactions, eliminating the problem of small samples.

A Few Results

The contributing libraries are currently a nonrepresentative sample of all U.S. libraries. Generally, they are bigger and have a larger income per capita than the average. Currently, there are 54 systems, comprising almost 500 libraries. SirsiDynix continues to add data from libraries to enrich NDP further.

The most popular titles at contributing libraries can be found through any of the dimensions of NDP data. To give a flavor of this capability, Table 1 shows the 10 most popular Chinese DVDs in a set of these libraries for a recent three-month timeframe. Table 2 shows popular cookbooks, and Table 3 lists popular audio cassettes.

Because the data on circulations are time-stamped, it is possible to calculate when items were circulated. Figures indicate that library users are taking advantage of the ILS's ability to transact business even during off hours.

Taking a broader view, in the second quarter of 2005 there were 26 million circulations recorded at these libraries, and the libraries held 39 million total copies, that is, materials individually bar-coded. These numbers can be examined

Table 1 / Top 10 Circulating Chinese DVD Titles, Second Quarter 2005*

Chinese Transliterated Title	English Title	Director	Rating
1 Ying Xiong	Hero	Yimou Zhang	PG-13
2 Wo Hu Cang Long	Crouching Tiger Hidden Dragon	Ang Lee	PG-13
3 Shi Mian Mai Fu	House of Flying Daggers	Yimou Zhang	PG-13
4 Shao Lin Zu Qiu	Shaolin Soccer	Xingchi Zhou	Unrated
5 Yin Shi Nan Nv	Eat Drink Man Woman	Ang Lee	Unrated
6 Ba Wang Bie Ji	Farewell My Concubine	Kaige Chen	R
7 Chong Qing Sen Lin	Chungking Express	Kar Wai Wong	PG-13
8 Xi Zao	Shower	Yang Zhang	PG-13
9 Shi Qi Sui De Dan Che	Beijing Bicycle	Xiaoshuai Wang	PG-13
10 Jian Gui	The Eye	Oxide Pang Chun, Danny Pang	R

* From 21 library systems representing 2,892,164 distinct titles and 13,471,271 checkouts in the second quarter of 2005.
Source: SirsiDynix

Table 2 / Top 10 Circulating Cookbooks, Second Quarter 2005*

Title	Author
1 *South Beach Diet Cookbook*	Arthur Agatston
2 *Rachael Ray's 30-Minute Get Real Meals: Eat Healthy Without Going to Extremes*	Rachael Ray
3 *Garlic and Sapphires: The Secret Life of a Critic in Disguise*	Ruth Reichl
4 *Rachael Ray's 30-Minute Meals 2*	Rachael Ray
5 *Jan Karon's Mitford Cookbook Kitchen Reader*	Jan Karon
6 *Ultimate Weight Solution Cookbook Recipes for Weight Loss*	Phillip C. McGraw
7 *Paula Deen & Friends Living It Up, Southern Style*	Paula H. Deen
8 *Atkins for Life Low-Carb Cookbook: More Than 250 Recipes for Every Occasion*	Veronica C. Atkins
9 *Joy of Cooking*	Irma von Starkloff Rombauer
10 *Barefoot in Paris: Easy French Food You Really Can Make at Home*	Ina Garten

* From 21 library systems representing 2,892,164 distinct titles and 13,471,271 checkouts in second quarter 2005.
Source: SirsiDynix

Table 3 / Top 10 Circulating Books on Audio Cassette, Second Quarter 2005*

1 *Harry Potter and the Order of the Phoenix*	J. K. Rowling
2 *Harry Potter and the Prisoner of Azkaban*	J. K. Rowling
3 *Da Vinci Code*	Dan Brown
4 *Harry Potter and the Sorcerer's Stone*	J. K. Rowling
5 *Harry Potter and the Chamber of Secrets*	J. K. Rowling
6 *Bad Beginning*	Lemony Snicket
7 *Austere Academy*	Lemony Snicket
8 *Reptile Room*	Lemony Snicket
9 *Harry Potter and the Goblet of Fire*	J. K. Rowling
10 *Little House on the Prairie*	Laura Ingalls Wilder

* From 21 library systems representing 2,892,164 distinct titles and 13,471,271 checkouts in second quarter 2005.
Source: SirsiDynix

Table 4 / Comparison of Ranks of Circulations and Holdings, Second Quarter 2005*

Dewey Classes	Rank of Circulations	Rank of Holdings	Difference in Ranks
(710) Civic and landscape art	40	63	23
(560) Paleontology Paleozoology	33	55	22
(460) Spanish and Portuguese languages	54	74	20
(690) Buildings	31	47	16
(510) Mathematics	25	40	15
(450) Italian, Romanian, Rhaeto-Romantic	80	92	12
(490) Other languages	61	73	12
(240) Christian moral and devotional theology	26	37	11
(440) Romance languages, French	73	83	10
(410) Linguistics	69	78	9
(060) General organization and museology	99	90	-9
(320) Political science	36	25	-11
(350) Public administration	42	29	-13
(500) Natural sciences and mathematics	43	30	-13
(030) General encyclopedic works	66	51	-15
(700) The arts	51	36	-15
(310) General statistics	98	82	-16
(020) Library and information sciences	63	41	-22
(920) Biography, genealogy, insignia	44	19	-25
(010) Bibliography	89	54	-35

* From 54 library systems and 425 libraries representing 39 million distinct titles and 26 million total circulations in second quarter 2005.
Source: SirsiDynix

in various ways—for example, by sorting the circulations and holdings by their Dewey classes. (Note that public libraries have many materials that are not classed in Dewey—fiction and books on paperback book racks, for instance. Forty-eight percent of the holdings that circulated in the second quarter of 2005 were unclassed, so these are excluded from the analysis that follows.)

Table 4 shows a comparison of 20 Dewey classes. These were selected by ranking each Dewey class by its circulation, and then by its holdings, and comparing the two ranks by subtracting them. The table lists the 10 Dewey classes where the rank of holdings exceeded the rank of circulations the most, and the 10 where circulations exceeded holdings the most. These are the extreme cases—most classes show a better balance between the ranks of holdings and of circulations.

What does this table tell us? We see that items in 710–719 were 63rd in holdings (of 99) but 40th in circulations. In effect, they were used more than the size of their collections would suggest. Bibliography (010) was 54th in holdings but 89th in circulations. Given that many bibliographies are reference materials, this result makes sense, as does that for general encyclopedic works (030) and for similar reasons, but in the case of circulating materials this analysis suggests an imbalance in collections.

One of the things known from the literature of library use is that English-language materials are overwhelmingly the largest in use and holdings, and in the second quarter of 2005, 98 percent of the materials where a language can be identified were in English. But note that four of the ten Dewey classes one might

Table 5 / Summary Data, Change in Circulations by Selected Formats*

Format	Total Increase (%)†	Total Circulations First Quarter 2005	Total Circulations First Quarter 2002– First Quarter 2005
Magazine	874	75,128	451,454
Book on CD	361	122,574	908,919
DVD	345	359,797	3,146,221
Paperback	132	667,171	5,960,166
Music on CD	108	248,461	2,129,209
Videocassette	56	659,854	6,848,567
Book	45	3,608,368	40,016,518

* From 11 library systems representing 55 million checkouts, first quarter 2002–first quarter 2005.
† Increase for first quarter 2005 over first quarter 2002.
Source: SirsiDynix

call "overused"—that is, the circulation rank is higher than the rank of the holdings of materials—deal with foreign languages, and a fifth is linguistics.

These results suggest a method for assessing a collection's balance, but it is only a first look as one is led to wonder more about the materials circulating in those language classes.

To go beyond this analysis a bit: A separate examination of the materials in Paleontology (the Dewey 560s) shows that almost all high-circulating items in this class in the second quarter of 2005 were children's books about dinosaurs.

Table 5 shows the change in total circulation over time by item format. For this analysis, the 11 libraries in NDP for the entire period from the first quarter of 2002 through the first quarter of 2005 were analyzed to compare the circulation change for selected formats of the more than 40 NDP tracks. The table reports the summary percent increases for first quarter 2005 over first quarter 2002, the total circulations for these seven formats in first quarter 2005, and the total circulations over the entire period.

The summary figures are based on totals for this set of libraries, which circulated almost 55 million items during this period. Clearly, magazines—at nearly 900 percent—grew the most, but number of circulations is smallest of the formats analyzed here.

Books-on-CD is the next category in terms of percent increase. The increase in this format's circulation, at 361 percent, is substantial although the number of circulations is low. The books-on-cassette category is not shown here because the increase over the period was less than 2 percent. However, there were 153,000 total circulations in first quarter 2005, a figure greater than books-on-CD. These two formats used for listening to books were responsible for 275,000 circulations at the end of the period and the books-on-CD category represents a growing segment.

DVD circulations increased 345 percent at these libraries over the period. Note that videocassettes grew by only 56 percent but that the totals are higher for the whole period. What this chart does not show is that in March of 2005, both for this set of libraries and for all libraries reporting to NDP, DVD circulations surpassed those of videocassettes and continued to do so through June 2005, indicating that the much-anticipated change in format has occurred.

Books, showing the smallest percent of increase of the formats here, nonetheless had more than twice the circulation number of the formats listed in this table both for the last quarter and as a total for the period. Books are what library users check out the most, although the growth of this format is lowest on this list.

Library Data from NCES

Surrounding this information from contributing libraries are data from the U.S. National Center for Education Statistics (NCES) on all public libraries in the United States. NCES has conducted a national library survey since 1987, and it currently publishes three series from that data-collection effort. Two of these are included in NDP. One is the state summary data, which summarizes data for the public libraries in the states and is the best series to compare state data and arrive at national assessments of the public library condition. The other is the public library data file, which presents more-detailed information on the 9,200 individual public library systems. In addition, the ratios used in the popular NCES State Rank Order Tables are available for every library system in the country, permitting close comparison of individual libraries.

By integrating these two sets of data, one can select "like libraries" for comparison. In the public library world, "like libraries" usually means libraries serving about the same number of people in their service areas, so one can find among all contributing libraries those of similar size to a target library and compare titles circulated. In addition, one can compare these similar libraries to find out, for example, if they have more income or staff per capita. An interface makes it easy to produce charts, graphs, and tables and to export the data to a spreadsheet for further analysis.

Geographic and Demographic Data

Of course, there is more to finding "like libraries" than population served because those populations vary so much. NDP includes demographic data on each of the nearly 17,000 library buildings in two ways.

SirsiDynix has partnered with GeoLib (http://www.geolib.org) of Florida State University to present basic demographic data for default market areas around each of these libraries. Analysis has shown differences in the way libraries are used, and the demographics of the people who live around the various libraries strongly influence which books circulate. With NDP, one cannot see who is checking out which books, but one does know the demographics of the library borrowers' neighborhoods. Matching demographic characteristics provides a new method of discovering "like libraries." For example, by comparing a library's demographic information with that of similar NDP contributing libraries, one has a more sophisticated way to compare titles circulated, circulation statistics, and per capitas.

An exploratory study examined how demographics might affect circulation at three NDP libraries in the Fairfax County, Virginia, system. In the market area surrounding two of the libraries (the Woodrow Wilson Community Library and the Thomas Jefferson Community Library) there is a low percentage of college graduates and a low percentage of high school graduates, according to U.S. Census reports; at the third (the Great Falls Community Library), there is a high percentage of college graduates and those with graduate degrees (with almost everyone at least finishing high school). Residents of the first two areas have a relatively low income; the second group of residents have a relatively high income.

What did people check out at these three libraries? At the two with few college graduates, of the top 100 circulating items, one had 24 foreign-language items and the other had 21. In each, Spanish-language materials had about half as many circulations as Vietnamese items. The high-college-demographic library had one foreign language item in the top 100. These results, while sparse, are reasonable and suggest that NDP data can supply a basis for predicting which titles will circulate at libraries with varying population demographics.

These results were for all circulations by any library user and they indicate that the two libraries with low-college demographics have a bit more than 20 percent of their highest-circulating titles in foreign languages. What about adult circulations? About the same 20 percent of high-circulating titles are foreign-language materials. A more interesting result came in seeing what the children were checking out. In the two low-college demographic libraries, 1 percent of the high-circulating titles were in a foreign language; all children are reading *Harry Potter*—and everything else—in English.

Number of Libraries in the United States and Canada

Statistics are from *American Library Directory (ALD) 2005–2006* (Information Today, Inc., 2005). Data are exclusive of elementary and secondary school libraries.

Libraries in the United States

Public Libraries	16,971 *
Public libraries, excluding branches	9,734 †
Main public libraries that have branches	2,385
Public library branches	7,237
Academic Libraries	3,698 *
Community college	1,125
Departmental	176
Medical	8
Religious	6
University and college	2,573
Departmental	1,463
Law	181
Medical	250
Religious	227
Armed Forces Libraries	314 *
Air Force	91
Medical	12
Army	143
Medical	29
Navy	65
Law	1
Medical	14
Government Libraries	1,225 *
Law	412
Medical	178
Special Libraries (excluding public, academic, armed forces, and government)	8,208 *
Law	969
Medical	1,644
Religious	580
Total Special Libraries (including public, academic, armed forces, and government)	9,526
Total law	1,563

Note: Numbers followed by an asterisk are added to find "Total libraries counted" for each of the three geographic areas (United States, U.S.-administered regions, and Canada). The sum of the three totals is the "Grand total of libraries listed" in *ALD*. For details on the count of libraries, see the preface to the 58th edition of *ALD—Ed.*

†Federal, state, and other statistical sources use this figure (libraries *excluding* branches) as the total for public libraries.

Total medical	2,135
Total religious	1,102
Total Libraries Counted(*)	30,416

Libraries in Regions Administered by the United States

Public Libraries	28*
Public libraries, excluding branches	10†
Main public libraries that have branches	3
Public library branches	18
Academic Libraries	36*
Junior college	6
Departmental	3
Medical	0
University and college	30
Departmental	22
Law	3
Medical	2
Religious	1
Armed Forces Libraries	2*
Air Force	1
Army	1
Navy	0
Government Libraries	7*
Law	2
Medical	2
Special Libraries (excluding public, academic, armed forces, and government)	9*
Law	3
Medical	1
Religious	1
Total Special Libraries (including public, academic, armed forces, and government)	19
Total law	8
Total medical	5
Total religious	2
Total Libraries Counted(*)	82

Libraries in Canada

Public Libraries	2,106*
Public libraries, excluding branches	807†
Main public libraries that have branches	165
Public library branches	1,299

Academic Libraries	352*
Junior college	89
Departmental	15
Medical	0
Religious	3
University and college	263
Departmental	195
Law	17
Medical	23
Religious	34
Government Libraries	310*
Law	25
Medical	5
Special Libraries (excluding public, academic, armed forces, and government)	1,030*
Law	112
Medical	195
Religious	26
Total Special Libraries (including public, academic, armed forces, and government)	1,137
Total law	154
Total medical	223
Total religious	98
Total Libraries Counted(*)	3,798

Summary

Total U.S. Libraries	30,416
Total Libraries Administered by the United States	82
Total Canadian Libraries	3,798
Grand Total of Libraries Listed	34,296

Library Acquisition Expenditures, 2004–2005: U.S. Public, Academic, Special, and Government Libraries

The information in these tables is taken from *American Library Directory* (*ALD*) *2005–2006* (Information Today, Inc., 2005). The tables report acquisition expenditures by public, academic, special, and government libraries.

The total number of libraries in the United States and in regions administered by the United States listed in this 58th edition of *ALD* is 30,498, including 16,999 public libraries, 3,734 academic libraries, 8,217 special libraries, 316 armed forces libraries, and 1,232 government libraries.

Understanding the Tables

Number of libraries includes only those U.S. libraries in *ALD* that reported annual acquisition expenditures (3,426 public libraries, 1,445 academic libraries, 311 special libraries, 119 government libraries). Libraries that reported annual income but not expenditures are not included in the count. Academic libraries include university, college, and junior college libraries. Special academic libraries, such as law and medical libraries, that reported acquisition expenditures separately from the institution's main library are counted as independent libraries.

The amount in the *total acquisition expenditures* column for a given state is generally greater than the sum of the categories of expenditures. This is because the total acquisition expenditures amount also includes the expenditures of libraries that did not itemize by category.

Figures in *categories of expenditure* columns represent only those libraries that itemized expenditures. Libraries that reported a total acquisition expenditure amount but did not itemize are only represented in the total acquisition expenditures column.

Table 1 / Public Library Acquisition Expenditures

State	Number of Libraries	Total Acquisition Expenditures	Books	Other Print Materials	Periodicals/ Serials	Manuscripts & Archives	AV Equipment	AV Materials	Microforms	Electronic Reference	Preservation
						Categories of Expenditure (in U.S. dollars)					
Alabama	46	7,161,415	2,208,809	33,937	202,135	—	30,206	314,709	211,000	117,185	3,200
Alaska	16	1,193,702	184,795	9,800	31,363	—	5,000	5,256	1,000	11,560	2,000
Arizona	33	13,831,440	8,778,671	976,486	1,316,254	—	1,500	1,261,871	27,500	1,525,592	40,423
Arkansas	19	5,353,605	3,208,965	4,200	144,301	—	1,061	264,358	21,314	260,723	6,517
California	120	93,885,470	42,736,157	1,121,189	6,092,798	194,041	538,526	7,371,779	742,861	7,776,293	232,268
Colorado	30	13,887,132	8,460,361	50,360	750,796	—	2,200	760,075	13,397	1,166,089	400
Connecticut	102	12,805,546	5,695,369	37,159	1,333,488	2,000	109,253	823,054	152,972	970,696	33,028
Delaware	9	1,079,518	645,093	5,000	53,889	2,000	1,000	82,466	17,500	3,500	3,500
District of Columbia	—	—	—	—	—	—	—	—	—	—	—
Florida	62	53,788,796	26,754,819	237,142	3,929,536	40,164	1,049,675	2,809,265	221,295	2,772,692	30,000
Georgia	23	8,882,491	5,291,947	47,113	291,164	—	4,954	983,395	26,391	563,522	8,266
Hawaii	1	5,621,005	3,201,881	—	833,066	—	—	—	828,058	758,000	—
Idaho	37	2,846,709	1,198,182	31,158	94,225	—	56,150	128,435	17,200	582,744	12,731
Illinois	224	49,028,551	18,396,438	86,853	1,700,296	13,800	261,251	3,923,744	174,778	4,828,590	63,156
Indiana	204	36,877,132	12,543,822	57,061	1,474,332	—	399,065	2,578,956	226,604	1,728,457	90,957
Iowa	147	12,381,317	4,144,515	131,481	512,503	1,430	61,258	910,556	16,233	328,464	350
Kansas	87	9,662,139	4,616,074	575,944	1,238,955	450	46,981	611,082	44,104	1,097,334	641
Kentucky	51	11,089,806	3,274,157	45,655	119,604	—	17,361	782,825	8,254	261,834	8,346
Louisiana	23	7,370,905	2,800,399	57,572	459,535	—	2,000	330,757	26,348	118,024	12,500
Maine	56	1,625,018	870,469	6,961	188,550	950	8,600	70,602	1,600	25,347	500
Maryland	20	20,093,508	11,560,163	134,807	215,229	—	94,400	792,736	—	703,812	500
Massachusetts	180	18,434,224	10,420,333	95,957	1,070,049	6,085	155,269	1,147,847	110,696	537,326	16,009
Michigan	154	49,674,203	14,981,246	43,735	1,954,799	4,200	279,214	3,245,763	93,533	2,367,189	120,739
Minnesota	56	16,890,572	6,373,853	2,086	482,078	—	23,739	1,693,886	3,194	718,242	260,369
Mississippi	21	4,459,996	1,507,430	83,046	99,467	—	1,200	273,133	11,077	101,392	2,408

	Count										
Missouri	96	24,830,638	12,293,157	46,557	1,275,149	—	102,579	2,787,208	357,049	3,499,827	28,825
Montana	29	1,797,450	947,787	2,253	121,277	6,700	50	30,650	3,047	99,944	53,865
Nebraska	56	4,734,866	1,755,915	774	236,230	—	12,237	250,086	33,408	695,012	6,848
Nevada	8	8,894,867	363,183	73,313	139,907	—	11,000	34,426	46,804	222,737	3,000
New Hampshire	94	3,499,360	1,578,303	20,952	193,249	717	3,754	309,084	36,819	119,256	16,718
New Jersey	116	31,728,174	17,780,012	103,273	2,260,495	—	119,731	2,850,717	226,514	1,556,284	11,331
New Mexico	13	3,842,777	2,888,614	427	36,488	875	1,054	434,258	2,494	197,822	3,500
New York	249	60,551,524	27,662,215	495,962	6,629,116	9,500	511,379	4,012,486	435,078	3,513,594	111,339
North Carolina	52	10,088,584	4,319,190	43,878	275,274	1,500	12,185	506,572	61,399	214,916	471
North Dakota	13	1,129,642	440,673	4,000	134,065		5,200	44,205	7,760	58,439	1,500
Ohio	105	87,744,454	29,936,299	293,075	6,357,331	2,000	714,299	10,560,980	480,978	4,590,457	375,766
Oklahoma	23	6,095,209	3,606,131	46,329	1,195,616	—	51,494	313,578	4,767	169,996	5,472
Oregon	63	14,296,396	7,706,577	24,312	1,369,784	7,000	44,290	2,383,921	16,682	871,204	41,607
Pennsylvania	206	29,988,855	6,249,865	33,583	890,945	250	25,527	1,111,078	144,914	811,580	304,333
Rhode Island	23	3,742,119	1,204,880	40,945	137,259	750	—	171,197	13,764	329,338	5,129
South Carolina	29	13,236,096	7,224,943	11,770	1,056,736	1,000	217,267	1,502,117	108,673	1,127,252	15,911
South Dakota	27	1,954,072	1,053,410	900	220,940	530	10,600	236,397	19,443	103,986	646
Tennessee	39	12,488,100	9,648,379	42,044	759,549	14,000	30,746	442,625	17,930	1,191,458	85,621
Texas	153	34,284,315	16,191,924	438,308	3,007,389	—	472,659	1,719,171	208,617	1,477,474	30,849
Utah	16	9,447,424	5,563,869	216,490	551,610			1,936,155	9,650	476,666	2,513
Vermont	51	1,099,953	660,743	10,987	82,737	120	2,500	76,421	1,050	46,095	125
Virginia	48	13,547,138	7,158,858	74,236	1,150,733	47,592	20,281	1,344,069	183,516	927,999	591,694
Washington	32	16,345,852	6,433,472	61,988	509,202	—		1,704,756	11,050	836,693	—
West Virginia	20	3,117,697	811,090	17,314	86,974	—	1,000	137,996	4,880	42,165	2,623
Wisconsin	122	16,731,629	8,361,852	107,472	2,029,067	—	413,451	1,486,655	74,684	394,847	216,339
Wyoming	21	1,832,764	363,453	409	47,107	—	6,000	53,508	185	72,431	2,800
U.S. Virgin Islands	1	8,000	7,000	—	1,000	—	—	—	—	—	—
Total	3,426	874,982,155	382,065,742	6,086,253	55,343,641	357,654	5,939,146	67,606,866	5,508,064	52,972,079	2,867,633
Estimated % of Acquisition Expenditures			44	0.70	6.33	0.04	0.68	7.73	0.63	6.05	0.33

Table 2 / Academic Library Acquisition Expenditures

State	Number of Libraries	Total Acquisition Expenditures	Books	Other Print Materials	Periodicals/ Serials	Manuscripts & Archives	AV Equipment	AV Materials	Microforms	Electronic Reference	Preservation
Alabama	26	22,028,910	4,631,621	100,401	14,193,442	3,000	28,056	125,782	128,267	1,533,752	195,193
Alaska	4	3,164,133	503,550	—	677,444	—	—	39,417	49,990	656,250	17,750
Arizona	17	15,339,758	1,520,852	54,604	1,804,316	20,048	13,122	127,247	61,686	1,320,888	16,481
Arkansas	13	10,501,110	1,773,809	38,485	6,593,953	1,864	47,796	126,616	193,139	964,774	150,163
California	99	93,942,512	18,708,437	447,272	32,633,853	—	200,674	717,665	1,508,646	11,434,096	1,029,821
Colorado	20	17,848,560	2,808,761	28,202	9,481,822	6,183	4,695	107,581	90,642	701,396	77,462
Connecticut	21	46,389,056	13,978,486	55,365	15,631,143	—	23,890	155,150	151,056	5,937,208	865,753
Delaware	3	338,763	80,000	—	39,386	—	14,476	—	5,901	19,000	—
District of Columbia	12	27,993,496	3,330,615	598,855	10,302,734	4,725	26,300	6,164	293,491	1,222,468	187,685
Florida	47	43,709,785	9,612,869	547,792	20,981,506	—	179,477	389,744	556,955	6,035,794	496,371
Georgia	33	36,305,444	3,954,577	94,189	10,649,290	—	38,887	49,831	166,659	684,219	773,333
Hawaii	4	760,347	172,306	500	238,299	—	18,000	18,216	50,126	108,585	19,000
Idaho	6	8,297,138	1,566,667	—	5,559,765	828	—	8,095	61,398	919,371	184,004
Illinois	61	84,647,738	17,197,792	1,323,164	33,931,473	5,845	346,406	465,116	354,635	5,062,664	1,846,262
Indiana	33	26,510,358	7,311,272	5,400	12,236,171	51,000	108,651	203,245	218,457	2,104,164	232,860
Iowa	32	18,187,043	3,912,502	505,948	10,248,415	275	32,797	111,817	443,522	1,763,690	161,916
Kansas	31	10,592,437	2,817,519	17,082	5,429,604	2,000	18,175	92,701	76,943	947,383	67,748
Kentucky	25	29,994,146	5,630,394	49,913	16,260,869	30,760	5,755	153,764	342,029	3,212,362	331,049
Louisiana	19	12,662,957	1,884,398	187,357	7,361,548	3,070	16,084	14,901	105,785	704,320	92,892
Maine	10	9,714,018	2,070,075	—	5,614,803	200	1,287	43,907	221,517	1,331,612	224,747
Maryland	32	26,800,991	4,526,311	78,688	8,257,425	1,704	91,372	164,597	543,664	1,789,984	238,018
Massachusetts	49	71,368,434	7,225,016	885,546	24,251,873	2,000	271,509	193,617	747,400	4,893,452	412,628
Michigan	43	40,646,919	9,819,012	130,916	21,374,446	11,700	74,678	149,466	391,635	3,788,684	348,527
Minnesota	25	28,186,843	5,140,932	502,423	4,540,741	—	21,006	226,212	171,782	1,690,531	134,201
Mississippi	12	9,481,829	407,588	3,257	1,658,938	—	106,156	32,950	130,159	576,753	61,119
Missouri	38	34,379,657	6,149,247	880,303	19,107,923	2,065	23,585	180,525	215,791	3,519,878	340,387

Categories of Expenditure (in U.S. dollars)

State	No.	Total									
Montana	13	5,978,040	1,254,993	—	4,478,007	—	50,121	17,495	—	123,225	54,199
Nebraska	17	11,665,834	1,472,405	68,929	3,209,120	—	59,051	85,716	90,962	433,493	108,607
Nevada	4	1,079,172	554,085	—	97,644	—	—	25,024	55,667	138,459	8,293
New Hampshire	6	5,831,117	1,347,777	—	2,959,523	3,000	2,686	34,149	7,000	637,405	75,529
New Jersey	25	22,717,975	2,299,932	121,768	2,747,296	—	35,559	36,303	148,867	1,255,903	139,943
New Mexico	16	11,171,445	2,977,142	146,625	5,873,017	—	24,537	24,985	108,077	954,165	227,932
New York	105	133,778,967	12,758,714	963,227	35,620,319	53,924	323,330	569,332	1,206,172	10,609,414	1,010,378
North Carolina	47	37,082,015	7,455,072	41,064	19,206,968	3,500	123,879	293,351	793,932	2,418,903	283,985
North Dakota	10	5,773,244	728,395	29,173	3,375,786	—	3,500	62,345	52,854	937,826	67,013
Ohio	53	45,894,744	8,010,921	122,281	13,544,304	2,235	101,408	399,376	565,245	3,980,388	616,796
Oklahoma	20	16,454,833	1,387,685	203,126	3,575,910	4,100	14,300	23,425	76,115	2,948,743	65,418
Oregon	30	19,421,134	3,184,053	153,943	7,777,519	—	141,334	176,783	90,899	1,318,264	213,087
Pennsylvania	71	70,347,300	14,695,570	3,682,435	27,988,013	5,922	169,050	601,874	904,678	16,755,737	663,563
Rhode Island	10	13,080,889	1,339,353	15,700	3,372,382	8,500	48,000	59,515	29,138	795,497	29,651
South Carolina	25	11,857,089	989,414	3,832	1,250,587	—	6,000	62,113	131,678	488,581	97,126
South Dakota	8	2,230,928	434,094	—	715,151	680	5,000	9,119	55,664	399,425	19,618
Tennessee	36	27,357,763	4,096,419	13,032	13,085,689	2,614	13,600	111,300	319,870	2,136,747	161,107
Texas	82	91,142,486	14,147,535	586,102	25,340,896	2,668	241,377	570,631	2,080,946	10,220,205	561,281
Utah	8	11,786,672	3,819,263	11,392	6,745,952	55,808	38,996	116,554	46,090	768,976	183,641
Vermont	13	8,261,702	1,940,246	21,040	3,259,325	3,000	13,093	98,177	65,993	1,588,378	142,837
Virginia	36	37,842,686	7,074,090	43,322	18,857,270	15,321	125,171	281,258	352,634	3,734,521	269,506
Washington	30	17,740,316	4,122,304	126,533	9,933,317	2,500	97,500	178,919	391,142	1,384,312	118,608
West Virginia	19	4,210,569	795,793	164,490	1,433,976	8,598	36,346	50,188	137,350	1,021,393	29,172
Wisconsin	36	15,208,888	3,512,632	49,210	8,083,171	918	61,023	318,809	299,685	2,428,860	134,399
Wyoming	3	3,338,426	376,747	1,000	2,458,322	—	9,845	57,335	293	374,104	60,780
American Samoa	1	5,000	1,000	—	3,000	—	—	1,000	—	—	—
Guam	1	5,000	—	—	—	—	—	—	—	—	—
Puerto Rico	4	1,625,173	287,673	1,366	1,011,753	500	21,000	18,925	—	217,456	3,500
U.S. Virgin Islands	1	230,045	—	—	—	—	—	—	—	—	—
Total	1,445	1,363,013,834	237,871,915	13,105,252	525,080,399	321,055	3,478,540	8,193,327	15,292,226	131,001,658	13,851,339
Estimated % of Acquisition Expenditures			17.45	0.96	38.52	0.02	0.26	0.60	1.12	9.61	1.02

Table 3 / Special Library Acquisition Expenditures

State	Number of Libraries	Total Acquisition Expenditures	Books	Other Print Materials	Periodicals/ Serials	Manuscripts & Archives	AV Equipment	AV Materials	Microforms	Electronic Reference	Preservation
Alabama	1	1,150	500	—	650	—	—	—	—	—	—
Alaska	0	—	—	—	—	—	—	—	—	—	—
Arizona	12	171,820	32,113	—	33,122	150	—	5,000	50	3,000	8,700
Arkansas	0	—	—	—	—	—	—	—	—	—	—
California	32	1,907,678	400,775	32,500	374,590	900	23,920	21,500	16,000	100,700	14,825
Colorado	3	13,260	9,000	—	1,760	—	—	2,000	—	—	—
Connecticut	5	102,273	59,913	383	6,200	19,431	702	—	1,000	3,000	6,894
Delaware	0	—	—	—	—	—	—	—	—	—	—
District of Columbia	6	1,603,250	191,225	35,000	190,025	18,000	—	—	25,000	625,000	500,000
Florida	14	396,924	112,835	3,250	96,532	1,200	7,000	4,000	700	12,600	11,003
Georgia	2	76,300	5,300	—	71,000	—	—	—	—	—	—
Hawaii	4	122,000	54,000	2,500	61,000	—	—	—	—	—	4,500
Idaho	2	1,000,100	—	—	—	—	—	—	—	—	—
Illinois	31	4,424,673	325,534	49,660	306,807	41,400	8,800	17,450	9,431	344,180	24,200
Indiana	6	336,515	36,024	—	3,500	—	525	1,000	3,350	1,000	1,500
Iowa	3	239,200	500	—	—	—	—	—	—	—	1,000
Kansas	5	44,174	5,301	—	2,923	100	—	—	—	—	100
Kentucky	2	24,834	14,804	—	8,679	—	—	—	—	—	962
Louisiana	0	—	—	—	—	—	—	—	—	—	—
Maine	2	4,297	2,673	—	1,500	—	—	—	—	—	124
Maryland	9	369,769	41,731	1,000	121,836	50	1,000	—	—	46,492	550
Massachusetts	13	1,238,103	487,042	2,000	126,750	5,500	—	16,500	500	365,400	49,950
Michigan	2	39,000	28,000	—	11,000	—	—	—	—	—	—
Minnesota	7	156,380	8,380	500	9,900	2,000	500	4,000	1,500	14,000	2,600
Mississippi	2	116,150	10,100	—	106,050	—	—	—	—	—	—

Missouri	5	194,247	39,514	2,000	41,207	—	35,695	—	200	3,886	71,495
Montana	3	44,000	13,500	3,000	5,000	—	—	—	19,000	2,000	—
Nebraska	3	7,950	5,500	500	1,700	—	—	—	—	—	—
Nevada	1	1,000	—	—	—	—	—	—	—	—	—
New Hampshire	2	230,825	—	—	—	—	—	—	—	—	—
New Jersey	10	381,580	35,900	2,000	15,150	—	7,050	6,000	—	2,700	—
New Mexico	4	35,500	10,900	4,000	3,900	—	300	200	500	1,100	2,800
New York	38	1,207,073	392,170	8,475	433,124	40,000	4,474	79,479	8,400	70,225	39,125
North Carolina	0	—	—	—	—	—	—	—	—	—	—
North Dakota	1	11,116	5,873	—	4,618	—	—	—	—	—	625
Ohio	16	1,242,098	195,996	18,630	814,328	1,800	3,000	12,622	1,639	169,849	11,634
Oklahoma	4	508,262	18,814	—	22,138	2,500	15,000	—	—	2,059	—
Oregon	5	7,800	1,900	100	2,250	—	—	—	50	—	—
Pennsylvania	17	1,223,277	184,410	49,945	187,598	29,012	240	5,599	1,800	196,500	10,281
Rhode Island	1	50,895	32,695	—	8,000	—	—	—	—	—	10,200
South Carolina	4	385,000	75,800	—	30,000	—	—	—	—	—	—
South Dakota	0	—	—	—	—	—	—	—	—	—	—
Tennessee	5	44,110	17,479	2,500	12,349	—	500	3,073	—	7,509	—
Texas	10	1,128,889	61,657	38,984	88,210	750	105	795	—	115,000	2,500
Utah	1	1,000	—	—	—	—	—	—	—	—	—
Vermont	0	—	—	—	—	—	—	—	—	—	—
Virginia	8	394,418	102,928	32,900	43,215	23,150	41,470	3,135	3,000	24,500	101,160
Washington	2	7,500	2,500	—	650	—	—	—	—	2,000	200
West Virginia	2	110,000	2,500	—	7,250	107,000	—	500	—	30,000	—
Wisconsin	6	173,245	62,550	—	89,000	—	1,595	1,000	—	18,900	—
Wyoming	0	—	—	—	—	—	—	—	—	—	—
Total	311	19,777,635	3,088,336	289,827	3,343,511	292,943	151,876	183,853	92,120	2,161,600	876,928
Estimated % of Acquisition Expenditures			15.62	1.47	16.91	1.48	0.77	0.93	0.47	10.93	4.43

Table 4 / Government Library Acquisition Expenditures

State	Number of Libraries	Total Acquisition Expenditures	Books	Other Print Materials	Periodicals/ Serials	Manuscripts & Archives	AV Equipment	AV Materials	Microforms	Electronic Reference	Preservation
Alabama	2	664,299	370,233	—	22,770	6,000	21,244	218	11,880	210,788	21,166
Alaska	0	—	—	—	—	—	—	—	—	—	—
Arizona	1	11,697	5,000	3,000	3,697	—	—	—	—	—	—
Arkansas	1	45,000	35,000	—	10,000	—	—	—	—	—	—
California	18	4,759,199	607,221	121,836	622,779	—	5,000	28,682	52,193	107,959	20,556
Colorado	2	140,000	—	—	—	—	—	—	—	—	—
Connecticut	0	—									
Delaware	0	—									
District of Columbia	3	3,322,784	36,000	—	20,000	—	—	—	52,000	23,000	5,000
Florida	3	399,500	97,000	—	208,500	—	—	32,000	14,000	48,000	—
Georgia	0	—									
Hawaii	2	1,139,106	382,746	—	753,360	—	—	—	3,000	—	—
Idaho	0	—									
Illinois	2	26,100	—	—	—	—	—	—	—	—	—
Indiana	0	—									
Iowa	1	50,000	—	—	—	—	—	—	—	—	—
Kansas	2	667,572	305,477	197,768	118,029	—	—	—	—	35,444	10,854
Kentucky	0	—									
Louisiana	6	4,520,565	5,745	—	143,557	—	—	—	—	12,045	—
Maine	2	389,866	—	—	—	—	—	—	—	—	—
Maryland	7	8,054,975	565,000	8,000	3,646,500	—	5,000	—	—	1,445,000	72,000
Massachusetts	6	553,303	140,000	—	45,000	—	—	—	—	42,000	7,500
Michigan	2	52,270	19,982	5,000	22,592	—	—	4,696	—	—	—
Minnesota	5	1,196,414	21,000	—	61,500	—	—	—	—	52,000	—
Mississippi	1	2,500	—	—	—	—	—	—	—	—	—

State	No.	Total									
Missouri	0	—	—	—	—	—	—	—	—	—	—
Montana	4	531,192	16,640	—	203,490	—	—	—	—	865	12,000
Nebraska	0	—	—	—	—	—	—	—	—	—	—
Nevada	2	603,966	393,711	—	69,230	—	2,414	—	4,662	133,949	—
New Hampshire	1	45,995	5,548	—	30,135	—	—	—	9,887	425	—
New Jersey	0	—	—	240,000	—	—	—	—	—	—	—
New Mexico	1	633,000	25,000	—	121,000	—	2,630	—	2,000	230,000	15,000
New York	8	2,290,823	1,169,070	—	107,800	—	—	5,300	1,000	50,324	5,300
North Carolina	3	468,960	412,410	3,000	22,320	—	5,000	—	7,700	7,300	11,230
North Dakota	1	43,000	8,000	—	30,000	—	—	—	—	5,000	—
Ohio	2	180,296	124,836	—	13,000	—	—	—	—	42,460	—
Oklahoma	1	30,033	1,399	171	15,065	500	—	—	—	12,081	1,317
Oregon	4	169,567	48,400	—	78,167	—	1,000	10,000	—	30,000	—
Pennsylvania	10	1,512,402	1,175,375	—	4,500	—	3,500	—	—	183,533	8,000
Rhode Island	2	897,000	663,827	—	66,087	—	—	669	4,000	162,417	—
South Carolina	1	48,450	—	—	—	—	—	—	—	—	—
South Dakota	0	—	—	—	—	—	—	—	—	—	—
Tennessee	2	245,625	110,342	4,531	19,351	—	—	11,401	—	—	—
Texas	3	221,445	155,783	—	35,811	—	—	13,351	1,500	—	15,000
Utah	1	100,000	—	—	100,000	—	—	—	—	—	—
Vermont	0	—	—	—	—	—	—	—	—	—	—
Virginia	2	80,579	34,510	—	39,114	—	—	1,446	—	5,400	109
Washington	1	4,000	2,000	—	2,000	—	—	—	—	—	—
West Virginia	0	—	—	—	—	—	—	—	—	—	—
Wisconsin	3	202,100	34,100	—	83,000	—	—	—	—	46,000	1,000
Wyoming	1	229,000	190,000	—	24,000	—	—	—	10,000	—	5,000
Total	119	34,532,583	7,161,355	583,306	6,742,354	6,500	45,788	107,763	172,322	2,887,490	211,032
Estimated % of Acquisition Expenditures			20.74	1.69	19.52	0.02	0.13	0.31	0.50	8.36	0.61

Highlights of NCES Surveys

Public Libraries

The following are highlights from the E.D. Tab publication *Public Libraries in the United States: Fiscal Year 2003,* released in September 2005. The data were collected by the National Center for Education Statistics (NCES). For more information on NCES surveys, see the article "National Center for Education Statistics Library Statistics Program" in Part 1.

Number of Public Libraries and Population of Legal Service Area

- There were 9,211 public libraries (administrative entities) in the 50 states and the District of Columbia in fiscal year (FY) 2003.
- Public libraries served 97 percent of the total population of the states and the District of Columbia, either in legally established geographic service areas or in areas under contract.
- Eleven percent of the public libraries served 72 percent of the population of legally served areas in the United States; each of these public libraries had a legal service area population of 50,000 or more.

Service Outlets

- In FY 2003, 81 percent of public libraries had one single direct-service outlet (an outlet that provides service directly to the public). Nineteen percent had more than one direct-service outlet. Types of direct-service outlets include central library outlets, branch library outlets, and bookmobile outlets.
- A total of 1,547 public libraries (17 percent) had one or more branch library outlets, with a total of 7,479 branch outlets. The total number of central library outlets was 9,062. The total number of stationary outlets (central library outlets and branch library outlets) was 16,541. Eight percent of public libraries had one or more bookmobile outlets, with a total of 864 bookmobiles.
- Eleven percent of public libraries had an average number of weekly public service hours per outlet of less than 20 hours, 38 percent had weekly public service hours per outlet of 20 to 39 hours, and 51 percent had weekly public service hours per outlet of 40 hours or more.

Legal Basis and Interlibrary Relationships

- In FY 2003, 53 percent of public libraries were part of a municipal government, 10 percent were part of a county or parish, 15 percent were nonprofit association libraries or agency libraries, 14 percent were separate government units known as library districts, 3 percent had multi-jurisdictional legal basis under an intergovernmental agreement, 2 percent were part of a school district, 1 percent were part of a city or county, and 1 percent reported their legal basis as "other."

- Seventy-six percent of public libraries were members of a federation or cooperative service, while 23 percent were not. One percent served as the headquarters of a federation or cooperative service.

Library Services

Total Circulation, Interlibrary Loans, Reference Transactions, and Library Visits

- Total nationwide circulation of public library materials was 2 billion, or 7 materials circulated per capita.
- Among the 50 states and the District of Columbia, the highest circulation per capita was 14.7, and the lowest was 2.1.
- Nationwide, 26.7 million library materials were loaned by public libraries to other libraries.
- Nationwide, reference transactions in public libraries totaled 302.3 million, or 1.1 reference transactions per capita.
- Nationwide, library visits to public libraries totaled 1.3 billion, or 4.6 library visits per capita.

Children's Services

- Nationwide, circulation of children's materials was 699.9 million, or 36 percent of total circulation, in FY 2003. Attendance at children's programs was 53.2 million.

Internet Access and Electronic Services

- Nationwide, uses of electronic resources per year totaled 331.9 million, or 1.2 uses of electronic resources per capita.
- Internet terminals available for public use in public libraries nationwide numbered 157,000, or 2.8 per 5,000 population. The average number of Internet terminals available for public use per stationary outlet was 9.5.
- Ninety-nine percent of the unduplicated population of legal service areas had access to the Internet through their local public library.

Collections

- Nationwide, public libraries had 802 million print materials in their collections, or 2.9 volumes per capita, in FY 2003. By state, the number of print materials per capita ranged from 1.7 to 5.2.
- Public libraries nationwide had 37.4 million audio materials and 32.6 million video materials in their collections.

Staff

- Public libraries had a total of 136,000 paid full-time-equivalent (FTE) staff in FY 2003, or 12.1 paid FTE staff per 25,000 population. Of the total FTE staff, 22 percent, or 2.7 per 25,000 population, had master's degrees from programs of library and information studies accredited by the American Library Association (ALA-MLS degrees), 11 percent were librarians by title but did not have an ALA-MLS degree, and 67 percent were in other positions.

- Forty-five percent of all public libraries, or 4,182 libraries, had librarians with ALA-MLS degrees.

Operating Revenue and Expenditures

Operating Revenue

- In FY 2003, 80 percent of public libraries' total operating revenue of about $8.7 billion came from local sources; 11 percent from state sources; 1 percent from federal sources; and 9 percent from other sources, such as monetary gifts and donations, interest, library fines, fees, or grants.
- Nationwide, the average total per capita14 operating revenue for public libraries was $31.18. Of that, $24.93 was from local sources, $3.39 from state sources, $0.17 from federal sources, and $2.68 from other sources.
- Per capita operating revenue from local sources was under $3.00 for 8 percent of public libraries, $3.00 to $14.99 for 33 percent of libraries, $15.00 to $29.99 for 33 percent of libraries, and $30.00 or more for 26 percent of libraries.

Operating Expenditures

- Total operating expenditures for public libraries were $8.3 billion in FY 2003. Of this, 66 percent was expended for paid staff and 14 percent for the library collection.
- Twenty-nine percent of public libraries had operating expenditures of less than $50,000, 41 percent expended $50,000 to $399,999, and 30 percent expended $400,000 or more.
- Nationwide, the average per capita operating expenditure for public libraries was $29.60. By state, the highest average per capita operating expenditure was $53.94 and the lowest was $13.09.
- Expenditures for library collection materials in electronic format were 1 percent of total operating expenditures for public libraries.

State Library Agencies

The following are highlights from the E.D. Tab publication *State Library Agencies: Fiscal Year 2003,* released in December 2004.

Governance

- Nearly all state library agencies (49 agencies) are located in the executive branch of government. Two state library agencies are located in the legislative branch.
- Sixteen state library agencies are independent agencies within the executive branch. Of the state library agencies located in the executive branch, almost two thirds (33 agencies) are part of a larger agency.

- Of the 33 state library agencies that were part of a larger state agency, 14 were part of the state department of education. Four state library agencies were located in a department of cultural resources, and five were part of a department of state.

Collections and Services

- State library agency collections averaged 531,000 uncataloged government documents. The agencies averaged 457,000 book and serial volumes. The median number of books and serial volumes held was 179,000.
- State library agencies also held audio or visual materials or serial subscriptions. The average number of such materials held was 3,700 audio materials, 3,000 video materials, and 1,300 serial subscriptions.
- State library agencies averaged 37,000 library visits and 61,000 circulation transactions during the fiscal year; the median number of circulation transactions was 9,400. State library agency staff responded to an average of 26,000 reference transactions; the median number of reference transactions was 14,000.

Services to Public Libraries

- All state library agencies provided the following types of services to public libraries: administration of Library Services and Technology Act (LSTA) grants; collection of library statistics; continuing education programs; and library planning, evaluation, and research. Nearly all state library agencies (47 to 50 agencies) provided consulting services, interlibrary loan referral services, library legislation preparation or review, and review of technology plans for the E-rate discount program.
- Services to public libraries provided by 40 to 45 state library agencies were administration of state aid, reference referral services, state standards or guidelines, statewide public relations or library promotion campaigns, and summer reading program support. Three fourths of state library agencies (39) provided literacy program support to public libraries.
- Thirteen state library agencies reported accreditation of public libraries, and 24 reported certification of public librarians.

Services to Academic Libraries

- Over two thirds of state library agencies (35 to 41 agencies) provided the following services to academic libraries: administration of LSTA grants, continuing education, interlibrary loan referral services, or reference referral services. Thirty-two state library agencies provided consulting services, 26 provided union list development, and 23 provided statewide public relations or library promotion campaigns to academic libraries.
- Services to academic libraries provided by four to six state library agencies were administration of state aid, certification of academic librarians, literacy program support, and state standards/guidelines . No state library agency accredited academic libraries.

Services to School Library Media Centers

- Nearly two thirds or more of state library agencies (33 to 41) provided administration of LSTA grants, continuing education, interlibrary loan referral services, or reference referral services to school library media centers (LMCs).
- Twenty-nine state library agencies provided consulting services to school libraries, 24 provided library planning or evaluation research or statewide public relations and library promotions campaigns to LMCs, 21 supported union list development, and 20 provided library legislative preparation or review.
- No state library agency reported accreditation of school library media centers. Three agencies administered state aid to LMCs, four reported certification of library media specialists, six reviewed technology plans for the E-rate discount program, and eight reported retrospective conversion of bibliographic records.

Services to Special Libraries

- Two thirds or more of state library agencies (34 to 43 agencies) served special libraries through administration of LSTA grants, consulting services, continuing education, interlibrary loan referral services, and reference referral services.
- Twenty-six state library agencies provided union list development; 25 agencies supported special library planning, evaluation, and research; and 20 offered statewide public relations or library program campaigns.
- Six state library agencies administered state aid to special libraries, maintained state standards/guidelines, or reviewed technology plans for the E-rate discount program. Five state library agencies supported special library summer reading programs, and four reported certification of librarians of special libraries. No state library agency accredited special libraries.

Services to Systems

- Two thirds of state library agencies (34 agencies) administered LSTA grants to library systems.
- At least half of state library agencies (26 to 31 agencies) provided the following services to library systems: administration of state aid, collection of library statistics, consulting services, continuing education, interlibrary loan referral, library legislation preparation or review, library planning, evaluation and research, and review of technology plans for the E-rate discount program.
- Six state library agencies reported library system accreditation and seven reported certification of librarians of library systems.

Service Outlets and Staff

- State library agencies reported a total of 134 service outlets—47 main or central outlets, 71 other outlets (excluding bookmobiles), and 16 bookmobiles. The user groups receiving library services through these outlets, and the number of outlets serving them, included the general public (95 outlets); state government employees (77 outlets); the blind and physically handicapped (56 outlets); residents of state correctional institutions (31 outlets); and residents of other state institutions (27 outlets).

- The total number of budgeted FTE positions in state library agencies was 3,600. Librarians with ALA-MLS degrees were in 1,100 positions, other professionals accounted for 718 FTE positions, and other paid staff were in 1,700 FTE positions.

- Most of the budgeted FTE positions in state library agencies (55 percent) provided library services; 19 percent were in library development; and 13 percent of budgeted FTE positions were in administration or other services.

Revenue

- State library agencies reported a total revenue of $1.1 billion in FY 2003. The states provided $916 million, $154 million came from federal sources, and $33 million came from other sources.

- Among states with populations of 2.6 million to 5 million, 18 percent of state library agencies' revenue came from LSTA. State library agencies in states with fewer than 800,000 residents received 8 percent of their revenue from LSTA. The state library agencies in the remaining population categories received between 12 and 14 percent of their federal funds from LSTA.

- States designated $595 million of state library agency revenue for state aid to libraries. Revenue from state sources for state aid to libraries varied by population categories from $2.44 per capita for states with 10 million or more residents to $0.37 per capita among states with fewer than 800,000 residents.

Expenditures

- State library agencies reported total expenditures of $1.1 billion in FY 2003. Of those expenditures, $301 million were operating expenditures, representing 28 percent of total expenditures, and $764 million were financial assistance to libraries, or 70 percent of total expenditures.

- Among states with $50 million or more in revenue, 84 percent ($3.94 per capita) of state library agency expenditures were for financial assistance to libraries, and 13 percent of expenditures ($0.61 per capita) were for operating expenditures. States with less than $4 million in revenue used 85 percent ($2.86 per capita), of their expenditures for operating costs and 12 percent ($0.40 per capita) of expenditures was for financial assistance to libraries.

- State library agencies reported that $172 million of their operating expenditures was for employee salaries and wages and benefits. State library agencies with the largest total revenue ($50 million or more) had employee costs of $38.7 million. The state library agencies with the smallest total revenue (less than $4 million) had operating expenditures for salaries and benefits of $9.6 million. State library agencies' total staffing costs ranged, by revenue category, from 53 percent to 62 percent of the total operating expenditures for FY 2003.
- Of the financial assistance to libraries provided by state library agencies in 2003, 50 percent ($385 million) was targeted to individual public libraries and 21 percent ($163 million) went to public library systems.

Academic Libraries

The following are highlights taken from the E.D. Tab publication *Academic Libraries: 2000,* released in November 2003.

Services

- In FY 2000, of the 3,923 two-year and four-year degree-granting postsecondary institutions in the United States, 3,527 reported that they had their own academic library. Of these 3,527 libraries, 87 percent responded to the NCES-sponsored Academic Libraries Survey.
- In FY 2000 academic libraries at degree-granting postsecondary institutions in the United States reported a total of about 194 million circulation transactions, including reserves.
- In FY 2000 academic libraries provided a total of about 9.5 million interlibrary loans to other libraries (both academic libraries and other types of libraries) and received about 7.7 million loans.
- Twenty-five libraries reported that they were open 168 hours a week (24 hours a day, 7 days a week). Overall, the largest percentage of academic libraries (44 percent) reported providing 60 to 79 hours of public service per typical week in fall 2000. In addition, 40 percent provided 80 or more public-service hours per typical week. The percentage of institutions providing 80 or more public-service hours ranged from 6 percent in less-than-four-year institutions to 81 percent in doctorate-granting institutions.
- In total, academic libraries reported a gate count of about 16.5 million visitors per typical week in fall 2000 (about 1.6 visits per total FTE enrollment).
- About 1.6 million reference transactions were reported in a typical week in fall 2000 by all academic libraries.
- In FY 2000 academic libraries reported about 432,000 presentations to groups serving about 7.5 million.

Collections

- Together, the nation's 3,527 academic libraries at degree-granting post-secondary institutions reported inventories totaling 913.5 million paper volumes (books, bound serials, and government documents) at the end of FY 2000.

- Of the total paper volumes held at the end of FY 2000, 43 percent (396.8 million) were held by 4 percent (126) of the institutions, which are those categorized under the Carnegie Classification as Research I or Research II institutions. Fifty-five percent of the volumes were at those institutions classified as either Research or Doctoral in the Carnegie Classification.

- The median number of paper volumes held per FTE student was 53.2 volumes. Median volumes held ranged from 18.1 per FTE in less-than-four-year institutions to 116 in doctorate-granting institutions.

- In FY 2000 the median number of paper volumes added to collections per FTE student was 1.5. The median number added ranged from 0.7 per FTE student in less-than-four-year institutions to 2.7 in doctorate-granting institutions.

Staff

- A total of 95,665 FTE staff were working in academic libraries in FY 2000. Of these, 31,016 (32 percent) were librarians or other professional staff; 37,899 (40 percent) were other paid staff; 229 (less than 0.5 percent) were contributed services staff; and 26,521 (28 percent) were student assistants.

- Excluding student assistants, the median number of academic library FTE staff per 1,000 FTE students was 5.6. The median ranged from 3.7 in less-than-four-year institutions to 8.5 in doctorate-granting institutions.

Expenditures

- In FY 2000 total expenditures for the 3,527 libraries at degree-granting postsecondary institutions were $5 billion. The three largest expenditure items for all academic libraries were salaries and wages at $2.5 billion (50 percent); current paper and electronic serial subscriptions at $1.1 billion (23 percent); and paper books and bound serials at $552.1 million (11 percent).

- The 568 libraries at doctorate-granting institutions (16 percent of the total institutions) accounted for $3.3 billion, or 65 percent of the total expenditure dollars at all academic libraries at degree-granting postsecondary institutions.

- In FY 2000 the median amount for total operating expenditures per FTE student was $326.46, and the median for information resource expenditures was $90.91.

Electronic Services

- In FY 2000, 94 percent of degree-granting postsecondary institutions with an academic library had access from within the library to an electronic catalog of the library's holdings, 99 percent had Internet access within the library, 73 percent had library reference service by e-mail within the library, and 72 percent had access to library reference service by e-mail from elsewhere on campus. Ninety-eight percent had instruction by library staff on the use of Internet resources within the library.

- In FY 2000, 58 percent of academic libraries had technology within the library to assist persons with disabilities, and 49 percent had access to this service from elsewhere on campus. Ninety-four percent provided services to distance-education students.

- More than four fifths (82 percent) of academic libraries had computers not dedicated to library functions for patron use inside the library. Less than one fifth (18 percent) had video/desktop conferencing by or for the library within the library, and about one fourth (26 percent) had access from elsewhere on campus. Twenty-one percent had satellite broadcasting by or for the library within the library, and 29 percent had access from elsewhere on campus.

- Nearly one-half (49 percent) of academic libraries provided electronic document delivery to patrons' accounts.

Public Library State Rankings, Preliminary Data for 2003

	Library Visits per Capita*	Reference Transactions per Capita	Circulation Transactions per Capita	Interlibrary Loans per 1,000 Population	Terminals per 5,000 Population**
Alabama	48	34	49	36	17
Alaska	24	51	30	23	5
Arizona	34	22	22	35	43
Arkansas	47	46	45	46	45
California	32	19	36	25	47
Colorado	3	9	7	22	28
Connecticut	2	10	11	13	18
Delaware	36	47	29	5	47
District of Columbia***	38	1	51	51	50
Florida	34	5	37	33	45
Georgia	41	18	42	37	24
Hawaii	27	32	38	50	51
Idaho	7	27	16	26	16
Illinois	13	4	17	8	21
Indiana	4	8	4	32	9
Iowa	16	40	12	20	7
Kansas	8	11	6	10	4
Kentucky	40	48	35	42	41
Louisiana	50	12	48	31	36
Maine	20	34	24	19	6
Maryland	22	7	10	30	38
Massachusetts	15	29	20	4	20
Michigan	31	32	31	7	15
Minnesota	23	24	9	11	25
Mississippi	51	49	50	47	33
Missouri	29	31	18	24	18
Montana	37	49	34	27	26
Nebraska	18	37	14	29	3
Nevada	33	44	33	39	49
New Hampshire	26	39	23	17	9
New Jersey	21	23	28	18	31
New Mexico	43	44	43	40	26
New York	14	6	27	9	32
North Carolina	39	16	39	48	42
North Dakota	27	41	21	16	13
Ohio	1	2	1	6	11
Oklahoma	25	38	32	34	22
Oregon	5	19	2	3	29
Pennsylvania	42	41	40	12	30
Rhode Island	9	26	26	2	14
South Carolina	44	14	41	45	35
South Dakota	6	27	13	15	1
Tennessee	46	34	47	49	44

	Library Visits per Capita*	Reference Transactions per Capita	Circulation Transactions per Capita	Interlibrary Loans per 1,000 Population	Terminals per 5,000 Population**
Texas	49	14	44	41	34
Utah	11	3	3	44	37
Vermont	19	30	25	14	2
Virginia	30	13	15	43	39
Washington	17	16	5	28	23
West Virginia	45	43	46	38	40
Wisconsin	9	25	8	1	12
Wyoming	12	21	19	21	8

	Book and Serial Volumes per Capita	Audio Materials per 1,000 Population	Video Materials per 1,000 Population	Current Serials Subscriptions per 1,000 Population	Paid FTE Staff per 25,000 Population
Alabama	41	42	43	51	41
Alaska	21	24	6	9	27
Arizona	50	39	38	44	39
Arkansas	39	51	49	48	48
California	38	43	39	39	46
Colorado	31	22	8	28	17
Connecticut	12	12	4	16	5
Delaware	43	37	31	26	51
District of Columbia***	8	30	51	18	4
Florida	46	33	30	40	35
Georgia	49	49	47	50	44
Hawaii	34	6	45	41	31
Idaho	23	28	26	33	24
Illinois	17	14	9	3	7
Indiana	11	3	2	10	2
Iowa	15	13	11	2	18
Kansas	6	10	3	12	6
Kentucky	42	40	41	43	33
Louisiana	35	48	35	27	25
Maine	1	27	17	15	11
Maryland	27	18	29	29	14
Massachusetts	4	21	15	4	12
Michigan	22	20	27	25	28
Minnesota	24	19	22	20	26
Mississippi	44	50	44	47	32
Missouri	19	23	25	19	20
Montana	25	36	35	30	43
Nebraska	9	11	13	7	13
Nevada	51	34	28	35	41
New Hampshire	7	17	12	6	16
New Jersey	18	25	23	22	9
New Mexico	36	41	50	38	40
New York	14	2	19	14	8
North Carolina	46	47	48	44	47

	Book and Serial Volumes per Capita	Audio Materials per 1,000 Population	Video Materials per 1,000 Population	Current Serials Subscriptions per 1,000 Population	Paid FTE Staff per 25,000 Population
North Dakota	13	29	24	17	37
Ohio	10	1	1	8	1
Oklahoma	37	35	33	34	34
Oregon	28	7	16	24	23
Pennsylvania	30	8	32	32	36
Rhode Island	16	32	18	23	10
South Carolina	40	44	40	37	38
South Dakota	2	26	7	11	15
Tennessee	48	46	46	49	50
Texas	45	45	42	46	49
Utah	31	5	20	31	30
Vermont	5	16	14	1	22
Virginia	33	31	37	36	29
Washington	26	15	21	21	21
West Virginia	28	38	34	42	45
Wisconsin	20	9	5	5	19
Wyoming	3	4	10	13	3

	Paid FTE Librarians per 25,000 Population	ALA-MLIS Librarians per 25,000 Population	Other Paid FTE Staff per 25,000 Population	Total Operating Income per Capita	State Income per Capita
Alabama	32	42	46	47	26
Alaska	25	20	23	12	23
Arizona	43	27	29	35	43
Arkansas	46	51	40	48	34
California	47	24	38	27	18
Colorado	28	15	13	6	46
Connecticut	6	2	6	5	34
Delaware	44	43	47	38	8
District of Columbia***	7	1	4	2	50
Florida	41	22	31	30	15
Georgia	50	28	33	41	7
Hawaii	38	10	27	39	2
Idaho	34	43	14	33	31
Illinois	11	9	5	3	10
Indiana	12	8	2	11	9
Iowa	3	30	37	29	29
Kansas	8	23	8	13	30
Kentucky	20	45	41	37	23
Louisiana	23	31	23	26	21
Maine	10	16	22	31	42
Maryland	15	17	16	14	5
Massachusetts	9	6	25	16	12
Michigan	24	11	26	17	20
Minnesota	30	21	18	20	19

	Paid FTE Librarians per 25,000 Population	ALA-MLIS Librarians per 25,000 Population	Other Paid FTE Staff per 25,000 Population	Total Operating Income per Capita	State Income per Capita
Mississippi	29	49	32	51	13
Missouri	35	40	12	18	27
Montana	21	50	51	42	33
Nebraska	4	32	28	22	38
Nevada	49	37	30	24	44
New Hampshire	1	13	39	21	48
New Jersey	27	5	7	7	22
New Mexico	33	39	43	44	36
New York	19	4	9	4	11
North Carolina	51	34	35	43	16
North Dakota	22	48	49	45	25
Ohio	14	7	1	1	1
Oklahoma	17	37	48	36	32
Oregon	30	14	15	10	41
Pennsylvania	39	26	36	34	3
Rhode Island	15	3	11	9	4
South Carolina	42	25	34	40	17
South Dakota	13	41	19	23	50
Tennessee	47	47	44	49	45
Texas	45	33	44	46	40
Utah	40	36	21	28	36
Vermont	2	29	41	32	49
Virginia	37	19	17	25	14
Washington	36	11	10	8	39
West Virginia	26	45	50	50	6
Wisconsin	18	18	20	19	27
Wyoming	5	34	3	15	47

	Local Income per Capita	Other Income per Capita	Operating Expenditures per Capita	Collection Expenditures per Capita	Staff Expenditures per Capita	Salary and Wages Expenditures per Capita
Alabama	44	38	46	45	46	45
Alaska	11	23	10	17	14	16
Arizona	28	51	35	32	32	33
Arkansas	43	43	50	47	50	49
California	26	30	30	40	26	29
Colorado	4	15	11	6	12	11
Connecticut	7	5	6	4	4	3
Delaware	38	16	37	28	38	38
District of Columbia***	1	19	2	24	1	1
Florida	29	44	33	29	36	36
Georgia	42	48	41	43	39	39
Hawaii	51	33	38	50	34	24
Idaho	31	22	34	41	31	32
Illinois	2	10	5	3	6	5

	Local Income per Capita	Other Income per Capita	Operating Expenditures per Capita	Collection Expenditures per Capita	Staff Expenditures per Capita	Salary and Wages Expenditures per Capita
Indiana	10	20	4	2	8	9
Iowa	27	21	27	22	28	28
Kansas	12	8	14	12	17	15
Kentucky	33	30	40	39	43	42
Louisiana	22	39	31	37	35	35
Maine	34	7	29	34	29	23
Maryland	23	6	15	8	13	13
Massachusetts	14	17	16	7	15	6
Michigan	13	18	19	25	20	21
Minnesota	18	28	18	25	16	17
Mississippi	49	48	51	51	51	51
Missouri	16	12	21	10	24	25
Montana	37	24	44	46	44	43
Nebraska	20	29	22	9	25	26
Nevada	32	4	25	15	27	31
New Hampshire	17	13	20	19	19	18
New Jersey	5	26	7	13	5	7
New Mexico	39	47	42	38	42	46
New York	6	2	3	11	3	4
North Carolina	41	40	43	42	41	41
North Dakota	47	27	45	36	47	47
Ohio	48	9	1	1	2	2
Oklahoma	30	46	36	33	37	37
Oregon	8	14	9	16	9	14
Pennsylvania	46	11	32	30	33	34
Rhode Island	24	1	12	18	10	10
South Carolina	36	45	39	35	40	40
South Dakota	19	35	26	21	21	22
Tennessee	45	33	48	49	48	48
Texas	40	50	47	43	45	44
Utah	21	36	23	14	23	30
Vermont	35	3	28	31	30	27
Virginia	25	41	24	27	22	20
Washington	3	37	8	5	7	8
West Virginia	50	42	49	48	49	49
Wisconsin	15	25	17	20	18	19
Wyoming	9	32	13	23	11	12

FTE = Full-time equivalent

* Per capita is based on the unduplicated population of legal service areas.

** Average number of public-use terminals per 5,000 population.

***The District of Columbia, while not a state, is included in the state rankings. Special care should be using in comparing its data to state data.

Source: Compiled by Catherine Barr from *Public Libraries in the United States: Fiscal Year 2003*, National Center for Education Statistics (2005).

Library Buildings 2005:
A Storm Rains on Our Parade

Bette-Lee Fox

Managing Editor, *Library Journal*

A year that features 185 completed public library projects should be cause for celebration, and likely those constituencies that now have access to these 91 new buildings and 94 added-to/renovated facilities no doubt have been pleased with the outcome. Yet, underlying all this solid library construction news is a sadness over the devastation suffered by other libraries and their communities following Hurricane Katrina and her sister storms.

Library Journal (*LJ*) has covered the aftermath of the hurricane in news stories in print and on its Web site. Perhaps some of the affected libraries would have appeared in this year's roundup of projects completed between July 1, 2004 and June 30, 2005. But with the chaos of the storm itself and the impact on information delivery, data on those projects did not reach us or no longer seemed a priority to those involved. The usual abundance of Louisiana construction projects has dwindled in this year's coverage to two. Other states that generally have significant building programs also seem to be underrepresented. Perhaps 2005 will go down as not only the year of Katrina but as the anomaly in our statistics as well.

The projects we are featuring include big and bold design. They deserve all the fanfare they can endure. Among the biggest is the Fayetteville Public Library in Arkansas, *LJ*'s 2005 Library of the Year, which includes an 88,000 square foot parking garage in addition to the 88,000 square foot building. Other large buildings include Cherry Hill (New Jersey) Public Library ($21.6 million); Columbus (Georgia) Public Library ($40 million); and Evansville Vanderburgh Public Library Central Library in Indiana ($33.6 million).

The jim-dandiest addition/renovation is the $57.6 million work done to the Akron-Summit County (Ohio) Public Library main branch, which now encompasses 270,000 square feet.

Joint use between public and academic facilities and libraries and other service centers seems to have hit its stride, with several projects combining audiences.

The 31 college and university libraries include the new building at Vermont's Middlebury College, costing $40 million; the Hannon Library addition/ renovation at Southern Oregon University in Ashland, $23.2 million; and the Gottesman Libraries at Columbia's Teachers College in New York, a renovation that came in at $18.8 million.

Despite all the bad weather, total expenditures for this year's projects tallied just over $832.5 million, with local funding, as always, taking up the bulk of it, but with gifts and fund-raising efforts paying off. The library future remains bright—no storm clouds on this horizon.

Adapted from *Library Journal*, December 2005.

Table 1 / New Academic Library Buildings, 2005

Name of Institution	Project Cost	Gross Area (Sq. Ft.)	Sq. Ft. Cost	Construction Cost	Equipment Cost	Book Capacity	Architect
Middlebury College Library, VT	$40,000,000	138,000	$217.39	$30,000,000	$2,115,000	700,000	Gwathmey Siegel
Christopher Center for Library and Information Resources, Valparaiso University, IN	33,000,000	105,000	285.71	30,000,000	3,000,000	600,000	Esherick Homsey Dodge...
Marlene and Nathan Addlestone Library, College of Charleston, SC	33,000,000	144,555	183.32	26,500,000	4,600,000	1,000,000	Enwright Associates
Indiana Univ. Purdue Univ. Columbus	30,000,000	130,000	192.31	25,000,000	4,700,000	75,000	KPF Associates
Wm. T. Boyce Library, Fullerton Community College, CA	23,978,841	67,680	254.89	17,251,003	2,214,500	103,000	TBP Architecture
Indiana University Southeast Library, New Albany	15,500,000	75,000	188	14,100,000	1,100,000	500,000	MSKTD & Associates
Peter H. Armacost Library, Eckerd College, St. Petersburg, FL	13,500,000	49,393	208.13	10,280,000	1,599,000	250,000	Canerday, Belfsky & Arroyo; Ayers Saint...
West St. Petersburg Community Library,* St. Petersburg College, FL	11,400,000	53,439	189	10,100,000	1,300,000	125,000	Canerday, Belfsky & Arroyo; Creative Arts
Prim Library, Sierra Nevada College, Incline Village, NV	10,150,000	32,000	296.88	9,500,000	650,000	100,000	Lake Flato
Boyd Tenney Library and Computer Commons, Yavapai College, Prescott, AZ	9,758,644	59,094	143.23	8,463,992	1,294,652	95,000	DLR Group
St. John the Evangelist Library, Christendom College, Front Royal, VA	8,150,907	40,000	174.46	6,978,214	1,172,693	150,000	O'Brien & Keane
Prescott College Information Commons at the Crossroads Center, AZ	3,900,000	22,000	127.27	2,800,000	410,000	n.a.	Weddle-Gilmore
Leech Lake Tribal College Lib., Cass Lake, MN	3,100,000	7,900	352.03	2,781,000	96,000	n.a.	AmerIndian Architects
Library Depository/Retrieval Facility, University of Nebraska–Lincoln	2,997,000	10,149	255.38	2,591,900	45,000	800,000	Clark Enersen Partners
Roy Row Sr. and Imogene Row Johns Library and Academic Building, Univ. of Arkansas Community College at Batesville	2,500,000	17,400	116.55	2,028,000	288,000	14,800	Fennell Purifoy Hammock
Architecture and Landscape Architecture Lib.,** Penn State University, University Park	1,580,000	7,000	200	1,400,000	180,000	40,000	WTW Architects

*A joint-use project between the college and the community, it includes a café.
**Part of larger Stukeman Family Building School of Architecture and Landscape Architecture.

Table 2 / Academic Library Buildings, Additions and Renovations, 2005

Name of Institution	Status	Project Cost	Gross Area (Sq. Ft.)	Sq. Ft. Cost	Construction Cost	Equipment Cost	Book Capacity	Architect
Hannon Library, Southern Oregon University, Ashland	Total	$23,200,000	125,700	$135.63	$17,049,043	$2,405,803	397,584	SRG Partnership
	New	n.a.	61,700	182.37	11,252,368	n.a.	99,396	
	Renovated	n.a.	64,000	90.57	5,796,675	n.a.	298,188	
James B. Duke Library, Furman University, Greenville, SC	Total	21,642,000	139,441	137.75	19,208,000	2,434,000	800,000	Shepley Bulfinch Richardson...
	New	11,192,300	53,884	183.59	9,892,300	1,300,000	700,000	
	Renovated	10,449,700	85,557	108.88	9,315,700	1,134,000	100,000	
David Bishop Skillman Library, Lafayette College, Easton, PA	Total	20,600,000	107,000	161.68	17,300,000	559,000	859,000	Ann Beha Architects
	New	9,300,000	30,000	255.83	7,675,000	454,000	186,000	
	Renovated	11,300,000	77,000	125	9,625,000	105,000	673,000	
Donnelley and Lee Library, Lake Forest College, IL	Total	18,000,000	72,000	194.44	14,000,000	4,000,000	375,000	Shepley Bulfinch Richardson...
	New	8,500,000	27,000	259.26	7,000,000	1,500,000	230,000	
	Renovated	9,500,000	45,000	155.56	7,000,000	2,500,000	145,000	
Tusculum College Library, Greeneville, TN	Total	7,925,000	42,403	160.37	6,800,000	1,125,000	69,000	Hecht, Burdeshaw, Johnson...; Fisher & Associates
	New	n.a.	29,191	n.a.	n.a.	n.a.	59,000	
	Renovated	n.a.	13,212	n.a.	n.a.	n.a.	10,000	
Technical Resource Center and Library, Eastern Maine Community College, Bangor	Total	4,000,000	38,250	89.87	3,437,714	95,000	25,000	WBRC Architects/Engineers
	New	n.a.	n.a.	n.a.	n.a.	n.a.	n.a.	
	Renovated	n.a.	n.a.	n.a.	n.a.	n.a.	n.a.	
Middle Georgia Technical College Library, Warner Robins	Total	859,000	7,000	104.86	734,000	125,000	20,000	JMA Architecture
	New	n.a.	5,000	n.a.	n.a.	n.a.	n.a.	
	Renovated	n.a.	2,000	n.a.	n.a.	n.a.	n.a.	

n.a. = not available

Table 3 / Academic Library Buildings, Renovations Only, 2005

Name of Institution	Project Cost	Gross Area (Sq. Ft.)	Sq. Ft. Cost	Construction Cost	Equipment Cost	Book Capacity	Architect
Gottesman Libraries, Teachers College, Columbia University, New York	$18,800,000	55,000	$225.45	$12,400,000	$1,600,000	500,000	Shepley Bulfinch Richardson Abbott; FxFowle
Johnston Memorial Library, Virginia State University, Petersburg	12,074,036	103,190	66.87	6,900,000	1,282,972	400,000	Livas Group Architects
Moraine Valley Community College Library/Learning Resources Center, Palos Hills, IL	2,066,785	32,000	34.4	1,100,000	966,785	90,000	Legat Architects
Peabody Library, Vanderbilt University, Nashville	1,500,000	38,477	32.49	1,250,000	250,000	250,000	Johnson Johnson Crabtree
Learning Commons at Tutt Library, Colorado College, Colorado Springs	1,082,000	7,489	93.95	703,593	314,866	457,600*	LKA Partners, Inc.
Blinn College Library, Bryan Campus, TX	862,535	18,234	42.26	770,535	92,000	65,000	SHW Group, Inc.
Spahr Engineering Library, University of Kansas, Lawrence	350,000	14,840	18.19	270,000	80,000	100,000	Gould Evans
Earl K. Oldham Library, Arlington Baptist College, TX	42,500	10,800	3.94	42,500	0	35,000	none

*Counted in documents volumes.

Table 4 / New Public Library Buildings, 2005

Community	Pop. ('000)	Code	Project Cost	Const. Cost	Gross Sq. Ft.	Sq. Ft. Cost	Equip. Cost	Site Cost	Other Costs	Volumes	Federal Funds	State Funds	Local Funds	Gift Funds	Architect
Arizona															
Anthem	100	M	$3,600,010	$2,921,000	23,000	$127.00	$739,010	Owned	$0	77,000	$0	$0	$3,220,010	$440,000	DLR Group
Phoenix	46	B	6,180,664	3,126,485	15,000	208.43	2,297,058	Owned	757,121	76,000	0	0	6,180,664	0	Richard & Bauer
Sun Lakes	15	B	1,373,396	1,206,250	9,650	125.00	0	152,000	15,146	20,000	0	0	499,562	873,834	not reported
Arkansas															
Fayetteville	66	M	23,341,655	18,762,925	88,000	213.22	2,194,334	268,000	2,116,396	300,000	0	0	20,500,000	2,841,655	Meyer, Scherer...
Little Rock	14	B	2,861,078	2,049,679	13,500	151.82	222,220	396,234	192,945	50,000	0	0	2,861,078	0	AMR Architects
Little Rock	20	B	3,738,732	2,828,511	10,700	264.35	247,679	425,714	236,828	40,000	0	0	3,738,732	0	Stocks-Mann
California															
Chatsworth	56	B	5,638,890	3,800,000	12,500	304.00	250,010	1,223,880	365,000	50,000	0	0	5,638,890	0	GA Design
Cuppertino	57	M	21,300,000	15,000,000	54,300	276.24	1,000,000	Owned	5,300,000	400,000	0	0	20,850,000	450,000	SMWM
Julian	12	B	3,606,000	2,570,000	9,540	269.39	120,000	400,000	516,000	42,000	398,000	2,280,000	770,000	158,000	NTD/Stichler
Los Angeles	63	B	8,135,981	6,099,844	26,300	231.93	630,000	Owned	1,406,137	170,935	0	0	8,135,981	0	CWA AIA, Inc.
Los Angeles	46	B	5,758,165	3,870,000	10,500	368.57	224,060	1,337,762	326,343	40,000	0	0	5,758,165	0	Hodgetts & Fung
Millbrae	21	M	14,437,400	10,529,675	49,271	404.99	800,000	Owned	3,107,725	100,000	0	0	14,187,400	250,000	Field Paoli
National City	63	M	17,406,637	12,596,317	49,271	255.65	1,780,439	1,055,881	1,974,000	175,400	0	11,112,814	6,293,823	0	Carrier Johnson
San Jose	49	B	12,154,084	7,948,904	24,000	331.20	412,887	1,118,533	2,673,760	91,000	0	0	12,106,634	47,450	Anderson Brule
Vacaville	87	B	6,500,000	5,300,000	25,000	212.00	450,000	Owned	750,000	100,000	0	0	6,500,000	0	Dean F. Unger
Westwood	48	B	10,681,970	6,760,000	12,500	540.80	261,850	3,010,120	650,000	50,000	0	0	10,681,970	0	Steven Ehrlich
Connecticut															
Salem	4	M	1,722,000	1,336,292	7,000	190.89	206,188	Owned	179,520	26,928	0	500,000	1,100,000	123,000	Noyes Vogt
Florida															
Eatonville	25	B	40,000	0	6,000	0.00	40,000	Leased	0	20,000	0	0	40,000	0	Rhodes & Brito
Largo	73	M	20,787,294	15,990,100	90,300	177.08	2,453,194	Owned	2,344,000	400,000	357,660	500,000	18,029,634	1,900,000	Collman...; Daly
Lauderhill	94	B	1,983,347	1,431,409	10,000	143.14	374,405	Owned	177,533	40,000	0	0	1,983,347	0	Ian Nestor/PGAL
Tampa	38	B	5,466,375	2,320,930	15,000	154.73	624,541	1,470,000	1,050,904	70,000	0	500,000	4,966,375	0	FleischmanGarcia
Valrico	40	B	4,513,000	2,358,000	15,000	157.20	626,654	283,412	1,244,934	70,000	0	500,000	4,013,000	0	FleischmanGarcia
Georgia															
Atlanta	17	B	4,845,175	2,798,300	8,000	349.79	400,000	403,148	1,243,727	40,000	0	0	4,845,175	0	Cheeks/Hornbein
Columbus	276	MS	40,000,000	23,551,287	100,000	235.51	3,457,640	7,500,000	5,491,073	500,000	0	0	40,000,000	0	Robert A.M. Stern
Suwanee	38	B	4,011,000	3,145,000	20,477	153.59	502,000	Owned	364,000	57,000	0	0	4,011,000	0	Lindsay, Pope....

Symbol Code: B=Branch Library; BS=Branch and System Headquarters; M=Main Library; MS=Main and System Headquarters; S=System Headquarters; n.a.=not available

Location	#	Code													Firm
Illinois															
Chicago	37	B	6,219,024	4,090,825	14,500	282.13	140,549	436,306	1,551,344	60,000	0	2,000,000	4,219,024	0	Parkman & Weston
Orland Park	57	M	21,086,372	16,444,893	93,000	176.82	1,713,668	Owned	2,927,811	324,000	0	0	21,086,372	0	Lohan Anderson
Indiana															
Evansville	171	MS	33,652,000	25,125,000	147,000	170.92	3,223,000	1,865,000	3,439,000	541,000	0	0	33,652,000	0	Engberg
Anderson															
Evansville	173	B	4,699,000	3,483,408	20,130	173.05	390,000	127,800	697,792	80,000	0	0	4,698,000	1,000	Veazey Parrott...
Fort Wayne	25	B	2,249,028	1,696,165	10,500	161.54	143,281	197,270	212,312	28,000	0	0	2,249,028	0	Grinsfelder Assocs.
Fort Wayne	60	B	3,122,101	2,603,049	20,000	130.15	261,144	Owned	257,908	77,284	0	0	3,122,101	0	Moake Park Group
Grabill	20	B	1,371,105	918,297	7,500	122.44	146,911	164,821	141,076	33,000	0	0	1,371,105	0	Design Collaborative
West Lafayette	28	M	8,709,959	6,364,680	58,658	108.50	604,400	1,206,800	534,079	162,500	0	0	8,684,959	25,000	K.R. Montgomery
Iowa															
Anamosa	5	M	2,224,732	1,863,954	14,298	130.36	100,000	90,000	170,778	50,000	0	200,000	425,000	1,599,732	OPN
Polk City	2	M	984,395	847,493	6,000	141.25	66,414	22,500	47,988	30,007	0	0	657,823	326,572	FEH Assocs.
Louisiana															
Monroe	10	B	1,938,876	1,450,600	10,000	145.06	204,000	80,000	204,276	35,000	0	0	1,858,876	80,000	Herbert Land
Maryland															
Odenton	152	B	10,695,271	6,449,064	38,000	169.70	1,351,000	1,500,000	1,395,207	110,000	0	0	10,695,271	0	Lukmire Group
Massachusetts															
Boxborough	5	M	3,754,866	2,842,626	12,000	236.89	333,700	Owned	578,540	49,584	0	1,588,634	2,166,232	0	J. Stewart Roberts
Gardner	21	M	7,703,595	6,272,219	32,000	196.01	344,324	275,000	812,052	112,184	0	2,586,043	1,750,000	3,367,552	Burt Hill Kosar...
Palmer	13	M	5,913,893	4,155,620	30,054	138.27	557,123	273,000	928,150	90,000	0	1,768,018	2,847,033	1,298,842	Alfred P. Casella
Michigan															
Grosse Pt. Park	54	B	6,203,850	4,610,797	15,800	291.82	344,681	530,000	718,372	38,000	0	0	6,203,850	0	David Milling
Howard City	7	M	1,442,000	1,150,000	9,200	125.00	100,000	Owned	192,000	33,000	0	0	819,000	623,000	Capital Consultants
Redford Twp.	52	M	9,480,072	6,853,345	65,000	105.43	929,461	500,000	1,197,266	166,000	0	0	8,955,072	525,000	Merritt McPherson...
Missouri															
Kansas City	60	B	1,970,500	1,187,500	35,000	33.93	709,000	Leased	74,000	131,000	0	0	1,970,500	0	BNIM
St. Joseph	69	B	4,472,960	3,369,748	27,800	121.21	306,600	528,254	268,358	150,000	0	0	4,472,960	0	Ellison-Auxier
Montana															
Darby	4	M	877,227	674,600	5,000	134.92	88,400	35,000	79,227	16,500	95,000	10,444	8,000	763,783	L'Heureux Page...
Nevada															
Incline Village	12	M	4,900,000	3,600,000	11,404	315.68	265,000	Owned	1,035,000	50,000	0	0	4,868,200	31,800	Hershenow...: Daly
Sparks	60	M	7,008,079	5,783,015	30,000	192.77	384,532	Owned	840,532	83,000	0	0	6,878,079	130,000	Leo A. Daly

Symbol Code: B=Branch Library; BS=Branch and System Headquarters; M=Main Library; MS=Main and System Headquarters; S=System Headquarters; n.a.=not available

Table 4 / New Public Library Buildings, 2005 *(cont.)*

Community	Pop. ('000)	Code	Project Cost	Const. Cost	Gross Sq. Ft.	Sq. Ft. Cost	Equip. Cost	Site Cost	Other Costs	Volumes	Federal Funds	State Funds	Local Funds	Gift Funds	Architect
New Jersey															
Cherry Hill	70	M	21,600,000	16,500,000	72,500	227.59	1,675,000	1,300,000	2,125,000	200,000	0	2,700,000	18,900,000	0	Beatty, Harvey
Gillette	9	M	3,405,782	2,797,400	16,115	173.59	365,882	Owned	242,500	72,000	0	547,210	2,512,790	452,006	RBA Group
New York															
So. Huntington	37	M	12,657,280	8,460,000	45,000	188.00	1,212,000	Owned	2,985,280	150,000	0	0	12,657,280	0	Beatty, Harvey
North Carolina															
China Grove	45	B	3,390,000	2,325,393	23,505	98.93	650,000	159,402	255,205	70,000	24,843	0	3,014,800	350,357	Ramsey Burgin Smith
Greensboro	70	B	2,861,364	1,766,431	15,000	117.76	484,194	200,000	410,739	45,000	0	0	2,397,261	464,103	Teague Freyaldenhoven
Statesville	113	MS	6,653,030	4,358,170	54,000	80.71	1,332,500	496,250	466,110	240,000	92,000	0	6,361,030	200,000	Craig Gaulden Davis
Ohio															
Akron	25	B	2,276,000	1,626,000	12,000	135.50	200,000	150,000	300,000	68,000	0	0	2,276,000	0	Moody•Nolan
Cedarville	11	B	720,278	509,278	5,003	101.79	211,000	Leased	0	44,000	239,000	0	300,278	181,000	Brentwood Builders
Hudson	22	M	13,615,000	9,543,200	52,360	182.26	1,182,700	1,175,300	1,713,800	142,000	0	0	12,215,000	1,400,000	Meehan Architects
Painesville	47	M	11,741,000	9,446,000	65,935	143.26	1,338,000	Owned	957,000	140,000	0	0	11,591,000	150,000	Meehan Architects
Toledo	9	B	1,821,646	1,354,205	8,010	169.06	101,619	195,000	170,822	54,520	0	0	1,821,646	0	Duket/Porter Assocs.
Oklahoma															
Hugo	15	B	2,251,503	1,721,808	13,500	127.54	178,800	155,109	195,786	38,000	0	0	14,751	2,236,752	J3 Architecture Inc.
Oregon															
Alsea	2	B	749,110	593,010	4,400	134.78	63,100	50,000	3,000	14,000	350,000	90,000	37,300	271,810	Richard P. Turi
Eagle Point	7	B	1,710,085	1,228,602	8,512	144.34	112,025	85,000	284,458	28,200	0	0	1,593,554	116,531	Skelton, Straus…
Gold Hill	5	B	1,201,778	853,366	4,982	171.29	83,403	118,264	146,745	13,440	0	0	1,071,778	130,000	Skelton, Straus…
Prospect	1	B	625,451	483,634	2,400	201.51	58,140	Leased	83,677	4,410	0	0	625,451	0	Skelton, Straus…
Tigard	68	M	13,664,288	8,611,551	48,430	177.81	997,731	2,201,860	1,853,146	250,000	0	0	13,424,288	240,000	SRG Partnership
Pennsylvania															
Philadelphia	38	B	3,523,330	2,859,261	10,812	264.45	353,569	65,200	245,300	55,000	0	0	3,367,950	155,380	Buell Kratzer Powell
Rhode Island															
Exeter	6	M	1,612,590	1,293,138	6,400	202.05	73,760	87,009	158,683	22,000	0	645,825	300,000	691,000	Prout, Robert & Elias

Symbol Code: B=Branch Library; BS=Branch and System Headquarters; M=Main Library; MS=Main and System Headquarters; S=System Headquarters; n.a.=not available

South Carolina														
Easley	110	MS	6,900,000	6,200,000	63,000	109.52	700,000	Owned	n.a.	85,000	0	0	6,900,000	0	McMillan Smith
Greenville	29	B	2,481,074	1,484,102	11,500	129.05	253,337	440,000	303,635	65,000	0	0	1,635,407	845,667	Design Strategies
John's Island	24	B	4,600,500	2,847,000	16,839	169.08	521,000	Owned	1,232,500	50,000	0	0	4,563,000	37,500	McKellar & Assocs.
McCormick	9	M	1,236,516	1,016,908	8,400	121.06	83,153	50,500	85,955	43,300	11,580	894,298	225,000	105,638	James, DuRant...
Taylors	36	B	1,892,293	1,277,099	11,306	112.96	210,845	301,071	103,278	65,000	0	0	1,546,626	345,667	Design Strategies
South Dakota														
Sioux Falls	26	B	2,325,299	1,688,978	14,900	113.35	429,185	Owned	207,136	40,000	0	0	2,325,299	0	FEH; Van de Walle
Tennessee														
Cordova	65	B	6,371,700	4,133,000	30,000	137.77	1,825,700	Owned	413,000	150,000	0	0	6,371,700	0	FORMUS
Knoxville	54	B	2,369,297	1,685,324	12,000	140.44	212,571	298,000	173,402	55,000	0	0	2,289,297	80,000	Lewis Group
Memphis	51	B	6,371,700	4,133,000	30,000	137.77	1,825,700	Owned	413,000	125,000	0	0	6,371,700	0	Fleming Assocs.
Texas														
Allen	65	M	11,856,318	7,378,853	53,060	139.07	1,345,010	2,199,962	932,493	175,000	0	0	11,756,818	99,500	pro•forma
Alvarado	4	M	623,110	573,110	10,000	57.31	38,000	Owned	12,000	30,000	0	0	505,784	117,326	Norman Patten
El Paso	60	B	4,098,860	3,100,000	23,000	134.78	533,860	Owned	465,000	100,000	0	0	4,098,860	0	Perspectiva; Frye...
Houston	48	B	6,555,225	3,392,357	20,550	165.08	1,576,950	1,000,000	585,918	66,000	693,750	0	4,297,917	1,600,000	Bailey Architects
San Antonio	82	B	2,444,999	1,945,500	14,567	133.56	263,400	42,999	193,100	45,000	1,020,000	0	1,424,999	0	Sprinkle Robey
Utah														
Heber City	16	M	5,114,201	3,981,201	21,000	189.58	298,000	535,000	300,000	88,900	50,363	5,466	5,000,000	192,000	VCBO Architecture
Vermont														
Craftsbury	3	M	600,000	493,000	3,100	159.03	30,000	54,000	23,000	12,000	0	30,000	131,000	439,000	Sandra Vitzthum
Virginia														
Chesapeake	20	B	4,016,700	2,000,000	16,981	117.78	340,000	Owned	1,676,700	70,000	0	0	3,991,700	25,000	Design Collaborative
Virginia Beach	30	B	3,115,256	2,060,000	16,000	128.75	400,000	330,000	325,256	75,000	0	0	3,105,256	10,000	Design Collaborative
Washington														
Seattle	32	B	5,752,481	3,276,539	10,800	303.38	346,583	1,350,977	778,382	40,200	0	0	5,732,481	20,000	Carlson Architects
Seattle	35	B	7,248,776	5,323,135	15,000	354.88	472,367	315,309	1,137,965	66,700	0	0	7,223,776	25,000	Buffalo Design
Seattle	4	B	1,042,415	629,188	3,800	165.58	163,200	Leased	250,027	12,000	0	0	773,371	269,044	Miller Hayashi
Seattle	37	B	12,698,257	7,124,289	18,100	393.61	432,933	3,559,984	1,581,051	66,700	0	0	12,473,257	225,000	Bohlin Cywinski...
Wisconsin														
Hatley	3	B	984,036	756,713	7,344	103.03	63,518	100,000	63,805	16,351	325,000	0	525,786	133,250	River House
New Berlin	44	M	9,070,300	7,273,479	55,177	131.82	1,092,828	Owned	703,993	155,000	0	0	9,070,300	0	Plunkett Raysich

Symbol Code: B=Branch Library; BS=Branch and System Headquarters; M=Main Library; MS=Main and System Headquarters; S=System Headquarters; n.a.=not available

Table 5 / Public Library Buildings, Additions and Renovations, 2005

Community	Pop. ('000)	Code	Project Cost	Const. Cost	Gross Sq. Ft.	Sq. Ft. Cost	Equip. Cost	Site Cost	Other Costs	Volumes	Federal Funds	State Funds	Local Funds	Gift Funds	Architect
Alabama															
Robertsdale	83	S	$803,706	$503,706	7,600	$66.28	$60,000	$86,000	$154,000	n.a.	$0	$0	$787,706	$16,000	Gatlin Hudson
Arizona															
Chino Valley	8	M	94,500	80,500	1,000	80.50	5,000	Owned	9,000	4,500	0	8,500	60,000	30,000	Alliance Architecture
California															
Burlingame	5	B	1,233,000	973,000	3,000	324.33	149,000	Owned	111,000	1,225	0	0	155,000	1,078,000	Dahanukar Brandes
Coronado	27	M	9,364,815	7,032,965	40,000	175.82	891,542	Owned	1,440,308	225,000	0	0	8,760,399	604,416	M.W. Steele Group
Loma Linda	20	B	53,087	23,338	6,000	3.88	29,749	Owned	0	50,000	0	0	53,087	0	not reported
Sacramento	50	B	861,472	399,882	12,686	31.52	152,492	Owned	309,098	63,000	0	0	564,645	96,827	Moniz & Rusconi
Stockton	591	MS	1,584,085	1,269,682	20,479	62.00	237,353	Owned	77,050	500,000	200,000	0	1,538,054	46,031	Wenell Mattheis Bowe
Torrance	147	M	1,209,648	505,250	16,000	31.58	577,769	Owned	126,629	140,000	0	524,343	323,104	362,201	Deems Lewis....
Victorville	78	B	106,000	59,000	7,500	7.86	47,000	Leased	0	65,000	76,000	0	0	30,000	not reported
Wrightwood	4	B	125,000	90,303	4,000	22.57	34,697	Leased	0	15,000	0	0	125,000	0	not reported
Colorado															
Cascade	3	B	209,477	153,345	1,900	80.71	35,086	Leased	21,046	9,000	0	0	187,477	22,000	Gifford-Spurck
Colorado Springs	117	B	500,451	359,086	10,000	35.91	91,836	Leased	49,529	65,000	0	0	488,714	11,737	E. Wright Ingraham
Littleton	43	M	714,067	580,975	5,300	109.62	33,532	Owned	99,560	1,500	0	0	409,426	304,641	Brendle APV
Parachute	4	B	356,605	296,420	2,000	148.21	39,604	Leased	20,581	15,810	0	160,260	185,095	11,250	C.F. Brenner, Inc.
Connecticut															
Greenwich	61	M	3,060,546	2,785,803	n.a.	n.a.	0	Owned	274,743	n.a.	0	0	3,060,546	0	Cesar Pelli
Plainville	17	M	5,199,179	3,728,000	30,000	124.27	300,000	361,000	810,179	129,000	0	500,000	4,400,000	300,000	Tuthill & Wells
Florida															
Ft. Lauderdale	56	B	848,629	477,178	14,500	32.91	239,664	Leased	131,787	60,000	0	0	848,629	0	Martin Moul & Wilkin
Margate	70	B	2,692,513	1,978,072	15,800	125.19	353,584	Leased	360,857	50,000	0	0	2,692,513	0	ACAI Assocs.
Georgia															
Nashville	16	B	1,187,030	945,616	12,300	76.88	100,000	Owned	141,414	40,000	0	788,500	398,530	0	J. Glenn Gregory
Illinois															
Chicago	55	B	6,754,660	3,855,980	14,500	265.93	152,539	1,082,747	1,663,394	75,000	0	0	6,754,660	0	Stephen Rankin
Palos Heights	12	M	4,990,711	3,945,712	31,448	125.47	489,087	Owned	555,912	85,000	0	0	4,990,711	0	Engberg Anderson
St. Charles	48	M	14,400	14,400	120	120.00	0	Owned	0	n.a.	0	0	14,400	0	none

Symbol Code: B=Branch Library; BS=Branch and System Headquarters; M=Main Library; MS=Main and System Headquarters; S=System Headquarters; n.a.=not available

Location															
Indiana															
Akron	3	M	1,826,419	1,361,347	11,910	114.30	100,592	138,000	226,480	40,000	490,000	0	1,309,419	27,000	Morrison, Kattman…
Angola	14	M	3,330,032	3,150,086	35,000	90.00	36,983	Owned	142,963	110,000	0	0	3,330,032	0	Morrison, Kattman…
Indianapolis	13	B	16,074	16,074	5,000	3.21	0	Owned	0	n.a.	0	0	16,074	0	none
Indianapolis	62	B	39,880	39,880	12,000	3.32	0	Owned	0	n.a.	0	0	39,880	0	none
Indianapolis	52	B	24,670	24,670	13,500	1.83	0	Owned	0	n.a.	0	0	24,670	0	none
Indianapolis	39	B	53,567	53,567	6,500	8.25	0	Owned	0	n.a.	0	0	53,567	0	none
Indianapolis	45	B	256,305	288,194	18,500	13.85	0	Owned	31,889	n.a.	0	0	288,194	0	Rosk Group
Sullivan	22	B	24,489	24,839	1,080	22.68	0	Owned	350	n.a.	0	0	24,839	0	not reported
Terre Haute	106	M	110,000	175,000	3,600	30.56	0	Leased	0	20,112	0	0	175,000	0	not reported
Thorntown	5	M	1,665,312	1,999,582	14,900	111.77	65,000	Owned	334,270	50,000	0	0	1,999,582	0	Veazey Parrott…
Walton	3	M	1,423,000	1,100,000	10,500	104.76	95,000	Owned	228,000	30,000	0	454,000	944,000	25,000	Prince Alexander
Waynedale	30	B	1,591,424	1,183,443	13,300	88.98	202,727	36,390	168,864	80,412	0	0	1,591,424	0	Kelty Tappy Design
Iowa															
Mt. Pleasant	n.a.	M	6,450,000	5,450,000	70,000	77.85	450,000	Owned	550,000	70,100	0	1,000,000	3,000,000	2,500,000	Howard R. Green Co.
Kentucky															
Lexington	250	B	398,859	156,363	7,000	22.33	203,856	Leased	38,640	14,215	0	0	388,859	10,000	Brandstetter; Vitetta
Paducah	65	M	725,440	569,923	5,000	113.98	105,261	Owned	50,256	n.a.	0	0	700,440	25,000	Kerr Architects Inc.
Louisiana															
Baton Rouge	32	B	3,316,135	2,775,232	19,267	144.04	298,688	Owned	242,215	100,000	0	0	3,316,135	0	Washer-Hill Lipscomb
Maryland															
Cumberland	30	MS	1,350,000	1,100,000	11,500	95.65	130,000	Leased	120,000	n.a.	0	100,000	870,000	380,000	Eads Group
Massachusetts															
Concord	16	M	7,820,000	6,163,700	46,035	133.89	262,497	Owned	1,393,803	244,000	0	0	400,000	7,420,000	J. Stewart Roberts
North Adams	15	M	4,214,500	3,800,000	27,270	139.35	85,000	Owned	329,500	100,000	0	1,890,000	1,500,000	1,000,000	Best Joslin
Provincetown	3	M	4,372,516	3,849,525	15,250	252.43	4,974	Owned	518,017	39,455	0	1,878,456	1,820,000	674,065	Perry Dean Rogers
Michigan															
Howell	42	M	340,055	101,011	3,201	31.56	199,543	Owned	39,501	29,500	0	0	122,682	217,373	Riemenschneider
Midland	76	M	144,465	107,959	1,846	58.48	18,506	Owned	18,000	9,040	0	0	0	144,465	Dow-Howell-Gilmore
Portland	12	M	3,605,335	2,975,780	14,866	200.17	274,563	Owned	354,992	40,830	0	0	3,485,335	120,000	David W. Osler
Temperance	31	B	4,250,000	3,270,000	30,000	109.00	540,000	Owned	440,000	n.a.	0	0	4,230,000	20,000	The Collaborative
Minnesota															
Minneapolis	24	B	4,800,000	3,772,000	14,600	258.36	300,000	Owned	728,000	35,000	0	150,000	4,400,000	250,000	KKE Architects
Mississippi															
Olive Branch	35	B	1,169,967	916,043	19,000	48.21	204,009	Owned	49,915	100,000	0	500,000	669,967	0	O. Marvin Johnson

Symbol Code: B=Branch Library; BS=Branch and System Headquarters; M=Main Library; MS=Main and System Headquarters; S=System Headquarters; n.a.=not available

Table 5 / Public Library Buildings, Additions and Renovations, 2005 *(cont.)*

Community	Pop. ('000)	Code	Project Cost	Const. Cost	Gross Sq. Ft.	Sq. Ft. Cost	Equip. Cost	Site Cost	Other Costs	Volumes	Federal Funds	State Funds	Local Funds	Gift Funds	Architect
Montana															
Colstrip	5	B	313,000	296,000	2,300	128.69	13,000	Owned	4,000	20,000	0	0	300,000	13,000	Stevenson Design
New Hampshire															
Farmington	7	M	201,507	145,042	1,420	102.14	42,687	Owned	13,778	8,500	22,500	0	87,360	91,647	CMK Architects
New Jersey															
Bergenfield	26	M	3,420,756	2,713,445	32,312	83.98	300,000	Owned	407,311	190,000	0	744,864	2,634,592	41,300	Arcari + Iovino
Chester	9	M	2,859,325	2,277,052	15,000	151.80	208,624	Owned	373,649	60,000	0	478,695	2,300,630	80,000	Dennis Kowal
Clark Twp.	15	M	2,197,265	1,942,000	22,881	84.87	148,000	Owned	107,265	75,000	0	0	2,197,265	0	Arcari + Iovino
Closter	9	M	2,500,000	1,900,000	16,000	118.75	160,000	Owned	440,000	80,000	0	500,000	1,700,000	300,000	Arcari + Iovino
Florham Park	9	M	2,552,091	2,122,455	15,533	136.64	290,636	Owned	139,000	56,000	0	486,251	1,315,840	750,000	Faridy Veisz Fraytak
Hillsborough	18	M	4,500,000	3,600,000	20,400	176.47	150,000	400,000	350,000	85,000	0	445,792	4,054,208	0	Goldstein Partners...
Linden	38	M	334,000	290,000	34,000	85.29	0	Owned	44,000	n/a	0	0	334,000	0	Potter Architects
Little Ferry	9	M	1,335,718	1,147,000	7,765	147.71	65,000	Owned	123,718	25,000	129,835	234,000	971,883	0	Arcari + Iovino
Maywood	10	M	1,444,210	1,240,122	14,372	86.29	104,676	Owned	99,412	83,450	0	285,161	170,000	989,049	Arcari + Iovino
Middletown Twp.	70	MS	8,477,950	5,513,861	39,000	141.38	1,225,058	Owned	1,739,031	250,000	248,300	1,170,711	6,408,939	650,000	Beatty Harvey
New Providence	1	M	1,017,748	934,912	3,838	243.59	0	Owned	82,836	84,510	0	237,012	515,000	265,736	Arcari + Iovino
Washington Twp.	9	M	1,152,332	1,035,525	12,337	92.42	12,200	Owned	104,607	40,147	150,858	149,576	851,898	0	Arcari + Iovino
New York															
Brooklyn	63	B	2,056,158	1,482,000	18,500	80.11	383,000	Owned	191,158	90,000	0	0	2,056,158	0	Sen Architects LLP
Corona	44	B	2,860,000	2,225,000	8,370	265.83	225,000	Owned	410,000	58,380	0	0	2,860,000	0	Gruzen Samton
Valley Stream	50	M	818,750	519,500	14,100	36.84	247,750	Owned	51,500	n/a	0	10,000	808,450	300	Wiedersum Assocs.
North Carolina															
Andrews	8	B	127,863	98,660	5,800	17.01	20,703	Owned	8,500	25,104	0	0	37,800	90,063	Dechant Architecture
Wilson	76	M	5,300,000	4,124,578	43,740	94.30	747,156	Owned	428,266	140,000	0	0	5,300,000	0	Ramsay Burgin Smith
Ohio															
Akron	386	MS	57,600,000	46,400,000	270,000	171.85	4,200,000	Owned	7,000,000	800,000	0	0	57,600,000	0	Fleischman; Gwath...
McComb	6	M	131,261	106,525	900	118.36	8,158	Owned	16,578	n/a	0	0	0	131,261	Bruce Wobser
Waterville	13	B	1,330,083	1,074,542	12,194	88.12	169,135	Leased	86,406	107,692	0	0	1,330,083	0	Buehrer Group
Woodsfield	15	M	958,910	758,128	2,737	276.99	86,359	Owned	114,423	4,400	0	0	958,910	0	Domokur, Robinson...

Symbol Code: B=Branch Library; BS=Branch and System Headquarters; M=Main Library; MS=Main and System Headquarters; S=System Headquarters; n.a.=not available

State / City	No.	Symbol	Col1	Col2	Col3	Col4	Col5	Status	Col6	Col7	Col8	Col9	Col10	Col11	Architect
Oklahoma															
Tulsa	27	B	2,087,432	1,610,196	15,500	103.88	348,548	Owned	128,688	60,000	0	0	2,067,432	20,000	Dewberry
Watonga	4	M	141,750	120,000	1,500	80.00	0	Owned	21,750	n/a	0	70,875	70,875	0	not reported
Oregon															
Enterprise	2	M	33,000	28,000	n/a	n/a	0	Owned	5,000	17,000	0	0	6,000	27,000	WC Construction
Pennsylvania															
Philadelphia	26	B	4,173,439	3,537,796	11,000	321.62	375,640	Owned	260,003	65,000	0	0	3,981,141	192,298	Buell Kratzer Powell
Pittsburgh	50	B	806,000	403,000	12,300	32.76	248,000	Leased	155,000	48,000	0	0	806,000	0	Burt, Hill
Pittsburgh	459	M	5,860,000	3,730,000	18,000	207.22	500,000	Owned	1,630,000	21,000	0	0	0	5,860,000	Edge Studio
Pittsburgh	36	B	6,780,000	4,611,000	24,833	185.68	828,000	Leased	1,341,000	111,000	77,800	0	6,617,656	84,544	Arthur Lubetz
Tennessee															
Memphis	25	B	1,000,000	800,000	10,000	80.00	150,000	Owned	50,000	50,000	0	0	1,000,000	0	Self Tucker
Texas															
Austin	20	B	2,883,211	2,119,913	16,000	132.49	287,336	Owned	475,962	40,000	0	0	2,868,211	15,000	Lawrence; Carter
Coppell	39	M	472,965	286,986	28,000	10.25	108,874	Owned	77,105	120,000	0	0	472,965	0	PSA-Dewberry Inc.
Denton	106	M	2,662,428	1,257,222	22,876	54.96	470,000	Owned	935,206	85,345	0	0	2,662,428	0	Booziotis & Co.
Houston	30	B	1,100,635	862,363	9,265	93.08	58,400	Owned	179,872	29,000	865,000	0	235,635	0	English + Assocs.
Houston	28	B	792,182	635,800	4,524	140.54	32,800	Owned	123,582	30,000	255,000	0	537,182	0	English + Assocs.
Houston	11	B	662,337	509,843	4,560	111.81	48,300	Owned	104,194	25,000	260,000	0	402,337	0	English + Assocs.
Houston	26	B	1,181,580	866,193	12,252	70.70	174,607	Owned	140,780	41,000	547,000	0	693,400	0	STOA International
Utah															
Tremonton	7	M	194,646	152,302	3,115	48.89	38,669	Owned	3,675	27,000	0	0	172,791	21,855	Cooper Roberts…
Vermont															
Newport	7	M	648,450	624,396	11,700	53.37	8,054	Owned	16,000	22,000	370,000	50,000	130,000	98,450	MGSArchitects
Virginia															
Altavista	21	B	362,882	332,015	2,640	125.76	8,497	Owned	22,370	7,295	0	0	203,992	158,890	Winthrop, Jenkins
Washington															
Seattle	34	B	3,630,178	2,518,509	12,420	202.78	282,806	Owned	828,863	40,200	0	0	3,560,178	70,000	Cardwell Architects
Seattle	10	B	1,000,237	690,295	6,840	100.92	90,731	Owned	219,211	26,000	0	0	251,600	749,267	Hoshide Williams
Wisconsin															
Gilman	1	M	86,000	82,000	1,000	82.00	1,000	Leased	3,000	5,000	0	0	85,300	700	not reported
Sheboygan	50	M	153,360	83,430	1,800	46.35	59,305	Owned	10,625	n/a	0	0	0	153,360	LJM Architects

Symbol Code: B=Branch Library; BS=Branch and System Headquarters; M=Main Library; MS=Main and System Headquarters; S=System Headquarters; n.a.=not available

Table 6 / Public Library Buildings, Six-Year Cost Summary

	Fiscal 2000	Fiscal 2001	Fiscal 2002	Fiscal 2003	Fiscal 2004	Fiscal 2005
Number of new buildings	114	80	101	103	99	91
Number of ARRs*	127	132	111	92	102	94
Sq. ft. new buildings	1,752,395	1,924,548	2,144,185	2,340,374	3,178,027	2,349,670
Sq. ft. ARRs	2,272,684	2,215,702	2,351,100	1,725,902	2,096,243	1,530,382
New Buildings						
Construction cost	$232,832,870	$275,404,635	$303,284,460	$420,486,065	$655,261,309	$420,241,028
Equipment cost	36,127,111	51,445,962	44,985,041	51,738,413	72,422,017	57,152,920
Site cost	28,655,584	33,375,676	28,523,513	30,095,454	30,873,801	43,892,631
Other cost	39,878,940	39,511,803	48,115,515	69,981,113	157,419,044	75,384,007
Total—Project cost	331,345,167	400,838,076	429,787,571	573,531,535	916,026,171	596,670,586
ARRs—Project cost	301,200,950	285,583,407	358,658,087	263,624,575	326,410,267	235,915,173
New & ARR Project cost	$632,546,117	$686,421,483	$788,445,658	$837,156,110	$1,242,436,438	$832,585,759
Fund Sources						
Federal, new buildings	$7,598,492	$2,687,151	$5,395,598	$9,106,615	$3,765,492	$3,657,196
Federal, ARRs	2,600,334	6,959,013	5,197,596	6,482,225	6,202,088	3,692,293
Federal, total	$10,198,826	$9,646,164	$10,593,194	$15,588,840	$9,967,580	$7,349,489
State, new buildings	$12,456,471	$6,696,211	$13,745,400	$18,465,123	$115,846,277	$28,458,752
State, ARRs	36,982,165	19,396,775	18,874,053	16,090,024	24,889,690	12,816,996
State, total	$49,438,636	$26,092,986	$32,619,453	$34,555,147	$140,735,967	$41,275,748
Local, new buildings	$287,118,370	$356,563,114	$363,288,508	$507,445,956	$703,245,493	$537,391,416
Local, ARRs	220,776,786	211,059,513	312,253,572	207,977,217	237,027,037	193,115,934
Local, total	507,895,156	567,622,627	675,542,080	715,423,173	940,272,530	730,507,350
Gift, new buildings	$26,544,144	$34,923,118	$39,257,565	$39,094,374	$93,284,817	$27,464,751
Gift, ARRs	33,309,803	43,344,138	20,795,667	31,972,475	58,402,733	26,579,726
Gift, total	$59,853,947	$78,267,256	$60,053,232	$71,066,849	$151,687,550	$54,044,477
Total funds used	$627,386,565	$681,629,033	$778,807,959	$836,634,009	$1,242,663,627	$833,177,064

*ARR: Additions, Renovations, and Remodels

Book Trade Research and Statistics

Prices of U.S. and Foreign Published Materials

Janet Belanger Morrow

Editor, ALA ALCTS Library Materials Price Index Group

The Library Materials Price Index Group (LMPI) of the American Library Association's Association for Library Collections and Technical Services' Publications Committee continues to monitor library prices for a range of library materials from sources within North America and from other key publishing centers around the world. During 2004 price increases for library materials were mixed, with five categories underperforming the U.S. Consumer Price Index (CPI).

Periodicals and serials significantly outperformed the CPI, as usual, but, surprisingly, so did college books. In the past, books have not usually been subject to the inflationary activity seen in the serials industry. Preliminary data for 2005 show a slight increase in the CPI, and periodicals are again showing a significant increase from the previous year, but college books have dropped back down to a more normal inflation rate. CPI data are obtained from the Bureau of Labor Statistics Web site at http://www.bls.gov/cpi.

Some indexes have not been updated and are repeated from last year. Several factors have hampered index preparation in recent years. These include mergers and acquisitions in the publishing and distribution world that make it more difficult to determine what is published in a foreign country by "multinational" firms, the conversion of several key countries to the euro, and migrations by vendors to new internal systems. Several compilers are in active discussion with vendors to obtain data to revive their indexes.

	Percent Change				
Index	2001	2002	2003	2004	2005
CPI	1.6	2.4	1.9	3.3	3.4
Periodicals	8.6	7.55	8.2	6.5	7.8
Serial services	5.8	5.1	7.2	7.1	n.a
Hardcover books	15.1	-10.3	0.8	-3.17	n.a.
Academic books	0.4	2.0	1.3	1.9	n.a.
College books	1.9	-0.07	4.8	4.4	1.7
Mass market paperbacks	9.4	1.27	0.3	2.51	n.a
Trade paperbacks	22.9	-18.0	4.9	2.74	n.a.
Newspapers	2.9	3.6	3.5	2.1	-0.9

n.a. = not available

U.S. Published Materials

Tables 1 through 8B indicate average prices and price indexes for library materials published primarily in the United States. These indexes are U.S. Periodicals (Table 1), U.S. Serial Services (Table 2), U.S. Hardcover Books (Table 3), North American Academic Books (Table 4), U.S. College Books (Table 5), U.S. Mass Market Paperback Books (Table 6), U.S. Paperbacks (Excluding Mass Market) (Table 7), and U.S. Daily Newspapers and International Newspapers (Tables 8A and 8B). A table on U.S. Nonprint Media is no longer included.

Periodical and Serial Prices

The LMPI Group and Swets Information Services jointly produce the U.S. Periodical Price Index (USPPI) (Table 1). The subscription prices shown are publishers' list prices, excluding publisher discount or vendor service charges. This report includes 2004, 2005, and 2006 data indexed to the base year of 1984.

Compiled by Brenda Dingley, this table shows that U.S. periodical prices, excluding Russian translations, increased by 7.8 percent from 2005 to 2006. This figure represents a 1.3 percent increase in the overall rate of inflation from the 6.5 percent figure posted from 2004 to 2005. Including the Russian translation category, the single-year increase was only slightly lower, at 7.7 percent for 2006. This figure is 0.7 percent higher than the rate of 7.0 percent for the entire sample in 2005. In 2005 the overall greatest price increases were in the social sciences. The 2006 prices show the overall greatest price increases in the sciences, as has been more usual. Unlike last year, when no subject category showed the double-digit increases seen in previous years, the Home Economics category this year posted an increase of 11.8 percent. Zoology posted the second-highest increase at 9.5 percent, and Sociology and Anthropology posted the third-highest increase at 9.0 percent. Children's Periodicals, as usual, showed the lowest increase, at 0.1 percent.

More extensive reports from the periodical price index were published annually in the April 15 issue of *Library Journal* through 1992, in the May issue of *American Libraries* from 1993 to 2002, and in the October 2003 issue of *Library Resources and Technical Services*. All subsequent reports are available on the ALCTS Web site at http://www.ala.org/ala/alcts/alctspubs/pubsresources/resources.htm. Future editions of the USPPI will also be posted on the ALCTS Web site as they are completed.

The U.S. Serial Services Index (Table 2) has been updated through 2004. Compiler Nancy Chaffin noted that titles continued to experience migration from print to electronic format. As the index is built only of printed products, the e-only titles were dropped from the various subject indexes. As this trend continues, it becomes more difficult to identify new titles that are print subscriptions.

All areas of serial services saw increases in prices for 2004, with the highest a tie between General and Humanities and U.S. Documents (both at 11.3 percent) and the lowest (5.2 percent) in Science and Technology. The average increase was 7.1 percent for all subject categories. More extensive reports on serial ser-

(text continues on page 502)

Table 1 / U.S. Periodicals: Average Prices and Price Indexes, 2004–2006
Index Base: 1984 = 100

Subject Area	1984 Average Price	2004 Average Price	2004 Index	2005 Average Price	2005 Index	2006 Average Price	2006 Index
U.S. Periodicals excluding Russian translations	$54.97	$328.47	597.5	$349.79	636.3	$377.08	686.0
U.S. Periodicals including Russian translations	72.47	420.14	579.8	449.69	620.5	484.18	668.1
Agriculture	24.06	134.15	557.6	141.46	587.9	148.86	618.7
Business and Economics	38.87	196.04	504.4	205.85	529.6	218.33	561.7
Chemistry and physics	228.90	1,765.20	771.2	1,879.56	821.1	2,045.12	893.5
Children's periodicals	12.21	28.23	231.2	28.62	234.4	28.63	234.5
Education	34.01	175.10	514.9	190.32	559.6	203.07	597.1
Engineering	78.70	509.73	647.7	552.02	701.4	592.99	753.5
Fine and applied arts	26.90	68.77	255.6	70.93	263.7	76.24	283.4
General interest periodicals	27.90	52.32	187.5	54.47	195.2	57.53	206.2
History	23.68	85.09	359.3	89.65	378.6	93.92	396.6
Home economics	37.15	159.40	388.4	171.03	416.7	191.25	466.0
Industrial arts	30.40	140.28	461.5	144.97	476.9	148.05	487.0
Journalism and communications	39.25	149.77	381.6	160.88	409.9	168.67	429.7
Labor and industrial relations	29.87	163.80	548.4	168.73	564.9	183.77	615.2
Law	31.31	115.91	370.2	120.95	386.3	126.25	403.2
Library and information sciences	38.85	127.07	327.1	136.99	352.6	145.61	374.8
Literature and language	23.02	76.16	330.8	80.39	349.2	87.54	380.3
Mathematics, botany, geology, general science	106.56	704.12	660.8	729.15	684.3	788.55	740.0
Medicine	125.57	895.72	713.3	962.83	766.8	1,034.83	824.1
Philosophy and religion	21.94	77.16	351.7	81.11	369.7	87.28	397.8
Physical education and recreation	20.54	64.25	312.8	69.77	339.7	72.82	354.5
Political science	32.43	176.12	543.1	189.87	585.5	205.29	633.0
Psychology	69.74	454.84	652.2	496.41	711.8	539.07	773.0
Russian translations	381.86	2,288.20	599.2	2,496.09	653.7	2,677.92	701.3
Sociology and anthropology	43.87	261.86	596.9	284.18	647.8	309.70	706.0
Zoology	78.35	632.61	807.4	680.81	868.9	745.61	951.6
Total number of periodicals							
Excluding Russian translations	3,731	3,729		3,728		3,728	
Including Russian translations	3,942	3,912		3,910		3,910	

Compiled by Brenda Dingley, University of Missouri, Kansas City, based on subscription information supplied by Swets Information Services.

Table 2 / U.S. Serial Services: Average Price and Price Indexes 2002–2004

Index Base: 1984 = 100

Subject Area	1984 Average Price	2002 Average Price	2002 Index	2003 Average Price	2003 Percent Increase	2003 Index	2004 Average Price	2004 Percent Increase	2004 Index
U.S. serial services*	$295.13	$747.16	253.2	$800.74	7.2	271.3	$857.96	7.1	290.7
Business	437.07	849.65	194.4	911.89	7.3	208.6	975.45	7.0	223.2
General and humanities	196.55	569.02	289.5	596.50	4.8	303.5	663.75	11.3	337.7
Law	275.23	839.65	305.1	916.06	9.1	332.8	975.82	6.5	354.5
Science and technology	295.36	975.49	330.3	1,054.03	8.1	356.9	1,108.86	5.2	375.4
Social sciences	283.82	656.54	231.3	698.13	6.3	246.0	768.44	10.1	270.7
U.S. documents	97.37	202.60	208.1	189.05	-6.7	194.2	210.39	11.3	216.1
Total number of services	1,537	1,311		1,310			1,326		

Compiled by Nancy J. Chaffin, Arizona State University (West) from data suppled by the Faxon Company, publishers' list prices, and library acquisitions records.
The definition of a serial service has been taken from *American National Standard for Library and Information Services and Related Publishing Practices—Library Materials—Criteria for Price Indexes* (ANSI Z39.20 - 1983).
*Excludes Wilson Index; excludes Russian translations as of 1988.

Table 3 / U.S. Hardcover Books: Average Prices and Price Indexes, 2003–2005
Index Base: 1997 = 100

Category	1997 Average Price	2003 Final			2004 Final			2005 Preliminary		
		Volumes	Average Price	Index	Volumes	Average Price	Index	Volumes	Average Price	Index
Agriculture	$63.70	615	$55.50	87.1	522	$67.99	106.7	396	$66.59	104.5
Arts	55.99	3,094	50.97	91.0	3,361	57.13	102.0	2,625	60.18	107.5
Biography	54.78	4,849	78.82	143.9	3,167	49.92	91.1	2,070	50.64	92.4
Business	99.34	2,050	99.61	100.3	2,126	100.67	101.3	1,688	102.21	102.9
Education	85.74	2,566	82.58	96.3	1,369	66.85	78.0	804	76.45	89.2
Fiction	24.97	5,728	27.46	110.0	7,506	26.53	106.2	4,789	26.59	106.5
General works	108.87	832	142.96	131.3	834	234.71	215.6	538	185.21	170.1
History	62.81	4,361	73.27	116.7	4,339	57.16	91.0	3,198	67.26	107.1
Home economics	36.79	1,393	29.78	80.9	1,603	34.45	93.6	1,012	39.62	107.7
Juveniles	19.25	15,316	28.11	146.0	13,013	27.85	144.7	9,884	31.62	164.3
Language	71.90	2,766	86.56	120.4	1,247	77.06	107.2	922	100.48	139.7
Law	109.95	1,289	102.92	93.6	1,340	120.37	109.5	1,153	118.32	107.6
Literature	62.07	2,231	73.64	118.6	2,157	66.03	106.4	1,438	80.09	129.0
Medicine	111.88	3,440	93.84	83.9	3,038	96.46	86.2	2,664	103.72	92.7
Music	57.87	985	51.05	88.2	1,020	46.04	79.6	825	40.58	70.1
Philosophy, psychology	59.87	2,871	57.15	95.5	3,113	59.84	99.9	2,067	67.68	113.0
Poetry, drama	46.99	1,198	48.42	103.0	1,457	41.75	88.8	833	58.25	124.0
Religion	54.32	4,043	45.43	83.6	5,772	42.07	77.4	2,805	56.25	103.6
Science	103.54	5,052	110.00	106.2	4,652	117.17	113.2	3,811	116.78	112.8
Sociology, economics	79.32	8,727	75.53	95.2	7,625	76.96	97.0	6,202	84.42	106.4
Sports, recreation	46.97	1,677	42.39	90.2	1,802	42.60	90.7	1,283	48.66	103.6
Technology	133.58	3,541	93.35	69.9	3,373	115.93	86.8	2,354	128.63	96.3
Travel	44.87	779	49.78	110.9	1,024	44.69	99.6	641	48.55	108.2
Totals	$72.67	79,403	$63.33	87.1	75,460	$61.32	84.4	54,002	$68.20	93.8

Compiled by Catherine Barr from data supplied by the R. R. Bowker Company's Books in Print database.
Final data include items listed between January of that year and June of the following year with an imprint date of the specified year.

Table 4 / North American Academic Books: Average Prices and Price Indexes 2002–2004
(Index Base: 1989 = 100)

Subject Area	LC Class	1989		2002		2003		2004			
		No. of Titles	Average Price	No. of Titles	Average Price	No. of Titles	Average Price	No. of Titles	Average Price	% Change 2003–2004	Index
General works	A	333	$134.65	85	$69.17	68	$56.87	209	$136.89	140.7	101.7
Philosophy and religion	B	3,518	29.06	5,091	45.02	5,230	46.12	5,026	48.63	5.4	167.3
Psychology	BF	890	31.97	1,008	44.85	982	50.79	954	46.91	-7.6	146.7
History	C-D-E-F	5,549	31.34	7,771	40.68	7,957	42.04	7,811	43.26	2.9	138.0
Geography	G	396	47.34	772	64.91	741	64.51	699	69.05	7.0	145.9
Anthropology	GN	406	32.81	573	50.87	530	49.25	344	57.32	16.4	174.7
Physical education and recreation	GV	814	20.38	1,028	28.58	1,052	29.37	1,281	36.73	25.1	180.2
Business and economics	H	5,979	41.67	6,047	58.93	6,050	62.30	5,900	70.21	12.7	168.5
Sociology	HM	2,742	29.36	4,030	45.84	4,059	47.76	3,935	49.26	3.1	167.8
Political science	J	1,650	36.76	1,771	50.83	1,803	52.09	1,762	55.56	6.7	151.1
Law	K	1,252	51.10	2,047	71.12	2,029	75.40	2,009	81.90	8.6	160.3
Education	L	1,685	29.61	2,390	42.30	2,643	45.08	2,536	46.45	3.0	156.9
Fine and applied arts	M-N	3,040	40.72	5,274	58.19	4,839	58.61	3,728	48.41	-17.4	118.9
Literature and language	P	10,812	24.99	12,645	35.83	15,695	32.48	15,242	33.33	2.6	133.4

Subject	LC	No.	Price	No.	Price	No.	Price	No.	Price	% Change	Index
Science (general)	Q	433	56.10	400	86.72	372	80.97	343	95.60	18.1	170.4
Mathematics and computer science	QA	2,707	44.68	4,206	66.47	3,894	72.15	3,278	74.59	3.4	166.9
Physics and astronomy	QB	1,219	64.59	1,219	88.94	1,221	90.38	1,077	100.27	10.9	155.2
Chemistry	QD	577	110.61	458	147.20	470	152.78	450	166.26	8.8	150.3
Geology	QE	303	63.49	237	69.20	225	75.74	222	92.33	21.9	145.4
Zoology	QH,L,P,R	1,967	71.28	2,280	81.91	2,029	81.58	1,765	91.56	12.2	128.5
Botany	QK	251	69.02	225	80.54	189	87.20	134	96.08	10.2	139.2
Medicine	R	5,028	58.38	5,682	72.04	7,940	75.06	5,596	69.69	-7.2	119.4
Agriculture	S	897	45.13	1,194	72.28	1,072	63.80	1,057	68.45	7.3	151.7
Engineering and technology	T	4,569	64.94	5,688	88.12	5,650	94.08	4,933	100.09	6.4	154.1
Industrial arts	TT	175	23.89	229	30.02	221	28.69	230	30.13	5.0	126.1
Home economics	TX	535	27.10	665	31.85	631	30.38	652	34.07	12.1	125.7
Military and naval science	U-V	715	33.57	579	56.26	502	62.19	502	47.78	-23.2	142.3
Library and information science	Z	857	44.51	575	60.37	529	79.71	547	101.74	27.6	228.6
Average for all subjects		59,299	$41.69	74,169	$55.90	78,623	$56.62	72,222	$57.71	1.9	138.4

Compiled by Stephen Bosch, University of Arizona, from electronic data provided by Baker and Taylor, Blackwell North America, and Yankee Book Peddler. The data represent all titles (hardcover, trade, and paperback books, as well as annuals) treated for all approval plan customers serviced by the three vendors. Due to the merger between Yankee and Baker and Taylor, Baker and Taylor no longer services approval accounts so the B&T data represent imprints in their database. This table covers titles published or distributed in the United States and Canada during the calendar years listed.

This index does include paperback editions. The overall average price of materials is lower than if the index consisted only of hardbound editions.

(text continued from page 496)

vices pricing are available on the ALCTS Web site at http://www.ala.org/ala/alcts/alctspubs/pubsresources/resources.htm.

Book Prices

Average book prices continue to be mixed in 2004. Hardcover books (Table 3) showed a decrease of 3.17 percent, which is not as dramatic a decrease as in 2002, but still significant after last year's small increase.

The average price of North American Academic Books in 2004 (Table 4) increased by 1.9 percent, a slightly higher increase than was seen in preceding years, which showed 0.4 and 1.3 overall percent increases in pricing. The data used for this index is derived from titles treated by Blackwell North America and Yankee Book Peddler in their approval plans during the calendar years listed and titles treated by Baker and Taylor through all order types during the calendar years listed. The index does include paperback editions as supplied by these vendors, and the recent increases in the number of paperbacks distributed as part of the approval plans has clearly influenced the prices reflected in the index figures. Blackwell's showed an increase in the number of paperbacks during the past several years and they now constitute 33 percent of the titles listed by Blackwell's. In 2003 to 2005 the number of paperbacks treated in the approval plan increased 6 percent and the number of hardbacks decreased 2 percent. Other vendors are showing similar impacts from the growth of paperback publishing. Paperbacks will continue to be a part of this index, as they are included in the approval plan data and represent a viable part of the North American book market. The direct impact on inflation caused by hardback/paperback pricing continues to be unquantifiable, but it is clear that the modest increases in overall price inflation for academic books during the past few years seem to correlate to increases in paperback numbers. This may change as publishers have started to "up" the size of paperbacks as well as the price.

Other factors are also certainly at work contributing to the overall average price seeing a modest increase. Analysis of the data as it is processed shows that the overlap titles that are excluded from the index tend to be more expensive than the unique titles processed by each vendor. This fact will tend to hold down the average price and increases in the index. In all cases the average price of a book for each vendor is 4 percent to 6 percent higher than the aggregate average price. This shows that when the titles are combined in the aggregate index the unique titles each vendor handles tend to be cheaper than the titles that overlap. This makes sense since publications from small publishers tend to be cheaper than those of mainstream publishers and the small publishers will tend to make up more of the unique titles handled by each vendor. The vendors will all carry the full title list from Macmillan or Oxford University Press, but a small regional press may not be supplied by all three vendors. Current trends reported by vendors indicate that increases are going to grow in 2005, and there should also be increases in the titles available.

Price changes vary, as always, among subject areas. This year there were several double-digit increases in subject areas and several areas saw prices decrease. The areas of Science, Technology, and Medicine (STM) are again showing large price increases. Last year few STM areas showed double-digit increases. This year Botany, Physics and Astronomy, Zoology, Geology, and Science (general) all showed double-digit increases. Social Sciences also had several areas with double-digit inflation. These included Home Economics, Business and Economics, Anthropology, Physical Education and Recreation, and Library and Information Science. The humanities were spared large increases as the fine arts area and literature showed either a minimal increase or an actual decrease.

It is good to remember that price indexes become less accurate at describing price changes the smaller the sample becomes. The General Works area showed a 140 percent increase in prices, but to conclude that all books in the area increased 140 percent is not correct. This area has a small sample size of only 209 books and since it also includes the Class A area, the presence of just a few large expensive bibliographic sets or encyclopedias can have a major impact on prices for the category. Last year General Works prices dropped 17 percent after a 36 percent increase the year before. As this area has a relatively small number of titles, but large numbers of expensive encyclopedic sets, prices will always be volatile. It only takes a handful of titles to change these numbers drastically.

Table 5 (U.S. College Books), prepared by Frederick C. Lynden, reappears after a three-year absence, bringing up-to-date the index published earlier based on titles reviewed during 2000 in *Choice* magazine, a publication of ALA's Association of College and Research Libraries. This updated College Book Price Index covers the years 2002 to 2005. The index base has been changed to 1989 to match the index base of the North American Academic Book Price Index.

For 2005 the average price for books (including reference books) was $60.33. This represents a 1.71 percent increase over 2004 when reference books are included. Reference titles had the highest average price, $123.72. The average price for non-reference titles was $54.43 or a 1.84 percent increase over 2004. Data for this index were compiled from 6,524 reviews published in *Choice* during 2005 (because expensive titles—$500 or more—and non-book titles were omitted, the total of titles reported is smaller). Prices in 2002 through 2005 were indexed to the 1989 base year. As in the case of North American Academic Books, the index includes some paperback prices, and as a result the average price of books is less than if only hardcover books were included.

The average prices for Humanities titles decreased slightly from the previous year (-0.5 percent). Prices for Science and Technology titles showed a 7.6 percent increase, whereas Social and Behavioral Sciences titles increased by only 0.55 percent. Excluding Reference titles, the average price for all books grew by only 1.8 percent. The average prices for all books, including Reference, increased by 1.7 percent. Since 1989 there has been an overall 49 percent increase in the average price of college books.

(text continues on page 509)

Table 5 / U.S. College Books: Average Prices and Price Indexes 1989, 2001–2005
(Index base for all years; 1989=100)

Subject	1989 No. of Titles	1989 Avg. Price Per Title	2001 No. of Titles	2001 Avg. Price Per Title	2002 No. of Titles	2002 Avg. Price Per Title	2002 Indexed to 1989	2002 Indexed to 2001	2003 No. of Titles	2003 Avg. Price Per Title	2003 Indexed to 1989	2003 Indexed to 2002	2004 No. of Titles	2004 Avg. Price Per Title	2004 Indexed to 1989	2004 Indexed to 2003	2005 No. of Titles	2005 Avg. Price Per Title	2005 Indexed to 1989	2005 Indexed to 2004
General	19	$40.19	n.a.	n.a.	n.a.	n.a.	n.a.	n.a.	n.a.	n.a.	n.a.	n.a.	n.a.	n.a.	n.a.	n.a.	n.a.	n.a.	n.a.	n.a.
Humanities	21	32.33	41	$48.69	38	$47.57	147.14	97.70	43	$50.24	155.40	105.61	50	$51.18	158.30	101.87	64	$49.04	151.69	95.82
Art and architecture	276	55.56	130	49.73	157	53.42	96.15	107.42	141	52.45	94.40	98.18	160	53.22	95.79	101.47	145	52.26	94.06	98.20
Fine arts	n.a.	n.a.	151	59.09	181	55.26	n.a.	93.52	168	56.90	n.a.	102.97	152	59.81	n.a.	105.11	167	58.85	n.a.	98.39
Architecture	n.a.	n.a.	69	51.51	61	56.09	n.a.	108.89	51	61.16	n.a.	109.04	86	57.14	n.a.	93.43	83	54.62	n.a.	95.59
Photography	24	44.11	30	53.32	24	54.09	122.63	101.44	34	52.00	117.89	96.14	38	45.00	102.02	86.54	31	57.24	129.77	127.20
Communication	42	32.70	63	49.90	81	47.90	146.48	95.99	70	51.67	158.01	107.87	78	53.40	163.30	103.35	99	50.74	155.17	95.02
Language and literature	110	35.17	98	51.23	75	56.02	159.28	109.35	81	55.96	159.11	99.89	98	60.14	171.00	107.47	86	56.85	161.64	94.53
African and Middle Eastern	n.a.	n.a.	30	44.89	28	43.00	n.a.	95.79	25	58.62	n.a.	136.33	16	53.52	n.a.	91.30	19	57.69	n.a.	107.79
Asian and Oceanian	n.a.	n.a.	23	42.26	16	49.74	n.a.	117.70	27	47.49	n.a.	95.48	30	50.54	n.a.	106.42	17	44.17	n.a.	87.40
Classical	75	43.07	20	51.94	22	62.74	145.67	120.79	27	58.43	135.66	93.13	24	61.97	143.88	106.06	31	57.26	132.95	92.40
English and American	547	30.27	530	47.06	498	49.62	163.92	105.44	457	53.42	176.48	107.66	419	52.14	172.25	97.60	418	53.92	178.13	103.41
Germanic	38	32.18	42	46.39	27	52.81	164.11	113.84	31	53.55	166.41	101.40	28	57.01	177.16	106.46	38	63.44	197.14	111.28
Romance	97	30.30	86	46.80	88	50.23	165.78	107.33	70	51.64	170.43	102.81	73	52.18	172.21	101.05	76	60.10	198.35	115.18
Slavic	41	27.92	22	52.00	18	52.21	187.00	100.40	17	48.81	174.82	93.49	14	48.15	172.46	98.65	15	44.85	160.64	93.15
Performing arts	20	29.41	15	44.75	17	51.34	174.57	114.73	18	39.36	133.83	76.67	22	38.81	131.96	98.60	22	35.10	119.35	90.44
Film	82	33.00	90	50.46	110	49.60	150.30	98.30	105	51.96	157.45	104.76	98	52.63	159.48	101.29	109	43.95	133.18	83.51
Music	156	35.34	115	50.67	130	53.95	152.66	106.47	147	53.46	151.27	99.09	166	55.79	157.87	104.36	140	52.15	147.57	93.48
Theater and dance	58	34.18	53	50.94	53	45.54	133.24	89.40	47	48.14	140.84	105.71	60	56.61	165.62	117.59	51	56.42	165.07	99.66
Philosophy	185	37.25	158	45.80	177	44.98	120.75	98.21	189	50.06	134.39	111.29	182	49.91	133.99	99.70	178	49.01	131.57	98.20
Religion	174	33.49	222	37.94	249	40.25	120.19	106.09	260	40.96	122.31	101.76	267	45.33	135.35	110.67	251	46.95	140.19	103.57
Total Humanities	1,946	$36.09	1,988	$48.05	2,050	$49.57	137.35	103.16	2,008	$51.49	142.67	103.87	2,061	$52.64	145.86	102.23	2,040	$52.37	145.11	99.49
Science/Technology	99	$46.90	55	$43.14	57	$41.46	88.40	96.11	59	$43.41	92.56	104.70	57	$39.38	83.97	90.72	51	$46.65	99.47	118.46

History of science, technology	74	40.56	75	47.06	107	40.33	99.43	85.70	109	42.94	105.87	106.47	128	43.11	106.29	100.40	118	45.53	112.25	105.61
Astronautics/astronomy	22	50.56	57	43.96	51	38.31	75.77	87.15	42	34.54	68.31	90.16	60	56.10	110.96	162.42	43	50.93	100.73	90.78
Biology	97	51.01	129	46.98	100	55.85	109.49	118.88	128	61.57	120.70	110.24	152	61.17	119.92	99.35	142	65.61	128.62	107.26
Botany	29	63.91	75	59.21	90	58.47	91.49	98.75	83	53.25	83.32	111.07	54	58.88	92.13	110.57	63	57.47	89.92	97.61
Zoology	53	49.21	71	56.62	65	47.62	96.77	84.10	70	57.54	116.93	120.83	79	66.35	134.83	115.31	97	65.55	133.20	98.79
Chemistry	21	70.76	47	82.99	40	90.75	128.25	109.35	47	101.29	143.15	111.61	65	114.08	161.22	112.63	73	121.84	172.19	106.80
Earth science	34	79.44	59	72.64	50	51.42	64.73	70.79	49	57.92	72.91	112.64	57	66.75	84.03	115.25	52	82.73	104.14	123.94
Engineering	87	66.74	70	77.66	75	80.62	120.80	103.81	69	69.63	104.33	86.37	76	92.90	139.20	133.42	92	108.88	163.14	117.20
Health sciences	94	34.91	138	49.67	169	47.91	137.24	96.46	121	46.23	132.43	96.49	142	46.12	132.11	99.76	136	45.91	131.51	99.54
Information/computer science	70	40.35	35	53.12	51	50.36	124.81	94.80	35	55.16	136.70	109.53	57	62.36	154.55	113.05	65	63.16	156.53	101.28
Mathematics	60	48.53	84	55.91	93	62.59	128.97	111.95	110	54.90	113.13	87.71	95	65.70	135.38	119.67	90	73.39	151.23	111.70
Physics	22	43.94	57	47.71	42	61.51	139.99	128.92	47	52.47	119.41	85.30	49	77.26	175.83	147.25	63	73.85	168.07	95.59
Sports/physical education	18	27.46	47	37.73	73	39.10	142.39	103.63	63	40.00	145.67	102.30	61	43.63	158.89	109.08	65	36.04	131.25	82.60
Total Science/Technology	780	$49.54	999	$54.51	1063	$53.41	107.81	97.98	1,032	$54.24	109.49	101.55	1,132	$61.77	124.69	113.88	1,150	$66.44	134.11	107.56
Social/Behavioral Sciences	92	$37.09	86	$52.42	107	$47.55	128.20	90.71	130	$49.13	132.46	103.32	123	$48.01	129.44	97.72	119	$50.19	135.32	104.54
Anthropology	96	39.94	152	50.52	146	53.77	134.63	106.43	112	55.83	139.78	103.83	109	54.45	136.33	97.53	132	56.13	140.54	103.09
Business, management/labor	145	35.72	140	44.37	139	43.52	121.84	98.08	146	44.34	124.13	101.88	129	44.69	125.11	100.79	144	51.75	144.88	115.80
Economics	332	40.75	256	50.00	267	50.36	123.58	100.72	267	54.18	132.96	107.59	249	52.38	128.54	96.68	228	56.85	139.51	108.53
Education	71	34.50	162	47.61	171	48.16	139.59	101.16	164	47.54	137.80	98.71	153	45.27	131.22	95.23	175	49.02	142.09	108.28
History, geography/area studies	59	42.10	88	44.85	122	48.91	116.18	109.05	97	49.10	116.63	100.39	118	53.04	125.99	108.02	108	46.11	109.52	86.93
Africa	44	34.85	23	56.62	28	54.24	155.64	95.80	47	58.61	168.18	108.06	31	61.57	176.67	105.05	33	50.74	145.60	82.41
Ancient history	n.a.	n.a.	26	48.23	47	51.64	n.a.	107.07	47	63.44	n.a.	122.85	48	65.49	n.a.	103.23	45	60.48	n.a.	92.35
Asia and Oceania	76	34.75	80	49.27	93	51.68	148.72	104.89	88	49.22	141.64	95.24	97	53.90	155.11	109.51	74	56.91	163.77	105.58
Central and Eastern Europe	n.a.	n.a.	61	46.41	184	22.34	n.a.	48.14	59	50.88	n.a.	227.75	62	53.84	n.a.	105.82	57	51.89	n.a.	96.38
Latin America and Caribbean	42	37.23	49	47.76	57	51.50	138.33	107.83	66	53.83	144.59	104.52	45	51.34	137.90	95.37	69	52.20	140.21	101.68
Middle East and North Africa	30	36.32	39	51.94	54	51.41	141.55	98.98	45	51.23	141.05	99.65	40	52.00	143.17	101.50	45	50.22	138.27	96.58
North America	349	30.56	364	40.33	348	40.61	132.89	100.69	388	42.93	140.48	105.71	413	42.32	138.48	98.58	380	40.79	133.48	96.38
United Kingdom	n.a.	n.a.	104	55.81	84	54.40	n.a.	97.47	84	52.79	n.a.	97.04	99	57.01	n.a.	107.99	82	52.11	n.a.	91.41

Table 5 / U.S. College Books: Average Prices and Price Indexes 1989, 2001–2005 (cont.)
(Index base for all years; 1989=100)

Subject	1989		2001		2002				2003				2004				2005			
	No. of Titles	Avg. Price Per Title	No. of Titles	Avg. Price Per Title	No. of Titles	Avg. Price Per Title	Indexed to 1989	Indexed to 2001	No. of Titles	Avg. Price Per Title	Indexed to 1989	Indexed to 2002	No. of Titles	Avg. Price Per Title	Indexed to 1989	Indexed to 2003	No. of Titles	Avg. Price Per Title	Indexed to 1989	Indexed to 2004
Western Europe	287	42.08	156	48.71	132	52.49	124.74	107.76	147	51.74	122.96	98.57	127	52.74	125.33	101.93	142	58.09	138.05	110.14
Political science	28	33.56	31	48.37	25	48.56	144.70	100.39	29	57.88	172.47	119.19	22	63.77	190.02	110.18	25	52.31	155.87	82.03
Comparative politics	236	37.82	170	51.12	189	52.81	139.64	103.31	206	55.31	146.25	104.73	193	55.86	147.70	100.99	189	57.10	150.98	102.22
International relations	207	35.74	160	50.78	169	49.11	137.41	96.71	179	52.89	147.99	107.70	182	50.43	141.10	95.35	155	50.08	140.12	99.31
Political theory	59	37.76	55	48.90	70	52.18	138.19	106.71	48	49.65	131.49	95.15	60	55.48	146.93	111.74	70	48.71	129.00	87.80
U.S. politics	212	29.37	146	42.43	171	45.70	155.60	107.71	183	46.25	157.47	101.20	170	46.54	158.46	100.63	178	44.80	152.54	96.26
Psychology	179	36.36	106	49.65	124	50.22	138.12	101.15	137	54.44	149.72	108.40	152	55.37	152.28	101.71	116	54.47	149.81	98.37
Sociology	178	36.36	193	50.61	146	49.87	137.16	98.54	155	48.72	133.99	97.69	167	51.56	141.80	105.83	182	52.76	145.10	102.33
Total Social/Behavioral Sciences	2,722	$36.43	2,647	$47.93	2,873	$47.10	129.29	98.27	2,824	$50.34	138.18	106.88	2,789	$50.66	139.06	100.64	2,748	$50.94	139.83	100.55
Total General, Humanities, Science/Technology, Social Science (excl. Reference)	5,530	$38.16	5,634	$49.14	5,986	$49.07	128.59	99.86	5,864	$51.42	134.75	104.79	5,982	$53.45	140.07	103.95	5,938	$54.43	142.64	101.83
Reference	636	61.02	n.a.	n.a.	n.a.	n.a.	n.a.	n.a.	n.a.	n.a.	n.a.	n.a.	n.a.	n.a.	n.a.	n.a.	n.a.	n.a.	n.a.	n.a.
General	n.a.	n.a.	109	84.57	79	91.90	n.a.	108.67	80	74.96	n.a.	81.57	57	86.37	n.a.	115.22	52	86.72	n.a.	100.41
Humanities	n.a.	n.a.	177	94.47	165	107.13	n.a.	113.40	173	103.95	n.a.	97.03	183	94.42	n.a.	90.83	137	125.31	n.a.	132.72
Science/Technology	n.a.	n.a.	82	103.90	99	116.02	n.a.	111.67	119	121.65	n.a.	104.85	128	112.45	n.a.	92.44	97	127.71	n.a.	113.57
Social/Behavioral	n.a.	n.a.	266	107.83	233	109.67	n.a.	101.71	231	119.21	n.a.	108.70	270	134.70	n.a.	112.99	267	128.65	n.a.	95.51
Total Reference	636	$61.02	634	$99.59	576	$107.59	176.32	108.03	603	$109.44	179.35	101.72	638	$114.36	187.41	104.50	553	$123.72	202.75	108.18
Grand Total (incl. Ref.)	6,166	$40.52	6,268	$54.24	6,562	$54.20	133.76	99.93	6,467	$56.83	140.25	104.85	6,620	$59.32	146.40	104.38	6,491	$60.33	148.89	101.70

Compiled by Frederick C. Lynden.

Table 6 / U.S. Mass Market Paperbacks Average Per-Volume Prices, 2003–2005
Index Base: 1997 = 100

Category	1997 Average Prices	2003 Final Volumes	2003 Final Average Prices	2003 Final Index	2004 Final Volumes	2004 Final Average Prices	2004 Final Index	2005 Preliminary Volumes	2005 Preliminary Average Prices	2005 Preliminary Index
Agriculture	$7.50	1	$7.95	106.0	0	n.a.	n.a.	1	$7.99	106.5
Arts	6.54	4	7.86	120.2	8	$7.50	114.7	7	7.47	114.2
Biography	6.46	44	7.39	114.4	43	7.86	121.7	38	7.49	115.9
Business	6.51	9	8.96	137.6	8	9.59	147.3	5	9.37	143.9
Education	7.32	25	6.86	93.7	16	7.36	100.6	18	8.87	121.2
Fiction	5.40	2,348	6.72	124.4	2,477	6.83	126.5	2,441	7.00	129.6
General works	7.48	13	7.90	105.6	10	8.23	110.0	7	8.04	107.5
History	6.13	38	7.13	116.3	49	7.90	128.9	21	7.20	117.5
Home economics	6.89	25	7.62	110.6	22	7.84	113.8	18	8.06	117.0
Juveniles	4.69	2,054	5.60	119.4	2,086	5.79	123.5	2,122	5.91	126.0
Language	5.92	53	4.01	67.7	49	5.42	91.6	11	7.52	127.0
Law	6.69	3	7.48	111.8	3	8.96	133.9	1	6.99	104.5
Literature	6.72	71	7.58	112.8	49	7.41	110.3	52	7.12	106.0
Medicine	6.53	19	7.54	115.5	27	7.36	112.7	27	7.90	121.0
Music	7.97	7	6.77	84.9	4	7.48	93.9	10	8.49	106.5
Philosophy, psychology	6.52	111	7.69	117.9	107	8.46	129.8	105	8.41	129.0
Poetry, drama	6.41	27	7.30	113.9	23	7.19	112.2	18	7.13	111.2
Religion	6.99	166	8.10	115.9	120	7.98	114.2	143	8.31	118.9
Science	5.17	29	6.04	116.8	12	6.97	134.8	13	8.40	162.5
Sociology, economics	6.76	74	7.67	113.5	71	8.11	120.0	53	8.16	120.7
Sports, recreation	6.43	44	7.34	114.2	36	8.12	126.3	62	8.14	126.6
Technology	6.87	11	6.66	96.9	3	8.64	125.8	10	6.34	92.3
Travel	8.75	1	5.99	68.5	5	8.56	97.8	2	8.95	102.3
Totals	$5.36	5,177	$6.37	118.8	5,228	$6.53	121.8	5,185	$6.68	124.6

Compiled by Catherine Barr from data supplied by the R. R. Bowker Company's Books in Print database.
Final data include items listed between January of that year and June of the following year with an imprint date of the specified year.

Table 7 / U.S. Paperbacks (Excluding Mass Market): Average Prices and Price Indexes, 2003–2005
Index Base: 1997 = 100

Category	1997 Average Price	2003 Final Volumes	2003 Final Average Price	2003 Final Index	2004 Final Volumes	2004 Final Average Price	2004 Final Index	2005 Preliminary Volumes	2005 Preliminary Average Price	2005 Preliminary Index
Agriculture	$28.50	562	$26.73	93.8	578	$28.21	99.0	553	$29.83	104.7
Arts	27.78	3,447	29.48	106.1	3,465	31.68	114.0	3,250	28.46	102.5
Biography	19.83	2,824	21.86	110.2	4,663	23.48	118.4	3,319	23.08	116.4
Business	128.45	3,354	59.21	46.1	3,638	55.05	42.9	3,572	51.98	40.5
Education	27.41	3,640	35.88	130.9	2,941	39.04	142.4	2,936	36.22	132.1
Fiction	16.22	9,547	18.42	113.6	18,054	19.05	117.5	13,641	17.78	109.6
General works	199.57	1,096	48.04	24.1	2,669	176.71	88.6	710	48.14	24.1
History	26.24	6,459	29.03	110.6	6,067	32.31	123.1	4,781	27.89	106.3
Home economics	25.16	1,639	20.78	82.6	2,230	21.02	83.6	2,333	21.40	85.1
Juveniles	19.26	2,855	26.17	135.9	6,531	23.69	123.0	4,085	29.72	154.3
Language	28.98	2,460	34.20	118.0	2,264	34.15	117.8	2,153	32.71	112.9
Law	44.78	1,801	51.21	114.4	1,838	56.60	126.4	1,931	73.81	164.8
Literature	20.98	2,625	26.05	124.2	3,159	26.47	126.2	2,127	28.49	135.8
Medicine	47.25	4,044	41.77	88.4	4,570	40.33	85.4	4,736	43.50	92.1
Music	22.18	1,688	26.14	117.9	1,840	22.82	102.9	1,561	25.16	113.4
Philosophy, psychology	23.72	4,200	24.64	103.9	5,620	24.75	104.3	4,883	26.56	112.0
Poetry, drama	17.00	3,185	19.04	112.0	5,443	18.23	107.2	4,131	18.02	106.0
Religion	20.03	6,203	22.73	113.5	8,143	22.25	111.1	6,276	20.69	103.3
Science	48.57	4,458	40.04	82.4	4,117	43.31	89.2	3,935	48.27	99.4
Sociology, economics	31.23	9,974	39.51	126.5	9,687	37.81	121.1	9,260	35.51	113.7
Sports, recreation	23.56	3,002	22.13	93.9	3,139	22.27	94.5	3,179	25.47	108.1
Technology	69.52	5,721	65.04	93.6	6,000	57.65	82.9	4,871	69.35	99.8
Travel	20.13	2,074	22.76	113.1	2,734	20.84	103.5	2,664	21.08	104.7
Totals	$38.45	86,858	$32.85	85.4	109,390	$33.75	87.8	90,887	$31.97	83.2

Compiled by Catherine Barr from data supplied by the R. R. Bowker Company's Books in Print database.
Final data include items listed between January of that year and June of the following year with an imprint date of the specified year.

(text continued from page 503)

Calculated separately, Reference titles showed an 8.2 percent increase over the previous year. There has been a steady increase in the price of reference books from $107.59 in 2002 to $123.72 in 2005. Since 1989 there has been a 102 percent overall increase in the average price of reference books.

Prices of mass market paperback books (Table 6) rose 2.51 percent between 2003 and 2004, a much steeper increase than the 0.3 percent increase recorded for 2003. On the other hand, trade and other paperback prices (Table 7) rose only 2.74 percent, slightly less than the 4.9 percent increase from 2002 to 2003.

Newspaper Prices

The indexes for U.S. (Table 8A) and international (Table 8B) newspapers compiled by Genevieve Owens and Wilba Swearingen show decreases for the year. For international newspapers, it is the first decrease since 2001, and the U.S. newspapers have not shown a decrease in more than 20 years. This reflects a market that is still struggling with the advent of the World Wide Web and may be reluctant to raise prices due to the perceived competition. The decrease of 3.4 percent for international newspapers is more difficult to explain. Two titles were lost from the index in the past year, which, considering the size of the index list, may have more of an impact on the average than actual market fluctuations. Data are compiled with the assistance of EBSCO Subscription Services.

Table 8A / U.S. Daily Newspapers:
Average Prices and Price Indexes, 1990–2006

Year	Number of Titles	Average Price	Percent Change	Index
1990	165	$189.58	0.0	100.0
1991	166	198.13	4.5	104.5
1992	167	222.68	12.4	117.5
1993	171	229.92	3.3	121.3
1994	171	261.91	13.9	138.2
1995	172	270.22	3.2	142.5
1996	166	300.21	11.1	158.4
1997	165	311.77	3.9	164.5
1998	163	316.60	1.5	167.0
1999	162	318.44	0.6	168.0
2000	162	324.26	1.8	171.0
2001	160	330.78	2.0	174.5
2002	158	340.38	2.9	179.5
2003	156	352.65	3.6	186.0
2004	154	364.97	3.5	192.5
2005	154	372.64	2.1	196.6
2006	154	369.24	-0.9	194.8

Compiled by Genevieve S. Owens, Williamsburg Regional Library, and Wilba Swearingen, Louisiana State University Health Sciences Center Library, New Orleans, from data supplied by EBSCO Information Services. We thank Kathleen Born of EBSCO for her assistance with this project.

Table 8B / International Newspapers:
Average Prices and Price Indexes, 1993–2006
(Index Base: 1993 = 100)

Year	Number of Titles	Average Price	Percent Change	Index
1993	46	$806.91	0.0	100.0
1994	46	842.01	4.3	104.3
1995	49	942.13	11.9	116.3
1996	50	992.78	5.4	123.0
1997	53	1,029.49	3.7	127.6
1998	52	1,046.72	1.7	129.7
1999	50	1,049.13	0.2	130.0
2000	50	1,050.88	0.2	130.2
2001	50	1,038.26	-1.2	128.7
2002	49	1,052.69	+1.4	130.5
2003	46	1,223.31	+16.2	151.6
2004	43	1,301.71	+6.4	161.3
2005	47	1,352.23	+3.9	167.6
2006	45	1,306.79	-3.4	161.9

Compiled by Genevieve S. Owens, Williamsburg Regional Library, and Wilba Swearingen, Louisiana State University Health Sciences Center Library, New Orleans, from data supplied by EBSCO Information Services. We thank Kathleen Born of EBSCO for her assistance with this project.

Prices of Other Media

The U.S. nonprint media index (former Table 9) does not appear this year. Those wishing historical information can find data for 1997 and 1998, indexed to a base of 1980, in the 2001 edition of the *Bowker Annual*. The database, compiled in previous years by Dana Alessi, collects information from titles reviewed in *Booklist, Library Journal, School Library Journal,* and *Video Librarian.*

The CD-ROM price inventory that formerly appeared as Table 10 has also been discontinued. As with U.S. Serial Services, many of the titles that were published in CD-ROM format have migrated to Web editions. Additionally, the changes from single workstation pricing to network pricing or site licenses made it difficult to track prices for this category of material.

Efforts to develop a price index for electronic journals are still under discussion, but many factors have hindered progress in this area, not the least of which are the continued volatility of pricing models, consortial pricing, and institution-specific package deals. The Association of Research Libraries is also considering ways to gather this important economic data for libraries.

Foreign Prices

Exchange rates were closely watched during 2005 and the dollar showed some improvement against the euro, the pound, and the yen for the first time in two years. This should have resulted in improved buying power for materials priced in those currencies, though the overall increase in average book prices may be working against the slight advantage in currency exchange.

Dates	12/31/00	12/31/01	12/31/02	12/31/03	12/31/04	12/31/05
Canada	1.5219*	1.5925*	1.5592*	1.2958*	1.1880**	1.1680**
Euro	1.0666*	1.1322*	0.9414*	0.7913*	0.7530**	0.8470**
U.K.	0.6836*	0.6938*	0.6182*	0.5478*	0.5240**	0.5820**
Japan	112.22	127.59*	121.89*	106.27*	103.11**	117.94**

* Data from the regional Federal Reserve Bank of St. Louis (http://www.stls.frb.org/fred/data/exchange.html).
**Data from Financial Management Services. U.S. Treasury Department (http://fms.treas.gov/intn.html). The change is due to the Federal Reserve Bank of St. Louis no longer reporting euro to U.S. and U.K. to U.S. rates.

The foreign price indexes that follow are British Academic Books (Table 9), and Latin American Periodicals (Tables 10A and 10B). Tables showing prices for German academic books, German academic periodicals, and Dutch English-language periodicals have not been updated and are not included in this volume. Please refer to earlier editions of the *Bowker Annual* for historical information.

British Prices

The price index for British academic books (Table 9) is compiled by Curt Holleman from information supplied by Blackwell's Book Services. The average price in pounds of a British book went from £40.85 in 2004 to £43.37 in 2005, an increase of 6.2 percent. Book production went from 12,825 titles to 14,260, an increase of 11.2 percent. Although the pound fell about 1.3 percent against the dollar, the cost for U.S. libraries of keeping up with British books clearly went up substantially in 2005.

Latin American Prices

Scott Van Jacob compiles the Latin American Periodicals indexes (Tables 10A and 10B, former Tables 14A and 14B) with prices provided by Blackwell's Book Services, the Library of Congress's Rio Office and the University of Texas, Austin.

Due to loss of the vendor providing data, the Latin American Periodicals Price Index will not be updated this year and the 2002–2003 index is shown again. Based on that data, the weighted overall mean for Latin American periodicals including newspapers rose 13.8 percent in 2002–2003, a significant increase from the 3.7 percent of the previous period. When newspapers are not included, the increase was 9.5 percent, again much higher than the 1.6 percent of the previous period. However, increases varied widely by region and especially by country. Currency fluctuations may well account for much of this variation.

The most recent Latin American book price index was published in 1997. A new index based on data provided by Latin American book vendors is expected to replace that index, but is not yet available.

(text continues on page 515)

Table 9 / British Academic Books: Average Prices and Price Indexes, 2003–2005

(Index Base: 1985 = 100; prices listed are pounds sterling)

Subject Area	1985 No. of Titles	1985 Average Price	2003 No. of Titles	2003 Average Price	2003 Index	2004 No. of Titles	2004 Average Price	2004 Index	2005 No. of Titles	2005 Average Price	2005 Index
General works	29	£30.54	32	£42.20	138.2	33	£28.22	92.4	26	£33.59	110.0
Fine arts	329	21.70	490	31.14	143.5	518	32.41	149.4	603	29.94	138.0
Architecture	97	20.68	153	35.74	172.8	143	39.85	192.7	199	36.38	175.9
Music	136	17.01	137	37.59	221.0	142	36.78	216.2	134	38.44	226.0
Performing arts except music	110	13.30	208	33.35	250.8	225	29.98	225.4	290	31.42	236.2
Archaeology	146	18.80	100	44.84	238.5	104	42.88	228.1	129	40.87	217.4
Geography	60	22.74	38	60.51	266.1	46	43.66	192.0	55	50.01	219.9
History	1,123	16.92	1,041	34.30	202.7	1,164	32.87	194.3	1,198	36.02	212.9
Philosophy	127	18.41	306	42.87	232.9	303	40.19	218.3	359	43.54	236.5
Religion	328	10.40	579	38.35	368.8	691	34.23	329.1	601	40.00	384.6
Language	135	19.37	210	48.60	250.9	228	42.87	221.3	292	45.68	235.8
Miscellaneous humanities	59	21.71	33	33.49	154.3	29	31.56	145.4	37	37.92	174.7
Literary texts (excluding fiction)	570	9.31	976	14.68	157.7	1,292	13.64	146.5	1,138	14.68	157.7
Literary criticism	438	14.82	485	39.22	264.6	533	39.76	268.3	619	43.62	294.3
Law	188	24.64	552	55.97	227.2	580	55.19	224.0	674	63.17	256.4
Library science and book trade	78	18.69	62	36.88	197.3	70	47.01	251.5	65	40.65	217.5
Mass communications	38	14.20	113	35.51	250.1	137	39.25	276.4	170	41.68	293.5
Anthropology and ethnology	42	20.71	52	49.68	239.9	58	48.64	234.9	72	50.57	244.2
Sociology	136	15.24	205	47.07	308.9	209	41.35	271.3	276	47.74	313.3
Psychology	107	19.25	131	44.63	231.8	156	42.41	220.3	156	42.56	221.1
Economics	334	20.48	556	56.20	274.4	520	55.54	271.2	603	56.20	274.4
Political science, international relations	314	15.54	724	41.33	266.0	744	42.57	273.9	879	46.23	297.5
Miscellaneous social sciences	20	26.84	31	44.53	165.9	44	55.33	206.1	33	65.90	245.5
Military science	83	17.69	62	38.66	218.5	80	36.35	205.5	58	40.48	228.8
Sports and recreation	44	11.23	79	32.75	291.6	105	41.69	371.2	131	37.23	331.5
Social service	56	12.17	83	32.04	263.3	88	33.52	275.4	99	40.41	332.0
Education	295	12.22	369	39.14	320.3	376	41.76	341.7	429	38.92	318.5
Management and business administration	427	19.55	849	42.67	218.3	781	44.79	229.1	890	47.74	244.2
Miscellaneous applied social sciences	13	9.58	25	55.07	574.8	29	45.79	478.0	28	39.90	416.5
Criminology	45	11.45	128	33.55	293.0	119	35.44	309.5	150	43.17	377.0

Applied interdisciplinary social sciences	254	14.17	528	42.86	302.5	517	45.54	595	47.20	333.1
General science	43	13.73	46	37.55	273.5	37	40.95	59	38.57	280.9
Botany	55	30.54	21	61.71	202.1	25	69.77	38	53.26	174.4
Zoology	85	25.67	40	51.99	202.5	42	53.30	51	59.64	232.3
Human biology	35	28.91	32	52.76	182.5	24	56.43	45	50.65	175.2
Biochemistry	26	33.57	13	57.23	170.5	27	70.82	19	69.10	205.8
Miscellaneous biological sciences	152	26.64	110	52.13	195.7	118	56.36	138	54.08	203.0
Chemistry	109	48.84	72	72.41	148.3	71	78.59	70	69.91	143.1
Earth sciences	87	28.94	76	64.19	221.8	72	61.57	87	63.34	218.9
Astronomy	43	20.36	59	50.33	247.2	54	51.99	74	42.92	210.8
Physics	76	26.58	184	61.89	232.8	179	61.85	185	56.22	211.5
Mathematics	123	20.20	224	50.87	251.8	192	48.75	225	49.39	244.5
Computer sciences	150	20.14	138	39.66	196.9	139	42.51	142	41.49	206.0
Interdisciplinary technical fields	38	26.14	42	50.12	191.7	45	57.20	36	51.61	197.4
Civil engineering	134	28.68	73	72.71	253.5	103	83.35	128	80.38	280.3
Mechanical engineering	27	31.73	38	89.25	281.3	30	83.34	24	54.62	172.1
Electrical and electronic engineering	100	33.12	107	62.41	188.4	106	58.01	126	65.63	198.2
Materials science	54	37.93	42	82.24	216.8	48	89.62	48	90.58	238.8
Chemical engineering	24	40.48	5	77.89	192.4	21	64.21	30	77.60	191.7
Miscellaneous technology	217	36.33	239	52.82	145.4	223	55.15	286	54.89	151.1
Food and domestic science	38	23.75	33	51.08	215.1	38	46.72	90	30.98	130.4
Non-clinical medicine	97	18.19	169	37.11	204.0	183	43.09	181	43.80	240.8
General medicine	73	21.03	63	46.04	218.9	61	46.34	87	50.53	240.2
Internal medicine	163	27.30	178	55.26	202.4	152	56.35	185	60.74	222.5
Psychiatry and mental disorders	71	17.97	199	30.50	169.7	211	33.21	238	34.42	191.5
Surgery	50	29.37	41	63.20	215.2	43	71.39	57	67.95	231.4
Miscellaneous medicine	292	22.08	276	50.24	227.5	254	45.74	318	49.31	223.3
Dentistry	20	19.39	22	40.30	207.8	20	37.61	17	34.86	179.8
Pharmacy*	n.a.	n.a.	16	48.52	n.a.	7	36.42	5	29.79	n.a.
Nursing	71	8.00	82	25.08	313.5	79	24.43	105	29.42	367.8
Agriculture and forestry	78	23.69	68	59.97	253.1	7	56.00	63	48.47	204.6
Animal husbandry and veterinary medicine	34	20.92	35	50.34	240.6	46	54.92	59	43.88	209.8
Natural resources and conservation	58	22.88	60	49.44	216.1	57	52.57	50	60.39	263.9
Total, all books	9,049	£19.07	12,145	£41.62	218.2	12,825	£40.85	14,260	£43.37	227.4

Compiled by Curt Holleman, Southern Methodist University, from data supplied by B. H. Blackwell and the Library and Information Statistics Unit at Loughborough University.
* New category introduced in 2001.

Table 10A / Latin American Periodical Price Index, 2002–2003 Country and Region Index

	Total Titles	Mean w/o newspapers	Index (1992 = 100)	Weighted mean w/o newspapers	Index (1992 = 100)
Country					
Argentina	149	$103.14	107	$85.32	104
Bolivia	5	42.16	69	32.84	29
Brazil	301	41.81	81	37.54	82
Caribbean	29	40.80	96	41.60	98
Chile	33	162.30	85	60.89	82
Colombia	57	84.28	107	109.24	105
Costa Rica	23	42.83	104	51.36	100
Cuba	15	61.93	114	46.46	87
Ecuador	18	73.78	111	79.81	99
El Salvador	8	57.38	106	54.51	85
Guatemala	12	141.67	101	178.88	102
Honduras	n.a.	n.a.	n.a.	n.a.	n.a.
Jamaica	12	43.08	93	68.85	122
Mexico	210	117.05	97	93.75	105
Nicaragua	7	28.58	116	32.37	136
Panama	11	38.77	108	39.46	113
Paraguay	7	19.33	95	30.85	101
Peru	50	131.59	106	117.98	109
Uruguay	22	84.13	98	56.82	94
Venezuela	37	100.49	95	80.59	82
Region					
Caribbean	56	46.23	98	48.13	100
Central America	63	59.93	103	78.85	105
South America	676	76.26	107	77.60	110
Mexico	210	117.05	97	93.75	105
Latin America	1,005	82.52	99	79.53	110

Subscription information provided by Blackwell North America, Library of Congress Rio Office, and the University of Texas. Index based on 1992 LAPPI mean prices. The 2001/2002 subscription prices were included in this year's index if a new subscription price was not available.

Compiled by Scott Van Jacob, University of Notre Dame.

n.a. = fewer than five subscription prices were found

Table 10B / Latin American Periodical Price Index, 2002–2003: Subject Index

Subjects	Mean	Index (1992 = 100)	Weighted mean	Index (1992 = 100)
Social sciences	$87.96	99	$81.33	104
Humanities	46.11	88	51.80	117
Science/technology	66.44	89	94.10	118
General	108.51	79	84.00	80
Law	111.15	101	137.32	153
Newspapers	678.33	144	763.27	197
Totals w/o newspapers	82.52	96	79.53	104
Total with newspapers	117.44	115	98.42	120
Total titles w/o newspapers = 1,005				
Total titles with newspapers = 1,070				

(text continued from page 511)

Using the Price Indexes

Librarians are encouraged to monitor trends in the publishing industry and changes in economic conditions when preparing budget forecasts and projections. The ALA ALCTS Library Materials Price Index Group endeavors to make information on publishing trends readily available by sponsoring the annual compilation and publication of price data contained in Tables 1 to 10. The indexes cover newly published library materials and document prices and rates of percent changes at the national and international level. They are useful benchmarks against which local costs can be compared, but because they reflect retail prices in the aggregate, they are not a substitute for cost data that reflect the collecting patterns of individual libraries, and they are not a substitute for specific cost studies.

Differences between local prices and those found in national indexes arise partially because these indexes exclude discounts, service charges, shipping and handling fees, and other costs that the library might incur. Discrepancies may also relate to a library's subject coverage; mix of titles purchased, including both current and backfiles; and the proportion of the library's budget expended on domestic or foreign materials. These variables can affect the average price paid by an individual library, although the individual library's rate of increase may not differ greatly from the national indexes.

LMPI is interested in pursuing studies that would correlate a particular library's costs with the national prices. The group welcomes interested parties to its meetings at ALA Annual Conference and Midwinter Meeting.

The current LMPI Group consists of compilers Catherine Barr, Ajaye Bloomstone, Stephen Bosch, Nancy Chaffin, Brenda Dingley, Virginia Gilbert, Curt Holleman, Frederick Lynden, Genevieve Owens, Wilba Swearingen, Steven Thompson, and Scott van Jacob, and editor Janet Belanger Morrow.

Book Title Output and Average Prices: 2004 Final and 2005 Preliminary Figures

Andrew Grabois

Research Consultant for R. R. Bowker

For the second year in a row, American book title output increased by double-digit percentages, reaching another record-setting total of 190,078 new titles and editions published in 2004, according to figures compiled by R. R. Bowker. The final total for 2004 showed an increase of 19,017 new titles and editions, or 11.12 percent, over the 171,061 reported in 2003. More than half of the total increase in U.S. title output in 2004 was accounted for by the 59.16 percent growth in new adult fiction titles and editions. The huge increase in output for adult fiction follows an increase of only 1.71 percent in 2003 and three straight years of flat output during the nonfiction boom that followed the terrorist attacks of September 11, 2001. Growth in juvenile title output continued, exceeding the previous year's record total by 7.3 percent. Preliminary figures for total book output for 2005 show that there will be a modest increase at best, so we will have to wait another year to cross the threshold of 200,000 new titles and editions.

Table 1 / American Book Production, 2002–2005

Category	2002 Final	2003 Final	2004 Final	2005 Preliminary
Agriculture	921	1,174	1,099	948
Arts	5,107	6,541	6,826	5,887
Biography	5,306	7,706	7,872	5,426
Business	5,028	5,399	5,765	5,262
Education	4,723	6,213	4,336	3,747
Fiction	17,303	17,599	28,010	20,865
General works	1,644	1,996	3,509	1,255
History	7,929	10,824	10,451	8,003
Home economics	2,183	3,059	3,846	3,360
Juveniles	11,208	20,187	21,661	15,982
Language	13,452	5,284	3,559	3,084
Law	2,715	3,109	3,152	3,091
Literature	4,609	4,948	5,364	3,614
Medicine	6,574	7,483	7,629	7,397
Music	1,920	2,574	2,850	2,381
Philosophy, psychology	6,663	7,187	8,829	7,027
Poetry, drama	3,328	4,391	6,920	4,982
Religion	7,436	10,343	14,009	9,222
Science	7,804	9,512	8,772	7,745
Sociology, economics	15,327	18,701	17,518	15,513
Sports, recreation	4,086	4,718	4,962	4,514
Technology	9,239	9,253	9,376	7,249
Travel	2,615	2,860	3,763	3,305
Totals	147,120	171,061	190,078	149,859

As explained in the 2000 edition of the *Bowker Annual,* the title output and average price figures are now compiled from Bowker's *Books In Print* database, resulting in a more accurate and comprehensive picture of American book publishing.

Output by Format and by Category

Book title output for 2004 showed an extraordinary increase for trade and other paperbacks, a decline for hardcovers, and virtually the same output for mass market. Excluding mass market, paperback output (Table 5) increased by 22,532 (25.94 percent), hardcover output (Table 2) decreased by 3,943 titles (4.96 percent), and mass market paperback output (Table 4) increased by 51 titles (0.99 percent). Hardcovers priced at less than $81 constituted 80.57 percent of all hardcovers, an increase of 3.19 percent over 2003.

The year 2004 was a mixed bag for adult nonfiction categories. The nonfiction categories that experienced the largest year-over-year increases in new titles were religion with an increase of 3,666 titles (35.44 percent), philosophy and psychology with an increase of 1,642 titles (22.85 percent), general works with an increase of 1,513 titles (75.80 percent), and travel with an increase of 903 titles (31.57 percent). Categories with the largest declines were education with 1,877 fewer titles (30.21 percent), language with a decline of 1,725 titles (32.65 per-

Table 2 / Hardcover Average Per-Volume Prices, 2003–2005

Category	2003 Prices	2004 Final			2005 Preliminary		
		Vols.	$ Total	Prices	Vols.	$ Total	Prices
Agriculture	$55.50	522	$35,491.20	$67.99	396	$26,370.85	$66.59
Arts	50.97	3,361	192,019.57	57.13	2,625	157,976.96	60.18
Biography	78.82	3,167	158,110.39	49.92	2,070	104,825.47	50.64
Business	99.61	2,126	214,025.15	100.67	1,688	172,527.37	102.21
Education	82.58	1,369	91,515.94	66.85	804	61,469.36	76.45
Fiction	27.46	7,506	199,169.64	26.53	4,789	127,343.33	26.59
General works	142.96	834	195,749.55	234.71	538	99,642.30	185.21
History	73.27	4,339	248,022.40	57.16	3,198	215,095.45	67.26
Home economics	29.78	1,603	55,215.36	34.45	1,012	40,097.99	39.62
Juveniles	28.11	13,013	362,412.05	27.85	9,884	312,485.20	31.62
Language	86.56	1,247	96,089.23	77.06	922	92,643.06	100.48
Law	102.92	1,340	161,302.48	120.37	1,153	136,420.44	118.32
Literature	73.64	2,157	142,419.84	66.03	1,438	115,175.56	80.09
Medicine	93.84	3,038	293,046.52	96.46	2,664	276,305.09	103.72
Music	51.05	1,020	46,960.59	46.04	825	33,474.96	40.58
Philosophy, psychology	57.15	3,113	186,271.70	59.84	2,067	139,896.62	67.68
Poetry, drama	48.42	1,457	60,825.07	41.75	833	48,519.76	58.25
Religion	45.43	5,772	242,831.64	42.07	2,805	157,781.62	56.25
Science	110.00	4,652	545,092.35	117.17	3,811	445,060.13	116.78
Sociology, economics	75.53	7,625	586,820.00	76.96	6,202	523,553.98	84.42
Sports, recreation	42.39	1,802	76,761.88	42.60	1,283	62,429.71	48.66
Technology	93.35	3,373	391,031.32	115.93	2,354	302,784.57	128.63
Travel	49.78	1,024	45,766.44	44.69	641	31,122.44	48.55
Totals	$63.33	75,460	$4,626,950.31	$61.32	54,002	$3,683,002.22	$68.20

cent), and sociology and economics with a decrease of 1,183 titles (6.33 percent).

Fiction, a traditional measure of the overall health of the publishing industry, experienced a huge increase of 10,411 titles (59.16 percent) between 2003 and 2004, following an increase of just 296 titles (1.71 percent) in 2003. Growth in this category was driven by an 89.12 percent increase in non-mass market paperbacks, and a 31.04 percent increase in hardcovers. Even the output of mass market fiction titles grew in 2004, but by a much more modest 5.49 percent. The preliminary 2005 figures for fiction seem to indicate that only the mass market format will show any growth. The juveniles category (children's and young adult titles), also seen by the publishing industry as a bellwether category, increased by 1,474 titles (7.30 percent) between 2003 and 2004, following the historic increase of 8,979 titles (80.11 percent) between 2002 and 2003. A 15.04 percent decrease in the output of juvenile hardcovers was more than offset by a 128.76 percent increase in non-mass market paperbacks.

Average Book Prices

Average book prices were mixed in 2004, with some subject categories showing price increases and others recording decreases. The overall average price for all hardcover books (Table 2) decreased by $2.01 (3.18 percent) between 2003 and

Table 3 / Hardcover Average Per-Volume Prices, Less Than $81, 2003–2005

Category	2003 Prices	2004 Final Vols.	2004 Final $ Total	2004 Final Prices	2005 Preliminary Vols.	2005 Preliminary $ Total	2005 Preliminary Prices
Agriculture	$34.65	390	$14,610.59	37.46	288	$10,300.92	$35.77
Arts	38.37	2,938	113,163.47	38.52	2,245	92,391.34	41.15
Biography	37.02	2,841	89,898.74	31.64	1,819	58,995.68	32.43
Business	40.17	1,308	50,933.82	38.94	1,018	40,596.14	39.88
Education	40.28	998	38,341.96	38.42	510	20,548.25	40.29
Fiction	25.55	7,468	193,025.77	25.85	4,752	120,666.46	25.39
General works	41.37	450	16,771.10	37.27	298	11,927.28	40.02
History	39.40	3,639	140,460.44	38.60	2,576	107,637.30	41.78
Home economics	26.01	1,521	39,794.08	26.16	925	24,551.43	26.54
Juveniles	19.74	12,728	258,026.95	20.27	9,533	197,409.10	20.71
Language	35.46	803	32,866.71	40.93	509	22,373.52	43.96
Law	48.32	587	27,454.73	46.77	474	22,222.21	46.88
Literature	41.53	1,716	72,331.52	42.15	1,083	46,140.16	42.60
Medicine	41.07	1,756	69,137.51	39.37	1,297	56,959.53	43.92
Music	35.78	887	27,787.74	31.33	742	20,262.76	27.31
Philosophy, psychology	38.46	2,472	87,862.54	35.54	1,529	60,150.83	39.34
Poetry, drama	35.04	1,314	40,808.84	31.06	745	24,606.41	33.03
Religion	30.28	5,194	148,910.59	28.67	2,350	76,840.98	32.70
Science	38.85	2,130	89,916.60	42.21	1,628	68,902.92	42.32
Sociology, economics	43.65	5,574	246,629.37	44.25	3,994	178,465.79	44.68
Sports, recreation	33.35	1,676	55,230.58	32.95	1,177	42,142.56	35.81
Technology	43.84	1,483	69,476.80	46.85	1,015	46,579.56	45.89
Travel	31.13	922	25,758.37	27.94	567	16,982.30	29.95
Totals	$32.67	60,795	$1,949,198.82	$32.06	41,074	$1,367,653.43	$33.30

2004, following an increase of 49 cents (0.78 percent) between 2002 and 2003. Hardcovers priced at less than $81 (Table 3), which constitute 80.57 percent of all hardcovers, decreased by 61 cents (1.87 percent) in 2004, following a decrease of $3.07 (8.59 percent) in 2003.

The overall average price for mass market paperback books (Table 4) recorded an increase of 16 cents (2.57 percent) between 2003 and 2004, following a decrease of 2 cents (0.31 percent) between 2002 and 2003. Paperbacks other than mass market (Table 5) registered an increase of 90 cents (2.74 percent), following an increase of $1.52 (4.85 percent), recorded between 2002 and 2003.

The average book prices for fiction titles, usually considered a bellwether for book prices in the trade, were again mixed in 2004. Hardcover fiction titles decreased 93 cents (3.39 percent), following a much larger decrease of $2.89 (9.52 percent) recorded in 2003. Mass market fiction increased 11 cents (1.64 percent), while trade and other paperbacks increased 63 cents (3.42 percent), following an increase of 32 cents (1.77 percent) recorded in 2003.

Hardcover children's books (juveniles) decreased 26 cents (0.93 percent), reversing the increase of $5.55 (24.6 percent) in 2003. Children's mass market paperbacks increased 19 cents (3.39 percent), reversing the decrease of 13 cents (2.19 percent) reported in 2003, while trade and other paperback children's titles decreased by $2.48 (9.48 percent), reversing the increase of $6.84 (35.39 per-

Table 4 / Mass Market Paperbacks Average Per-Volume Prices, 2003–2005

Category	2003 Prices	2004 Final			2005 Preliminary		
		Vols.	$ Total	Prices	Vols.	$ Total	Prices
Agriculture	$7.95	0	0.00	0.00	1	$7.99	$7.99
Arts	7.86	8	59.96	7.50	7	52.32	7.47
Biography	7.39	43	337.97	7.86	38	284.44	7.49
Business	8.96	8	76.68	9.59	5	46.83	9.37
Education	6.86	16	117.72	7.36	18	159.70	8.87
Fiction	6.72	2,477	16,905.65	6.83	2,441	17,095.30	7.00
General works	7.90	10	82.33	8.23	7	56.28	8.04
History	7.13	49	387.12	7.90	21	151.18	7.20
Home economics	7.62	22	172.58	7.84	18	145.05	8.06
Juveniles	5.60	2,086	12,086.44	5.79	2,122	12,550.74	5.91
Language	4.01	49	265.66	5.42	11	82.73	7.52
Law	7.48	3	26.89	8.96	1	6.99	6.99
Literature	7.58	49	363.22	7.41	52	370.26	7.12
Medicine	7.54	27	198.61	7.36	27	213.37	7.90
Music	6.77	4	29.92	7.48	10	84.86	8.49
Philosophy, psychology	7.69	107	905.41	8.46	105	882.90	8.41
Poetry, drama	7.30	23	165.40	7.19	18	128.38	7.13
Religion	8.10	120	957.31	7.98	143	1,187.72	8.31
Science	6.04	12	83.68	6.97	13	109.15	8.40
Sociology, economics	7.67	71	575.99	8.11	53	432.36	8.16
Sports, recreation	7.34	36	292.25	8.12	62	504.86	8.14
Technology	6.66	3	25.93	8.64	10	63.37	6.34
Travel	5.99	5	42.79	8.56	2	17.90	8.95
Totals	$6.37	5,228	$34,159.51	$6.53	5,185	$34,634.68	$6.68

cent) reported in 2003.

As always, many of the other subject categories recorded mixed average prices in 2004, showing considerable volatility in year-to-year price increases and decreases across formats. Sociology and economics, for example, shows an average price increase of $1.43 (1.89 percent) for hardcover titles, an increase of 44 cents (5.74 percent) for mass market paperback titles, and a decrease of $1.70 (4.30 percent) for trade and other paperback titles. History recorded an average price decrease of $16.11 (21.99 percent) for hardcover titles, an increase of 77 cents (10.80 percent) for mass market paperback titles, and an increase of $3.28 (11.30 percent) for trade and other paperback titles.

Each of the 23 standard subject groups used here represents one or more specific Dewey Decimal Classification numbers, as follows: Agriculture, 630–699, 712–719; Art, 700–711, 720–779; Biography, 920–929; Business, 650–659; Education, 370–379; Fiction; General Works, 000–099; History, 900–909, 930–999; Home Economics, 640–649; Juveniles; Language, 400–499; Law, 340–349; Literature, 800–810, 813–820, 823–899; Medicine, 610–619; Music, 780–789; Philosophy, Psychology, 100–199; Poetry, Drama, 811, 812, 821, 822; Religion, 200–299; Science, 500–599; Sociology, Economics, 300–339, 350–369, 380–389; Sports, Recreation, 790–799; Technology, 600–609, 620–629, 660–699; Travel, 910–919.

Table 5 / Other Paperbacks Average Per-Volume Prices, 2003–2005

Category	2003 Prices	2004 Final			2005 Preliminary		
		Vols.	$ Total	Prices	Vols.	$ Total	Prices
Agriculture	$26.73	578	$16,308.12	28.21	553	$16,496.96	$29.83
Arts	29.48	3,465	109,753.89	31.68	3,250	92,504.88	28.46
Biography	21.86	4,663	109,477.55	23.48	3,319	76,603.71	23.08
Business	59.21	3,638	200,263.68	55.05	3,572	185,672.66	51.98
Education	35.88	2,941	114,813.70	39.04	2,936	106,352.84	36.22
Fiction	18.42	18,054	344,006.98	19.05	13,641	242,566.70	17.78
General works	48.04	2,669	471,629.29	176.71	710	34,178.78	48.14
History	29.03	6,067	196,028.65	32.31	4,781	133,364.89	27.89
Home economics	20.78	2,230	46,879.47	21.02	2,333	49,935.07	21.40
Juveniles	26.17	6,531	154,708.29	23.69	4,085	121,388.11	29.72
Language	34.20	2,264	77,322.42	34.15	2,153	70,433.09	32.71
Law	51.21	1,838	104,030.10	56.60	1,931	142,519.34	73.81
Literature	26.05	3,159	83,627.05	26.47	2,127	60,592.05	28.49
Medicine	41.77	4,570	184,319.05	40.33	4,736	206,037.39	43.50
Music	26.14	1,840	41,984.18	22.82	1,561	39,277.14	25.16
Philosophy, psychology	24.64	5,620	139,072.00	24.75	4,883	129,700.91	26.56
Poetry, drama	19.04	5,443	99,249.23	18.23	4,131	74,460.77	18.02
Religion	22.73	8,143	181,141.62	22.25	6,276	129,834.84	20.69
Science	40.04	4,117	178,314.18	43.31	3,935	189,941.24	48.27
Sociology, economics	39.51	9,687	366,312.91	37.81	9,260	328,792.91	35.51
Sports, recreation	22.13	3,139	69,897.08	22.27	3,179	80,976.59	25.47
Technology	65.04	6,000	345,907.53	57.65	4,871	337,813.27	69.35
Travel	22.76	2,734	56,987.70	20.84	2,664	56,151.29	21.08
Totals	$32.85	109,390	$3,692,034.67	$33.75	90,887	$2,905,595.43	$31.97

Book Sales Statistics, 2005: AAP Preliminary Estimates

Association of American Publishers

Net sales for the United States publishing industry are estimated to have increased by 9.9 percent from 2004 to 2005 to a grand total of $25.1 billion, according to figures released by the Association of American Publishers (AAP).

Trade sales rose at a compound annual growth rate of 9.1 percent from 2002 to 2005, with sales of $7.83 billion in 2005. The largest increase in the trade category over that four-year period came from juvenile hardbound books, which rose at a compound growth rate of 19.6 percent.

El-hi (elementary and high school) sales—now inclusive of standardized tests—were up by 4.3 percent annually compounded from 2002 to 2005, reaching $6.6 billion in 2005, while higher education sales rose 3.6 percent annually compounded over the same period, with sales of $3.4 billion in 2005. Sales of professional and scholarly books were up 1.5 percent compounded annually from 2002 to 2005 with total sales of $3.3 billion in 2005.

Book clubs and mail order publications (down 8.2 percent annually compounded 2002–2005, with sales of $1.50 billion) and mass market paperback publications (down 3.5 percent compounded 2002–2005, with sales of $1.08 billion) lost ground in 2005. Sales of religious books, a category that includes many self-help texts, grew 14.2 percent compounded annually from 2002 to 2005, totaling $876 million in 2005.

Table 1 gives complete details. Please note that the table is not directly comparable with those in editions of the *Bowker Annual* previous to 2004 because of a change in the way in which the statistics are analyzed and reported; AAP decided two years ago that the size of the market had been overstated since 1997. The updated statistics also reflect changes in some reporting segments. The book club and mail order segments have been combined, the subscription reference category eliminated, and the "all other" segment significantly expanded.

The sales figures in this report are based on year-to-date data in the AAP 2005 December Monthly Sales Report, the U.S. Department of Commerce's Census Bureau Report, and other statistical data. The report and accompanying table were prepared for AAP by Management Practice, Inc.

For more information, contact Tina Jordan, AAP New York (212-255-0200 ext. 263, e-mail tjordan@publishers.org).

Table 1 / Estimated Book Publishing Industry Sales, 2002, 2003–2005
(figures in thousands of dollars)

| | 2002 Census | 2003 | | 2004 | | 2005 | | Compound Growth Rate 2002–2005 |
			% Change		% Change		% Change	
Trade (total)	$6,027,658	$6,534,828	8.4	$6,267,199	-4.1	$7,828,050	24.9	9.1
Adult hardbound	2,111,628	2,060,949	-2.4	2,190,788	6.3	2,221,700	1.4	1.7
Adult paperbound	1,020,015	1,013,895	-0.6	1,042,284	2.8	1,140,989	9.5	3.8
Juvenile hardbound	2,114,091	2,718,721	28.6	2,264,695	-16.7	3,614,748	59.6	19.6
Juvenile paperbound	781,924	741,264	-5.2	769,432	3.8	850,613	10.6	2.8
Book clubs and mail order	1,946,640	1,771,443	-9.0	1,613,784	-8.9	1,505,661	-6.7	-8.2
Mass market paperback	1,207,630	1,187,100	-1.7	1,081,448	-8.9	1,083,611	0.2	-3.5
Audiobooks	143,410	161,049	12.3	159,922	-0.7	206,299	29.0	12.9
Religious	588,153	883,406	50.2	932,877	5.6	875,971	-6.1	14.2
E-books	29,979	80,793	169.5	123,695	53.1	179,110	44.8	81.5
Professional	3,155,191	3,268,778	3.6	3,334,153	2.0	3,300,812	-1.0	1.5
El-Hi (K–12 education)	5,795,044	5,939,920	2.5	5,945,860	0.1	6,570,175	10.5	4.3
Higher education	3,025,029	3,133,930	3.6	3,190,340	1.8	3,359,428	5.3	3.6
All other	136,488	153,932	12.8	161,629	5.0	158,558	-1.9	5.1
Total	$22,055,222	$23,115,180	4.8	$22,810,907	-1.3	$25,067,676	9.9	4.4

Source: Association of American Publishers

The Market for U.S. Book Exports and Imports, 2005: Dynamic Changes

Albert N. Greco

Senior Researcher
The Institute for Publishing Research
angreco@aol.com

Is globalization good or bad for U.S. book publishers?

At first glance, most individuals would support international trade because it opens up viable channels of distribution and produces new or additional revenue streams that augment traditional domestic U.S. business opportunities. Clearly, international trade has proven to be a bonanza for many book publishing firms able to develop effective marketing campaigns to sell foreign book rights as well as the exportation of book units. In addition, certain business firms in the entertainment industry (such as those producing motion pictures and television programs) with holdings in book publishing provided global support services for some publishers.

Some individuals, on the other hand, have expressed concern about the debilitating impact of globalization, specifically the impact of outsourcing on local communities and employment declines in certain manufacturing industries.

These issues have been explored by a number of major academics interested in the vagaries of international trade. General macroeconomic analyses of trade were undertaken by Nayyar (2006), Mah (2006), and Besedes (2006). For further discussion of the importance of both exports and imports, see *The Book Publishing Industry* (A. N. Greco, 2005), which augmented the research released by the Book Industry Study Group (2006) and the work of Clark and Bruce (2006).

Ellner's research (2006) on the emerging Latin American markets shed light on this pivotal region. Whereas Tong (2006) and Sharma (2006) concentrated on China's significant market, Wilson (2006) analyzed the Indian market, which is active in both book printing and book typesetting for U.S. firms.

Hau and Ray (2006) investigated the relationship between exchange rates and capital flows. Outsourcing, now a major political topic, was addressed by Ramanujan and Jane (2006). The ravages of book piracy were evident in the research released by the International Intellectual Property Alliance (2006).

A review of data released by the U.S. Department of Commerce indicated that the current U.S. international trade account deficit (the imbalance between exports and imports) topped $804.9 billion in 2005, up a sharp 20.48 percent since 2004 ($668.1 billion). Book imports contributed to that imbalance, jumping 4.75 percent (2004, $1,934.4 million; 2005, $2,026.3 million). While this book import trend has to cause concern in publishing circles, not all of the news was bleak. Book exports surged 8.84 percent, growing from $1,740.5 million in 2004 to $1,894.3 million in 2005 (the highest level since 1997). Overall, the ratio of book exports to imports stood at 0.93 in 2005, somewhat better than 2004's 0.90 mark.

Historical Background, 1970–2005

Book exports increased steadily between 1970 and 1997, growing 984.39 percent during those years. Yet there were some substantive econometric indicators that far too many industry analysts failed to grasp. First, book imports were increasing at a faster pace, topping 1,310 percent during the same period. Second, many of the books imported into the United States were printed abroad for U.S. firms, thereby allowing these publishers to reduce their paper, printing, and binding (PPB) unit manufacturing costs. Third, certain publishers took advantage of competitive foreign typesetting costs, which also increased profits. Fourth, the book export-import ratio fell from 1.90 in 1970 to 1.46 in 1997. Fifth, exports as a percentage of total U.S. book shipments (that is, net publishers' revenues) dropped from a high of 9.4 percent in 1990 to 6.6 percent in 2004 and were at 6.8 percent in 2005.

As for the years since 1997, exports sagged 11.36 percent between 1997 and 2002 while imports grew by 28 percent, and the export-import ratio declined precipitously to a marginal 1.01. By 2005 the export-import ratio rebounded slightly to 0.93.

Table 1 outlines the book export and import trends since 1970, and Table 2 contains information regarding exports as a percentage of total book shipments.

Table 1 / U.S. Trade in Books: 1970–2005
($ million)

Year	U.S. Book Exports	U.S. Book Imports	Ratio: U.S. Book Exports/Imports
1970	$174.9	$92.0	1.90
1975	269.3	147.6	1.82
1980	518.9	306.5	1.69
1985	591.2	564.2	1.05
1990	1,415.1	855.1	1.65
1995	1,779.5	1,184.5	1.50
1996	1,775.6	1,240.1	1.43
1997	1,896.6	1,297.5	1.46
1998	1,841.8	1,383.7	1.33
1999	1,871.1	1,441.4	1.30
2000	1,877.0	1,590.5	1.18
2001	1,712.3	1,627.8	1.05
2002	1,681.2	1,661.2	1.01
2003	1,693.6	1,755.9	0.96
2004	1,740.5	1,934.4	0.90
2005	1,894.3	2,026.3	0.93

Source: U.S. Department of Commerce, International Trade Administration. All totals are rounded to one decimal point. Data for individual categories may not add to totals due to statistical rounding. Due to changes in the classification of "U.S. traded products" and what constitutes products classified as "books," data prior to 1990 are not strictly comparable to data beginning in 1990.

Table 2 / U.S. Book Industry Shipments
Compared to U.S. Book Exports: 1970–2005
($ million)

Year	Total Shipments	U.S. Book Exports	Exports as a Percent of Total Shipments
1970	$2,434.2	$174.9	7.2
1975	3,536.5	269.3	7.6
1980	6,114.4	518.9	8.5
1985	10,165.7	591.2	5.8
1990	14,982.6	1,415.1	9.4
1995	19,471.0	1,779.5	9.1
1996	20,285.7	1,775.6	8.8
1997	21,131.9	1,896.6	9.0
1998	22,507.0	1,841.8	8.2
1999	23,926.9	1,871.1	7.8
2000	24,749.0	1,877.0	7.6
2001	24,742.6	1,712.3	6.9
2002	25,270.2	1,681.2	6.7
2003	25,998.5	1,693.6	6.5
2004	26,450.9	1,740.5	6.6
2005	27,804.2	1,894.3	6.8

Source: U.S. Department of Commerce, International Trade Administration; and the Book Industry Study Group (BISG). BISG's totals were used for shipments beginning in 1985 through 2004. Commerce totals were used for 1970–1980. Because of changes in the classification of U.S. traded products and what constitutes products classified as "books," data prior to 1990 are not strictly comparable to data beginning in 1990. All totals are rounded to one decimal point. Data for individual categories may not add to totals due to statistical rounding.

Market for U.S. Book Exports, 2005

While China emerged as a major supplier of manufactured goods in the 1990s, it was not one of the ten major book export destinations between 1996 and 2005.

Canada remained the United States' biggest export partner, at $866.2 million in 2005, up 17 percent since 1996. Other important destinations included the United Kingdom (up 25.9 percent between 1996 and 2005), Mexico (up 65.5 percent, an indicator that NAFTA was working), and Australia (approaching $100.8 million in 2005).

Rounding out the top ten were Japan (slipping about $5 million in 2005), Singapore (up 48.2 percent since 1996 but down nearly $5 million in 2005), Germany (up $8 million), South Korea (up nearly $12 million), Hong Kong (down $6 million), and India (up $3.5 million).

Data on the top 25 export destinations revealed the staggering importance of this small cluster of countries, which accounted for $1,784,398,000 in 2005 (up 8.5 percent from 2004); all other nations generated an additional $109,946,000 (up 15.4 percent), so these 25 countries accounted for 94.2 percent of all exports. In 2004 the top 25 nations accounted for $1,645,273,000 and 94.7 percent of all exports.

Table 3 / Top Ten Exports Destinations for U.S. Books: 1996–2005
($'000)

Country	1996	1997	1998	1999	2000	2001	2002	2003	2004	2005	Percent Change 1996–2005
Canada	740,393	823,614	807,583	807,541	756,667	727,698	742,619	776,441	812,833	866,173	17.0
United Kingdom	226,309	254,441	237,062	253,646	264,230	250,031	270,622	274,596	289,196	284,993	25.9
Japan	129,515	120,262	133,281	101,146	123,100	129,316	100,804	95,835	98,436	93,394	-27.9
Australia	118,076	138,070	157,928	139,588	116,302	66,010	70,806	76,067	78,549	100,769	-14.7
Mexico	62,011	58,239	58,770	65,599	73,886	63,804	64,938	68,132	66,087	102,658	65.5
Singapore	36,024	36,851	26,536	41,135	60,669	48,985	49,570	48,358	57,974	53,395	48.2
Germany	42,365	48,847	40,671	43,134	34,341	34,007	29,081	34,128	27,174	35,789	-15.5
South Korea	33,978	29,196	16,106	24,627	36,793	35,499	29,131	24,698	26,670	38,557	13.5
Hong Kong	21,949	23,923	21,292	20,667	32,492	29,409	31,559	19,234	22,936	16,636	-24.2
India	14,599	17,838	12,286	11,954	14,430	15,992	19,513	16,807	18,967	22,497	54.1

Source: U.S. Department of Commerce, International Trade Administration.

Note: Individual shipments are excluded from the foreign trade data if valued under $2,500. All totals are rounded to one decimal point. Data for individual categories may not add to totals due to statistical rounding.

Overall, exports increased a modest 2.9 percent to these 25 nations in 2004 as compared with an 8.5 percent increase in 2005. Markets posting impressive gains in 2005 included Australia (up 28.3 percent), the Philippines (up 43.2 percent), France (up 29.1 percent), Malaysia (up 63.5 percent), and Argentina (up 137.6 percent). A few overseas markets showed declines, including Singapore (down 7.9 percent), Hong Kong (down 27.5 percent), the Netherlands (down 14.9 percent), and, surprisingly, China (down 8.7 percent). Table 4 lists data on these 25 nations.

Table 4 / U.S. Book Exports to 25 Principal Countries: 2004–2005
($'000)

Country	Value		Percent Change 2004–2005
	2004	2005	
Canada	$812,833	$866,173	6.6
United Kingdom	289,196	284,993	-1.5
Japan	98,436	93,394	-5.1
Australia	78,549	100,769	28.3
Mexico	66,087	102,658	55.3
Singapore	57,974	53,395	-7.9
Germany	27,174	35,789	31.7
South Korea	26,670	38,557	44.6
Hong Kong	22,936	16,636	-27.5
India	18,967	22,497	18.6
China	18,110	16,532	-8.7
South Africa	17,966	19,279	7.3
Taiwan	15,966	14,489	-9.2
Netherlands	15,877	13,518	-14.9
Philippines	13,395	19,177	43.2
New Zealand	10,643	12,958	21.8
Brazil	8,930	9,610	7.6
France	8,168	10,545	29.1
Belgium	6,619	9,098	37.5
Malaysia	6,463	10,567	63.5
Nigeria	6,371	6,324	-0.7
Thailand	6,065	7,448	22.8
Spain	4,523	6,002	32.7
Sweden	4,477	7,149	59.7
Argentina	2879	6,841	137.6
Total, Top 25 Countries	$1,645,273	$1,784,398	8.5
All Others	$95,246	$109,946	15.4
Grand Total	$1,740,519	$1,894,344	8.8

Source: U.S. Department of Commerce, International Trade Administration. Note: Individual shipments are excluded from the foreign trade data if valued under $2,500. All totals are rounded to one decimal point. Data for individual categories may not add to totals due to statistical rounding.

As expected, the export of dictionaries and thesauruses continued to experience market fluctuations, dropping 24.3 percent in revenues and 18 percent in units, although encyclopedias exhibited an impressive pattern of growth (up 11 percent in revenues, and up 12.9 percent in units). Other categories on the upswing included technical, scientific, and professional books and hardcover books. The performance of religious books and textbooks was modest, with declines in the mass market paperback segment. Table 5 contains detailed data on revenues and units.

Table 5 / U.S. Exports of Books: 2005

Category	Value ($'000)	Percent Change 2004–2005	Units ('000)	Percent Change 2004–2005
Dictionaries and thesauruses	$2,236	-24.3	507	-18.0
Encyclopedias	9,204	11.0	1,776	12.9
Textbooks	413,408	2.8	65,410	0.2
Religious books	83,303	2.3	58,857	-8.5
Technical, Scientific, and Professional	475,407	21.4	86,139	13.9
Hardcover books, n.e.s.	164,373	12.1	39,291	13.7
Mass market paperbacks	216,541	-5.4	107,234	-22.0
Total, All books	$1,894,344	8.8	721,321	-12.6

Source: U.S. Department of Commerce, International Trade Administration.
Note: Individual shipments are excluded from the foreign trade data if valued under $2,500. All totals are rounded to one decimal point. Data for individual categories may not add to totals due to statistical rounding.
n.e.s. = not elsewhere specified.

Of the top ten exports markets for mass market paperbacks, seven recorded declines in 2005, with large reversals in the United Kingdom, Australia, Singapore, and Malaysia. Overall, this segment dropped 5.4 percent in revenues and 22 percent in unit sales. Table 6 outlines these trends.

Table 6 / U.S. Book Exports of Mass Market Paperbacks (Rack Size): Top Ten Markets 2005

Country	Value ($'000)	Percent Change 2004–2005	Units ('000)	Percent Change 2004–2005
Canada	$117,310	-4.9	57,449	-25.0
United Kingdom	20,678	-35.6	9,349	-50.4
Japan	14,468	-0.5	10,979	-2.3
Philippines	11,563	114.0	5,032	91.6
South Africa	10,618	13.2	3,315	17.5
Australia	5,967	-2.3	3,021	-25.0
Singapore	4,805	6.6	1,416	-47.3
China	2,834	0.7	1,844	18.7
Brazil	2,381	-3.7	1,455	-1.8
Malaysia	2,352	-3.1	1,006	-30.9

Source: U.S. Department of Commerce, International Trade Administration. All totals are rounded to one decimal point. Data for individual categories may not add to totals due to statistical rounding.

As for the other book export categories, technical, scientific, and professional books continued to post impressive tallies in terms of revenues (up 21.4 percent), with Canada, Mexico, Belgium, and Germany eager for these titles. Table 7 covers this category.

Table 7 / U.S. Exports of Technical, Scientific, and Professional Books: Top Ten Markets 2005

Country	Value ($'000)	Percent Change 2004–2005	Units ('000)	Percent Change 2004–2005
Canada	$148,376	7.8	15,651	5.9
United Kingdom	87,801	24.3	7,231	3.8
Mexico	41,351	167.9	32,445	45.8
Japan	40,895	-4.1	2,742	-15.9
Australia	30,514	57.6	7,520	29.2
Germany	18,973	49.5	2,274	52.1
South Korea	15,803	129.5	2,850	304.4
Singapore	13,732	1.4	2,787	-13.1
Belgium	7,758	49.9	877	67.9
India	7,633	16.6	887	-85.6

Source: U.S. Department of Commerce, International Trade Administration. All totals are rounded to one decimal point. Data for individual categories may not add to totals due to statistical rounding.

The textbook market sagged in 2005, with revenues up 2.8 percent and units barely posting any gain. While the United Kingdom remained the principal export market, Australia and Taiwan generated impressive gains. Unfortunately, a methodological problem exists in this book category. El-hi (K–12 education) textbooks and supplements are included, but the U.S. Department of Commerce does not provide separate totals for el-hi titles. Table 8 lists the growth recorded by textbooks.

Table 8 / U.S. Exports of Textbooks 2005: Top Ten Markets

Country	Value ($'000)	Percent Change 2004–2005	Units ('000)	Percent Change 2004–2005
United Kingdom	$107,355	-4.4	20,746	-1.0
Canada	73,832	-0.4	6,157	-15.3
Australia	36569	29.6	6,144	41.8
Singapore	31,492	-13.7	4,553	-29.5
Japan	28,322	-12.6	2,632	-18.2
South Korea	16,844	2.8	3,364	-6.9
Mexico	10,595	-28.6	2,720	-16.4
Taiwan	7,871	42.6	1,197	31.1
Hong Kong	7,864	4.3	1,201	-11.6
Germany	7,161	55.9	809	26.2

Source: U.S. Department of Commerce, International Trade Administration. All totals are rounded to one decimal point. Data for individual categories may not add to totals due to statistical rounding.

Over the last five years, the domestic religious book market has been buoyant, posting large annual increases in both revenues and units. This has slackened somewhat, and a similar pattern was evident in the export sector. While strong double-digit increases were registered by Canada, Australia, Argentina, and Ghana, overall export units declined 8.5 percent. Table 9 shows the performance of this category.

Table 9 / U.S. Exports of Religious Books 2005: Top Ten Markets

Country	Value ($'000)	Percent Change 2004–2005	Units ('000)	Percent Change 2004–2005
Canada	$16,765	29.5	5,277	24.6
United Kingdom	13,804	-35.9	7,810	-22.6
Australia	11,677	47.2	4,806	44.2
Mexico	6,997	0.2	3,622	-46.3
Nigeria	5,369	-3.3	2,849	-18.5
Argentina	4,043	147.7	2,912	62.7
Kenya	2,551	70.7	1,400	16.9
Jamaica	2,101	14.8	1,321	2.7
Ghana	1,635	-2.2	2,709	18.2
Dominican Republic	1,598	59.9	2,333	12.5

Source: U.S. Department of Commerce, International Trade Administration. All totals are rounded to one decimal point. Data for individual categories may not add to totals due to statistical rounding.

Table 10 / U.S. Exports of Hardbound Books 2005: Top Ten Markets

Country	Value ($'000)	Percent Change 2004–2005	Units ('000)	Percent Change 2004–2005
Canada	$103,306	13.4	20,437	13.8
United Kingdom	24,569	0.6	6,736	13.0
Australia	8,236	-12.9	1,982	-3.8
India	4,749	10.7	1,860	8.7
Japan	3,714	149.3	738	24.6
Philippines	1,699	-18.6	1,427	-10.7
New Zealand	1,606	-48.1	289	-32.9
Singapore	1,581	63.5	374	38.8
France	1,345	908.4	817	1,777.9
Sweden	1,179	302.9	n.a.	n.a.

Source: U.S. Department of Commerce, International Trade Administration. All totals are rounded to one decimal point. Data for individual categories may not add to totals due to statistical rounding.
n.a. = not available

Although Americans have little appetite for foreign books, even in translation, the foreign market is eager for hardcover books in English, and the impressive growth in revenues (up 12.1 percent) in 2005 was paced by the performance of a number of markets, including France (up 1,777.9 percent), Singapore (up 38.8 percent), and Japan (up 24.6 percent). The strong appeal of the fantasy market, driven by the popularity of the Harry Potter books, as well as new titles by

James Patterson, Mary Higgins Clark, Janet Evanovich, and John Grisham (aided by a cluster of other "big book" authors) continued, and the export market for hardbound books remains impressive. Table 10 lists information about hardbound sales for 2004.

In recent years encyclopedias and dictionaries and thesauruses have been underperforming book categories in both the domestic and export markets. The reason was clear: with the proliferation of computers with "tools" applications, individuals used printed encyclopedias, dictionaries, and thesauruses considerably less. However, the 2005 export market for encyclopedias was up a robust 11 percent in revenues and 12.9 percent in units, with large surges reported in the United Kingdom (up 571.8 percent), the Philippines (up 129.3 percent), and Venezuela (up 1707.3 percent). Table 11 outlines these developments.

Table 11 / U.S. Exports of Encyclopedias and Serial Installments: Top Ten Markets 2005

Country	Value ($'000)	Percent Change 2004–2005	Units ('000)	Percent Change 2004–2005
Mexico	$2,150	6.7	501	7.3
Canada	1,611	-15.8	428	0.7
Japan	1,256	15.9	180	15.4
Australia	976	100.3	116	44.7
United Kingdom	423	591.0	87	571.8
Venezuela	355	126.7	75	1,707.3
Philippines	350	64.7	87	129.3
South Africa	328	-36.1	37	-30.3
Colombia	275	-12.1	49	-29.3
India	314	241.4	22	104.5

Source: U.S. Department of Commerce, International Trade Administration. All totals are rounded to one decimal point. Data for individual categories may not add to totals due to statistical rounding.

Table 12 / U.S. Exports of Dictionaries (Including Thesauruses) 2005: Top Ten Markets

Country	Value ($'000)	Percent Change 2004–2005	Units ('000)	Percent Change 2004–2005
Canada	$854	-30.3	216	-29.9
United Kingdom	365	142.7	84	209.7
Mexico	323	-47.2	83	-18.0
Colombia	115	n.a.	6	n.a.
Philippines	76	127.5	13	60.6
Japan	65	104.0	11	74.9
Australia	53	-86.7	8	-88.9
Kenya	44	n.a.	12	n.a.
India	39	179.9	22	2,728.5
Costa Rica	33	n.a.	5	n.a.

Source: U.S. Department of Commerce, International Trade Administration. All totals are rounded to one decimal point. Data for individual categories may not add to totals due to statistical rounding.

n.a. = not available

Dictionaries and thesauruses, on the other hand, fell into an abyss, with units declining 18 percent and revenues off 24.3 percent. Unimpressive results were evident in most markets, including Canada, Mexico, and Australia. Sales to the other countries were marginal at best.

If this depressing trend continues, we may be compelled to drop this category from future studies. This year, however, detailed information can be found in Table 12.

Market for U.S. Book Imports, 2005

In 1996 China was ranked ninth among the top ten sources of U.S. book imports. By 2005 it was the principal source of imported books for the U.S. market with a staggering $605,229,000 in revenues (up 954.4 percent between 1996 and 2005). The United Kingdom was a distant second with $307,517,000 (up 10 percent between 1996 and 2005).

The empirical research indicated conclusively that China prints books (and in many instance also sets the type) for U.S. publishers in almost every book category. Table 13 outlines these trends.

To place this trend in perspective, China's market share of all U.S. book imports in 2005 was 29.87 percent, making it the market leader in the following book categories: textbooks (third); religious books (second); technical, scientific, and professional books (first); hardbound books (first); mass market paperbacks (first); and encyclopedias (first).

According to the latest statistics released by the International Intellectual Property Alliance (IIPA, 2006), China was on the "priority watch list" for $2,366 million worth of piracy in the following categories for 2005:

- Business software, $1,276 million
- Records and music, $204 million
- Motion pictures, $244 million
- Entertainment software, $590 million
- Books, $52 million

Based on a review of the IIPA methodology, it appears the figure for book piracy is a remarkably low estimate.

Other nations made major inroads into the U.S. market. The United Kingdom, the traditional leader (until 2002), had a 15.18 percent share in 2005, although this was only a 1 percent increase over 2004. Other major players were Germany (up 18.9 percent), Mexico (up 81 percent), India (up 52.2 percent, and also active in typesetting), Russia (up 47.7 percent), and Sweden (up 74.2 percent).

Overall, the top 25 nations accounted for 97.83 percent of all imports. Table 14 lists data on these nations for 2004 and 2005. Table 15 lists the value of imports for 2004 and 2005 by book categories that posted impressive results in those two years.

Table 13 / Top Ten Import Sources of Books, 1996–2005
($'000)

Country	1996	1997	1998	1999	2000	2001	2002	2003	2004	2005	Percent Change 1996–2005
China	$57,402	$73,310	$101,012	$142,459	$220,895	$267,582	$338,489	$413,065	$533,524	$605,229	954.4
United Kingdom	279,532	283,380	314,290	278,252	317,660	303,897	267,853	287,972	304,619	307,517	10.0
Canada	146,009	189,413	215,825	221,462	229,045	243,689	251,085	275,053	289,423	281,120	92.5
Hong Kong	221,894	203,243	200,242	229,293	224,834	229,719	223,452	189,783	185,963	176,079	-20.6
Singapore	96,124	92,134	94,672	89,000	86,630	96,325	100,610	103,383	113,900	115,314	20.0
Italy	91,268	85,514	102,525	100,475	94,983	87,779	83,360	84,167	78,567	69,463	-23.9
Germany	54,147	57,536	63,066	57,082	57,345	53,092	55,993	52,055	57,353	68,.211	26.0
Spain	31,375	36,673	37,596	46,590	55,506	50,474	50,994	48,407	49,330	38,725	28.4
Japan	66,034	66,281	58,775	55,087	59,268	49,956	47,198	45,277	48,726	50,765	-23.1
South Korea	21,229	17,544	25,816	29,728	29,430	35,559	40,459	39,083	46,265	54,303	155.8

Source: U.S. Department of Commerce, International Trade Administration. All totals are rounded to one decimal point. Data for individual categories may not add to totals due to statistical rounding.

Table 14 / U.S. Book Imports from 25 Principal Countries: 2004–2005

Country	Value ($'000) 2004	Value ($'000) 2005	Percent Change 2004–2005
China	$533,524	$605,229	13.4
United Kingdom	304,619	307,517	1.0
Canada	289,423	281,120	-2.9
Hong Kong	185,963	176,079	-5.3
Singapore	113,900	115,314	1.2
Italy	78,567	69,463	-11.6
Germany	57,353	68,211	18.9
Spain	49,330	38,725	-21.5
Japan	48,726	50,765	4.2
South Korea	46,265	54,303	17.4
France	24,508	29,790	21.5
Mexico	22,627	40,956	81.0
Belgium	19,912	22,557	13.3
Colombia	16,860	19,324	14.6
Israel	14,508	12,687	-12.6
Netherlands	13,483	8,200	-39.2
Malaysia	10,800	13,097	21.3
Australia	10,545	8,680	-17.7
Thailand	9,953	12,839	29.0
India	8,222	12,512	52.2
Taiwan	7,469	7,322	-2.0
United Arab Emirates	7,142	7,309	2.3
Brazil	6,703	6,138	-8.4
Russia	5,067	7,485	47.7
Sweden	3,857	6,717	74.2
Total Top 25 Countries:	1,893,256	1,982,340	4.9
All Others:	45,022	43,980	-2.3
Grand Total:	$1,934,350	$2,026,320	4.8

Source: U.S. Department of Commerce, International Trade Administration. All totals are rounded to one decimal point. Data for individual categories may not add to totals due to statistical rounding. Individual shipments are excluded from the foreign trade data if valued under $2,500.

Table 15 / U.S. Imports of Books: 2004–2005

Category	Value ($'000) 2004	Value ($'000) 2005	Percent Change 2004–2005
Encyclopedias	$6,458	6,057	-6.2
Textbooks	217,413	232,518	6.9
Religious books	99,478	108,631	9.2
Technical, Scientific, and Professional	265,561	291,244	9.7
Hardcover books, n.e.s.	577,274	596,036	3.3
Mass market paperbacks	128,727	112,633	-12.5
Total, All books	$1,934,350	$2,026,320	4.8

Source: U.S. Department of Commerce, International Trade Administration. All totals are rounded to one decimal point. Data for individual categories may not add to totals due to statistical rounding. Individual shipments are excluded from the foreign trade data if valued under $2,500.

One of the most successful book categories in the past decade has been textbooks, both el-hi and college level. Overall, imports (primarily books printed abroad but not published and printed abroad) posted an impressive 6.9 percent increase in revenues between 2004 and 2005. Nations exceptionally active in this sector included the United Kingdom (still the leader although revenues declined 18.5 percent in 2005), Canada (up 99.5 percent), and China (also off a surprisingly 2 percent). Latin America was well represented, with Mexico up 51.2 percent and Colombia up 18.1 percent, but Hong Kong (up 39.2 percent) and Singapore (up 112 percent) generated larger revenues. Table 16 provides data on this major category.

Sooner or later, U.S.-based printers will address the growing impact of offshore printing of books (particularly in China, Indonesia, and India).

Table 16 / U.S. Imports of Textbooks: Top Ten Markets 2005

Country	Value ($'000)	Percent Change 2004–2005	Units ('000)	Percent Change 2004–2005
United Kingdom	$81,929	10.2	4,450	-18.5
Canada	36,652	26.8	11,552	99.4
China	33,942	-34.8	12,381	-2.0
Hong Kong	26,147	69.5	9,006	39.2
Singapore	10,013	-8.2	4,635	112.0
Italy	4,567	8.4	755	-37.5
Mexico	4,485	7.2	940	51.2
Germany	3,938	54.7	475	123.1
Colombia	3,862	17.8	2,221	18.1
Spain	3,796	18.4	593	-4.4

Source: U.S. Department of Commerce, International Trade Administration. All totals are rounded to one decimal point. Data for individual categories may not add to totals due to statistical rounding.

The importation of printed religious books—most of which are printed but not published and printed abroad—surged 9.2 percent in 2005 to $108.6 million. As in previous years, South Korea and China were the two most active nations in this book category (accounting for 41.89 percent of all religious book imports), with Israel, Belgium, and Colombia (an emerging printing powerhouse) rounding out the top five. Table 17 outlines these revenue and unit developments.

In 2005 additional attempts were made in the United States and abroad to offer electronic versions of religious books, notably Bibles and commentaries. Little empirical data exists on this trend, but reports indicate a lackluster response from consumers, so it remains unlikely that electronic religious books will emerge as a significant format in the next decade.

However, while technical, scientific, and professional books continue to grow in importance, as evidenced by the 9.7 percent increase in imports, this sector is unquestionably positioned to witness a migration to the electronic distribution of content (especially in the legal and business subcategories) by the end of this decade. Nonetheless, imports from China were up 19.9 percent because of its dominant 24.89 percent of the market. Other principal countries included Canada and the United Kingdom, both of which lost market shares to China. Mexico (up

Table 17 / U.S. Imports of Bibles, Testaments, Prayer Books, and Other Religious Books, 2005: Top Ten Markets

Country	Value ($'000)	Percent Change 2004–2005	Units ('000)	Percent Change 2004–2005
South Korea	$23,511	30.8	15,075	-17.8
China	21,994	26.6	11,028	5.8
Israel	11,604	-10.4	2,438	-31.6
Belgium	9,966	14.8	2,853	12.3
Colombia	5,769	-23.5	7,138	5.5
Spain	3,780	19.4	839	-17.5
United Kingdom	3,675	-17.9	978	-1.1
Hong Kong	3,602	-3.6	4,459	12.6
Singapore	2,627	21.6	925	-12.3
Canada	2,242	32.3	1,839	26.6

Source: U.S. Department of Commerce, International Trade Administration. All totals are rounded to one decimal point. Data for individual categories may not add to totals due to statistical rounding.

Table 18 / U.S. Imports of Technical, Scientific, and Professional Books, 2005: Top Ten Markets

Country	Value ($'000)	Percent Change 2004–2005	Units ('000)	Percent Change 2004–2005
China	$72,488	114.9	9,154	19.9
Canada	53,040	-20.5	12,189	-69.1
United Kingdom	44,875	-32.4	2,813	-49.6
Germany	33,625	31.7	1,957	-5.8
Mexico	20,288	137.3	26,274	129.1
Hong Kong	10,610	43.9	1,818	-16.1
Japan	10,292	24.9	1,054	-10.1
Belgium	5,699	13.5	n.a.	n.a.
Singapore	5,516	53.3	1,576	54.1
Sweden	3,817	32.3	1,657	39.5

Source: U.S. Department of Commerce, International Trade Administration. All totals are rounded to one decimal point. Data for individual categories may not add to totals due to statistical rounding.
n.a. = not available

129.1 percent; another growing printing exporter to the United States) was ranked in the top five. Sweden (up 39.5 percent) emerged as a new player in this field. See Table 18 for details on revenues and units.

China's position in the hardbound book import sector is $243,441,000, accounting for 40.84 percent of all imported hardbound books. The United Kingdom and Hong Kong were distant rivals (but both lost market share to China between 2004 and 2005). Other competitors (all of whom sustained declines in business levels in 2005) included Singapore, Canada, Italy, Japan, and Spain. Only Germany posted any increase (35.9 percent), although France was able to move into the top ten. Table 19 lists data on this niche.

Table 19 / U.S. Imports of Hardbound Books, 2005: Top Ten Markets

Country	Value ($'000)	Percent Change 2004–2005	Units ('000)	Percent Change 2004–2005
China	$243,441	11.8	105,995	4.2
United Kingdom	78,283	9.6	9,072	-20.8
Hong Kong	72,793	-9.1	29,061	-17.7
Singapore	49,639	3.0	20,996	-4.6
Canada	35,112	6.1	8,475	-9.8
Italy	29,469	-8.7	7,682	-6.7
Japan	11,510	-27.4	2,601	-13.6
France	13,757	58.6	n.a.	n.a.
Spain	9,374	-51.9	1,990	-40.0
Germany	8,912	13.5	1,671	35.9

Source: U.S. Department of Commerce, International Trade Administration. All totals are rounded to one decimal point. Data for individual categories may not add to totals due to statistical rounding.
n.a. = not available

E-books continue to receive a great deal of attention in the United States, especially with the 2006 launch of Sony's new hand-held device, but sales remain marginal (estimated to be at about $15 million in 2005). Print will remain the dominant format for the foreseeable future.

Mass market paperbacks struggled in 2005 and imports reflected this trend, with overall revenues sagging 12.5 percent. China was again the primary source of these books, with a 28.89 percent market share. However, even China sustained an 18.9 percent drop in business, as did Canada, Singapore, Spain, and Hong Kong. Strong gains were posted by Indonesia, Japan, and Thailand, although they remain small players in this area. Table 20 outlines developments in this category.

Table 20 / U.S. Imports of Mass Market Paperbacks (Rack Size), 2005: Top Ten Markets

Country	Value ($'000)	Percent Change 2004–2005	Units ('000)	Percent Change 2004–2005
China	$32,544	-6.6	27,232	-18.9
Canada	22,386	29.5	13,648	-21.0
United Kingdom	18,347	-17.3	4,079	1.2
Singapore	10,401	-15.7	6,025	-30.1
Italy	8,903	-27.0	3,052	-29.6
Spain	4,460	-10.8	1,713	-33.0
Hong Kong	4,031	-61.1	2,604	-56.3
Indonesia	1,911	263.7	2,881	353.9
Japan	1,295	-17.8	257	24.1
Thailand	822	-4.7	707	137.2

Source: U.S. Department of Commerce, International Trade Administration. All totals are rounded to one decimal point. Data for individual categories may not add to totals due to statistical rounding.

The last category, encyclopedias, remains an exceptionally small one, with only $6,057,000 in total imports. Two nations, China (with a 26.17 percent market share) and Colombia (17.98 percent share), dominate this category, which may be dropped from future studies. Table 21 outlines the trends of this niche.

Table 21 / U.S. Imports of Encyclopedias and Serial Installments, 2005: Top Ten Markets

Country	Value ($'000)	Percent Change 2004–2005	Units ('000)	Percent Change 2004–2005
China	$1,585	36.4	350	-9.4
Colombia	1,089	6,758.9	560	4,1374.1
Mexico	754	9.4	165	33.9
Singapore	519	265.0	136	117.3
Italy	400	109.1	21	-57.4
Hong Kong	382	-51.7	65	-47.7
Canada	299	-62.5	48	-33.6
Slovak Republic	297	46.4	54	80.1
United Kingdom	249	-71.2	39	-75.1
Spain	234	-57.6	32	22.3

Source: U.S. Department of Commerce, International Trade Administration. All totals are rounded to one decimal point. Data for individual categories may not add to totals due to statistical rounding. Calculations used two decimal points because of the size of the totals.

Conclusions

In spite of the positive impacts associated with globalization, and the inherent corporate partnerships available to global media and entertainment corporations active in book publishing, exports continue to remain a small fraction of all book revenues. To address this situation, the industry has yet to grapple with the substantive issues relating to the following:

- Distribution of books from the United States to foreign markets, which has been hampered by inefficient export operations; significant attention should be paid to what has emerged as a serious bottleneck
- Creation of a central office monitoring, on a monthly basis, export sales, changes in book category imports, and the daily impact of currency changes on the bottom line
- The pernicious impact of book piracy
- The need to pay more attention to collecting and analyzing basic, critical macroeconomic data

References

Besedes, T. "Ins, Outs, and the Duration of Trade." *Canadian Journal of Economics* 39, 1 (February 2006): 266.

Book Industry Study Group, Inc. (2006). *Book Industry Trends 2006*. Book Industry Study Group, Inc.

Clark, D. P., and D. Bruce. "On the Incidence of U.S. Tariffs." *World Economy* 29, 2 (February 2006): 123.

Ellner, S. "Macroeconomic Policies and Latin American Democracy," *Latin American Politics and Society* 48, 1 (Spring 2006): 175–189

Greco, A. N. (2005). *The Book Publishing Industry*. Lawrence Erlbaum Associates.

Hau, H., and H. Ray. "Exchange Rates, Equity Prices and Capital Flows." *Review of Financial Studies* 19, 1 (Spring 2006): 273.

International Intellectual Property Alliance (2006). "Appendix A: IIPA 'Special 301' Recommendations; International Intellectual Property Alliance 2006 'Special 301 Report' Appendix B: Methodology." http://www.iipa.com.

Mah, J. S. "Export Promotion and Economic Development." *Journal of World Trade* 40, 1 (February 2006): 153–167.

Nayyar, D. "Globalization, History, and Development: A Tale of Two Centuries." *Cambridge Journal of Economics* 30, 1 (January 2006): 137.

Ramanujan, S., and S. Jane. "A Legal Perspective on Outsourcing and Offshoring." *Journal of the American Academy of Business* 8, 2 (March 2006): 51–59.

Sharma, S. D. "Money Talks: Revaluing China's Currency." *Georgetown Journal of International Affairs* 7, 1 (Winter 2006): 59–65.

Tong, Z. "The Development of China and World Trade." *Journal of World Trade* 40, 1 (February 2006): 129–137.

Wilson, B. A. "India and the Global Economy." *Business Economics* 41,1 (January 2006): 28–37.

Number of Book Outlets in the United States and Canada

The *American Book Trade Directory* (Information Today, Inc.) has been published since 1915. Revised annually, it features lists of booksellers, wholesalers, periodicals, reference tools, and other information about the U.S. and Canadian book markets. The data shown in Table 1, the most current available, are from the 2006–2007 edition of the directory.

The 22,705 stores of various types shown are located throughout the United States, Canada, and regions administered by the United States. "General" bookstores stock trade books and children's books in a general variety of subjects. "College" stores carry college-level textbooks. "Educational" outlets handle school textbooks up to and including the high school level. "Mail order" outlets sell general trade books by mail and are not book clubs; all others operating by mail are classified according to the kinds of books carried. "Antiquarian" dealers sell old and rare books. Stores handling secondhand books are classified as "used." "Paperback" stores have more than 80 percent of their stock in paperbound books. Stores with paperback departments are listed under the appropriate major classification ("general," "department store," "stationer," and so forth.). Bookstores with at least 50 percent of their stock on a particular subject are classified by subject.

Table 1 / Bookstores in the United States and Canada, 2005

Category	United States	Canada
Antiquarian General	1,063	88
Antiquarian Mail Order	407	12
Antiquarian Specialized	198	6
Art Supply Store	77	1
College General	3,282	179
College Specialized	119	10
Comics	225	23
Computer Software	2	0
Cooking	313	8
Department Store	1,692	2
Educational*	187	37
Federal Sites†	246	1
Foreign Language*	31	3
General	5,211	746
Gift Shop	179	14
Juvenile*	175	24
Mail Order General	191	16
Mail Order Specialized	514	24
Metaphysics, New Age, and Occult	198	26
Museum Store and Art Gallery	531	36
Nature and Natural History	148	8
Newsdealer	61	4
Office Supply	24	4
Other‡	2,112	384

Paperback§	164	8
Religious*	2,741	231
Self Help/Development	27	10
Stationer	7	7
Toy Store	41	20
Used*	501	96
Totals	20,677	2,028

* Includes Mail Order Shops for this topic, which are not counted elsewhere in this survey.

† National Historic Sites, National Monuments, and National Parks.

‡ Stores specializing in subjects or services other than those covered in this survey.

§ Includes Mail Order. Excludes used paperback bookstores, stationers, drugstores, or wholesalers handling paperbacks.

Review Media Statistics

Compiled by the staff of the *Bowker Annual*

Number of Books and Other Media Reviewed by Major Reviewing Publications 2004–2005

	Adult		Juvenile		Young Adult		Total	
	2004	2005	2004	2005	2004	2005	2004	2005
Booklist[1]	5,128	5,067	3,456	3,139	—	—	8,674	8,206
BookPage[2]	765	669	132	95	31	45	928	809
Bulletin of the Center for Children's Books[3]	—	—	840	886	—	—	840	886
Chicago Sun Times	550	540	80	85	—	—	630	625
Chicago Tribune Sunday Book Section	600	600	275	275	25	25	900	900
Choice[4]	7,538	7,519	—	—	—	—	7,538	7,519
Horn Book Guide	—	—	4,429	3,472	—	570	4,429	4,042
Horn Book Magazine	5	1	306	330	107	75	418	406
Kirkus Reviews[5]	2,474	2,278	1,590	1,791	—	—	4,064	4,069
Library Journal[6]	6,210	5,967	—	—	—	—	6,210	5,967
Los Angeles Times	1,200	n.a.	—	—	—	—	1,200	n.a.
New York Times Sunday Book Review[5]	1,060	1,070	130	140	—	—	1,190	1,210
Publishers Weekly[7]	6,160	6,646	2,143	1,843	—	—	8,303	8,489
School Library Journal[5]	387	249	4,339,	4,446	—	—	4,726	4,695
Washington Post Book World	1,500	1,500	150	150	50	50	1,700	1,700

n.a.=not available

1 All figures are for a 12-month period from September 1, 2004 to August 31, 2005 (vol. 101). YA books are included in the juvenile total. *Booklist* also reviewed 715 other media.

2 *BookPage* also reviewed 46 audiobooks.

3 All figures are for 12-month period beginning September and ending July/August. YA books are included in the juvenile total. The *Bulletin* also reviewed 10 professional books.

4 All materials reviewed in *Choice* are scholarly publications intended for undergraduate libraries. Total includes 986 Internet sites, 6 CD-ROMs, and 3 DVDs.

5 YA books are included in the juvenile total.

6 In addition *LJ* reviewed 304 audiobooks, 340 videos/DVDs, 55 magazines, 318 books in "Collection Development," 68 online databases and CD-ROMs, and previewed 1,186 books and audiobooks in "Prepub Alert," "Prepub Mystery," and "Prepub Audio."

7 Adult figure includes 137 audiobooks and 1,273 online reviews; juvenile figure includes 456 notes and 287 reprint notices.

Part 5
Reference Information

Bibliographies

The Librarian's Bookshelf

Cathleen Bourdon, MLS

Executive Director, Reference and User Services Association, American Library Association

Most of the books on this selective bibliography have been published since 2003; a few earlier titles are retained because of their continuing importance.

General Works

American Library Directory, 2006–2007. 2v. Information Today, Inc. 2006. $299.95

Annual Review of Information Science and Technology (ARIST). Vol. 40. Ed. by Blaise Cronin. Information Today, Inc. 2005. $99.95.

The Bowker Annual Library and Book Trade Almanac, 2006. Information Today, Inc. 2006. $199.95

Encyclopedia of Library and Information Science. 2nd ed. Ed. by Miriam A. Drake. Marcel Dekker, 2003. $1,500.

International Encyclopedia of Information and Library Science. Ed. by John Feather and Paul Sturges. Routledge, 2003. $195.

Library Literature and Information Science Index. H. W. Wilson, 1921–. Also available online, 1984–.

The Oxford Guide to Library Research. 3rd ed. By Thomas Mann. Oxford University Press, 2005. Paper $16.95.

The Whole Library Handbook. 4th ed. Ed. by George Eberhart. American Library Association, 2006. Paper $42.

Academic Libraries

Academic Library Trends and Statistics, 2004. 3 vols. Association of College and Research Libraries/American Library Association, 2005. $240.

ARL Statistics. Association of Research Libraries. Annual. 1964–. $120.

The Changing Academic Library: Operations, Cultures, Environments. By John M. Budd. Association of College and Research Libraries/American Library Association, 2005. Paper $35.

CLIP (College Library Information Packet) Notes. Association of College and Research Libraries/American Library Association, 1980–. Most recent volume is No. 35, 2005. $29.

Digital Resources and Librarians: Case Studies in Innovation, Invention, and Implementation. Ed. by Patricia O'Brien Libutti. Association of College and Research Libraries/American Library Association, 2004. Paper $35.50.

Human Resource Management in Today's Academic Library: Meeting Challenges and Creating Opportunities. By Janice Simmons-Welburn and Beth McNeil. Libraries Unlimited, 2004. $45.

SPEC Kits. Association of Research Libraries. 1973–. 10/yr. $260.

Survey of the State of Audio Collections in Academic Libraries. By Abby Smith, David Randal Allen, and Karen Allen. Council on Library and Information Resources, 2004. Paper $20.

Administration and Personnel

Access in the Future Tense. Council on Library and Information Resources, 2004. Paper $20.

The Accidental Library Manager. By Rachel Singer Gordon. Information Today, Inc. 2005. Paper $29.50.

Advances in Library Administration and Organization. Most recent volume is No. 23. Ed. by Edward D. Garten and Delmus E. Williams. Elsevier Science, 2006. $94.95.

Business Planning for Cultural Heritage Institutions. By Liz Bishoff and Nancy Allen. Council on Library and Information Resources, 2004. Paper $20.

Conflict Management for Libraries: Strategies for a Positive, Productive Workplace. By Jack G. Montgomery and Eleanor I. Cook. American Library Association, 2005. Paper $42.

Fundamentals of Library Supervision. By Joan Giesecke and Beth McNeil. American Library Association, 2005. Paper $42.

Managing Budgets and Finance: A How-to-Do-It Manual for Librarians and Information Professionals. By Arlita W. Hallam and Teresa R. Dalston. Neal-Schuman, 2005. Paper $59.95.

Managing Outsourcing in Library and Information Services. By Sheila Pantry and Peter Griffiths. Facet Publishing, 2004. Paper $75.

The Neal-Schuman Directory of Public Library Job Descriptions. By Rebecca Brumley. Neal-Schuman, 2005. Paper and CD-ROM $125.

Planning and Evaluating Networked Services and Resources. Ed. by John Carlo Bertot and Denise M. Davis. Libraries Unlimited, 2005. Paper $45.

RFID in Libraries. Library Video Network, 2004. DVD or VHS $75.

Risk and Insurance Management Manual for Libraries. By Mary Breighner, William Payton, and Jeanne M. Drewes. Library Administration and Management Association/American Library Association, 2005. Paper $40.

Staff Planning in a Time of Demographic Change. Ed. by Vicki Whitmel. Scarecrow Press, 2005. Paper $40.

Strategic Planning and Management for Library Managers. By Joseph R. Matthews. Libraries Unlimited, 2005. Paper $40.

Transitioning from Librarian to Middle Manager. By Pixey Ann Mosley. Libraries Unlimited, 2004. Paper $40.

The 2003 OCLC Environmental Scan: Pattern Recognition. By Cathy De Rosa, Lorcan Dempsey, and Alane Wilson. OCLC, 2004. Paper $15.

Advocacy

The Essential Friends of Libraries: Fast Facts, Forms and Tips. By Sandy Dolnick. American Library Association, 2004. Paper and CD-ROM $42.

Lobbying for Libraries and the Public's Access to Government Information: An Insider's View. By Bernadine E. Abbott-Hoduski. Scarecrow Press, 2003. $39.95.

Lobbying for Public and School Libraries: A History and Political Playbook. By Richard S. Halsey. Scarecrow Press, 2003. Paper $36.

Making Our Voices Heard: Citizens Speak Out for Libraries. By Sally Gardner Reed and Beth Nawalinski. Friends of Libraries U.S.A., 2004. Notebook and CD-ROM $30.

101+ Great Ideas for Libraries and Friends. By Sally Gardner Reed, Beth Nawalinski, and Alexander Peterson. Neal-Schuman, 2004. Paper $65.

Partnering with Purpose: A Guide to Strategic Partnership Development for Libraries and Other Organizations. By Janet L. Crowther and Barry Trott. Libraries Unlimited, 2004. Paper $32.

Political Advocacy for School Librarians: You Have the Power! By Sandy Schuckett. Linworth Publishing, 2004. Paper $39.95.

The Successful Library Trustee Handbook. By Mary Y. Moore. American Library Association, 2004. Paper $32.

Why Libraries Matter: A Story Long Overdue. By the Alliance Library System. TumbleBooks, 2005. Animated online book, http://www.LibrariesMatter.com/books/index.cfm.

Buildings and Space Planning

Energy Management Strategies in Public Libraries. By Edward Dean. Libris Design, 2002. Paper $35.

Libraries Designed for Users: A 21st Century Guide. By Nolan Lushington. Neal-Schuman, 2002. Paper $99.95.

Library as Place: Rethinking Roles, Rethinking Space. Council on Library and Information Resources, 2005. Download pdf from http://www.clir.org/pubs/abstract/pub/29abst.html.

The Library as Place: Symposium on Building and Revitalizing Health Sciences Libraries in the Digital Age. National Library of Medicine and Association of Academic Health Sciences Libraries, 2004. DVD $10 or download from http//:www.aahsl.org/building.

The Most Beautiful Libraries in the World. By Jacques Bosser. Abrams, 2003. $50.

Cataloging and Classification

Authority Control in Organizing and Accessing Information: Definition and International Experience. Ed. by Arlene G. Taylor and Barbara B. Tillett. Haworth Press, 2005. Paper $34.95.

Cataloging and Organizing Digital Resources: A How-to-Do-It Manual for Librarians. By Anne M. Mitchell and Brian E. Surratt. Neal-Schuman, 2005. Paper $75.

Cataloging Correctly for Kids: An Introduction to the Tools. 4th ed. Ed. by Sheila S. Intner, Joanna F. Fountain, and Jane E. Gilchrist. American Library Association, 2005. Paper $32.

Cataloging with AACR2 and MARC21: For Books, Electronic Resources, Sound Recordings, Videorecordings, and Serials. 2nd ed. By Deborah A. Fritz. American Library Association, 2004. Loose-leaf $68.

The Concise AACR2. 4th ed. By Michael Gorman. American Library Association, 2004. Paper $40.

Maxwell's Handbook for AACR2: Explaining and Illustrating the Anglo-American Cataloguing Rules Through the 2003 Update. 4th ed. By Robert L. Maxwell. American Library Association, 2004. Paper $65.

Metadata: A Cataloger's Primer. Ed. by Richard P. Smiraglia. Haworth Press, 2005. Paper $39.95.

Metadata in Practice. Ed. by Diane I. Hillman and Elaine L. Westbrooks. American Library Association, 2004. Paper $50.

Understanding Metadata. National Information Standards Organization, 2004. Free pdf download file from http://www.niso.org.

Wynar's Introduction to Cataloging and Classification. Revised 9th ed. By Arlene G. Taylor. Libraries Unlimited, 2004. $49.50.

Children's and Young Adult Services and Materials

Boys and Literacy: Practical Strategies for Librarians, Teachers and Parents. By Elizabeth Knowles and Martha Smith. Libraries Unlimited, 2005. Paper $35.

Collection Management for Youth: Responding to the Needs of Learners. By Sandra Hughes-Hassell and Jacqueline C. Mancall. American Library Association, 2005. Paper $35.

Cool Story Programs for the School-Age Crowd. By Rob Reid. American Library Association, 2004. Paper $32.

Digital Inclusion, Teens, and Your Library: Exploring the Issues and Acting on Them. By Lesley S. J. Farmer. Libraries Unlimited, 2005. Paper $39.

Early Literacy Storytimes @ your library: Partnering with Caregivers for Success. By Saroj Nadkarni Ghoting and Pamela Martin-Diaz. American Library Association, 2005. Paper $45.

Fiore's Summer Reading Program Handbook: A How-to-Do-It Manual. By Carole D. Fiore. Neal-Schuman, 2005. Paper $65.

Fundamentals of Children's Services. By Michael Sullivan. American Library Association, 2005. Paper $45.

Hooking Teens with the Net. By Linda W. Braun. Neal-Schuman, 2003. Paper $45.

I Found it on the Internet: Coming of Age Online. By Frances Jacobson Harris. American Library Association, 2005. Paper $35.

Library Teen Advisory Groups. By Diane P. Tuccillo. Scarecrow Press, 2005. $29.95.

Neal-Schuman Guide to Celebrations and Holidays Around the World: The Best Books, Media, and Multicultural Learning Activities. By Kathryn I. Matthew and Joy L. Lowe. Neal-Schuman, 2004. Paper $65.

The Newbery and Caldecott Awards: A Guide to the Medal and Honor Books. By the Association for Library Service to Children/American Library Association, 2005. Paper $19.

Rhyming, Writing, and Role-Play: Quick and Easy Lessons for Beginning Readers. By Mary A. Lombardo. Linworth Publishing, 2004. Paper $15.95.

Twenty Tellable Tales: Audience Participation Folktales for the Beginning Storyteller. By Margaret Read MacDonald. American Library Association, 2004. Paper $28.

Collection Development

Collection Management and Strategic Access to Digital Resources: The New Challenges for Research Libraries. Ed. by Sul H. Lee. Haworth Press, 2005. Paper $19.95.

The Coretta Scott King Awards: 1970–2004. 3rd ed. Ed. by Henrietta M. Smith. American Library Association, 2004. Paper $35.

From A to Zine: Building a Winning Zine Collection in Your Library. By Julie Bartel. American Library Association, 2004. Paper $35.

Graphic Novels in Your Media Center: A Definitive Guide. By Allison A. W. Lyga and Barry Lyga. Libraries Unlimited, 2004. Paper $35.

Graphic Novels Now: Building, Managing and Marketing a Dynamic Collection. By Francisca Goldsmith. American Library Association, 2005. Paper $35.

Guide to Licensing and Acquiring Electronic Information. By Stephen Bosch, Patricia A. Promis, and Chris Sugnet. Scarecrow Press, 2005. Paper $40.

The Kovacs Guide to Electronic Library Collection Development: Essential Core Subject Collections, Selection Criteria, and Guidelines. By Diane Kovacs and Kara L.

Robinson. Neal-Schuman, 2004. Paper $125.

Licensing in Libraries: Practical and Ethical Aspects. Ed. by Karen Rupp-Serrano. Haworth Press, 2005. Paper $29.95.

Reference Collection Development: A Manual. Ed. by Alice J. Perez. Reference and User Services Association/American Library Association, 2004. Paper $27.

Success by the Numbers: Statistics for Business Development. Ed. by Ryan Womack. Reference and User Services Association/American Library Association, 2005. Paper $24.

Copyright

Acquiring Copyright Permission to Digitize and Provide Open Access to Books. By Denise Troll Covey. Council on Library and Information Resources, 2006. Paper $25.

Carmack's Guide to Copyright and Contracts: A Primer for Genealogists, Writers, and Researchers. By Sharon DeBartolo Carmack. Genealogical Publishing, 2005. Paper $15.95.

Complete Copyright: An Everyday Guide for Librarians. By Carrie Russell. American Library Association, 2004. Paper $50.

Copyright: The Impact of Digital Networks and Technological Controls on Copyright and the Dissemination of Information in Higher Education. Association of College and Research Libraries/American Library Association, 2005. Paper $28.

Copyright Catechism: Practical Answers to Everyday School Dilemmas. By Carol Simpson. Linworth Publishing, 2005. Paper $36.95.

Copyright for Schools: A Practical Guide. 4th ed. By Carol Simpson. Linworth Books, 2005. Paper $44.95.

Copyright for Teachers and Librarians. By Rebecca P. Butler. Neal-Schuman, 2004. Paper $59.95.

Copyright Law and the Distance Education Classroom. By Thomas A. Lipinski. Scarecrow Press, 2005. Paper $37.50.

Copyright Law for Librarians and Educators: Creative Strategies and Practical

Solutions. 2nd ed. By Kenneth D. Crews. American Library Association, 2005. Paper $45.

Intellectual Property Rights: A Critical History. By Christopher May and Susan K. Sell. Lynne Rienner Publishers, 2006. $52.

Reserves, Electronic Reserves, and Copyright: The Past and the Future. By Brice Austin. Haworth Press, 2005. Paper $19.95.

Customer Service

Creating the Customer-Driven Library: Building on the Bookstore Model. By Jeannette Woodward. American Library Association, 2004. Paper $38.

Face It! Using Your Face to Sell Your Message. By Arch Lustberg. Library Video Network, 2002. Video $75.

High Tech, High Touch: Library Customer Service Through Technology. By Lynn Jurewicz and Todd Cutler. American Library Association, 2003. Paper $38.

Distance Education

Attracting, Educating, and Serving Remote Users Through the Web: A How-to-Do-It Manual for Librarians. Ed. by Donnelyn Curtis. Neal-Schuman, 2002. Paper $55.

Libraries Without Walls 5: The Distributed Delivery of Library and Information Services. Ed. by Peter Brophy, Shelagh Fisher, and Jenny Craven. Facet Publishing, 2004. $125.

Supporting E-Learning: A Guide for Library and Information Managers. Ed. by Maxine Melling. Facet, 2005. $99.95.

The Electronic Library

Building an Electronic Resource Collection: A Practical Guide. By Stuart D. Lee and Frances Boyle. Facet Publishing, 2004. Paper $75.

The Changing Landscape for Electronic Resources: Content, Access, Delivery, and Legal Issues. Ed. by Yem S. Fong and Suzanne M. Ward. Haworth Press, 2004. Paper $29.95.

E-Book Functionality: What Libraries and Their Patrons Want and Expect from Electronic Books. By Susan Gibbons, Thomas A. Peters, and Robin Bryan. Library and Information Technology Association/ American Library Association, 2003. Paper $34.99.

Electronic Theses and Dissertations: A Sourcebook for Educators, Students and Librarians. By Edward A. Fox, Shahrooz Feizabadi, Joseph M. Moxley, and Christian R. Weisser. Marcel Dekker, 2004. $79.75.

EScholarship: A LITA Guide. Ed. by Debra Shapiro. Library and Information Technology Association/American Library Association, 2005. Paper $32.

The Information Commons: A Public Policy Report. By Nancy Kranich. Brennan Center for Justice, New York University of Law, 2004. Free pdf download from http://brennancenter.org/resources/books.html.

Virtual Inequality: Beyond the Digital Divide. By Karen Mossberger, Caroline J. Tolbert, and Mary Stansbury. Georgetown University Press, 2003. Paper $19.95.

Evaluation of Library Services

Demonstrating Results: Using Outcome Measurement in Your Library. By Rhea Joyce Rubin. American Library Association, 2006. Paper $50.

How Libraries and Librarians Help: A Guide to Identifying User-Centered Outcomes. By Joan C. Durrance and Karen E. Fisher. American Library Association, 2004. Paper $42.

Libraries Act on Their LibQUAL+ Findings: From Data to Action. Ed. by Fred M. Heath, Martha Kyrillidou, and Consuella A. Askew. Haworth Press, 2004. Paper $29.95.

Library Collection Assessment Through Statistical Sampling. By Brian J. Baird. Scarecrow Press, 2004. Paper $29.95.

The Library's Continuous Improvement Fieldbook: 29 Ready-to-Use Tools. By Sara Laughlin, Denise Sisco Shockley, and Ray Wilson. American Library Association, 2003. Paper $35.

Measuring for Results: The Dimensions of Public Library Effectiveness. By Joseph R. Matthews. Libraries Unlimited, 2004. Paper $40.

Outcomes Assessment in Higher Education: Views and Perspectives. Ed. by Peter Hernon and Robert E. Dugan. Libraries Unlimited, 2004. Paper $50.

Fund Raising

Big Book of Library Grant Money, 2006. American Library Association, 2006. Paper $275.

Getting Grants in Your Community. By Sally Gardner Reed and Beth Nawalinski. Friends of Libraries U.S.A., 2005. Paper and CD-ROM $40.

Made Possible: Succeeding with Sponsorships. By Patricia Martin. Jossey-Bass, 2003. Paper $30.

National Guide to Funding for Libraries and Information Services. 8th ed. Ed. by Jeffrey A. Falkenstein. The Foundation Center, 2005. Paper $125.

History

A Brief History of the Future of Libraries. By Gregg Sapp. Scarecrow Press, 2003. $65.

The Encyclopedia of the Library of Congress: For Congress, the Nation and the World. Ed. by John Y. Cole and Jane Aikin. Bernan Press, 2005. $125.

Library: An Unquiet History. By Matthew Battles. W. W. Norton, 2003. $24.95.

The Road Home: My Life and Times. By Vartan Gregorian. Simon & Schuster, 2003. $29.95.

Wrestling with the Muse: Dudley Randall and the Broadside Press. By Melba Joyce Boyd. Columbia University Press, 2004. $29.50.

Information Literacy

Educating the Net Generation. Ed. by Diana G. Oblinger and James L. Oblinger. Download pdf from EDUCAUSE, http://www.educause.edu/books/educatingthenetgen/5989.

Information Literacy: Essential Skills for the Information Age. 2nd ed. By Michael B. Eisenberg, Carrie A. Lowe, and Kathleen L. Spitzer. Libraries Unlimited, 2004. Paper $48.

Integrating Information Literacy into the Higher Education Curriculum: Practical Models for Transformation. By Ilene F. Rockman. Jossey-Bass, 2004. $36.

Learning to Lead and Manage Information Literacy Instruction. By Esther S. Grassian and Joan R. Kaplowitz. Neal-Schuman, 2005. Paper and CD-ROM $75.

Library Anxiety: Theory, Research, and Application. By Anthony J. Onwuegbuzie, Qun G. Jiao, and Sharon L. Bostick. Scarecrow Press, 2004. Paper $39.50.

Media Literacy: Activities for Understanding the Scripted World. By Roberta S. Endich. Linworth Publishing, 2004. Paper $29.95.

Music Library Instruction. Ed. by Deborah Campana. Scarecrow Press, 2004. Paper $34.95.

Teaching Information Skills: Theory and Practice. By Jo Webb and Chris Powis. Facet Publishing, 2004. $99.95.

Teaching with Computers: Strategies That Work in Grades K–6. By M. Ellen Jay and Hilda L. Jay. Neal-Schuman, 2003. Paper $59.95.

Information Science

Introduction to Modern Information Retrieval. 2nd ed. By G. G. Chowdhury. Facet Publishing, 2004. Paper $89.95.

Spanning the Theory-Practice Divide in Library and Information Science. By Bill Crowley. Scarecrow Press, 2005. Paper, $45.

Understanding Information Systems: What They Do and Why We Need Them. By Lee Ratzan. American Library Association, 2004. Paper $58.

Intellectual Freedom

Banned Books Resource Guide. Office for Intellectual Freedom/American Library Association, 2004. Paper $35.

IFLA/FAIFE World Report on Libraries and Intellectual Freedom. IFLA/FAIFE, 2005. Paper 27 euros.

Intellectual Freedom Manual. 7th ed. ALA Office for Intellectual Freedom/American Library Association, 2006. Paper $52.

Libricide: The Regime-Sponsored Destruction of Books and Libraries in the Twentieth Century. By Rebecca Knuth. Praeger, 2003. $39.95.

Patriot Debates: Experts Debate the USA Patriot Act. Ed. by Stewart A. Baker and John Kavanagh. American Bar Association, 2005. Paper $29.95.

Privacy in the 21st Century: Issues for Public, School and Academic Libraries. By Helen R. Adams, Robert F. Bocher, Carol A. Gordon, and Elizabeth Barry-Kessler. Libraries Unlimited, 2005. Paper $40.

Refuge of a Scoundrel: The Patriot Act in Libraries. By Herbert N. Foerstel. Libraries Unlimited, 2004. $35.

Safeguarding Our Patrons' Privacy: What Every Librarian Needs to Know About the USA Patriot Act and Related Anti-Terrorism Measures. Association of Research Libraries, 2003. Video and manual $35.

Saving Our Children from the First Amendment. By Kevin W. Saunders. New York University Press, 2004. $48.

Interlibrary Loan, Document Delivery, and Resource Sharing

Interlibrary Loan and Document Delivery in the Larger Academic Library: A Guide for University, Research, and Larger Public Libraries. By Lee Andrew Hilyer. Haworth Press, 2002. Paper $24.95.

Interlibrary Loan Policies Directory. 7th ed. Ed. by Leslie R. Morris. Neal-Schuman, 2002. Paper $199.95.

Legal Solutions in Electronic Reserves and the Electronic Delivery of Interlibrary Loan. By Janet Brennan Croft. Haworth Press, 2004. Paper $19.95.

The Internet/Web

The Accidental Webmaster. By Julie M. Still. Information Today, Inc. 2003. Paper $29.50.

Internet and Personal Computing Fads. By Mary Ann Bell, Mary Ann Berry, and James L. Van Roekel. Haworth Press, 2004. Paper $15.95.

The Internet Under the Hood: An Introduction to Network Technologies for Information Professionals. By Robert E. Molyneux. Libraries Unlimited, 2003. Paper $40.

Library Web Sites: Creating Online Collections and Services. By A. Paula Wilson. American Library Association, 2004. Paper $35.

Net Effects: How Librarians Can Manage the Unintended Consequences of the Internet. Ed. by Marylaine Block. Information Today, Inc. 2003. $39.50.

Web-Based Instruction: A Guide for Libraries. 2nd ed. By Susan Sharpless Smith. American Library Association, 2005. Paper $52.

The Web Library: Building a World Class Personal Library with Free Web Resources. By Nicholas G. Tomaiuolo. Information Today, Inc. 2004. Paper $29.95.

Web Site Design with the Patron in Mind: A Step-by-Step Guide for Libraries. By Susanna Davidsen and Everyl Yankee. American Library Association, 2004. Paper $40.

XML: A Guide for Librarians. By Ron Gilmour. Library and Information Technology Association/American Library Association, 2003. Paper $29.

Knowledge Management

Knowledge Management: Libraries and Librarians Taking Up the Challenge. Ed. by Hans-Christoph Hobohm. K. G. Saur, 2004. 74 euros.

Knowledge Management Lessons Learned: What Works and What Doesn't. By Michael E. D. Koenig and T. Kanti Srikantaiah. Information Today, Inc. 2004. $44.50.

Librarians and Librarianship

The ALA Survey of Librarian Salaries 2005. American Library Association, 2005. Paper $70.

ARL Annual Salary Survey, 2003–2004. Association of Research Libraries, 2004. Paper $130.

Dewey Need to Get Organized? A Time Management and Organization Guide for School Librarians. By J'aimé L. Foust. Linworth Publishing, 2003. Paper $39.95.

Dismantling the Public Sphere: Situating and Sustaining Librarianship in the Age of the New Public Philosophy. By John E. Buschman. Libraries Unlimited, 2003. Paper $60.

Expectations of Librarians in the 21st Century. Ed. by Karl Bridges. Greenwood, 2003. $67.95.

The Image of Librarians in Cinema, 1917–1999. By Ray and Brenda Tevis. McFarland, 2005. Paper $45.

Jeremiad Jottings. By Blaise Cronin. Scarecrow Press, 2004. Paper $24.95.

Last One Out Turn Off the Lights: Is This the Future of American and Canadian Libraries? Ed. by Susan E. Cleyle and Louise M. McGillis. Scarecrow Press, 2005. Paper $45

The Librarian's Guide to Writing for Publication. By Rachel Singer Gordon. Scarecrow Press, 2004. Paper $34.95.

Librarianship and Information Science in the Islamic World, 1966–1999: An Annotated Bibliography. By Sterling Joseph Coleman, Jr. Scarecrow Press, 2005. Paper $60.

Our Own Selves: More Meditations for Librarians. By Michael Gorman. American Library Association, 2004. Paper $28.

Perspectives, Insights and Priorities: Seventeen Leaders Speak Freely of Librarianship. Ed. by Norman Horrocks. Scarecrow Press, 2005. Paper $24.95.

Public Speaking Handbook for Librarians and Information Professionals. By Sarah R. Statz. McFarland, 2003. Paper $39.95.

Reflecting on Leadership. By Karin Wittenborg, Chris Ferguson, and Michael Keller. Council on Library and Information Resources, 2004. Paper $15.

The Romance of Libraries. By Madeleine Lefebvre. Scarecrow Press, 2006. Paper $25.

Unfinished Business: Race, Equity and Diversity in Library and Information Science Education. Ed. by Maurice B. Wheeler. Scarecrow Press, 2005. Paper $38.

Women's Issues at IFLA: Equality, Gender and Information on Agenda: Papers from the Programs of the Round Table on Women's Issues at IFLA Annual Conferences, 1993–2002. Ed. by Leena Siitonen. K. G. Saur, 2004. $78.

Museums/Archives

Developing and Maintaining Practical Archives: A How-to-Do-It Manual for Archivists and Librarians. 2nd ed. By Gregory S. Hunter. Neal-Schuman, 2003. Paper $65.

Moving Archives: The Experience of Eleven Archivists. Ed. by John Newman and Walter Jones. Scarecrow Press, 2003. $35.

Thirty Years of Electronic Records. Ed. by Bruce I. Ambacher. Scarecrow Press, 2003. Paper $42.

Preservation

Assessing Preservation Needs: A Self-Survey Guide. By Beth Patkus. Northeast Document Conservation Center, 2003. Paper $15.

Developing Print Repositories: Models for Shared Preservation and Access. By Bernard Reilly, Jr. Council on Library and Information Resources, 2003. Paper $20.

National Digital Preservation Initiatives: An Overview of Developments in Australia, France, the Netherlands, and the United Kingdom and of Related International Activity. By Neil Beagrie. Council on Library and Information Resources, 2003. Paper $20.

Preparing for the Worst, Planning for the Best: Protecting our Cultural Heritage from Disaster. Ed. by Johanna G. Wellheiser and Nancy E. Gwinn. K. G. Saur, 2005. 78 euros.

Preservation and Conservation for Libraries and Archives. By Nelly Balloffet and Jenny Hille. American Library Association, 2005. $125.

Protecting Your Library's Digital Sources: The Essential Guide to Planning and Preservation. By Miriam B. Kahn. American Library Association, 2004. Paper $40.

Public Libraries

Author Day Adventures: Bringing Literacy to Life with an Author Visit. By Helen Foster James. Scarecrow Press, 2003. Paper $19.95.

Creating Policies for Results: From Chaos to Clarity. By Sandra Nelson and June Garcia. American Library Association, 2003. Paper $50.

Cultural Programming for Libraries: Linking Libraries, Communities, and Culture. By Deborah A. Robertson. American Library Association, 2005. Paper $35.

Exemplary Public Libraries: Lessons in Leadership, Management and Service. By Joy M. Greiner. Libraries Unlimited, 2004. $45.

Hennen's Public Library Planner: A Manual and Interactive CD-ROM. By Thomas J. Hennen, Jr. Neal-Schuman, 2004. Paper and CD-ROM $125.

Introduction to Public Librarianship. By Kathleen de la Peña McCook. Neal-Schuman, 2004. Paper $59.95.

The Public Library Manager's Forms, Policies and Procedures Handbook with CD-ROM. By Rebecca Brumley. Neal-Schuman, 2004. Paper with CD-ROM $125.

Public Library Data Service Statistical Report. Public Library Association/American Library Association, 2005. Paper $80.

The Public Library Start-Up Guide. By Christine Lind Hage. American Library Association, 2003. Paper $42.

Public Relations/Marketing

Blueprint for Your Library Marketing Plan: A Guide to Help You Survive and Thrive. By Patricia H. Fisher and Marseille M.

Pride. American Library Association, 2005. Paper $45.

Going Places with Youth Outreach: Smart Marketing Strategies for Your Library. By Angela B. Pfeil. American Library Association, 2005. Paper $32.

Library Marketing That Works! By Suzanne Walters. Neal-Schuman, 2004. Paper and CD-ROM $65.

Library Public Relations, Promotions and Communication: A How-to-Do-It Manual. 2nd ed. By Lisa A. Wolfe. Neal-Schuman, 2005. Paper $65.

Marketing Your Library. By Peggy Barber and Linda Wallace. Library Video Network, 2005. 20-minute video, VHS or DVD, $99.

Merchandising Strategies. Library Video Network, 2005. 22-minute video, VHS or DVD, $120.

Readers' Advisory

ALA's Guide to Best Reading. American Library Association, 2005. Kit $34.95. Camera-ready lists of the year's best books for children, teens, and adults.

The Booktalker's Bible: How to Talk About the Books You Love to Any Audience. By Chapple Langemack. Libraries Unlimited, 2003. Paper $30.

Booktalks and More: Motivating Teens to Read. By Lucy Schall. Libraries Unlimited, 2003. Paper $35.

The Horror Readers' Advisory: The Librarian's Guide to Vampires, Killer Tomatoes, and Haunted Houses. By Becky Siegel Spratford and Tammy Hennigh Clausen. American Library Association, 2004. Paper $36.

Readers' Advisory Service in the Public Library. By Joyce G. Saricks. American Library Association, 2005. Paper $38.

Reading and Reader Development: The Pleasure of Reading. By Judith Elkin, Briony Train, and Debbi Denham. Facet Publishing, 2003. $85.

Reference Services

Conducting the Reference Interview. Library Video Network, 2004. VHS or DVD $99.

Digital Reference Services. Ed. by Bill Katz. Haworth Press, 2004. Paper $34.95.

Digital Versus Non-Digital Reference: Ask a Librarian Online and Offline. Ed. by Jessamyn West. Haworth Press, 2004. Paper $29.95.

Going Live: Starting and Running a Virtual Reference Service. By Steve Coffman. American Library Association, 2003. Paper $42.

Introduction to Reference Work in the Digital Age. By Joseph Janes. Neal-Schuman, 2003. Paper $59.95.

The Librarian's Guide to Genealogical Services and Research. By James Swan. Neal-Schuman, 2004. Paper $75.

Puzzles and Essays from "The Exchange": Tricky Reference Questions. By Charles R. Anderson. Haworth Press, 2003. Paper $14.95.

Reading and the Reference Librarian: The Importance to Library Service of Staff Reading Habits. By Juris Dilevko and Lisa Gottlieb. McFarland, 2004. Paper $45.

The Virtual Reference Desk: Creating a Reference Future. Ed. by R. David Lankes, Eileen G. Abels, Marilyn Domas White, and Saira N. Haque. Neal-Schuman, 2006. Paper $75.

Virtual Reference Training: The Complete Guide to Providing Anytime, Anywhere Answers. By Buff Hirko and Mary Bucher Ross. American Library Association, 2004. Paper $42.

School Libraries/Media Centers

District Library Administration: A Big Picture Approach. By Cynthia Anderson. Linworth Publishing, 2005. Paper $44.95.

Essential Documents for School Libraries: I've-Got-It! Answers to I-Need-It-Now! Questions. By Colleen MacDonell. Linworth Publishing, 2005. Paper $44.95.

Guiding Students from Cheating and Plagiarism to Honesty and Integrity: Strategies for Change. By Ann Lathrop and Kathleen Foss. Libraries Unlimited, 2005. Paper $35.

The Power of Reading: Insights from the Research. 2nd. ed. By Stephen D. Krashen. Libraries Unlimited, 2004. Paper $25.

Power Tools Recharged: 125+ Essential Forms and Presentations for Your School Library Information Program. By Joyce Kasman Valenza. American Library Association, 2004. Loose-leaf with CD-ROM $55.

Redefining Literacy for the 21st Century. By David F. Warlick. Linworth Publishing, 2004. Paper $44.95.

Reference Skills for School Library Media Specialists: Tools and Tips. 2nd ed. By Ann Riedling. Linworth Publishing, 2005. Paper $44.95.

Seven Steps to an Award-Winning School Library Program. By Ann M. Martin. Libraries Unlimited, 2005. Paper $35.

The Whole School Library Handbook. Ed. by Blanche Woolls and David V. Loertscher. American Library Association, 2005. Paper $45.

Serials

Do We Want to Keep Our Newspapers? Ed. by David McKitterick. King's College London, 2003. Paper £15.

E-Journals: A How-to-Do-It Manual for Building, Managing, and Supporting Electronic Journal Collection. By Donnelyn Curtis. Neal-Schuman, 2005. Paper $75.

Introduction to Serials Work for Library Technicians. By Scott Millard. Haworth Press, 2004. $39.95.

The Nonsubscription Side of Periodicals: Changes in Library Operations and Costs Between Print and Electronic Formats. By Roger C. Schonfeld, Donald W. King, Ann Okerson, and Eileen Gifford Fenton. Council on Library and Information Resources, 2004. Paper $20.

Open Access Bibliography: Liberating Scholarly Literature with E-Prints and Open Access Journals. By Charles W. Bailey, Jr. Download pdf from http://info.lib.uh.edu/cwb/oab.pdf or $45 from Association of Research Libraries.

Serials in the Park. Ed. by Patricia Sheldahl French and Richard L. Worthing. Haworth Press, 2004. Paper $34.95.

Services for Special Groups

¡Bienvenidos! ¡Welcome! A Handy Resource Guide for Marketing Your Library to Latinos. By Susannah Mississippi Byrd. American Library Association, 2005. Paper $20.

Bridging the Digital Divide in the Spanish Speaking Community. Colorado State Library. Library Video Network, 2004. DVD $40.

From Outreach to Equity: Innovative Models of Library Policy and Practice. Ed. by Robin Osborne. American Library Association, 2004. Paper $32.

Improving the Quality of Library Services for Students with Disabilities. Ed. by Peter Hernon. Libraries Unlimited, 2006. Paper $45.

Library Services to Indigenous Populations: Viewpoints and Resources. Ed. by Kelly Webster. American Library Association, 2005. Paper $23.

Serving Seniors: A How-to-Do-It Manual for Librarians. By RoseMary Honnold and Saralyn A. Mesaros. Neal-Schuman, 2004. Paper $59.95.

Still Struggling for Equality: American Public Library Services with Minorities. By Plummer Alston Jones, Jr. Libraries Unlimited, 2005. $65.

Technical Services

The Complete Guide to Acquisitions Management. By Frances C. Wilkinson and Linda K. Lewis. Libraries Unlimited, 2003. Paper $45.

Guide to Out-of-Print Materials (ALCTS Acquisitions Guides Series #12). By Narda Tafuri, Anna Seaberg, and Gary Handman. Scarecrow Press, 2004. Paper $18.50.

In-House Book Binding and Repair. By Sharon McQueen. Scarecrow Press, 2005. Paper $35.

Innovative Redesign and Reorganization of Library Technical Services: Paths for the Future and Case Studies. Ed. by Bradford Lee Eden. Libraries Unlimited, 2004. Paper $45.

Integrating Print and Digital Resources in Library Collections. Ed. by Audrey Fenner. Haworth Press, 2006. Paper $29.95.

Technology

Directory of Library Automation Software, Systems, and Services. Ed. by Pamela Cibbarelli. Information Today, Inc. 2006. Paper $89. Published biennially.

Neal-Schuman Directory of Management Software for Public Access Computers. By Michael P. Sauers and Louise E. Alcorn. Neal-Schuman, 2003. Paper $99.95.

Technology for Results: Developing Service-Based Plans. By Diane Mayo. American Library Association, 2005. Paper $50.

Technology Planning: Preparing and Updating a Library Technology Plan. By Joseph R. Matthews. Libraries Unlimited, 2005. Paper $45.

Using PDAs in Libraries: A How-to-Do-It Manual. By Colleen Cuddy. Neal-Schuman, 2005. Paper $65.

Periodicals and Periodical Indexes

Acquisitions Librarian
Advanced Technology Libraries
Against the Grain
American Archivist
American Libraries
Behavioral and Social Sciences Librarian
Book Links
Booklist
Bookmobile and Outreach Services
The Bottom Line
Cataloging and Classification Quarterly
Catholic Library World
Children and Libraries: The Journal of the Association for Library Services to Children
CHOICE
Collection Management
College and Research Libraries
College and Undergraduate Libraries
Community and Junior College Libraries
Computers in Libraries

Criticas

DTTP: Documents to the People

Information Technology and Libraries

Information Outlook (formerly Special Libraries)

Interface

Journal of Academic Librarianship

Journal of Education for Library and Information Science

Journal of Information Ethics

Journal of Interlibrary Loan, Document Delivery and Information Supply

Journal of Library Administration

Journal of the American Society for Information Science and Technology

Journal of the Medical Library Association

Knowledge Quest

Law Library Journal

Legal Reference Services Quarterly

Libraries & Culture

Library Administration and Management

Library and Archival Security

Library and Information Science Research (LIBRES)

Library Hi-Tech News

Library Hotline

Library Issues: Briefings for Faculty and Academic Administrators

Library Journal

Library Media Connection (formerly Book Report and Library Talk)

The Library Quarterly

Library Resources and Technical Services

Library Technology Reports

Library Trends

Medical Reference Services Quarterly

MultiMedia and Internet @ Schools

Music Library Association Notes

Music Reference Services Quarterly

Net Connect

The One-Person Library

Portal: Libraries and the Academy

Progressive Librarian

Public Libraries

Public Library Quarterly

RBM: A Journal of Rare Books, Manuscripts, and Cultural Heritage

Reference and User Services Quarterly (formerly RQ)

Reference Librarian

Resource Sharing & Information Networks

RSR: Reference Services Review

Rural Libraries

School Library Journal

Science & Technology Libraries

Searcher

Serials Librarian

Serials Review

Technical Services Quarterly

Technicalities

Video Librarian

Voice of Youth Advocates (VOYA)

World Libraries

Young Adult Library Services

Ready Reference

How to Obtain an ISBN

Doreen Gravesande

Director
United States ISBN/SAN Agency

The International Standard Book Numbering (ISBN) system was introduced into the United Kingdom by J. Whitaker & Sons Ltd. in 1967 and into the United States in 1968 by R. R. Bowker. The Technical Committee on Documentation of the International Organization for Standardization (ISO TC 46) is responsible for the international standard.

The purpose of this standard is to "establish the specifications for the International Standard Book Number (ISBN) as a unique international identification system for each product form or edition of a monographic publication published or produced by a specific publisher." The standard specifies the construction of an ISBN, the rules for assignment and use of an ISBN, and all metadata associated with the allocation of an ISBN.

Types of monographic publications to which an ISBN may be assigned include printed books and pamphlets (in various product formats); electronic publications (either on the Internet or on physical carriers such as CD-ROMs or diskettes); educational/instructional films, videos and transparencies; educational/instructional software; audio books on cassettes or CD or DVD; braille publications; and microform publications.

Serial publications, printed music, and musical sound recordings are excluded from the ISBN standard as they are covered by other identification systems.

The ISBN is used by publishers, distributors, wholesalers, bookstores, and libraries, among others, in 217 countries and territories as an ordering and inventory system. It expedites the collection of data on new and forthcoming editions of monographic publications for print and electronic directories used by the book trade. Its use also facilitates rights management and the monitoring of sales data for the publishing industry.

The current ISBN consists of 10 digits. On January 1, 2007, a revised ISBN standard will change the ISBN to a 13-digit identifier that will substantially increase the numbering capacity of the worldwide ISBN system.

All existing 10-digit ISBNs at that time will be converted to a 13-digit ISBN by the addition of the Bookland EAN prefix 978 (as is currently done when a 10-digit ISBN is converted to a 13-digit bar code).

Once all 10-digit ISBNs have been exhausted by national ISBN agencies, the International ISBN Agency will begin allocating new complete 13-digit ISBNs with the EAN prefix 979.

Construction of an ISBN

An ISBN currently consists of 10 digits separated into the following parts:

1 Group identifier: national, regional, or geographic area
2 Publisher or producer identifier
3 Title identifier
4 Check digit

When an ISBN is written or printed, it should be preceded by the letters ISBN, and each part should be separated by a space or hyphen. In the United States, the hyphen is used for separation, as in the following example: ISBN 1-879500-01-9. In this example, 1 is the group identifier, 879500 is the publisher identifier, 01 is the title identifier, and 9 is the check digit. The group of English-speaking countries, which includes the United States, Australia, Canada, New Zealand, and the United Kingdom, uses the group identifiers 0 and 1.

The ISBN Organization

The administration of the ISBN system is carried out at three levels—through the International ISBN Agency in Berlin, through the national agencies, and through the publishing houses themselves. The International ISBN Agency in Berlin, which is responsible for assigning country prefixes and for coordinating the worldwide implementation of the system, has an advisory panel that represents the International Organization for Standardization (ISO), publishers, and libraries. The International ISBN Agency publishes the *Publishers International ISBN Directory,* which is a listing of all national agencies' publishers with their assigned ISBN publisher prefixes. R. R. Bowker, as the publisher of *Books In Print* with its extensive and varied database of publishers' addresses, was the obvious place to initiate the ISBN system and to provide the service to the U.S. publishing industry. To date, the U.S. ISBN Agency has entered more than 170,000 publishers into the system.

ISBN Assignment Procedure

Assignment of ISBNs is a shared endeavor between the U.S. ISBN Agency and the publisher. Publishers can make online application through the ISBN Agency's Web site, or by phone or fax. After an application is received and processed by the agency, an ISBN Publisher Prefix is assigned, along with a computer-generated block of ISBNs that is mailed or e-mailed to the publisher. The publisher then has the responsibility to assign an ISBN to each title, keep an accurate record of each number assigned, and register each title in the *Books In Print* database at http://www.bowkerlink.com. It is the responsibility of the ISBN Agency to validate assigned ISBNs and keep a record of all ISBN publisher prefixes in circulation.

ISBN implementation is very much market-driven. Major distributors, wholesalers, retailers, and so forth recognize the necessity of the ISBN system and request that publishers register with the ISBN Agency. Also, the ISBN is a mandatory bibliographic element in the International Standard Bibliographical Description (ISBD). The Library of Congress Cataloging in Publication (CIP) Division directs publishers to the agency to obtain their ISBN prefixes.

Location and Display of the ISBN

On books, pamphlets, and other printed material, the ISBN shall be printed on the verso of the title leaf or, if this is not possible, at the foot of the title leaf itself. It should also appear on the outside back cover or on the back of the jacket if the book has one (the lower right-hand corner is recommended). The ISBN shall also appear on any accompanying promotional materials following the provisions for location according to the format of the material.

On other monographic publications, the ISBN shall appear on the title or credit frames and any labels permanently affixed to the publication. If the publication is issued in a container that is an integral part of the publication, the ISBN shall be displayed on the label. If it is not possible to place the ISBN on the item or its label, then the number should be displayed on the bottom or the back of the container, box, sleeve, or frame. It should also appear on any accompanying material, including each component of a multi-type publication.

Printing of ISBN in Machine-Readable Coding

All books should carry ISBNs in Bookland EAN bar code machine-readable format. All ISBN Bookland EAN bar codes start with the EAN prefix 978 for books (see Figure 1).

The 978 ISBN Bookland/EAN prefix is followed by the first nine digits of the ISBN. The check digit of the ISBN is dropped and replaced by a check digit calculated according to the EAN rules.

Figure 1 / Printing the ISBN in Bookland/EAN Symbology

The following is an example of the conversion of the ISBN to ISBN Bookland/EAN:

ISBN	1-879500-01-9
ISBN without check digit	1-879500-01
Adding EAN flag	978187950001
EAN with EAN check digit	9781879500013

After January 1, 2007, publishers with existing 10-digit ISBNs will need to convert them to a 13-digit ISBN by the addition of the EAN prefix 978 (see Figure 1 above).

It is recommended that the ISBN-13 and ISBN-10 should be printed on the copyright page on publications from now until the transition to the ISBN-13 has been made final. There is no need to print the ISBN-13 and ISBN-10 on the back of the publications, provided there is an EAN-13 bar code. If an EAN bar code is not printed on the back cover, it is recommended that both the ISBN-13 and ISBN-10 should also be printed there in addition to the copyright page. This procedure, when implemented, will allow the ISBN 10 to be easily deleted from reprints after 2007 with little or no cost to the publisher/printer. Below is an example of how the ISBN 13 and ISBN 10 should now be printed on publications (please note that this is a sample ISBN only):

ISBN-13: 978-1-873671-00-9

ISBN-10: 1-873671-00-8

A new 13-digit ISBN beginning with the EAN prefix 979 and issued by the International ISBN Agency will not require conversion.

Five-Digit Add-On Code

In the United States, a five-digit add-on code is used for additional information. In the publishing industry, this code is used for price information. The lead digit of the five-digit add-on has been designated a currency identifier, when the add-on is used for price. Number 5 is the code for the U.S. dollar; 6 denotes the Canadian dollar; 1 the British pound; 3 the Australian dollar; and 4 the New Zealand dollar. Publishers that do not want to indicate price in the add-on should print the code 90000 (see Figure 2).

Figure 2 / Printing the ISBN Bookland/EAN Number in Bar Code with the Five-Digit Add-On Code

978 = ISBN Bookland/EAN prefix
5 + Code for U.S. $
0995 = $9.95

90000 means no information
in the add-on code

Reporting the Title and the ISBN

After the publisher reports a title to the ISBN Agency, the number is validated and the title is listed in the many R. R. Bowker hard-copy and electronic publications, including *Books in Print; Forthcoming Books; Paperbound Books in Print; Books in Print Supplement; Books Out of Print; Books in Print Online; Books in Print Plus-CD ROM; Children's Books in Print; Subject Guide to Children's Books in Print; Books Out Loud: Bowker's Guide to AudioBooks; Bowker's Complete Video Directory; The Software Encyclopedia; Software for Schools;* and other specialized publications.

For ISBN application and information, visit the ISBN Agency Web site at http://www.isbn.org, call the toll free number 877-310-7333, fax 908-219-0188, or write to the United States ISBN Agency, 630 Central Ave., New Providence, NJ 07974.

How to Obtain an ISSN

National Serials Data Program
Library of Congress

In the early 1970s the rapid increase in the production and dissemination of information and an intensified desire to exchange information about serials in computerized form among different systems and organizations made it increasingly clear that a means to identify serial publications at an international level was needed. The International Standard Serial Number (ISSN) was developed and has become the internationally accepted code for identifying serial publications.

The number itself has no significance other than as a brief, unique, and unambiguous identifier. It is an international standard, ISO 3297, as well as a U.S. standard, ANSI/NISO Z39.9. The ISSN consists of eight digits in Arabic numerals 0 to 9, except for the last, or check, digit, which can be an X. The numbers appear as two groups of four digits separated by a hyphen and preceded by the letters ISSN—for example, ISSN 1234-5679.

The ISSN is not self-assigned by publishers. Administration of the ISSN is coordinated through the ISSN Network, an intergovernmental organization within the UNESCO/UNISIST program. The network consists of national and regional centers, coordinated by the ISSN International Centre, located in Paris. Centers have the responsibility to register serials published in their respective countries.

Because serials are generally known and cited by title, assignment of the ISSN is inseparably linked to the key title, a standardized form of the title derived from information in the serial issue. Only one ISSN can be assigned to a title in a particular medium. For titles issued in multiple media, e.g., print, online, CD-ROM, a separate ISSN is assigned to each medium version. If a title change occurs or the medium changes, a new ISSN must be assigned. Centers responsible for assigning ISSNs also construct the key title and create an associated bibliographic record.

The ISSN International Centre handles ISSN assignments for international organizations and for countries that do not have a national center. It also maintains and distributes the collective ISSN database that contains bibliographic records corresponding to each ISSN assignment as reported by the rest of the network. The database contains more than 1 million ISSNs.

In the United States, the National Serials Data Program at the Library of Congress is responsible for assigning and maintaining the ISSNs for all U.S. serial titles. Publishers wishing to have an ISSN assigned should request an application form from the program, or download one from the program's Web site, and ask for an assignment. Assignment of the ISSN is free, and there is no charge for its use.

The ISSN is used all over the world by serial publishers to distinguish similar titles from each other. It is used by subscription services and libraries to manage files for orders, claims, and back issues. It is used in automated check-in systems by libraries that wish to process receipts more quickly. Copyright centers use the ISSN as a means to collect and disseminate royalties. It is also used as an identification code by postal services and legal deposit services. The ISSN is included as a verification element in interlibrary lending activities and for union catalogs as a collocating device. In recent years, the ISSN has been incorporated into bar codes for optical recognition of serial publications and into the standards for the identification of issues and articles in serial publications. Another recent use for the ISSN is as a linking mechanism in online systems where the ISSN can serve to connect catalog records or citations in abstracting and indexing databases with full-text journal content via OpenURL resolvers or reference linking services.

For further information about the ISSN or the ISSN Network, U.S. libraries and publishers should contact the National Serials Data Program, Library of Congress, Washington, DC 20540-4160; 202-707-6452; fax 202-707-6333; e-mail issn@loc.gov. ISSN application forms and instructions for obtaining an ISSN are also available via the Library of Congress World Wide Web site, http://lcweb.loc.gov/issn.

Non-U.S. parties should contact the ISSN International Centre, 20 rue Bachaumont, 75002 Paris, France; telephone (33-1) 44-88-22-20; fax (33-1) 40-26-32-43; e-mail issnic@issn.org; World Wide Web http://www.ISSN.org.

How to Obtain an SAN

Doreen Gravesande

Director
United States ISBN/SAN Agency

SAN stands for Standard Address Number. It is a unique identification code for addresses of organizations that are involved in or served by the book industry, and that engage in repeated transactions with other members within this group. It is recognized as the identification code for electronic communication within the industry.

For purposes of this standard, the book industry includes book publishers, book wholesalers, book distributors, book retailers, college bookstores, libraries, library binders, and serial vendors. Schools, school systems, technical institutes, and colleges and universities are not members of this industry, but are served by it and therefore included in the SAN system.

The purpose of SAN is to facilitate communications among these organizations, of which there are several hundreds of thousands, that engage in a large volume of separate transactions with one another. These transactions include purchases of books by book dealers, wholesalers, schools, colleges, and libraries from publishers and wholesalers; payments for all such purchases; and other communications between participants. The objective of this standard is to establish an identification code system by assigning each address within the industry a unique code to be used for positive identification for all book and serial buying and selling transactions.

Many organizations have similar names and multiple addresses, making identification of the correct contact point difficult and subject to error. In many cases, the physical movement of materials takes place between addresses that differ from the addresses to be used for the financial transactions. In such instances, there is ample opportunity for confusion and errors. Without identification by SAN, a complex record-keeping system would have to be instituted to avoid introducing errors. In addition, problems with the current numbering system—such as errors in billing, shipping, payments, and returns—are significantly reduced by using the SAN system. SAN will also eliminate one step in the order fulfillment process: the "look-up procedure" used to assign account numbers. Previously a store or library dealing with 50 different publishers was assigned a different account number by each of the suppliers. SAN solved this problem. If a publisher indicates its SAN on its stationery and ordering documents, vendors to whom it sends transactions do not have to look up the account number, but can proceed immediately to process orders by SAN.

Libraries are involved in many of the same transactions as book dealers, such as ordering and paying for books and charging and paying for various services to other libraries. Keeping records of transactions, whether these involve buying, selling, lending, or donations, entails similar operations that require an SAN. Having the SAN on all stationery will speed up order fulfillment and eliminate errors in shipping, billing, and crediting; this, in turn, means savings in both time and money.

History

Development of the Standard Address Number began in 1968 when Russell Reynolds, general manager of the National Association of College Stores (NACS), approached R. R. Bowker and suggested that a "Standard Account Number" system be implemented in the book industry. The first draft of a standard was prepared by an American National Standards Institute (ANSI) Committee Z39 subcommittee, which was co-chaired by Russell Reynolds and Emery Koltay of Bowker. After Z39 members proposed changes, the current version of the standard was approved by NACS on December 17, 1979.

Format

The SAN consists of six digits plus a seventh *Modulus 11* check digit; a hyphen follows the third digit (XXX-XXXX) to facilitate transcription. The hyphen is to be used in print form, but need not be entered or retained in computer systems. Printed on documents, the Standard Address Number should be preceded by the identifier "SAN" to avoid confusion with other numerical codes (SAN XXXXXXX).

Check Digit Calculation

The check digit is based on *Modulus 11,* and can be derived as follows:

1. Write the digits of the basic number.   2 3 4 5 6 7
2. Write the constant weighting factors associated with each position by the basic number.   7 6 5 4 3 2
3. Multiply each digit by its associated weighting factor.   14 18 20 20 18 14
4. Add the products of the multiplications.   14 + 18 + 20 + 20 + 18 + 14 = 104
5. Divide the sum by *Modulus 11* to find the remainder.   104 -: 11 = 9 plus a remainder of 5
6. Subtract the remainder from the *Modulus 11* to generate the required check digit. If there is no remainder, generate a check digit of zero. If the check digit is 10, generate a check digit of X to represent 10, since the use of 10 would require an extra digit. 11 - 5 = 6
7. Append the check digit to create the standard seven-digit Standard Address Number.   SAN 234-5676

SAN Assignment

R. R. Bowker accepted responsibility for being the central administrative agency for SAN, and in that capacity assigns SANs to identify uniquely the addresses of organizations. No SANs can be reassigned; in the event that an organization should cease to exist, for example, its SAN would cease to be in circulation entirely. If an organization using an SAN should move or change its name with no change in ownership, its SAN would remain the same, and only the name or address would be updated to reflect the change.

The SAN should be used in all transactions; it is recommended that the SAN be imprinted on stationery, letterheads, order and invoice forms, checks, and all other documents used in executing various book transactions. The SAN should always be printed on a separate line above the name and address of the organization, preferably in the upper left-hand corner of the stationery to avoid confusion with other numerical codes pertaining to the organization, such as telephone number, zip code, and the like.

SAN Functions

The SAN is strictly a Standard Address Number, becoming functional only in applications determined by the user; these may include activities such as purchasing, billing, shipping, receiving, paying, crediting, and refunding. It is the system used by Pubnet, a leading publishing industry e-commerce exchange, and is required in all electronic data interchange communications using the Book Industry Systems Advisory Committee (BISAC) EDI formats. Every department that has an independent function within an organization could have a SAN for its own identification.

For additional information or suggestions, write to Paula Kurdi, ISBN/SAN Agency, R. R. Bowker, LLC, 630 Central Ave., New Providence, NJ 07974, call 908-219-0283, or fax 908-219-0188. The e-mail address is ISBN-SAN@bowker.com. The SAN Web site for online applications is at http://www.isbn.org.

Distinguished Books

Notable Books of 2005

The Notable Books Council of the Reference and User Services Association, a division of the American Library Association, selected these titles for their significant contribution to the expansion of knowledge or for the pleasure they can provide to adult readers.

Fiction

Bates, Judy Fong. *Midnight at the Dragon Café*. Perseus (1-58243-189-2).

Foer, Jonathan Safran. *Extremely Loud and Incredibly Close*. Houghton Mifflin (0-618-32970-6).

Gaitskill, Mary. *Veronica*. Pantheon (0-375-42145-9).

Ghosh, Amitav. *Hungry Tide*. Houghton Mifflin (0-618-32997-8).

Ishiguro, Kazuo. *Never Let Me Go*. Knopf (1-4000-4339-5).

Iweala, Uzodinma. *Beasts of No Nation*. HarperCollins (0-06-079867-X).

McCarthy, Cormac. *No Country for Old Men*. Knopf (0-375-40677-8).

McEwan, Ian. *Saturday*. Doubleday (0-385-51180-9).

Murakami, Haruki. *Kafka on the Shore*, translated by Philip Gabriel. Knopf (1-4000-4366-2).

Robinson, Marilynne. *Gilead*. Farrar, Straus & Giroux (037-415389-2).

Urrea, Luis Alberto. *The Hummingbird's Daughter*. Little, Brown (0-316-74546-4).

Nonfiction

Alexievich, Svetlana. *Voices from Chernobyl: The Oral History of a Nuclear Disaster*, translated by Keith Gessen. Dalkey Archive (1-56478-401-0).

Philip Boehm. *A Woman in Berlin: Eight Weeks in the Conquered City*. Henry Holt (0-8050-7540-2).

Bordewich, Fergus. *Bound for Canaan: The Underground Railroad and the War for the Soul of America*. Amistad (0-06-052430-8).

Cathcart, Brian. *The Fly in the Cathedral*. Farrar, Straus & Giroux (0-374-15716-2).

Diamond, Jared. *Collapse: How Societies Choose to Fail or Succeed*. Viking (0-670-03337-5).

Eichenwald, Kurt. *Conspiracy of Fools: A True Story*. Broadway (0-7679-1178-4).

Lepore, Jill. *New York Burning: Liberty, Slavery, and Conspiracy in Eighteenth-Century Manhattan*. Knopf (1-4000-4029-9).

Moorehead, Caroline. *Human Cargo: A Journey Among Refugees*. Henry Holt (0-8050-7443-0).

Packer, George. *The Assassins' Gate: America in Iraq*. Farrar, Straus & Giroux (0-374-29963-3).

Reiss, Tom. *The Orientalist: Solving the Mystery of a Strange and Dangerous Life*. Random (1-4000-6265-9).

Reynolds, David S. *John Brown, Abolitionist: The Man Who Killed Slavery, Sparked the Civil War, and Seeded Civil Rights*. Knopf (0-375-41188-7).

Walker, Steven. *Shockwave: Countdown to Hiroshima*. HarperCollins (0-06-074284-4).

Walls, Jeannette. *The Glass Castle*. Simon & Schuster (0-7432-4754-X).

Poetry

Alexander, Elizabeth. *American Sublime*. Graywolf (1-55597-432-5).

Dybek, Stuart. *Streets in Their Own Ink*. Farrar, Straus & Giroux (0-374-27095-3).

Best Books for Young Adults

Each year a committee of the Young Adult Library Services Association (YALSA), a division of the American Library Association, compiles a list of the best fiction and nonfiction appropriate for young adults ages 12 to 18. Selected on the basis of each book's proven or potential appeal and value to young adults, the titles span a variety of subjects as well as a broad range of reading levels.

Fiction

Adlington, L. J. *The Diary of Pelly D.* Greenwillow (0-06-076615-8).

Bechard, Margaret. *Spacer and Rat.* Roaring Brook (1-59643-058-3).

Black, Holly. *Valiant: A Modern Tale of Faerie.* Simon & Schuster (0-689-86822-7).

Bray, Libba. *Rebel Angels.* Delacorte (0-385-73029-2).

Bruchac, Joseph. *Code Talker: A Novel About the Navajo Marines of World War Two.* Dial (0-8037-2921-9).

Buckhanon, Kalisha. *Upstate.* St. Martin's (0-312-33268-8).

Castellucci, Cecil. *Boy Proof.* Candlewick (0-7636-2333-4).

Coburn, Jake. *LoveSick.* Dutton (0-525-47383-1).

Cummings, Priscilla. *Red Kayak.* Dutton (0-525-47317-3).

De la Peña, Matt. *Ball Don't Lie.* Delacorte (0-385-73232-5).

Delaney, Joseph. *Revenge of the Witch.* Greenwillow (0-06-076618-2).

Every Man for Himself: Ten Short Stories About Being a Guy. Ed. by Nancy E. Mercado. Dial (0-8037-2896-4).

Flake, Sharon G. *Bang!* Hyperion (0-7868-1844-1).

Fleischman, Paul. *Zap.* Candlewick (0-76362-774-7).

Frank, E. R. *Wrecked.* Simon & Schuster (0-689-87383-2).

Gaiman, Neil. *Anansi Boys.* HarperCollins (0-06-051518-X).

Galloway, Gregory. *As Simple as Snow.* Putnam (0-399-15231-8).

Green, John. *Looking for Alaska.* Dutton (0-525-47506-0).

Griffin, Adele. *Where I Want to Be.* Putnam (0-399-23783-6).

Grimes, Nikki. *Dark Sons.* Hyperion (0-786-81888-3).

Gruber, Michael. *The Witch's Boy.* HarperTempest (0-06-076164-4).

Halam, Ann. *Siberia: A Novel.* Random (0-385-74650-4).

Hartnett, Sonya. *Stripes of the Sidestep Wolf.* Candlewick (0-7636-2644-9).

Hautman, Pete. *Invisible.* Simon & Schuster (0-689-86800-6).

Hearn, Julie. *The Minister's Daughter.* Simon & Schuster (0-689-87690-4).

Hiaasen, Carl. *Flush.* Knopf (0-375-92182-6).

Holub, Josef. *An Innocent Soldier,* translated by Michael Hofmann. Scholastic (0-439-62771-0).

Jacobson, Jennifer Richard. *Stained.* Simon & Schuster (0-689-86745-X).

Johnson, Maureen. *13 Little Blue Envelopes.* HarperCollins (0-06-054141-5).

Kass, Pnina Moed. *Real Time.* Clarion (0-618-44203-0).

Kibuishi, Kazu. *Daisy Kutter: The Last Train.* Viper (0-9754193-2-3).

Krovatin, Christopher. *Heavy Metal and You.* Scholastic (0-439-73648-X).

Lanagan, Margo. *Black Juice.* HarperCollins (0-06-074390-5).

Larbalestier, Justine. *Magic or Madness.* Penguin (1-59514-022-0).

Larochelle, David. *Absolutely Positively Not.* Scholastic (0-439-59109-0).

Lester, Julius. *Day of Tears: A Novel in Dialogue.* Hyperion (0-7868-0490-4).

Levithan, David. *Are We There Yet?* Knopf (0-375-82846-X).

Lubar, David. *Sleeping Freshmen Never Lie: A Novel.* Dutton (0-525-47311-4).

Lynch, Chris. *Inexcusable.* Simon & Schuster (0-689-84789-0).

Lynch, Jim. *The Highest Tide: A Novel.*

Bloomsbury (1-58234-605-4).

Martinez, A. Lee. *Gil's All Fright Diner.* Tor (0-765-31471-1).

McGhee, Alison. *All Rivers Flow to the Sea.* Candlewick (0-7636-2591-4).

Meyer, Stephanie. *Twilight: A Novel.* Little, Brown (0-316-16017-2).

Myers, Walter Dean. *Autobiography of My Dead Brother.* HarperCollins (0-06-058291-X).

Oppel, Kenneth. *Skybreaker.* HarperCollins (0-06-053227-0).

Pearson, Mary E. *A Room on Lorelei Street.* Holt (0-8050-7667-0).

Peet, Mal. *Keeper.* Candlewick (0-7636-2749-6).

Perkins, Lynne Rae. *Criss Cross.* Greenwillow (0-06-009272-6).

Qualey, Marsha. *Just Like That.* Dial (0-8037-2840-9).

Riordan, Rick. *The Lightning Thief: Percy Jackson and the Olympians.* Hyperion (0-7868-5629-7).

Rowling, J. K. *Harry Potter and the Half-Blood Prince.* Scholastic (0-439-78454-9).

Salisbury, Graham. *Eyes of the Emperor.* Random (0-385-72971-5).

Spillebeen, Geert. *Kipling's Choice,* translated by Terese Edelstein. Houghton (0-618-43124-1).

Staples, Suzanne Fisher. *Under the Persimmon Tree.* Farrar (0-374-38025-2).

Stein, Tammar. *Light Years: A Novel.* Knopf (0-375-83023-5).

Thal, Lilli. *Mimus,* translated by John Brownjohn. Annick (1-55037-925-9).

Tiffany, Grace. *Ariel.* HarperCollins (0-06-075327-7).

Tingle, Rebecca. *Far Traveler.* Putnam (0-399-23890-5).

Tullson, Diane. *Red Sea.* Orca (1-55143-331-1).

Vaughan, Brian K. *Runaways: Volume 1,* illus. by Adrian Alphona. Marvel (0-7851-1876-4).

Vaught, Susan. *Stormwitch.* Bloomsbury (1-58234-952-5).

Volponi, Paul. *Black and White.* Viking (0-670-06006-2).

Waid, Mark, and others. *Superman: Birthright.* DC Comics (1-4012-0251-9).

Weaver, Will. *Full Service.* Farrar (0-374-32485-9).

Westerfeld, Scott. *Peeps.* Penguin (1-59514-031-X).

Westerfeld, Scott. *Uglies.* Simon & Schuster (0-689-86538-4).

Whitcomb, Laura. *A Certain Slant of Light.* Houghton (0-618-58532-X).

Wittlinger, Ellen. *Sandpiper.* Simon & Schuster (0-689-86802-2).

Wooding, Chris. *Poison.* Scholastic (0-439-75570-0).

Wynne-Jones, Tim. *A Thief in the House of Memory.* Farrar (0-374-37478-3).

Zusak, Markus. *I Am the Messenger.* Knopf (0-375-83099-5).

Nonfiction

Akbar, Said Hyder, and Burton, Susan. *Come Back to Afghanistan: A California Teenager's Story.* Bloomsbury (1-58234-520-1).

Bartoletti, Susan Campbell. *Hitler Youth: Growing Up in Hitler's Shadow.* Scholastic (0-439-35379-3).

Blumenthal, Karen. *Let Me Play: The Story of Title IX—The Law That Changed the Future of Girls in America.* Simon & Schuster (0-689-85957-0).

Bolden, Tonya. *Maritcha: A Nineteenth Century American Girl.* Abrams (0-8109-5045-6).

Deem, James M. *Bodies From the Ash: Life and Death in Ancient Pompeii.* Houghton (0-618-47308-4).

Delisle, Guy. *Pyongyang: A Journey in North Korea.* Drawn and Quarterly (1-896597-89-0).

Dendy, Leslie, and Boring, Mel. *Guinea Pig Scientists: Bold Self-Experimenters in Science and Medicine.* Holt (0-8050-7316-7).

Eisner, Will. *The Plot: The Secret Story of the Protocols of the Elders of Zion.* Norton (0-393-06045-4).

Farrell, Jeanette. *Invisible Allies: Microbes That Shape Our Lives.* Farrar (0-374-33608-3).

Fleming, Candace. *Our Eleanor: A Scrapbook Look at Eleanor Roosevelt's Remarkable Life.* Simon & Schuster (0-689-86544-9).

Frank, Mitch. *Understanding the Holy Land:*

Answering Questions About the Israeli-Palestinian Conflict. Viking (0-670-06032-1).

Giblin, James Cross. *Good Brother, Bad Brother: The Story of Edwin Booth and John Wilkes Booth.* Clarion (0-618-09642-6).

Growing Up in Slavery: Stories of Young Slaves as Told by Themselves, ed. by Yuval Taylor. Lawrence Hill (1-55652-548-6).

Jurmain, Suzanne. *The Forbidden Schoolhouse: The True and Dramatic Story of Prudence Crandall and Her Students.* Houghton (0-618-47302-5).

Lavender, Bee. *Lessons in Taxidermy.* Akashic (1-888451-79-3).

Nelson, Marilyn. *Fortune's Bones: The Manumission Requiem.* Front Street (1-932425-12-8).

Nelson, Marilyn. *A Wreath for Emmett Till,* illus. by Philippe Lardy. Houghton (0-618-39752-3).

O'Donnell, Joe. *Japan 1945: A U.S. Marine's Photographs from Ground Zero.* Vanderbilt (0-8265-1467-7).

Partridge, Elizabeth. *John Lennon: All I Want Is the Truth.* Viking (0-670-05954-4).

Zenatti, Valérie. *When I Was a Soldier: A Memoir.* Bloomsbury (1-58234-978-9).

Quick Picks for Reluctant Young Adult Readers

The Young Adult Library Services Association, a division of the American Library Association, annually chooses a list of outstanding titles that will stimulate the interest of reluctant teen readers. This list is intended to attract teens who, for whatever reason, choose not to read.

The list, compiled by a 12-member committee, includes fiction and nonfiction titles published from late 2004 through 2005.

Fiction

Adoff, Jaime. *Jimi and Me.* Hyperion (0-7868-5214-3).

Black, Holly. *Valiant: A Modern Tale of Faerie.* Simon & Schuster (0-689-86822-7).

Arakawa, Hiromu. *Fullmetal Alchemist.* Vol. 1, Viz Media (1-59116-920-8); Vol. 2 (1-59116-923-2); Vol. 3 (1-59116-925-9); Vol. 4 (1-59116-929-1).

Bradley, Alex. *24 Girls in 7 Days.* Dutton (0-525-47369-6).

Brown, Tracy. *Criminal Minded.* St. Martin's (0-312-33646-2).

Burke, Morgan. The Party Room Trilogy: *Get It Started.* Simon Pulse (0-689-87225-9); *After Hours* (0-689-87226-7); *Last Call* (0-689-87227-5).

Cary, Kate. *Bloodline.* Razorbill (1-59514-012-3).

Castellucci, Cecil. *Boy Proof.* Candlewick (0-7636-2333-4).

Clugston, Chynna. *Queen Bee.* Scholastic Graphix (0-439-70987-3).

Coy, John. *Crackback.* Scholastic (0-439-69733-6).

Dean, Zoey. *Blonde Ambition.* Little, Brown (0-316-73474-8).

Delaney, Joseph. *Revenge of the Witch: Book One—The Last Apprentice.* Greenwillow (0-06-076618-2).

De la Peña, Matt. *Ball Don't Lie.* Delacorte (0-385-73232-5).

Deuker, Carl. *Runner.* Houghton Mifflin (0-618-54298-1).

Flake, Sharon. *Bang!* Hyperion (0-7868-1844-1).

Flanagan, John. *Ranger's Apprentice: Book One—The Ruins of Gorlan.* Philomel/Putnam (0-399-24454-9).

Friedman, Aimee. *South Beach.* Scholastic (0-439-70678-5).

Goobie, Beth. *Something Girl.* Orca Soundings (1-55143-347-8).

Grant, Vicki. *Dead-End Job.* Orca Soundings (1-55143-378-8).

Green, John. *Looking for Alaska.* Dutton (0-525-47506-0).

Hiaasen, Carl. *Flush.* Random (0-375-92182-6).

Horowitz, Anthony. *Raven's Gate.* Scholastic (0-439-67995-8).

Horowitz, Anthony. *Scorpia.* Philomel (0-399-24151-5).

Kirkman, Robert. *Invincible: The Ultimate Collection, Vol. 1.* Image Comics (1-58240-500-X.

Klass, David. *Dark Angel.* Farrar, Straus & Giroux (0-374-39950-6).

Krovatin, Christopher. *Heavy Metal and You.* Scholastic (0-439-73648-X).

Lockhart, E. *The Boyfriend List: 15 Guys, 11 Shrink Appointments, 4 Ceramic Frogs, and Me, Ruby Oliver.* Random (0-385-73206-6).

Loeb, Jeph. *Superman/Batman: Vol. 1—Public Enemies.* DC Comics (1-4012-0220-9).

Mac, Carrie. *Charmed.* Orca Soundings (1-55143-321-4).

Mayer, Melody. *The Nannies.* Delacorte (0-385-73283-X).

Meyer, Adam. *The Last Domino.* Penguin Putnam (0-399-24332-1).

Meyer, Stephenie. *Twilight.* Little, Brown (0-316-16017-2).

Newman, Leslea. *Jailbait.* Delacorte (0-385-90230-1).

Olin, Sean. *Killing Britney.* Simon Pulse (0-689-87778-1).

Patterson, James. *Maximum Ride: The Angel Experiment.* Little, Brown (0-316-15556-X).

Riley, Andy. *Return of the Bunny Suicides.* Penguin (0-452-28623-9).

Rose, Malcolm. *Traces: Framed!* Kingfisher (0-7534-5829-2); *Traces: Lost Bullet* (0-7534-5830-6); *Traces: Roll Call* (0-7534-5923-X).

Shan, Darren. *Lord Loss.* Little, Brown (0-316-11499-5).

Shaw, Susan. *The Boy from the Basement.* Dutton (0-525-47223-1).

Shusterman, Neal. *Dread Locks: Dark Fusion, Book One.* Dutton (0-525-47554-0); *Red Rider's Hood: Dark Fusion, Book Two* (0-525-47562-1).

Sloan, Brian. *A Really Nice Prom Mess.* Simon & Schuster (0-689-87438-3).

Sorrells, Walter. *Fake ID: The Hunted—Book One.* Dutton (0-525-47514-1).

Standiford, Natalie. *The Dating Game.* Little, Brown (0-316-11040-X); *The Dating Game: Breaking Up Is Really, Really Hard to Do* (0-316-11041-8).

Stone, Jeff. *The Five Ancestors: Monkey.* Random (0-375-83073-1); *The Five Ancestors: Tiger* (0-375-83071-5).

Tiernan, Cate. *Balefire: A Chalice of Wind.* Penguin (1-59514-045-X); *Balefire: A Circle of Ashes* (1-59514-046-8).

Volponi, Paul. *Black and White.* Penguin (0-670-06006-2).

Whyman, Matt. *Boy Kills Man.* Harper (0-06-074664-5).

Williams, Lori Aurelia. *Broken China.* Simon & Schuster (0-689-86878-2).

Nonfiction

Baltin, Steve. *From the Inside: Linkin Park's Meteora.* Bradson Press (0-9603574-1-6).

Benton, Jim. *It's Happy Bunny: Life. Get One.* Scholastic (0-439-69346-2); *It's Happy Bunny: Love Bites* (0-439-69345-4).

Buckley, James Jr. *Scholastic Book of Firsts.* Scholastic (0-439-67607-X).

Caldwell, Ben. *Fantasy! Cartooning.* Sterling (1-4027-1612-5).

Caprio, Robert. *Are We There Yet? Tales from the Never-Ending Travels of WWE Superstars.* Simon & Schuster (0-7434-9041-X).

Carlson, Lori. *Red Hot Salsa: Bilingual Poems on Being Young and Latino in the United States.* Henry Holt (0-8050-7616-6).

Cosmo Girl Quiz Book: Discover Your Personality. Sterling (1-58816-489-6).

Davis, James. *Skateboarding Is Not a Crime: 50 Years of Street Culture.* Firefly (1-55407-001-5).

Edgar, Jim. *Bad Cat.* Workman (0-7611-3619-3).

50 Cent *From Pieces to Weight: Once Upon a Time in Southside, Queens.* MTV/Pocket Books (0-7434-8644-7).

Finkel, Jon. *Greatest Stars of the NBA: Jason Kidd.* Tokyopop (1-59532-183-7); *Great-*

est Stars of the NBA: Kevin Garnett (1-59532-184-5); *Greatest Stars of the NBA: Shaquille O'Neal* (1-59532-181-0); *Greatest Stars of the NBA: Tim Duncan* (1-59532-182-9).

Flaherty, Mike. *American Chopper: At Full Throttle.* Meredith (0-696-22165-9).

Foxworthy, Jeff. *Jeff Foxworthy's Redneck Dictionary: Words You Thought You Knew the Meaning Of.* Villard (1-4000-6465-1).

Ganz, Nicholas. *Graffiti World: Street Art from Five Continents.* Harry N. Abrams (0-8109-4979-2).

Grandberry, Omari. *O.* MTV Books (1-4165-0328-5).

Haab, Sherri. *The Hip Handbag Book: 25 Easy-to-Make Totes, Purses and Bags.* Watson-Guptill (0-8230-2263-3).

Happy Kitty Bunny Pony: A Saccharine Mouthful of Super Cute. Abrams (0-8109-9200-0).

Hart, Christopher. *Manhwa Mania: How to Draw Korean Comics.* Watson-Guptill (0-8230-2976-X).

Hee-Joon, Son. *PHD: Phantasy Degree* Vol. 1. Tokyopop (1-59532-319-8); Vol. 2 (1-59532-320-1).

Hess, Jared, and Jerusha Hess. *Napoleon Dynamite: The Complete Quote Book.* Simon Spotlight (1-4169-1391-2).

Keys, Alicia. *Tears for Water: Songbook of Poems and Lyrics.* Penguin Putnam (0-399-15257-1).

Kilpatrick, Nancy. *The Goth Bible: A Compendium for the Darkly Inclined.* St. Martin's (0-312-30696-2).

Lane, Billy. *Chop Fiction: It's Not a Motorcycle, Baby, It's a Chopper.* Motorbooks International (0-7603-2011-X).

Lee, Lela. *Angry Little Girls.* Abrams (0-8109-5868-6).

Mad About the '90s: The Best of the Decade. DC Comics (1-4012-0660-3).

Miller, Steve, and Brian Baugh. *Scared! How to Draw Fantastic Horror Comic Characters.* Watson-Guptill (0-8230-1664-1).

Oh, Minya. *Bling Bling: Hip Hop's Crown Jewels.* Wenner *1-932958-02-9.*

Ohba, Tsugumi. *Deathnote: Volume I—Boredom.* Viz (1-4215-0168-6).

Palmer, Chris. *Streetball: All the Ballers, Moves, Slams and Shine.* Harper (0-06-072444-7).

Perel, David. *Bat Boy Lives! The Weekly World News Guide to Politics, Culture, Celebrities, Alien Abductions, and the Mutant Freaks that Shape our World.* Sterling (1-4027-2823-9).

Polhemus, Ted. *Hot Bodies, Cool Styles.* Thames and Hudson (0-500-28500-4).

Powell, Michael. *Superhero Handbook.* Sterling (1-4027-2991-X).

The RZA. *The Wu Tang Manual.* Riverhead (1-59448-018-4).

Seventeen Magazine's Traumarama! Real Girls Share Their Most Embarrassing Moments. Hearst Books (1-58816-517-5).

Steffans, Karine. *Confessions of a Video Vixen.* Amistad (0-06-084242-3).

Sugiyama, Rika. *Comics Artists—Asia: Manga Manhwa Manhua.* Harper (0-06-058924-8).

Teen People Celebrity Beauty Guide: Star Secrets for Gorgeous Hair, Makeup, Skin and More! Time, Inc. (1-932273-39-5).

Wilson, Daniel. *How to Survive a Robot Uprising: Defending Yourself Against the Coming Rebellion.* Bloomsbury (1-58234-592-9).

Audiobooks for Young Adults

Each year a committee of the Young Adult Library Services Association, a division of the American Library Association, compiles a list of the best audiobooks for young adults ages 12 to 18. The titles are selected for their teen appeal and recording quality, and because they enhance the audience's appreciation of any written work on which the recordings may be based. While the list as a whole addresses the interests and needs of young adults, individual titles need not appeal to this entire age range but rather parts of it.

Acceleration, by Graham McNamee, read by Scott Brick. Listening Library, 5 hours and 30 minutes, 5 discs (0-3072-0733-1) or 4 cassettes (0-3072-0732-3).

Around the World in 80 Days, by Jules Verne, read by Jim Dale. Listening Library, 7 hours and 53 minutes, 7 discs (0-3072-0682-3) or 5 cassettes (0-3072-0628-9).

Artemis Fowl: The Opal Deception, by Eoin Colfer, read by Nathaniel Parker. Listening Library, 7 hours and 30 minutes, 6 discs (0-3072-4333-8) or 5 cassettes (0-3072-4331-1).

Bindi Babes, by Narinder Dhami, read by Nina Wadia. Listening Library, 4 hours and 21 minutes, 4 cassettes (1-4000-8538-1).

Bird, by Angela Johnson, read by Chantale Hosein, Kamahl Palmer, and Matthew Pavich. Listening Library, 2 hours and 10 minutes, 2 discs (1-4000-9926-9) or 2 cassettes (1-4000-9925-0).

Bras & Broomsticks, by Sarah Mlynowski, read by Arlene Meyers. Listening Library, 8 hours and 11 minutes, 7 discs (0-3072-0684-X) or 6 cassettes (1-4000-9879-3).

Buddha Boy, by Kathe Koja, read by Spencer Murphy. Full Cast Audio, 2 hours and 45 minutes, 3 discs (1-9320-7653-0).

Colibrí, by Ann Cameron, read by Jacqueline Kim. Listening Library, 4 hours and 45 minutes, 5 discs (1-4000-8993-X) or 3 cassettes (1-4000-8536-5).

Cruise Control, by Terry Trueman, read by Andy Paris. Recorded Books, 3 hours and 30 minutes, 3 cassettes (1-4193-3109-4).

Dear Zoe: A Novel, by Philip Beard, read by Cassandra Morris. HighBridge, 4 hours and 45 minutes, 5 discs (1-56511-942-8).

Fish, by L. S. Matthews, read by J. Lamia. Listening Library, 3 hours and 13 minutes, 3 discs (1-4000-8988-3) or 2 cassettes (1-4000-8521-7).

Flush, by Carl Hiaasen, read by Michael Welch. Listening Library, 5 hours and 23 minutes, 5 discs (0-307-28290-2) or 4 cassettes (0-307-28289-9).

Inventing Elliot, by Graham Gardner, read by Dominic Taylor. Listening Library, 4 hours and 45 minutes, 4 cassettes (1-8072-2320-4).

Lizzie Bright and the Buckminster Boy, by Gary D. Schmidt, read by Sam Freed. Listening Library, 6 hours and 49 minutes, 6 discs (0-307-28183-3).

Norman Tuttle on the Last Frontier: A Novel in Stories, by Tom Bodett, read by the author. Listening Library, 4 hours and 40 minutes, 4 discs (1-4000-9495-X) or 3 cassettes (1-4000-9057-1).

Pendragon, Book 1: The Merchant of Death, by D. J. MacHale, read by William Dufris. Brilliance, 12 hours, 10 discs (1-59737-238-2).

Princess in Training, by Meg Cabot, read by Clea Lewis. Listening Library, 6 hours and 17 minutes, 6 discs (0-307-20670-X) or 4 cassettes (1-4000-9876-9).

Prom, by Laurie Halse Anderson, read by Katherine Kellgren. Recorded Books, 5 hours and 45 minutes, 5 discs (1-4193-5610-0) or 4 cassettes (1-419-35097-8).

The Sea of Trolls, by Nancy Farmer, read by Gerard Doyle. Recorded Books, 14 hours, 12 discs (1-419-3082-03) or 10 cassettes (1-419-3209-04).

The Teacher's Funeral: A Comedy in Three Parts, by Richard Peck, read by Dylan

Baker. Listening Library, 4 hours and 42 minutes, 5 discs (1-4000-9496-8) or 4 cassettes (1-4000-9103-9).

Tiger, Tiger, by Lynne Reid Banks, read by Jan Francis. Listening Library, 5 hours and 3 minutes, 4 discs (0-3072-4638-0) or 3 cassettes (0-3072-4546-2).

The Truth About Forever, by Sara Dessen, read by Stina Nielsen. Recorded Books, 12 hours and 30 minutes, 8 discs (1-419-3387-9X) or 9 cassettes (1-4193-2648-1).

The Truth About Sparrows, by Marian Hale, read by Emily Janice Card. Listening Library, 5 hours and 36 minutes, 4 cassettes (0-3072-0720-X).

Whale Rider, by Witi Ihimaera, read by Jay Laga'aia. Bolinda Audio, 3 hours and 40 minutes, 4 discs (1-7409-3558-6).

The Young Man and the Sea, by Rodman Philbrick, read by Kirby Heyborne. Listening Library, 3 hours and 48 minutes, 3 cassettes (1-4000-9460-7).

Notable Recordings for Children

This list of notable recordings for children was selected by the Association for Library Service to Children, a division of the American Library Association. Recommended titles are chosen by children's librarians and educators on the basis of their originality, creativity, and suitability.

"Artemis Fowl, Book 4: The Opal Deception." Listening Library. Elementary–middle school. Nathaniel Parker reads this addition to Eoin Colfer's Artemis Fowl saga.

"A Bear Called Paddington." Harper Children's Audio. All ages. Michael Bond's classic story is told by Stephen Fry.

"Blues Journey." Live Oak Media. Backed by harmonica and guitar, Richard Allen brings alive Walter Dean Myers's poems.

"The Cay." Listening Library. Elementary–middle school. Michael Boatman narrates Theodore Taylor's survival story.

"Chronicles of Ancient Darkness 1: Wolf Brother." Harper Children's Audio. Elementary–middle school. Ian McKellen reads Michelle Paver's story of a mystical ancient world.

"Giddyup!" Prairie Dog Entertainment. All ages. A sing-along CD featuring western swing and bluegrass.

"The Goose Girl." Full Cast Audio. Middle school. Cynthia Bishop narrates Shannon Hale's retelling of the Grimm fairy tale.

"Gregor the Overlander." Listening Library. Elementary–middle school. Suzanne Collins's story is told by Paul Boehmer.

"Ish." Weston Woods. Preschool and up. Chester Gregory reads Peter Reynolds's fable of the creative power of "ish."

"Judy Moody Declares Independence." Recorded Books. Elementary. Kate Forbes is the voice of Judy in this version of Megan McDonald's story.

"The Last Apprentice: Revenge of the Witch." Harper Children's Audio. Middle school. Christopher Evan Welch narrates Joseph Delaney's fantasy, the first book in the Last Apprentice series.

"The Man Who Walked Between the Towers." All ages. Live Oak Media. Author Mordicai Gerstein narrates his Caldecott-winning chronicle of Philippe Petit's high-wire feat.

"The Minister's Daughter." Listening Library. Middle school–young adult. Heather O'Neill narrates Julie Hearn's story, set in the era of the English Civil War.

"The Old Country." Listening Library. Elementary–middle school. Mordicai Gerstein's novella is read by Tovah Feldshuh.

"A Pack of Lies." BBC/Chivers Children's Audio Books. Middle school–young adult. Andrew Sachs creates voices for such diverse characters as a crusty Chinese potter and a vain teenage girl in Geraldine McCaughrean's story.

"Private Peaceful." Recorded Books. Middle school–young adult. Michael Morpurgo's story of a family caught up in World War I is read by Jeff Woodman.

"Raven's Gate." Recorded Books. Middle school–young adult. Simon Prebble tells Anthony Horowitz's tale of supernatural suspense.

"Revenge of the Whale: The True Story of the Whaleship Essex." Audio Bookshelf. The true story of the whaler *Essex*, rammed and sunk by an enraged whale, is told by Taylor Mali.

"Scat Like That!" Rounder Records. All ages. Cathy Fink and Marcy Marxer blend music and education.

"Some Assembly Required." Razor & Tie. All ages. Tom Chapin leads a team of musicians in a collection of songs for the whole family.

"Songs from the Neighborhood." Memory Lane Syndication. All ages. Songs by Fred Rogers, television's "Mr. Rogers," are sung by musical celebrities including Jon Secada, Amy Grant, Ricky Skaggs, and Roberta Flack.

"The Star of Kazan." Recorded Books. Elementary–middle school. Patricia Conolly reads Eva Ibbotson's old-fashioned novel set in Vienna a century ago.

"Tiger, Tiger." Listening Library. Middle school–young adult. Lynne Reid Banks's novel, set in ancient Rome, is read by Jan Francis.

"Urchin of the Riding Stars." Listening Library. Elementary–middle school. Andrew Sachs tells M. I. McAllister's fable of treachery and intrigue set in a medieval animal kingdom.

"Will You Sign Here, John Hancock?" Weston Woods. Narrator Jeff Brooks echoes author Jean Fritz's light touch and gentle humor in this biography of the founding father.

Notable Children's Books

A list of notable children's books is selected each year by the Notable Children's Books Committee of the Association for Library Service to Children, a division of the American Library Association. Recommended titles are selected by children's librarians and educators based on originality, creativity, and suitability for children. [See "Literary Prizes, 2005" later in Part 5 for Caldecott, Newbery, and other award winners—*Ed.*]

Books for Younger Readers

Agee, Jon. *Terrific.* Illus. Hyperion (0-7868-5184-8).

Arnold, Katya. *Elephants Can Paint Too!* Illus. Simon & Schuster (0-689-86985-1).

Arnold, Tedd. *Hi! Fly Guy.* Illus. Scholastic (0-439-63903-4).

Beaumont, Karen. *I Ain't Gonna Paint No More!* Illus. by David Catrow. Harcourt (0-15-202488-3).

Bloom, Suzanne. *A Splendid Friend, Indeed.* Illus. Boyds Mills (1-59078-286-0).

Del Negro, Janice. *Willa and the Wind.* Illus. by Heather Solomon. Marshall Cavendish (0-7614-5232-X).

DiCamillo, Kate. *Mercy Watson to the Rescue.* Illus. by Chris Van Dusen. Candlewick (0-7636-2270-2).

Ehlert, Lois. *Leaf Man.* Illus. Harcourt (0-15-205304-2).

Graham, Bob. *Oscar's Half Birthday.* Illus. Candlewick (0-7636-2699-6).

Grey, Mini. *Traction Man Is Here!* Illus. Knopf (0-375-83191-6).

Guy, Ginger Foglesong. *Siesta.* Illus. by René King Moreno. Greenwillow (0-06-056061-4).

Hicks, Barbara Jean. *Jitterbug Jam: A Monster Tale.* Illus. by Alexis Deacon. Farrar (0-374-33685-7).

Juster, Norton. *The Hello, Goodbye Window.* Illus. by Chris Raschka. Hyperion (0-7868-0914-0).

Karas, G. Brian. *On Earth.* Illus. Putnam (0-399-24025-X).

Kerley, Barbara. *You and Me Together: Moms, Dads, and Kids Around the World.* Illus. National Geographic (0-7922-8297-3).

Mora, Pat. *Doña Flor: A Tall Tale About a Giant Woman with a Great Big Heart.* Illus. by Raúl Colón. Random/Knopf (0-375-82337-9).

Muth, Jon J. *Zen Shorts.* Illus. Scholastic (0-439-33911-1).

Park, Linda Sue, and Julia Durango. *Yum! Yuck! A Foldout Book of People Sounds.* Illus. by Sue Ramá. Charlesbridge (1-57091-659-4).

Priceman, Marjorie. *Hot Air: The (Mostly) True Story of the First Hot-Air Balloon Ride.* Illus. Simon & Schuster (0-689-82642-7).

Richardson, Justin, and Peter Parnell. *And Tango Makes Three.* Illus. by Henry Cole. Simon & Schuster (0-689-87845-1).

Rohmann, Eric. *Clara and Asha.* Illus. Roaring Brook (1-59643-031-1).

Rylant, Cynthia. *Henry and Mudge and the Great Grandpas.* Illus. by Suçie Stevenson. Simon & Schuster (0-689-81170-5).

Sayre, April Pulley. *Stars Beneath Your Bed: The Surprising Story of Dust.* Illus. by Ann Jonas. Greenwillow (0-06-057189-6).

Seeger, Laura Vaccaro. *Walter Was Worried.* Illus. Roaring Brook (1-59643-068-0).

Shannon, George. *White Is for Blueberry.* Illus. by Laura Dronzek. Greenwillow (0-06-029275-X).

Silverman, Erica. *Cowgirl Kate and Cocoa.* Illus. by Betsy Lewin. Harcourt (0-15-202124-8).

Van Leeuwen, Jean. *Amanda Pig and the Really Hot Day.* Illus. by Ann Schweninger. Dial (0-8037-2887-5).

Willems, Mo. *Leonardo the Terrible Monster.* Illus. Hyperion (0-7868-5294-1).

Winthrop, Elizabeth. *Squashed in the Middle.* Illus. by Pat Cummings. Henry Holt (0-8050-6497-4).

Middle Readers

Alarcón, Francisco X. *Poems to Dream Together/Poemas para Soñar Juntos.* Illus. by Paula Barragán. Lee & Low (1-58430-233-X).

Anderson, M. T. *Whales on Stilts.* Illus. by Kurt Cyrus. Harcourt (0-15-205340-9).

Armstrong, Alan. *Whittington.* Illus. by S. D. Schindler. Random (0-375-82864-8).

Birdsall, Jeanne. *The Penderwicks: A Summer Tale of Four Sisters, Two Rabbits, and a Very Interesting Boy.* Knopf (0-375-83143-6).

Borden, Louise. *The Journey that Saved Curious George: The True Wartime Escape of Margret and H. A. Rey.* Illus. by Allan Drummond. Houghton (0-618-33924-8).

Burleigh, Robert. *Toulouse-Lautrec: The Moulin Rouge and the City of Light.* Illus. Abrams (0-8109-5867-8).

Collard, Sneed B. *The Prairie Builders: Reconstructing America's Lost Grasslands.* Photographs by the author. Houghton (0-618-39687-X).

Delano, Marfé Ferguson. *Genius: A Photobiography of Albert Einstein.* National Geographic (0-7922-9544-7).

Erdrich, Louise. *The Game of Silence.* Illus. HarperCollins (0-06-029789-1).

Giovanni, Nikki. *Rosa.* Illus. by Bryan Collier. Holt (0-8050-7106-7).

Goscinny, René. *Nicholas.* Trans. by Anthea Bell, illus. by Jean-Jacques Sempé. Phaidon (0-71484-529-9).

Greene, Stephanie. *Queen Sophie Hartley.* Clarion (0-618-49461-8).

Himelblau, Linda. *The Trouble Begins.* Delacorte (0-385-73273-2).

Holm, Jennifer L., and Matthew Holm. *Babymouse: Queen of the World!* Illus. by Matthew Holm. Random (0-375-93229-1 hardcover, 0-375-83229-7 paperback).

Johnson-Davies, Denys. *Goha the Wise Fool.* Illus. by Hag Hamdy Mohamed Fattouh and Hany El Saed Ahmed. Philomel (0-399-24222-8).

Kerrin, Jessica Scott. *Martin Bridge, Ready for Takeoff!* Illus. by Joseph Kelly. Kids Can (1-55337-688-9).

A Kick in the Head: An Everyday Guide to Poetic Forms. Ed. by Paul B. Janeczko, illus. by Chris Raschka. Candlewick (0-7636-0662-6).

McKissack, Patricia C., and Onawumi Jean Moss. *Precious and the Boo Hag*. Illus. by Kyrsten Brooker. Simon & Schuster (0-689-85194-4).

Menchú, Rigoberta, with Dante Liano. *The Girl from Chimel*. Illus. by Domi, trans. by David Unger. Groundwood (0-88899-666-7).

Napoli, Donna Jo. *The King of Mulberry Street*. Random (0-385-74653-9).

Russo, Marisabina. *Always Remember Me: How One Family Survived World War II*. Illus. Simon & Schuster (0-689-86920-7).

Sabuda, Robert, and Matthew Reinhart. *Dinosaurs: Encyclopedia Prehistorica*. Illus. Candlewick (0-7636-2228-1).

Say, Allen. *Kamishibai Man*. Illus. Houghton Mifflin (0-618-47954-6).

Sidman, Joyce. *Song of the Water Boatman and Other Pond Poems*. Illus. by Beckie Prange. Houghton Mifflin (0-618-13547-2).

Singer, Marilyn. *Central Heating: Poems About Fire and Warmth*. Illus. by Meilo So. Knopf (0-375-82912-1).

Taback, Simms. *Kibitzers and Fools: Tales My Zayda Told Me*. Illus. Viking (0-670-05955-2).

Turner, Pamela S. *Gorilla Doctors: Saving Endangered Great Apes*. Illus. Houghton Mifflin (0-618-44555-2).

Williams, Mary. *Brothers in Hope: The Story of the Lost Boys of Sudan*. Illus. by R. Gregory Christie. Lee & Low (1-58430-232-1).

Winter, Jeanette. *The Librarian of Basra: A True Story from Iraq*. Illus. Harcourt (0-15-205445-6).

Winter, Jonah. *Roberto Clemente: Pride of the Pittsburgh Pirates*. Illus. by Raúl Colón. Simon & Schuster (0-689-85643-1).

Woodson, Jacqueline. *Show Way*. Illus. by Hudson Talbott. Putnam (0-399-23749-6).

Older Readers

Armstrong, Jennifer. *Photo by Brady: A Picture of the Civil War*. Illus. Simon & Schuster (0-689-85785-3).

Bartoletti, Susan Campbell. *Hitler Youth: Growing Up in Hitler's Shadow*. Scholastic (0-439-35379-3).

Blumenthal, Karen. *Let Me Play: The Story of Title IX, the Law That Changed the Future of Girls in America*. Illus. Simon & Schuster (0-689-85957-0).

Bolden, Tonya. *Maritcha: A Nineteenth-Century American Girl*. Illus. Abrams (0-8109-5045-6).

Broach, Elise. *Shakespeare's Secret*. Holt (0-8050-7387-6).

Bruchac, Joseph. *Code Talker: A Novel About the Navajo Marines of World War Two*. Dial (0-8037-2921-9).

Canales, Viola. *The Tequila Worm*. Random (0-385-74674-1).

Carvell, Marlene. *Sweetgrass Basket*. Dutton (0-525-47547-8).

Dowell, Frances O'Roark. *Chicken Boy*. Simon & Schuster (0-689-85816-7).

Ellis, Deborah. *Our Stories, Our Songs: African Children Talk About AIDS*. Fitzhenry and Whiteside (1-55041-913-7).

Fleming, Candace. *Our Eleanor: A Scrapbook Look at Eleanor Roosevelt's Remarkable Life*. Illus. Simon & Schuster (0-689-86544-9).

Frank, Mitch. *Understanding the Holy Land: Answering Questions About the Israeli-Palestinian Conflict*. Illus. Viking (0-670-06032-1).

Freedman, Russell. *Children of the Great Depression*. Illus. Clarion (0-618-44630-3).

Funke, Cornelia. *Inkspell*. Trans. by Anthea Bell. Scholastic (0-439-55400-4).

García, Laura Gallego. *The Legend of the Wandering King*. Trans. by Dan Bellm. Scholastic (0-439-58556-2).

Giblin, James Cross. *Good Brother, Bad Brother: The Story of Edwin Booth and John Wilkes Booth*. Illus. Clarion (0-618-09642-6).

Gruber, Michael. *The Witch's Boy*. Harper (0-06-076164-4).

Guys Write for Guys Read. Ed. by Jon Scieszka. Illus. Viking (0-670-06007-0 hardcover, 0-670-06027-5 paperback).

Hale, Shannon. *Princess Academy*. Bloomsbury (1-58234-993-2).

Hiaasen, Carl. *Flush*. Knopf (0-375-82182-1).

Holub, Josef. *An Innocent Soldier*. Trans. by Michael Hofmann. Scholastic (0-439-62771-0).

Howe, James. *Totally Joe.* Simon & Schuster (0-689-83957-X).

Jurmain, Suzanne. *The Forbidden Schoolhouse: The True and Dramatic Story of Prudence Crandall and Her Students.* Illus. Houghton Mifflin (0-618-47302-5).

Krull, Kathleen. *Leonardo da Vinci.* Illus. by Boris Kulikov. Viking (0-670-05920-X).

Lester, Julius. *Day of Tears: A Novel in Dialogue.* Hyperion (0-7868-0490-4).

Mwangi, Meja. *The Mzungu Boy.* Groundwood (0-88899-653-5).

Nelson, Marilyn. *A Wreath for Emmett Till.* Illus. by Philippe Lardy. Houghton Mifflin (0-618-39752-3).

Nye, Naomi Shihab. *A Maze Me: Poems for Girls.* Illus. by Terre Maher. Greenwillow (0-06-058189-1).

Perkins, Lynne Rae. *Criss Cross.* Illus. Greenwillow (0-06-009273-4).

Riordan, Rick. *The Lightning Thief.* Hyperion (0-7868-5629-7).

Salisbury, Graham. *Eyes of the Emperor.* Random (0-385-72971-5).

Staples, Suzanne Fisher. *Under the Persimmon Tree.* Farrar (0-374-380252).

Stauffacher, Sue. *Harry Sue.* Knopf (0-375-83274-2).

Varmer, Hjørdis. *Hans Christian Andersen: His Fairy Tale Life.* Trans. by Tiina Nunnally, illus. by Lilian Brøgger. Groundwood (0-88899-690-X).

Walker, Sally M. *Secrets of a Civil War Submarine: Solving the Mysteries of the H. L. Hunley.* Illus. Carolrhoda (1-57505-830-8).

Wilson, Jacqueline. *The Illustrated Mum.* Delacorte (0-385-73237-6).

Yee, Lisa. *Stanford Wong Flunks Big-Time.* Scholastic (0-439-62247-6).

Zenatti, Valérie. *When I Was a Soldier.* Trans. by Adriana Hunter. Bloomsbury (1-58234-978-9).

Zevin, Gabrielle. *Elsewhere.* Farrar (0-374-32091-8).

All Ages

A Family of Poems: My Favorite Poetry for Children. Ed. by Caroline Kennedy. Illus. by Jon J Muth. Hyperion (0-7868-5111-2).

Notable Children's Videos

These titles are selected by a committee of the Association for Library Service to Children, a division of the American Library Association. Recommendations are based on originality, creativity, and suitability for young children.

Boxes for Katje. Spoken Arts. Ages 5–9.

Ella the Elegant Elephant. Spoken Arts. Ages 4–6.

Ellington Was Not a Street. Weston Woods. Ages 5–12.

Ish. Weston Woods. Ages 4–9.

The Journey of Oliver K. Woodman. Nutmeg Media. Ages 5–9.

Kidnapped. WGBH Boston Video. Ages 10–14.

Kids Talkin' About Death. National Film Board of Canada. Ages 9–12.

The Man Who Walked Between the Towers. Weston Woods. Ages 8–14.

Peep and His Pals. WGBH Boston Video. Ages 3–6.

Portion Distortion: Seeing the Healthy Way to Eat. Human Relations Media. Ages 7–12.

Rainbows in the Sea. Earthwise Media. Ages 11 and up.

Roberto the Insect Architect. Weston Woods. Ages 5–8.

Stars! Stars! Stars! Weston Woods. Ages 5–9.

Wild About Books. Weston Woods. Ages 3–8.

Notable Software and Online Subscription Services for Children

This list is chosen by a committee of the Association for Library Service to Children, a division of the American Library Association. Titles are chosen on the basis of their originality, creativity, and suitability for young children.

Software

Alphabet Track, Eye Track, Phoneme Track. SEMERC (http://www.semerc.com). Ages 5 and up. Three programs designed for children with dyslexia, dyspraxia, and other learning problems. Windows/Macintosh.

Charles W. Morgan: Voyages of the Past, Present and Future. Mystic Seaport Museum (http://www.mysticseaport.org). Ages 8 and up. The whaling ship *Charles W. Morgan* comes alive in virtual 3D tours, detailed plans of the ship, video clips, games, and music. Windows/MacIntosh.

Essay Express: Strategies for Successful Essay Writing FableVision (http://www.fable vision.com/essayexpress). Ages 9 and up. The Rotten Green Peppers band leads a tour of essay writing with humor, music, and graphics. Windows/MacIntosh.

Britannica 2006. Encyclopedia Britannica (http://www.britannica.com). All ages. Three interactive reference libraries aimed at elementary and secondary students and adults include an encyclopedia, dictionary, thesaurus, timelines, a research organizer, audio clips, videos, and Web links. The elementary level also features games and activities. Windows/MacIntosh.

Subscription Services

Grolier Online. Grolier (http://go.grolier. com). This upgraded version features age-appropriate home pages, enhanced graphics, and updated and expanded content. Two encyclopedia interfaces are provided, for grades 3–5 and grades 6 and up. Activities include science projects, recipes, and puzzles and games. Windows/MacIntosh.

Bestsellers of 2005

Hardcover Bestsellers: Truth Is Stronger Than Fiction

Daisy Maryles
Executive Editor, *Publishers Weekly*

A year or so ago Kevin Trudeau and Alliance Publishing weren't on anyone's bestsellers radar screen. Not so in 2005: *Natural Cures "They" Don't Want You to Know About* was the leading hardcover adult bestseller, with sales of more than 3.7 million copies. If you factor in direct-to-customer sales via TV infomercials, the number goes even higher.

Says Alliance spokesperson Neil Sant: "Traditional methods of selling books through retail stores, although an important method of book distribution, is fast becoming only one of a growing number of viable channels for reaching potential book buyers." And this was another bestseller where controversy reigned, especially regarding many of Trudeau's medical pronouncements. But it didn't matter—consumers kept buying.

Most of the other nonfiction top sellers had the usual credentials: earlier bestselling titles, including some that won major book prizes; visible platforms, e.g., national print journalists, hosts, and regulars on national and cable TV shows, and beloved celebrities. *The Purpose-Driven Life* is on our year-end chart for the third time—the first two years it led the nonfiction lists and for 2005 it lands at No. 3. *Your Best Life Now* is No. 2; in 2004 it was No. 9. And while these two books led the religion and inspirational book parade, they were part of a larger group of such titles—24, a record for these annual lists. Warner Faith placed six books by Joyce Meyer, who was named one of the top 25 evangelical leaders in America by *Time* magazine.

Another category that enjoyed strong sales was cookbooks. Several of the top sellers, including Giada De Laurentiis and Paula Deen, drew fans from their shows on the Food Network. Leading the pack was Mireille Guiliano, No. 11 on our year-end list with about 970,000 copies sold—her winning diet allows chocolate and wine!

Biography and autobiography enjoyed lots of bestseller play this year, too. For the most part, historical biographies outsold books by and about contemporary figures.

On the fiction side, John Grisham is back in the top spot with *The Broker* (which garnered some of his best reviews, including a *Publishers Weekly* star); Dan Brown, who held the top rank in 2003 and 2004 with *The Da Vinci Code*, moves down a slot. James Patterson is the dominant author, with four books in the top 15—a record for these year-end charts. And while debut fiction took fewer slots among the year's bestsellers (five in 2005 vs. eight to ten in the past three years), the category was well represented by Elizabeth Kostova's *The Historian*, a book the author spent ten years researching and writing; it sold more than 850,00 copies. The only other newcomer to the top 15 is David Baldacci,

Adapted from *Publishers Weekly*, March 27, 2006.

Publishers Weekly 2005 Bestsellers

FICTION

1. **The Broker** by John Grisham. Doubleday (1/05) 1,827,877
2. **The Da Vinci Code** by Dan Brown. Doubleday (3/03) *1,576, 342
3. **Mary, Mary** by James Patterson. Little, Brown (11/05) 1,103,036
4. **At First Sight** by Nicholas Sparks. Warner (10/05) 1,093,717
5. **Predator** by Patricia Cornwell. Putnam (10/05) 1,040,250
6. **True Believer** by Nicholas Sparks. Warner (4/05) 1,039,065
7. **Light from Heaven** by Jan Karon. Viking (11/05) 872,000
8. **The Historian** by Elizabeth Kostova. Little, Brown (6/05) 853,676
9. **The Mermaid Chair** by Sue Monk Kidd. Viking (4/05) 872,000
10. **Eleven on Top** by Janet Evanovich. St. Martin's (6/05) 853,000
11. **Honeymoon** by James Patterson and Howard Roughan. Little, Brown (2/05) 797,046
12. **4th of July** by James Patterson and Maxine Paetro. Little, Brown (5/05) 745,227
13. **Lifeguard** by James Patterson and Andrew Gross. Little, Brown (7/05) 741,652
14. **S Is for Silence** by Sue Grafton. Putnam (12/05) 665,919
15. **The Camel** Club by David Baldacci. Warner (10/05) 634,054

NONFICTION

1. **Natural Cures "They" Don't Want You to Know About** by Kevin Trudeau. Alliance Publishing (6/05) 3,724,422
2. **Your Best Life Now: 7 Steps to Living at Your Full Potential** by Joel Osteen. Warner Faith (9/04) *2,562,906
3. **The Purpose-Driven Life** by Rick Warren. Zondervan (10/02) *2,500,015
4. **You: The Owner's Manual** by Michael F. Roizen, M.D., and Mehmet C. Oz, M.D. HarperResource (5/05) 2,000,000
5. **1776** by David McCullough. Simon & Schuster (**1,730,000)
6. **The World Is Flat** by Thomas L. Friedman. Farrar, Straus & Giroux (4/05) 1,535,731
7. **Love Smart: Find the One You Want—Fix the One You Got** by Dr. Phil McGraw. Free Press (12/05) **1,200,000
8. **Blink: The Power of Thinking Without Thinking** by Malcolm Gladwell. Little, Brown (1/05) 1,179,023
9. **Freakonomics: A Rogue Economist Explores the Hidden Side of Everything** by Stephen D. Levitt and Stephen J. Dubner. Morrow (5/05) 1,150,765
10. **Guinness World Records 2006** by Guinness World Records. Guinness Publishing (8/05) 983,000
11. **French Women Don't Get Fat** by Mireille Guiliano. Knopf (12/04) *970,000
12. **Teacher Man** by Frank McCourt. Scribner (11/05) 872,000
13. **Our Endangered Values** by Jimmy Carter. S&S (11/05) (**686,981)
14. **700 Sundays** by Billy Crystal. Warner (10/05) 685,000
15. **Team of Rivals: The Political Genius of Abraham Lincoln** by Doris Kearns Goodwin. S&S (10/05) **620,000

* All sales figures reflect books sold only in calendar year 2005. ** Sales figures were submitted to *Publishers Weekly* in confidence, for use in placing titles on the lists. Numbers shown are rounded down to indicate relationship to sales figures for other titles.

Note: Rankings are determined by sales figures provided by publishers; the numbers generally reflect reports of copies "shipped and billed" in calendar year 2005. Publishers were instructed to adjust sales figures to include returns through January 31, 2006. Publishers did not at that time know what total returns would be—indeed, the majority of returns occur after that cutoff date—so none of these figures should be regarded as final net sales. (Dates in parentheses indicate month and year of publication.)

Nonfiction: What's on Second?

How *Publishers Weekly* bestsellers compared with the rankings
at major chains, independents and wholesalers

PW Rankings	Sales Outlets*										
	BN/BNC.	W	B	BT	O	TC	E	BB	H	AM.C	BKS
1. Natural Cures . . .	7	1	3	3	—	—	—	—	2	27	14
2. Your Best Life Now	5	3	10	17	19	—	—	—	—	23	—
3. The Purpose-Driven Life	3	4	8	19	37	29	—	—	34	9	7
4. You: The Owner's Manual	8	5	4	4	—	15	37	—	3	2	9
5. 1776	1	2	1	2	3	3	11	16	4	5	1
6. The World Is Flat	2	6	2	1	1	2	3	9	21	1	2
7. Love Smart	56	—	—	—	—	—	—	—	49	—	—
8. Blink	4	10	6	5	2	1	2	—	56	4	3
9. Freakonomics	6	12	5	7	4	4	6	12	29	—	5
10. Guinness World Records	39	—	—	47	—	—	—	—	—	—	—
11. French Women . . .	9	15	9	11	6	12	—	—	23	11	4
12. Teacher Man	14	9	15	10	13	24	—	—	38	24	—
13. Our Endangered Values	11	11	13	9	—	14	26	—	17	22	—
14. 700 Sundays	—	—	—	—	—	—	—	—	—	—	—
15. Team of Rivals	13	8	7	14	7	7	7	8	—	17	—

Fiction: Who's on First?

How *Publishers Weekly* bestsellers compared with the rankings
at major chains, independents and wholesalers

PW Rankings	Sales Outlets*										
	BN/BNC.	W	B	BT	O	TC	E	BB	H	AM.C	BKS
1. The Broker	3	3	2	4	25	46	—	39	1	5	5
2. The Da Vinci Code	2	1	1	20	7	13	33	12	3	2	2
3. Mary, Mary	8	4	8	8	—	—	—	—	22	12	—
4. At First Sight	9	2	11	18	—	17	—	—	21	28	—
5. Predator	11	11	16	14	—	—	—	—	27	20	—
6. True Believer	7	5	7	13	—	—	—	—	12	25	9
7. The Mermaid Chair	4	18	5	3	19	3	43	6	34	4	1
8. Light from Heaven	18	13	18	29	—	—	—	—	26	18	—
9. The Historian	6	10	3	5	10	1	4	19	35	3	3
10. Eleven on Top	17	20	17	11	—	—	—	—	11	17	—
11. Honeymoon	10	8	10	10	—	—	—	—	—	—	—
12. 4th of July	12	7	9	12	—	—	—	—	41	26	—
13. Lifeguard	15	12	12	16	—	—	—	—	—	—	—
14. S Is for Silence	22	16	20	6	—	—	—	—	43	21	—
15. The Camel Club	14	21	14	24	26	—	—	—	—	27	—

* **BN/BN.C**	Barnes & Noble & B&N.com	**WB**	Waldenbooks
B	Borders	**BT**	Baker & Taylor
O	Olsson's	**TC**	Tattered Cover
E	Elliott Bay	**BB**	Books & Books
H	Hastings	**AM.C**	Amazon.com
BKS	Book Sense		

whose sales figures have been on an upward trend; *The Camel Club* sold more than 634,000 copies.

Missing in Action

More new nonfiction titles sold 100,000+ copies in 2005 than in fiction—154 vs. 136. Also, in nonfiction, nine books reported sales of 1 million+; four of those were in the 2 million+ range. In fiction, only six books had sales of more than 1 million (and two of those were by Nicholas Sparks).

Our weekly bestseller charts do not reflect sales through price clubs and major discounters, so sales in these outlets may have been stronger than in traditional stores. The charts on the previous page offer some insight on how the top 15 hardcovers in fiction and nonfiction fared in different kinds of retail outlets. In fiction, only four chart toppers—*The Broker*, *The Da Vinci Code*, *The Mermaid Chair* and *The Historian*—sold well in all venues. In nonfiction, *1776* and *The World Is Flat* were top sellers in all outlets polled; *700 Sundays* did not rank among the top 50 at any of these retailers.

As always, all our calculations are based on shipped-and-billed figures supplied by publishers for new books released in 2004 and 2005 (a few books published earlier that continued their tenures on our 2005 weekly lists and/or our monthly religion lists are included). These figures reflect only 2005 sales, and publishers were instructed not to include book club and overseas transactions. We also asked publishers to take into account returns through January 31; it would be safe to surmise that not all did. Sales figures on these pages should not be considered final. For many of these books, especially those published in the final third of the year, returns are not yet calculated.

The figures for all books listed below with a pound symbol (#) were submitted to *Publishers Weekly* in confidence, for use in placing titles on the lists. Numbers are rounded down to indicate relationship to sales figures of other titles.

The Fiction Runners-Up

16. *Blue Smoke* by Nora Roberts. Putnam (620,107)
17. *Toxic Bachelors* by Danielle Steel. Delacorte (#620,000)
18. *Forever Odd* by Dean Koontz. Bantam (#580,000)
19. *The Rising (Before They Were Left Behind)* by Tim LaHaye and Jerry B. Jenkins. Tyndale (532,409)
20. *Knife of Dreams* by Robert Jordan. Tor (514,833)
21. *The Regime: Evil Advances (Before They Were Left Behind)* by Tim LaHaye and Jerry B. Jenkins. Tyndale (480,442)
22. *The Interruption of Everything* by Terry McMillan. Viking (470,000)
23. *Saving Fish from Drowning* by Amy Tan. Putnam (466,547)
24. *Gabriel's Angel* by Nora Roberts. Harlequin/Silhouette (465,000)
25. *Impossible* by Danielle Steel. Delacorte (#450,000)
26. *Miracle* by Danielle Steel. Delacorte (#450,000)

27. *Lincoln Lawyer* by Michael Connelly. Little, Brown (439,446)
28. *No Place Like Home* by Mary Higgins Clark. Simon & Schuster (#433,000)
29. *Star Wars, Episode III: Revenge of the Sith* by Matthew Woodring Stover. Del Rey (431,426)
30. *Broken Prey* by John Sandford. Putnam (402,063)

300,000+

Polar Shift by Clive Cussler. Putnam (380,514)

The Da Vinci Code: Special Illustrated Edition by Dan Brown. Doubleday (379,700)

Two of a Kind by Nora Roberts. Harlequin/Silhouette, (375,000)

Ordinary Heroes by Scott Turow. Farrar, Straus & Giroux, (#370,000+)

A Breath of Snow and Ashes by Diana Gabaldon. Delacorte (#370,000)

Christ the Lord by Ann Rice. Knopf (361,000)

Son of a Witch by Gregory Maguire. Regan Books (350,000)

The Five People You Meet in Heaven by Mitch Albom. Hyperion (348,012; total sales, 6,464,395)

Point Blank by Catherine Coulter. Putnam (342,166)

Consent to Kill by Vince Flynn. Atria (342,000)

A Feast for Crows by George R. R. Martin. Bantam (#325,000)

Velocity by Dean Koontz. Bantam (#325,000)

Origin in Death by J. D. Robb. Putnam (321,452)

The Ambler Warning by Robert Ludlum. St. Martin's (310,152)

The Undomestic Goddess by Sophie Kinsella. Dial (#310,000)

Amazing Peace: A Celebration by Maya Angelou. Random House (301,420)

200,000+

The Divide by Nicholas Evans. Putnam (296,686)

The Closers by Michael Connelly. Little, Brown (291,194)

A Wedding in December by Anita Shreve. Little, Brown (285,295)

Every Breath You Take by Judith McNaught. Ballantine (283,940)

A Long Way Down by Nick Hornby. Riverhead (278,929)

Until I Find You by John Irving. Random House (265,797)

The Christmas Hope by Donna Van Liere. Integrity (262,176)

Chill Factor by Sandra Brown. Simon & Schuster (#255,000+)

Unexpected Blessings by Barbara Taylor Bradford. St. Martin's (253,388)

The March by E. L. Doctorow. Random House (248,926)

The Hostage by W. E. B. Griffin. Putnam (242,037)

Goodnight Nobody by Jennifer Weiner. Atria (242,000)

The Widow of the South by Robert Hicks. Warner (233,193)

The Lighthouse by P. D. James. Knopf (231,000)

There's Something About Christmas by Debbie Macomber. Mira (223,000)

On the Run by Iris Johansen. Bantam (#220,000)

The Wonder Spot by Melissa Bank. Viking (215,000)

Angels & Demons: Special Illustrated Edition by Dan Brown. Atria (214,000)

Everyone Worth Knowing by Lauren Weisberger. Simon & Schuster (#213,250)

In the Company of Cheerful Ladies by Alexander McCall Smith. Pantheon (213,000)

Rage by Jonathan Kellerman. Ballantine (212,473)

Saturday by Ian McEwan. Doubleday (207,096)

Prince of Fire by Daniel Silva. Putnam (204,989)

150,000+

Cold Service by Robert B. Parker. Putnam (199,081)

The Scorpion's Gate by Richard A. Clarke. Putnam (198,495)

Lipstick Jungle by Candace Bushnell. Hyperion (193,987)

Slow Burn by Julie Garwood. Ballantine (191,671)

Sunflower by Richard Paul Evans. Simon & Schuster (#190,000)

Two-Dollar Bill by Stuart Woods. Putnam (189,175)

Turning Angel by Greg Iles. Scribner (#188,000)

Memories of My Melancholy Whores by Gabriel García Márquez. Knopf (183,500)

Countdown by Iris Johansen. Bantam (#180,000)

Friends, Lovers, Chocolate by Alexander McCall Smith. Pantheon (180,000)

Marker by Robin Cook. Putnam (173,371)

Ya-Yas in Bloom by Rebecca Wells. HarperCollins (169,032)

The Innocent by Harlan Coben. Dutton (168,913)

Sweetwater Creek by Anne Rivers Siddons. HarperCollins (166,226)

No Country for Old Men by Cormac McCarthy. Knopf (165,500)

Prep by Curtis Sittenfeld. Random House (163,263)

Without Mercy by Jack Higgins. Putnam (162,329)

Haunted: A Novel by Chuck Palahniuk. Doubleday (161,797)

Iron Orchid by Stuart Woods. Putnam (157,661)

Vanish by Tess Gerritsen. Ballantine (157,383)

School Days by Robert B. Parker. Putnam (153,062)

A Good Yarn by Debbie Macomber. Mira (153,000)

Anansi Boys by Neil Gaiman. Morrow (150,335)

125,000+

Double Tap by Steve Martini. Putnam (148,310)

The Constant Princess by Philippa Gregory. Touchstone (#147,222)

First Impressions by Jude Deveraux. Atria (145,000)

All Night Long by Jayne Ann Krentz. Putnam (144,902)

The Christmas Blessing by Donna Van Liere. St. Martin's (141,213)

Match Me if You Can by Susan Elizabeth Phillips. Morrow (140,000)

Vanishing Acts by Jodi Picoult. Atria (140,000)

Gilead by Marilynne Robinson. Farrar, Straus & Giroux (139,376)

Star Wars: Dark Lord, the Rise of Darth Vader by James Luceno. Del Rey (137,661)

Remains Silent by Michael Baden and Linda Kenney. Knopf (134,000)

Zorro by Isabel Allende. HarperCollins (130,632)

Dance of Death by Douglas Preston & Lincoln Child. Warner (128,498)

The Twelfth Card: A Lincoln Rhyme Novel by Jeffery Deaver. Simon & Schuster (#125,750)

The Cat Who Dropped a Bombshell by Lillian Jackson Braun. Putnam (125,419)

The Simple Truth About Love by Bradley Trevor Grieve. Andrew McMeel (125,030)

The Truth About Diamonds by Nicole Richie. Regan Books (125,000)

100,000+

Marriage Most Scandalous by Johanna Lindsey. Pocket (#124,000)

One Shot by Lee Child. Delacorte (#120,000)

Conviction: A Novel by Richard North Patterson. Random House (119,672)

Straken by Terry Brooks. Del Rey (118,467)

Extremely Loud and Incredibly Close by Jonathan Safran Foer. Houghton Mifflin (114,566)

The Christmas Shoes by Donna Van Liere. St. Martin's (114,510)

Lie by Moonlight by Amanda Quick. Putnam (113,162)

Pretty Woman by Fern Michaels. Pocket (#112,000)

Killing Time by Linda Howard. Ballantine (111,634)

Company Man by Joseph Finder. St. Martin's (111,510)

Babylon Rising: The Europa Conspiracy by Tim LaHaye with Bob Phillips. (#110,000)

The Collected Stories of Louis L'Amour, Vol. III by Louis L'Amour. Bantam (#110,000)

Tyrannosaur Canyon by Douglas Preston. Forge (110,000)

A Stroke of Midnight by Laurell K. Hamilton. Ballantine (109,830)

The Assassins by Oliver North. Broadman & Holman (#109,800)

Cross Bones by Kathy Reichs. Scribner (#107,000)

Devil's Corner by Lisa Scottoline. Harper-Collins (105,241)

Always Time to Die by Elizabeth Lowell. Morrow (104,750)

History of Love by Nicole Krauss. Norton (104,564)

Pawley's Island by Dorothea Benton Frank. Berkley (103,581)

Long Time Gone by J. A. Jance. Morrow (102,818)

Superstition by Karen Robards. Putnam (102,800)

Fire Sale by Sara Paretsky. Putnam (102,412)

Blood Memory by Greg Iles. Scribner (#102,000)

Something Blue by Emily Griffin. St. Martin's (101,867)

Genevieve by Eric Jerome Dickey. Dutton (101,782)

The Ezekiel Option by Joel C. Rosenberg. Tyndale (100,711)

Straight into Darkness by Faye Kellerman. Warner (100,350)

Never Call Retreat: Lee and Grant: The Final Victory by Newt Gingrich and William Forstchen. St. Martin's/Thomas Dunne (100,199)

The Nonfiction Runners-up

16. *Winning* by Jack Welch. Harper Business (605,000)

17. *Captivating: Unveiling the Mystery of a Woman's Soul* by John and Stasi Eldredge. Nelson (595,058)

18. *Marley & Me* by John Grogan. Morrow (569,101)

19. *The Truth (with jokes)* by Al Franken. Dutton (560,163)

20. *Everyday Italian: 125 Simple and Delicious Recipes* by Giada De Laurentiis. Clarkson Potter (545,062)

21. *Daily Readings from Your Best Life Now* by Joel Osteen. Warner Faith (522,167)

22. *Good to Great: Why Some Companies Make the Leap . . . and Others Don't* by Jim Collins. Collins (500,000)

23. *Paula Deen & Friends: Living It Up, Southern Style* by Paula Deen with Martha Nesbit. Simon & Schuster (#498,000)

24. *Secrets of the Millionaire Mind: Mastering the Inner Game of Wealth* by T. Harv Eker. Collins (450,000)

25. *The Year of Magical Thinking* by Joan Didion. Knopf (440,000)

26. *100 People Who Are Screwing Up America (and Al Franken Is #37)* by Bernard Goldberg. HarperCollins (406,663)

27. *Your Best Life Now Journal: A Guide to Reaching Your Full Potential* by Joel Osteen. Warner Faith (401,013)

28. *The Money Book* by Suze Orman. Riverhead (394,615)

29. *And One More Thing Before You Go . . .* by Maria Shriver. Free Press (#394,000)

30. *Jeff Foxworthy's Redneck Dictionary* by Jeff Foxworthy. Villard (393,473)

300,000+

Talk to the Hand: The Utter Bloody Rudeness of the World Today, or Six Good Reasons to Stay Home and Bolt the Door by Lynne Truss. Gotham (391,632)

On Bullshit by Harry Frankfurt. Princeton Univ. Press (391,629)

Betty Crocker Cookbook: Everything You Need to Know to Cook Today 10th Ed. (binder) by Kristi Hart, ed. Wiley (351,604)

Juiced by Jose Canseco. Regan Books (365,000)

The FairTax Book by Neal Boortz. Regan Books (350,000)

Exercise and Nutrition for Maximum Results in Minimum Time by Bob Greene. Simon & Schuster (#344,000)

The Daily Show with Jon Stewart Presents America (the Book) by Jon Stewart and the writers of *The Daily Show*. Warner (339,250)

Start Late Finish Rich by David Bach. Broadway (#334,000)

The Perricone Weight-Loss Diet: A Simple 3-Part Plan to Lose the Fat, the Wrinkles, and the Years by Nicholas Perricone, M.D. Random House (325,473)

Driven from Within by Michael Jordan. Atria (315,000)

Blood Brother by Anne Bird. Regan Books (310,000)

Approval Addiction: Overcoming Your Need to Please Everyone by Joyce Meyer. Warner Faith (309,434)

It's Called a Break Up Because It's Broken by Greg Behrendt and Amiira Ruotola-Behrendt. Broadway (#305,500)

For Women Only: What You Need to Know About the Inner Lives of Men by Shaunti Feldhahn. Multnomah (305,139)

The Little Book That Beats the Market by Joel Greenblatt and Andrew Tobias. Wiley (303,846)

The South Beach Diet Quick and Easy Cookbook by Arthur Agatston, M.D. Rodale (300,376)

200,000+

Collapse: How Societies Choose to Fail or Succeed by Jared Diamond. Viking (290,000)

He's Just Not That into You by Greg Behrendt and Liz Tuccillo. Simon Spotlight (290,000)

The Five Dysfunctions of a Team by Patrick Lencioni. Wiley (284,477)

My Friend Leonard by James Frey. Riverhead (278,929)

The 3-Hour Diet: How Low-Carb Diets Make You Fat and Timing Makes You Thin by Jorge Cruise. Collins (275,000)

Jim Cramer's Real Money: Sane Investing in an Insane World by James J. Cramer. Simon & Schuster (#270,000+)

Martha Stewart's Baking Handbook by Martha Stewart. Clarkson Potter (267,079)

Who Moved My Cheese? by Spencer Johnson. Putnam (267,043)

Witness by Amber Frey. Regan Books (265,000)

My Life So Far by Jane Fonda. Random House (250,697)

The Complete Calvin and Hobbes by Bill Watterson. Andrews McMeel (250, 085)

Straight Talk: Overcoming Emotional Battles with the Power of God's Word by Joyce Meyer. Warner Faith (232,961)

For Laci: A Mother's Story of Love, Loss, and Justice by Sharon Rocha. Crown (228,220)

Wild at Heart: Discovering the Secret of a Man's Soul by John Eldredge. Nelson (226,594)

My FBI: Bringing Down the Mafia, Investigating Bill Clinton, and Fighting the War on Terror by Louis Freeh. St. Martin's (225,774)

It's Not Easy Being Green: And Other Things to Consider by Jim Henson. Hyperion (220,576)

Coming Home to Myself by Wynonna Judd with Patsi Bale Cox. NAL (216,256)

Ending Your Day Right: Devotions for Every Evening of the Year by Joyce Meyer. Warner Faith (215,508)

Are Men Necessary? by Maureen Dowd. Putnam (214,980)

A Deadly Game by Catherine Cryer. Regan Books. (210,000)

The Beatles: The Biography by Bob Spitz. Little, Brown (209,164)

Confessions of a Video Vixen by Karrine Steffans. Amistad (207,834)

Body for Life for Women: 12 Weeks to a Firm, Fit, Fabulous Body at Any Age by Pamela Peeke, M.D. Rodale (203,952)

A Lotus Grows in the Mud by Goldie Hawn. Putnam (201,700)

Be Honest, You're Not That into Him Either by Ian Kerner. Regan Books (200,000)

Mother-Daughter Wisdom by Christiane Northrup, M.D. Bantam (#200,000)

150,000+

Between You and Me: A Memoir by Mike Wallace. Hyperion (199,075)

New Rules: Polite Musings from a Timid Observer by Bill Maher. Rodale (197,640)

The Education of a Coach by David Halberstam. Hyperion (197,169)

Starting Your Day Right: Devotions for Each Morning of the Year by Joyce Meyer. Warner Faith (190,717)

Home Rules: Transform The Place You Live into a Place You'll Love by Nate Berkus. Hyperion (190,626)

Coach: Lessons on the Game of Life by Michael Lewis. Norton (187,211)

Total Money Makeover: A Proven Plan for Financial Success by Dave Ramsey. Nelson (186,075)

The Secret Man: The Story of Watergate's Deep Throat by Bob Woodward (with "A Reporter's Assessment" by Carl Bernstein). Simon & Schuster (#185,254)

Character Is Destiny: Inspiring Stories Every Young Person Should Know and Every Adult Should Remember by John McCain. Random House (183,683)

Never Have Your Dog Stuffed: And Other Things I've Learned by Alan Alda. Random House (183,504)

Secrets and Mysteries of the World by Sylvia Browne. Hay House (183,022)

A Crack in the Edge of the World: America and the Great California Earthquake of 1906 by Simon Winchester. HarperCollins (182,069)

The Martha Rules: 10 Essentials for Achieving Success as You Start, Build, or Manage a Business by Martha Stewart. Rodale (179,719)

Men in Black: How the Supreme Court Is Destroying America by Mark R. Levin. Regnery (177,559)

Phenomenon: Everything You Need to Know About the Other Side and What It Means to You by Sylvia Browne. Dutton (177,300)

The Cosmo Kama Sutra: 77 Mind-Blowing Sex Positions. Hearst (177,151)

The Planets by Dava Sobel. Viking (176,000)

Plan B by Anne Lamott. Riverhead (172,671)

Git-R-Done by Larry the Cable Guy. Crown (167,543)

The Tender Bar by J. R. Moehringer. Hyperion (164,081)

Why Do I Love These People? Honest and Amazing Stories of Real Families by Po Bronson. Random House (163,331)

Paula Deen's Kitchen Classics by Paula H. Deen. Random House (157,583)

Do As I Say (Not As I Do): Profiles in Liberal Hypocrisy by Peter Schweizer. Doubleday (153,734)

Where God Was Born: A Journey by Land to the Roots of Religion by Bruce Feiler. Morrow (153,025)

John Paul the Great: Remembering a Spiritual Father by Peggy Noonan. Viking (151,000)

125,000+

Betty Crocker Cookbook Bridal Edition by Betty Crocker. Wiley (149,879)

Suzanne Somers' Slim and Sexy Forever: The Hormone Solution for Permanent Weight Loss and Optimal Living by Suzanne Somers. Crown (149,243)

A Million Little Pieces by James Frey. Doubleday (149,041)

Dean & Me: (A Love Story) by Jerry Lewis with James Kaplan. Doubleday (148,477)

What Remains by Carole Radziwill. Scribner (148,000)

Bait and Switch: The Futile Pursuit of the American Dream by Barbara Ehrenreich. Henry Holt (146,229)

Conspiracy of Fools by Kurt Eichenwald. Broadway (#141,000)

SuperFoods HealthStyle by Steven G. Pratt and Kathy Matthews. Morrow (140,961)

Mother Angelica: The Remarkable Story of a Nun, Her Nerve, and a Network of Miracles by Raymond Arroyo. Doubleday (137,641)

Battlefield of the Mind Devotional by Joyce Meyer. Warner Faith (135,072)

Younger Next Year by Chris Crowley and Henry S. Lodge, M.D. Workman (129,683)

The Lost Painting: The Quest for a Caravaggio Masterpiece by Jonathan Harr. Random House (129,280)

From Pieces to Weight: Once Upon a Time in Southside Queens by 50 Cent. Pocket (128,478)

The Bob Dylan Scrapbook, 1956–1966 by Bob Dylan. Simon & Schuster (#125,500)

Being Perfect by Anna Quindlen. Random House (125,235)

The Game by Neil Strauss. Regan Books (125,000)

100,000+

Sinatra by Anthony Summers and Robbyn Swan. Knopf (123,000)

Baby Laughs: The Naked Truth About the First Year of Mommyhood by Jenny McCarthy. Dutton (120,093)

Down Came the Rain: My Journey Through Postpartum Depression by Brooke Shields. Hyperion (119,151)

The Power of Intention: Learning to Co-create Your World, Your Way by Dr. Wayne W. Dyer. Hay House (119,022)

Sylvia Browne's Lessons for Life by Sylvia Browne. Hay House (118,988)

Smashed: Story of a Drunken Girlhood by Koren Zailckas. Viking (117,000)

1491 by Charles C. Mann. Knopf (116,000)

The Perricone Promise by Nicholas Perricone, M.D. Warner (115,000)

Never Eat Alone: And Other Secrets to Success, One Relationship at a Time by Keith Ferrazzi with Tahl Raz. Doubleday (114,049)

Poker: The Real Deal by Phil Gordon. Simon Spotlight (113,000)

The Glass Castle: A Memoir by Jeannette Walls. Scribner (112,000)

Next Man Up: A Year Behind the Lines in Today's NFL by John Feinstein. Little, Brown (111,852)

Under and Alone: The True Story of the Undercover Agent Who Infiltrated America's Most Violent Outlaw Motorcycle Gang by William Queen. Random House (111,475)

The Complete Cartoons of the New Yorker by Robert Mankoff. Black Dog & Leventhal (111,348)

Elvis by the Presleys by Priscilla Presley and Lisa Marie Presley; edited by David Ritz. Crown (110,654)

Heaven by Randy Alcorn. Tyndale (110,631)

Don't Kiss Them Good-bye by Allison DuBois. Fireside (110,235)

Japanese Women Don't Get Old or Fat by Naomi Moriyama and William Doyle. Delacorte (#110,000)

One Soldier's Story: A Memoir by Bob Dole. HarperCollins (109,338)

Busting Vegas: The MIT Whiz Kid Who Brought the Casinos to Their Knees by Ben Mezrich. Morrow (108,056)

The Best Recipes in the World by Mark Bittman. Broadway (#106,000)

The One Thing You Need to Know: . . . . About Great Managing, Great Leading, and Sustained Individual Success by Marcus Buckingham. Free Press (#105,750)

Being Dead Is No Excuse: The Official Southern Ladies Guide to Hosting the Perfect Funeral by Charlotte Hays and Gayden Metcalfe. Miramax (105,596)

Molto Italiano: 327 Simple Italian Recipes to Cook at Home by Mario Batali. Ecco (104,773)

The Power of Being Positive by Joyce Meyer. Warner Faith (104,376)

Spook: Science Tackles the Afterlife by Mary Roach. Norton (103,976)

Life Is Not a Fairy Tale by Fantasia. Fireside (103,105)

6-Day Body Makeover: Drop One Whole Dress or Pant Size in Just 6 Days—and Keep It Off by Michael Thurmond. Warner (103,038)

He-Motions by T. D. Jakes. Putnam (102,746)

Lance Armstrong's War by Daniel Coyle. HarperCollins (101,741)

The One Minute Manager Anniversary Edition by Ken Blanchard and Spencer Johnson. Morrow (101,633)

Symptoms of Withdrawal: A Memoir of Snapshots and Redemption by Christopher Kennedy Lawford. Morrow (101,086)

Julie and Julia: 365 Days, 524 Recipes, 1 Tiny Apartment Kitchen by Julie Powell. Little, Brown (101,021)

Eats, Shoots & Leaves: The Zero Tolerance Approach to Punctuation by Lynne Truss. Gotham (100,737)

The Superbowl: An Official Retrospective by Ken Leiker. Ballantine (100,694)

102 Minutes: The Untold Story of the Fight to Survive Inside the Twin Towers by Jim Dwyer and Kevin Flynn. Holt (100,617)

Never Call Retreat: Lee and Grant by Newt Gingrich and William Forstchen. St. Martin's (100,199)

The River of Doubt: Theodore Roosevelt's Darkest Journey by H. W. Brands. Doubleday (100,044)

A Briefer History of Time by Stephen Hawking with Leonard Mlodinow. Bantam (#100,000)

Condi vs. Hillary by Dick Morris. Regan Books (100,000)

Talking Back . . . to Presidents, Dictators, and Assorted Scoundrels by Andrea Mitchell. Viking (100,000)

Paperback Bestsellers: Something New, Something Old

Dermot McEvoy

Contributing Editor, *Publishers Weekly*

In early 2006 James Frey was chastised, ostracized, and perhaps indelibly stigmatized by Oprah Winfrey's public humiliation of him on national TV. But that was this year. Last year, thanks in major part to Oprah's impassioned support for *A Million Little Pieces*, the now-alleged memoir racked up enough sales to lead all trade paperbacks in the United States, with more than 3 million units sold. And in the first three months of this year, *Pieces* continued strong, riding high on both *Publishers Weekly*'s and the *New York Times*' bestseller lists. "The controversy," according to Russell Perreault, v-p/director of publicity for Anchor, "actually propelled sales."

Do You Sudoku?

The big news of 2005 was the emergence of sudoku titles. According to its fans, sudoku is the new crossword puzzle, Rubik's Cube and Bridge column all rolled into one. We encountered 23 sudoku titles, with total sales nearing the 5,700,000 mark. St. Martin's/Griffin author Will Shortz was the most prolific, with six titles, ranging from the easy-to-do to the master category.

Eat, Then Diet

Cooking and dieting seem to go together. So it's no surprise that both are well represented for 2005. The new cooking wizard is Food Network's starlet Rachael Ray. She weighed in with two new titles and three backlist favorites. In all, she sold more than 2 million copies in 2005. Good Books was also well represented, with three titles in the Fix-It and Forget-It line. Paula Deen, another Food Network star, sold a whopping 634,403 copies of *Lady & Sons: Savannah Country Cookbook*. And once you pack those pounds on, they gotta come off. It seems that with the death of Dr. Robert Atkins, his diet books also took a hit. The new diet guru is Dr. Arthur Agatston and his South Beach Diet titles. Three trade titles sold nearly 1,680,000 copies and the mass market of the *South Beach Diet* added another 1,800,000.

Tie-Ins Diversify

In the old days, tie-ins were strictly related to motion pictures and TV movies. Now they've branched out into the Broadway theater, too, with tie-ins of "Wicked" and "The Color Purple" leading the way. The hottest show on television was represented by a "Desperate Housewives" tie-in, while "Capote," which won Philip Seymour Hoffman an Oscar, also breathed new life into Truman's Capote 1966 classic, *In Cold Blood*. "Brokeback Mountain," the most controversial movie of the year, also was represented in sales. The most successful tie-in was *Memoirs of a Geisha* by Arthur Golden. Three Vintage editions (trade reprint, trade tie-in, mass market tie-in) sold in excess of 1,720,000 copies.

Mass Market: Novels Are Us

Mass market has become the home of genre fiction. Mass market sales were heavily influenced by novelists with very familiar names. John Grisham led the charge, and was followed in the multiples by Nora Roberts (11 times), Janet Evanovich (6), Dan Brown, and Dean Koontz (3 each). Mass market nonfiction was few and far between, represented most notably by *The South Beach Diet* and the two volumes of former President Clinton's *My Life*.

Rules for Inclusion

Listed on the following pages are trade paperbacks and mass market titles published in 2004 and 2005; the rankings are based only on 2005 sales. To qualify, trade paperbacks had to have sold more than 100,000 copies in 2005; for mass markets, sales of more than 500,000 were required. A single asterisk (*) indicates the book was published in 2004; a double asterisk (**) means the book was published earlier but either remained or reappeared on *PW*'s bestseller charts in 2005. These reappearances are most often movie tie-ins. A pound symbol (#) indicates that the shipped-and-billed figure was rounded down to the nearest 5,000 to indicate the book's sales relationship to other titles. The actual figures were given to *PW* in confidence for use only in placing titles on these lists.

Trade Paperbacks

One Million+

A Million Little Pieces. James Frey. Rep. Anchor (3,057,707)

**The Kite Runner.* Khaled Hosseini. Rep. Riverhead (2,092,805)

***Guns, Germs and Steel.* Jared Diamond. Rep. Norton (2,000,000)

Rachael Ray 365. Rachael Ray. Orig. Clarkson Potter (1,037,321)

***Wicked.* Gregory Maguire. Rep. Regan Books (1,000,000)

700,000+

The Secret Life of Bees. Sue Monk Kidd. Rep. Penguin (940,046)

Curious Incident/Dog in Night. Mark Haddon. Rep. Vintage (756,976)

**The Tipping Point.* Malcolm Gladwell. Rep. Little, Brown/Back Bay Books (730,687)

South Beach Diet. Arthur Agatston, M.D. Rep. St. Martin's/Griffin (700,000)

500,000+

My Sister's Keeper. Jodi Picoult. Rep. Washington Square Press (693,000)

**Bad Cat.* Jim Edgar. Orig. Workman (689,139)

Lady & Sons: Savannah Country. Paula H. Deen. TV tie-in. Random (634,403)

Sudoku Easy Vol. 1. Will Shortz. Orig. St. Martin's/Griffin (625,000)

Memoirs of a Geisha. Arthur Golden. Movie tie-in. Vintage (609,346)

Why Do Men Have Nipples? Mark Leyner and Billy Goldberg, M.D. Orig. Three Rivers (584,952)

***Their Eyes Were Watching God.* Zora Hurston. Rep. HarperPerennial (537,854)

Rachael Ray's 30-Minute Get Real Meals. Rachael Ray. Orig. Clarkson Potter (526,337)

Sam's Letters to Jennifer. James Patterson. Rep. Warner (524,784)

As I Lay Dying, The Sound and the Fury, Light in August Boxed Set. William Faulkner. Oprah Book Club reissue. Vintage (518,049)

Light on Snow. Anita Shreve. Rep. Little, Brown (508,726)

South Beach Diet Good Fats/Good Carbs Guide. Arthur Agatston, M.D. Revised. Rodale (506,825)

Sudoku Easy-to-Hard Vol. 2. Will Shortz. Orig. St. Martin's/Griffin (500,000)

250,000+

**The Devil in the White City.* Erik Larson. Rep. Vintage (475,968)

South Beach Diet Dining Guide. Arthur Agatston, M.D. Orig. Rodale (473,378)

Su Doku for Dummies. Andrew Heron. Orig. Wiley (466,073)

***Rich Dad, Poor Dad.* Robert T. Kiyosaki and Sharon L. Lechter. Orig. Warner (440,755)

Dress Your Family in Corduroy and Denim. David Sedaris. Rep. Little, Brown (430,743)

New York Post Su Doku 1. Wayne Gould. Orig. Collins (423,498)

Dark Watch. Clive Cussler. Orig. Berkley (414,602)

***Tuesdays with Morrie.* Mitch Albom. Rep. Broadway (413,000)

The Book of Sudoku #1. Michael Mepham. Orig. Overlook (409,000)

#O'Hurley's Return. Nora Roberts. Reissue. Harlequin/Silhouette (406,000)

***The Alchemist.* Paulo Coelho. Rep. Harper San Francisco (403,098)

#Rules of Play. Nora Roberts. Reissue. Harlequin/Silhouette (400,100)

Can You Keep a Secret? Sophie Kinsella. Rep. Dial (400,000)

**The Time Traveler's Wife.* Audrey Niffenegger. Rep. Harvest (395,000)

Bad Dog. R. D. Rosen, Harry Prichett, and Rob Battles. Orig. Workman (387,376)

**90 Minutes in Heaven.* Don Piper with Cecil Murphey. Orig. Revell (386,816)

**The Wedding.* Nicholas Sparks. Rep. Warner (379,177)

**The Known World.* Edward Jones. Rep. Amistad (377,711)

The Shadow of the Wind. Carlos Ruiz Zafon. Rep. Penguin (372,652)

***The Life of Pi.* Yann Martel. Rep. Harvest (368,000)

***Fix-It and Forget-It Cookbook: Feasting with Your Slow Cooker.* Dawn J. Ranck and Phyllis Pellman Good. Orig. Good Books (358,175)

**The Lovely Bones.* Alice Sebold. Rep. Little, Brown (353,752)

Skinny Dip. Carl Hiaasen. Rep. Warner (344,227)

Little Earthquakes. Jennifer Weiner. Rep. Washington Square Press (343,000)

***Reading Lolita in Tehran.* Azar Nafisi. Rep. Random (342,769)

***Memoirs of a Geisha.* Arthur Golden. Rep. Vintage (336,809)

A Salty Piece of Land. Jimmy Buffett. Rep. Little, Brown (332,692)

Sudoku Easy-to-Hard Vol. 3. Will Shortz. Orig. St. Martin's/Griffin (325,000)

The Revelation. Beverly Lewis. Rep. Bethany (313,183)

*The 7 Habits of Highly Effective People 15th Anniv. Ed. Stephen R. Covey. Rep. Free Press (303,773)

**30-Minute Meals 2. Rachael Ray. Orig. Lake Isle (300, 000)

Supernanny. Jo Frost. Rep. Hyperion (297,293)

The Preacher's Daughter. Beverly Lewis. Rep. Bethany (295,583)

The Full Cupboard of Life. Alexander McCall Smith. Rep. Anchor (290,054)

Bergdorf Blondes. Plum Sykes. Rep. Miramax (283,695)

*Finally. Boston Globe. Orig. Triumph (283,000)

New York Post Su Doku 2. Wayne Gould. Orig. Collins (268,323)

Vanishing Acts. Jodi Picoult. Rep. Washington Square Press (267,000)

*The Birth of Venus. Sarah Dunant. Rep. Random (260,415)

I Am Charlotte Simmons. Tom Wolfe. Rep. Picador (260,000)

The Plot Against America. Philip Roth. Rep. Vintage (259,237)

The Jane Austen Book Club. Karen Joy Fowler. Rep. Plume (257,939)

Su Doku for Dummies 2. Andrew Heron. Orig. Wiley (253,399)

Something Borrowed. Emily Giffin. Rep. St. Martin's/Griffin (250,000)

**Blue Like Jazz. Donald Miller. Orig. Nelson (250,000)

100,000+

My Life. Bill Clinton. Rep. Vintage (248,806)

O'Reilly Factor for Kids. Bill O'Reilly. Rep. Harper (247,189)

The Great Influenza. John M. Barry. Rep. Penguin (247,000)

**In Cold Blood. Truman Capote. Reissue. Vintage (236,436)

Good Grief. Lolly Winston. Rep. Warner (235,506)

The Book of Sudoku #2. Michael Mepham. Orig. Overlook (235,000)

Shopaholic & Sister. Sophie Kinsella. Rep. Dial (230,000)

*The Devil Wears Prada. Lauren Weisberger. Rep. Broadway (226,000)

The Essential Book of Su Doku. Pete Sinden. Orig. Atria (226,000)

*Fix-It and Forget-It Lightly: Healthy, Low-Fat Recipes for Your Slow Cooker. Phyllis Pellman Good. Orig. Good Books (225,770)

**The Power of a Praying Wife. Stormie Omartian. Rep. Harvest (225,028)

*Caring for Your Baby and Young Child. Steven P. Shelov, M.D. Revised. Bantam (220,000)

New York Post Su Doku 3. Wayne Gould. Orig. Collins (218,492)

**It's Not About the Bike. Lance Armstrong. Rep. Berkley (218,173)

Dark Tower V: Wolves of the Calla. Stephen King. Rep. Scribner (215,000)

**Mere Christianity. C. S. Lewis. Rep. Harper San Francisco (215,000)

What You Wear Can Change Your Life. Susannah Constantine and Trinny Woodall. Orig. Riverhead (213,542)

The Notebook. Nicholas Sparks. Movie tie-in. Warner (213,532)

Robert Ludlum's The Moscow Vector. Robert Ludlum and Patrick Larkin. Orig. St. Martin's/Griffin (210,000)

Collapse. Jared Diamond. Orig. Penguin (209,417)

*Cooking 'Round the Clock. Rachael Ray. Orig. Lake Isle (208,000)

Deliver Us from Evil. Sean Hannity. Rep. Regan Books (205,000)

The Official Book of Sudoku: Book 1. Rep. Plume (204,285)

Giant Book of Sudoku. Will Shortz. Orig. St. Martin's/Griffin (200,000)

Family First. Dr. Phil McGraw. Rep. Free Press (199,430)

The Power of Intention. Wayne Dyer. Rep. Hay House (196,285)

American Soldier. Gen. Tommy Franks. Rep. Regan Books (195,000)

The Maker's Diet. Dr. Jordan Rubin. Rep. Berkley (193,191)

The Red Hat Society's Laugh Lines. Sue Ellen Cooper. Orig. Warner (191,802)

**Everything Is Illuminated. Jonathan Foer. Rep. HarperPerennial (189,592)

**In Her Shoes. Jennifer Weiner. Movie tie-in. Washington Square Press (187,000)

The Fabric of the Cosmos. Brian Greene. Rep. Vintage (185,225)

Prep. Curtis Sittenfeld. Rep. Random (184,573)

Moonlight on the Millpond. Lori Wick. Orig. Harvest (182,269)

**Confessions of an Ugly Stepsister.* Gregory Maguire. Rep. Regan Books (180,000)

A Little Fate. Nora Roberts. Reissue. Berkley (173,618)

Shoot the Moon. Billie Letts. Rep. Warner (173,447)

The Perricone Promise. Nicholas Perricone, M.D. Rep. Warner (173,333)

His Excellency. Joseph Ellis. Rep. Vintage (172,628)

Alexander Hamilton. Ron Chernow. Rep. Penguin (172,593)

**The Passion of Christ.* John Piper. Orig. Crossway (172,514)

Dark Tower VI: Song of Susannah. Stephen King. Rep. Scribner (172,000)

**Under the Banner of Heaven.* Jon Krakauer. Rep. Anchor (171,792)

Fame. Karen Kingsbury. Orig. Tyndale (170,451)

Just Above a Whisper. Lori Wick. Orig. Harvest (170,167)

Jonathan Strange & Mr. Norrell. Susanna Clarke. Rep. Bloomsbury (170,000)

True Betrayals. Nora Roberts. Reissue. Berkley (169,418)

When Will Jesus Bring the Pork Chops? George Carlin. Rep. Hyperion (167,096)

**The Dante Club.* Matthew Pearl. Rep. Random (166,935)

***Screwtape Letters.* C. S. Lewis. Reissue. Harper San Francisco (166,747)

The Virgin's Lover. Philippa Gregory. Rep. Touchstone (166,444)

The Namesake. Jhumpa Lahiri. Rep. Mariner (164,188)

Dark Tower VII. Stephen King. Rep. Scribner (164,000)

The Book of Sudoku #3. Michael Mepham. Orig. Overlook (164,000)

*** The Power of a Praying Woman.* Stormie Omartian. Rep. Harvest (161,850)

Ultimate Hitchhiker's Guide. Douglas Adams. Movie tie-in. Del Rey (158,231)

Forgiven. Karen Kingsbury. Orig. Tyndale (156,056)

Believe It. Chicago Tribune. Orig. Triumph (155,000)

Desperate Housewives. Orig. TV tie-in. Hyperion (153,999)

You Can Do It! Lauren Catuzzi Grandcolas. Orig. Chronicle (153,749)

***The Color Purple.* Alice Walker. Rep. Broadway Harvest (153,000)

The ABS Diet Eat Right Every Time Guide. David Zinczenko with Ted Spiker. Orig. Rodale (152,897)

Chicken Soup for the Dog Lover's Soul. Jack Canfield and Mark Victor Hansen. Orig. HCI (152,891)

The Essential Book of Su Doku, Vol. 2. Pete Sinden. Orig. Atria (152,000)

The Biggest Loser. The Biggest Loser Experts and Cast with Maggie Greenwood Robinson. Orig. Rodale (151,560)

The Essential Book of Su Doku, Vol. 3. Pete Sinden. Orig. Atria (151,000)

Chicken Soup for Every Mom's Soul. Jack Canfield and Mark Victor Hansen. Orig. HCI (147,235)

Su Doku for Dummies 3. Andrew Heron. Orig. Wiley (146,461)

The Sunday Philosophy Club. Alexander McCall Smith. Rep. Anchor (146,352)

Founding Mothers. Cokie Roberts. Rep. HarperPerennial (144,885)

**Kalahari Typing School for Men.* Alexander McCall Smith. Rep. Anchor (144,302)

Cupcakes: From the Cake Mix Doctor. Anne Byrn. Rep. Workman (144,214)

**The Queen's Fool.* Philippa Gregory. Rep. Touchstone (144,187)

**Mountains Beyond Mountains.* Tracy Kidder. Rep. Random (143,545)

The Lost Chronicles. Mark Cotta Vaz. Orig. TV tie-in. Hyperion (143,400)

The True and Outstanding Adventures of the Hunt Sisters. Elisabeth Robinson. Rep. Little, Brown (141,066)

Knowing Aslan. Thomas Williams. Orig. W (141,000)

Chicken Soup for the Soul: The Book of Christmas Virtues. Jack Canfield and Mark Victor Hansen. Orig. HCI (140,815)

**Dreams from My Father.* Barack Obama. Orig. Three Rivers (139,654)

**Ask and It Is Given.* Esther and Jerry Hicks. Rep. Hay House (136,743)

Nightmare in Wichita. Robert Beattie. Orig. NAL (136,553)

*The Bookseller of Kabul. Asne Seierstad. Rep. Little, Brown (136,382)

*Mirror Mirror. Gregory Maguire. Rep. Regan Books (135,000)

The Sudoku Gift Box. Michael Mepham. Orig. Boxed set. Overlook (135,000)

Love. Toni Morrison. Rep. Vintage (134,865)

The Official Book of Sudoku: Book 2. Rep. Plume (133,187)

The Princes of Ireland. Edward Rutherfurd. Rep. Ballantine (133,014)

Olivia Joules and the Overactive Imagination. Helen Fielding. Orig. Penguin (132,877)

Battle Ready. Tom Clancy. Rep. Berkley (132,811)

Chronicles of Narnia. Perry Moore. Orig. Harper San Francisco (131,835)

Pregnancy Journal. A. Christine Harris. Revised. Chronicle (129,597)

*Flyboys. James Bradley. Rep. Little, Brown (129,503)

Master Sudoku. Carol Vorderman. Orig. Three Rivers (129,410)

Chicken Soup for the Father & Daughter Soul. Jack Canfield and Mark Victor Hansen. Orig. HCI (123,620)

Your Best Life Now Study Guide. Joel Osteen. Orig. Warner Faith (121,322)

Extreme Makeover: Home Edition. Madison Press. Orig. Hyperion (120,932)

The End of Faith. Sam Harris. Rep. Norton (120,000)

Bringing Up Boys. Dr. James Dobson. Rep. Tyndale (119,541)

Even Now. Karen Kingsbury. Orig. Zondervan (118,285)

*Leap of Faith. Queen Noor. Rep. Miramax (116,756)

*Angry Housewives Eating Bon Bons. Lorna Landvik. Rep. Ballantine (116,408)

*Flowers for Algernon. Daniel Keyes. Rep. Harvest (116,000)

Fix-It and Forget-It Diabetic Cookbook. Phyllis Pellman Good with the American Diabetes Association. Orig. Good Books (115,725)

Snow. Orhan Pamuk. Rep. Vintage (115,063)

*Chicken Soup for the Teenage Soul IV. Jack Canfield and Mark Victor Hansen. Orig. HCI (115,023)

**Get Togethers. Rachael Ray. Orig. Lake Isle (115,000)

*Every Young Woman's Battle. Shannon Ethridge and Stephen Arterburn. Orig. WaterBrook (113,325)

Mother to Daughter. Harry H. Harrison, Jr. Orig. Workman (112,857)

Must Love Dogs. Claire Cook. Movie tie-in. NAL (111,733)

**Lucky. Alice Sebold. Rep. Little, Brown (111,540)

Truth and Beauty. Ann Patchett. Rep. HarperPerennial (111,362)

Shadow Divers. Robert Kurson. Rep. Random (111,093)

Prophecy. Sylvia Browne. Rep. NAL (111,064)

Shopgirl. Steve Martin. Movie tie-in. Hyperion (110,890)

*Beloved. Toni Morrison. Reissue. Vintage (110,453)

Magical Thinking. Augusten Burroughs. Rep. Picador (110,000)

Sudoku for Your Coffee Break. Will Shortz. Orig. St. Martin's/Griffin (110,000)

The Rising. Tim LaHaye and Jerry B. Jenkins. Rep. Tyndale (109,861)

Hypocrite in a Puffy White Dress. Susan Jane Gilman. Orig. Warner (109,803)

ABS Diet Paperback. David Zinczenko with Ted Spiker. Rep. Rodale (109,467)

The Queen of the Big Time. Adriana Trigiani. Rep. Ballantine (109,381)

How to Talk to a Liberal (if You Must). Ann Coulter. Rep. Three Rivers (109,105)

Brokeback Mountain. Annie Proulx. Movie tie-in. Scribner (109,000)

**Wild at Heart. John Eldredge. Rep. Nelson (108,000)

Jarhead. Anthony Swofford. Movie tie-in. Scribner (107,500)

Sarah. Marek Halter. Rep. Three Rivers (106,832)

*Reading Group. Elizabeth Noble. Orig. Harper (106,020)

Breakers Reef. Terri Blackstock. Orig. Zondervan (105,451)

44 Scotland Street. Alexander McCall Smith. Orig. Anchor (105,096)

Ultimate Sudoku Challenge. Will Shortz. Orig. St. Martin's/Griffin (105,000)

*Sideways. Rex Pickett. Movie tie-in. St. Martin's/Griffin (105,000)

Will in the World. Stephen Greenblatt. Rep. Norton (105,000)

The Art of Mending. Elizabeth Berg. Rep. Ballantine (104,610)

Best American Short Stories 2005. Ed. by Michael Chabon. Orig. Houghton Mifflin (104,022)

Runaway. Alice Munro. Rep. Vintage (103,985)

**Empire Falls. Richard Russo. Rep. Vintage (103,451)

**Positions of the Day. Lorelei Sharkey and Emma Taylor. Orig. Chronicle (102,344)

*Chicken Soup for the Girlfriend's Soul. Jack Canfield and Mark Victor Hansen. Orig. HCI (102,557)

Chicken Soup for the Girl's Soul. Jack Canfield and Mark Victor Hansen. Orig. HCI (102,224)

*The Motorcycle Diaries. Che Guevara. Movie tie-in. Ocean Press (101,399)

Sudoku. Nikoli Publishing. Orig. Workman (100,576)

The Kite Runner (Essential Edition). Khaled Hosseini. Rep. Riverhead (100,126)

The Case for a Creator. Lee Strobel. Orig. Zondervan (100,088)

Shantaram. Gregory Roberts. Rep. St. Martin's/Griffin (100,000)

Playing with Boys. Alisa Valdez-Rodriguez. Rep. St. Martin's/Griffin (100,000)

**Shopaholic Takes Manhattan. Sophie Kinsella. Orig. Dial (100,000)

He's Just Not That into You (Abridged). Greg Behrendt and Liz Tuccillo. Rep. Simon Spotlight (100,000)

Size 12 Is Not Fat. Meg Cabot. Orig. Avon (100,000)

*Searching for God Knows What. Donald Miller. Orig. Nelson (100,000)

Almanacs, Atlases & Annuals

The World Almanac and Book of Facts 2006. Edited by Ken Park. Annual. World Almanac (436,639)

J. K. Lasser's Your Income Tax 2006. Orig. Wiley (249,685)

The Old Farmer's Almanac 2006. Annual. Yankee (235,887)

Turbotax 2006 Income Tax Guide. Intuit. Orig. St. Martin's/Griffin (210,000)

Europe TravelBook. Annual. Orig. AAA (200,000)

2006 AAA North American Road Atlas. Annual. AAA (170,500)

What Color Is Your Parachute? 2006. Richard Nelson Bolles. Orig. Ten Speed (137,500)

Mass Market

Two Million+

#The Broker. John Grisham. Rep. Dell (3,620,000)

Red Lily. Nora Roberts. Orig. Jove (2,609,515)

Black Rose. Nora Roberts. Orig. Jove (2,445,574)

#**Angels and Demons. Dan Brown. Reissue. Pocket (2,201,000)

One Million+

3rd Degree. James Patterson and Andrew Gross. Rep. Warner (1,964,441)

#Life Expectancy. Dean Koontz. Rep. Bantam (1,800,000)

South Beach Diet. Arthur Agatston, M.D. Rep. St. Martin's (1,800,000)

Trace. Patricia Cornwell. Rep. Berkley (1,751,971)

State of Fear. Michael Crichton. Rep. Avon (1,700,000)

London Bridges. James Paterson. Rep. Warner Vision (1,682,185)

Northern Lights. Nora Roberts. Rep. Jove (1,630,034)

#Nighttime Is My Time. Mary Higgins Clark. Rep. Pocket (1,563,000)

#The Calhouns: Catherine, Amanda and Lilah. Nora Roberts. Reissue. Harlequin/Silhouette (1,406,900)

#The Calhouns: Suzanna & Megan. Nora Roberts. Reissue. Harlequin/Silhouette (1,398,400)

Hour Game. David Baldacci. Rep. Warner Vision (1,393,957)

Blowout. Catherine Coulter. Rep. Jove (1,383,808)

#Night Tales: Night Shield & Night Moves. Nora Roberts. Reissue. Harlequin/Silhouette (1,333,100)

The Wedding. Nicholas Sparks. Rep. Warner (1,333,071)

#Night Tales: Night Shift and Night Shadow. Nora Roberts. Reissue. Harlequin/Silhouette (1,330,200)

Ten Big Ones. Janet Evanovich. Rep. St. Martin's (1,300,000)

#Going Home. Nora Roberts. Reissue. Harlequin/Silhouette (1,296,600)

#Night Tales: Nightshade and Night Smoke. Nora Roberts. Reissue. Harlequin/Silhouette (1,292,200)

Are You Afraid of the Dark? Sidney Sheldon. Rep. Warner (1,283,869)

R Is for Ricochet. Sue Grafton. Rep. Berkley (1,185,493)

Hidden Prey. John Sandford. Rep. Berkley (1,140,180)

White Hot. Sandra Brown. Rep. Pocket (1,121,855)

#The Taking. Dean Koontz. Rep. Bantam (1,100,000)

*Digital Fortress. Dan Brown. Rep. St. Martin's (1,100,000)

Full Bloom. Janet Evanovich. Orig. St. Martin's (1,100,000)

The Narrows. Michael Connelly. Rep. Warner (1,078,805)

#The Rule of Four. Ian Caldwell and Dustin Thomason. Rep. Dell (1,070,000)

Night Fall. Nelson DeMille. Rep. Warner (1,064,617)

#*Deception Point. Dan Brown. Reissue (1,051,000)

#Dean Koontz's Frankenstein: Prodigal Son. Dean Koontz and Kevin J. Anderson. Orig. Bantam (1,050,000)

#Alone. Lisa Gardner. Rep. Bantam (1,040,000)

#Echoes. Danielle Steel. Rep. Dell (1,030,000)

#Divine Evil. Nora Roberts. Reissue. Bantam (1,020,000)

#The Ultimate Weight Solution. Dr. Phil McGraw. Rep. Pocket (1,010,000)

Metro Girl. Janet Evanovich. Rep. Harper-Torch (1,000,000)

750,000+

Robert Ludlum's The Bourne Legacy. Robert Ludlum and Eric Van Lustbader. Rep. St. Martin's (1,000,000)

Love Overboard. Janet Evanovich. Revision. Harper Torch (960,000)

Whiteout. Ken Follett. Rep. Signet (959,273)

#Nosy Neighbor. Fern Michaels. Rep. Pocket (954,000)

#Carolina Isle. Jude Deveraux. Orig. Pocket (953,000)

Survivor in Death. J. D. Robb. Rep. Berkley (932,179)

*What on Earth Am I Here For? Rick Warren. Rep. Zondervan (920,539)

Atkins for Life. Robert C. Atkins, M.D. Rep. St. Martin's (900,000)

#50 Harbor Street. Debbie Macomber. Orig. Mira (890,000)

Manhunt. Janet Evanovich. Revision. Harper-Torch (890,000)

Twisted. Jonathan Kellerman. Rep. Random (883,599)

Lost City. Clive Cussler. Rep. Berkley (863,160)

#Loving Scoundrel. Johanna Lindsey. Rep. Pocket Star (857,000)

#Silver Bells. Luanne Rice. Rep. Bantam (850,000)

#The Shop on Blossom Street. Debbie Macomber. Rep. Mira (840,000)

Visions in Death. J. D. Robb. Rep. Berkley (834,416)

#Family Blessings. Fern Michaels. Rep. Pocket (829,000)

The Zero Game. Brad Meltzer. Rep. Warner Vision (829,556)

#Random. Danielle Steel. Rep. Dell (810,000)

Unexpected Blessings. Barbara Taylor Bradford. Rep. St. Martin's (800,000)

#Blind Alley. Iris Johansen. Rep. Bantam (780,000)

#Dean Koontz's Frankenstein: City of Night. Dean Koontz and Ed Gorman. Orig. Bantam (780,000)

#The Summer I Dared. Barbara Delinsky. Rep. Pocket (766,000)

#Firestorm. Iris Johansen. Rep. Bantam (760,000)

Back to the Bedroom. Janet Evanovich. Revision. HarperTorch (755,000)

#*Summer's Child.* Luanne Rice. Orig. Bantam (750,000)

500,000+

Memoirs of a Geisha. Arthur Golden. Movie tie-in. Vintage (774,628)

The Colorado Kid. Stephen King. Orig. Hard Case Crime (762,000)

Just One Look. Harlan Coben. Rep. Signet (749,544)

Double Tap. Steve Martini. Rep. Jove (735,245)

Tom Clancy's Splinter Cell: Operation Barracuda. David Michaels. Orig. Berkley (724,910)

Therapy. Jonathan Kellerman. Rep. Random (717,013)

Double Homicide. Jonathan Kellerman and Faye Kellerman. Rep. Warner (715,876)

At Home in Mitford. Jan Karon. Rep. Penguin (710,127)

Lyon's Gate. Catherine Coulter. Orig. Jove (697,177)

#*Home for the Holidays.* Debbie Macomber. Rep. Mira (691,300)

#*Blood Memory.* Greg Iles. Rep. Pocket Star (676,000)

#*Holly.* Jude Deveraux. Rep. Pocket Star (673,000)

#*Second Chance.* Danielle Steel. Rep. Dell (660,000)

#*Memorial Day.* Vince Flynn. Rep. Pocket Star (658,000)

A Light in the Window. Jan Karon. Orig. Penguin (657,207)

Nights of Rain and Stars. Maeve Binchy. Rep. Signet (655,542)

#*Garden of Beasts.* Jeffery Deaver. Rep. Pocket (654,000)

The Lazarus Vendetta. Robert Ludlum and Patrick Larkin. Rep. St. Martin's (650,000)

Murder List. Julie Garwood. Rep. Random (640,853)

The Paid Companion. Amanda Quick. Rep. Jove (631,214)

Sleeping Beauty. Phillip Margolin. Rep. HarperTorch (630,000)

**The Notebook.* Nicholas Sparks. Movie tie-in. Warner (624,226)

The Prince of Beverly Hills. Stuart Woods. Rep. Signet (605,617)

The Nanny Diaries. Emma McLaughlin and Nicola Kraus. Rep. St. Martin's (600,000)

#*Worth More Dead.* Ann Rule. Orig. Pocket (597,000)

Op-Center XII: War of Eagles. Tom Clancy. Orig. Berkley (591,261)

The Color of Death. Elizabeth Lowell. Rep. Avon (585,000)

#*Green River, Running Red.* Ann Rule. Rep. Pocket (582,000)

Bait. Karen Robards. Rep. Signet (578,143)

Edge of Evil. J. A. Jance. Orig. Avon (575,000)

#*Ghost Walk.* Heather Graham. Orig. Mira (572,100)

Shem Creek. Dorothea Benton Frank. Rep. Berkley (562,494)

These High, Green Hills. Jan Karon. Orig. Penguin (560,322)

Hunting Fear. Kay Hooper. Rep. Bantam (560,000)

Two Dollar Bill. Stuart Woods. Rep. Signet (556,866)

Ain't She Sweet. Susan Elizabeth Phillips. Rep. Avon (555,000)

The Day of the Dead. J. A. Jance. Rep. Avon (555,000)

Wait Until Midnight. Amanda Quick. Orig. Jove (550,482)

#*Demon Rumm.* Sandra Brown. Rep. Bantam (550,000)

It's in His Kiss. Julia Quinn. Orig. Avon (550,000)

#*Child of Darkness.* V. C. Andrews. Orig. Pocket Star (549,000)

Final Scream. Lisa Jackson. Reissue. Zebra (544,600)

#*Next Mrs. Blackthorne.* Joan Johnston. Orig. Pocket (536,000)

The Motive. John Lescroart. Rep. Signet (536,067)

Payback. Fern Michaels. Rep. Zebra (531,800)

The Ideal Bride. Stephanie Laurens. Rep. Avon (530,000)

#*See Jane Die.* Erica Spindler. Rep. Mira (526,100)

Liars & Thieves. Stephen Coonts. Rep. St. Martin's (525,000)

Blue Dahlia. Nora Roberts. Orig. Jove (521,321)

My Life (Vol. 1). Bill Clinton. Rep. Vintage (508,434)

Hot Target. Suzanne Brockmann. Rep. Random (508,041)

Tuesdays with Morrie. Mitch Albom. Rep. Anchor (507,713)

Deep Freeze. Lisa Jackson. Orig. Zebra (507,400)

A Fine Passion. Stephanie Laurens. Orig. Avon (505,000)

Body Double. Tess Gerritsen. Rep. Random (503,234)

Picture Perfect. Fern Michaels. Reissue. Zebra (502,100)

Conviction. Richard N. Patterson. Rep. Random (501,779)

Kiss Me While I Sleep. Linda Howard. Rep. Random (501,375)

Temptress. Lisa Jackson. Orig. Onyx (501,321)

My Life (Vol. 2). Bill Clinton. Rep. Vintage (500,434)

Sandstorm. James Rollins. Rep. Avon (500,000)

The Secret Sister. Elizabeth Lowell. Reissue. Avon (500,000)

It Happened One Autumn. Lisa Kleypas. Orig. Avon (500,000)

The Goodbye Summer. Patricia Gaffney. Rep. HarperTorch (500,000)

Killer Smile. Lisa Scottoline. Rep. HarperTorch (500,000)

Hide Yourself Away. Mary Jane Clark. Rep. St. Martin's (500,000)

Children's Bestsellers: Potter Leads the Pack

Diane Roback

Senior Editor, Children's Books, *Publishers Weekly*

Many a children's book over the years has hinged on a piece of magic—a potion, a princess, a pebble. The story in children's publishing this year hinged on two particularly magic words: fantasy and sequel. And when it's a year that has a new Harry Potter title, the numbers soar off the charts into a realm all their own.

In 2005 the sixth and penultimate Harry Potter book far outsold any other book in America—13.5 million copies. Runnerup on the hardcover list: another penultimate title—Lemony Snicket's *The Penultimate Peril* (No. 12 in the projected series of 13), which came in at just under 1.8 million copies sold, followed closely by Christopher Paolini's *Eragon* sequel, *Eldest*, at 1.75 million.

Several other followups to previous hits also sold in big numbers: *Girls in Pants* (777,000); *If You Give a Pig a Party* (480,000); the fourth Artemis Fowl book (450,000); *Snowmen at Christmas*, followup to 2002's sleeper *Snowmen at Night* (309,000); *Jingle Bells, Batman Smells*, the latest Junie B. Jones title (307,000); Cornelia Funke's *Inkspell*, sequel to *Inkheart* (246,000); and *Flush* (209,000), Carl Hiaasen's next kids' novel after his Newbery Honor-winning *Hoot*.

Narnia was the big story in paperbacks: 9.8 million copies of the seven backlist titles flew off the shelves, thanks to the December movie (worldwide gross: $692 million), as well as 3.9 million other Narnia titles in various formats, for a grand total of 13.7 million books sold.

Elsewhere on the charts, Shel Silverstein had a posthumous hit in *Runny Babbit* (469,000), Eric Carle's *10 Little Rubber Ducks* racked up big sales (374,000); James Patterson kicked off a series for kids with *Maximum Ride* (302,000); and Robert Sabuda's newest pop-up was *Winter's Tale* (285,000).

Notable this year was the dearth of big celebrity books; only Caroline Kennedy's poetry collection, *A Family of Poems* (275,000), and Paul McCartney's foray into picture books, *High in the Clouds* (206,000), made top-selling showings.

For the full set of numbers, read on.

Children's Hardcover Frontlist

300,000+

1. *Harry Potter and the Half-Blood Prince.* J. K. Rowling. Scholastic/Levine (13,500,000)
2. *The Penultimate Peril (A Series of Unfortunate Events #12).* Lemony Snicket, illus. by Brett Helquist. HarperCollins (1,765,315)
3. *Eldest.* Christopher Paolini. Knopf (1,752,753)
4. *Girls in Pants: The Third Summer of the Sisterhood.* Ann Brashares. Delacorte (776,839)
5. *If You Give a Pig a Party.* Laura Numeroff, illus. by Felicia Bond. HarperCollins/Geringer (479,589)
6. *Runny Babbit.* Shel Silverstein. HarperCollins (469,373)
7. *Artemis Fowl: The Opal Deception.* Eoin Colfer. Hyperion/Miramax (450,000)
8. *10 Little Rubber Ducks.* Eric Carle. HarperCollins (373,862)
9. *Snowmen at Christmas.* Caralyn Buehner, illus. by Mark Buehner. Dial (309,373)
10. *Jingle Bells, Batman Smells! (P.S. So Does May) (Junie B. Jones #25).* Barbara Park, illus. by Denise Brunkus. Random (307,232)
11. *Maximum Ride.* James Patterson. Little, Brown (301,747)

200,000+

12. *Winter's Tale.* Robert Sabuda. Little Simon, 2003 (285,090)
13. *Carnival at Candlelight (Magic Tree House #33).* Mary Pope Osborne, illus. by Sal Murdocca. Random (281,841)
14. *A Family of Poems.* Caroline Kennedy, illus. by Jon J Muth. Hyperion (275,000)
15. *The Lion, the Witch and the Wardrobe.* Kate Egan. HarperKidsEntertainment (271,480)
16. *Dora's Big Book of Stories.* Simon Spotlight (266,805)
17. *Diary of a Spider.* Doreen Cronin, illus. by Harry Bliss. HarperCollins/Cotler (259,524)
18. *Belly Button Book* (board book). Sandra Boynton. Workman (254,514)
19. *The Cranium Big Book of Outrageous Fun.* Little, Brown (254,325)
20. *Inkspell.* Cornelia Funke. Chicken House/Scholastic (245,738)
21. *Fairyopolis.* Inspired by Cicely Mary Barker. Frederick Warne (242,331)
22. *Madagascar: It's a Zoo in Here.* Michael Steele. Scholastic (232,923)

23. *Cinderella.* Golden/Disney (227,343)

24. *Season of the Sandstorms (MTH #34).* Mary Pope Osborne, illus. by Sal Murdocca. Random (226,921)

25. *Walt Disney's Cinderella.* Lara Bergen. Disney (225,000)

26. *A Series of Unfortunate Events: The Ominous Omnibus (Books 1–3).* Lemony Snicket, illus. by Brett Helquist. HarperKidsEntertainment (217,694)

27. *Are You My Mother?* (cloth edition) P. D. Eastman. Golden (211,608)

28. *Flush.* Carl Hiaasen. Knopf (208,642)

29. *High in the Clouds.* Paul McCartney, Geoff Dunbar, and Philip Ardagh, illus. by Geoff Dunbar. Dutton (205,519)

100,000+

30. *The Little Engine That Could.* Watty Piper, illus. by Loren Long. Philomel (188,751)

31. *The Happy Man and His Dump Truck.* Miryam, illus. by Tibor Gergely. Golden (186,860)

32. *Honey . . . Honey . . . Lion!* Jan Brett. Putnam (175,050)

33. *Fairy Dust and the Quest for the Egg.* Gail Carson Levine, illus. by David Christiana. Disney (175,000)

34. *Dora the Explorer Movie Theater Storybook & Movie Projector.* Reader's Digest (174,941)

35. *Mary Engelbreit's Mother Goose.* Mary Engelbreit. HarperCollins (168,135)

36. *Hugs and Kisses (Dora the Explorer).* Christine Ricci. Simon Spotlight (161,844)

37. *Charlie Bone and the Castle of Mirrors.* Jenny Nimmo. Scholastic/ Orchard (160,748)

38. *Disney's Chicken Little.* Golden/Disney (158,039)

39. *Berry Princess* (board book). Megan Bryant. Grosset & Dunlap (150,038)

40. *Septimus Heap, Book One: Magyk.* Angie Sage. HarperCollins/ Tegen (136,870)

41. *Read and Learn Bible.* Scholastic/Little Shepherd (136,445)

42. *Arthur Spiderwick's Field Guide to the Fantastical World Around You.* Tony DiTerlizzi and Holly Black. Simon & Schuster (132,950)

43. *The Princess Diaries, Vol. VI: Princess in Training.* Meg Cabot. Harper-Collins (130,126)

44. *Here Come the Backyardigans!* Janice Burgess. Simon Spotlight (129,539)

45. *Rough Weather Ahead for Walter the Farting Dog.* William Kotzwinkle, Glenn Murray and Elizabeth Gundy, illus. by Audrey Coleman. Dutton (122,285)

46. *Russell the Sheep.* Rob Scotton. HarperCollins (121,423)

47. *Disney's Chicken Little (Read-Aloud Storybook).* Random/Disney (114,561)

48. *Who's Under That Hat?* Sarah Weeks, illus. by David A. Carter. Harcourt/ Red Wagon (110,000)

49. *The Rivers of Zadaa (Pendragon #6).* D. J. MacHale. Simon & Schuster (109,856)

50. *Ready or Not.* Meg Cabot. HarperCollins (107,204)

51. *Cinderella.* Matthew Reinhart. Little Simon (104,863)

52. *Zathura the Movie: Deluxe Storybook.* Houghton Mifflin (104,516)

53. *Then He Ate My Boy Entrancers.* Louise Rennison. HarperTempest (103,029)

54. *My Grandpa's Briefcase.* P. H. Hanson. Workman (101,638)

55. *The Fairy Tale Detectives (The Sisters Grimm Book 1).* Michael Buckley, illus. by Peter Ferguson. Abrams/ Amulet (101,243)

56. *Disney Once Upon a Time.* Disney (100,000)

57. *Disney Princess: Time for the Ball.* Lara Bergen. Disney (100,000)

75,000+

58. *The Turkey Ball* (board book). David Steinberg, illus. by Liz Conrad. Price Stern Sloan (98,149)

59. *Nurse Nancy.* Kathryn Jackson, illus. by Corinne Malvern. Golden (97,649)

60. *One Fish, Two Fish, Three, Four, Five Fish.* Dr. Seuss. Random (97,529)

61. *Can You See What I See?* Walter Wick. Scholastic/Cartwheel (96,581)

62. *I Love You Through and Through* (board book). Bernadette Rossetti Shustak, illus. by Caroline Jay Church. Scholastic/Cartwheel (95,045)

63. *The Chronicles of Narnia Full-Color Gift Edition Box Set.* C. S. Lewis, illus. by Pauline Baynes. HarperCollins (94,237)

64. *How Do Dinosaurs Eat Their Food?* Jane Yolen, illus. by Mark Teague. Scholastic/Blue Sky (93,201)

65. *Dog Train.* Sandra Boynton. Workman (93,010)

66. *High Rhulain.* Brian Jacques. Philomel (92,671)

67. *Thomas & Friends: Railway Rhymes.* R. Schuyler Hooke, illus. by Richard Courtney. Random (92,184)

68. *Beyond the Valley of Thorns (Land of Elyon #2).* Patrick Carman. Scholastic/Orchard (91,970)

69. *Pooh's Easter Basket.* Random/Disney (89,496)

70. *Thomas & Friends: Go, Train, Go!* Rev. W. Awdry, illus. by Tommy Stubbs. Random (89,338)

71. *A Time for Freedom.* Lynne Cheney. Simon & Schuster (86,954)

72. *The Adventures of Captain Underpants Collectors Edition.* Dav Pilkey. Scholastic/Blue Sky (85,588)

73. *My Very First Book of Colors.* Eric Carle. Philomel (85,452)

74. *Bears.* Ruth Krauss, illus. by Maurice Sendak. HarperCollins (85,276)

75. *Leonardo the Terrible Monster.* Mo Willems. Hyperion (85,000)

76. *Click, Clack, Quackity Quack.* Doreen Cronin, illus. by Betsy Lewin. Simon & Schuster (84,992)

77. *Dick and Jane: We Play Outside.* Grosset & Dunlap (84,298)

78. *Scorpia.* Anthony Horowitz. Philomel (83,280)

79. *The Dark Hills Divide (Land of Elyon #1).* Patrick Carman. Scholastic/ Orchard (79,975)

80. *Sesame Street Elmo's Easy as ABC.* Reader's Digest (78,614)

81. *The Unusual Suspects (The Sisters Grimm Book 2).* Michael Buckley, illus. by Peter Ferguson. Abrams/Amulet (78,113)

82. *My Fuzzy Valentine.* Naomi Kleinberg, illus. by Louis Womble. Random (77,987)

83. *My Very First Book of Shapes* (board book). Eric Carle. Philomel (77,803)

84. *Biscuit Storybook Collection.* Alyssa Satin Capucilli, illus. by Pat Schories. HarperFestival (77,379)

85. *Rebel Angels.* Libba Bray. Delacorte (77,095)

86. *It's Happy Bunny: Love Bites.* Jim Benton. Scholastic (76,871)

87. *The Curse of the Gloamglozer (The Edge Chronicles #4).* Paul Stewart and Chris Riddell. Random/Fickling (76,274)

88. *Rotten School #1.* R. L. Stine, illus. by Trip Park. HarperCollins (75,931)

89. *Prayers for Children.* Golden (75,337)

90. *Zen Shorts.* Jon J Muth. Scholastic (75,298)

91. *The Penderwicks.* Jeanne Birdsall. Knopf (75,087)

Children's Hardcover Backlist

300,000+

1. *The Polar Express.* Chris Van Allsburg. Houghton Mifflin, 1985 (898,187)

2. *Goodnight Moon* (board book). Margaret Wise Brown, illus. by Clement Hurd. HarperFestival, 1991 (627,169)

3. *The Bad Beginning (A Series of Unfortunate Events #1).* Lemony Snicket, illus. by Brett Helquist. HarperCollins, 1999 (567,754)

4. *The Miserable Mill (A Series of Unfortunate Events #4).* Lemony Snicket, illus. by Brett Helquist. HarperCollins, 2000 (532,787)

5. *The Austere Academy (A Series of Unfortunate Events #5).* Lemony Snicket, illus. by Brett Helquist. HarperCollins, 2000 (527,009)

6. *The Grim Grotto (A Series of Unfortunate Events #11).* Lemony Snicket, illus. by Brett Helquist. HarperCollins, 2004 (495,717)

7. *The Ersatz Elevator (A Series of Unfortunate Events #6).* Lemony Snicket, illus. by Brett Helquist. HarperCollins, 2001 (483,676)

8. *Brown Bear, Brown Bear, What Do You See?* (board book) Bill Martin Jr., illus. by Eric Carle. Holt, 1996 (474,276)

9. *The Reptile Room (A Series of Unfortunate Events #2)*. Lemony Snicket, illus. by Brett Helquist. HarperCollins, 1999 (474,138)

10. *The Wide Window (A Series of Unfortunate Events #3)*. Lemony Snicket, illus. by Brett Helquist. HarperCollins, 2000 (454,709)

11. *The Slippery Slope (A Series of Unfortunate Events #10)*. Lemony Snicket, illus. by Brett Helquist. HarperCollins, 2003 (443,912)

12. *The Very Hungry Caterpillar* (board book). Eric Carle. Philomel, 1994 (427,351)

13. *The Vile Village (A Series of Unfortunate Events #7)*. Lemony Snicket, illus. by Brett Helquist. HarperCollins, 2001 (423,905)

14. *Green Eggs and Ham*. Dr. Seuss. Random, 1960 (416,264)

15. *The Hostile Hospital (A Series of Unfortunate Events #8)*. Lemony Snicket, illus. by Brett Helquist. HarperCollins, 2001 (403,607)

16. *Oh, the Places You'll Go!* Dr. Seuss. Random, 1990 (385,026)

17. *The Carnivorous Carnival (A Series of Unfortunate Events #9)*. Lemony Snicket, illus. by Brett Helquist. HarperCollins, 2002 (384,506)

18. *One Fish, Two Fish, Red Fish, Blue Fish*. Dr. Seuss. Random, 1960 (331,809)

19. *The Poky Little Puppy*. Janette Sebring Lowrey. Golden, 2001 (323,972)

200,000+

20. *Dr. Seuss's ABC* (board book). Dr. Seuss. Random, 1996 (299,361)

21. *Thomas' Magnetic Playbook*. Illus. by Ted Gadecki. Random, 2001 (295,000)

22. *Mr. Brown Can Moo, Can You?* (board book) Dr. Seuss. Random, 1996 (285,919)

23. *Thomas and the Big, Big Bridge*. Rev. W. Awdry. Golden, 2003 (279,984)

24. *Dora's Storytime Collection*. Simon Spotlight, 2003 (268,021)

25. *The Going-to-Bed Book* (board book). Sandra Boynton. Little Simon, 1982 (263,338)

26. *The Giving Tree*. Shel Silverstein. HarperCollins, 1964 (259,021)

27. *Disney's Storybook Collection*. Disney, 1998 (250,000)

28. *Barnyard Dance!* (board book) Sandra Boynton. Workman, 1993 (235,203)

29. *The Cat in the Hat*. Dr. Seuss. Random, 1957 (226,831)

30. *Harry Potter and the Sorcerer's Stone*. J. K. Rowling. Scholastic/Levine, 1998 (220,428)

31. *Snuggle Puppy* (board book). Sandra Boynton. Workman, 2003 (218,414)

32. *The Little Red Hen*. J.P. Miller. Golden, 2001 (215,069)

33. *Harry Potter and the Goblet of Fire*. J. K. Rowling. Scholastic/Levine, 2000 (211,674)

34. *Harry Potter and the Order of the Phoenix*. J. K. Rowling. Scholastic/Levine, 2003 (210,677)

35. *Tails.* Matthew Van Fleet. Harcourt/Red Wagon, 2003 (210,000)
36. *Five Little Monkeys Jumping on the Bed* (board book). Eileen Christelow. Clarion, 1998 (203,885)
37. *Fisher Price Cars, Trucks, Planes & Trains.* Reader's Digest, 2004 (200,916)
38. *Polar Bear, Polar Bear, What Do You Hear?* (board book) Bill Martin Jr., illus. by Eric Carle. Holt, 1997 (200,377)

100,000+

39. *Are You My Mother?* (board book) P. D. Eastman. Random, 1998 (197,759)
40. *Hop on Pop.* Dr. Seuss. Random, 1963 (193,646)
41. *Disney Princess Music Player Storybook.* Reader's Digest, 2004 (193,405)
42. *Where the Sidewalk Ends (30th anniversary edition).* Shel Silverstein. HarperCollins, 2004 (193,137)
43. *Harry Potter and the Prisoner of Azkaban.* J. K. Rowling. Scholastic/Levine, 1999 (189,336)
44. *Moo, Baa, La La La!* (board book) Sandra Boynton. Little Simon, 1982 (184,150)
45. *Harry Potter and the Chamber of Secrets.* J. K. Rowling. Scholastic/Levine, 1999 (182,359)
46. *Put Me in the Zoo* (board book). Robert Lopshire. Random, 2001 (177,307)
47. *The Field Guide (The Spiderwick Chronicles #1).* Tony DiTerlizzi and Holly Black. Simon & Schuster, 2003 (174,847)
48. *My Little Golden Book About God.* Eloise Wilkin. Golden, 2000 (173,742)
49. *The Foot Book* (board book). Dr. Seuss. Random, 1996 (170,845)
50. *Are You My Mother?* P. D. Eastman. Random, 1960 (170,466)
51. *I'm a Big Sister.* Joanna Cole, illus. by Maxie Chambliss. HarperCollins, 1997 (169,219)
52. *Zathura.* Chris Van Allsburg. Houghton Mifflin, 2002 (168,793)
53. *Go, Dog, Go!* P. D. Eastman. Random, 1961 (167,868)
54. *Dr. Seuss ABC.* Dr. Seuss. Random, 1960 (165,262)
55. *Dragon Rider.* Cornelia Funke. Scholastic/Chicken House, 2004 (164,277)
56. *Clap Your Hands.* Random, 2002 (163,132)
57. *I'm a Big Brother.* Joanna Cole, illus. by Maxie Chambliss. HarperCollins, 1997 (161,948)
58. *Eragon.* Christopher Paolini. Knopf, 2003 (161,331)
59. *The Chronicles of Narnia.* C. S. Lewis, illus. by Pauline Baynes. HarperCollins, 2004 (160,307)
60. *The Shy Little Kitten.* Cathleen Schurr. Golden, 1999 (158,566)
61. *Walt Disney's Scamp.* Golden/Disney, 2004 (158,036)
62. *Disney/Pixar's Finding Nemo.* Golden/Disney, 2003 (157,724)
63. *The Three Little Pigs.* Golden/Disney, 2004 (157,598)

64. *Kitten's First Full Moon.* Kevin Henkes. Greenwillow, 2004 (155,974)

65. *There's a Wocket in My Pocket!* (board book) Dr. Seuss. Random, 1996 (155,030)

66. *My Granny's Purse.* P. H. Hanson. Workman, 2003 (153,546)

67. *Disney's Princess Storybook Collection.* Sarah Heller. Disney, 1999 (150,000)

68. *Elmo's Big Left-and-Look Book.* Anna Ross, illus. by Joe Mathieu. Random, 1994 (149,998)

69. *Summer of the Sea Serpent (MTH #31).* Mary Pope Osborne, illus. by Sal Murdocca. Random/Stepping Stone, 2004 (147,118)

70. *Disney Princess: Happily Ever After Stories.* Disney, 2004 (145,000)

71. *Storybook Treasury of Dick and Jane and Friends.* Grosset & Dunlap, 2003 (144,713)

72. *Kira-Kira.* Cynthia Kadohata. Atheneum, 2004 (144,648)

73. *Dick and Jane: A Christmas Story.* Grosset & Dunlap, 2004 (143,453)

74. *The Runaway Bunny* (board book). Margaret Wise Brown, illus. by Clement Hurd. HarperFestival, 1991 (141,045)

75. *The Jolly Barnyard.* Annie North Bedford, illus. by Tibor Gergely. Golden, 2004 (139,704)

76. *It's Hard to Be Five.* Jamie Lee Curtis, illus. by Laura Cornell. HarperCollins/Cotler, 2004 (137,290)

77. *Where Is Baby's Belly Button?* (board book) Karen Katz. Little Simon, 2000 (136,647)

78. *The Lion, the Witch and the Wardrobe* (picture book). C. S. Lewis, illus. by Tudor Humphries. HarperCollins, 2004 (133,918)

79. *Good Night, Gorilla* (board book). Peggy Rathmann. Putnam, 1996 (132,752)

80. *The Complete Chronicles of Narnia.* C. S. Lewis, illus. by Pauline Baynes. HarperCollins, 1998 (131,978)

81. *A Treasury of Curious George.* H. A. and Margret Rey. Houghton Mifflin, 2004 (130,814)

82. *Haunted Castle on Hallow's Eve (MTH #30).* Mary Pope Osborne, illus. by Sal Murdocca. Random/Stepping Stone, 2003 (130,797)

83. *Disney Princess Movie Theater Storybook & Movie Projector.* Reader's Digest, 2002 (128,487)

84. *The Seeing Stone (The Spiderwick Chronicles #2).* Tony DiTerlizzi and Holly Black. Simon & Schuster, 2003 (127,791)

85. *Hand, Hand, Fingers, Thumb.* Al Perkins. Random, 1998 (126,679)

86. *Thomas the Tank Engine's Big Lift-and-Look Book.* Rev. W. Awdry, illus. by Owain Bell. Random, 1996 (124,911)

87. *Pajama Time!* (board book) Sandra Boynton. Workman, 2000 (122,095)

88. *Go, Dog, Go!* (board book) P. D. Eastman. Random, 1997 (121,660)

89. *Olivia* (board book). Ian Falconer. Atheneum/Schwartz, 2004 (120,169)

90. *The Complete Adventures of Curious George.* Margret and H. A. Rey. Houghton Mifflin, 2001 (119,945)

91. *Old MacDonald.* Illus. by Michelle Berg. Scholastic, 2004 (117,988)

92. *Hop on Pop* (board book). Dr. Seuss. Random, 2004 (116,730)

93. *Winter of the Ice Wizard (MTH #32).* Mary Pope Osborne, illus. by Sal Murdocca. Random/Stepping Stone, 2004 (116,692)

94. *Put Me in the Zoo.* Robert Lopshire. Random, 1960 (115,046)

95. *Fisher-Price Christmastime Is Here!* Reader's Digest, 2002 (114,786)

96. *Doctor Dan the Bandage Man.* Helen Gaspard, illus. by Corinne Malvern. Golden, 2004 (114,677)

97. *If You Give a Mouse a Cookie.* Laura Numeroff, illus. by Felicia Bond. HarperCollins/Geringer, 1985 (114,402)

98. *Al Capone Does My Shirts.* Gennifer Choldenko. Putnam, 2004 (113,902)

99. *Fox in Socks.* Dr. Seuss. Random, 1965 (113,142)

100. *Where the Wild Things Are.* Maurice Sendak. HarperCollins, 1963 (112,924)

101. *How the Grinch Stole Christmas.* Dr. Seuss. Random, 1957 (112,405)

102. *Doggies* (board book). Sandra Boynton. Little Simon, 1984 (110,670)

103. *Jesus and the 12 Dudes Who Did.* Mindy MacDonald. Multnomah, 2004 (110,442)

104. *Knuffle Bunny.* Mo Willems. Hyperion, 2004 (110,000)

105. *Peter and the Starcatchers.* Ridley Pearson and Dave Barry. Disney, 2004 (110,000)

106. *Dora's Halloween Adventure.* Sarah Willson. Simon Spotlight, 2003 (109,414)

107. *The Ironwood Tree (Spiderwick Chronicles #4).* Tony DiTerlizzi and Holly Black. Simon & Schuster, 2004 (108,668)

108. *I Love You, Mommy.* Edie Evans. Golden, 1999 (107,119)

109. *Lucinda's Secret (Spiderwick Chronicles #3).* Tony DiTerlizzi and Holly Black. Simon & Schuster, 2003 (105,964)

110. *Dick and Jane: Fun with Our Family.* Grosset & Dunlap, 2004 (104,706)

111. *Top-Secret, Personal Beeswax: A Journal by Junie B. and Me.* Barbara Park, illus. by Denise Brunkus. Random/Stepping Stone, 2003 (104,580)

112. *Christmas in Camelot (MTH #29).* Mary Pope Osborne, illus. by Sal Murdocca. Random/Stepping Stone, 2001 (104,542)

113. *But Not the Hippopotamus* (board book). Sandra Boynton. Little Simon, 1982 (103,696)

114. *Mister Seahorse.* Eric Carle. Philomel, 2004 (101,830)

115. *The Little Engine That Could.* Watty Piper, illus. by Doris and George Hauman. Grosset & Dunlap, 1978 (101,685)

116. *The Alphabet Book* (board book). P. D. Eastman. Random, 2000 (101,056)

117. *The Very Lonely Firefly* (board book). Eric Carle. Philomel, 1999 (100,598)

118. *I Love You, Daddy.* Edie Evans. Golden, 2001 (100,229)
119. *Disney Princess Dress-Up.* Disney, 2004 (100,000)
120. *Don't Let the Pigeon Drive the Bus!* Mo Willems. Hyperion, 2003 (100,000)

75,000+

121. *Walter the Farting Dog: Trouble at the Yard Sale.* William Kotzwinkle, and Glenn Murray, illus. by Audrey Coleman. Dutton, 2004 (98,953)
122. *Dick and Jane: Fun Wherever We Are.* Grosset & Dunlap, 2004 (98,049)
123. *Pinocchio.* Steffi Fletcher. Golden/Disney, 2002 (97,629)
124. *Valentines for Everyone!* (*Dora the Explorer* board book) Chris Gifford and Christine Ricci. Simon Spotlight, 2003 (97,626)
125. *Toes, Ears, & Nose!* (board book) Marian Dane Bauer, illus. by Karen Katz. Little Simon, 2003 (96,789)
126. *Homeward Bound* (*Dora the Explorer* board book). Sonali Fry. Simon Spotlight, 2004 (96,624)
127. *Fisher-Price My Little People Farm.* Reader's Digest, 1997 (96,582)
128. *Blue Hat, Green Hat* (board book). Sandra Boynton. Little Simon, 1984 (95,239)
129. *How Do Dinosaurs Clean Their Rooms?* (board book) Jane Yolen, illus. by Mark Teague. Scholastic/Blue Sky, 2004 (94,384)
130. *The Sisterhood of the Traveling Pants.* Ann Brashares. Delacorte, 2001 (93,148)
131. *A Light in the Attic.* Shel Silverstein. HarperCollins, 1981 (92,300)
132. *Diary of a Worm.* Doreen Cronin, illus. by Harry Bliss. HarperCollins/ Cotler, 2003 (91,584)
133. *Elmo Loves You.* Sarah Albee, illus. by Maggie Swanson. Random, 2002 (91,360)
134. *Ten Apples Up on Top!* (board book) Dr. Seuss. Random, 1998 (91,295)
135. *The World of Dick and Jane and Friends.* Grosset & Dunlap, 2004 (91,103)
136. *Dora Discovers.* Lauren Silverhardt. Simon Spotlight, 2004 (90,838)
137. *Walt Disney's Bambi.* Golden Books. Golden/Disney, 2004 (90,392)
138. *The Secret of the Old Clock (Nancy Drew #1).* Carolyn Keene. Grosset & Dunlap, 1930 (90,573)
139. *So Big!* Anna Jane Hays, illus. by Christopher Moroney. Random, 2003 (89,657)
140. *Counting Kisses* (board book). Karen Katz. Little Simon, 2003 (89,611)
141. *I Can Read with My Eyes Shut!* Dr. Seuss. Random, 1978 (89,281)
142. *The Night Before Christmas Pop-Up.* Robert Sabuda. Little Simon, 2002 (88,768)
143. *The Very Busy Spider.* Eric Carle. Philomel, 1995 (88,504)

144. *Philadelphia Chickens.* Sandra Boynton. Workman, 2002 (88,173)
145. *The Lion, the Witch and the Wardrobe.* C. S. Lewis, illus. by Pauline Baynes. HarperCollins, 2003 (88,131)
146. *The Night Before Christmas.* Clement C. Moore, illus. by Mary Engelbreit. HarperCollins, 2002 (88,053)
147. *I Spy Treasure Hunt.* Jean Marzollo and Walter Wick, illus. by Walter Wick., 1999 (86,530)
148. *A to Z* (board book). Sandra Boynton. Little Simon, 1984 (85,542)
149. *I Spy Christmas.* Jean Marzollo, illus. by Walter Wick. Scholastic/Cartwheel, 1992 (85,531)
150. *Mother Goose.* Golden/Disney, 2004 (83,270)
151. *Ten Apples Up on Top!* Theo. LeSieg, illus. by Roy McKie. Random, 1961 (82,721)
152. *Falling Up.* Shel Silverstein. HarperCollins, 1996 (82,153)
153. *Walt Disney's Dumbo.* Golden/ Disney, 2004 (81,574)
154. *Wonderful Wizard of Oz.* Robert Sabuda. Little Simon, 2000 (81,178)
155. *The Wrath of Mulgarath (Spiderwick Chronicles #5).* Tony DiTerlizzi and Holly Black. Simon & Schuster, 2004 (80,263)
156. *The Hidden Staircase (Nancy Drew #2).* Carolyn Keene. Grosset & Dunlap, 1930 (79,416)
157. *Elmo's World: Love!* Kara McMahon, illus. by Mary Beth Nelson. Random, 2004 (79,276)
158. *Scholastic Children's Dictionary.* Scholastic, 2002 (79,059)
159. *Time for Bed* (board book). Mem Fox, illus. by Jane Dyer. Harcourt/Red Wagon, 1997 (79,000)
160. *The Nose Book* (board book). Al Perkins, illus. by Joe Mathieu. Random, 2003 (78,461)
161. *If You Take a Mouse to School.* Laura Numeroff, illus. by Felicia Bond. HarperCollins/Geringer, 2002 (77,987)
162. *The Saggy Baggy Elephant.* Kathryn Jackson, illus. by Gustaf Tenggren. Golden, 1999 (77,554)
163. *I Am Not Going to Get Up Today!* Dr. Seuss, illus. by James Stevenson. Random, 1987 (77,071)
164. *Stop, Train, Stop!* (board book) Rev. W. Awdry. Random, 1998 (76,931)
165. *Snowmen at Night.* Caralyn Buehner, illus. by Mark Buehner. Dial, 2002 (76,776)
166. *Disney's The Little Mermaid.* Golden, 2003 (76,498)
167. *The Little Red Caboose.* Marian Potter. Golden, 2000 (75,779)
168. *If You Give a Pig a Pancake.* Laura Numeroff, illus. by Felicia Bond. HarperCollins/Geringer, 1998 (75,779)
169. *I'll Teach My Dog a Lot of Words* (board book). Michael Frith, illus. by P. D. Eastman. Random, 1999 (75,562)
170. *The Very Hungry Caterpillar.* Eric Carle. Philomel, 1981 (75,529)

171. *Click, Clack Moo: Cows That Type.* Doreen Cronin, illus. by Betsy Lewin. Simon & Schuster, 2000 (75,467)

172. *Oh, the Thinks You Can Think!* Dr. Seuss. Random, 1975 (75,244)

173. *Opposites* (board book). Sandra Boynton. Little Simon, 1982 (75,202)

174. *How I Became a Pirate.* Melinda Long, illus. by David Shannon. Harcourt, 2003 (75,000)

Children's Paperback Frontlist

300,000+

1. *The Lion, the Witch and the Wardrobe Movie* (movie tie-in). C. S. Lewis, illus. by Pauline Baynes. HarperKidsEntertainment (996,122)

2. *Eragon.* Christopher Paolini. Knopf (887,901)

3. *The Chronicles of Narnia Movie* (tie-in edition). C. S. Lewis, illus. by Pauline Baynes. HarperKidsEntertainment (886,272)

4. *Charlie & the Chocolate Factory* (movie tie-in). Roald Dahl, illus. by Quentin Blake. Puffin (795,925)

5. *The Sisterhood of the Traveling Pants* (movie tie-in). Ann Brashares. Dell (534,313)

6. *Strawberry Shortcake: Berry Fairy Tales Cinderella.* Megan E. Bryant, illus. by Scott Neely. Grosset & Dunlap (343,139)

7. *Bambi II.* Random/Disney (330,000)

200,000+

8. *Big Sister Dora (Dora the Explorer).* Adapted by Alison Inches, illus. by Dave Aikins. Simon Spotlight (295,375)

9. *Star Wars: Episode II Revenge of the Sith.* Patricia Wredge. Scholastic (294,275)

10. *Disney's Chicken Little: The Sky Is Falling!* Random/Disney (273,042)

11. *Katie Kazoo, Switcheroo Super Special: Whirlwind Vacation.* Nancy Krulik, illus. by John and Wendy. Grosset & Dunlap (260,778)

12. *Dance to the Rescue (Dora the Explorer).* Adapted by Laura Driscoll, illus. by Dave Aikins. Simon Spotlight (259,044)

13. *The Lion, the Witch and the Wardrobe: The Creatures of Narnia.* Scout Driggs, illus. by Justin Sweet. HarperKidsEntertainment (258,640)

14. *Disney's Chicken Little: The Big Game!* Random/Disney (236,452)

15. *The Lion, the Witch and the Wardrobe: Welcome to Narnia.* Jennifer Frantz. HarperTrophy (235,630)

16. *Nobody Does It Better (Gossip Girl #7).* Cecily Von Ziegesar. Little, Brown (234,493)

17. *Junie B., First Grader: Boo . . . and I Mean It!* Barbara Park, illus. by Denise Brunkus. Random (230,012)

18. *Barbie: The Magic of Pegasus.* Mary Man-Kong. Golden (229,952)

19. *Junie B., First Grader: Shipwrecked.* Barbara Park, illus. by Denise Brunkus. Random (228,686)
20. *Madagascar: It's a Zoo in Here.* Michael Steele. Scholastic (218,501)
21. *Madagascar: Fearless Foursome.* Apple Jordan. Scholastic (215,017)
22. *Inkheart.* Cornelia Funke. Scholastic/Chicken House (213,463)
23. *Star Wars Revenge of the Sith* (movie storybook). Random (212,707)
24. *The Revenge of the Wannabes (The Clique #3).* Lisi Harrison. Little, Brown (203,444)

100,000+

25. *Strawberry Shortcake's Ballet Recital.* Grosset & Dunlap (196,508)
26. *Strawberry Shortcake: Strawberry Shortcake and the Butterfly Garden.* Kelli Curry. Grosset & Dunlap (192,526)
27. *Thomas Goes Fishing.* Rev. W. Awdry, illus. by Richard Courtney. Random (192,280)
28. *Madagascar: Born to Be Wild.* Erica David. Scholastic (191,709)
29. *The Lion, the Witch and the Wardrobe.* C. S. Lewis. HarperCollins (189,758)
30. *Madagascar: Bungle in the Jungle.* Apple Jordan. Scholastic (187,054)
31. *Strawberry Shortcake: Strawberry Shortcake's Seaberry Mystery.* Sonia Sander, illus. by Josie Yee and Jim Durk. Grosset & Dunlap (184,648)
32. *A Dream for a Princess.* Random/Disney (183,718)
33. *Barbie and the Magic of Pegasus.* Random (181,744)
34. *Dora's Pirate Adventure.* Adapted by Leslie Valdes. Simon Spotlight (180,555)
35. *ttyl.* Lauren Myracle. Abrams/Amulet (178,265)
36. *Thomas & Friends: Calling All Engines.* Rev. W. Awdry, illus. by Richard Courtney. Random (177,391)
37. *Dora's Costume Party.* Christine Ricci. Simon Spotlight (176,849)
38. *Strawberry Shortcake: Filly Show.* Grosset & Dunlap (175,189)
39. *Nothing Can Keep Us Together (Gossip Girl #8).* Cecily Von Ziegesar. Little, Brown (172,701)
40. *The World Almanac for Kids 2006.* Edited by Ken Park. World Almanac (168,012)
41. *The Lion, the Witch and the Wardrobe: Tea with Mr. Tumnus.* Jennifer Frantz. HarperTrophy (166,915)
42. *My Little Pony: The Missing Recipe.* Ruth Benjamin, illus. by Angel Rodriguez. HarperFestival (166,366)
43. *Strawberry Shortcake: The Halloween Play.* Eva Mason, illus. by John Huxtable. Grosset & Dunlap (165,026)
44. *The Lion, the Witch and the Wardrobe: The Quest for Aslan.* Jasmine Jones. HarperKidsEntertainment (163,274)
45. *Revenge of the Sith Scrapbook.* Ryder Windham. Random (158,151)

46. *The Invasion of the Boy Snatchers (The Clique #4).* Lisi Harrison. Little, Brown (156,152)

47. *The Lion, the Witch and the Wardrobe: Edmund and the White Witch.* Scout Driggs, illus. by Justin Sweet. HarperKidsEntertainment (155,912)

48. *Thomas & Friends: Hooray for Thomas!* Based on the stories of Rev. W. Awdry. Random (151,048)

49. *Artemis Fowl.* Eoin Colfer. Hyperion/Miramax (150,000)

50. *Star Wars Revenge of the Sith: Obi-Wan's Foe.* Jane Mason and Sarah Stephens, illus. by Tommy Lee Edwards. LucasBooks (148,762)

51. *Charlie & the Chocolate Factory* (movie picture book). Puffin (146,804)

52. *Disney/Pixar's Finding Nemo.* Random/Disney (145,160)

53. *Madagascar: Alex and Marty Run Wild.* Marcie Aboff. Scholastic (138,900)

54. *A Great and Terrible Beauty.* Libba Bray. Delacorte (137,552)

55. *My Little Pony: Rose Blossom's First Christmas.* Ann Maria Capalija, illus. by Carlo LoRaso. HarperFestival (137,378)

56. *Chasing Vermeer.* Blue Balliett, illus. by Brett Helquist. Scholastic (133,106)

57. *The Curse of Ravenscourt.* Sarah Masters Buckey, illus. by Jean-Paul Tibbles. Pleasant Company, (132,798)

58. *Christmas Is Here!* Siobhan Ciminera. Grosset & Dunlap (130,091)

59. *Tall Cool One (The A-List #4).* Zoey Dean. Little, Brown (126,756)

60. *The Magician's Nephew.* C. S. Lewis. HarperCollins (125,934)

61. *Travel Team.* Mike Lupica. Puffin (124,995)

62. *Dora's Starry Christmas.* Christine Ricci. Simon Spotlight (124,919)

63. *Robots: Meet the Robots.* Acton Figueroa, illus. by Phil Mendez. HarperKidsEntertainment (124,159)

64. *Barbie Fairytopia.* Mary Man-Kong. Golden (123,005)

65. *Eggs for Everyone! (Dora the Explorer).* Laura Driscoll. Simon Spotlight (122,944)

66. *The Princess Diaries, Vol. V.* Meg Cabot. HarperTrophy (120,416)

67. *The Amulet of Samarkand.* Jonathan Stroud. Hyperion/Miramax, 2004 (120,000)

68. *At the Carnival (Dora the Explorer).* Laura Driscoll. Simon Spotlight (119,482)

69. *Just Like Me.* Random/Disney (118,780)

70. *The Batman: Severe Gear.* Devan Aptekar. Scholastic (118,387)

71. *The Batman: Above the Law.* Devan Aptekar. Scholastic (117,582)

72. *Madagascar Play Along Storybook.* J. E. Bright. Scholastic (117,564)

73. *Miss Spider: The Sunny Patch.* David Kirk. Grosset & Dunlap (117,272)

74. *Charlie and the Chocolate Factory* (movie joke book). Puffin (115,085)

75. *Winx Club: What Are Friends For?* Ellie Oryan, illus. by Santanach. Scholastic (114,712)

76. *Katie Kazoo, Switcheroo 16: Bad Rap.* Nancy Krulik, illus. by John and Wendy. Grosset & Dunlap (114,640)

77. *Strawberry Shortcake: Meet Rainbow Sherbet.* Sudipta Bardhan-Quallen, illus. by Josie Yee. Grosset & Dunlap (114,589)

78. *Robots: The Movie Novel.* Nancy Krulik. HarperKidsEntertainment (114,245)

79. *Harry Potter and the Goblet of Fire Poster Book.* Marie Morreale. Scholastic (113,060)

80. *Show Me Your Smile! A Visit to the Dentist (Dora the Explorer).* Simon Spotlight (111,542)

81. *A Pet for a Princess.* Random/Disney (111,235)

82. *Fantastic Four.* Stephen Sullivan. HarperKidsEntertainment (111,018)

83. *Madagascar* (junior novelization). Louise Gikow. Scholastic (110,769)

84. *March of the Penguins.* National Geographic (110,194)

85. *Artemis Fowl: The Eternity Code.* Eoin Colfer. Hyperion/Miramax, 2004 (110,000)

86. *Batman Begins: Training Bruce Wayne.* Holly Kowitt. Scholastic (108,437)

87. *The People of Sparks.* Jeanne DuPrau. Random (107,587)

88. *Strawberry Shortcake's Show-and-Tell Surprise.* Megan E. Bryant, illus. by Scott Neely. Grosset & Dunlap (106,836)

89. *Artemis Fowl: The Arctic Incident.* Eoin Colfer. Hyperion/Miramax, 2003 (105,000)

90. *The It Girl.* Cecily Von Ziegesar. Little, Brown (104,751)

91. *Herbie: Fully Loaded.* Irene Trimble. Random/Disney (104,307)

92. *The Batman: Cave of Wonders.* Ben Harper. Scholastic (103,086)

93. *The Apprentice Mad Libs.* Roger Price, illus. by Leonard Stern. Price Stern Sloan (102, 783)

94. *Disney's Chicken Little* (junior novelization). Random/Disney (102,782)

95. *Dora's Ready-to-Read Adventures.* Simon Spotlight (101,662)

96. *The Horse and His Boy.* C. S. Lewis. HarperCollins (101,348)

97. *Danger at the Zoo.* Kathleen Ernst, illus. by Jean-Paul Tibbles. Pleasant Company (100,938)

98. *A Bug-a-Boo Day Play (Miss Spider's Sunny Patch Friends).* David Kirk. Grosset & Dunlap (100,501)

99. *King Kong: Journey to Skull Island.* Jennifer Frantz, illus. by Peter Bollinger. HarperTrophy (100,410)

100. *The Secret Life of a Ping-Pong Wizard (Hank Zipzer #9).* Henry Winkler and Lin Oliver. Grosset & Dunlap (100,329)

Children's Paperback Backlist

500,000+

1. *The Lion, the Witch and the Wardrobe.* C. S. Lewis, illus. by Pauline Baynes. HarperTrophy, 1994 (1,964,428)

2. *The Magician's Nephew.* C. S. Lewis, illus. by Pauline Baynes. HarperTrophy, 1994 (1,520,158)

3. *The Horse and His Boy.* C. S. Lewis, illus. by Pauline Baynes. HarperTrophy, 1994 (1,178,103)

4. *Prince Caspian.* C. S. Lewis, illus. by Pauline Baynes. HarperTrophy, 1994 (1,058,351)

5. *The Voyage of the Dawn Treader.* C. S. Lewis, illus. by Pauline Baynes. HarperTrophy, 1994 (1,032,330)

6. *The Silver Chair.* C. S. Lewis, illus. by Pauline Baynes. HarperTrophy, 1994 (1,029,914)

7. *The Last Battle.* C. S. Lewis, illus. by Pauline Baynes. HarperTrophy, 1994 (1,015,383)

8. *The Chronicles of Narnia.* C. S. Lewis, illus. by Pauline Baynes. HarperTrophy, 2001 (987,612)

9. *The Sisterhood of the Traveling Pants.* Ann Brashares. Laurel-Leaf, 2003 (887,574)

10. *Harry Potter and the Goblet of Fire.* J. K. Rowling. Scholastic, 2002 (771,676)

11. *The Second Summer of the Sisterhood.* Ann Brashares. Delacorte, 2004 (719,745)

12. *Harry Potter and the Sorcerer's Stone.* J. K. Rowling. Scholastic, 1999 (622,290)

13. *Harry Potter and the Order of the Phoenix.* J. K. Rowling. Scholastic, 2004 (553,642)

14. *Harry Potter and the Chamber of Secrets.* J. K. Rowling. Scholastic, 2000 (545,557)

15. *The Outsiders.* S. E. Hinton. Puffin, 1997 (536,906)

16. *Harry Potter and the Prisoner of Azkaban.* J. K. Rowling. Scholastic, 2001 (506,883)

300,000+

17. *Charlie and the Chocolate Factory.* Roald Dahl, illus. by Quentin Blake. Puffin, 1998 (486,507)

18. *The Giver.* Lois Lowry. Laurel-Leaf, 2002 (452,949)

19. *Dinosaurs Before Dark (MTH #1).* Mary Pope Osborne, illus. by Sal Murdocca. Random/Stepping Stone, 1992 (397,270)

20. *Where the Wild Things Are.* Maurice Sendak. HarperCollins, 1988 (378,044)

21. *Holes.* Louis Sachar. Yearling and Laurel-Leaf, 2000 (349,674)

22. *Dora's Picnic.* Christine Ricci, illus. by Susan Hall. Simon Spotlight, 2003 (344,388)

23. *What Is a Princess?* Random/Disney, 2004 (331,683)

24. *The Care and Keeping of You.* Valorie Schaefer, illus. by Norm Bendell. Pleasant Company, 1998 (325,661)

25. *The Knight at Dawn (MTH #2).* Mary Pope Osborne. Random/Stepping Stone, 1993 (310,910)

26. *Mummies in the Morning (MTH #3).* Mary Pope Osborne, illus. by Sal Murdocca. Random/Stepping Stone, 1993 (309,238)

27. *Dora in the Deep Sea.* Christine Ricci, illus. by Robert Roper. Simon Spotlight, 2003 (303,703)

200,000+

28. *Pirates Past Noon (MTH #4).* Mary Pope Osborne, illus. by Sal Murdocca. Random/Stepping Stone, 1994 (294,501)

29. *Thomas and the Magic Railroad: Little Engines Can Do Big Things.* Illus. by Ted Gadecki. Random, 2000 (290,859)

30. *Speak.* Laurie Halse Anderson. Puffin, 2001 (281,219)

31. *Follow Those Feet! (Dora the Explorer).* Christine Ricci, illus. by Susan Hall. Simon Spotlight, 2003 (279,629)

32. *Junie B. Jones and the Stupid Smelly Bus (Junie B. Jones #1).* Barbara Park, illus. by Denise Brunkus. Random/Stepping Stone, 1992. (257,782)

33. *Lil' Bratz: Dancin' Divas.* Grosset & Dunlap, 2004 (257,449)

34. *I Love My Papi! (Dora the Explorer).* Alison Inches, illus. by Dave Aikins. Simon Spotlight, 2004 (255,093)

35. *Junie B. Jones and a Little Monkey Business (Junie B. Jones #2).* Barbara Park, illus. by Denise Brunkus. Random/Stepping Stone, 1993. (237,739)

36. *Night of the Ninjas (MTH #5).* Mary Pope Osborne, illus. by Sal Murdocca. Random/Stepping Stone, 1995 (234,348)

37. *Thomas Comes to Breakfast.* Based on the stories of Rev. W. Awdry, illus. by Richard Courtney. Random, 2004 (229,012)

38. *Hoot.* Carl Hiaasen. Knopf, 2004 (228,299)

39. *Afternoon on the Amazon (MTH #6).* Mary Pope Osborne. Random/Stepping Stone, 1995 (227,952)

40. *Junie B. Jones and Some Sneaky Peeky Spying (Junie B. Jones #4).* Barbara Park, illus. by Denise Brunkus. Random/Stepping Stone, 1995 (227,726)

41. *Junie B. Jones and Her Big Fat Mouth (Junie B. Jones #3).* Barbara Park, illus. by Denise Brunkus. Random/Stepping Stone, 1993 (226,276)

42. *Midnight on the Moon (MTH #8).* Mary Pope Osborne, illus. by Sal Murdocca. Random/Stepping Stone, 1996 (224,410)

43. *Charlotte's Web.* E. B. White, illus. by Garth Williams. HarperTrophy, 1988 (223,403)

44. *A Wrinkle in Time.* Madeleine L'Engle. Yearling and Laurel-Leaf, 1973 (223,180)

45. *Thomas's ABC Book.* Based on the stories of Rev. W. Awdry. Random, 1998 (222,809)

46. *Dolphins at Daybreak (MTH #9).* Mary Pope Osborne, illus. by Sal Murdocca. Random/Stepping Stone, 1997 (220,872)

47. *Thomas & Friends: Down at the Docks.* Rev. W. Awdry, illus. by Richard Courtney. Random, 2003 (215,547)

48. *Say "Cheese!" (Dora the Explorer).* Christine Ricci, illus. by Steven Savitsky. Simon Spotlight, 2004 (213,093)

49. *Hatchet.* Gary Paulsen. Aladdin, 1996 (208,418)

50. *Sunset of the Sabertooth (MTH #7).* Mary Pope Osborne, illus. by Sal Murdocca. Random/Stepping Stone, 1996 (208,306)

51. *Catch Me, Catch Me!* Based on the stories of Rev. W. Awdry, illus. by Owain Bell. Random, 1990 (206,476)

100,000+

52. *High Tide in Hawaii (MTH #28).* Mary Pope Osborne, illus. by Sal Murdocca. Random/Stepping Stone, 2003 (194,208)

53. *Ghost Town at Sundown (MTH #10).* Mary Pope Osborne, illus. by Sal Murdocca. Random/Stepping Stone, 1997 (190,519)

54. *Charlie and the Great Glass Elevator.* Roald Dahl, illus. by Quentin Blake. Puffin, 1998 (184,462)

55. *Junie B. Jones Has a Monster Under Her Bed (Junie B. Jones #8).* Barbara Park, illus. by Denise Brunkus. Random/Stepping Stone, 1997 (179,900)

56. *Where the Red Fern Grows.* Wilson Rawls. Yearling and Laurel-Leaf, 1997 (178,187)

57. *Junie B. Jones Is a Party Animal (Junie B. Jones #10).* Barbara Park, illus. by Denise Brunkus. Random/Stepping Stone, 1997 (176,504)

58. *Thomas and the Magic Railroad Diesel: 10 Means Trouble.* Illus. by Richard Courtney. Random, 2000 (175,490)

59. *The Watsons Go to Birmingham—1963.* Christopher Paul Curtis. Yearling and Laurel-Leaf, 1997 (173,933)

60. *Junie B. Jones and the Yucky Blucky Fruitcake (Junie B. Jones #5).* Barbara Park, illus. by Denise Brunkus. Random/Stepping Stone, 1995 (172,788)

61. *Lions at Lunchtime (MTH #11).* Mary Pope Osborne. illus. by Sal Murdocca. Random/Stepping Stone, 1998 (172,689)

62. *Junie B. Jones Is Not a Crook (Junie B. Jones #9).* Barbara Park, illus. by Denise Brunkus. Random/Stepping Stone, 1997 (172,645)

63. *Junie B. Jones Is Almost a Flower Girl.* Barbara Park, illus. by Denise Brunkus. Random/Stepping Stone, 1999 (171,483)

64. *Disney/Pixar's The Incredibles: The Incredible Dash.* Random/Disney, 2004 (169,471)

65. *Junie B. Jones Loves Handsome Warren (Junie B. Jones #7).* Barbara Park, illus. by Denise Brunkus. Random/Stepping Stone, 1996 (169,443)

66. *Junie B. Jones Is Beauty Shop Guy (Junie B. Jones #11).* Barbara Park, illus. by Denise Brunkus. Random/Stepping Stone, 1998 (167,420)

67. *Polar Bears Past Bedtime (MTH #12).* Mary Pope Osborne, illus. by Sal Murdocca. Random/Stepping Stone, 1998 (166,435)

68. *Walt Disney's Cinderella.* Random/Disney, 2002 (166,406)

69. *Island of the Blue Dolphins.* Scott O'Dell. Yearling, 1971 (165,104)

70. *Junie B. Jones and That Meanie Jim's Birthday (Junie B. Jones #6).* Barbara Park, illus. by Denise Brunkus. Random/Stepping Stone, 1996 (164,820)

71. *Dora's Backpack.* Sarah Willson, illus. by Robert Roper. Simon Spotlight, 2002 (164,459)

72. *Number the Stars.* Lois Lowry. Yearling, 1990 (164,057)

73. *Maniac Magee.* Jerry Spinelli. Little, Brown, 1999 (163,238)

74. *Tonight on the Titanic (MTH #17).* Mary Pope Osborne, illus. by Sal Murdocca. Random/Stepping Stone, 1999 (161,158)

75. *Tales of a Fourth Grade Nothing.* Judy Blume. Puffin, 2003 (159,627)

76. *Thomas and Percy and the Dragon.* Rev. W. Awdry, illus. by Richard Courtney. Random, 2003 (159,251)

77. *Monster.* Walter Dean Myers. Amistad, 2001 (158,274)

78. *Thomas & Friends: The Special Delivery.* Rev. W. Awdry, illus. by Richard Courtney. Random, 2002 (158,081)

79. *Junie B., First Grader: Toothless Wonder (Junie B. Jones #20).* Barbara Park, illus. by Denise Brunkus. Random/Stepping Stone, 2003 (156,770)

80. *James Goes Buzz Buzz.* Rev. W. Awdry, illus. by Richard Courtney. Random, 2004 (156,708)

81. *Vacation Fun Mad Libs.* Roger Price, illus. by Leonard Stern. Price Stern Sloan, 1987 (155,837)

82. *Best Dad in the Sea.* Random/Disney, 2003 (155,079)

83. *The Original Mad Libs 1.* Roger Price, illus. by Leonard Stern. Price Stern Sloan, 1974 (154,433)

84. *Just Me and My Dad.* Mercer Mayer. Golden, 2001 (153,883)

85. *Are You There God? It's Me, Margaret.* Judy Blume. Yearling, 1986 (153,515)

86. *Artemis Fowl.* Eoin Colfer. Hyperion/Miramax, 2002 (150,000)

87. *I Like Bugs.* Margaret Wise Brown. Random, 1999 (149,824)

88. *Vacation Under Volcano (MTH #13).* Mary Pope Osborne, illus. by Sal Murdocca. Random/Stepping Stone, 1998 (148,344)

89. *The Clique.* Lisi Harrison. Little, Brown, 2004 (147,130)

90. *Frog and Toad Are Friends.* Arnold Lobel. HarperTrophy, 1979 (146,633)

91. *Among the Hidden.* Margaret Peterson Haddix. Aladdin, 1998 (145,474)

92. *The Berenstain Bears and Too Much TV.* Stan Berenstain and Jan Berenstain. Random, 1984 (145,295)

93. *Best Friends for Never (The Clique #2).* Lisi Harrison. Little, Brown, 2004 (144,342)

94. *Little Star (Dora the Explorer).* Sarah Willson. Simon Spotlight, 2002 (144,041)

95. *Junie B. Jones and the Mushy Gushy Valentine (Junie B. Jones #14).* Barbara Park, illus. by Denise Brunkus. Random/Stepping Stone, 1999 (143,907)

96. *Bridge to Terabithia.* Katherine Paterson. HarperTrophy, 1987 (142,824)

97. *The City of Ember.* Jeanne DuPrau. Random, 2004 (142,244)

98. *Just Me and My Mom.* Mercer Mayer. Golden, 2001 (141,820)

99. *Thomas & Friends: Percy's Chocolate Crunch.* Random, 2003 (137,677)

100. *Goofy Mad Libs.* Roger Price, illus. by Leonard Stern. Price Stern Sloan, 1993 (133,773)

101. *Danny and the Dinosaur.* Syd Hoff. HarperTrophy, 1992 (133,612)

102. *Junie B., First Grader: At Last! (Junie B. Jones #18).* Barbara Park, illus. by Denise Brunkus. Random/Stepping Stone, 2002 (133,095)

103. *Gossip Girl (Gossip Girl #1).* Cecily Von Ziegesar. Little, Brown, 2002 (132,275)

104. *Good Morning, Gorillas (MTH #26).* Mary Pope Osborne, illus. by Sal Murdocca. Random/Stepping Stone, 2002 (131,942)

105. *Junie B., First Grader: Cheater Pants (Junie B. Jones #21).* Barbara Park, illus. by Denise Brunkus. Random/Stepping Stone, 2004 (131,837)

106. *Oh, Yuck! The Encyclopedia of Everything Nasty.* Joy Masoff. Workman, 2000 (130,824)

107. *Tigers at Twilight (MTH #19).* Mary Pope Osborne, illus. by Sal Murdocca. Random/Stepping Stone, 1999 (130,140)

108. *Junie B. Jones Smells Something Fishy (Junie B. Jones #12).* Barbara Park, illus. by Denise Brunkus. Random/Stepping Stone, 1998 (129,527)

109. *Amelia Bedelia.* Peggy Parish, illus. by Fritz Siebel. HarperTrophy, 1992 (129,022)

110. *Frindle.* Andrew Clements. Aladdin, 1996 (127,723)

111. *A Pony for Success.* Andrea Posner-Sanchez, illus. by Francesc Mateu. Random/Disney, 2002 (127,710)

112. *Bud, Not Buddy.* Christopher Paul Curtis. Yearling, 2002 (126,521)

113. *Junie B. Jones Has a Peep in Her Pocket (Junie B. Jones #15).* Barbara Park, illus. by Denise Brunkus. Random/Stepping Stone, 2000 (126,053)

114. *Stage Fright on a Summer Night (MTH #25).* Mary Pope Osborne, illus. by Sal Murdocca. Random/Stepping Stone, 2002 (125,934)

115. *Dora Loves Boots.* Alison Inches, illus. by Zina Saunders. Simon Spotlight, 2004 (124,952)

116. *Junie B. Jones Is a Graduation Girl (Junie B. Jones #17).* Barbara Park, illus. by Denise Brunkus. Random/Stepping Stone, 2001 (124,472)

117. *Dora's Book of Manners.* Christine Ricci, illus. by Susan Hall. Simon Spotlight, 2004 (123,542)

118. *The Adventures of Captain Underpants.* Dav Pilkey. Scholastic, 1997 (123,014)

119. *Fun with Dick and Jane.* Grosset & Dunlap, 2004 (122,481)

120. *Day of the Dragon-King (MTH #14).* Mary Pope Osborne, illus. by Sal Murdocca. Random/Stepping Stone, 1998 (121,794)

121. *Junie B., First Grader: Boss of Lunch (Junie B. Jones #19).* Barbara Park, illus. by Denise Brunkus. Random/Stepping Stone, 2003 (121,707)

122. *Read with Dick and Jane: Jump and Run.* Grosset & Dunlap, 2003 (121,631)

123. *The Night Before Kindergarten.* Natasha Wing, illus. by Julie Durrell. Grosset & Dunlap, 2001 (121,371)

124. *Goodnight Moon.* Margaret Wise Brown, illus. by Clement Hurd. Harper-Trophy, 1977 (121,332)

125. *Dingoes at Dinnertime (MTH #20).* Mary Pope Osborne, illus. by Sal Murdocca. Random/Stepping Stone, 2000 (120,823)

126. *Walk Two Moons.* Sharon Creech. HarperTrophy, 1996 (120,585)

127. *Captain Underpants and the Perilous Plot of Professor Poopypants.* Dav Pilkey. Scholastic, 2000 (120,009)

128. *Stargirl.* Jerry Spinelli. Laurel-Leaf, 2002 (119,155)

129. *Dora Goes to School.* Adapted by Leslie Valders, illus. by Robert Roper. Simon Spotlight, 2004 (118,286)

130. *Dinosaur Days.* Joyce Milton. Random, 1985 (116,959)

131. *Captain Underpants and the Wrath of the Wicked Wedgie Woman.* Dav Pilkey. Scholastic, 2001 (116,919)

132. *Care Bears.* Nancy Parent, illus. by Jay Johnson. Scholastic (116,351)

133. *Spider-Man: I Am Spider-Man.* Acton Figueroa. HarperFestival, 2002 (116,212)

134. *Mad Mad Mad Mad Mad Libs.* Roger Price, illus. by Leonard Stern. Price Stern Sloan, 1998 (115,972)

135. *Nate the Great.* Marjorie Weinman Sharmat, illus. by Marc Simont. Yearling, 1977 (115,831)

136. *Biscuit.* Alyssa Satin Capucilli, illus. by Pat Schories. HarperTrophy, 1997 (115,595)

137. *Revolutionary War on Wednesday (MTH #22).* Mary Pope Osborne, illus. by Sal Murdocca. Random/Stepping Stone, 2000 (114,374)

138. *Go Ask Alice.* Anonymous. Aladdin, 1971 (114,373)

139. *Matilda.* Roald Dahl, illus. by Quentin Blake. Puffin, 1998 (114,315)

140. *Earthquake in the Early Morning (MTH #24).* Mary Pope Osborne, illus. by Sal Murdocca. Random/Stepping Stone, 2001 (114,304)

141. *Viking Ships at Sunrise (MTH #15).* Mary Pope Osborne, illus. by Sal Murdocca. Random/Stepping Stone, 1998 (113,624)

142. *Captain Underpants and the Attack of the Talking Toilets.* Dav Pilkey. Scholastic, 1999 (113,344)

143. *Tangerine.* Edward Bloor. Scholastic, 2001 (113,263)

144. *Mad Libs on the Road.* Roger Price, illus. by Leonard Stern. Price Stern Sloan, 1999 (112,689)

145. *The Sign of the Beaver.* Elizabeth George Speare. Yearling, 1984 (112,265)

146. *The Best Christmas Pageant Ever.* Barbara Robinson. HarperTrophy, 1988 (112,236)

147. *Who Can Help?* Grosset & Dunlap, 2004 (110,295)

148. *Junie B. Jones Is Captain Field Day (Junie B. Jones #16).* Barbara Park, illus. by Denise Brunkus. Random/Stepping Stone, 2001 (110,059)

149. *Read with Dick and Jane: Something Funny.* Grosset & Dunlap, 2003 (109,760)

150. *Sooper Dooper Mad Libs.* Roger Price, illus. by Leonard Stern. Price Stern Sloan, 1974 (108,703)

151. *Twister on Tuesday (MTH #23).* Mary Pope Osborne, illus. by Sal Murdocca. Random/Stepping Stone, 2001 (108,643)

152. *Tuck Everlasting.* Natalie Babbitt. FSG/Sunburst, 2005 (107,749)

153. *Captain Underpants and the Big, Bad Battle of the Bionic Booger Boy, Part 2.* Dav Pilkey. Scholastic, 2003 (107,452)

154. *The Thief Lord.* Cornelia Funke. Scholastic/Chicken House (107,311)

155. *Buffalo Before Breakfast (MTH #18).* Mary Pope Osborne, illus. by Sal Murdocca. Random/Stepping Stone, 1999 (107,296)

156. *The BFG.* Roald Dahl, illus. by Quentin Blake. Puffin, 1998 (106,963)

157. *Thanksgiving on Thursday (MTH #27).* Mary Pope Osborne, illus. by Sal Murdocca. Random/Stepping Stone, 2002 (106,918)

158. *The Little Old Lady Who Was Not Afraid of Anything.* Linda Williams, illus. by Megan Lloyd. HarperTrophy, 1988 (106,880)

159. *Frog and Toad All Year.* Arnold Lobel. HarperTrophy, 1984 (106,662)

160. *Good Night, Dora!* Christine Ricci, illus. by Susan Hall. Simon Spotlight, 2002 (106,403)

161. *Freak the Mighty.* Rodman Philbrick. Scholastic, 2001 (106,241)

162. *The Mouse and the Motorcycle.* Beverly Cleary, illus. by Tracy Dockray. HarperTrophy, 1990 (105,935)

163. *Warriors #1.* Erin Hunter. Avon, 2004 (105,839)

164. *Frog and Toad Together.* Arnold Lobel, HarperTrophy, 1979 (105,463)

165. *Sarah, Plain and Tall.* Patricia MacLachlan. HarperTrophy, 1987 (105,207)

166. *Alexander and the Terrible, Horrible, No Good, Very Bad Day.* Judith Viorst, illus. by Ray Cruz. Aladdin, 1987 (104,917)

167. *James and the Giant Peach.* Roald Dahl, illus. by Quentin Blake. Puffin, 2001 (104,507)
168. *Seedfolks.* Paul Fleischman, illus. by Judy Pedersen. HarperTrophy, 1999 (103,989)
169. *Hour of the Olympics (MTH #16).* Mary Pope Osborne, illus. by Sal Murdocca. Random/Stepping Stone, 1998 (103,386)
170. *Civil War on Sunday (MTH #21).* Mary Pope Osborne, illus. by Sal Murdocca. Random/Stepping Stone, 2000 (102,758)
171. *Caps for Sale.* Esphyr Slobodkina. HarperTrophy, 1987 (102,636)
172. *Chicka Chicka Boom Boom.* Bill Martin Jr. and John Archambault. Aladdin, 1989 (102,415)
173. *The Feelings Book.* Lynda Madison, illus. by Norm Bendell. Pleasant Company, 2002 (102,364)
174. *My Little Pony: Belle of the Ball.* Ruth Benjamin, illus. by Ken Edwards. HarperFestival, 2004 (101,806)
175. *You're the One I Want (Gossip Girl #6).* Cecily Von Ziegesar. Little, Brown, 2004 (101,621)
176. *Touching Spirit Bear.* Ben Mikaelsen. HarperTrophy, 2002 (101,589)
177. *Blubber.* Judy Blume. Yearling, 1986 (101,528)
178. *Junie B., First Grader: One-Man Band (Junie B. Jones #22).* Barbara Park, illus. by Denise Brunkus. Random/Stepping Stone, 2004 (101,386)
179. *The Phantom Tollbooth.* Norton Juster. Yearling, 1988 (100,735)
180. *Dinosaur Babies.* Lucille Recht Penner. Random, 1991 (100,152)
181. *Off-the-Wall Mad Libs.* Roger Price, illus. by Leonard Stern. Price Stern Sloan, 1978 (100,120)
182. *Monster Mad Libs.* Roger Price, illus. by Leonard Stern. Price Stern Sloan, 1974 (100,038)

Literary Prizes, 2005

Gary Ink

Library Services Manager, *Publishers Weekly, Library Journal*

Academy of American Poets Academy Fellowship. For distinguished poetic achievement. *Offered by:* Academy of American Poets. *Winner:* Claudia Rankine.

Ambassador Book Awards. To honor an exceptional contribution to the interpretation of life and culture in the United States. *Offered by:* English-Speaking Union. *Winners:* (poetry) Donald Justice for *Collected Poems* (Knopf); (fiction) Marilynne Robinson for *Gilead* (Farrar, Straus & Giroux); (American studies) David Hackett Fischer for *Washington's Crossing* (Oxford).

American Academy of Arts and Letters Awards in Literature. To honor writers of exceptional achievement. *Offered by:* American Academy of Arts and Letters. *Winners:* (poetry) Joseph Harrison, Charles Martin, Burton Watson; (fiction) Jim Grimsley, Edward P. Jones.

American Academy of Arts and Letters Rome Fellowships. For a one-year residency at the American Academy in Rome for young writers of promise. *Offered by:* American Academy of Arts and Letters. *Winners:* Craig Arnold, Aaron Hamburger.

American Book Awards. For literary achievement by people of various ethnic backgrounds. *Offered by:* Before Columbus Foundation. *Winners:* (fiction) Julie Chibbaro for *Redemption* (Atheneum); Ralph Flores for *The Horse in the Kitchen* (University of New Mexico); Don Lee for *Country of Origin* (Norton); (poetry) Lamont Steptoe for *A Long Movie of Shadows* (Whirlwind); Don West for *No Lonesome Road* (University of Illinois).

Rudolfo and Patricia Anaya Premio Atzlan Literary Prize. To honor a Chicano or Chicana fiction writer who has published no more than two books. *Offered by:* University of New Mexico. *Winner:* Mary Helen Lagasse for *The Fifth Sun* (Curbstone).

Hans Christian Andersen Awards. To an author and an illustrator whose body of work has made an important and lasting contribution to children's literature. *Offered by:* International Board of Books for Young People (IBBY). *Winners:* Not awarded in 2005.

Bancroft Prizes. For books of exceptional merit and distinction in American history, American diplomacy, and the international relations of the United States. *Offered by:* Columbia University. *Winners:* Melvin Patrick Ely for *Israel on the Appomattox* (Knopf); Michael J. Klarman for *From Jim Crow to Civil Rights* (Oxford); Michael O'Brien for *Conjectures of Order* (University of North Carolina).

Barnes & Noble Discover Great New Writers Awards. To honor a first novel and a first work of nonfiction by American authors. *Offered by:* Barnes & Noble. *Winners:* (fiction) John Dalton for *Heaven Lake* (Scribner); (nonfiction) Alison Smith for *Name All the Animals* (Scribner).

Mildred L. Batchelder Award. For an American publisher of a children's book originally published in a foreign country and subsequently published in English in the United States. *Offered by:* American Library Association, Association for Library Service to Children. *Winner:* Catherine Tenerson for *The Shadows of Ghadames* by Joelle Stolz (Delacorte).

Pura Belpré Awards. To a Latino/Latina writer and illustrator whose work portrays, affirms, and celebrates the Latino cultural experience in an outstanding work of literature for children and youth. *Offered by:* American Library Association, Association for Library Service to Children and REFORMA (the National Association to Promote Library and Information Services to Latinos and the Spanish-Speaking). *Winners:* (writer) Viola Canales for *The Tequila Worm* (Random House); (illustrator) Raul Colón for *Doña Flor: A Tall Tale About a Giant Woman with a Great Big Heart* by Pat Mora (Alfred A. Knopf).

Curtis Benjamin Award for Creative Publishing. To a U.S. publisher who has demonstrated exceptional creativity and innovation in publishing. *Offered by:* Association of American Publishers. *Winner:* Lawrence Ferlinghetti.

Helen B. Bernstein Award. For excellence in journalism. *Offered by:* New York Public Library. *Winner:* Jason DeParle for *American Dreams* (Viking).

Book Sense Book of the Year Awards. To honor titles that member stores have most enjoyed handselling during the past year. *Offered by:* American Booksellers Association. *Winners:* (fiction) Susanna Clarke for *Jonathan Strange and Mr. Norrell* (Bloomsbury); (nonfiction) Robert Kurson for *Shadow Divers* (Random House); (children's literature) Blue Balliett for *Chasing Vermeer,* illus. by Brett Helquist (Scholastic); (children's illustrated) Betsy Lewin for *Duck for President,* text by Doreen Cronin (Simon & Schuster).

Boston Globe/Horn Book Awards. For excellence in children's literature. *Offered by: Boston Globe* and *Horn Book Magazine. Winners:* (fiction) Neal Shusterman for *The Schwa Was Here* (Dutton); (nonfiction) Phillip Hoose for *The Race to Save the Lord God Bird* (Kroupa/Farrar); (picture book) Mini Grey for *Traction Man Is Here* (Knopf).

W. Y. Boyd Literary Novel Award. To honor a novel set in a period when the United States was at war. *Offered by:* American Library Association. *Winner:* Jeff Shaara for *To the Last Man* (Ballantine).

Michael Braude Award. For light verse. *Offered by:* American Academy of Arts and Letters. *Winner:* Not awarded in 2005.

Randolph Caldecott Medal. For the artist of the most distinguished picture book. *Offered by:* American Library Association, Association for Library Service to Children. *Winner:* Kevin Henkes for *Kitten's First Full Moon* (Greenwillow).

California Book Awards. To California residents to honor books of fiction and poetry published in the previous year. *Offered by:* Commonwealth Club of California. *Winners:* (Gold Medal for Poetry) Adrienne Rich for *The School Among the Ruins* (Norton); (Gold Medal for Fiction) Andrew Sean Greer for *The Confessions of Max Tivoli* (Farrar, Straus & Giroux).

John W. Campbell Memorial Award. For science fiction writing. *Offered by:* Center for the Study of Science Fiction. *Winner:* Elizabeth Bear.

Carnegie Medal (United Kingdom). For the outstanding children's book of the year. *Offered by:* The Library Association. *Winner:* Frank Cotrell Boyce for *Millions* (Macmillan).

Chicago Tribune Literary Prize. For a lifetime of literary achievement by an author whose body of work has had great impact on American society. *Offered by: Chicago Tribune. Winner:* Margaret Atwood.

Chicago Tribune Young Adult Fiction Prize. For a fiction work of high literary merit that addresses themes especially relevant to adolescents, and speaks to their role and significance in society. *Offered by: Chicago Tribune. Winner:* Linda Sue Park for *Project Mulberry* (Clarion Books).

Arthur C. Clarke Award (United Kingdom). For the best science fiction novel published in the United Kingdom. *Offered by:* British Science Fiction Association. *Winner:* China Mieville for *Iron Council* (Del Rey).

Matt Cohen Award (Canada). To a Canadian author whose life has been dedicated to writing as a primary pursuit, for a body of work. *Offered by:* Writers' Trust of Canada. *Winner:* Howard Engel.

Commonwealth Writers' Prize (United Kingdom). To reward and encourage new Commonwealth fiction and ensure that works of merit reach a wider audience outside their country of origin. *Offered by:* Commonwealth Institute. *Winner:* Andrea Levy for *Small Island* (Review).

Benjamin H. Danks Award. To a promising young writer of fiction, creative nonfiction, or poetry. *Offered by:* American Academy of Arts and Letters. *Winner:* Edwidge Danticat.

Philip K. Dick Award. For a distinguished science fiction paperback original published in the United States. *Offered by:* Norwescon. *Winner:* Gwyneth Jones for *Life* (Aqueduct).

Emily Dickinson First Book Award. To a writer over the age of 50 who has never published a book. *Offered by:* The Poetry Foundation. *Winner:* Landis Everson.

Draine-Taylor Biography Prize (Canada). To a Canadian author of a biography, autobiography, or memoir. *Offered by:* Claire Draine Taylor and Nathan A. Taylor. *Winner:* Peter C. Newman for *Here Be Dragons* (McClelland & Stewart).

Margaret A. Edwards Award. For lifetime contribution to writing for young adults. *Offered by:* American Library Association, Young Adult Library Services Association. *Winner:* Francesca Lia Block.

Marian Engel Award (Canada). To a female Canadian writer in mid-career for a body of work. *Offered by:* Writers' Trust of Canada. *Winner:* Dianne Warren.

Clifton Fadiman Medal for Excellence in Fiction. To honor the most memorable book published at least a decade ago. *Offered by:* Mercantile Library of New York. *Winner:* James Purdy for *Eustace Chisholm and the Works* (Carroll & Graf).

Timothy Findley Award (Canada). To a male Canadian author in mid-career for a body of work. *Offered by:* Writers' Trust of Canada. *Winner:* David Adams Richards.

E. M. Forster Award. To a young writer from England, Ireland, Scotland, or Wales for a stay in the United States. *Offered by:* American Academy of Arts and Letters. *Winner:* Dennis O'Driscoll.

Forward Prize (United Kingdom). For poetry. *Offered by: The Forward. Winners:* (best collection) David Harsent for *Legion* (Faber & Faber); (best first collection) Helen Farish for *Intimates* (Jonathan Cape); (best single poem) Paul Farley for "Liverpool Disappears for a Billionth of a Second."

Frost Medal. To recognize distinguished achievement in poetry over a lifetime. *Offered by:* Poetry Society of America. *Winner:* Marie Ponsot.

Lewis Galantiere Award. For a literary translation into English from any language other than German. *Offered by:* American Translators Association. *Winner:* Roger Greenwald for *North in the World: Selected Poems of Rolf Jacobsen* (University of Chicago).

Giller Prize (Canada). For the best novel or short story collection written in English. *Offered by:* Giller Prize Foundation and Scotiabank. *Winner:* David Bergen for *The Time in Between* (Random House).

Gold Medal for Belles Lettres. To honor the distinguished career of a novelist or short story writer. *Offered by:* American Academy of Arts and Letters. *Winner:* Joan Didion.

Golden Kite Awards. For children's books. *Offered by:* Society of Children's Book Writers and Illustrators. *Winners:* (fiction) Christopher Paul Curtis for *Bucking the Sarge* (Wendy Lamb Books); (nonfiction) Michael L. Cooper for *Dust to Eat* (Clarion); (picture book text) Deborah Hopkinson for *Apple to Oregon* (Atheneum); (picture book illustration) Jean Cassels for *The Mysterious Collection of Dr. David Harleyson* (Walker).

Kate Greenaway Medal (United Kingdom). For children's book illustration. *Offered by:* The Library Association. *Winner:* Chris Riddell for *Jonathan Swift's Gulliver* (Walker).

Gryphon Award. To the author of the best book for kindergarten through fourth-grade readers. *Offered by:* Center for Children's Books, University of Illinois. *Winner:* Monika Bang-Campbell for *Little Rat Rides,* illus. by Molly Bang (Harcourt).

Guardian Children's Fiction Prize (United Kingdom). For an outstanding children's novel. *Offered by: The Guardian. Winner:* Kate Thompson for *The New Policeman* (Bodley Head)

Guardian First Book Award (United Kingdom). For recognition of a first book. *Offered by: The Guardian. Winner:* Alexander Masters for *Stuart: A Life Backwards.*

O. B. Hardison, Jr. Poetry Prize. To a U.S. poet who has published at least one book in the last five years, and has made important contributions as a teacher, and is committed to furthering the understanding of poetry. *Offered by:* Folger Shakespeare Library. *Winner:* Tony Hoagland.

Heartland Prizes. To recognize an outstanding work of fiction and an outstanding work of nonfiction, each about people and places in America's heartland. *Offered by: Chicago Tribune. Winners:* (fiction) Marilynne Robinson for *Gilead* (Farrar, Straus & Giroux); (nonfiction) Kevin Boyle for *Arc of Justice* (Henry Holt).

Ernest Hemingway Foundation Award. For a distinguished work of first fiction by an American. *Offered by:* PEN New England. *Winner:* Chris Abani for *Graceland* (Farrar, Straus & Giroux).

William Dean Howells Medal. In recognition of the most distinguished novel published in the preceding five years. *Offered by:* American Academy of Arts and Letters. *Winner:* Shirley Hazzard for *The Great Fire* (Farrar, Straus & Giroux).

Hugo Awards. For outstanding science fiction writing. *Offered by:* World Science Fiction Convention. *Winners:* (best novel) Susanna Clarke for *Jonathan Strange and Mr. Norrell* (Bloomsbury); (best related book) *The Cambridge Companion to Science Fiction,* Edward James and Farah Mendlesohn, eds. (Cambridge University); (best editor) Ellen Datlow; (best artist) Jim Burns.

Hurston/Wright Legacy Awards. To writers of African American descent for a book of fiction, a book of first fiction, and a book of nonfiction. *Offered by:* Hurston/Wright Foundation and Borders Books. *Winners:* (fiction) Maryse Conde for *Who Slashed Celanire's Throat?* (Atria); (nonfiction) Alexis De Veaux for *Warrior Poet* (Norton); (debut fiction) Chris Abani for *Graceland* (Farrar, Straus & Giroux); (contemporary fiction) Tracy Price-Thompson for *A Woman's Worth* (One World).

IMPAC Dublin Literary Award (Ireland). For a book of high merit, written in English or translated into English. *Offered by:* IMPAC Corp. and the City of Dublin. *Winner:* Edward P. Jones for *The Known World* (Amistad Press).

Rona Jaffe Writers Awards. To identify and support women writers of exceptional talent in the early stages of their careers. *Offered by:* Rona Jaffee Foundation. *Winners:* Nan Cohen, Averill Curdy, Rebecca Curtis, Frances Hwang, Aryn Kyle, Asali Solomon.

Jerusalem Prize (Israel). To a writer whose works best express the theme of freedom of the individual in society. *Offered by:* Jerusalem International Book Fair. *Winner:* Antonio Lobo Antunes.

Samuel Johnson Prize for Nonfiction (United Kingdom). For an outstanding work of nonfiction. *Offered by:* British Broadcasting Corporation. *Winner:* Jonathan Coe for *Like a Fiery Elephant* (Picador).

Sue Kaufman Prize for First Fiction. For a first novel or collection of short stories. *Offered by:* American Academy of Arts and Letters. *Winner:* John Dalton for *Heaven Lake* (Scribner).

Ezra Jack Keats Awards. For children's picture books. *Offered by:* New York Public Library and the Ezra Jack Keats Foundation. *Winners:* (new writer award) Janice N. Harrington for *Going North* (Farrar, Straus & Giroux); (new illustrator award) Ana Juan for *The Night Eater* (Scholastic).

Coretta Scott King Awards. For works that promote the cause of peace and brotherhood. *Offered by:* American Library Association, Social Responsibilities Roundtable. *Winners:* (author) Toni Morrison for *Remember: The Journey to School Integration* (Houghton Mifflin); (illustrator) Kadir Nelson for *Ellington Was Not a Street,* written by Ntozake Shange (Simon & Schuster).

Kiriyama Pacific Rim Book Prizes. For a book of fiction and a book of nonfiction that best contribute to a fuller understanding among the nations and peoples of the Pacific Rim. *Offered by:* Kiriyama Pacific Rim Institute. *Winners:* (fiction) Nadeem Aslam for *Maps for Lost Lovers* (Knopf); (nonfiction) Suketu Mehta for *Maximum City* (Knopf).

Robert Kirsch Award. To a living author whose residence or focus is the American West, and whose contributions to American letters clearly merits body-of-work recognition. *Offered by: Los Angeles Times. Winner:* Tony Hillerman.

Koret Jewish Book Awards. To underline the centrality of books in Jewish culture and to encourage serious readers to seek the best of Jewish books. *Offered by:* Koret Foundation. *Winners:* (biography) Amos Oz for *A Tale of Love and Darkness* (Harcourt); (history) Elisheva Baumgarten for *Mothers and Children* (Princeton); (fiction) Tony Eprile for *The Persistence of Memory* (Norton); (philosophy) Steven Greenberg for *Wrestling with God and Men* (University of Wisconsin); (translation) Robert Alter for *The Five Books of Moses* (Norton); (children's literature) Karen Hesse for *The Cats of Krasinski Square* (Scholastic).

Koret Young Writer on Jewish Themes Award. To a poet, fiction writer, or creative nonfiction writer age 35 or younger who has published no more than one book. *Offered by:* Koret Foundation. *Winner:* Tim Bradford for a work-in-progress.

Harold Morton Landon Translation Award. For a book of verse translated into English by a single translator. *Offered by:* Academy of American Poets. *Winner:* Daryl Hine for *Works of Hesiod and the Homeric Hymns* (University of Chicago).

James Laughlin Award. To commend and support a second book of poetry. *Offered by:* Academy of American Poets. *Winner:* Barbara Jane Reyes for *Poeta en San Francisco* (Tinfish Press).

Ruth Lilly Poetry Prize. To a United States poet whose accomplishments warrant extraordinary recognition. *Offered by:* The Poetry Foundation. *Winner:* C. K. Williams.

Astrid Lindgren Award (Sweden). In memory of Astrid Lindgren to honor outstanding children's book writing. *Offered by:* Government of Sweden. *Winners:* (illustrator) Ryôji Arai; (writer) Philip Pullman.

Locus Awards. For science fiction writing. *Offered by:* Locus Publications. *Winners:* (best novel) Neal Stephenson for *The Baroque Cycle: The Confusion; The System of the World* (Morrow); (best fantasy novel) China Mieville for *Iron Council* (Del Rey); (best first novel) Susanna Clarke for *Jonathan Strange and Mr. Norrel* (Bloomsbury); (best young adult) Terry Pratchett for *A Hatful of Sky* (HarperCollins); (best anthology) *The Year's Best Science Fiction: Twenty-First Annual Collection,* Gardner Dozois, ed. (St. Martin's); (best collection) John Varley for *The John Varley Reader* (Ace); (best nonfiction book) Ursula K. Le Guin for *The Wave in the Mind* (Shambhala); (best art book) *Spectrum 11: The Best in Contemporary Fantastic Art,* Cathy and Arnie Fenner, eds.; (best editor) Ellen Datlow; (best artist) Michael Whelan; (best book publisher) Tor.

Los Angeles Times Book Prizes. To honor literary excellence. *Offered by: Los Angeles Times. Winners:* (fiction) Colm Toibin for *The Master* (Scribner); (current interest) Evan Wright for *Generation Kill* (Putnam); (biography) Mark Stevens and Annalyn Swan for *De Kooning* (Knopf); (history) Geoffrey R. Stone for *Perilous Times* (Norton); (poetry) Richard Howard for *Inner Voices* (Farrar, Straus & Giroux); (mystery/thriller) Kem Nunn for *Tijuana Straits* (Scribner); (science/technology) Charles Wohlforth for *The Whale and the Supercomputer* (North Point); (young adult fiction) Melvin Burgess for *Doing It* (Henry Holt); (Art Seidenbaum Award for First Fiction) Lorriane Adams for *Harbor* (Knopf).

Amy Lowell Poetry Traveling Scholarship. For a U.S. poet to spend one year outside North America in a country the recipient feels will most advance his or her work. *Offered by:* Amy Lowell Poetry Travelling Scholarship. *Winner:* Geri Ann Doran.

Anthony J. Lukas Prizes. For nonfiction writing that demonstrates literary grace, serious research, and concern for an important aspect of American social or political life. *Offered by:* Columbia University Graduate School of Journalism and the Nieman Foundation. *Winners:* (book prize) Evan Wright for *Generation Kill* (Putnam); (work-in-progress) Joan Quigley for *Home Fires* (Random House).

Mark Lynton History Prize. For history writing that demonstrates literary grace and serious research. *Offered by:* Columbia University Graduate School of Journalism and the Nieman Foundation. *Winner:* Richard Steven Street for *Beasts of the Field* (Stanford University Press).

James Madison Book Award. To honor books representing excellence in bringing knowledge and understanding of American history to children ages 5 to 14. *Offered by:* Lynne Cheney. *Winner:* Albert Marrin for *Old Hickory: Andrew Jackson and the American People* (Dutton Children's).

Man Booker International Literary Prize (United Kingdom). For a significant contribution to world literature. *Offered by:* Man Group. *Winner:* Ismail Kadare.

Man Booker Prize (United Kingdom). For the best novel written in English by a Commonwealth author. *Offered by:* Booktrust and the Man Group. *Winner:* John Banville for *The Sea* (Pan Macmillan).

Lenore Marshall Poetry Prize. For an outstanding book of poems published in the United States. *Offered by:* Academy of American Poets. *Winner:* Donald Revell for *My Mojave* (Alice James Books).

Addison M. Metcalf Award. To a young writer of great promise. *Offered by:* American Academy of Arts and Letters. *Winner:* Ilya Kaminsky.

Vicky Metcalf Award for Children's Literature (Canada). To a Canadian writer of children's literature for a body of work. *Offered by:* George Cedric Metcalf Foundation. *Winner:* Deborah Ellis.

National Arts Club Medal of Honor for Literature. *Offered by:* National Arts Club. *Winner:* P. D. James.

National Book Awards. For the best books of the year published in the United States. *Offered by:* National Book Foundation. *Winners:* (fiction) William T. Vollmann for *Europe Central* (Viking); (nonfiction) Joan Didion for *The Year of Magical Thinking* (Knopf); (poetry) W. S. Merwin for *Migration* (Copper Canyon); (young people's literature) Jeanne Birdsall for *The Penderwicks* (Knopf); (Literarian award) Lawrence Ferlinghetti.

National Book Critics Circle Awards. For literary excellence. *Offered by:* National Book Critics Circle. *Winners:* (fiction) Marilynne Robinson for *Gilead* (Farrar, Straus & Giroux); (nonfiction) Diarmaid MacCulloch for *The Reformation* (Viking); (biography/autobiography) Mark Stevens and Annalyn Swan for *De Koon-*

ing (Knopf); (criticism) Patrick Neate for *Where You're At* (Riverhead); (poetry) Adrienne Rich for *The School Among the Ruins* (Norton); (Ivan Sandrof lifetime achievement award) Louis D. Rubin; (Nona Balakian citation for excellence in reviewing) David Orr.

National Book Foundation Medal for Distinguished Contribution to American Letters. To a person who has enriched the nation's literary heritage over a life of service or corpus of work. *Offered by:* National Book Foundation. *Winner:* Norman Mailer.

National Translation Award. To honor a translator whose work has made the most valuable contribution to literary translation into English. *Offered by:* American Literary Translators Association. *Winner:* Aron Aji for *The Garden of Departed Cats* by Bilge Karasu (New Directions).

Nebula Awards. For science fiction writing. *Offered by:* Science Fiction and Fantasy Writers of America. *Winners:* (best novel) Lois McMaster Bujold for *Paladin Of Souls* (Eos); (Grand Master) Anne McCaffrey.

Nestlé Children's Book Prizes (formerly Smarties Book Prizes) (United Kingdom). To encourage high standards and to stimulate interest in books for children. *Offered by:* Nestlé UK Ltd. *Winners:* (9–11 years) Sally Gardner for *I, Coriander* (Orion); (6–8 years) Nick Butterworth for *The Whisperer* (HarperCollins); (5 and younger) Oliver Jeffers for *Lost and Found* (HarperCollins).

John Newbery Medal. For the most distinguished contribution to literature for children. *Offered by:* American Library Association, Association for Library Service to Children. *Winner:* Cynthia Kadohata for *Kira-Kira* (Atheneum).

Nimrod/Hardman Katherine Anne Porter Award. To a prose writer of demonstrated achievement. *Offered by:* American Academy of Arts and Letters. *Winner:* Thomas Gough.

Nobel Prize in Literature (Sweden). For the total literary output of a distinguished career. *Offered by:* Swedish Academy. *Winner:* Harold Pinter.

Flannery O'Connor Awards for Short Fiction. For collections of short fiction. *Offered by:* PEN American Center. *Winners:* Brad Vice for *The Bear Bryant Funeral Train* (University of Georgia); David Crouse for *Copy Cats* (University of Georgia).

Scott O'Dell Award. For historical fiction. *Offered by: Bulletin of the Center for Children's Books,* University of Chicago. *Winner:* A. LaFaye for *Worth* (Simon & Schuster).

Orange Award for New Writers (United Kingdom). For a first novel or short story collection by a woman, written in English and published in the United Kingdom. *Offered by:* Orange PLC. *Winner:* Diana Evans for *26a* (Chatto & Windus).

Orange Prize for Fiction (United Kingdom). For the best novel written by a woman and published in the United Kingdom. *Offered by:* Orange PLC. *Winner:* Lionel Shriver for *We Need to Talk About Kevin* (Serpent's Tail).

Pearson Writers' Trust Non-Fiction Prize (Canada). To a Canadian author of a non-fiction book. *Offered by:* Pearson Canada. *Winner:* Elaine Dewar for *The Second Tree* (Random House).

PEN Award for Poetry in Translation. For a book-length translation of poetry from any language into English and published in the United States. *Offered by:* PEN American Center. *Winner:* Pierre Joris for *Lightduress* by Paul Celan (Green Integer).

PEN/Martha Albrand Award for the Art of the Memoir. To honor a U.S. author's first book-length memoir. *Offered by:* PEN American Center. *Winner:* Nick Flynn for *Another Bullshit Night in Suck City* (Norton).

PEN/Book-of-the-Month Club Translation Award. For a book-length literary translation from any language into English. *Offered by:* PEN American Center. *Winner:* Tim Wilkinson for *Fatelessness* by Imre Kertesz (Vintage).

PEN/Faulkner Award for Fiction. To honor the best work of fiction published by an American. *Offered by:* PEN American Center. *Winner:* Ha Jin for *War Trash* (Pantheon).

PEN/Malamud Award. To an author who has demonstrated long-term excellence in short fiction. *Offered by:* PEN American Center. *Winner:* Lorrie Moore.

PEN/Newman's Own First Amendment Award. To honor a U.S. resident who has fought courageously to safeguard the First Amendment right to freedom of expression. *Offered by:* PEN American Center. *Winner:* Joan Airoldi.

PEN/Joyce Osterweil Prize for Poetry. To honor an emerging poet. *Offered by:* PEN American Center. *Winner:* Yerra Sugarman for *Forms of Gone* (Sheep Meadow Press).

Maxwell E. Perkins Award for Distinguished Achievement in Fiction. To honor an editor, publisher, or agent who has nurtured or championed U.S. fiction writers. *Offered by:* Mercantile Library of New York. *Winner:* Nan Talese.

Edgar Allan Poe Awards. For outstanding mystery, suspense, and crime writing. *Offered by:* Mystery Writers of America. *Winners:* (novel) T. Jefferson Parker for *California Girl* (Morrow); (first novel) Don Lee for *Country of Origin* (Norton); (paperback original) Domenic Stansberry for *The Confession* (Hard Case Crime); (critical/biographical) Leslie S. Klinger, ed., for *The New Annotated Sherlock Holmes* (Norton); (fact crime) Leonard Levitt for *Conviction: Solving the Moxley Murder* (Regan Books); (young adult) Dorothy and Thomas Hoobler for *In Darkness, Death* (Philomel); (juvenile) Blue Balliett for *Chasing Vermeer* (Scholastic); (Grand Master) Marcia Muller; (Ellery Queen) Carolyn Marino, HarperCollins; (Mary Higgins Clark) Rochelle Krich for *Grave Endings* (Ballantine); (Robert L. Fish) Thomas Morrissey for *Can't Catch Me* (Akashic Books)

Michael L. Printz Award for Excellence in Literature for young adults. *Offered by:* American Library Association, Association for Library Service to Children. *Winner:* Meg Rosoff for *How I Live Now* (Random House).

Pulitzer Prizes in Letters. To honor distinguished work by American writers, dealing preferably with American themes.

Offered by: Columbia University Graduate School of Journalism. *Winners:* (fiction) Marilynne Robinson for *Gilead* (Farrar, Straus & Giroux); (history) David Hackett Fischer for *Washington's Crossing* (Oxford University); (biography) Mark Stevens and Annalyn Swan for *De Kooning* (Knopf); (poetry) Ted Kooser for *Delights and Shadows* (Copper Canyon); (nonfiction) Steve Coll for *Ghost Wars* (Penguin).

Raiziss/De Palchi Translation Award. For a translation into English of a significant work of modern Italian poetry by a living translator. *Offered by:* Academy of American Poets. *Winner:* Ann Snodgrass for *The Selected Poems of Vittorio Sereni* (work-in-progress)

Rea Award for the Short Story. To honor a living writer who has made a significant contribution to the short story as an art form. *Offered by:* Dungannon Foundation. *Winner:* Ann Beattie.

Arthur Rense Poetry Prize. To an exceptional poet. *Offered by:* American Academy of Arts and Letters. *Winner:* Daniel Hoffman.

Rita Awards. *Offered by:* Romance Writers of America. *Winners:* (best traditional romance) Jessica Hart for *Christmas Eve Marriage* (Harlequin); (best regency romance) Sophia Nash for *A Passionate Endeavor* (Signet); (best short contemporary series) Barbara McCauley for *Miss Pruitt's Private Life* (Silhouette); (best short historical romance) Susan Kay Law for *A Wanted Man* (Avon); (best long contemporary series) Inglath Cooper for *John Riley's Girl* (Harlequin); (best historical romance) Laura Kinsale for *Shadowheart* (Berkley); (best paranormal romance) Lori Handeland for *Blue Moon* (St. Martin's); (best romantic suspense) Karen Rose for *I'm Watching You* (Warner Books); (best inspirational romance) Shelley Bates for *Grounds To Believe* (Steeple Hill); (best contemporary single title Jennifer Crusie for *Bet Me* (St. Martin's); (best romantic novella) Maggie Shayne for "Her Best Enemy" in *Night's Edge* (Harlequin); (novel with strong romantic elements) Evelyn Vaughn for *A.K.A. Goddess* (Silhouette); (best first book) Lani Diane Rich for *Time Off for Good Behavior* (Warner).

John Llewellyn Rhys Prize (United Kingdom). For a work of literature by a British or Commonwealth author 35 or younger and published in the United Kingdom. *Offered by:* Booktrust. *Winner:* Charlotte Mendelson for *Daughters of Jerusalem* (Picador).

Rogers Writers' Trust Fiction Prize (Canada). To a Canadian author of a novel or short story collection. *Offered by:* Rogers Communications. *Winner:* Alice Munro for *Runaway* (McClelland & Stewart).

Richard and Hinda Rosenthal Foundation Award. For a work of fiction that is a considerable literary achievement though not necessarily a commercial success. *Offered by:* American Academy of Arts and Letters. *Winner:* Jeff Talarigo for *The Pearl Diver* (Doubleday/Talese).

Juan Rulfo International Latin American and Caribbean Prize (Mexico). *Offered by:* Juan Rulfo International Latin American and Caribbean Prize Committee. *Winner:* Tomas Segovia.

Schneider Family Book Awards. To honor authors and illustrators for books that embody artistic expressions of the disability experience of children and adolescents. *Offered by:* American Library Association. *Winners:* (ages 0–10) *My Pal, Victor/Mi Amigo, Victor* by Diane Gonzales Bertrand, illus. by Robert L. Sweetland (Raven Tree); (ages 11–13) *Becoming Naomi León* by Pam Muñoz Ryan (Scholastic); (ages 13–18) *My Thirteenth Winter: A Memoir* by Samantha Abeel (Orchard Books).

Shelley Memorial Award. To a poet living in the United States who is chosen on the basis of genius and need. *Offered by:* Poetry Society of America. *Winner:* Lyn Hejinian.

Robert F. Sibert Award. For the most distinguished informational book for children. *Offered by:* American Library Association, Association for Library Service to Children. *Winner:* Russell Freedman for *The Voice That Challenged a Nation: Marian Anderson and the Struggle for Equal Rights* (Clarion).

WHSmith Literary Award (United Kingdom). For an author whose book makes, in the opinion of the judges, the most significant contribution to literature. *Offered by:* WHSmith, PLC. *Winner:* Philip Roth for *The Plot Against America* (Houghton Mifflin).

Spur Awards. *Offered by:* Western Writers of America. *Winners:* (best first novel) D. L. Birchfield for *Field of Honor* (University of Oklahoma Press); (best original mass-market paperback) Richard S. Wheeler for *Vengeance Valley* (Pinnacle); (best western juvenile nonfiction) Ednah New Rider Weber for *Rattlesnake Mesa: Stories from a Native American Childhood* (Lee & Low); (best western novel under 90,000 words) Rick Steber for *Buy the Chief a Cadillac* (Bonanza); (best novel of the West) Kathleen O'Neal Gear and W. Michael Gear for *People of the Raven* (Forge); (nonfiction—biography) Thom Hatch for *Black Kettle: The Cheyenne Chief Who Sought Peace but Found War* (John Wiley & Sons); (nonfiction—contemporary) Charles H. Harris, III and Louis R. Sadler for *The Texas Rangers and the Mexican Revolution* (University of New Mexico Press); (nonfiction—historical) Richard Steven Street for *Beasts of the Field* (Stanford University Press); (short nonfiction) Jim Doherty for "Blood for Oil" in *Just the Facts* (Deadly Serious Press); (short fiction) Larry D. Sweazy for "The Promotion" from the anthology *Texas Rangers* (Berkley); (juvenile fiction) Mary Cronk Farrell for *Fire in the Hole* (Clarion); (illustrated children's book) Deborah Hopkinson for *Apples to Oregon,* illus. by Nancy Carpenter (Simon and Schuster); (drama script) John Fusco for "Hidalgo" (Touchstone Pictures); (documentary script) Laura Verklan for "Wild West Tech Deadwood Tech" (The History Channel); (poetry) Walt McDonald for *A Thousand Miles of Stars* (Texas Tech University Press).

Wallace Stevens Award. To recognize outstanding and proven mastery in the art of poetry. *Offered by:* Academy of American Poets. *Winner:* Gerald Stern.

Stonewall Book Awards. *Offered by:* Gay, Lesbian, Bisexual, and Transgendered Round Table, American Library Association. *Winners:* (Barbara Gittings Literature Award) Colm Tóibín for *The Master: A Novel* (Scribner); (Israel Fishman Nonfiction Award) Joan Roughgarden for *Evolution's Rainbow: Diversity, Gender, and Sexuality in Nature and in People* (University of California Press).

The Story Prize. For the best short story collection of the year. *Offered by: Story* magazine. *Winner:* Edwidge Danticat for *The Dew Breaker* (Knopf).

Charles Taylor Prize for Literary Nonfiction (Canada). To honor a book of creative nonfiction widely available in Canada and written by a Canadian citizen or landed immigrant. *Offered by:* Charles Taylor Foundation. *Winner:* Charles Montgomery for *The Last Heathen* (Douglas & McIntyre).

Sydney Taylor Children's Book Awards. For a distinguished contribution to Jewish children's literature. *Offered by:* Association of Jewish Libraries. *Winners:* (older readers) Sarah Littman for *Confessions of a Closet Catholic* (Dutton); (younger readers) Erica Silverman for *Sholom's Treasure: How Sholom Aleichem Became a Writer,* illus. by Mordicai Gerstein (Farrar, Straus and Giroux).

Thurber Prize. For a humorous book of fiction or nonfiction. *Offered by:* Thurber House. *Winner:* Christopher Buckley for *No Way to Treat a First Lady* (Random House).

Kate Frost Tufts Discovery Award. For a first or very early book of poetry by an emerging poet. *Offered by:* Claremont Graduate School. *Winner:* Patrick Phillips for *Chattahoochee* (University of Arkansas).

Kingsley Tufts Poetry Award. For a book of poetry by a mid-career poet. *Offered by:* Claremont Graduate School. *Winner:* Michael Ryan for *New and Selected Poems* (Houghton Mifflin).

Harold D. Vursell Memorial Award. To a writer whose work merits recognition for the quality of its prose style. *Offered by:* American Academy of Arts and Letters. *Winner:* Ann Patchett.

George Washington Book Prize. To recognize published works about George Washington or the founding era. *Offered by:* Washington College and the Gilder Lehman Institute of American History. *Winner:* Ron Chernow for *Alexander Hamilton* (Penguin).

Whitbread Book Awards (United Kingdom). For literature of merit that is readable on a wide scale. *Offered by:* Booksellers Association of Great Britain. *Winners:* (first novel) Tash Aw for *The Harmony Silk Factory* (RIverhead); (children's) Kate Thompson for *The New Policeman* (Gardners Books); (novel) Ali Smith for *The Accidental* (Pantheon); (biography) Hilary Spurling for *Matisse the Master* (Part 2) (Knopf); (poetry) Christopher Logue for *Cold Calls* (Faber & Faber); (book of the year) Hilary Spurling for *Matisse the Master* (Part 2) (Knopf).

Whiting Writers' Awards. For emerging writers of exceptional talent and promise. *Offered by:* Mrs. Giles Whiting Foundation. *Winners:* (plays) Rinne Groff; (poetry) Thomas Sayers Ellis; Ilya Kaminsky, Dana Levin, Spencer Reece, Tracy K. Smith; (fiction) Sarah Shun-lien Bynum, Nell Freudenberger, Seth Kantner; (fiction/poetry) John Keene.

Walt Whitman Award. To a U.S. poet who has not published a book of poems in a standard edition. *Offered by:* Academy of American Poets. *Winner:* Mary Rose O'Reilley for *Half Wild* (Louisiana State University).

Laura Ingalls Wilder Award. For an author or illustrator whose books have made a substantial and lasting contribution to children's literature. *Offered by:* American Library Association, Association for Library Service to Children. *Winner:* Laurence Yep.

Robert H. Winner Memorial Award. To a mid-career poet over 40 who has published no more than one book of poetry. *Offered by:* Poetry Society of America. *Winner:* Julie Sheehan.

L. L. Winship Award. For a book of poetry, fiction, or creative nonfiction with a New England subject or written by a New England author. *Offered by:* PEN New England. *Winners:* Kevin Goodan for *In the Ghost-House Acquainted* (Alice James); Edward Delaney for *Warp and Weft* (Permanent Press).

Thomas Wolfe Award. To honor writers with distinguished bodies of work. *Offered by:* Thomas Wolfe Society and the University of North Carolina at Chapel Hill. *Winner:* Fred Cappell.

Helen and Kurt Wolff Translator's Prize. For an outstanding translation from German into English, published in the United States. *Offered by:* Goethe Institut Inter Nationes Chicago. *Winner:* Michael Henry Heim for *Death in Venice* by Thomas Mann (HarperCollins).

World Fantasy Convention Awards. For outstanding fantasy writing. *Offered by:* World Fantasy Convention. *Winners:* (novel) Susanna Clarke for *Jonathan Strange and Mr. Norrell* (Bloomsbury); (anthology) Barbara and Christopher Roden, eds., for *Acquainted with the Night* (Ash-Tree Press); Sheree R. Thomas, ed., for *Dark Matter: The Reading of Bones* (Warner); (collection) Margo Lanagan for *Black Justice* (Allen & Unwin); (lifetime achievement) Tom Doherty, Carol Emshwiller.

Writers' Trust of Canada/McClelland & Stewart Journey Prize (Canada). To a new, developing Canadian author for a short story or an excerpt from a novel-in-progress. *Offered by:* McClelland & Stewart and James A. Michener. *Winner:* Devin Krukoff for the short story "The Last Spark."

Young Lions Fiction Award. For a novel or collection of short stories by an American under the age of 35. *Offered by:* Young Lions of the New York Public Library. *Winner:* Andrew Sean Greer for *The Confessions of Max Tivoli* (Farrar, Straus & Giroux).

Part 6
Directory of Organizations

Directory of Library and Related Organizations

Networks, Consortia, and Other Cooperative Library Organizations

United States

Alabama

Alabama Health Libraries Assn. (ALHeLa), Baugh Medical Libs., Mobile 36688-0002. SAN 372-8218. Tel. 251-460-7043, fax 251-471-7857. *Dir.* Tom Williams.

Jefferson County Hospital Librarians Assn., Brookwood Medical Center, Birmingham 35209. SAN 371-2168. Tel. 205-877-1131, fax 205-877-1267.

Library Management Network (LMN), 110 Johnston St. S.E., Decatur 35601. SAN 322-3906. Tel. 256-308-2529, fax 256-308-2533. *System Coord.* Charlotte Moncrief.

Marine Environmental Sciences Consortium, Dauphin Island Sea Lab, Dauphin Island 36528. SAN 322-0001. Tel. 251-861-2141, fax 251-861-4646, e-mail disl@disl.org. *Dir.* George Crozier.

Network of Alabama Academic Libraries, c/o Alabama Commission on Higher Education, Montgomery 36130-2000. SAN 322-4570. Tel. 334-242-2164, fax 334-242-0270. *Dir.* Sue O. Medina.

Alaska

Alaska Library Network (ALN), 344 W. Third Ave., Ste. 125, Anchorage 99501. SAN 371-0688. Tel. 907-269-6570, fax 907-269-6580, e-mail aslanc@eed.state.ak.us.

Arizona

Maricopa County Community College District/Lib. Technical Services, 2411 W. 14 St., Tempe 85281-6942. SAN 322-0060. Tel. 480-731-8774, fax 480-731-8787. *Head, Technical Services* Vince Jenkins.

Arkansas

Arkansas Area Health Education Center Consortium (AHEC), Sparks Regional Medical Center, Fort Smith 72901-4992. SAN 329-3734. Tel. 479-441-5337, fax 479-441-5339. *Dir.* Grace Anderson.

Arkansas Independent Colleges and Universities, 1 Riverfront, Ste. 610, North Little Rock 72114. SAN 322-0079. Tel. 501-378-0843, fax 501-374-1523. *Pres.* Kearney E. Dietz.

Northeast Arkansas Hospital Library Consortium, 223 E. Jackson, Jonesboro 72401. SAN 329-529X. Tel. 870-972-1290, fax 870-931-0839. *Dir.* Karen Crosser.

South Arkansas Film Coop, c/o Malvern-Hot Spring County Lib., Malvern 72104. SAN 321-5938. Tel. 501-332-5441, fax 501-332-6679, e-mail hotspringcountylibrary@yahoo.com.

California

Bay Area Library and Information Network (BAYNET), 672 Prentiss St., San Francisco 94110-6130. SAN 371-0610. Tel. 415-826-2464, e-mail infobay@baynetlibs.org.

Central Associatio of Libraries (CAL), 605 N. El Dorado St., Stockton 95202-1999. SAN 322-0125. Tel. 209-937-8649, fax 209-937-8292, e-mail 4999@ci.stockton. ca.us. *Dir.* Darla Gunning.

Consortium for Open Learning, 333 Sunrise Ave., No. 229, Roseville 95661-3479. SAN 329-4412. Tel. 916-788-0660, fax 916-788-0696, e-mail cdl@calweb.com. *Manager* Sandra Scott-Smith.

Consumer Health Information Program and Services (CHIPS), County of Los Angeles Public Lib., Carson 90745. SAN 372-8110. Tel. 310-830-0909, fax 310-834-4097, e-mail chips@colopl.org. *Libn.* Scott A. Willis.

Gold Coast Library Network, 4882 McGrath St., Ste. 230, Ventura 93003-7721. Tel. 805-650-7732, fax 805-642-9095, e-mail goldcln@rain.org. *Dir.* Vincent Schmidt.

Hewlett-Packard Library Information Network, 1501 Page Mill Rd., Palo Alto 94304. SAN 375-0019. Tel. 650-857-3091, fax 650-852-8187. *Dir.* Eugenie Prime.

Kaiser Permanente Library System—Southern California Region (KPLS), Health Sciences Lib., Riverside 92505. SAN 372-8153. Tel. 951-353-3659, fax 951-353-3262. *Dir.* William Paringer.

Metropolitan Cooperative Library System (MCLS), 3675 E. Huntington Dr., Ste. 100, Pasadena 91107. SAN 371-3865. Tel. 626-683-8244, fax 626-683-8097, e-mail mclshq@mcls.org. *Exec. Dir.* Barbara Custen.

National Network of Libraries of Medicine—Pacific Southwest Region (NN-LM PSRML), Louise M. Darling Biomedical Lib., Los Angeles 90095-1798. SAN 372-8234. Tel. 310-825-1200, fax 310-825-5389, e-mail psr-nnlm@library.ucla.edu. *Dir.* Judy Consales.

Nevada Medical Library Group (NMLG), Barton Memorial Hospital Lib., South Lake Tahoe 96150. SAN 370-0445. Tel. 530-542-3000 ext. 2903, fax 530-541-4697. *In Charge* Laurie Anton.

Northern California Assn. of Law Libraries (NOCALL), PMB 336, San Francisco 94105. SAN 323-5777. E-mail admin@ nocall.org. *Pres.* Tina Dumas.

Northern California Consortium of Psychology Libraries (NCCPL), Saybrook Graduate School and Research Center, San Francisco 94133. SAN 371-9006. Tel. 415-394-5062, fax 415-433-9271, e-mail nccpl-d@ jfku.edu. *Dir., Lib. Services* Annemarie Welteke.

OCLC Western Service Center, 3281 E. Guasti Rd., Ste. 560, Ontario 91761. SAN 370-0747. Tel. 909-937-3300, fax 909-937-3384. *Dir.* Pamela Bailey.

Peninsula Libraries Automated Network (PLAN), 2471 Flores St., San Mateo 94403-4000. SAN 371-5035. Tel. 650-358-6714, fax 650-358-6715. *Database Manager* Susan Yasar.

Research Libraries Group (RLG), 2029 Stierlin Ct., Ste. 100, Mountain View 94043-4684. SAN 322-0206. Fax 650-964-0943, e-mail ric@notes.rlg.org. *Pres.* James Michalko.

San Bernardino, Inyo, Riverside Counties United Library Services (SIRCULS), 3581 Mission Inn Ave., Riverside 92501-3377. SAN 322-0222. Tel. 909-369-7995, fax 909-784-1158, e-mail sirculs@inlandlib. org. *Exec. Dir.* Kathleen F. Aaron.

San Francisco Biomedical Library Network (SFBLN), H. M. Fishbon Memorial Lib., San Francisco 94115. SAN 371-2125. Tel. 415-885-7378, e-mail fishbon@itsa.ucfs. edu.

Santa Clarita Interlibrary Network (SCIL-NET), Powell Lib., Santa Clarita 91321. SAN 371-8964. Tel. 661-259-3540, fax 661-222-9159. *Libn.* John Stone.

Serra Cooperative Library System, 820 E St., San Diego 92101. SAN 372-8129. Tel. 619-232-1225, fax 619-696-8649, e-mail serral@sbcglobal.net. *System Coord.* Susan Swisher.

Substance Abuse Librarians and Information Specialists (SALIS), P.O. Box 9513, Berkeley 94709-0513. SAN 372-4042. Tel. 510-642-5208, fax 510-642-7175, e-mail salis@arg.org. *Chair* Stephanie Asteriadis.

Colorado

Bi-State Academic Libraries (BI-SAL), c/o Marycrest International Univ., Denver 80236-2711. SAN 322-1393. Tel. 563-

326-9254, fax 563-326-9250. *Libn.* Mary Edwards.

Bibliographical Center for Research, Rocky Mountain Region (BCR), 14394 E. Evans Ave., Aurora 80014-1478. SAN 322-0338. Tel. 303-751-6277, fax 303-751-9787, e-mail admin@bcr.org. *Exec. Dir.* David H. Brunell.

Colorado Alliance of Research Libraries, 3801 E. Florida Ave., Ste. 515, Denver 80210. SAN 322-3760. Tel. 303-759-3399, fax 303-759-3363.

Colorado Assn. of Law Libraries, P.O. Box 13363, Denver 80201. SAN 322-4325. Tel. 303-492-7312, fax 303-713-6218. *Pres.* Dan Cordova.

Colorado Council of Medical Librarians (CCML), P.O. Box 101058, Denver 80210-1058. SAN 370-0755. Tel. 303-837-7375, fax 303-837-7977. *Pres.* Joyce Condon.

Colorado Library Consortium (CLiC), 770 W. Hampden Ave., Ste. 340, Englewood 80110. SAN 371-3970. Tel. 303-422-1150, fax 303-431-9752. *Dir.* Valerie Horton.

Peaks and Valleys Library Consortium, c/o Arkansas Valley Regional Lib. Service System, Pueblo 81004. SAN 328-8684. Tel. 719-542-2156, fax 719-542-3155. *Dir.* Donna Jones Morris.

Connecticut

Capital Area Health Consortium, 270 Farmington Ave., Ste. 352, Farmington 06032-1994. SAN 322-0370. Tel. 860-676-1110, fax 860-676-1303, e-mail info@cahc.org. *Pres.* Karen Goodman.

Connecticut Library Consortium, 2911 Dixwell Ave., Ste. 201, Hamden 06518-3130. SAN 322-0389. Tel. 203-288-5757, fax 203-287-0757. *Exec. Dir.* Bradley Christine.

Council of State Library Agencies in the Northeast (COSLINE), Connecticut State Lib., Hartford 06106. SAN 322-0451. Tel. 860-757-6510, fax 860-757-6503.

CTW Library Consortium, Olin Memorial Lib., Middletown 06459-6065. SAN 329-4587. Tel. 860-685-3889, fax 860-685-2661. *System Libn.* Alan E. Hagyard.

Hartford Consortium for Higher Education, 950 Main St., Ste. 314, Hartford 06103. SAN 322-0443. Tel. 860-906-5016, fax

860-906-5118. *Exec. Dir.* Rosanne Druckman.

LEAP, 110 Washington Ave., North Haven 06473. SAN 322-4082. Tel. 203-239-1411, fax 203-239-9458. *Exec. Dir.* Diana Sellers.

Libraries Online (LION), 100 Riverview Center, Ste. 252, Middletown 06457. SAN 322-3922. Tel. 860-347-1704, fax 860-346-3707. *Exec. Dir.* Joan Gillespie.

Library Connection, 599 Matianuck Ave., Windsor 06095-3567. Tel. 860-298-5322, fax 860-298-5328. *Exec. Dir.* George Christian.

North Atlantic Health Sciences Libraries (NAHSL), Medial Lib. CB-3, Hartford 06102. SAN 371-0599. Tel. 508-856-6099, fax 508-856-5899. *Chair* Edward Donnald.

Delaware

Central Delaware Library Consortium, Dover Public Lib., Dover 19901. SAN 329-3696. Tel. 302-736-7030, fax 302-736-5087. *Dir.* Sheila B. Anderson.

Delaware Library Consortium (DLC), Delaware Academy of Medicine, Wilmington 19806. SAN 329-3718. Tel. 302-656-6398, fax 302-656-0470, e-mail library@delamed.org. *In Charge* Gail P. Gill.

District of Columbia

Council for Christian Colleges and Universities, 321 Eighth St. N.E., Washington 20002. SAN 322-0524. Tel. 202-546-8713, fax 202-546-8913, e-mail council@cccu.org. *Pres.* Robert C. Andringa.

District of Columbia Area Health Science Libraries (DCAHSL), American College of Obstetrics and Gynecology Resource Center, Washington 20024. SAN 323-9918. Tel. 202-863-2518, fax 202-484-1595, e-mail resources@acog.org. *Dir.* Mary Hyde.

EDUCAUSE, c/o 1150 18th St. N.W., Ste. 1010, Washington 20036. SAN 371-487X. Tel. 202-872-4200, fax 202-872-4318. *Pres.* Brian Hawkins.

Fedlink/Federal Library and Information Network, c/o Federal Library and Information Center Committee, Washington 20540-

4935. SAN 322-0761. Tel. 202-707-4800, fax 202-707-4818, e-mail flicc@loc.gov. *Exec. Dir.* Roberta I. Shaffer.

Interlibrary Users Assn. (IUA), c/o Urban Institute Lib., Washington 20037. SAN 322-1628. Tel. 202-261-5534, fax 202-223-3043. *Pres.* Nancy Minter.

Library of Congress, National Lib. Service for the Blind and Physically Handicapped (NLS), 1291 Taylor St. N.W., Washington 20542. SAN 370-5870. Tel. 202-707-5100, fax 202-707-0712, e-mail nls@loc.gov. *Dir.* Frank Kurt Cylke.

OCLC CAPCON Service Center, 1990 M St. N.W., Ste. 200, Washington 20036-3430. SAN 321-5954. Tel. 202-331-5771, fax 202-331-5788, e-mail capcon@oclc.org. *Exec. Dir.* Katherine Blauer.

Transportation Research Board, 500 Fifth St. N.W., Washington 20001. SAN 370-582X. Tel. 202-334-2990, fax 202-334-2527. *Dir.* Barbara Post.

Veterans Affairs Library Network (VALNET), Lib. Programs Office 19E, Washington 20420. SAN 322-0834. Tel. 202-273-8523, fax 202-273-9386. *Network Services* Ginny DuPont.

Washington Theological Consortium, 487 Michigan Ave. N.E., Washington 20017-1585. SAN 322-0842. Tel. 202-832-2675, fax 202-526-0818, e-mail wtconsort@aol.com. *Dir.* John Crossin.

Florida

Central Florida Library Cooperative (CFLC), 431 E. Horatio Ave., Ste. 230, Maitland 32751. SAN 371-9014. Tel. 407-644-9050, fax 407-644-7023. *Exec. Dir.* Marta Westall.

Florida Library Information Network, R. A. Gray Bldg., Tallahassee 32399-0250. SAN 322-0869. Tel. 850-245-6600, fax 850-245-6744, e-mail library@dos.state.fl.us.

Miami Health Sciences Library Consortium (MHSLC), KBI/IDM (142D), Miami 33125-1673. SAN 371-0734. Tel. 786-596-6506, fax 786-596-5910. *Pres.* Devica Samsundar.

Palm Beach Health Sciences Library Consortium (PBHSLC), c/o Good Samaritan Medical Center Medical Lib., West Palm

Beach 33402. SAN 370-0380. Tel. 561-650-6315, fax 561-650-6417.

Panhandle Library Access Network (PLAN), Five Miracle Strip Loop, Ste. 8, Panama City Beach 32407-3850. SAN 370-047X. Tel. 850-233-9051, fax 850-235-2286. *Exec. Dir.* William P. Conniff.

Southeast Florida Library Information Network (SEFLIN), 100 S. Andrews Ave., Fort Lauderdale 33301. SAN 370-0666. Tel. 954-334-1280, fax 954-334-1295. *Pres.* William Miller.

Southwest Florida Library Network, Bldg. III, Unit 7, Fort Myers 33913. Tel. 239-225-4225, fax 239-225-4229. *Exec. Dir.* Barbara J. Stites.

Tampa Bay Library Consortium, 1202 Tech Blvd., Ste. 202, Tampa 33619. SAN 322-371X. Tel. 813-740-3963, fax 813-628-4425.

Tampa Bay Medical Library Network (TABAMLN), Orlando Regional Health Care-Health Science Lib., Orlando 32806-2134. SAN 322-0885. Tel. 321-841-5878, fax 321-843-6825.

Georgia

Assn. of Southeastern Research Libraries (ASERL), c/o SOLINET, Atlanta 30309-2955. SAN 322-1555. Tel. 404-892-0943, fax 404-892-7879. *Exec. Dir.* John Burger.

Atlanta Health Science Libraries Consortium, Atlanta Medical Center, Atlanta 30312. SAN 322-0893. Tel. 404-265-4605, fax 404-265-3559. *Manager* Tara Douglas-Williams.

Atlanta Regional Consortium for Higher Education, 50 Hurt Plaza, Ste. 735, Atlanta 30303-2923. SAN 322-0990. Tel. 404-651-2668, fax 404-651-1797, e-mail arche@atlantahighered.org. *Pres.* Michael Gerber.

Georgia Interactive Network for Medical Information (GAIN), c/o Med. Lib., Mercer Univ., Macon 31207. SAN 370-0577. Tel. 478-301-2515, fax 478-301-2051. *Dir.* Jan H. LaBeause.

Georgia Online Database (GOLD), c/o Public Lib. Services, Atlanta 30345-4304. SAN 322-094X. Tel. 404-982-3560, fax 404-982-3563.

Metro Atlanta Library Assn. (MALA), c/o Atlanta Fulton Public Lib.-ILC, Atlanta 30303-1089. SAN 378-2549. Tel. 404-730-1733, fax 404-730-1988. *Pres.* Rick L. Wright.

Southeastern Library Network (SOLINET), 1438 W. Peachtree St. N.W., Ste. 200, Atlanta 30309-2955. SAN 322-0974. Tel. 404-892-0943, fax 404-892-7879. *Exec. Dir.* Kate Nevins.

SWGHSLC, Colquitt Regional Medical Center Health Sciences Lib., Moultrie 31776. SAN 372-8072. Tel. 229-890-3460, fax 229-891-9345. *Libn.* Susan Leik.

Hawaii

Hawaii-Pacific Chapter of the Medical Library Assn. (HPC-MLA), 1301 Punchbowl St., Honolulu 96813. SAN 371-3946. Tel. 808-547-4300, fax 808-547-4019. *Chair* Mabel Trafford.

Idaho

Canyon Owyhee Library Group, 203 E. Idaho Ave., Homedale 83628. Tel. 208-337-4613, fax 208-337-4933. *Media Specialist* Sherry Thomas.

Cooperative Information Network (CIN), 8385 N. Government Way, Hayden 83835-9280. SAN 323-7656. Tel. 208-772-5612, fax 208-772-2498, e-mail hay@cin.kcl. org. *In Charge* John W. Hartung.

Gooding County Library Consortium, c/o Gooding H.S., Gooding 83330. SAN 375-0094. Tel. 208-934-4831, fax 208-934-4347. *Head Libn.* Cora Caldwell.

Grangeville Cooperative Network, c/o Grangeville Centennial Lib., Grangeville 83530-1729. SAN 375-0108. Tel. 208-983-0951, fax 208-983-2336, e-mail library@grangeville.us.

Idaho Health Information Assn. (IHIA), Kootenai Medical Center, W. T. Wood Medical Lib., Coeur d'Alene 83814. SAN 371-5078. Tel. 208-666-3498, fax 208-666-2948. *Dir.* Marcie Horner.

Library Consortium of Eastern Idaho, 457 Broadway, Idaho Falls 83402. SAN 323-7699. Tel. 208-612-8450, fax 208-529-1467. *System Admin.* Roger Evans.

Lynx, c/o Boise Public Lib., Boise 83702-7195. SAN 375-0086. Tel. 208-384-4238, fax 208-384-4025. *Dir.* Stephen Cottrell.

Southwest Library Cooperative, c/o Boise State Univ., Albertsons Lib., Boise 83725-1430. SAN 375-0078. Tel. 208-426-4231; 208-426-4024; 208-426-1234, fax 208-426-1885. *Univ. Libn.* Timothy A. Brown.

VALNet, Lewis Clark State College Lib., Lewiston 83501. SAN 323-7672. Tel. 208-792-2227, fax 208-792-2831.

Illinois

Alliance Library System, 600 High Point Lane, East Peoria 61611. SAN 371-0637. Tel. 309-694-9200, fax 309-694-9230. *Exec. Dir.* Kitty Pope.

American Theological Library Assn. (ATLA), 250 S. Wacker Dr., Ste. 1600, Chicago 60606-5889. SAN 371-9022. Tel. 312-454-5100, fax 312-454-5505, e-mail atla@ atla.com. *Exec. Dir.* Dennis A. Norlin.

Areawide Hospital Library Consortium of Southwestern Illinois (AHLC), c/o St. Elizabeth Hospital Health Science Lib., Belleville 62222. SAN 322-1016. Tel. 618-234-2120, fax 618-222-4614.

Assn. of Chicago Theological Schools, Catholic Theological Union, Paul Bechtold Lib., Chicago 60615-5698. SAN 370-0658. Tel. 773-753-5322, fax 773-753-5340. *Dir.* Kenneth O'Malley.

Capital Area Consortium, Decatur Memorial Hospital-Health Science Lib., Decatur 62526. Tel. 217-876-2940, fax 217-876-2945. *Coord.* Karen Stoner.

Center for Research Libraries, 6050 S. Kenwood, Chicago 60637-2804. SAN 322-1032. Tel. 773-955-4545, fax 773-955-4339. *Pres.* Bernard F. Reilly.

Chicago and South Consortium, Governors State Univ. Lib., University Park 60466. SAN 322-1067. Tel. 708-534-5000 ext. 5142, fax 708-534-8454.

Consortium of Museum Libraries in the Chicago Area, c/o Morton Arboretum, Sterling Morton Lib., Lisle 60532-1293. SAN 371-392X. Tel. 630-719-7932, fax 630-719-7950. *Chair* Michael T. Stieber.

Council of Directors of State University Libraries in Illinois (CODSULI), Univ. of Illinois at Springfield, Springfield 62794.

SAN 322-1083. Tel. 217-206-6597, fax 217-206-6354.

East Central Illinois Consortium, Carle Foundation Hospital Lib., Urbana 61801. SAN 322-1040. Tel. 217-383-3456, fax 217-383-3452. *Manager* Gerald Dewitt.

Fox Valley Health Science Library Consortium, Provena St. Joseph Hospital Medical Lib., Elgin 60123. SAN 329-3831. Tel. 847-695-3200, fax 847-888-3532, e-mail fuhslc@uic.edu.

Heart of Illinois Library Consortium, 210 W. Walnut St., Canton 61520. SAN 322-1113. *Chair* Michelle Quinones.

Illinois Library and Information Network (ILLINET), c/o Illinois State Lib., Springfield 62701-1796. SAN 322-1148. Tel. 217-782-2994, fax 217-785-4326. *Dir.* Jean Wilkins.

Illinois Library Computer Systems Organization (ILCSO), Univ. of Illinois, Lib. and Information Science Bldg., Ste. 228, Champaign 61820-6211. SAN 322-3736. Tel. 217-244-7593, fax 217-244-7596, e-mail oncall@listserv.ilcso.uiuc.edu. *Dir.* Kristine Hammerstrand.

Illinois Office of Educational Services, 2450 Foundation Dr., Ste. 100, Springfield 62703-5464. SAN 371-5108. Tel. 217-786-3010, fax 217-786-3020, e-mail oesiscc@siu.edu.

LIBRAS, Judson College, Elgin 60123. SAN 322-1172. Tel. 847-628-2036, fax 847-628-2045, e-mail librasweb@libras-inc.org. *Pres.* Larry Wild.

Metropolitan Consortium of Chicago, Chicago School of Professional Psychology, Chicago 60610. SAN 322-1180. Tel. 312-329-6633, fax 312-644-6075. *Coord.* Margaret White.

National Network of Libraries of Medicine-Greater Midwest Region (NN-LM GMR), c/o Lib. of Health Science, Univ. Illinois at Chicago, Chicago 60612-4330. SAN 322-1202. Tel. 312-996-2464, fax 312-996-2226, e-mail gmr@uic.edu. *Dir.* Susan Jacobson.

Private Academic Libraries of Illinois (PALI), c/o Wheaton College Lib., Franklin and Irving, Wheaton 60187. SAN 370-050X. E-mail crflatzkehr@curf.edu. *Pres.* P. Paul Snezek.

Quad Cities Libraries in Cooperation (Quad-LINC), 220 W. 23 Ave., Coal Valley 61240. SAN 373-093X. Tel. 309-799-3155 ext. 3254, fax 309-799-7916. *Assistant Dir., Technical Services and Automation* MaryAnne Stewart.

River Bend Library System (RBLS), 220 W. 23 Ave., Coal Valley 61240-9624. SAN 371-0653. Tel. 309-799-3155, fax 309-799-7916.

Sangamon Valley Academic Library Consortium, MacMurray College, Henry Pfeiffer Lib., Jacksonville 62650. SAN 322-4406. Tel. 217-479-7110, fax 217-245-5214.

Indiana

American Zoo and Aquarium Assn. (AZA-LSIG), Indianapolis Zoo, Indianapolis 46222. SAN 373-0891. Tel. 317-630-5110, fax 317-630-5114.

Central Indiana Health Science Libraries Consortium, Indiana Univ. School of Medicine Lib., Indianapolis 46202. SAN 322-1245. Tel. 317-274-8358, fax 317-274-4056. *Pres.* Elaine Skopelja.

Collegiate Consortium Western Indiana, c/o Cunningham Memorial Lib., Terre Haute 47809. SAN 329-4439. Tel. 812-237-3700, fax 812-237-3376.

Evansville Area Library Consortium, 3700 Washington Ave., Evansville 47750. SAN 322-1261. Tel. 812-485-4151, fax 812-485-7564. *Coord.* Jane Saltzman.

Indiana Cooperative Library Services Authority (INCOLSA), 6202 Morenci Trail, Indianapolis 46268-2536. SAN 322-1296. Tel. 317-298-6570, fax 317-328-2380.

Indiana State Data Center, Indiana State Lib., Indianapolis 46204-2296. SAN 322-1318. Tel. 317-232-3733, fax 317-232-3728. *Coord.* Frank H. Wilmot.

Northeast Indiana Health Science Libraries Consortium (NEIHSL), Univ. Saint Francis Health Sciences Lib., Fort Wayne 46808. SAN 373-1383. Tel. 260-434-7691, fax 260-434-7695. *Coord.* Lauralee Aven.

Northwest Indiana Health Science Library Consortium, c/o NW Center for Medical Educ., Gary 46408-1197. SAN 322-1350. Tel. 219-980-6852; 219-980-6709, fax

219-980-6524; 219-980-6566. *Libn.* Felicia A. Young.

Iowa

Consortium of College and University Media Centers (CCUMC), Instructional Tech Center, Iowa State Univ., Ames 50011-3243. SAN 322-1091. Tel. 515-294-1811, fax 515-294-8089, e-mail ccumc@ccumc. org. *Exec. Dir.* Don A. Rieck.

Dubuque (Iowa) Area Library Information Consortium, c/o NE Iowa Community College, Burton Payne Lib., Peosta 52068. Tel. 563-556-5110 ext. 269, fax 563-557-0340. *Coord.* Deb Seiffert.

Iowa Private Academic Library Consortium (IPAL), c/o Buena Vista Univ. Lib., Storm Lake 50588. SAN 329-5311. Tel. 712-749-2127; 712-749-2203, fax 712-749-2059, e-mail library@bvu.edu. *Univ. Libn.* Jim Kennedy.

Linn County Library Consortium, Hiawatha Public Lib., Hiawatha 52233. SAN 322-4597. Tel. 319-393-1414, fax 319-393-6005. *Pres.* Jeaneal Weeks.

Polk County Biomedical Consortium, c/o Des Moines Area Community College, Ankeny Campus, Ankeny 50021. SAN 322-1431. Tel. 515-964-6573, fax 515-965-7126. *In Charge* Diane Messersmith.

Quad City Area Biomedical Consortium, Great River Medical Center Lib., West Burlington 52655. SAN 322-435X. Tel. 319-768-4075, fax 319-768-4080. *Coord.* Judy Hawk.

Sioux City Library Cooperative (SCLC), c/o Sioux City Public Lib., Sioux City 51101-1203. SAN 329-4722. Tel. 712-255-2933 ext. 251, fax 712-279-6432. *Chair* Peg Brady.

State of Iowa Libraries Online (SILO), State Lib. of Iowa, Des Moines 50319. SAN 322-1415. Tel. 515-281-4105, fax 515-281-6191. *State Libn.* Mary Wegner.

Kansas

Associated Colleges of Central Kansas, 210 S. Main St., McPherson 67460. SAN 322-1474. Tel. 620-241-5150, fax 620-241-5153.

Dodge City Library Consortium, c/o Central Elementary School, Dodge City 67801. SAN 322-4368. Tel. 620-227-1601, fax 620-227-1721. *Chair* Linda Zupancic.

Kansas Library Network Board, 300 S.W. 10 Ave., Rm. 343 N, Topeka 66612-1593. SAN 329-5621. Tel. 785-296-3875, fax 785-296-6650. *Exec. Dir.* Eric Hansen.

Kentucky

Assn. of Independent Kentucky Colleges and Universities, 484 Chenault Rd., Frankfort 40601. SAN 322-1490. Tel. 502-695-5007, fax 502-695-5057. *Pres.* Gary S. Cox.

Eastern Kentucky Health Science Information Network (EKHSIN), c/o Camden-Carroll Lib., Morehead 40351. SAN 370-0631. Tel. 606-783-6860, fax 606-784-2178. *Interim Dir.* Elsie Pritchard.

Kentuckiana Metroversity, 200 W. Broadway, Ste. 700, Louisville 40202. SAN 322-1504. Tel. 502-897-3374, fax 502-895-1647.

Kentucky Health Science Libraries Consortium, VA Medical Center, Lib. Services 142D, Louisville 40206-1499. SAN 370-0623. Tel. 502-287-6240, fax 502-287-6134. *Head Libn.* Gene M. Haynes.

Theological Education Assn. of Mid America (TEAM-A), c/o Southern Baptist Theological Seminary, Louisville 40280-0294. SAN 322-1547. Tel. 502-897-4807, fax 502-897-4600. *Libn.* Bruce Keisling.

Louisiana

Central Louisiana Medical Center Library Consortium (CLMLC), VA Medical Center 142D, Alexandria 71306. Tel. 318-619-9102, fax 318-619-9144, e-mail clmlc@yahoo.com. *Coord.* Miriam J. Brown.

Health Sciences Library Assn. of Louisiana (HSLAL), Tulane Health Sciences Lib., New Orleans 70112-2632. SAN 375-0035. Tel. 504-988-2404, fax 504-988-2412. *Chair* Susan Dorsey.

Loan SHARK, State Lib. of Louisiana, Baton Rouge 70802. SAN 371-6880. Tel. 225-342-4918, 225-342-4920, fax 225-219-4725. *Coord.* Virginia R. Smith.

Louisiana Government Information Network (LaGIN), c/o State Lib. of Louisiana, Baton Rouge 70802. SAN 329-5036. Tel. 225-342-4920, e-mail lagin@pelican.state.lib.la.us. *Coord.* Virginia Smith.

New Orleans Educational Telecommunications Consortium, 2 Canal St., Ste. 2038, New Orleans 70130. SAN 329-5214. Tel. 504-524-0350, fax 504-524-0327, e-mail noetc_inc@excite.com. *Exec. Dir.* Michael Adler.

Maine

Health Science Library Information Consortium (HSLIC), 211 Marginal Way, No. 245, Portland 04101. SAN 322-1601. Tel. 207-871-4081. *Chair* John Hutchinson.

Maryland

ERIC Project, 4483-A Forbes Blvd., Lanham 20706. SAN 322-161X. Tel. 301-552-4200, fax 301-552-4700, e-mail info@ericfac.piccard.csc.com. *Dir.* Lawrence Henry.

Library Video Network (LVN), 320 York Rd., Towson 21204. SAN 375-5320. Tel. 410-887-2090, fax 410-887-2091, e-mail lvn@bcpl.net. *Manager* Carl Birkmeyer.

Maryland Interlibrary Loan Organization (MILO), c/o Enoch Pratt Free Lib., Baltimore 21201-4484. SAN 343-8600. Tel. 410-396-5498, fax 410-396-5837, e-mail milo@epfl.net. *Manager* Emma E. Beaven.

National Network of Libraries of Medicine (NN-LM), National Lib. of Medicine, Bethesda 20894. SAN 373-0905. Tel. 301-496-4777, fax 301-480-1467. *Dir.* Angela Ruffin.

National Network of Libraries of Medicine— Southeastern Atlantic Region (NNLM-SEA), Univ. of Md. Health Sciences and Human Services Lib., Baltimore 21201-1512. SAN 322-1644. Tel. 410-706-2855, fax 410-706-0099. *Dir.* Mary J. Tooey.

Regional Alcohol and Drug Abuse Resource Network (RADAR), National Clearinghouse Alcohol and Drug Info., Rockville 20852. SAN 377-5569. Tel. 301-468-2600, fax 301-468-6433, e-mail info@health.org. *Coord.* Marion Pierce.

U.S. National Library of Medicine (NLM), 8600 Rockville Pike, Bethesda 20894. SAN 322-1652. Tel. 301-594-5983, fax 301-402-1384, e-mail custserv@nlm.nih.gov.

Washington Research Library Consortium (WRLC), 901 Commerce Dr., Upper Marlboro 20774. SAN 373-0883. Tel. 301-390-2031, fax 301-390-2020. *Exec. Dir.* Lizanne Payne.

Massachusetts

Boston Biomedical Library Consortium (BBLC), c/o Percy R. Howe Memorial Lib., Boston 02115. SAN 322-1725. Tel. 617-262-5200, fax 617-262-4021.

Boston Library Consortium, McKim Bldg., Boston 02117. SAN 322-1733. Tel. 617-262-0380, fax 617-262-0163. *Exec. Dir.* Barbara G. Preece.

Cape Libraries Automated Materials Sharing (CLAMS), 270 Communication Way, Unit 4E-4F, Hyannis 02601. SAN 370-579X. Tel. 508-790-4399, fax 508-771-4533. *Exec. Dir.* Monica Grace.

Catholic Library Assn., 100 North St., Ste. 224, Pittsfield 01201-5109. SAN 329-1030. Tel. 413-443-2252, fax 413-442-2252, e-mail cla@cathla.org. *Exec. Dir.* Jean R. Bostley, SSJ.

Central and Western Massachusetts Automated Resource Sharing (CW MARS), 67 Millbrook St., Ste. 201, Worcester 01606. SAN 322-3973. Tel. 508-755-3323 ext. 30, fax 508-755-3721. *Exec. Dir.* Joan Kuklinski.

Cooperating Libraries of Greater Springfield (CLIC), Springfield College, Springfield 01109. SAN 322-1768. Tel. 413-748-3502, fax 413-748-3631. *Dir.* Andrea Taupier.

Fenway Libraries Online (FLO), c/o Wentworth Institute Technology, Boston 02115. SAN 373-9112. Tel. 617-442-2384, fax 617-442-1519. *Dir.* Jamie Ingram.

Fenway Library Consortium, Univ. of Massachusetts, Boston 02125. SAN 327-9766. Tel. 617-521-2741, 617-573-8536, fax 617-521-3093. *Dir.* David Ortiz.

Massachusetts Health Sciences Libraries Network (MAHSLIN), Brigham and Women's Hospital, Boston 02115. SAN 372-8293.

Tel. 617-525-6787, fax 617-975-0890. *Pres.* Anne Fladger.

Merrimack Valley Library Consortium, 123 Tewksbury St., Andover 01810. SAN 322-4384. Tel. 978-475-7632, fax 978-475-7179. *Exec. Dir.* Lawrence Rungren.

METROWEST Massachusetts Regional Library System, 135 Beaver St., Waltham 02452. Tel. 781-398-1819, fax 781-398-1821. *Admin.* Sondra H. Vandermark.

Minuteman Library Network, 10 Strathmore Rd., Natick 01760-2419. SAN 322-4252. Tel. 508-655-8008, fax 508-655-1507. *Exec. Dir.* Carol B. Caro.

National Network of Libraries of Medicine— New England Region (NN-LM NER), Univ. of Massachusetts Medical School, Shrewsbury 01545-2732. SAN 372-5448. Tel. 508-856-5979, fax 508-856-5977. *Dir.* Elaine Martin.

NELINET, 153 Cordaville Rd., Southborough 01772. SAN 322-1822. Tel. 508-460-7700 ext. 1934, fax 508-460-9455. *Exec. Dir.* Arnold Hirshon.

North of Boston Library Exchange (NOBLE), 26 Cherry Hill Dr., Danvers 01923. SAN 322-4023. Tel. 978-777-8844, fax 978-750-8472. *Exec. Dir.* Ronald A. Gagnon.

Northeast Consortium of Colleges and Universities in Massachusetts (NECCUM), Northern Essex Community College, Haverhill 01830. SAN 371-0602. Tel. 978-556-3400, fax 978-556-3738. *Dir.* Linda Hummel-Shea.

Northeastern Consortium for Health Information (NECHI), Lowell General Hospital Health Science Lib., Lowell 01854. SAN 322-1857. Tel. 978-937-6247, fax 978-937-6855. *Libn.* Donna Beales.

SAILS, 547 W. Groves St., Ste. 4, Middleboro 02346. SAN 378-0058. Tel. 508-946-8600, fax 508-946-8605. *Pres.* Robin Glasser.

Southeastern Massachusetts Consortium of Health Science Libraries (SEMCO), South Shore Hospital, South Weymouth 02190. SAN 322-1873. Tel. 781-340-8528, fax 781-331-0834. *Dir.* Kathy McCarthy.

Southeastern Massachusetts Regional Library System (SEMLS), 10 Riverside Dr., Lakeville 02347. Tel. 508-923-3531, fax 508-923-3539, e-mail semls@semls.org. *Admin.* Cynthia A. Roach.

West of Boston Network (WEBNET), Horn Lib.-Babson College, Babson Park 02457. SAN 371-5019. Tel. 781-239-4308, fax 781-239-5226. *Pres.* Marilyn Bregoli.

Western Massachusetts Health Information Consortium, Baystate Medical Center Health Sciences Library, Springfield 01199. SAN 329-4579. Tel. 413-794-1291, fax 413-794-1978. *Pres.* Karen Dorval.

Michigan

Berrien Library Consortium, c/o William Hessel Lib., Lake Michigan College, Benton Harbor 49022-1899. SAN 322-4678. Tel. 269-927-8605, fax 269-927-6656. *Pres.* Diane Baker.

Detroit Area Consortium of Catholic Colleges, c/o Sacred Heart Seminary, Detroit 48206. SAN 329-482X. Tel. 313-883-8500, fax 313-868-6440. *Dir.* Herman Peterson.

Kalamazoo Consortium for Higher Education (KCHE), Kalamazoo College, Kalamazoo 49006. SAN 329-4994. Tel. 269-337-7220, fax 269-337-7219. *Pres.* Eileen B. Wilson-Oyelaran.

Lakeland Library Cooperative, 4138 Three Mile Rd. N.W., Grand Rapids 49534. SAN 308-132X. Tel. 616-559-5253, fax 616-559-4329. *Dir.* Daniel J. Siebersma.

Michigan Assn. of Consumer Health Information Specialists (MACHIS), Bronson Methodist Hospital, Kalamazoo 49007. SAN 375-0043. Tel. 269-341-8627, fax 269-341-8828. *Dir.* Marge Kars.

Michigan Health Sciences Libraries Assn. (MHSLA), 1407 Rensen St., Ste. 4, Lansing 48910. SAN 323-987X. *Pres.* Jennifer Barlow.

Michigan Library Consortium (MLC), 1407 Rensen St., Ste. 1, Lansing 48910-3657. SAN 322-192X. Tel. 517-394-2420, fax 517-394-2096, e-mail reception@mlcnet.org. *Contact* Diana Mitchell.

Northland Interlibrary System (NILS), 316 E. Chisholm St., Alpena 49707. SAN 329-4773. Tel. 989-356-1622, fax 989-354-3939. *Interim Dir.* Christine Johnson.

Southeastern Michigan League of Libraries (SEMLOL), Lawrence Technological

Univ., Southfield 48075. SAN 322-4481. Tel. 248-204-3000, fax 248-204-3005. *Contact* Gary Cocozzoli.

Southwest Michigan Library Cooperative (SMLC), 305 Oak St., Paw Paw 49079. SAN 371-5027. Tel. 269-657-4698, fax 269-657-4494. *Dir.* Alida L. Geppert.

Suburban Library Cooperative (SLC), 16480 Hall Rd., Clinton Township 48038. SAN 373-9082. Tel. 586-286-5750, fax 586-286-8951. *Dir.* Tammy L. Turgeon.

The Library Network (TLN), 13331 Reeck Rd., Southgate 48195-3054. SAN 370-596X. Tel. 734-281-3830, fax 734-281-1817. *Dir.* A. Michael Deller.

Upper Peninsula of Michigan Health Science Library Consortium, c/o Marquette Health System Hospital, Marquette 49855. SAN 329-4803. Tel. 906-225-3429, fax 906-225-3524. *In Charge* Janis Lubenow.

Upper Peninsula Region of Library Cooperation, 1615 Presque Isle Ave., Marquette 49855. SAN 329-5540. Tel. 906-228-7697, fax 906-228-5627. *In Charge* Suzanne Dees.

Valley Library Consortium, 3210 Davenport Ave., Saginaw 48602-3495. Tel. 989-497-0925, fax 989-497-0918. *Exec. Dir.* Karl R. Steiner.

Minnesota

Arrowhead Health Sciences Library Network, Univ. of Minnesota Duluth Lib., Duluth 55812. SAN 322-1954. Tel. 218-726-8104, fax 218-726-6205. *Coord.* Adele Krusz.

Capital Area Library Consortium (CALCO), c/o Minnesota Dept. of Transportation, Lib. MS155, Saint Paul 55155. SAN 374-6127. Tel. 651-296-5272, fax 651-297-2354. *Libn.* Shirley Sherkow.

Central Minnesota Libraries Exchange (CMLE), Miller Center, Rm. 130-D, Saint Cloud 56301-4498. SAN 322-3779. Tel. 320-255-2950, fax 320-654-5131, e-mail cmle@stcloudstate.edu. *Dir.* Patricia A. Post.

Community Health Science Library, c/o Saint Francis Medical Center, Breckenridge 56520. SAN 370-0585. Tel. 218-643-7542, fax 218-643-7452. *Dir.* Kristi Kaseman.

Cooperating Libraries in Consortium (CLIC), 1619 Dayton Ave., Ste. 204, Saint Paul 55104. SAN 322-1970. Tel. 651-644-3878, fax 651-644-6258. *Exec. Dir.* Chris Olson.

Metronet, 1619 Dayton Ave., Ste. 314, Saint Paul 55104. SAN 322-1989. Tel. 651-646-0475, fax 651-649-3169, e-mail info@metronet.lib.mn.us. *Exec. Dir.* Tom Shaughnessy.

Metropolitan Library Service Agency (MELSA), 1619 Dayton Ave., No. 314, Saint Paul 55104-6206. SAN 371-5124. Tel. 651-645-5731, fax 651-649-3169, e-mail melsa@melsa.org. *Exec. Dir.* Marlene Moulton Janssen.

MINITEX Library Information Network, Univ. of Minnesota–Twin Cities, 15 Andersen Lib., Minneapolis 55455-0439. SAN 322-1997. Tel. 612-624-4002, fax 612-624-4508. *Dir.* William DeJohn.

Minnesota Theological Library Assn. (MTLA), c/o Bethel Seminary Lib., Saint Paul 55112. SAN 322-1962. Tel. 651-638-6184, fax 651-638-6006. *Pres.* Sandy Oslund.

North Country Library Cooperative, 5528 Emerald Ave., Mountain Iron 55768-2069. SAN 322-3795. Tel. 218-741-1907, fax 218-741-1908. *Dir.* Linda J. Wadman.

Northern Lights Library Network, 103 Graystone Plaza, Detroit Lakes 56501-3041. SAN 322-2004. Tel. 218-847-2825, fax 218-847-1461, e-mail nloffice@nlln.org. *Dir.* Ruth Solie.

SMILE (Southcentral Minnesota Inter-Library Exchange), 1400 Madison Ave., No. 622, Mankato 56001. SAN 321-3358. Tel. 507-625-7555, fax 507-625-4049, e-mail smile@tds.lib.mn.us. *Dir.* Nancy Katharine Steele.

Southeastern Libraries Cooperating (SELCO), 2600 19th St N.W., Rochester 55901-0767. SAN 308-7417. Tel. 507-288-5513, fax 507-288-8697. *Exec. Dir.* Ann B. Hutton.

Southwest Area Multicounty Multitype Interlibrary Exchange (SAMMIE), 109 S. 5 St., Ste. 30, Marshall 56258. SAN 322-2039. Tel. 507-532-9013, fax 507-532-2039, e-mail sammie@starpoint.net. *Dir.* Robin Chaney.

Twin Cities Biomedical Consortium (TCBC), c/o Fairview Univ. Medical Center, Minneapolis 55455. SAN 322-2055. Tel. 612-273-6595, fax 612-273-2675. *Chair* Michael Scott.

Valley Medical Network, Lake Region Hospital Lib., Fergus Falls 56537. SAN 329-4730. Tel. 218-736-8158, fax 218-736-8731. *In Charge* Connie Schulz.

Waseca Interlibrary Resource Exchange (WIRE), c/o Waseca High School Media Center, Waseca 56093. SAN 370-0593. Tel. 507-835-5470 ext. 218, fax 507-835-1724, e-mail tlol@waseca.k12.mn.us.

West, P.O. Box 64526, Saint Paul 55164-0526. SAN 322-4031. Tel. 651-687-7000, fax 651-687-5614, e-mail west.customer.service@thomson.com.

Mississippi

Central Mississippi Library Council (CMLC), c/o Millsaps College Lib., Jackson 39210. SAN 372-8250. Tel. 601-974-1070, fax 601-974-1082. *Admin.* Tom Henderson.

Mississippi Biomedical Library Consortium, c/o College of Veterinary Medicine, Mississippi State Univ., Mississippi State 39762. SAN 371-070X. Tel. 662-325-1240, fax 662-325-1141, e-mail library@cvm.msstate.edu.

Missouri

Health Sciences Library Network of Kansas City (HSLNKC), Univ. of Missouri, Kansas City Health Sciences Lib., Kansas City 64108-2792. SAN 322-2098. Tel. 816-235-1880, fax 816-235-6570. *Dir.* Peggy Mullaly-Quijas.

Kansas City Metropolitan Library and Information Network, 15624 E. 24 Hwy., Independence 64050. SAN 322-2101. Tel. 816-521-7257, fax 816-461-0966. *Exec. Dir.* Susan Burton.

Kansas City Regional Council for Higher Education, Park Univ., Parkville 64152-3795. SAN 322-211X. Tel. 816-741-2816, fax 816-741-1296, e-mail kcrche@kcrche.com. *Dir.* Gloria Brady.

Library Systems Service, Bernard Becker Medical Lib., Saint Louis 63110. SAN 322-2187. Tel. 314-362-2778, fax 314-362-0190. *Manager* Russ Monika.

Missouri Library Network Corp., 8045 Big Bend Blvd., Ste. 202, Saint Louis 63119-2714. SAN 322-466X. Tel. 314-918-7222, fax 314-918-7727. *Acting Dir.* Tracy Byerly.

Saint Louis Regional Library Network, 341 Sappington Rd., Saint Louis 63122. SAN 322-2209. Tel. 314-395-1305.

Nebraska

Lincoln Health Sciences Library Group (LHSLG), Univ. of Nebraska–Lincoln, Lincoln 68588-4100. SAN 329-5001. Tel. 402-472-2554, fax 402-472-5131.

NEBASE, c/o Nebraska Lib. Commission, Lincoln 68508-2023. SAN 322-2268. Tel. 402-471-2045, fax 402-471-2083.

Southeast Nebraska Library System, 5730 R St., Ste. C-1, Lincoln 68505. SAN 322-4732. Tel. 402-467-6188, fax 402-467-6196.

Nevada

Information Nevada, Interlibrary Loan Dept., Nevada State Lib. and Archives, Carson City 89701-4285. SAN 322-2276. Tel. 775-684-3326, fax 775-684-3330. *Head of ILL* Mona Reno.

New Hampshire

Carroll County Library Cooperative, c/o Madison Lib., Madison 03849. SAN 371-8999. Tel. 603-367-8545, fax 603-367-4479, e-mail librarian@madison.lib.nh.us.

Health Science Libraries of New Hampshire and Vermont, Lakes Region General Hospital, Laconia 03246. SAN 371-6864. Tel. 603-527-2837, fax 603-527-7197.

Hillstown Cooperative, Three Meetinghouse Rd., Bedford 03110. SAN 371-3873. Tel. 603-472-2300, fax 603-472-2978.

Librarians of the Upper Valley Cooperative (LUV Coop), 1173 U.S. Rte. 4, Canaan 03741. SAN 371-6856. Tel. 603-523-9650, e-mail canaantownlibrary@hotmail.com. *In Charge* Amy Thurber.

Merri-Hill-Rock Library Cooperative, c/o Sandown Public Lib., Sandown 03873-

0580. SAN 329-5338. Tel. 603-887-3428, fax 603-887-0590, e-mail sandownlibrary @comcast.net. *Dir., Lib. Services* Diane Heer.

New England Law Library Consortium (NELLCO), 9 Drummer Rd., Keene 03431. SAN 322-4244. Tel. 603-357-3385, fax 603-357-2075. *Exec. Dir.* Tracy L. Thompson.

New Hampshire College and University Council, 3 Barrell Ct., Ste. 100, Concord 03301-8543. SAN 322-2322. Tel. 603-225-4199, fax 603-225-8108. *Exec. Dir.* Thomas R. Horgan.

Nubanusit Library Cooperative, c/o Peterborough Town Lib., Peterborough 03458. SAN 322-4600. Tel. 603-924-8040, fax 603-924-8041.

Scrooge and Marley Cooperative, 695 Main St., Laconia 03246. SAN 329-515X. Tel. 603-524-4775. *Chair* Randy Brough.

Seacoast Cooperative Libraries, North Hampton Public Lib., North Hampton 03862. SAN 322-4619. Tel. 603-964-6326, fax 603-964-1107, e-mail coop@hampton.lib. nh.us. *Dir.* Pamela Schwotzer.

New Jersey

Basic Health Sciences Library Network (BHSL), Mountainside Hospital Health Science Lib., Montclair 07042. SAN 371-4888. Tel. 973-429-6240, fax 973-680-7850. *Coord.* Pat Regenberg.

Bergen Passaic Health Sciences Library Consortium, c/o Englewood Hospital and Medical Center, Health Sciences Lib., Englewood 07631. SAN 371-0904. Tel. 201-894-3069, fax 201-894-9049, e-mail lia.sabbagh@ehmc.com.

Central New Jersey Health Science Libraries Consortium (CNJHSLA), Saint Francis Medical Center Medical Lib., Trenton 08629. SAN 370-0712. Tel. 609-599-5068, fax 609-599-5773. *Libn.* Donna Barlow.

Central New Jersey Regional Library Cooperative, 4400 Rte. 9 S., Ste. 3400, Freehold 07728-1383. SAN 370-5102. Tel. 732-409-6484, fax 732-409-6492. *Dir.* Connie S. Paul.

Consortium of Foundation Libraries, Robert Wood Johnson Foundation, Princeton

08543. SAN 322-2462. Tel. 609-452-8701. *Chair* Hinda Greenberg.

Cosmopolitan Biomedical Library Consortium (CBLC), Overlook Hospital Medical Lib., Summit 07902. SAN 322-4414. Tel. 908-522-2699. *In Charge* Vicki Sciuk.

Health Sciences Library Assn. of New Jersey (HSLANJ), Saint Michaels Medical Center, Newark 07102. SAN 370-0488. Tel. 973-877-5471, fax 973-877-5378. *Dir.* Larry Dormer.

Highlands Regional Library Cooperative, 66 Ford Rd., Ste. 124, Denville 07834. SAN 329-4609. Tel. 973-664-1776, fax 973-664-1780. *Exec. Dir.* Joanne P. Roukens.

INFOLINK/Eastern New Jersey Regional Library Cooperative, Inc., 44 Stelton Rd., Ste. 330, Piscataway 08854. SAN 371-5116. Tel. 732-752-7720, fax 732-752-7785. *Exec. Dir.* Cheryl O'Connor.

Integrated Information Solutions, 600 Mountain Ave., Rm. 6A-200, Murray Hill 07974. SAN 329-5400. Tel. 908-582-4840, fax 908-582-3146, e-mail libnet@library. lucent.com. *Manager* M. E. Brennan.

Libraries of Middlesex Automation Consortium (LMxAC), 1030 Saint George, Ste. 203, Avenel 07001. SAN 329-448X. Tel. 732-750-2525, fax 732-750-9392.

Monmouth-Ocean Biomedical Information Consortium (MOBIC), Community Medical Center, Toms River 08755. SAN 329-5389. Tel. 732-557-8117, fax 732-557-8354. *Libn.* Reina Reisler.

Morris Automated Information Network (MAIN), c/o Morris County Lib., 30 East Hanover Ave., Whippany 07981. SAN 322-4058. Tel. 973-631-5353, fax 973-631-5366. *Network Admin.* Ellen L. Sleeter.

Morris-Union Federation, 214 Main St., Chatham 07928. SAN 310-2629. Tel. 973-635-0603, fax 973-635-7827.

New Jersey Health Sciences Library Network (NJHSN), Mountainside Hospital, Montclair 07042. SAN 371-4829. Tel. 973-429-6240, fax 973-680-7850, e-mail pat. regenberg@ahsys.org.

New Jersey Library Network, Lib. Development Bureau, Trenton 08608. SAN 372-8161. Tel. 609-984-3293, fax 609-633-3963.

South Jersey Regional Library Cooperative, Paint Works Corporate Center, Gibbsboro 08026. SAN 329-4625. Tel. 856-346-1222, fax 856-346-2839. *Exec. Dir.* Karen Hyman.

Virtual Academic Library Environment (VALE), William Paterson Univ. Lib., Wayne 07470-2103. Tel. 973-720-3179, fax 973-720-3171. *Chair* Judy Cohn.

New Mexico

Alliance for Innovation in Science and Technology Information (AISTI), 369 Montezuma Ave., No. 156, Santa Fe 87501. E-mail info@aisti.org. *Chair* Margaret Alexander.

New Mexico Consortium of Academic Libraries, Dean's Office, Albuquerque 87131-0001. SAN 371-6872. Tel. 505-277-5057, fax 502-277-7196. *Dean* Camila Alire.

New Mexico Consortium of Biomedical and Hospital Libraries, Albuquerque Regional Medical Center/Lib., Albuquerque 87102. SAN 322-449X. Tel. 505-727-8291, fax 505-727-8190, e-mail medicall@sjhs.org. *Libn.* Marian Frear.

New York

Academic Libraries of Brooklyn, Long Island Univ. Lib.-LLC 517, Brooklyn 11201. SAN 322-2411. Tel. 718-488-1081, fax 718-780-4057. *Dean* Constance Woo.

Associated Colleges of the Saint Lawrence Valley, State Univ. of New York College at Potsdam, Potsdam 13676-2299. SAN 322-242X. Tel. 315-267-3331, fax 315-267-2389. *Exec. Dir.* Anneke J. Larrance.

Brooklyn-Queens-Staten Island-Manhattan-Bronx Health Sciences Librarians (BQSIMB), 121 DeKalb Ave., Brooklyn 11201. SAN 370-0828. Tel. 718-630-7200, fax 718-630-8918. *Pres.* Luda Dolinsky.

Capital District Library Council for Reference and Research Resources, 28 Essex St., Albany 12206. SAN 322-2446. Tel. 518-438-2500, fax 518-438-2872. *Exec. Dir.* Jean K. Sheviak.

Central New York Library Resources Council (CLRC), 6493 Ridings Rd., Syracuse 13206-1195. SAN 322-2454. Tel. 315-446-5446, fax 315-446-5590, e-mail mclane@clrc.org. *Exec. Dir.* Michael J. McLane.

Council of Archives and Research Libraries in Jewish Studies (CARLJS), 330 Seventh Ave., 21st fl., New York 10001. SAN 371-053X. Tel. 212-629-0500, fax 212-629-0508, e-mail nfjc@jewishculture.org. *Assoc. Dir.* Dana Schneider.

Library Consortium of Health Institutions in Buffalo (LCHIB), 155 Abbott Hall, SUNY at Buffalo, Buffalo 14214. SAN 329-367X. Tel. 716-829-3900 ext. 143, fax 716-829-2211. *Exec. Dir.* Martin E. Mutka.

Long Island Library Resources Council (LILRC), Melville Lib. Bldg, Ste. E5310, Stony Brook 11794-3399. SAN 322-2489. Tel. 631-632-6650, fax 631-632-6662. *Dir.* Herbert Biblo.

Medical and Scientific Libraries of Long Island (MEDLI), c/o Palmer School of Lib. and Info. Science, Brookville 11548. SAN 322-4309. Tel. 516-299-2866; 516-299-4110, fax 516-299-4168. *Pres.* Mary Westermann-Cicio.

Medical Library Center of New York, 220 Fifth Ave., 7th fl., New York 10001-7708. SAN 322-3957. Tel. 212-427-1630, fax 212-876-6697. *Dir.* William Self.

Metropolitan New York Library Council (METRO), 57 E. 11 St., 4th fl., New York 10003-4605. SAN 322-2500. Tel. 212-228-2320 ext. 10, fax 212-228-2598. *Exec. Dir.* Dottie Hiebing.

National Network of Libraries of Medicine-Middle Atlantic Region (NN-LM MAR), New York Academy of Medicine, New York 10029-5293. Tel. 212-822-7396, fax 212-534-7042, e-mail rml1@nyam.org. *Assoc. Dir.* Naomi Adelman.

Northeast Foreign Law Libraries Cooperative Group, Columbia Univ. Lib., New York 10027. SAN 375-0000. Tel. 212-854-1411, fax 212-854-3295. *Coord.* Silke Sahl.

Northern New York Library Network, 6721 U.S. Hwy. 11, Potsdam 13676. SAN 322-2527. Tel. 315-265-1119, fax 315-265-1881, e-mail info@nnyln.org. *Exec. Dir.* John J. Hammond.

Nylink, 74 N. Pearl St., 5th fl., Albany 12207. SAN 322-256X. Tel. 518-443-

5444, fax 518-432-4346, e-mail nylink@ nylink.org. *Exec. Dir.* Mary-Alice Lynch.

Research Library Assn. of South Manhattan, New York Univ., Bobst Lib., New York 10012. SAN 372-8080. Tel. 212-998-2477, fax 212-995-4366. *Dean of Lib.* Carol Mandel.

Rochester Regional Library Council, 390 Packetts Landing, Fairport 14450. SAN 322-2535. Tel. 585-223-7570, fax 585-223-7712, e-mail rrlc@rrlc.org. *Exec. Dir.* Kathleen M. Miller.

South Central Regional Library Council, 215 N. Cayuga St., Ithaca 14850. SAN 322-2543. Tel. 607-273-9106, fax 607-272-0740, e-mail scrlc@lakenet.org. *Exec. Dir.* Jean Currie.

Southeastern New York Library Resources Council (SENYLRC), 21 S. Elting Corners Rd., Highland 12528-2805. SAN 322-2551. Tel. 845-883-9065, fax 845-883-9483. *Exec. Dir.* John L. Shaloiko.

United Nations System Electronic Information Acquisitions Consortium (UNSEIAC), c/o Dag Hammarskjold Lib., Rm. L-166A, New York 10017. SAN 377-855X. Tel. 212-963-7440, fax 212-963-2608. *Head Libn.* Linda Stoddart.

Western New York Library Resources Council, 4455 Genesee St., Buffalo 14225. SAN 322-2578. Tel. 716-633-0705, fax 716-633-1736. *Exec. Dir.* Gail M. Staines.

North Carolina

Cape Fear Health Sciences Information Consortium, c/o Ervin J Biggs Lib., Lumberton 28358. SAN 322-3930. Tel. 910-671-5046, fax 910-671-5337.

Consortium of Southeastern Law Libraries (COSELL), Kathrine R. Everett Law Lib., Chapel Hill 27599. SAN 372-8277. Tel. 919-962-6202, fax 919-962-1193.

Dialog Corp, 11000 Regency Pkwy., Ste. 10, Cary 27511. SAN 322-0176. Tel. 919-462-8600, fax 919-468-9890.

North Carolina Area Health Education Centers, UNC Health Science Lib., CB 7585, Chapel Hill 27599-7585. SAN 323-9950. Tel. 919-962-0700. *Dir.* Diana McDuffee.

North Carolina Community College System, 200 W. Jones St., Raleigh 27603-1379.

SAN 322-2594. Tel. 919-807-7100, fax 919-807-7164. *Admin. Dir.* Sharon Rasazo.

North Carolina Library and Information Network, State Lib. of North Carolina, Raleigh 27699-4640. SAN 329-3092. Tel. 919-807-7400, fax 919-733-8748. *State Libn.* Sandra M. Cooper.

Northwest AHEC Library at Hickory, Catawba Medical Center, Hickory 28602. SAN 322-4708. Tel. 828-326-3662, fax 828-326-3484. *Dir.* Karen Lee Martinez.

Northwest AHEC Library at Salisbury, c/o Rowan Regional Medical Center, Salisbury 28144. SAN 322-4589. Tel. 704-210-5069, fax 704-636-5050.

Northwest AHEC Library Information Network, Wake Forest Univ. School of Medicine, Winston-Salem 27157-1049. SAN 322-4716. Tel. 336-713-7009, fax 336-713-7028. *Senior Libn.* Julie Richardson.

Triangle Research Libraries Network, Wilson Lib., Chapel Hill 27514-8890. SAN 329-5362. Tel. 919-962-8022, fax 919-962-4452.

Western North Carolina Library Network (WNCLN), Univ. of North Carolina at Asheville, Asheville 28804-3299. SAN 376-7205. Tel. 828-232-5095, fax 828-232-5137. *Dir.* Mark A. Stoffan.

North Dakota

Dakota West Cooperating Libraries (DWCL), c/o Mandan Public Lib., Mandan 58554-3149. SAN 373-1391. *Dir.* Kelly Steckler.

Mid-America Law School Library Consortium (MALSLC), Univ. of North Dakota School of Law, Grand Forks 58202. SAN 371-6813. Tel. 701-777-2535, fax 701-777-2219. *Chair* Gary Gott.

Tri-College University Libraries Consortium, 650 NP Ave., Fargo 58102. SAN 322-2047. Tel. 701-231-8170, fax 701-231-7205.

Ohio

Central Ohio Hospital Library Consortium, 127 S. Davis Ave., Columbus 43222. SAN 371-084X. Tel. 614-234-5214, fax 614-234-1257. *Dir.* Rebecca Ayers.

Cleveland Area Metropolitan Library System (CAMLS), 20600 Chagrin Blvd., Ste. 500,

Shaker Heights 44122-5334. SAN 322-2632. Tel. 216-921-3900, fax 216-921-7220. *Exec. Dir.* Michael G. Snyder.

Columbus Area Library and Information Council of Ohio (CALICO), c/o Westerville Public Lib., Westerville 43081. SAN 371-683X. Tel. 614-882-7277, fax 614-882-5369.

Consortium of Popular Culture Collections in the Midwest (CPCCM), c/o Popular Culture Lib., Bowling Green 43403-0600. SAN 370-5811. Tel. 419-372-2450, fax 419-372-7996. *In Charge* Nancy Down.

Greater Cincinnati Library Consortium, 2181 Victory Pkwy., Ste. 214, Cincinnati 45206-2855. SAN 322-2675. Tel. 513-751-4422, fax 513-751-0463, e-mail gclc@gclc-lib.org. *Exec. Dir.* Michael R. McCoy.

Molo Regional Library System, 123 N. Bridge St., Newcomerstown 43832-1093. SAN 322-2705. Tel. 330-364-8535, fax 330-364-8537, e-mail molo@molorls.org.

NEOUCOM Council of Associated Hospital Librarians, Oliver Ocasek Regional Medical Info. Center, Rootstown 44272. SAN 370-0526. Tel. 330-325-6616; 330-325-6600, fax 330-325-0522. *Dir.* Thomas C. Atwood.

NOLA Regional Library System, 4445 Mahoning Ave. N.W., Warren 44483. SAN 322-2713. Tel. 330-847-7744, fax 330-847-7704, e-mail nola@nolanet.org. *Dir.* Paul Pormen.

Northwest Library District (NORWELD), 1811/2 S. Main St., Bowling Green 43402. SAN 322-273X. Tel. 419-352-2903, fax 419-353-8310. *Dir.* Allan Gray.

OCLC Online Computer Library Center, 6565 Frantz Rd., Dublin 43017-3395. SAN 322-2748. Tel. 614-764-6000, fax 614-718-1017, e-mail oclc@oclc.org. *Pres./CEO* Jay Jordan.

Ohio Library and Information Network (Ohio-LINK), 2455 N. Star Rd., Ste. 300, Columbus 43221. SAN 374-8014. Tel. 614-728-3600, fax 614-728-3610, e-mail info@ohiolink.edu. *Exec. Dir.* Thomas J. Sanville.

Ohio Network of American History Research Centers, Ohio Historical Society Archives-Lib., Columbus 43211-2497. SAN 323-9624. Tel. 614-297-2510, fax 614-297-

2546, e-mail ohsref@ohiohistory.org. *Research* Louise Jones.

Ohio Valley Area Libraries, 252 W. 13 St., Wellston 45692. SAN 322-2756. Tel. 740-384-2103, fax 740-384-2106, e-mail ovalrls@oplin.lib.oh.us; oval@oplin.lib.oh.us. *Dir.* Marion J. Cochran.

OHIONET, 1500 W. Lane Ave., Columbus 43221-3975. SAN 322-2764. Tel. 614-486-2966, fax 614-486-1527. *Exec. Dir./ CEO* Michael P. Butler.

Southwestern Ohio Council for Higher Education, 3155 Research Blvd., Ste. 204, Dayton 45420-4015. SAN 322-2659. Tel. 937-258-8890, fax 937-258-8899, e-mail soche@soche.org.

State Assisted Academic Library Council of Kentucky (SAALCK), c/o GCLC, Cincinnati 45206. SAN 371-2222. Fax 513 751-0463, e-mail saalck@saalck.org. *Exec. Dir.* Michael McCoy.

Oklahoma

Greater Oklahoma Area Health Sciences Library Consortium (GOAL), Mercy Memorial Health Center—Resource Center, Ardmore 73401. SAN 329-3858. Tel. 580-220-6625, fax 580-220-6599. *Pres.* Catherine Ice.

Oklahoma Health Sciences Library Assn. (OHSLA), Univ. of Oklahoma—HSC Bird Health Science Lib., Oklahoma City 73190. SAN 375-0051. Tel. 405-271-2285 ext. 48755, fax 405-271-3297. *Dir.* Clinton M. Thompson.

Oregon

Chemeketa Cooperative Regional Library Service, c/o Chemeketa Community College, Salem 97305-1453. SAN 322-2837. Tel. 503-399-5105, fax 503-399-7316, e-mail cocl@chemeketa.edu. *Coord.* Linda Cochrane.

Coos County Library Service District, Extended Service Office, Tioga 104, 1988 Newmark, Coos Bay 97420. SAN 322-4279. Tel. 541-888-7260, fax 541-888-7285. *Dir.* Mary Jane Fisher.

Library Information Network of Clackamas County, 16239 S.E. McLoughlin Blvd., Ste. 208, Oak Grove 97267-4654. SAN

322-2845. Tel. 503-723-4888, fax 503-794-8238. *Manager* Joanna Rood.

Orbis Cascade Alliance, 1501 Kincaid, No. 4, Eugene 97401-4540. SAN 377-8096. Tel. 541-346-1832, fax 541-346-1968, e-mail orbcas@uoregon.edu. *Chair* Susan Barnes Whyte.

Oregon Health Sciences Libraries Assn. (OHSLA), Oregon Health and Science Univ. Lib., Portland 97239-3098. SAN 371-2176. Tel. 503-494-3462, fax 503-494-3322, e-mail library@ohsu.edu. *Dir.* James Morgan.

Southern Oregon Library Federation, c/o Klamath County Lib., Klamath Falls 97601. SAN 322-2861. Tel. 541-882-8894, fax 541-882-6166. *Dir.* Andy Swanson.

Southern Oregon Library Information System (SOLIS), 724 S. Central Ave., Ste. 112, Medford 97501. Tel. 541-772-2141, fax 541-772-2144, e-mail solis97501@yahoo. com. *Assistant Admin.* Sylvia Lee.

Washington County Cooperative Library Services, 111 N.E. Lincoln St., MS No. 58, Hillsboro 97124-3036. SAN 322-287X. Tel. 503-846-3222, fax 503-846-3220. *Manager* Eva Calcagno.

Pennsylvania

Associated College Libraries of Central Pennsylvania, c/o Commonwealth Libs., Harrisburg 17126-1745. Tel. 717-783-5968, fax 717-783-2070. *Pres.* Janet Hurlbert.

Berks County Library Assn. (BCLA), Albright College Lib., Reading 19612-5234. SAN 371-0866. Tel. 610-921-7212. *Pres.* Joan King.

Central Pennsylvania Consortium, Dickinson College, Carlisle 17013-2896. SAN 322-2896. Tel. 717-245-1515, fax 717-245-1807, e-mail cpc@dickinson.edu.

Central Pennsylvania Health Sciences Library Assn. (CPHSLA), Memorial Medical Center Health Sciences Lib., Johnstown 15905. SAN 375-5290. Tel. 814-534-9413, fax 814-534-3244. *Pres.* Kris Kalina.

Consortium for Health Information and Library Services, 1 Medical Center Blvd., Upland 19013-3995. SAN 322-290X. Tel. 610-447-6163, fax 610-447-6164, e-mail chi@hslc.org.

Cooperating Hospital Libraries of the Lehigh Valley Area, Saint Luke's Hospital, Estes Lib., Bethlehem 18015. SAN 371-0858. Tel. 610-954-3407, fax 610-954-4651. *Chair* Sharon Hrabina.

Delaware Valley Information Consortium (DEVIC), St. Mary Medical Center Medical Lib., Langhorne 19047. Tel. 215-710-2012, fax 215-710-4638. *Dir.* Ann B. Laliotes.

Eastern Mennonite Associated Libraries and Archives (EMALA), 2215 Millstream Rd., Lancaster 17602. SAN 372-8226. Tel. 717-393-9745, fax 717-393-8751. *Chair* Edsel Burdge.

Erie Area Health Information Library Cooperative (EAHILC), UPMC Northwest Medical Lib., Franklin 16323. SAN 371-0564. Tel. 814-437-7000 ext. 5331, fax 814-437-4538, e-mail nwmc@mail. cosmosbbs.com. *Chair* Ann L. Lucas.

Greater Philadelphia Law Library Assn. (GPLLA), P.O. Box 335, Philadelphia 19105-0335. SAN 373-1375. E-mail gpllal@hslc.org. *Pres.* Jeffrey W. Kreiling.

Health Sciences Libraries Consortium, 3600 Market St., Ste. 550, Philadelphia 19104-2646. SAN 323-9780. Tel. 215-222-1532, fax 215-222-0416, e-mail support@hslc. org. *Exec. Dir.* Joseph C. Scorza.

Interlibrary Delivery Service of Pennsylvania (IDS), c/o Bucks County IU, No. 22, Doylestown 18901. SAN 322-2942. Tel. 215-348-2940 ext. 1620, fax 215-348-8315, e-mail ids@bucksiu.org. *Admin. Dir.* Beverly J. Carey.

Keystone Library Network, Dixon Univ. Center, 2986 N. 2 St., Harrisburg 17110-1201. Tel. 717-720-4088, fax 717-720-4453. *Coord.* Mary Lou Sowden.

Laurel Highlands Health Science Library Consortium, 116 Luna Lane, Johnstown 15904. SAN 322-2950. Tel. 814-341-0242, fax 814-266-8230. *Dir.* Heather W. Brice.

Lehigh Valley Assn. of Independent Colleges, 130 W. Greenwich St., Bethlehem 18018. SAN 322-2969. Tel. 610-625-7888, fax 610-625-7891. *Exec. Dir.* Tom A. Tenges.

Northeastern Pennsylvania Library Network, c/o Marywood Univ. Lib., Scranton 18509-

1598. SAN 322-2993. Tel. 570-348-6260, fax 570-961-4769. *Dir.* Catherine H. Schappert.

Northwest Interlibrary Cooperative of Pennsylvania (NICOP), Edinboro Univ. of Pennsylvania, Edinboro 16444. SAN 370-5862. Tel. 814-454-1813 ext. 26, fax 814-732-2883. *Dir.* Donald Dilmore.

PALINET, 3000 Market St., Ste. 200, Philadelphia 19104-2801. SAN 322-3000. Tel. 215-382-7031, fax 215-382-0022, e-mail palinet@palinet.org. *Exec. Dir.* Catherine C. Wilt.

Pennsylvania Library Assn., 220 Cumberland Pkwy, Ste. 10, Mechanicsburg 17055. Tel. 717-766-7663, fax 717-766-5440. *Exec. Dir.* Glenn R. Miller.

Philadelphia Area Consortium of Special Collections Libraries (PACSCL), Historical Society of Pennsylvania, Philadelphia 19107. SAN 370-7504. Tel. 215-985-1445, fax 215-985-1446, e-mail info@pacscl.org. *Chair* David Moltke-Hansen.

Southeastern Pennsylvania Theological Library Assn. (SEPTLA), c/o Lancaster Theological Seminary, Lancaster 17603. SAN 371-0793. Tel. 717-290-8755. *Chair* Marsha Blake.

State System of Higher Education Library Cooperative (SSHELCO), c/o Bailey Lib., Slippery Rock 16057. Tel. 724-738-2630, fax 724-738-2661. *Dir.* Philip Tramdack.

Susquehanna Library Cooperative (SLC), Harvey A. Andruss Lib., Bloomsburg Univ., Bloomsburg 17815-1301. SAN 322-3051. Tel. 570-389-4224. *Chair* John B. Pitcher.

Tri-State College Library Cooperative (TCLC), c/o Rosemont College Lib., Rosemont 19010-1699. SAN 322-3078. Tel. 610-525-0796, fax 610-525-1939, e-mail tclc@hslc.org. *Coord.* Ellen Gasiewski.

Rhode Island

Cooperating Libraries Automated Network-CLAN (Rhode Island), 600 Sandy Lane, Warwick 02886. SAN 329-4560. Tel. 401-738-2200, fax 401-736-8949. *Chair* Susan Reed.

Library of Rhode Island (LORI), c/o Office of Lib. and Info. Services, Providence 02908-5870. SAN 371-6821. Tel. 401-

222-2726, fax 401-222-4195. *Lib. Services Dir.* Anne Parent.

South Carolina

Charleston Academic Libraries Consortium (CALC), Trident Technical College, Charleston 29423. SAN 371-0769. Tel. 843-574-6088, fax 843-574-6484. *Chair* Drucie Raines.

Columbia Area Medical Librarians' Assn. (CAMLA), Professional Lib., Columbia 29201. SAN 372-9400. Tel. 803-898-1735, fax 803-898-1712. *Coord.* Neeta N. Shah.

South Carolina AHEC, c/o Medical Univ. of South Carolina, Charleston 29425. SAN 329-3998. Tel. 843-792-4431, fax 843-792-4430. *Exec. Dir.* David Garr.

South Carolina State Library/South Carolina Library Network, 1430 and 1500 Senate St., Columbia 29201. SAN 322-4198. Tel. 803-734-8666, fax 803-734-8676, e-mail webadm@leo.scsl.state.sc.us. *Dir.* Patti J. Butcher.

South Dakota

South Dakota Library Network (SDLN), 1200 University, Unit 9672, Spearfish 57799-9672. SAN 371-2117. Tel. 605-642-6835, fax 605-642-6472. *Dir.* Gary Johnson.

Tennessee

Assn. of Memphis Area Health Science Libraries (AMAHSL), c/o Methodist Healthcare Nursing Lib., Memphis 38104. SAN 323-9802. Tel. 901-726-8862, fax 901-726-8807. *Libn.* Denise Fesmire.

Consortium of Southern Biomedical Libraries (CONBLS), Meharry Medical College, Nashville 37208. SAN 370-7717. Tel. 615-327-6728, fax 615-327-6448. *Acting Dir.* Marvelyn E. Thompson.

Knoxville Area Health Sciences Library Consortium (KAHSLC), Univ. of Tennessee Medical Center, Knoxville 37920. SAN 371-0556. Tel. 865-544-9525, fax 865-544-9527. *In Charge* Martha Earl.

Mid-Tennessee Health Science Librarians Assn., VA Medical Center, Nashville

37212. SAN 329-5028. Tel. 615-327-4751 ext. 5523, fax 615-321-6336.

Tennessee Health Science Library Assn. (THeSLA), Holston Valley Medical Center Health Sciences Lib., Kingsport 37660. SAN 371-0726. Tel. 423-224-6870, fax 423-224-6014, e-mail sharon_m_brown@wellmont.org.

Tri-Cities Area Health Sciences Libraries Consortium, East Tennessee State Univ., James H. Quillen College of Medicine, Johnson City 37614. SAN 329-4099. Tel. 423-439-6252, fax 423-439-7025. *Dir.* Biddanda Ponnappa.

West Tennessee Academic Library Consortium, Lambuth Univ. Lib., Jackson 38301. SAN 322-3175. Tel. 731-425-3479, fax 731-425-3200. *Dir.* Pamela R. Dennis.

Texas

Abilene Library Consortium, 241 Pine St., Ste. 15C, Abilene 79601. SAN 322-4694. Tel. 325-672-7081, fax 325-672-7084. *Exec. Dir.* Robert Gillette.

Amigos Library Services, 14400 Midway Rd., Dallas 75244-3509. SAN 322-3191. Tel. 972-851-8000, fax 972-991-6061, e-mail amigos@amigos.org. *Exec. Dir.* Bonnie Juergens.

Council of Research and Academic Libraries (CORAL), P.O. Box 290236, San Antonio 78280-1636. SAN 322-3213.

Del Norte Biosciences Library Consortium, El Paso Community College, El Paso 79998. SAN 322-3302. Tel. 915-831-4149, fax 915-831-4639. *Coord.* Becky Perales.

Harrington Library Consortium, 2201 Washington, Amarillo 79109. SAN 329-546X. Tel. 806-371-5135, fax 806-371-5119. *Manager* Roseann Perez.

Health Libraries Information Network (Health LINE), UT Southwestern Medical Center Lib., Dallas 75390-9049. SAN 322-3299. Tel. 214-648-2626, fax 214-648-2826. *In Charge* Brian Bunnett.

Houston Area Research Library Consortium (HARLiC), c/o Moody Medical Lib., Galveston 77555-1035. SAN 322-3329. Tel. 409-772-2371, fax 409-762-9782. *Pres.* Brett Kirkpatrick.

National Network of Libraries of Medicine—South Central Region (NNLM SCR), c/o HAM-TMC Lib., Houston 77030-2809. SAN 322-3353. Tel. 713-799-7880, fax 713-790-7030, e-mail nnlmscr@library.tmc.edu. *Assoc. Dir.* Renee Bougard.

Northeast Texas Library System (NETLS), 625 Austin St., Garland 75040-6365. SAN 370-5943. Tel. 972-205-2566, fax 972-205-2767. *Dir.* Claire Bausch.

South Central Academic Medical Libraries Consortium (SCAMeL), c/o Lewis Lib.-UNTHSC, Fort Worth 76107. SAN 372-8269. Tel. 817-735-2380, fax 817-735-5158.

Texas Council of State University Librarians, Texas Lib. Assn., Austin 78746-6763. SAN 322-337X. *Pres.* Kathy Hoffman.

Texnet, P.O. Box 12927, Austin 78711. SAN 322-3396. Tel. 512-463-5406, fax 512-936-2306, e-mail ill@tsl.state.tx.us.

Utah

Forest Service Library Network, Rocky Mountain Research Station, Ogden 84401. SAN 322-032X. Tel. 801-625-5445, fax 801-625-5129, e-mail rmrs_library@fs.fed.us.

National Network of Libraries of Medicine—MidContinental Region (NN-LM MCR), Univ. of Utah, Spencer S. Eccles Health Science Lib., Salt Lake City 84112-5890. SAN 322-225X. Tel. 801-587-3412, fax 801-581-3632. *Dir.* Wayne J. Peay.

Utah Academic Library Consortium (UALC), Univ. of Utah, Salt Lake City 84112-0731. SAN 322-3418. Tel. 801-581-3386, 801-581-6594, fax 801-585-3033. *Dir.* Rita Reusch.

Utah Health Sciences Library Consortium, c/o Univ. of Utah, Spencer S. Eccles Health Science Lib., Salt Lake City 84112. SAN 376-2246. Tel. 801-408-1054.

Vermont

Vermont Resource Sharing Network, c/o Vermont Dept. of Libs., Montpelier 05609-0601. SAN 322-3426. Tel. 802-828-3261, fax 802-828-2199. *Dir., Lib. Services* Marjorie Zunder.

Virginia

American Indian Higher Education Consortium (AIHEC), 121 Oronoco St., Alexandria 22314. SAN 329-4056. Tel. 703-838-0400, fax 703-838-0388, e-mail aihec@aihec.org. *Pres.* James Shanley.

Defense Technical Information Center, 8725 John J. Kingman Rd., Ste. 1948, Fort Belvoir 22060-6218. SAN 322-3442. Tel. 703-767-9100, fax 703-767-9183. *Acting Admin.* Paul Ryan.

Lynchburg Area Library Cooperative, Randolph Macon Woman's College, Lynchburg 24503. SAN 322-3450. Tel. 434-947-8133, fax 434-947-8134.

Lynchburg Information Online Network (LION), 2315 Memorial Ave., Lynchburg 24503. SAN 374-6097. Tel. 434-381-6311, fax 434-381-6173. *Dir.* John G. Jaffee.

NASA Libraries Information System—NASA Galaxie, NASA Langley Research Center, MS 185, Technical Lib., Hampton 23681-2199. SAN 322-0788. Tel. 757-864-2356, fax 757-864-2375, e-mail tech-library@larc.nasa.gov. *Branch Manager* Carolyn L. Helmetsie.

Richmond Academic Library Consortium (RALC), Virginia Commonwealth Lib., Richmond 23284-2033. SAN 322-3469. Tel. 804-828-1107, fax 804-862-6125. *Pres.* John E. Ulmschneider.

Southside Virginia Library Network (SVLN), Longwood Univ., Farmville 23909-1897. SAN 372-8242. Tel. 434-395-2633, fax 434-395-2453. *Dir.* Wendell Barbour.

Southwestern Virginia Health Information Librarians (SWVAHILI), Carilion Health Sciences Lib., Roanoke 24033. SAN 323-9527. Tel. 540-981-8039, fax 540-981-8666, e-mail kdillon@carilion.com. *Chair* Kelly Near.

United States Army Training and Doctrine Command (TRADOC)/Lib. Program Office, U.S. Army Hq. TRADOC, Fort Monroe 23651. SAN 322-418X. Tel. 757-788-2909, fax 757-788-2931. *Dir.* Janet Scheitle.

Virginia Independent College and University Library Assn., c/o Mary Helen Cochran Lib., Sweet Briar 24595. SAN 374-6089.

Tel. 434-381-6138, fax 434-381-6173. *Dir.* John Jaffee.

Virginia Tidewater Consortium for Higher Education, 1417 43rd St., Norfolk 23529-0293. SAN 329-5486. Tel. 757-683-3183, fax 757-683-4515, e-mail lgdotolo@aol.com. *Pres.* Lawrence G. Dotolo.

Virtual Library of Virginia (VIVA), George Mason Univ., Fairfax 22030. Tel. 703-993-4652, fax 703-993-4662. *Chair* Ralph Alberico.

Washington

Cooperating Libraries in Olympia (CLIO), Evergreen State College Lib. L2300, Olympia 98505. SAN 329-4528. Tel. 360-866-6000 ext. 6260, fax 360-867-6790. *Dean* Lee Lyttle.

Inland NorthWest Health Sciences Libraries (INWHSL), P.O. Box 10283, Spokane 99209-0283. SAN 370-5099. Tel. 509-324-7344, fax 509-324-7349. *Contact* Robert Pringle.

National Network of Libraries of Medicine—Pacific Northwest Region (NN-LM PNR), Univ. of Washington, Seattle 98195-7155. SAN 322-3485. Tel. 206-543-8262, fax 206-543-2469, e-mail nnlm@u.washington.edu. *Dir.* Sherrilynne S. Fuller.

Palouse Area Library Information Services (PALIS), c/o Neill Public Lib., Pullman 99163. SAN 375-0132. Tel. 509-334-3595, fax 509-334-6051. *Dir.* Andriette Pieron.

Washington Idaho Network (WIN), Gonzaga Univ., Spokane 99258. Tel. 509-323-6545, fax 509-324-5398, e-mail winsupport@gonzaga.edu. *Pres.* Eileen Bell-Garrison.

West Virginia

Huntington Health Science Library Consortium, Marshall Univ. Health Science Libs., Huntington 25701-3655. SAN 322-4295. Tel. 304-691-1753, fax 304-691-1766. *Dir.* Edward Dzierzak.

Mid-Atlantic Law Library Cooperative (MALLCO), College of Law Lib., Morgantown 26506. SAN 371-0645. Tel. 304-293-7641; 304-293-7775, fax 304-293-6020. *In Charge* Camille M. Riley.

Wisconsin

Fox River Valley Area Library Consortium (FRVALC), Moraine Park Technical College, Fond Du Lac 54935. SAN 322-3531. Tel. 920-924-3112, 920-922-8611, fax 920-924-3117. *In Charge* Charlene Pettit.

Fox Valley Library Council, c/o OWLS, Appleton 54911. SAN 323-9640. Tel. 920-832-6190, fax 920-832-6422. *Pres.* Joy Schwarz.

Library Council of Southeastern Wisconsin, 814 W. Wisconsin Ave., Milwaukee 53233-2309. SAN 322-354X. Tel. 414-271-8470, fax 414-286-2798, e-mail lcomm@execpc.com. *Exec. Dir.* Susie M. Just.

North East Wisconsin Intertype Libraries (NEWIL), 515 Pine St., Green Bay 54301. SAN 322-3574. Tel. 920-448-4412, fax 920-448-4420. *Coord.* Terrie Howe.

Northwestern Wisconsin Health Science Library Consortium, Wausau Hospital, Dr. Joseph F Smith Medical Lib., Wausau 54401. Tel. 715-847-2184, fax 715-847-2183. *In Charge* Jan Kraus.

South Central Wisconsin Health Science Library Consortium, c/o Fort Healthcare Medical Lib., Fort Atkinson 53538. SAN 322-4686. Tel. 920-568-5194, fax 920-568-5195. *Coord.* Carrie Garity.

Southeastern Wisconsin Health Science Library Consortium, VA Center Medical Lib., Milwaukee 53295. SAN 322-3582. Tel. 414-384-2000 ext. 42342, fax 414-382-5334. *Dir.* Janice Curnes.

Southeastern Wisconsin Information Technology Exchange (SWITCH), 6801 N. Yates Rd., Milwaukee 53217-3985. SAN 371-3962. Tel. 414-351-2423, fax 414-228-4146. *Coord.* William A. Topritzhofer.

University of Wisconsin System School Library Education Consortium (UWSSLEC), Graduate and Continuing Educ., Univ. of Wisconsin–Whitewater, Whitewater 53190. Tel. 262-472-1463, 262-472-5208, fax 262-472-5210, e-mail lenchoc@uww.edu. *Co-Dir.* E. Anne Zarinnia.

Wisconsin Area Research Center Network/ ARC Network, Wisconsin Historical Society, Madison 53706. SAN 373-0875. Tel. 608-264-6477, fax 608-264-6486. *Head of Public Services* Richard Pifer.

Wisconsin Library Services (WILS), 728 State St., Rm. 464, Madison 53706-1494. SAN 322-3612. Tel. 608-263-4981, 608-263-4962, fax 608-262-6067, 608-263-3684. *Dir.* Kathryn Schneider Michaelis.

Wisconsin Valley Library Service (WVLS), 300 N. 1 St., Wausau 54403. SAN 371-3911. Tel. 715-261-7250, fax 715-261-7259. *Dir.* Heather Ann Eldred.

WISPALS Library Consortium, c/o Gateway Technical College, Kenosha 53144-1690. Tel. 262-564-2602, fax 262-564-2787. *Coord.* Ellen J. Pedraza.

Wyoming

University of Wyoming Information Network Plus (UWIN Plus), Coe Lib., Rm 104A, Laramie 82071. SAN 371-4861. Tel. 307-766-5379, fax 307-766-5368, e-mail uwinplus@uwyo.edu. *Coord.* Jenny Garcia.

Western Council of State Libraries, Supreme Court and State Lib. Bldg., Cheyenne 82002. SAN 322-2314. Tel. 307-777-5911. *Pres.* Lesley Boughton.

WYLD Network, c/o Wyoming State Lib., Cheyenne 82002-0060. SAN 371-0661. Tel. 307-777-6339, fax 307-777-6289. *Automation System Coord./Manager* Brian A. Greene.

Virgin Islands

VILINET/Virgin Islands Library and Information Network, c/o Div. of Libs., Archives, and Museums, Saint Thomas 00802. SAN 322-3639. Tel. 340-773-5715, fax 340-773-3257. *Dir.* Wallace Williams.

Canada

Alberta

Alberta Assn. of College Librarians (AACL), Lakeland College Learning Resources Centre, Vermillion T9X 1K5. SAN 370-0763. Tel. 780-853-8468, fax 780-853-8662. *Acting Dir.* Greg Michaud.

Northern Alberta Health Libraries Assn. (NAHLA), Inst. of Health Economics Lib.,

Edmonton T5J 3N4. SAN 370-5951. Tel. 780-448-4881, e-mail nahla@freenet. edmonton.ab.ca. *Pres.* Janice Varney.

British Columbia

BC Electronic Library Network (ELN), Simon Fraser Univ., Burnaby V5A IS6. Tel. 604-268-7003, fax 604-291-3023, e-mail eln@ola.bc.ca or office@eln.bc.ca. *Manager* Anita Cocchia.

British Columbia College and Institute Library Services, Langara College Lib., Vancouver V5Y 2Z6. SAN 329-6970. Tel. 604-323-5237, fax 604-323-5544, e-mail cils@langara.bc.ca. *Dir.* Mary Anne Epp.

Manitoba

Manitoba Government Libraries Council (MGLC), c/o Instructional Resources Unit, Winnipeg R3G 0T3. SAN 371-6848. Tel. 204-945-7833, fax 204-945-8756. *Chair* John Tooth.

Manitoba Library Consortium (MLCI), c/o Lib. Admin., Univ. of Winnipeg, Winnipeg R3B 2E9. SAN 372-820X. Tel. 204-786-9801, fax 204-783-8910. *Chair* Mark Leggott.

New Brunswick

Maritimes Health Libraries Assn. (MHLA-ABSM), c/o Region 7 Hospital Corp., Miramich E1V 3G5. SAN 370-0836. Tel. 506-623-3215, fax 506-623-3280. *Libn.* Nancy McAllister.

Nova Scotia

NOVANET, 1550 Bedford Hwy, No. 501, Bedford B4A 1E6. SAN 372-4050. Tel. 902-453-2470, fax 902-453-2369, e-mail office@novanet.ns.ca. *Contact* Dylan Boudreau.

Ontario

Bibliocentre, 31 Scarsdale Rd., North York M3B 2R2. SAN 322-3663. Tel. 647-722-9300, fax 647-722-9301. *Exec. Dir.* Janice Hayes.

Canadian Assn. of Research Libraries, Univ. of Ottawa, Morisset Hall, Rm. 239, Ottawa

K1N 9A5. SAN 323-9721. Tel. 613-562-5385, fax 613-562-5195, e-mail carladm@ uottawa.ca. *Exec. Dir.* Timothy Mark.

Canadian Health Libraries Assn. (CHLA-ABSC), 39 River St., Toronto M5A 3P1. SAN 370-0720. Tel. 416-646-1600, fax 416-646-9460, e-mail info@chla-absc.ca. *Pres.* Penny Logan.

Hamilton and District Health Library Network, c/o St. Joseph's Hospital, Hamilton L8N 4A6. SAN 370-5846. Tel. 905-522-1155 ext. 3410. *Coord.* Jean Maragno.

Health Science Information Consortium of Toronto, c/o Gerstein Science Info. Center, Univ. of Toronto, Toronto M5S 1A5. SAN 370-5080. Tel. 416-978-6359, fax 416-971-2637. *Exec. Dir.* Laurie Scott.

Ontario Health Libraries Assn. (OHLA), c/o Lakeridge Health, Oshawa L1G 2B9. SAN 370-0739. Tel. 905-576-8711 ext. 3334, fax 905-721-4759.

Ontario Library Consortium (OLC), Owen Sound and North Grey Union Public Lib., Owen Sound N4K 4K4. *Pres.* Judy Armstrong.

Shared Library Services (SLS), South Huron Hospital, Shared Lib. Services, Exeter N0M 1S2. SAN 323-9500. Tel. 519-235-4002 ext. 249, fax 519-235-4476, e-mail shha.sls@hphp.org. *Libn.* Linda Wilcox.

Toronto Health Libraries Assn. (THLA), 3324 Yonge St., Toronto M4N 3R1. SAN 323-9853. Tel. 416-485-0377, fax 416-485-6877, e-mail medinfoserv@rogers.com.

Toronto School of Theology, 47 Queen's Park Crescent E., Toronto M5S 2C3. SAN 322-452X. Tel. 416-978-4039, fax 416-978-7821. *Chair* Noel S. McFerran.

Quebec

Assn. des Bibliothèques de la Santé Affiliées à l'Université de Montréal (ABSAUM), c/o Health Lib., Univ. of Montreal, Montreal H3C 3J7. SAN 370-5838. Tel. 514-343-6826, fax 514-343-2350. *Dir.* Diane Raymond.

Canadian Heritage Information Network (CHIN), 15 Eddy St., 4th fl., Gatineau K1A 0M5. SAN 329-3076. Tel. 819-994-1200, fax 819-994-9555, e-mail service@ chin.gc.ca. *Manager* Patricia Young.

National Library and Information-Industry Associations, United States and Canada

American Association of Law Libraries

Executive Director, Susan E. Fox
53 W. Jackson Blvd., Ste. 940, Chicago, IL 60604
312-939-4764, fax 312-431-1097
World Wide Web http://www.aallnet.org

Object

The American Association of Law Libraries (AALL) is established for educational and scientific purposes. It shall be conducted as a nonprofit corporation to promote and enhance the value of law libraries to the public, the legal community, and the world; to foster the profession of law librarianship; to provide leadership in the field of legal information; and to foster a spirit of cooperation among the members of the profession. Established 1906.

Membership

Memb. 5,000+. Persons officially connected with a law library or with a law section of a state or general library, separately maintained. Associate membership available for others. Dues (Indiv., Indiv. Assoc., and Inst.) $145; (Inst. Assoc.) $256 times the number of members; (Retired) $36; (Student) $36; (SIS Memb.) $12 each per year. Year. July 1–June 30.

Officers

Pres. Claire M. Germain, Cornell Univ. Law Lib. E-mail cmg13@cornell.edu; *V.P.* Sarah G. Holterhoff; *Secy.* Darcy Kirk; *Treas.* Joyce Manna Janto; *Past Pres.* Victoria K. Trotta.

Executive Board

Steven P. Anderson, Kathy Carlson, Lyonette Louis-Jacques, Anne K. Myers, Merle J. Slyhoff, Kathie J. Sullivan.

Committees

AALL Archives Policy Review (Special).
AALL Centennial Celebration (Special).
AALL LexisNexis Call for Papers Committee.
AALLNET (Advisory).
AALL Vendor Relations Task Force.
Access to Electronic Legal Information.
Annual Meeting Local (Advisory).
Annual Meeting Program.
Awards.
Bylaws.
Citation Formats.
Copyright.
Council of Chapter Presidents.
Council of Newsletter Editors.
Council of SIS Chairs.
CRIV (Relations with Information Vendors).
Diversity.
Economic Status of Law Librarianship.
Executive Board Finance and Budget.
Fair Business Practices Implementation Task Force.
Gen X Gen Y Task Force.
George Strait Fund-Raising.
Government Relations.
Graduate Education for Law Librarianship.
Grants.
Index to Foreign Legal Periodicals (Advisory).
Indexing of Periodical Literature (Advisory).
LLJ and AALL Spectrum Editorial Board (Advisory).
Membership and Retention.
Mentoring.
Nominations.

Open Access Task Force.
Permanent Public Access to Legal Information Special Committee.
Placement.
Price Index for Legal Publications (Advisory).
Promoting Law Librarians to the Legal Community (Special).

Public Relations.
Publications.
Recruitment to Law Librarianship.
Research.
Scholarships.
Training the Next Generation of Law Librarians (Special).

American Library Association

Executive Director, Keith Michael Fiels
50 E. Huron St., Chicago, IL 60611
800-545-2433, 312-280-1392, fax 312-440-9374
World Wide Web http://www.ala.org

Object

The mission of the American Library Association (ALA) is to provide leadership for the development, promotion, and improvement of library and information services and the profession of librarianship in order to enhance learning and ensure access to information for all. Founded 1876.

Membership

Memb. (Indiv.) 61,767; (Inst.) 4,088; (Corporate) 272; (Total) 66,127 (as of July 31, 2005). Any person, library, or other organization interested in library service and librarians. Dues (Indiv.) 1st year, $50; 2nd year, $75; 3rd year and later, $100; (Trustee and Assoc. Memb.) $45; (Student) $25; (Foreign Indiv.) $60; (Other) $35; (Inst.) $110 and up, depending on operating expenses of institution.

Officers (2005–2006)

Pres. Michael Gorman, dean of lib. services, CSU–Fresno, 5200 N. Barton, Fresno, CA 93740-0001. Tel. 559-278-2403, fax 559-278-6952, e-mail michaelg@csufresno.edu; *Pres.-Elect* Leslie B. Burger, director, Princeton Public Lib., 65 Witherspoon St., Princeton, NJ 08542-3214. Tel. 609-924-8822 ext. 253,

fax 609-924-7937, email lburger@princeton library.org; *Immediate Past Pres.* Carol Brey-Casiano, dir. of libs., El Paso Public Library, City Hall no. 2, Civic Center Plaza, 501 N. Oregon St., El Paso, TX 79901-1103. Tel. 915-541-4098, fax 915-541-4945, e-mail breycx@elpasotexas.gov; *Treas.* Teri R. Switzer, assoc. dean, research, operations and document delivery services, Univ. of Colorado at Denver and Health Science Center, 1100 Lawrence St., Denver, CO 80204-2041. Tel. 303-556-3523, fax 303-556-3528, e-mail teri.switzer@cudenver.edu; *Exec. Dir.* Keith Michael Fiels, ALA Headquarters, 50 E. Huron St., Chicago, IL 60611. Tel. 312-280-1392, fax 312-944-3897, e-mail kfiels@ala.org.

Executive Board

Francis J. Buckley, Jr. (2008), Michael A. Golrick (2006), Janet Swan Hill (2007), Nann Blaine Hilyard (2007), Terri G. Kirk (2006), June A. Pinnell-Stephens (2008), James R. Rettig (2006), Patricia H. Smith (2008).

Endowment Trustees

Robert R. Newlen, Rick J. Schwieterman, Carla J. Stoffle; *Exec. Board Liaison* Teri R. Switzer; *Staff Liaison* Gregory L. Calloway.

Divisions

See the separate entries that follow: American Assn. of School Libns.; Assn. for Lib. Collections and Technical Services; Assn. for Lib. Service to Children; Assn. for Lib. Trustees and Advocates; Assn. of College and Research Libs.; Assn. of Specialized and Cooperative Lib. Agencies; Lib. Admin. and Management Assn.; Lib. and Info. Technology Assn.; Public Lib. Assn.; Reference and User Services Assn.; Young Adult Lib. Services Assn.

Publications

ALA Handbook of Organization (ann.).
American Libraries (11 a year; memb.; organizations $60; foreign $70; single copy $6).
Book Links (6 a year; U.S. $29.95; foreign $36; single copy $6).
Booklist (22 a year; U.S. and possessions $89.95; foreign $105; single copy $6).

Round Table Chairpersons

(ALA staff liaison is given in parentheses.)
Continuing Library Education Network and Exchange. Judy Card (Lorelle R. Swader).
Ethnic and Multicultural Information Exchange. Plummer Alston Jones, Jr. (Satia M. Orange).
Exhibits. Amy Rosenbaum (Deidre I. Ross).
Federal and Armed Forces Libraries. Georgette Harris (Reginald Scott).
Gay, Lesbian, Bisexual, Transgendered. Anne L. Moore, Norman J. Eriksen (Satia M. Orange).
Government Documents. Arlene A. Weible (Reginald Scott).
Intellectual Freedom. Pamela R. Klipsch (Nanette Perez).
International Relations. Jeannette E. Pierce (Michael P. Dowling, Delin R. Guerra).
Library History. Christine J. Pawley (Denise M. Davis).
Library Instruction. Carol Lynn Schuetz (Lorelle R. Swader).
Library Research. Jo Bell Whitlatch (Denise M. Davis).

Library Support Staff Interests. Alice L. Poffinberger (Lorelle R. Swader).
Map and Geography. Tsering Wangyal Shawa (Danielle M. Alderson).
New Members. Nadine M. Flores (Kimberly Sanders).
Social Responsibilities. Elaine M. Harger (Satia M. Orange).
Staff Organizations. Virginia L. Fore (Lorelle R. Swader).
Video. Mary S. Laskowski (Danielle M. Alderson).

Committee Chairpersons

(ALA staff liaison is given in parentheses.)
Accreditation (Standing). Thomas W. Leonhardt (Karen L. O'Brien).
American Libraries Advisory (Standing). Helen Ruth Adams (Leonard Kniffel).
Appointments (Standing). Leslie B. Burger (Lois Ann Gregory-Wood).
Awards (Standing). Timothy P. Grimes (Cheryl Malden).
Budget Analysis and Review (Standing). Patricia M. Wong (Gregory L. Calloway).
Chapter Relations (Standing). Ann Hamilton (Michael P. Dowling).
Committee on Committees (Elected Council Committee). Leslie B. Burger (Lois Ann Gregory-Wood).
Conference Committee (Standing). To be appointed (Deidre I. Ross).
Conference Program Coordinating Team. Donald L. Roalkvam (Deidre I. Ross).
Constitution and Bylaws (Standing). Norman Horrocks (JoAnne M. Kempf).
Council Orientation (Standing). Joseph M. Eagan (Lois Ann Gregory-Wood).
Diversity (Standing). V. Tessa Perry (Gwendolyn Prellwitz).
Education (Standing). Loriene Roy (Lorelle R. Swader).
Election (Standing). Peggy Sullivan (Al Companio, Eileen Mahoney).
Human Resource Development and Recruitment (Standing). Olivia M. A. Madison (Lorelle R. Swader).
Information Technology Policy Advisory. Sherrie Schmidt (Frederick W. Weingarten).

Intellectual Freedom (Standing). Kenton L. Oliver (Judith F. Krug).

International Relations (Standing). Ismail Abdullahi (Michael P. Dowling).

Legislation (Standing). Larry Romans (Lynne E. Bradley).

Literacy (Standing). Vivian R. Wynn (Dale P. Lipschultz).

Literacy and Outreach Services Advisory (Standing). Robin Osborne (Satia M. Orange).

Membership (Standing). Marcia L. Boosinger (To be appointed).

Organization (Standing). Melora Ranney Norman (Lois Ann Gregory-Wood).

Orientation, Training and Leadership Development. Donna O. Dziedzic (Dorothy H. Ragsdale).

Pay Equity (Standing). To be appointed (Lorelle R. Swader).

Policy Monitoring (Standing). Stephen L. Matthews (Lois Ann Gregory-Wood).

Professional Ethics (Standing). Sarah M. Pritchard (Beverley Becker, Judith F. Krug).

Public Awareness (Standing). Sally Gardner Reed (Mark R. Gould).

Publishing (Standing). Norman L. Maas (Donald E. Chatham).

Research and Statistics (Standing). Daniel O. O'Connor (Denise M. Davis).

Resolutions. Larry L. Hardesty (Lois Ann Gregory-Wood).

Status of Women in Librarianship (Standing). To be appointed (Lorelle R. Swader).

Web Site Advisory. Michelle L. Frisque (Debi Lewis, Sherri L. Vanyek).

Joint Committee Chairpersons

ALA/SAA/AAM: American Library Association–Society of American Archivists–American Association of Museums. Beverly P. Lynch (ALA); Deborra Richardson (SAA); To be appointed (AAM).

American Federation of Labor/Congress of Industrial Organizations–ALA, Library Service to Labor Groups, RUSA. Kay K. Ikuta (ALA); Pamela Wilson (AFL/CIO).

Association of American Publishers–ALA. Michael Gorman (ALA); To be appointed (AAP).

Association of American Publishers–ALCTS. To be appointed (ALCTS); To be appointed (AAP).

Children's Book Council–ALA. Julie A. Cummins (ALA); Elise Supovitz (CBC).

American Library Association
American Association of School Librarians

Executive Director, Julie A. Walker
50 E. Huron St., Chicago, IL 60611
312-280-2433, 800-545-2433 ext. 4382, fax 312-664-7459
E-mail aasl@ala.org, World Wide Web http://www.ala.org/aasl

Object

The American Association of School Librarians (AASL) is interested in the general improvement and extension of library media services for children and young people. AASL has specific responsibility for planning a program of study and service for the improvement and extension of library media services in elementary and secondary schools as a means of strengthening the educational program; evaluation, selection, interpretation, and utilization of media as they are used in the context of the school program; stimulation of continuous study and research in the library field and establishing criteria of evaluation; synthesis of the activities of all units of the American Library Association in areas of mutual concern; representation and interpretation of the need for the function of school libraries to other educational and lay groups; stimulation of professional growth, improvement of the status of school librarians, and encouragement of participation by members in appropriate type-of-activity divisions; and conducting activities and projects for improvement and extension of service in the school library when such projects are beyond the scope of type-of-activity divisions, after specific approval by the ALA Council.

Established in 1951 as a separate division of ALA.

Membership

Memb. 9,900+. Open to all libraries, school library media specialists, interested individuals, and business firms with requisite membership in ALA.

Officers (2005–2006)

Pres. J. Linda Williams; *Pres.-Elect* Cynthia A. Jones Phillip; *Treas./Financial Officer* Dennis J. LeLoup; *Past Pres.* Dawn P. Vaughn.

Board of Directors

Officers; Cassandra G. Barnett, Dolores D. Gwaltney, Terri G. Kirk, Kathleen V. Ellis, Eloise M. Long, A. Elaine Twogood, Alison E. Almquist, Mary Ann Harlan, Sara Kelly Johns, Melissa P. Johnston, Irene Kwidzinski, Floyd Clark Pentlin, Joanne M. Proctor, Virginia L. Wallace, Jan Weber, Julie A. Walker (ex officio).

Publications

Knowledge Quest (5 a year; memb.; nonmemb. $40). *Ed.* Debbie Abilock. E-mail kq@abilockl.net.

School Library Media Research (nonsubscription electronic publication available to memb. and nonmemb. at http://www. ala.org/aasl/slmr). *Ed.* Daniel Callison, School of Lib. and Info. Sciences, 10th and Jordan, Indiana Univ., Bloomington, IN 47405. E-mail callison@indiana.edu.

AASL Hotlinks (monthly electronic newsletter automatically sent to members).

Committee Chairpersons

AASL/ACRL Joint Information Literacy Committee. Melinda Greenblatt, Amy L. Deuink.

AASL/ELMS Executive Committee. Lesley S. J. Farmer.

AASL/Highsmith Research Grant. Laura Richardson.

AASL/ISS Executive Committee. Linell Wootton Ela.

AASL/SPVS Executive Committee. Sylvia K. Norton.

ABC/CLIO Leadership Grant. Amy Elinor Cass.

Affiliate Assembly. Diane R. Chen.

Alliance for Association Excellence. Dennis J. LeLoup.

American University Press Book Selection. Judith McGowan.

Annual Conference. Floyd Clark Pentlin, Vicki M. Emery.

Appointments. M. Veanna Baxter.

Awards. Ann M. Martin.

Bylaws and Organization. Carolyn L. Cain.

Collaborative School Library Media Award. Melissa P. Johnston.

Distinguished School Administrator Award. Marsha B. Haseldon.

Distinguished Service Award. Cara Cavin.

Frances Henne Award. Nancy Heiniger.

ICONnect Online Courses for Professionals and Families. Sara Wolf.

Information Technology Pathfinder Award. Joyce Kasman Valenza.

Intellectual Freedom. To be announced.

Intellectual Freedom Award. Debra A. Bashaw.

International Relations Committee. Johan Koren.

Knowledge Quest Editorial Board. Debbie Abilock.

Legislation. Diane R. Chen.

National Conference, 2007. Carl A. Harvey, Allison G. Kaplan.

National School Library Media Program of the Year Award. Gail K. Dickinson.

NCATE Coordinating Committee. Judi Repman.

New Member Mentoring Task Force. Frances R. Roscello.

Nominating 2006. Nancy Everhart.

Publications. Clara L. Sitter.

Reading for Understanding Special Committee. Sharon Coatney.

Recruitment for the Profession Task Force. Sallie H. Barringer.

Research/Statistics. Keith Curry Lance.

School Librarians Workshop Scholarship. Sara Wolf.

SLMR Electronic Editorial Board. Daniel J. Callison.

Teaching for Learning Committee. Catherine E. Marriott.

Web Advisory. Constance J. Champlin, Joette Stefl-Mabry.

Web Site Resource Guides Editorial Board. Rebecca Wojahn.

American Library Association
Association for Library Collections and Technical Services

Executive Director, Charles Wilt
50 E. Huron St., Chicago, IL 60611
800-545-2433 ext. 5030, fax 312-280-5033
E-mail cwilt@ala.org
World Wide Web http://www.ala.org/alcts

Object

The Association for Library Collections and Technical Services (ALCTS) envisions an environment in which traditional library roles are evolving. New technologies are making information more fluid and raising expectations. The public needs quality information anytime, anyplace. ALCTS provides frameworks to meet these information needs.

ALCTS provides leadership to the library and information communities in developing principles, standards, and best practices for creating, collecting, organizing, delivering, and preserving information resources in all forms. It provides this leadership through its members by fostering educational, research, and professional service opportunities. ALCTS is committed to quality information, universal access, collaboration, and life-long learning.

Standards: Develop, evaluate, revise, and promote standards for creating, collecting, organizing, delivering, and preserving information resources in all forms.

Best practices: Research, develop, evaluate, and implement best practices for creating, collecting, organizing, delivering, and preserving information resources in all forms.

Education: Assess the need for, sponsor, develop, administer, and promote educational programs and resources for life-long learning.

Professional development: Provide opportunities for professional development through research, scholarship, publication, and professional service.

Interaction and information exchange: Create opportunities to interact and exchange information with others in the library and information communities.

Association operations: Ensure efficient use of association resources and effective delivery of member services.

Established 1957; renamed 1988.

Membership

Memb. 4,865. Any member of the American Library Association may elect membership in this division according to the provisions of the bylaws.

Officers (2005–2006)

Pres. Rosann V. Bazirjian, Walter Clinton Jackson Lib., Univ. of North Carolina–Greensboro, 1000 Spring Garden St., Greensboro, NC 27402. Tel. 336-334-5880, fax 336-334-5399, e-mail rvbazirj@uncg.edu; *Pres.-Elect* Bruce Chr. Johnson, Cataloging Distribution Service, Lib. of Congress, Washington, DC 20540-0001. Tel. 202-707-1652, fax 202-707-3959, e-mail bjoh@loc.

gov; *Past Pres.* Carol Pitts Diedrichs, Univ. of Kentucky Lib., 1-85 William T. Young Lib., Lexington, KY 40506-0456. Tel. 859-257-0500 ext. 2087, fax 859-257-8379, e-mail diedrichs@uky.edu; *Councilor* Diane Dates Casey, Governors State Univ. Lib., 1 University Pkwy., University Park, IL 60466. Tel. 708-534-4110, fax 708-534-4564, e-mail d-casey@govst.edu.

Address correspondence to the executive director.

Board of Directors

Larry Alford, Rosann V. Bazirjian, Diane Dates Casey, Karen Darling, Karl Debus-Lopez, Carol Pitts Diedrichs, John Duke, Jill Emery, Elaine Franco, Joan Gatewood, Dina Giambi, Bruce Chr. Johnson, Cheryl Kern-Simirenko, Dustin Larmore, Helen Reed, Mary Beth Weber, Cynthia Whitacre, Charles Wilt.

Publications

ALCTS Newsletter Online (bimonthly; free). *Ed.* Mary Beth Weber, Cataloging Dept., Rutgers Univ. Libs., 47 Davidson Rd, Piscataway, NJ 08854. Tel. 732-445-0500, fax 732-445-5888, e-mail mbfecko@rci.rutgers.edu. Posted to http://www.ala.org/alcts.

Library Resources & Technical Services (q.; memb.; nonmemb. $75). *Ed.* Peggy Johnson, Univ. of Minnesota Libs., 499 Wilson Lib., 309 19th Ave. S., Minneapolis, MN 55455. Tel. 612-624-2312, fax 612-626-9353, e-mail m-john@tc.umn.edu.

Section Chairpersons

Acquisitions. Karl Debus-Lopez.
Cataloging and Classification. Cynthia Whitacre.
Collection Management and Development. Larry P. Alford.
Preservation and Reformatting. Joan Gatewood.
Serials. Jill Emery.

Committee Chairpersons

Hugh C. Atkinson Memorial Award (ALCTS/ACRL/LAMA/LITA). Karen Williams.
Association of American Publishers/ALCTS Joint Committee. To be announced.
Paul Banks and Carolyn Harris Preservation Award Jury. Patricia Selinger.
Best of *LRTS* Award Jury. Lori Osmus Kappmeyer.
Blackwell's Scholarship Award Jury. Deborah Thomas.
Budget and Finance. Cheryl Kern-Simirenko.
Education. Karen M. Letarte.
Fund Raising. Jennifer F. Paustenbaugh.
International Relations. Wanda Dole.
Leadership Development. Betsy Simpson.
LRTS Editorial Board. Peggy Johnson.
MARBI. Martha Yee.
Membership. Sheila A. Smyth.
Nominating. Brian E. C. Schottlaender.
Organization and Bylaws. Dustin Larmore.
Esther J. Piercy Award Jury. Larry Heiman.
Planning. Helen Reed.
Program. Genevieve Owens.
Publications. Narda Tafuri.

Discussion Groups

Authority Control in the Online Environment (ALCTS/LITA). Linda Ballinger.
Automated Acquisitions/In-Process Control Systems. Katharine Treptow Farrell.
Creative Ideas in Technical Services. Kalyani Parthasarathy.
Electronic Resources. Angelo Riggio.
MARC Formats (ALCTS/LITA). Helen E. Gbala.
Newspapers. Lydia Sue Kellerman.
Out of Print. Maria Kuhn.
Pre-Order and Pre-Catalog Searching. Mark Kendall.
Role of the Professional in Academic Research Technical Service Departments. Lisa Robinson.
Scholarly Communications. Brad Eden.
Technical Services Administrators of Medium-Sized Research Libraries. Elizabeth Brice.
Technical Services Directors of Large Research Libraries. Karen Calhoun.
Technical Services Workstations (ALCTS/LITA). Birong A. Ho.

American Library Association
Association for Library Service to Children

Executive Director, Diane Foote
50 E. Huron St., Chicago, IL 60611
312-280-2162, 800-545-2433 ext. 2162
E-mail dfoote@ala.org
World Wide Web http://www.ala.org/alsc

Object

Interested in the improvement and extension of library services to children in all types of libraries. Responsible for the evaluation and selection of book and nonbook materials for, and the improvement of techniques of, library services to children from preschool through eighth grade or junior high school age, when such materials or techniques are intended for use in more than one type of library. Founded 1901.

Membership

Memb. 3,943. Open to anyone interested in library services to children. For information on dues, see ALA entry.

Address correspondence to the executive director.

Officers

Pres. Ellen G. Fader; *V.P./Pres.-Elect* Kathleen T. Horning; *Past Pres.* Gretchen Wronka.

Directors

Carol Edwards, Molly S. Kinney, Starr LaTronica, Jane Marino, Kathryn McClelland, Judith O'Malley, Pat Scales, Kathy Toon, Rose Trevino.

Publications

Children and Libraries: The Journal of the Association for Library Service to Children (q.; memb.; nonmemb. $40; foreign $50).

Committee Chairpersons

ALSC @ your library Advocacy Campaign Task Force. Stephanie Bange.

ALSC BWI Summer Reading Grant. Jill Walker.

Arbuthnot Honor Lecture 2006. Jean Gaffney.

Mildred L. Batchelder Award 2006. Karen Breen.

Bechtel Fellowship. Debra Gold.

Pura Belpré Award 2006. Barbara Scotto.

Pura Belpré Fund Raising Task Force. Caroline Ward.

Randolph Caldecott Award 2006. Gratia Banta.

Andrew Carnegie Award 2006. Susan Pine.

Children and Libraries Advisory Committee. Jerianne Kladder.

Children and Technology. Bruce Farrar.

Distinguished Service Award 2006. Therese Bigelow.

Early Childhood Programs and Services. Linda Ernst.

Education. Joyce Laiosa.

Theodor Seuss Geisel Award 2006. Caroline Ward.

Great Web Sites. Maren Ostergard, Janet Sarratt.

Maureen Hayes Award. Floyd Dickman.

Intellectual Freedom. Michael Santangelo.

International Relations. Charlene McKenzie.

Legislation. Bessie Condos-Tichauer.

Liasion with National Organizations. Rebecca Purday, Myrna Allen.

Library Service to Special Population Children and their Caregivers. Carrie Banks.

Local Arrangements (New Orleans). Pabby Arnold.

Managing Children's Services. Susan Pannebaker.

Membership. Sarah English.

National Institute Planning Task Force 2006. Hedra Packman, Crystal Faris.

National Planning of Special Collections. Mary Beth Dunhouse.

John Newbery Award 2006. Barbara Barstow.

Nominating 2006. Margaret Tice.

Notable Children's Books. Rita Auerbach.

Notable Children's Recordings. Mary Burkey.

Notable Children's Software. Kirsten Cutler.

Notable Children's Videos. Lucinda Whitehurst.

Organization and Bylaws. Roxanne Feldman Hsu.

Penguin Young Readers Group Award. Patricia Gonzales.

Planning and Budget. Rhonda Puntney.

Program Coordinating. Marian Creamer.

Publications. Amanda Williams.

Quicklists Consulting. Lisa Dennis, Tali Balas.

Research and Development. Eliza Dresang.

Charlemae Rollins President's Program 2006. Nell Colburn.

Sagebrush Award. Patricia Dollisch.

Scholarships. Mary Cissell.

School Age Programs and Service. Leslie Jacobs.

Robert F. Sibert Award 2006. Kathy Simonetta.

Laura Ingalls Wilder Award 2007. Roger Sutton.

American Library Association
Association for Library Trustees and Advocates

Executive Director, Kerry Ward
50 E. Huron St., Chicago, IL 60611-2795
312-280-2160, 800-545-2433 ext. 2161, fax 312-280-3256
E-mail kward@ala.org
World Wide Web http://www.ala.org/alta

Object

The Association for Library Trustees and Advocates (ALTA) was founded in 1890 as the American Library Trustee Association. It is the only division of the American Library Association dedicated to promoting and ensuring outstanding library service through educational programs that develop excellence in trusteeship and actions that advocate access to information for all. ALTA represents library trustees, advocates, volunteers, and friends through the United States and Canada. It became an ALA division in 1961.

Membership

Memb. 1,200. Open to all interested persons and organizations. For dues and membership year, see ALA entry.

Officers (2005–2006)

Pres. Jane Rowland. E-mail jrowland@calumetcitypl.org; *1st V.P./Pres.-Elect* Anne D. Sterling. E-mail nimbleleap@aol.com; *2nd V.P.* Donald L. Roalkvam. E-mail droalkva@allstate.com; *Councilor* Shirley Bruursema; *Past Pres.* Marguerite E. Ritchey. E-mail margueritemr@hotmail.com.

Publication

The Voice (q.; memb.).

American Library Association
Association of College and Research Libraries

Executive Director, Mary Ellen K. Davis
50 E. Huron St., Chicago, IL 60611-2795
312-280-2523, 800-545-2433 ext. 2523, fax 312-280-2520
E-mail acrl@ala.org, World Wide Web http://www.ala.org/acrl

Object

The Association of College and Research Libraries (ACRL) leads academic and research librarians and libraries in advancing learning and scholarship. Founded 1938.

Membership

Memb. 13,118. For information on dues, see ALA entry.

Officers

Pres. Camila A. Alire, dean, Univ. Libs. MSC 05 3020, Univ. of New Mexico, Albuquerque, NM 87131-0001. Tel. 505-277-2678, fax 505-277-7196, e-mail calire@umn.edu; *Pres.-Elect* Pamela Snelson, college libn., Shadek-Fackenthal Lib., Franklin & Marshall College, P.O. Box 3003, Lancaster, PA 17604-3003. Tel. 717-291-3896, fax 717-291-4160, e-mail pamela.snelson@fandm.edu; *Past Pres.* Frances J. Maloy, leader, access services, Woodruff Lib., Emory Univ., 540 Asbury Circle, Atlanta, GA 30322. Tel. 404-727-0126, fax 404-727-1655, e-mail libfm@emory.edu; *Budget and Finance Chair* Susan M. Kroll, associate v.p., Health Sciences Center for Knowledge Management, Ohio State Univ., 376 W. 10 Ave., Columbus, OH 43210-1240. Tel. 614-292-4852, fax 614-292-1920, e-mail kroll.1@osu.edu; *ACRL Councilor* Elaine Didier, director, Gerald R. Ford Lib. and Museum, 1000 Beal Ave., Ann Arbor, MI 48109. Tel. 734-205-0566, fax 734-205-0571 e-mail elaine.didier@nara.gov.

Board of Directors

Officers; Nancy H. Allen, Janis M. Bandelin, Lori A. Goetsch, Rita Jones, Lynne King, W. Bede Mitchell, Dorothy A. Washington, Karen A. Williams.

Publications

Choice (11 a year; $285; foreign $335). *Ed.* Irving Rockwood.

Choice Reviews-on-Cards ($370; foreign $430).

ChoiceReviews.online ($325).

College & Research Libraries (C&RL) (6 a year; memb.; nonmemb. $65). *Ed.* William Gray Potter.

College & Research Libraries News (11 a year; memb.; nonmemb. $44). *Ed.* Stephanie D. Orphan.

Publications in Librarianship (formerly *ACRL Monograph Series*) (occasional). *Ed.* Charles A. Schwartz.

RBM: A Journal of Rare Books, Manuscripts, and Cultural Heritage (2 a year; $40). *Ed.* Richard Clement.

List of other publications and rates available through the ACRL office.

Committee and Task Force Chairpersons

AASL/ACRL Information Literacy (interdivisional). Melinda Dale Greenblatt, Amy L. Deuink.

Academic/Research Librarian of the Year Award Selection. Leslie J. Canterbury.

ACRL/Harvard Leadership Institute Advisory. John William Collins, III.

Advocacy Coordinating. Helen H. Spalding.

Appointments. Laverna M. Saunders.

Hugh C. Atkinson Memorial Award. Karen A. Williams.

Awards. Larry L. Hardesty.

Blog Advisory Board. Steven J. Bell.

Budget and Finance. Susan M. Kroll.

Bylaws. Michelle M. Reid.

Choice Editorial Board. Joan L. Heath.

Colleagues. Stella Bentley.

College & Research Libraries Editorial Board. William Gray Potter.

College & Research Libraries News Editorial Board. Joan L. Lippincott.

Conference Program Planning, New Orleans (2006). Camila Alire.

Conference Program Planning, Washington, D.C. (2007). Pamela Snelson.

Copyright. Donna L. Ferullo.

Council of Liaisons. Julie B. Todaro.

E. J. Josey Spectrum Scholar Mentor. Theresa S. Byrd.

Doctoral Dissertation Fellowship. Teresa Y. Neely.

Effective Practices Review Committee. Jo Davies.

Ethics. Phillip J. Jones.

Excellence in Academic Libraries Award (Nominations). Susan K. Nutter.

Excellence in Academic Libraries Award (Selection). Tyrone Heath Cannon.

Friends Fund. John Popko.

Government Relations. W. Lee Hisle.

Grassroots Library Advocacy. Nancy A. Davenport, Patricia H. Smith.

Guidelines for Media Resources in Academic Libraries Review. William N. Nelson.

Information Literacy Advisory. Elizabeth A. Dupuis.

Institute for Information Literacy Executive. Terese Heidenwolf.

Intellectual Freedom. Robert P. Holley.

International Relations. Nicoletta C. Hary.

Samuel Lazerow Fellowship. Anne Campbell Moore.

Leadership Recruitment and Nomination. Tyrone Heath Canon.

Marketing Academic and Research Libraries. Frank A. D'Andraia.

Membership Advisory. Christie J. Flynn.

National Conference Executive Committee, Baltimore 2007. Mary Reichel.

New Publications Advisory. Jan H. Kemp.

President's Program Planning Committee, New Orleans, 2006. Lynn S. Connaway, Louise S. Sherby.

President's Program Planning Committee, Washington, D.C., 2007. Michael J. LaCrox, Lisa M. Stillwell.

Professional Development Coordinating. Evelyn V. Blount.

Publications Coordinating. Catherine A. Lee.

Publications in Librarianship Editorial Board. Charles A. Schwartz.

Racial and Ethnic Diversity. Elizabeth Chisato Uyeki.

RBM Editorial Board. Richard W. Clement.

Research. James L. Mullins.

Resources for College Libraries Editorial Board. Carolyn A. Sheehy.

Review and Revision of the Guidelines for the Preparation of Policies on Library Access. Norice Lee.

Scholarly Communications. Ray English.

Standards and Accreditation. William N. Nelson.

Statistics. Leslie A. Manning.

Status of Academic Librarians. Carolyn H. Allen.

Discussion Group Chairpersons

Academic Library Outreach. Stephanie R. Davis-Kahl.

Alliances for New Directions in Teaching/ Learning. Mark Horan.

Australian-Canadian-New Zealand Studies. Faye Christenberry.

Consumer and Family Studies. Priscilla C. Geahigan.

Electronic Reserves. Laureen Esser.

Electronic Text Centers. Robert H. Scott.

Fee-Based Information Service Centers in Academic Libraries. Steve Coffman.

Information Commons. Caroline Patricia Crouse, Michael Whitchurch.

Libraries and Information Science. Susan E. Searing.

Library Development. Kimberly Anice Hale.

Media Resources. Monique L. Threatt.

MLA International Bibliography. John L. Novak.

Partnership Librarians. Mary Stahley.

Personnel Administrators and Staff Development Officers. Jenifer S. Abramson, Laine Stambaugh.
Philosophical, Religious, and Theological Studies. Celestina Wroth.
Popular Cultures. Sandra Sue Ballasch.
Regional Campus Libraries. Darby Syrkin.
Scholarly Communications. Bonnie MacEwan.
Sports and Recreation. Mila C. Su.
Team-Based Organizations. Robert Patrick Mitchell.
Undergraduate Libraries. Leah G. McGinnis.

Section Chairpersons

African-American Studies Librarians. Heather Martin.
Anthropology and Sociology. Shawn W. Nicholson.

Arts. Jane E. Sloan.
Asian, African, and Middle Eastern. Cynthia A. Tysick.
College Libraries. Robin Wagner.
Community and Junior College Libraries. Christine Godin.
Distance Learning. Jack Fritts.
Education and Behavioral Sciences. Douglas L. Cook.
Instruction. Lisa J. Hinchliffe.
Law and Political Science. Connie S. Stoner.
Literatures in English. Susanna Van Sant.
Rare Books and Manuscripts. Katherine Reagan.
Science and Technology. Julia M. Gelfand.
Slavic and East European. Daniel M. Pennell.
University Libraries. Sandra Yee.
Western European Studies. Helene S. Baumann.
Woman's Studies. Megan M. Adams.

American Library Association
Association of Specialized and Cooperative Library Agencies

Executive Director, Cathleen Bourdon
50 E. Huron St., Chicago, IL 60611-2795
312-280-4398, 800-545-2433 ext. 4398, fax 312-944-8085
World Wide Web http://www.ala.org/ascla

Object

Represents state library agencies, specialized library agencies, multitype library cooperatives, and independent librarians. Within the interests of these types of library organizations, the Association of Specialized and Cooperative Library Agencies (ASCLA) has specific responsibility for

1. Development and evaluation of goals and plans for state library agencies, specialized library agencies, and multitype library cooperatives to facilitate the implementation, improvement, and extension of library activities designed to foster improved user services, coordinating such activities with other appropriate ALA units

2. Representation and interpretation of the role, functions, and services of state library agencies, specialized library agencies, multitype library cooperatives, and independent librarians within and outside the profession, including contact with national organizations and government agencies

3. Development of policies, studies, and activities in matters affecting state library agencies, specialized library agencies, multitype library cooperatives, and independent librarians relating to (a) state and local library legislation, (b) state grants-in-aid and appropriations, and (c) relationships among state, federal, regional, and local governments, coordinating such activities with other appropriate ALA units

4. Establishment, evaluation, and promotion of standards and service guidelines relating to the concerns of this association

5. Identifying the interests and needs of all persons, encouraging the creation of services to meet these needs within the areas of concern of the association, and promoting the use of these services provided by state library agencies, specialized library agencies, multitype library cooperatives, and independent librarians

6. Stimulating the professional growth and promoting the specialized training and continuing education of library personnel at all levels in the areas of concern of this association and encouraging membership participation in appropriate type-of-activity divisions within ALA

7. Assisting in the coordination of activities of other units within ALA that have a bearing on the concerns of this association

8. Granting recognition for outstanding library service within the areas of concern of this association

9. Acting as a clearinghouse for the exchange of information and encouraging the development of materials, publications, and research within the areas of concern of this association

Membership

Memb. 917.

Board of Directors (2005–2006)

Pres. Diana M. Paque; *Pres.-Elect* Marilyn M. Irwin; *Past Pres.* Peggy D. Rudd; *Dirs.- at-Large* Lori A. Bell, Carol Ann Desch, Sarah E. Hamrick, Stephen Prine; *Div. Councilor* Cynthia Roach; *Newsletter Editor* Sara G. Laughlin; *Section Reps.* Brenda K. Bailey-Hainer, Mimi McCain, Connie S. Paul, Jean F. Porter, Rahye L. Puckett.

Publications

Interface (q.; memb.; single copies $7). *Ed.* Sara G. Laughlin, 1616 Treadwell La., Bloomington, IN 47408. Tel. 812-334-8485.

Committee Chairpersons

Accessibility Assembly. Rhea Joyce Rubin.
Advocacy Group. Sarah E. Harmick.
American Correctional Association/ASCLA Joint Committee on Institution Libraries. Jean Clancy Botta.
Awards. Ruth E. O'Donnell.
Chapter Relations. Sondra L. Taylor-Furbee.
Conference Program Team 2006. Beverley R. Shirley.
Conference Program Team 2007. Sarah E. Hamrick.
Education Assembly. Rachel E. Mosman.
Freedom to Read Foundation. Jane Kolbe.
Intellectual Freedom. Kendall F. Wiggin.
Interagency Council on Information Resources for Nursing. Frederick Pattison.
Legislation. Barratt Wilkins.
Literacy Assembly. Kathleen Ann Baxter.
Membership Promotion (task force). Ronald P. Leonard.
Planning and Budget Assembly. Marilyn M. Irwin.
Professional Ethics. Jean F. Porter.
Publications. Jean Currie.
Recruitment Assembly. Cheryl G. Bryan.
Standards Review. Rod Wagner.
Web Site Advisory. Brian A. Greene.

American Library Association
Library Administration and Management Association

Executive Director, Lorraine Olley
50 E. Huron St., Chicago, IL 60611
312-280-5032, 800-545-2433 ext. 5032, fax 312-280-5033
Marketing Specialist, Fred Reuland. E-mail freuland@ala.org
World Wide Web http://www.ala.org/lama

Object

LAMA's Strategic Plan (2006–2010), adopted by its board of directors in January 2006, sets out the following:

Mission: The Library Administration and Management Association encourages and nurtures current and future leaders, and develops and promotes outstanding leadership and management practices.

Vision: LAMA will be the foremost organization developing present and future leaders in library and information services.

Image: LAMA is a welcoming community where aspiring and experienced leaders from all types of libraries, as well as those who support libraries, come together to gain skills in a quest for excellence in library management, administration and leadership.

In addition,

- LAMA will be an organization in which value to its members drives decisions.

- LAMA will expand and strengthen leadership and management expertise at all levels for all libraries.

- LAMA will facilitate professional development opportunities to enhance leadership and management.

- LAMA will be the preeminent professional organization that develops and supports library leaders and managers.

Established 1957.

Membership

Memb. 4,800.

Officers (July 2005–June 2006)

Pres. Catherine Murray-Rust; *Pres.-Elect* Andrea Lapsley; *Secy.* Emily Bergman; *Division Councilor* Sue H. MacTavish; *Past Pres.* Virginia Steel.

Address correspondence to the executive director.

Publications

Library Administration and Management (q.; memb.; nonmemb. $65; foreign $75). *Ed.* Gregg Sapp.

LEADS from LAMA (approx. biweekly; free through Internet). *Ed.* Lorraine Olley. To subscribe, send to listproc@ala.org the message *subscribe lamaleads [first name last name]*.

Committee Chairpersons

Budget and FInanace. Janice L. Flug.

Cultural Diversity Grant. Sylvia Y. Sorinkle-Hamlin.

Editorial Advisory Board. Paul M. Anderson.

Leadership and Development. Karen Holloway, Cathy C. Miesse.

Membership. Shawn Tonner.

Nominating. Janice D. Simmons-Welburn.

Organization. Lynn K. Chmelir.

President's Program. Patricia A. Schafer.

Program. Thomas E. Schneiter.

Publishing. Alfred Willis.

Recognition of Achievement. Carol L. Anderson.

Special Conferences and Programs. Laura Bayard.

Strategic Planning Implementation. Dana M. Sally.

Web Site Advisory Board. Diane B. Bisom.

Section Chairpersons

Buildings and Equipment. Drew Harrington.
Fund Raising and Financial Development. Elizabeth A. Titus.

Human Resources. Jeanne F. Voyles.
Library Organization and Management. Eric C. Shoaf.
Measurement, Assessment, and Evaluation. Bonnie J. Allen.
Public Relations and Marketing. Michele C. Russo.
Systems and Services. Susan H. Anthes.

American Library Association
Library and Information Technology Association

Executive Director, Mary C. Taylor
50 E. Huron St., Chicago, IL 60611
312-280-4267, 800-545-2433
E-mail mtaylor@ala.org
World Wide Web http://www.lita.org

Object

As a center of expertise about information technology, the Library and Information Technology Association (LITA) leads in exploring and enabling new technologies to empower libraries. LITA members use the promise of technology to deliver dynamic library collections and services.

LITA educates, serves, and reaches out to its members, other ALA members and divisions, and the entire library and information community through its publications, programs, and other activities designed to promote, develop, and aid in the implementation of library and information technology.

Membership

Memb. 4,800.

Officers (2005–2006)

Pres. Patrick Mullin; *V.P./Pres.-Elect* Bonnie Postlethwaite; *Past Pres.* Colby Mariva Riggs.

Directors

Officers; Kristin A. Antelman, Amira Aaron, Mark A. Beatty, Michelle L. Frisque, Peter Murray, Jennie L. McKee, Andrew K. Pace, Bonnie S. Postlethwaite; *Councilor* Karen G. Schneider; *Bylaws and Organization* Maribeth Manoff; *Exec. Dir.* Mary C. Taylor.

Publication

Information Technology and Libraries (*ITAL*) (q.; memb.; nonmemb. $55; single copy $20). *Ed.* John P. Webb. For information or to send manuscripts, contact the editor.

Committee Chairpersons

Budget Review. Colby Mariva Riggs.
Bylaws and Organization. Maribeth Manoff.
Committee Chair Coordinator. Scott P. Muir.
Education. Tara Lee Dirst.
Executive. Patrick J. Mullin.
International Relations. David J. Nutty.
ITAL Editorial Board. John P. Webb.
Legislation and Regulation. Eulalia A. Roel.
LITA/Brett Butler Entrepreneurship Award. Judith Carter.

LITA/Endeavor Student Writing Award. James R. Kennedy.

LITA/Library Hi Tech Award. Jeffrey G. Trzeciak.

LITA/LSSI and LITA/OCLC Minority Scholarships. Debra Ann Hanken Kurtz.

LITA National Forum 2006. Dale Poulter.

LITA National Forum 2007. Mary LaMarca.

LITA/OCLC Kilgour Award. Qiang Jin.

LITA/Christian Larew Scholarship. Eva Sorrell.

Membership Development. Navjit K. Brar.

Nominating. Flo J. Wilson.

Program Planning. David W. Bretthauer.

Publications. Nancy N. Colyar.

Regional Institutes. Susan Logue.

Technology and Access. Aimee Fifarek.

Top Technology Trends. Jennifer Ward.

TER Board. Sharon Rankin.

Web Coordinating. Michelle L. Frisque.

Interest Group Coordinators

Authority Control in the Online Environment (LITA/ALCTS). Leah Manon Theroux.

Blogs, Interactive Media, Groupware, and Wikis IG. Karen G. Schneider.

Digital Library Technologies. Martin Halbert.

Electronic Publishing/Electronic Journals. Lloyd Davidson.

Electronic Resources Management (LITA/ALCTS) Timothy D. Jewell.

Emerging Technologies. Rose Nelson.

Heads of Library Technology. Susan M. Thompson.

Human/Machine Interface. Nancy B. Turner.

Imagineering. Catherine Wagner.

Internet Portals. Harrison Dekker.

Internet Resources. Laura B. Cohen.

JPEG 2000 in Archives and Libraries. Peter Murray.

MARC Formats (LITA/ALCTS). Mark Truitt.

Open Source Systems. Gwendolyn J. Reece.

Personal Computing. Florence Ye Tang.

RFID Technology. Qing Haley.

Secure Systems and Services. George J. Harmon.

Standards. Nathan D. M. Robertson.

Technical Services Workstations (LITA/ALCTS). Birong Ho.

American Library Association
Public Library Association

Executive Director, Greta K. Southard
50 E. Huron St., Chicago, IL 60611
312-280-5752, 800-545-2433, ext. 5752, fax 312-280-5029
E-mail pla@ala.org
World Wide Web http://www.pla.org

Object

The Public Library Association (PLA) has specific responsibility for

1. Conducting and sponsoring research about how the public library can respond to changing social needs and technical developments

2. Developing and disseminating materials useful to public libraries in interpreting public library services and needs

3. Conducting continuing education for public librarians by programming at national and regional conferences, by publications such as the newsletter, and by other delivery means

4. Establishing, evaluating, and promoting goals, guidelines, and standards for public libraries

5. Maintaining liaison with relevant national agencies and organizations engaged in public administration and human services, such as the National Association of Counties, the

Municipal League, and the Commission on Post-Secondary Education

6. Maintaining liaison with other divisions and units of ALA and other library organizations, such as the Association of American Library Schools and the Urban Libraries Council

7. Defining the role of the public library in service to a wide range of user and potential user groups

8. Promoting and interpreting the public library to a changing society through legislative programs and other appropriate means

9. Identifying legislation to improve and to equalize support of public libraries

PLA enhances the development and effectiveness of public librarians and public library services. This mission positions PLA to

- Focus its efforts on serving the needs of its members
- Address issues that affect public libraries
- Commit to quality public library services that benefit the general public

The goals of PLA are

Advocacy and recognition. Public libraries will be recognized as the destination for a wide variety of valuable services and their funding will be a community priority.

A literate nation. PLA will be a valued partner of public library initiatives to create a nation of readers.

Staffing and recruitment. Public libraries will be recognized as exciting places to work and will be staffed by skilled professionals who are recognized as the information experts, are competitively paid, and reflect the demographics of their communities.

Training and knowledge transfer. PLA will be nationally recognized as the leading source for continuing education opportunities for public library staff and trustees.

Membership

Memb. 10,000+. Open to all ALA members interested in the improvement and expansion of public library services to all ages in various types of communities.

Officers (2005–2006)

Pres. Daniel L. Walters, Las Vegas–Clark County Public Lib., 833 Las Vegas Blvd. N., Las Vegas, NV 89101-2030. Tel. 702-507-3611, fax 702-507-3609, e-mail waltersd@lvccld.org; *Pres.-Elect* Susan H. Hildreth, California State Lib., P.O. Box 942837, Sacramento, CA 94237-0001. Tel. 916-654-0174, fax 916-654-0064, e-mail shhildreth@concast.net; *Past-Pres.* Clara Nalli Bohrer, West Bloomfield Township Public Lib., 4600 Walnut Lake Rd., W. Bloomfield, MI 48323-2557. E-mail bohrercn@wblib.org.

Publication

Public Libraries (bi-mo.; memb.; nonmemb. $50; foreign $60; single copy $10). *Managing Ed.* Kathleen Hughes, PLA, 50 E. Huron St., Chicago, IL 60611.

Cluster Chairpersons

Issues and Concerns Steering Committee. Wayne M. Crocker.

Library Development Steering Committee. Nicola K. Stanke.

Library Services Steering Committee. Carol L. Sheffer.

Committee Chairs

Issues and Concerns Cluster

Intellectual Freedom. Penelope Jeffrey.
International Relations. Kathleen Imhoff.
Legislation. Mark Smith.
Library Confidentialty Task Force. Catherine O'Connell.
Public Policy in Public Libraries. Kathryn Robinson.
Recruitment of Public Librarians. Monique Le Conge.
Research and Statistics. Rochelle Logan.
Workload Measures and Staffing Patterns. Regina Cooper.

Library Development Cluster

Branch Libraries. Cheryl Smith.
Marketing Public Libraries. Mary Fran Bennett.
Metropolitan Libraries. Therese Bigelow.
Practical Applications of Technology in Public Libraries. Sharon R. Castleberry.
Public Library Systems. Rhonda Puntney.
Rural Library Services. Lawrence Grieco.
Small and Medium-Sized Libraries. Mark Pumphrey.
Technology in Public Libraries. Douglas Bailey.

Library Services Cluster

Adult Continuing and Independent Learning Services. Carol Marlowe.
Audiovisual. Jana Prock.
Basic Education and Literarcy Services. Virginia McHenry-Hepner.
Career and Business Services. Barbara Spruill.
Cataloging Needs of Public Libraries. Vivian Bordeaux.

Collection Management Committee. Mary Wallace.
Community Information Services. Margaret Gillis Bruni.
Reader's Advisory. Madlyn Schneider.
Services to Elementary-School-Age Children and Their Caregivers. Barbara H. Fischer.
Services to Multicultural Populations. Mary Louise Daneri.
Services to Preschool Children and Their Caregivers. Penny Neef.
Services to Teenagers and Their Caregivers. Bill Stack.

Business Committees

Annual Conference Coordinating Committee 2006. Bruce Schauer.
Annual Conference Coordinating Committee 2007. Claudia Sumler.
Assessing for Results Book Review Committee. Sandra Nelson.
Awards. Jean M. Tabor.
Budget and Finance. Clara Nalli Bohrer.
Bylaws and Organization. Rivkah K. Sass.
Leadership Development 2006. William Knott.
Leadership Development 2007. Anne Marie Gold.
National Conference 2006. Toni Garvey.
National Conference (Program) 2006. Sandra Nelson.
Membership. Albert Tovar.
PLA Partners. David Paynter.
President's Events 2006. Rivkah K. Sass.
Publications, Electronic Communications Advisory. Steven Cohen.
Publications, PLA Monographs. Margaret Smith.
Publications, *Public Libraries* Advisory. Marcia G. Schneider.
Publications, *Statistical Report* Advisory. Louise A Sevold.
Publications, University Press Books for Public Libraries. Saul Amdursky.

American Library Association
Reference and User Services Association

Executive Director, Cathleen Bourdon
50 E. Huron St., Chicago, IL 60611-2795
312-280-4398, 800-545-2433 ext. 4398, fax 312-944-8085
E-mail rusa@ala.org, World Wide Web http://www.ala.org/rusa

Object

The Reference and User Services Association (RUSA) is responsible for stimulating and supporting in every type of library the delivery of reference/information services to all groups, regardless of age, and of general library services and materials to adults. This involves facilitating the development and conduct of direct service to library users, the development of programs and guidelines for service to meet the needs of these users, and assisting libraries in reaching potential users.

The specific responsibilities of RUSA are

1. Conduct of activities and projects within the association's areas of responsibility

2. Encouragement of the development of librarians engaged in these activities, and stimulation of participation by members of appropriate type-of-library divisions

3. Synthesis of the activities of all units within the American Library Association that have a bearing on the type of activities represented by the association

4. Representation and interpretation of the association's activities in contacts outside the profession

5. Planning and development of programs of study and research in these areas for the total profession

6. Continuous study and review of the association's activities

Membership

Memb. 5,110.

Officers (July 2005–June 2006)

Pres. Diane M. Zabel; *Pres.-Elect* Diana D. Shonrock; *Secy.* William Alfred McHugh; *Past Pres.* Gwen Arthur.

Directors-at-Large

Denise Beaubien Bennett, Linda Friend, Cynthia R. Levine, Carla Rickerson, Cathleen Alice Towe, Amy Tracy Wells; *Councilor* Neal Wyatt; *Eds.* Connie J. Van Fleet, Danny P. Wallace; *Ex Officio* Daniel C. Mack; *Exec. Dir.* Cathleen Bourdon.

Publication

RUSQ (q.; memb. $50, foreign memb. $60, single copies $15). *Eds.* Connie J. Van Fleet, Danny P. Wallace.

Section Chairpersons

Business Reference and Services. Jennifer C. Boettcher.

Collection Development and Evaluation. Steve Alleman.

History. Andrew M. Smith.

Machine-Assisted Reference. Mary Pagliero Popp.

Reference Services. David A. Tyckoson.

Sharing and Transforming Access to Resources. Anne Kathleen Beaubien.

Committee Chairpersons

Access to Information. Justina Osatohanmwen Osa.

AFL/CIO Joint Committee on Library Services to Labor Groups. Kay K. Ikuta, Pamela Wilson.

Awards Coordinating. Neal Wyatt.

Conference Program. Muzette Z. Diefenthal.

Conference Program Coordinating. Corinne M. Hill.

Membership. Lori S. Thornton.

Margaret E. Monroe Adult Services Award. Susan Herzog.

Isadore Gilbert Mudge/R. R. Bowker Award. Jerilyn A. Marshall.

Nominating 2006. A. Craig Hawbaker.

Organization. Kay A. Cassell.

Planning and Finance. Gwen Arthur.

Professional Development. Bobray J. Bordelon.

Publications. Joseph E. Straw.

Reference Services Press Award. Susan J. Beck.

John Sessions Memorial Award. Dan D. Golodner.

Standards and Guidelines. Ronald Wayne Bivens-Tatum.

Thomson Gale Research Award for Excellence in Reference and Adult Services. Teresa A. Beck.

Walgreens Consumer Health Advisory. Carla D. Hayden.

White House Conference on Aging (task force). Allan Martrin Kleiman.

American Library Association
Young Adult Library Services Association

Executive Director, Beth Yoke
50 E. Huron St., Chicago, IL 60611
312-280-4390, 800-545-2433 ext. 4390, fax 312-664-7459
E-mail yalsa@ala.org, World Wide Web http://www.ala.org/yalsa

Object

In every library in the nation, quality library service to young adults is provided by a staff that understands and respects the unique informational, educational, and recreational needs of teenagers. Equal access to information, services, and materials is recognized as a right, not a privilege. Young adults are actively involved in the library decision making process. The library staff collaborates and cooperates with other youth-serving agencies to provide a holistic, communitywide network of activities and services that support healthy youth development. To ensure that this vision becomes a reality, the Young Adult Library Services Association (YALSA)

1. Advocates extensive and developmentally appropriate library and information services for young adults, ages 12 to 18

2. Promotes reading and supports the literacy movement

3. Advocates the use of information and communications technologies to provide effective library service

4. Supports equality of access to the full range of library materials and services, including existing and emerging information and communications technologies, for young adults

5. Provides education and professional development to enable its members to serve as effective advocates for young people

6. Fosters collaboration and partnerships among its individual members with the library community and other groups involved in providing library and information services to young adults

7. Influences public policy by demonstrating the importance of providing library and information services that meet the unique needs and interests of young adults

8. Encourages research and is in the vanguard of new thinking concerning the provision of library and information services for youth

Membership

Memb. 4,089. Open to anyone interested in library services and materials for young adults. For information on dues, see ALA entry.

Officers

Pres. Pam Spencer Holley. E-mail pamsholley@aol.com; *V.P./Pres.-Elect* Judy Nelson. E-mail jnelson@pcl.lib.wa.us; *Past Pres.* David Mowery. E-mail d.mowery@brooklynpubliclibrary.org.

Directors

Nick Buron. E-mail nick.h.buron@queens library.org; Sarah Cornish. E-mail cornish sarah@hotmail.com; Sarah Flowers. E-mail sflowers@library.sccgov.org; Maria Gentle. E-mail mgentl@arlingtonva.us; Francisca Goldsmith. E-mail goldson@pacbell.net; Jessica Mize. E-mail jmize@wideopenwest.com.

Publication

Young Adult Library Services (quarterly) (memb.; nonmemb. $40; foreign $50). *Ed.* Linda Johns.

Committee Chairpersons

Alex Awards. Ann Theis.
Audio Books and Media Exploration. Carly Wiggins.
Audio Books Preconference. Francisca Goldsmith, Jamie Watson.

Best Books for Young Adults. Lynn Rutan.
Division and Membership Promotion. Anne Heidemann.
Margaret Edwards Award 2006. Maria Gentle.
Margaret Edwards Award 2007. Mary Hastler.
Graphic Novels (task force). Kat Kan.
Intellectual Freedom. Barbara Conkin.
Legislation. Laurel Sandor.
New Directions Implementation (task force). Anthony Bernier.
Nominating. Sara Ryan.
Organization and Bylaws. Stacy Creel Chavez.
Outreach to Young Adults with Special Needs. Kristin Fletcher-Spear.
Partnerships Advocating for Teens. Sandra Payne.
Popular Paperbacks for Young Adults. Walter Mayes.
President's Program 2006. Michael Cart, Susan Raboy.
Michael L. Printz Award 2006. Michael Cart.
Michael L. Printz Award 2007. Ed Sullivan.
Professional Development. Mary Hastler.
Program Planning Clearinghouse and Evaluation. Erin Downey Howerton.
Publications. Julie Bartel.
Publishers Liaison. David Hrivnak.
Quick Picks for Young Adult Readers. Jamie Watson.
Regional Institute (task force). Linda Braun.
Research. Jami Jones.
Selected DVDs and Videos for Young Adults. Shawn Thrasher.
Serving Young Adults in Large Urban Populations. Kathleen Degyansky, Sandra Payne.
Strategic Planning. Audra Caplan.
Teaching Young Adult Literature. Teri Lesesne, Shannan Sword.
Technology for Young Adults. Connie Repplinger.
Teen Advisory Group Site (TAGS). Paula Brehm-Heeger.
Teen Read Week. Lorraine Squires.
YA Galley. Tracey Firestone.
Youth Participation. Melissa Rabey.
Youth Participation Coordinator. Donna McMillan.

American Indian Library Association (AILA)

President, Carlene Engstrom, Director, D'Arcy McNickle Library,
Salish Kootenai College, Pablo, Montana
E-mail carlene_engstrom@skc.edu
World Wide Web http://www.ailanet.org

Object

To promote the development of and access to library and information services by American Indian people.

Founded 1979; affiliated with American Library Association 1985.

Membership

Any person, library, or other organization interested in promoting the development of and access to library and information services by American Indian people may become a member.

Dues (Inst.) $30; (Indiv.) $15; (Student) $10.

Officers (July 2005–June 2006)

Pres. Carlene Engstrom. E-mail carlene_ engstrom@skc.edu; *V.P./Pres.-Elect* Karen Letarte. E-mail karen_letarte@ncsu.edu; *Secy.* Richenda Wilkinson. E-mail richenda. wilkinson@oregonstate.edu; *Treas.* Joan Howland. E-mail howla001@tc.umn.edu;

Past Pres. Kelly Webster. E-mail kellypw7@ hotmail.com.

Publication

AILA Newsletter (q.). *Ed.* Rhonda Harris Taylor, assoc. professor, School of Lib. and Info. Studies, Univ. of Oklahoma, 401 W. Brooks, Norman, OK 73019. E-mail rtaylor @ou.edu.

Committee Chairs

Bylaws and Constitution. David Ongley.
Childrens' Literature Award. Victor Schill, Naomi Caldwell.
Communications and Publications. Kathleen Burns.
Development and Fund Raising. Jacquie Samples.
Distinguished Service Award. Victor Schill.
Nominating. Lotsee Patterson.
Scholarship Review Board. Joan Howland, Lotsee Patterson.
Subject Access and Classification. John Berry.
Programming. Kelly Webster.

American Merchant Marine Library Association

(An affiliate of United Seamen's Service)
Executive Director, Roger T. Korner
125 Maiden Lane, 14th fl., New York, NY 10038
212-269-0711, e-mail ussammla@ix.netcom.com
World Wide Web http://uss-ammla.com

Object

Provides ship and shore library service for American-flag merchant vessels, the Military Sealift Command, the U.S. Coast Guard, and other waterborne operations of the U.S. government. Established 1921.

Officers (2005–2006)

Pres. Talmage E. Simpkins; *Chair, Executive Committee* Edward R. Morgan; *V.P.s* John M. Bowers, Capt. Timothy A. Brown, James Capo, David Cockroft, Ron Davis, Capt. Remo Di Fiore, John Halas, Sakae Idemoto, Rene Lioeanjie, Michael R. McKay, George E. Murphy, Capt. Gregorio Oca, Michael Sacco, John J. Sweeney; *Secy.* Donald E. Kadlac; *Treas.* William D. Potts; *Gen. Counsel* John L. DeGurse, Jr.; *Exec. Dir.* Roger T. Korner.

American Society for Information Science and Technology

Executive Director, Richard B. Hill
1320 Fenwick Lane, Ste. 510, Silver Spring, MD 20910
301-495-0900, fax 301-495-0810, e-mail asis@asis.org
World Wide Web http://www.asis.org

Object

The American Society for Information Science and Technology (ASIS&T) provides a forum for the discussion, publication, and critical analysis of work dealing with the design, management, and use of information, information systems, and information technology.

Membership

Memb. (Indiv.) 3,500; (Student) 800; (Inst.) 250. Dues (Indiv.) $140; (Student) $40; (Inst.) $650 and $800.

Officers

Pres. Michael Leach, Harvard Univ.; *Pres.-Elect* Edie Rasmussen, Univ. of British Columbia; *Treas.* June Lester, Oklahoma Univ.; *Past Pres.* Nicholas J. Belkin, Rutgers Univ.

Address correspondence to the executive director.

Board of Directors

Dirs.-at-Large Marianne Afifi, Suzie Allard, Carol Barry, Donald Case, Vicki Gregory, Gail Hodge, Beata Panagopoulos, Dietmar

Wolfram; *Deputy Dirs.* Pascal Calarco, Amy Wallace; *Exec. Dir.* Richard B. Hill.

Publications

Advances in Classification Research, vols. 1–10. Available from Information Today, Inc., 143 Old Marlton Pike, Medford, NJ 08055.

Annual Review of Information Science and Technology. Available from Information Today, Inc.

ASIS Thesaurus of Information Science and Librarianship. Available from Information Today, Inc.

Bulletin of the American Society for Information Science and Technology. Available from ASIS&T.

Editorial Peer Review: Its Strengths and Weaknesses by Ann C. Weller. Available from Information Today, Inc.

Electronic Publishing: Applications and Implications. Eds. Elisabeth Logan and Myke Gluck. Available from Information Today, Inc.

Evaluating Networked Information Services: Techniques, Policy and Issues by Charles R. McClure and John Carlo Bertot. Available from Information Today, Inc.

From Print to Electronic: The Transformation of Scientific Communication. Susan Y. Crawford, Julie M. Hurd, and Ann C. Weller. Available from Information Today, Inc.

Historical Studies in Information Science. Eds. Trudi Bellardo Hahn and Michael Buckland. Available from Information Today, Inc.

Information Management for the Intelligent Organization: The Art of Environmental Scanning, 2nd edition, by Chun Wei Choo, Univ. of Toronto. Available from Information Today, Inc.

Intelligent Technologies in Library and Information Service Applications by F. W. Lancaster and Amy Warner. Available from Information Today, Inc.

Introductory Concepts in Information Science by Melanie J. Norton. Available from Information Today, Inc.

Journal of the American Society for Information Science and Technology. Available from John Wiley and Sons, 605 Third Ave., New York, NY 10016.

Knowledge Management for the Information Professional. Eds. T. Kanti Srikantaiah and Michael Koenig. Available from Information Today, Inc.

Knowledge Management: The Bibliography. Compiled by Paul Burden. Available from Information Today, Inc.

Proceedings of ASIS&T Annual Meetings. Available from Information Today, Inc.

Scholarly Publishing: The Electronic Frontier. Eds. Robin P. Peek and Gregory B. Newby. Available from MIT Press, Cambridge, Massachusetts.

Statistical Methods for the Information Professional by Liwen Vaughan. Available from Information Today, Inc.

Studies in Multimedia. Eds. Susan Stone and Michael Buckland. Based on the Proceedings of the 1991 ASIS Mid-Year Meeting. Available from Information Today, Inc.

The Web of Knowledge: A Festschrift in Honor of Eugene Garfield. Eds. Blaise Cronin and Helen Barsky Atkins. Available from Information Today, Inc.

Committee Chairpersons

Awards and Honors. Stephanie Wright.
Budget and Finance. June Lester.
Constitution and Bylaws. K. T. Vaughan.
Education. To be announced.
Leadership Development. Allison Brueckner.
Membership. Kris Liberman.
Nominations. Nicholas Belkin.
Standards. Gail Thornburg.

American Theological Library Association

300 S. Wacker Dr., Ste. 1200, Chicago, IL 60606-5889
Tel. 888-665-2852, 312-454-5100, fax 312-454-5505
E-mail atla@atla.com
World Wide Web http://www.atla.com/atlahome.html

Mission Statement

The mission of the American Theological Library Association (ATLA) is to foster the study of theology and religion by enhancing the development of theological and religious libraries and librarianship. In pursuit of this mission, the association undertakes

• To foster the professional growth of its members, and to enhance their ability to serve their constituencies as administrators and librarians

• To advance the profession of theological librarianship, and to assist theological librarians in defining and interpreting the proper role and function of libraries in theological education

• To promote quality library and information services in support of teaching, learning, and research in theology, religion, and related disciplines and to create such tools and aids (including publications) as may be helpful in accomplishing this

• To stimulate purposeful collaboration among librarians of theological libraries and religious studies collections, and to develop programmatic solutions to information-related problems common to those librarians and collections

Membership

(Inst.) 265; (International Inst.) 13; (Indiv.) 492; (Student) 67; (Lifetime) 90; (Affiliates) 71.

Officers (2004–2007)

Pres. Christine Wenderoth, JKM Lib., 1100 E. 55 St., Chicago, IL 60615. Tel. 773-256-0735, fax 773-256-0737, e-mail cwendero@lstc.edu; *V.P.* Duane Harbin, Bridwell Lib., Southern Methodist Univ., P.O. Box 750133, Dallas, TX 75275-0133. Tel. 214-768-2663, fax 214-213-2117; *Secy.* Roberta A. Schaafsma, Duke Univ. Divinity School Lib., Box 90972, Durham, NC 27708-0972. Tel. 919-660-3491; fax 919-681-7594; *Past Pres.* Paul F. Stuehrenberg, Yale Univ. Divinity School Lib., 409 Prospect St., New Haven, CT 06511. Tel. 203-432-5292, fax 203-432-3906, e-mail paul.stuehrenberg@yale.edu; *Exec. Dir.* Dennis A. Norlin, American Theological Lib. Assn., 300 S. Wacker Drive, Ste. 1200, Chicago, IL 60606-5889. Tel. 312-454-5100, fax 312-454-5505, e-mail dnorlin@atla.com.

Board of Directors

Officers; William B. Badke, Assoc. Canadian Theological Schools Lib.; Eileen Crawford, Vanderbilt Univ. Divinity Lib.; Howertine L. Farrell Duncan, Wesley Theological Seminary Lib.; M. Patrick Graham, Pitts Theology Lib., Emory Univ.; Paula Hamilton, Sanctuary for Sacred Arts; James C. Pakala, Covenant Theological Seminary; Marsha Lund Smalley, Yale Univ. Divinity School Lib.; David R. Stewart, Luther Seminary Lib.

Publications

ATLA Indexes in MARC Format (2 a year).

ATLA Religion Database on CD-ROM, 1949–.
ATLA Religion Database: Ten Year Subset on CD-ROM, 1993–.
Biblical Studies on CD-ROM (ann.).
Catholic Periodical and Literature Index on CD-ROM (ann.).
Index to Book Reviews in Religion (ann.).

Newsletter (q.; memb.; nonmemb. $50). *Ed.* Jonathan West.
Old Testment Abstracts on CD-ROM (ann.).
Proceedings (ann.; memb.; nonmemb. $50). *Ed.* Jonathan West.
Religion Index One: Periodicals (2 a year).
Research in Ministry: An Index to Doctor of Ministry Project Reports (ann.), and online.

Archivists and Librarians in the History of the Health Sciences

President, Lilla Vekerdy
Rare Book Librarian, Bernard Becker Medical Library
Washington University School of Medicine
660 S. Euclid Ave., St. Louis, MO 63110
314-362-4235, e-mail vekerdyl@wustl.edu
World Wide Web http://www.library.ucla.edu/libraries/biomed/alhhs

Object

This association was established exclusively for educational purposes to serve the professional interests of librarians, archivists, and other specialists actively engaged in the librarianship of the history of the health sciences by promoting the exchange of information and by improving the standards of service.

Membership

Memb. 170. Dues $15 (Americas), $21 (other countries).

Officers (May 2005–May 2006)

Pres. Lilla Vekerdy; *Secy.-Treas.* Patricia Gallagher, special project coord., New York Academy of Medicine, 1216 Fifth Ave., New York, NY 10029. Tel. 212-822-7324, fax 212-423-0266, e-mail pgallagher@nyam.org.

Publication

The Watermark (q.; memb.). *Co-Eds.* Linda Lohr, History of Medicine Collection, Health Sciences Lib., Univ. of Buffalo, B5 Abbott Hall, 3455 Main St., Buffalo, NY 14214-3002. Tel. 716-829-3900 ext. 136, fax 716-829-2211, e-mail lalohr@buffalo.edu; Eric v.d. Luft, SUNY Upstate Medical Univ., Health Sciences Lib., 766 Irving Ave. Syracuse, NY 13210. Tel. 315-464-4585, e-mail lifte@upstate.edu.

ARMA International–The Association for Information Management Professionals

Executive Director/CEO, Peter R. Hermann
13725 W. 109 St., Ste. 101, Lenexa, KS 66215
800-422-2762, 913-341-3808, fax 913-341-3742
E-mail hq@arma.org, World Wide Web http://www.arma.org

Object

To advance the practice of records and information management as a discipline and a profession; to organize and promote programs of research, education, training, and networking within that profession; to support the enhancement of professionalism of the membership; and to promote cooperative endeavors with related professional groups.

Membership

Annual dues $150 for international affiliation. Chapter dues vary.

Officers (July 2005–June 2006)

Pres. Cheryl L. Pederson, Cargill, Inc., P.O. Box 5716, Minneapolis, NM 55440-5716. Tel. 952-742-6363, e-mail cheryl_pederson @cargill.com; *Pres.-Elect* Susan McKinney, dir., records and info. mgt., Univ. of Minnesota, 502 Morrill Hall, 100 Church St. S.E., Minneapolis MN 55455. Tel. 612-625-3497, e-mail susanmckinney@mail.ogc.

umn.edu; *Chair* David McDermott, J. R. Simplot Co., 5369 Irving St., Boise, ID 83706. Tel. 208-327-3209, e-mail dave. mcdermott@simplot.com; *Treas.* Fred A. Pulzello, Morgan Stanley, 180 Varick St., New York, NY 10014. Tel. 917-606-8423, e-mail fred.pulzello@morganstanley.com; *Dirs.* Douglas Allen. E-mail doug.allen@ eistream.com; Sonia A. Black. E-mail sa black@uwimona.edu.jm; William S. Gaskill. E-mail wsgaskill@jonesday.com; Steven Gray. E-mail steve_gray@wvi.org; Dianne Hagan. E-mail dianne.hagan@carrier.utc .com; Deborah Marshall. E-mail deborah. marshall@pb.com; Bonnie Nadler. E-mail bonnien_crm@msn.com; John T. Phillips. E-mail john@infotechdecisions.com; Roberta Shaffer. E-mail rsha@loc.gov; Marry-Ellyn Strauser. E-mail Marry-Ellyn.Strauser@ shawinc.com; Judy Tyler. E-mail judy.tyler@ cen.amedd.army.mil; Richard Weinholdt. E-mail rweinholdt@shaw.cam.

Publication

Information Management Journal. Ed. Jody Becker.

Art Libraries Society of North America (ARLIS/NA)

Executive Director, Elizabeth Clarke
329 March Rd., Ste. 232, Box 11, Ottawa, ON K2K 2E1, Canada
800-817-0621, fax 613-599-7027, e-mail eclarke@igs.net
World Wide Web http://www.arlisna.org

Object

To foster excellence in art librarianship and visual resources curatorship for the advancement of the visual arts. Established 1972.

Membership

Memb. 1,100. Dues (Inst./Business Affiliate) $145; (Indiv.) $85; (Student) $45; (Retired/ Unemployed) $45; (Sustaining) $250; (Sponsor) $500; (Overseas) $65. Year. Jan. 1–Dec. 31. Membership is open to all those interested in visual librarianship, whether they be professional librarians, students, library assistants, art book publishers, art book dealers, art historians, archivists, architects, slide and photograph curators, or retired associates in these fields.

Officers

Pres. Margaret Webster, Knight Visual Resources Facility, B-56 Sibley Hall, Cornell Univ., Ithaca, NY 14853-0001. Tel. 607-255-3300, fax 607-255-1900, e-mail mnw3@ cornell.edu; *V.P./Pres.-Elect* Ann Baird Whiteside, Fine Arts Lib., Fiske Kimball Lib., Univ. of Virginia, P.O. Box 400131, Charlottesville, VA 22904-4131. Tel. 434-924-6601, fax 434-982-2678, e-mail awhiteside@virginia.edu; *Secy.* Eumie Imm-Stroukoff, Research Center, Georgia O'Keefe Museum, 217 Johnson St., Santa Fe, NM 87501. Tel. 505-946-1011, fax 505-9461093, e-mail eumie@okeefemuseum.org; *Treas.* Lynda White, Alderman Lib., Univ. of Virginia, P.O. Box 400114, Charlottesville, VA 22904-4114. Tel. 434-924-3240, fax 434-924-1431, e-mail lsw6y@virginia.edu; *Past Pres.* Jeanne Brown, Architecture Studies Lib., Univ. of Nevada–Las Vegas, Box 45-4049, Las Vegas, NV 89154-4049. Tel. 702-895-4369, fax 702-895-1975, e-mail jeanneb

@unlv.nevada.edu; *Assoc. Admin.* Vicky Roper, ARLIS/NA, 329 March Rd., Ste. 232, Box 11, Ottawa, ON K2K 2E1, Canada. Tel. 800-817-0621, fax 613-599-7027, e-mail vicky@mcphersonclarke.com.

Address correspondence to the executive director.

Publications

ARLIS/NA Update (bi-mo.; memb.).
Art Documentation (2 a year; memb., subscription).
Handbook and List of Members (ann.; memb.).
Occasional Papers (price varies).
Miscellaneous others (request current list from headquarters).

Committee Chairpersons

ARLIS/NA and VRA Summer Educational Institute for Visual Resources and Image Management. Karin Whalen, Trudy Jacoby.
Awards. Daniel Starr.
Cataloging Advisory. Kay Teel.
Development. Kim Collins, Allen Townsend.
Distinguished Service Award. Barbara Polowy.
Diversity. Vanessa Kam, Laurel Bliss.
Finance. Phil Heagy.
International Relations. Hugh Wilburn.
Membership. Janine Henri.
Gerd Muehsam Award. Jeff Ross.
Nominating. Deborah Kempe.
Professional Development. Heidi Hass.
Public Policy. Tim Shipe, Cara List.
Publications. Jack Robertson.
Research Awards. John Hagood, Terry Wilson.
Standards. Donald Juedes.
Strategic Planning. Leslie Abrams, Lucie Stylianopoulos.
Travel Awards. Kitty Chibnik, Nensi Brailo.
George Wittenborn Award. Barbara Prior.

Asian/Pacific American Librarians Association (APALA)

Executive Director, Gary Colmenar
World Wide Web http://www.apalaweb.org

Object

To provide a forum for discussing problems and concerns of Asian/Pacific American librarians; to provide a forum for the exchange of ideas by Asian/Pacific American librarians and other librarians; to support and encourage library services to Asian/Pacific American communities; to recruit and support Asian/Pacific American librarians in the library/information science professions; to seek funding for scholarships in library/information science programs for Asian/Pacific Americans; and to provide a vehicle whereby Asian/Pacific American librarians can cooperate with other associations and organizations having similar or allied interests. Founded 1980; incorporated 1981; affiliated with American Library Association 1982.

Membership

Open to all librarians and information specialists of Asian/Pacific descent working in U.S. libraries and information centers and other related organizations, and to others who support the goals and purposes of APALA. Asian/Pacific Americans are defined as those who consider themselves Asian/Pacific Americans. They may be Americans of Asian/Pacific descent, Asian/Pacific people with the status of permanent residency, or Asian/Pacific people living in the United States. Dues (Inst.) $50; (Indiv.) $20; (Students/Unemployed Librarians) $10.

Officers (July 2005–June 2006)

Pres. Ganga Dakshinamurti, Univ. of Manitoba Lib., Winnipeg. E-mail ganga_dakshinamurti@umanitoba.ca; *V.P./Pres.-Elect* Vacant; *Secy.* Joy Chase. E-mail joy.chase@evc.edu; *Treas.* Buenaventura ("Ven") Basco. E-mail bbasco@mail.ucf.edu; *Past Pres.* Heawon Paick. E-mail hwpaick@netscape.net.

Publication

APALA Newsletter (q.).

Committee Chairs

Awards Committee. Dora Ho, Cathy Lu.
Constitution and Bylaws. Thaddeus Bejnar.
Finance. Buenaventura Basco.
Membership and Recruitment. Mohoko Hosoi.
Newsletter and Publications. Kenneth Yamashita.
Nomination. Gary Colmenar.
Program. Heawon Paick.
Publicity. Smiti Gandhi.
Scholarship. Sandy Wee.
Web. May Chang.

AIIM—The Enterprise Content Management Association

President, John F. Mancini
1100 Wayne Ave., Ste. 1100, Silver Spring, MD 20910
800-477-2446, 301-587-8202, fax 301-587-2711
E-mail aiim@aiim.org, World Wide Web http://www.aiim.org
European Office: The IT Centre, 8 Canalside, Lowesmoor Wharf, Worcester WR1 2RR,
England. Tel. 44-1905-727600, fax 44-1905-727609, e-mail info@aiim.org.uk.

Object

AIIM is an international authority on enterprise content management, the tools and technologies that capture, manage, store, preserve, and deliver content in support of business processes. Founded 1943 as the Association for Information and Image Management.

Officers

Chair Larry Wischerth, TIAA-CREF; *V. Chair* Don McMahan, Visioneer Inc.; *Treas.* Baron Gemmer, Innovative Corporate Solutions; *Past Chair* A. J. Hyland, Hyland Software.

Publication

AIIM E-DOC Magazine (bi-mo.; memb.).

Association for Library and Information Science Education

Executive Director, Deborah York
1055 Commerce Park Drive, Tech Center 1, Oak Ridge, TN 37830
Tel. 865-425-0155, fax 865-481-0390, e-mail contact@alise.org
World Wide Web http://www.alise.org

Object

The Association for Library and Information Science Education (ALISE) is devoted to the advancement of knowledge and learning in the interdisciplinary field of information studies. Established 1915.

Membership

Memb. 500. January–December. Any library/information science school with a program accredited by the ALA Committee on Accreditation may become an institutional member. Any school that offers a graduate degree in librarianship or a cognate field but whose program is not accredited by the ALA Committee on Accreditation may become an institutional member at a lower rate. Any school outside the United States and Canada offering a program comparable to that of institutional membership may become an international affiliate institutional member. Any organizational entity wishing to support LIS education may become an associate institutional member. Any faculty member, administrator, librarian, researcher, or other individual employed full time may become a personal member. Any retired or part-time faculty member, student, or other individual employed less than full time may become a personal member. Any student may become a member at a lower rate.

Officers (2006–2007)

Pres. John Budd, Univ. of Missouri–Columbia. E-mail buddj@missouri.edu; *Pres.-Elect* Connie Van Fleet, Univ. of Oklahoma. E-mail cvanfleet@ou.edu; *Secy.-Treas.* Lisa

Given, Univ. of Alberta. E-mail given@
ualberta.ca; *Past Pres.* Ken Haycock, San
Jose State Univ. E-mail khaycock@slis.sjsu.
edu.

Directors

Officers; Gloria Leckie, Univ. of Western
Ontario; Heidi Julian, Univ. of Alberta; Julie
Hersberger, Univ. of North Carolina–Greens-
boro.

Publications

*ALISE Library and Information Science Edu-
cation Statistical Report* (ann.; $65).
*Journal of Education for Library and Infor-
mation Science* (4 a year; $150; foreign

$175).
Membership Directory (ann.; $40).
*Directory of LIS Programs and Faculty in the
United States and Canada* (ann.; $50).

Committee Chairpersons

Awards and Honors. Mark Winston.
Budget and Finance. Lisa Given.
Conference Planning. Michele Besant, Melis-
sa Gross.
Governance. Ken Haycock.
International Relations. Susan Higgins.
Membership. John Agada.
Nominating. Bernie Sloan.
Publications. Christine Pawley.
Recruitment. Lynda Baker.
Research. Lynne McKechnie.

Association of Academic Health Sciences Libraries

Executive Director, Shirley Bishop
2150 N. 107 St., Ste. 205, Seattle, WA 98133
206-367-8704, fax 206-367-8777
E-mail aahsl@sbims.com, World Wide Web http://www.aahsl.org

Object

The Association of Academic Health Sciences Libraries (AAHSL) is composed of the
directors of libraries of more than 140 accredited U.S. and Canadian medical schools
belonging to the Association of American
Medical Colleges. Its goals are to promote
excellence in academic health science libraries
and to ensure that the next generation of
health practitioners is trained in information-
seeking skills that enhance the quality of
healthcare delivery, education, and research.
Founded 1977.

Membership

Memb. 140+. Regular membership is available to nonprofit educational institutions
operating a school of health sciences that has

full or provisional accreditation by the Association of American Medical Colleges. Regular members shall be represented by the chief
administrative officer of the member institution's health sciences library. Associate
membership (and nonvoting representation)
is available at $600 to organizations having
an interest in the purposes and activities of
the association.

Officers (2005–2006)

Pres. Logan Ludwig, Medical Center Lib.,
Loyola Univ.; *Pres.-Elect* Elaine Martin,
Lamar Soutter Lib., Univ. of Massachusetts;
Secy.-Treas. Ruth Riley, School of Medicine
Lib., Univ. of South Carolina; *Past Pres.* J.
Michael Homan, Mayo Medical Lib., Mayo
Foundation.

Association of Independent Information Professionals (AIIP)

8550 United Plaza Blvd., Ste. 1001, Baton Rouge, LA 70809
225-408-4400, fax 225-922-4611, e-mail info@aiip.org
World Wide Web http://www.aiip.org

Object

AIIP's members are owners of firms providing such information-related services as online and manual research, document delivery, database design, library support, consulting, writing, and publishing. The objectives of the association are

- To advance the knowledge and understanding of the information profession
- To promote and maintain high professional and ethical standards among its members
- To encourage independent information professionals to assemble to discuss common issues
- To promote the interchange of information among independent information professionals and various organizations
- To keep the public informed of the profession and of the responsibilities of the information professional

Membership

Memb. 650+.

Officers (2005–2006)

Pres. Jodi Gregory, Access Information Services. Tel. 937-439-0418, e-mail access@access-inform.com; *Pres.-Elect* Crystal Sharp, Sharp Information Systems, Ltd. Tel. 519-495-2889; *Secy.* Debbie Wynot, Library Consultants. Tel. 504-885-5926; *Treas.* Theresa Buiel, ThinkLink. Tel. 781-963-2251.

Publications

Connections (q.).
Membership Directory (ann.).
Professional Paper series.

Association of Jewish Libraries (AJL)

c/o NFJC, 330 Seventh Ave., 21st fl., New York, NY 10001
212-725-5359, e-mail ajlibs@osu.edu
World Wide Web http://www.jewishlibraries.org

Object

Mission

The Association of Jewish Libraries promotes Jewish literacy through enhancement of libraries and library resources and through leadership for the profession and practitioners of Judaica librarianship. The association fosters access to information, learning, teaching, and research relating to Jews, Judaism, the Jewish experience, and Israel.

Goals

- Maintain high professional standards for Judaica librarians and recruit qualified individuals into the profession
- Facilitate communication and exchange of information on a global scale
- Encourage quality publication in the field in all formats and media

- Stimulate publication of high-quality children's literature
- Facilitate and encourage establishment of Judaica library collections
- Enhance information access for all through application of advanced technologies
- Publicize the organization and its activities in all relevant venues
- Stimulate awareness of Judaica library services among the public at large
- Promote recognition of Judaica librarianship within the wider library profession
- Encourage recognition of Judaica library services by other organizations and related professions
- Ensure continuity of the association through sound management, financial security, effective governance, and a dedicated and active membership

Membership

Memb. 1,400. Dues $50; (Student/Retired) $30. Year. July 1–June 30.

Officers (July 2004–June 2006)

Pres. Ronda Rose, Kosofsky Lib., Temple Emanuel, Beverly Hills; *V.P./Pres.-Elect* Laurel Wolfson, Hebrew Union College; *V.P. Memb.* Joseph Galron, Ohio State Univ., Columbus; *V.P. Publications* Elana Gensler, Hebrew Academy of Long Beach (New York); *Treas.* Schlomit Schwartzer, Univ. of Miami; *Recording Secy.* Susan Dubin, Off-the-Shelf Lib. Services; *Corresponding Secy.* Noreen Wachs, Ramaz Middle School, New York; *Past Pres.* Pearl Berger, Yeshiva Univ. Libs., New York.

Address correspondence to the association.

Publications

AJL Newsletter (q.). *Ed.* Libby K. White. Baltimore Hebrew Univ., 5800 Park Heights Ave., Baltimore, MD 21215

Judaica Librarianship (irreg.). *Ed.* Zachary M. Baker, Area Studies Resource Group, Green Lib., Stanford Univ., 557 Escondido Mall, Stanford, CA 94305.

Division Presidents

Research and Special Library. Peggy Pearlstein, Lib. of Congress.

Synagogue, School, and Center Libraries. Linda R. Silver, Jewish Education Center of Cleveland.

Association of Research Libraries

Executive Director, Duane E. Webster
21 Dupont Circle N.W., Ste. 800, Washington, DC 20036
202-296-2296, fax 202-872-0884
E-mail arlhq@arl.org, World Wide Web http://www.arl.org

Object

The Association of Research Libraries (ARL) influences the changing environment of scholarly communication and the public policies that affect research libraries and the communities they serve. ARL pursues this mission by advancing the goals of its member research libraries, providing leadership in public and information policy to the scholarly and higher education communities, fostering the exchange of ideas and expertise, and shaping a future environment that leverages its interests with those of allied organizations.

Membership

Memb. 123. Membership is institutional. Dues $20,750 for 2006.

Officers

Pres. Brian E. C. Schottlaender, Univ. of California–San Diego; *Pres.-Elect* Sherrie Schmidt, Arizona State Univ.; *Past Pres.* Ann Wolpert, MIT.

Board of Directors

Camila Alire, Univ. of New Mexico; Brinley Franklin, Univ. of Connecticut; Joyce Garnett, Univ. of Western Ontario; Marianne Gaunt, Rutgers Univ.; Tom Leonard, Univ. of California–Berkeley; Charles B. Lowry, Univ. of Maryland; Sherrie Schmidt, Arizona State Univ.; Brian E. C. Schottlaender, Univ. of California–San Diego; Suzanne Thorin, Indiana; Betsy Wilson, Univ. of Washington; Ann Wolpert, MIT; Jennifer Younger, Univ. of Notre Dame.

Publications

ARL: A Bimonthly Report on Research Libraries Issues and Actions from ARL, CNI, and SPARC (bi-mo.).
ARL Academic Health Sciences Library Statistics (ann.).
ARL Academic Law Library Statistics (ann.).
ARL Annual Salary Survey (ann.).
ARL Preservation Statistics (ann.).
ARL Statistics (ann.).
SPEC Kits (6 a year).

Committee and Work Group Chairpersons

ACLS Cyberinfrastructure Report Task Force. Karin Wittenborg, Univ. of Virginia.

Finance. Ann Wolpert, MIT.

New Ways of Measuring Collections Task Force. Brinley Franklin, Univ. of Connecticut.

Membership. Paula Kaufman, Illinois at Urbana-Champaign.

Public Policies Affecting Research Libraries. Winston Tabb, Johns Hopkins.

Research, Teaching, and Learning. Betsy Wilson, Univ. of Washington.

Scholarly Communication. Carol Mandel, New York Univ.

Special Collections Task Force. Joe Hewitt, Univ. of North Carolina.

Statistics and Assessment. Colleen Cook, Texas A&M.

Digitizing Government Document Collections Working Group. Kenneth Frazier, Wisconsin–Madison.

ARL Membership

Nonuniversity Libraries

Boston Public Lib., Canada Inst. for Scientific and Technical Info., Center for Research Libs., Lib. of Congress, Lib. and Archives Canada, National Agricultural Lib., National Lib. of Medicine, New York Public Lib., New York State Lib., Smithsonian Institution Libs.

University Libraries

Alabama, Alberta, Arizona, Arizona State, Auburn, Boston College, Boston Univ., Brigham Young, British Columbia, Brown, California–Berkeley, California–Davis, California–Irvine, California–Los Angeles, California–Riverside, California–San Diego, California–Santa Barbara, Case Western Reserve, Chicago, Cincinnati, Colorado, Colorado State, Columbia, Connecticut, Cornell, Dartmouth, Delaware, Duke, Emory, Florida, Florida State, George Washington, Georgetown, Georgia, Georgia Inst. of Technology, Guelph, Harvard, Hawaii, Houston, Howard, Illinois–Chicago, Illinois–Urbana-Champaign, Indiana, Iowa, Iowa State, Johns Hopkins, Kansas, Kent State, Kentucky, Laval, Louisiana State, Louisville, McGill, McMaster, Manitoba, Maryland, Massachusetts, Massachusetts Inst. of Technology, Miami (Florida), Michigan, Michigan State, Minnesota, Missouri, Montreal, Nebraska–Lincoln, New Mexico, New York, North Carolina, North Carolina State, Northwestern, Notre Dame, Ohio, Ohio State, Oklahoma, Oklahoma State, Oregon, Pennsylvania, Pennsylvania State, Pittsburgh, Princeton, Purdue, Queen's (Kingston, Ontario, Canada), Rice, Rochester, Rutgers, Saskatchewan, South Carolina, Southern California, Southern Illinois, SUNY–Albany, SUNY–Buffalo, SUNY–Stony Brook, Syracuse, Temple, Tennessee, Texas, Texas A&M, Texas Tech, Toronto, Tulane, Utah, Vanderbilt, Virginia, Virginia Tech, Washington, Washington (Saint Louis, Missouri), Washington State, Waterloo, Wayne State, Western Ontario, Wisconsin, Yale, York.

Association of Vision Science Librarians

Chair 2004–2006, Pamela C. Sieving
National Institutes of Health Library, 10 Center Drive, Rm. 1L09G,
Bethesda, MD 20892-1150
301 451-5862, e-mail PamSieving@nih.gov
World Wide Web http://spectacle.berkeley.edu/~library/AVSL.HTM

Object

To foster collective and individual acquisition and dissemination of vision science information, to improve services for all persons seeking such information, and to develop standards for libraries to which members are attached. Founded 1968.

Membership

Memb. (U.S.) 85; (Foreign) 35.

Publications

Core List of Audio-Visual Related Serials.

Guidelines for Vision Science Libraries.

Opening Day Book, Journal and AV Collection—Visual Science.

Ph.D. Theses in Physiological Optics (irreg.).

Publication Considerations in the Age of Electronic Opportunities.

Standards for Vision Science Libraries.

Union List of Vision-Related Serials (irreg.).

Meetings

Annual meeting held in December in connection with the American Academy of Optometry; midyear mini-meeting with the Medical Library Association.

Beta Phi Mu
(International Library and Information Studies Honor Society)

Executive Director, Wayne Wiegand
College of Information, Florida State University, Tallahassee, FL 32306-2100
850-644-3907, fax 850-644-9763
E-mail beta_phi_mu@ci.fsu.edu
World Wide Web http://www.beta-phi-mu.org

Object

To recognize and encourage scholastic achievement among library and information studies students and to sponsor appropriate professional and scholarly projects. Founded at the University of Illinois in 1948.

Membership

Memb. 23,000. Open to graduates of library school programs accredited by the American Library Association who fulfill the following requirements: complete the course requirements leading to a fifth year or other advanced degree in librarianship with a scholastic average of 3.75 where A equals 4 points (this provision shall also apply to planned programs of advanced study beyond the fifth year that do not culminate in a degree but that require full-time study for one or more academic years) and in the top 25 percent of their class; receive a letter of recommendation from their respective library schools attesting to their demonstrated fitness for successful professional careers.

Officers

Pres. Anna Perrault, Univ. of South Florida, 4202 Fowler Ave. E., CIS 1040, Tampa, FL 33620-7800; *Exec. Dir.* Wayne Wiegand, College of Information, Florida State Univ., Tallahassee, FL 32306-2100. Tel. 850-644-3907, fax 850-644-9763, e-mail beta_phi_mu @lis.fsu.edu.

Directors

Nicholas C. Burckel, Michael Carpenter, Timothy Sineath, Danny P. Wallace, Blanche Woolls.

Publications

Beta Phi Mu Monograph Series. Book-length scholarly works based on original research in subjects of interest to library and information professionals. Available from Greenwood Press, 88 Post Rd. W., Box 5007, Westport, CT 06881-9990.

Chapbook Series. Limited editions on topics of interest to information professionals.

Newsletter. (Electronic only). *Ed.* Harla J. Frank.

Chapters

Alpha. Univ. of Illinois, Grad. School of Lib. and Info. Science; *Beta.* (Inactive) Univ. of Southern California, School of Lib. Science; *Gamma.* Florida State Univ., School of Lib. and Info. Studies; *Delta.* (Inactive) Loughborough College of Further Educ., School of Libnship., Loughborough, England; *Epsilon.* Univ. of North Carolina, School of Lib. Science; *Zeta.* Atlanta Univ., School of Lib. and Info. Studies; *Theta.* Pratt Inst., Grad. School of Lib. and Info. Science; *Iota.* Catholic Univ. of America, School of Lib. and Info. Science; Univ. of Maryland, College of Lib. and Info. Services; *Kappa.* (Inactive). Western Michigan Univ., School of Libnship.; *Lambda.* Univ. of Oklahoma, School of Lib. Science; *Mu.* Univ. of Michigan, School of Lib. Science; *Xi.* Univ. of Hawaii, Grad. School of Lib. Studies; *Omicron.* Rutgers Univ., Grad. School of Lib. and Info. Studies; *Pi.* Univ. of Pittsburgh, School of Lib. and Info. Science; *Rho.* Kent State Univ., School of Lib. Science; *Sigma.* Drexel Univ., School of Lib. and Info. Science; *Tau.* (Inactive). State Univ. of New York at Genesee, School of Lib. and Info. Science; *Upsilon.* (Inactive). Univ. of Kentucky, College of Lib. Science;

Phi. Univ. of Denver, Grad. School of Libn-ship. and Info. Mgt.; *Chi.* Indiana Univ., School of Lib. and Info. Science; *Psi.* Univ. of Missouri at Columbia, School of Lib. and Info. Sciences; *Omega.* (Inactive). San Jose State Univ., Div. of Lib. Science; *Beta Alpha.* Queens College, City College of New York, Grad. School of Lib. and Info. Studies; *Beta Beta.* Simmons College, Grad. School of Lib. and Info. Science; *Beta Delta.* State Univ. of New York at Buffalo, School of Info. and Lib. Studies; *Beta Epsilon.* Emporia State Univ., School of Lib. Science; *Beta Zeta.* Louisiana State Univ., Grad. School of Lib. Science; *Beta Eta.* Univ. of Texas at Austin, Grad. School of Lib. and Info. Science; *Beta Theta.* (Inactive). Brigham Young Univ., School of Lib. and Info. Science; *Beta Iota.* Univ. of Rhode Island, Grad. Lib. School; *Beta Kappa.* Univ. of Alabama, Grad. School of Lib. Service; *Beta Lambda.* North Texas State Univ., School of Lib. and Info. Science; Texas Woman's Univ., School of Lib. Science; *Beta Mu.* Long Island Univ., Palmer Grad. Lib. School; *Beta Nu.* Saint John's Univ., Div. of Lib. and Info. Science; *Beta Xi.* North Carolina Central Univ., School of Lib. Science; *Beta Omicron.* (Inactive) Univ. of Tennessee at Knoxville, Grad. School of Lib. and Info. Science; *Beta Pi.* Univ. of Arizona, Grad. Lib. School; *Beta Rho.* Univ. of Wisconsin at Milwaukee, School of Lib. Science; *Beta Sigma.* (Inactive) Clarion State College, School of Lib. Science; *Beta Tau.* Wayne State Univ., Div. of Lib. Science; *Beta Upsilon.* (Inactive) Alabama A&M Univ., School of Lib. Media; *Beta Phi.* Univ. of South Florida, Grad. Dept. of Lib., Media, and Info. Studies; *Beta Psi.* Univ. of Southern Mississippi, School of Lib. Service; *Beta Omega.* Univ. of South Carolina, College of Libnship.; *Beta Beta Alpha.* Univ. of California at Los Angeles, Grad. School of Lib. and Info. Science; *Beta Beta Gamma.* Rosary College, Grad. School of Lib. and Info. Science; *Beta Beta Delta.* Univ. of Cologne, Germany; *Beta Beta Epsilon.* Univ. of Wisconsin at Madison, Lib. School; *Beta Beta Zeta.* Univ. of North Carolina at Greensboro, Dept. of Lib. Science and Educational Technology; *Beta Beta Theta.* Univ. of Iowa, School of Lib. and Info. Science; *Beta Beta Iota.* State Univ. of New York, Univ. at Albany, School of Info. Science and Policy; *Beta Beta Kappa.* Univ. of Puerto Rico Grad. School of Info. Sciences and Technologies; *Pi Lambda Sigma.* Syracuse Univ., School of Info. Studies.

Bibliographical Society of America

Executive Secretary, Michèle E. Randall
Box 1537, Lenox Hill Station, New York, NY 10021
212-452-2710 (tel./fax), e-mail bsa@bibsocamer.org
World Wide Web http://www.bibsocamer.org

Object

To promote bibliographical research and to issue bibliographical publications. Organized 1904.

Membership

Memb. 1,200. Dues $65. Year. Jan.–Dec.

Officers

Pres. John Bidwell. E-mail jbidwell@morgan library.org; *V.P.* Irene Tichenor. E-mail itichenor@earthlink.net; *Secy.* David R. Whitesell. E-mail whitesel@fas.harvard.edu; *Treas.* R. Dyke Benjamin. E-mail dyke. benjamin@lazard.com.

Council

(2006) Susan M. Allen, John N. Hoover, Mark S. Lasner, Bruce Whiteman; (2007) Eric Holzenberg, Hope Mayo, Justin G. Schiller, Arthur L. Schwarz.

Publication

Papers of the Bibliographical Society of America (q.; memb.). *Ed.* Trevor Howard-Hill, Thomas Cooper Lib., Univ. of South Carolina, Columbia, SC 29208. Tel./fax 803-777-7046, e-mail RalphCrane@msn.com.

Black Caucus of the American Library Association (BCALA)

President, Andrew Jackson (Sekou Molefi Baako)
Executive Director, Langston Hughes Community Library Cultural Center
Queens Borough Public Library, 100-01 Northern Blvd., Corona, NY 11368
718 651-1100 ext. 210, fax 718 651-6258, e-mail andrew.p.jackson@queenslibrary.org,
World Wide Web http://www.bcala.org

Mission

The Black Caucus of the American Library Association serves as an advocate for the development, promotion, and improvement of library services and resources to the nation's African American community, and provides leadership for the recruitment and professional development of African American librarians. Founded in 1970.

Membership

Membership is open to any person, institution, or business interested in promoting the development of library and information services for African Americans and other people of African descent and willing to maintain good financial standing with the organization. The membership is currently composed of librarians and other information professionals, library support staff, libraries, publishers, authors, vendors, and other library-related organizations in the United States and abroad. Dues (Corporate) $200; (Institutional) $60; (Regular) $45; (Student) $10.

Officers

Pres. Andrew Jackson (Sekou Molefi Baako). E-mail andrew.p.jackson@queenslibrary.org; *V.P./Pres.-Elect* Wanda Brown. E-mail brownw@wfu.edu; *Secy.* Ira Revels. E-mail ir33@cornell.edu; *Treas.* Stanton F. Biddle. E-mail treasurer@bcala.org; *Past Pres.* Bobby Player. E-mail bplayer@howard.edu.

Executive Board

Rochelle Ballard, Trevor A. Dawes, Sharon K. Epps, George C. Grant, Emily Guss, Ernestine L. Hawkins, Jos N. Holman, Jennifer Lang, Rhea Brown Lawson, Karen Lemmons, Sibyl E. Moses, LeRoy Robinson, Karolyn S. Thompson, Roberta V. Webb, Lainey Westbrooks.

Publication

BCALA Newsletter. Managing Ed. Roland Barksdale-Hall, Ste. 1, 939 Baldwin Ave., Sharon, PA 16146. Tel. 724-346-0459, e-mail newsletter@bcala.org.

Committee Chairpersons

Affiliated Chapters. Sylvia Sprinkle Hamlin, Lainey Westbrooks.
Affirmative Action. Jane Moore McGinn, Howard F. McGinn.
ALA Relations. Gloria J. Leonard.
Awards. ayo dayo.
History. Reinette F. Jones, Sibyl E. Moses.

Budget/Audit. Jos N. Holman.

Constitution and Bylaws. Brenda Hunter, Rhea Brown Lawson.

E. J. Josey Scholarship. Rochelle Ballard, Michael C. Walker.

Fund Raising. Carolyn L. Garnes.

International Relations. Lavonda K. Broadnax, V. Tessa Perry.

John C. Tyson Memorial Scholarship. Em Claire Knowles.

Literary Awards. John Page.

Membership. Gladys Smiley Bell, Tiffeni Fontno.

Newsletter. Roland Barksdale-Hall, S. D. Harris.

Nominations/Elections. Bobby Player.

Programs. Wanda Brown.

Public Relations. Valerie Bell, Rose T. Dawson.

Recruitment and Professional Development. LeRoy ("Lee") LaFleur, Allison Sutton.

Services to Children of Families of African Descent. Khafre K. Abif, Karen Lemmons.

Technology Advisory. Ira Revels, H. Jamane Yeager.

Sixth National Conference. Richard Bradberry, Carolyn Norman.

Awards

BCALA Literary Awards.

E. J. Josey Scholarship Award.

DEMCO/ALA Black Caucus Award for Excellence in Librarianship.

BCALA Trailblazer's Award.

Distinguished Service Award.

John Tyson Award.

Smiley Student Fund.

Canadian Association for Information Science (CAIS) (Association Canadienne des Sciences de l'Information)

University of Toronto, Faculty of Info. Studies, Toronto, ON M5S 3G6
416-978-4666, fax 416-971-1399
World Wide Web http://www.cais-acsi.ca/home.htm

Object

To promote the advancement of information science in Canada and encourage and facilitate the exchange of information relating to the use, access, retrieval, organization, management, and dissemination of information.

Membership

Institutions and individuals interested in information science and involved in the gathering, organization, and dissemination of information (such as information scientists, archivists, librarians, computer scientists, documentalists, economists, educators, journalists, and psychologists) who support CAIS's objectives can become association members.

Dues (Inst.) $165; (Personal) $75; (Senior) $40; (Student) $25.

Directors

Pres. Lynne Howarth, Univ. of Toronto; *V.P.* Lisa Given, Univ. of Alberta; *Treas.* Donna Chan, Univ. of Western Ontario; *Dir.,* Communications Haidar Moukdad, Dalhousie Univ.; *Dir., Membership* Clément Arsenault, Univ. de Montréal; *Secy.* Kimiz Dalkir, McGill Univ.; *Past Pres.* Louise Spiteri, Dalhousie Univ.

Publication

Canadian Journal of Information and Library Science

Canadian Library Association (CLA)

Executive Director, Don Butcher
328 Frank St., Ottawa, ON K2P 0X8
613-232-9625 ext. 306, fax 613-563-9895
E-mail dbutcher@cla.ca, World Wide Web http://cla.ca

Object

CLA is its members' advocate and public voice, educator and network. It builds the Canadian library and information community by promoting, developing, and supporting library and information services and advancing today's information professionals, through cooperation with all who share its values. The association represents Canadian librarianship to the federal government and media, carries on international liaison with other library associations and cultural agencies, offers professional development programs, and supports such core library values as intellectual freedom and access to information, particularly for disadvantaged populations. Founded in 1946, CLA is a nonprofit voluntary organization governed by an elected executive council.

Membership

Memb. (Indiv.) 2,000; (Inst.) 460. Open to individuals, institutions, and groups interested in librarianship and in library and information services.

Officers

Pres. Barbara Clubb, chief libn., Ottawa Public Lib.; *V.P./Pres.-Elect* Linda Cook, dir., Edmonton Public Lib.; *Treas.* A. A. ("Sandy") Cameron.

Publications

Feliciter: Linking Canada's Information Professionals (6 a year; magazine/journal); *CLA Digest* (bi-weekly; electronic newsletter).

Divisions

Canadian Association of College and University Libraries (CACUL).

Canadian Association of Public Libraries (CAPL).

Canadian Association of Special Libraries and Information Services (CASLIS).

Canadian Library Trustees Association (CLTA).

Canadian Association for School Libraries (CASL).

Catholic Library Association

Executive Director, Jean R. Bostley, SSJ
100 North St., Ste. 224, Pittsfield, MA 01201-5109
413-443-2252, fax 413-442-2252, e-mail cla@cathla.org
World Wide Web http://www.cathla.org

Object

The promotion and encouragement of Catholic literature and library work through cooperation, publications, education, and information. Founded 1921.

Membership

Memb. 1,000. Dues $45–$300. Year. July–June.

Officers (2005–2007)

Pres. Kenneth O'Malley, CP, Paul Bechtold Lib., Catholic Theological Union, 5401 S. Cornell Ave., Chicago, IL 60615-5698. Tel. 772-753-5322, fax 773-753-5440, e-mail omalleyk@ctu.edu; *V.P./Pres.-Elect* Catherine M. Fennell, Gertrude Kistler Memorial Lib., Rosemont College, 1400 Montgomery Ave., Rosemont, PA 19010; *Past Pres.* M. Dorothy Neuhofer, OSB, St. Leo Univ., Box 6665 MC 2128, Saint Leo, FL 33574-6665. Tel. 352-588-8260, fax 352-588-8484, e-mail dorothy.neuhofer@saintleo.edu.

Address correspondence to the executive director.

Executive Board

Officers; Kathy C. Born, Public Lib. of Cincinnati and Hamilton County, Delhi Branch, 5095 Foley Rd., Cincinnati, OH 45238. E-mail kathyborn@peoplepc.com; John R. Edson, Hamburg Public Lib., 102 Buffalo St., Hamburg, NY 14075; Anne LeVeque, research libn., Washington, D.C. E-mail anne.leveque@gmail.com; Maxine C. Lucas, Harvard-Westlake Middle School, 700 N. Faring Rd., Los Angeles, CA 90077. E-mail maxine.lucas@sbcglobal.net; Malachy R. McCarthy, Claretian Missionaries Archives, 205 W. Monroe St., Chicago, IL 60606. E-mail malachy@claret.org; Annette B. Thibodeaux, Archbishop Chapelle H.S., 8800 Veterans Blvd., Metairie, LA 70003. E-mail jthibod885@aol.com.

Publications

Catholic Library World (q.; memb.; nonmemb. $60). *General Ed.* Mary E. Gallagher, SSJ; *Production Ed.* Allen Gruenke.
Catholic Periodical and Literature Index (*CLPI*) (q.; $400 calendar year; abridged ed., $125 calendar year; *CPLI* on CD-ROM, inquire). *Ed.* Kathleen Spaltro.

Center for the Study of Rural Librarianship

Department of Library Science, Clarion University of Pennsylvania,
840 Wood St., Clarion, PA 16214
Tel. 814-393-2014, fax 814-393-2150, e-mail vavrek@clarion.edu or csrl@clarion.edu
World Wide Web http://jupiter.clarion.edu/~csrl/csrlhom.htm

Object

The Center for the Study of Rural Librarianship (CSRL) is a research, publishing, consultative, and continuing education facility established in the Department of Library Science at Clarion University of Pennsylvania in 1978. CSRL is concerned with the development and use of information technology in rural communities. Its mission is to extend knowledge relative to the nature and role of rural and small libraries on a global basis. Its recent endeavors include library outreach and particularly bookmobile services in the United States and overseas.

Its objectives are

- To stimulate imaginative thinking relative to rural library services
- To identify problems endemic with library services—for those currently being served and those who are unserved
- To provide consultative services in designing new service patterns in rural libraries
- To conduct and/or coordinate research relative to identifiable library problems
- To stimulate continuing education
- To coordinate physical and human resources which could be lent to analyze library services
- To collect data relevant to the needs of rural libraries

Two virtual associations are part of CSRL: the Association of Rural and Small Libraries and the Association of Bookmobile and Outreach Services.

The Association of Rural and Small Libraries (http://arsl.clarion.edu) is comprised of libraries of all types including public, school, small urban branches, special and corporate, and small academic. The defining characteristics are a library with a limited budget and a diverse clientele. Librarians, support staff, governmental officials, trustees, friends of libraries, and professionals from other fields comprise this association, which has a membership of about 250. Officers of the association are *Pres.* Colleen Carney, *V.P.* Ken Davenport, and *Secy.-Treas.* Mary Pasek Williams.

The Association of Bookmobile and Outreach Services (http://abos.clarion.edu) encompasses libraries of all types. It also has a membership of about 250, made up of library administrators, support staff, governmental officials, trustees, friends of libraries, and professionals from other fields. Officers of the association are *Pres.* Marilyn Kaeckmeister, *V.P.* Jeannie Dilger-Hill, and *Secy.-Treas.* MaryAnne Marjama.

Both endeavors are supported by CSRL in cooperation with the H. W. Wilson Foundation. Membership of each is open to individuals and institutions at $39 a year.

Publications

Since 1980 the journal *Rural Libraries* has been published by CSRL twice a year. An annual subscription is $20 for domestic and $30 for international subscribers. Back copies are available at $10 each, and the full text of *Rural Libraries* articles is available at http://jupiter.clarion.edu/~csrl/rural.htm. A second semiannual publication, *Bookmobile and Outreach Services,* has been offered since 1998 at the same subscription rates.

To provide a forum for discussion, the listservs arsl-l, abos-l, and rurlib-l are maintained as a service for bookmobile/outreach specialists and those interested in the services of rural libraries. CSRL also publishes a variety of monographs.

Chief Officers of State Library Agencies (COSLA)

201 E. Main St., Ste. 1405, Lexington, KY 40507
859-514-9151, fax 859-514-1966, e-mail ttucker@amrms.com

Object

To provide a means of cooperative action among its state and territorial members, to strengthen the work of the respective state and territorial agencies, and to provide a continuing mechanism for dealing with the problems faced by the heads of these agencies, which are responsible for state and territorial library development.

Membership

COSLA is an independent organization of the men and women who head the state and territorial agencies responsible for library development. Its membership consists solely of the top library officers of the 50 states, the District of Columbia, and the territories, variously designated as state librarian, director, commissioner, or executive secretary.

Officers (2005–2006)

Pres. J. Gary Nichols, state libn., Maine State Lib., 64 State House Sta., Augusta, ME 04333. Tel. 207-287-5600, fax 207-287-5615, e-mail gary.nichols@state.me.us; *V.P./Pres Elect* Susan McVey, dir., State of Oklahoma Dept. of Libs., 200 N.E. 18 St., Oklahoma City, OK 73105-3298. Tel. 405-521-3173, fax 405-525-7804, e-mail smcvey @oltn.odl.state.ok.us; *Secy.* Michael York, state libn., New Hampshire State Lib., 20 Park St., Concord, NH 03301-6316. Tel. 603-271-2392, fax 603-271-6826, e-mail myork@ library.state.nh.us; *Treas.* Peggy D. Rudd, dir. and libn., Texas Lib. and Archives Commission, P.O. Box 12927, Austin, TX 78711-2927. Tel. 512-463-5460, fax 512-463-5436, e-mail prudd@tsl.state.tx.us; *Past Pres.* GladysAnn Wells, dir., State Lib. of Arizona, State Capitol, 1700 W. Washington, Rm. 200, Phoenix, AZ 85007. Tel. 602-542-4035, fax 602-542-4972, e-mail gawells@lib.az.us; *Dirs.* Christie Pearson Brandau, state libn., Kansas State Lib., 300 S.W. 10, Topeka, KS 66612. Tel. 785-296-3296, fax 785-296-6650, e-mail christieb@kslib.info; Ann Joslin, state libn., State Lib., 325 W. State St., Boise, ID 83702. Tel. 208-334-2150, fax 208-334-4016, e-mail ajoslin@isl.state.id.us; *Assn. Dir.* Tracy Tucker. Tel. 859-514-9210, e-mail ttucker@amrms.com.

Chinese American Librarians Association (CALA)

Executive Director, Sally C. Tseng
949-552-5615, fax 949-857-1988, e-mail sctseng888@yahoo.com
World Wide Web http://www.cala-web.org

Object

To enhance communications among Chinese American librarians as well as between Chinese American librarians and other librarians; to serve as a forum for discussion of mutual problems and professional concerns among Chinese American librarians; to promote Sino-American librarianship and library services; and to provide a vehicle whereby Chinese American librarians can cooperate with other associations and organizations having similar or allied interests.

Membership

Memb. 1,100+ Open to anyone who is interested in the association's goals and activities. Dues (Regular) $30; (International/Student/Nonsalaried) $15; (Inst.) $100; (Life) $400.

Officers

Pres. Haipeng Li. E-mail haipeng.li@oberlin.edu; *V.P./Pres.-Elect/Treas.* Dora Ho. E-mail doraho@yahoo.com; *Past Pres.* Diana Wu. E-mail diana.wu@sjsu.edu; *Exec. Dir.* Sally C. Tseng. E-mail sctseng888@yahoo.com.

Publications

Journal of Library and Information Science (2 a year; memb.; nonmemb. $15). *Ed.* Zhijia Shen. E-mail shen@colorado.edu.

Membership Directory (memb.).

Newsletter (3 a year; memb.; nonmemb. $10). *Ed.* Shinxing Wen. E-mail shwen@umich.edu.

Committee Chairpersons

Awards. Ying Shen, Priscilla Yu.
Constitution and Bylaws. Harriet Ying.
Finance. Cathy Lu.
International Relations. Connie Haley, Susana Liu.
Local Arrangement. Amy Su Liu, Tina Soong.
Membership. Minmin Qin.
Nomination. Shixing Wen.
Public Relations/Fund Raising. Linna Yu, Esther Lee.
Publication. Sha-Li Zhang.
Scholarship. Holly Yu.

Ad Hoc Committees and Task Forces

Best Book Award. Yi Liang, Julia Tung.
Mentorship Program. Rosa Hsu.
Officer's Handbook. Dora Ho.
2006 Conference Program Planning. Haipeng Li.
Sally C.Tseng's Professional Development Grant. Manuel Urrizola.
Webmaster. Shixing Wen.

Chapter Presidents

California. Kuei Chiu.
Florida. To be announced.
Greater Mid-Atlantic. Helen Wang.
Midwest. Fu Li.
Northeast. Zheng Wang.
Southwest. Klarion Tang.

Church and Synagogue Library Association (CSLA)

Box 19357, Portland, OR 97280-0357
503-244-6919, 800-542-2752, fax 503-977-3734
E-mail CSLA@worldaccessnet.com
World Wide Web http://www.csla.info

Object

To act as a unifying core for the many existing church and synagogue libraries; to provide the opportunity for a mutual sharing of practices and problems; to inspire and encourage a sense of purpose and mission among church and synagogue librarians; to study and guide the development of church and synagogue librarianship toward recognition as a formal branch of the library profession. Founded 1967.

Membership

Memb. 1,800. Dues (Inst.) $200; (Affiliated) $95; (Church/Synagogue) $55 ($60 foreign); (Indiv.) $35 ($40 foreign). Year. Jan.–Dec.

Officers (July 2005–July 2006)

Pres. Evelyn Pockrass; *Pres.-Elect* Maryann Barth; *2nd V.P.* Craig Kubic; *Treas.* Warren Livingston; *Admin.* Judith Janzen; *Past Pres.* Rod McClendon; *Ed., Church and Syna-* *gogue Libraries* Karen Bota, 490 N. Fox Hills Dr., No. 7, Bloomfield Hills, MI 48304; *Book Review Ed.* Monica Tenney, 399 Blenheim Rd., Columbus OH 43214-3219. E-mail motenney@aol.com.

Executive Board

Officers; committee chairpersons.

Publications

Bibliographies (1–5; price varies).
Church and Synagogue Libraries (bi-mo.; memb.; nonmemb. $45; Canada $55).
CSLA Guides (1–20; price varies).

Committee Chairpersons

Awards. Kay Mowery.
Conference. Sarah Gramley.
Library Services. Judy Livingston.
Nominations and Elections. Marjorie Smink.
Publications. Alice Hamilton.

Coalition for Networked Information

Executive Director, Clifford A. Lynch
21 Dupont Circle, Ste. 800, Washington, DC 20036
202-296-5098, fax 202-872-0884
E-mail info@cni.org, World Wide Web http://www.cni.org

Mission

The Coalition for Networked Information (CNI) is an organization to advance the transformative promise of networked information technology for the advancement of scholarly communication and the enrichment of intellectual productivity.

Membership

Memb. 208. Membership is institutional. Dues $5,975. Year. July–June.

Officers (July 2005–June 2006)

Duane Webster, exec. dir., Association of Research Libraries; Brian L. Hawkins, pres., EDUCAUSE.

Steering Committee

Richard P. West, California State Univ. (*Chair*); Daniel E. Atkins, Univ. of Michigan; Brian L. Hawkins, EDUCAUSE; Fred M. Heath, Univ. of Texas, Austin; Vace Kundakci, Columbia Univ.; Ronald L. Larsen, Univ. of Pittsburgh; Clifford Lynch, CNI; Roy Rosenzweig, George Mason Univ.; Donald J. Waters, Andrew W. Mellon Foundation; Duane Webster, ARL; Karin Wittenborg, Univ. of Virginia; Ann J. Wolpert, MIT.

Publication

CNI-Announce (subscribe by e-mail to cni-announce-subscribe@cni.org).

Council on Library and Information Resources

1755 Massachusetts Ave. N.W., Ste. 500, Washington, DC 20036-2124
202-939-4750, fax 202-939-4765
World Wide Web http://www.clir.org

Object

In 1997 the Council on Library Resources (CLR) and the Commission on Preservation and Access (CPA) merged and became the Council on Library and Information Resources (CLIR). CLIR's mission is to expand access to information, however recorded and preserved, as a public good. CLIR is an independent, nonprofit organization. CLIR identifies and defines the key emerging issues related to the welfare of libraries and the constituencies they serve, convenes the leaders who can influence change, and promotes collaboration among the institutions and organizations that can achieve change. The council's interests embrace the entire range of information resources and services from traditional library and archival materials to emerging digital formats. It assumes a particular interest in helping institutions cope with the accelerating pace of change associated with the transition into the digital environment.

CLIR is an independent nonprofit organization. While maintaining appropriate collaboration and liaison with other institutions and organizations, the council operates independently of any particular institutional or vested interests.

Through the composition of its board, it brings the broadest possible perspective to bear upon defining and establishing the priority of the issues with which it is concerned.

Board

CLIR's Board of Directors currently has 18 members.

Officers

Chair Charles Phelps; *Pres.* Nancy A. Davenport. E-mail ndavenport@CLIR.org; *Treas.* Herman Pabbruwe.

Address correspondence to headquarters.

Publications

Annual Report.
CLIR Issues (bi-mo.).
Technical reports.

Council on Library/Media Technicians

President, Jackie Lakatos
630-257-6541, fax 630-257-7737, e-mail jlakatos@lemontlibrary.org

The Council on Library/Media Technicians (COLT), an affiliate of the American Library Association, is an international organization that works to address the issues and concerns of library and media support staff personnel.

Since 1967 COLT has addressed issues covering such areas as technical education, continuing education, certification, job description uniformity, and the more elusive goals of gaining recognition and respect for the professional work that its members do.

Objectives

COLT's objectives are

- To function as a clearinghouse for information relating to library support staff personnel
- To advance the status, employment, and certification of library staff
- To promote effective communication and cooperation with other organizations whose purposes and objectives are similar to those of COLT

COLT's Web site, http://colt.ucr.edu, provides information on library technician programs, a speaker exchange listing for help in organizing workshops and conferences, bibliographies on needed resources, and jobline resource links.

COLT holds an annual conference, generally immediately preceding the American Library Association Annual Conference.

Membership

Membership is open to all library employees. Dues (Inst.) $70 ($95 foreign); (Indiv.) $45 ($70 foreign); (Student) $35. Year Jan.–Dec.

Officers (2005–2006)

Pres. Jackie Lakatos. E-mail jlakatos@ lemontlibrary.org; *Acting V.P./Training and Event Mgr.* Rita McGeary. E-mail ritam@ palsnet.info; *Secy.* Kristen Fiato. E-mail fiato@law.stetson.edu; *Treas.* Stan Cieplinski. E-mail stan.cieplinski@domail.maricopa. edu.

Federal Library and Information Center Committee

Executive Director, Roberta I. Shaffer
Library of Congress, Washington, DC 20540-4935
202-707-4800, World Wide Web http://www.loc.gov/flicc

Object

The Federal Library and Information Center Committee (FLICC) makes recommendations on federal library and information policies, programs, and procedures to federal agencies and to others concerned with libraries and information centers. The committee coordinates cooperative activities and services among federal libraries and information centers and serves as a forum to consider issues and policies that affect federal libraries and information centers, needs and priorities in providing information services to the government and to the nation at large, and efficient and cost-effective use of federal library and information resources and services. Furthermore, the committee promotes improved access to information, continued development and use of the Federal Library and Information Network (FEDLINK), research and development in the application of new technologies to federal libraries and information centers, improvements in the management of federal libraries and information centers, and relevant education opportunities. Founded 1965.

Membership

Libn. of Congress, Dir. of the National Agricultural Lib., Dir. of the National Lib. of Medicine, Dir. of the National Lib. of Educ., representatives of each of the cabinet-level executive departments, and representatives of each of the following agencies: National Aeronautics and Space Admin., National Sci-ence Foundation, Smithsonian Institution, U.S. Supreme Court, National Archives and Records Admin., Admin. Offices of the U.S. Courts, Defense Technical Info. Center, Government Printing Office, National Technical Info. Service (Dept. of Commerce), Office of Scientific and Technical Info. (Dept. of Energy), Exec. Office of the President, Dept. of the Army, Dept. of the Navy, Dept. of the Air Force, and chair of the FEDLINK Advisory Council. Fifteen additional voting member agencies are selected on a rotating basis by the voting members of FEDLINK. These rotating members serve a three-year term. One representative of each of the following agencies is invited as an observer to committee meetings: Government Accountability Office, General Services Admin., Joint Committee on Printing, National Commission on Libs. and Info. Science, Office of Mgt. and Budget, Office of Personnel Mgt., and U.S. Copyright Office.

Officers

Chair James H. Billington, Libn. of Congress; *Chair Designate* Deanna Marcum, Assoc. Libn. for Lib. Services, Lib. of Congress; *Exec. Dir.* Roberta I. Shaffer.

Address correspondence to the executive director.

Publications

FEDLINK Technical Notes (bi-mo.).
FLICC Newsletter (q.).

Federal Publishers Committee

Chair, Glenn W. King
Bureau of the Census, Washington, DC 20233
301-763-4176, fax 301-457-4707
E-mail glenn.w.king@census.gov

Object

To foster and promote effective management of data development and dissemination in the federal government through exchange of information, and to act as a focal point for federal agency publishing.

Membership

Memb. 500. Membership is available to persons involved in publishing and dissemination in federal government departments, agencies, and corporations, as well as independent organizations concerned with federal government publishing and dissemination. Some key federal government organizations represented are the Joint Committee on Printing, Government Printing Office, National Technical Info. Service, National Commission on Libs. and Info. Science, and the Lib. of Congress.

Officers

Chair Glenn W. King; *V. Chair, Programs* Sandra Smith; *Dirs.* John Ward, Leslie M. Greenberg.

Publication

Guide to Federal Publishing (occasional).

Friends of Libraries U.S.A. (FOLUSA)

Executive Director, Sally Gardner Reed
1420 Walnut St., Ste. 450, Philadelphia, PA 19102-4017
800-936-5872, 215-790-1674, fax 215-545-3821
E-mail friends@folusa.org, World Wide Web http://www.folusa.org

Object

Friends of Libraries U.S.A. (FOLUSA) is a national nonprofit organization providing networking opportunities and educational support for local friends-of-libraries groups. Membership includes more than 2,000 friends groups, libraries, and individuals.

FOLUSA was established in 1979 as a committee of the Library Administration and Management Association of the American Library Association. Its mission is to motivate and support local friends groups in their efforts to preserve and strengthen libraries, and to create awareness and appreciation of library services by assisting in developing friends groups; providing guidance, education, and counsel throughout the friends network; promoting the development of strong library-advocacy programs; serving as a clearinghouse of information and expertise; promoting early-childhood literacy; and promoting appreciation of the nation's literary heritage.

FOLUSA provides consulting services, training, and workshops at the regional, state, and national levels focusing on developing friends groups, fund raising, and advocacy. It works with local and state friends groups to enhance their efforts as advocates, volunteers, program and community-outreach catalysts, and as fund-raisers in support of their local and state libraries.

Since 1989 FOLUSA has presented an annual public service award to a member of Congress who has shown leadership and support of library issues. The award presentation is part of Library Legislative Day in Washington, D.C. Awards for friends groups annually total more than $15,000 and recognize outstanding community and volunteer involvement.

Membership

Membership is open to all friends of libraries groups, libraries, and individuals who support libraries. Dues (indiv.) $35 up; (small libraries, budgets under $1 million) $50; (large libraries, budgets over $1 million) $100; (small friends groups, fewer than 100 members) $40; (medium friends groups, 100 to 499 members) $65; (large friends groups, 500+ members) $100.

Officers (2005–2006)

Pres. Douglas Roesemann; *V.P./Pres.-Elect* Mary K. Dodge; *Secy.* Margaret Schuster; *Treas.* Amy Doughtery; *Past Pres.* Susan Schmidt.

Directors

Jeff Bantly, Peggy Barber, John Barnes, John Carson, George Coe, Martin Covert, Mary Dodge, Rodrigue Gauvin, Martin Gomez, William Gordon, Barbara Hoffert, Robin Hoklotubbe, Cherine Janzen, Stephen Klein, Mary D. Lankford, Deborah Loeding, Margaret Murray, Veronda Pitchford, Eva Poole, Robert Rotello, Kay Runge, Laura Salmon, Virginia Stanley, David Warren, Joe Weed.

Publications

NewsUpdate, (bi-mo.)
Making Our Voices Heard: Citizens Speak Out for Libraries
Getting Grants in Your Community
101+ Great Ideas for Libraries and Friends

Medical Library Association

Executive Director, Carla Funk
65 E. Wacker Place, Ste. 1900, Chicago, IL 60601-7298
312-419-9094, fax 312-419-8950
E-mail info@mlahq.org, World Wide Web http://www.mlanet.org

Object

MLA, a nonprofit educational organization, is composed of health sciences information professionals with more than 4,700 members worldwide. Through its programs and services, MLA provides lifelong educational opportunities, supports a knowledge base of health information research and works with a global network of partners to promote the importance of quality information for improved health to the healthcare community and the public.

Membership

Memb. (Inst.) 884; (Indiv.) 3,664. Institutional members are medical and allied scientific libraries. Individual members are people who are (or were at the time membership was established) engaged in professional library or bibliographic work in medical and allied scientific libraries or people who are interested in medical or allied scientific libraries. Dues (Student) $40; (Emeritus) $55; (International) $110; (Indiv.) $165; and (Inst.) $255–$600, based on the number of the library's periodicals subscriptions. Members may be affiliated with one or more of MLA's 23 special interest sections and 14 regional chapters.

Officers

Pres. Mary Joan ("M. J.") Tooey, Health Sciences and Human Services Lib., Univ. of Maryland, 601 W. Lombard St., Baltimore, MD 21201; *Pres-Elect.* Jean Shipman; *Past Pres.* Joanne G. Marshall, Univ. of North

Carolina at Chapel Hill, Chapel Hill, NC 27514-3360.

Directors

Margaret Bandy (2008), Nancy W. Clemmons (2006), Sarah H. Gable (2007), Craig C. Haynes (2008), Dixie A. Jones (2007), Rosalind K. Lett (2006), Faith Meakin (2007), Tovah Reis (2008), Connie Schardt (2008).

Publications

Journal of the Medical Library Association (q.; $163).
MLA News (10 a year; $58).
Miscellaneous (request current list from association headquarters).

Music Library Association

8551 Research Way, Ste. 180, Middleton, WI 53562
608-836-5825, World Wide Web http://www.musiclibraryassoc.org

Object

To promote the establishment, growth, and use of music libraries; to encourage the collection of music and musical literature in libraries; to further studies in musical bibliography; to increase efficiency in music library service and administration; and to promote the profession of music librarianship. Founded 1931.

Membership

Memb. 1,177. Dues (Inst.) $125; (Indiv.) $90; (Retired) $60; (Student) $35. Year. July 1–June 30.

Officers

Pres. Bonna J. Boettcher, Music Lib. and Sound Recordings Archives, William T.

Jerome Lib., 3rd fl., Bowling Green State Univ., Bowling Green, OH 43403-0179. Tel. 419-372-9929, fax 419-372-2499, e-mail bboettc@bgnet.bgsu.edu; *Rec. Secy.* Michael Colby, Catalog Dept., Shields Lib., 100 N. West Quad, Univ. of California–Davis, Davis, CA 95616-5292. Tel. 530-752-0931, fax 530-754-8785, e-mail mdcolby@ucdavis. edu; *Treas./Exec. Secy.* Nancy B. Nuzzo, Music Lib., Univ. at Buffalo, 112 Baird Hall, Buffalo, NY 14260-4750. Tel. 716-645-2924, fax 716-645-3906, e-mail nuzzo@buffalo. edu.

Members-at-Large

Linda Blair, Eastman School of Music; Pamela Bristah, Wellesley College; Paul Cauthen, Univ. of Cincinnati; Ruthan Boles McTyre, Univ. of Iowa; Amanda Maple, Penn State Univ.; Matthew Wise, New York Univ.

Special Officers

Advertising Mgr. Susan Dearborn, 1572 Massachusetts Ave., No. 57, Cambridge, MA 02138. Tel. 617-876-0934; *Business Mgr.* Jim Zychowicz, 8551 Research Way, Ste. 180, Middleton, WI 53562. Tel. 608-836-5825; *Asst. Convention Mgr.* Gordon Rowley, Box 395, Bailey's Harbor, WI 54202. Tel. 920-839-2444, e-mail baileysbreeze@itol.com; *Convention Mgr.* Annie Thompson, 435 S. Gulfstream Ave., Apt. 506, Sarasota, FL 34236. Tel. 941-955-5014, fax 941-316-0468, e-mail figarotu@msn.com; *Placement* Jennifer Ottervik, Univ. of South Carolina Music Lib., 813 Assembly St., Columbia, SC 29208. Tel. 803-777-5425, fax 803-777-1426, e-mail ottervikj@gwm.sc.edu; *Publicity* Kenneth Calkins, Music Lib., Univ. of California–San Diego, 9500 Gilman Dr., No 0175Q, La Jolla, CA 92093. Tel. 858-534-1267, fax 858-534-0189, e-mail kcalkins@ucsd.edu.

Publications

MLA Index and Bibliography Series (irreg.; price varies).
MLA Newsletter (q.; memb.).

MLA Technical Reports (irreg.; price varies).
Music Cataloging Bulletin (mo.; $25).
Notes (q.; indiv. $85; inst. $100).

Committee and Roundtable Chairpersons

Administration. Paula Elliot, Washington State Univ.

Bibliographic Control. Nancy Lorimer, Stanford Univ.

Development. Allie Wise Goudy, Western Illinois Univ.

Education. Holling J. Smith-Borne, DePauw Univ.

Finance. Pamela Bristah, Wellesley College.

Legislation. Gordon Theil (UCLA).

Membership. Michael Rogan, Tufts Univ.

Preservation. Alice Carli, Eastman School of Music.

Public Libraries. Steven Landstreet, Free Lib. of Philadelphia.

Publications. Karen Little, Univ. of Louisville.

Reference and Public Service. Paul Cary, Baldwin-Wallace College.

Resource Sharing and Collection Development. Brian Doherty, Arizona State Univ.

National Association of Government Archives and Records Administrators (NAGARA)

90 State St., Albany, NY 12207
518-463-8644, fax 518-463-8656
E-mail nagara@caphill.com
World Wide Web http://www.nagara.org

Object

Founded in 1984, NAGARA is a growing nationwide association of local, state, and federal archivists and records administrators, and others interested in improved care and management of government records. NAGARA promotes public awareness of government records and archives management programs, encourages interchange of information among government archives and records management agencies, develops and implements professional standards of government records and archival administration, and encourages study and research into records management problems and issues.

Membership

Most NAGARA members are federal, state, and local archival and records management agencies.

Officers

Pres. Timothy A. Slavin, Div. of Historical and Cultural Affairs, 21 The Green, Dover, DE 19901. Tel. 302-739-5314, fax 302-739-2578, e-mail timothy.slavin@state.de.us; *V.P.* Preston Huff, National Archives and Records Admin., Southwest Region, 501 W. Felix St., Bldg. 1, Fort Worth, TX 76115. Tel. 817-831-5627, e-mail preston.huff@nara.gov; *Secy.* Caryn Wojcik, Michigan Records Mgt. Services, Michigan Historical Center, 3405 N. Martin Luther King, Jr. Blvd., Lansing, MI 48909. Tel. 517-335-8222, fax 517-335-9418, e-mail wojcikc@michigan.gov; *Treas.* John Stewart, National Archives and Records Admin., Great Lakes Region, 7358 S. Pulaski Rd., Chicago, IL 60629-5898. Tel. 773-581-7816, fax 312-886-7883, e-mail john.stewart@nara.gov.

Directors

Paul Bergeron, City of Nashua (New Hampshire); Jelain Chubb, Missouri State Archives; Terry B. Ellis, County Records Mgr., Salt Lake County Records Mgt. and Archives; Nancy Fortna, National Archives and Records Admin., Washington, D.C.; Mary Beth Herkert, Oregon State Archives; Richard Hite, Rhode Island State Archives; Kay Lanning Minchew, Troup County (Georgia) Archives; Barbara Voss, National Archives and Records Admin., Rocky Mountain Region.

Publications

Clearinghouse (q.; memb.).
Crossroads (q.; memb.).
Government Records Issues (series).
Preservation Needs in State Archives (report).
Program Reporting Guidelines for Government Records Programs.

National Church Library Association

Executive Director, Susan Benish
275 S. Third St., Ste. 101A, Stillwater, MN 55082
651-430-0770, e-mail info@churchlibraries.org
World Wide Web http://www.churchlibraries.org

Object

The National Church Library Association (NCLA, formerly the Lutheran Church Library Association) is a nonprofit organization that serves the unique needs of congregational libraries and those who manage them. NCLA provides inspiration, solutions, and support to church librarians in the form of printed manuals and guidelines, booklists, a quarterly journal (*Libraries ALIVE*), national conferences, a mentoring program, online support, and personal advice. Regional chapters operate throughout the country.

Membership

Memb. 800 churches, 100 personal. Dues $40, $55. Year. Jan.–Jan.

Officers

Pres. Barbara Livdahl; *V.P.* Karen Gieseke; *Secy.* Brenda Langerud; *Treas.* Esther Bunch; *Past Pres.* Bonnie McLellan.

Address correspondence to the executive director.

Directors

Gerrie Buzard, Sandra Cully, Rachel Riensche, Violet Russell.

Publication

Libraries ALIVE (q.; memb.).

Committee Chairpersons

Advisory. Mary Jordan.
Librarian Resources. Marlys Johnson.

NFAIS

Executive Director, Bonnie Lawlor
1518 Walnut St., Ste. 1004, Philadelphia, PA 19102
215-893-1561, fax 215-893-1564
E-mail nfais@nfais.org
World Wide Web http://www.nfais.org

Object

NFAIS (formerly the National Federation of Abstracting and Information Services) is an international nonprofit membership organization composed of leading information providers. Its membership includes government agencies, nonprofit scholarly societies, and private sector businesses. NFAIS serves groups that aggregate, organize, or facilitate access to information. To improve members' capabilities and to contribute to their ongoing success, NFAIS provides a forum to address common interests through education and advocacy. Founded 1958.

Membership

Memb. 50+. Full members: regular and government organizations that provide information services, primarily through organizing, compiling, and providing access to original or source materials. Examples of full members: organizations that assemble tables of contents, produce abstract and indexing services, provide library cataloging services, or generate numeric or factual compilations. Associate members are organizations that operate or manage online information services, networks, in-house information centers, and libraries; undertake research and development in information science or systems; are otherwise involved in the generation, promotion, or distribution of information products under contract; or publish original information sources. To be a corporate affiliated member, another member of the corporation or government agency must already be a NFAIS member paying full dues.

Officers (2005–2006)

Pres. Lucian Parziale; *Pres.-Elect* Linda Beebe; *Treas.* Kevin Bouley; *Secy.* Terence Ford; *Past Pres.* Linda Sacks.

Directors

David Brown, Matt Dunie, David Gillikin, Marjorie M. K. Hlava, Janice Mears, John Regazzi, Judith Russell.

Staff

Exec. Dir. Bonnie Lawlor. E-mail blawlor@nfais.org; *Dir., Planning and Communications* Jill O'Neill. E-mail jilloneill@nfais.org; *Customer Service* Margaret Manson. E-mail mmanson@nfais.org.

Publications

NFAIS Newsletter (mo.; North America $120/yr.; elsewhere $135).

For a detailed list of NFAIS publications, see the NFAIS Web site (http://www.nfais.org).

National Information Standards Organization

Interim Executive Director, Patricia Stevens
4733 Bethesda Ave., Ste. 300, Bethesda, MD 20814
301-654-2512, fax 301-654-1721
E-mail nisohq@niso.org, World Wide Web http://www.niso.org

Object

NISO, the National Information Standards Organization, a nonprofit association accredited by the American National Standards Institute (ANSI), identifies, develops, maintains, and publishes technical standards to manage information in our changing and ever-more-digital environment. NISO standards apply both traditional and new technologies to the full range of information-related needs, including retrieval, repurposing, storage, metadata, and preservation.

Experts from the information industry, libraries, and publishing participate in the development of NISO standards. The standards are approved by the consensus body of NISO's voting membership, which consists of more than 90 voting members representing libraries, government, associations, and private businesses and organizations. NISO is supported by its membership and corporate grants. NISO is a nonprofit educational organization. NISO is accredited by ANSI and serves as the U.S. Technical Advisory Group to ISO/TC 46 Information and documentation.

Membership

Memb. 90+. Open to any organization, association, government agency, or company willing to participate in and having substantial concern for the development of NISO standards. Libraries support NISO as members of the Library Standards Alliance.

Officers

Chair Carl Grant, pres. and COO, VTLS, Inc., Blacksburg, Virginia; *V. Chair/Chair-Elect* Robin Murray, managing dir. and CEO, Fretwell-Downing Informatics, Sheffield, England; *Secy.* Patricia Stevens, NISO, Bethesda, Maryland; *Treas.* Doug Cheney, V.P., Product Master, Barnes & Noble, New York; *Past Chair* Jan Peterson, V.P., content development, Infotrieve, Los Angeles.

Publications

Information Standards Quarterly (U.S $92/year, foreign $134).

NISO Newsline (free monthly e-letter released on the first Wednesday of each month. See the NISO Web site for details on subscribing and archived issues).

For additional NISO publications, see "National Information Standards Organization (NISO) Standards" later in Part 6.

NISO published standards are available free of charge as downloadable pdf files from the NISO Web site http://www.niso.org). Standards in hard copy are available for sale on the Web site. The *NISO Annual Report* is available on request.

Patent and Trademark Depository Library Association

http://www.ptdla.org

Object

The Patent and Trademark Depository Library Association (PTDLA) provides a support structure for the 84 patent and trademark depository libraries (PTDLs) affiliated with the U.S. Patent and Trademark Office (USPTO). The association's mission is to discover the interests, needs, opinions, and goals of the PTDLs and to advise USPTO in these matters for the benefit of PTDLs and their users, and to assist USPTO in planning and implementing appropriate services. Founded in 1983 as the Patent Depository Library Advisory Council; name changed to Patent and Trademark Depository Library Association in 1988; became an American Library Association affiliate in 1996.

Membership

Open to any person employed in a patent and trademark depository library whose responsibilities include the patent collection. Affiliate membership is also available. Dues $25.

Officers (2005–2006)

Pres. Nan Myers. E-mail nan.myers@wichita.edu; *V.P./Pres.Elect* Jan Comfort. E-mail comfortj@clemson.edu; *Secy.* Leena Lalwani. E-mail llalwani@umich.edu; *Treas.*

Suzanne Holcombe. E-mail sholcom@okstate.edu; *Past Pres.* Charlotte Erdmann. E-mail cerdmann@purdue.edu.

Regional Representatives

Region 1, Leonard Adams. E-mail len.adams@library.umass.edu; Region 2, Deb Leary. E-mail dleary@libraryweb.org; Region 3, Marion Armour Gemmen. E-mail marmour@wvu.edu; Region 4, Jan Comfort. E-mail comfortj@clemson.edu; Region 5, Robert Klein. E-mail patents@mdpls.org; Region 6, Tom Rohrig. E-mail tom.rohrig@ttu.edu; Region 7, Ran Raider. E-mail ran.raider@wright.edu; Region 8, Nancy Spitzer. E-mail spitzer@engr.wisc.edu; Region 9, Suzanne Holcombe. E-mail sholcom@okstate.edu.

Publication

Intellectual Property Journal of the PTDLA. Electronic at http://www.ptdla.org/ipjournal. html. *Eds.* Claudine Jenda, Auburn Univ. Libs., 231 Mell St., Auburn, AL 36849-5606. Tel. 334-844-1658, e-mail jendaca@auburn. edu; Andrew Wohrley, Auburn Univ. Libs. Tel. 334-844-4461, e-mail wohrlaj@auburn. edu; Esther Crawford, Fondren Lib., Rice Univ., P.O. Box 1892, Houston, TX 77251-1892. Tel. 713-348-6212, crawford@rice.edu.

REFORMA (National Association to Promote Library and Information Services to Latinos and the Spanish-Speaking)

President, Ana Elba Pavón
World Wide Web http://www.reforma.org

Object

Promoting library services to the Spanish-speaking for more than 30 years, REFORMA, an affiliate of the American Library Association, works in a number of areas to promote the development of library collections to include Spanish-language and Latino-oriented materials; the recruitment of more bilingual and bicultural professionals and support staff; the development of library services and programs that meet the needs of the Latino community; the establishment of a national network among individuals who share its goals; the education of the U.S. Latino population in regard to the availability and types of library services; and lobbying efforts to preserve existing library resource centers serving the interest of Latinos.

Membership

Memb. 800+. Any person who is supportive of the goals and objectives of REFORMA.

Officers

Pres. Ana Elba Pavón, San Mateo Public Lib., 1100 Park Place, San Mateo, CA 94403. Tel. 650-522-7805, fax 650-522-7801, e-mail apvp0405@yahoo.com; *V.P./Pres.-Elect* Roxana Benavides, Brooklyn Public Lib., Sunset Park Branch, 5108 4th Ave., Brooklyn, NY 11220. Tel. 718-567-2806 ext. 117, fax 718-567-2810, e-mail r.benavides@brooklynpubliclibrary.org; *Secy.* Delores Carlito, Mervyn H. Sterne Lib., Univ. of Alabama. Tel. 205-934-6364, e-mail delo@uab.edu; *Treas.* Adalín Torres Zayas, Inglewood Public Lib., 101 W. Manchester Blvd., Inglewood, CA. 90301-1753. Tel. 310-412-8734, fax 310-412-8848, e-mail aitorres@cityofinglewood.org; *Memb.-At-Large* Mary Callaghan ("Cal") Zunt, Carnegie West Branch, Cleveland Public Lib., 1900 Fulton Rd., Cleveland, OH 44113-3346. Tel. 216-623-6927, e-mail cal.zunt@cpl.org; *Past Pres.* José Ruiz-Alvarez, Arlington Public Lib., 1624 New York Ave., Arlington, TX 76010. Tel. 817-275-3321, e-mail reformista4ever@hotmail.com; *Chapter Reps.* Hal Bright, Farmington Lib., P.O. Box 407, Farmington, CT 06034. Tel. 860-673-6791, fax 860-675-7148, e-mail phxmars@yahoo.com; Barbara Miller, Fullerton Pollak Lib., California State Univ., P.O. Box 4150, Fullerton, CA 92834-4150. Tel. 714-278-4460, e-mail bmiller@fullerton.edu; Leslie Monsalve-Jones, New Mexico State Lib., 1209 Camino Carlos Rey, Santa Fe, NM 87504. Tel. 505-476-9718, e-mail leslie@stlib.state.nm.us.

Committees

Pura Belpré Award. Rose Treviño.
Children's and Young Adult Services. Rose Treviño.
Education. Denise Adkins.
Finance. José Ruiz-Alvarez.
Information Technology. Francisco Garcia.
International Relations. Armando Trejo.
Legislative. Mario A. Ascencio.
Membership. Robin Imperial.
Mora Award. Ruth Mitchel.
Nominations. Maria Kramer.
Organizational Development. Patricia Clark.
Public Relations. Selina Gómez-Beloz.
Recruitment and Mentoring. Toni Anaya, Gwen Gregory.

Publication

REFORMA Newsletter (q.; memb.).

Meetings

General membership and board meetings take place at the American Library Association Midwinter Meeting and Annual Conference.

RLG

Senior Account Manager, Sharon Vaughn-Lahman
2029 Stierlin Court, Suite 100, Mountain View, CA 94043-4684. Tel. 650-691-2276, fax 650-964-0943, e-mail svl@rlg.org, World Wide Web http://www.rlg.org

Object

Incorporated as the Research Libraries Group in 1975, RLG is a not-for-profit membership organization of libraries, archives, museums, and other memory institutions with remarkable collections for research and learning. RLG and its members collaborate on standards and specific projects to bring these collections online, help deliver them around the world, and support their preservation in digital form. As part of this work, RLG offers Internet-based services to institutions and individuals for improving information discovery and use. RLG's main classes of information, available on the Internet, are international union catalogs (e.g., RedLightGreen, RLG Union Catalog, Hand Press Books database); article- and chapter-level indexes to journals and books (e.g., Anthropology Plus or History of Science, Technology, and Medicine); *RLG Archival Resources* (full-text finding aids and archival collections cataloging); and digital-image sources of art and objects from museums and other heritage collections (e.g., RLG Cultural Materials, Trove.net, and CAMIO). In addition, the RLIN21 service includes a Web interface to find and download cataloging copy from RLG catalogs, as well as a PC-based client to create and maintain records in these catalogs. RLG's ILL Manager is peer-to-peer PC-based software for handling ILL traffic.

Membership

Memb. 150+. Membership is not a requirement to use RLG services. Membership is open to any nonprofit institution with an educational, cultural, or scientific mission. Annual dues, based on the size of institution-al operating budget, support RLG member programs and projects.

Directors

RLG is governed by a board of up to 19 directors: 12 elected from and by RLG's member institutions, up to six at-large directors elected by the board itself, and the president. The board is responsible for the organization's governance and for ensuring that RLG fulfills its purpose and goals. Annual board elections are held each spring. In 2006 the board's chair is James G. Neal, vice president for information services and university librarian, Columbia University. For a current list of directors, see http://www.rlg.org/en/page.php?Page_ID=122.

Staff

Pres. and CEO James Michalko; *Chief Operating Officer* Molly Singer; *Dir., Member Programs and Services* James Michalko; *Dir., Product Management* Susan Yoder; *Dir., Systems* David Richards; *Dir., Marketing and Sales* Karen Carbonnet.

Publications

RLG regularly issues Web-based informational, research, and user publications. See http://www.rlg.org/en/page.php?Page_ID=5 or contact RLG for more information. RLG newsletters include *RLG DigiNews* (bi-mo.; Web-based newsletter to help keep pace with preservation uses of digitization).

RLG Focus (bi-mo.; Web-based user services newsletter).

RLG News (quarterly magazine).

Scholarly Publishing and Academic Resources Coalition (SPARC)

Executive Director, Heather Joseph
21 Dupont Circle, Ste. 800, Washington, DC 20036
202-296-2296, fax 202-872-0884
E-mail sparc@arl.org
World Wide Web http://www.arl.org/sparc

SPARC (the Scholarly Publishing and Academic Resources Coalition) is an international alliance of research libraries and library associations fostering change in scholarly communication. SPARC was founded to address serious problems caused by the soaring cost of scientific, technical, and medical journals, and to unleash the potential of the digital networked environment for enhancing the scholarly communication process.

SPARC pursues its objectives by pursuing three strategic directions:

- Advocating for changes at the public policy level that create a culture supportive of access

- Educating stakeholders in scholarly communication about available tools, resources, contributors, and SPARC support

- Incubating alternative publishing models

Founded in 1997, SPARC has expanded to represent nearly 100 libraries in Europe. Several national organizations and institutions sponsor SPARC Europe, including the Joint Information Systems Committee (JISC) in Britain; the Society of College, National, and University Libraries (SCONUL) in Britain and Ireland; and UKB, the Netherlands Cooperative of Research Libraries. The Ligue des Bibliothèques Européennes de Recherche (LIBER) also participates.

Catalyst for Change

SPARC is a visible advocate for changes in scholarly communication that benefit more than the academic community alone. For example, in 2004 SPARC brought together patient advocates with library groups and other stakeholders to form the Alliance for Taxpayer Access (http://www.taxpayeraccess.org). This group was key in rallying support for Congress and the National Institutes of Health (NIH) in creating their public access policy. The policy encourages researchers to deposit the results of research funded by taxpayer dollars in an NIH-maintained online archive as part of their grant. The NIH put this policy in place to enhance their investment in biomedical research. SPARC is now working to capitalize on this success by advocating for public access programs in other grant-issuing federal agencies.

In addition, SPARC continues to work with major library groups in the development of its Open Access and Create Change programs (http://www.createchange.org). These and other resources are tools to help librarians and researchers to learn, educate, and advocate for effective scholarly communication in their communities.

Exploring New Models

SPARC is a leading proponent of reducing or removing barriers to access peer-reviewed literature. SPARC works with universities and libraries to enhance awareness of the new roles we can play to support information dissemination, including:

- Hosting an institutional repository (IR)

- Providing infrastructure support for scholar-led innovations in scholarly communication

- Developing new digital-publishing enterprises and models

SPARC has worked to share information and expertise in these areas by organizing a series of workshops and producing position papers, including "The Case for Institutional Repositories." SPARC continues to work in collaboration with Creative Commons and other groups to craft an addendum to standard publishers' agreements that authors can use as a model in retaining copyright to their published works.

Publisher Partnerships

SPARC influences the journals marketplace by fostering competition in academic disciplines where prices are too high. SPARC has focused largely on the scientific, technical, and medical (STM) fields, where the situation is worst and the economic benefits of change are greatest. However, the latest SPARC publisher partnerships have been in economics, social sciences, and the humanities. All academic disciplines are adversely affected by imbalances in the scholarly publishing marketplace and should have an equal opportunity to exploit the Internet's potential.

Membership

SPARC and SPARC Europe are supported by a membership of more than 300 libraries. Several major library organizations around the world are SPARC affiliate members. Membership is institutional. Full North American member dues are $5,000 a year, with a $7,500 purchase commitment. Other membership categories are available. SPARC Europe members are listed at http://www.sparceurope.org.

For library membership information, contact SPARC at sparc@arl.org or visit the SPARC Web site at http://www.arl.org/sparc.

Publications

SPARC Open Access Newsletter. This free monthly electronic newsletter provides news and analysis of the open access movement. To subscribe, send an e-mail to SPARC-OANews-feed@arl.org.

SPARC E-news (http://www.arl.org/sparc/pubs/enews).

See http://www.arl.org/sparc/pubs/index.html for a complete list of SPARC publications.

Society for Scholarly Publishing

Executive Directors, Francine Butler, Jerry Bowman
10200 W. 44 Ave., Ste. 304, Wheat Ridge, CO 80033
303-422-3914, fax 303-422-8894
E-mail ssp@resourcenter.com
World Wide Web http://www.sspnet.org

Object

To draw together individuals involved in the process of scholarly publishing. This process requires successful interaction of the many functions performed within the scholarly community. The Society for Scholarly Publishing (SSP) provides the leadership for such interaction by creating opportunities for the exchange of information and opinions among scholars, editors, publishers, librarians, printers, booksellers, and all others engaged in scholarly publishing.

Membership

Memb. 800. Open to all with an interest in the scholarly publishing process and dissemination of information. Dues (Indiv.) $115; (Supporting) $1,100; (Sustaining) $2,750. Year. Jan. 1–Dec. 31.

Executive Committee

Pres. Norman Frankel, American Medical Assn. E-mail norman_frankel@ama-assn.org; *Pres.-Elect* Judy Luther, Informed Strategies. E-mail judy.luther@informedstrategies.com; *Past Pres.* Heather Joseph, Assn. of Research Libs.; *Secy.-Treas.* Ray Fastiggi, Rockefeller Univ. Press.

Meetings

An annual meeting is conducted in late May/early June; the location changes each year. SSP also conducts several seminars throughout the year and a Top Management Roundtable each fall.

Society of American Archivists

Executive Director, Nancy Perkin Beaumont
527 S. Wells St., Fifth Floor, Chicago, IL 60607
312-922-0140, fax 312-347-1452
World Wide Web http://www.archivists.org

Object

Provides leadership to ensure the identification, preservation, and use of records of historical value. Founded 1936.

Membership

Memb. 4,325. Dues (Indiv.) $70–$180, graduated according to salary; (Assoc.) $70, domestic; (Student) $40; (Inst.) $225; (Sustaining) $440.

Officers (2005–2006)

Pres. Richard Pearce-Moses; *V.P.* Elizabeth Adkins; *Treas.* Fynnette Eaton.

Council

Mark Duffy, Aimee Felker, Peter Gottlieb,

Kathryn Neal, Christopher Paton, Ben Primer, Carla Summers, Sheryl K. Williams, Peter Wosh.

Staff

Exec. Dir. Nancy Perkin Beaumont; *Memb. Services Coord.* Jeanette Spears; *Publishing Dir.* Teresa Brinati; *Educ. Dir.* Solveig DeSutter; *Memb. and Technical Services Dir.* Brian Doyle; *Meetings Program Coord.* Carlos Salgado; *Educ. Program Coord.* Vacant.

Publications

American Archivist (q.; $85; foreign $90). *Ed.* Mary Jo Pugh, *Managing Ed.* Teresa Brinati. Books for review and related correspondence should be addressed to the managing editor.
Archival Outlook (bi-mo.; memb.). *Ed.* Teresa Brinati.

Software and Information Industry Association (SIIA)

1090 Vermont Ave. N.W., Washington, DC 20005
Tel. 202-289-7442, fax 202-289-7097
World Wide Web http://www.siia.net

Membership

Memb. 600 companies. Formed January 1, 1999, through the merger of the Software Publishers Association (SPA) and the Information Industry Association (IIA). Open to companies involved in the creation, distribution, and use of software, information products, services, and technologies. For details on membership and dues, see the SIIA Web site.

Staff

Pres. Kenneth Wasch. E-mail kwasch@siia.net.

Officers

Chair Mark H. Webbink, Red Hat; *V. Chair* Jessica Perry, Dow Jones; *Treas.* Daniel Cooperman, Oracle; *Secy.* Robert Merry, Congressional Quarterly.

Board of Directors

Cindy Braddon, McGraw-Hill; John Brigden, Veritas; Daniel Cooperman, Oracle; Clare Hart, Factiva; R. Douglas Kemp, Bloomberg; Edward S. Knight, NASDAQ; Steven Manzo, Reed Elsevier; Bernard McKay, Intuit; Robert Merry, Congressional Quarterly; Jessica Perry, Dow Jones; Gail Pierson, Riverdeep; Jack Sabo, New York Board of Trade; Larry Snowhite, Houghton Mifflin; Jason Stewart, Thomson; Mark Webbink, Red Hat; Ken Wasch, SIIA.

Special Libraries Association (SLA)

Chief Executive Officer, Janice R. Lachance
331 S. Patrick St., Alexandria, VA 22314
703-647-4900, fax 703-647-4901
E-mail sla@sla.org, World Wide Web http://www.sla.org

Mission

To advance the leadership role of the association's members in putting knowledge to work for the benefit of decision makers in corporations, government, the professions, and society; to shape the destiny of our information- and knowledge-based society.

Membership

Memb. 11,000. Dues (Organizational) $500; (Indiv.) $166/$99; (Student/Retired) $35.

Officers (July 2005–June 2006)

Pres. Pamela Rollo; *Pres.-Elect* Ethel Salonen; *Treas.* Gloria Zamora; *Chapter Cabinet Chair* Patricia Cia; *Chapter Cabinet Chair-Elect* Anne Caputo; *Div. Cabinet Chair* Brent Mai; *Div. Chapter Chair-Elect* Agnes Mattis; *Past Pres.* Ethel Salonen.

Directors

Officers; Susan Klopper, Lynn McCay, Renee Massoud, Cindy Romaine, Roberto Sarmiento, Dan Trefethen.

Publication

Information Outlook (mo.) (memb., non-memb. $125/yr.)

Committee Chairpersons

Association Office Operations. Ethel Salonen.
Awards and Honors. Cindy Hill.
Bylaws. Marjorie Hlava.
Cataloging. Buzz Haughton.
Committees. Wei Wei.
Conference Planning (2005). Karen Reczek.

Diversity Leadership Development. Vandana Ranjan, Jeffrey Dreiblatt.
Finance. Gloria Zamora.
Nominating. Wilda Newman.
Professional Development. Dee Magnoni.
Public Policy. Pat Wilson.
Public Relations. Kate Arnold.
Research. Sylvia James.
SLA Endowment Fund Grants. Susan DiMattia.
SLA Scholarship. Ailya Rose.
Student and Academic Relations. Linda Drake.
Technical Standards. Julie-Mae Stanley.

Theatre Library Association (TLA)

c/o The New York Public Library for the Performing Arts,
40 Lincoln Center Plaza, New York, NY 10023
World Wide Web http://tla.library.unt.edu

Object

To further the interests of collecting, preserving, and using theater, cinema, and performing arts materials in libraries, museums, and private collections. Founded 1937.

Membership

Memb. 375. Dues (Indiv.) $30, (Inst.) $40. Year. Jan. 1–Dec. 31.

Officers

Pres. Martha S. LoMonaco, Fairfield Univ.; *V.P.* Kenneth Schlesinger, LaGuardia Community College/CUNY; *Exec. Secy.* Nancy Friedland, Columbia Univ.; *Treas.* Paul Newman, private collector.

Executive Board

Susan Brady, Nena Couch, James Fisher, Mark Maniak, Judith S. Markowitz, Julian Mates, Robert W. Melton, Tobin Nellhaus, Catherine Ritchie, Jason Rubin, Angela Weaver, Don B. Wilmeth; *Honorary* Paul Myers, Marian Seldes; *Historian* Louis A. Rachow; *Legal Counsel* Madeleine Nichols.

Publications

Broadside (q.; memb.). *Ed.* Ellen Truax.
Performing Arts Resources (occasional; memb.).
Membership Directory. Ed. Maryann Chach.

Committee Chairpersons

Conference Planning. Kenneth Schlesinger.
Membership. Judy Markowitz.
Nominating. Kevin Winkler.
Professional Award. Camille Dee.
Publications. Robert Melton.
Strategic Planning. Kenneth Schlesinger.
TLA/Freedley Awards. Richard Wall.

Urban Libraries Council (ULC)

President, Martín Gómez
1603 Orrington Ave., Ste. 1080, Evanston, IL 60201
847-866-9999, fax 847-866-9989
E-mail info@urbanlibraries.org
World Wide Web http://www.urbanlibraries.org

Object

To identify and make known the opportunities for urban libraries serving cities of 100,000 or more individuals, located in a Standard Metropolitan Statistical Area; to provide information on state and federal legislation affecting urban library programs and systems; to facilitate the exchange of ideas and programs of member libraries and other libraries; to develop programs that enable libraries to act as a focus of community development and to supply the informational needs of the new urban populations; to conduct research and educational programs that will benefit urban libraries and to solicit and accept grants, contributions, and donations essential to their implementation.

ULC currently receives core funding from membership dues. Current major projects supported by grant funding from a variety of sources include: Librarians for America's Neighborhoods (funded by a grant from the Institute for Museum and Library Services), and Learning in Libraries (funded by the Wallace Foundation). ULC is a 501(c)(3) not-for-profit corporation based in the state of Illinois.

Membership

Membership is open to public libraries serving populations of 100,000 or more located in a Standard Metropolitan Statistical Area and to corporations specializing in library-related materials and services. Annual dues are based on the size of the library's operating budget, according to the following schedule: under $2 million to $10 million, $4,500; over $10 million, $7,500. In addition, ULC member libraries may choose Sustaining or Contributing status (Sustaining, $14,000; Contributing, $10,000). Corporate membership dues are $7,500.

Officers (2005–2006)

Chair Jane Light, dir., San Jose Public Lib., 150 E. San Fernando St., San Jose, CA 95112. Tel. 408-808-2150; *V. Chair/Chair-Elect* Mary Dempsey, dir., Chicago Public Lib., 400 S. State St., Chicago, IL 60605. Tel. 312-747-4090; *Secy./Treas.* Charles Higueras, San Francisco Public Lib. Friends and Foundation, 100 Larkin St., San Francisco, CA 94102; *Past Chair* Donna Nicely, dir., Nashville Public Lib., 615 Church St., Nashville, TN 37219-2314. Tel. 615-862-5760.

Officers serve one-year terms, members of the executive board two-year terms. New officers are elected and take office at the summer annual meeting of the council.

Executive Board

Marie Harris Aldridge. E-mail maldridge1@prodigy.net; Ginnie Cooper. E-mail g.cooper@brooklynpubliclibrary.org; Mary Dempsey. E-mail mdempsey@chipublib.org; Duncan Highsmith. E-mail dhighsmith@highsmith.com; Charles Higueras. E-mail chigueras@vbnarch.com; John Kretzmann. E-mail j-kretzmann@northwestern.edu; Patricia Lasher. E-mail pjl@fullenweider.com; Wai-Fong Lee. E-mail wflee@sccd.ctc.edu; Jane Light. E-mail jane.light@sjlibrary.org; Rosalind McGee. E-mail rozmcgee@xmission.com; Michael Morand. E-mail michael.morand@yale.edu; Donna Nicely. E-mail donna.nicely@nashville.gov; Clement Price. E-mail caprice@andromeda.rutgers.edu; Dot Ridings. E-mail dridings@aol.com; Raymond Santiago. E-mail santiagor@mdpls.org.

Key Staff

Pres. Martín Gómez; *Senior V.P., Admin./Member Services* Bridget A. Bradley; *V.P., Program/Development* Danielle Milam.

State, Provincial, and Regional Library Associations

The associations in this section are organized under three headings: United States, Canada, and Regional. Both the United States and Canada are represented under Regional associations.

United States

Alabama

Memb. 1,200. Term of Office. Apr. 2005–Apr. 2006. Publication. *The Alabama Librarian* (q.).

Pres. Jane Garrett, Baldwin Middle Magnet School, Montgomery 36102. Tel. 334-279-0022, e-mail rjgarrett_1991@yahoo.com; *Pres.-Elect* Bettye Forbus, Houston-Love Memorial Lib., P.O. Box 1369, Dothan 36302. Tel. 334-793-9767, e-mail blforbus@yahoo.com; *Secy.* Theresa C. Trawick, Lurleen B. Wallace Community College, MacArthur Campus, P.O. Drawer 910, Opp 36467. Tel. 334-493-5368, e-mail ttrawick@lbwcc.edu; *Treas.* Vivian B. White, Montgomery City-County Public Lib., P.O. Box 1950, Montgomery 36102. Tel. 334-240-4300, fax 334-240-4977; *Past Pres.* Tim Dodge, Auburn Univ. Libs., 213 Mell St., Auburn Univ., Auburn 36849-5606. Tel. 334-844-1729, fax 334-844-4461, e-mail dodgeti@auburn.edu; *Assoc. Admin.* Steve Chew, Professional Services Group, Bailey Building, 400 S. Union St., Ste. 395, Montgomery 36104. Tel. 877-563-5146 (toll-free), 334-263-1272, fax 334-265-1281, fax 334-265-1281, e-mail mdginc@bellsouth.net.

Address correspondence to the association administrator.

World Wide Web http://allanet.org.

Alaska

Memb. 450+. Publication. *Newspoke* (bi-mo.).

Pres. Ann Myren. E-mail amyren@apt alaska.net; *V.P./Committees* Amelia Jenkins. E-mail jnarj20@mail.uas.alaska.edu; *Co.-V.P.s/Conference* Colleen Tyrell. E-mail ctyrrell@chartercollege.edu; Judy Green. E-mail afjfg@uaa.alaska.edu; *Secy.* Caitlin Dixon. E-mail caitlinedixon@hotmail.com;

Treas. Diane Ruess. E-mail ffder@uaf.edu; *Past Pres.* Judith Anglin. E-mail juditha@firstcitylibraries.org; *Exec. Officer* Mary Jennings. E-mail maryj@gci.net.

Address correspondence to the secretary, Alaska Lib. Assn., P.O. Box 81084, Fairbanks 99708. Fax 877-863-1401, e-mail akla@akla.org.

World Wide Web http://www.akla.org.

Arizona

Memb. 1,000. Term of Office. Nov. 2005–Nov. 2006. Publication. *AzLA Newsletter* (mo.).

Pres. Deborah Tasnadi, Peoria Public Lib. Tel. 623-773-7555, e-mail DeborahT@peoria az.com; *Pres.-Elect* Ann Dutton Ewbank. E-mail adutton1@cox.net; *Secy.* Louisa Aikin, Mustang Lib. Tel. 480-312-6035, e-mail laikin@scottsdaleaz.gov; *Treas.* Denise Keller, Pinal County Lib. Tel. 520-866-6457, e-mail denise.keller@co.pinal.az.us; *Past Pres.* Thomas Sullivan, Tucson-Pima Public Lib. Tel. 520-791-4391, e-mail laura.sullivan @tucsonaz.gov; *Admin. Asst.* Courtney LeVinus. E-mail admin@azla.org.

Address correspondence to the administrative assistant, AzLA, 2302 N. 3 St., Ste. F, Phoenix 85004.

World Wide Web http://www.azla.org.

Arkansas

Memb. 600. Term of Office. Jan.–Dec. 2006. Publication. *Arkansas Libraries* (bi-mo.).

Pres. Diane Hughes, Lake Hamilton Junior H.S., 281 Wolf St., Pearcy 71964. Tel. 501-767-2731, fax 501-767-1711, e-mail diane.hughes@lh.dsc.k12.ar.us; *V.P.* Ashley Burris, Lawrence County Lib., 1315 W. Main St., Walnut Ridge, 72476. Tel. 870-886-3222, fax 870-886-9520, e-mail akburris@hotmail.com; *Secy.-Treas.* Jamie Melson, Main Lib., Central Arkansas Lib. System,

100 Rock St., Little Rock 72201. Tel. 501-918-3074, fax 501-376-1830, e-mail jamiem @cals.lib.ar.us; *Past Pres.* Art Lichtenstein, Torreyson Lib., Univ. of Central Arkansas, 201 Donaghey Ave., Conway 72035. Tel. 501-450-5203, e-mail artl@uca.edu; *Exec. Admin.* Barbara Martin, P.O. Box 958, Benton 72018-0958. Tel. 501-860-7585, fax 501-776-9709, e-mail brmassocmgt@sbcglobal. net.

Address correspondence to the executive administrator.

World Wide Web http://www.arlib.org.

California

Memb. 2,500. Publication. *California Libraries* (bi-mo., print and online).

Pres. Margaret Miles, Plumas County Lib. Tel. 530-283-6269, e-mail margaretmiles@ countyofplumas.com; *V.P./Pres.-Elect* Margaret Todd, County of Los Angeles Public Lib. Tel. 562-940-8400, e-mail mdtodd@gw. colapl.org; *Treas.* Annette Milliron DeBacker, North Bay Cooperative Lib. System. Tel. 707-544-0142, e-mail annetnbc@sonic.net; *Past Pres.* Danis Kreimeier, Yorba Linda Public Lib. Tel. 714-777-2873 ext. 121, e-mail danisk@ylpl.lib.ca.us; *Exec. Dir./Secy.* Susan E. Negreen, California Lib. Assn., 717 20th St., Ste. 200, Sacramento 95814. Tel. 916-447-8541 ext. 2, fax 916-447-8394, e-mail snegreen@cla-net.org.

Address correspondence to the executive director.

World Wide Web http://www.cla-net.org.

Colorado

Memb. 1,100. Term of Office. Oct. 2005–Oct. 2006. Publication. *Colorado Libraries* (q.). *Co-Eds.* Janet Lee, Dayton Memorial Lib., Regis Univ., 3333 Regis Blvd., D-20, Denver 80221. Tel. 303-458-3552, fax 303-964-5143, e-mail jlee@regis.edu; Eileen Dumas, Aurora Public Lib., 14949 E. Alameda Pkwy., Aurora 80012. Tel. 303-739-6637, fax 303-739-6579, e-mail edumas@ci.aurora. co.us.

Pres. Judy Barnett, Wasson H.S., 2115 Afton Way, Colorado Springs 80909. Tel. 719-328-2024, e-mail barnejm@d11.org.; *V.P./Pres.-Elect* Beth Wrenn-Estes; *Secy.*

Abby Hoverstock; *Treas.* Shannon Cruthers; *Past Pres.* Ellen Greenblatt; *Exec. Dir.* Kathleen Sagee Noland, Colorado Association of Libs., 12081 W. Alameda Pkwy., No. 427, Lakewood 80228. Tel. 303-463-6400, e-mail kathleen@cal-webs.org.

Address correspondence to the executive director.

World Wide Web http://www.cal-webs. org.

Connecticut

Memb. 1,100. Term of Office. July 2005–June 2006. Publication. *Connecticut Libraries* (11 a year). *Ed.* David Kapp, 4 Llynwood Dr., Bolton 06040. Tel. 203-647-0697.

Pres. Alice Knapp, Ferguson Lib., Stamford 06904. Tel. 203-964-1000, fax 203-357-9098, e-mail aknapp@ferg.lib.ct.us *V.P./ Pres.-Elect* Tom Geoffino, Fairfield Public Lib. Tel. 203-256-3155, fax 203-256-3162, e-mail tgeoffino@fplct.org; *Treas.* Jan Fisher, Bridgeport Public Lib., Bridgeport 06604. Tel. 203-576-7777, fax 203-333-0253, e-mail jfisher@bridgeportpubliclibrary.org; *Past Pres.* Christine Bradley, Connecticut Lib. Consortium, 2911 Dixwell Ave., Hamden 06518-3130. Tel. 203-288-5757; *Admin. Asst.* Pam Najarian, Connecticut Library Assn., P.O. Box 85, Willimantic, CT 06226-0085. Tel. 860-465-5006, fax 860-465-5004, e-mail cla@ctlibrarians.org.

Address correspondence to the assistant administrator.

World Wide Web http://cla.uconn.edu.

Delaware

Memb. 300. Term of Office. Apr. 2005–Apr. 2006. Publication. *DLA Online Bulletin* (electronic only at http://www.dla.lib.de.us/ bulletin.shtml).

Pres. Hilary Welliver, Dover Public Lib. 45 S. State St., Dover 19901. Tel. 302-736-7034, fax 302-736-5087, e-mail hwell@lib. de. us; *V.P.* Paul Anderson, Univ. of Delaware Lib., 181 S. College Ave., Newark 19717-5267. Tel. 302-831-2231, e-mail pa@udel. edu; *Treas.* Michael Gutierrez, Univ. of Delaware Lib., 181 S. College Ave., Newark 19717-5267. Tel. 302-831-6076, fax 302-831-1631, e-mail mgutierrez@udel.edu;

Secy. Dianne McKellar, Univ. of Delaware Lib., 181 S. College Ave., Newark 19717-5267. Tel. 302-831-6076, fax 302-831-1631, e-mail mckellar@udel.edu; *Past Pres.* Margaret Prouse, Delaware Tech, Terry Campus, 100 Campus Dr., Dover 19904. Tel. 302-857-1060, fax 302-857-1099, e-mail mprouse@college.dtec.edu.

Address correspondence to the association, Box 816, Dover 19903-0816. E-mail dla@dla.lib.de.us.

World Wide Web http://www.dla.lib.de.us.

District of Columbia

Memb. 300+. Term of Office. July 2005–June 2006. Publication. *Intercom* (mo.).

Pres. Kathryn Ray, American Univ. Lib. Tel. 202-885-3238, e-mail ray@american.edu; *V.P./Pres.-Elect* Elaine Cline. Tel. 202 647-3002, e-mail ClineCE@state.gov; *Secy.* Bill Tuceling. Tel. 202 512-5025, e-mail tucelingw@gao.gov; *Treas.* Sara Striner. Tel. 202-707-2957, e-mail sstr@loc.gov; *Past Pres.* Noel Rutherford, District of Columbia Public Lib. Tel. 202-282-0213, fax 202-282-2326, e-mail nrutherf@yahoo.com.

Address correspondence to the association, Box 14177, Benjamin Franklin Sta., Washington, DC 20044. Tel. 202-872-1112.

World Wide Web http://www.dcla.org.

Florida

Memb. (Indiv.) 1,400+. Term of Office. April 2005–March 2006. Publication. *Florida Libraries* (s. ann.). *Ed.* Gloria Colvin, Florida State Univ. Libs. E-mail gpcolvin@yahoo.com.

Pres. Nancy Pike, Sarasota County Lib. System, 6700 Clark Rd., Sarasota 34241. Tel. 941-861-9842, fax 941-861-9855, e-mail nmpike@scgov.net; *Pres.-Elect* Sol M. Hirsch, Alachua County Lib. District, 401 E. University Ave., Gainesville 32601. Tel. 352-334-3910, fax 352-334-3918, e-mail shirsch@aclib.us; *Secy.* Lisa Manners, Broward County West Regional Lib., 8601 W. Broward Blvd., Plantation 33324. Tel. 954-831-3306, fax 954-831-3326, e-mail lmanners@browardlibrary.org; *Treas.* Shannon Bennett-Manross, M. M. Bennett Lib., Gibbs Campus, St. Petersburg College, 6605

Fifth Ave. N., St. Petersburg 33781. Tel. 727-341-3517, fax 727-341-4654, e-mail Manross.Shannon@spcollege.edu; *Past Pres.* Derrie Perez, USF Lib. System, 4202 E. Fowler St., Lib. 122, Tampa 33620-5400. Tel. 813-974-1642, fax 813-974-5153, e-mail dperez@lib.usf.edu; *Exec. Dir.* Ruth O'Donnell, 3509 Trillium Court, Tallahassee 32312. Tel. 850-668-6911, e-mail flaexecutivedirector@comcast.net.

Address correspondence to the executive director.

World Wide Web http://www.flalib.org.

Georgia

Memb. 1,080. Term of Office. Dec. 2005–Dec. 2006. Publication. *Georgia Library Quarterly.* *Ed.* Susan Cooley, Sara Hightower Regional Lib., 205 Riverside Pkwy., Rome 30161. Tel. 706-236-4621, fax 706-236-4631, e-mail cooleys@mail.floyd.public.lib.ga.us.

Pres. Bob Fox, Clayton College and State Univ. Lib., P.O. Box 285, Morrow 30260. Tel. 770-961-3520, e-mail bob.fox@library.gatech.edu; *1st V.P./Pres.-Elect* JoEllen Ostendorf. E-mail jostendorf@thclibrary.net; *2nd V.P.* Elaine Yontz. E-mail eyontz@valdosta.edu; *Secy.* Carolyn Fuller. E-mail cfuller@henry.public.lib.ga.us; *Treas.* Carol Stanley. E-mail cstanley@athenstech.edu; *Past Pres.* Julie Walker. E-mail jwalker@georgialibraries.org.

Address correspondence to the president, c/o Georgia Lib. Assn., Box 793, Rex 30273-0793.

World Wide Web http://gla.georgialibraries.org.

Hawaii

Memb. 320. Publication. *HLA Newsletter* (3 a year).

Pres. Carol Kellett, Univ. of Hawaii at Manoa. E-mail president@hlaweb.org; *V.P.* Keiko Okuharat, Univ. of Hawaii at Manoa. E-mail vicepresident@hlaweb.org; *Secy.* Nancy Sack, Univ. of Hawaii at Manoa. E-mail secretary@hlaweb.org; *Co-Treas.* Kuang-Tien ("KT") Yao, Xin Li. E-mail treasurer@hlaweb.org; *Past Pres.* A. Lee Adams. E-mail pastpresident@hlaweb.org.

Address correspondence to the president.

Idaho

Memb. 500. Term of Office. Oct. 2005–Oct. 2006.

Pres. Val Fenske, Curriculum and Technology Center, Idaho Dept. of Educ., P.O. Box 83720, Boise 83720. Tel. 208-332-6967, e-mail vafenske@sde.idaho.gov; *V.P./Pres.-Elect* Tamra Hawley-House, Boise Public Lib., 715 S. Capitol Blvd., Boise 83702. Tel. 208-384-4200, e-mail thawley@cityofboise.org; *Secy.* Lynne Bidwell, Lewis-Clark State College Lib., 500 Eighth Ave., Lewiston 83501-2698. Tel. 208-792-2438, e-mail lbidwell@lcsc.edu; *Treas.* Pam Bradshaw, Idaho State Lib., 325 W. State St., Boise 82702. Tel. 208-334-2150, e-mail pbradsha@isl.state.id.us; *Past Pres.* Barbara Greever, Univ. of Idaho Lib., Box 442350, Moscow 83844-2350. Tel. 208-885-2510, e-mail bgreever@uidaho.edu.

Address correspondence to the president.

World Wide Web http://www.idaho libraries.org.

Illinois

Memb. 3,000. Term of Office. July 2005–July 2006. Publication. *ILA Reporter* (bi-mo.).

Pres. Allen Lanham, Booth Lib., Eastern Illinois Univ., 600 Lincoln Ave., Charleston 61920; *V.P./Pres.-Elect* Dianne C. Harmon, Black Road Branch, Joliet Public Lib., 3395 Black Rd., Joliet 60431; *Treas.* Christopher Bowen, Downers Grove Public Lib., 1050 Curtiss, Downers Grove 60515-4606; *Past Pres.* Nancy M. Gillfillan, Fondulac District Lib., 140 E. Washington St., East Peoria 61611-2526; *Exec. Dir.* Robert P. Doyle, 33 W. Grand Ave., Ste. 301, Chicago 60610-4306. Tel. 312-644-1896, fax 312-644-1899, e-mail ila@ila.org.

Address correspondence to the executive director.

World Wide Web http://www.ila.org.

Indiana

Memb. 3,000+. Term of Office. March 2005–April 2006. Publication. *Indiana Libraries* (s. ann.). *Ed.* Alberta Davis Comer, Cunningham Memorial Lib., Indiana State Univ., 650 Sycamore St., Terre Haute 47809. E-mail libcomer@isugw.indstate.edu.

Pres. Wendy Phillips. Tel. 317-814-3901, fax 317-571-4285, e-mail wphillips@carmel.lib.in.us; *1st V.P.* Sara Laughlin. Tel. 812-334-8485, fax 812-336-2215, e-mail laughlin@bluemarble.net; *2nd V.P.* Jeff Lorenzo. Tel. 812-524-9000, fax 812-524-9001, e-mail jlorenzo@jefflorenzo.com; *Secy.* Nancy Wootton Colborn. Tel. 574-237-4321, fax 574-237-4472, e-mail ncolborn@iusb.edu; *Treas.* David Eisen. Tel. 574-259-5277, fax 574-255-8489, e-mail d.eisen@mppl.lib.in.us; *Past Pres.* John Robson. Tel. 812-877-8365, fax 812-877-8175, e-mail john.m.robson@rose-hulman.edu; *Exec. Dir.* Linda Kolb. E-mail lkolb@ilfonline.org.

Address correspondence to Indiana Lib. Federation, 941 E. 86 St., Ste. 260, Indianapolis 46240. Tel. 317-257-2040, fax 317-257-1389, e-mail ilf@indy.net.

World Wide Web http://www.ilfonline.org.

Iowa

Memb. 1,700. Term of Office. Jan.–Dec. Publication. *The Catalyst* (bi-mo.). *Ed.* Laurie Hews.

Pres. Susan Craig, Iowa City Public Lib., 123 S. Linn St., Iowa City 52240. Tel. 319-356-5200 ext. 153, fax 319-365-5495, e-mail scraig@icpl.org; *V.P./Pres.-Elect* Sheryl Bissen, Grinnell College Libs., 1111 Sixth Ave., Grinnell 50112. Tel. 641-269-3359, fax 641-269-4283, e-mail bissen@grinnell.edu; *Secy.* Marilyn Murphy, Busse Center Lib., Mt. Mercy College, 1330 Elmhurst Dr. N.E., Cedar Rapids 52402. Tel. 319-363-8213 ext. 1244, fax 319-363-9060, e-mail marilyn@mmc.mtmercy.edu; *Past Pres.* Katherine F. Martin, Rod Lib., Univ. of Northern Iowa, Cedar Falls 50613-3675. Tel. 319-273-7255, fax 319-273-2913, e-mail katherine.martin@uni.edu; *Exec. Dir.* Laurie Hews. Tel. 515-273-5322, fax 515-309-4576, e-mail ialibrary@mcleodusa.net.

Address correspondence to the association, 3636 Westown Pkwy., Ste. 202, West Des Moines 50266.

World Wide Web http://www.iowalibrary association.org.

Kansas

Memb. 1,500. Term of Office. July 2005–June 2006. Publication. *KLA Newsletter* (q.). *Pres.* Tim Rogers, Johnson County Lib., Box 2933, Shawnee Mission 66201. E-mail rogers@jocolibrary.org; *1st V.P.* Michelle Swain, Arkansas City Public Lib., 120 E 5 Ave, Arkansas City 67005. Tel. 620-442-1280, e-mail mswain@acpl.org; *Secy.* Kristen Becker, Liberal Memorial Lib., 509 N. Kansas, Liberal 67901; *Past Pres.* Bob Walter, Axe Lib., Pittsburg State Univ., Pittsburg 66762; *Exec. Dir.* Rosanne Siemens, Kansas Lib. Assn., 1020 Washburn, Topeka 66604. Tel. 866-552-4636, 785-235-1383, fax 785-235-1383, e-mail kansaslibraryassociation@yahoo.com.

Address correspondence to the executive director.

World Wide Web http://skyways.lib.ks.us/KLA.

Kentucky

Memb. 1,900. Term of Office. Oct. 2005–Oct. 2006. Publication. *Kentucky Libraries* (q.).

Pres. Christine McIntosh, Bernheim Middle School, 700 Audubon Dr., Shepherdsville 40165. Tel. 502-543-7614, fax 502-543-8295, e-mail cmcintosh@bullitt.k12.ky.us; *V.P./Pres.-Elect* Laura Davison, Univ. of Kentucky Medical Center Lib., Lexington 40526-0298. Tel. 859-323-6138, fax 859-323-1040, e-mail davison@email.uky.edu; *Secy.* Matt Onion, Ashland Community and Technical College, 1400 College Dr., Ashland 41101. Tel. 606-326-2113, e-mail matt.onion@kctcs.edu; *Past Pres.* Linda Kompanik, Logan County Public Lib., 201 W. Sixth St., Russellville 42276. Tel. 270-726-6129, fax 270-726-6127, e-mail lindak@loganlibrary.org; *Exec. Secy.* Tom Underwood, 1501 Twilight Trail, Frankfort 40601. Tel. 502-223-5322, fax 502-223-4937, e-mail info@kylibasn.org.

Address correspondence to the executive secretary.

World Wide Web http://www.kylibasn.org.

Louisiana

Memb. (Indiv.) 1,170; (Inst.) 56. Term of Office. July 2005–June 2006. Publication. *Louisiana Libraries* (q.). *Ed.* Vivian Solar. Tel. 225-647-8924, fax 225-644-0063, e-mail vsolar@state.lib.la.us.

Pres. Jackie Choate. Tel. 337-893-2655, fax 337-898-0526, e-mail jchoate@state.lib.la.us; *1st V.P./Pres.-Elect* Beth Paskoff. Tel. 225-578-1480, fax 225-578-4581, e-mail bpaskoff@lsu.edu; *2nd V.P.* Mary Cosper LeBoeuf. Tel. 985-876-5861, fax 985-876-5864, e-mail mcosperl@state.lib.la.us; *Secy.* Betsy Miguez. Tel. 337-482-1173, fax 337-482-5841, e-mail bbmiguez@louisiana.edu; *Past Pres.* Terry Thibodeaux. Tel./fax 225-621-8281, e-mail thibodeaux@cox.net.

Address correspondence to Louisiana Lib. Assn., 421 S. Fourth St., Eunice 70535. Tel. 337-550-7890, fax 337-550-7846, e-mail office@llaonline.org.

World Wide Web http://www.llaonline.org.

Maine

Memb. 950. Term of Office. (Pres., V.P.) July 2005–July 2006. Publication. *Maine Memo* (mo.).

Pres. Pamela Turner, Baxter Memorial Lib., 71 South St., Gorham 04038. Tel. 207-839-5031, e-mail pturner@baxter-memorial.lib.me.us; *V.P./Pres.-Elect* Nikki Maounis, Rockland Public Lib., 80 Union St., Rockland 04841. Tel. 207-594-0310, fax 207-594-0333, e-mail nmaounis@rockland.me.us; *Secy.* Sarah Sugden, Waterville Public Lib., 73 Elm St., Waterville 04901. Tel. 207-872-5433, fax 207-873-4779, e-mail ssugden@waterville.lib.me.us; *Treas.* Marian Peterson, South Portland Public Lib., 482 Broadway, South Portland 04106. Tel. 207-767-7662, fax 207-767-76726, e-mail mpeterson@south portland.org; *Past Pres.* Steve Norman, Belfast Free Lib., 106 High St., Belfast 04915. Tel. 207-338-3884, e-mail snorman@belfast library.org.

Address correspondence to the association, 60 Community Dr., Augusta 04330. Tel. 207-623-8428, fax 207-626-5947. World Wide Web http://mainelibraries.org.

Maryland

Memb. 1,000. Term of Office. July 2005–July 2006. Publications. *Happenings* (mo.), *The Crab* (q.).

Pres. Kay Bowman, Davis Community Lib., Montgomery County Public Lib.; *1st V.P./Pres.-Elect* Michael Gannon, Anne Arundel County Public Lib.; *2nd V.P.* Valerie Piechocki, Prince Georges County Public Lib; *Secy.* Monica McAbee, Prince Georges County Public Lib.; *Treas.* Beth Pelle, Frederick County Public Libs.; *Past Pres.* Raineyl Coiro, Eastern Shore Regional Lib.; *Exec. Dir.* Margaret Carty.

Address correspondence to the association, 1401 Hollins St., Baltimore 21223. Tel. 410-947-5090, fax 410-947-5089, e-mail mla@mdlib.org.

World Wide Web http://mdlib.org.

Massachusetts

Memb. (Indiv.) 950; (Inst.) 100. Term of Office. July 2005–June 2006. Publication. *Bay State Libraries* (4 a year).

Pres. Kathleen Baxter. Tel. 781-320-7230, fax 781-320-7230, e-mail katie_baxter-fac@nobles.edu; *V.P./Pres.-Elect* Kathy Glick Weil. Tel. 617-796-1400, fax 617-965-8457, e-mail glickweil@minlib.net; *Secy.* Marnie Warner. Tel. 617-878-0338, fax 617-723-8821, e-mail warner_m@jud.state.ma.us; *Treas.* Ann Parsons Wirtanen. Tel. 978-433-0330, fax 978-723-8821, e-mail aparsons@cwmars.org; *Past Pres.* Carolyn Noah. Tel. 508-757-4110 ext.305, fax 508-757-4370, e-mail cnoah@cmrls.org; *Exec. Mgr.* Diane Klaiber, Massachusetts Lib. Assn., P.O. Box 1445, Marstons Mills 02648. Tel. 508-428-5865, fax 508-428-5865, e-mail malibraries@comcast.net.

Address correspondence to the executive manager.

World Wide Web http://www.masslib.org.

Michigan

Memb. (Indiv.) 1,850; (Inst.) 375. Term of Office. July 2005–June 2006 Publications. *Michigan Librarian Newsletter* (6 a year), *Michigan Library Association Forum* e-journal (2 a year).

Pres. Michael McGuire, Traverse Area District Lib., 610 Woodmere Ave., Traverse City 49686. Tel. 616-932-8500, fax 616-932-8538, e-mail mlaprez@tcnet.org; *Pres.-Elect* Leah Black, Michigan State Univ., 11595 Chandler Rd., DeWitt 48820-9710. Tel. 517-432-6123, fax 517-353-8969, e-mail blackl@msu.edu; *V.P.* Julia Nims, Eastern Michigan Univ., EMU Halle Lib., Ypsilanti 48197. Tel. 734-487-0020, fax 734-487-8861, e-mail julia.nims@emich.edu; *Secy.* Sheryl Vanderwagen, Lakeland Lib. Cooperative, 4138 Three Mile Rd., Grand Rapids 49544. Tel. 616-559-5253, fax 616-559-4329, e-mail sheryl@llcoop.org; *Past Pres.* Linda Farynk, Saginaw Valley State Univ., 415 W. Main St., Midland 48640. Tel. 989-964-4236, fax 989-964-2003, e-mail lfarynk@svsu.edu.

Address correspondence to Gretchen Couraud, Exec. Dir., Michigan Lib. Assn., 1407 Rensen St., Ste. 2, Lansing 48910. Tel. 517-394-2774, fax 517-394-2675, e-mail mla@mlcnet.org.

World Wide Web http://www.mla.lib.mi.us.

Minnesota

Memb. 900. Term of Office. (Pres., Pres.-Elect) Jan.–Dec. 2006.

Pres. Audrey Betcher. Tel. 507-285-8011, fax 507-287-1910, e-mail audrey@rochester.lib.mn.us; *Pres.-Elect* Heidi Hoks. Tel. 320-650-2500, fax 320-650-2501, e-mail heidih@grrl.lib.mn.us; *Secy.* Michele McGraw. Tel. 952-847-5931, e-mail mmcgraw@hclib.org; *Treas.* Ann Hokanson. Tel. 507-433-2391, e-mail ahokanson@selco.info; *Past Pres.* Marlene Moulton Janssen. Tel. 763-785-3695, fax 763-717-3262, e-mail marlene.moultonjanssen@anoka.lib.mn.us; *Exec. Dir.* Barbara Vaughan, Minnesota Lib. Assn., 1619 Dayton Ave., Ste. 314, Saint Paul 55104. Tel. 651-641-0982, fax 651-641-3169, e-mail barbara@mnlibraryassociation.org.

Address correspondence to the executive director.

World Wide Web http://www.mnlibraryassociation.org.

Mississippi

Memb. 600. Term of Office. Jan.–Dec. 2006. Publication. *Mississippi Libraries* (q.). *Pres.* Susan S. Cassagne, Natchez Adams Wilkinson Lib. Service. Tel. 601-445-8862, fax 601-446-7795, e-mail scassagne@naw. lib.ms.us; *V.P./Pres.-Elect* Catherine A. Nathan, First Regional Lib. System. Tel. 662-429-4439, e-mail cnathan@first.lib.ms.us; *Secy.* Linda Milner, Mid Mississippi Library System. Tel. 662-289-5151, e-mail asst director@midmissregional.lib.ms.us; *Treas.* Carol D. Green, Univ. of Southern Mississippi. Tel. 601-266-4476, e-mail carol.green@ usm.edu; *Past Pres.* Juanita Flanders, Hinds Community College, Box 1100, Raymond 39154-1100. Tel. 601-857-3380, fax 601-857-3293, e-mail hjflanders@hinds.cc.ms.us; *Exec. Secy.* Mary Julia Anderson, P.O. Box 13687, Jackson 39236-3687. Tel. 601-981-4586, fax 601-981-4501, e-mail info@miss lib.org.

Address correspondence to the executive secretary.

World Wide Web http://www.misslib.org/index.php.

Missouri

Memb. 812. Term of Office. Jan.–Dec. 2006. Publication. *MO INFO* (bi-mo.). *Ed.* Margaret Booker.

Pres. Wicky Sleight, Kirkwood Public Lib., 140 E. Jefferson Ave., Kirkwood 63122. Tel. 314-821-5770, fax 314-822-3755, e-mail wsleight@real.more.net; *Pres.-Elect* Karen Horny, Missouri State Univ. Libs., 901 S. National Ave., Springfield 65897. Tel. 417-836-4525, fax 417-836-4764, e-mail karen horny@missouristate.edu; *Secy.* Carrie Cline, McDonald County Lib., 808 Bailey Rd., Pineville 64856. Tel. 417-223-4489, fax 417-223-4011, e-mail carrie@librarymail.org; *Treas.* Catherine Craven, Health Management and Information–UMC, P.O. Box 7702, Columbia 65205. Tel. 573-882-1542, e-mail cravenc@health.missouri.edu; *Past Pres.* Ann Campion Riley, Lovejoy Lib., Southern Illinois Univ.–Edwardsville, 14140 Cross Trails Dr., Chesterfield 63017-3309. Tel. 618-650-2779, e-mail anriley@siue.edu; *Exec. Dir.* Margaret Booker, Missouri Lib.

Assn., 3212-A LeMone Industrial Blvd., Columbia 65201. Tel. 573-449-4627, fax 573-449-4655, e-mail mla001@more.net.

Address correspondence to the executive director.

World Wide Web http://www.molib.org.

Montana

Memb. 600. Term of Office. July 2005–June 2006. Publication. *Montana Library Focus* (bi-mo.).

Pres. Milla L. Cummins, Livingston-Park County Public Lib., 228 W. Callender St., Livingston 59047-2618. Tel. 406-222-0862, fax 406-222-6522, e-mail mcummins@ycsi. net; *V.P./Pres.-Elect* Lyn McKinney; *Secy./Treas.* Debbi Kramer, Judith Basin County Lib., P.O. Box 486, Standford 59479. Tel. 406-566-2277 ext. 123, e-mail spclk@ 3rivers.net; *Past Pres.* Richard Wojtowicz, MSU Libs., Box 173320, Bozeman 59717-3320. Tel. 406-994-1873, fax 406-994-2851, e-mail richw@montana.edu; *Exec. Dir.* Ilene Casey, P.O. Box 1085, Manhattan 59741-1085. Tel. 406-284-6646, e-mail mla_icasey @mtlib.org.

Address correspondence to the executive director.

World Wide Web http://www.mtlib.org.

Nebraska

Term of Office. Jan.–Dec. 2006. Publication. *Nebraska Library Association Quarterly (NLAQ)* (q.). *Ed.* John Bernardi. E-mail bernardj@omaha.lib.ne.us.

Pres. Joan Birnie, Broken Bow Public Lib. E-mail bbpl@kdsi.net; *V.P./Pres.-Elect* Beth Goble, Nebraska Lib. Commission. E-mail bgoble@nlc.state.ne.us; *Secy.* Julie Simpson, Lincoln City Libs. E-mail j.simpson@mail. lcl.lib.ne.us; *Treas.* Devra Dragos, Nebraska Lib. Commission. E-mail ddragos@nlc.state. ne.us; *Past Pres.* Brenda Ealey, Southeast Lib. System. E-mail bsealey@alltel.net; *Exec. Dir.* Maggie Harding. E-mail gh12521 @alltel.net.

Address correspondence to the executive director.

World Wide Web http://www.nebraska libraries.org.

Nevada

Memb. 450. Term of Office. Jan.–Dec. 2006. Publication. *Nevada Libraries* (q.).

Pres. Kim Clanton-Green, Las Vegas-Clark County Lib. Dist. E-mail clanton-greenk@lvccld.org; *V.P./Pres.-Elect* Debbie Jacobs, Clayton Middle School. E-mail djacobs@washoe.k12.nv.us; *Treas.* Joanne Ross, Spring Valley Lib., Las Vegas-Clark County Lib. Dist. E-mail rossj@lvccld.org; *Past Pres.* Ian Campbell, Washoe County Lib. System. E-mail idcampbe@mail.co.washoe.nv.us; *Exec. Secy.* Tamara Gieseking, Enterprise Lib., Las Vegas-Clark County Lib. Dist., 25 E. Shelbourne Ave., Las Vegas 89123. Tel. 702-507-3779, fax 702-507-3779, e-mail giesekingt@lvccld.org.

Address correspondence to the executive secretary.

World Wide Web http://www.nevada libraries.org.

New Hampshire

Memb. 700. Publication. *NHLA News* (q.).

Pres. Doris Mitton, Dalton Public Lib., 741 Dalton Rd., Unit 2, Dalton 03598. Tel. 603-837-2751, e-mail daltonpl@ncia.net; *V.P./Pres.-Elect* Ann Donohue, Manchester Lib., Univ. of New Hampshire, 400 Commercial St., Manchester 03101. Tel. 603-641-4173, e-mail annie.donohue@unh.edu; *Secy.* Dianne Hathaway, Goffstown Public Lib., 2 High St., Goffstown 03045. Tel. 603-497-2102, e-mail dianneh@goffstown.lib.nh.us; *Past Pres.* Catherine Redden, Lane Memorial Lib., 2 Academy Ave., Hampton 03842. Tel. 603-926-3368, e-mail director@hampton.lib.nh.us.

Address correspondence to the association, Box 2332, Concord 03302.

World Wide Web http://webster.state.nh.us/nhla.

New Jersey

Memb. 1,700. Term of Office. July 2005–June 2006. Publication. *New Jersey Libraries Newsletter* (mo.).

Pres. April Judge, West Caldwell Public Lib., 30 Clinton Rd., West Caldwell 07006. Tel. 973-226-5441, fax 973-228-7578, e-mail judge@bccls.org; *V.P.* Joan Bernstein, Mount Laurel Lib., 100 Walt Whitman Ave., Mount Laurel 08054. Tel. 856-234-7319 ext. 303, fax 856-234-6916, e-mail jeb@mtlaurel.lib.nj.us; *2nd V.P.* Mary Mallery, Sprague Lib., Montclair State Univ., 1 Normal Ave., Montclair 07043. Tel. 973-655-7150, fax 973-655-7780, e-mail mallerym@mail.montclair.edu; *Secy.* Margery Kirby Cyr, Old Bridge Public Lib., 1 Old Bridge Plaza, Old Bridge 08857. Tel. 732-721-5600 ext. 5014, fax 732-679-0556, e-mail mcyr@lmxac.org; *Treas.* Keith McCoy, Roselle Public Lib., 104 W. 4 Ave., Roselle 07203. Tel. 908-245-5809, fax 908-298-8881, e-mail wkmccoy@lmxac.org; *Past Pres.* Carol Phillips, East Brunswick Public Lib., 2 Jean Walling Civic Center, East Brunswick 08816. Tel. 732-390-6789, fax 732-390-6796, e-mail cphillips@ebpl.org; *Exec. Dir.* Patricia Tumulty, NJLA, Box 1534, Trenton 08607. Tel. 609-394-8032, fax 609-394-8164, e-mail ptumulty@njla.org.

Address correspondence to the executive director.

World Wide Web http://www.njla.org.

New Mexico

Memb. 550. Term of Office. Apr. 2005–Apr. 2006. Publication. *New Mexico Library Association Newsletter* (6 a year).

Pres. Kathy Matter. E-mail matterkathy@aol.com; *V.P.* Anne Lefkofsky. E-mail lefkofsky@cabq.gov; *Secy.* Julia Clarke. E-mail jclarke@cabq.gov; *Treas.* Joe Becker. E-mail jbecke@nmsu.edu; *Past Pres.* Heather Gallegos-Rex. E-mail heather.gallegos-rex@nm.state.us.

Address correspondence to the association, Box 26074, Albuquerque 87125. Tel. 505-400-7309, fax 505-891-5171, e-mail admin@nmla.org.

World Wide Web http://www.nmla.org.

New York

Memb. 3,000. Term of Office. Oct. 2005–Oct. 2006. Publication. *NYLA Bulletin* (6 a year). *Ed.* Michael J. Borges.

Pres. Jennifer Morris. Tel. 585-394-8260, e-mail jmorris@pls-net.org; *Pres.-Elect* Rachel Baum. Tel. 518-442-5110, e-mail rrbaum@uamail.albany.edu; *Treas.* Christine

McDonald. Tel. 518-92-6508, e-mail mcdonald@crandalllibrary.org; *Past Pres.* Rocco Staino. Tel. 914-669-5414, e-mail stainor@northsalem.k12.ny.us; *Exec. Dir.* Michael J. Borges. E-mail director@nyla.org.

Address correspondence to the executive director, New York Lib. Assn., 252 Hudson Ave., Albany 12210. Tel. 800-252-6952 or 518-432-6952, fax 518-427-1697, e-mail director@nyla.org.

World Wide Web http://www.nyla.org.

North Carolina

Memb. 1,100. Term of Office. Oct. 2005–Oct. 2007. Publication. *North Carolina Libraries* (q.). *Ed.* Ralph Schott, Academic Lib. Services, 4016 Joyner Lib., East Carolina Univ., Greenville 27858. Tel. 252-328-0265, fax 252-328-0268, e-mail scottr@mail.ecu.edu.

Pres. Robert Burgin, North Carolina Central Univ., 307 Swiss Lake Dr., Cary 27513. Tel. 919-462-0134, fax 919-380-8074, e-mail rburgin@mindspring.com; *V.P./Pres.-Elect* Phil Barton, Rowan Public Lib., P.O. Box 4039, Salisbury 28145. Tel. 704-216-8229, e-mail bartonp@co.rowan.nc.us; *Secy.* Paula Hinton, P.O. Box 1148, Buies Creek 27506. Tel. 919-962-1151, e-mail pphinton@email.unc.edu; *Treas.* Tina Stepp, 212 Newman Dr., Hendersonville 28792. Tel. 828-697-4725, e-mail tstepp@Henderson.lib.nc.us; *Past Pres.* Pauletta Brown Bracy, North Carolina Central Univ., SLIS, Box 19586, Durham 27707. Tel. 919-560-6401, fax 919-560-6402, e-mail pbracy@wpo.nccu.edu; *Admin. Asst.* Kim Parrott, North Carolina Lib. Assn., 1811 Capital Blvd., Raleigh 27604. Tel. 919-839-6252, fax 919-839-6253, e-mail nclaonline@ibiblio.org.

Address correspondence to the administrative assistant.

World Wide Web http://www.nclaonline.org.

North Dakota

Memb. (Indiv.) 400; (Inst.) 18. Term of Office. Sept. 2005–Sept. 2006. Publication. *The Good Stuff* (q.). *Ed.* Marlene Anderson, Bismarck State College Lib., Box 5587, Bismarck 58506-5587. Tel. 701-224-5578.

Pres. Jeanne Narum, Minot Public Lib., 516 Second Ave. S.W., Minot 58701. Tel. 701-852-1045, fax 701-852-2595, e-mail jnarum@srt.com; *Pres.-Elect* Beth Postema, Fargo Public Lib., 102 N. Third St., Fargo 58102. Tel. 701-241-1491, fax 701-241-8581, e-mail bepostema@ci.fargo.nd.us; *Treas.* Michael Safratowich, Harley French Lib. of the Health Sciences, Univ. of North Dakota, Box 9002, Grand Forks 58202-9002. Tel. 701-777-2602, fax 701-777-4790, e-mail msafrat@medicine.nodak.edu; *Past Pres.* Marlene Anderson, Bismarck State College Lib., Box 5587, Bismarck 58506-5587. Tel. 701-224-5578, fax 701-224-5551, e-mail marlene.anderson@bsc.nodak.edu.

Address correspondence to the president.

World Wide Web http://www.ndla.info.

Ohio

Memb. 3,400+. Term of Office. Jan.–Dec. 2006. Publications. *Access* (mo.) (q.).

Pres. J. Craig Miller, Holmes County Dist. Public Lib., Millersburg; *V.P./Pres.-Elect* Cindy Lombardo, Tuscaraws County Public Lib., New Philadelphia; *Secy.-Treas.* Carlton Sears, Public Lib. of Youngstown and Mahoning County, Youngstown; *Past Pres.* Pam Hickson-Stevenson, Portage County Dist. Lib., Garrettsville; *Exec. Dir.* Douglas S. Evans.

Address correspondence to the executive director, OLC, 2 Easton Oval, Ste. 525, Columbus 43219-7008. Tel. 614-416-2258, fax 614-416-2270, e-mail olc@olc.org.

World Wide Web http://www.olc.org.

Oklahoma

Memb. (Indiv.) 1,050; (Inst.) 60. Term of Office. July 2005–June 2006. Publication. *Oklahoma Librarian* (bi-mo.). *Ed.* Christine Detlaff. E-mail dettlaffc@redlandscc.edu.

Pres. Jeanie Johnson. E-mail jeanie_johnson@oc.edu; *V.P./Pres.-Elect* Pat Weaver-Meyers. E-mail plweaver-meyers@noble.org; *Secy.* Sarah Robbins. E-mail srobbins@ou.edu; *Treas.* Deborah Willis. E-mail dwillis@mls.lib.ok.us; *Past Pres.* Lynn

McIntosh. E-mail crlsdir@oltn.odl.state.ok. us; *Exec. Dir.* Kay Boies, 300 Hardy Dr., Edmond 73013. Tel. 405-348-0506, fax 405-348-1629, e-mail kboies@coxinet.net. Address correspondence to the executive director.

World Wide Web http://www.oklibs.org.

Oregon

Memb. (Indiv.) 1,000+. Publications. *OLA Hotline* (bi-w.), *OLA Quarterly.*
Pres. Leah Griffith, Newberg Public Lib. Tel. 503-537-1256, e-mail leahg@ccrls.org *V.P./Pres.-Elect* Aletha Bonebrake, Baker County Public Lib. Tel. 541-523-6419, e-mail alethab@oregontrail.net; *Secy.* Steven Engelfried, Beaverton City Lib. Tel. 503-526-2599, e-mail sengelfried@ci.beaverton. or.us; *Treas.* Julia Longbrake, Mt. Hood Community College. Tel. 503-491-7693, e-mail longbraj@mhcc.edu; *Past Pres.* Maureen Cole, Northwest Christian College. Tel. 541-684-7237, e-mail mcole@nwcc.edu. Address correspondence to Oregon Lib. Assn., P.O. Box 2042, Salem 97308. E-mail ola@olaweb.org.

World Wide Web http://www.olaweb.org.

Pennsylvania

Memb. 1,800. Term of Office. Jan.–Dec. 2006. Publication. *PaLA Bulletin* (10 a year).
Pres. Evelyn Minick, St. Joseph's Univ. E-mail minick@sju.edu; *1st V.P.* Janice Trapp, J. V. Brown Lib. E-mail jtrapp@jvbrown. edu; *2nd V.P.* Dana Krydick, WCFLS. E-mail dkrydick@comcast.net; *Treas.* Rob Lesher, Adams County Lib. System. E-mail robin1@ adamslibrary.org; *Past Pres.* Cathi Alloway, Dauphin County Lib. System, 101 Walnut St., Harrisburg 17101. Tel. 717-234-4961, fax 717-234-7479, e-mail calloway@dcls. org; *Exec. Dir.* Glenn R. Miller, Pennsylvania Lib. Assn., 220 Cumberland Pkwy., Ste. 10, Mechanicsburg 17055. Tel. 717-766-7663, fax 717-766-5440, e-mail glenn@pa libraries.org.

Address correspondence to the executive director.

World Wide Web http://www.palibraries. org.

Rhode Island

Memb. (Indiv.) 350+; (Inst.) 50+. Term of Office. June 2005–June 2007. Publication. *Rhode Island Library Association Bulletin.* Ed. Leslie McDonough.
Pres. Cindy Lunghofer, East Providence Public Lib., 41 Grove Ave., East Providence 02914. Tel. 401 434-2453, e-mail book_n@ yahoo.com; *V.P./Pres.-Elect* Chris La Roux, Greenville Public Lib., 573 Putnam Pike, Greenville 02828. Tel. 401-949-3630, e-mail chrislx@lori.state.ri.us; *Secy.* Hope Houston, Office of Lib. and Info. Services, 1 Capitol Hill, Providence 02908. Tel. 401-222-5770, e-mail hhouston@gw.doa.state.ri.us; *Treas.* Janet A. Levesque, Cumberland Public Lib., 1464 Diamond Hill Rd., Cumberland 02864. Tel. 401-333-2552 ext. 5, e-mail jlevesque@ cumberlandlibrary.org; *Past Pres.* Derryl R. Johnson, 10 Midway St., North Scituate 02857. Tel. 401-258-7443, e-mail dejohnson 2@earthlink.net.

World Wide Web http://www.uri.edu/ library/rila/rila.html.

South Carolina

Memb. 550+. Term of Office. Jan.–Dec. 2006. Publication. *News and Views.*
Pres. Joyce Durant, Rogers Lib., Francis Marion Univ., P.O. Box 100547, Florence 29501. Tel. 843-661-1304, fax 843-661-1309, e-mail jdurant@fmarion.edu; *1st V.P./Pres.-Elect* Quincy Pugh, Richland County Public Lib., 1431 Assembly St., Columbia 29201. Tel. 803-929-3449, fax 803-929-3448, e-mail qpugh@richland.lib. sc.us; *2nd V.P. for Membership* Debbie Vaughn, College of Charleston, 66 George St., Charleston 29424. Tel. 843-953-5477, fax 843-953-8019, e-mail vaughnd@cofc. edu; *Secy.* Clo Cammarata, Richland County Public Lib., 1431 Assembly St., Columbia 29201. Tel. 803-929-3400, fax 803-929-3476, e-mail ccammarata@richland.lib.sc.us; *Treas.* Libby Young, Furman Univ., 10 W. Earle St., Greenville 29609. Tel. 864-294-2260, fax 864-294-3004, e-mail libby.young @furman.edu; *Past Pres.* Elizabeth Shuping, Horry County Memorial Lib., 1603 Fourth Ave., Conway 29526. Tel. 843-248-1550, fax

843-248-1549. e-mail eshuping@excite.com; *Exec. Secy.* Gabrielle Barnes, South Carolina Lib. Assn., P.O. Box 1763, Columbia 29202. Tel. 803-252-1087, fax 803-252-0589, e-mail scla@capconsc.com.

Address correspondence to the executive secretary.

World Wide Web http://www.scla.org.

South Dakota

Memb. (Indiv.) 470; (Inst.) 62. Term of Office. Oct. 2005–Oct. 2006. Publication. *Book Marks* (bi-mo.). *Ed.* Lisa Brunick, Augustana College. E-mail lisa_brunick@augie.edu.

Pres. Kevin Kenkel, Dakota Weslyan Univ. E-mail kekenkel@dwu.edu; *V.P./Pres.-Elect* Greta Chapman, Rapid City Public Lib. E-mail gchapman@rcplib.org; *Secy.* LaVera Rose, South Dakota State Lib., Pierre. E-mail lavera.rose@state.sd.us; *Exec. Secy./Treas.* Brenda Hemmelman, Rapid City Public Lib. E-mail bkstand@rap.midco.net; *Past Pres.* Deb Hagemeier, Augustana College. E-mail debh@augie.edu.

Address correspondence to the executive secretary, SDLA, Box 1212, Rapid City 57709-1212. Tel. 605-394-3169 ext. 501, e-mail bkstand@rap.midco.net.

World Wide Web http://www.sdlibrary association.org.

Tennessee

Memb. 725. Term of Office. July 2005–June 2006. Publications. *Tennessee Librarian* (q.), *TLA Newsletter* (bi-mo.) (both electronic only at http://www.tnla.org).

Pres. Cathy T. Farley, White County Public Lib., Sparta 38583. E-mail cathymt@charter.net; *V.P./Pres.-Elect* Pat Thompson, Blount County Public Lib., Maryville 37804. E-mail tlathompat@yahoo.com; *Recording Secy.* Sue Knoche, Quillen College of Medicine Lib., East Tennessee State Univ., Johnson City 37604. E-mail knoches@mail.etsu.edu; *Past Pres.* Kay Due, Memphis Public Lib., Memphis 38103. E-mail duek@memphislibrary.org; *Exec. Dir.* Annelle R. Huggins, Tennessee Lib. Assn., Box 241074, Memphis 38124. Tel. 901-485-6952, e-mail ahuggins@midsouth.rr.com.

Address correspondence to the executive director.

World Wide Web http://tnla.org.

Texas

Memb. 7,300. Term of Office. Apr. 2005–Apr. 2006. Publications. *Texas Library Journal* (q.), *TLACast* (9 a year).

Pres. Gretchen McCord Hoffmann. E-mail ghoffmann@fulbright.com; *Pres.-Elect* Jana Knezek. Tel. 210-522-8190, fax 210-706-8974, e-mail janaknezek@nisd.net; *Treas.* Janet Key. E-mail janet.key@tccd.edu; *Past Pres.* Dana C. Rooks. E-mail drooks@uh.edu; *Exec. Dir.* Patricia H. Smith, TXLA, 3355 Bee Cave Rd., Ste. 401, Austin 78746-6763. Tel. 512-328-1518, fax 512-328-8852, e-mail pats@txla.org.

Address correspondence to the executive director.

World Wide Web http://www.txla.org.

Utah

Memb. 650. Term of Office. May 2005–May 2006. Publication. *UTAH Libraries News* (bi-mo.) (electronic at http://www.ula.org/newsletter).

Pres. Hikmet Loe, Salt Lake City Public Lib., 210 E. 400 S., Salt Lake City 84111. Tel. 801-322-8155, e-mail nhloe@slcpl.org; *Treas./Exec. Secy.* Christopher Anderson.

Address correspondence to the executive secretary, 2150 S. 1300 E., Ste. 500, Salt Lake City 84106. Tel. 801-273-8150, e-mail admin@ula.org.

World Wide Web http://www.ula.org.

Vermont

Memb. 400. Publication. *VLA News* (6 a year).

Pres. Daisy Benson, Bailey/Howe Lib., Univ. of Vermont, Burlington 05405. Tel. 802-656-0636, fax 802-656-4038, e-mail daisy.benson@uvm.edu; *V.P./Pres.-Elect* Lisa von Kann, St. Johnsbury Athenaeum, 1171 Main St., St. Johnsbury 05819. Tel. 802-748-8291, e-mail lvkann@stjathenaeum.org; *Secy.* Teresa Faust, Burlington College., 95 North Ave., Burlington 05401. Tel. 802-862-9616, e-mail tfaust@burlcol.edu; *Treas.*

Donna Edwards, Samuel Read Hall Lib., Lyndon State College, P.O. Box 919, Lyndonville 05851. Tel. 802-626-6447, fax 802-626-6331, e-mail donna.edwards@lsc.vsc.edu; *Past Pres.* David Clark, Ilsley Public Lib., 75 Main St., Middlebury 05753. Tel. 802-388-4095, fax 802-388-4367, e-mail dclark@myriad.middlebury.edu.

Address correspondence to VLA, Box 803, Burlington 05402.

World Wide Web http://www.vermontlibraries.org.

Virginia

Memb. 1,100+. Term of Office. Oct. 2005–Oct. 2006. Publications. *Virginia Libraries* (q.); *VLA Newsletter* (10 a year).

Pres. Ruth Arnold, Staunton Public Lib., 1 Churchville Ave., Staunton 24401. Tel. 540-332-3902, fax 540-332-3906, e-mail arnoldrs@ci.staunton.va.us; *V.P./Pres.-Elect* Pat Howe, Longwood Univ. Lib., Redford and Pine Sts., Farmville 23909. Tel. 434-395-2443, fax 434-395-2453, e-mail howepa@longwood.edu; *2nd V.P.* Libby Lewis, Lib. of Virginia, 800 E. Broad St., Richmond 23219. Tel. 804-692-3762, fax 804-692-3771, e-mail elewis@lva.lib.va.us; *Secy.* Lydia Williams, Longwood Univ. Lib., Redford and Pine Sts., Farmville 23909. Tel. 434-395-2432, e-mail lwilliam@longwood.edu; *Treas.* Sue Burton, Portsmouth Public Libs., 601 Court St., Portsmouth 23704. Tel. 757-393-8365, fax 757-393-5107, e-mail burtonsu@portsmouthva.gov; *Past Pres.* Sam Clay, Fairfax County Public Lib., 1200 Government Center Pkwy., Ste. 324, Fairfax 22035. Tel. 703-324-8308, fax 703-222-3193, e-mail edwin.clay@fairfax.gov; *Exec. Dir.* Linda Hahne, P.O. Box 8277, Norfolk 23503-0277. Tel. 757-583-0041, fax 757-583-5041, e-mail lhahne@coastalnet.com.

Address correspondence to the executive director.

World Wide Web http://www.vla.org.

Washington

Memb. 1,200. Term of Office. Apr. 2005–Apr. 2007. Publication. *ALKI* (3 a year). Ed. Cameron Johnson, Everett Public Lib., 2702 Hoyt Ave., Everett 98201. Tel. 425-257-7640, e-mail alkieditor@wla.org.

Pres. Carolynne Myall, John F. Kennedy Lib., Eastern Washington Univ., 816 F St., Cheney 99004. Tel. 509-359-6967, fax 509-359-2476, e-mail cmyall@ewu.edu; *V.P./Pres.-Elect* Martha Parsons, WSU Energy Program Lib., 925 Plum St. S.E., Olympia 98501. Tel. 360-956-2159, fax 360-236-2159, e-mail parsonsm@energy.wsu.edu; *Secy.* Nancy Slote, Fairwood Lib./KCLS, 17009 140th S.E., Renton 98058. Tel. 425-226-0522, fax 206-296-8115, e-mail nslote@kcls.org; *Treas.* Priscilla Ice, Valley Lib./SCLD, 12004 E. Main, Spokane 99206. Tel. 509-922-1371, fax 509-892-5570, e-mail pice@scld.org; *Past Pres.* John Sheller, Federal Way 320th/KCLS, 848 S. 320, Federal Way 98003. Tel. 253-839-0257, fax 206-296-5053, e-mail jsheller@wla.org; *Assn. Coord.* Gail E. Willis, 4016 First Ave. N.E., Seattle 98105-6502. Tel. 206-545-1529, fax 206-545-1543, e-mail washla@wla.org.

Address correspondence to the association coordinator.

World Wide Web http://www.wla.org.

West Virginia

Memb. 650+. Term of Office. Dec. 2005–Nov. 2006. Publication. *West Virginia Libraries* (6 a year). *Ed.* Pamela Coyle, Martinsburg Public Lib., 101 W. King St., Martinsburg 25401 Tel. 304-267-8933, e-mail pcoyle@martin.lib.wv.us.

Pres. Martha C. Yancey, Evansdale Lib., West Virginia Univ. Libs., P.O. Box 6105, Morgantown 26505. Tel. 304-293-5039 ext. 5118, e-mail myancey@wvu.edu; *1st V.P./Pres.-Elect* Ann Farr, Greenbrier County Public Lib., 301 Courtney Dr., Lewisburg 24901. Tel. 304-647-7568, e-mail farrann@mail.mln.lib.wv.us; *2nd V.P.* Olivia L. Bravo, Kanawha County Public Lib., 123 Capitol St., Charleston 25301. Tel. 304-343-4646, e-mail olivia.bravo@kanawha.lib.wv.us; *Secy.* Margaret Smith, Hamlin-Lincoln County Public Lib., 7999 Lynn Ave., Hamlin 25523. Tel. 304-824-5481, fax 304-824-7014, e-mail msmith@cabell.lib.wv.us; *Treas.* Jewell Ayers, Raleigh County Public Lib., 221 N. Kanawha St., Beckley 25801. Tel. 304-255-0511 ext. 316, e-mail jewell@raleight.lib.

wv.us; *Past Pres.* Penny Pugh, West Virginia Univ. Libs., P.O. Box 6069, West Virginia Univ., Morgantown 26506. Tel. 304-293-4040 ext. 4043, e-mail ppugh@wvu.edu. Address correspondence to the president. World Wide Web http://www.wvla.org.

Wisconsin

Memb. 1,800. Term of Office. Jan.–Dec. 2006. Publication. *WLA Newsletter* (q.). *Pres.* David Weinhold, Eastern Shores Lib. System, 4632 S. Taylor Dr., Sheboygan 53081. E-mail weinhold@esls.lib.wi.us; *Pres.-Elect* Becca Berger, Door County Lib., 107 S. Fourth Ave., Sturgeon Bay 54235. E-mail rberger@mail.nfls.lib.wi.us; *Secy.* Genevieve Foskett, Highsmith Corporate Lib., P.O. Box 800, Fort Atkinson 53538-0800. E-mail gfoskett@highsmith.com; *Treas.* Gayle Falk, Burlington Public Lib., 166 E. Jefferson St., Burlington 53105-1491. Tel. 262-763-7623, fax 262-763-1938, e-mail gafalk@burlington.lib.wi.us; *Past Pres.* Terry Dawson, Appleton Public Lib., 225 N. Oneida St., Appleton 54911-4780. Tel. 920-832-6170, fax 920-832-6182, e-mail tdawson @apl.org; *Exec. Dir.* Lisa K. Strand. Tel. 608-245-3640, fax 608-245-3646, e-mail strand@scls.lib.wi.us.

Address correspondence to the association, 5250 E. Terrace Dr., Ste. A1, Madison 53718-8345.

World Wide Web http://www.wla.lib.wi.us.

Wyoming

Memb. 450+. Term of Office. Oct. 2005–Oct. 2006. *Pres.* Erin Kinney, Wyoming State Lib. Tel. 307-777-6332, fax 307-777-5920, e-mail ekinne@state.wy.us; *V.P./Pres.-Elect* Ara Anderson, Campbell County Public Lib. System. Tel. 307-687-9210, fax 307-686-4009, e-mail aanderson@will.state.wy.us; *Recording Secy.* Patty Myers, Campbell County Public Lib. System. Tel. 307-687-0009, e-mail pmyers@will.state.wy.us; *Past Pres.* Deb Schlinger. E-mail dschling@will.state. wy.us; *Exec. Secy.* Laura Grott, Box 1387, Cheyenne 82003. Tel. 307-632-7622, fax 307-638-3469, e-mail grottski@aol.com.

Address correspondence to the executive secretary.

World Wide Web http://www.wyla.org.

Canada

Alberta

Memb. 500. Term of Office. May 2005–Apr. 2006. Publication. *Letter of the LAA* (4 a year).

Pres. Judy Moore, Centre for Reading and the Arts, Edmonton Public Lib., 7 Sir Winston Churchill Sq., Edmonton T5J 2V4. Tel. 780-496-7062, fax 780-944-7570, e-mail jmoore@epl.ca; *1st V.P.* Anne Carr-Wiggin, NEOS Lib. Consortium, Ring House No. 1, Univ. of Alberta, Edmonton T6G 2E1. E-mail anne.carr-wiggin@ualberta.ca; *2nd V.P.* Connie Forst, RR 1, Willingdon T0B 0R0. Tel. 780-459-1681, fax 780-458-5772, e-mail cforst@nlls.ab.ca; *Treas.* Rachel Sarjeant-Jenkins, Medicine Hat Public Lib., 352 First St. S.E., Medicine Hat T1A 0A6. Tel. 403-502-8528, fax 403-502-8529, e-mail racsar@ medicinehat.ca; *Past Pres.* Pam Ryan, Univ. of Alberta Libs., 5-02 Cameron Lib., Edmonton T6G 2J8. E-mail pam.ryan@ualberta.ca; *Exec. Dir.* Christine Sheppard, 80 Baker Crescent N.W., Calgary T2L 1R4. Tel. 403-284-5818, fax 403-282-6646, e-mail christine. sheppard@shaw.ca.

Address correspondence to the executive director.

World Wide Web http://www.laa.ab.ca.

British Columbia

Memb. 750. Term of Office. Apr. 2005–Apr. 2006. Publication. *BCLA Reporter.* Ed. Ted Benson.

Pres. Melanie Houlden, Surrey Public Lib., 13742 72nd Ave., Surrey V3W 2P4. Tel. 604-572-8269, fax 604-596-8523, e-mail mghoulden@surrey.ca; *V.P./Pres.-Elect* Inba Kehoe, McPherson Lib., Univ. of Victoria, P.O. Box 1800, Sta. CSC, Victoria V8W 3H5. Tel. 250-472-5017, fax 250-721-8235, e-mail ikehoe@uvic.ca; *Treas.* Andree Duval, Port Moody Public Lib., 100 Newport Dr., Port Moody V3H 3E1. Tel. 604-469-4690, fax 604-469-4576, e-mail andree.duval@ cityofportmoody.com; *Past Pres.* Diana

Guinn, Port Moody Public Lib., 100 Newport Dr., Port Moody V3H 3E1. Tel. 604-469-4580, fax 604-469-4576, e-mail diana.guinn @cityofportmoody.com; *Exec. Dir.* Michael Burris.

Address correspondence to the association, 900 Howe St., Ste. 150, Vancouver V6Z 2M4. Tel. 604-683-5354, fax 604-609-0707, e-mail office@bcla.bc.ca.

World Wide Web http://www.bcla.bc.ca.

Manitoba

Memb. 500+. Term of Office. May 2005–May 2006. Publication. *Newsline* (mo.).

Pres. Michael Hohner, Univ. of Winnipeg Lib., 515 Portage Ave., Winnipeg R3B 2E9. Tel. 204-786-9812, fax 204-786-8910, e-mail m.honner@uwinnipeg.ca; *V.P.* Betty Braaksma, Elizabeth Dafoe Lib., Univ. of Manitoba, Winnipeg. R3T 2N2. Tel. 204-474 7193, fax 204-474-7597, e-mail braaksma@cc. umanitoba.ca; *Secy.* Lori Giles-Smith, Neil John Maclean Health Sciences Lib., 770 Bannatyne Ave., Winnipeg R3E 0W3. Tel. 204-789-3344, fax 204-789-3922, e-mail lori_giles-smith@umanitoba.ca; *Treas.* Larry Laliberte, Elizabeth Dafoe Lib., Univ. of Manitoba, Winnipeg R3T 2N2. Tel. 204-480-1439, fax 204-989-8476, e-mail laliber@cc. umanitoba.ca; *Past Pres.* Linwood DeLong, Univ. of Winnipeg Lib., 515 Portage Ave., Winnipeg R3B 2E9. Tel. 204-786-9124, fax 204-786-1824, e-mail l.delong@uwinnipeg. ca.

Address correspondence to the association, 606-100 Arthur St., Winnipeg R3B 1H3. Tel. 204-943-4567, fax 204-942-1555, e-mail mla@uwinnipeg.ca.

World Wide Web http://www.mla.mb.ca.

Ontario

Memb. 4,000+. Term of Office. Jan. 2005–Jan. 2006. Publications. *Access* (q.); *Teaching Librarian* (q.).

Pres. Janet Kaufman, Univ. of Guelph. E-mail jkaufman@uoguelph.ca; *V.P./Pres.-Elect* Esther Rosenfeld. E-mail esther. rosenfeld@sympatico.ca; *Treas.* Roderick McLean. E-mail rodm@vianet.on.ca; *Past Pres.* Cynthia Archer, York Univ. Lib. E-mail carcher@yorku.ca; *Exec. Dir.* Larry Moore. E-mail lmoore@accessola.com.

Address correspondence to the association, 100 Lombard St., Ste. 303, Toronto M5C 1M3. Tel. 416-363-3388, fax 416-941-9581, e-mail info@accessola.com.

World Wide Web http://www.accessola. com.

Quebec

Memb. (Indiv.) 120; (Inst.) 18; (Commercial) 2. Term of Office. June 2005–May 2006. Publication. *ABQLA Bulletin* (3 a year).

Pres. Wendy Wayling. E-mail wwayling@ westmount.org; *V.P.* Mary Jane O'Neill. E-mail oneillmj@ville.pointe-claire.qc.ca; *Treas.* Kay Turner. E-mail kturner@emsb.qc. ca; *Past Pres.* Ann Moffat. E-mail amoffat@ westmount.org; *Exec. Secy.* Janet Ilavsky, Box 1095, Pointe-Claire H9S 4H9. Tel. 514-697-0146, e-mail abqla@abqla.qc.ca.

Address correspondence to the executive secretary.

World Wide Web http://www.abqla.qc.ca.

Saskatchewan

Memb. 225. Term of Office. May 2005–May 2006. Publication. *Forum* (4 a year).

Pres. Colleen Murphy, Dr. John Archer Lib., Univ. of Regina, Regina S4S 0A2. Tel. 306-585-4028, fax 306-585-4493, e-mail colleen.murphy@uregina.ca; *V.P.* Carol Shepstone, Univ. of Saskatchewan Lib., 145 Murray Building, 3 Campus Drive, Saskatoon S7N 5A4. Tel. 306-966-5960, fax 306-966-6040, e-mail carol.shepstone@usask.ca; *Treas.* Rosemary Loeffler, La Ronge Public Lib., Box 5680, La Ronge S0J 1L0. Tel. 306-425-2160, fax 306-425-3883, e-mail r.loeffler.sla@pnls.lib.sk.ca; *Past Pres.* Michael Keaschuk, Chinook Regional Lib., 1240 Chaplin St. W., Swift Current S9H 0G8. Tel. 306-773-3186, fax 306-773-0434, e-mail mkeaschuk@chinook.lib.sk.ca; *Exec. Dir.* Judith Silverthorne, 2010 Seventh Ave., No. 15, Regina S4R 1C2. Tel. 306-780-9413, fax 306-780-9447, e-mail slaexdir@sasktel. net.

Address correspondence to the executive director.

World Wide Web http://www.lib.sk.ca/sla.

Regional

Atlantic Provinces: N.B., N.L., N.S., P.E.

Memb. (Indiv.) 200+; (Inst.) 26. Term of Office. May 2005–May 2006. Publications. *APLA Bulletin* (bi-mo.), *Membership Directory* (ann.).

Pres. Jennifer Richard, Vaughan Memorial Lib., Acadia Univ., Wolfville, NS B4P 2R6. Tel. 902-585-1403, fax 902-585-1748, e-mail jennifer.richard@acadiau.ca; *V.P./Pres.-Elect* Ivan Douthwright, George A. Rawlyk Lib., Atlantic Baptist Univ., P.O. Box 6004, Moncton, NB E1C 9L7. Tel. 506-863-6443, fax 506-858-9694, e-mail ivan.douthwright @abu.nb.ca; *Secy.* Jennifer Adams, Vaughan Memorial Lib., Acadia Univ., Wolfville NS B4P 2R6. Tel. 902-585-1718, fax 902-585-1748, e-mail jennifer.adams@acadiau.ca; *Treas.* Ewa Piorko. E-mail empiorko@ hotmail.com; *Past Pres.* Allan Groen, Provincial Libn., Province of Prince Edward Island, Box 7500, Morell, PE C0A 1S0. Tel. 902-961-7316, fax 902-961-7322, e-mail ajgroen@gov.pe.ca.

Address correspondence to Atlantic Provinces Lib. Assn., c/o School of Info. Management, Faculty of Management, Kenneth C. Rowe Management Bldg., 6100 University Ave., Halifax, NS B3H 3J5.

World Wide Web http://www.apla.ca.

Mountain Plains: Ariz., Colo., Kan., Mont., Neb., Nev., N.Dak., N.M., Okla., S.Dak., Utah, Wyo.

Memb. 820. Publications. *MPLA Newsletter* (bi-mo.), *Ed. and Adv. Mgr.* Judy Zelenski, 14293 W. Center Dr., Lakewood, CO 80228. Tel. 303-985-7795, e-mail mpla_exec secretary@operamail.com.

Pres. Sharon Osenga, Meridian Lib. System, 3519 Second Ave., Kearney, NE 68847. Tel. 308-234-2087, fax 308-234-4040, e-mail sosenga@frontiernet.net; *V.P./Pres.-Elect* Wayne Hanway, Southeastern Public Lib. System, 401 N. 2 St., McAlester, OK 74501. Tel. 918-426-0456, fax 918-766-2510, e-mail whanway@sepl.lib.ok.us; *Past Pres.* Beth Avery, Leslie J. Savage Lib., Western State

Collegel of Colorado, Gunnison, CO 81231, e-mail bavery@western.edu; *Acting Exec. Secy.* Judy Zelenski, 14293 W. Center Dr., Lakewood, CO 80228. Tel. 303-985-7795, fax 303-573-4927, e-mail mpla_exec secretary@operamail.com.

Address correspondence to the executive secretary, Mountain Plains Lib. Assn.

World Wide Web http://www.mpla.us.

New England: Conn., Maine, Mass., N.H., R.I., Vt.

Memb. (Indiv.) 1,300; (Inst.) 100. Term of Office. Nov. 2005–Oct. 2006. Publication. *New England Libraries* (bi-mo.). *Ed.* David Bryan, 157 S. Orleans Rd., Orleans, MA 02653. Tel. 508-240-2357, e-mail publications manager@nelib.org.

Pres. Janice Wilbur, d'Alzon Lib., Assumption College, 500 Salisbury St., Worcester, MA 01609. Tel. 508-767-7271, fax 508-767-7374, e-mail president@nelib.org; *V.P./ Pres.-Elect* Susan Raskin Abrams, Newton Free Lib., 330 Homer St., Newton, MA 02459-1429. Tel. 617-796-1370, fax 617-964-9549, e-mail vicepresident@nelib.org; *Secy.* Esme Green, Westfield Athenaeum, 6 Elm St., Westfield, MA 01085. Tel. 413-568-0638, fax 413-568-1558, e-mail secretary@ nelib.org; *Treas.* Camille Close, Eugene Smith Lib., Eastern Connecticut State Univ., 83 Windham St., Willimantic, CT 06226. Tel. 860-465-5566, e-mail treasurer@nelib. org; *Past Pres.* Joanne Lamothe, Tufts Lib., 46 Broad St., Weymouth, MA 02188. Tel. 781-337-1402, fax 781-682-6123, e-mail pastpresident@nelib.org.

Address correspondence to New England Lib. Assn., 14 Pleasant St., Gloucester, MA 01930. Tel. 972-282-0787, fax 978-282-1304, e-mail office@nelib.org.

World Wide Web http://www.nelib.org.

Pacific Northwest: Alaska, Idaho, Mont., Ore., Wash., Alberta, B.C.

Memb. (Active) 550; (Subscribers) 100. Term of Office. Aug. 2005–Aug. 2006. Publication. *PNLA Quarterly. Ed.* Mary Bolin 319A Love Lib., University of Nebraska,

P.O. Box 881140, Lincoln, NE 68588-4100. Tel. 402-472-4281, e-mail mbolin2@unl.edu. *Pres.* Charlotte Glover, Ketchikan Public Lib., 629 Dock St., Ketchikan, AK 99904. Tel. 907-225-0370, fax 907-225-0153, e-mail charg@firstcitylibraries.org; *1st V.P./Pres.-Elect* Jason Openo, Salem Public Lib., P.O. Box 14810, 585 Liberty St. S.E., Salem, OR 97309. Tel. 503-588-6183, fax 503-588-6055, e-mail jopeno@cityofsalem.net; *2nd V.P.* Christine Sheppard, Lib. Assn. of Alberta, 80 Baker Crescent N.W., Calgary, AB T2L 1R4. Tel. 403-284-5818, e-mail christine.sheppard@shaw.ca; *Secy.* Marg Anderson, Southern Alberta Institute of Technology (SAIT), 1301 16th Ave. N.W., Calgary, AB T2M 0L4. Tel. 403-284-7016, fax 403-284-7127, e-mail marg.anderson@sait.ca; *Treas.* Kay Vynanek, Washington State Univ., Pullman, WA 99164-5610. Tel. 509-335-9514, e-mail kayv@wsu.edu; *Past Pres.* Jan Zauha, Montana State Univ.–Bozeman, Box 173320, Bozeman, MT 59717-3320. Tel. 406-994-6554, fax 406-994-2851, e-mail alijz@montana.edu.

Address correspondence to the president, Pacific Northwest Lib. Assn.

World Wide Web http://www.pnla.org.

Southeastern: Ala., Ark., Fla., Ga., Ky., La., Miss., N.C., S.C., Tenn., Va., W.Va.

Memb. 500. Term of Office. Nov. 2004–Oct. 2006. Publication. *The Southeastern Librarian* (q.).

Pres. Judith A. Gibbons, Kentucky Dept. for Libs. and Archives, P.O. Box 537, Frankfort, KY 40602. Tel. 502-564-8300, fax 502-564-5773, e-mail judith.gibbons@ky.gov; *1st V.P./Pres.-Elect* Faith A. Line, Sumter County Lib., 111 N. Harvin St., Sumter, SC 29150. Tel. 803-773-7273, fax 803-773-4875, e-mail linef@infoave.net; *Secy.* Carol S. Brinkman, Kersey Lib., Univ. of Louisville, 3426 Warner Ave., Louisville, KY 40207. Tel. 502-852-1008, fax 502-852-0020, e-mail csbrin01@gwise.louisville.edu; *Treas.* William N. Nelson, Augusta State Univ. Lib., 3317 Sugar Mill Rd., Augusta, GA 30907. Tel. 706-737-1745, fax 706-667-4415, e-mail wnelson@aug.edu.

Address correspondence to Gordon N. Baker, Southeastern Library Association, Administrative Services, P.O. Box 950, Rex, GA 30273-0950. Tel. 678-466-4325, fax 770-961-3712, e-mail gordonbaker@clayton.edu.

State and Provincial Library Agencies

The state library administrative agency in each of the U.S. states will have the latest information on its state plan for the use of federal funds under the Library Services and Technology Act (LSTA). The directors and addresses of these state agencies are listed below.

Alabama

Rebecca Mitchell, Dir., Alabama Public Lib. Service, 6030 Monticello Dr., Montgomery 36130. Tel. 334-213-3902, fax 334-213-3993, e-mail rmitchell@apls.state.al.us.

Alaska

Kathryn H. Shelton, Acting Dir., Alaska Dept. of Educ., Div. of Libs., Archives, and Museums, Box 110571, Juneau 99811-0571. Tel. 907-465-2912, fax 907-465-2151, e-mail kay_shelton@eed.state.ak.us.

Arizona

GladysAnn Wells, Dir., Arizona State Lib., Archives and Public Records, Rm. 200, 1700 W. Washington, Phoenix 85007-2896. Tel. 602-542-4035, fax 602-542-4972, e-mail gawells@lib.az.us.

Arkansas

Carolyn Ashcraft, State Libn., Arkansas State Lib., 1 Capitol Mall, 5th fl., Little Rock 72201-1081. Tel. 501-682-1526, fax 501-682-1899, e-mail cashcraft@asl.lib.ar.us.

California

Susan Hildreth, State Libn., California State Lib., P.O. Box 942837, Sacramento 94237-0001. Tel. 916-654-0266, fax 916-653-7818, e-mail shildreth@library.ca.gov.

Colorado

Eugene Hainer, State Libn., Colorado State Lib., Rm. 309, 201 E. Colfax Ave., Denver 80203. Tel./fax 303-866-6940, e-mail hainer_g@cde.state.co.us.

Connecticut

Kendall F. Wiggin, State Libn., Connecticut State Lib., 231 Capitol Ave., Hartford 06106. Tel. 860-757-6510, fax 860-757-6503, e-mail kwiggin@cslib.org.

Delaware

Anne Norman, State Libn., Div. of Libs., 43 S. DuPont Hwy., Dover 19901. Tel. 302-739-4748 ext. 126, fax 302-739-6787, e-mail norman@lib.de.us.

District of Columbia

Francis Buckley, Interim Dir., District of Columbia Public Lib., 901 G St. N.W., Ste. 400, Washington 20001. Tel. 202-727-1101, fax 202-727-1129, e-mail francis.buckley@dc.gov.

Florida

Judith A. Ring, State Libn., Div. of Lib. and Info. Services, R. A. Gray Bldg., 500 S. Bronough St., Tallahassee 32399-0250. Tel. 850-245-6604, fax 850-488-2746, e-mail jring@mail.dos.state.fl.us.

Georgia

Lamar Veatch, State Libn., Georgia Public Lib. Services, 1800 Century Place, Ste. 150, Atlanta 30345. Tel. 404-982-3569, fax 404-982-3563, e-mail lveatch@state.lib.ga.us.

Hawaii

Jo Ann Schindler, State Libn., Hawaii State Public Lib. System, 44 Merchant St., Honolulu 96813. Tel. 808-586-3704, fax 808-586-3715, e-mail joann@lib.state.hi.us.

Idaho

Ann Joslin, State Libn., Idaho State Lib., 325 W. State St., Boise 83702-6072. Tel. 208-334-2150, fax 208-334-4016, e-mail ajoslin @isl.state.id.us.

Illinois

Anne Craig, Dir., Illinois State Lib., 300 S. 2 St., Springfield 62701-1796. Tel. 217-524-4200, fax 217-782-6062, e-mail acraig@ ilsos.net.

Indiana

Barbara Maxwell, Dir., Indiana State Lib., 140 N. Senate Ave., Indianapolis 46204. Tel. 317-232-3692, fax 317-232-0002, e-mail bmaxwell@statelib.lib.in.us.

Iowa

Mary Wegner, State Libn., State Lib. of Iowa, E. 12 and Grand, Des Moines 50319. Tel. 515-281-4105, fax 515-281-6191, e-mail mary.wegner@lib.state.ia.us.

Kansas

Christie Pearson Brandau, State Libn., Kansas State Lib., Rm. 343N, 300 S.W. 10 Ave., Topeka 66612-1593. Tel. 785-296-3296, fax 785-296-6650, e-mail christie@ kslib.info.

Kentucky

Jim Nelson, State Libn./Commissioner, Kentucky Dept. for Libs. and Archives, 300 Coffee Tree Rd., Frankfort 40602-0537. Tel. 502-564-8300 ext. 312, fax 502-564-5773, e-mail jim.nelson@ky.gov.

Louisiana

Rebecca Hamilton, State Libn., State Lib. of Louisiana, P.O. Box 131, Baton Rouge 70821-0131. Tel. 225-342-4923, fax 225-219-4804, e-mail rhamilton@crt.state.la.us.

Maine

J. Gary Nichols, State Libn., Maine State Lib., 64 State House Sta., Augusta 04333-0064. Tel. 207-287-5600, fax 207-287-5615, e-mail gary.nichols@maine.gov.

Maryland

Irene Padilla, Asst. State Superintendent for Libs., Maryland State Dept. of Educ., 200 W. Baltimore St., Baltimore 21201. Tel. 410-767-0435, fax 410-333-2507, e-mail ipadilla @msde.state.md.us.

Massachusetts

Robert C. Maier, Dir., Massachusetts Board of Lib. Commissioners, 648 Beacon St., Boston 02215. Tel. 617-267-9400, fax 617-421-9833, e-mail robert.maier@state.ma.us.

Michigan

Nancy Robertson, Interim State Libn., Lib. of Michigan, 717 W. Allegan St., P.O. Box 30007, Lansing 48909-7507. Tel. 517-373-7513, fax 517-373-4480, e-mail nrobertson @michigan.gov.

Minnesota

Suzanne Miller, State Libn., Lib. Development and Services, Minnesota Dept. of Educ., 1500 Hwy. 36 W., Roseville 55113-4266. Tel. 651-582-8722, fax 651-582-8897, e-mail suzanne.miller@state.mn.us.

Mississippi

Sharman Smith, Exec. Dir., Mississippi Lib. Commission, 1221 Ellis Ave., Jackson 39289-0700. Tel. 601-961-4039, fax 601-354-6713, e-mail sharman@mlc.lib.ms.us.

Missouri

Sara Parker, State Libn., Missouri State Lib., 600 W. Main, P.O. Box 387, Jefferson City 65102-0387. Tel. 573-751-2751, fax 573-751-3612, e-mail parkes@sosmail.state.mo.gov.

Montana

Darlene Staffeldt, State Libn., Montana State Lib., 1515 E. 6 Ave., P.O. Box 201800, Helena 59620-1800. Tel. 406-444-3115, fax 406-444-0266, e-mail dstaffeldt@mt.us.

Nebraska

Rod Wagner, Dir., Nebraska Lib. Commission, 1200 N St., Ste. 120, Lincoln 68508-2023. Tel. 402-471-2045, fax 402-471-2083, e-mail rwagner@nlc.state.ne.us.

Nevada

Sara Jones, State Libn., Nevada State Lib. and Archives, 100 N. Stewart St., Carson City 89710-4285. Tel. 775-684-3315, fax 775-684-3311, e-mail sfjones@clan.lib.nv.us.

New Hampshire

Michael York, State Libn., New Hampshire State Lib., 20 Park St., Concord 03301-6314. Tel. 603-271-2397, fax 603-271-6826, e-mail myork@library.state.nh.us.

New Jersey

Norma E. Blake, State Libn., New Jersey State Lib., P.O. Box 520, Trenton 08625-0520. Tel. 609-292-6200, fax 609-292-2746, e-mail nblake@njstatelib.org.

New Mexico

Richard Akeroyd, State Libn., New Mexico State Lib., 1209 Camino Carlos Rey, Santa Fe 87505-6980. E-mail rakeroyd@stlib.state.nm.us.

New York

Janet M. Welch, State Libn./Asst. Commissioner for Libs., New York State Lib., 10C34 Cultural Educ. Center, Albany 12230. Tel. 518-474-5930, fax 518-486-6880, e-mail jwelch2@mail.nysed.gov.

North Carolina

Mary L. Boone, State Libn., State Lib. of North Carolina, 4640 Mail Service Center, 109 E. Jones St., Raleigh 27699-4640. Tel. 919-807-7410, fax 919-733-8748, e-mail mboone@library.dcr.state.nc.us.

North Dakota

Doris Ott, State Libn., North Dakota State Lib., 604 E. Boulevard Ave., Bismarck 58505-0800. Tel. 701-328-2492, fax 701-328-2040, e-mail dott@state.nd.us.

Ohio

Jo Budler, State Libn., State Lib. of Ohio, 274 E. 1 Ave., Columbus 43201. Tel. 614-644-6843, fax 614-466-3584, e-mail jbudler@sloma.state.ohio.us.

Oklahoma

Susan McVey, Dir., Oklahoma Dept. of Libs., 200 N.E. 18 St., Oklahoma City 73105-3298. Tel. 405-522-3173, fax 405-525-7804, e-mail smcvey@oltn.odl.state.ok.us.

Oregon

James B. Scheppke, State Libn., Oregon State Lib., 250 Winter St. N.E., Salem 97310-0640. Tel. 503-378-4367, fax 503-585-8059, e-mail jim.b.scheppke@state.or.us.

Pennsylvania

M. Clare Zales, Deputy Secy. of Educ. and Commissioner of Libs., Office of Commonwealth Libs., 333 Market St., Harrisburg 17105. Tel. 717-787-2646, fax 717-772-3265, e-mail mzales@state.pa.us.

Rhode Island

Anne T. Parent, Chief of Lib. Services, Office of Lib. and Info. Services, 1 Capitol Hill, Providence 02908. Tel. 401-222-5763, fax 401-222-4195, e-mail Anne_Parent@gw.doa.state.ri.us.

South Carolina

Patti J. Butcher, Dir., South Carolina State Lib., P.O. Box 11469, Columbia 29211. Tel. 803-734-8666, fax 803-734-8676, e-mail patti@leo.scsl.state.sc.us.

South Dakota

Dorothy M. Liegl, State Libn., South Dakota State Lib., 800 Governors Dr., Pierre 57501-2294. Tel. 605-773-3131, fax 605-773-6962, e-mail dorothy.liegl@state.sd.us.

Tennessee

Jeanne D. Sugg, State Libn. and Archivist, Tennessee State Lib. and Archives, 403 Seventh Ave. N., Nashville 37243-0312. Tel. 615-741-7996, fax 615-741-6471, e-mail Jeanne.Sugg@state.tn.us.

Texas

Peggy D. Rudd, Dir./Libn., Texas State Lib. and Archives Commission, P.O. Box 12927, Austin 78711-2927. Tel. 512-463-5460, fax 512-463-5436, e-mail peggy.rudd@tsl.state. tx.us.

Utah

Donna Jones Morris, State Libn./Dir., Utah State Lib. Div., 250 N. 1950 W., Salt Lake City 84115-7901. Tel. 801-715-6770, fax 801-715-6767, e-mail dmorris@utah.gov.

Vermont

Sybil Brigham McShane, State Libn., Vermont Dept. of Libs., Pavillion Office Bldg., 109 State St., Montpelier 05609-0601. Tel. 802-828-3265, fax 802-828-2199, e-mail sybil.mcshane@dol.state.vt.us.

Virginia

Nolan T. Yelich, Libn. of Virginia, Lib. of Virginia, 800 E. Broad St., Richmond 23219-8000. Tel. 804-692-3535, fax 804-692-3594, e-mail nyelich@lva.lib.va.us.

Washington

Jan Walsh, State Libn., Washington State Lib., P.O. Box 42460, Olympia 98504-2460. Tel. 360-704-5253, fax 360-586-7575, e-mail jwalsh@secstate.wa.gov.

West Virginia

J. D. Waggoner, Secy., West Virginia Lib. Commission, 1900 Kanawha Blvd. E., Charleston 25305-0620. Tel. 304-558-2041, fax 304-558-2044, e-mail waggoner@wvlc. lib.wv.us.

Wisconsin

Richard Grobschmidt, State Libn./Asst. Superintendent, Div. for Libs. and Community Learning, Dept. of Public Instruction, P.O. Box 7841, Madison 53707-7841. Tel. 608-266-2205, fax 608-267-1052, e-mail richard. grobschmidt@dpi.state.wi.us.

Wyoming

Lesley Boughton, State Libn., Wyoming State Lib., 2301 Capitol Ave., Cheyenne 82002. Tel. 307-777-5911, fax 307-777-6289, e-mail lbough@state.wy.us.

American Samoa

Cheryl Morales, Territorial Libn., Feleti Barstow Public Lib., P.O. Box 997687, Pago Pago, AS 96799. Tel. 11-684-633-5816, fax 11-684-633-5823, e-mail feletibarstow@ yahoo.com.

Federated States of Micronesia

Eliuel K. Pretrict, Secy., Dept. of Health, Educ., and Social Affairs, FSM Div. of Educ., P.O. Box PS 70, Pallikir Sta., Pohnpei, FM 96941. Tel. 11-691-320-2619, fax 11-691-320-5500, e-mail fsmhealth@mail.fm.

Guam

(Position vacant) Dir./Territorial Libn., Guam Public Lib. System, 254 Martyr St., Agana 96910. Tel. 671-475-4753, fax 671-477-9777.

Northern Mariana Islands

Kevin Latham, Dir., Commonwealth Public Lib., Box 501092, Saipan 96950. Tel. 670-235-7322, fax 670-235-7550, e-mail kclatham @gmail.com.

Palau

Mario Katosang, Minister of Educ., Republic of Palau, Box 7080, Koror, PW 96940. Tel. 11-680-488-2973, fax 11-680-488-2930, e-mail mariok@palaumoe.net.

Puerto Rico

Miguel A. Hernandez, Acting Dir., Lib. Services and Info. Program, Box 190759, San Juan, PR 00919-0759. Tel. 787-759-1120, fax 787-754-0843, e-mail Hernandez_Mi@de.gobierno.pr.

Republic of the Marshall Islands

Lenest Lanki, Secy., Internal Affairs, Marshall Islands, Box 629, Majuro, MH 96960. Tel. 11-692-625-5024, fax 11-692-625-5353, e-mail ltlanki@hotmail.com.

Virgin Islands

Claudette C. Lewis, Exec. Asst. Commissioner, Div. of Libs., Archives, and Museums, Cyril E. King Airport Terminal Bldg., St. Thomas, VI 00802. Tel. 340-774-3320, fax 809-775-5706.

Canada

Alberta

Bonnie Gray, Mgr., Public Lib. Services, Alberta Community Development, 803 Standard Life Centre, 10405 Jasper Ave., Edmonton T5J 4R7. Tel. 780-415-0295, fax 780-415-8594, e-mail bonnie.gray@gov.ab.ca.

British Columbia

Maureen Woods, Dir., Public Lib. Services Branch, Ministry of Community, Aboriginal and Women's Services, 800 Johnson St., Victoria BC V8W 1N3. Tel. 250-356-1791, fax 250-953-3225, e-mail maureen.woods@gems8.gov.bc.ca.

Manitoba

Maureen Cubberley, Dir., Public Library Services, Manitoba Dept. of Culture, Heritage and Tourism, Unit 200, 1525 First St., Brandon R7A 7A1. Tel. 204-726-6590, e-mail mcubberley@gov.mb.ca.

New Brunswick

Sylvie Nadeau, Exec. Dir., New Brunswick Public Lib. Service, 250 King St., Place 6000, Fredericton E3B 9M9. Tel. 506-453-2354, fax 506-444-4064, e-mail Sylvie.Nadeau@gnb.ca. World Wide Web http://www.gnb.ca/publiclibraries.

Newfoundland and Labrador

Shawn Tetford, Exec. Dir., Provincial Info. and Lib. Resources Board of Newfoundland and Labrador, 48 St. George's Ave., Stephenville A2N 1K9. Tel. 709-643-0900, fax 709-643-0925, e-mail shawntetford@nlpublic libraries.ca, World Wide Web http://www.nlpubliclibraries.ca.

Northwest Territories

Alison Hopkins, Territorial Libn., NWT Lib. Services, 75 Woodland Dr., Hay River X0E 1G1. Tel. 867-874-6531, fax 867-874-3321, e-mail Alison_Hopkins@gov.nt.ca. World Wide Web http://www.nwtpls.gov.nt.ca.

Nova Scotia

Jennifer Evans, Dir., Nova Scotia Provincial Lib., 3770 Kempt Rd., Halifax B3K 4X8. Tel. 902-424-2455, fax 902-424-0633, e-mail evansjl@gov.ns.ca.

Nunavut

Robin Brown, Mgr., Lib. Policy, Baker Lake Headquarters, Nunavut Public Lib. Services, Box 270, Baker Lake X0C 0A0. Tel. 867-793-3326, fax 867-793-3332, e-mail rbrown2@gov.nu.ca.

Ontario

Rita Scagnetti, Dir., Heritage and Libs. Branch, Ontario Government Ministry of Culture, 400 University Ave., 4th fl., Toronto M7A 2R9. Tel. 416-314-7342, fax 416-314-7635, e-mail rita.scagnetti@mcl.gov.on.ca.

Prince Edward Island

Allan Groen, Provincial Libn., Province of Prince Edward Island, P.O. Box 7500, Morell C0A 1S0. Tel. 902-961-7320, fax 902-961-7322, e-mail ajgroen@gov.pe.ca.

Quebec

André Couture, Dir., Direction des Politiques et de la Coordination des Programmes, Gouvernement du Quebec, 225 Grande Allée Est, RC-C, Quebec G1R 5G5. Tel. 418-644-0485, fax 418-643-4080, e-mail andre.couture@mcc.gouv.qc.ca.

Saskatchewan

Joylene Campbell, Provincial Libn., Saskatchewan Learning, 1945 Hamilton St., Regina S4P 2C8. Tel. 306-787-2972, fax 306-787-2029, e-mail jcampbell@library.gov.sk.ca. World Wide Web http://www.sasked.gov.sk.ca/branches/prov_library/index.shtml.

Yukon Territory

Julie Ourom, Mgr., Public Libs., Dept. of Community Services, Box 2703, Whitehorse Y1A 2C6. Tel. 867-667-5447, fax 867-393-6333, e-mail julie.ourom@gov.yk.ca.

State School Library Media Associations

Alabama

Children's and School Libns. Div., Alabama Lib. Assn. Memb. 650. Publication. *The Alabama Librarian* (q.).

Chair Sharon Townson. E-mail townsonsd@ccpls.com; *V. Chair/Chair-Elect* Jessica E. Platt. E-mail jessica.platt@mps.k12.al.us; *Exec. Dir.* Steve Chew, Professional Services Group, Bailey Bldg., 400 S. Union St., Ste. 395, Montgomery 36104. Tel. 334-263-1272, fax 334-265-1281, e-mail mdginc@bellsouth.net.

Address correspondence to the executive director.

World Wide Web http://allanet.org.

Alaska

Alaska Assn. of School Libns. Memb. 200+. Term of Office. Mar. 2005–Mar. 2006. Publication. *Puffin* (3 a year).

Pres. Valerie Oliver. E-mail oliver_valerie@asd.k12.org; *Pres.-Elect* Barb Bryson. E-mail barb_bryson@valdez.cc; *Secy.* Tiki Levinson. E-mail tlevinson@dgsd.k12.ak.us; *Treas.* Kirk Thompson. E-mail kirk.thompson@matsuk12.ak.us; *Past Pres.* Karen J. Davis. E-mail kjdavis@edulynx.com; *School Lib. Coord. for Alaska State Lib.* Sue Sherif. E-mail sue_sherif@eed.state.ak.us.

World Wide Web http://www.akla.org/akasl.

Arizona

Teacher-Librarian Div., Arizona Lib. Assn. Memb. 1,000. Term of Office. Dec. 2004–Dec. 2006. Publication. *AZLA Newsletter*.

Chair Ann Dutton Ewbank, Cholla Middle School. Tel. 602-896-5409, e-mail adutton@ch.wesd.k12.az.us.

Address correspondence to the chairperson.

World Wide Web http://www.azla.affiniscape.com.

Arkansas

Arkansas Assn. of Instructional Media. Term of Office. Apr. 2005–April 2006.

Pres. Rachel Shankles. E-mail Shankles@cablelynx.com; *Pres.-Elect* Evelyn McFadden. E-mail e_mcfadden@yahoo.com; *Secy.* Karen Richardson. E-mail richark@jessie1.k12.ar.us; *Treas.* Lawanda Dale. E-mail dalej@yahoo.com; *Past Pres.* Djuna Dudeck. E-mail ddudeck@yahoo.com.

Address correspondence to the president.

World Wide Web http://aaimonline.net.

California

California School Lib. Assn. Memb. 2,200. Publication. *CSLA Journal* (2 a year); *CSLA Bulletin* (9 a year).

Pres. Kathryn Matlock, 1336 La Loma Dr., Redlands 92373. Tel. 909-792-0895, e-mail kmatlock@rialto.k12.ca.us; *Pres.-Elect* Martha Rowland, 1845 Commercial Way, Sacramento 95818. Tel. 916-492-2756, e-mail martha-rowland@sac-city.k12.ca.us; *Secy.* Marianne Newman, 352 N. California St., Los Angeles 91775-2309. Tel. 626-309-9112, e-mail msnewm@aol.com; *Treas.* Theo Palmer, 6797 Western Ave., Riverside 92505. Tel. 951-687-0418, e-mail tpalmer@alvord.k12.ca.us; *Past Pres.* Ann H. Wick, 28266 Twin Ponds Rd., Clovis 93611. Tel. 559-855-2709, e-mail awick@sierra.k12.ca.us; *Office Mgr.* Sue Dalrymple, 1001 26th St., Sacramento 95816. Tel. 916-447-2684, fax 916-447-2695, e-mail csla@pacbell.net; *Exec. Dir.* Penny Kastanis. Tel. 916.447.2684, e-mail pkastanis@pacbell.net.

World Wide Web http://www.schoolibrary.org.

Address correspondence to the office manager.

Colorado

Colorado Assn. of School Libns. Memb. 500. Term of Office. Oct. 2005–Oct. 2006. Publication. *Newsletter* (5 a year).

Pres. Kim Meyer, Marshdale Elementary, 26663 N. Turkey Creek Rd., Evergreen 80439. Tel. 303-982-5188, fax 303-982-5187, e-mail kmeyer@jeffco.k12.co.us; *V.P./Pres.-Elect* Gwen Giddens, Colorado Springs School Dist. 11, 711 San Rafael,

Colorado Springs 80903. Tel. 719-520-2254, e-mail giddegb@d11.org; *Secy.* Sherry Crow, Midland International Elementary, 2110 W. Broadway, Colorado Springs 80904. Tel. 719-328-4524, e-mail crowsr@d11.org; *Past Pres.* Dave Sanger, 12162 Tenderfoot Trail, Parker 80138. Tel. 303-841-9535, e-mail dsanger401@aol.com; *Exec. Dir.* Kathleen Sagee Noland, Colorado Assn. of Libs., 12081 W. Alameda Pkwy., No. 427, Lakewood 80228. Tel. 303-463-6400, fax 303-798-2485, e-mail kathleen@cal-webs.org.

World Wide Web http://www.cal-webs.org.

Connecticut

Connecticut Educational Media Assn. Memb. 550. Term of Office. July 2005–June 2006. Publications. *CEMA Update* (q.); *CEMA Gram* (mo.).

Pres. Dianne Kimball, 42 Carriage Dr., Meriden 06450. Tel. 203-639-7578, e-mail dkimball@wallingford.k12.ct.us; *V.P.* Janet Roche. E-mail jroche@simsbury.k12.ct.us; *Recording Secy.* Christopher Barlow, e-mail christophbarlow@sbcglobal.net; *Treas.* Sewell Pruchnik. E-mail spruchnik@snet.net; *Past Pres.* Jerilyn Van Leer. E-mail jeri_vanleer@whps.org; *Admin. Secy.* Anne Weimann, 25 Elmwood Ave., Trumbull 06611. Tel. 203-372-2260, e-mail aweimann@snet.net.

Address correspondence to the administrative secretary.

World Wide Web http://www.ctcema.org.

Delaware

Delaware School Lib. Media Assn., Div. of Delaware Lib. Assn. Memb. 100+. Term of Office. Apr. 2005–Apr. 2006. Publications. *DSLMA Newsletter* (electronic; irreg.); column in *DLA Bulletin* (3 a year) (electronic at http://www.dla.lib.de.us/bulletin.shtml).

Pres. Christine Payne, Olive B. Loss Elementary School, 200 Brennan Blvd., Bear 19701. Tel. 302-832-1343, e-mail christine.payne@appo.k12.de.us; *V.P./Pres.-Elect* Jamie Alascia, William Henry Middle School, 65 Carver Rd., Dover 19904. E-mail jalascia@apital.k12.de.us; *Secy.* Cristina Smith, Silver Lake Elementary School, 200 E. Cochran St., Middletown 19709. Tel. 302-378-5023, e-mail cristina.smith@appo.k12.de.us

Address correspondence to the president.

World Wide Web http://www.udel.edu/erc/dslma.

District of Columbia

District of Columbia Assn. of School Libns. Memb. 35. Publication. *Newsletter* (4 a year).

Pres. André Maria Taylor. E-mail divalibrarian2@aol.com.

Florida

Florida Assn. for Media in Education. Memb. 1,450. Term of Office. Nov. 2005–Oct. 2006. Publication. *Florida Media Quarterly.* *Ed.* Nancy Pelser-Borowicz.

Pres. Sandra Dunnavant. E-mail president@floridamedia.org; *Pres.-Elect* Belinda Vose. E-mail vose_b@firn.edu; *V.P.* James Carey. E-mail jcarey@chuma1.cas.usf.edu; *Secy.* Vange Scivally. E-mail scivale@ocps.net; *Treas.* Sherie Bargar. E-mail bargars@osceola.k12.fl.us.

Address correspondence to FAME, P.O. Box 560787, Orlando 32856-0787. E-mail info@floridamedia.org.

World Wide Web http://www.floridamedia.org.

Georgia

Georgia Lib. Assn., School Lib. Media Division.

Chair Pam Nutt, Moore Elementary School, 201 Cabin Creek Dr., Griffin 30223. Tel. 770-229-3756, e-mail pnutt@spalding.k12.ga.us

Georgia Lib. Media Assn. Memb. 701. Term of Office. Jan. 2006–Jan. 2007.

Pres. Donna Milner. E-mail donnamilner@yahoo.com; *Pres.-Elect* Rosalind L. Dennis. E-mail rosalind_l_dennis@fc.dekalb.k12.ga.us; *Secy.* Kathleen Disney. E-mail kathleen_r_disney@fc.dekalb.k12.ga.us; *Treas.* Rebecca Amerson. E-mail rebecca.amerson@cherokee.k12.ga.us; *Past Pres.* Cawood Cornelius. E-mail ccornelius@gcbe.org.

World Wide Web http://www.glma-inc.org.

Hawaii

Hawaii Assn. of School Libns. Memb. 200+. Term of Office. June 2005–July 2006. Publication. *HASL Newsletter* (4 a year).

Pres. Loraine Hotoke, Liholiho Elementary. E-mail loraine_hotoke@notes.k12.hi.us; *V.P., Programming* Jo-An Goss, Hawaiian Studies and Language Programs Section, OCISS Annex. E-mail jo-an_goss@notes. k12.hi.us; *V.P., Membership* Kristen Kawasaki. Kalani H.S. E-mail kkawasaki@hawaii. rr.com; *Recording Secy.* Deb Peterson, Punahou (Cooke Lib.). E-mail dpeterson@ punahou.edu; *Corresponding Secy.* Elissa Pickard, Dole Middle School. E-mail elissa_ pickard@notes.k12.hi.us; *Treas.* Linda Marks, Kalihi Uka Elementary. E-mail flcadiz@ aol.com; *Dir. of Nominations* Susan Yokota, Moanalua H.S. E-mail yokotas001@hawaii. rr.com; *Past Pres.* Jo-An Goss. E-mail jo-an_ goss@notes.k12.hi.us.

Address correspondence to the association, Box 235019, Honolulu 96823.

World Wide Web http://www.k12.hi.us/ ~hasl.

Idaho

Educational Media Div., Idaho Lib. Assn. Term of Office. Oct. 2005–Oct. 2007. Publication. Column in *The Idaho Librarian* (q.).

Chair Pam Juel, Meridian School Dist., 911 Meridian Rd., Meridian 83642. Tel. 208-855-4500, fax 208-888-6700, e-mail julep@ meridianschools.org; *Past Chair* Norma Jean Sprouffske, Caldwell School Dist. 132, 1101 Cleveland Blvd., Caldwell 83605. Tel. 208-455-3305, e-mail njsprouffske@earthlink.net.

Address correspondence to the chairperson.

Illinois

Illinois School Lib. Media Assn. Memb. 1,000. Term of Office. July 2005–June 2006. Publications. *ISLMA News* (4 a year); *ISLMA Membership Directory* (ann.); *Linking for Learning: the Illinois School Library Media Program Guidelines* (2005); *Powerful Libraries Make Powerful Learners: The Illinois Study* (2005).

Pres. Leslie Forsman, Triopia CUSD No. 27, 2204 Concord-Arenzville Rd., Concord 62631. Tel. 217-457-2284 or 217-457-2281, fax 217-457-2277, e-mail lforsman@hotmail. com; *Pres.-Elect* Becky Robinson, Lombard Middle School, 1220 E. Knox St., Galesburg 61401. Tel. 309-341-1099 or 309-342-9171 ext. 238, fax 309-342-7135, e-mail rrobins1 @roe33.k12.il.us; *Exec. Secy.* Kay Maynard, ISLMA, P.O. Box 598, Canton 61520. Tel. 390-649-0911, e-mail islma@islma.org.

World Wide Web http://www.islma.org.

Indiana

Assn. for Indiana Media Educators. Term of Office. May 2005–Apr. 2006. Publications. *FOCUS on Indiana Libraries* (mo.); *Indiana Libraries* (q.).

Pres. Rick A. Jones, Eastbrook H.S., Marion 46953. Tel. 765-664-1214 ext. 104, fax 765-664-1216, e-mail rajones@eastbrook. k12.in.us; *Pres.-elect.* Kimberly Carr, Burris Laboratory School, Muncie 47306. Tel. 765-285-2342, fax 765-285-8620, e-mail 01kcarr @bsu.edu; *Secy.* Beth Slightom, Fall Creek Valley Middle School, Indianapolis 46236. Tel. 317-823-5490, fax 317-823-5497, e-mail bethslightom@msdlt.k12.in.us; *Treas.* Sue Jones, Tecumseh Middle School, Lafayette 47905-2096. Tel. 765-772-4750, fax 765-772-4763, e-mail sjones@lsc.k12.in.us.

Address correspondence to the association, 941 E. 86 St., Ste. 260, Indianapolis 46240. Tel. 317-257-2040, fax 317-257-1389, e-mail ilf@indy.net.

World Wide Web http://www.ilfonline. org/AIME/index.htm.

Iowa

Iowa Assn. of School Libns. Memb. 300. Term of Office. Jan.–Jan. Publication. *The Advocate* (electronic, 4 a year). *Ed.* Becky Stover Johnson. E-mail bcjohnson@cr.k12. ia.us.

Pres. Jill Hofmockel. E-mail jhofmockel @ccs.k12.ia.us; *V.P./Pres.-Elect* Kristin Steingraeber. E-mail steingraeberk@aea15.k12. ia.us; *Secy./Treas.* Debra Dorzweiler. E-mail ddorzweiler@west-branch.k12.ia.us; *Exec. Dir., Iowa Lib. Assn.* Laurie Hews, 3636

Westown Pkwy., West Des Moines 50266. Tel. 800-452-5507, e-mail ialib@mcleoud usa.net.

Address correspondence to the executive director.

World Wide Web http://www.iema-ia.org.

Kansas

Kansas Assn. of School Libns. Memb. 650. Term of Office. Aug. 2005–July 2006. Publication. *KASL News* (online; q.).

Pres. Linda Roberts. Tel. 620-347-4115, e-mail lroberts@usd246.org; *Pres.-Elect* Martha House. Tel. 620-767-5149, e-mail mhouse@cgrove417.org; *Secy.* Nora Jones. Tel. 620-241-9560, e-mail nora.jones@ mcpherson.com; *Treas.* Anita Brozik. Tel. 316-788-8500 ext. 251, e-mail abrozik@ usd260.com; *Past Pres.* Ann Schuster. Tel. 913-239-6010, e-mail aschuster@bluevalley k12.org; *Exec. Secy.* Judith Eller, 8517 W. Northridge, Wichita 67205. Tel. 316-773-6723, e-mail judy.eller@wichita.edu.

Address correspondence to the executive secretary.

World Wide Web http://www.skyways. org/KASL.

Kentucky

Kentucky School Media Assn. Memb. 620. Term of Office. Oct. 2005–Oct. 2006. Publication. *KSMA Newsletter* (q.).

Chair Angie Hawkins, South Heights Elementary School, 1199 Madison St., Henderson 42420. Tel. 270-831-5080, fax 270-831-5082, e-mail ahawkins@henderson.k12.ky. us; *Past Chair* Lisa Hughes, Heath H.S., 4330 Metropolis Lake Rd., West Paducah 42086. Tel. 270-538-4104, fax 270-538-4091, e-mail lhughes@mccracken.k12.ky.us.

Address correspondence to the chairperson.

World Wide Web http://www.kysma.org.

Louisiana

Louisiana Assn. of School Libns. Memb. 249. Term of Office. July 2005–June 2006.

Pres. Kathryn Arrington. E-mail karrington @ebrschools.org; *1st V.P./Pres.-Elect* Susan Cheshire. E-mail scheshire@bellsouth.net; *2nd V.P.* Peggy Wheelis. E-mail wheelis@ bayou.com; *Secy.* Anne Maverick. E-mail amaverick@ebrschools.org; *Past Pres.* Linda Holmes. E-mail holmesl@wfpsb.org.

Address correspondence to the association, c/o Louisiana Lib. Assn., 421 S. 4 St., Eunice 70535. Tel. 337-550-7890, fax 337-550-7846, e-mail office@llaonline.org.

World Wide Web http://www.llaonline. org/sig/lasl.

Maine

Maine School Lib. Assn. Memb. 350. Term of Office. May 2003–May 2005. Publication. *Maine Entry* (with the Maine Lib. Assn.; q.).

Pres. Terri Caouette, Lincoln Middle School. E-mail tcaouette@yahoo.com; *1st V.P.* Jeff Small, Cony H.S., Augusta. E-mail jsmall@augustaschools.org; *2nd V.P.* Donna Chale, Warsaw Middle School. E-mail dchale @warsaw-ms.sad53.k12.me.us; *Secy.* Joyce Lewis, Winslow H.S. E-mail jlucas@ winslowk12.org; *Treas.* Pam Goucher, Freeport Middle School. E-mail pam_goucher@ coconetme.org; *Past Pres.* Gretchen Asam, Presque Isle H.S. E-mail asamg1@yahoo. com; *Exec. Secy.* Edna Comstock. E-mail empoweredna@gwi.net.

Address correspondence to the president.

World Wide Web http://www.mas libraries.org.

Maryland

Maryland Educational Media Organization. Term of Office. July 2005–June 2006.

Pres. Dorothy P. D'Ascanio, Jackson Road Elementary School, 900 Jackson Rd., Silver Spring 20904. E-mail dorothy_p._ d'ascanio@fc.mcps.k12.md.us; *Secy.* Patricia Goff, Kenwood H.S., Baltimore County. E-mail pgoff@bcps.org; *Treas.* Sandra Bicksler, Professional Lib., Anne Arundel County. E-mail sbicksler@aacps.org; *Past Pres.* Jay Bansbach, Severn Elementary School, Severn 21144. E-mail cjbansbach@yahoo.com.

Address correspondence to the association, Box 21127, Baltimore 21228.

World Wide Web http://mdedmedia.org.

Massachusetts

Massachusetts School Lib. Media Assn. Memb. 800. Term of Office. June 2005–May 2006. Publication. *Media Forum* (online, q.). *Pres.* Kathy Lowe, Boston Arts Academy, Fenway H.S., Boston. Tel. 617-635-6470 ext. 236, fax 617-635-9204, e-mail kathylowe @verizon.net; *Secy.* Carol Klatt, Northeast Elementary, Waltham. Tel. 781-314-5747, e-mail klattc@k12.waltham.ma.us; *Treas.* Barbara Andrews. E-mail bandrews4@rcn.com; *Past Pres.* Ann Perham, Needham H.S. Tel. 781-455-0800 ext. 1708, e-mail ann_perham @needham.k12.ma.us; *Exec. Dir.* Doris Smith, MSLMA, P.O. Box 505, Bedford 01730. Tel. 781-275-2551, e-mail dsmith@ mslma.org.

Address correspondence to the executive director.

World Wide Web http://www.mslma.org.

Michigan

Michigan Assn. for Media in Education. Memb. 1,200. Term of Office. Jan.–Dec. 2006. Publications. *Media Spectrum* (2 a year); *MAME Newsletter* (4 a year). *Pres.* Marcia Lambert, Marshall Middle School, 100 E. Green St., Marshall 49068. Tel. 269-781-1251 ext. 1209, e-mail mlambert @marshall.k12.mi.us; *Pres.-Elect* Josephine Kirkbride, Chippewa Hills School Dist., 350 E. Wheatland Ave., Remus 49340. Tel. 989-967-8230, e-mail jkirkbride@chsd.us; *Secy.* Sue Taylor, Birmingham School Dist., Derby Middle School, 1300 Derby Rd., Birmingham 48009. Tel. 248-203-5052, e-mail st03bps@ birmingham.k12.mi.us; *Treas.* Bruce Pope-joy, East Jackson Community Schools, 4340 Walz Rd., Jackson 49201. Tel. 517-764-6010, fax 517-764-6081, e-mail mame exhibits@aol.com; *Past Pres.* Joanne Steckling, Sashabaw Middle School, 5565 Pine Knob Lane, Clarkston 48346. Tel. 248-623-4261, fax 248-623-4262, e-mail joanne@ jsteckling.com; *Exec. Dir.* Roger Ashley, MAME, 1407 Rensen, Ste. 3, Lansing 48910. Tel. 517-394-2808, fax 517-394-2096, e-mail ashleymame@aol.com.

Address correspondence to the executive director.

World Wide Web http://www.mame.gen. mi.us.

Minnesota

Minnesota Educational Media Organization. Memb. 625. Term of Office. July 2005–July 2006. Publications. *Minnesota Media*; *MEMOrandom*; *MTNews*. *Co-Pres.* Mary Garlie, Park Rapids H.S., 401 Huntsinger, Park Rapids 56470. Tel. 218-237-6499, e-mail mgarlie@parkrapids. k12.mn.us; Laurie Conzemius, Pine Meadow Elementary, 1029 Fifth St. N., Sartell 56377. Tel. 320-656-3701 ext. 811, e-mail conzemius@sartell.k12.mn.us; *Co-Pres.-Elect* Gina Light, Pearson Elementary, 917 Dakota St. S., Shakopee 55379. Tel. 952-496-5852 ext. 6841, e-mail gmlight@chaska. net; Barb Theirl, College of St. Catherine, 2004 Randolph Ave., No. 4125, St. Paul 55105. Tel. 651-690-6607, e-mail bhtheirl@ stkate.edu; *Secy.* Leslie Yoder, SPPS, 1930 Como Ave., St. Paul 55108. Tel. 651-603-4923, e-mail leslie.yoder@spps.org; *Treas.* Margaret Meyer, Becker Primary School, 12050 Hancock St., Becker 55308. Tel. 763-261-6324, e-mail mmeyer@becker.k12.mn. us; *Past Pres.* Jane Prestebak, Media Services and Instruction Technology, 8301 47th Ave. N., New Hope 55428. Tel. 763-504-4921, e-mail jane_prestebak@rdale.k12.mn. us; *Admin. Asst.* Deanna Sylte, P.O. Box 130555, Roseville 55113-0005. Tel./fax 651-771-8672, e-mail dsylte@tcq.net.

World Wide Web http://memoweb.org.

Mississippi

School Section, Mississippi Lib. Assn. Memb. 1,300. *Chair* Bettie Cox, Mississippi School of the Arts. Tel. 601-823-1340, e-mail betcox@ mde.k12.ms.us; *V. Chair* Diane B. Willard, Franklin County School Dist. Tel. 601-384-2441, e-mail dwillard@fcsd.k12.ms.us; *Exec. Secy.* Mary Julia Anderson.

Address correspondence to School Section, Mississippi Lib. Assn., P.O. Box 13687, Jackson 39236-3687. Tel. 601-981-4586, fax 601-981-4501, e-mail info@misslib.org.

World Wide Web http://www.misslib.org

Missouri

Missouri Assn. of School Libns. Memb. 1,000. Term of Office. June 2005–JUNE 2006. Publications. *Connections* (q.). *Pres.* Susan Rundel; *1st V.P./Pres.-Elect* Linda Weatherspoon; *2nd V.P.* Dea Borneman; *Secy.* Michelle Schmitt; *Treas.* Sandy Roth; *Past Pres.* Patricia Bibler.

Address correspondence to the association, 925 Madison St., Jefferson City 65101. Tel. 573-893-4155, fax 573-632-6678, e-mail masl_org@earthlink.net.

World Wide Web http://maslonline.org.

Montana

Montana School Lib. Media Div., Montana Lib. Assn. Memb. 200+. Term of Office. July 2005–June 2006. Publication. *FOCUS* (published by Montana Lib. Assn.) (q.).

Co-Chairs Colet Bartow, Manhattan H.S., P.O. Box 425, Manhattan 59741. Tel. 406-284-3341, fax 406-284-3104, e-mail cbartow @manhattan.k12.mt.us; Barb Oriet, Longfellow School, 516 S. Tracy, Bozeman 59815. Tel. 406-522-6174, e-mail boriet@bozeman. k12.mt.us; *Past Chair* Yvette Majerus, Moore Public Schools, 509 Highland Ave., Moore 59464. Tel. 406-374-2231, e-mail ymajerus @moore.k12.mt.us; *Exec. Dir., Montana Lib. Assn.* Ilene Casey, P.O. Box 1085, Manhattan 59741-1085. Tel. 406-284-6646, e-mail mla_icasey@mtlib.org.

World Wide Web http://www.mtlib.org/ slmd/slmd.html.

Nebraska

Nebraska Educational Media Assn. Memb. 370. Term of Office. July 2005–June 2006. Publication. *NEMA News* (q.).

Pres. Donna Helvering. E-mail dhelveri@ mpsomaha.org; *Pres.-Elect* Pam Springer. E-mail pspringer@paplv.esu3.org; *Secy.* Jayne Engel Hlavac. E-mail jengel@esu7.org; *Treas.* Mary Reiman. E-mail mreiman@lps. org; *Past Pres.* Gail Formanack. E-mail gail.formanack@ops.org; *Exec. Secy.* Trudy Pedley. E-mail trpedley@ellipse.net.

Address correspondence to the executive secretary.

World Wide Web http://nema.k12.ne.us.

Nevada

Nevada School and Children's Libs. Section, Nevada Lib. Assn. Memb. 120.

Chair Ann Aas; *Exec. Secy.* Patrick Dunn, Elko-Lander-Eureka Counties Lib., 720 Court St., Elko 89801. Tel. 775-738-3066, fax 775-738-8262, e-mail pfdunn@clan.lib. nv.us.

Address correspondence to the executive secretary.

World Wide Web http://www.nevada libraries.org/publications/handbook/nscls.html.

New Hampshire

New Hampshire Educational Media Assn., Box 418, Concord 03302-0418. Memb. 265. Term of Office. June 2005–June 2006. Publication. *Online* (irreg., electronic only).

Pres. Dorothy Grazier, Winnacunnet H.S., 1 Alumni Dr., Hampton 03842. Tel. 603-926-3395, e-mail dgrazier@winnacunnet.k12. nh.us; *Pres.-Elect* Diane Beaman, Belmont H.S., 255 Seavey Rd., Belmont 03220. Tel. 603-267-6525, e-mail dbeaman@shaker.k12. nh.us; *Recording Secy.* Mimi Crowley, Amherst St. School, 71 Amherst St., Nashua 03064. E-mail crowleym@nashua.edu; *Treas.* Jeff Kent, Beaver Meadow School, Concord 03301. Tel. 603-225-0854, e-mail jkent@csd. k12.nh.us; *Past Pres.* Linda Sherouse, North Hampton School, 201 Atlantic Ave., North Hampton 03862. Tel. 603-964-5501 ext. 230, fax 603-964-9018, e-mail lsherouse@sau21. k12.nh.us.

Address correspondence to the president.

World Wide Web http://www.nhema.net.

New Jersey

New Jersey Association of School Librarians (NJASL). Memb. 1,100. Term of Office. Aug. 2005–July 2006. Publication. *Bookmark* (mo.).

Pres. LaDawna Harrington, Avenel Middle School, 85 Woodbine Ave., Avenel 07001. Tel. 732-396-7028, e-mail ladawna. harrington@woodbridge.k12.nj.us; *V.P./ Pres.-Elect* Mary Moyer, Delsea H.S., Box 405, Fries Mill Rd., Franklinville 08322. Tel. 856-694-0100 ext. 239, fax 856-694-3146, e-mail mmoyerlib@comcast.net; *Correspond-*

ing Secy. Pat Massey, South Plainfield H.S., 200 Lake St., South Plainfield 07080. Tel. 908-754-4620 ext. 286, fax 908-756-7659, e-mail pmassey@spnet.k12.nj.us; *Past Pres.* Mary Lewis, David Brearley Middle/H.S., 401 Monroe Ave., Kenilworth 07033. Tel. 908-931-9696 ext. 319, fax 908-931-1618, e-mail maryklewis@optonline.net.

Address correspondence to the president-elect, NJASL, Box 610, Trenton 08607. Tel. 609-394-8032.

World Wide Web http://www.njasl.org.

New York

School Lib. Media Section, New York Lib. Assn., 252 Hudson St., Albany 12210. Tel. 518-432-6952. Memb. 880. Term of Office. Oct. 2005–Oct. 2006. Publications. *SLMS-Gram* (q.); participates in *NYLA Bulletin* (mo. except July and Aug.).

Pres. Marcia Eggleston. E-mail megglest @nncsk12.org; *Pres.-Elect* Sally Daniels. E-mail sallydaniels@twcny.rr.com; *V.P., Communications* Ellen Rubin. E-mail erubin@ wallkillcds.k12.ny.us; *V.P., Conferences* Bernie Tomasso. E-mail btomasso@twcny. rr.com; *Secy.* Anne Hegel. E-mail ahegel@ caz.cnyric.org; *Treas.* Rebecca Gerald. E-mail rgerald@its.dcboces.org; *Past Pres.* Patricia Shanley. Tel. 845-783-9574, e-mail pshanley@frontiernet.net.

Address correspondence to the president.

World Wide Web http://www.nyla.org

North Carolina

North Carolina School Lib. Media Assn. Memb. 1,100+. Term of Office. Oct. 2005–Oct. 2006.

Pres. Sandra D. Andrews, UNC Dept. of Lib. and Info. Studies, 349 Curry Bldg., Univ. of North Carolina at Greensboro, Greensboro 27402. Tel. 336-334-5738, e-mail sdandre2@uncg.edu; *V.P./Pres.-Elect* Jackie Pierson, Winston-Salem/Forsyth County Schools, 1605 Miller St., Winston-Salem 27101. Tel. 336-727-2373, e-mail jpierson@triad.rr.com; *Secy.* Corine Warren, J. W. Coon Elementary School, 905 Hope Mills Rd., Fayetteville 28304. Tel. 910-425-6141, fax 910-425-0878, e-mail corine

warren@ccs.k12.nc.us; *Treas.* Libby Oxenfeld, Guilford County Schools, 120 Franklin Blvd. Greensboro 27401. Tel. 336-370-2310, fax 336-370-2363, e-mail oxenfee@gcsnc. com; *Past Pres.* Karen Lowe, Northwest RESA, 808 Green Acres, Myers St., Millers Creek 28651. Tel. 336-667-1754, fax 336-667-0503, e-mail lowekr@charter.net.

Address correspondence to the president.

World Wide Web http://www.ncslma.org.

North Dakota

School Lib. and Youth Services Section, North Dakota Lib. Assn. Memb. 100. Term of Office. Sept. 2005–Sept. 2006. Publication. *The Good Stuff* (q).

Chair Glenda Westman, White Shield School, 1747 40th Ave. N.W., Garrison 58540-9440. Tel. 701-743-4350, fax 701-743-4501, e-mail glenda.westman@sendit. nodak.edu.

Address correspondence to the chairperson.

Ohio

Ohio Educational Lib. Media Assn. Memb. 1,000. Term of Office. Jan.–Dec. 2006. Publication. *Ohio Media Spectrum* (q.).

Pres. Sue Rahn. E-mail suerahn@ trotwood.k12.oh.us; *V.P.* Vicky Schmarr. E-mail schmarrv@aol.com; *Treas.* Sue Subel. E-mail smsubel@aol.com; *Past Pres.* Christine Findlay. E-mail christine.findlay@ centerville.k12.oh.us; *Dir. of Services* Kate Brunswick, 17 S. High St., Ste. 200, Columbus 43215. Tel. 614-221-1900, fax 614-221-1989, e-mail kate@assnoffices.com.

Address correspondence to the director of services.

World Wide Web http://www.oelma.org.

Oklahoma

Oklahoma Assn. of School Lib. Media Specialists. Memb. 300+. Term of Office. July 2005–June 2006. Publication. *Oklahoma Librarian.*

Pres. Deborah Maehs. E-mail maehsville @aol.com; *Pres.-Elect* Stephanie McDaniel. E-mail mcdanst@tulsaschools.org; *Secy.* Connie Wise. E-mail wise@woodwardps.net;

Treas. Bonnie Brown. E-mail brownbo@ tulsaschools.org; *Past Pres.* Margo Canaday. E-mail mcanaday@bps.k12.ok.us.

Address correspondence to the president, c/o Oklahoma Lib. Assn., 300 Hardy Dr., Edmond 73013. Tel. 405-348-0506.

World Wide Web http://www.oklibs.org/ oaslms.

Oregon

Oregon Educational Media Assn. Memb. 600. Term of Office. July 2005–June 2006. Publication. *OEMA Newsletter* (electronic).

Pres. Jim Tindall. E-mail tindallj@nwasco. k12.or.us; *Pres.-Elect* Allen Kopf. E-mail kopf@umatilla.k12.or.us; *Secy.* Jenny Takeda. E-mail jenny_takeda@beavton.k12.or.us; *Treas.* Merrie Olson. E-mail molson@epud. net; *Past Pres.* Martha Decherd. E-mail martha_decherd@ddouglas.k12.or.us; *Exec. Dir.* Jim Hayden, Box 277, Terrebonne 97760. Tel./fax 541-923-0675, e-mail j23 hayden@aol.com.

Address correspondence to the executive director.

World Wide Web http://www.oema.net.

Pennsylvania

Pennsylvania School Libns. Assn. Memb. 1,500+. Term of Office. July 2004–June 2006. Publication. *Learning and Media* (q.).

Pres. Anita Vance. E-mail alv@lion.crsd. k12.pa.us; *V.P./Pres.-Elect* Margaret Foster. E-mail mfoster@northallegheny.org; *Secy.* Carolyn Walsh. E-mail cwalsh6946@aol. com; *Treas.* Connie Roupp. E-mail croupp@ stny.rr.com; *Past Pres.* Geneva Reeder. E-mail greeder@dejazzd.com.

Address correspondence to the president. World Wide Web http://www.psla.org.

Rhode Island

Rhode Island Educational Media Assn. Memb. 350+. Term of Office. June 2005– May 2006.

Pres. Phyllis Humphrey. E-mail rid04893 @ride.ri.net; *Secy.* Sue Fleisig. E-mail sue fleisig@aol.com; *Treas.* Judi O'Brien. E-mail obrienj@ride.ri.net; *Past Pres.* Holly Barton. E-mail bartonh@ride.ri.net.

Address correspondence to the association, Box 470, East Greenwich 02818.

World Wide Web http://www.ri.net/ RIEMA.

South Carolina

South Carolina Assn. of School Libns. Memb. 1,100. Term of Office. June 2005–May 2006. Publication. *Media Center Messenger* (4 a year).

Pres. Lawren Hammond. E-mail lhammond @aiken.k12.sc.us; *V.P./Pres.-Elect* Carolyn P. Jenkins. E-mail cpjenkins30@hotmail. com; *Secy.* Valerie Byrd Fort. E-mail val_ byrd@yahoo.com; *Treas.* Stephen Reed. E-mail screed3103@aol.com; *Past Pres.* Martha Taylor. E-mail martha_taylor@charter.net.

Address correspondence to the president. World Wide Web http://www.scasl.net.

South Dakota

South Dakota School Lib. Media Assn., Section of the South Dakota Lib. Assn. and South Dakota Education Assn. Memb. 140+. Term of Office. Oct. 2005–Oct. 2006.

Chair Lee Crary, Bison School Lib. E-mail lee.crary@k12.sd.us.

Tennessee

Tennessee Assn. of School Libns. Memb. 450. Term of Office. Jan.–Dec. 2006. Publication. *Footnotes* (q.).

Pres. Brenda Moriarty, Lincoln Elementary School, 1000 Summer St., Kingsport 37664. Tel. 423-378-2367, e-mail bmoriarty @k12.tn.com; *V.P./Pres.-Elect* Margaret Hausauer, Kenwood Elementary School, 1101 Peachers Mill Rd., Clarksville 37042. E-mail margaret.hausauer@cmcss.net; *Secy.* Carol Burr, Goodlettsville Elementary School, 514 Donald St., Goodlettsville 37072. E-mail carol.burr@mnps.org; *Treas.* Lynn Caruthers, Joseph Brown Elementary School, 301 Cord Dr., Columbia 38401. Tel. 931-388-3601, e-mail lcaruth@charter.net; *Past Pres.* Allison Roberts, Barger Academy of Fine Arts, 4808 Brainerd Rd., Chattanooga 37411. Tel. 423-493-0348, e-mail roberts_allison@hcde.org.

Address correspondence to the president.

World Wide Web http://www.korrnet.org/tasl.

Texas

Texas Assn. of School Libns. (Div. of Texas Lib. Assn.). Memb. 4,051. Term of Office. Apr. 2005–Apr. 2006. Publication. *Media Matters* (3 a year).

Chair Tanya Tullos, Sherwood Elementary, 1700 Sherwood Forest Dr., Houston 77043. Tel. 713-365-4800, fax 325-365-4808, e-mail tullost@springbranchisd.com; *Chair-Elect* Jack Strawn, O'Connor H.S., 7722 Cascade Oak Dr., San Antonio 78249. Tel. 210-695-4800 ext. 2230, fax 210-695-4804, e-mail e028015@nisd.net; *Secy.* Charlyn Trussell, Mission CISD, 2207 Clinton St., Mission 78572. Tel. 956-580-5605; *Past Chair* Janice Richardson, Leander Middle School, 18215 Lura Lane, Jonestown 78645. Tel. 512-434-7840, fax 512-434-7805, e-mail janice.richardson@leanderisd.org.

Address correspondence to the Texas Library Association, 3355 Bee Cave Rd., Ste. 401, Austin 78746. Tel. 512-328-1518, fax 512-328-8852, e-mail tla@txla.org.

World Wide Web http://www.txla.org/groups/tasl/index.html.

Utah

Utah Educational Lib. Media Assn. Memb. 390. Term of Office. Mar. 2005–Feb. 2006. Publication. *UELMA Newsletter* (q.).

Pres. Nan Allsen, North Sanpete H.S., 390 E. 700 S., Mount Pleasant 84647. Tel. 435-462-2452 ext. 216, fax 435-462-3112, e-mail nan@nsanpete.k12.ut.us; *Pres.-Elect* Cindy Mitchell, South Jordan Middle School, 10245 S. 2700 W., South Jordan 84095. Tel. 801-412-2917, fax 801-412-2930, e-mail cindy.mitchell@jordan.k12.ut.us; *Secy.* Diana Hanke, Duchesne School Dist., P.O. Box 446, Duchesne 84021. Tel. 435-738-1249, e-mail dhanke@dcsd.org; *Past Pres.* Fawn Morgan, Layton H.S., 440 Lancer Lane, Layton 84041. Tel. 801-402-4996, fax 801-402-4801, e-mail fmorgan@dsdmail.net; *Exec. Dir.* Larry Jeppesen, Cedar Ridge Middle School, 65 N. 200 W., Hyde Park 84318. Tel.

435-563-6229, fax 435-563-3914, e-mail larry.jeppesen@cache.k12.ut.us.

Address correspondence to the executive director.

World Wide Web http://www.uelma.org.

Vermont

Vermont Educational Media Assn. Memb. 200+. Term of Office. May 2005–May 2006. Publication. *VEMA News* (q.).

Pres. Dan Greene, U32 Junior-Senior H.S., Montpelier. E-mail dgreen@u32.org; *Pres.-Elect* Anne Gallivan, Barstow Memorial School, Chittenden. E-mail agallivan@barstow.k12.vt.us; *Secy.* Marsha Middleton, North Country Union H.S., Newport. E-mail mmiddleton@ncuhs.org; *Treas.* Donna Smyth, Proctor Elementary School, Proctor. E-mail dsmyth@proctorelem.org; *Past Pres.* Angel Harris, Alburg Community Educ. Center. E-mail angharr@gisu.org.

Address correspondence to the president.

World Wide Web http://www.vema-online.org.

Virginia

Virginia Educational Media Assn. Memb. 1,700. Term of Office. (Pres., Pres.-Elect) Nov. 2005–Nov. 2006; (other offices 2 years in alternating years). Publication. *Mediagram* (q.).

Pres. Dee Griffith, Mountain View Elementary, Loudoun County. E-mail dgriffit@loudoun.k12.va.us; *Pres.-Elect* Laurel Morgan, Lake Taylor Middle School, Norfolk. E-mail lmorgan@nps.k12.va.us; *Secy.* Beverly Shearon, Brunswick Senior H.S., Brunswick County. E-mail bev.shearon@brun.k12.va.us; *Treas.* Kathy Meredith, Tomahawk Elementary, Hampton. E-mail kmeredith@campbell.k12.va.us; *Past Pres.* Kathy Lehman, Thomas Dale H.S., Chesterfield County. E-mail kathy_lehman@ccpsnet.net; *Exec. Dir.* Jean Remler. Tel./fax 703-764-0719, e-mail jremler@pen.k12.va.us.

Address correspondence to the association, Box 2743, Fairfax 22031-0743.

World Wide Web http://vema.gen.va.us.

Washington

Washington Lib. Media Assn. Memb. 1,450+. Term of Office. Oct. 2005–Oct. 2006. Publications. *The Medium* (3 a year); *The Message* (2 a year).

Pres. Sarah Applegate. E-mail sapplegate @nthurston.k12.wa.us; *Pres.-Elect* Marianne Hunter. E-mail mhunter@nthurston.k12.wa. us; *V.P.* Karen Williams. E-mail karen. williams@kent.k12.wa.us; *Secy.* Teresa McCausland. E-mail tmccausland@nsd.org; *Treas.* Kathy Kugler. E-mail kkugler@ mindspring.com; *Past Pres.* Kay Evey. E-mail eveyk@tukwila.wednet.edu.

Address correspondence to the association, Box 50194, Bellevue 98015-0194. E-mail wlma@wlma.org.

World Wide Web http://www.wlma.org.

West Virginia

School Library Division, West Virginia Lib. Assn. Memb. 50. Term of Office. Nov. 2005–Nov. 2006. Publication. *WVLA School Library News* (5 a year).

Chair Pat Ramsburg. E-mail pramsbur@ access.k12.wv.us; *Chair-Elect* Ginny Frank. E-mail vfrank@access.k12.wv.us; *Secy.* Kathy Bargeloh. E-mail kbargelo@access. k12.wv.us

Address correspondence to the chairperson.

Wisconsin

Wisconsin Educational Media Assn. Memb. 1,100+. Term of Office. Apr. 2005–Apr. 2006. Publication. *Dispatch* (7 a year).

Pres. Kate Bugher. E-mail kbugher@ madison.k12.wi.us; *Pres.-Elect* Annette Smith. E-mail smitha@mail.milton.k12.wi. us; *Secy.* Kathy Boguszewski. E-mail kboguszewski@janesville.k12.wi.us; *Treas.* Mike Weber. E-mail weber@hartfordjt1.k12. wi.us; *Past Pres.* Mary Lou Zuege. E-mail zuegmar@sdmf.k12.wi.us.

Address correspondence to Courtney Rounds, WEMA Assn. Mgr., P.O. Box 206, Boscobel 53805. Tel. 608-375-6020, e-mail wema@centurytel.net.

World Wide Web http://www.wema online.org.

Wyoming

Section of School Library Media Personnel, Wyoming Lib. Assn. Memb. 90+. Term of Office. Oct. 2005–Oct. 2006. Publications. *WLA Newsletter*; *SSLMP Newsletter*.

Chair Jan Segerstrom, Jackson Hole H.S. E-mail jasegerstrom@teton1.k12.wy.us; *Chair-Elect* Mary Jayne Jordan, Sundance H.S. E-mail jordanmj@hms.crooknet.k12. wy.us; *Secy.* Deb Lanthier. E-mail deb_ lanthier@hotmail.com. Address correspondence to the chairperson.

International Library Associations

International Association of Agricultural Information Specialists (IAALD)

Peter Ballantyne, President
P.O. Box 63, Lexington, KY 40588-0063
E-mail peter.ballantyne@iaald.org
World Wide Web http://www.iaald.org

Object

The association facilitates professional development of and communication among members of the agricultural information community worldwide. Its goal is to enhance access to and use of agriculture-related information resources. To further this mission, IAALD will promote the agricultural information profession, support professional development activities, foster collaboration, and provide a platform for information exchange. Founded 1955.

Membership

Memb. 400+. Dues (Inst.) $US110; (Indiv.) $US50.

Officers

Pres. Peter Ballantyne (The Netherlands). E-mail peter.ballantyne@iaald.org; *1st V.P.* Stephen Rudgard (Italy). E-mail stephen.rudgard@iaald.org; *2nd V.P.* Dorothy Mukhebi (Uganda). E-mail dorothy.mukhebi@iaald.org; *Secy.-Treas.* Antoinette P. Greider (USA). E-mail toni.greider@iaald.org.

Publications

Quarterly Bulletin of the IAALD (memb.).

International Association of Law Libraries (IALL)

Box 5709, Washington, DC 20016-1309
Tel. 804-924-3384, fax 804-924-7239
World Wide Web http://www.iall.org

Object

IALL is a worldwide organization of librarians, libraries, and other persons or institutions concerned with the acquisition and use of legal information emanating from sources other than their jurisdictions, and from multinational and international organizations.

IALL's basic purpose is to facilitate the work of librarians who must acquire, process, organize, and provide access to foreign legal materials. IALL has no local chapters but maintains liaison with national law library associations in many countries and regions of the world.

Membership

More than 800 members in more than 50 countries on five continents.

Officers (2005–2006)

Pres. Jules Winterton (Great Britain); *1st V.P.* Richard A. Danner (USA); *2nd V.P.* Jarmila Looks (Switzerland); *Secy.* Ann Morrison (Canada); *Treas.* Gloria F. Chao (USA); *Past Pres.* Holger Knudsen (Germany).

Board Members

Jennefer Aston (Ireland); Amanda Barratt (South Africa); Marie-Louise H. Bernal (USA); James Butler (Australia); Mark D. Engsberg (USA); Giina Kaskla (Belgium); Petal Kinder (Australia); Halvor Kongshavn (Norway); Bettina Picone-Maxion (Italy); Silke A. Sahl (USA).

Publication

International Journal of Legal Information (3 a year; $US60 for individuals; $US95 for institutions).

International Association of Music Libraries, Archives and Documentation Centres (IAML)

c/o Roger Flury, IAML Secretary General
Music Room, National Library of New Zealand
Box 1467, Wellington, New Zealand
Tel. 64-4-474-3039, fax 64-4-474-3035
World Wide Web http://www.iaml.info

Object

To promote the activities of music libraries, archives, and documentation centers and to strengthen the cooperation among them; to promote the availability of all publications and documents relating to music and further their bibliographical control; to encourage the development of standards in all areas that concern the association; and to support the protection and preservation of musical documents of the past and the present.

Membership

Memb. 2,000.

Board Members

Pres. Massimo Gentili-Tedeschi, Biblioteca Nazionale Braidense, Ufficio Ricerca Fondi Musicali, via Conservatorio, 12, I-20122 Milano, Italy. Tel. 39-02-7601-1822, fax 39-02-7600-3097, e-mail president@iaml.info; *Past Pres.* John H. Roberts, Music Lib., 240 Morrison Hall, Univ. of California, Berkeley, CA 94720. Tel. 510-642-2428, fax 510-642-8237, e-mail jroberts@library.berkeley.edu; *V.P.s* James P. Cassaro, Theodore M. Finney Music Lib., Univ. of Pittsburgh, B28 Music Bldg., Pittsburgh, PA 15260. Tel. 412-624-4130, fax 412-624-4180, e-mail cassaro@pitt.edu; Dominique Hausfater, Mediathèque Hector Berlioz, Conservatoire National Supérieur de Musique et de Danse de Paris, 209 Ave. Jean-Jaurès, F-75019 Paris, France. Tel. 33-1-40-40-46-28, fax 33-1-40-40-45-34, e-mail dhausfater@cnsmdp.fr; Ruth Hellen, Audio Visual Services, Enfield Libs., Town Hall, Green Lane, London N13 4XD, England. Tel. 44-208-379-2760, fax 44-208-379-2761, e-mail r-hellen@enfield.gov.uk; Federica Riva, Bibliotecario del Conservatorio Sezione Musicale della Biblioteca Palatina, Nel Conservatorio di Musica Arrigo Boito, via Conservatorio 27/a, I-43100 Parma, Italy. Tel. 39-0521-381-958, fax 39-0521-200-398, e-mail f.riva@agora.it; *Treas.* Martie Severt, MCO Muziekbibliotheek, Postbus 125, NL-1200 AC Hilversum, Netherlands. E-mail m.severt@mco.nl.

Publication

Fontes Artis Musicae (4 a year; memb.). *Ed.* John Wagstaff, Music Faculty Lib., Oxford Univ., St. Aldate's, Oxford OX1 1DB, England.

Professional Branches

Archives and Documentation Centres. Judy Tsou, Univ. of Washington, Seattle, WA 98145.

Broadcasting and Orchestra Libraries. Jutta Lambrecht, Westdeutscher Rundfunk, Dokumentation und Archive, Appellhofplatz 1, D-50667 Köln, Germany.

Libraries in Music Teaching Institutions. Anne Le Lay, Bibliothèque du CNR, 22 rue de la Belle Feuille, F-92100 Boulogne-Billancourt, France.

Public Libraries. Kirsten Husted, Biblioteket for Vejle By og Amt, Willy Sørensen Plads 1, Vejle, Denmark.

Research Libraries. Joachim Jaenecke, Staatsbibliothek zu Berlin, 10102 Berlin, Germany.

International Association of School Librarianship (IASL)

Karen Bonanno, Executive Secretary
P.O. Box 83, Zillmere, Qld. 4034, Australia
Fax 617-3633-0570, e-mail iasl@kb.com.au
World Wide Web http://www.iasl-slo.org

Object

The objectives of the International Association of School Librarianship are to advocate the development of school libraries throughout all countries; to encourage the integration of school library programs into the instructional and curriculum development of the school; to promote the professional preparation and continuing education of school library personnel; to foster a sense of community among school librarians in all parts of the world; to foster and extend relationships between school librarians and other professionals connected with children and youth; to foster research in the field of school librarianship and the integration of its conclusions with pertinent knowledge from related fields; to promote the publication and dissemination of information about successful advocacy and program initiatives in school librarianship; to share information about programs and materials for children and youth throughout the international community; and to initiate and coordinate activities, conferences, and other projects in the field of school librarianship and information services. Founded 1971.

Membership

Memb. 600.

Officers and Executive Board

Pres. Peter Genco, USA; *V.P.s* James Henri, Hong Kong; Judy O'Connell, Australia; Dilgit Singh, Malaysia; *Treasurer* Anne Lockwood, Australia; *Dirs.* Margaret Baffour-Awuah, Africa–Sub-Sahara; Lourense Das, Europe; Rose Dotten, Canada; Eleanor Howe, USA; Elizabeth Greef, Oceania; Angel Leung Yuet Ha, East Asia; Colleen MacDonell, International Schools; Katharina B. L. Berg, Latin America; Jagtar Singh, Asia; John Royce, North Africa/Middle East.

Publications

Selected Papers from Proceedings of Annual Conferences:

21st Annual Conference, 1992, Belfast, Northern Ireland. *Toward the 21st Century: Books and Media for the Millennium.* $US25.

22nd Annual Conference, 1993, Adelaide, Australia. *Dreams and Dynamics.* $US25.

23rd Annual Conference, 1994, Pittsburgh. *Literacy: Traditions, Cultures, Technology.* $US25.

24th Annual Conference, 1995, Worcester, England. *Sustaining the Vision.* $US25.

25th Annual Conference, 1996, Ocho Rios, Jamaica. *School Libraries Imperatives for the 21st Century.* $US25.

26th Annual Conference, 1997, Vancouver, Canada. *Information Rich But Knowledge Poor?* $US25.

27th Annual Conference, 1998, Ramat-Gan, Israel. *Education for all: Culture, Reading and Information.* $US25.

28th Annual Conference, 1999, Birmingham, Alabama. *Unleash the Power: Knowledge, Technology, Diversity.* $US25.

29th Annual Conference, 2000, Malmo, Sweden. *Information Literacy: Key to the Future.* $US25.

30th Annual Conference, 2001, Auckland, New Zealand. *Inspiring Connections: Learning, Libraries and Literacy.* $US25.

31st Annual Conference, 2002, Petaling Jaya, Malaysia. *School Libraries for a Knowledge Society.* $US40.

32nd Annual Conference, 2003, Durban, South Africa. *School Libraries: Breaking Down Barriers.* $US45.

33rd Annual Conference, 2004, Dublin, Ireland. *From Aesop to E-Book: The Story Goes On.* $US45.

34th Annual Conference, 2005, Hong Kong. *Information Leadership in a Culture of Change.* $US25.

International Association of Technological University Libraries (IATUL)

President, Gaynor Austen, Library, Queensland University of Technology, GPO Box 2434, Brisbane, Qld. 4001, Australia
Tel. 61-7-3864-2560, fax 61-7-3864-1823, e-mail g.austen@qut.edu.au
World Wide Web http://www.iatul.org

Object

To provide a forum where library directors can meet to exchange views on matters of current significance in the libraries of universities of science and technology. Research projects identified as being of sufficient interest may be followed through by working parties or study groups.

Membership

Ordinary, associate, sustaining, and honorary. Membership fee 75–150 euros a year, sustaining membership 500 euros a year. Memb. 232 (in 42 countries).

Officers and Executives

Membs. Ana Azevedo, Biblioteca Faculdade de Engenharia Universidade do Porto, R. Roberto Frias 4200-465, Porto, Portugal. E-mail ana@fe.up.pt; Arja-Riitta Haarala, Tempere Univ. of Technology Lib., Tempere FIN-33101, Finland. E-mail arja-riitta.haarala @tut.fi; Catherine J. Matthews, Lib., Ryerson Polytechnic Univ., 340 Victoria St., Toronto, Ontario M5B 2K3, Canada. E-mail cmatthew @acs.ryerson.ca; Judith Palmer, Radcliffe Science Lib., Oxford Univ., Parks Rd., Oxford OX1 3QP, England. E-mail judith. palmer@bodley.ox.ac.uk; Alice Trussell, Fiedler Engineering Lib., Kansas State Univ.,

Manhattan, KS 66506. E-mail alitrus@lib.
ksu.edu; Sohair Wastawy, Lib. of Alexandria,
El Shatby, Alexandria 21526, Egypt. E-mail
sohair.wastawy@bibalex.org; *Past Pres.*
Michael Breaks, Heriot-Watt Univ. Lib.,
Edinburgh EH14 4AS, Scotland. Tel. 44-131-
451-3570, fax 44-131-451-3164, e-mail
m.l.breaks@hw.ac.uk.

Publication

IATUL Proceedings on CD-ROM (ann.).

International Council on Archives (ICA)

Joan van Albada, Secretary-General
60 Rue des Francs-Bourgeois, F-75003 Paris, France
Tel. 33-1-40-27-63-06, fax 33-1-42-72-20-65, e-mail ica@ica.org
World Wide Web http://www.ica.org

Object

To establish, maintain, and strengthen relations among archivists of all lands, and
among all professional and other agencies or
institutions concerned with the custody, organization, or administration of archives, public
or private, wherever located. Established
1948.

Membership

Memb. c. 1,700 (representing c. 180 countries and territories).

Officers

Secy.-Gen. Joan van Albada; *Deputy Secy.-*
Gen. Perrine Canavaggio; *Office Mgr.* Annick
Carteret.

Publications

Comma (memb.).
Flash (3 a year; memb.).
Guide to the Sources of the History of Nations
(Latin American Series, 11 vols. pub.;
Africa South of the Sahara Series, 20 vols.
pub.; North Africa, Asia, and Oceania
Series: 15 vols. pub.).
Guide to the Sources of Asian History (Eng-
lish-language series [India, Indonesia,
Korea, Nepal, Pakistan, Singapore], 14
vols. pub.; National Language Series
[Indonesia, Korea, Malaysia, Nepal, Thai-
land], 6 vols. pub.; other guides, 3 vols.
pub.).

International Federation of Film Archives (FIAF)

Secretariat, 1 Rue Defacqz, B-1000 Brussels, Belgium
Tel. 32-2-538-3065, fax 32-2-534-4774, e-mail info@fiafnet.org
World Wide Web http://www.fiafnet.org

Object

Founded in 1938, FIAF brings together not-for-profit institutions dedicated to rescuing films and any other moving-image elements considered both as cultural heritage and as historical documents.

FIAF is a collaborative association of the world's leading film archives whose purpose has always been to ensure the proper preservation and showing of motion pictures. A total of 141 archives in more than 70 countries collect, restore, and exhibit films and cinema documentation spanning the entire history of film.

FIAF seeks to promote film culture and facilitate historical research, to help create new archives around the world, to foster training and expertise in film preservation, to encourage the collection and preservation of documents and other cinema-related materials, to develop cooperation between archives, and to ensure the international availability of films and cinema documents.

Officers

Pres. Eva Orbanz; *Secy.-Gen.* Meg Labrum; *Treas.* Karl Griep; *Membs.* Magdalena Acosta, Jan-Erik Billinger, Vittorio Boarini, Sylvia Frank, Gregory Lukow, Eric Le Roy, Patrick Loughney, Hisashi Okajima, Vladimir Opela, Yolande Racine.

Address correspondence to Christian Dimitriu, senior administrator, c/o the FIAF Secretariat. E-mail info@fiafnet.org.

Publications

Journal of Film Preservation.
FIAF International Filmarchive Database
For other FIAF publications, see the Web site http://www.fiafnet.org.

International Federation of Library Associations and Institutions (IFLA)

P.O. Box 95312, 2509 CH The Hague, Netherlands
Tel. 31-70-314-0884, fax 31-70-383-4827
E-mail ifla@ifla.org, World Wide Web http://www.ifla.org

Object

To promote international understanding, cooperation, discussion, research, and development in all fields of library activity, including bibliography, information services, and the education of library personnel, and to provide a body through which librarianship can be represented in matters of international interest. Founded 1927.

Officers and Governing Board

Pres. Alex Byrne, Univ. of Technology, Sydney, Australia; *Pres.-Elect* Claudia Lux, Zentral- und Landesbibliothek, Berlin, Germany; *Treas.* Gunnar Sahlin, National Lib. of Sweden, Stockholm, Sweden; *Governing Board* Nancy Bold, Nancy Bold and Assoc., Golden, Colorado; Maria Isabel Carbal da Franca, Grupo de Information e Documentation,

Juridica Do RJ, Rio de Janeiro, Brazil; Gwynneth Evans, Ottawa, Canada; Barbara Ford, Univ. of Illinois at Urbana-Champaign; Nancy E. Gwinn, Smithsonian Inst. Lib., Chevy Chase, Maryland; Torny Kjekstad, Baerum Public Lib., Bekkestua, Norway; Sang-wan Han, Korean Lib. Assn., Seoul, Korea; Bob McKee, Cilip, London, England; Vinyet Panyella, Parlament de Catalunya, Barcelona, Spain; Adolfo Rodriguez Gallardo, National Univ. of Mexico, Mexico DF; Shawky Salem, ACML–Egypt, Alexandria, Egypt; Réjean Savard, Université de Montréal, Montreal, Canada; Donna W. Scheeder, Lib. of Congress, Washington, D.C.; Edward Swanson, MINITEX Lib. Info. Network, Minneapolis; Barbara Tillet, Lib. of Congress; Tiiu Valm, Nat. Lib. of Estonia, Tallinn, Estonia; Jacinta Were, Univ. of Nairobi Lib., Nairobi, Kenya; Zhang Xiaolin, Lib. of Chinese Academy of Sciences, Beijing, China; *Secy.-Gen.* Peter Johan Lor; *Coord. Professional Activities* Sjoerd M. J. Koopman.

Publications

IFLA Annual Report
IFLA Directory (bienn.).
IFLA Journal (4 a year).
IFLA Professional Reports.
IFLA Publications Series.
International Cataloguing and Bibliographic Control (q.).
International Preservation News.

American Membership

American Assn. of Law Libs.; American Lib. Assn.; Assn. for Lib. and Info. Science Educ.; Assn. of Research Libs.; International Assn. of Law Libs.; International Assn. of School Libns.; Medical Lib. Assn.; Special Libs. Assn. *Institutional Membs.* There are 123 libraries and related institutions that are institutional members or consultative bodies and sponsors of IFLA in the United States (out of a total of 1,646), and 124 personal affiliates (out of a total of 352).

International Organization for Standardization (ISO)

ISO Central Secretariat, 1 rue de Varembé, Case Postale 56,
CH-1211 Geneva 20, Switzerland
41-22-749-0111, fax 41-22-733-3430, e-mail central@iso.org
World Wide Web http://www.iso.org

Object

A worldwide federation of national standards bodies, founded in 1947, at present comprising some 156 members, one in each country. The object of ISO is to promote the development of standardization and related activities in the world with a view to facilitating international exchange of goods and services, and to developing cooperation in the spheres of intellectual, scientific, technological, and economic activity. The scope of ISO covers international standardization in all fields except electrical and electronic engineering standardization, which is the responsibility of the International Electrotechnical Commis-

sion (IEC). The results of ISO technical work are published as International Standards.

Officers

Pres. Masami Tanaka, Japan; *V.P. (Policy)* Torsten Bahke, Germany; *V.P. (Technical Management)* Ziva Patir, Israel; *Secy.-Gen.* Alan Bryden.

Technical Work

The technical work of ISO is carried out by some 190 technical committees. These include:

ISO/TC 46–Information and documentation (Secretariat, Association Française de Normalization, 11 Ave. Francis de Pressensé, 93571 Saint-Denis La Plaine, Cedex, France). Scope: Standardization of practices relating to libraries, documentation and information centers, indexing and abstracting services, archives, information science, and publishing.

ISO/TC 37–Terminology and language and content resources (Secretariat, INFO-TERM, Aichholzgasse 6/12, 1120, Vienna, Austria, on behalf of Österreichisches Normungsinstitut). Scope: Standardization of principles, methods, and applications relating to terminology and other language and content resources in the contexts of multilingual communication and cultural diversity.

ISO/IEC JTC 1–Information technology (Secretariat, American National Standards Institute, 25 W. 43 St., fourth fl., New York, NY 10036). Scope: Standardization in the field of information technology.

Publications

ISO Annual Report.

ISO Focus (11 a year).

ISO CataloguePlus on CD-ROM (combined catalog of published standards and technical work program) (ann.).

ISO International Standards.

ISO Management Systems (bi-mo.).

ISO Memento (ann.).

ISO Online information service on World Wide Web (http://www.iso.org).

Foreign Library Associations

The following is a list of regional and national library associations around the world. A more complete list can be found in *International Literary Market Place* (Information Today, Inc.).

Regional

Africa

Standing Conference of Eastern, Central, and Southern African Lib. and Info. Assns., c/o Tanzania Library Assn., P.O. Box 33433, Dar es Salaam, Tanzania. Tel. 255-22-2775411, e-mail tla_tanzania@yahoo.com, World Wide Web http://www.scecsal.org.

The Americas

Asociación de Bibliotecas Universitarias, de Investigación e Institucionales del Caribe (Assn. of Caribbean Univ., Research, and Institutional Libs.), Box 23317, UPR Sta., San Juan, PR 00931-3317. Tel. 787-790-8054, 787-764-0000, e-mail acuril@rrpac. upr.clu.edu, World Wide Web http://acuril.rrp.upr.edu/que.htm. *Pres.* Astrid J. T. Britten, Biblioteca Nacional de Aruba, George Madurostraat 13, Oranjestad, Aruba. Tel. 297-582-1580, fax 297-582-5493, e-mail astridbritten@hotmail.com; *Exec. Secy.* Oneida Rivera de Ortiz.

Seminar on the Acquisition of Latin American Lib. Materials, c/o *Exec. Secy.* Laura Gutiérrez-Witt, SALALM Secretariat, Benson Latin American Collection, Sid Richardson Hall 1.109, Univ. of Texas, Austin, TX 78713. Tel. 512-495-4471, fax 512-495-4488, e-mail sandyl@mail.utexas. edu, World Wide Web http://www.lib. utexas.edu/benson/secretariat.

Asia

Congress of Southeast Asian Libns. (CONSAL), c/o *Secy.-Gen.* Tay Ai Cheng, c/o National Lib. Board, Marine Parade Community Lib., 278 Marine Parade Community Bldg., No. B-01, Singapore 449282. Tel. 65-6342-4200, fax 65-6342-4222, e-mail aicheng@nlb.gov.sg, World Wide Web http://www.consal.org.sg.

The Commonwealth

Commonwealth Lib. Assn., Univ. of the West Indies, Bridgetown Campus, Learning Resources Center, P.O. Box 64, Bridgetown, Barbados. Tel. 246-417-4201, fax 246-424-8944, e-mail watsone@ uwichill.edu.bb. *Pres.* Elizabeth Watson.

Standing Conference on Lib. Materials on Africa, Commonwealth Secretariat, Marlborough House, Pall Mall, London SW1Y 5HX, England. Tel. 020-7747-6253, fax 020-7747-6168, e-mail scolma@hotmail. com, World Wide Web http://www.lse.ac. uk/library/scolma. *Chair* David Blake; *Secy.* Iain Cooke.

Europe

Ligue des Bibliothèques Européennes de Recherche (LIBER) (Assn. of European Research Libs.), c/o Erland Kolding Nielsen, Dir.-Gen., Royal Lib., Box 2149, DK-1016 Copenhagen, Denmark. Tel. 45-33-47-4301, fax 45-33-32-98-46, e-mail ekn@kb.dk, World Wide Web http://www. kb.dk/guests/intl/liber.

National

Argentina

Asociación de Bibliotecarios Graduados de la República Argentina (ABGRA) (Assn. of Graduate Libns. of Argentina), Tucuman 1424, 8 piso D, C1050AAB Buenos Aires. Tel./fax 11-4371-5269, e-mail info@ abgra.org.ar, World Wide Web http:// www.abgra.org.ar. *Pres.* Ana Maria Peruchena Zimmermann; *Exec. Secy.* Rosa Emma Monfasani.

Australia

Australian Lib. and Info. Assn., Box 6335, Kingston, ACT 2604. Tel. 2-6215-8222, fax 2-6282-2249, e-mail enquiry@alia. org.au, World Wide Web http://www.alia. org.au. *Pres.* Christine Mackenzie; *Exec. Dir.* Jennifer Nicholson.

Australian Society of Archivists, c/o Queensland State Archives, Box 1397, Sunnybank Hills, Qld. 4109. E-mail info@archives. qld.gov.au, World Wide Web http://www. archives.qld.gov.au. *Pres.* Kathryn Dan; *Secy.* Fiona Burn.

Council of Australian State Libs., c/o State Lib. of Victoria, 328 Swanston St., Melbourne, Vic. 3000. Tel. 3-8664-7512, fax 3-9639-4737, e-mail casl@slv.vic.gov.au, World Wide Web http://www.casl.org.au. *Chief Exec. Officer* Marie Schwirtlich.

Austria

Österreichische Gesellschaft für Dokumentation und Information (Austrian Society for Documentation and Info.), c/o Wirtschaftuniversitaet Wein, Augasse 9, 1090 Vienna. E-mail oegdi@termnet.at, World Wide Web http://www.oegdi.at. *Pres.* Gerhard Richter.

Vereinigung Österreichischer Bibliothekarinnen und Bibliothekare (Assn. of Austrian Libns.), Voralberger Federal State Lib., Fluherstr. 4, 6900 Bregenz. E-mail voeb@ uibk.ac.at, World Wide Web http://voeb. uibk.ac.at. *Pres.* Harald Weigel; *Secy.* Werner Schlacher.

Bangladesh

Lib. Assn. of Bangladesh, c/o Inst. of Lib. and Info. Science, Bangladesh Central Public Lib. Bldg., Shahbagh, Dacca 1000. Tel. 2-863-1471, e-mail msik@icddrb.org. *Pres.* M. Shamsul Islam Khan; *Gen. Secy.* Kh. Fazlur Rahman.

Barbados

Lib. Assn. of Barbados, Box 827E, Bridgetown. *Pres.* Shirley Yearwood; *Secy.* Hazelyn Devonish.

Belgium

Archief- en Bibliotheekwezen in België (Belgian Assn. of Archivists and Libns.), Ruisbroekstr. 2-10, B-1000 Brussels. Tel. 2-519-5351, fax 2-519-5533, e-mail wim. devos@kbr.be. *Gen. Secy.* Wim De Vos.

Association Belge de Documentation/Belgische Vereniging voor Documentatie (Belgian Assn. for Documentation), chaussée de Wavre 1683, Waversesteenweg, B-1160 Brussels. Tel. 2-675-58-62, fax 2-672-74-46, e-mail info@abd-bvd.be, World Wide Web http://www.abd-bvd.be. *Pres.* Philippe Laurent; *Secy.* Vincent Maes.

Association Professionnelle des Bibliothécaires et Documentalistes (Assn. of Libns. and Documentation Specialists), 30 rue Rêve d'Or, 7100 La Louvière. Tel. 064-22-18-34, fax 064-21-28-50, e-mail biblio. hainaut@skynet.be, World Wide Web http://www.apbd.be. *Pres.* Jean-Claude Trefois; *Secy.* Laurence Hennaux.

Vlaamse Vereniging voor Bibliotheek-, Archief-, en Documentatiewezen (Flemish Assn. of Libns., Archivists, and Documentalists), Statiestraat 179, B-2600 Berchem, Antwerp. Tel. 3-281-4457, fax 3-218-8077, e-mail vvbad@vvbad.be, World Wide Web http://www.vvbad.be. *Pres.* Geert Puype; *Exec. Dir.* Marc Storms.

Belize

Belize Lib. Assn., c/o Central Lib., Bliss Inst., Box 287, Belize City. Tel. 2-7267, fax 2-34246. *Pres.* H. W. Young; *Secy.* Robert Hulse.

Bolivia

Asociación Boliviana de Bibliotecarios (Bolivian Lib. Assn.), c/o Efrain Virreria Sanchez, Casilla 992, Cochabamba. *Dir.* Gunnar Mendoza.

Bosnia and Herzegovina

Drustvo Bibliotekara Bosne i Hercegovine (Libns. Society of Bosnia and Herzegovina), Zmaja od Bosne 8B, 71000 Sarajevo. Tel. 33-275-312, fax 33-218-431, e-mail nubbih@nub.ba, World Wide Web http://www.nub.ba. *Pres.* Nevenka Hajdarovic.

Botswana

Botswana Lib. Assn., Box 1310, Gaborone. Tel. 31-355-2295, fax 31-357-291. *Chair* Bobana Badisang; *Secy.* Peter Tshukudu.

Brazil

Associação dos Arquivistas Brasileiros (Assn. of Brazilian Archivists), Av. Presidente Vargas 1733, Sala 903, 20210-030 Rio de Janiero RJ. Tel. 21-2507-2239, fax 21-3852-2541, e-mail aab@aab.org.br, World Wide Web http://www.aab.org.br. *Pres.* Lucia Maria Vellosode Oliveira; *Secy.* Laura Regina Xavier.

Brunei Darussalam

Persatuan Perpustakaan Kebangsaan Negara Brunei (National Lib. Assn. of Brunei), Perpustakaan Universiti Brunei Darussalam, Jalan Tungku Link Gadong BE 1410. Tel. 2-223-060, e-mail chieflib@lib.ubd.edu.bn, World Wide Web http://www.ppknbd.org.bn. *Pres.* Puan Nellie bte Dato Paduka Haji Sunny.

Cameroon

Association des Bibliothécaires, Archivistes, Documentalistes et Muséographes du Cameroun (Assn. of Libns., Archivists, Documentalists, and Museum Curators of Cameroon), B.P. 4609, Yaoundé, Nlongkak Centre Province. Tel. 222-6362, fax 222-4785, e-mail abadcam@yahoo.fr. *Pres.* Hilaire Omokolo.

Canada

Bibliographical Society of Canada/La Société Bibliographique du Canada, Box 575, Postal Sta. P, Toronto, ON M5S 2T1. E-mail mcgaughe@yorku.ca, World Wide Web http://www.library.utoronto.ca/bsc. *Pres.* Carl Spadoni; *Secy.* Anne McGaughey.

Canadian Assn. for Info. Science/Association Canadienne des Sciences de l'Information, c/o Lynne Howarth, CAIS president, Faculty of Information Studies, Univ. of Toronto,

140 St. George St., Toronto, ON M5S 3G6. Tel. 416-978-4666, fax 416-971-1399, e-mail lynne.howarth@utoronto.ca. World Wide Web http://www.cais-acsi.ca.

Canadian Assn. for School Libraries (CASL), 328 Frank Street, Ottawa, ON K2P 0X8. *Pres.* Marlene Turkington, Thames Valley District School Board, 1250 Dundas St., London, ON N5W 5P2. Tel. 519-452-2530, e-mail m.turkington@tvdsb.on.ca. World Wide Web http://www.caslibraries.ca.

Canadian Assn. of Research Libraries/Association des Bibliothèques de Recherche du Canada (CARL/ABRC), Rm. 239, 65 University St., Ottawa, ON K1N 9A5. Tel. 613-562-5385, fax 613-562-5195, World Wide Web http://www.uottawa.ca/library/carl.

Canadian Lib. Assn., c/o *Exec. Dir.* Don Butcher, 328 Frank St., Ottawa, ON K2P 0X8. Tel. 613-232-9625, fax 613-563-9895, e-mail dbutcher@cla.ca. (For detailed information on the Canadian Lib. Assn. and its divisions, see "Canadian Library Association" in Part 1 and "National Library and Information-Industry Associations, United States and Canada" earlier in Part 6. For information on the library associations of the provinces of Canada, see "State, Provincial, and Regional Library Associations.")

Chile

Colegio de Bibliotecarios de Chile AG (Chilean Lib. Assn.), Paraguay 383, Torre 11, Oficina 122, 6510017 Santiago. Tel. 2-222-5652, fax 2-635-5023, e-mail cbc@bibliotecarios.cl, World Wide Web http://www.bibliotecarios.cl. *Pres.* Marcia Marinovic Simunovic; *Secy.* Ana Maria Pino Yanez.

China

China Society for Lib. Science, 33 Zhongguancum (S), Beijing 100081. Tel. 10-6841-9270, fax 10-6841-9271, e-mail ztxhmsc@pulicf.nls.cov.cn, World Wide Web http://www.nlc.gov.cn. *Secy.-Gen.* Gulian Li; *Pres.* Liu Deyou.

Colombia

Asociación Colombiana de Bibliotecarios y Documentalistas (Colombian Assn. of Libns. and Documentalists), Carrera 50, 27-70, Modulo 1 Nivel 4, Bloque C, Colceincias, Bogotá. Tel. 1-360-3077 ext. 326, World Wide Web http://www.ascolbi.org/acerca.htm. *Pres.* Carlos Alberto Zapata.

Congo, Democratic Republic

Association Zaïroise des Archivistes, Bibliothécaires et Documentalistes (Zaire Association of Archivists, Librarians, and Documentalists), BP 805, Kinshasa X1. Tel. 012-30123. *Exec. Secy.* E. Kabeba-Bangasa.

Costa Rica

Asociación Costarricense de Bibliotecarios (Costa Rican Assn. of Libns.), Apdo. 3308, San José. Tel. 234-9989, e-mail info@cesdepu.com, World Wide Web http://www.cesdepu.com. *Secy.-Gen.* Rodolfo Saborio Valverde.

Côte d'Ivoire

Association pour le Développement de la Documentation, des Bibliothèques et Archives de la Côte d'Ivoire, c/o Bibliothèque Nationale, BPV 180, Abidjan. Tel. 32-38-72. *Secy.-Gen.* Cangah Guy; *Dir.* Ambroise Agnero.

Croatia

Hrvatsko Knjiznicarsko Drustvo (Croatian Lib. Assn.), Ulica Hrvatske bratske zajednice 4, 10 000 Zagreb. Tel. 1-615-93-20, fax 1-616-41-86, e-mail hbd@nsk.hr, World Wide Web http://www.hkdrustvo.hr. *Pres.* Alemka Belan-Simic; *Secy.* Ana-Marija Dodigovic.

Cuba

Lib. Assn. of Cuba, c/o Direccion de Relaciones Internacionales, Ministerio de Cultura, Calle 4 e/m 11y13, Vedado, Havana.

Tel. 7-55-2244, fax 7-66-2053. *Dir.* Marta Terry González.

Cyprus

Kypriakos Synthesmos Vivliothicarion (Lib. Assn. of Cyprus), Box 1039, 1434 Nicosia. Tel. 22-404-849. *Pres.* Costas D. Stephanov; *Secy.* Paris G. Rossos.

Czech Republic

Svaz Knihovniku Informachnich Pracovniku Ceske Republiky (Assn. of Lib. and Info. Professionals of the Czech Republic), National Lib., Klementinum 190, 11001 Prague. Tel. 2-2166-3111, fax 2-2166-3261, e-mail vit.richter@nkp.cz, World Wide Web http://www.nkp.cz. *Pres.* Vit Richter.

Denmark

Arkivforeningen (Archives Society), c/o Landsarkivet for Sjaelland, jagtvej 10, 22 Copenhagen N. Tel. 31-39-35-20, fax 33-15-32-39. *Pres.* Tyge Krogh; *Secy.* Charlotte Steinmark.

Danmarks Biblioteksforening (Danish Lib. Assn.), Vesterbrogade 20/5, 1620 Copenhagen V. Tel. 33-25-09-35, fax 33-25-79-00, World Wide Web http://www.dbf.dk. *Dir.* Winnie Vitzansky.

Danmarks Forskningsbiblioteksforening (Danish Research Lib. Assn.), c/o Statsbiblioteket, Universitetsparken 8000, Århus C. Tel. 45-89-46-22-07, fax 45-89-46-22-20, e-mail df@statsbiblioteket.dk, World Wide Web http://www.dfdf.dk. *Pres.* Erland Kolding Neilsen; *Secy.* Hanne Dahl.

Kommunernes Skolebiblioteksforening (formerly Danmarks Skolebiblioteksforening) (Assn. of Danish School Libs.), Krimsveg 29B 1, DK-2300 Copenhagen S. Tel. 33-11-13-91, fax 33-11-13-90, e-mail kom skolbib@ksbf.dk, World Wide Web http://www.ksbf.dk. *Chief Exec.* Paul Erik Sorensen.

Dominican Republic

Asociación Dominicana de Bibliotecarios (Dominican Assn. of Libns.), c/o Biblioteca Nacional, Plaza de la Cultura, Cesar Nicolás Penson 91, Santo Domingo. Tel. 688-4086, e-mail biblioteca.nacional@ dominicana.com. *Pres.* Prospero J. Mella-Chavier; *Secy.-Gen.* V. Regús.

Ecuador

Asociación Ecuatoriana de Bibliotecarios (Ecuadoran Lib. Assn.), c/o Casa de la Cultura Ecuatoriana Benjamin Carrión, Ave. 12 de Octubre 555, Quito. Tel. 2-528-840, fax 2-223-391, e-mail asoebfp@ hotmail.com, World Wide Web http://www.reicyt.org.ec/aeb. *Pres.* Wilson Vega.

Egypt

Egyptian Assn. for Lib. and Info. Science, c/o Dept. of Archives, Libnship., and Info. Science, Faculty of Arts, Univ. of Cairo, Cairo. Tel. 2-567-6365, fax 2-572-9659. *Pres.* S. Khalifa; *Secy.* Hosam El-Din.

El Salvador

Asociación de Bibliotecarios de El Salvador (El Salvador Lib. Assn.), Apdo 2923, San Salvador. Tel. 216-312, fax 225-0278, World Wide Web http://ues.edu.sv/abes. *Pres.* Carmen Salinas de Salinas.

Asociación General de Archivistas de El Salvador (Assn. of Archivists of El Salvador), Edificio Comercial San Francisco No. 214, ga. C Ote y 2a Ave. Nte, San Salvador. Tel. 222-94-18, fax 281-58-60, e-mail agnes@agn.gob.sv, World Wide Web http://www.agn.gob.sv.

Ethiopia

Ye Ethiopia Betemetshaft Serategnoch Mahber (Ethiopian Lib. and Info. Assn.), Box 30530, Addis Ababa. Tel. 1-511-344, fax 1-552-544. *Pres.* Mulugeta Hunde; *Secy.* Girma Makonnen.

Finland

Suomen Kirjastoseura (Finnish Lib. Assn.), Kansakoulukatu 10 A 19, FIN-00100 Helsinki. Tel. 9-694-1858, fax 9-694-1859, e-mail fla@fla.fi, World Wide Web http://www.kaapeli.fi/~fla/presentation. html. *Pres.* Mirja Ryynanen; *Secy.-Gen.* Tuula Haavisto.

France

Association des Archivistes Français (Assn. of French Archivists), 9 rue Montcalm, F-75018 Paris. Tel. 1-46-06-39-44, fax 1-46-06-39-52, e-mail secretariat@archivistes. org, World Wide Web http://www. archivistes.org. *Pres.* Henri Zuber; *Secy.* Agnès Dejob.

Association des Bibliothécaires Français (Assn. of French Libns.), 31 rue de Chabrol, F-75010 Paris. Tel. 1-55-33-10-30, fax 1-55-30-10-31, e-mail abf@abf.asso.fr, World Wide Web http://www.abf.asso.fr. *Pres.* Gérard Briand; *Gen. Secy.* Jean-François Jacques.

Association des Professionnels de l'Information et de la Documentation (Assn. of Info. and Documentation Professionals), 25 rue Claude Tillier, F-75012 Paris. Tel. 1-43-72-25-25, fax 1-43-72-30-41, e-mail adbs @adbs.fr, World Wide Web http://www. adbs.fr. *Pres.* Florence Wilhelm.

Germany

Arbeitsgemeinschaft der Spezialbibliotheken (Assn. of Special Libs.), c/o Forschungszentrum, Jülich GmbH, Zentralbibliothek, 52426 Jülich. Tel. 2461-61-2907, fax 2461-61-6103, World Wide Web http:// www.aspb.de. *Chair* Rafael Ball.

Berufsverband Information Bibliothek (Assn. of Info. and Lib. Professionals), Gartenstr. 18, 72764 Reutlingen. Tel. 7121-3491-0, fax 7121-300-433, e-mail mail@bib-info.de, World Wide Web http://www.bib-info.de. *Pres.* Klaus Peter Boettger; *Secy.* Katharina Boulanger.

Deutsche Gesellschaft für Informationswissenschaft und Informationspraxis eV (German Society for Info. Science and Practice), Ostbahnhofstr. 13, 60314 Frankfurt-am-Main 1. Tel. 69-43-03-13, fax 69-49-09-09-6, e-mail mail@dgi-info.de, World Wide Web http://www.dgd.de. *Pres.* Gabriele Beger.

Deutscher Bibliotheksverband eV (German Lib. Assn.), Strasse des 17 Juni 114,

10623 Berlin. Tel. 30-39-00-14-80, fax 30-39-00-14-84, e-mail dbv@bibliotheks verband.de, World Wide Web http://www. bibliotheksverband.de. *Pres.* Brigitte Scherer.

VdA—Verband Deutscher Archivarinnen und Archivare (Assn. of German Archivists), Postfach 2119, 99402 Weimar. Tel. 03643-870-235, fax 03643-870-164, e-mail info@vda.archiv.net, World Wide Web http://www.vda.archiv.net. *Chair* Volker Wahl.

Verein der Diplom-Bibliothekare an Wissenschaftlichen Bibliotheken (Assn. of Certified Libns. at Academic Libs.), c/o Stadtbuecherei Muelheim an der Ruhr, Friedrich-Ebert Str. 47, 45468 Muelheim an der Ruhr. Tel. 221-574-7161, fax 221-574-7110, World Wide Web http://www. bibliothek.uni-regensburg.de/vddb. *Chair* Klaus-Peter Boettger.

Verein Deutscher Bibliothekare (Assn. of German Libns.), Unter den Linden 8, 10117 Berlin. Tel. 30-266-1728, fax 30-266-1717, e-mail olaf.hanann@sbb.spk-berlin.de. *Pres.* Daniela Luelfing; *Secy.* Thomas Elsmann.

Ghana

Ghana Lib. Assn., Box 5015, Accra. Tel. 21-764-822. *Pres.* E. S. Asiedo; *Secy.* A. W. K. Insaidoo.

Greece

Enosis Hellinon Bibliothekarion (Greek Lib. Assn.), 4 Skoulenion St., 105 61 Athens. Tel. 210-322-6625. *Pres.* K. Xatzopoulou; *Gen. Secy.* E. Kalogeraky.

Guyana

Guyana Lib. Assn., c/o National Lib., 76-77 Church and Main Sts., Georgetown. Tel. 0226-2690, fax 0227-4053, e-mail natlib@sdnp.org.gy, World Wide Web http:// www.natlib.gov.gy. *Pres.* Ivor Rodriguez; *Secy.* Gwyneth George.

Honduras

Asociación de Bibliotecarios y Archiveros de Honduras (Assn. of Libns. and Archivists of Honduras), 11a Calle, 1a y 2a Avdas., No. 105, Comayagüela DC, Tegucigalpa. *Pres.* Francisca de Escoto Espinoza; *Secy.-Gen.* Juan Angel R. Ayes.

Hong Kong

Hong Kong Lib. Assn., GPO 10095, Hong Kong. E-mail hkla@hkla.org.hk, World Wide Web http://www.hklib.org. *Pres.* Julia Chan.

Hungary

Magyar Könyvtárosok Egyesülete (Assn. of Hungarian Libns.), Hold u 6, H-1054 Budapest. Tel./fax 1-311-8634, e-mail mke@oszk.hu, World Wide Web http:// www.mke.oszk.hu. *Pres.* Bakos Klara; *Exec. Secy.* Eva Jaki.

Iceland

Upplysing—Felag bokasafns-og upplysingafraeoa (Information—the Icelandic Lib. and Info. Science Assn.), Lagmuli 7, 108 Reykjavik. Tel. 553-7290, fax 588-9239, e-mail upplysing@bokis.is, World Wide Web http://www.bokis.is. *Pres.* H. A. Hardarson; *Secy.* A. Agnarsdottir.

India

Indian Assn. of Academic Libns., c/o Jawaharlal Nehru Univ. Lib., New Mehrauli Rd., New Delhi 110067. Tel. 11-683-1717. *Secy.* M. M. Kashyap.

Indian Assn. of Special Libs. and Info. Centres, P-291, CIT Scheme 6M, Kankurgachi, Calcutta 700054. Tel. 33-2352-9651, e-mail iaslic@vsnl.net, World Wide Web http://www.iaslic.org. *Publisher* J. M. Das.

Indian Lib. Assn., A/40-41, Flat 201, Ansal Bldg., Mukerjee Nagar, Delhi 110009. Tel. 11-326-4748, e-mail ilanet1@nda.vsnl.net.in. *Pres.* Kalpana Dasgsupta.

Indonesia

Ikatan Pustakawan Indonesia (Indonesian Lib. Assn.), Jalan Merdeka Selatan No. 11, 10110 Jakarta, Pusat. Tel./fax 21-385-5729. *Pres.* S. Kartosdono.

Iraq

Iraq Archivists Institute, c/o National Centre of Archives, National Lib. Bldg., Bab-Al-Muaddum, Baghdad. Tel. 1-416-8440. *Dir.* Salim Al-Alousi.

Ireland

Cumann Leabharlann Na h-Eireann (Lib. Assn. of Ireland), 53 Upper Mount St., Dublin. Tel. 1-6120-2193, fax 1-6121-3090, e-mail president@libraryassociation. ie, World Wide Web http://www.library association.ie. *Pres.* Ruth Flanagan; *Hon. Secy.* Denise Murphy.

Israel

Israel Libns. and Info. Specialists Assn., 9 Beit Hadfus St., Givaat Shaul, Jerusalem. Tel. 2-658-9515, fax 2-625-1628, e-mail icl@icl.org.il, World Wide Web http://www.icl.org.il. *Pres.* Benjamin Schachter.

Israel Society of Libs. and Info. Centers, P.O. Box 28273, 91282 Jerusalem. Tel./fax 2-624-9421, e-mail asmi@asmi.org.il, World Wide Web http://www.asmi.org.il. *Chair* Shoshana Langerman.

Italy

Associazione Italiana Biblioteche (Italian Lib. Assn.), C.P. 2461, 00100 Rome. Tel. 6-446-3532, fax 6-444-1139, e-mail aib@aib.it, World Wide Web http://www.aib.it. *Pres.* Mauro Guerrini; *Secy.* Gianfranco Crupi.

Jamaica

Jamaica Lib. Assn., P.O. Box 125, Kingston 5. Tel./fax 876-927-1614, e-mail liaja president@yahoo.com, World Wide Web http://www.liaja.org.jm. *Pres.* Byron Palmer; *Secy.* F. Salmon.

Japan

Joho Kagaku Gijutsu Kyokai (Info. Science and Technology Assn.), Sasaki Bldg., 2-5-7 Koisikawa, Bunkyo-ku, Tokyo 112-0002. Tel. 3-3813-3791, fax 3-3813-3793, e-mail infosta@infosta.or.jp, World Wide Web http://www.infosta.or.jp. *Pres.* T. Gondoh; *Gen. Mgr.* Yukio Ichikawa.

Nihon Toshokan Kyokai (Japan Lib. Assn.), 1-11-14 Shinkawa, Chuo-ku, Tokyo 104 0033. Tel. 3-3523-0811, fax 3-3523-0841, e-mail info@jla.or.jp, World Wide Web http://www.jla.or.jp. *Secy.-Gen.* Reiko Sakagawa.

Senmon Toshokan Kyogikai (Japan Special Libs. Assn.), c/o Japan Lib. Assn., Bldg. F6, 1-11-14 Shinkawa, Chuo-ku, Tokyo 104-0033. Tel. 3-3537-8335, fax 3-3537-8336, e-mail jsla@jsla.or.jp, World Wide Web http://www.jsla.or.jp. *Pres.* Kousaku Inaba; *Exec. Dir.* Fumihisa Nakagawa.

Jordan

Jordan Lib. Assn., P.O. Box 6289, Amman. Tel./fax 6-462-9412, e-mail info@jorla. org, World Wide Web http://www.jorla. org. *Pres.* Anwar Akroush; *Secy.* Yousra Abu Ajamieh.

Kenya

Kenya Lib. Assn., Box 46031, Nairobi. Tel. 2-334-244, fax 2-336-885, e-mail jwere@ ken.healthnet.org. *Chair* Jacinta Were; *Secy.* Alice Bulogosi.

Korea (Republic of)

Korean Lib. Assn., 1-KA, Hoehyun-Dong, Choong-ku, Seoul 100-177. Tel. 02-535-4868, fax 2-535-5616, e-mail klanet@ hitel.net, World Wide Web http://korla.or. kr. *Pres.* Ki Nam Shin; *Exec. Dir.* Won Ho Jo.

Laos

Association des Bibliothécaires Laotiens (Assn. of Laotian Libns.), c/o Direction de la Bibliothèque Nationale, Ministry of Info. and Culture, B.P. 122, Vientiane. Tel. 21-2452, fax 21-2408, e-mail pfd-mill@pan.laos.net.la.

Latvia

Lib. Assn. of Latvia, Latvian National Lib., Kr. Barona 14, 2 Stavs, 205 telpa, 1423 Riga. Tel. 371-728-7620, fax 371-728-0851, e-mail lnb@lbi.lnb.lv, World Wide Web http://www.lnb.lv. *Pres.* Aldis Abele.

Lebanon

Lebanese Lib. Assn., c/o American Univ. of Beirut, Univ. Lib./Serials Dept., Box 11-0236, Beirut. Tel. 1-350-000, fax 1-351-706, World Wide Web http://www.aub.edu.lb. *Pres.* Fawz Abdalleh; *Exec. Secy.* Rudaynah Shoujah.

Lesotho

Lesotho Lib. Assn., Private Bag A26, Maseru. Tel./fax 340-601, e-mail mmc@doc.isas.nul.ls, World Wide Web http://www.sn.apc.org. *Chair* S. M. Mohai; *Secy.* N. Taole.

Lithuania

Lithuanian Libns. Assn., Sv. Ignoto 6-108, LT-2600, Vilnius. Tel./fax 2-750-340, e-mail lbd@vpu.lt, World Wide Web http://www.lbd.lt. *Pres.* Vida Garunkstyte.

Macedonia

Bibliotekarsko Drustvo na Makedonija (Union of Libns.' Assns. of Macedonia), Box 566, 91000 Skopje. Tel. 91-226-846, fax 91-232-649, e-mail mile@nubsk.edu.mk or bmile47@yahoo.com. *Pres.* Mile Boseki; *Secy.* Poliksena Matkovska.

Malawi

Malawi Lib. Assn., Box 429, Zomba. Tel. 50-522-222, fax 50-523-225. *Chair* Joseph J. Uta; *Secy.* Vote D. Somba.

Malaysia

Persatuan Perpustakaan Malaysia (Lib. Assn. of Malaysia), 232 Jalan Tun Razak, 50572 Kuala Lumpur. Tel. 3-2687-1700, fax 3-2694-2490, e-mail pnmweb@pnm.my, World Wide Web http://www.pnm.my.

Pres. Chew Wing Foong; *Secy.* Leni Abdul Latif.

Mali

Association Malienne des Bibliothécaires, Archivistes et Documentalistes (Mali Assn. of Libns., Archivists, and Documentalists), rue Kasse Keita, Bamako. Tel. 22-49-63. *Dir.* Mamadou Konoba Keiita.

Malta

Malta Lib. and Info. Assn. (MaLIA), c/o Univ. of Malta Lib., Tal-Qroqq, Msida MSD 06. Tel. 2132-2054, e-mail mpar1@lib.um.edu.mt, World Wide Web http://www.malia-malta.org. *Chair* Robert Mizzi.

Mauritania

Association Mauritanienne des Bibliothécaires, Archivistes, et Documentalistes (Mauritanian Assn. of Libns., Archivists, and Documentalists), c/o Bibliothèque Nationale, B.P. 20, Nouakchott. *Pres.* O. Diouwara; *Secy.* Sid'Ahmed Fall dit Dah.

Mauritius

Mauritius Lib. Assn., c/o The British Council, Royal Rd., P.O. Box 111, Rose Hill. Tel. 454-9550, fax 454-9553, e-mail ielts@mu.britishcouncil.org, World Wide Web http://www.britishcouncil.org/mauritius. *Pres.* K. Appadoo; *Secy.* S. Rughoo.

Mexico

Asociación Mexicana de Bibliotecarios (Mexican Assn. of Libns.), Apdo. 80-065, Administracion de Correos 80, 06001 México DF 06760. Tel. 55-55-75-33-96, fax 55-55-75-11-35, e-mail correo@ambac.org.mx, World Wide Web http://www.ambac.org.mx. *Pres.* Felipe Becerril Torres; *Secy.* Elias Cid Ramirez.

Myanmar

Myanmar Lib. Assn., c/o National Lib., Strand Rd., Yangon. *Chief Libn.* U Khin Maung Tin.

Nepal

Nepal Lib. Assn., Box 2773, Kathmandu. Tel. 1-331-316, fax 1-483-720. *Contact* Rudra Prasad Dulal.

The Netherlands

Nederlandse Vereniging voor Beroepsbeoefenaren in de Bibliotheek-Informatie-en Kennissector (Netherlands Assn. of Libns., Documentalists, and Info. Specialists), NVB-Nieuwegracht 15, 3512 LC Utrecht. Tel. 30-231-1263, fax 30-231-1830, e-mail info@nvbonline.nl, World Wide Web http://www.nvb-online.nl. *Pres.* J. S. M. Savenije.

New Zealand

Lib. and Info. Assn. of New Zealand Aotearoa, Old Wool House, Level 5, 139-141 Featherston St., Box 12-212, Wellington 6038. Tel. 4-473-5834, fax 4-499-1480, e-mail office@lianza.org.nz, World Wide Web http://www.lianza.org.nz. *Pres.* Steven Lulich.

Nicaragua

Asociación Nicaraguense de Bibliotecarios y Profesionales a Fines (Nicaraguan Assn. of Libns.), Apdo. 3257, Managua. *Exec. Secy.* Susana Morales Hernández.

Nigeria

Nigerian Lib. Assn., c/o National Lib. Assn., Sanusi Dantata House, Business Central District, Garki District, Abuja 900001. Tel. 8055-365245, fax 9-234-6773, e-mail info@nla-ng.org, World Wide Web http://www.nla-ng.org. *Pres.* A. O. Banjo; *Secy.* D. D. Bwayili.

Norway

Arkivarforeningen (Assn. of Archivists), Postboks 4015, Ulleval Sta., 0806 Oslo. Tel. 22-022-657, fax 22-237-489, e-mail synne.stavheim@riksarkivaren.dep.no, World Wide Web http://www.forsker forbundet.no.

Norsk Bibliotekforening (Norwegian Lib. Assn.), Malerhaugveien 20, N-0661 Oslo. Tel. 2324-3430, fax 2267-2368, e-mail nbf@norskbibliotekforening.no, World Wide Web http://www.norskbibliotek forening.no. *Dir.* Berit Aaker.

Pakistan

Pakistan Lib. Assn., c/o Pakistan Inst. of Development Economics, P.O. Box 1091, Islamabad 44000. Tel. 51-921-4523, fax 51-922-1375, e-mail nlpiba@isb.paknet. com.pk, World Wide Web http://www.nlp. gov.pk. *Pres.* Sain Malik; *Secy.-Gen.* Atta Ullah.

Panama

Asociación Panameña de Bibliotecarios (Panama Lib. Assn.), c/o Biblioteca Interamericana Simón Bolivar, Estafeta Universitaria, Panama City. *Pres.* Bexie Rodriguez de León.

Paraguay

Asociación de Bibliotecarios Universitarios del Paraguay (Assn. of Paraguayan Univ. Libns.), c/o Yoshiko M. de Freundorfer, Escuela de Bibliocelogia, Universidad Nacional de Asunción, Casilla 910, 2064 Asunción. *Pres.* Gloria Ondina Ortiz; *Secy.* Celia Villamayor de Diaz.

Peru

Asociación de Archiveros del Perú (Peruvian Assn. of Archivists), Archivo Central Salaverry, 2020 Jesús Mario, Universidad del Pacifico, Lima 11. Tel. 1-219-0100, fax 1-472-9635, e-mail dri@u8p.edu.pe, World Wide Web http://www.up.edu/pe. *Pres.* José Luis Abanto Arrelucea.

Asociación Peruana de Bibliotecarios (Peruvian Assn. of Libns.), Bellavista 561 Miraflores, Apdo. 995, Lima 18. Tel. 1-474-869. *Pres.* Martha Fernandez de Lopez; *Secy.* Luzmila Tello de Medina.

Philippines

Assn. of Special Libs. of the Philippines, Rm. 301, National Lib. Bldg., T. M. Kalaw St.,

2801 Ermita, Manila. Tel. 2-893-9590, fax 2-893-9589, e-mail vvtl26_ph@yahoo. com. *Pres.* Valentina Tolentino; *Secy.* Socorro G. Elevera.

Bibliographical Society of the Philippines, National Lib. of the Philippines, T. M. Kalaw St., 1000 Ermita, Manila. Tel. 2-583-252, fax 2-502-329, e-mail amb@nlp. gov.ph, World Wide Web http://www.nlp. gov.ph. *Chief* Leticia D. A. Tominez.

Philippine Libns. Assn., Rm. 301, National Lib. of the Philippines, T. M. Kalaw St., 1000 Ermita, Manila. Tel. 2-523-0068, e-mail libfamv@mail.dlsu.edu.ph, World Wide Web http://www.dlsu.eduph/library/ plai. *Pres.* Fe Angelo Verosa; *Secy.* Shirley L. Nava.

Poland

Stowarzyszenie Bibliotekarzy Polskich (Polish Libns. Assn.), al Niepodleglosci 213, 02-086 Warsaw. Tel. 22-608-2256, fax 22-825-9157, e-mail biurozgsbp@wp.pl, World Wide Web http://ebib.oss.wroc.pl/ sbp. *Chair* Jan Wolosz; *Secy.-Gen.* Elzbieta Stefanczyk.

Portugal

Associação Portuguesa de Bibliotecários, Arquivistas e Documentalistas (Portuguese Assn. of Libns., Archivists, and Documentalists), R. Morais Soares, 43C-1 DTD, 1900-341 Lisbon. Tel. 21-816-1980, fax 21-815-4508, e-mail bad@apbad.pt, World Wide Web http://www.apbad.pt. *Pres.* Antonio Jose de Pina Falcao.

Puerto Rico

Sociedad de Bibliotecarios de Puerto Rico (Society of Libns. of Puerto Rico), P.O. Box 22898, Universidad de Puerto Rico, San Juan 00931. Tel. 787-764-0000 ext. 5205, fax 787-763-0000 ext. 5204, e-mail vtorres@upracd.upr.clu.edu, World Wide Web http://www.geocities.com/sociedads bpr. *Pres.* Victor Federico Torres; *Secy.* Doris E. Rivera Marrero.

Russia

Rossiiskaya Bibliotechnaya Assotsiatsiya (Russian Lib. Assn.), 18 Sadovaya St., St. Petersburg 191069. Tel. 812-118-85-36, fax 812-110-58-61, e-mail rba@nlr.ru, World Wide Web http://www.rba.ru. *Exec. Secy.* Maya Shaparneva.

Senegal

Association Sénégalaise des Bibliothécaires, Archivistes et Documentalistes (Senegalese Assn. of Libns., Archivists, and Documentalists), BP 3252, Dakar. Tel. 221-864-2773, fax 221-824-2379, e-mail ebad@ebad.ucad.sn, World Wide Web http://www.ebad.ucad.sn. *Pres.* Ndiaye Djibril.

Serbia and Montenegro

Jugoslovenski Bibliografsko Informacijski Institut, Terazije 26 11000 Belgrade. Tel. 11-687-836, fax 11-687-760, e-mail yubin @jbi.bg.ac.yu, World Wide Web http:// www.yu-yubin.org. *Dir.* Radomir Glavicki.

Sierra Leone

Sierra Leone Assn. of Archivists, Libns., and Info. Scientists, 7 Percival St., Freetown. Tel. 22-22-0758. *Pres.* Deanna Thomas.

Singapore

Lib. Assn. of Singapore, Geyland East Community Lib., 50 Geyland East Ave. 1, 3rd fl., Singapore 389777. Tel. 6749-7990, fax 6749-7480, World Wide Web http://www. las.org.sg.

Slovenia

Zveza Bibliotekarskih Druötev Slovenije (Union of Assns. of Slovene Libns.), Turjaška 1, 1000 Ljubljana. Tel. 01-20-01-193, fax 01-42-57-293, e-mail zveza-biblio. ds-nuk@quest.arnes.si, World Wide Web http://www.zbds-zveza.si. *Pres.* Melita Ambrožič. E-mail melita.ambrozic@nuk. uni-lj.si.

South Africa

Lib. and Info. Assn. of South Africa, P.O. Box 1598, Pretoria 0001. Tel. 12-481-2870, fax 12-481-2873, e-mail liasa@liasa.org.za, World Wide Web http://www.liasa.org.za. *Pres.* Robert Moropa.

Spain

Asociación Española de Archiveros, Bibliotecarios, Museólogos y Documentalistas (Spanish Assn. of Archivists, Libns., Curators, and Documentalists), Recoletos 5, 28001 Madrid. Tel. 91-575-1727, fax 91-578-1615, e-mail anabad@anabad.org, World Wide Web http://www.anabad.org. *Pres.* Julia M. Rodriguez Barrero.

Sri Lanka

Sri Lanka Lib. Assn., Professional Center, 275/75 Bauddhaloka Mawatha, Colombo 7. Tel./fax 1-258-9103, e-mail slla@opera mail.com, World Wide Web http://www.naresa.ac.lk/slla. *Pres.* Deepali Talagala.

Swaziland

Swaziland Lib. Assn., Box 2309, Mbabane. Tel. 404-2633, fax 404-3863, e-mail sd nationalarchives@realnet.co.sz, World Wide Web http://www.swala.sz. *Chair* Nomsa Mkhwanazi; *Secy.* Sibongile Nxumaloi.

Sweden

Svensk Biblioteksförening (Swedish Lib. Assn.), Saltmätargatan 3A, P.O. Box 3127, S-10362 Stockholm. Tel. 8-545-132-30, fax 8-545-132-31, e-mail info@biblioteks foreningen.org, World Wide Web http://www.biblioteksforeningen.org. *Secy.-Gen.* Niclas Lindberg.

Svenska Arkivsamfundet (Swedish Assn. of Archivists), c/o Landsarkivet i Lund, Anna-Christina Ulfsparre, Box 2016, S-22002 Lund. Tel. 46-197-000, fax 46-197-070, e-mail info@arkivsamfundet.org, World Wide Web http://www.arkivsamfundet.org. *Pres.* Berndt Fredriksson; *Secy.* Julia Aslund.

Switzerland

Association des Bibliothèques et Bibliothécaires Suisses/Vereinigung Schweizerischer Bibliothekare/Associazione dei Bibliotecari Svizzeri (Assn. of Swiss Libs. and Libns.), Hallestr. 58, CH-3012 Bern. Tel. 31-382-42-40, fax 31-382-46-48, e-mail bbs@bbs.ch, World Wide Web http://www.bbs.ch. *Gen. Secy.* Rosemarie Simmen.

Schweizerische Vereinigung für Dokumentation/Association Suisse de Documentation (Swiss Assn. of Documentation), Schmidgasse 4, Postfach 601, CH-6301 Zoug. Tel. 41-726-45-05, fax 41-726-45-09, e-mail svd-asd@hispeed.ch, World Wide Web http://www.svd-asd.org. *Pres.* Urs Naegeli, *Secy.* M. Harald Schwenk.

Verein Schweizerischer Archivarinnen und Archivare (Assn. of Swiss Archivists), Schweizerisches Bundesarchiv, Archivstr. 24, 3003 Bern. Tel. 31-322-89-89, e-mail andreas.kellerhals@bar.admin.ch, World Wide Web http://www.staluzern.ch/vsa. *Pres.* Andreas Kellerhals.

Taiwan

Lib. Assn. of China, c/o National Central Lib., 20 Chungshan S. Rd., Taipei 100-01. Tel. 2-2331-2475, fax 2-2370-0899, e-mail lac@msg.ncl.edu.tw, World Wide Web http://www.lac.ncl.edu.tw. *Pres.* Huang Shih-wson; *Secy.-Gen.* Teresa Wang Chang.

Tanzania

Tanzania Lib. Assn., P.O. Box 3433, Dar es Salaam. Tel. 22-277-5411, e-mail tla_tanzania@yahoo.com, World Wide Web http://www.tlatz.org. *Chair* Alli Mcharazo.

Thailand

Thai Lib. Assn., 1346 Akarnsongkrau Rd. 5, Klongchan, Bangkapi, 10240 Bangkok. Tel. 2-734-8022, fax 2-734-8024, World Wide Web http://tla.or.th. *Pres.* Khunying Maenmas Chawalit; *Exec. Secy.* Vorrarat Srinamngern.

Trinidad and Tobago

Lib. Assn. of Trinidad and Tobago, Box 1275, Port of Spain. Tel. 868-687-0194, e-mail secretary@latt.org.tt, World Wide Web http://www.latt.org.tt/cms. *Pres.* Lillibeth S. V. Ackbarali; *Secy.* Sally Anne Montserin.

Tunisia

Association Tunisienne des Documentalistes, Bibliothécaires et Archivistes (Tunisian Assn. of Documentalists, Libns., and Archivists), Centre de Documentation Nationale 8004, rue Sidi El Benna R P, 1000 Tunis. Tel. 651-924. *Pres.* Ahmed Ksibi.

Turkey

Türk Küüphaneciler Dernegi (Turkish Libns. Assn.), Elgün Sok-8/8, 06440 Kizilay/Ankara. Tel. 312-230-13-25, fax 312-232-04-53. *Pres.* A. Berberoglu; *Secy.* A. Kaygusuz.

Uganda

Uganda Lib. Assn., P.O. Box 8147, Kampala. Tel. 141-256-77-467698, World Wide Web http://ou.edu/cas/slis/ULA_index. *Editor* Matthew Lubuulwa. E-mail nlubuulwa@yahoo.com.

Ukraine

Ukrainian Lib. Assn., 14 Chigorina St., Kiev 252042. Tel./fax 380-44-268-05-33, e-mail pashkova@uba.kiev.ua, World Wide Web http://www.uba.org.ua. *Pres.* Valentyna S. Pashkova.

United Kingdom

ASLIB (Assn. for Info. Management), Holywell Centre, 1 Phipp St., London EC2A 4PS, England. Tel. 20-7613-3031, fax 20-7613-5080, e-mail aslib@aslib.com, World Wide Web http://www.aslib.co.uk. *Dir.* R. B. Bowes.

Bibliographical Society, Institute of English Studies, Senate House, Rm. 304, Malet St., London WC1E 7HU, England. Tel. 20-7611-7244, fax 20-7611-8703, e-mail secretary@bibsoc.org.uk, World Wide Web http://www.bibsoc.org.uk/bibsoc.htm. *Pres.* John Flood.

Chartered Inst. of Lib. and Info. Professionals (formerly the Lib. Assn.), 7 Ridgmount St., London WC1E 7AE, England. Tel. 20-7255-0500, fax 20-7255-0501, e-mail info@cilip.org.uk, World Wide Web http://www.cilip.org.uk. *Chief Exec.* Bob McKee.

School Lib. Assn., Unit 2, Lotmead Business Village, Lotmead Farm, Wanborough, Swindon, Wilts. SN4 0UY, England. Tel. 1793-791-787, fax 1793-791-786, e-mail info@sla.org.uk, World Wide Web http://www.sla.org.uk. *Pres.* Aidan Chambers; *Chief Exec.* Kathy Lemaire.

Scottish Lib. Assn., 1st fl., Bldg. C, Brandon Gate, Leechlee Rd., Hamilton ML3 6AU, Scotland. Tel. 1698-458-888, fax 1698-283-170, e-mail sla@slainte.org.uk, World Wide Web http://www.slainte.org.uk. *Dir.* Elaine Fulton.

Society of Archivists, Prioryfield House, 20 Canon St., Taunton, Somerset TA1 1SW, England. Tel. 1823-327-030, fax 1823-371-719, e-mail offman@archives.org.uk, World Wide Web http://www.archives.org.uk. *Exec. Secy.* Patrick S. Cleary.

Society of College, National, and Univ. Libs (SCONUL) (formerly Standing Conference of National and Univ. Libs.), 102 Euston St., London NW1 2HA, England. Tel. 20-7387-0317, fax 20-7383-3197, e-mail info@sconul.ac.uk, World Wide Web http://www.sconul.ac.uk. *Exec. Secy.* A. J. C. Bainton.

Welsh Lib. Assn., c/o Publications Office, Dept. of Info. and Lib. Studies, Llanbadarn Fawr, Aberystwyth, Dyfed SY23 3AS, Wales. Tel. 1970-622-174, fax 1970-622-190, e-mail hle@aber.ac.uk, World Wide Web http://www.dil.aber.ac.uk/holi/wla/wla.htm. *Pres.* Andrew Green.

Uruguay

Agrupación Bibliotecológica del Uruguay (Uruguayan Lib. and Archive Science Assn.), Cerro Largo 1666, 11200 Montevideo. Tel. 2-400-57-40. *Pres.* Luis Alberto Musso.

Asociación de Bibliotecólogos del Uruguay, Eduardo V. Haedo 2255, Box 1315, 11000 Montevideo. Tel./fax 2-4099-989, e-mail abu@adinet.com.uy. *Pres.* Eduardo Correa.

Vatican City

Biblioteca Apostolica Vaticana, Cortile del Belvedere, 00120 Vatican City, Rome. Tel. 6-6987-9402, fax 6-6988-4795, e-mail bav@librs6k.vatlib.it. *Prefect* Don Raffaele Farina.

Venezuela

Colegio de Bibliotecólogos y Archivólogos de Venezuela (Venezuelan Lib. and Archives Assn.), Apdo. 6283, Caracas. Tel. 212-572-1858. *Pres.* Elsi Jimenez de Diaz.

Vietnam

Hôi Thu-Vien Viet Nam (Vietnamese Lib. Assn.), National Lib. of Vietnam, 31 Trang Thi, 10000 Hanoi. Tel. 4-824-8051, fax 4-825-3357, e-mail info@nlv.gov.vn, World Wide Web http://www.nlv.gov.vn.

Zambia

Zambia Lib. Assn., Box 38636, Lusaka. *Chair* Benson Njobvu. E-mail benson njobvu@hotmail.com.

Zimbabwe

Zimbabwe Lib. Assn., Box 3133, Harare. *Chair* Driden Kunaka; *Hon. Secy.* Albert Masheka.

Directory of Book Trade and Related Organizations

Book Trade Associations, United States and Canada

For more extensive information on the associations listed in this section, see the annual edition of *Literary Market Place* (Information Today, Inc.).

AIGA (American Institute of Graphic Arts), 164 Fifth Ave., New York, NY 10010. Tel. 212-807-1990, fax 212-807-1799, e-mail info@aiga.org, World Wide Web http://www.aiga.org. *Pres.* Bill Grant, Grant Design Collaborative, P.O. Box 1910, Canton, GA 30169. Tel. 770-479-8280, e-mail bill@grantcollaborative.com; *Exec. Dir.* Richard Grefe. E-mail grefe@aiga.org.

American Booksellers Assn., 200 White Plains Rd., Tarrytown, NY 10591. Tel. 800-637-0037, 914-591-2665, fax 914-591-2720, World Wide Web http://www.bookweb.org. *Pres.* Mitchell Kaplan, Books & Books, 265 Aragon Ave., Coral Gables, FL 33134-5009. Tel. 305-442-4408, fax 305-444-9751, e-mail kaplan296@aol.com; *V.P./Secy.* Russ Lawrence, Chapter One Book Store, 252 Main St., Hamilton, MT 59840-2552. Tel. 406-363-5220, fax 406-363-5003, e-mail russ@chapter1bookstore.com; *Chief Exec. Officer* Avin Mark Domnitz. E-mail avin@bookweb.org.

American Literary Translators Assn. (ALTA), Univ. of Texas–Dallas, MC35, Box 830688, Richardson, TX 75083-0688. Tel. 972-883-2093, fax 972-883-6303, e-mail jdickey@utdallas.edu, World Wide Web http://www.literarytranslators.org. *Pres.* John Balcom. E-mail balcom@redshift.com; *Contact* Jessie Dickey.

American Medical Publishers Assn. (AMPA), c/o Barbara J. Meredith, V.P., Professional/Scholarly Publishing Div., Assn. of American Publishers, 71 Fifth Ave., New York, NY 10003-3004. Tel. 212-255-0200 ext. 223, fax 212-255-7007, e-mail bmeredith@publishers.org.

American Printing History Assn., Box 4519, Grand Central Sta., New York, NY 10163-4519. World Wide Web http://www.printinghistory.org. *Pres.* Eric Holzenberg; *Exec. Secy.* Stephen Crook. E-mail sgcrook@printinghistory.org.

American Society of Indexers, 10200 W. 44 Ave., Ste. 304, Wheat Ridge, CO 80033. Tel. 303-463-2887, fax 303-422-8894, e-mail info@asindexing.org, World Wide Web http://www.asindexing.org/site. *Pres.* Maria Coughlin; *V.P.* Seth Maislin; *Exec. Dirs.* Francine Butler, Jerry Bowman.

American Society of Journalists and Authors, 1501 Broadway, Ste. 302, New York, NY 10036. Tel. 212-997-0947, fax 212-937-3215, e-mail execdir@asja.org, World Wide Web http://www.asja.org. *Pres.* Jack El-Hai; *Exec. Dir.* Brett Harvey.

American Society of Magazine Editors, 810 Seventh Ave., 24th fl., New York, NY 10019. Tel. 212-872-3735, e-mail asme@magazine.org. *Exec. Dir.* Marlene Kahan.

American Society of Media Photographers, 150 N. Second St., Philadelphia, PA 19106. Tel. 215-451-2767, fax 215-451-0880, e-mail mopsik@asmp.org, World Wide Web http://www.asmp.org. *Pres.* Susan Carr. E-mail president@asmp.org; *Exec. Dir.* Eugene Mopsik.

American Society of Picture Professionals, 409 S. Washington St., Alexandria, VA 22314. Tel. 703-299-0219, fax 703-299-0219, e-mail cathy@aspp.com, World Wide Web http://www.aspp.com. *Pres.* Eileen Flanagan; *Exec. Dir.* Cathy D.-P. Sachs.

American Translators Assn., 225 Reinekers Lane, Ste. 590, Alexandria, VA 22314. Tel. 703-683-6100, fax 703-683-6122, e-mail ata@atanet.org, World Wide Web http://www.atanet.org. *Pres.* Marian S. Greenfield; *Pres.-Elect* Jiri Stejskal; *Secy.* Alan K. Melby; *Treas.* Peter Krawutschke; *Exec. Dir.* Walter W. Bacak, Jr. E-mail walter@atanet.org.

Antiquarian Booksellers Assn. of America, 20 W. 44 St., 4th fl., New York, NY 10036-6604. Tel. 212-944-8291, fax 212-944-8293, e-mail inquiries@abaa.org, World Wide Web http://www.abaa.org. *Pres.* John Crichton, Brick Row Book Shop; *V.P.* Forrest Proper, Joslin Hall Rare Books; *Exec. Dir.* Liane Thomas Wade. E-mail hq@abaa.org.

Assn. of American Publishers, 71 Fifth Ave., New York, NY 10003. Tel. 212-255-0200, fax 212-255-7007. *Washington Office* 50 F St. N.W., Washington, DC 20001-1564. Tel. 202-347-3375, fax 202-347-3690. *Pres./CEO* Patricia S. Schroeder; *V.P.s* Allan Adler, Tina Jordan, Barbara Meredith; *Dir., Communications and Public Affairs* Judith Platt; *Exec. Dir., School Div.* Stephen D. Driesler; *Exec. Dir., Higher Education* Bruce Hildebrand; *Chair* Anthony Lucki, Houghton Mifflin.

Assn. of American Univ. Presses, 71 W. 23 St., Ste. 901, New York, NY 10010. Tel. 212-989-1010, e-mail info@aaupnet.org, World Wide Web http://aaupnet.org. *Pres.* Lynne Withey, Univ. of California Press; *Exec. Dir.* Peter Givler. E-mail pgivler@aaupnet.org.

Assn. of Authors' Representatives, Box 237201, Ansonia Sta., New York, NY 10023. E-mail info@aar-online.org, World Wide Web http://aar-online.org.

Association of Booksellers for Children, 3900 Sumac Circle, Middleton, WI 53562. Tel. 608-836-6050, fax 608-836-1438, World Wide Web http://www.abfc.com. *Exec. Dir.* Kristen McLean.

Assn. of Canadian Publishers, 161 Eglinton Ave. E., Ste. 702, Toronto, ON M4P 1J5. Tel. 416-487-6116, fax 416-487-8815, e-mail admin@canbook.org, World Wide Web http://www.publishers.ca. *Pres.* Kirk Howard, Dundurn Press. Tel. 416-214-5544, e-mail jkh@dundurn.com; *V.P.* Todd Besant, Turnstone Press. Tel. 204-947-1555, e-mail editor@turnstonepress. com; *Exec. Dir.* Margaret Eaton.

Assn. of Educational Publishers (AEP), 510 Heron Dr., Ste. 201, Logan Township, NJ 08085. Tel. 856-241-7772, fax 856-241-0709, e-mail mail@edpress.org, World Wide Web http://www.edpress.org. *Pres.* Keith Garton; *Pres.-Elect* Jo-Ann McDevitt; *V.P.* Rachelle Cracchiolo; *Treas.* Richard Casabonne; *Past Pres.* Hugh Roome; *CEO/Exec. Dir.* Charlene F. Gaynor. E-mail cgaynor@edpress.org.

Assn. of Graphic Communications, 330 Seventh Ave., 9th fl., New York, NY 10001-5010. Tel. 212-279-2100, fax 212-279-5381, World Wide Web http://www. agcomm.org. *Pres./CEO* Susan Greenwood. E-mail susie@agcomm.org.

Authors Guild, 31 E. 28 St., 10th flr., New York, NY 10016-7923. Tel. 212-563-5904, fax 212-564-5363, e-mail staff@authorsguild.org. *Pres.* Nick Taylor; *V.P.s* Judy Blume, James B. Stewart; *Treas.* Peter Petre; *Secy.* Pat Cummings.

Book Industry Study Group, 19 W. 21 St., Ste. 905, New York, NY 10010. Tel. 646-336-7141, fax 646-336-6214, e-mail info @bisg.org, World Wide Web http://www. bisg.org. *Exec. Dir.* Jeff Abraham. E-mail jeff@bisg.org.

Book Manufacturers' Institute, 2 Armand Beach Drive, Ste. 1B, Palm Coast, FL 32137. Tel. 386-986-4552, fax 386-986-4553, e-mail info@bmibook.com, World Wide Web http://www.bmibook.org. *Pres.* William L. Upton, Malloy, Inc.; *V.P./Pres.-Elect* Ken Fultz, Mazer Corp.; *Treas.* John J. Edwards, Edwards Brothers; *Exec.*

V.P./Secy. Bruce W. Smith. Address correspondence to the executive vice president.

Bookbuilders of Boston, 44 Highland Circle, Halifax, MA 02338. Tel. 781-293-8600, fax 866-820-0469, e-mail office@bb boston.org, World Wide Web http://www. bbboston.org. *Pres.* Victor Curran, DS Graphics; *1st V.P.* Marty Rabinowitz, Addison-Wesley Professional; *2nd V.P.* Carol Heston, Victor Graphics; *Treas.* Larry Bisso, Bradford & Bigelow; *Secy.* Kim Boedigheimer, Addison-Wesley Professional.

Bookbuilders West, 1032 Irving St., No. 602, San Francisco, CA 94122-2200. E-mail president@bookbuilders.org, World Wide Web http://www.bookbuilders.org. *Pres.* Elise Gochberg, Transcontinental Printing Services; *Secy.* Anne Fuzellier, McGraw-Hill Higher Education; *Treas.* Michael O'Brien, TechBooks/GTS.

Canadian Booksellers Assn., 789 Don Mills Rd., Ste. 700, Toronto, ON M3C 1T5. Tel. 416-467-7883, fax 416-467-7886, e-mail enquiries@cbabook.org, World Wide Web http://www.cbabook.org. *Pres.* Paul McNally, McNally Robinson Booksellers. E-mail paul@grant.mcnallyrobinson.ca; *V.P.* Steve Budnarchuk, Audreys Books. E-mail stevebudnarchuk@audreysbooks. com; *Exec. Dir.* Susan Dayus. E-mail sdayus@cbabook.org.

Canadian ISBN Agency, c/o Published Heritage, Library and Archives Canada, 395 Wellington St., Ottawa, ON K1A 0N4. Tel. 819-994-6872, fax 819-997-7517, e-mail isbn@lac-bac.gc.ca.

Canadian Printing Industries Association, 75 Albert St., Ste. 906, Ottawa, ON K1P 5E7. Tel. 613-236-7208, fax 613-236-8169, e-mail belliott@cpia-aci.ca, World Wide Web http://www.cpia-aci.ca. *Pres.* Bob Elliott; *Chair* Ward Griffin.

Catholic Book Publishers Assn., 8404 Jamesport Dr., Rockford, IL 61108. Tel. 815-332-3245, e-mail cbpa3@aol.com, World Wide Web http://cbpa.org. *Pres.* Jill Kurtz; *V.P.* Mary Carol Kendzia; *Secy.* Jean Larkin; *Treas.* Therese Brown; *Exec. Dir.* Terry Wessels.

Chicago Book Clinic, 5443 N. Broadway, Ste. 101, Chicago, IL 60640. Tel. 773-561-4150, fax 773-561-1343, e-mail chgo bookclinic@aol.com, World Wide Web http://www.chicagobookclinic.org. *Pres.* Tammy Levy, McGraw-Hill, 130 E. Randolph, Ste. 400, Chicago, IL 60601. Tel. 312-233-7804, fax 312-233-6763, e-mail tammy_levy@mcgraw-hill.com; *V.P.* Jen Thomas, FiberMark, 916 Ascot Dr., Elgin, IL 60123. Tel. 847-630-0244, e-mail jthomas@fibermark.com; *Admin.* Kevin G. Boyer. E-mail kgboyer@ix.netcom.com.

Children's Book Council, 12 W. 37 St., 2nd fl., New York, NY 10018-7480. Tel. 212-966-1990, fax 212-966-2073, World Wide Web http://www.cbcbooks.org. *Chair* Simon Boughton; *V. Chair/Chair-Elect* Doug Whiteman; *Secy.* Brenda Bowen; *Treas.* Suzanne Murphy.

Copyright Society of the USA. *Pres.* Barry Slotnick; *V.P./Pres.-Elect* Helene Blue; *Secy.* Jay Kogan; *Treas.* Gloria Phares; *Admin.* Amy Nickerson. E-mail amy@ csusa.org, World Wide Web http://www. csusa.org.

Council of Literary Magazines and Presses, 154 Christopher St., Ste. 3C, New York, NY 10014. Tel. 212-741-9110, fax 212-741-9112, e-mail info@clmp.org, World Wide Web http://www.clmp.org. *Pres.* Ira Silverberg; *Exec. Dir.* Jeffrey Lependorf. E-mail jlependorf@clmp.org.

Educational Paperback Assn., Box 1399, East Hampton, NY 11937. Tel. 631-329-3315, e-mail edupaperback@aol.com, World Wide Web http://www.edupaperback.org. *Pres.* Dick Tinder; *V.P.* Jean Srnecz; *Treas.* Anne Sterling; *Exec. Secy.* Marilyn Abel.

Evangelical Christian Publishers Assn., 4816 S. Ash Ave., Ste. 101, Tempe, AZ 85282. Tel. 480-966-3998, fax 480-966-1944, e-mail mkuyper@ecpa.org, World Wide Web http://www.ecpa.org. *Pres./CEO* Mark W. Kuyper; *Chair* Mark D. Taylor, Tyndale House Publishers; *V. Chair* Mike Hyatt, Thomas Nelson Publishers; *Secy.* Robert Fryling, InterVarsity Press; *Treas.* John Howard, Howard Publishers; *Memb.-at-Large* Kent R. Wilson, NavPress.

Graphic Artists Guild, 90 John St., Ste. 403, New York, NY 10038. Tel. 212-791-3400, fax 212-792-0333, e-mail admin@gag.org,

World Wide Web http://www.gag.org. *Pres.* John Schmelzer. E-mail president@gag.org; *Admin. Dir.* Patricia McKiernan. E-mail admin@gag.org.

Great Lakes Booksellers Assn., c/o *Exec. Dir.* Jim Dana, Box 901, 208 Franklin St., Grand Haven, MI 49417. Tel. 616-847-2460, fax 616-842-0051, e-mail glb@books-glba.org, World Wide Web http://www.books-glba.org. *Pres.* Nicola Rooney, Nicola's Books, Ann Arbor, Michigan. E-mail nicolasbooks@sbcglobal.net; *V.P.* Carol Besse, Carmichael's Bookstore, Louisville, Kentucky. E-mail csbesse@bellsouth.net; *Past Pres.* Sue Boucher, Lake Forest Book Store, Lake Forest, Illinois. E-mail lfbooks@aol.com.

Guild of Book Workers, 521 Fifth Ave., New York, NY 10175. Tel. 212-292-4444, e-mail publicity@guildofbookworkers.allmail.net, World Wide Web http://palimpsest.stanford.edu/byorg/gbw. *Pres.* Betsy Palmer Eldridge; *V.P.* James Reid-Cunningham.

Horror Writers Assn., Box 50577, Palo Alto, CA 94303. E-mail hwa@horror.org, World Wide Web http://www.horror.org. *Pres.* Gary Braunbeck; *V.P.* Judi Rohrig; *Secy.* Nancy Etchemendy; *Treas.* Lisa Morton.

International Assn. of Printing House Craftsmen (IAPHC), 7042 Brooklyn Blvd., Minneapolis, MN 55429. Tel. 800-466-4274, 763-560-1620, fax 763-560-1350, World Wide Web http://www.iaphc.org. *Chair* Bill Leahy; *V. Chair* Eric Olsen; *Pres./CEO* Kevin Keane. E-mail kkeane1069@aol.com.

International Standard Book Numbering U.S. Agency, 630 Central Ave., New Providence, NJ 07974. Tel. 877-310-7333, fax 908-219-0188, e-mail isbn-san@bowker.com, World Wide Web http://www.isbn.org. *Dir.* Doreen Gravesande; *ISBN/SAN Managing Ed.* Paula Kurdi.

Jewish Book Council, 15 E. 26 St., 10th fl., New York, NY 10010. Tel. 212-532-4949 ext. 297, fax 212-481-4174, World Wide Web http://www.jewishbookcouncil.org. *Exec. Dir.* Carolyn Starman Hessel.

Library Binding Institute, 14 Bay Tree Lane, Tequesta, FL 33469. Tel. 561-745-6821, fax 561-745-6813, e-mail info@lbinders.

org, World Wide Web http://www.lbinders.org. *Exec. Dir.* Debra Nolan. E-mail dnolan@lbinders.org.

Magazine Publishers of America, 810 Seventh Ave., 24th fl., New York, NY 10019. Tel. 212-872-3700, e-mail mpa@magazine.org, World Wide Web http://www.magazine.org. *Pres./CEO* Nina B. Link. Tel. 212-872-3710, e-mail president@magazine.org.

Midwest Independent Publishers Assn., Box 581432, Minneapolis, MN 55458-1432. Tel. 651-917-0021, World Wide Web http://www.mipa.org. *Pres.* Sybil Smith. E-mail smithseprs@aol.com; *V.P. Memb.* Pat Bell. E-mail patjbell@aol.com.

Miniature Book Society. World Wide Web http://www.mbs.org. *Pres.* Eileen Cummings. E-mail inkydew@aol.com; *V.P.* Pat Pistner. E-mail pistner@comcast.net; *Secy.* Twyla Racz. E-mail tracz@emich.edu; *Treas.* Kathy King. E-mail kking@midohio.net; *Past Pres.* Neale Albert. E-mail nalbert@paulweiss.com.

Minnesota Book Publishers Roundtable. *Pres.* Susan Doerr, Univ. of Minnesota Press, 111 Third Ave. S., Ste. 290, Minneapolis, MN 55401. Tel. 612-627-1967, fax 612-627-1980, e-mail doer0012@umn.edu. World Wide Web http://www.publishersroundtable.org.

Mountains and Plains Booksellers Assn., 19 Old Town Sq., Ste. 238, Fort Collins, CO 80524. Tel. 970-484-5856, fax 970-407-1479, e-mail info@mountainsplains.org, World Wide Web http://www.mountainsplains.org.

National Assn. for Printing Leadership, 75 W. Century Rd., Paramus, NJ 07652. Tel. 800-642-6275, 201-634-9600, fax 201-986-2976, e-mail info@napl.org, World Wide Web http://www.napl.org. *Pres./CEO* Joseph P. Truncale; *Chair* Joan B. Davidson; *V. Chair* Stephen L. Johnson; *Secy./Treas.* William F. Woods, Jr.

National Assn. of College Stores, 500 E. Lorain St., Oberlin, OH 44074-1294. Tel. 800-622-7498, 440-775-7777, fax 440-775-4769, e-mail info@nacs.org, World Wide Web http://www.nacs.org. *CEO* Brian Cartier.

National Coalition Against Censorship (NCAC), 275 Seventh Ave., New York, NY 10001. Tel. 212-807-6222, fax 212-807-6245, e-mail ncac@ncac.org, World Wide Web http://www.ncac.org. *Exec. Dir.* Joan E. Bertin.

New Atlantic Independent Booksellers Assn. (NAIBA), 2667 Hyacinth St., Westbury, NY 11590. Tel. 516-333-0681, fax 516-333-0689, e-mail info@naiba.com. *Pres.* Lynn Gonchar, Tudor Bookshop and Cafe, 651 Wyoming Ave., Kingston, PA 18704. Tel. 570-288-9697, fax 570-288-9601; *Exec. Dir.* Eileen Dengler.

New England Booksellers Assn., 1770 Massachusetts Ave., Ste. 332, Cambridge, MA 02140. Tel. 800-466-8711, 617-576-3070, fax 617-576-3091, e-mail rusty@neba.org, World Wide Web http://www.newengland books.org. *Pres.* Allan Schmid; *V.P.* Penny McConnel; *Treas.* Mitch Gaslin; *Exec. Dir.* Wayne A. Drugan, Jr.

North American Bookdealers Exchange, Box 606, Cottage Grove, OR 97424. Tel./fax 541-942-7455, e-mail nabe@bookmarketing profits.com, World Wide Web http://bookmarketingprofits.com. *Dir.* Al Galasso.

Northern California Independent Booksellers Assn., The Presidio, 1007 General Kennedy Ave., Box 29169, San Francisco, CA 94129. Tel. 415-561-7686, fax 415-561-7685, e-mail office@nciba.com, World Wide Web http://www.nciba.com. *Pres.* Nick Setka; *V.P.* Judy Wheeler; *Exec. Dir.* Hut Landon.

Pacific Northwest Booksellers Assn., 317 W. Broadway, Ste. 214, Eugene, OR 97401-2890. Tel. 541-683-4363, fax 541-683-3910, e-mail info@pnba.org, World Wide Web http://www.pnba.org. *Pres.* Pat Rutledge, A Book for All Seasons, 703 Hwy. 2, Leavenworth, WA 98826-1354. Tel. 509-548-1451, fax 509-548-2062, e-mail abookfor@earthlink.net; *Exec. Dir.* Thom Chambliss.

PEN American Center, Div. of International PEN, 568 Broadway, Ste. 303, New York, NY 10012. Tel. 212-334-1660, fax 212-334-2181, e-mail pen@pen.org, World Wide Web http://www.pen.org. *Pres.* Salman Rushdie; *V.P.s* Paul Auster, Jhum-pa Lahiri; *Treas.* Wendy Gimbel; *Secy.* Rick Moody.

Periodical and Book Assn. of America, 481 Eighth Ave., Ste. 826, New York, NY 10001. Tel. 212-563-6502, fax 212-563-4098, e-mail info@pbaa.net, World Wide Web http://www.pbaa.net. *Pres.* Robert Kerekes. E-mail bob.kerekes@ingram periodicals.com; *Chair* William Michalo-poulos. E-mail william_michalopoulos@ businessweek.com; *Exec. Dir.* Lisa W. Scott. E-mail lscott@pbaa.net or lisaw scott@hotmail.com.

Publishers Marketing Assn., 627 Aviation Way, Manhattan Beach, CA 90266. Tel. 310-372-2732, fax 310-374-3342, e-mail info@pma-online.org, World Wide Web http://www.pma-online.org. *Pres.* Kent Sturgis; *Exec. Dir.* Jan Nathan.

Romance Writers of America, 16000 Stuebner Airline Dr., Ste. 140, Spring, TX 77379. Tel. 832-717-5200, fax 832-717-5201, e-mail info@rwanational.com, World Wide Web http://www.rwanational.com. *Pres.* Gayle Wilson; *Pres.-Elect* Jill Limber; *Past Pres.* Tara Taylor Quinn; *Exec. Dir.* Allison Kelley. E-mail akelley@rwa national.org.

Science Fiction and Fantasy Writers of America, P.O. Box 877, Chestertown, MD 21620. E-mail execdir@sfwa.org, World Wide Web http://www.sfwa.org. *Pres.* Robert Wayne Bailey; *V.P.* Howard V. Hendrix; *Treas.* Justin Stanchfield; *Secy.* Catherine Mintz; *Exec. Dir.* Jane Jewell.

Small Press Center for Independent Publishing, 20 W. 44 St., New York, NY 10036. Tel. 212-764-7021, fax 212-354-5365, e-mail info@smallpress.org, World Wide Web http://www.smallpress.org. *Chair* Mary Bertschmann; *V. Chair* Lloyd Jassin; *Exec. Dir.* Karin Taylor.

Small Publishers Assn. of North America (SPAN), 1618 W. Colorado Ave., Colorado Springs, CO 80904. Tel. 719-475-1726, fax 719-471-2182, e-mail span@ spannet.org, World Wide Web http://www. spannet.org. *Exec. Dir.* Scott Flora.

Society of Children's Book Writers and Illustrators (SCBWI), 8271 Beverly Blvd., Los Angeles, CA 90048. Tel. 323-782-1010, fax 323-782-1892, World Wide Web http://

www.scbwi.org. *Pres.* Stephen Mooser. E-mail stephenmooser@scbwi.org; *Exec. Dir.* Lin Oliver.

Society of Illustrators (SI), 128 E. 63 St., New York, NY 10021. Tel. 212-838-2560, fax 212-838-2561, e-mail info@society illustrators.org, World Wide Web http://www.societyillustrators.org.

Society of National Association Publications (SNAP), 8405 Greensboro Dr., Ste. 800, McLean, VA 22102. Tel. 703-506-3285, fax 703-506-3266, e-mail snapinfo@snaponline.org, World Wide Web http://www.snaponline.org. *Pres.* Larry Price. E-mail lprice@aba.com; *V.P.* Robert Fromberg. E-mail rfromberg@hfma.org.

Southern Independent Booksellers Alliance, 2611 Forest Dr., No.124, Columbia, SC 29204. Tel. 800-331-9617 or 803-779-0118, fax 803-779-0113, e-mail info@sibaweb.org, World Wide Web http://www.sibaweb.org. *Pres.* Sally Brewster, Park Road Books.

Technical Assn. of the Pulp and Paper Industry, 15 Technology Pkwy. S., Norcross, GA 30092 (P.O. Box 105113, Atlanta, GA 30348). Tel. 770-446-1400, fax 770-446-6947, World Wide Web http://www.tappi.org. *Pres.* Willis J. Potts, Jr., Inland Paperboard and Packaging; *V.P.* Mark R. McCollister, C. A. Lawton Company.

Western Writers of America, c/o *Exec. Dir.* James A. Crutchfield, 1012 Fair St., Franklin, TN 37064. E-mail tncrutch@aol.com. World Wide Web http://www.western writers.org. *Pres.* Rita Cleary; *V.P.* Cotton Smith.

Women's National Book Assn., c/o Susannah Greenberg Public Relations, 2166 Broadway, Ste. 9-E, New York, NY 10024. Tel./fax 212-208-4629, e-mail publicity@bookbuzz.com, World Wide Web http://www.wnba-books.org. *Pres.* Jill A. Tardiff, Bamboo River Assocs., 625 Madison St., Unit B, Hoboken, NJ 07030. Tel. 201-656-7220, fax 201-792-0254, e-mail jtardiff-wnbanyc@worldnet.att.net; *V.P./Pres.-Elect* Laurie Beckelman, Prentice Associates, 160 Tea Rock Lane, Marshfield, MA 02050. Tel. 781-834-8002, e-mail lbeckelman@aol.com; *Secy.* Michele Leber, 1805 Crystal Dr., No. 911, Arlington, VA 22202-4420. Tel. 703-920-2010, fax 703-979-6372, e-mail michele.leber @comcast.net; *Treas.* Amy Barden, 3101 Ravensworth, Alexandria, VA 22302. Tel. 703-578-4023, e-mail amyb3cat@yahoo.com.

International and Foreign Book Trade Associations

For Canadian book trade associations, see the preceding section, "Book Trade Associations, United States and Canada." For a more extensive list of book trade organizations outside the United States and Canada, with more detailed information, consult *International Literary Market Place* (Information Today, Inc.), which also provides extensive lists of major bookstores and publishers in each country.

International

African Publishers' Network, BP 3429, Abidjan 01, Côte d'Ivoire. Tel. 04-20-21-18-01, fax 04-20-21-18-03, e-mail apnetes@yahoo.com, World Wide Web http://www.freewebs.com/africanpublishers. *Chair* Mamadou Aliou Sow; *Exec. Secy.* Akin Fasemore.

Afro-Asian Book Council, 4835/24 Ansari Rd., Daryaganj, New Delhi 110002, India. Tel. 11-326-1487, fax 11-326-7437, e-mail sdas@ubspd.com. *Secy.-Gen.* Sukumar Das; *Dir.* Abul Hasan.

Centre Régional pour la Promotion du Livre en Afrique (Regional Center for Book Promotion in Africa), P.O. Box 1646, Yaoundé, Cameroon. Tel. 22-4782. *Secy.* William Moutchia.

Centro Régional para el Fomento del Libro en América Latina y el Caribe (CERLALC) (Regional Center for Book Promotion in Latin America and the Caribbean), Calle 70, No. 9-52, Apdo. Aéreo 57348, Santafé de Bogotá 2, Colombia. Tel. 1-212-6056, fax 1-255-4614, e-mail libro@cerlalc.com, World Wide Web http://www.cerlalc.com. *Dir.* Carmen Barvo.

Federation of European Publishers, Ave. de Tervueren 204, B-1150 Brussels, Belgium. Tel. 2-770-11-10, fax 2-771-20-71, e-mail abergman@fep-fec.be, World Wide Web http://www.fep-fee.be. *Pres.* Arne Bach; *Dir.-Gen.* Anne Bergman-Tahon.

International Assn. of Scientific, Technical and Medical Publishers (STM), POB 90407, NL-2509 LK The Hague, Netherlands. Tel. 70-314-09-30, fax 70-314-09-40, e-mail info@stm-assoc.org, World Wide Web http://www.stm-assoc.org. *Chair* Eric Swanson; *Secy.* Lex Lefebvre.

International Board on Books for Young People (IBBY), Nonnenweg 12, CH-4055 Basel, Switzerland. Tel. 61-272-2917, fax 61-272-2757, e-mail ibby@ibby.org, World Wide Web http://www.ibby.org. *Exec. Dir.* Kimete Basha; *Admin. Dir.* Elizabeth Page.

International Booksellers Federation, Chaussée de Charleroi 51b, Boîte 1, 1060 Brussels, Belgium. Tel. 2-223-49-40, fax 2-223-49-38, e-mail ibf.booksellers@skynet.be, World Wide Web http://www.ibf-booksellers.org. *Pres.* Eric Hardin; *Dir.* Françoise Dubruille.

International League of Antiquarian Booksellers, 400 Summit Ave., Saint Paul, MN 55102. Tel. 800-441-0076, 612-290-0700, fax 612-290-0646, e-mail info@ilab-lila.com, World Wide Web http://www.ilab.org. *Pres.* Robert D. Fleck; *Secy.-Gen.* Steven Temple.

International Publishers Assn. (Union Internationale des Editeurs), Ave. Miremont 3, CH-1206 Geneva, Switzerland. Tel. 22-346-3018, fax 22-347-5717, e-mail secretariat@ipa-uie.org, World Wide Web http://www.ipa-uie.org. *Pres.* Pere Vicens Rahola; *Secy.-Gen.* Jens Bammel.

National

Argentina

Cámara Argentina del Libro (Argentine Book Assn.), Avda. Belgrano 1580, 4 piso, 1093 Buenos Aires. Tel. 1-4381-8383, fax 1-4381-9253, e-mail cal@editores.com, World Wide Web http://www.editores.org.ar. *Dir.* Norberto J. Pou.

Fundación El Libro (Book Foundation), Hipolito Yrigoyen 1628, 5 piso, 1089

Buenos Aires. Tel. 11-4374-3288, fax 11-4375-0268, e-mail fundacion@el-libro.com.ar, World Wide Web http://www.el-libro.com.ar. *Pres.* Carlos Alberto Pazos; *Dir.* Marta V. Diaz.

Australia

Australian and New Zealand Assn. of Antiquarian Booksellers, 604 High St., Prahran, Vic. 3181. Tel. 3-9525-1649, e-mail admin@anzaab.com, World Wide Web http://www.anzaab.com.au. *Pres.* Lovella Kerr.

Australian Booksellers Assn., 828 High St., Unit 9, Kew East, Vic. 3102, Australia. Tel. 3-9859-7322, fax 3-9859-7344, e-mail mail@aba.org.au, World Wide Web http://www.aba.org.au. *Pres.*Tim Peach; *Exec. Dir.* Celia Pollock.

Australian Publishers Assn., 60/89 Jones St., Ultimo, NSW 2007. Tel. 2-9281-9788, fax 2-9281-1073, e-mail apa@publishers.asn.au, World Wide Web http://www.publishers.asn.au. *Chief Exec.* Susan Bridge.

Austria

Hauptverband des Österreichischen Buchhandels (Austrian Publishers and Booksellers Assn.), Grünangergasse 4, A-1010 Vienna. Tel. 1-512-15-35, fax 1-512-84-82, e-mail hvb@buecher.at, World Wide Web http://www.buecher.at. *Pres.* Alexander Potyka.

Verband der Antiquare Österreichs (Austrian Antiquarian Booksellers Assn.), Grünangergasse 4, A-1010 Vienna. Tel. 1-512-15-35, fax 1-512-84-82, e-mail sekretariat@hvb.at, World Wide Web http://www.antiquare.at. *Pres.* Norbert Donhofer.

Belarus

National Book Chamber of Belarus, 11 Masherow Ave., 220600 Minsk, Belarus. Tel. 172-235-839, fax 172-235-825, e-mail palata@palata.belpak.minsk.by. *Contact* Anatoli Voronko.

Belgium

Vlaamse Boekverkopersbond (Flemish Booksellers Assn.), Hof ter Schriecklaan 17, 2600 Berchem/Antwerp. Tel. 3-230-89-23, fax 3-281-22-40, e-mail info@boek.be, World Wide Web http://www.boek.be. *Gen. Secy.* Luc Tessens.

Bolivia

Cámara Boliviana del Libro (Bolivian Booksellers Assn.), Calle Capitan Ravelo No. 2116, 682 La Paz. Tel. 2-44-4339, fax 2-44-1523, e-mail cabolib@ceibo.entelnet.bo. *Pres.* Rolando Condori Salinas; *Secy.* Teresa G. de Alvarez.

Brazil

Cámara Brasileira do Livro (Brazilian Book Assn.), Cristiano Viana 91, 05411-000 Sao Paulo-SP. Tel. /fax 11-3069-1300, e-mail cbl@cbl.org.br, World Wide Web http://www.cbl.org.br. *Pres.* Oswaldo Siciliano; *Gen. Mgr.* Aloysio T. Costa.

Sindicato Nacional dos Editores de Livros (Brazilian Publishers Assn.), Av. Rio Branco 37, Sala 1.504, 20090-003 Rio de Janeiro-RJ. Tel. 21-2233-6481, fax 21-2253-8502, e-mail snel@snel.org.br, World Wide Web http://www.snel.org.br. *Pres.* Paulo Roberto Rocco.

Chile

Cámara Chilena del Libro AG (Chilean Assn. of Publishers, Distributors, and Booksellers), Av. Libertador Bernardo O'Higgins 1370, Oficina 501, Santiago de Chile. Tel. 56-2-698-9519, fax 56-2-698-9226, e-mail prolibro@tie.cl, World Wide Web http://www.camlibro.cl. *Pres.* Eduardo Castillo Garcia.

Colombia

Cámara Colombiana del Libro (Colombian Book Assn.), Calle 40, No. 21-31, Bogotá DC. Tel. 1-288-6188, fax 1-287-3320, e-mail camlibro@camlibro.com.co, World Wide Web http://www.camlibro.com.co.

Czech Republic

Svaz českých knihkupcu a nakladatelů (Czech Publishers and Booksellers Assn.), Jana Masaryka 56, 120 00 Prague 2. Tel. 2-24-

219-944, fax 2-24-219-942, e-mail sckn@
sckn.cz, World Wide Web http://www.
sckn.cz. *Chair* Jitka Undeova.

Denmark

Danske Boghandlerforening (Danish Booksellers Assn.), Siljangade 6.3, DK 2300
Copenhagen S. Tel. 32-54-22-55, fax 32-
54-00-41, e-mail ddb@bogpost.dk, World
Wide Web http://www.bogguide.dk. *Pres.*
Jesper Moller.
Danske Forlaeggerforening (Danish Publishers Assn.), 18/1 Kompagnistr. 1208, Copenhagen K. Tel. 33-15-66-88, fax 33-15-
65-88, e-mail publassn@webpartner.dk.
Dir. Tune Olsen.

Ecuador

Cámara Ecuatoriana del Libro, Núcleo de
Pichincha, Avda. Eloy Alfaro, N29-61 e
Inglaterra piso N 9, Quito. Tel. 2-553-311,
fax 2-222-150, e-mail celnp@hoy.net,
World Wide Web http://celibro.org.ec.
Pres. Luis Mora Ortega.

Egypt

General Egyptian Book Organization, Cor-
niche el-Nil–Ramlet Boulac, Cairo 11221.
Tel. 2-5775-436, fax 2-5765-058, e-mail
info@egyptianbook.org, World Wide Web
http://www.egyptianbook.org. *Chair* Nass-
er El Ansary.

Estonia

Estonian Publishers Assn., Roosikrantsi 6,
10119 Tallinn. Tel. 2-644-9836, fax 2-
641-1443, e-mail astat@eki.ee. *Dir.* A.
Trummal.

Finland

Kirjakauppaliitto Ry (Booksellers Assn. of
Finland), Eerikinkatu 15-17 D 43-44, FIN-
00100 Helsinki. Tel. 9-6859-9110, fax 9-
6859-9119, e-mail toimisto@kirjakaup
paliitto.fi, World Wide Web http://www.
kirjakauppaliitto.fi. *Dir.* Olli Erakivi.
Suomen Kustannusyhdistys (Finnish Book
Publishers Assn.), P.O. Box 177, FIN-
00121 Helsinki. Tel. 9-2287-7250, fax 9-

6121-226, e-mail veikko.sonninen@
skyry.net, World Wide Web http://www.
skyry.net. *Dir.* Veikko Sonninen.

France

Cercle de la Librairie (Circle of Professionals
of the Book Trade), 35 rue Grégoire-de-
Tours, F-75006 Paris. Tel. 1-44-41-28-00,
fax 1-44-41-28-65, e-mail commercial@
electre.com, World Wide Web http://www.
electre.com. *Pres.* Charles Henri Flammar-
ion.
Fédération Française des Syndicats de
Libraires (FFSL) (French Booksellers
Assn.), 43 rue de Châteaudun, F-75009
Paris. Tel. 1-42-82-00-03, fax 1-42-82-10-
51. *Pres.* Jean-Luc Dewas.
France Edition, 115 blvd. Saint-Germain, F-
75006 Paris. Tel. 1-44-41-13-13, fax 1-46-
34-63-83, e-mail info@franceedition.org,
World Wide Web http://www.france
edition.org. *Pres.* Liana Levi; *Dir.-Gen.*
Jean-Guy Boin. *New York Branch* French
Publishers Agency, 853 Broadway, Ste.
1509, New York, NY 10003-4703. Tel.
212-254-4540, fax 212-979-6229, World
Wide Web http://frenchpubagency.com.
Syndicat National de la Librairie Ancienne et
Moderne (National Assn. of Antiquarians
and Modern Booksellers), 4 rue Gît-le-
Coeur, F-75006 Paris. Tel. 1-43-29-46-38,
fax 1-43-25-41-63, e-mail slam-livre@
wanadoo.fr, World Wide Web http://www.
slam-livre.fr. *Pres.* Alain Marchiset.
Syndicat National de l'Edition (National
Union of Publishers), 115 blvd. Saint-Germain, F-75006 Paris. Tel. 1-44-41-40-50,
fax 1-44-41-40-77, World Wide Web http://
www.snedition.fr. *Pres.* Serge Eyrolles.
Union des Libraires de France (Union of
French Booksellers), 40 rue Grégoire-de-
Tours, F-75006 Paris. Tel./fax 1-43-29-88-
79. *Pres.* Eric Hardin; *Gen. Delegate*
Marie-Dominique Doumenc.

Germany

Börsenverein des Deutschen Buchhandels
e.V. (Stock Exchange of German Booksellers), Grosser Hirschgraben 17-21,
60313 Frankfurt-am-Main. Tel. 69-1306-0,
fax 69-1306-201, e-mail info@boev.de,

World Wide Web http://www.boev.de. *Gen. Mgr.* Harald Heker.

Verband Deutscher Antiquare e.V. (German Antiquarian Booksellers Assn.), Geschaftsstelle, Herr Norbert Munsch, Seeblick 1, 56459 Elbingen. Tel. 6535-909-147, fax 6435-909-148, e-mail buch@antiquare.de, World Wide Web http://www.antiquare.de. *Pres.* Joechen Granier.

Ghana

University Bookshop (formerly West African University Booksellers Assn.), Univ. of Ghana, P.O. Box 25, Legon. Tel./fax 21-500-398, unibks@ug.gn.apc.org. *Mgr.* Emmanuel K. H. Tonyigah.

Greece

Hellenic Federation of Publishers and Booksellers, Themistocleous 73, 10683 Athens. Tel. 2103-300-924, fax 2133-00-926, e-mail poev@otenet.gr. *Pres.* Georgios Dardanos.

Hungary

Magyar Könyvkiadók és Könyvterjesztök Egyesülése (Assn. of Hungarian Publishers and Booksellers), Kertesz u 41, 1073 Budapest. Tel. 1-343-25-40, fax 1-343-25-41, e-mail mkke@mkke.hu, World Wide Web http://www.mkke.hu. *Pres.* István Bart; *Secy.-Gen.* Péter Zentai.

Iceland

Félag Islenskra Bókaútgefenda (Icelandic Publishers Assn.), Baronsstig 5, 101 Reykjavik. Tel. 511-8020, fax 511-5020, e-mail baekur@mmedia.is. *Chair* Sigurdur Svavarsson; *Gen. Mgr.* Vilborg Hardardóttir.

India

Federation of Indian Publishers, Federation House, 18/1-C Institutional Area, Aruna Asaf Ali Marg, New Delhi 110067. Tel. 11-2696-4847, 11-2685-2263, fax 11-2686-4054, e-mail fip1@satyam.net.in, World Wide Web http://www.fiponweb.com. *Pres.* Shri Anand Bhushan.

Indonesia

Ikatan Penerbit Indonesia (Assn. of Indonesian Book Publishers), Jl. Kalipasir 32, Jakarta 10330. Tel. 21-314-1907, fax 21-314-6050, e-mail sekretariat@ikapi.or.id, World Wide Web http://www.ikapi.or.id. *Pres.* Arselan Harahap; *Secy.-Gen.* Robinson Rusdi.

Ireland

CLE: The Irish Book Publishers Assn., 43/44 Temple Bar, Dublin 2. Tel. 1-670-7393, fax 1-670-7642, e-mail info@publishing ireland.com, World Wide Web http://www.publishingireland.com. *Pres.* Tony Farmar.

Israel

Book and Printing Center, Israel Export Institute, 29 Hamered St., P.O. Box 50084, Tel Aviv 61500. Tel. 3-514-2830, fax 3-514-2902, e-mail export-institute@export.gov.il or pama@export.gov.il, World Wide Web http://www.export.gov.il. *Dir.-Gen.* Yechiel Assia.

Book Publishers Assn. of Israel, P.O. Box 20123, Tel Aviv 61201. Tel. 3-561-4121, fax 3-561-1996, e-mail info@tbpai.co.il, World Wide Web http://www.tbpai.co.il. *Managing Dir.* Amnon Ben-Shmuel; *Chair* Shay Hausman.

Italy

Associazione Italiana Editori (Italian Publishers Assn.), Via delle Erbe 2, 20121 Milan. Tel. 2-86-46-3091, fax 2-89-01-0863, e-mail aie@aie.it, World Wide Web http://www.aie.it. *Dir.* Ivan Cecchini.

Associazione Librai Antiquari d'Italia (Antiquarian Booksellers Assn. of Italy), Via del Parione, 11, 50123 Florence. Tel. 55-282-635, fax 55-214-831, e-mail alai@alai.it, World Wide Web http://www.alai.it. *Pres.* Umberto Pregliasco.

Jamaica

Booksellers' Assn. of Jamaica, c/o Novelty Trading Co. Ltd., Box 80, Kingston. Tel.

876-922-5883, fax 876-922-4743. *Pres.* Keith Shervington.

Japan

Japan Assn. of International Publications (formerly Japan Book Importers Assn.), Chiyoda Kaikan 21-4, Nihonbashi 1-chome, Chuo-ku, Tokyo 103-0027. Tel. 3-3271-6901, fax 3-3271-6920, e-mail jaip@poppy.ocn.ne.jp, World Wide Web http://www.jaip.gr.jp. *Chair* Seishiro Murata; *Secy.-Gen.* Hiroshi Takahashi.

Japan Book Publishers Assn., 6 Fukuromachi, Shinjuku-ku, Tokyo 162-0828. Tel. 3-3268-1301, fax 3-3268-1196, e-mail rd@jbpa.or.jp, World Wide Web http://www.jbpa.or.jp. *Pres.* Kunizo Asakura; *Exec. Dir.* Tadashi Yamashita.

Kenya

Kenya Publishers Assn., P.O. Box 42767, Nairobi 00100. Tel. 20-375-2344, fax 20-375-4076, e-mail kenyapublishers@wananchi.com, World Wide Web http://www.kenyabooks.org. *Exec. Secy.* Lynnette Kariuki.

Korea (Republic of)

Korean Publishers Assn., 105-2 Sagan-dong, Jongro-gu, Seoul 110-190. Tel. 2-735-2701, fax 2-738-5414, e-mail kpa@kpa21.or.kr, World Wide Web http://www.kpa21.or.kr. *Pres.* Choon Ho Na; *Secy.-Gen.* Jong Jin Jung.

Latvia

Latvian Publishers Assn., K Barona iela 36-4, LV-1011 Riga. Tel. 371-728-2392, fax 371-728-0549, e-mail lga@gramatizdeveji.lv, World Wide Web http://www.gramatizdeveji.lv. *Exec. Dir.* Dace Pugaca.

Lithuania

Lithuanian Publishers Assn., Ave. Jaksto 22-13, 01105 Vilnius. Tel./fax 5-261-7740, e-mail lla@centras.lt, World Wide Web http://www.lla.lt. *Pres.* Arvydas Andrijauskas.

Malaysia

Malaysian Book Publishers' Assn., No. 39 Jln Nilam 1/2, Subang Sq., Subang High-Tech Industrial Park Batutiga, 40000 Shah Alam, Selangor. Tel. 3-5637-9044, fax 3-5637-9043, e-mail inquiry@cerdik.com.my, World Wide Web http://www.mabopa.com.my. *Pres.* Ng Tieh Chuan.

Mexico

Cámara Nacional de la Industria Editorial Mexicana (Mexican Publishers' Assn.), Holanda No. 13, CP 04120, Mexico 21. Tel. 55-5688-24-34, fax 55-5604-43-47, e-mail cepromex@caniem.com, World Wide Web http://www.caniem.com. *Co-Pres.* A. H. Gayosso, J. C. Cramerez.

The Netherlands

KVB (formerly Koninklijke Vereeniging ter Bevordering van de Belangen des Boekhandels) (Royal Dutch Book Trade Assn.), Postbus 15007, 1001 MA Amsterdam. Tel. 20-624-02-12, fax 20-620-88-71, e-mail info@kvb.nl, World Wide Web http://www.kvb.nl. *Exec. Dir.* C. Verberne.

Nederlands Uitgeversverbond (Royal Dutch Publishers Assn.), Postbus 12040, 1100 AA Amsterdam. Tel. 20-43-09-150, fax 20-43-09-179, e-mail info@nuv.nl, World Wide Web http://www.nuv.nl. *Pres.* Henk J. L. Vonhoff.

Nederlandsche Vereeniging van Antiquaren (Netherlands Assn. of Antiquarian Booksellers), Postbus 364, 3500 AJ Utrecht. Tel. 30-231-92-86, fax 30-234-33-62, e-mail bestbook@wxs.nl, World Wide Web http://nvva.nl. *Pres.* Ton Kok.

Nederlandse Boekverkopersbond (Dutch Booksellers Assn.), Prins Hendriklaan 72, 3721 AT Bilthoven. Tel. 30-228-79-56, fax 030-228-45-66, e-mail nbb@boekbond.nl, World Wide Web http://www.boekbond.nl. *Pres.* W. Karssen; *Exec. Secy.* A. C. Doeser.

New Zealand

Booksellers New Zealand, Box 13-248, Wellington. Tel. 4-478-5511, fax 4-478-5519, e-mail enquiries@booksellers.co.nz,

World Wide Web http://www.booksellers. co.nz. *Chair* Tony Moores; *Chief Exec.* Alice Heather.

Nigeria

Nigerian Publishers Assn., GPO Box 2541, Ibadan. Tel. 2-241-4427, fax 2-241-3396, e-mail nigpa@skannet.com or nigpa@ steineng.net. *Pres.* V. Nwankwo.

Norway

Norske Bokhandlerforening (Norwegian Booksellers Assn.), Øvre Vollgate 15, 0158 Oslo 1. Tel. 22-00-75-80, fax 22-33-38-30, e-mail dnf@forleggerforeningen. no, World Wide Web http://www. forleggerforeningen.no. *Dir.* Kristin C. Slordahl.

Norske Forleggerforening (Norwegian Publishers Assn.), Øvre Vollgate 15, 0158 Oslo 1. Tel. 22-00-75-80, fax 22-33-38-30, e-mail dnf@forleggerforeningen.no, World Wide Web http://www.forlegger foreningen.no. *Contact* Kristin C. Slordahl.

Peru

Cámara Peruana del Libro (Peruvian Publishers Assn.), Av.Abancay 4ta cuadra, Lima. Tel. 1-428-7690, fax 1-427-7331, e-mail dn@binape.gob.pe, World Wide Web http://www.binape.gob.pe. *Pres.* Julio Cesar Flores Rodriguez; *Exec. Dir.* Dra Loyda Moran Bustamente.

Philippines

Philippine Educational Publishers Assn., 84 P. Florentino St., 3008 Quezon City. Tel. 2-712-4106, e-mail dbuhain@cnl.net, World Wide Web http://nbdb.gov/ph/ publindust.htm. *Pres.* Dominador D. Buhain.

Poland

Polskie Towarzystwo Wydawców Ksiazek (Polish Society of Book Editors), ul. Mazowiecka 2/4, 00048 Warsaw. Tel. 22-826-72-71, fax 22-826-07-35. *Pres.* Janusz Fogler; *Gen. Secy.* Donat Chruscicki.

Stowarzyszenie Ksiegarzy Polskich (Assn. of Polish Booksellers), ul. Mokotowska 4/6, 00641 Warsaw. Tel. 22-252-874, World Wide Web http://www.bookweb.org/orgs/ 1322.html. *Pres.* Tadeusz Hussak.

Portugal

Associação Portuguesa de Editores e Livreiros (Portuguese Assn. of Publishers and Booksellers), Av. dos Estados Unidas da America 97, 6 Esq., 1700-167 Lisbon. Tel. 21-843-51-80, fax 21-848-93-77, e-mail geral@apel.pt, World Wide Web http://www.apel.pt. *Pres.* Graca Didier.

Russia

Publishers Assn., B. Nikitskaya St. 44, 121069 Moscow. Tel. 95-202-11-74, fax 95-202-39-89. *Dir.* V. Shibaev; *Contact* I. Laptev.

Russian Book Chamber, ul Ostozhenka d ya, 119034 Moscow. Tel. 95-291-12-78, fax 95-291-96-30, e-mail bookch@postman. ru, World Wide Web http://www. bookchamber.ru.

Serbia and Montenegro

Assn. of Serbia and Montenegro Publishers and Booksellers, POB 570, 11000 Belgrade. Tel. 11-2642-533, fax 11-2686-539, e-mail uijk@eunet.yu, World Wide Web http://www.beobookfair.co.yu. *Gen. Dir.* Zivadin Mitrovic.

Singapore

Singapore Book Publishers Assn., c/o Cannon International, 86 Marine Parade Centre, No. 03-213, Singapore 440086. Tel. 65-344-7801, fax 65-447-0897, e-mail twcsbpa@singnet.com.sg. *Pres.* K. P. Siram.

Slovenia

Zdruzenie Zaloznikov in Knjigotrzcev Slovenije Gospodarska Zbornica Slovenije (Assn. of Publishers and Booksellers of Slovenia), Dimiceva 13, 1504 Ljubljana. Tel. 1-5898-474, fax 1-5898-100, e-mail

info@gzs.si, World Wide Web http://
www.gzs.si. *Pres.* Milan Matos.

South Africa

Publishers Assn. of South Africa, Centre for
the Book, 62 Queen Victoria St., Cape
Town 8000. Tel. 21-426-2728, fax 21-426-
1733, e-mail pasa@publishsa.co.za, World
Wide Web http://www.publishsa.co.za.
Admin. Desiree Murdoch.
South African Booksellers Assn. (formerly
Associated Booksellers of Southern Africa),
P.O. Box 870, Bellville 7530. Tel. 21-918-
8616, fax 21-951-4903, e-mail fnel@
naspers.com, World Wide Web http://sa
booksellers.com. *Pres.* Guru Redhi; *Secy.*
Peter Adams.

Spain

Federación de Gremios de Editores de Es-
paña (Federation of Spanish Publishers
Assns.), Cea Bermdez 44-2 Dche, 2003
Madrid. Tel. 91-534-51-95, fax 91-535-
26-25, e-mail fgee@fge.es, World Wide
Web http://www.federacioneditores.org.
Pres. D. Emiliano Martinez; *Exec. Dir.*
Antonio Ma Avila.

Sri Lanka

Sri Lanka Assn. of Publishers, 112 S. Mahin-
da Mawatha, Colombo 10. Tel. 1-695-773,
fax 1-696-653, e-mail dayawansajay@
hotmail.com. *Dir.* Dayawansa Jayakody;
Gen. Secy. Gamini Wijesuriya.

Sudan

Sudanese Publishers Assn., c/o Institute of
African and Asian Studies, Khartoum
Univ., P.O. Box 321, Khartoum 11115.
Tel. 249-11-778-0031, fax 249-11-770-
358, e-mail makkawi@sudanmail.net. *Dir.*
Abel Rahim Makkawi.

Sweden

Svenska Förläggareföreningen (Swedish Publishers Assn.), Drottninggatan 97, S-11360
Stockholm. Tel. 8-736-19-40, fax 8-736-
19-44, e-mail info@forlaggareforeningen,

World Wide Web http://www.forlaggare
foreningen.se. *Dir.* Kristina Ahlinder.

Switzerland

Association Suisse des Éditeurs de Langue
Française (ASELF) (Swiss Assn. of English-Language Publishers), 2 Ave. Agas-
siz, 1001 Lausanne. Tel. 21-319-71-11,
fax 21-319-79-10, World Wide Web http://
www.culturactif.ch/editions/asef1.htm.
Secy. Gen. Philippe Schibli.
Schweizerischer Buchhandler- und Verleger-
Verband (Swiss German-Language Booksellers and Publishers Assn.), Alderstr. 40,
8034 Zurich. Tel. 1-421-28-00, fax 1-421-
28-18, e-mail sbvv@swissbooks.ch, World
Wide Web http://www.swissbooks.ch.
Exec. Dir. Martin Jann.

Thailand

Publishers and Booksellers Assn. of Thailand, 947/158-159 Moo 12, Bang Na-Trad
Rd., Bang Na, Bangkok 10260. Tel. 2-954-
9560-4, fax 2-954-9565-6, e-mail info@
pubat.or.th, World Wide Web http://www.
pubat.or.th.

Uganda

Uganda Publishers and Booksellers Assn.,
P.O. Box 7732, Kampala. Tel. 41-259-163,
fax 41-251-160, e-mail mbd@infocom.
co.ug. *Contact* Martin Okia.

United Kingdom

Antiquarian Booksellers Assn., Sackville
House, 40 Piccadilly, London W1J 0DR,
England. Tel. 20-7439-3118, fax 20-7439-
3119, e-mail info@aba.org.uk, World
Wide Web http://www.aba.org.uk. *Pres.*
Jonathan Potter.
Assn. of Learned and Professional Society
Publishers, South House, The Street,
Clapham, Worthing, West Sussex BN13
3UU, England. Tel. 1903-871-686, fax
1903-871-457, World Wide Web http://
www.alpsp.org/default.htm. *Secy.-Gen.*
Sally Morris. E-mail sally.morris@alpsp.
org
Booktrust, 45 East Hill, Wandsworth, Lon-
don SW18 2QZ, England. Tel. 20-8516-

2977, fax 20-8516-2978, World Wide Web http://www.booktrust.org.uk.

Educational Publishers Council, 29B Montague St., London WC1B 5BH, England. Tel. 20-7691-9191, fax 20-7691-9199, e-mail mail@publishers.org.uk, World Wide Web http://www.publishers.org.uk. *Chair* Philip Walters; *Dir.* Graham Taylor.

Publishers Assn., 29B Montague St., London WC1B 5BH, England. Tel. 20-7691-9191, fax 20-7691-9199, e-mail mail@publishers. org.uk, World Wide Web http://www. publishers.org.uk. *Pres.* Anthony Forbes-Watson; *Chief Exec.* Ronnie Williams.

Scottish Book Trust, Sandeman House, Trunk's Close, 55 High St., Edinburgh EH1 1SR, Scotland. Tel. 131-524-0160, fax 131-524-0161, e-mail info@scottish booktrust.com, World Wide Web http:// www.scottishbooktrust.com. *Chief Exec. Officer* Marc Lambert.

Scottish Publishers Assn., Scottish Book Centre, 137 Dundee St., Edinburgh EH11 1BG, Scotland. Tel. 131-228-6866, fax 131-228-3220, e-mail info@scottishbooks. org, World Wide Web http://www.scottish books.org. *Dir.* Lorraine Fannin; *Chair* Timothy Wright.

Welsh Books Council (Cyngor Llyfrau Cymru), Castell Brychan, Aberystwyth, Ceredigion SY23 2JB, Wales. Tel. 1970-624-151, fax 1970-625-385, e-mail castel brychan@wbc.org.uk, World Wide Web http://www.cllc.org.uk. *Dir.* Gwerfyl Pierce Jones.

Uruguay

Cámara Uruguaya del Libro (Uruguayan Publishers Assn.), Juan D. Jackson 1118, 11 200 Montevideo. Tel. 82-41-57-32, fax 82-41-18-60, e-mail camurlib@adinet. com.uy. *Pres.* Ernesto Sanjines.

Venezuela

Cámara Venezolana del Libro (Venezuelan Publishers Assn.), Av. Andrés Bello, Edificio Centro Andrés Bello, Torre Oeste 11, piso 11, Of. 112-0, Caracas 1050. Tel. 212-793-1347, fax 212-793-1368, e-mail cavelibro@cantv.net. *Dir.* M. P. Vargas.

Zambia

Booksellers and Publishers Assn. of Zambia, Box 31838, Lusaka. Tel. 1-255-282, fax 1-255-195, e-mail bpaz@zamnet.zm, World Wide Web http://africanpublishers.org. *Exec. Dir.* Basil Mbewe.

Zimbabwe

Zimbabwe Book Publishers Assn., P.O. Box 3041, Harare. Tel./fax 4-754-256, e-mail engelbert@collegepress.co.zw.

National Information Standards Organization (NISO) Standards

Information Retrieval

Z39.2-1994 (R2001)	Information Interchange Format
Z39.47-1993 (R2003)	Extended Latin Alphabet Coded Character Set for Bibliographic Use (ANSEL)
Z39.50-2003	Information Retrieval (Z39.50) Application Service Definition and Protocol Specification
Z39.53-2001	Codes for the Representation of Languages for Information Interchange
Z39.64-1989 (R2002)	East Asian Character Code for Bibliographic Use
Z39.76-1996 (R2002)	Data Elements for Binding Library Materials
Z39.84-2005	Syntax for the Digital Object Identifier
Z39.88-2004	The OpenURL Framework for Context-Sensitive Services
Z39.89-2003	The U.S. National Z39.50 Profile for Library Applications

Library Management

Z39.7-2004	Information Services and Use: Metrics and Statistics for Libraries and Information Providers—Data Dictionary
Z39.20-1999	Criteria for Price Indexes for Print Library Materials
Z39.71-1999	Holdings Statements for Bibliographic Items
Z39.73-1994 (R2001)	Single-Tier Steel Bracket Library Shelving
Z39.83-2002	Part 2: Protocol Implementation

Preservation and Storage

Z39.32-1996 (R2002)	Information on Microfiche Headers
Z39.48-1992 (R2002)	Permanence of Paper for Publications and Documents in Libraries and Archives
Z39.62-2000	Eye-Legible Information on Microfilm Leaders and Trailers and on Containers of Processed Microfilm on Open Reels
Z39.74-1996 (R2002)	Guides to Accompany Microform Sets
Z39.77-2001	Guidelines for Information About Preservation Products
Z39.78-2000	Library Binding
Z39.79-2001	Environmental Conditions for Exhibiting Library and Archival Materials

Publishing and Information Management

Z39.9-1992 (R2001)	International Standard Serial Numbering (ISSN)
Z39.14-1997 (R2002)	Guidelines for Abstracts
Z39.18-2005	Scientific and Technical Reports—Preparation, Presentation, and Preservation
Z39.19-2005	Guidelines for the Construction, Format, and Management of Monolingual Controlled Vocabularies
Z39.23-1997 (R2002)	Standard Technical Report Number Format and Creation
Z39.26-1997 (R2002)	Micropublishing Product Information
Z39.29-2005	Bibliographic References
Z39.41-1997 (R2002)	Printed Information on Spines
Z39.43-1993 (R2001)	Standard Address Number (SAN) for the Publishing Industry
Z39.56-1996 (R2002)	Serial Item and Contribution Identifier (SICI)
Z39.82-2001	Title Pages for Conference Publications
Z39.85-2001	Dublin Core Metadata Element Set
Z39.86-2005	Specifications for the Digital Talking Book
ANSI/NISO/ISO 10283-1995 (R2002)	Electronic Manuscript Preparation and Markup

In Development/NISO Initiatives

NISO examines new areas for standardization, reports, and best practices on a continuing basis to support its ongoing standards development program. NISO working groups are exploring these areas:

- Digital Rights Expression
- Identifiers for Digital Content
- Exchange of Serial Subscription Information Serials JWP—(NISO and EDItEUR)
- License Expression
- Metasearch Initiative—Access Management, Collection Description, and Search/Retrieve
- Networked Reference Services
- Standardized Usage Statistics Harvesting Initiative
- Technical Metadata for Digital Still Images
- Version of Journal Articles (NISO and ALPSP)
- Web Services and Practices
- ISBN revision—13-digit ISBN approved for transition by January 1, 2007

NISO Technical Reports and Other Publications

Environmental Guidelines for the Storage of Paper Records (TR01-1995)

Guidelines for Indexes and Related Information Retrieval Devices (TR02-1997)

Guidelines to Alphanumeric Arrangement and Sorting of Numerals and Other Symbols (TR03-1999)

Information Standards Quarterly (ISQ) (NISO quarterly newsletter)
A Framework of Guidance for Building Good Digital Collections
The RFP Writer's Guide to Standards for Library Systems
Metadata Demystified: A Guide for Publishers
Understanding Metadata
Up and Running: Implementing Z39.50—Proceedings of a Symposium Sponsored by the State Library of Iowa
Z39.50: A Primer on the Protocol
Z39.50 Implementation Experiences

Workshop reports and white papers are available on the NISO Web site at http://www.niso.org/standards/std_resources.html.

For more information, contact NISO, 4733 Bethesda Ave., Suite 300, Bethesda, MD 20814. Tel. 301-654-2512, fax 301-654-1721, e-mail nisohq@niso.org, World Wide Web http://www.niso.org.

Calendar, 2006–2014

The list below contains information on association meetings or promotional events that are, for the most part, national or international in scope. State and regional library association meetings are also included. To confirm the starting or ending date of a meeting, which may change after the *Bowker Annual* has gone to press, contact the association directly. Addresses of library and book trade associations are listed in Part 6 of this volume. For information on additional book trade and promotional events, see *Literary Market Place* and *International Literary Market Place*, published by Information Today, Inc., and other library and book trade publications such as *Library Journal, School Library Journal,* and *Publishers Weekly*. An Information Today events calendar can be found at http://www.infotoday.com/calendar.shtml.

2006

June

1–2	Rhode Island Library Assn.	Smithfield
1–3	Canadian Assn. for Information Science	Toronto
3–6	North American Fuzzy Information Processing Society	Montreal
5–11	International Council for Scientific and Technical Information (ICSTI)	Washington, DC
7–9	Society for Scholarly Publishing	Crystal City, VA
8–12	American Assn. of Law Libraries	St. Louis
9–12	BookExpo Canada	Toronto
11–13	Global Information Technology Management Association (GITMA) World Conference	Orlando
11–14	Special Libraries Assn.	Baltimore
11–15	Joint Conference on Digital Libraries	Chapel Hill
14–15	International Conference on Information Literacy	Kuala Lumpur, Malaysia
14–17	Canadian Library Assn.	Ottawa
15–17	American Society of Indexers/Abstracting Society of Canada	Toronto
15–17	Assn. of Canadian Archivists	St. John's, NL
18–21	Assn. of Jewish Libraries	Cambridge, MA
18–23	International Assn. of Music Libraries, Archives, and Documentation Centers	Göteborg, Sweden
21–24	American Theological Library Assn.	Chicago

June 2006 *(cont.)*

22–28	American Library Assn. Annual Conference	New Orleans
26–29	International Conference on Data Mining	Las Vegas

July

3–7	International Association of School Librarians	Lisbon, Portugal
4–7	International Society for Knowledge Organization	Vienna, Austria
6–7	European and Mediterranean Conference on Information Systems	Alicante, Spain
6–9	Tokyo International Book Fair	Tokyo, Japan
8–12	American Assn. of Law Libraries	St. Louis
31–8/6	Society of Amercan Archivists	Washington, DC

August

1–2	Third International Conference on Knowledge Management (ICKM)	London, England
2–6	Society of American Archivists, National Association of Government Archives and Records Administrators, Council of State Archivists	Washington, DC
4–6	Americas Conference on Information Systems	Acapulco, Mexico
4–6	Wikimedia Foundation Conference (Wikimania 2006)	Boston
9–12	Pacific Northwest Library Assn.	Eugene, OR
12–18	Edinburgh International Book Festival	Edinburgh, Scotland
15–19	Nevada Library Assn.	Las Vegas
20–24	World Library and Information Conference (IFLA General Conference)	Seoul, Korea
30–9/2	Beijing International Book Fair	Beijing, China

September

6–8	I-KNOW (Sixth International Conference on Knowledge Management)	Graz, Austria
9–13	International League of Antiquarian Booksellers	Philadelphia
11–16	Tenth European Conference of Medical and Health Libraries	Cluj-Napoca, Romania
14–16	Assn. for Library Service to Children Institute	Pittsburgh
17–19	Maine Library Assn.	Augusta
18–19	Web Search University Place	Washington, DC
20–22	Georgia Library Assn.	Athens
20–22	North Dakota Library Assn.	Fargo
20–22	South Dakota Library Assn.	Rapid City
21–24	Göteborg Book Fair	Göteborg, Sweden

27–29	Minnesota Library Assn.	St. Cloud
27–30	Kentucky Library Assn.	Louisville
27–30	Wyoming Library Assn.	Gillette

October

2–4	West Virginia Library Assn.	Huntington
3–6	Illinois Library Assn	Chicago
4–5	Idaho Library Assn.	Moscow
4–6	Missouri Library Assn.	Columbus
4–7	International Association of Computer Information Systems (IACIS)	Reno
4–8	Frankfurt Book Fair	Frankfurt, Germany
7–10	Arkansas Library Assn.	Fayetteville
8–16	Istanbul Book Fair	Istanbul, Turkey
10–13	EDUCAUSE	Dallas
10–13	Michigan Library Assn.	Detroit
10–15	Joint Conference of Librarians of Color	Dallas
11–13	Iowa Library Assn.	Council Bluffs
11–13	Iowa Library Assn.	Council Bluffs
16–17	Internet Librarian International	London, England
22–24	New England Library Assn.	Burlington, VT
22–25	ARMA International	San Antonio
23–26	Internet Librarian 2006	Monterey, CA
24–27	Mississippi Library Assn.	Tunica
25–27	Nebraska Library Assn.	Omaha
26–29	Library and Information Technology Assn. (LITA) National Forum	Nashville
28–30	Boston International Antiquarian Book Fair	Boston
31–11/2	Wisconsin Library Assn.	Wisconsin Dells

November

1–4	New York Library Assn.	Saratoga Springs
3–9	American Society for Information Science and Technology	Austin
8–10	Virginia Library Assn.	Williamsburg
8–12	Colorado Assn. of Libraries	Denver
10–13	California Library Assn.	Sacramento
11–15	American Medical Informatics Assn.	Washington, DC
11–21	Puerto Rico International Book Fair	San Juan
12–15	Pennsylvania Library Assn.	Pittsburgh
14–16	Arizona Library Assn.	Mesa
17–19	Miami Book Fair International	Miami
28–30	Online Information 2006	London, England
28–30	South Carolina Library Assn.	Hilton Head

December 2006

5–8	International Conference on Digital Libraries	New Delhi, India
10–13	First International Information Literacy Coalition Conference	St. Thomas, Virgin Islands

2007

January

16–19	Assn. for Library and Information Science Education	Seattle
19–24	American Library Assn. Midwinter Meeting	Seattle

February

1–3	Ontario Library Assn.	Toronto

March

6–8	Louisiana Library Assn.	Baton Rouge
7–9	Tennessee Library Assn.	Nashville
12–17	Texas Library Assn.	San Antonio
29–4/1	ACRL National Conference	Baltimore

April

9–13	Florida Library Assn.	Orlando
11–13	Kansas Library Assn.	Topeka
11–14	Texas Library Assn.	San Antonio
18–20	Tennessee Library Assn.	Chattanooga
24–25	New Jersey Library Assn.	Long Branch

May

15–17	Utah Library Assn.	Provo
18–23	Medical Library Assn.	Philadelphia
23–26	Canadian Library Assn.	St. John's, NL

June

1–3	BookExpo America	New York
3–6	Special Libraries Assn.	Denver
21–27	American Library Assn. Annual Conference	Washington, DC
30–7/6	International Assn. of Music Libraries, Archives, and Documentation Centers	Sydney, Australia

July

14–18	American Assn. of Law Libraries	New Orleans
19–24	Hong Kong Book Fair	Hong Kong

August

27–9/2	Society of American Archivists	Chicago
TBA	73rd World Library and Information	
	Congress/IFLA Annual Conference	Durban, South Africa

September

26–28	North Dakota Library Assn.	Jamestown

October

3–5	Missouri Library Assn.	Springfield
3–5	South Dakota Library Assn.	Watertown
3–5	West Virginia Library Assn.	Morgantown
4–7	LITA National Forum	Denver
6–10	Arkansas Library Assn.	Little Rock
7–10	ARMA International	Baltimore
10–14	Frankfurt Book Fair	Frankfurt, Germany
14–16	New England Library Assn.	Sturbridge, MA
16–19	Wisconsin Library Assn.	Green Bay
22–25	Music Library Assn./Society for American	
	Music	Pittsburgh
24–26	Minnesota Library Assn.	Mankato
24–26	Nebraska Library Assn.	Kearney

November

1–2	Virginia Library Assn.	Hot Springs
10–14	American Medical Informatics Assn.	Chicago

2008

January

11–16	American Library Assn. Midwinter Meeting	Philadelphia

March

25–29	Public Library Assn.	Minneapolis

April

9–11	Kansas Library Assn.	Wichita
15–18	Texas Library Assn.	Dallas
30–5/3	Utah Library Assn./Mountain Plains Library	
	Assn.	Salt Lake City

May

16–21	Medical Library Assn.	Chicago
21–24	Canadian Library Assn.	Vancouver

May 2008 *(cont.)*

30–6/1	BookExpo America	Los Angeles

June

2–4	Canadian Assn. for Information Science	Vancouver
26–2/7	American Library Assn. Annual Conference	Anaheim

July

12–16	American Assn. of Law Libraries	Portland, OR
26–31	Special Libraries Assn.	Seattle

August

23–31	Society of American Archivists	San Francisco

October

3–4	Arkansas Library Assn.	Little Rock
8–10	Minnesota Library Assn.	Twin Cities
15–17	Nebraska Library Assn.	Lincoln
20–23	ARMA International	Las Vegas

December

3–5	West Virginia Library Assn.	White Sulphur Springs

2009

January

23–28	American Library Assn. Midwinter Meeting	Denver

April

1–3	Kansas Library Assn.	Overland Park
20–25	Texas Library Assn.	Houston

May

29–31	BookExpo America	New York

June

13–18	Special Libraries Assn.	Washington, DC

July

9–15	American Library Assn. Annual Conference	Chicago

October

7–9   Minnesota Library Assn.   Duluth

2010

January

15–20   American Library Assn. Midwinter Meeting   Boston

April

12–16   Texas Library Assn.   San Antonio

June

24–30   American Library Assn. Annual Conference   Orlando

October

6–8   Minnesota Library Assn.   Rochester

2011

January

28–2/2   American Library Assn. Midwinter Meeting   Chicago

April

12–15   Texas Library Assn.   Austin

June

23–29   American Library Assn. Annual Conference   New Orleans

October

5–7   Minnesota Library Assn.   Twin Cities

2012

January

20–25   American Library Assn. Midwinter Meeting   San Antonio

April

17–20   Texas Library Assn.   Dallas

June

21–27   American Library Assn. Annual Conference   Anaheim

2013

January

25–30   American Library Assn. Midwinter Meeting   Seattle

April

8–12   Texas Library Assn.   San Antonio

June

20–26   American Library Assn. Annual Conference   Washington, DC

2014

January

24–29   American Library Assn. Midwinter Meeting   Philadelphia

June

26–2/7   American Library Assn. Annual Conference   Las Vegas

Acronyms

A

AALL. American Association of Law Libraries

AAP. Association of American Publishers

AASL. American Association of School Librarians

ABA. American Booksellers Association

ABFFE. American Booksellers Foundation for Free Expression

ACRL. Association of College and Research Libraries

ADA. Anti-Deficiency Act

AgNIC. Agriculture Network Information Center

AIIM. The Enterprise Content Management Association

AIIP. Association of Independent Information Professionals

AILA. American Indian Library Association

AJL. Association of Jewish Libraries

ALA. American Library Association

ALCTS. Association for Library Collections and Technical Services

ALIC. Archives Library Information Center

ALISE. Association for Library and Information Science Education

ALSC. Association for Library Service to Children

ALTA. Association for Library Trustees and Advocates

AMMLA. American Merchant Marine Library Association

APALA. Asian/Pacific American Librarians Association

ARC. National Archives and Records Administration, Archival Research Catalog

ARL. Association of Research Libraries

ARLIS/NA. Art Libraries Society of North America

ASCLA. Association of Specialized and Cooperative Library Agencies

ASIS&T. American Society for Information Science and Technology

ATLA. American Theological Library Association

B

BCALA. Black Caucus of the American Library Association

BEA. BookExpo America

BISG. Book Industry Study Group

BRD. American Booksellers Association, Booksellers Resource Directory

BSA. Bibliographical Society of America

C

CAIS. Canadian Association for Information Science

CALA. Chinese-American Librarians Association

CAPL. Canadian Association of Public Libraries

CARE. Charity Aid, Recovery, and Empowerment Act

CARL. Canadian Association of Research Libraries

CASL. Canadian Association for School Libraries

CASLIS. Canadian Association of Special Libraries and Information Services

CD-ROM. Compact Disc Read-Only Memory

CDNL. Conference of Directors of National Libraries

CIA. Central Intelligence Agency

CIPA. Children's Internet Protection Act

CLA. Canadian Library Association; Catholic Library Association

CLTA. Canadian Library Trustees
Association
CNI. Coalition for Networked Information
COLT. Council on Library/Media
Technicians
COSLA. Chief Officers of State Library
Agencies
CPCC. Canadian Private Copying Collective
CRS. Congressional Research Service
CSLA. Church and Synagogue Library
Association
CSRL. Center for the Study of Rural
Librarianship

D

DLF. Digital Library Federation
DMCA. Digital Millennium Copyright Act
DMCRA. Digital Media Consumers' Rights
Act
DOE. Education, U.S. Department of
DREI. Digital reference, Digital Reference
Education Initiative
DRM. Digital rights management
DTB. Digital talking book (DTB) technology
DTIC. Defense Technical Information Center

E

EAR. National Technical Information
Service, Export Administration
Regulations
EDB. Energy, Science and Technology
Database
EMIERT. American Library Association,
Ethnic and Multicultural Information and
Exchange Round Table
EPA. Environmental Protection Agency
ERA. Electronic Records Archives
ERAL. National Agricultural Library,
Electronic Repository of Agricultural
Literature
ERIC. Educational Resources Information
Center
ERMI. Council on Library Information
Resources, E-Resources Management
Initiative

F

FAFLRT. American Library Association,
Federal and Armed Forces Librarians
Round Table
FCC. Federal Communications Commission
FDLP. Government Printing Office, Federal
Depository Library Program
FDsys. Government Printing Office, Future
Digital System
FECA. Family Entertainment and Copyright
Act
FEDRIP. National Technical Information
Service, FEDRIP (Federal Research in
Progress Database)
FIAF. International Federation of Film
Archives
FLICC. Federal Library and Information
Center Committee
FOIA. Freedom of Information Act
FOLUSA. Friends of Libraries U.S.A.
FPC. Federal Publishers Committee
FRANAR. International Federation of
Library Associations and Institutions,
FRANAR Working Group

G

GATS. General Agreement on Trade in
Services
GLBT. American Library Association, Gay,
Lesbian, Bisexual, and Transgendered
Round Table
GODORT. American Library Association,
Government Documents Round Table
GPO. Government Printing Office
GRC. National Technical Information
Service, GOV.Research Center

I

IAALD. International Association of
Agricultural Information Specialists
IACs. Defense Technical Information Center,
Information Analysis Centers
IALL. International Association of Law
Libraries

IAML. International Association of Music
Libraries, Archives and Documentation
Centres

IASL. International Association of School
Librarianship

IATUL. International Association of
Technological University Libraries

ICABS. IFLA-CDNL Alliance for
Bibliographic Standards

ICBS. International Committee of the Blue
Shield

IFLA. International Federation of Library
Associations and Institutions

IFRT. American Library Association,
Intellectual Freedom Round Table

ILL/DD. Interlibrary loan/document delivery

ILS. Library of Congress, Integrated Library
System

IMLS. Institute of Museum and Library
Services

ISBN. International Standard Book Number

ISCAP. Interagency Security Classification
Appeals Panel

ISO. International Organization for
Standardization

ISSN. International Standard Serial Number

L

LAC. Library and Archives Canada

LAMA. Library Administration and
Management Association

LC. Library of Congress

LCA. Library Copyright Alliance

LHRT. American Library Association,
Library History Round Table

LIS. Library of Congress, Legislative
Information System or Library/informa-
tion science

LITA. Library and Information Technology
Association

LJ. Library Journal

LOCKSS. Government Printing Office,
LOCKSS (Lots of Copies Keep Stuff Safe)

LRRT. American Library Association,
Library Research Round Table

LSP. National Center for Education
Statistics, Library Statistics Program

LSTA. Library Services and Technology Act

LWB. Librarians Without Borders

M

MAGERT. American Library Association,
Map and Geography Round Table

MLA. Medical Library Association; Music
Library Association

N

NAGARA. National Association of
Government Archives and Records
Administrators

NAL. National Agricultural Library

NARA. National Archives and Records
Administration

NASTA. National Association of State
Textbook Administrators

NCES. National Center for Education
Statistics

NCLA. National Church Library Association

NCLB. No Child Left Behind

NCLIS. National Commission on Libraries
and Information Science

NDIIPP. National Digital Information
Infrastructure and Preservation Program

NDP. Normative Data Project for Libraries

NEH. National Endowment for the
Humanities

NFAIS. NFAIS (National Federation of
Abstracting and Information Services)

NGA. National Geospatial-Intelligence
Agency

NIH. National Institutes of Health

NIMAS. Standards, National Instructional
Materials Accessibility Standard

NIOSH. National Institute for Occupational
Safety and Health

NISO. National Information Standards
Organization

NLE. National Library of Education

NLM. National Library of Medicine

NMRT. American Library Association, New
Members Round Table

NSA. National Security Agency

NTIS. National Technical Information
Service

O

OAI. Open Archives Initiative
OGI. People's Republic of China, Open Government Information

P

PIRG. Public Interest Research Group
PLA. Public Library Association
PLGDB. Databases, Public Library Geographic Database Mapping project
PLUS. Photographs, PLUS (Picture Licensing Universal System)
PTDLA. Patent and Trademark Depository Library Association
PW. Publishers Weekly

R

RTECS. Databases, Registry of Toxic Effects of Chemical Substances
RUSA. Reference and User Services Association

S

SAA. Society of American Archivists
SAN. Standard Address Number
SARS. Sudden Acute Respiratory Syndrome
SBU. Government documents, "Sensitive But Unclassified"
SIIA. Software and Information Industry Association
SLA. Special Libraries Association
SPARC. Scholarly Publishing and Academic Resources Coalition
SRIM. National Technical Information Service, Selected Research in Microfiche

SRRT. American Library Association, Social Responsibilities Round Table
SSP. Society for Scholarly Publishing
STINET. Scientific and Technical Information Network
StLA. State libraries and library agencies, NCES State Library Agencies survey

T

TLA. Theatre Library Association
TRI. Environmental Protection Agency, Toxic Release Inventory

U

ULC. Urban Libraries Council
USPS. Postal Service, U.S.

V

VHP. Veterans History Project
VR. Virtual reference

W

WIPO. World Intellectual Property Organization
WNC. World News Connection
WSIS. World Summit on the Information Society

Y

YALSA. Young Adult Library Services Association
YPG. Association of American Publishers, Young to Publishing Group

Index of Organizations

Please note that many cross-references refer to entries in the Subject Index.

Subject Index

Please note that many cross-references refer to entries in the Index of Organizations.

A

Academic books
  college textbooks, 161–162, 165, 495
  electronic resources, 255–256
  prices and price indexes
    British averages, 512–513(table)
    North American, 500–501(table), 502
    U.S. college books, 504–506(table)
  sales, 19
  See also Association of American Publishers, Professional/Scholarly Publishing; Society for Scholarly Publishing; Textbooks
Academic libraries, *see* College and research libraries
Access, open, 183
Acquisitions
  expenditures, 459–467
    academic libraries, 462–463(table)
    government libraries, 466–467(table)
    public libraries, 460–461(table)
    special libraries, 464–465(table)
  See also specific types of libraries, e.g., Public libraries
Adults, services for, 323
  best books, 567–579
  readers' advisory, bibliography for librarians, 553
  See also Literacy programs; Reference and User Services Association
Advocacy; bibliography for librarians, 546
Agencies, library, *see* Library associations and agencies
Agricultural libraries, *see* International Association of Agricultural Information Specialists; National Agricultural Library
ALA v. FCC, 329–330

Alabama
  humanities councils, 352
  library associations, 720
  networks and cooperative library organizations, 635
  school library media associations, 742
Alaska
  humanities councils, 352
  library associations, 730
  networks and cooperative library organizations, 635
  school library media associations, 742
Almanacs, bestselling, 596
American Center for Cures Act, 329
American Libraries, 146
American Samoa; humanities council, 357
Anti-Deficiency Act (ADA), 326
Archives
  acquisition expenditures
    academic libraries, 462–463(table)
    government libraries, 466–467(table)
    public libraries, 460–461(table)
    special libraries, 464–465(table)
  bibliography for librarians, 552
  open archives initiative, 121, 203
  People's Republic of China, 302
  See also Archives Library Information Center; Electronic Records Archives; Library and Archives Canada; National Archives and Records Administration; Open Archives Initiative
Arizona
  humanities councils, 352
  library associations, 720
  networks and cooperative library organizations, 635
  school library media associations, 742
Arkansas
  Fayetteville Public Library, 482
  humanities councils, 352

Toxins, 70–71, 88, 334
Tsunami, 10

U

UMG v. MP3.com, 262
United States
  associations
    book trade, 773–778
    library/information industry, 656–719
  book exports, 523–538
    destinations, 526(table)
    dictionaries, 528(table), 531–532,
      531(table)
    encyclopedias and serial installments,
      528(table), 531–532
    hardcover books, 528(table), 530(table)
    market for, 525, 527–532
    paperbacks, mass market, 528(table)
    to principal countries, 527(table)
    religious, 528(table), 530(table)
    shipments, 525(table)
    technical, scientific, professional,
      528(table), 529(table)
    textbooks, 528(table), 529(table)
    trade balance, 524(table)
    See also Books, exports, U.S.
  book imports, 523–538, 534(table)
    encyclopedias and serial installments,
      538(table)
    hardcover, 537(table)
    import sources, 533(table)
    paperbacks, mass market, 537(table)
    from principal countries, 534(table)
    religious, 536(table)
    technical, scientific, professional,
      536(table)
    textbooks, 535, 535(table)
    See also Books, imports, U.S.
  book production, 516(table)
  bookstores, 540–541(table)
  government information, *see* Government
    information, access to
  libraries, number of, 456–458(table)
  networks and cooperative library organiza-
    tions, 635–655
  postal service, *see* Postal issues; Postal Ser-
    vice, U.S.
  prices and price indexes, *see under* Acade-
    mic books; Audiovisual materials;
    Books; CD-ROM; Hardcover books;

Microforms; Paperback books; Peri-
  odicals and serials
published materials, *see* Government Print-
  ing Office
*Universal Music v. Sharman License Hold-
  ings*, 259
University libraries, *see* College and research
  libraries
Urban libraries, *see* Urban Libraries Council
USA Patriot Act, 46
  AAP activities, 158–159
  ABA activities, 178, 180–181
  ALA activities, 136–137, 330–332
  amendments, proposed, 338–339
  Improvement and Reauthorization Act, 5,
    158, 330, 339
  national security letters, 330–331
  Sanders amendment, 158
Utah
  humanities council, 356
  library associations, 730
  networks and cooperative library organiza-
    tions, 652
  school library media associations, 750

V

Valenza, Joyce, 14–15
Vendor services
  FEDLINK, 55–56
  salaries, 401(table)
Vermont
  humanities council, 356
  library associations, 730–731
  networks and cooperative library organiza-
    tions, 652–653
  school library media associations, 750
Veterans History Project (VHP), 36
Videocassettes, children's; notable, 578
"The View," book club, 173
Virgin Islands
  humanities council, 357
  networks and cooperative library organiza-
    tions, 654
Virginia
  humanities council, 356
  library associations, 731
  networks and cooperative library organiza-
    tions, 653
  school library media associations, 750
Virtual reference (VR), 311–319
  ALA guidelines, 316–317

chat software, features, 312–313
conference, 318
consortia, 314–315
copyright issues and document delivery, 317
critics/closures, 314
defined, 311–312
e-mail reference, 313
education/professional development, 318
expanding area of service, 313–314
instant messaging, 316
market trends, software, 316
privacy/legal issues, 317
starting a new service, 316–317
Visually handicapped, library services for, *see* Blind, services for the
The Voice that Challenged a Nation . . . (Freedman), 149

W

Warlick, David, 15–16
Warren, Rick, 23, 580
Washington, D.C., *see* District of Columbia
Washington
humanities council, 356
library associations, 731
"library value" studies, 440–441
networks and cooperative library organizations, 653
school library media associations, 751
Washington Post, 161
West Virginia
humanities council, 356

library associations, 731-732
networks and cooperative library organizations, 653
school library media associations, 751
Wikis, 7, 14
Winfrey, Oprah, *see* Oprah Book Club
Wisconsin
humanities council, 356
library associations, 732
networks and cooperative library organizations, 654
school library media associations, 751
Workforce Investment Act, 325
Wyoming
humanities council, 356
library associations, 732
networks and cooperative library organizations, 654
school library media associations, 751

Y

Young adults, 442
bibliography for librarians, 547–548
books, best books, 149, 568–570
audiobooks, 573–574
reluctant readers, 570–572
Generation M, 13
information-seeking behavior, 443
services history, 443
Teen Read Week, 139
See also Children and young adults; Young Adult Library Services Association